0   2.99

SECOND EDITION THE
EUROPEAN
WORLD
A HISTORY

SECOND EDITION THE
EUROPEAN
WORLD
A HISTORY

JEROME BLUM *Princeton University*
RONDO CAMERON *Emory University*
THOMAS G. BARNES *University of California, Berkeley*

LITTLE, BROWN AND COMPANY
BOSTON

LIBRARY OF CONGRESS CATALOG CARD NUMBER 76-81160

THIRD PRINTING

Published simultaneously in Canada by Little, Brown & Company (Canada) Limited

PRINTED IN THE UNITED STATES OF AMERICA

PREFACE

The intermixture in our own time of European, or Western, civilization with non-Western civilizations and cultures is producing a new, global civilization. It is the purpose of this book to tell the story of Western civilization from the "Dark Ages" when Europe emerged as a cultural entity up to the transmutation of Western civilization in the twentieth century. It is not a story of continual progress. Throughout its history the European world has experienced fluctuations of fortune and circumstance, periods of harmony and periods of strife and discord. Nor does the story have a simple, obvious moral. The attentive reader, however, can learn much about his own cultural heritage and so arrive at a better understanding of the world in which he lives and his own place in it.

We owe many acknowledgments for help that we have received in the writing of this book; so many, indeed, that we cannot name them all. A complete listing would have to begin with the teachers who introduced us to the study of history, would include the many historians whose works we have used, and would end with the students in the classes that we ourselves have taught and who did much to shape our conception of the kind of book we wanted to write. The first edition benefited from the comments and suggestions of Professors William J. Bouwsma, University of California, Berkeley; Roderic H. Davidson, George Washington University; Charles F. Delzell, Vanderbilt University; the late Klaus Epstein, Brown University; Franklin L. Ford, Harvard University; Leonard Krieger, University of Chicago; George L. Mosse, the late Robert L. Reynolds, and Philip D. Curtin, all of the University of Wisconsin; Herbert H. Rowen, Rutgers University; Robert Lindsay, Ohio University; James Sturm, Richmond College of the City University of New York; and Reese Jenkins, Case Western Reserve University.

In this revised edition we have been able to incorporate numerous suggestions made by users of the first edition. We are particularly grateful to the scores of anonymous (to us) college and university professors who filled out a long questionnaire based on their experience with the first edition; we only hope the improvements they suggested will merit their continued use of the new edition. Finally, we wish to express again our indebtedness to the editorial staff of the publisher, and especially to Charles Christensen and Miss Lynne S. Marcus.

J.B.
R.C.
T.G.B.

CONTENTS

List of Maps and Charts

List of Illustrations

SECOND EDITION **THE EUROPEAN WORLD** A HISTORY

THE EMERGENCE OF THE EUROPEAN WORLD
PART ONE

INTRODUCTION: THE FOUNDATIONS

Europe is the smallest of the five major continents, contains less than 10 per cent of the world's land area and, in the mid-twentieth century, had about 20 per cent of the world's population. In quantitative terms Europe may appear of slight importance in our global age.

The European world, however, is more than a matter of numbers and geography. It is a concept of civilization. It includes European culture in the Western Hemisphere and also outposts of European culture in Asia, Africa, and Australasia. The history of the European world, in short, is the history of Western civilization.

As a distinctly human attribute culture is as old as man himself, but the earliest civilizations for which we have evidence apparently originated in the fourth or fifth millennium before Christ, in association with the development of settled agriculture and the domestication of animals. This occurred first in western Asia, perhaps along the fertile crescent, the semicircle stretching from Egypt to the Persian Gulf. The early civilizations of Babylonia, Egypt, and probably that of the Indus valley in India, were offshoots of this cradle of civilization. The only other known civilization with definitely independent origins was that of the pre-Columbian inhabitants of America that evolved in the first millennium after Christ, although the origins of Chinese civilization (second or third millennium B.C.) may have been mostly independent of the original center in western Asia. All other civilizations were, in some measure, derived from these first civilizations.

As a social phenomenon, civilization grows and is transmitted by means of social processes. The growth of civilization is essentially the proliferation and elaboration of all the elements of which civilization is

1

THE PHYSICAL FEATURES OF EUROPE

ICELAND

FAEROE IS.

0   300   600
Miles

SHETLAND IS.

KJOLEN

SCANDINAVIAN
PENINSULA

HEBRIDES

ATLANTIC

GRAMPIAN MTS.

North

BRITISH

Sea

JUTLAND
PENINSULA

Irish
Sea

PENNINES

OCEAN

ISLES

GREAT

LOW

Thames R.

English Channel

Seine R.

Rhine R.

Elbe R.

Oder

Loire R.

Bay of Biscay

Garonne R.

CENTRAL
MASSIF

Saône R.

Rhône R.

ALPS

PO VALLEY

Po R.

Danu

Drava

CANTABRIAN MTS.

PYRENEES

DINAR

Douro R.

SPANISH

Ebro R.

APENNINE MTS.

Adriatic

Tagus R.
PLATEAU

CORSICA

S

SA. MORENA

BALEARIC IS.

Guadalquivir R.

SA. NEVADA

SARDINIA
Tyrrhenian Sea

Strait of   Gibraltar

Strait of
Messina

SICILY

AFRICA

Mediterranea

2

composed. New elements enter the stream by means of chance discovery, and even more by novel combinations of existing elements. These discoveries or new combinations are usually the result of social interaction, as is the transmission of civilization from one generation to another.

The diffusion of civilization is also the result of social interaction, especially through trade, conquest, and mass migration. The confrontation of a relatively primitive society by an advanced or civilized society usually results in at least a partial adoption by the former of the civilization of the latter. If, however, the civilized society is feeble it may succumb and its civilization may expire. A civilization is seldom completely obliterated; some of its elements are incorporated into the culture of the more primitive society and help bring about the evolution of a new civilization.

In a very real sense all civilization is a single entity, the civilization of man. But civilization is in a constant state of change and is never quite the same from place to place or at successive points in time, so that it is customary to speak of civilizations as well as civilization. European, or Western, civilization originated from the fusion of German (barbarian) culture and Roman civilization during the so-called Dark Ages from the fifth to the tenth century A.D. Roman civilization, in turn, was descended from the earliest civilizations of western Asia and Egypt by way of the Greeks. Since the process of civilization is cumulative, each of these predecessors contributed important elements to the European heritage.

EARLY EXPANSION AND DECLINE

From the beginning of their civilization Europeans have been aggressive and expansionist, conquering, colonizing, trading, proselytizing, and ultimately spreading their culture to every part of the world. Initially this cultural expansion owed much to the vigorous propagation of the Christian faith. Christianization gave to the European world a unity and cultural cohesiveness that was the ideological foundation of its civilization. The first phase of expansion reached its apogee in the period from the beginning of the tenth to the beginning of the fourteenth century. During those centuries European culture spread from its initial centers between the Loire and Rhine rivers in present-day northern France, Belgium, and western Germany throughout the continent, from Spain to Scandinavia, from Iceland to southern Italy, from England to Russia, and even briefly, during the Crusades, to Palestine. The central political fact of European expansion in the early phase was the system of interdependence called feudalism, which knitted diverse and often discordant petty political entities into a defensive posture sufficiently strong to preserve internal order and to withstand threats from without. Economic growth was part of the expansion, and the twelfth and thirteenth centuries witnessed the crest of a wave of material prosperity of the European world with burgeoning towns and cities as the centers of trade.

In the fourteenth century Europe descended into an era of crisis and contraction that lasted more than a hundred years. Economic life was overcome by stagnation and decline. Population declined and great stretches of land lay empty and untilled. Civil wars among ruling cliques of feudal lords and petty princes proved the beginning of the end of the old political structure; feudalism, which in preceding centuries had been the bulwark of internal order had become the greatest threat to order. Mass insurrections of discontented peasants and urban workers broke out in every part of Europe. Civil commotion was joined by a grass-roots protest against the increasing materialism and decreasing spirituality of the Roman Catholic Church. The papacy, at the pinnacle of its power in the twelfth and thirteenth centuries, now reached the low ebb of its fortunes, and the pope himself for a time became a tool of the French king.

AN AGE OF RENEWED CONFIDENCE

The way out of the morass of decay was indicated by emerging national monarchies, by a new wave of economic expansion, and by a revitalization of European intellectual life. At the expense of the political power of the old aristocracy, kings succeeded in the fifteenth and sixteenth centuries in fashioning nation-states, challenging the interference of both church and lords in internal affairs and each other in state rivalries productive of wars. Economic revival, buttressed by increasing population, began in the latter part of the fifteenth century. Demand grew, commerce and industry expanded, gold and silver poured into Europe from the New World, prices rose, and there began to emerge a worldwide pattern of trade with Europe as its center. Starting in the fourteenth century in the Italian city-states the intellectual and artistic revival of the Renaissance spread to northwestern Europe in the fifteenth and sixteenth centuries and touched every institution and facet of contemporary Europe. It was much more than a new conception of man, a revival of classical learning, and an artistic flowering without parallel in history. It was the expression of a confident civilization prepared for change and demanding expansion.

The confidence of the European world as it broadened its horizons found new outlets beyond the frontiers of Europe. Bold and skillful navigators journeyed to far-off places. Their discoveries, followed by colonization and exploitation, gave a stake in the greater, once unknown, world to the maritime states of the Atlantic seaboard of Europe and confirmed the shift in the focal point of the European world from the Mediterranean to western Europe.

The unified Christian faith of western Europe fell victim to the new confidence. Beginning with Martin Luther's challenge in 1517 to abuses long evident in the Roman Catholic Church, the Protestant Reformation soon became a revolt against ecclesiastical authority, producing theological variety and denominational atomism and ultimately assuring the triumph of secularism. The key to the success of the Protestant reformers lay in the leverage that their revolt presented to secular rulers for the aggrandizement of their power and property. The net gain of the age of the Reformation went to the rulers of the emerging nation-states, whether Protestant or Catholic, who were already fashioning the absolutism that would dominate the European world from the mid-seventeenth to the end of the eighteenth century.

Finally, in perhaps the supreme achievement of the epoch, European man evolved a new way of looking at himself, the world, and the universe. New attitudes of secularism and individualism produced new patterns of thought that made possible new approaches to old problems. Above all, a great outburst of scientific speculation in the sixteenth century heralded the beginning of the revolution in science that is still not ended.

The attainments of the European world during this great age of expansion have about them the aura of modernity. So, too, has the sense of crisis which dominated the first six decades of the seventeenth century. A series of destructive wars, compounded of religious motives and dynastic ambitions, filled most of that period and brought in its wake civil commotion and revolution. The simple confidence of the Renaissance and the spiritual exhilaration of the Reformation evaporated. The beneficiaries were the new absolutist monarchs under whose rule order was once more regained.

THE HERITAGE OF THE EUROPEAN WORLD
CHAPTER ONE

Europe is as much a geographical as a historical fact, and its history has been conditioned by the physical theater in which it has unfolded. Europe forms the westernmost fifth of Eurasia, the greatest land mass on earth, and no definite boundary marks it off from Asia. In contrast to the rest of Eurasia, Europe resembles a peninsula. The Atlantic Ocean on its west, connecting four continents — Europe, North America, South America, and Africa — provided the avenue for the political, cultural, and economic expansion of Europe from the fifteenth century onward. Bays and inlets cut deep incisions into the seacoasts of Europe, and it has many straits, such as those commanding the entrances to the Mediterranean, the Baltic Sea, the Black Sea, and the North Sea. In the power struggles of the European states the straits and narrow seas have been of major strategic importance.

A mountain spine, dominated by the Alps, separates the Mediterranean region from the great plain that extends from the Atlantic coast of France through the Low Countries (Belgium and Holland) across northern Germany and Poland, into Russia as far as the Ural Mountains, and merges with the Great Siberian Plain at the southern end of the Urals. This fertile plain with its many gentle hills has simplified the movements of armies bent on conquest in the wars that have marred Europe's history.

The navigable rivers that lace the continent had much to do with the growth of trade and communications, the establishment of cities, and the formation of the states of modern Europe. In northwestern and central Europe they flow northward into the Atlantic and its subsidiary seas, except for the Danube, which runs into the Black Sea. In eastern Europe the great plainland is drained by rivers flowing into the Black and Caspian seas. In southern Europe, because of the sharp changes in elevation, there are few navigable streams.

THE LEGACY OF ANCIENT CIVILIZATION

Western civilization claims a distinguished lineage. Its immediate forerunners were the civilizations of classical Greece and Rome. These, in turn, were built on the achievements of Egypt, Mesopotamia, and other ancient civilizations of the Near East, as southwestern Asia and the northeastern corner of Africa are sometimes called. Behind the emergence of these first civilizations lay a long period of cultural development, during which decisive changes in technology and attitude occurred with gradually increasing frequency.

One of the distinctive features of human culture is the use of tools; man is sometimes called, in fact, a tool-using animal. Since tools are usually made of durable materials, it is possible to trace the development of culture by means of those which have survived. The earliest recognizable tools (as distinguished from sticks and stones appropriated from nature on the occasion of their use) are chipped flints and other stones in a variety of sizes and shapes, used as crude axes, knives, scrapers, and so forth. The period in which they constituted the most important tools of man is called the Paleolithic or Old Stone Age. It lasted well over half a million years, until about 8000 B.C. in southwestern Asia, and even longer in other parts of the world. Paleolithic man probably developed other elements of culture that have entered into our heritage, such as primitive notions of art, religion, and social organization (the family and the tribe, for instance). Unfortunately, apart from magnificent but rare cave paintings in France and Spain, there is little direct testimony to these epochal inventions; our knowledge of them consists largely of educated guesses based on the equivocal evidence of graves and buried settlements.

THE BIRTH OF CIVILIZATION

Between about 8000 B.C. and about 4000 B.C. men in various parts of the Old World gradually perfected the technique of making stone tools by polishing instead of chipping them. This period of prehistory is called the Neolithic or New Stone Age. People in the region between the Tigris and Euphrates rivers and the Mediterranean developed settled agriculture (wheat or barley), domesticated animals (pigs, goats, and sheep), and invented pottery. They probably also invented textiles, since basket weaving almost certainly preceded pottery, but no material evidence survives. These various developments are sometimes referred to collectively as the Neolithic Revolution. By permitting the regular production and accumulation of food, they made possible the growth of permanent urban settlements, or cities, and a more complex social organization and culture.

During the next four thousand years the region west of the Indus River, including the Mediterranean basin, produced other major elements of civilization that entered into the heritage of the European world. These included the development of new varieties of plants and domesticated animals, fermented beverages, metallurgy (especially the use of copper, bronze, and iron), and architecture, as well as the invention of the wheel, writing, the sailing ship, and money. It is not possible to say precisely when or where most of them were invented or discovered, much less who was responsible. In only a few instances can one link special achievements with particular peoples.

Empires rose and fell in Egypt and Mesopotamia, Iran, Syria, Asia Minor, and the islands of the eastern Mediterranean. The arts of government, including terrorism and torture as well as codified civil law, were refined. Not all improvements in civilization came from the great and powerful. The Phoenicians, a seafaring people from the region of modern Lebanon, ranged from the eastern Mediterranean to modern Britain, where they traded Eastern manufactures for the tin of Cornwall. They also colonized extensively in the western Mediterranean at Carthage, across the bay from modern Tunis, in Marseilles, and on the Iberian peninsula. Their most important contribution to civilization, which grew out of their trading habits, was the invention of the first alphabet. Another Semitic people from the eastern Mediterranean who enjoyed a brief period of earthly glory in the tenth century B.C. made a far more lasting contribution to civilization than the fabulous temple of their King Solomon. The monotheistic religion of the ancient Hebrews provided the foundation for Christianity and Islam as well as modern Judaism.

CLASSICAL GREECE

Greece was the earliest direct ancestor of European civilization. A turbulent society developed rapidly between about 800 and 600 B.C. This was the great period of maritime and colonial expansion of the Greek city-states, which ultimately numbered over one hundred autonomous units located on the Grecian peninsula, nearby islands, and other coastal areas from the Crimea to southern Spain.

Small, independent, and vigorous, the city-states defy generalization. Sparta and Athens, the two most important, represent the extremes. Sparta was militaristic and autocratic in social and political structure. In contrast, Athens developed a system of government that was broadly based on consent, and during its Golden Age, 600 to 400 B.C., it introduced a rational legal system, representative assemblies, the election of military leaders, and other features of an open society. Both city-states produced leaders of great capacity; but there is historic irony in the fact that Pericles of Athens (d. 429 B.C.), who presided over the period of greatest democracy and cultural vitality in Athens, was also the leader who provoked the strife between Athens and Sparta that led to the Peloponnesian Wars (431–404 B.C.), a general Greek conflagration. The Greek city-states were so weakened by the fighting that a half-century later Philip of Macedon and his son Alexander the Great (d. 323 B.C.) were able to erect a huge, if short-lived, empire on their remains.

The most durable glory of classical Greece lay in the realm of artistic and intellectual achievement. Her architecture, sculpture, and crafts have been imitated but seldom equaled. Her tragedians — Aeschylus, Sophocles, and Euripides — cast the bravery of the human spirit, the dilemma of power, and the destructiveness of self-consuming arrogance in terms that still move men. Rarely, for example, has the tension between the need for public order and the demands of private conscience — a moral paradox defying easy practical solution that has arisen time and time again in critical periods of Western history — been presented more acutely and painfully than in the play *Antigone,* composed by Sophocles in 442 B.C. The satirical drama of Aristophanes, pillorying contemporary mores, and the histories of Herodotus and Thucydides testify to the range and critical insight of Greek literature. Greek scientific genius remained unequaled for two thousand years and Socrates (d. 399 B.C.), Plato (d. 347 B.C.), and Aristotle (d. 322 B.C.) established a general framework for philosophical inquiry that remained the accepted model until the nineteenth century.

Under the sponsorship of Alexander's empire and the Hellenistic kingdoms that succeeded it, Greek culture spread over the whole Mediterranean world, and in the first century B.C. achieved a thorough intellectual conquest of the imperial Roman republic, its military conqueror. In the four following centuries many elements of Greek thought, especially the Platonic tradition, deeply affected the character of early Christianity. The rediscovery of Aristotle's works in twelfth-century western Europe led to his domination of the philosophy and much of the theology of the later Middle Ages. The men of the Renaissance recovered the bulk of Greek culture and passionately sought to fashion European civilization on it. Ever since, the classical glory of Greece has had a hold on European man's sensibilities unmatched by any other cultural influence except the Judeo-Christian religious tradition. The glory that was Greece has proven to be the richest intellectual inheritance of the European world.

ROMAN CIVILIZATION

In 509 B.C., in the bright morning of Greece's Golden Age, a small city-state in Italy won its independence from the militaristic northerners who had ruled it for a century. Within 250 years Rome became master of all Italy and within another 250 years of the whole of the Mediterranean world and nearly all of Europe west of the Rhine and south of the

Danube. For nearly 500 years more the Roman Empire constituted a monument to military prowess, statesmanship, administrative capacity, and engineering skill.

The Roman heritage has survived because of the solidity and durability with which the Romans built. Aqueducts, straight roads, and domed and barrel-vaulted buildings of towns and villas still exist. More subtle were the grammatical foundations that enabled Latin to survive, to be parent to five modern languages, and to condition the crude language of our Anglo-Saxon linguistic forebears. Roman law was a masterful combination of precedent, decrees, and scholarly creation. Informed by equitable practice, and rationalized and codified by Emperor Justinian in the sixth century A.D., Roman law became the basis of the Church's canon law, and the handmaiden of early modern absolutism. It was ultimately the basis of the law of most European nations from France to Russia, of international law, and one of the founts of our own Anglo-American law. The Roman *jus naturale* (natural or fundamental law) nurtured the constitutionalism of European civilization; its concern with right and justice as practical and attainable objects, not abstract ideals, has been one of the great civilizing influences of all time. Roman law served to keep alive the memory of the Roman genius for good government and contributed to Europe's nostalgia for Rome's order and grandeur.

THE ADVENT AND RISE OF CHRISTIANITY

During the five centuries from the ministry of Christ to the fall of Rome, Christianity grew from a small band of persecuted followers of a publicly executed and repudiated messiah of the Jewish people to become the great unifying force in Western society. Christianity derived from its Judaic origins the idea of one universal God and the law of Moses. The unique contribution of the New Testament was the idea of the redemption of mankind from sin to life everlasting through the love of God in Christ's sacrifice. The Christians' claim of Christ's divinity put them outside the pale of Judaism, but it did not alter the basic contribution of Judaism to the new faith.

Decisive to the future success of Christianity was the work of Saul of Tarsus, or St. Paul, a Jew and a Roman Citizen, who had never known Christ personally but who, following a miraculous conversion, broadened the new faith to attract non-Jews. Propagandist, organizer, and mediator, Paul's zeal and common sense, his mysticism and practicality, won converts and created cells of believers throughout the eastern part of the empire and in Rome itself. The promise of a better life in the next world, the equality of all men in the sight of God, and the expression of love in Christ's sacrifice appealed strongly to the poor, whose lives were hard and empty of hope.

Great variety existed in the Church's organization in the first century, with major responsibilities resting in the hands of laymen. As communication between the cells increased, episcopacy (the institution in which bishops claim spiritual descent from the original Apostles) and a professional priesthood developed. Episcopacy followed the Roman administrative pattern: bishops exercised authority over a city and its environs (a diocese) and archbishops oversaw a number of bishops (a province), usually from the capital of a Roman province. A few archbishops, calling themselves "patriarchs," asserted even wider jurisdiction, which extended in some cases beyond the frontiers of the empire. The greatest prestige attached to the bishop of Rome, who was also an archbishop and patriarch of the West. Rome's growing claim to ultimate authority over all other bishoprics was resisted by the great Eastern patriarchates of Alexandria, Antioch (both founded, like Rome, in apostolic times), Constantinople (the new imperial capital after 330), and finally Jerusalem (made a patriarchate in 451 out of respect for its place in sacred history).

Harsh, though sporadic, persecution did much to strengthen Christianity. Alone among the popular religions Christianity forbade emperor worship, even to the point of death. This rigidity won admiration and respect. It also held tremendous attraction for responsible Romans who were shocked by the declining morality of the later empire. The last major phase of persecution, under Emperor Diocletian (A.D. 284–305), was followed by toleration of the faith under his successor, Constantine, who was formally converted to Christianity on his deathbed in 337. By A.D. 400 Christianity was the official religion of the empire; no other religions were tolerated.

The fourth and fifth centuries were the great formative era of Christian doctrine. There was no universally accepted central authority; no bishop yet exercised unquestioned primacy over the entire Church, which included peoples of differing cultural heritages and traditions. It was almost inevitable, then, that on many important religious issues respectable and responsible spokesmen of the Church found themselves in serious opposition to one another. These disagreements were further aggravated by the enigmatic blending of simplicity and subtlety that characterizes the language of the New Testament, which invited disparate interpretations. Thus arose the typical heresies of the classical age of Christianity: Donatism, a dispute in North Africa over sacramental discipline; Pelagianism, a theological controversy over the relationship between God's saving grace and man's free will; and the series of dogmatic disputes over the nature of Christ: Arianism (stressing His humanity), Monophysitism (stressing His divinity), Nestorianism, etc. Complicating the situation were competing sects such as the Gnostics and the Manichees, who strove to combine Christianity with the religious tradition of ancient Persia and a good deal of occult lore. Many of these heresies were never completely suppressed; the difficult questions of logic which gave rise to some of them appeared again in other contexts and centuries.

The fourth and fifth centuries were also the era of the great theologians called Fathers of the Church. Basil the Great (330–379) formulated the rule of Eastern monasticism and gave the Eastern Church the most commanding of its liturgies, or services of worship. Jerome (d. 420) translated the whole Bible into Latin; his work decisively shaped the sacred language of the medieval West and remained the authorized translation for Roman Catholics into the present century. Ambrose, archbishop of Milan (374–397), Christianized much of the ethical content of the classics, especially the works of Cicero, a Roman statesman-philosopher of the first century B.C. Ambrose was also an important channel for the doctrinal speculations of the Greek Fathers of his century, whom the Latin-speaking clergy of the Western Church had difficulty understanding. His pastoral example became a model for the later Latin episcopate. In one dramatic and memorable showdown with his old friend the Roman emperor Theodosius I, he successfully defended the principle that in spiritual matters a bishop was the judge of *any* layman, regardless of his temporal position.

Augustine (354–430), bishop of Hippo in North Africa, had been a Manichee and then philosophically skeptical of Christianity before he succumbed to the arguments of his mother Monica, Christian Neoplatonism, and Ambrose. He was the most dynamic, prolific, and in some ways most original of the Western Fathers. He argued that human knowledge depends in some way on divine illumination, he asserted the primacy of God's grace and the moral futility of unaided human effort in the scheme of salvation, and he stressed the paramount practical importance of unity in the Christian community. He proposed as the ideal form of Christian society an eternal City of God unattainable on earth and far transcending the visible Church as well as the secular state. In his *Confessions* he pioneered the tradition of individualistic self-examination which has become one of the most typical features of the Western mentality. Augustine's influence on Christian thought in the West was to be all-pervasive, even when misunderstood. It moved materialists and mystics, popes and the opponents of the papacy, and held special appeal in later centuries for ascetics, humanists, Calvinists, Counter-Reformation Catholics, and even existentialists of the twentieth century.

By 476, when the barbarian Odoacer deposed the last Western emperor, Christianity in the West possessed the institutions, the doctrine, the clergy, the unity, the discipline, and the zeal to bridge the wide gulf that was opening between the comfortable order of the Greco-Roman past and the unknown, unpromising future.

THE SLOW BIRTH OF EUROPE

Prior to the collapse of the Roman Empire in the West there had been no "Europe" except in a shadowy geographical sense. The frontiers of the empire had indeed extended to the highlands of Scotland, the mouths of the Rhine, and even across the Danube into what is now Rumania, whose name and language are indicative of its origins. But the empire also included large areas of North Africa and western Asia; the Mediterranean did not so much divide Europe from Africa as it united the disparate, far-flung provinces of the empire about the capital. As long as Rome remained the center of the ancient world, a truly European civilization could not emerge.

THE FALL OF ROME

The empire reached its peak of power and prosperity in the century before the reign of Emperor Marcus Aurelius, who died in 180. Thereafter its western portions underwent a gradual decline, politically, economically, and culturally. The removal of the capital to Constantinople (330) constituted a major watershed in the development of European civilization. It began the separation of the empire into East and West, with the East the wealthier, more advanced area and the West increasingly subject to incursions of barbarians from both within and without the empire. What remained of the empire in the West was a hollow shell, which finally crumbled under its own weight.

Although it is very difficult, perhaps impossible, to establish a generally recognized "cause" or sequence of causes for the fall of the Roman Empire and of classical civilization, the chief symptom of that collapse was probably the failure of the Romans to maintain, much less to improve upon, the institutions and organizations that had made them great. The Roman world paid a price for peace and order in the form of taxation to maintain the army and the imperial bureaucracy; it exchanged its economic surplus for stable government. With the growth of corruption and inefficiency in the central government, the price became too high. The always increasing burden of taxation varied inversely with the benefits that government conferred. The result was the inability to collect sufficient revenue to maintain essential services and order. With the decay of Roman power, transportation and trade became more hazardous and costly; pirates infested the Mediterranean and robber bands controlled the mountain passes. The great Roman roads fell into disrepair, and in some areas the pavement was even dug up for use as building material. Long-distance trade fell to a mere trickle.

Because of the decline in trade, the *latifundia* (large estates) that had once produced surpluses for urban markets became more self-sufficient, and cities dwindled in size. Rome itself, which had several hundred thousand inhabitants at its height in the second century, fell to but a few thousand at its nadir in the tenth. The decline in population, whatever its immediate causes, affected rural areas as well; by 476 the population of the western half of the empire may have been less than two-thirds of the population under Marcus Aurelius. In northwestern Europe a manorial system of economy characterized by self-sufficient villages began to take shape. Thus, a major feature of the decline of ancient civilization was the gradual reversal of economic life to a primitive subsistence basis.

THE GERMANIC INVASIONS

North of the Rhine and the Danube lived numerous Germanic tribes. Although the Romans called these people barbarians, the Germans were by no means naked savages. They practiced settled agriculture and had an intricate structure of social organization based on kinship and personal loyalty. They were also effective warriors. The defeat that they inflicted on Roman legions at the battle of Teutoberg Forest in A.D. 9 was so decisive that it caused the Emperor Augustus to give up permanently the idea of extending the boundaries of the empire beyond the Rhine.

In time the Romans and the immediately neighboring Germans settled down to generally peaceful relations. They traded with one another, and some German tribes moved inside the empire or settled down along its borders as allies (*foederati*) and border guards. The Romans also employed Germans as mercenaries in their legions, so that by the third century most of the soldiers and many of the generals were of German origin. In this way many Germans became partly Romanized, although they did not give up entirely their barbarian ways, such as an abhorrence of urban life. By the same token the empire became increasingly barbarized.

The gradual Germanic penetration of the empire was transformed into a mass movement by the sudden invasion of Europe by the Huns in the last quarter of the fourth century. These nomads poured out of central Asia and fell upon the Germanic tribes, thereby starting a great wave of migration from one end of Europe to the other. Many Germans looked for refuge behind the fortified frontiers of the empire. The Romans, unable to hold back the human flood, decided to admit the Germans as allies. This served only to hasten the disintegration of Rome, for the barbarian tribesmen swept through the empire, sacking Rome itself on several occasions. The various tribes finally settled in different sections of the empire, which they took over for themselves — the Visigoths in Spain, the Vandals in North Africa, the Franks in Gaul, the Burgundians in southeastern France, and the Angles and Saxons in Britain. In Italy German mercenaries under Odoacer deposed the Western emperor and set up their own king in 476 — a year that is often given as the traditional date for the end of the Western empire. The emperor in Constantinople sent the Ostrogoths, another Germanic people, to win back Italy for him, but the victorious Ostrogoth leader Theodoric took over Italy as his own kingdom. Emperor Justinian (527–565) made a last desperate bid to win back the West and restore the unity of the Mediterranean world. Although he at first enjoyed success, a new wave of barbarians, the Lombards, swept into the Italian peninsula, conquered most of it, and left only a few areas still under the rule of the emperor in Constantinople.

The ease with which the German invaders carved out kingdoms for themselves demonstrates the extent to which the empire had decayed. The invaders formed a minority — often a very small minority — in the lands they conquered; yet the Roman citizens who lived there offered little resistance. Apparently they had become so alienated from the Roman imperial government, and the conditions under which they lived had deteriorated so badly, that they saw no purpose in struggling to preserve the empire. Coming as warriors and frequently as conquerors, the Germans imposed themselves on the native inhabitants. They partially dispossessed and sometimes intermarried with the old Roman aristocracy, and exploited the common people, most of whom had already been reduced to serfdom.

The Germans had no purposeful intention of destroying Roman civilization. Even after the final overthrow of the Western empire they continued to acknowledge a vague allegiance to the emperor of Constantinople. Nevertheless, their triumph brought classical civilization in the West to an end. The German rulers lacked the political experience and the trained bureaucracy to preserve the Roman form of centralized government. Since German society was based upon tradition and custom, the conquerors would not accept the Roman system of written laws, courts, and administrative decisions; they supplanted Roman legal procedures with their own crude practices. The individual German was bound by ties of blood to a "folk" and considered himself responsible only to the customs and laws of his tribe, no matter where he went. He gave unpaid service to his king in war and peace out of personal loyalty, but he fully expected a tangible reward for this. Taxation he saw as a device for the personal enrichment of the king rather than a normal source of public revenue, so that the kings found it almost impossible to raise the money needed to run governments, and administration remained rudimentary.

The decline in economic life that had begun in imperial times continued. Similarly, the downward trend in intellectual activity was accelerated by the Germanic conquests. The Romans themselves showed little interest in the enrichment or even the survival of their own literature and art, while the Germans rarely mastered Latin and added nothing

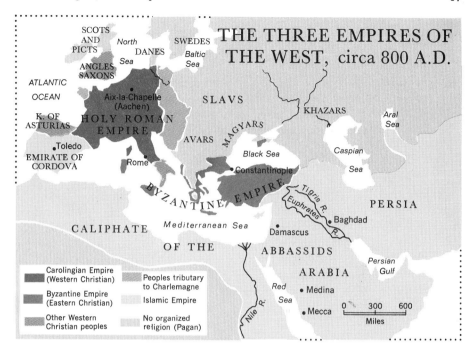

THE THREE EMPIRES OF THE WEST, circa 800 A.D.

SCOTS AND PICTS
ANGLES SAXONS
ATLANTIC OCEAN
DANES
North Sea
SWEDES
Baltic Sea
SLAVS
KHAZARS
Aral Sea
Aix-la-Chapelle (Aachen)
HOLY ROMAN EMPIRE
K. OF ASTURIAS
MAGYARS
AVARS
Toledo
EMIRATE OF CORDOVA
Rome
Black Sea
Caspian Sea
BYZANTINE EMPIRE
Constantinople
Tigris R.
Euphrates R.
PERSIA
CALIPHATE
Mediterranean Sea
Damascus
Baghdad
OF THE
ABBASSIDS
Nile R.
Red Sea
ARABIA
Medina
Mecca
Persian Gulf

Carolingian Empire (Western Christian)
Byzantine Empire (Eastern Christian)
Other Western Christian peoples
Peoples tributary to Charlemagne
Islamic Empire
No organized religion (Pagan)

0   300   600
Miles

to the cultural legacy of the ancient civilization. By the middle of the seventh century the Roman Empire was no more than a memory in most of western Europe and an ill-remembered one at that. It would be a long time, though, before thoughtful Europeans would be able to conceive of any other model for effective large-scale government.

CAROLINGIAN EUROPE

Of all the Germanic tribes the Franks created the strongest state. Led from the fifth to the early seventh centuries by a series of strong rulers of the Merovingian dynasty, they conquered much of France. Later Merovingian rulers were weaklings, but fortunately for the Franks a new line took power in the eighth century. This dynasty was called Carolingian from its greatest member, Charlemagne or Charles (Carolus) the Great. Charlemagne (768–814), the second king of his line, set out to create a European empire that would rival that of ancient Rome. He pushed beyond the Frankish frontiers to make himself ruler of what are today the Low Countries, Switzerland, most of Germany, Bohemia, Austria, and parts of Denmark and northern Spain. He overthrew the Lombard kings of Italy and conquered the peninsula down to and including Rome. His empire thus became the first broad-based European state. This fact received symbolic recognition when, on Christmas Day in 800, Pope Leo III crowned Charlemagne as emperor of the Romans in the huge basilica of

St. Peter built by Constantine. The so-called Holy Roman Empire, as Voltaire maliciously described it in the eighteenth century, was neither holy, nor Roman, nor an empire; but far outlasting Charlemagne's own Frankish territorial empire, it gave Europeans a sense of unity and coherence as well as continuity with a more glorious past. Its final dissolution occurred at the hands of Napoleon in 1806, after an existence of more than a thousand years — and Napoleon, who enjoyed being called a new Charlemagne, only dissolved that empire in order to clear the title for his own.

Charlemagne's policies encouraged the sense of European unity in other respects. A devout Christian, he supported the pope's claims to spiritual leadership over the entire Christian community, even though he insisted on maintaining personal control over the dispensing of ecclesiastical patronage. He subsidized scholars and artists and strongly supported the Church's efforts to revive classical learning. He tried to impose uniform liturgical practices and educational programs on all his lands and took advantage of any chance to reconcile the diverse legal traditions of his subject peoples. He succeeded in a sweeping monetary reform and established a system of coinage and accounting based on the silver standard, of which the pounds, shillings, and pence of Great Britain are direct — although of course greatly altered — descendants. On the other hand he continued the Germanic tradition of division of inheritance. Only the death of most of his sons before him saved his empire from immediate breakup, and civil war broke out during the reign of his only surviving son and successor, Louis the Pious (814–840). In 843 the empire disintegrated into three main parts, one approximating modern France, another western Germany, and the third an uncertain borderland between them extending southward into Italy. Charlemagne's ambitious but ambiguous legacy to Europe thus contained the seeds of both unity and strife.

THE THREAT OF ISLAM

The unity of fledgling Europe was endangered by the rapid advance of another new and even more vigorous civilization in the seventh century. Islamic or Moslem civilization, based on the religious teachings of the prophet Mohammed, exploded with the fury of a desert whirlwind from its home in the Arabian peninsula. Mohammed, who was a merchant before he became a religious leader, borrowed heavily from Judaism and early Christianity. Although he denied the divinity of Christ, he accepted Jesus and the ancient Hebrew prophets as spokesmen of the one true god, Allah. Mohammed regarded himself as the last and greatest of the prophets. In the Koran, the holy book of the Islamic religion, he stressed not only monotheism but also life after death, including the rewards of heaven and the punishment of hell. Another principle of Islam required the faithful to engage in the *jihad* or holy war against unbelievers.

By the time of his death in 632, only ten years after the beginning of his rise to power, Mohammed had established control over the principal cities of Arabia. The most spectacular phase in the expansion of Islam came immediately after his death. In less than two decades a few hundred thousand desert nomads from Arabia, proud and fanatical, wrested control of Syria, Egypt, and Libya from the Byzantine (Eastern Roman) Empire and overran the once formidable Persian Empire. Civil wars among rival Arab leaders slowed the pace of conquest for a time, but it accelerated again at the end of the seventh century, spreading Islam to the banks of the Indus River, central Asia, and along the shore of North Africa.

In the year 711 the Moslems, a mixed force of Arabs and Berbers, crossed the Strait of Gibraltar and invaded Visigothic Spain. It proved an easy conquest. In less than two years the Moslem forces extended their control to all but the most northern mountain fringes of the Iberian peninsula. Islamic armies also crossed the Pyrenees and invaded Frankish Gaul. Although turned back at Tours in 732 by Charles Martel, grandfather of Charlemagne, they continued to menace the Frankish state for many years.

As a result of their conquests in the Greek-speaking Eastern empire, the Arabs took over much of the learning of classical Greece. They drew great wealth from the control of trade routes between East and West, built great cities with spectacular palaces and mosques, and founded important schools. Moslems became the world's leaders in scientific and philosophic thought — a position that they held for several centuries. During the intellectual revival of western Europe in the eleventh and twelfth centuries many Christian scholars went to Moslem Spain to study classical philosophy and science. Modern mathematics is based upon the Arabic system of notation; algebra was an Arabic invention. Many ancient Greek authors are known to us today only through Arabic translations. Western civilization owes a large debt to Islam, her precocious and once threatening half-sister.

VIKINGS AND MAGYARS

While the Christians of western Europe were still defending themselves from Moslem attacks in the south, another fierce breed set upon them from the north. The Vikings or Northmen in Scandinavia were distant relatives of the Germanic tribes who had taken over the legacy of Rome. Late in the eighth century they began to pour out of their northern homeland.

Unlike other Germanic migrations, those of the Vikings took place by sea and were connected with both trade and piracy. The Vikings expanded in many directions, sometimes to make sudden piratical forays and return to their homeland, sometimes to settle permanently in distant lands. When they discovered uninhabited islands in the North Atlantic, including Iceland and Greenland, they colonized them, preserving their own language and customs in the new environment. Elsewhere they settled as conquerors over native populations and soon adopted the native culture. Vikings became rulers in Scotland, England, Ireland, France, and Russia. The province of Normandy in western France was named for the Northmen (Normans) who settled there in the tenth century, and in the next century their descendants established new Norman kingdoms in Sicily and England.

The Viking invasions began to taper off in the tenth century, and political conditions became more stable in both Scandinavia and western Europe. Christian missionaries penetrated the northern countries and by the year 1000 had made many converts. A century and a half later all the kings of the Viking homelands had become Christians, and Scandinavia entered the mainstream of European culture.

In the ninth century a nomadic people called Magyars, whose ancestors had come from central Asia, rode into the Danube valley and settled down on the alternating plains and marshes of what is now Hungary. From there they raided neighboring Germany and Italy and even went as far as eastern France. Shortly after the year 1000 they accepted Christianity and began to imitate the ways of European civilization.

MEDIEVAL CIVILIZATION IN ITS PRIME

At the beginning of the second millennium of the Christian era three competing civilizations occupied Europe and the Mediterranean basin: Islamic, Byzantine, and Western European. Of the three, the European was the most backward. The Arabs took over and built upon the civilizations of the lands that they conquered. The Byzantine or old Eastern Roman Empire had lost some of its former power and glory but remained an impressive center of culture. Its influence extended far beyond the contracted boundaries of the empire into Slavic lands and the Near East as well as western Europe. The emperor was universally regarded as pre-eminent among the world's rulers, and Byzantium itself (or Constantinople) was deemed to be the greatest, most brilliant city in the world. Western Europe, however, was on the eve of its first great age of expansion. Over the next three centuries it grew in population, wealth, and the arts of civilization and expanded territorially in both the south and east. Before the end of this age of expansion Western civilization equaled if it did not surpass its rivals in culture as well as in political and military power.

FEUDALISM

The political basis of medieval civilization was feudalism. Although historians and anthropologists have discovered similar systems of sociopolitical organization in many different parts of the world, to which they have extended the name feudalism, the feudalism of medieval western Europe was distinctive in both its origins and its manifestations.

Feudalism developed as a response to the peculiar conditions of western Europe from the ninth to the thirteenth centuries — specifically the breakdown of central authority, the increasing self-sufficiency of the economy, the ties of personal loyalty and dependence of the Germanic tribes, and the necessity for defense against invaders from all directions. Under feudalism a mounted fighting man, the knight, usually held a grant of land, called a fief or *beneficium,* from his superior or feudal lord. The grant gave him the right to receive an income from a particular estate or manor. In return he became the lord's vassal and had to swear oaths of homage and fealty which implied that he would at the lord's command present himself for military service, perhaps with a number of retainers, and provide his lord with certain other services. He had the duty of maintaining order on his estate and collecting various fees or feudal dues from his dependents. Subinfeudation was permitted; that is, a vassal could grant similar rights and privileges to those below him in the social scale. In short, feudalism was a method of government in which political authority was fragmented, with private individuals, the vassals, exercising public powers.

Two points about feudalism are of particular importance. In the first place, feudalism applied only to the ruling (and fighting) classes of medieval society — perhaps 5 per cent of the population. Although the common man, typically a peasant, was affected by the feudal system, he was not a part of it. Second, it is useful to distinguish feudalism from manorialism, a closely related but different institutional pattern.

ECONOMIC ORGANIZATION: THE MANORIAL SYSTEM

Throughout the Middle Ages — indeed, throughout the history of Europe until very recent times — most of the people obtained their basic subsistence from agriculture or related occupations. Therefore, climate and geography exercised a profound influence on individuals, communities, and entire societies. The characteristics of the terrain, the fertility of the soil, the amount of rain all combined to dictate the kinds of crops that could be grown. Along with the level of technology, they also dictated the productivity of the soil and thus the maximum density of the population.

The characteristic unit of settlement, especially in northwestern Europe, was the peasant village; the characteristic form of economic and social organization was the manorial system. This system began to take shape in the last centuries of the Roman Empire. It represented a remarkably successful adaptation of social and economic institutions to the peculiarities of soil and climate in a period characterized by local self-sufficiency. A typical village might contain from 20 to 200 households (perhaps 80 to 1,000 inhabitants). The majority of villagers were normally in a state of serfdom, that is, bound to the lord on whose land they lived and subject to him. Whether they were serfs or freemen (and there were numerous gradations within and between these two categories), the external features of their lives differed little. The houses were usually rude, one-room structures made of mud and wattle, thatched with straw, having a single low doorway, no windows, and a hole in the roof that served as a chimney. There were no barns, and in winter the livestock shared quarters with the family. The pace of life was determined by the rhythm of the seasons — punctuated, on occasion, by periods of famine, epidemic, and enemy invasion.

The villages usually lay in the midst of huge open fields. Within each field a peasant household cultivated a number of strips of land in common with other households with adjoining strips. The size of the strips varied greatly within villages or regions. A normal peasant holding was divided into dozens or scores of strips totalling about thirty acres. In addition to cultivated fields, each village possessed common pastureland and woodlands or forests. The church was the center of social life, and usually a crude mill, a smithy, a community oven, and a wine press supplied community necessities. Cloth was woven from yarn spun at home by women from local wool or flax by means of a distaff (hence the "distaff side"; the spinning wheel was a comparatively late invention). Most other commodities in common use were produced locally in household or village.

The relationship of villagers to the feudal nobility, their superiors in the social hierarchy, varied from place to place and time to time. Usually each village had near it a castle or manor house, in which the feudal lord or his representative lived. In principle the lord's function was to provide protection and enforce justice among the villagers. In return the villagers had to cultivate the demesne, the lord's land, give him various labor services and other dues, and be subject to his discipline. In practice such a relationship frequently degenerated into a system of outright exploitation. On some estates — especially in the vicinity of towns after the revival of commerce, where markets offered peasants the opportunity to sell surplus produce for money — the peasants gradually emancipated themselves from direct subservience, substituting payment of money rents for labor services or dues paid in produce.

ECONOMIC REVIVAL AND THE GROWTH OF TOWNS

In the second half of the eleventh century Europe entered upon an era of economic growth marked by improvements in farming techniques, a rise in population, the clearing of much new land for the production of food, an increase in the size and number of towns, and an expansion in trade, both local and international. Heavy wheeled plows drawn by teams of as many as eight oxen came into wide use to turn over the heavy soils of western Europe. Three-field rotation often replaced more wasteful systems of tillage by which each year villagers allowed half or more of their land to go unplanted. Under the three-field system the villagers planted a field for two years in succession and then fallowed it for a year to allow it to regain its fertility. The resulting increase in output and expansion of agriculture into newly cleared areas helped increase the population. The surplus production was exchanged for manufactures of the growing towns, breaking down the tendency toward manorial self-sufficiency.

New towns sprang up and old ones grew nearly everywhere in western and central Europe, but most strikingly in Flanders and northern Italy. The Flemish centers specialized in the manufacture of woolen cloth, while the town economy of Italy depended mainly on international trade, particularly of the importation of silks, spices, and other expensive wares from the Orient. Trade relations were soon established between Flanders and northern Italy, at first overland via the fairs of Champagne in northern France, later by sea through the Strait of Gibraltar. Trade continued to spread through western Europe, permitting greater local and regional specialization in production and larger accumulations of wealth.

The growth of towns and trade created a new element in European society. The people of the towns — the bourgeoisie (from *bourg,* town) — stood outside the existing social patterns. Most feudal lords did not understand or have sympathy with the needs of townspeople, although the Counts of Flanders and Champagne were outstanding exceptions. Feudal law was inadequate for handling commercial litigation, and the bonds of serfdom clashed with the personal freedom that townsmen needed to go about their business. Everywhere in western Europe the towns struggled to gain local autonomy and personal freedom for their citizens. Most of them succeeded, though some were more successful than others, depending upon the strength of their rulers; thus, the towns of France and England gained less autonomy than those of Germany and Italy. This difference turned out to be of much importance to later political development, for it allowed the monarchs of France and England to draw upon the wealth of the townspeople and build up centralized states, in contrast to the rulers of Germany and Italy.

THE CRUSADES

Between 1095 and 1270 the West launched a succession of expeditions to wrest the Holy Land from the Turkish Moslems. The Crusades were inspired by the popes, most of them were led by kings, and they attracted innumerable Europeans of the middle and lower classes, including women and children, as well as the flower of the nobility. They represented the first era of European expansion, a forerunner of the outward thrust of Europe in the fifteenth and sixteenth centuries.

Although ultimately unsuccessful in their primary aim, the Crusades affected most aspects of medieval civilization. Two major developments resulted. The first was increased trade between the East and Europe in luxury commodities, raising the standard of living in Europe and contributing to a more civilized life among its aristocrats. Carried on by such cities as Venice, Genoa, and Pisa, the trade stimulated navigation, cartography, and the new techniques of ship construction, and spurred manufacturing and banking in Italy, Flanders, and other parts of northern Europe. No less significant was the broadening of the West's horizons. European man came into contact with civilizations different from and even superior to his own. The Crusades perceptibly shifted European attention from its northern preoccupation, dating from Charlemagne's era, to a Mediterranean focus, restoring the Mediterranean world to a major creative role in Europe. All these changes added fresh excitement to native cultural development, and thereby contributed to the brilliance of the High Middle Ages and the Renaissance.

THE ROLE OF THE CHURCH

The Crusades illustrate only one facet of the effective power of the medieval Church. The Church provided the framework for medieval life. It was a pervasive, continually civilizing influence. It anointed the king at his coronation, sanctified the feudal contract in the vassal's oath to the lord, and blessed the fields of the manor. Its holy days provided the peasant respite from a hard life. To the castle it added the church as the dominant monuments of civilized man in an imperfectly civilized landscape. Its sacraments prepared king and cottager alike for salvation. It attempted to govern the rules of warfare. It provided resorts of spiritual rest and mills of spiritual exertion in monasteries and nunneries. It controlled a large part of the economy by its vast landed estates. Most of the art, literature, and music of the age awaited its inspiration and throve on its patronage. All knowledge was subject to its approval, and truth was its sole preserve. Its clergy was a privileged order, and the service of God was an avenue for social advancement, wealth, and power in both Church and state.

From the late ninth to the early eleventh century, the Latin clergy passed through an eclipse. The papacy was a pawn in local Italian politics, many bishops became satellites of vigorous lay noblemen, and the monasteries and parish churches were dominated by lay patrons. Clerical immorality, the sale of church offices, and inattention to clerical responsibilities were rife. In a little over a century the situation dramatically altered. From a monastery founded at Cluny in France in 910 there emanated a movement for reform of the Church that in the last half of the eleventh century "captured" the papacy itself in the person of Pope Gregory VII (1073–1085). The Gregorian reforms removed the election of the pope from the German emperor and Roman nobility to a college of cardinals, wrested the appointment of bishops from lay hands by a series of compromises in which appointment was shared by pope and lay ruler, and thoroughly purged the Church of most of the abuses that had reduced its effectiveness.

In the process of reform, the seeds of a greater papal ·ambition were planted. The papacy emerged as a territorial power in Italy and became involved in German imperial politics in a way that eventually proved more corrosive of its authority than its old subservience had been. Pope Innocent III (1198–1216) humbled the kings of France and England and emerged the arbiter of European politics. He bequeathed to his successors in the thirteenth century a constant struggle, first with the emperor and then with the emerging monarchies. The most extreme assertion of papal supremacy over secular rulers occurred during the pontificate of Innocent IV (1243–1254) who deposed both a king of Portugal and Emperor Frederick II in 1245.

The Gregorian reforms contributed to the revitalization of Western thought which made the twelfth and thirteenth centuries a golden age of learning and spirituality. Perhaps the most distinctive attribute of this creative period was the method of reasoning known as scholasticism. Profoundly shaped by the writings of Aristotle, which became once more available in Latin translations from the Arabic (through Spain) or the original Greek (from Byzantium), scholastic philosophy of the thirteenth century undertook a massive systematization of all serious thought about everything of importance. Stimulated and disturbed by their contact with the intellectual values of pagan antiquity and with the more recent doctrines of Moslem and Jewish thinkers, the Latin scholastics surpassed their masters in devising an institution for the support of sustained teaching and research — the university. The first universities evolved at Bologna, Paris, and Oxford in the half-century before 1215. Similar in their origins to artisan or merchant gilds, these associations of teachers and students were characterized by a degree of autonomy guaranteed by papal or royal charter (or both), and by detailed regulations concerning admission, courses of study, examinations, licensing, internal organization and behavior, and so on. Scattered throughout the Western world from Portugal and Scotland to Sweden and Hungary in the fifteenth century, the university pattern was exported to the Americans with the earliest waves of European colonization, and now covers the earth. Few other medieval inventions have proved so durable.

The most outstanding product of the university was the work of Thomas Aquinas (1226–1274), who wrote prolifically on a vast range of subjects. Thomas argued that man could arrive at truth by the two roads of revelation and reason. Revelation, he said, appeals to faith through the authoritative teaching of the Scriptures, the Fathers, and the living Church, while reason appeals to logical assent through the rigorous discipline of philosophy. The final statements of these two methods cannot really contradict one another, since both derive ultimately from God. Filled with lucid and dispassionate optimism, Aquinas died without quite finishing his *Summa Theologica,* which was to have summarized and reconciled all the major currents of theology and philosophy known to him.

Thomistic scholasticism never won universal assent even among the Catholic clergy, for parallel to the intellectual revival occurred a spiritual revival that was antagonistic to the spirit of Aquinas's synthesis. In Western Christendom the new piety created an emotional fervor that found outlets in an emphasis on love, devotional practices, and the cult of the Virgin Mary. Two great orders of begging friars, the Dominicans and the Franciscans, were founded on its principles. Dominic (1170–1221) and his friars turned to the towns, largely neglected by the existing church organization, to preach redemption and a return to orthodoxy. Francis of Assisi (1182–1226) embraced poverty in order to minister to the needs of all men in total self-effacing love, teaching men of God's love by example. The friars represented the opposite of scholasticism in original motivation. Yet Aquinas was a Dominican, and by the end of the thirteenth century the Dominicans and Franciscans dominated the universities.

MEDIEVAL CULTURE

Medieval culture appears at first sight to have been wholly dominated by the religious concerns of Western man. Cathedrals and abbeys are the material vestiges of medieval man's other-worldliness. Most of the music of the Middle Ages that has come to us had a liturgical use, either as the music of the Mass or as hymns of devotion. Sculpture and painting have survived as incidental decoration to a harmonious whole: statues of Christ, the saints, and the prophets graced the façades of churches; illumination of the initial letters of manuscripts graced the Word of God or books of devotion. Although much of the literature of the High Middle Ages is written in the vernacular (instead of Latin), it is often moralistic and didactic. The personalities and points of view that we encounter in literary forms as diverse as popular drama, Joinville's *Life of St. Louis,* Dante's monumental *Divine Comedy,* or Chaucer's *Canterbury Tales* all breathe the air and reflect the light of an unquestioned and unquestionably Christian cosmos.

Not that the daily life of Christendom is presented in a perfect or idealized form in these works — far from it. Medieval authors and audiences enjoyed scandalous and ribald tales as much as edifying ones, but the existence of the frivolous, obscene, or even evil faces of reality did not seem then to put the right order of the world in doubt. Serious literature dealing with predominantly secular material, such as the epic *Song of Roland,* Chrétien de Troyes's *Lancelot,* Gottfried von Strassburg's *Tristan,* or the rambling *Romance of the Rose,* paid close attention to those aspects of feudal and chivalric loyalty and honor and to those varieties of fantasy or allegory that devout churchmen were busily baptizing and absorbing. Even carnal love was increasingly recognized by the Church as a valid human attribute related to God's perfect love. Nor did the cruder Goliard poetry — doggerel composed by vagabond scholars and renegade priests mocking virtue, the pope, the clergy, even Scripture, and extolling vice — or the light Latin poetry of university students incur much wrath. The medieval Church, while it felt compelled to correct error and extirpate heresy, was not overly concerned with the vanities and verbal licentiousness of the orthodox.

The medieval church building can be seen as a symbolic reaching heavenward — especially the towering Gothic cathedral, which had been released from the more massive and fortresslike Romanesque by technical advances in the twelfth century. The history of Gothic architecture is marked by the use of more and more glass, fewer walls, richer colors, and increasing unconventionality of decorative forms. The asceticism and martial discipline of a civilization embattled by barbarians to the north, Moslems to the south, and the devil everywhere in the early Middle Ages gave way in the twelfth century to a society more sure of itself, less concerned with mere survival, and having greater room for love, compassion, lightness, and joy. Gothic architecture, the literature of romance, the growth of melody and polyphonic harmony in music following the earlier Gregorian chant — all testify to a civilization that had passed through the smoke and din of battle to the sights and sounds of joy. It is a sad axiom of human experience, however, that no joyous state is constant, and no balance of dynamic forces capable of long duration.

THE CRISIS OF THE MEDIEVAL ORDER

From the thirteenth to the end of the fifteenth century the history of medieval Europe was dominated by three major developments. The first was the destruction of Byzantium, the rise of its successors, and the impact that this had on western Europe. The second was the rise of national monarchies at the expense of the feudal lords and feudal system. The third was the progressive decline of the papacy's temporal influence over the emerging national monarchies and the reduction of its spiritual authority over individual Christians. These three developments amounted to a crisis of the established order of medieval Europe. They presaged the Renaissance, the Protestant Reformation, and the emergence of absolutism in early modern Europe.

THE ECLIPSE OF BYZANTIUM

As the twelfth century witnessed medieval civilization at its prime in the West, it also witnessed the beginning of the decline of Byzantium. The causes of decline stemmed from six centuries of almost continuous hostile invasions. The demands made by this long confrontation weakened the economy, induced corruption, and brought about political instability.

The Crusades accelerated the decline. The West's intervention did not seriously reduce Turkish pressure on Byzantium, and it introduced a discordant Western element in the persons of the ambitious feudal lords who seized and held Byzantium from 1204 to 1261. Even after the Byzantine Greeks had regained the empire, remnants of the Western lords retained control of a number of key regions of the empire. The Crusades also put Byzantium's trade in the hands of the northern Italian port cities.

In the mid-thirteenth century the Seljuk Turks, who had long mounted the Islamic attack on Byzantium and against whom the Crusades had been raised, were themselves defeated by a new wave of invaders from Asia, the Mongols. The Seljuk empire disintegrated, but over the next century the Ottoman dynasty organized a new Turkish empire which attacked Byzantium with new vigor. The Ottoman Turks absorbed the outer regions of Byzantium by a brilliant policy of aggression and conciliation. In 1453 they took Constantinople itself and the Byzantine Empire disappeared.

Politically the Ottoman Empire was the successor of Byzantium, but in a more subtle way Byzantium's successor was the Russians, a people who, though never colonized by Byzantium, accepted the Christian faith of Constantinople. Russia, in the centuries after the fall of Con-

---

St. Sophia

> "So the church has become a spectacle of marvellous beauty, overwhelming to those who see it, but to those who know it by hearsay altogether incredible. For it soars to a height to match the sky, and as if surging up from amongst the other buildings it stands on high and looks down upon the remainder of the city, adorning it, because it is a part of it, but glorifying in its own beauty, because, though a part of the city and dominating it, it at the same time towers above it to such a height that the whole city is viewed from there as a watch tower. Both its breadth and its length have been so carefully proportioned, that it may not improperly be said to be exceedingly long and at the same time unusually broad. And it exults in an indescribable beauty." Procopius (d. 562?) BUILDINGS, tr. H. B. Dewing and G. Downey (London, 1940).

Shostal

stantinople, exerted the formative influence on Slavic peoples and emerged as a major power in eastern Europe.

KIEVAN RUSSIA

Early in the first millennium of the Christian era nomadic Slavic tribes settled down in the valley of the Dnieper River. In time the tribes formed federations, each with a city as its center. In the eighth century Northmen — called Varangians in Russia — came down the Russian rivers from their northern homeland and hired themselves out to the cities as mercenaries. In time chieftains of the Varangian bands took over as rulers of the cities that had hired them. Early in the ninth century the Varangian ruler of Kiev succeeded in establishing his supremacy over the rulers of the other cities. Thus was created the loose union of semiautonomous city-states called the Kievan federation.

The Kievan state lay along one of Europe's most important trade routes — the river network that runs from Scandinavia to Constantinople and the East. Just as in the West, economic activity expanded, population rose, wealth increased, towns grew in size and importance, improvements were introduced into agriculture, and much new land was taken under the plow. As in western Europe, too, religion played an important part in the evolution of social and political life. The Russians became Christians late in the tenth century. Linked both economically and culturally to Constantinople, they chose to embrace the Eastern or Greek Church rather than Latin Christianity. This was a major determinant of future Russian history, for the split between the Greek and Latin Churches helped to alienate Russia from the intellectual and social currents of Western lands for centuries.

The growth and prosperity of Kievan Russia continued into the last part of the twelfth century, but the loose federation was fatally weakened by civil wars among rival princes. Then waves of nomad invaders from the Asian steppes, climaxed in the thirteenth century by a great invasion of the Mongols or Tatars, destroyed the Kievan federation. The great mass of the Russian people fled to the northeast into what is now the north-central part of European Russia. There, cut off almost entirely from Western contact, the Russians lived for the next two centuries in small principalities whose rulers constantly warred with one another. The principalities paid tribute to the Mongol conquerors, who ruled loosely over Russia from their headquarters in the southern steppe. During the era of the "Tartar Yoke," Russian political, economic, and intellectual life suffered a nearly disastrous decline.

In the fourteenth century the frontier principality of Moscow emerged as the dominant power in northern Russia. As the Mongol hegemony disintegrated, Moscow, supported by the Russian Orthodox Church, extended its power over the other principalities. Late in the fifteenth century the Muscovite ruler adopted the title "tsar" (caesar) of "all the Russias," began to assume Byzantine-like control over the church in Russia, and autocratically began the destruction of the old nobility's power from his seat in the Kremlin, a chilly bastion in the heart of Moscow.

THE EMERGENCE OF NATIONAL MONARCHIES

The king in feudal society was an anomaly, a leftover from an older tradition of centralization, such as that of the Carolingian Empire or of tribal chieftainship. Certain regalia and panoply surrounded him, he was solemnly anointed at his coronation, and his title "emperor" or "king" denoted a ruler who knew no lord on earth. His authority was limited, however, by the large areas of political, administrative, judicial, military, and economic power that both his vassals and the vassals of his vassals held.

During the eleventh century the French and English monarchies began a long campaign against the power of the great feudal nobles, which produced at the end of the Middle Ages two emergent nation-states unified around their royal governments. In Germany and Italy during the same period exactly the opposite occurred, although in Germany the monarch enjoyed initially a position more favorable than that of the king of France.

By the mid-eleventh century Anglo-Saxon England had experienced only a limited degree of feudalization. When William, duke of Normandy, conquered England from its last Anglo-Saxon king in 1066, he instituted full-fledged feudalism with three significant limitations: he succeeded in enforcing the principle that all land was held ultimately from him and military service was owed only to him; bishops and abbots were no different from lay nobles in their feudal obligations to him; and the assets of the Anglo-Saxon king were retained by the Conqueror. The latter included direct taxation, militia service outside the feudal web, communal courts of justice, and the office of the sheriff, a local official responsible solely to the king. From this advantageous position William and his successors for the next 150 years built up a bureaucracy, central and local, for the collection of taxes, defense, and the preservation of order or the "king's peace." Relying upon their feudal responsibility to do justice to their vassals and their regal responsibility to dispense justice to all others in the old communal courts, the Norman kings evolved a common law — common to all England. Litigants, seeking a more equitable justice, flocked to the king's courts, the only courts in which they could receive trial by jury and the courts with the most effective sanctions. This led to the eclipse of the feudal courts of the king's vassals, to his own profit, and to the enfeebling of the feudal nobles. By commuting feudal services due in kind into money, the monarch was strengthened

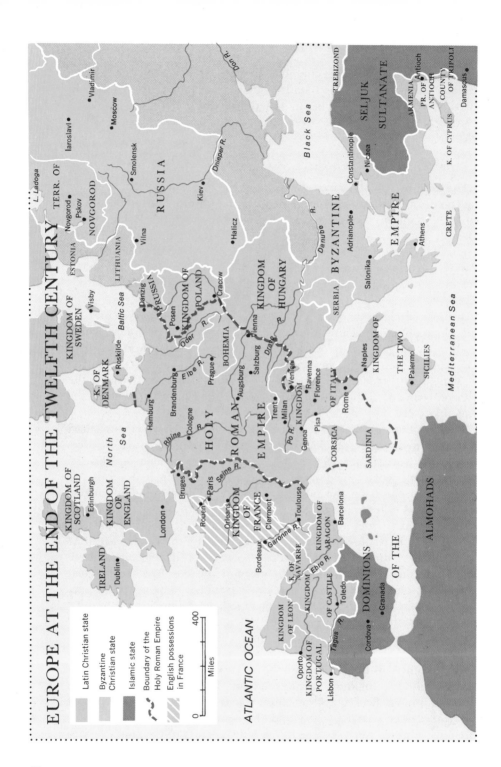

EUROPE AT THE END OF THE TWELFTH CENTURY

ATLANTIC OCEAN

Latin Christian state

Byzantine Christian state

Islamic state

— Boundary of the Holy Roman Empire

English possessions in France

0   400
Miles

KINGDOM OF SCOTLAND
Edinburgh

KINGDOM OF ENGLAND
London

IRELAND
Dublin

North Sea

KINGDOM OF SWEDEN
Visby

K. OF DENMARK
Roskilde

Baltic Sea

TERR. OF NOVGOROD
Novgorod
Pskov

ESTONIA

LITHUANIA
Vilna

L. Ladoga

Iaroslavl
Vladimir
Moscow

RUSSIA
Smolensk
Kiev
Halicz

Don R.

Dnieper R.

PRUSSIA
Danzig
Posen
KINGDOM OF POLAND
Cracow

Oder R.

BOHEMIA
Prague

Brandenburg
Elbe R.
Hamburg
Cologne
Rhine

HOLY ROMAN EMPIRE
Augsburg
Salzburg
Vienna
Trent
Milan
Po R.
Genoa

KINGDOM OF HUNGARY

Drave R.

Venice
Ravenna
Florence
Pisa

KINGDOM OF ITALY
Rome

SERBIA

Danube R.

BYZANTINE EMPIRE
Adrianople
Salonika
Athens

Black Sea

TREBIZOND
Constantinople
Nicaea

ARMENIA
PR. OF ANTIOCH
Antioch
COUNTY OF TRIPOLI
Damascus

SELJUK SULTANATE

K. OF CYPRUS

CRETE

Mediterranean Sea

KINGDOM OF FRANCE
Paris
Rouen
Orleans
Clermont
Seine R.
Bordeaux
Garonne R.
Toulouse

Bruges

KINGDOM OF NAVARRE
Ebro R.
Barcelona
KINGDOM OF ARAGON

KINGDOM OF LEON
KINGDOM OF CASTILE
Toledo
Cordova
Granada

KINGDOM OF PORTUGAL
Oporto
Lisbon
Tagus R.

ALMOHADS

DOMINIONS OF THE

CORSICA
SARDINIA
THE TWO SICILIES
Palermo
Naples
KINGDOM OF

32

fiscally. Despite occasional collisions with assertive popes or archbishops of Canterbury, the Norman kings generally had the support of the Church. They also forged an alliance with London and other developing towns of England, who depended upon the king for their liberties, the preservation of order, and the expansion of trade.

In the thirteenth century baronial reaction set in. The barons, the chief vassals of the king, wrested Magna Carta from King John in 1215, reforming specific abuses of royal power but not retracting those extensions of royal power that were already part of the fabric of government. A baronial rebellion placed John's successor under baronial control from 1258 to 1265 and resulted in the transformation of the feudal right of a vassal to be consulted in extraordinary circumstances into a parliament, a meeting of the king with the bishops, the barons, and representatives of the towns and the countryside. Both Magna Carta and Parliament had future potentialities for withstanding royal aggrandizement, but they did not check the centralizing tendency of the English monarchy. In the last quarter of the thirteenth century Edward I (1272–1307) brought the English medieval monarchy to the apex of power and, in turning Parliament into a tool of the monarchy, further reduced the nobles' strength. Parliament, as a tool of baronial faction, would play its part in the deposition and murder of four English monarchs during the fourteenth and fifteenth centuries, but by the beginning of the fourteenth century the English monarchy had already undermined feudalism as an institution capable of preventing the emergence of the monarchic nation-state.

The French kings of the Capetian dynasty between 987 and 1328 evolved many institutions and methods similar to those used by William the Conqueror and his successors to reduce the independence of the great feudal barons. The Capetians had further to go, however, and started from a smaller and feebler base. In 987 the domain of the king of France was a small nucleus of the whole kingdom, centered on Paris; he had vassals with domains many times greater than his own. By skillfully playing feudal politics, the Capetians advanced their regal power and expanded their domain.

The French development of centralized monarchy was slightly behind that of England, since it started from less favorable foundations and necessitated the acquisition of domain, whereas William took his domain entire at the Conquest. By the end of the Middle Ages, however, the French monarchy was in almost as favorable a position as the English, for in France there was no focus for feudal opposition to the centralizing tendency of the monarchy. French feudal opposition was based on provincial autonomy. It was not coordinated in the Estates-General, a representative assembly that developed tardily and rather haphazardly in the fourteenth century.

The Hundred Years' War, from 1338 to 1453, between English monarchs who claimed the throne of France and the Valois dynasty, successors of the Capetians, ultimately strengthened the hand of the French king by making him the center of patriotic resistance to English invasion. After Jeanne d'Arc (1412?–1431) rallied the French king and people to ultimate victory, the French monarchy was more powerful than ever. England's defeat helped to plunge that land into a civil war, the Wars of the Roses, from 1455 to 1485, that was the last disruptive shudder of the English feudal nobility.

The political development of Germany offers a striking contrast to that of England and France. In Germany the central power had to retreat before the demands and pressures of local lords and the Church. This withdrawal represented a reversal of the trend that had started in the tenth century when the Saxon dynasty established itself as ruler over a great part of Germany and managed to gain a large measure of control over the feudal nobility. Encouraged by their success in Germany, the Saxon kings tried to extend their rule to neighboring lands and succeeded in making themselves kings of Italy. In 962 Otto I was crowned emperor by the pope as the successor to Charlemagne, and the title lodged with German rulers for the next 850 years.

Otto's intervention in Italy proved a heavy burden on his successors, for they found themselves constantly involved in Italian and papal political conflicts and wars. Moreover, the emperor's power depended upon the continued support of the Church. As long as the Church had no quarrel with him, things went well. When Gregory VII launched the long struggle to free the papacy from imperial authority, the power of the emperor began to ebb. The rivalry between the Hohenstaufen and Welf families for the imperial throne in the twelfth century brought chaos, and feudalism took deeper root in Germany. During the twelfth century the emperors kept their German realm from disintegration, but by the middle of the thirteenth century all effective power in Germany was in the hands of the great lords and powerful churchmen. Germany, which in the tenth century had been moving toward centralization, broke down into a welter of independent principalities and cities and was destined to remain disunited for another six hundred years.

In Italy the growing strength of the towns, prospering from the expansion in economic life, had challenged the emperor's claims to dominate that land. In 1176 the cities of Lombard plain in northern Italy, supported by the pope, had defeated the feudal army of Emperor Frederick Barbarossa and won near-independence. In the first part of the thirteenth century Emperor Frederick II (1194–1250) seemed for a time on the verge of reestablishing imperial control over Italy. His ambitions ran counter to the wishes of the papacy, however, for Rome was determined that no secular ruler should be master of the whole peninsula. The pope rallied Frederick's enemies, made the war against him a holy crusade, summoned a council that deposed Frederick, and constantly stirred up public opinion against him. Frederick was never decisively defeated, but after his death the towns of northern and central Italy became completely independent of imperial authority. Sicily and Naples, acquired by the emperors through marriage, also were lost to them when, at the pope's invitation, Charles of Anjou, brother of France's King Louis IX, invaded Sicily and made himself ruler. The papacy's victory over the emperors meant that Italy became a land divided among many independent city-states in the north and center, the papacy at Rome, and the Angevin kingdom in the south. Like Germany, Italy was destined to remain disunited for another six hundred years.

DECLINE OF THE PAPACY

A head-on collision between the papacy and Philip IV of France, a monarch of the new style, resulted in the humiliation of Pope Boniface VIII in 1303 and the removal of the papacy to Avignon in the south of France in 1305. The issue was the right of the king to tax the clergy of his kingdom. The king won and the papacy lost. From 1305 to 1378, the so-called Babylonian Captivity of the papacy, seven popes resided in Avignon, and the pontiff was a tool of the French throne's ambitions and an object of contempt to France's enemies, England and the Holy Roman emperor. From 1378 to 1409 two popes presided simultaneously, and from 1409 to 1417 three popes vied for authority — the pawns of power politics, hurling anathemas at each other. The Great Schism was healed only by a return to the device that had brought unity to the early Church, the council. The Council of Constance (1414–1417), comprising all the bishops of the Western Church, restored the unity of the Church by electing a single new pope. Reform was postponed, but the council asserted that a council was superior to the pope and provided for regular councils. Successive popes stood in fear of councils, with their reforming zeal and their representation of secular national interests in the persons of bishops who were dependent upon their kings and princes. In the early fifteenth century the pope and councils effectively canceled each other out, and none of the reforms of the Church and its clergy that had been moved by the councils were implemented. After 1450 there were no more councils for a century — the next one was called to attempt to heal the breach known as the Protestant Reformation, which was provoked in part by the earlier failure to reform.

The era of the Babylonian Captivity and the Great Schism seriously weakened the prestige and authority of the papacy, and gave national monarchs the opportunity to erode the power of the Church as they had eroded the power of the feudal nobility. A more fundamental erosion was that of the allegiance of individual Christians to the Church of the papacy. The last quarter of the fourteenth century witnessed two heretical movements in two countries. In England the Oxford theologian John Wyclif argued for a church without property and attacked a wide range of clerical abuses. He enjoyed royal protection, although in the years following his death in 1384 his followers — called Lollards — were heavily persecuted. Wyclif's doctrines reached Bohemia and moved a professor-priest there, Jan Hus, to mount a similar attack. His movement was nationalistic, aimed at severing Bohemia's connection with the German emperor. Despite the burning of Hus as a heretic at the Council of Constance, his followers, the Hussites, fought the king of Bohemia and the papacy to a compromise which recognized as orthodox in Bohemia certain religious practices that were condemned everywhere else. In common with the earlier Albigensian and Waldensian heresies of the thirteenth century in southern Europe, the Lollards and Hussites advanced anticlericalism or opposition to the priest and his power as an intermediary between man and God. These heresies were popular, enjoying large followings. Moreover, the Hussite heresy was national, giving clear evidence of how far the Church had grown away from lay sentiments and aspirations. When popular anticlericalism, patriotism, and the ambitions of kings and princes coalesced, the stage was set for the Protestant Reformation of the sixteenth century.

ECONOMIC CHANGE AND
THE EXPANSION
OF EUROPE
CHAPTER TWO

The economic expansion of the twelfth and thirteenth centuries slowed down or leveled off in the first half of the fourteenth century and about the middle of the century gave way to economic stagnation, lasting in most parts of Europe approximately one hundred years. In spite of the depressed conditions, the period witnessed continued changes in economic organization and commercial institutions in the direction of modern capitalism. Meanwhile improvements in the techniques of shipbuilding and navigation facilitated a renewed interest in oceanic exploration and overseas trade. Toward the middle of the fifteenth century economic activity picked up and, reinforced by the progress of exploration and discovery, began a sustained expansion that carried on into the seventeenth century.

THE GREAT DEPRESSION OF
THE LATER MIDDLE AGES

Evidence of the great depression that began in the middle of the fourteenth century can be found in the movement of population and prices, in the changes in agriculture, commerce, and industry, and in social unrest and political disturbances. Although the depression varied in intensity in different parts of Europe and was broken by minor fluctuations, it was sufficiently general to be considered a European phenomenon. The evidence is not yet complete enough to establish with certainty the causes of the depression, but one of the most obvious symptoms (and a possible cause) was the great decline in population.

FAMINE, PLAGUE, AND WAR

The population expansion of the eleventh, twelfth, and thirteenth centuries had already begun to level off by 1300 for reasons that are still unclear. Probably the society had expanded to the limits of its food supply provided by the available technology. In any event, in the first half of the fourteenth century local famines became more and more frequent. Then came the greatest natural disaster of the Middle Ages — indeed, one of the greatest of all times — the Black Death or bubonic plague (although it may not have been the bubonic plague exclusively). It carried away as much as one-third of the total population and an even larger proportion in some localities.

The plague apparently reached Europe from central Asia, possibly even from China, but it spread first through the Genoese. Genoa had a colony on the Crimean peninsula in the Black Sea, which the Mongols besieged in 1347. Siege conditions alone would have been conducive to an epidemic; but there is a story that the Mongols, who were themselves afflicted by the plague, catapulted the bodies of men who had died of it into the fortress of the Genoese — an early form of biological warfare. Some of the survivors returned to Europe as unsuspecting carriers of the disease. It spread first along the main routes of communication and trade, afflicting mostly the thickly settled, highly urban areas of Europe. Italy, France, and England each apparently lost between one-third and one-half of its population in a very few years. The Italian city of Siena reportedly lost 70 per cent of its population in a single year; neighboring Florence lost 50 per cent. Peripheral areas of Europe off the main trade routes escaped the worst ravages of the plague. No area, however — from the Mediterranean to the Arctic, from Constantinople to Iceland — escaped it entirely. The disease became more or less endemic, breaking out again every ten or fifteen years for the remainder of the century.

Wars both civil and international added to the effects of plague and famine, further reducing population and causing disorganization and dislocation. Wars were standard in medieval Europe, but they increased in intensity in the fourteenth and fifteenth centuries. Domestic strife further weakened the already staggering economy and brought other social and political changes. The strife took two principal forms: civil war, such as the Wars of the Roses in England, between rival ruling groups or cliques, chiefly nobles and other aristocrats; and genuine social revolt in which the mass of the people rose against their rulers. The first type resembled a war between independent states (to which it was often related) and usually affected only those directly involved either as participants or as peasants whose land was fought over and ravaged. The social revolts, however, profoundly influenced the lives of the masses. They, in turn, broke down into two main varieties: peasant revolts and risings of urban workers.

In the 1320's the weavers of Ghent and other Flemish cities rose against their merchant employers and feudal lords, temporarily controlled the countryside, provoked the enmity of the peasants, and even formed an alliance with the English king. In 1358 the peasants of northern France, burdened with oppressive taxation by the Hundred Years' War, rose in a Jacquerie (from the name Jacques Bonhomme, meaning a common fellow, and applied to peasants indiscriminately). They burned chateaus and murdered feudal lords and royal officials. In Florence in 1378 the *ciompi,* workers in the woolen industry, waged a full-fledged class war against their masters and temporarily gained control of the city. Peasant unrest in England flamed into revolt in 1381, merging with the religious protest of the Lollards.

These are but a few examples of the social discontent that boiled over into rebellions and class wars. The majority were brought on by economic distress caused by the plague or declining markets and production and aggravated by oppressive taxation and other restrictions or regulations of the ruling classes. They resulted in arson, murder, pillage, and indiscriminate slaughter. Without exception avenging nobles or masters eventually put them down with equal or greater ferocity.

AGRARIAN CRISIS

The reduction in population and the dislocations caused by the wars resulted in a shortage of labor to till the soil and the resulting abandonment of much land. The labor shortage produced a rise in money wage rates and made it easier for the peasants to secure better terms from their lords, either by deserting their original holdings and going to another area, or by threatening to do so. Thus the labor shortage led both to the emancipation of serfs and to the commutation of traditional labor services and payments in kind into payments in money. Peasants rented the land for a fixed payment of money instead of giving labor service and a share of their produce to the lord. This process had already taken place to some extent in western Europe, but the depression following 1350 greatly hastened it throughout the area of manorial economy. Some lords who had formerly engaged in demesne farming — that is, who had cultivated their own demesne either for subsistence or for a marketable surplus — found it so difficult and expensive to get labor that they rented out their demesnes and became *rentiers* or rent receivers. These developments contributed in western Europe to liberation of the serfs and gradual decay of the institution of serfdom.

In eastern Europe a very different process took place. While the serfs in western Europe were being freed, the peasants in eastern Europe, who had been relatively free, were subjected to a process of enserfment that eventually developed into its worst form — that found in Poland and Russia in the eighteenth and early nineteenth centuries. Such town life as had existed in the past declined in eastern Europe. The lords became more powerful in society, at the expense of both the townsmen and their nominal sovereigns, and had a free hand to exploit the peasants. Although there were other factors, the growing political power of the lords in eastern Europe seems to have been the main reason for the paradox that serfdom there increased at the very time that serfdom in western Europe declined.

COMMERCIAL AND INDUSTRIAL DEPRESSION

The agrarian crisis and the decline in population were accompanied by a commercial and industrial depression. The demand for merchandise declined. Manufacturing became more expensive because of the shortage of labor and rising wage rates. The combination of these two factors led in the late fourteenth and early fifteenth centuries to increased regimentation and regulation of commerce and industry, as merchants and manufacturers sought to protect their shrunken markets and get the most from their expensive labor. The regimentation and regulation operated at both the local and the regional or international levels. At the local level the rules of the artisan associations, called gilds, became more restrictive as opportunities diminished. The gilds limited the number of master craftsmen who might belong; they exacted higher entrance fees, limited output (no master might produce more than a certain quota of goods), enforced strict working rules (no master might hire more than a given number of apprentices or do night work), and limited new members to the sons or relatives of deceased masters.

At the regional and international levels shrinking markets and declining profits produced a rivalry approaching open warfare, such as that between Venice and Genoa or Florence and Pisa. Florence increased its importance in this period of depression by crushing its rivals with superior political and military force and reducing them to the status of satellites.

Another result of the depression in industry was an attempt by manufacturers, especially those who were not among the favored few, to escape

---

Table 1   *Age of Economic Decline, 1300 to 1475*
Grain Prices in England, France, and Alsace
(1351–1375 = 100)

Period	England	France	Alsace
1351–1375	100	100	100
1376–1400	71	48	71
1401–1425	70	55	64
1426–1450	70	74	74
1451–1475	54	33	49

Source: W. Abel, *Agrarkrisen und Agrarkonjunktur in Mitteleuropa* (Berlin, 1935), p. 34.

from the higher labor costs and restrictive regulations of the gilds by moving their workshops to the countryside. There they obtained cheaper labor and could regulate industrial processes as they chose. This movement was especially successful in England, where the gilds and master manufacturers were not as powerful as elsewhere. They were powerful enough to regulate the trade in the city, but they could not prevent the development of industry in the countryside. A great woolen industry began to develop in England when the industrialists set up fulling mills on the streams in the west of England and in Yorkshire and induced the peasants to take up spinning and weaving in their cottages.

THE HANSEATIC LEAGUE

There were also attempts to regulate international trade. The Hanseatic League, the most famous attempt, was composed of German trading cities such as Lübeck, Hamburg, Bremen, Cologne, Danzig, Magdeburg, and Leipzig. The League grew out of the cooperation of merchants from these cities in foreign trading centers. In London all German traders lived together in the *Stalhof* or Steelyard, where they had special trading privileges and a certain amount of self-government free from the interference of the English king. They had a similar settlement in Bruges. In Venice at the *Fondaco dei Tedeschi,* the German factory or foundation, German merchants could get board and room in addition to special trading privileges. Bergen, Norway, was in effect a German city, as was Wisby on the island of Gothland in the Baltic. German colonies existed in several Russian cities. As a result of the increasing pressure on markets after the Black Death and the attempts of the Danish king to drive the German merchants out of Denmark, the cities from which the merchants came banded together in 1370 to establish the Hanseatic League as a formal political framework, although it was never more than a loose federation of independent towns.

The success of the league aroused the antagonism of other merchant groups, who eventually persuaded their governments to take positive action to break the League's power. With the return of prosperity in the latter half of the fifteenth century the component cities of the League, feeling that they had less to gain by subordinating their activities to group policy, began to break away and follow their individual interests. By the beginning of the sixteenth century the League had ceased to play an important role in European commercial affairs.

THE RISE OF MODERN CAPITALISM

It is impossible to give a precise definition of capitalism. Capitalism is a historical phenomenon, and historical phenomena do not have the neat precision of logical postulates or mathematical formulas. Without

FIORENZA

Florence in the Late Fifteenth Century

> *"Our beautiful Florence contains 270 shops belonging to the wool merchants'*
> *guild . . . also 83 rich and splendid warehouses of the silk merchants' guild.*
> *. . . The number of banks amounts to 33; the shops of the cabinetmakers . . .*
> *to 84; and the workshops of the stonecutters and marble workers . . . to 54.*
> *There are 44 goldsmiths' and jewelers' shops, 30 gold-beaters, silver wire-drawers,*
> *and a wax-figure maker . . . Sixty-six is the number of the apothecaries' and*
> *grocer shops; 70 that of the butchers, besides 8 large shops in which are sold*
> *fowl of all kind, as well as game and also the native wine called Trebbiano . . . ;*
> *it would awaken the dead in its praise."* From a letter of Benedetto Dei to a
> Venetian (1472), in G. R. B. Richards, ed., FLORENTINE MERCHANTS IN THE AGE
> OF THE MEDICI (Cambridge, 1932).

attempting a precise definition, therefore, we will simply list some of the
distinguishing features of modern capitalism.

BASIC CHARACTERISTICS OF CAPITALIST ECONOMY

Capitalism's most fundamental feature is private ownership of the
means of production, or private property. In this characteristic it differs
from collective or public ownership in the various forms of socialism and
from the extremely diffuse rights in property found in medieval Europe
in the period of manorial economy. Also significant is that capitalism
produces goods for sale on the market: it is an exchange economy, not
a subsistence economy. Private property and market-oriented production
bring out a third characteristic: economic decisions are in the hands of
private individuals who are primarily concerned with their own economic welfare. In this feature it differs from the centralized, compre-

hensive planning of production of socialism, and from the reliance of pre-capitalistic society upon custom or tradition for economic guidance.

Fourth, capitalism's market orientation leads to extensive use of money and credit and a system of prices. They are needed not only to facilitate exchange but also to quantify economic values and permit rational calculation. Such calculation — for example, of prospective profits and losses from alternative types of investment — is necessary to make the economy flexible and responsive to changes in consumer demand and the conditions of supply, as well as to stimulate the introduction of technological improvements. Although credit may not be strictly necessary to a capitalist economy, it is in fact an almost invariable accompaniment. It is usually by means of credit that the capitalistic entrepreneur (that is, the organizer of production) gains control over the resources, including labor, necessary for production.

Some authorities assert that a rational or predictable legal framework — a "government of laws, not of men" — is a prerequisite for the operation of capitalism. It is necessary, they maintain, in order to have laws that define and protect property, enforce contracts, settle disputes equitably, and prevent arbitrary interferences in private relationships by the sovereign power (whether he is a monarch or the head of a republican form of government). Such a legal framework greatly facilitates the operation of a capitalist system, and all fully developed capitalist systems operate in such an environment. A strong argument can be made from historical evidence, however, that capitalism contributed as much or more to the development of such a legal framework as the latter contributed to the growth of capitalism.

One aspect of a rational legal framework is a certain measure of equality before the law. This implies neither equality of economic circumstance nor political equality. It does mean, however, that if the greatest noble in the land owes a legally incurred debt to a petty tradesman and refuses to discharge it properly, the tradesman can force the noble to defend himself in a court of law. If this were not possible, capitalists would be wary of doing business with nobles — as, indeed, they have been throughout history, when political inequality has overridden legal equality.

Closely related to a rational legal framework is yet another characteristic, which is easily misunderstood: the necessity for at least a limited amount of personal freedom. This necessity raises certain questions in the study of capitalism: how much freedom is required, and what kind of freedom? Whose freedom? Need the workers be free? Is capitalism compatible with slavery? Obviously it is, for the American South before the Civil War was a capitalistic area, engaged in capitalistic agriculture, selling on a world market, and employing slaves. Nevertheless, for a capitalist system to operate there must be certain specific freedoms. Individuals must be free to dispose of their property; if a person owns property but is not free to sell it, he does not really have control of it. The freedom to enter into contracts — to agree to do certain things in return for certain considerations or rewards — is another essential freedom of capitalist organization. Substantial numbers of individuals must be legally free to go into any occupation or profession they choose. They must be free to undertake production — that is, to become entrepreneurs — if they can gain control of the necessary capital; and they must be legally free to seek employment from others. Geographical and social mobility — the freedom to move up (or down) through the various social ranks — are essential and are related to the concept of equality before the law. On the other hand, democracy or political freedom — the freedom of the masses to participate in elections and government — is not a necessary part of capitalism. Only very recently have the masses been able to participate in the process of government; and when they have, there have been frequent departures from the capitalist system.

These are a few of the distinguishing features of capitalism. They do not exhaust the list, nor can they be accepted without qualifications. Like civilization itself (and capitalism, as well as other forms of economic organization, is a part of modern civilization), they did not all come into existence at any one time and place. They developed gradually, piecemeal, along with the system itself.

HISTORICAL STAGES OF CAPITALISM

If the distinguishing features of capitalism did not all arise at once, can it be said when the system began? Certainly some of the features existed in the ancient world. The Greeks and other ancient peoples used money, possessed private property, and had an elaborate network of trade and markets. Roman law contained many of the concepts basic to modern capitalist legal doctrines. It might be claimed that capitalism has existed since the beginning of human history, or at least since the beginning of civilization. Such a statement is meaningless, however. Modern capitalism differs profoundly from the forms of economic organization of the ancient world and from those of the non-Western world in modern times. Modern capitalism is, in fact, a distinctive contribution of the Western world to modern civilization.

One historical description of modern capitalism is that it is a form of economic organization that developed gradually in Europe in the later Middle Ages, spread to the Western Hemisphere and other parts of the world in early modern times, and reached its peak development late in the nineteenth century. The rise of modern capitalism was not a specific episode in world history, for it had been growing more or less continuously — at least until the early twentieth century — since the early Middle Ages. Nevertheless, certain periods of history stand out as especially important for its development. One was the period of economic expansion of the twelfth and thirteenth centuries, which witnessed the birth of modern capitalism. The cities of northern Italy were its cradle. Another extremely important period lasted from the end of the eighteenth century to the beginning of the twentieth century, when capitalism became the dominant form of economic organization throughout the Western world and made significant penetrations into the non-Western world. A third period of crucial importance lasted roughly from the mid-fourteenth to the early or mid-seventeenth centuries, the era with which this chapter is concerned.

Although the great depression of the fourteenth century served in some ways as a check on the development of capitalism, in other respects it stimulated its development in western Europe. Under the pressure of increased competition the capitalist entrepreneurs further refined, rationalized, and elaborated the techniques and institutions that they had inherited from their Italian and Flemish predecessors of the twelfth and thirteenth centuries. Sometime in the fifteenth century a new period of expansion began. It is difficult to give the exact date of the revival because it varied from one region to another. The year 1475 might be used as an average date for the beginning of the upswing. This second great expansion of the economy, enormously stimulated by geographical discovery and overseas exploration, carried on through the sixteenth and into the seventeenth centuries, running down at different times in different parts of Europe.

The growth of population provides the clearest evidence of the economic expansion of the early modern period. After the Black Death the population continued to decline until near the end of the fourteenth century, when it finally stabilized at about 60 per cent of its maximum in the first half of the century. For reasons still not understood it began to grow again around the middle of the fifteenth century, surpassing its previous maximum early in the sixteenth century and pushing on to about one hundred million at the middle of the seventeenth century, when it leveled off again. At that time the population of Europe was over twice as large as it had been at its low point in the beginning of the fifteenth century.

THE ELABORATION OF CAPITALIST TECHNIQUE

All sectors of the economy — agriculture, industry, commerce, and finance — benefited from the general economic expansion, but commercial and financial developments were most significant for the progress of capitalism. As in the period of depression, merchants and financiers continued to improve and refine their techniques of doing business and introduced new institutions. Double-entry bookkeeping, introduced in the early fourteenth century in Italy, gave businessmen a method of keeping closer check on the status of their affairs and permitted them to calculate more accurately the possible outcomes of their ventures. Maritime insurance, utilized in a rudimentary fashion as early as the twelfth century, greatly reduced the hazards of loss faced by individual businessmen. Soon after the invention of printing in about 1450 merchants' newsletters — embryonic *Wall Street Journals* — appeared, helping merchants to keep abreast of prices in distant ports and of commercial and political developments that might have a bearing on their business.

As the scope of commerce widened and the volume of transactions increased, business organizations themselves became larger and more complex. During the expansion of trade in the twelfth and thirteenth centuries the typical merchant had been a traveling merchant, working on his own account and carrying his goods with him. The principal exception was a simple form of business association, the *commenda,* in which a man who did not travel provided the capital for an associate who did. Usually such partnerships were limited to a single voyage, although they could be renewed frequently. Even before the great depression a significant change in the organization of business had taken place with the rise of the resident or sedentary merchant, who conducted his business from a central office by means of numerous traveling employees, agents, and partners located in distant centers of commerce. In the course of the fourteenth and fifteenth centuries this form of organization became even more elaborate. The commenda took on new and more complex forms, and the "company" (*compagnia*), a forerunner of the modern corporation or joint-stock company, came into existence.

The sedentary merchant, unlike his peripatetic forebear, was in a position to extend his financial control over the processes of production as well as of distribution. The woolen industry of Florence, for example, employed as many as thirty thousand workers, mostly under the control of the great merchants. In some cases merchants accumulated so much wealth that they could no longer employ it themselves in their own businesses. They became bankers and financiers, financing the business of others, including that of popes, kings, and emperors. The famous Medici family of Florence was one example; the Fuggers of Augsburg in southern Germany were another.

The decline of the Champagne fairs in northeastern France in the early fourteenth century and the rise of Bruges in Flanders as the principal entrepôt for the Italian trade with northern Europe marked another stage in the development of capitalism. The city fathers of Bruges established a permanent, continuous *bourse* or market in place of periodic, temporary fairs. Other mercantile cities soon adopted this institution, notably Antwerp on the Scheldt River, which replaced Bruges as the major northern entrepôt near the end of the fifteenth century. The bankers of important commercial cities also established clearing houses to

AN EARLY FINANCIAL EMPIRE

★ Branch of the Medici Bank of Florence in 1455

▬ Boundary of The Holy Roman Empire

facilitate the payments of their clients, eliminating the need for coin in many transactions. Most bankers were private individuals or family firms who combined banking with money changing or mercantile operations, but in 1401 the city of Barcelona established the first public bank. It was followed by another in Genoa in 1407. The bankers also developed credit instruments, such as letters of credit and bills of exchange.

One of the factors contributing to economic expansion was an increase in the money supply. The output of the silver mines of central Europe declined in the fourteenth century, at first because the richest veins of ore had been worked out, then because of the ravages of the plague and the population decline. With the development of new mining techniques and the increasing demand for silver for both monetary and artistic uses, output increased once again after about 1450. The Portuguese brought back driblets of gold among the early fruits of their exploration of the African coast. The consequence of the increased supply of money, together with the continual debasement of coinage by sovereign rulers, was a gentle rise in prices. The largest increase in the money supply came in the sixteenth century, when an inflow of precious metals resulted from the discovery of the New World.

THE GREAT DISCOVERIES

The world in the second half of the twentieth century stands on the threshold of a great age of exploration, the exploration of space. Five hundred years ago, in the second half of the fifteenth century, Europe stood on the threshold of a great age of exploration also. The comparison presents some interesting parallels and contrasts.

Today it is a rare person who is not aware that great new discoveries are soon to be made in space. In the fifteenth century educated persons at least were aware of and curious about the possibility of discoveries of lands and peoples unknown to them or that they knew only through shadowy myths and legends. That is the principal similarity between the times; the differences are great. It is unlikely that astronautical explorers will discover new, hitherto unsuspected worlds in space that will compare in importance for us with the discovery of the Western Hemisphere, a new world for Europeans.

The risks involved for the men who made the first daring sea voyages into the unknown were much greater than for the first astronauts, brave though the latter may be. Magellan's expedition (1519–1522) set out with five ships and 243 men; three years later it returned without its commander — one ship and 18 half-starved, disease-ridden men. Nor was this an isolated example. Many expeditions did not return at all. If the expected losses in the exploration of space were anywhere near as great proportionately, it is most unlikely that the exploration would be undertaken.

Although the techniques were different and the risks were greater, the motives behind the explorations were quite similar to those of today. The rulers and statesmen who financed the explorations — then as now the cost was so great that only the resources of governments could suffice — sought wealth, power, and prestige for themselves and their countries. They were also moved by religious zeal, analogous to the ideological zeal that animates the race for space today, and by scientific curiosity. The brave but not necessarily virtuous men who actually made the discoveries were inspired by much the same motives. They also possessed the psychological trait essential to any hazardous undertaking, the spirit of adventure. Whatever the mixture of motives, the immediate goal of the early explorations was to find a sea route to the East.

EARLY CONTACTS WITH THE FAR EAST

In the thirteenth century, at the very time that the commercial revival reached its peak in Europe, the conquests of the Mongols created the largest empire thitherto recorded, stretching from Korea in the east to Poland and Hungary in the west. The pope and several European rulers sent emissaries to the court of the Great Khan, as the Mongol ruler was known, hoping to effect an alliance against the Moslems in the Near East. Although these attempts were fruitless, the Mongols willingly received European missionaries, craftsmen, and merchants. In 1289 the pope sent an Italian friar to assume the post of archbishop of Peking, where he built a flourishing Christian community and remained till his death in 1328. The Mongol rulers sent ambassadors to the kings of France and England and other European courts.

Conditions were therefore propitious for the establishment of direct contact with China, the heartland of the Mongol Empire. Among the earliest and most famous European merchants and travelers in China were members of the Polo family of Venice. In 1255 two brothers, Nicolo and Maffeo Polo, who had traded in the Black Sea area, traveled across central Asia, reaching China itself after several years and numerous adventures. They returned to Europe in 1269 but two years later again set out for China, this time accompanied by Nicolo's young son Marco. When they reached Peking in 1275, they received a gracious welcome from Kublai Khan (1214–1294), who proved to be a humane and enlightened ruler. For fifteen years Marco traveled throughout eastern Asia in the service of the Khan, returning to Italy in 1295. His book relating his adventures provided much information about Asia in that period. Meanwhile a lively trade had grown up between Europe and China, so that it became profitable to write and sell merchants' handbooks and travel guides describing the best routes, the chief commercial cities, and the principal goods in demand.

After about 1340 the Mongol Empire began to break up, and in 1368 a native, antiforeign dynasty, the Ming, overthrew the Mongols in China itself. The new dynasty excluded Europeans from China. Eastern products, especially pepper, cinnamon, and other spices from the Indies, continued to come into Europe, but at the eastern end of the route the trade was controlled by Arab merchants in the Indian Ocean, and at the western end by Venetians and Genoese in the Mediterranean. The trade was extremely lucrative, especially since the Venetians and Genoese followed monopolistic policies and excluded other Europeans from the eastern Mediterranean by diplomacy and force. Consequently, there was a persistent search for alternative routes to the East by land and sea. In the end the Portuguese finally achieved the breakthrough by finding an all-water route to the Indies.

BY SEA TO THE EAST

Notable technological developments in ship design, shipbuilding, and navigation took place in the later Middle Ages. The Mediterranean ships of Greco-Roman times had been mainly oared galleys with auxiliary sails. They were still a great factor in the Mediterranean commerce of the thirteenth and early fourteenth centuries, but their limitations for oceanic navigation are obvious. The early Norsemen performed heroic feats in similar, even smaller sail and oar-propelled boats when they discovered and settled Iceland, Greenland, and even (briefly) North America; but as events proved, their ships were quite incapable of sustaining large-scale overseas commerce.

The foremost improvements in ship design and shipbuilding were the replacement of the steering oar by a hinged rudder and the replacement of the single sail with five or six smaller, more easily handled sails. Together, these devices gave greater maneuverability and directional control and dispensed with the oarsmen. Ships became larger, more manageable, more seaworthy, and had greater cargo capacity, enabling them to make longer voyages. At about the same time a rudimentary magnetic compass, probably introduced from China, significantly reduced the large element of guesswork involved in navigation. Similar developments took place in cartography. Most medieval maps were highly stylized, not giving a true representation of distance and direction. Practical seamen began compiling books of sailing instructions, called portolans, including greatly improved charts.

The Italians had been leaders in the art of navigation. As early as 1291 the Vivaldi brothers of Genoa sailed down the Atlantic coast of Africa in an effort to reach India by sea, never to be seen again. In the thirteenth century Genoese and Venetian galleys began to make annual voyages through the Atlantic to Bruges and London. The Italians were conservative in ship design, however, and the lead was soon taken by seamen who sailed the open seas, especially the Flemish, Dutch, and Portuguese. The Portuguese, in particular, seized the initiative in all aspects of the sailor's art: ship design, navigation, and exploration. The vision and energy of one man, Prince Henry, called the Navigator, were chiefly responsible for the great progress in geographical knowledge and discovery made by Europeans in the fifteenth century.

Henry (1394–1460), a younger son of the king of Portugal, devoted himself to encouraging the exploration of the African coast with the ultimate object of reaching the Indian Ocean. At his castle on the promontory of Sagres at the southern tip of Portugal he established a sort of institute for advanced study to which he brought astronomers, geographers, cartographers, and navigators of all nationalities. From 1418 until the end of his life he sent out expeditions almost annually. Carefully and patiently his sailors charted the coast and currents, discovered or rediscovered and colonized the islands of the Atlantic, and established trade relations with the native chiefs of the African coast. Henry did not live to realize his greatest ambition. In fact, at the time of his death his sailors had gone little farther than Cape Verde, but the scientific and exploratory work carried out under his patronage laid the foundation for subsequent discoveries.

After Henry's death exploratory activity slackened somewhat for lack of royal patronage and because of the lucrative trade in ivory, gold, and slaves that Portuguese merchants carried on with the native kingdom of Ghana. King John II, who came to the throne in 1481, renewed the explorations at an accelerated pace. Within a few years his navigators pushed almost to the tip of Africa. Realizing that he was on the verge of success, John sent out two expeditions in 1487. Down the coast went Bartholomew Diaz, who rounded the Cape of Good Hope (which he at first named the Cape of Storms) in 1488; through the Mediterranean and overland to the Red Sea went Pedro de Covilhão, who reconnoitered the western edges of the Indian Ocean from Mozambique in Africa to the Malabar coast of India. The way was paved for the next and greatest voyage, that of Vasco da Gama from 1497 to 1499 around Africa to Calicut in India. As a result of disease, mutiny, storms, and difficulties with both his Hindu hosts and the numerous Arab merchants whom he encountered, da Gama lost two of his four ships and almost two-thirds of his crew. Nevertheless, the cargo of spices with which he returned sufficed to pay the cost of his voyage many times over, and was tangible proof of his success.

Seeing such profits the Portuguese lost no time in capitalizing on their advantage. Within a dozen years they had swept the Arabs off the Indian Ocean and established fortified trading posts from Mozambique and the Persian Gulf to the fabled Spice Islands or Moluccas. In 1513 one of their ships put in at Canton in South China, and by mid-century they had opened trading and diplomatic relations with Japan.

THE NEW WORLD

In 1483 or 1484, while the crews of John II were still working their way down the African coast, a Genoese who had sailed in Portuguese service and married a Portuguese presented himself at the Portuguese court. He came to ask the king to finance a voyage across the Atlantic in order to reach the East by sailing west. Such a proposal was not entirely novel. There was a general belief that the earth was a sphere. But was the plan feasible? Christopher Columbus, the Genoese, thought it was, although the weight of opinion was against him. John's advisers had a more nearly correct impression of the size of the globe than did Columbus, who thought that the distance from the Azores to the Spice Islands was little greater than the length of the Mediterranean. Although John had authorized privately financed expeditions west to the Azores, he concentrated his own resources on the more likely project of rounding Africa. His answer to Columbus was No!

Columbus persevered. He appealed to the Spanish monarchs, Ferdinand and Isabella. Although he impressed Isabella with his manner, his personality, and his ambitious ideas, she and her husband were engaged at the time in the last crusade, a war against the Moorish kingdom of Granada, and had no money to spare for such an unlikely scheme. Columbus tried to interest the realistic and economical King Henry VII of England, as well as the king of France, but in vain. At length, in 1492, Ferdinand and Isabella conquered the Moors. As a sort of victory celebration, and in hopes of scoring a triumph over their fellow monarch in Portugal, whose successes were becoming the envy of Europe, Isabella agreed to underwrite an expedition. In five small ships, by no means the equal of their Portuguese counterparts, Columbus and his crew set sail on August 3, 1492. After spending a month in the Canaries for repairs and losing two of its ships, the tiny fleet sailed westward for five weeks before sighting land on October 12.

For Columbus it was the culmination of a life's ambition. He thought he had reached the Indies. Though dismayed at their obvious poverty, he dubbed the inhabitants Indians. After a few weeks of reconnoitering amongst the islands, later called the West Indies, he returned to Spain to spread the joyful tidings. Since he had lost his flagship, the *Santa Maria*, by shipwreck in the islands, Columbus left some of his men in a fortified post on Santo Domingo. The following year he returned with 17 ships, 1,500 men, and enough equipment (including cattle and other livestock) to establish a permanent settlement. Within a few years the Spanish had several flourishing colonies. Altogether Columbus made four voyages to the western seas. He discovered the coasts of Central America and northern South America in addition to the islands, and persisted until the end of his days in believing that he had discovered a direct route to Asia.

Immediately following the return of the first expedition, Ferdinand and Isabella applied to the pope for a "line of demarcation" to confirm Spanish title to the newly discovered lands. This line, running from pole to pole at a longitude 100 leagues (about 330 nautical miles) west of the Azores and Cape Verde islands, divided the non-Christian world into two halves for purposes of further exploration, with the western half reserved for the Spanish and the eastern half reserved for the Portuguese. The next year, 1494, the Portuguese king in the Treaty of Tordesillas persuaded the Spanish rulers to set the line 370 leagues (about 1220 nautical miles) west of Cape Verde, the westernmost promontory of Africa — about 210 nautical miles further west than the 1493 line. This suggests that the Portuguese may have already known of the existence of the New World, for the new line placed the hump of South America — the beachhead that later became Brazil — in the Portuguese hemisphere. In 1500, on the first major Portuguese trading voyage after da Gama's return, Pedro de Cabral sailed directly for the hump and claimed it for Portugal before proceeding to India.

Cabral was not the first European to discover South America. Besides possible unidentified predecessors, Columbus himself had explored its coast in 1498, and several other explorers did likewise between 1498 and 1500. One of them, a Florentine agent of the Medici bank who resided in Seville, gave the new world his name. Amerigo Vespucci explored the northeast coast of South America in 1499 and discovered the mouth of the Amazon River. On subsequent voyages he concluded from studies of the flora and fauna that the continent could not be Asia. In letters to Europe he referred to it as the *Mundus Novus,* the New World. In 1507 a German geographer, Martin Waldseemüller, labeled it America in honor of Vespucci. At first the name referred only to South America. Both the Spanish and the Portuguese refused to use it, but the name caught on and was eventually applied to both continents of the Western Hemisphere.

Meanwhile explorers of other nations followed up the news of Columbus's discovery. In 1497 John Cabot, an Italian sailor who lived in England, secured the backing of Bristol merchants for a voyage on which he discovered Newfoundland and Nova Scotia. The following year he and his son Sebastian led a larger expedition to explore the northern coast of North America, but since they brought back no spices, precious metals, or other marketable commodities, their commercial backers lost interest. Cabot also failed to persuade Henry VII to provide financial support, though the king did give him a modest reward of ten pounds for planting the English flag in the New World. French merchants sent another Italian, Verrazano, to discover a western passage to India in the 1520's. A decade later the Frenchman Jacques Cartier made the first of three voyages that resulted in the discovery and exploration of the St. Lawrence River. Cartier also claimed for France the area later known as Canada; but, failing to find the hoped-for passage to India, the French, like the English, evinced no further immediate interest in the New World except for fishing on the Grand Banks of Newfoundland.

In 1513 the Spaniard Balboa discovered the "South Sea," as he called the Pacific Ocean, beyond the Isthmus of Panama. By the 1520's Spanish and other navigators had explored the entire eastern coast of the two Americas from Labrador to Rio de la Plata. It became increasingly clear not only that Columbus had not discovered the Indies but that there was no easy passage through the center of the new continent. In 1519 Ferdinand Magellan, a Portuguese who had sailed in the Indian Ocean, persuaded the king of Spain to let him lead an expedition to the Spice Islands by way of the South Sea. Magellan had no thought of circumnavigating the globe, for he expected to find Asia a few days' sailing beyond Panama, within the Spanish orbit as determined by the Tordesillas

Treaty. His main problem, as he saw it, was to find a passage through or around South America. This he did, and the stormy treacherous straits he discovered still bear his name. The "peaceful sea" (*Mare Pacificum*) into which he emerged, however, yielded not riches but long months of starvation, disease, and eventually death for him and most of his crew. The remnants of his fleet wandered aimlessly in the East Indies for several months. At length one of Magellan's lieutenants, Sebastian del Cano, took the one surviving ship and its skeleton crew through the Indian Ocean and home to Spain after three years — the first men to sail entirely around the earth.

OVERSEAS EXPANSION AND
ITS IMPACT ON EUROPE

The first century of European overseas expansion and colonial conquest — that is, the sixteenth century — belonged almost exclusively to Spain and Portugal. For Spain it was the *Siglo de Oro*, the golden century. The eminence that these two nations have achieved in history is due mainly to their pioneering in the discovery, exploration, and exploitation of the non-European world. Prior to the sixteenth century they had been outside the mainstream of European civilization; afterward their power and prestige declined rapidly until by the beginning of the nineteenth century they had sunk into a state of somnolence approaching suspended animation, from which they have not yet fully recovered. In the sixteenth century, however, their dominions were the most extensive and they were the wealthiest and most powerful nations in the world.

THE STAKES OF EMPIRE

By 1515 the Portuguese had made themselves masters of the Indian Ocean. Vasco da Gama returned to India in 1501 with instructions to halt the Arab trade to the Red Sea and Egypt, by which the Venetians had obtained spices for distribution in Europe. In 1505 Francisco de Almeida went out as first Portuguese viceroy of India. He captured or established several cities and forts on the East African and Indian coasts and in 1509 completely destroyed a large Moslem fleet in the battle of Diu. In the same year Alfonso de Albuquerque, greatest of the Portuguese viceroys, assumed his duties and completed the subjugation of the Indian Ocean. He captured Ormuz at the entrance to the Persian Gulf and established a fort at Malacca on the narrow strait between the Malay Peninsula and Sumatra, a post that controlled the passage to the Celebes and Moluccas islands from which the most valuable spices came. Finally in 1515 he captured Ceylon, the key to mastery of the Indian Ocean. His attempt to capture Aden at the entrance to the Red Sea was repulsed, and a small trickle of trade continued to take this old route, but it did not effectively interfere with the Portuguese monopoly. Albuquerque established his capital at Goa on the Malabar Coast; Goa and Diu remained Portuguese possessions until 1961. The Portuguese also established trade relations with Siam and Japan. In 1557 they established themselves at Macao on the south coast of China, which they still hold. Because of their small population they did not attempt to conquer or colonize the interior of India, Africa, or the islands but contented themselves with controlling the sea lanes from strategic forts and trading posts.

Although at first it looked less promising, the Spanish Empire eventually proved to be even more profitable than the Portuguese. Disappointed in their quest for spices and stimulated by a few trinkets plundered from the savages in the islands of the Caribbean, the Spanish quickly turned to a search for gold and silver. Their continued efforts to find a passage to India soon revealed the existence of wealthy civilizations on the mainland of Mexico and northern South America. Between 1519 and 1521 Hernando Cortez effected the conquest of the Aztec Empire in Mexico. Francisco Pizarro conquered the Inca Empire in Peru in the 1530's. By the end of the sixteenth century the Spanish wielded effective power over the entire hemisphere from Florida and southern California in the north to Chile and the Rio de la Plata in the south (with the exception of Brazil). At first they merely plundered the original inhabitants of their existing movable wealth; when this source was quickly exhausted, they introduced European mining methods to the rich silver mines of Mexico and the Andes.

The Spanish, unlike the Portuguese, undertook from the beginning to colonize and settle the areas that they conquered. They brought European techniques, equipment, and institutions (including their religion), which they imposed upon the native Indian population. Besides European culture and manufactures, the Spanish introduced natural products previously unknown to the Western Hemisphere, including wheat and other cereal grains (except corn, which traveled in the opposite direction), sugar cane, coffee, most common vegetables and fruits (including citrus fruits), and many other forms of plant life. The pre-Columbian Indians of America had no domesticated animals except dogs and llamas. The Spanish introduced horses, cattle, sheep, donkeys, goats, pigs, and most domesticated fowls.

Some of the other features of European civilization that were introduced into America, such as firearms, alcoholic liquors, and the European diseases of smallpox, measles, and typhus, spread with great rapidity and lethal effect. The native population may have numbered as many as 10 or 12 million at the time of Columbus — some scholarly estimates range much higher — but by the end of the century these killers had reduced it to but a few million. To remedy the shortage of labor and because Indians did not make good slaves, the Spanish introduced African slaves to the Western Hemisphere as early as 1501. By 1600 a majority of the population of the West Indies was composed of Negroes and people of mixed races; Negroes were not so important on the mainland, except in Brazil and northern South America.

ECONOMIC CONSEQUENCES

The transplantation of European culture, together with the modification and occasional extinction of non-Western cultures, were the most dramatic and important aspects of the expansion of Europe. Expansion also produced feedback. European culture itself underwent substantial modification as a result of expansion.

On the economic side expansion resulted in a great increase in the volume and variety of goods traded. In the sixteenth century spices from the East and bullion from the West accounted for an overwhelming proportion of imports from the colonial world. As late as 1594, for example, 95 per cent of the value of legal exports from the Spanish colonies in the New World consisted of gold and silver bullion. Nevertheless, other commodities entered the stream of trade, gradually expanded in volume, and by the seventeenth and eighteenth centuries overshadowed the original overseas exports to Europe. Exotic dyestuffs such as indigo and cochineal added color to European fabrics and made them gayer and more salable both in Europe and overseas. Coffee from Africa, cocoa from America, and tea from Asia became staple European beverages. Cotton and sugar, although they were known earlier in Europe, had never been produced or traded on a large scale. When sugar cane was transplanted to America, the production of sugar increased enormously and brought that delicacy within the budget of ordinary Europeans. The introduction of cotton goods from India, at first a luxury reserved for the wealthy, led eventually to the establishment of one of Europe's largest industries, dependent upon a raw material imported from America and catering especially to the masses. Chinese porcelain had a similar history. Tobacco, one of America's most celebrated and controversial contributions to civilization, grew rapidly in popularity in Europe in spite of determined efforts by both church and state to stamp it out. In later years tropical fruits and nuts supplemented European diets, and furs, hides, exotic woods, and new fibers constituted important additions to European supplies.

One very special branch of commerce dealt in human beings: the slave trade. It was dominated at first by the Portuguese, then in turn by the Dutch, the French, and the English. Although the Spanish colonies were among the largest purchasers of slaves, the Spanish themselves did not engage in the trade to any great extent but granted it by contract, or *asiento,* to the traders of other nations. Usually the trade was triangular in nature. A European ship carrying firearms, knives, other metalwares, beads and similar cheap trinkets, gaily colored cloth, and liquor would sail for the West African coast, where it exchanged its cargo with local African chieftains for slaves, either war captives or the chief's own people. When the slave trader had loaded as many chained and manacled Africans as his ship would carry, he sailed for the West Indies or the mainland of North or South America. There he exchanged his human cargo for one of sugar, tobacco, or other products of the Western Hemisphere, with which he returned to Europe. Although the death rate for slaves in transit from disease and other causes was dreadfully high (frequently 50 per cent and sometimes more), the profits of the slave trade were extraordinary. European governments took no effective steps to prohibit it until the nineteenth century.

Many foodstuffs previously unknown in Europe, although not imported in large quantities, were introduced and naturalized, eventually becoming important staples of diet. From America came potatoes, tomatoes, string beans, squash, red peppers, pumpkins, and corn (called maize by most Europeans), as well as the domesticated turkey, which in spite of its name reached Europe from Mexico. Rice, originally from Asia, became naturalized in Europe and America.

Trade within Europe also grew. For example, the Portuguese brought spices back to Lisbon and sold them to merchants from other countries for distribution throughout Europe. Moreover, the Portuguese and Spanish, concentrating on the exploitation of their overseas empires, could not produce all the manufactured goods that were in demand there. They purchased the goods from other European countries, stimulating industry and commerce even in countries without colonies of their own. Shipbuilding and the production of naval stores, firearms, and munitions were among the most important industries involved. The textile industries found new outlets and in turn borrowed new techniques and materials from the textile industries of Asia. Metalware for use as tools and implements and glassware in the form of mirrors, bottles, and scientific instruments were in great demand in Europe and overseas. The brewing and distilling industries created new products such as rum and gin and increased their output to supply both markets. New industries, including sugar refining, tobacco processing, and cotton textile manufacture, that depended on imported raw materials grew in importance. Other manufactures ranging from porcelain to snuff boxes developed to satisfy newly created tastes.

Along with the increase in trade and industry there was an increase in the number of merchants, shippers, manufacturers, wage laborers, and others involved in the market economy, as well as an increase in the number, variety, and strength of trading, or capitalistic, institutions, such as

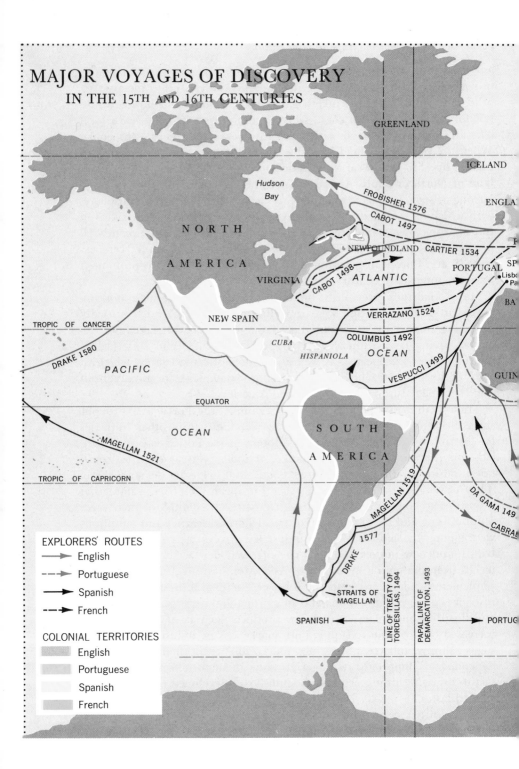

MAJOR VOYAGES OF DISCOVERY
IN THE 15TH AND 16TH CENTURIES

GREENLAND

ICELAND

ENGLA

Hudson
Bay

FROBISHER 1576

CABOT 1497

NORTH

NEWFOUNDLAND CARTIER 1534

AMERICA

PORTUGAL SP

Lisbo

VIRGINIA

CABOT 1498 ATLANTIC

Pa

TROPIC OF CANCER

NEW SPAIN

BA

VERRAZANO 1524

DRAKE 1580

CUBA

COLUMBUS 1492

OCEAN

PACIFIC

HISPANIOLA

GUIN

VESPUCCI 1499

EQUATOR

SOUTH

OCEAN

AMERICA

MAGELLAN 1521

MAGELLAN 1519

TROPIC OF CAPRICORN

DA GAMA 149

DRAKE

CABRA

1577

EXPLORERS' ROUTES
- → English
- --→ Portuguese
- → Spanish
- --→ French

STRAITS OF
MAGELLAN

LINE OF TREATY OF
TORDESILLAS, 1494

PAPAL LINE OF
DEMARCATION, 1493

COLONIAL TERRITORIES
- English
- Portuguese
- Spanish
- French

SPANISH ←

→ PORTUG

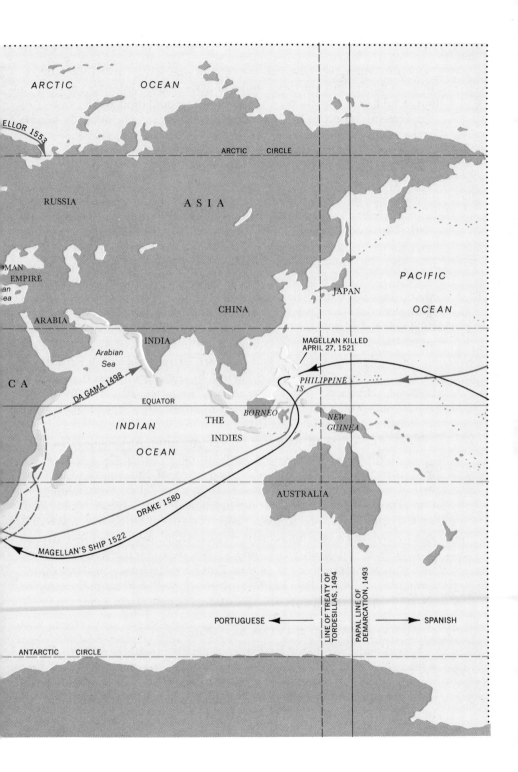

ARCTIC OCEAN

ELLOR 1553

ARCTIC CIRCLE

RUSSIA

ASIA

'MAN
EMPIRE
an
ea

ARABIA

PACIFIC

JAPAN

OCEAN

CHINA

INDIA

Arabian
Sea

MAGELLAN KILLED
APRIL 27, 1521

DA GAMA 1498

C A

PHILIPPINE
IS.

EQUATOR

INDIAN

THE

BORNEO

NEW
GUINEA

INDIES

OCEAN

DRAKE 1580

AUSTRALIA

MAGELLAN'S SHIP 1522

LINE OF TREATY OF
TORDESILLAS, 1494

PAPAL LINE OF
DEMARCATION, 1493

PORTUGUESE ◄─── ───► SPANISH

ANTARCTIC CIRCLE

stock exchanges, warehouses, banks, and the like. Capitalism, already well established in northern Italy and the Low Countries, took in a larger and larger fraction of the European population in the course of the sixteenth century. One important reason was the phenomenon known as the price revolution.

The flow of gold and silver from the Spanish colonies trebled Europe's supply of money metals in the course of the sixteenth century. As the quantity of money in circulation increased the prices of goods rose, so that the purchasing power of money decreased. In other words, the value of money measured in terms of the goods it could buy declined. The remarkable growth in population, however, seems to have been of greater importance in causing the rise in prices than the increase in the quantity of money. The constantly increasing population created an always mounting demand for the necessities of life, above all for food. The price of grain, the chief item by far in the diets of all Europeans, went up much more than did the prices of less vital commodities. In 1600 grain prices in England, Germany, and Poland were almost three times, and in France and Belgium about four times those in 1500. In this same period of time the price of manufactured goods increased by only about 100 per cent in France, Belgium, Germany, and Poland, by considerably less than that in England. Moreover, prices rose sharply in lands such as Russia and Sweden into which little American gold and silver had found its way but where population had increased.

The rising prices of foodstuffs made agriculture profitable. The new rural prosperity did not restrict itself to the people of the upper classes who owned most of the land. In many parts of Europe by the second half of the sixteenth century peasants who owned their own holdings or who rented sizable farms from noble, clerical, or bourgeois landowners, were sharing in the good times. Their standard of living rose markedly; in England and western Germany, for example, many peasants enlarged or otherwise improved their houses and acquired much better home furnishings. Everywhere in western Europe merchants, lawyers, government officials, and other wealthy townsmen, seeing the opportunity to profit from the prosperity of agriculture, bought farm land.

A SHIFT IN EUROPE'S CENTER OF GRAVITY

A final major economic consequence of the expansion of Europe — in a sense, the sum and culmination of all the other changes — was a pronounced shift in the location of the principal centers of economic activity within Europe. During the fifteenth century the cities of northern Italy retained the leadership in economic affairs that they had exercised throughout the Middle Ages. The Portuguese discoveries, however, deprived them of their monopoly of the spice trade. A series of wars involving the invasion and occupation of Italy by foreign armies further disrupted commerce and finance. The decline of Italy was not immediate or drastic, for the Italians had reservoirs of capital, entrepreneurial talent, and highly refined economic institutions to carry them through for several generations. Italy's decline was probably more relative than absolute, because of the great increase in the volume of European commerce. Nevertheless, the Venetians' famous Flanders fleet made its last voyage in 1532, and in the latter part of the century Venetian ambassadors complained of competition from cheaper French and English woolens in the markets of the Near East, which the Italians had regarded as their exclusive domain. By the early seventeenth century Italy had fallen into the backwaters of economic life, from which it did not emerge until the twentieth century.

Spain and Portugal enjoyed a fleeting glory as the leading economic powers of Europe. Lisbon replaced Venice as the great entrepôt of the spice trade. In 1521 the Portuguese king haughtily refused an offer of the Venetian Republic to purchase the entire annual import of spices. The Portuguese did not develop their commercial or capitalistic institutions, however. Instead, all trade with the East became a royal monopoly, strictly regulated for the benefit of the crown and royal favorites. Distribution of the spices and other exotic products in Europe was handled by the Dutch and Flemish in the north and by Italians in the Mediterranean. Their ships and merchants flocked to the harbor of Lisbon, sharing in the wealth of the Indies and building up stores of capital in their own countries. Thus, although the Portuguese monopoly was extremely lucrative for a time, in the long run it strengthened the capitalistic institutions of Portugal's trading partners more than those of Portugal itself. Both industry and agriculture declined in Portugal. Then, in 1580 the Portuguese crown fell to Philip II of Spain, who was more interested in protecting the Spanish Empire than the Portuguese one. By the end of the sixteenth century Dutch and English interlopers, who had been kept from trading with Portugal itself because of their hostility to Spain, began trading directly with the Orient — a portent of the imminent decline of the Portuguese Empire.

Spain, to which the American treasure first came, was the first to benefit from its effects. Spanish wealth and power became such that the legend of Spanish might did not die for more than two hundred years. Ironically, the seeds of its decline were sown by the same phenomenon that brought its wealth. The Spanish crown instituted a state monopoly over all trade in precious metals and foolishly tried to prevent their export from Spain to the rest of Europe. Other state policies proved equally unwise. Most of its expenditures went for war and war preparations or subsidies to idle aristocrats, who spent their incomes on luxurious consumption, including products purchased abroad. Much of the young manhood of Spain was recruited to fight dynastic wars in

THE MONETARY REVOLUTION:
SPANISH IMPORTS OF
AMERICAN GOLD AND SILVER

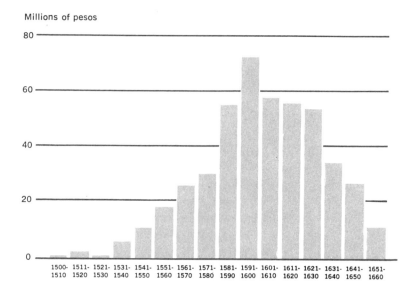

Source: E. J. Hamilton, "American Treasure
and the Price Revolution in Spain, 1501–1650"
(Cambridge: Harvard Univ. Press, 1934) p. 53.

Europe or to control the natives and direct mining operations in the
New World. The merchant class never had the opportunity to develop
that it had in other countries, and Spain did not become an important
nation commercially or industrially. Although it retained its extensive
colonial empire until the early nineteenth century, it was already in decline economically, politically, and militarily by the middle of the seventeenth century.

Central, eastern, and northern Europe did not participate significantly
in the commercial prosperity of the sixteenth century. The Hanseatic
League flourished in the fifteenth century but declined thereafter. Although the main causes of its decline were independent of the great
discoveries, the latter probably hastened the decline by strengthening
the commercial power of Dutch and English cities. Southern Germany
and Switzerland, which had also become commercially prominent in the
fifteenth century, retained their prosperity for a time; but since they
were no longer on the most important trade routes and had no ports to

benefit from the increase in seaborne trade, they slipped backward along with the rest of central and eastern Europe. All of central Europe soon plunged into religious and dynastic wars, which sapped its energy for economic activity.

The area that gained most from the economic changes associated with the great discoveries was the region bordering on the North Sea and the English Channel: the Low Countries, England, and northern France. This area, opening on the Atlantic and lying midway between northern and southern Europe, was clearly destined geographically for great prosperity in an age of worldwide oceanic commerce, especially after the economic decline of Spain and Portugal. The political development of these countries also contributed to making the area the focal point of capitalist economy — a position that it had distinctly gained by the end of the sixteenth century and continued to hold until the twentieth.

France, geographically contiguous with Spain, initially obtained Spanish gold and silver through the hands of merchants. Throughout the sixteenth century, France, too, engaged in dynastic and religious wars, and for the most part its government followed policies unfavorable to business interests. Therefore France did not gain as much as did the Netherlands and England, which benefited most from the increase in trade and the influx of precious metals.

Although Flanders never fully recovered from the great depression of the late Middle Ages, its neighboring provinces continued to prosper. Bruges gradually declined as the principal entrepôt for trade with southern Europe and Antwerp arose to take its place. All seventeen provinces of the Low Countries, from Flanders and Luxembourg in the south to Holland and Groningen in the north, fell to the crown of Spain early in the sixteenth century. They were therefore in an excellent position to capitalize on the trading opportunities of the Spanish Empire. In the second half of the sixteenth century the Netherlands revolted against Spanish domination. Although Spain repressed the revolt in the southern Netherlands (modern Belgium), the seven northern provinces won their independence. Economically this episode resulted in the decline of the southern provinces, partly because Spain enacted so many harsh punitive measures and partly because the Low Countries' maritime strength was based in the northern Netherlands. Trade shifted to the north, and Amsterdam became the great commercial and financial center of the seventeenth century.

England at the time of the great discoveries was just emerging from the status of a backward, raw materials-producing area into something of a manufacturing country. Its agriculture was also becoming more capitalistic and market-oriented. The Wars of the Roses decimated the ranks of the great nobility but left the urban middle classes and peasants almost untouched. The decline of the great nobility enhanced the importance of the lesser landed aristocracy, the gentry. The new Tudor dynasty, which came to the throne in 1485, depended heavily on gentry support and gave favors to it in return. The price revolution benefited English merchants, manufacturers, and progressive agriculturists at the expense of wage earners, small peasant farmers, and landowners temporarily unable to increase rents in line with rising prices. Although these factors produced a certain amount of social unrest, they also made the English social structure more fluid and flexible than that on the Continent and contributed to the strength of the institutions of capitalism.

POLITICAL, SOCIAL, AND CULTURAL CONSEQUENCES OF THE EXPANSION OF EUROPE

In hundreds of ways important and trivial, obvious and subtle, the great discoveries and overseas expansion of European civilization influenced the lives of Europeans. The shift in the center of economic activity entailed a shift in the locus of political power. In the sixteenth century the Hapsburgs, who ruled in Spain, central Europe, the Low Countries, and Spanish America, controlled the greatest concentration of political power that Europe had seen since Roman times. With the decline of Spain in the seventeenth century, the balance of power swung northward to countries with good harbors, large navies, and flourishing commerce: the United Netherlands, France, and England.

Among the social consequences of European expansion were an increase in wealth, luxury, the patronage of the arts, and in the political power and social influence of merchants and financiers. The discoveries provided new themes for art, new forms of luxury, and new areas for the exercise of wealth and power. Changes in diet and dress were accomplished by products imported from overseas. For the first time such things as sugar, spice, rum, and tobacco entered the diets of ordinary Europeans. The wealthy decked themselves in silks and exotic furs and plumes, weighted their fingers with precious stones, doused themselves with strong new perfumes, and consumed their highly spiced foods from utensils of silver and gold.

In science, knowledge of the world overseas provided facts to verify or refute existing theories and insights from which new theories grew. It revolutionized the study of geography. When Gerardus Mercator (1512–1594), inventor of the famous Mercator projection for showing the earth on a flat map, drew his map of the world less than fifty years after the first circumnavigation, he could present a reasonably accurate picture of at least the major continental outlines as we know them today. Astronomy, zoology, botany, and geology all received new data to digest and rationalize. The practice of medicine benefited directly from the introduction of new drugs such as quinine and camphor and was also misled by the introduction of many spurious ones.

In religion the immediate effect of the discoveries was to summon forth a vigorous missionary effort that ultimately carried Christianity to far corners of the world. A less obvious but ultimately deeply significant effect was the impetus the discoveries gave to the study of comparative religions and the challenge to long-accepted Christian dogma that resulted from this study. The institutions and behavior of hundreds of peoples who were previously unknown or slightly known to Europeans, from the most primitive and cannibalistic West Indians to the highly civilized Hindus and Chinese, provided food for thought for moralists, political philosophers, and proto-anthropologists. For at least three centuries the "noble savage" or "man in the state of nature" was used as the starting point for both democratic and authoritarian political thories. Those who dreamed of more nearly perfect societies, such as Thomas More in *Utopia* in the sixteenth century and Francis Bacon in *The New Atlantis* in the seventeenth, placed them in the newly discovered regions overseas.

The European world's knowledge of the greater world was still very limited, myth-ridden, unsophisticated, even credulous. As yet the new worlds were of only tertiary importance, at best, to European concerns. What was of immense significance was the limitless horizon of European consciousness, the advent of a sense of mastery over vast areas of land and water which hitherto had been a space of fearsome darkness. World maps of the early fifteenth century depicted the world as a small island comprising Europe, north Africa, and Asia set in an immense ocean inhabited by fierce, fanciful monsters dominating all but the island itself. Maps of the world of the late sixteenth century erred as far in the other direction, showing vast areas of land and much reduced belts of ocean. The monsters were still there, less fierce and less fanciful, but now reduced to mere decorations, conventional not fearsome. Europe had taken its first great steps to making the entire world an extension of the European world.

THE RENAISSANCE
CHAPTER THREE

For most of us the word Renaissance conjures up a vision of the magnificent art produced in northern Italy from the late fourteenth to the early sixteenth century. Actually artistic creativity was only one, albeit a major, aspect of the history of the era, and the Renaissance was not limited to Italy, though it began there. A greatly heightened interest in, and knowledge of, Greek and Roman classics also characterized the era. The new-found enthusiasm for antiquity had a profound influence on every aspect of intellectual and cultural life, affected religion, and brought about changes in man's attitude toward government. Finally, and above all, a new emphasis on the power of human creativity, a heady compound of individualism and secularism, underlay all intellectual and aesthetic achievements of the era.

THE RENAISSANCE IN ITALY

People in northern Italy during these years were certain that they were living in a time of intellectual revolution, marked by a rebirth (the meaning of *renaissance*) of the values of classical Greco-Roman civilization. They scorned the thousand years that separated them from the end of classical antiquity as the dark ages, in which they were convinced there had been no great cultural achievements. They were confident that the dark ages had ended and that they were living in a golden age. In the 1430's a Florentine named Matteo Palmieri wrote: "It is but in our own days that men dare boast they see the dawn of better things. . . . Now, indeed, may every thoughtful spirit thank God that it has been permitted him to be born in this new age, so full of hope and promise, which already rejoices in a greater array of nobly-gifted souls than the world has seen in the thousand years that preceded it." Palmieri's braggadocio was common currency among his contemporaries.

Historians have long debated whether the Italians of the Renaissance were right in their boast that their age broke abruptly with the immediately preceding centuries, or whether the Renaissance only continued trends that had already been much in evidence during the preceding three centuries of medieval civilization. It is now generally agreed that the Renaissance had firm roots in the Middle Ages. At the same time, most historians recognize the Renaissance as an age of transition in which individualism and secularism began to erode the corporate and religious world view that characterized the Middle Ages. In this sense the Renaissance in Italy marked the onset of the modern world.

The real problem in dealing with the Renaissance is to analyze the proportion of "modern individualism" to "medieval corporateness" or of "modern secularism" to "medieval religiosity" at any one point, and even to determine exactly what is meant by key concepts such as "modern individualism." The Swiss historian Jacob Burckhardt, in *The Civilization of the Renaissance in Italy* (1860), the foundation of modern histories of the subject, described the Italian Renaissance man as

the first born among the sons of modern Europe. In the Middle Ages both sides of human consciousness — that which was turned within and that which was turned without — lay dreaming or half awake beneath a common veil. The veil was woven of faith, illusion, and childish prepossession, through which the world and history was seen clad in strange hues. Man was conscious of himself only as a member of a race, people, party, family, or corporate body — only through some general category. In Italy this veil first melted into air; an *objective* treatment and consideration of the state and of all things of this world became possible. The *subjective* side at the same time asserted itself with corresponding emphasis; man became a spiritual *individual,* and recognized himself as such.

The school of Renaissance historians that evolved from Burckhardt's theories provoked a controversy with the medievalists that is still alive. The Dutch scholar Johan Huizinga, in *The Waning of the Middle Ages* (1919), argued that although the fourteenth and fifteenth centuries may for convenience's sake be called the Renaissance, they were the terminal centuries of the Middle Ages for Europe outside Italy. The exponents of these two points of view have sought either to extend Burckhardt to the north or to extend Huizinga to Italy, with the result that all of the hitherto vivid contrasts between Renaissance and medieval have tended to become blurred. As the Renaissance advocates have underestimated the importance of the survival of fundamental institutions and governmental practices from the Middle Ages, so the medievalists have strained to find Renaissance attributes in the twelfth century. As in any controversy, sound research has sometimes been overinflated and men have seemed to take extreme positions. The conflict might be resolved by a more vigorous investigation of how the Renaissance differed from modern times rather than from the Middle Ages. Then its transitional quality — the only point of agreement among most of the contestants — would perhaps be made more apparent.

The Italian Renaissance had substantial foundations. Political and social developments in northern Italy were among the most important. During the Middle Ages feudal lords held political and military leadership in most parts of Europe. In northern and central Italy, however, the long contest for power between papal and imperial forces promoted the emergence of independent city-states or communes. These small states were ruled by oligarchies composed of rich merchants and of nobles from the surrounding countryside who had moved into the cities. The fusion of the wealthy burghers and the nobility within the cities created a new social and political milieu, which was completely different from the feudal society dominant elsewhere in Europe. In this new milieu people had a civic consciousness, a pride in their city's particular qualities, and conceived of their city's glory as concrete and material. Secular interests were paramount. The city-states engaged in an intense rivalry with one another. Their competitiveness extended into the realm of culture. Rulers sought to exalt themselves and their states, and men of private means wanted to call attention to themselves. As a result they eagerly sponsored artists and scholars whose works were to enshrine for posterity the merits and glories of their patrons.

The competition in patronage presupposed the existence of surplus capital. Here again circumstances favored northern Italy. Although most of Europe had experienced an economic decline, hard times, and a fall in population during the century from about 1350 to 1450, Italians had amassed great riches during the preceding era of economic growth. They continued to be active in banking, trade, industry, and agriculture and, despite the depression, continued to pile up wealth, though probably at a slower rate. The decline in economic activity, however, meant that there were fewer opportunities for profitable investment in business enterprise. Consequently, wealthy men turned more of their surplus capital into works of art, handsome buildings, and the support of men of letters.

The political, social, and economic foundations of the Renaissance exhibited the elitist nature of the age. Political power, social prestige, and wealth were limited to the upper echelons of society — although these were a larger proportion of the whole population in northern Italian city-states than in most other areas in Europe — and there was nothing egalitarian about society. In every facet of the Renaissance, from humanism to art, the social presupposition of inequality was present. The Renaissance was a spiritual and aesthetic experience only for those who had arrived materially. It bore less relation to the real condition of most men than did the all-embracing order of medieval religion it scorned.

ITALIAN HUMANISM

The first historians of the Renaissance treated the revival of antiquity as a new phenomenon. Actually, many of the classical authors were known and read in medieval times. There was an important qualitative distinction, however, in the way a scholastic of the High Middle Ages and a scholar of the Renaissance used the ancient writings. Medieval scholastics tried to reconcile them with Christian theology and blend them with Christian ideals. To the scholars of the Renaissance, classical times seemed a golden age in which men, untroubled by concerns about salvation, were interested in man for man's sake alone. The secular and individualistic attitude that they found in the classics coincided with, and seemed to justify, their own conception of how men should live and act.

The study of the classics came to be known as humanism, from *studia humanitatis,* the Latin term for studies that give man the understanding to express his own individuality in his conduct, speech, and writing. Most of the humanists, as the men who pursued the classical studies were called, were laymen. Some were clerics, however, and included men who held high Church office. Other important churchmen gave their patronage to humanists. Thus, the secular influence of humanism was often sponsored and advanced by men of the Church.

PETRARCH

The first of the Renaissance humanists was Francesco Petrarca (1304–1374), or Petrarch as he is called in English. While still a boy, Petrarch became enamored of the classics, particularly the rhetorical works of Cicero. Compelled by his father to become a lawyer, Petrarch called his time at law school seven wasted years. After his father's death he gladly gave up his practice for the study of Latin classics. The great figures of antiquity became so real to him that he called Cicero his father and the poet Virgil his brother. He wrote extensively in classical Latin, searched tirelessly for classical Latin manuscripts, and spent long hours editing and ridding them of the errors of copyists. He could not read Greek — to his great sorrow — but he collected and preserved classical writings in that language, too. In his own Latin writings he did not slavishly imitate the ancients but developed his own flowing style.

Although he was happiest when he was working at his desk, Petrarch did not spend his life in the scholar's traditional ivory tower. He traveled widely and knew many of the important men of his time. Imitating his "brother" Virgil, he loved nature and wrote lyrically about rural sights and sounds. He eagerly sought personal glory and fame, and while still in his thirties won recognition throughout Italy and elsewhere in Europe as the foremost literary figure of the time.

Petrarch was the first to call the period since classical times the dark ages. He was certain that a new age of glory and light was dawning in which, he said, men "will be able to walk back into the pure radiance of the past." His enthusiasm and fame inspired others to seek out old manuscripts in monasteries and other repositories, to write treatises in Ciceronian Latin, and to sing the praises of classical antiquity. Many of these humanists were employed by rulers, popes, and men of wealth as secretaries, government officials, or teachers. Through such positions of influence they transmitted to others the view of life and the secularism that they found in the classics.

At the end of the fourteenth century several Greek scholars settled in Italy to teach classical Greek. Eager Italians soon learned to read and prize the writings of Greek antiquity. After the fall of Constantinople to the Turks in 1453, exiled Byzantines swelled the tide, bringing with them a number of new texts. In the second half of the fifteenth century a few humanists began to study Hebrew and other Oriental tongues. During this period printing was introduced into Italy from Rhineland Germany, where it had just been invented. Until then, copyists had laboriously transcribed the ancient writings. The printed editions of the Greek and Roman classics greatly stimulated their circulation.

HUMANIST TECHNIQUES OF SCHOLARSHIP

As they continued their intensive study of the ancient writings, the humanists developed new scholarly techniques that laid the foundation for modern methods of historical and literary analysis. They became skilled in the art of textual criticism and learned how to examine sources in order to make sure that they were genuine or were accurate copies. The most famous triumph of the new scholarly methods came in 1440 when Lorenzo Valla, one of the greatest Latinists of his day, proved spurious a document called the Donation of Constantine, which had long served as one of the main supports for the papacy's claim to spiritual and temporal sovereignty. The Church maintained that Emperor Constantine had given to the bishop of Rome spiritual supremacy over the other patriarchates of the Church and temporal dominion over Italy and western Europe in a charter, the Donation, shortly after his conversion to Christianity in the fourth century. On the basis of the language and anachronistic historical references in the charter, Valla proved that it was a forgery, probably written in the eighth century by someone in the papal chancery.

The humanists' enthusiasm for antiquity was also responsible for the development of the study of archaeology. People had used the ruins of ancient Rome as stone quarries and had stripped marble from the classical monuments to burn for lime. Humanists lamented the destruction of these ancient glories and wrote treatises on classical archaeology and epigraphy (the deciphering and interpretation of ancient inscriptions). In the second half of the fifteenth century the popes forbad further depredations and sponsored excavations that recovered ancient works of art, including such masterpieces as the Apollo Belvedere and the Laocoön statues of the Hellenistic period. In other cities of Italy wealthy men and scholars built up their own private collections of classical works of art and ancient objects.

HUMANIST EDUCATION

The achievements of the humanists included an almost total reconstruction of the theory and practice of education. In medieval Europe formal education had been limited mainly to the study of theology, medicine, and law. In the fifteenth century humanists, inspired by classical ideals, argued that the aim of education should be to produce men whose every action expresses their own individuality and who lead good and useful lives no matter what career they follow. They stressed the classics, mathematics, music, religion, and some science in order to teach the student intellectual discipline, stimulate his imagination, and provide him with guides to moral conduct. They maintained, however, that education was more than just book learning. They insisted on training in good manners. They also added athletics and outdoor activity in imitation of Greek educational philosophy, which held that both mind and body must be developed in harmony.

Only the sons of the rich could afford this kind of education. Nevertheless, the educational innovations lived on far beyond the era of the Renaissance. They persist today in our effort to give students a liberal education that will broaden their perspective, deepen their understanding, and develop their sense of civic responsibility.

The humanists did not restrict their educational work to youths. Many gave public lectures before large and appreciative audiences, often delivering a series of talks in one city and then moving on to another town. This method of adult education popularized the ideals of humanism. Humanists also taught one another by forming academies, supported by wealthy patrons, to discuss scholarly and philosophical problems. By the end of the fifteenth century nearly every Italian cultural center had its own academy. The Platonic Academy at Florence, founded by Cosimo de' Medici in 1459, was the most famous, especially during the reign of Cosimo's grandson, Lorenzo the Magnificent. As its name indicates, this academy devoted itself especially to the study of Plato and tried, among other things, to reconcile the tenets of Platonism with the theology of Christianity.

THE ITALIAN HUMANIST IMAGE OF MAN

The intellectual and political ferment of the Renaissance convinced men that they lived in a new era and gave them a feeling of freedom from traditional restraints and the old concern that life was only a preparation for salvation. Above all, it encouraged them to believe that man is the master of his own destiny, that there need be no limit to his ambitions and virtuosity, and that his purpose on earth is to develop himself to his fullest capacities.

A new, humanistic image of man is to be found in the writings of many men of the Italian Renaissance. In 1434 Leon Battista Alberti wrote that "men are themselves the source of their own fortune and misfortune." Fifty years later Giovanni Pico della Mirandola explained in an essay, *The Dignity of Man,* that God had put man in the center of the universe and said to him, "We have made you neither heavenly nor earthly, neither mortal nor immortal, so that, more freely and more honorably the molder and maker of yourself, you may fashion yourself in whatever form you shall prefer. . . . [T]o man it has been granted to have what he chooses, to be what he wills."

The emphasis upon man as his own master resulted in a revision of the old scale of social values. Success and fame were not dependent upon birth and social status but upon a man's native abilities. The man who began life as a peasant or worker could rise to the heights if he had talent, imagination, intelligence, self-reliance, and ambition — and luck. The men of the Renaissance summed up in one word the qualities that enabled the outstanding individual to shape his own destiny and achieve greatness in whatever field he chose. That word was *virtù,* from the Latin word for man (*vir*). It had nothing to do with virtue in the modern sense of moral rectitude, which was not considered necessary for the possession of *virtù.*

The new emphasis upon individuality also produced an intense self-consciousness. Renaissance men sought ceaselessly to prove themselves men of *virtù* in the eyes of their fellows. The rulers and the rich spent mightily on ostentatious display, on great public and private entertainments, and on works of art and buildings to call attention to their generosity and achievements. Men showed scant modesty in telling about their abilities and boasted publicly about their exploits. Their ideal was the universal man (*uomo universale*), that is, the man who excelled in many different fields.

The most famous of the universal men were Michelangelo (1475–1564), Leonardo da Vinci (1452–1519), and Leon Battista Alberti (1404–1472). Michelangelo's sculptures and frescoes are among the world's greatest artistic creations. He was also an architect, a military engineer and, when he was past the age of seventy, the author of beautiful sonnets.

Leonardo distinguished himself as painter, architect, anatomist, scientist, inventor, and engineer. Alberti commanded four skills — painting, architecture, poetry, and music — and was master of the traditional disciplines of mathematics, philosophy, and law. He wrote treatises on all of these subjects in pure and elegant prose.

Although these three men and a few others stand out as giants, many lesser men passed easily from one artistic or intellectual field to another — perhaps too easily. There was much superficial dazzle in the *universali* because many of the skills were highly related and based upon specific (classical) models that were limited in number and variety. Men believed that they could master many fields, and if their grasp outreached their capacity, their universality of interest produced the richness and excitement of Renaissance culture.

The self-confidence of these men and their conviction that a man should be judged by his accomplishments rather than his birth had practical limitations. Low-born and newly risen men successful in politics or business in Italian city-states were stalked by a sense of inferiority to the more established feudal aristocracies in the north. In search of recognition as aristocrats they sought to acquire the courtliness and fine manners of the natural born noble. Manuals on etiquette appeared in the late fifteenth and early sixteenth centuries to meet the demand. They analyzed proper behavior and laid down rules to transform the soldier of fortune or the newly rich merchant into a man of breeding and a connoisseur of taste. Some manuals contained elementary instructions, for their readers often started from scratch: for instance, a gentleman should not thrust a stinking thing under another man's nose to show him how bad it smells; nor should he spit, nor pare his nails in public.

A book called *The Courtier,* begun in 1510 and published in 1528, was the most famous of the manuals of etiquette. Its author, Baldassare Castiglione, belonged to an ancient but impoverished noble family. Having spent several years at the court of Urbino in northern Italy, he cast his book in the form of conversations among the highly cultivated members of that court. He pointed out that it was easier to become a gentleman if one was born into the nobility, but conceded that high birth was not essential. Despite his aristocratic bias, his conception of the gentleman corresponded with the Renaissance ideal of the well-rounded individual. The true gentleman had to have courage, skill in outdoor sports, knowledge of the classics, and eloquence in his speech. He must have polish and wit, grace and nonchalance. He must know something about the arts, especially music, and be adept in the social graces and the pursuit of love. He must wear his learning and his accomplishments lightly, as if they were perfectly natural to him, and must avoid pedantry and pomposity. Castiglione's book enjoyed great success in Italy and soon appeared in a number of foreign translations. It had an enormous and lasting influence in shaping the social behavior of Western man. Gross manners and vulgarity, of course, did not disappear, but *The Courtier* and its many imitators established the pattern for gentlemanly behavior.

The Courtier marked a peak in Italian Renaissance humanism; indeed, it marked the onset of a decline for the humanist man. Harking back to the feudal chivalric ideal of the High Middle Ages, it testified to the waning of the old civic pride that had nurtured the early humanism of Petrarch two centuries before in favor of a would-be *uomo universale,* who was more surface than substance, more manner than man.

ITALIAN ART

If Italians had done nothing else during the Renaissance, their painting, sculpture, and architecture would alone have made it one of the most brilliant epochs in the history of human achievement. Probably no other age has produced so much artistic genius. Their works, their techniques, and their themes set the standards for the art of the Western world until very recent times, and they provide the models to which modern art is invidiously compared.

The artists of the Renaissance shared to the full the self-confidence and egoism that typified the era. They were not content to be anonymous craftsmen, as most of their medieval predecessors had been. They passionately sought recognition, vied openly with fellow artists, and were often intensely jealous of one another. They demanded that their patrons accord them respect and honor and took quick offense if they felt that they had been slighted. The patrons readily acquiesced to the demands and accepted affronts from artists that they would not have taken from others. Patrons competed with one another for the services of artists, paid them extravagantly, and accepted them as equals. As Cosimo de' Medici said, "One must treat these people of extraordinary genius as if they were celestial spirits, and not like beasts of burden."

The artists shared the conviction that their era represented a complete break with the immediate past. They had utter contempt for the art of the Middle Ages (though they readily adopted techniques that had been developed by their "brutish predecessors") and admired only the art of classical antiquity. Their fondest hope was to equal and, if possible, to exceed the accomplishments of the ancients. In their self-conscious imitativeness and their aspiration to excel the imitated, the artists of the Italian Renaissance revealed both their power and their limitations.

PAINTING

Until the time of Giotto di Bondone (*c.* 1270–1337) Italian painting, dominated by Byzantine influences, had been flat and two-dimensional, though it was far more ambitious and highly developed than art elsewhere in Europe. Giotto broke away from this style and produced much more realistic paintings. Although his work seems primitive compared to later Renaissance art, his successful attempts to provide an illusion of depth by contrasting light and shade (*chiaroscuro*) and by varying the brightness of colors made him a revolutionary figure in the history of art.

A dramatic advance in the realism heralded by Giotto came nearly a century after his death when a great new wave of innovation and progress began in Florence. Masaccio (*c.* 1401–1429) was the first great figure of the outburst. He produced in a brief career works that were exceptional in their physical realism, organic unity, and portrayal of character and emotion. Their precise anatomical detail, representation of movement, and perspective and foreshortening set the pattern for Italian painting. After Masaccio's death artists traveled to Florence to study his murals and draw inspiration from them.

Painters conceived their problem to be the combination of a faithful portrayal of what they saw and beauty. To achieve realism, they made careful studies of nature. They also sought, and attained, technical mastery. They worked out theories of perspective based on experimentation and mathematical principles. They studied anatomy, botany, and zoology. They filled their sketchbooks with drawings of faces and the human figure, as well as with sketches and diagrams to illustrate perspective. Insisting that every part of a painting had to be in harmonious relation with every other part, they made systematic studies of the length of the hand, the width of the foot, or the relation of the thickness of the waist to the whole figure.

Despite the differences between Italian Renaissance and medieval art, the new artists remained closely linked to their predecessors in one very important respect: the choice of themes. Italian Renaissance art, like the medieval, was above all a religious art. By far the majority of the subjects selected came from the Bible. Traditional scenes of Christianity predominated — the Nativity, the Crucifixion, the Stations of the Cross, or the miracles of the saints. Renaissance artists, too, did much of their work for churches and monasteries. While retaining some of the religious symbols that had been so important in medieval art, they added their own genius and worldly outlook. The saints are recognizable human beings, the Madonnas are beautiful young women, the faces of patrons or of the artist and his friends often appear, and the biblical scenes somehow never seem far from scenes of contemporary Italian life.

With the notable exception of Michelangelo, the greatest artists engaged in portraiture. Their brushes were able to produce more than just the features of the subjects. They knew how to penetrate to the innermost qualities of personality. "Paint the face," urged Leonardo, "in such a way that it will be easy to understand what is going on in the mind."

Their portraits are dramatic character studies that reflect the Renaissance conception of man as an individual, noble, dignified, and free to make of himself what he wishes.

Landscape painting was another major innovation of Renaissance art. Often, landscapes were used as symbols. Forbidding rocks and mountains symbolized hell or terror; gardens represented paradise. As men became increasingly interested in the world in which they lived, painters introduced local Italian landscapes as background, even in paintings of biblical subjects. The revival of interest in Latin authors, especially Virgil, who proclaimed the beauties of country life also drew the attention of artists to rural scenes. Usually artists included landscape to give a painting the illusion of depth, and the landscape formed a minor part of the picture. Then, as they learned more about color, light, shadow, and perspective, they became ever more entranced with scenery, and landscapes began to dominate many paintings. Landscape emerged as a distinctive artistic genre, far removed from the original pictorial representations of sacred themes.

As artists grew more interested in portraying reality and learned more about the techniques of their craft, they made increasing use of the nude in their work. This was another great innovation. Like the ancient artists whom they admired, they realized that clothing masks the human form and prevents the artist from conveying to the observer the full sense of life and movement and energy. Above all others, Michelangelo mastered the nude as a medium of expression. His towering genius enabled him to make the male form seem superhuman in the heroic figures in the biblical scenes that he painted on the ceiling of the Sistine Chapel in the Vatican.

In the latter part of the fourteenth and in the early fifteenth centuries — the era that is often termed the High Renaissance — classical allegories became fashionable in art. They were essentially pagan in origin, drawn from classical mythology. Influenced by the metaphysical teachings of the Neo-Platonists in the Florentine Platonic Academy and by a renewal of interest in such esoteric studies as astrology, artists often intended several layers of meaning in their paintings. For example, Raphael (1483–1520) in a painting of Cupid and Psyche told the well-known story and also tried to show the ascent and ultimate deification of the human soul. Bandinelli portrayed the struggle between lust and reason by painting a battle scene between one group of gods, including Venus, Cupid, and Vulcan, who represented the baser instincts and another group of gods, led by Jupiter, Minerva, and Mercury, who symbolized man's higher nature. The use of this pictorial language, which was comprehensible to only a few, contributed to intellectual snobbery. Those who knew enough to understand what the artist meant felt superior to the many who did not share their knowledge and who saw only the literal meaning. The pious might justly fear that the ignorant would be seduced from faith by the pagan figures.

Brogi — Art Reference Bureau

Perseus, by Benvenuto Cellini (1500–1571)

"Now it pleased God that, on the instant of [the statue's] exposure to view, a shout of boundless enthusiasm went up in commendation of my work, which consoled me not a little. The folk kept on attaching sonnets to the posts of the door, which was protected with a curtain while I gave the last touches to the statue. . . . At last I brought the whole work to completion: and on a certain Thursday morning I exposed it to the public gaze. Immediately, before the sun was fully in the heavens, there assembled such a multitude of people that no words could describe them. All with one voice contended which should praise it most." From Cellini's autobiography, THE LIFE OF BENVENUTO CELLINI, tr. J. A. Symonds (New York, 1926).

SCULPTURE

Sculpture bore a close relationship to painting and followed a parallel course in its development. Some artists, including Leonardo and Michelangelo, excelled in both art forms. Like the painters, the sculptors carefully studied human anatomy, experimented with new techniques, used the nude, chose many of their themes from the Bible and classical literature, and developed the art of portraiture.

Donatello (*c.* 1386–1466) was the first major Renaissance sculptor. His work opened a new chapter in the history of sculpture, just as the work of his contemporary and fellow Florentine, Masaccio, started a new era in painting. Donatello freed sculpture from its medieval function of serving only to embellish architecture; it became an independent art. Donatello's sculptures combined realism, classical proportions, and harmony and had a dramatic and emotional effect.

Renaissance sculpture reached its zenith with the work of Michelangelo. He produced statues that many critics think have never been equaled. He began by consciously imitating the classical style and succeeded so well that a Roman art dealer buried one of his pieces, a sleeping Cupid, then dug it up and sold it as an antique. He soon passed through this imitative stage and at the age of twenty-three did the *Pietà*. In this work he demonstrated his full powers for the first time. Soon after its completion Michelangelo carved a gigantic nude of David out of a single block of marble that was sixteen feet in length. The statue of the young shepherd who had just slain Goliath was the embodiment of the daring, power, and confidence of youth. As Michelangelo grew older, a consciousness of man's struggle to free himself from sin and achieve immortality dominated his work. In his sculpture, as in his painting, he sought to harmonize the physical and the spiritual in order to show the indivisibility of body and soul.

ARCHITECTURE

In architecture, as in painting and sculpture, the Renaissance broke with medieval ideals and, even more than in the other arts, with the style of the Middle Ages. The Gothic was abandoned in favor of classical forms and classical decoration. Renaissance architects, however, did not raise servile imitations of ancient buildings. They adapted the domes, columns, rounded arches, and symmetry of classical architecture to their own purposes. This adaptation was necessary, since the city patronage that supported them required compact buildings in a limited space (often side by side, as along Venice's Grand Canal) in contrast to the more ample landscaping of the classical monuments that were their models. In an age of universal skills many architects were also painters or sculptors, and in their architecture they pursued the same goals of harmony and beauty that inspired the other arts. They insisted that each part of

Alinari — Art Reference Bureau

The Cathedral in Florence

"The extraordinary beauty of the structure is self-evident. Its height from the ground level to the lantern is 154 braccia [one braccio equals 23 inches], the lantern itself being 36 braccia, the copper ball 4 braccia, and the cross 8 braccia, making 202 braccia in all. It may safely be asserted that the ancients never raised their buildings so high or incurred such great risks in contending with the skies as this building appears to, for it rises to such a height that the mountains about Florence look like its fellows. Indeed one would say that the heavens are incensed against it since it is continually being struck by lightening." G. Vasari (1511–1574), THE LIVES OF THE PAINTERS, SCULPTORS AND ARCHITECTS, ed. W. Gaunt (London, 1963).

a building harmonize with every other part. Beauty was achieved if the parts were related so intimately that nothing could be added or taken away from the building without destroying its harmony. Like the ancients, they considered the circle to be a symbol of God because it had neither beginning nor end. Therefore, they built churches with the altar at or near the center of the building and crowned them with circular domes. They intended that everything in the church should be in perfect mathematical proportion in order to represent the closest human approximation of divine order and harmony. They also designed lavish palaces, private homes, and country villas for the rich and powerful.

Filippo Brunelleschi (1377–1446), a Florentine contemporary of Masaccio and Donatello, was the pioneer of the Renaissance architectural style. He went to Rome to study the ancient ruins and learn the techniques of classical Roman architecture. When he returned to Florence, he received a commission to build a dome for the cathedral. His creation became a model for many later domes, among them St. Peter's in Rome and the Capitol dome in Washington.

Florence remained the great center of architecture and the other arts until the end of the fifteenth century. Then artistic and cultural supremacy shifted to Rome. As far as architecture was concerned, one reason for the transfer was the fact that in 1499 Pope Julius II persuaded an architect named Bramante to move to Rome. Bramante's work in the capital of Christendom led Renaissance architecture into its greatest phase. His own greatest work, and the culmination of Renaissance architecture, was the basilica of St. Peter's. Bramante's plan called for a church in the shape of a huge Greek cross having arms of equal length and crowned with a vast dome. It would have covered an area nearly twelve thousand square yards larger than that actually covered by St. Peter's, still the largest church in Christendom. After his death in 1515 a series of other men took over and altered Bramante's plans. In 1546 Michelangelo, who was seventy-one years old, agreed to take charge. He returned to the main outlines of Bramante's plan but added many features of his own, including a new design for the dome. He died long before the building was completed and many of the details of his plan were changed, but the great dome followed his design.

THE NORTHERN RENAISSANCE

To fifteenth-century Italians the culture of the north seemed so far behind theirs that when the French king invaded Italy in 1494, they regarded the attack as a new barbarian invasion. One reason for the lag was the economic and political chaos of the late fourteenth and the fifteenth centuries in lands north of Italy. Princes and nobles lacked the time and money needed to patronize artists and scholars. The disruption of wars, brigandage, want, misery, social strife, and pestilence made men pessimistic and insecure, in striking contrast to the optimism of the Italians of the Renaissance. In Italy the fusion of the nobility and the upper bourgeoisie in the cities produced a changed milieu in which new ideas could flourish. In the north the nobility still dominated with its traditional value system, and tales of chivalry remained the favorite form of literature even among members of the merchant class. In Italy classical writings served as the inspiration for a new world view. In the north stories of ancient Troy, Greece, and Rome were woven into fanciful tales of chivalric derring-do. A deliberate effort was made to keep alive the exaggerated glories of the knightly past by the introduction of elaborate court ceremonials, royal sponsorship of chivalric love and poetry, tournaments, and the creation of new knightly orders, such as the English Order of the Garter and the Burgundian Order of the Golden Fleece.

The French invasion of Italy in 1494 permanently connected northern Europe with Italian culture. The invasion accelerated immeasurably the process of cultural interchange that had already begun with traveling scholars and artists, students, clergymen, and merchants. By the beginning of the sixteenth century Italian culture exercised an unprecedented and almost hypnotic influence over European cultural life. Northern princes sought the services of Italian scholars and artists, and the monarchs of France, England, and Spain, secure on their thrones and with large revenues at their disposal, could afford lavish patronage. Even the miserly Henry VII of England (1485–1509) had a tomb made for himself and his wife by a Florentine artist, Torrigiano, which was so elaborate that a century later Francis Bacon said of Henry that he "dwelleth more richly dead than he did alive in any of his palaces." The much more extravagant Francis I of France (1515–1547) persuaded Leonardo da Vinci to come to France by offering him 7,000 gold florins and a palace of his own choosing.

NORTHERN ART AND ARCHITECTURE

Northern artists combined the artistic traditions of their own lands with the style and techniques that they learned from the Italians. This was done most successfully by Albrecht Dürer (1471–1528). While he was still an apprentice painter in Germany being trained in the Gothic style, he saw some engravings of Italian paintings and copied them in an attempt to learn how to draw the human form. Later he traveled to Italy to study and do research in artistic techniques. Influenced by the Italians, he used classical themes, studied mathematics and art theory, and wrote treatises on perspective and proportion. Yet he remained faithful to his own German tradition. His works have an intensity and air of mysticism, as well as sometimes a gaunt, inhuman, allegorical terror, that clearly distinguish them from Italian works of art.

Courtesy of The Metropolitan Museum of Art,
Harris Brisbane Dick Fund, 1943

Melancholia I, by Albrecht Dürer

*"His engraving of the Melancholic Temperament, the temperament that is to
say of the student, the author, and the artist, was intended to express this
painfulness of intellectual conception. It is really a work of religious art and,
as such, it has taken and maintains an astonishing hold upon the minds of
thoughtful men."* William Martin Conway, LITERARY REMAINS OF ALBRECHT
DÜRER (Cambridge, Eng., 1889).

Dürer was the leading figure among the artists who made the era from the 1490's to the 1520's the greatest in the history of German creative art. Another major artist of the period, Hans Holbein the Younger (1497–1543), stands out as one of the greatest portrait painters of all time. In his early years he painted religious subjects, but later he devoted himself completely to the portrayal of secular society. The meticulous detail, simplicity of composition, and complete frankness of his portraits reveal the intermingling of the German and Italian elements, an amalgam of the two traditions, which also can be seen in the work of other important German painters of the era. For three-quarters of a century painting in England was conditioned by the impact that Holbein made on aristocratic taste during his two long sojourns there. He died in England while serving as court painter to Henry VIII.

The Germans had no rivals in their mastery of woodcuts and copper engravings. Dürer above all others excelled in these media; indeed, he owed his greatest fame to his graphic art. His prints and those of other German artists served as powerful weapons of propaganda in the Protestant Reformation. A plate or woodcut could turn out thousands of copies of a drawing of a religious subject illustrating a theme of the reformers, or it could reproduce a caricature satirizing the Roman Catholic priesthood.

In the late thirteenth and the fourteenth centuries Flanders, which was then a part of the duke of Burgundy's possessions, was the scene of a great artistic outburst. Flemish painting alone in all of Europe rivaled that of the Italian Renaissance. The Flemings, unlike the Italians, made no conscious effort to break with the medieval past. Instead, they moved easily and gradually from the medieval toward a modern style, and their painting remained deeply spiritual and symbolic in the medieval manner. They differed from the Italians, too, in that they did not develop systematic and scientific studies of anatomy, perspective, and composition. They arrived at technical mastery by practice and, later, by heavy borrowing from the Italians.

Flanders, like northern Italy, was a land of cities with a rich urban patriciate. The great Flemish artists, however, did not paint primarily for these people. Many of their major works were done for the court of the Burgundian dukes, which more than any other court in Europe retained the medieval traditions of chivalry. In their art the Flemings reflected these two currents — the urban milieu from which they sprang and the chivalric trappings of court life.

The van Eyck brothers, Hubert (*c.* 1370–1426) and Jan (*c.* 1390–1440), were the first great figures of the Flemish school. Their painting *The Adoration of the Lamb,* covering both sides of six wooden panels, became the inspiration and model for other Flemish artists, just as the paintings of their Italian contemporary Masaccio inspired Italian artists. It was painted in oils and established the superiority of that medium for portraying colors and color depth. Until then artists had preferred to mix colors with egg yolk thinned with water (tempera), though the use of oil as a binding fluid for colors had been known for centuries.[1] Improvements in the refinement of linseed oil and in solvents and thinners after 1400 made it possible for the van Eycks to perfect the use of oil paints.

Contact between Italy and Flanders greatly increased in the sixteenth century. Flemish artists came more under Italian influence, as evidenced by better composition and the introduction of nudes into painting. The overall quality of their work, however, declined.

France's invasion of Italy in 1494 also introduced the north to Renaissance architecture. The architectural theories that came to the north in the first quarter of the sixteenth century were already obsolete in Italy, and this cultural lag enabled northern craftsmen to absorb the new forms into the older local tradition and thoroughly domesticate the first stage of Italian architectural influence. The early sixteenth-century Renaissance buildings in France, the Low Countries, and Germany show a compromise between late Gothic structure and Renaissance proportions, with a tendency to use Renaissance decoration to give an overall effect of the new. In England the Renaissance made slight impact on building until the last half of the sixteenth century, when much architectural decorativeness was borrowed from the Low Countries and obtained from design hand-books or do-it-yourself manuals for English gentlemen.

[1] Italian artists also practiced fresco painting, in which the pigments were mixed with water only. The artist painted on wet lime-plaster walls, and the colors dried and set with the plaster to become a permanent part of the wall. The Sistine Chapel ceiling, painted by Michelangelo, is the most famous example of this technique.

The Creation of Man, by Michelangelo
detail from ceiling of Sistine Chapel

"Thus, singlehanded, he completed the work in twenty months, aided only by his mixer of colors. . . . He used no perspective or foreshortening, or any fixed point of view, devoting his energies rather to adapting the figures to the disposition than the disposition to the figures, contenting himself with the perfection of his nude and draped figures, which are of unsurpassed design and excellence. . . . The venerable majesty of God with the motion as He surrounds some of the cherubs with one arm and stretches the other to an Adam of marvellous beauty of attitude and outline, seem a new creation of the Maker rather than one of the brush and design of a man." G. Vasari (1511–1574), in THE LIVES OF THE PAINTERS, SCULPTORS AND ARCHITECTS, ed. W. Gaunt (London, 1963).

THE NATURE OF NORTHERN HUMANISM

Italian humanists held a fundamentally secular outlook; they rejected the medieval past and studied the classics to find models for the worldly life that they thought men should live. Like the Italians, the humanists of England, France, Germany, the Low Countries, and Spain believed that man as a rational being had the capacity to lead a good life, but unlike the Italians, they had a profoundly religious world view. They wanted to integrate the new learning with the Christian heritage, including the best of medieval scholarship. They believed that the literature of classical antiquity together with the literature of Christian antiquity (the writings of the early Church Fathers and the New Testament) contained a wisdom that would improve individual man and, far more important, revitalize the Christian society of their own time. Their intention to reconcile the new wave of classical heritage and Christianity was similar in motivation though not in method to that of Aquinas in the thirteenth century during the first revival of classical learning. Their religious orientation gained for them the name of Christian humanists.

A new pietism, which originated in a movement called *Devotio moderna* and centered in the Low Countries and Germany during the fifteenth century, put its religious stamp on Christian humanism. The movement had its immediate cause in the deep distaste felt by many devout Christians for the worldly preoccupations of the papacy and the clergy. The *Devotio moderna* pietists skirted heresy, but their quietism and social respectability allowed them to avoid provoking Church or state. The movement comprised communities of laymen and laywomen, called Brethren of the Common Life, who lived according to ascetic discipline but not under monastic vows of organization. They emphasized the direct relationship of the individual to God and thereby lessened the importance of the priesthood as an intermediary between man and his Creator. Study of the Bible and other religious texts and a love of learning were important features. Above all, they were interested in education and became associated with schools run by men who had studied in Italy and returned filled with humanist zeal. Through their influence the schools combined religious earnestness and discipline with a humanist education and came to be recognized as the best of the day. The most famous one, at Deventer in the Netherlands, had 2,000 students.

THE SPREAD OF HUMANISM IN THE NORTH

During the last quarter of the fifteenth century and the first decades of the sixteenth the impact of Italian humanism on northern Europe made itself felt through many channels. Monarchs and princes, impressed by the elegance of Italian courts, decided that they must have secretaries and diplomats who could write and speak polished Latin. The Italian humanists whom they named to these offices served as transmitters of humanist culture. Other Italians took posts at universities to teach Greek and Latin and classical literature. Northerners went to Italy to study in increasing numbers and returned home to write about and teach the new learning. Historians applied the critical methods of humanist scholarship to historical sources and repudiated long-believed legends. Schools and universities introduced humanist studies into their curricula — though not without bitter controversy with traditionalists — and new universities were founded in which the humanities held a central position. By 1520 most of the German universities, Oxford and Cambridge in England, Alcalá in Spain, Louvain in Brabant, and the University of Paris had introduced the teaching of Greek and the study of Greek texts.

The invention of printing from movable type in the Rhineland in the middle of the fifteenth century contributed greatly to the rapid spread of humanism in the north. This technological innovation reduced drastically the cost of books. Wood-block printing, invented by the Chinese, had reached the West by the early fifteenth century, when books of crude pictures and short texts began to appear, although Chinese experiments with movable type do not seem to have been known in the West. The Chinese had also invented paper made of fiber or rags, and by the twelfth century some paper was being made in Europe, but parchment (made from thinly sliced animal skin) continued in general use until the printing press replaced the medieval copyist. Traditionally the credit for the first printing by movable type goes to Johann Gutenberg of Mainz in the 1440's. The process spread rapidly, and by 1500 thousands of books had been issued by printers all over Europe. During the last half of the fifteenth century a growing proportion of printed books were classical texts, grammars, and humanist writings. The press immeasurably hastened humanism's conquest of learning in the north.

The early printers tried to make their books look like medieval manuscripts. They modeled type faces on the heavy black letters of the scribes, sometimes used hand-painted decorations and initial letters, and occasionally printed on vellum. By the early decades of the sixteenth century, however, leading Italian printers, influenced by the handwriting developed by the humanists, adopted the Roman and italic types that are familiar today. The new typography soon spread to northern Europe.

THE CHRISTIAN HUMANISTS

The Christian humanists hoped that their study of the early texts of Christianity, particularly the Bible, based on the humanist techniques of textual criticism and philology, would enable them to purge Christian doctrine of the obscurities and errors added through the centuries by theologians who had not read the original texts. They argued that once the texts were published, they would reveal Christianity in its purest form. The abuses and materialism that had turned men from the Church and saddened the faithful would disappear, and the Church would gain renewed strength, vitality, and inspiration. They believed, too, that secular learning would increase the piety of the individual and enable him by the use of reason to improve his nature because, as the English humanist Thomas More put it, education in Latin and Greek "doth train the soul in virtue."

Learned men in all the lands of Europe shared these opinions to a greater or lesser degree. They motivated the Christian humanist movement in Spain, centering on the newly founded university of Alcalá, where the first translation of the New Testament drawn from Greek manuscripts, known as the Complutensian Bible, was completed in 1514. They also motivated the work of three outstanding Christian humanists, who illustrated the similarities and differences among Christian humanists generally.

Lefèvre d'Étaples (*c.* 1450–1536), the most brilliant French thinker of his time, studied in Italy and then lectured on classical philosophy at the University of Paris. He was an intensely religious man with strong mystical leanings, who put less emphasis upon human reason and more upon divine intercession than did most of his fellow Christian humanists. He wrote many treatises on religious philosophy, published commentaries on biblical texts, and in 1523 put out a French translation of the Bible. His views anticipated principles that were soon to be enunciated by the Protestant reformers, particularly the doctrine of justification by faith. Yet, like other Christian humanists, Lefèvre repudiated the reformers and remained loyal to Catholicism, even though the theological faculty of the University of Paris condemned him as a heretic.

Thomas More (1478–1535), the most prominent figure in English humanism, was the only one of the great humanists who was not a professional scholar or teacher. He had a brilliant career as a lawyer, diplomat, and politician, and rose to the high office of Lord Chancellor of England. He was almost unique among humanists in that he never studied in Italy. His brilliance won him the attention of his elders, and he advanced rapidly. Despite worldly success he practiced a rigorous medieval piety. He long wore a hair shirt next to his skin, and sometimes the blood that it drew stained his outer clothing. As Lord Chancellor, he repressed Protestants as heretics. Later he himself died on the scaffold for his Roman faith.

More wrote somber devotional works that warned of the need to prepare for death, but his most famous book was in a very different vein. Called *Utopia,* the Greek word for nowhere, the book was first printed in Latin in 1516 and was soon translated into other languages. More wrote it to criticize the evils of contemporary society and show men the way things might be if they lived according to the social and political ideals of Christianity and followed the counsels of reason. Utopia was a mythical island in the New World where property was held communally and each individual received as many goods as he needed. The government regulated economic life, education, and public health. There were only a few simple laws, the work day was limited to six hours, and every religious creed was tolerated except atheism. Everyone on the happy island lived in peace and prosperity — in contrast to the Europe of More's day.

Of all the Christian humanists, none had greater influence and fame than Desiderius Erasmus (1466–1536). He dominated the intellectual life of northern Europe to an extent unequaled by any man until Voltaire in the eighteenth century. He had disciples in every land of Europe, was on intimate terms with nearly all the great men of his time, and maintained a voluminous correspondence. He owed his reputation to his prodigious literary output, his vast erudition, his polished and persuasive literary style, his clarity and wit, his moderation, and his abundant common sense. He loved learning for its own sake but felt it must be used to combat ignorance, superstition, corruption, and violence. His books had enormous popularity; they were the first best sellers in the history of printing.

Erasmus was born in Rotterdam, the younger of two sons of a Catholic priest. He received his education at the famous Brethren of the Common Life school at Deventer and then was persuaded to accept ordination as a priest. He soon regretted this decision and set forth as a free-lance scholar and writer on travels that carried him through many lands. His distaste for clerical life and his love for the classics did not diminish his deep piety and devotion to Christianity. He believed that Christianity, stripped of the gloss and interpretations of theologians and restored to its original form, offered the perfect guide for both the individual and society. He wrote for the general reader in the hope of spreading this message, and he longed for the day when the Bible would be translated into every language, so that everyone could read and understand it for himself. He had nothing but contempt for the people and practices that he felt perverted the true nature of Christianity. He poured ridicule and scorn on the ignorance and venality of priests, the worship of relics, the exaggerated veneration of saints, and many other abuses in the Catholic Church.

Erasmus's views and influence made him a leader in the movement for reform of the Catholic Church. For a time he went along with Martin Luther, the great German reformer, but he could not go all the way. He wanted to reform the Church from within, not break away and start a new church. Erasmus and the other great Christian humanists treasured the unity of Christendom above any difference of opinion about doctrine. When Europe finally split between Catholic and Protestant, Erasmus and most of the other Christian humanists remained within the Catholic fold. The irony was that in their efforts to reform the Church they loved, they unwittingly helped to undermine it and to bring about a revolution.

RENAISSANCE SCIENCE

One of the current battlegrounds for Renaissance historians is this question: was the Renaissance era productive of scientific advance? Historians usually have drawn a clear distinction between Aristotelian metaphysics, the science of the Middle Ages, and the experimentally oriented natural philosophy of the late sixteenth and seventeenth centuries, which was basic to the development of modern science. The Renaissance seems to have little or no place in this pattern. Caught between two eras of science, it was neither the culmination of one nor the origin of the other. Copernicus (1473–1543), the greatest scientific figure of the era, exemplifies the problem. He was not an experimental scientist, but he was the point of origin for the great revolution on which modern science is founded. (See pp. 202–204.) He was very much a Renaissance humanist, yet he is most meaningfully treated in relation to the scientists of the late sixteenth and seventeenth centuries. Here again the Renaissance manifested itself as an age of transition.

In the Middle Ages the study of the physical world was dictated by the categories laid down centuries before by Aristotle. Such was the authority of Aristotle that medieval scientists believed they did not need data derived empirically, by experimentation. This does not mean that the Middle Ages were scientifically sterile. Alchemy, the attempted transmutation of base metals into gold, and astrology were practically motivated studies of the physical world. These studies grew rapidly in the fifteenth century, but it is difficult to assess precisely their contribution to modern science. Humanism acted as a powerful solvent of Aristotelianism by re-establishing the classical tension between Aristotle's materialism and Plato's idealism. This resulted in the growth of a Neo-Platonic movement in Italian humanism, which was associated with Marsilio Ficino (1433–1499) and the influential Platonic Academy in Florence. The Neo-Platonists reintroduced Plato's passion for numbers and harmonics, which probably contributed to awakening an interest in geometry and higher mathematics.

Renaissance humanists contributed to later scientific advances by uncovering and editing previously unknown works of classical science and by making accurate translations from the original Greek of texts that had been known only from Arabic or earlier imperfect Latin translations. Admiration for antiquity and philological scholarship, rather than scientific curiosity, inspired this work. Yet it made available ancient scientific knowledge that might otherwise have taken European scientists a long time to rediscover. In addition, the humanists' intensive examination of the original classical texts produced an intimate knowledge of ancient science that led ultimately to the recognition by scientists of both

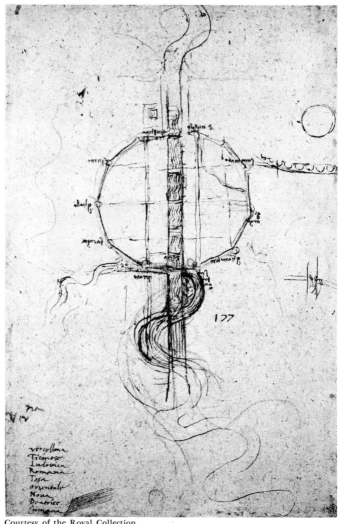

A Project for Regularizing the River Arno,
by Leonardo da Vinci

"That a river which has to be diverted from one place to another ought to be coaxed and not coerced with violence; and in order to do that it is necessary to build a sort of dam projecting into the river and then to throw another one below it projecting farther; and by proceeding in this way with a third, a fourth, a fifth, the river will discharge itself to the channel allotted to it, or by this means it may be turned away from the place where it has caused damage."
Edward MacCurdy, ed., THE NOTEBOOKS OF LEONARDO DA VINCI (New York, 1938), Vol. II.

the truth and the errors of ancient science and that suggested new avenues of scientific investigation.

The interest of Renaissance artists in the human body, which resulted from their efforts to achieve naturalistic portraiture, encouraged anatomical research. Anatomical study and dissection became accepted parts of the artist's training. The most famous and skilled of the artist-anatomists was Leonardo da Vinci. His notebooks contain hundreds of drawings and comments based upon his careful dissections of human and animal cadavers (they also include designs for submarines, airplanes, machine guns, and other modern inventions). Leonardo never published his anatomical investigations; his findings, therefore, probably had no influence on subsequent anatomical study.

The credit for the pioneering work in anatomy goes to Andreas Vesalius (1514–1564), a Fleming who taught anatomy at the University of Padua in Italy. His university became the chief center of scientific study, especially of medical science. Vesalius, like all medical men of that era, followed the teachings of Galen, who around A.D. 150 had summed up most of ancient Greek medical knowledge in several treatises. Galen had long been considered the final authority in medical science just as Aristotle was in physical science. When Vesalius's dissections showed that Galen's work contained many errors he decided to write his own textbook. Called *On the Structure of the Human Body*, it appeared in 1543 — the same year that saw the publication of Copernicus's book on the heliocentric theory. Vesalius illustrated his findings with beautifully executed woodcuts in which the anatomical drawings stood out against a background of Renaissance landscapes.

The book dealt with the relationship between the individual organ and the body as a whole. Vesalius showed that anatomy could be learned only by actual dissection, not by reading Galen. Although some scholars refused to be convinced, in time more open-minded men realized that Vesalius made Galen obsolete. They followed his technique of meticulous observation, and as a result a stream of important discoveries in human anatomy were made.

The very elusiveness of Renaissance science affords insight into some of the limitations of the period. For all its glory, the Renaissance did better in heralding the brave new world than in determining its course. Petrarch's words, "that to things transitory things eternal should succeed," seemed almost prophetic of the Renaissance's fate. Renaissance endeavor was too diffuse to be systematic; Renaissance man was too enamored of classical beauty to look beyond it. The high level at which the Renaissance operated, its preoccupation with a classical ideal that had only limited relevance to the contemporary condition of man, and the narrowness of its social base divorced it from reality. For historians, the unrealistic quality of so much of the Renaissance makes the age elusive, transitional, even transitory.

THE POLITICS OF
THE RENAISSANCE
CHAPTER FOUR

Politica est res dura (politics is a hard business) was a Roman maxim rediscovered by the Renaissance and much favored in discussion of contemporary politics. Medieval politics, of course, had not been soft, as the feudal lords in France and England discovered, as King John realized when forced to accept the humiliation of Magna Carta, and as Pope Boniface VIII learned when agents of the French king burst in upon him in his residence and put him under arrest. Yet in politics, as in art and letters, the Renaissance image of man brought about a changed emphasis and a new departure in theory and practice, both domestic and international. *Virtù* was not confined to artists — indeed, it was most clearly enunciated in the Renaissance conception of the statesman. Italian politics of the fourteenth and fifteenth centuries was dominated by men of *virtù* who with brutal realism consciously fashioned the techniques of statecraft and raised it to an art.

POLITICAL THEORY

Political theorists of the High Middle Ages had ranged over a wide area of thought and had often disagreed with their fellows. Still, they nearly all agreed on certain fundamental assumptions. They maintained that all authority derived ultimately from God, that monarchy was the best form of political organization, that the monarch must exercise his power in subjection to God's will, and that no human authority, whether religious or secular, could be unlimited. The monarch must rule for the common good, and his laws were valid only if they were designed for the welfare of the whole community in accordance with the dictates of reason or natural law. Democracy found no place in the writings of these men, but neither did authoritarianism or absolutism.

In the fourteenth century there was a discernible shift away from this concern with the duties and limitations of the governing authorities to an analysis of the structure of social institutions and the nature of government. In what has been called the most important political treatise of the later Middle Ages, the *Defensor Pacis* (1324), the joint authors, Marsiglio of Padua and John of Jandun, argued that organized religion in the form of the Church was only one form of social activity, and like all other social activities should be subordinate to the state. This first clear assertion of the supremacy of the secular over the spiritual power was destined to become a source book for all opponents of the papal power for the next two centuries. By the fifteenth century the secularism that had been a bold innovation in the *Defensor Pacis* became the common coin of political theory. Political philosophers ceased to regard politics as a human activity ultimately subject to theology. Instead, they saw it as a study of practical importance based on practical experience.

NICCOLÒ MACHIAVELLI

Niccolò Machiavelli (1469–1527) was the greatest of the new political philosophers. It is accurate to credit him with the founding of modern political theory, based on his observations of Italian Renaissance politics in action. Machiavelli served from 1498 to 1512 as an official and diplomat of the republican government of Florence. The work provided him with a close knowledge of the operation of government and the whole spectrum of attitudes and activities of contemporary Italian politicians at a time of great vitality and stress. In 1512 the overthrow of the republican government by the Medici cost him his post, and for the remaining fourteen years of his life he tried unsuccessfully to get back into the government. He filled his years of involuntary retirement with study and writing. In the breadth of his literary accomplishments — political and military treatises, histories, plays, poems, and stories — he demonstrated the proper Renaissance versatility.

Machiavelli was a child of the Italian Renaissance at its peak. Italian politics was one foundation of his political education; the other was a classicist's knowledge of the political history of Rome, especially under the republic. His long treatise called *Discourses on the First Ten Books of Livy* (a Roman historian) was based upon Roman history and was less explicitly related to practical experience than to classical times. In the *Discourses* he attempted a systematic analysis of six specific forms of government, which he argued followed one another in cyclical order: monarchy, tyranny, aristocracy, oligarchy, democracy, and mob rule.

Machiavelli owed his undying fame to his pamphlet *The Prince,* written in 1513 and addressed to the Medici ruler of Florence in 1515 in the hope that the prince would recognize and employ his talent. *The Prince* did not accomplish what its author had hoped, but it long out-

Brown Brothers

Niccolò Machiavelli

"The principal study and care and the especial province of a prince should be warfare and its attendant rules and discipline. . . . he must never let his mind be turned from the study of warfare and in times of peace he must concern himself with it more than in those of war. . . . As for the exercise of the mind, the prince should read the histories of all peoples and ponder on the actions of the wise men therein recorded." Niccolò Machiavelli, THE PRINCE (1532).

lived his ambitions and became the guidebook to power politics in future centuries. Because of it, Machiavelli's name became a synonym for political cunning and unscrupulous behavior — an identification that does less than justice to the man and to the sublety of his argument.

Machiavelli conceived of the state as a work of art, the creation of a leader who by the imposition of his *virtù* on the state and society increased the *virtù* of the mass of the people. *The Prince* has as its theme the doctrine that the ruler should use any means, however unprincipled, to win and hold power, to create a strong central government, and to preserve the state. The prince should keep his word or break it, be just or unjust, reward his supporters or sacrifice them, depending upon whichever action best suits the interests of the state. Men in general are "ungrateful, fickle, false, cowards, and covetous" and will not keep faith with the ruler, so that he need not keep faith with them. "The experience of our times," Machiavelli wrote, "shows those princes to have done great things who have no regard for their promises, who have been able by craftiness to confuse men's brains, and who have conquered over those who put their reliance on good faith." Machiavelli's cynicism and low opinion of mankind grew out of his own experiences in the world of Italian politics. Yet he had an idealistic end in view. He hoped that a ruler who followed his advice would be able to unite all Italy and drive out the foreign armies that had invaded the peninsula. He believed that good could come out of evil: the unprincipled despot could achieve desirable social ends more easily than could a just ruler.

Machiavelli placed the state and its preservation in the center of political theory. Machiavelli's empiricism — that the prince should do what he has learned by experience is best — was a powerful solvent to the accepted, static, hierarchic pattern of medieval thinking about political order. Since for Machiavelli the exact structure of the state was secondary and its preservation primary, his argument fitted the political systems that he had dealt with in the *Discourses*. Once Machiavelli had postulated necessity as the governing cause of political action, *raison d'état*, reason of state as the justification for any course of action no matter how immoral, was just around the corner.

ITALIAN POLITICS

In Machiavelli were present most of the theoretical ingredients for the best and the worst in European politics. The first manifestation of both ingredients was in the Italian politics of the Renaissance that schooled Machaivelli. This brand of politics stemmed principally from the growth of the city-states of northern Italy in the late Middle Ages. The conflict rising out of German imperial attempts to control Italy and the papacy's moves to counter them gave the city-states the opportunity to emerge

ITALIAN STATES IN 1494

SWITZERLAND

KINGDOM OF HUNGARY

DUCHY OF MILAN

KINGDOM D. OF SAVOY

OF M. OF ASTI MONTFERRAT

M. OF MANTUA

VENETIAN

M. OF SALUZZO

D. OF MODENA

D. OF FERRARA

FRANCE

R. OF GENOA

R. OF LUCCA

REPUBLIC OF FLORENCE

R. OF SAN MARINO

OTTOMAN EMPIRE

REPUBLIC

R. OF SIENA

PAPAL

Adriatic Sea

Ragusa

CORSICA
(TO GENOA)

STATES

Rome •

BENEVENTO

SARDINIA
(TO SPAIN)

Naples

KINGDOM

Tyrrhenian Sea

OF NAPLES

Republics

Feudal States

Papal States

Palermo •

D. = Duchy

M. = Marquisate

0   150

Miles

in the thirteenth century as independent political entities. Their near-monopoly of trade with the East provided the economic base for independence and determined the social composition of the oligarchies that ruled them.

Factionalism was endemic in most of the city-states, splitting the oligarchies and nurturing a constant struggle for power. The factions first grew out of the political alignments within each city by which one side supported the claims of the German emperors and their opponents supported the papacy. The imperial party was called the Ghibellines, and the papal party the Guelphs. These party names soon lost their original connotations and, instead, were applied to factions that were divided over more basic and less exalted causes. Class distinctions dividing the wealthy merchants and bankers from the shopkeepers, craftsmen, and professional men who made up the lesser bourgeoisie, as well as from the wage earners who formed the mass of the city population, added to the internal strife. Each class suspected the other and wanted to gain control of the government. Most of the time the wealthy oligarchs (in Florence they were called *popolo grasso,* fat people) managed to keep control. However, the unceasing social and political discord persuaded many city dwellers by the end of the thirteenth century that the only way to achieve internal order was by one-man rule. Sometimes this was done by turning the government over to the head of a political faction or the leader of a social class. In other cases an ambitious man assumed dictatorial power by a coup d'état. Sometimes an outsider was asked to take over in the hope that he would not be tied to any of the contesting groups within the city. In still other instances a mercenary captain hired to defend the city seized power for himself.

In this way, many of the northern Italian cities came under the rule of despots. The circumstances by which the despots came to power made their tenure insecure. They could not depend upon the traditional loyalty of their subjects, as legitimate monarchs could in other lands. Rivals never ceased plotting to overthrow them; they lived in the shadow of assassination and revolution. They had to be ruthless, cunning, and coldly rational to win and hold power. The stories of their atrocities and their craftiness are legion. To give only two examples, in 1409 Giovanni Maria Visconti, ruler of Milan, loosed mercenaries against his subjects, massacring two hundred Milanese, because people cried out to him in the streets to end the war that he was waging. Again in another city, a soldier of fortune named Oliverotto invited all the leading men, including the uncle who had raised him, to a banquet. After a sumptuous dinner and elaborate entertainment, he gave a signal to hidden confederates to rush out and kill the guests. He then made himself dictator.

RENAISSANCE DESPOTISM

Despite the constant wars among the city-states, the rulers, whether oligarchs or despots, were afraid to arm their subjects lest they be overthrown. The people, for their part, had no desire to fight for rulers whom they distrusted or despised. Therefore the rulers hired mercenary captains, called *condottieri* (singular, *condottiere*), who had their own bands of troops. The mercenaries had no loyalty to their employer, and fought for the highest bidder and changed sides without compunction. They preferred long wars to ensure their employment; the consequences were indecisive battles and prolonged sieges. Since his soldiers were his capital assets, the condottiere avoided wasting them in frontal assaults. Nor did he want to kill the opposing mercenaries, preferring to capture them for ransom. To minimize the loss of personnel, the mercenaries developed a code of military etiquette that disapproved of such practices as night battles or the use of artillery.

Sometimes the condottieri seized power from their employers and established themselves as tyrants. Some of these men had begun life as the sons of humble peasants or tradesmen. Not all of them, however, had lowly origins. Some came from backgrounds of wealth and culture, and a few were actually rulers of petty city-states seeking greater fortunes. Among the aristocratic condottieri was Federigo da Montefeltro (1422–1482), duke of Urbino, who was one of the most cultured and admired men of his time.

The despots were aware that ruthlessness alone would not keep them in power and that they must satisfy the demands of their subjects or be overthrown. They often improved methods of taxation, ordered the construction of public works and buildings to give people employment and beautify the city, built canals, promoted irrigation projects to increase farm production in the countryside around the city, enforced impartial justice (except where their own interests were involved), and followed policies to encourage business enterprise.

They made a major and lasting contribution in the inspiration that their success provided to other men. Their careers represented a triumph of individualism — of *virtù*. They demonstrated that a man of ability and determination could win fame, power, and wealth regardless of birth or social status. The more intelligent despots surrounded themselves with men of their own stamp, with whom they could establish rapport, rather than with simpering courtiers. Thus the intellectual and social climate of the despot's entourage proved highly favorable to the advancement of creativity and individual ability.

Finally, the despots distinguished themselves as patrons of art and culture. Many of them possessed a genuine appreciation of beauty and learning. All craved lasting fame and knew that they could gain it by commissioning magnificent buildings, pictures, and other artistic works as perpetual monuments to their greatness. They hoped to win the respect and support of their subjects by surrounding themselves with the luxury and glamor expected of a prince. Their sponsorship of art and learning brought fame to the state and appealed to civic pride and loyalty. Without them, the Renaissance in culture was inconceivable.

Though the future of most Italian city-states lay with the despots, the civic consciousness of the cities must not be overlooked. There was explicit in the invitation to the despot, and implicit in the coup d'état of a condottiere, a commitment to rule the city-state for the benefit of the city. Machiavelli presupposed this commitment in his prince — and it was a quality usually to be found in the despots, whatever their faults.

ITALIAN POLITICS IN THE FIFTEENTH CENTURY

By the fifteenth century five states had emerged as the dominant powers of the peninsula. They were Milan, Florence, and Venice in the north, the Papal States in the center, and the kingdom of Naples in the south. Almost unconsciously the five developed a balance of power principle among themselves by which they tacitly agreed that no one state would gain a preponderance of power and, if one tried, the others would war against it. This was the first example in modern times of a group of states using the balance of power principle as a guide in mutual relations. They maintained permanent ambassadors at one another's capitals so that each ruler could keep in constant touch with what was happening in the other states. They also employed secret agents and depended upon merchants and bankers to gather information. Several states, notably Venice, drew up regulations for the training of diplomats and their conduct abroad. The Italian system of diplomacy became the norm for all of Europe in the sixteenth century.

Milan, which had long been an important economic center with territory covering a large part of Lombardy, was one of the first city-states to succumb to despotism. In 1277 the Visconti, a noble Milanese family, seized power and ruled arbitrarily for almost two hundred years. Around 1400 Gian Galeazzo Visconti tried to unite northern and central Italy in an absolute monarchy under his scepter. The determined resistance of Florence and Venice shattered his plans, and the Milanese state was restricted to Lombardy. When the direct Visconti line ran out in 1447, the Milanese tried to regain their freedom by establishing a republic. The new government hired Francesco Sforza (1402–1466), a condottiere, to defend it. Sforza, the illegitimate son of a condottiere, had married the illegitimate daughter of the last Visconti ruler. In 1450 he overthrew the republic and made himself despot. His dynasty lasted fifty years. Ludovico, last of the Sforza rulers, was one of the most famous princes of his time. Called *il Moro,* he won renown for his intelligence, political acumen, and sponsorship of the arts and learning. During his reign (1479–1500) he surrounded himself with scholars and artists, including the famous Leonardo da Vinci. His court was one of the most brilliant and luxurious in Europe.

Florence was the chief city of Tuscany and, until the end of the fifteenth century, the great center of Renaissance culture. It lay on the banks of the Arno halfway between Milan and Rome. The city owed its economic strength to banking families and manufacturers, especially those from the woolen cloth industry. From the thirteenth century on, the Florentine Republic was torn by struggles between political parties and between social and economic classes. After long years of struggle and experiments with different kinds of governments, ranging from radical democracy to dictatorship, Cosimo de' Medici (1389–1464) took over power. Cosimo was the head of the Medici banking and mercantile clan, the wealthiest family in Italy and probably in Europe. He kept himself in the background and seldom took public office. Instead, like a modern American political boss, he ruled the city by controlling the elections so that only men who took orders from him were chosen for public office. He gained and kept power by the typical political boss tactic of siding with the poor against the rich. He showed great skill in conducting the foreign affairs of his state, and he was a great patron of culture. When he died in 1464, the grateful Florentines inscribed on his tomb the title *Pater Patriae,* Father of the Country.

Cosimo's son, who succeeded to the rule of Florence, reigned for only five years. In 1469 Cosimo's grandson, the twenty-year-old Lorenzo (1449–1492), took over power. Lorenzo, known as the Magnificent, became the most famous of all the Medicis. In 1478 his rule was challenged by a powerful conspiracy led by the Pazzi, one of the great families of Florence. He overcame the threat and, to prevent its recurrence, adopted despotic measures. He tightened his control over the state by making the councils that governed the city responsible to him alone, and he cruelly punished those who plotted against him. Once he had established despotic rule, he devoted himself to his great passion — patronage of arts and letters. His great liberality, his intellectual interests, his own ability as a poet, and his excellent taste did much to make Florence one of the greatest centers of arts and letters known to history.

During Lorenzo's reign expensive wars, heavy taxation, lavish spending, and new and vigorous foreign competition brought on a serious decline in Florence's economic life. Lorenzo, who lacked the business acumen of his forebears, made matters worse by using state money for his own business purposes. His reputation became tarnished, and the Florentines turned against him and his family. A Dominican friar named Girolamo Savonarola (1452–1498) entranced great crowds with denunciations of Lorenzo's corruption, preached against the luxury and paganism of the Renaissance, and prophesied the ruin of Italy unless people mended their ways. After Lorenzo's death in 1492 Savonarola won a wide following that included some of the greatest figures of the Renaissance. In 1496 Lorenzo's son, who had succeeded him as head of state, was driven into exile and Savonarola became the virtual dictator of Florence. Under the spell of his sermons huge bonfires were fed with what he called "vanities" — books, paintings, luxurious clothes, and wigs — and laws were passed to forbid gambling, horse racing, profanity, and coarse songs. Savonarola bitterly attacked the pope, Alexander VI, for his immoral life and the corruption at Rome. Alexander replied by excommunicating him.

The Florentines soon found that the rigors of puritanism were ill-suited to their tastes. Political factions who were hostile to Savonarola, Franciscan monks who opposed him because of the old rivalry between their order and the Dominicans, and pressure from the papacy succeeded in bringing about the friar's downfall. In 1498 he was arrested, tortured, and burned at the stake in the great square of Florence. After a period of internal strife the Medicis returned to power in 1512.

The political history of Venice, or the Republic of St. Mark as it was called, stood in sharp contrast to the internal turmoil of Milan and Florence. An oligarchy of merchant aristocrats gained control of the state in the thirteenth century and retained power almost without challenge. The aristocrats, who formed about 2 per cent of the republic's population, transformed the general assembly of all citizens into a Great Council and restricted membership to their own group. The doge, the nominal head of state, who formerly had been elected by popular vote, was named by the council and became a figurehead. Smaller councils, of which the Council of Ten was the most important, handled the actual affairs of government.

Although they allowed no opposition, the Venetian oligarchs ruled wisely and did much to improve the economic welfare of the people. Venice, long one of the great trading centers of the world, continued to gain most of its wealth from sea commerce. All merchant galleys belonged to the state, which built the ships in the arsenal, a huge shipyard that was probably the largest industrial establishment of its time in Europe.

Until the fifteenth century the Venetians showed little interest in Italian politics. They directed their statecraft to the extension of maritime trade and to the conquest of territory in the eastern Mediterranean. The Venetians looked upon their policy of isolation from the rest of Italy as the foundation of their strength. The advances of the Ottoman Turks in the Mediterranean region, however, made it more difficult to trade with the East and cost the Venetians some of their overseas possessions, while the growing power of Milan and Florence threatened Venetian overland trade routes into Italy and Europe. These developments persuaded the oligarchs that their state must plunge into Italian political affairs. As a result, Venice pushed out her frontiers, became one of the largest of the city-states, and played a major role in the wars and politics of the peninsula.

The Papal States, the fourth of the chief powers of Italy, almost disintegrated as a political unit during the Babylonian Captivity and Great Schism (1305–1417). The accession of Martin V to the throne of St. Peter in 1417 marked the beginning of the restoration of papal sovereignty. His successors reestablished papal control over central Italy and took an active part in Italian political life. They also distinguished themselves as patrons of art and learning and once again made Rome a renowned center of culture. In their concern with power politics, art, and learning the Renaissance popes — as the pontiffs from Nicholas V (1447–1455) to Clement VII (1523–1534) are sometimes called — relegated their religious duties to second place. Their worldliness and the flagrant immorality of some of them occasioned criticism throughout Europe.

The kingdom of Naples-Sicily (later the kingdom of the Two Sicilies) comprised the southernmost parts of Italy and the islands of Sicily. In the thirteenth century the realm had been divided, and Sicily was governed by the ruler of Aragon (Spain) and the mainland by a prince of Anjou (France). From 1435 to 1458 the two parts were united under a single monarch, only to be divided again and then finally reconstituted as one kingdom by Spain in 1504. The kingdom never regained the political importance and prosperity that it had known in its medieval period of glory, and it lagged far behind the rest of Italy in culture.

The success of Renaissance politics in forging a balance of power that prevented the ascendancy of any single state preserved the territorial integrity of the major Italian states almost to the end of the fifteenth century. Then in 1494 Ludovico Sforza of Milan invited French assistance to counter an expected attack from Naples. The need to preserve the Italian balance of power became the excuse for a northern European monarchic nation-state to plunge Europe into its first general war, with Italy as the battlefield.

THE RISE OF THE NATION-STATES

The emergence of strong monarchies in medieval France and England centralized government at the expense of the feudal nobility. During the troubled times of the fourteenth and fifteenth centuries, when economic decline, wars, rebellions, and social unrest racked most of Europe, the chances for continuing the evolution of strong centralized states seemed doomed. Central governments became powerless, or nearly so, as feudal lords contested with their kings and with one another for domination. Then in the second half of the fifteenth century the trend toward decentralization was dramatically reversed. Strong kings in France, England, and Spain, who are sometimes referred to collectively as the New Monarchs, put an end to the internal disorders in their lands, restrained the power of the feudal nobility, extended the royal power and domain, and gained a wider sphere of action and greater control over their subjects. Their achievements led to the establishment of the national territorial state as we know it today.

Behind the success of these monarchs was the realization by most of their subjects that internal order depended upon the curbing of feudal power. This feeling was strongest in the middle classes in the towns. The growth of trade in the fifteenth century strengthened their position and encouraged them to supply the taxes to support monarchic power. The taxes enabled the monarchs to dispense with armies that had been based on feudal military service by armed retainers of the great feudal lords. As tactical developments reduced the military necessity for mounted knights and castles, it became feasible to destroy the castles of the feudal lords. Many of the nobility, particularly the smaller landed proprietors, concluded that the authority of the monarch was not easily withstood and that cooperation with him might secure lucrative offices and honors and preserve their privileges and immunities. The kings drew strong support from lawyers who were trained in the Roman law and who held posts in the government. They argued that the king incorporated within himself the will of the people and that he had the power to enact laws by his own authority. Their argument provided legal justification for the monarchs to disregard the feudal and customary laws that had protected the rights of the nobility and other special groups against royal encroachment. Now the will of the king was regarded as the law.

The monarchs of the new nation-states did not consciously intend to create anything like a modern national territorial state. They were motivated by dynastic ambitions and wanted to build up the power and glory of their families and ensure their continuation. Their states differed greatly from the states of today. Much that was medieval still remained, and they had only begun to evolve the administrative techniques and trained bureaucracy that characterize the modern state. The monarchs did not claim absolute power nor did they seek to establish uniformity in administration. The Church, feudal lords, and other privileged groups still enjoyed special powers and immunities, and newly annexed lands were often allowed to keep their own governing institutions. Nonetheless, one clearly sees the outlines of the modern state in the governmental structure of these monarchies. In fact, the word state in its modern sense of a land, its people, and its government first came into use in the first half of the sixteenth century. The transition from medieval to modern political organization that began in this era presents one of the most significant evidences that Europe had entered into a new stage of its history.

The final stages of the transition from feudal monarchy to the monarchic nation-state in France and England and the first stages in Spain occurred during the reigns of Louis XI, Henry VII, and Ferdinand of Aragon, respectively. A century later Francis Bacon, English philosopher and statesman, called these monarchs the "Three Magi" among the kings of their time.

LOUIS XI OF FRANCE

Louis XI inherited the throne of France in 1461. He was a cynical, brutal, and suspicious man, meticulously scrupulous in religious observances, but with absolutely no moral sensibilities. People were pawns

Courtesy of The Louvre

Louis XI of France, by Lugardon

*"I knew him, and was entertained in his service in the flower of his age, and at
the height of his prosperity, yet I never saw him free from labor and care. . . .
When his body was at rest his mind was at work, for he had affairs at several
places at once, and would concern himself as much with those of his neighbors as
in his own, putting officers of his own over all the great families, and
endeavoring to divide their authority as much as possible. When he was at war
he labored for a peace or truce, and when he had obtained it, he was impatient
for war again. He troubled himself with many trifles in his government, which he
had better have left alone: but it was his temper, and he could not help it."*
Philip de Commines (1447?–1511?), in his MEMOIRS (London, 1856).

to him, to be used to serve his own ends. His craftiness and intrigues won him the nickname "the Spider." Shabbily dressed and miserly, he shunned ceremony. At the same time he was highly intelligent, imaginative, and alert, and he never lost sight of the ambitious goals he set for himself and his country. He was a skilled negotiator and outstanding administrator, and he learned from his mistakes. Perhaps most important, fortune favored him. His opponents could not compare in ability, his feudal enemies died without heirs so that their lands reverted to him, and his people craved a strong king who could keep peace and order.

The provincial autonomy retained by the greater feudal lords within the kingdom posed a constant threat to Louis's authority. Their connection with him was still feudal, excluding him from direct governance of their provinces. Only by bringing their provinces within his own domain could he exercise effective sovereignty over all of France. The opportunity presented itself when the duke of Burgundy, Louis's most unmanageable and dangerous vassal, made a vigorous bid for complete independence.

In the fourteenth century the dukes of Burgundy had begun to acquire territory and to create a centralized state, at the expense of the French monarch, from their base in Franche-Comté between France and Switzerland. Through marriages, treaties, and conquests they gained control of most of the Low Countries. By 1450 the duke of Burgundy, who was nominally a vassal of both the king of France and the Holy Roman Emperor, had become one of Europe's most powerful rulers. Duke Charles the Bold (1467–1477) dreamed of adding more territory to link up the Low Countries and Franche-Comté, thereby creating a middle kingdom between France and Germany. Charles's dream came to nothing in 1477 when he died in battle against the Swiss, who were threatened by Charles's ambitions and were subsidized by Louis. Since Charles left no male heirs, all of his possessions except the Low Countries, which went to his daughter Mary, reverted to the French throne. A few years later the lands of the house of Anjou also came to Louis when the last of that line died. By the time of his death in 1484 Louis had greatly increased the size of his kingdom; its boundaries approximated those of modern France. Of the great feudal domains, only Brittany remained outside his sovereignty, and that was soon to fall to France through marriage.

To win and hold the support of the middle class, and at the same time to increase the prosperity of the realm so that he could get more tax revenues, Louis promoted the economic interests of the upper bourgeoisie. He regulated trade and industry to their advantage, encouraged the development of new manufactures, improved harbors and river channels, and took an active part in restoring and expanding French foreign trade and shipping. He chose many advisors and officials from the bourgeoisie.

He permitted the provincial estates and the Estates-General to remain

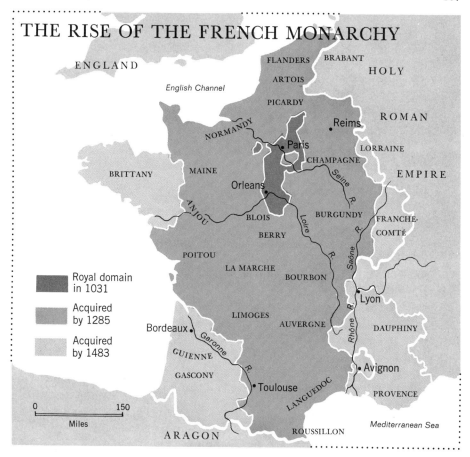

THE RISE OF THE FRENCH MONARCHY

ENGLAND

English Channel

FLANDERS BRABANT

ARTOIS

HOLY

PICARDY

NORMANDY

Reims

ROMAN

Paris

LORRAINE

CHAMPAGNE

BRITTANY MAINE

Orleans

EMPIRE

ANJOU

BLOIS

BERRY

BURGUNDY

FRANCHE-COMTÉ

POITOU

LA MARCHE

BOURBON

Seine R.

Loire R.

Saône R.

Royal domain in 1031

Acquired by 1285

Acquired by 1483

Bordeaux

LIMOGES

AUVERGNE

Lyon

DAUPHINY

GUIENNE

Garonne R.

GASCONY

Avignon

0   150

Miles

Toulouse

LANGUEDOC

PROVENCE

Rhône R.

ARAGON

ROUSSILLON

Mediterranean Sea

in existence but paid little attention to them. The Estates-General, the chief parliamentary body of France, met only once, in 1468, and then only to give formal approval of certain decisions Louis had already made. He restricted the power of the *parlements,* the high courts of justice. He held the clergy in check by intimidation and made himself master of the distribution of high clerical offices. He extracted ever increasing amounts of money from his subjects to pay the costs of government and the army. When he ascended the throne, the government's regular revenues amounted to 1.8 million livres; at the time of his death they had risen to 4.5 million livres. In addition to the regular revenues, he raised large sums by special subsidies, forced-loans from townspeople, and the sale of offices.

During the reign of Louis's son and heir, Charles VIII (1483–1498), who was a far less able man, the feudal nobility tried to regain some of its lost powers but Louis had built so well that the nobles could not

organize effectively against the throne. The long French involvement in
war in Italy, which began in 1494, also served to hold down feudal unrest, for the military campaigns drained off their energies. The royal
bureaucracy continued to grow and took over more and more of the
functions of local government, the fiscal system became more efficient, and
taxes kept rising. By the Concordat of Bologna in 1516 King Francis I
won recognition from Pope Leo X of the throne's almost complete control
of Church wealth in France and the right to appoint bishops and abbots.
The French clergy became in effect a national clergy principally controlled by the king.

HENRY VII OF ENGLAND

An intermittent series of armed clashes between rival groups of barons
seeking control of the central government kept England in turmoil from
1455 to 1485. The ostensible reason for the conflict was the rivalry between two dynasties, York and Lancaster, for the throne of England. The
Wars of the Roses — the emblem of the Yorkists was a white rose, that of
the Lancastrians was a red rose — seemed to result in a victory for the
Yorkists, who managed to keep the throne from 1461 to 1485. Then in
1485 the Yorkist king, Richard III, who had ascended the throne only two
years before, was killed in battle in a military invasion mounted by the
Welsh duke of Richmond, Henry Tudor, the Lancastrian claimant.
Henry assumed the throne as Henry VII, the first of an able dynasty that
ruled England for almost a century and a quarter.

Displaying characteristic political acumen, Henry reinforced his military conquest by marrying Elizabeth, heiress of the York dynasty, thereby
uniting the Lancaster and York claims. Some of the Yorkists continued
to oppose him and rebelled several times during the first half of his reign,
but Henry moved ruthlessly against his foes and in 1497 smashed the last
armed challenge to his supremacy.

He took other firm measures to break the power of the barons. During
the Hundred Years' War and the troubles of the fifteenth century, English
lords had almost of necessity kept armed forces, sometimes numbering
several thousand men who wore the livery (coat of arms) of their employers. These private armies made it impossible to preserve internal order
and the rule of law. Earlier kings had passed legislation against the
practice, but when offending barons were brought into court for trial,
judges were over-awed, witnesses feared to testify, and juries were afraid
to convict. By legislation and the use of every instrument of law, Henry
repressed abuses of the legal system by his "overmighty subjects" and
effectively reestablished public peace and royal authority. Because many
noble families had been wiped out in the Wars of the Roses or their
lands had been seized for treason, his position was further strengthened
by the reduced estates of his enemies. A thoroughgoing pragmatist and

legalist, Henry recognized that rebellion could be avoided by moving disputes from the field of battle into the courtroom. In this he was no innovator: as in most other aspects of government, his contribution rested in using to the full the institutions and procedures that were already in existence. His emphasis on making court cases out of what might otherwise have become private wars, and his assurance of the integrity of the courts and the enforcement of their decisions, established a rule of law that was the Tudor dynasty's firmest support.

Henry leaned heavily for support on the upper middle class and the untitled, landed lesser nobility or gentry, as they were called in England. He chose most of his counselors from these groups instead of from the great nobility, as earlier rulers had done. He used them in the increasingly efficient central bureaucracy, which he oversaw personally. Dependent upon unpaid justices of the peace, chosen from the gentry, to represent the royal power in local government, Henry accelerated the process that placed nearly all local administration in their hands. The institution of justice of the peace dated back to earlier centuries, but under Henry and his Tudor successors the office gained new powers and importance. A paid, professional, local bureaucracy such as France's might have been more efficient, but the justices of the peace, who were loyal servants of the king as long as their interests coincided, admirably suited Henry's purpose.

In the first half of his reign Henry summoned Parliament ten times to provide legislation to establish his supremacy and to grant the extraordinary revenue required to withstand the threats to his throne. After 1497 he convened it only once. He felt strong enough to rule alone, and his remarkable financial talents enabled him to meet the costs of government without new taxes voted by Parliament. When he mounted the throne, he had an empty treasury. Knowing that as long as he lacked money or had to depend upon others for it he would not have his own way, he economized, took back royal lands that had passed to others, confiscated the land and wealth of his enemies, enforced taxes, levied heavy fines and forced-loans, set up a more efficient government revenue office, and carefully checked the accounts himself. When he died, it was said that he had "the richest treasury in Christendom."

One reason he could amass so much wealth was that he did not have to maintain a standing army. Except for the 250 or so men in the Yeomen of the Guard (which he established) and a few small garrisons scattered throughout his possessions, Henry had no professional soldiers. He depended upon the patriotic support of his subjects, for every able-bodied Englishman was supposed to fight for the king when called.

Henry knew that it served his interests to promote the prosperity of the people, especially the merchant class. He encouraged foreign trade with continental Europe by treaties that afforded more favorable conditions for English merchants and the export of English wool and woolen cloth. He protected home industry by import and export restrictions. To promote English shipping, he restricted the importation of certain goods to English ships.

Through his forcefulness and wise policies, Henry ended a century of strife. Under his rule Englishmen enjoyed peace, confidence, and a growing prosperity. To his young son, Henry VIII, he left a united country, a degree of control over the people and Parliament that no other English king had ever had, and a full treasury. Henry VIII would soon dissipate the latter, but he never wasted the royal control and the unity of the nation.

FERDINAND AND ISABELLA OF SPAIN

By the fifteenth century the Christian kingdoms of the Iberian peninsula had been consolidated into four monarchies: Castile in the center and northwest, Aragon in the east, Portugal in the west, and the tiny mountain kingdom of Navarre in the north. Castile was by far the largest; it held two-thirds of the peninsula. The Moorish (Islamic) kingdom of Granada on the southern tip of the peninsula was all that remained of the Moslem Empire that had once held most of Spain.

In 1469 a marriage was arranged between Isabella, heiress of Castile, and Ferdinand, heir of Aragon. The marriage proved to be a turning point in the history of the Spanish state. Yet it did not by itself create a unified monarchy. Though both kingdoms accepted the two monarchs as their rulers, each kingdom kept its own laws, courts, parliaments, army, taxation, coinage, and tariff barriers, and the citizens of one kingdom were considered aliens in the other. Spanish nationalism scarcely existed.

In view of these circumstances the establishment of a unified national state seemed unlikely, but Ferdinand and Isabella had one extremely important factor that worked in their favor: the deep and traditional loyalty of the Spanish to the Church, the one institution common to, and venerated by, all Christian Spaniards. The new monarchs, who were themselves so devout that the pope gave them the title "the Catholic Sovereigns," deliberately built their policy of unification around the Church. To do so, they had to control the Church in Spain. Despite papal objections, they successfully asserted their right to appoint prelates, tax the Church, rid it of abuses, and curtail the right of ecclesiastical appeal to Rome.

As part of the policy of identification of loyalty to the throne with loyalty to Catholicism, the monarchs insisted upon religious uniformity among their subjects. The first victims were the Jews. During the Moorish era and for some time thereafter Jews had lived happily in Spain. In the fourteenth century anti-Semitism took on new proportions, and in 1391

Christian mobs in Castile murdered thousands of Jews. To save themselves, some of the survivors became Christians. They were called *conversos* (converts) or *Maranos*. A number of the converts secretly remained Jews. In 1478 the monarchs received permission from the pope to establish a special church court called the Inquisition to ferret out, punish, and confiscate the property of these people. In earlier times courts of inquisition had been subject to the ecclesiastical authorities; this one was established by Ferdinand "according to my pleasure and will in this kingdom and my lands." It represented the union of political and religious power in the hands of the throne and became a powerful instrument of the monarchs in their drive to gain control of the Church and exercise authority over their lay subjects. The throne appointed its officials and drafted its instructions, and for many years it remained the only royal institution that had equal power in both Aragon and Castile. The fanaticism and tortures of the Spanish Inquisition gave it an undying notoriety, and its name became a synonym for unfair and cruel judicial bodies. The zeal of its officers arose in part from the fact that one-third of the property confiscated from its victims went to the inquisitors and two-thirds to the king.

Many of Spain's Jews refused to be cowed into conversion and remained openly loyal to their faith. In 1492 the throne issued an ultimatum that offered Jews the choice of Christian baptism or exile and confiscation of their property. An estimated 150,000 to 200,000 people chose exile, depriving Spain of many of its leaders in the professions, learning, and economic life. Most of the refugees settled in the Near East, where they called themselves Sephardim and retained the language and customs of Spain until recent times.

The other victims of the drive for religious uniformity in Spain were the Moors. In 1492 the kingdom of Granada fell to the armies of Ferdinand and Isabella, bringing to an end the Christian reconquest of Spain that had started centuries before. The treaty of annexation guaranteed the Moslem Moors freedom of religion, but very soon pressure was exerted upon them to become Catholics. Some Moors revolted, whereupon the government decided that their action nullified the treaty. In 1502 a royal decree ordered all Moslems to become Catholics or leave Spain. Those who forsook Mohammedanism for Christianity were called Moriscos.

Like the other monarchs of nation-states, Ferdinand and Isabella faced the problem of controlling an unruly nobility. By skillful manipulation and the judicious use of force they regained much land for the crown. They outlawed private wars, destroyed many castles, forbade the building of new ones, and appointed men of middle-class origin to high government posts.

To aid in the restoration of internal order, the throne in 1476 revived

THE CHRISTIAN RE-CONQUEST OF SPAIN • 910-1492

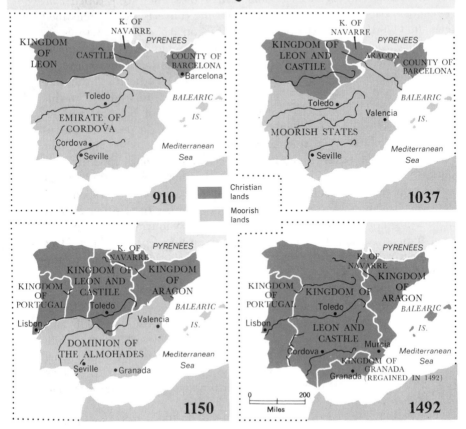

an old institution called the *Hermandad* (Brotherhood), an association of cities to maintain a constabulary and courts to preserve internal order. The new Hermandad, financed by the cities but under royal control and outside the regular legal system, dealt ruthlessly with rebels and lawbreakers. In twenty years it achieved its aim of restoring internal order and gaining universal respect for the authority of the throne, whereupon its powers were greatly reduced to prevent it from becoming a new threat to the throne.

The sovereigns established control over the cities by naming their own men to the once autonomous city councils and appointing an inspector, called a *corregidor,* to keep close watch on town governments in the interest of the throne. They paid little attention to the once-powerful *cortes* (parliamentary assemblies), summoning them irregularly and then only to give approval to proposed royal actions.

GERMANY AND THE HAPSBURG DYNASTY

The contrast between the development of the monarchic nation-state in France, England, and Spain and the continuing princely particularism in Germany was marked. There was, however, a growing nationalist sentiment in Germany, which tended to identify the empire and the emperor with Germany. But the new nationalist sentiment could not overcome the greater forces of disunity. The emperor, from 1438 on always the head of the House of Hapsburg, was chosen by the majority vote of seven electors — the count palatine of the Rhine, the margrave of Brandenburg, the king of Bohemia, the elector of Saxony, and the archbishops of Mainz, Trier, and Cologne — and had little real authority. Actual power resided in the hands of about 2,500 local and regional authorities. They included 50 ecclesiastical princes, 30 secular princes, over 100 counts, about 70 prelates, 66 imperial cities, and about 2,000 imperial knights who together owned less than 250 square miles of land. The emperor could levy a very limited amount of taxes, and his title carried with it no land from which to draw revenues. He therefore had to pay most of the costs of the imperial government from his own possessions. The other chief central authority of the empire, the Imperial Diet (Reichstag), represented the electors, the princes, and the cities. These groups knew that any increase in the central power would be at their expense, so they adamantly opposed any efforts in that direction.

Though German nationalist sentiment could identify the empire with Germany, it could not identify Germany with the empire, for the empire included non-Germans, such as the Czechs of Bohemia-Moravia and the Swiss. The religious movement led by Jan Hus in Bohemia in the early fifteenth century was nationalistic as well as heretical, and it left a legacy of Bohemian national separatism that the incorporation of Bohemia into the Hapsburg domain in the early sixteenth century did not immediately destroy. The Swiss also champed at the imperial bit. Resenting increased imperial taxes to strengthen the emperor's administration over them, they rebelled. They defeated the imperial army in 1499 and declared their independence although they did not win formal recognition of their independence by the empire until 1648. Each of the thirteen cantons that made up the Swiss confederation was itself an almost independent state. Each sent two delegates to a federal diet that met regularly to decide matters affecting the confederation as a whole. All acts of the diet had to have unanimous approval. Even when such unanimity was achieved, a canton could refuse to implement the legislation because there was no central executive authority to enforce the diet's decisions.

The general feudal disorder in fifteenth-century Europe was especially severe in Germany. For a time it seemed as if the individual German states of the empire would themselves fall apart. By the latter part of the century the rulers of Brandenburg, Bavaria, Saxony, and a few other princedoms overcame these dangers. On a small scale they emulated the accomplishments of the centralizing monarchs, restoring internal order, increasing revenues, and gaining recognition of their sovereignty. With their positions strengthened, the princes were able strongly to oppose any increase in the power of the imperial government. Emperor Maximilian (1486–1519), who seemed to many Germans the ideal monarch, met with rebuffs in his efforts to unite the empire and build up the central power. He had to yield to a group that demanded constitutional changes to weaken the power of the emperor even more.

In contrast to his failure to win greater power for the emperor, Maximilian enjoyed spectacular success in establishing the fortunes of his family, the Hapsburgs. Their possessions already included much of modern Austria. By a series of marriages Maximilian vastly increased the territories of his house and created a new family empire for his descendants. He himself married Mary of Burgundy, and so gained the Netherlands for his dynasty. His greatest coup came when he arranged a marriage between his son, Philip, and Joanna, heiress of Ferdinand and Isabella. The son of the marriage, Charles V, ultimately inherited the Austrian, Burgundian, and Spanish possessions, including Spain's enormous empire in the New World. Maximilian also arranged marriages between others of his progeny and the ruling family of Hungary and Bohemia, thereby securing the thrones of those lands for his dynasty. The Hapsburgs gained far more power and fame by nuptial diplomacy than they ever won in battle. An often quoted Latin verse put it well:

> Bella gerant alii, tu felix Austria nube
> Nam quae Mars aliis dat tibi donat Venus.
>
> (Others may wage war, you happy Austria marry;
> What Mars gives others, Venus gives to you.)

The new Hapsburg empire, built on marriages and family alliances, was a purely dynastic state. A common ruler provided the only bond that held together the scattered territories and heterogeneous peoples who made up the realm. It differed radically from the national territorial states established by the centralizing monarchs. The latter, motivated in their state-making policies by the desire to increase the power and glory of their dynasties, built on the foundation of a homogeneous population and compact territory. Their national territorial states — France, England, and Spain — rather than the supranational state of the Hapsburgs set the pattern for the future evolution of the European state system. With the emergence of the monarchic nation-states and the dynastic power of the Hapsburg emperor, the prerequisites were present for a new kind of statecraft: general European war.

THE ITALIAN WARS

In 1494 Charles VIII of France led his army across the Alps into Italy. Charles had a tenuous hereditary claim to the throne of Naples, which he used as the pretext for his invasion, although his plans went far beyond the conquest of Naples. He hoped to establish domination over all of Italy and then lead a crusade against the Turks, recapture the Holy Sepulcher in Jerusalem, and win the imperial crown for himself. The turmoil of Italian domestic policies gave him the opportunity for invasion. Ludovico Sforza of Milan had reason to believe that Naples would lead a coalition of Italian states against Milan. To ward off this threat, Sforza invited Charles to invade Italy and claim the crown of Naples. At the start of the campaign Charles won easy victories. An alliance called the Holy League formed against him. Its members ultimately included Spain, the empire, Venice, Milan, the papacy, and England. Each of the states felt its interests involved and damaged by the French conquests. The Holy League was the first of the great coalitions of states that have become standard features of international relations.

The allies drove Charles out of Italy in 1495. The French, however, would not give up their dream of domination in Italy and under Charles's successors returned again and again to the attack. Each time they were rebuffed by a coalition in which Spain usually took the lead. States entered and withdrew from the conflict, changed sides without compunction, and sought allies wherever they could find them; the French even leagued with the Turks, who until then had been regarded as the common enemy of all Christian states. Italy became a battleground for foreign armies and the war spread into France and Germany. Periods of uneasy truce punctuated the long struggle, but the conflict ended only in 1559 when by the Treaty of Cateau-Cambrésis the French finally abandoned their Italian ambitions and Spain (by this time ruled by the Hapsburgs) emerged as the dominant power in Italy.

THE RESULTS OF THE ITALIAN WARS

The Italian wars disrupted Italy economically and politically. The most notable victim was the Italian Renaissance. By the mid-sixteenth century, when Spain gained ascendancy in Italy and rigorous Catholic orthodoxy stifled the secular spirit of the Italian Renaissance, Italian creativity was already in sharp decline.

The Italian wars also completed a revolution in military tactics. For five hundred years heavily armored cavalrymen had dominated the battlefields of Europe. That predominance was ended not only by firearms but also by a new kind of infantry tactic. In 1476 and 1477 in three successive battles Swiss infantrymen, armed with eighteen-foot pikes, halberds (ax-head pikes), and broadswords, smashed the charge of the knights of Burgundy. The Swiss fought in compact squares of over 6,000 men, 85 men across and 75 ranks deep. Their success depended upon strict discipline. They had to ignore their wounded and close up the gaps caused by enemy action, since their strength lay in their massed impact. Bowmen and gunners preceded them in the attack to harass the enemy, then fell back to let through the pikemen and halberdiers.

The military prowess of Swiss infantrymen made them the most respected fighting men in Europe. Monarchs eagerly sought Swiss soldiers to fight for them. Providing mercenaries became a sort of state monopoly, in which the diet of the Swiss Confederation or the government of one of the cantons gave outsiders permission to recruit soldiers in return for cash, commercial privileges, shipments of grain, or other forms of payment. The Swiss Guards, who have patrolled the Vatican since 1510 in the brilliantly colored uniforms designed by Michelangelo, are the last reminders of the days when soldiers were Switzerland's chief export. Other armies soon copied the Swiss tactics, and by 1560 formations of massed pikemen surrounded by men armed with muskets were standard. The day of the mounted soldier, however, was not yet over. Heavy cavalry, charging in groups of 400 to 500, lances at tilt, and supported by armed crossbowmen, still presented a formidable fighting force, while light cavalry was indispensable for raiding and foraging.

During this era firearms underwent important changes. In artillery attention was drawn away from huge pieces to the development of readily portable, accurate cannon and improved gun carriages to transport them. In musketry, the invention of the matchlock and the wheel lock — firing mechanisms that did away with the need to hold a match to a touchhole to fire the weapon — and new designs in gun stocks improved efficiency. The musket displaced the bow as the chief battle weapon. Curiously enough, the spread of firearms reduced firepower. The longbowman could get off six arrows a minute, and the crossbowman one a minute, but it took the musketeer several minutes to load and fire his weapon, and accuracy was considerably less than with a bow. Nevertheless, the heavy ball that the gun fired made it a much more effective and brutal weapon, especially in the close-in, massed fighting which made accuracy irrelevant.

Charles VIII began his invasion in 1494 in a medieval spirit — as the first step in a chivalric crusade against the infidel. Instead, his invasion marked the opening of the modern era of international relations. In previous conflicts only immediate neighbors had usually been involved, such as the English and the French, the Florentines and the Milanese. The various disputes and wars among states had few cross-relations with one another. It was almost as if they were shut up in so many watertight compartments. Now for the first time all the major states found that their interests were enmeshed in a single issue of international relations:

the French scheme to dominate Italy. Combinations of powers emerged that had not been known before. The balance of power concept, by which states combine to check the ambitions of the most powerful among them, came into operation among the major European powers. The price for the preservation of that balance would be recurrent wars. The Italian wars established for centuries the basic pattern of European alignments, pivoting on a dynastic rivalry between the Hapsburgs and the ruling house of France. All that was lacking to give the Italian wars the full flavor of modernity was an ideological conflict. The Protestant Reformation and the Catholic reaction soon supplied it.

REFORMATIONS, PROTESTANT AND CATHOLIC
CHAPTER FIVE

In 1500 Europeans generally still spoke of Christendom rather than Europe to denote the greater entity to which they belonged. The distinction is significant. Europe is a secular concept that came into vogue only in the late seventeenth and eighteenth centuries; Christendom was a spiritual concept, ideationally, not geographically, descriptive. It bore witness to the unity of Western men under the apostolic Church of Rome. All except pockets of religious minorities — the Jews, Eastern Orthodox Christians in eastern Europe, Moslems — worshiped according to the same basic rites, accepted the Church's claim that it alone held the keys to salvation, and recognized the pope as the final authority on matters of Church government, faith, and morals. Within little more than a generation after 1500 that religious unity had vanished, obliterated by the Protestant Reformation. Northern Germany, Scandinavia, the Dutch Netherlands, parts of Switzerland, Scotland, and England permanently seceded from the Roman Church; large minorities in France, Bohemia, Poland, and Hungary subscribed to the new creeds and the old faith was barely able to contain Protestantism in those countries.

THE ELEVENTH HOUR OF THE MEDIEVAL CHURCH

The unity of medieval Christendom can be overstressed, especially if the medieval Church is equated with the present-day Roman Catholic Church. The price paid by Catholicism for survival in the face of the Protestant challenge has been a tight organization autocratically dominated by the papacy, allowing for only slight variation from place to place in a few relatively non-essential practices. The medieval Church was indeed a monolith, the "Rock of Peter," its unity and hierarchic structure capped by papal authority. Yet it was a rock incised by local particularism. There were local variations in the details of liturgical practice, significant differences in ecclesiastical organization, and restrictions on the exercise of papal authority over clergy and laity of varying force from one region to another. Areas farthest from Rome were least susceptible to continuous papal influence. The more highly developed medieval monarchies had wrested control from the papacy over many facets of ecclesiastical government. By 1500 most of the countries of Europe had witnessed attacks on the existing order of the Church, ranging from withdrawal into personal piety, through vigorous intellectual criticism, to outright revolt. The virulence, even the success, of movements demanding reform of the Church in the later Middle Ages were conditioned by the strength of local particularism. A reformer such as the Oxford theologian John Wyclif escaped condemnation as a heretic and died a natural death in 1384 because he enjoyed the protection of the king of England. The Bohemian reformer Jan Hus died at the stake in 1415 because he was not similarly favored, but his movement enjoyed such a popular following that Hussitism survived to merge with sixteenth-century Protestantism. The depth of the incisions varied, but generally where they were deepest the monolith stood in greatest danger of crumbling.

What is initially most arresting about the Protestant Reformation is that it did not take place a century earlier. Nonetheless, Wyclif and Hus were only heralds of reformation, and though both were theologically more advanced than Luther, the Church surmounted their challenges. Hus's burning lighted a general council of the Church that ended the disunity of the Great Schism and restored a unitary papacy. The Council of Constance in 1415 gave the medieval Church just one century in which to put its house in order. The history of this eleventh hour of the medieval Church is the history of the papacy's failure to correct abuses in face of the mounting attack of concerned Christians, clerical and lay, on those abuses, and increasing anti-clerical sentiment, which was almost universal among European laymen by the eve of the Protestant Reformation.

THE ABUSES

The ecclesiastical abuses were many and some were major. Three constituted corruption even by existing Church law. Simony, the sale of the entire range of Church offices, including bishoprics, made the clergyman's vocation a commodity, his duties a matter of profit. Pluralism, the simultaneous holding of several major Church offices, bred indifference to responsibility, non-residence of clergy, and the execution of the cure of souls by deputy. For example, the Italian cardinal Lorenzo Campeggio, Bishop of Bologna, also held the English see of Salisbury from 1524 to 1534 — he visited England only once, as the Pope's legate in 1528 to hear Henry VIII's divorce suit. Relatives of princes, popes, and bishops received lucrative and influential offices in the Church, a practice called nepotism from *nepos*, Latin for nephew and a euphemism for the illegitimate sons of supposedly celibate prelates.

While drawing the fire of those who urged reform, corruption was more symptomatic of spiritual laxity than of depravity. The monastic clergy were at the end of a long road of decline from the spiritual vitality of the monasteries in the early and high Middle Ages. Monasteries were less mills of spiritual exercise than retirement homes for wealthy and noble old folk served by the poorer lay brothers, whose status was little better than that of domestics. Their educational role had long since been taken over by schools and universities. Their charitable work was less pronounced in 1500 than at any earlier time. Most monastic houses were overly preoccupied with their landed estates, though they were heavily reliant on lay stewards and officials. In most of Europe the number of monks and nuns had declined in the late middle ages. While contemporary detractors of the monastic orders made much of supposed unchastity among monks and nuns, the monasteries were not so much dens of vice as they were no longer the spiritual powerhouses of the countryside, Christendom at prayer and work. The great orders of begging friars were a far cry from the ideals of St. Francis of Assisi or St. Dominic, but they were in better health than the contemplative, monastic orders. The friars contributed a large percentage of the faculties of the universities, and if they were too involved in ecclesiastical politics they still attracted men of capacity, dedication, and devotion. Some of their number were vociferous for reform. The Dominican friar, Girolamo Savonarola of Florence, prophet and demagogue, was also a genuine reformer whose burning in 1498 caused the most corrupt of the age's popes, Alexander VI, and his court to breathe easier. The Spanish Franciscans on the eve of the Protestant Reformation were kindled by a new fire for the purification of the Church and the conversion of the heathen in Spain's New World colonies. The Augustinian friar of Wittenberg, Martin Luther, proved the most influential of all friar-critics of the Church.

The secular (non-monastic) clergy were probably no worse with respect to ability, learning, devotion, and morality in 1500 than at any other time in the Middle Ages. That says very little in their favor, however. Those who were educated in divinity and canon law were drawn off into lucrative and powerful careers in Church and state. From them came the bishops and higher clergy. The bulk of the secular clergy were ill-educated and poor, and most of them worked their fields like common peasants, living lives neither longer nor less brutish than peasants. Too often an ignorant priest mumbled the mass deadened to its meaning and deaf to its drama.

All that was feeble, corrupt, and scandalous in the clergy as a whole appeared to be epitomized in the Pope and his court. The prestige, moral rectitude, fiery righteousness, and sense of mission of Innocent III and Boniface VIII (see p. 25) were never recovered after the Babylonian Captivity, when the popes lived in Avignon as clients of the king of France, or after the even more damaging Great Schism from 1378 to 1417, when there were first two and then three claimants to the papal throne. The schism was a mockery of papal authority: three sets of keys to the Kingdom of Heaven was absurd.

The popes who ruled after the schism, particularly the Renaissance popes, were far more concerned with establishing the papacy as an Italian political power, patronizing arts and learning, living in splendor, and enriching their relatives and favorites than they were with fulfilling their apostolic duty. Nicholas V (1447–1455), first of the Renaissance popes, loved books so much that he spent great sums for ancient and modern works and offered 10,000 gold pieces for a translation of Homer. Sixtus IV (1471–1484) showered wealth and power on his nephews and lived in sensuous luxury. The deeds of Rodrigo Borgia, Alexander VI (1492–1503), made his name a byword for lust and cruelty. During his pontificate the immorality and venality of the papacy knew no bounds. Much of the money that poured into Rome from Catholic Christendom was spent on an attempt to create an Italian kingdom for his beloved son Cesare. Julius II (1503–1513) was the favorite nephew of Pope Sixtus IV. His doting uncle made him a cardinal at twenty-eight, endowing him with twelve bishoprics, one archbishop, and three abbeys. As pope, Julius made his chief task the expansion of the temporal power of the papacy. In pursuit of this ambition he engaged in a number of wars and sometimes personally led his troops into combat, thereby winning the nickname, the Warrior Pope. Leo X (1513–1521), son of Lorenzo de' Medici, used the wealth of the Church for magnificent pageantry and patronage of the arts.

ANTI-CLERICALISM

The ever-increasing press of the popes for money, their worldliness, and their immorality had their counterparts down the ladder of the Church hierarchy. Bishops, whether or not they were princes in their own right — as were a number in Germany — were heavily involved in affairs of the secular state and were subsidized by the faithful to do the work of princes. Many laymen were jealous of the lucrative offices monopolized by clerics. A wider resentment grew from the arrogance of the higher clergy, the ostentatiousness of their wealth and power, their large jurisdiction in moral matters, and always their apparent greed. This resentment merged with contempt for a clergy that appeared to have lost its vocation, the cure of souls. By 1500 anti-clericalism was rife. It was a wholly negative sentiment, largely irrational, blanket in its condemnation. The virulent English anti-cleric, Simon Fish, merely echoed a common bitterness in characterizing the clergy "not as shepherds, but the ravenous wolves going in shepherds' clothing, devouring the flock."

THE OLD ORDER ATTACKED

The negativeness of anti-clericalism limited its destructiveness; it would prove a force only when the reformers openly attacked the Church to rally the masses behind them. Far more serious in effecting the erosion of the Church's authority on the eve of the Reformation was the attack of the devout, the learned, and the mighty in a three-pronged assault on the old ecclesiastical order.

The widespread religious revival that began in the fifteenth century was one manifestation of discontent with the Church. Pious clergy and laity organized movements such as the Brethren of the Common Life in the Rhineland and the Low Countries to revitalize popular interest in faith and salvation. The new printing presses turned out devotional books written for popular consumption as guides to pious living. There was a new interest in mysticism — the belief that by giving up all earthly desires and yielding completely to God man could commune directly with the Creator. While those who were caught up in the wave of popular pietism remained devout communicants of the Church, faced with the worldliness of the Church they felt that they knew better than prelates how to lead Christian lives and attain eternal salvation. This presumption was close to heresy in the eyes of the authorities. From it emerged a way of spiritual life that was increasingly independent of the organized Church and prepared many for the Protestant reformers' message, especially in Germany, England, the Low Countries, and France.

While the pietists expressed the discontent of the devout, a number of the Christian humanists enunciated the discontent of the intelligentsia, clerical and lay, with the medieval Church. The more outspoken of them, epitomized by the great Erasmus, scathingly attacked virtually every aspect of the contemporary Church. Such criticism aside, the overall effect of Christian humanism was still erosive of ecclesiastical authority. The Christian humanists sought to purify Christian doctrine of the errors accreted through centuries of theological activity by directing theological scholarship to the original texts. (See pp. 87–89.) They believed ardently that Christianity would be revived by finding its roots in the primitive Church, the Church of the Apostles and the early Church Fathers. With sublime naivety they assumed that investigation would establish one true doctrine in one true primitive Church. In fact their efforts uncovered a multiplicity of valid doctrinal positions, and insofar as their primitivism managed to reconstruct the early Church, its diversity in organization, practice, and creed emerged more clearly than its unity. And always implicit, sometimes explicit, in their writings was the invidious contrast of the present Church — corrupt, materialistic, abuse-ridden — with the supposedly pure primitive Church.

The secular rulers of the early sixteenth century required neither piety nor learning — though some of them were not lacking in either — to grasp the opportunity to press the Church in the interests of their own power. The abler monarchs sought to extend their dominion over all institutions within their realms, including the Church. Ferdinand and Isabella in effect controlled appointments to Church office in Spain, taxation by the Church, and ecclesiastical jurisdiction. In France King Francis I gained almost the same powers by the Concordat of Bologna in 1516, in return for his renunciation of the once popular doctrine of the supremacy of a Church council over the pope. The English king in the mid-fourteenth century secured laws limiting the papal power of appointment to Church offices in England and restricting the legal jurisdiction of the Church. The statutes were not vigorously enforced, and the pope exercised somewhat more influence in England than he did in Spain and France until Henry VIII demonstrated the power of the monarchy by reviving the statutes and reducing the English clergy to obedience.

Each attack, from widely differing quarters, weakened the Church. The Christian humanists comprised the luminaries of the Church and the world of letters, and their well-intentioned, often well-informed, criticism of the Church undermined the easy acceptance of the traditional authority of the ecclesiastical establishment by the learned and powerful clergy upon whom rested the responsibility for defending and advancing the Church. The growing dominance of secular rulers in the international Church within their national boundaries raised the prospect of an alternative to the pope as the supreme authority over the Church: the secular monarch. All together, popular piety, humanistic scholarship and criticism, and monarchial ambition cut deep into the monolith of the medieval Church. The hammer that shattered it was a German friar bent on debating the abuses of the Church.

LUTHER AND THE GERMAN REFORMATION

In Germany, where a strong central power did not emerge, there were fewer limitations on papal powers of appointment, ecclesiastical jurisdiction, and taxation. Rome drew enormous sums of money from Germany. The situation aroused the envy and cupidity of minor German rulers, the influence of the Christian humanists, and widespread popular piety, and together with the low moral prestige of the Church, made the German people and their rulers more receptive to revolt.

The signal for revolt came in 1517 from the small university town of

Wittenberg in Saxony. Following a standard academic practice, a friar named Martin Luther posted on a church door a challenge to other scholars to debate certain theological propositions. This seemingly insignificant act triggered the forces that wrecked the unity of Western Christendom.

Luther (1483–1546) came from a moderately prosperous family of peasant origin and received a university education. His father wanted him to become a lawyer, but after a mystical religious experience Luther decided to become a friar of the Augustinian order. He dedicated himself to theological studies and in a few years became professor of biblical exegesis at the University of Wittenberg. He held a number of other responsible offices, including that of district vicar of his religious order.

Although Luther might have congratulated himself on a modestly successful career, terrible doubts about his worthiness gnawed at his conscience and an unshakable burden of guilt overwhelmed his spirit. He prayed, fasted, scourged himself, and confessed for as much as six hours at a time, and still he could not free himself from his spiritual agony. He could not see how man, abject creature that he is, could overcome by his own efforts his inherent sinfulness. Through study of the Bible, Luther found an answer. Man must throw himself on God's mercy and accept His grace, realizing that he is too sinful to merit it by his own acts. Then can man be saved. Good works, such as prayers, fasts, pilgrimages, veneration of relics, and monastic asceticism, will avail him nothing. God gives His grace as a reward for faith alone, and man must rejoice in God's mercy and love, gratefully do His will, and follow His commandments.

The doctrine of "justification by faith" struck at the heart of the Catholic belief that man is saved by faith and good works. If faith alone saves, and if man himself can do nothing to merit salvation, he does not need the mediation of the Church and its priests between himself and God. All man needs is faith in God and the Bible to give him God's word so that he can live according to God's will. Luther did not at first realize the revolutionary nature of his teaching. He sought only to give the Bible a larger place in the theological curriculum of his university.

Luther was moved to challenge the Church by the activities of a Dominican friar, Johann Tetzel, who in 1517 began a massive sale of papal indulgences in Germany. The Church taught that men were so sinful that they could not do penance for all their sins in this life and that after death the soul would spend a period in a temporary place of penitence, purgatory. Since Christ and the saints had amassed an infinite surplus of good works, the pope could draw on this storehouse of good works — the Treasury of Merits — for the benefit of both the living and the dead, and by granting indulgences for sins shorten or forego entirely the soul's sojourn in purgatory. Theoretically the pope freely gave the indulgence and the recipient made a voluntary offering. In fact, indulgences were

Courtesy of the Fogg Art Museum, Harvard University,
Meta and Paul J. Sachs Collection

Luther, by Lucas Cranach

*"And so it will profit nothing that the body should be adorned with sacred
vestments, or dwell in holy places, or be occupied in sacred offices, or pray, fast,
and abstain from certain meats, or do whatever works can be done through the
body and in the body. Something widely different will be necessary for the
justification and liberty of the soul, since the things I have spoken of can be done
by an impious person, and only hypocrites are produced by devotion to these
things. . . . One thing, and one alone, is necessary for life, justification, and
Christian liberty; and that is the most holy word of God, the Gospel of Christ.
. . . For the word of God cannot be received and honored by any works, but by
faith alone."* From Luther, ON CHRISTIAN LIBERTY (1520).

sold and large-scale issue of them frequently coincided with a papal drive to raise money. Tetzel's indulgences were ostensibly to raise money to build St. Peter's in Rome. However, much of the money was to go to young Albert of Brandenburg to help him repay a loan to the Fuggers contracted by him to buy the archbishopric of Mainz from the pope.

RELIGIOUS REVOLT

Luther knew nothing of these behind-the-scene arrangements, but he had strong doubts about the efficacy of indulgences. As a professor, he decided that the matter should be discussed in proper academic fashion by writing a statement in Latin of his views and inviting other scholars to debate with him. On October 31, 1517, he posted ninety-five theses on the Wittenberg church door, the university's bulletin board. Three basic points underlay his ninety-five propositions. First, the pope should not take money from Germany to build St. Peter's; second, the pope did not control purgatory, and if he did, he should release everyone from it; and third, the Treasury of Merits did not exist, so that the pope did not have any superfluous good works at his disposal.

Luther had not expected any reaction outside the university community. To his great astonishment his theses, printed in Latin and German, spread rapidly throughout Germany. The sale of indulgences fell off. Albert of Brandenburg and the Dominican Order to which Tetzel belonged pressed the pope to discipline Luther. For political reasons Pope Leo did not want to antagonize Luther's prince, the Elector Frederick the Wise of Saxony, and delayed taking punitive action. Meanwhile, the attacks leveled at Luther by defenders of the Church compelled him to work out the implications of his theological position. He moved further and further away from orthodox doctrine. In a public debate at Leipzig in 1519 with Johann Eck, a German theologian of renown, he asserted that the bishop of Rome had not been recognized as head of the Church in the early days of Christianity and he admitted to sympathy with some of the doctrines of Jan Hus, burned as a heretic a century before. By that admission Luther identified himself as a heretic.

In the face of Luther's avowal of heresy and his growing popular following Pope Leo could delay no longer. In 1520 he issued a bull (letter) that gave Luther sixty days to recant. Luther replied by burning the document in public, together with the books of the Church's canon law, and by writing three pamphlets on his program of religious revolution. The first pamphlet, *Address to the Christian Nobility of the German Nation,* advanced his thesis of the "priesthood of all believers." The priesthood was no more sacred in the eyes of God than any other occupation or "calling." Every Christian had the right to interpret the Bible according to his own lights rather than accept the Church's interpretation; the Bible, not the Church, was the final authority on doctrine. Since the

Church had failed to reform itself, the secular government had to do it. Luther called upon the German nobility to take part in establishing a national church, free of abuses and severed from Rome. In the second treatise, *The Babylonian Captivity of the Church,* he denied the authority of the priesthood to mediate between the individual and God, asserting that the sacraments are useful only as aids to faith rather than the means of grace and the way to salvation. In *On Christian Liberty* he restated his basic tenet that faith alone makes the true Christian. If a man has faith, he will do good works automatically, for as Luther quoted from the Bible, "a good tree bringeth not forth corrupt fruit, neither doth a corrupt tree bring forth good fruit."

Pope Leo X had no choice but to excommunicate Luther and request the civil authority to punish him as a heretic. Luther had become a national figure, however, and the religious issues he raised had become national issues. Elector Frederick of Saxony and other German princes insisted that he could not be condemned without a hearing by the civil authority. In 1521 they persuaded Emperor Charles V to summon Luther before the Imperial Diet at Worms and to assure him safety while there. At the Diet, Luther refused to repudiate a word of what he had written or said. He explained that only the "Scriptures or right reason" could convince him that he was wrong. "I trust neither popes nor councils, since they have often erred and contradicted themselves." He ended his speech with the famous words, "On this I stand, I can do no other. God help me. Amen."

The Diet declared Luther a heretic and outlaw. Elector Frederick hid him in Wartburg Castle, where Luther spent his time translating the New Testament into German and writing religious tracts. After almost a year in Wartburg he decided to take his chances in the world. He returned to Wittenberg, and gathering together a band of followers including a number of fellow priests, he established the first Protestant church.

SOCIAL AND ECONOMIC REVOLT

As Luther's doctrines swept across Germany, they became intertwined with revolutionary social and economic ideas. Minor nobles saw in the religious confusions a chance to improve their economic position and increase their political importance. In 1522 under the leadership of Franz von Sickingen and the humanist Ulrich von Hutten they started a conflict, called the Knights' War, against the Catholic ecclesiastical princes in the hope of winning more land and power for themselves. The rulers of the larger states joined forces and crushed the rising.

In 1524 a peasants' revolt provoked a far more serious and bitter struggle. A deterioration in their social and economic position during the generation before the Reformation had produced unrest among the peasants, as well as among many townsmen. The new Lutheran ideas appealed strongly to them on religious grounds and afforded them the opportunity to make their economic and social demands part of the national movement for religious reform. In the most widely accepted statement of their program, called *Twelve Articles,* they utilized the teachings of religion to support their demands. They asked for the abolition of serfdom where it still existed, limitations on the tithes paid to the Church and the rents and services paid to the lords, an end to the seizure of common land by the nobles, and an extension of their traditional right to hunt, fish, and cut wood in the forests for their own use. They were the first, but not the last, to attempt to forge a bond between Protestantism and social amelioration.

The peasants and their town allies looked in vain to Luther for sympathy and support. When they employed violence against constituted authority, Luther passionately denounced them. In the pamphlet *Against the Thieving and Murderous Peasants* he urged the princes to wipe out the rebels as if they were mad dogs. His advice was superfluous. The princes suppressed the revolt with barbarity; an estimated 100,000 rebels lost their lives in battle and on the scaffold. Luther's recommendation for mercy after the revolt went unheeded. Luther's belief that civil government must always be obeyed both reduced the social base of his movement and tied it to the fortunes of the princes of Germany. Lutheranism ceased to be a national movement based on broad class support.

THE RELIGIOUS RADICALS

The disgruntled followers of Luther wanted to carry reform much further. Radical sects, called Anabaptists (re-baptizers), believed that infant baptism had no scriptural warrant and that the true Christian must be baptized as an adult, just as early Christians had been. They argued that both Luther and the Catholics erred in having the Church include all believers, since the Church should be a "company of saints" with strict requirements for membership. It should be limited to Christians who had experienced a spiritual regeneration and received baptism as adults. The Church should be independent of the state, and the government should have no power over religion.

The radical sects drew most of their members from the peasantry and the urban artisans. These pious, hard-working people believed that God had chosen them for suffering and martyrdom, but a few believed that they as God's instruments must enforce His will, by violence if necessary. They followed democratic procedure in the administration of their churches, and some of them advocated communal ownership in accordance with the Biblical description of the earliest Christians.[1]

---

[1] "All whose faith had drawn them together held everything in common; they would sell their property and possessions and make a general distribution as the need of each required." Acts 2:44–45.

The Anabaptists offered both a religious and a political threat to established society. Catholic and Protestant governments alike persecuted them. In 1535 rulers of the two faiths joined forces to besiege the town of Münster, where some of the more fanatical Anabaptists had taken over, abolished private property, and introduced polygamy on Biblical authority. The besiegers showed no mercy when they finally captured the city. In succeeding years thousands of Anabaptists died for their faith. The remnants of the movement lived on, stripped of its violent elements, under the leadership of Menno Simons, who died in 1561. The people today called Mennonites still live in simple biblical piety and reject worldly concerns, as urged by the original Anabaptists. Though stoutly condemned, the Anabaptist doctrines did in some instances creep into Protestant theology, most notably in the exclusive notion of the "company of saints" in English puritanism in the seventeenth century.

THE SPREAD OF LUTHERANISM

In contrast to the failures of the knights, the peasants, and the religious radicals, the rulers of Germany drew great advantage from the religious revolt. Conversion to Lutheranism enabled a German prince to repudiate the emperor's orthodox Catholicism and so further enhance the prince's political distinctiveness and power. Conversion ended the annoying interference of the pope, stopped the flow of gold to Rome, and allowed the prince to confiscate Church property. Lutheranism which stressed social conservatism and obeisance to civil authority, was safe and appealing to ambitious princes. The free cities of western Germany became Lutheran within a few months after Luther's appearance at the Diet of Worms in 1521, and soon a number of secular principalities followed their example. Catholicism persisted in most of the principalities ruled by churchmen, but even in them there were desertions, above all in Prussia, the territory of the Order of the Teutonic Knights. Albert of Hohenzollern, Grand Master of the Order, left his clerical calling in 1525 to become a Lutheran, secularized the domain of the order, and declared himself duke of Prussia. By the time Luther died in 1546, most of northern Germany had become Lutheran.

The new religion similarly appealed to the Scandinavian kings. The Swedish king Gustavus Vasa become a convert, and the national assembly declared Lutheranism the state religion and placed all Church property at the disposal of the king. In Denmark Frederick I adopted Lutheranism in 1527, making it the official religion of his state as well as of Norway and Iceland, then possessions of the Danish crown.

Lutheranism suffered a serious intellectual loss in the defection of many of the Christian humanists. The humanists led by Erasmus, early hailed Luther for his efforts to reform the abuses in the Church and return Christianity to its original principles. As time went on, however, they found themselves repelled by Luther's dogmatism, his intolerance of any views other than his own, his violent and often vulgar language, and his sweeping denunciations of the Church and the pope. After trying for several years to mediate between Luther and Rome and suffering the disfavor of both, Erasmus openly broke with Luther in 1524. Most other Christian humanists followed his lead.

During the years of gains and setbacks Luther continued the work of establishing his new church. He replaced the Latin liturgy with a service in German, consisting mainly of preaching, Bible reading, and hymn singing. Luther himself wrote a number of hymns, among which was the stirring "A Mighty Fortress Is Our God," sometimes called "the *Marseillaise* of the Reformation." Of the seven sacraments he retained only baptism and communion. He published a long and a short catechism to indoctrinate church members in Lutheran doctrine (they proved so successful that the Church of Rome soon imitated them and put out its own catechism), and he wrote many biblical commentaries. He made Lutheranism a state church, in which the government had supreme power over the church except in matters of doctrine. Monasticism was abolished, and the state supported the church with income from the monastic and other confiscated property. The state appointed ministers and certified their competence. Luther ended clerical celibacy and in 1525 he married a former nun.

THE SWISS REFORMATION AND THE RISE OF CALVINISM

As early as 1519 an independent Protestant movement arose in Zurich, Switzerland. Its leader, Ulrich Zwingli, was deeply influenced by the writings of the Christian humanists. He started on his career as a reformer before he knew of Luther. When he did read Luther's writings, he found himself in close agreement except on the issue of the "real presence." Luther maintained that in the Holy Communion the bread and wine remained bread and wine but Christ was present in them. This doctrine, known as "consubstantiation" (united in one common substance), differed from the orthodox Catholic doctrine called "transubstantiation" (changed into another substance), which held that the bread and wine became in substance the flesh and blood of Christ. Zwingli took a third position, namely, that the bread and wine served merely as symbols of Christ's flesh and blood and as a commemoration of the Last Supper. Zwingli's definition of the Communion greatly influenced other reformers, notably Calvin.

In 1529 Zwingli met with Luther to try to iron out doctrinal differences. Because they could not reach common ground, two separate branches of Protestantism developed: the Lutheran and the Reformed.

Their failure to agree was the first in the long series of schisms productive of so many different denominations in Protestantism. The name Protestant itself did not come into general use until 1529, when it was applied to a group of Lutheran German princes who presented a protest at the Imperial Diet against a new law that they thought operated against the further growth of their religion.

Reformed Protestantism spread into other parts of Switzerland until the country was divided between Catholic and Protestant. War broke out between the two camps, and Zwingli lost his life in battle in 1531. Soon after his death the combatants made a peace agreement that allowed each Swiss canton to choose its own religion. Protestantism made no further gains, and Switzerland settled into the division that for the most part still exists, with Catholicism dominant in the more mountainous regions and Protestantism in the cities and more fertile parts of the country.

CALVIN AND GENEVA

The city of Geneva, not then part of the Swiss Confederation, adopted Protestantism in the 1530's largely as a political expedient to rid itself of the domination of the neighboring Catholic state of Savoy. Most of the 13,000 Genevans remained Catholics, and many of those who chose Protestantism saw no necessity for basic theological changes. William Farel, chief Protestant preacher of the city, was outraged at this attitude but was unable to cope with it. In 1536 he called on Jean Calvin, a young French scholar who had already achieved modest fame as a Protestant theologian, to help him enforce the new orthodoxy in Geneva.

Calvin (1509–1564), son of a prosperous French lawyer, first studied for the priesthood, but at his father's insistence he turned from theology to law. While a student, he became interested in humanist learning and steeped himself in the writings of the early Church Fathers, especially St. Augustine. To his humanist and legal education he owed a mastery of Latin and French prose, an interest in ethical problems, and the legalistic cast of his thought.

In 1533 Calvin converted to Protestantism and decided to spend his life as a scholar and writer. He lived for a time in Basel, a sanctuary for Protestants and an intellectual center of the new faith. There in 1536 he published in six chapters the first version of his great work, *Institutes of the Christian Religion,* a treatise on the principles of Christianity. In later editions Calvin expanded the book until the last edition in 1559 had eighty chapters. The book's merit hardly lay in its originality. Calvin drew heavily from other reformers, particularly Luther, from the Church Fathers, especially St. Augustine, and from the Bible itself. Calvin's great contribution was his synthesis and logical presentation of hitherto unsystematized doctrines. Calvin's role in Protestant theology

Brown Brothers

John Calvin

"When we attribute foreknowledge to God, we mean that all things always were, and perpetually remain, under his eyes, so that to his knowledge there is nothing future or past, but all things are present. . . . And this foreknowledge is extended throughout the universe to every creature. We call predestination God's eternal decree, by which he determined with himself what he willed to become of each man. For all are not created in equal condition; rather, eternal life is foreordained for some, eternal damnation for others. Therefore, as any man has been created to one or another of these ends, we speak of him as predestined to life or to death." John Calvin, INSTITUTES OF THE CHRISTIAN RELIGION (Philadelphia, 1960).

can be justly compared to that of Thomas Aquinas, who three centuries before had performed much the same service for Catholic theology with his synthesis.

Calvin, like Luther, insisted that man is saved by faith alone. However, he shifted emphasis from God's love and the saving power of man's faith to the omnipotence of God. As punishment for Adam and Eve's transgression God had condemned man to live in perpetual sin; no one deserves to be saved. Yet God in His infinite mercy decreed that He would save some men for eternal life: "the elect." The rest of mankind was condemned to eternal damnation. Since past, present, and future are one to God, His decree had always existed; everyone was foreordained to heaven or hell from the beginning of time. This was the doctrine of "predestination." Luther and other reformers had professed this fatalistic and awesome doctrine, which originated with St. Augustine in the fifth century; Calvin made it dominate his entire theology.

If by human standards it seemed unjust for God to save or condemn without regard to merit, Calvin explained that whatever God does is the highest form of justice. Acceptance of the doctrine of predestination might have made men immoral, since whatever they did could have no effect on their salvation or damnation. Instead, Calvin's followers believed that the ability to live by a strict moral and religious code is a "sign of election"; as Calvin said, "Who are chosen unto eternal life are chosen unto good works." Even if a pious life does not guarantee membership in the elect, an immoral life certainly argues that one is not among the chosen. Acceptance of the doctrine thus operated in favor of a sober, industrious, and upright life. In an era when anxiety about salvation pressed heavily on men, Calvin's theology had an enormous appeal. It relieved believers of concern about their eternal destiny. Assuming that they were among the elect, they gained an unbounded self-confidence and self-righteousness that won them the dislike as well as the grudging admiration of men less certain of salvation.

Calvin also differed from Luther in the emphasis he put on Scripture. To Luther the Bible was the vehicle for the teachings of Christ. To Calvin it served as the immediate supreme authority in every aspect of life; man must live in strict obedience to its precepts. He differed even more markedly from Luther on the relations between church and state. Luther accepted the supremacy of the state. Calvin asserted that the church, or more precisely its ministers, must dominate, for the sovereignty of God comes before the sovereignty of man. Unlike Lutheranism and Zwinglianism, Calvinism provided — in principle at least — for relatively broad-based lay participation in church government. It had no place for prelates, and its government by both ministers and lay elders gave some measure of reality to the "priesthood of all believers." Among later generations of Calvinists this democratic orientation and the emphasis on God's sovereignty led to defiance of political-ecclesiastical despotism in

Scotland, England, the Netherlands, and North America and contributed significantly to the development of constitutional government.

When Calvin took over Protestant leadership in Geneva, he applied his ideas to the government of the city and organized it as a theocracy. The chief governing body, called the Consistory or Presbytery, consisted of six (later twelve) ministers and twelve laymen or elders. The Consistory both made and enforced the laws, which regulated with severity every aspect of human conduct including speech, dress, and manners. Calvin literally had a captive audience for his sermons, for failure to attend services, as well as sleeping or laughing in church, was punishable by a jail sentence. Calvin's powerful personality dominated the Consistory and made him virtual dictator of the city during his lifetime, except for a short period when a revolt against the severity of his rule drove him from the city. He enforced his stern moral code with the assistance of gossips, informers, and spies, and he did not hesitate to use torture, exile, and execution to compel adherence to the new orthodoxy. In 1553 Michael Servetus, a Spanish scholar fleeing Catholic persecution for denying the doctrine of the Trinity, sought refuge in Geneva. Calvin had him arrested, tried, and burned at the stake for heresy.

THE SPREAD OF CALVINISM

The close relationship of Lutheranism with German nationalism and the political ambitions of German princes made Lutheranism a faith largely confined to Teutonic lands. Calvinism was not associated with the political ambitions of rulers and was related only tangentially to the nationalist strivings of peoples. It became the international form of Protestantism, leaping over national boundaries and spreading throughout the Western world, impelled by the militancy, dedication, and sense of destiny of its adherents. As long as Calvin lived, Calvinists looked to Geneva for guidance and kept in constant touch with each other through the agency of Geneva. The Genevan church, which was organized according to the constitution drawn up by Calvin, served as the model for Calvinist churches everywhere long after Calvin's death.

Calvin hoped to achieve the greatest success in his own country, France, and the first French edition (1541) of the *Institutes* was dedicated to Francis I of France in the hope of converting him. Although unsuccessful in this ambition, Calvin wielded enormous influence over the Huguenots, as French Protestants were called, and was the principal architect of the French Reformed Church. During his brief exile from Geneva (1538–1541) Calvin resided in Strasbourg, where he planted the seeds of the new faith. It soon spread throughout the Rhineland and to other parts of Germany. It also spread to the Netherlands, superseding Lutheranism, which had earlier made inroads, and proved a potent weapon in the Dutch struggle for independence from Catholic Spain.

Calvinism achieved two of its most notable triumphs in English-speaking countries. In the sixteenth century Scotland went through a long period of political turmoil in which Protestantism became an ally of the nobles opposed to French influence, exercised notably by Mary of Lorraine, widowed mother of and regent for the infant Mary Queen of Scots. In 1559 John Knox, a former priest who had converted to Protestantism and spent several years in exile studying under Calvin in Geneva, returned to Scotland just as the anti-French party gained the upper hand. In 1560 Knox persuaded the Scottish Parliament to sever all ties with Rome and set up the Church of Scotland according to the Calvinist model. Calvinism also deeply influenced theology in the Church of England in the last half of the sixteenth century and formed the basis of Puritan belief and church order. Several colonial settlements in New England began as Calvinist theocracies, as interpreted by the Puritans.

THE REFORMATION IN ENGLAND

In the 1520's Luther's movement won a small following in Oxford and particularly Cambridge, the two English universities. In parts of England the followers of Wyclif, called Lollards, still survived underground as a proto-Protestant group. Yet the Reformation in England in its first stage had little to do with religion as such and was not anti-Catholic. The explanation for the anomaly lay principally in the character and ambitions of England's king, Henry VIII of the House of Tudor. In 1521 Henry, who had received some training in theology, wrote a refutation of Luther in Latin. Pope Leo X rewarded him with the title "Defender of the Faith," still borne by England's monarchs. According to his own definition Henry remained a Catholic to his death. But after 1534 there was no place for the pope in Henry's Catholicism.

HENRY'S DIVORCE

Soon after ascending the throne in 1509, for dynastic purposes Henry married Catherine of Aragon, his brother's widow. Canon law, based on Scripture (Lev. 20:21), forbade marriage to the widow of a brother, but Pope Julius II accommodatingly granted a dispensation for the marriage. In eighteen years of married life Catherine bore one surviving child, Mary. Henry wanted a male heir to ensure the stability of his dynasty. He had fallen in love with a young lady, Anne Boleyn. In 1527 he petitioned Pope Clement VII to annul his marriage to Catherine on the grounds that Julius II had exceeded his authority in granting the dispensation.

Under ordinary circumstances the pope probably would have obliged. He had recently granted similar favors to two of Henry's kin. Catherine of Aragon, however, was the aunt of Emperor Charles V, who occupied

Rome at the time and controlled the papacy. If Clement agreed to Henry's request he would incur Charles's wrath. On the other hand Henry's chief minister, Cardinal Wolsey, warned the pope that if he refused Henry England might defect from Rome. Clement temporized and even suggested that Henry follow Old Testament practice and take two wives.

During the early negotiations Henry never wavered in his religious orthodoxy, but in 1529 he decided upon a course of action that ultimately made his orthodoxy irrelevant. He summoned Parliament and kept it in session for seven years, playing on the members' loyalty to the dynasty and their anti-clericalism to move them to pass the statutes needed to make England independent of Rome. It is unlikely that Henry had a more far-reaching strategy than to pressure the pope into granting the annulment by progressively drying up the flow of papal revenue from England, subjugating the English clergy, and reducing papal power over the English church. When these tactics failed, Henry had the spiritual and legal responsibilities of the pope transferred to his pliant new archbishop of Canterbury, Thomas Cranmer, who in 1533 annulled the marriage of Henry to Catherine and declared valid his earlier, secret marriage to an already pregnant Anne Boleyn. In 1534 Henry and Parliament took the decisive step with the Act of Supremacy, which declared that the king, not the pope, was supreme head of the Church of England.

Most Englishmen, lay and clergy, confused by the course of events and moved by patriotism, dynastic loyalty, or fear, accepted the break without protest. A few stalwarts refused to renounce their allegiance to Rome and recognize the validity of Henry's marriage to Anne. Among them was Sir Thomas More, humanist luminary and formerly Henry's chief minister. He was beheaded for treason in 1535.

THE HENRICIAN REFORMATION

Henry moved next against England's eight hundred monasteries and nunneries. In 1536 and 1539 Parliament passed acts of dissolution enabling Henry to close the religious houses and confiscate their lands, ostensibly because the monks and nuns led sinful and useless lives. But Henry had other, more pressing reasons. As long as the monasteries existed, they were potential centers of papal influence. More important, Henry needed money badly to pay off debts and finance his policies. The lands he seized and sold ultimately came to rest in the hands of the rising landed gentry, who became stout defenders of Henry, his Protestant successors, and the Anglican Church, for fear that if Roman Catholicism came back they would lose their newly acquired properties.

Although the king rather than the pope headed the Anglican Church, doctrine and practice remained largely unchanged. At one time Henry moved cautiously toward Protestantism, but when a Catholic uprising, the Pilgrimage of Grace, broke out in the north of England in 1536, he retreated. In 1539, at Henry's behest Parliament passed the Act of the Six Articles, which required compliance under pain of death with the orthodox doctrines of the sacraments, the mass, auricular confession, and clerical celibacy.

Anne Boleyn had one daughter, Elizabeth, born in 1533. Henry, weary of Anne, unjustly accused her of adultery, and tried and beheaded her in 1536. The day after her execution Henry married Jane Seymour, one of Anne's maids-in-waiting, who died the following year after giving birth to a son, the future Edward VI. In quick succession Henry took three more wives: Anne of Cleves, a pawn in an abortive Protestant alliance against the emperor and whom Henry soon divorced; Catherine Howard, beheaded on charges of adultery when Henry thought his dynasty threatened by her powerful noble family; and Catherine Parr, a twice-widowed gentlewoman, who was widowed a third time by Henry's death.

PROTESTANTISM IN ENGLAND

Despite Henry's determination to keep Protestantism out of England, a small but influential group of Protestants formed, led by Thomas Cranmer, archbishop of Canterbury. The reformers' chance came with Henry's death in 1547 and the accession of his ten-year-old son Edward VI, for they dominated the council of regency that ruled for Edward. The new government repealed the Act of the Six Articles, made English the language of religious services in place of Latin, abolished many Catholic ceremonies and practices, and allowed clergymen to marry. In 1549 Archbishop Cranmer composed the Book of Common Prayer to replace the Catholic orders of worship. After approving the book, Parliament ordered its use in every church in the kingdom. In its first edition the Book of Common Prayer contained much that was Catholic, but a new edition issued three years later emphasized Protestant, almost Zwinglian, doctrine. The eloquence and solemn beauty of the Book of Common Prayer gave added strength to the cause of Anglicanism and emphasized its Protestant nature.

THE BRIEF RETURN TO ROME

Protestantism received a severe setback in 1553 when Edward died and was succeeded by his half-sister Mary. A plot to exclude Mary and give the crown to the Protestant Lady Jane Grey, grand-niece of Henry VIII, met with failure. The people of England accepted Mary Tudor as their rightful sovereign despite her religion. Mary's fondest ambition was to return England to the old faith and eradicate Protestantism. She pushed legislation through Parliament to repeal the religious changes of Henry VIII and Edward VI. In theory England was once more a Roman Catholic state reconciled with the papacy.

The queen and her advisers made no attempt at a genuine spiritual revival of Catholicism. Theirs was an archaic Catholicism, unaffected by the still nascent Catholic Reformation, which twenty years later would vigorously regain areas all over Europe for Rome and contain Protestantism. All moves to reclaim the confiscated monastic lands and other church endowments that had been settled in the gentry's hands met strong opposition. Mary did not have the money to reestablish medieval Catholicism in its full panoply, nor did she have the foresight to establish the new reformed Catholicism. In her determination to suppress heresy Mary executed hundreds of Protestants, most of them obscure artisans and many of them women. Her efforts gained her the name of "Bloody Mary" and an abiding hatred for Roman Catholicism among the English; the persecutions accomplished little else.

Mary forfeited much of the customary popular support for Tudor monarchs when she married Philip, son of Emperor Charles V and soon to be king of Spain. Charles saw the marriage as an opportunity to make England a part of the empire that the Hapsburgs had acquired through marriage. The English, moved both by the fear that their country would lose its independence and by a growing patriotism that included suspicion of all foreigners, especially those who were Roman Catholics, despised the marriage. The marriage itself was not successful. Mary, eleven years older than Philip, was in love with her husband, but he did not return her affection and spent as little time with her as possible. When she failed to produce an heir Roman Catholicism in England was doomed. In 1558 Mary died, a sad, disillusioned woman, well aware that her successor, her half-sister Elizabeth, the daughter of Anne Boleyn, was a Protestant.

THE CATHOLIC REFORMATION

Not all who sought to end the abuses in the Roman Catholic Church became Protestants. Those who remained loyal to the old faith continued to press for change from within, by no means in vain. Indeed, the first successful Catholic reform began in Spain over twenty years before Luther posted his theses. It furnished many of the most zealous combatants in the war against Protestantism in the sixteenth century.

Ferdinand and Isabella's resolve to establish control over the church in Spain and to weed out corruption in it was executed by Cardinal Francisco Ximenes de Cisneros, archbishop of Toledo, Grand Inquisitor, and their confessor and closest adviser. An investigation of conditions in the monasteries and nunneries persuaded Ximenes that drastic action was needed, and in 1494 he obtained a papal order empowering him to regulate all Spanish monasteries. He instituted stern disciplinary measures, reintroduced the ascetic rules of the religious orders, and exiled to

Morocco monks who remained incorrigible. Ximenes had a more difficult time in reforming the secular clergy, but as head of the Inquisition he exercised general supervision over the Spanish church and succeeded in raising the moral condition of the Spanish clergy higher than that of most of Europe's clergy. Protestant attacks on the corruption of the priesthood in other countries had little pertinence to Spain. In 1508 Ximenes established a university at Alcalá which served as the training ground for many of the next generation of bishops and made an important contribution to the overall improvement in the scholarly standards of the Spanish church. Reflecting the humanist interests of its founder, the new university had chairs in Greek and Hebrew in addition to the more traditional subjects.

ROMAN CATHOLIC REACTION TO THE PROTEST REFORMATION

The amazing speed with which Protestantism won converts put the Church very much on the defensive. After an initial attempt to suppress the revolt by force, more and more leaders realized that if the Church was to check the expansion of Protestantism, it would have to remove the offending abuses and, above all, it would have to develop and strengthen its spiritual resources. The reform movement in the Catholic Church developed as a counterreformation, designed to counteract the Protestant Reformation.

Shortly before 1517 a handful of prominent churchmen and laymen in Rome formed the Oratory of the Divine Love and through example and exhortation wielded enormous influence in reducing clerical abuses and monastic corruption throughout Italy. Stimulated by these developments, the papacy directed serious attention to reform. The era of the Renaissance papacy ended; beginning with Paul III (1534–1549) men of higher moral and religious standards were elevated to the throne of St. Peter and took the lead in reforming the Church "in head and members." In this work the papacy received invaluable assistance from new religious orders in which the members lived out in the world and were freed of the time-consuming communal obligations of monastic clergy, while disciplined and educated to resist the temptations of worldly life that beset ordinary pastoral clergy. The Capuchins, the Theatines, the Ursuline nuns, and most important, the Jesuits, founded in 1540 by Ignatius Loyola, served the Church and the papacy with untiring devotion and unquestioning obedience.

LOYOLA AND THE SOCIETY OF JESUS

In 1531 Loyola (1491–1556), scion of a noble Spanish family and a military officer, was seriously wounded in battle against the French. During a long and painful convalescence and after a period of agonized soul-

Ignatius Loyola

*"All members [of the Society of Jesus] shall be aware — and that not only at the
time of their first profession but as long as they live, and shall daily keep it in
mind — that this entire Society and its members serve as soldiers in faithful
obedience to the most holy lord Pope Paul III and his successors. We are
subject to the rule and divinely instituted authority of Christ's vicar to such a
degree that we not only obey him according to the general duty owed by all the
clergy but are so tied to him by the bond of an oath that whatever his Holiness
may ordain for the profit of souls and the propagation of the faith we are bound
to carry out instantly, as far as in us lies, without any evasion or excuse;
whether he sends us to the Turks, or into the New World, or to the Lutherans,
or into any other realm of infidels or unbelievers."* Foundation Charter of the
Society of Jesus, August 1539, in G. R. Elton, ed., RENAISSANCE AND REFORMATION
1300–1648 (New York, 1963).

searching, he became convinced that he must give up his career as a soldier of the king of Spain and become a soldier of Christ. In order to drive sin out of his mind and body, he lived nearly a year in rigorous asceticism in the town of Manresa. Following a pilgrimage to Jerusalem, Loyola decided to train his mind and spent nearly a decade studying at Alcalá and Paris.

At Manresa Loyola began to work on *The Spiritual Exercises,* a manual for those who wanted to share his experience. He felt that just as physical exercises develop the body, spiritual exercises like prayer, meditation, and examination of conscience "prepare and dispose the soul to rid itself of all inordinate attachments . . . and to seek and find the will of God." Complete obedience was due to the Roman Catholic Church as God's representative on earth: "To attain the truth in all things, we ought always to hold that we believe what seems to be white to be black, if the Hierarchal Church so defines it."

At Paris, Loyola attracted a small group of disciples, and after offering themselves to the pope for any service he might assign them, in 1540 Pope Paul III gave his approval for the establishment of the order. Loyola, the old soldier, insisted upon a military form of organization, with a general as commander of the Company of Jesus, afterward the Society of Jesus, and he required the unhesitating obedience that is characteristic of soldiers. Organized "to employ itself in the defense of the Holy Catholic faith," the Jesuit order threw itself into the struggle to stem Protestantism and win converts to Catholicism. Jesuit schools were founded to train the young in the traditional religion as well as in secular subjects; they dominated the educational system of Catholic Europe for the next two centuries. Cognizant of the importance of influence, the Jesuits managed to become the confessors for men of the ruling elite and mingled actively with the great of the world. Through their foreign missions they won thousands of converts in lands across the sea: a year after the order was founded, Francis Xavier sailed to the Orient to blaze the way for Jesuit missionaries. Within Europe they took their place in the front line of the Catholic counterattack against Protestantism. Through their fervor, diplomacy, and flexibility they played a major role in holding southern Germany, Austria, and France for Catholicism and winning back Poland and much of Hungary to the old religion, and they spearheaded a valiant if unsuccessful attempt to regain England for Catholicism.

THE COUNCIL OF TRENT (1545–1563)

The Church's traditional mode of dealing with a major crisis was to summon a general council of all the bishops. In the Reformation era the papacy's almost pathological fear of a council circumscribing the pope's power — as in the early fifteenth century — was joined by the fear that a council would compromise the faith in reaching an accommodation with Protestantism. Even the mighty voice of Emperor Charles V could not persuade successive popes to convoke a council until the first reform-minded pope, Paul III, summoned a general council to meet in Trent, an Austrian town near the Italian border, in 1545.

During the council's three sessions (1545 to 1547, 1551 to 1552, and 1562 to 1563) the number of bishops attending was never large and the Italian prelates formed a majority because of their relative nearness to Trent. The Italian prelates' dependency on the papacy assured the pope control of the council, and the papacy capitalized on the erudition and orthodoxy of a group of able Jesuits who worked on its behalf in the lobbies, winning over many delegates to the papal viewpoint. So guided, the council rejected all compromise with Protestantism and denounced the theology of the reformers. The dogmas and doctrines of the faith challenged by the reformers were tightly defined and reaffirmed: salvation by faith and good works not faith alone, the validity of the seven sacraments, transubstantiation, the sole authority of the Church not the individual to interpret the Bible and that in the light of the Church's traditions. The council declared the Vulgate, the Latin translation of the Bible that had been made by St. Jerome in the late fourth century, to be the only authoritative version of Scripture, ordered that only Latin be used in the mass, and gave approval to the veneration of saints and relics, the use of images, the cult of the Virgin, pilgrimages, and indulgences as spiritually rewarding acts. It revised the Index, the list of books that Catholics were forbidden to read, and drafted rules by which to judge books in the future. Subsequently the Index was kept up to date by a special Congregation of the Index, composed of cardinals and formed in 1571.

While the council found it easier to refute Protestant and define Catholic theology than to root out the many abuses within the Church, it did prescribe drastic reform of the monastic orders, directed that bishops reside in their dioceses and better control the clergy within their dioceses, denounced the appointment of immoral and incompetent men to high church office, decreed the elimination of abuses in the granting of indulgences, enacted a series of measures to improve the morals and discipline of the clergy, and ordered the establishment of a seminary in every diocese to train priests.

The council itself did not enforce its decrees; that was left to the pope. Throughout, the council acknowledged subordination to the pope, left the final decisions in difficult matters to him, and agreed that he was not bound by a majority vote of the delegates. Thus the council served to extend the papacy's influence and domination. Under energetic papal leadership the Roman Catholic Church regenerated itself and carried through moral and administrative reforms, took the offensive against Protestantism and not only stopped its further expansion but won back lands that had seemed irretrievably lost.

THE CONFRONTATION OF TWO REFORMATIONS

Max Weber, a German sociologist, has argued that Protestantism, especially Calvinism, stimulated the development of capitalism because of its emphasis on serving God in a secular occupation and on the virtues of sobriety, hard work, and thrift as signs of election. The "Protestant ethic" provided the religious justification for the "spirit of capitalism." According to R. H. Tawney's elaboration of Weber's thesis, "the tonic that braced" the new capitalists for the conflict with the entrenched aristocracy "was a new conception of religion, which taught them to regard the pursuit of wealth as, not merely an advantage, but a duty." The controversy over Weber's thesis has been considerable, and his most trenchant critics have pointed to the existence of the spirit of capitalism in Europe before Calvin and in Catholic societies after him. Yet the connection between English and Dutch economic vitality and Calvinism, and between the French Huguenots' prosperity and Calvinism, seems more than coincidental. Perhaps the Weber thesis makes more sense when stood on its head: many aspiring capitalists of Europe may have found Calvinism congenial, thus accounting for its widespread acceptance in the economically more progressive societies.

Nevertheless, the principal factor in determining whether or not Protestantism took root in a country seems to have been the attitude of the country's ruler. Where the monarch favored Protestantism, the country became Protestant, as in northern Germany, Scandinavia, and England. Where the monarch opposed Protestantism, as in Spain, Italy, Austria, and France, the country remained Catholic. Since everywhere in Europe religious uniformity was held to be the bulwark of political loyalty, the most important converts to Protestantism were the rulers, for their conversion led to the establishment of Protestantism as the religion of their subjects. Sometimes genuine religious sentiments drew rulers to the reform movement. More often, the prospect of confiscation of Church lands and the desire to curb the power of the Church and establish full control of their states proved stronger attractions and helped persuade them to break the connection with Rome.

Popular pressure became critical only in those instances when the prince remained Catholic but extended a measure of toleration to Protestants, or when he embraced a conservative Protestantism and then attempted to hold the line against further reform. In these situations Calvinism in particular proved destructive of continued monarchic determination to preserve uniformity. Certain German principalities and England, Scotland, and France serve to illustrate the point.

Calvinism provided a continuing provocation to Catholicism of a kind

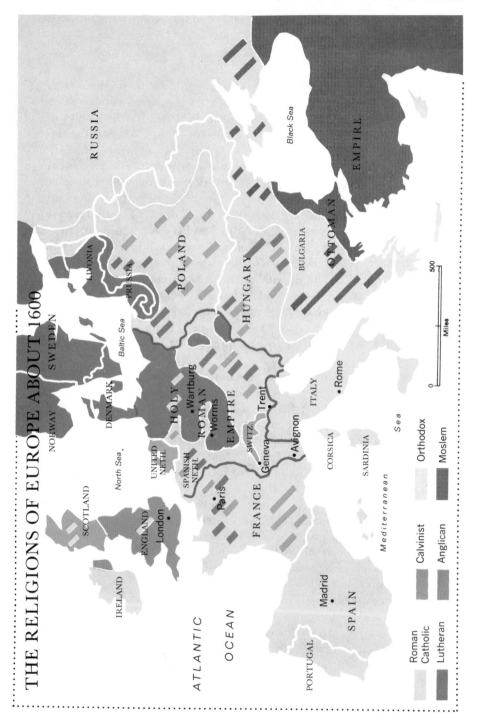

THE RELIGIONS OF EUROPE ABOUT 1600

RUSSIA

SWEDEN

NORWAY

DENMARK

SCOTLAND

IRELAND

ENGLAND
London

PORTUGAL

SPAIN
Madrid

FRANCE
Paris

ATLANTIC OCEAN

North Sea

Baltic Sea

LIVONIA

PRUSSIA

POLAND

HUNGARY

BULGARIA

OTTOMAN EMPIRE

Black Sea

UNITED NETH.

SPANISH NETH.

HOLY ROMAN EMPIRE
Wartburg
Worms

SWITZ.
Geneva

Trent

Avignon

ITALY
Rome

CORSICA

SARDINIA

Mediterranean Sea

500
Miles
0

Roman Catholic

Lutheran

Calvinist

Anglican

Orthodox

Moslem

not offered by Lutheranism and Anglicanism after the mid-sixteenth century. A Roman Catholicism refurbished, rigidified, and armed by the Council of Trent conceived its prime enemy to be Calvinism. As early as 1542, Cardinal Caraffa (later Pope Paul IV) instructed the Roman Inquisition that "none is to lower himself by showing toleration towards any sort of heretic, least of all a Calvinist." The confrontation of the two disciplined and ideologically zealous antagonists merged with the dynastic and political ambitions of princes and nationalist loyalties to keep Europe in turmoil for a century in a seemingly endless series of international wars and civil conflicts.

THE POLITICS OF
THE REFORMATION
CHAPTER SIX

The last half of the sixteenth century was an era of ideological conflict of a particularly vicious sort. While dynastic rivalry and power struggles remained prime motives for European war, international and internecine, war was made more terrible and more complicated by religious antagonism. The conflict was not only between Catholic and Protestant; it was often between differing factions of Protestants, sometimes differing groups of Catholics. Inquisitors, pursuivants, informers, and the public executioners of Europe became the hammers of orthodoxy, all orthodoxies. Flames consecrated "God's elect" from such unlikely stuff as shoemakers, the ax released the souls of bookish bishops and worldly lawyers, the noose drew heavenward elegant and genteel Jesuits who could (and did) pass for foppish youths on tour. Winston Churchill's chilling axiom, that flowers grow on the battlefield before they grow under the gallows, was proven by three centuries of religious hatred and its residual distrust to our own day. Much war was civil war. All war took on the nature of civil war, as Europeans rallied as "saints in arms" to battle old enemies and new, indiscriminately dubbed the "anti-Christ."

THE EMPIRE OF CHARLES V

In 1519 the seven electors of the Holy Roman Empire unanimously chose Charles I of Spain and Burgundy as successor to Emperor Maximilian. Charles spent 850,000 florins, more than half of it borrowed from the Fugger bankers, to bribe the electors to vote for him rather than the other candidates, who were not able or willing to spend as much.

The nineteen-year-old victor became Emperor Charles V. The imperial honor that he sought at such expense represented only a part of his dignity and power, for Charles's father was the heir of Emperor Maximilian

Charles V, by Titian

"Charles V carried the Hapsburg dynasty to the height of its greatness. He united and completed its possessions. . . . At the same time . . . he formed a world empire dependent for the first time in history not on conquest, still less on geographical interdependence, but on dynastic theory and unity of faith." Karl Brandi, THE EMPEROR CHARLES V, tr. C. V. Wedgwood (London, 1939).

and Mary of Burgundy, and his mother was the heiress of Ferdinand and Isabella. While he was still a boy, his father had died and his mother, known as Joanna the Mad (*la Loca*), had to be confined. From his father the youthful Charles inherited the Hapsburg possessions in central Europe and the Burgundian domains of the Low Countries and Franche-Comté; through his mother he inherited Spain, its dominions in Italy, and its vast new possessions in America. The marriage alliances that had been so skillfully negotiated by his grandfather Maximilian had paid off handsomely.

With all this, the most richly endowed monarch of Europe was not satisfied. He sought to enhance his power and enlarge the territories ruled by the House of Hapsburg. His plans went beyond mere dynastic ambitions, for his ultimate aim was the medieval ideal of the unification of all Christendom under one scepter, a hopeless anachronism in the age of the Reformation.

Charles was a man of great perseverance, patience, and common sense, but the obstacles were too formidable to admit of success. He could not even mobilize for a common policy all of the lands over which he already ruled. His empire was a purely dynastic creation, a group of states held together not by any common interests but by the single fact that all of them had the same ruler. Moreover, he was plagued by three great problems: the religious revolt in Germany and the German princes' opposition to Hapsburg domination; the threat of Turkish aggression; and a seemingly endless war with France. Perhaps Charles could have handled any one of these three successfully, but throughout his reign these and many lesser problems competed for his attention — and for his limited resources. Although gold and silver streamed into his treasury from the New World, there was never enough to cover all the expenses of a man who, in the words of one of his enemies, wanted "to be master everywhere."

LUTHERANISM AND THE GERMAN PRINCES

Napoleon Bonaparte once remarked that if Charles had allied himself with Lutheranism instead of combating it, he could have created a united Germany that included Austria and the Netherlands and could thus have conquered Europe. Instead, during the 1520's when Luther's reformation took shape, Charles, preoccupied with other matters, did not even visit Germany, much less take a personal part in its religious and social problems. Neither did his regent for Germany, his brother Ferdinand, who in 1526 became king of Hungary and of Bohemia and was compelled to battle the Turks continuously in defense of his new kingdoms.

Free to visit Germany for the first time in ten years, Charles summoned the Imperial Diet to meet in Augsburg in 1530 to discuss the religious problem. Since Luther was still under imperial ban and could not attend, his associate and friend, Philip Melancthon, served as chief advocate of the new faith. More conciliatory than Luther, Melancthon drafted a creed of Lutheran beliefs in which he toned down or omitted such key doctrines as the priesthood of all believers, the repudiation of papal supremacy, and the denial of the existence of purgatory. His compromise failed to win acceptance by the Catholic princes, and the Protestant princes retired from the Diet while the Catholics passed decrees to extirpate Lutheranism. Melancthon's creed, the Augsburg Confession, remains the official credo of orthodox Lutheranism.

The Lutheran princes formed a mutual defense coalition, the Schmalkaldic League. Turkish aggression distracted Charles's attention before he could mount his crusade, and in 1532 the adversaries agreed to the so-called Nuremberg Standstill, a truce by which the Lutherans made common cause with the emperor against the Turks. During the fifteen years the Standstill lasted, Lutheranism made great gains in Germany. Charles, determined to smash Lutheranism, took the offensive against the league in 1546. The Lutherans' defeat merely forced them in 1552 into an alliance with France, and a new round of war. Charles's failure to gain a decisive victory brought him to realize, reluctantly, that he could not destroy Lutheranism. In 1555 the Imperial Diet again met at Augsburg. By the Religious Peace of Augsburg each German prince was free to choose Catholicism or Lutheranism (but not Calvinism, or Anabaptism) and his subjects were obliged to follow suit. "Cuius regio, eius religio" (whose kingdom, his religion) preserved the unity of religion in each German state; but it was the death knell of the imperial pretension to unify Germany. Though the Holy Roman Empire lasted another 250 years, Charles's failure to establish the religious supremacy of Catholicism and with it his political hegemony was the end of the imperial idea. The empire survived as the shadow of a dynasty over a conglomeration of independent and religiously diverse states.

The Religious Peace of Augsburg brought over a half-century of uneasy religious truce to Germany. It was remarkable that the truce lasted so long. The rapid growth of Calvinism in Germany in the last half of the sixteenth century threatened the formula of the Peace of Augsburg, for the Calvinists were not a party to the peace and by their proselytizing zeal were a constant provocation to resurgent Catholicism. Though the Lutherans disliked the Calvinists intensely, they were forced to recognize that the mounting success of the Jesuits in the era of Catholic reform in winning converts from Calvinism was a threat to all Protestantism. Early in the seventeenth century, both sides coalesced into separate armed camps and almost went to war in 1610. Less than a decade later, events on the very frontier of the struggle between Catholic and Protestant, Bohemia, touched off the Thirty Years' War. (See pp. 219–226.)

THE TURKISH MENACE

In 1520 the Turks under the leadership of a new sultan, Suleiman II "the Magnificent," launched an advance along the Danube. In 1526 at Mohács in southern Hungary they routed the Hungarians. Three years later they stood at the gates of Vienna. Charles, who till then had left the defense of central Europe to his brother Ferdinand, had to shift troops from the west to repulse this threat. In 1532 the Turks again invaded Austria and again they were pushed back. Other troubles drew Charles away from the conflict and Ferdinand, who was then king of Hungary, carried on alone. He was defeated in his attempt to drive the Turks out of Hungary by Suleiman, who occupied most of the country. Finally in 1547 Ferdinand had to sign a truce recognizing the Turkish conquest of Hungary and agreeing to pay the Turks tribute for the small western strip that he still held. Meanwhile pirate chiefs who ruled in Algiers and Tunis and were under the protection of Turkey made the waters of the western Mediterranean unsafe for European shipping. Charles, who in his war against the Turk called himself "God's standard bearer," made two campaigns to northern Africa in an unsuccessful attempt to stamp out the pirates.

HAPSBURG VERSUS VALOIS

The Italian wars, which began when France invaded the peninsula in 1494, broke off temporarily in 1516. With his acquisition of the imperial crown in 1519, Charles V was able to encircle France by means of his control of Spain, the Netherlands, and Germany. France did not accept containment readily. The kings of the Valois dynasty, who had ruled France since 1328, had their own imperial ambitions that conflicted with Hapsburg aspirations not only in Italy but also in the Netherlands, northern Spain, and even Germany. In fact, Francis I of France (1515–1547) had been Charles's chief rival for election as Holy Roman Emperor. The many clashes of interest between Hapsburg and Valois made war inevitable. Other states, recognizing that the victor in this battle of giants would dominate Europe, entered the struggle first on one side and then on the other in hopes of maintaining the balance of power, so that neither Hapsburg nor Valois would crush the other.

In Francis I Charles had a formidable foe. Brilliant, learned, artistic, witty, Francis was also capricious, inconsistent, and extravagant. Yet he was masterful in furthering monarchic supremacy within France. He won from the papacy the appointment of French bishops. He further restricted the political powers of the *parlements,* the law courts that were bulwarks of the power of the nobility. He refined and strengthened the central bureaucracy, broadened its base of recruitment, centralized finance, and built a first-class war machine. He absorbed the nobility into a splendid court and occupied them with the externals of government — a policy that was the keystone of French absolutism until the French Revolution. In 1515 he reconquered Milan in a glorious victory over Swiss mercenaries; by 1520 he had diplomatically outmaneuvered Cardinal Wolsey, the capable viceroy of England's Henry VIII.

War between Francis and Charles began in 1522. In 1525 imperial troops destroyed the French army at the battle of Pavia in Italy, and Francis himself was taken prisoner. He was held in a Spanish prison until he agreed by the Treaty of Madrid in 1526 to renounce his claims in Italy, Burgundy, and the Netherlands.

Instead of ending the war, Charles's victory at Pavia only served to extend it. Francis never intended to keep the pledges extorted from him in the Madrid treaty, even though the Spanish retained his two sons as hostages. He found it easy to win allies against Charles, for other states feared that the Hapsburgs had grown too powerful. Charles, who had to divert many of his resources to meet renewed Turkish aggression in central Europe, found himself hard pressed both militarily and financially. In 1527 his unpaid troops in Italy mutinied; forty thousand of them descended upon Rome and sacked it, killing 4,000 people and leaving the city two-thirds destroyed. The Eternal City has fallen to invaders many times in its long history, but never has it suffered a worse fate. The sack of Rome ended the artistic and cultural pre-eminence of the city, firmly established Spanish control over the papacy, and ended forever the political independence of the popes.

From 1526 to 1559 the war raged intermittently. At one point Charles called Francis "a coward and a rogue" and the duel that almost ensued would have marked the first time that a European war was settled by personal combat between kings. The duel was never fought, however, and armies, not kings, clashed. A humiliating treaty imposed on Francis in 1529 at Cambrai, negotiated by his mother and Charles's aunt, though freeing Francis's two hostage-sons for an enormous ransom, did not bring peace. Francis's alliances with German Lutheran princes, even with the Turkish infidel, were calculated to embarrass and distract Charles. Francis's son Henry II took up where his father left off at his death in 1547, and in 1552 Henry attacked Charles. Six more years of war brought bankruptcy to both France and Spain, and in 1559 by the Treaty of Cateau-Cambrésis, France renounced its claims in Italy, the Low Countries, and Spain while retaining some minor border territories and Calais, captured from Spain's ally, England, in 1558.

The Hapsburgs had finally triumphed over the Valois. After decades of war they had won domination of Italy and had kept France out of the Low Countries and the empire. Spain emerged the dominant power of Europe while France sank into thirty years of anarchy and civil war. Under the Spanish yoke Italy exchanged the intellectual excitement and

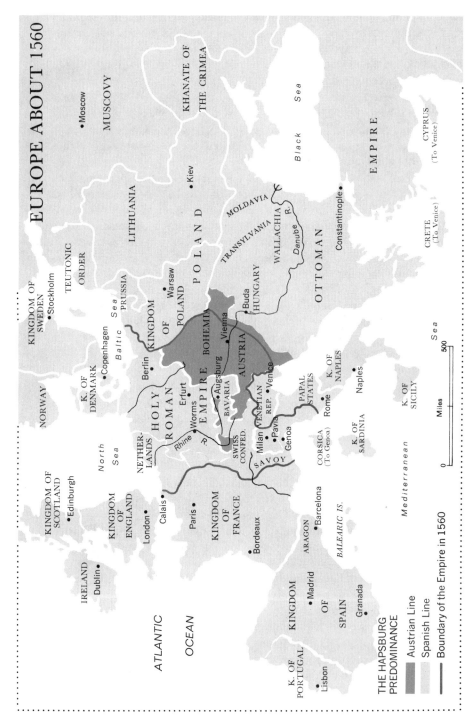

EUROPE ABOUT 1560

THE HAPSBURG
PREDOMINANCE

Austrian Line
Spanish Line
Boundary of the Empire in 1560

freedom of the Renaissance for rigorous Catholic orthodoxy, intellectual degeneration, and thought control. Of the once independent Italian states only the Republic of Venice preserved its freedom; all the others fell under Spanish suzerainty.

DIVISION OF THE HAPSBURG DOMAIN

In 1555 Charles, tired, discouraged, and prematurely aged, decided that the time had come to rid himself of his responsibilities. He wanted his son Philip to succeed him as ruler of both the Hapsburg and the Spanish possessions, but Charles's brother Ferdinand would not agree. After bitter discussions the emperor divided his realm. He turned over the Hapsburg patrimony in central Europe to Ferdinand, who was elected emperor, and to Philip he gave Spain, the Low Countries, and the Spanish possessions in Italy and the New World. After his abdication Charles retired to luxurious quarters that he had built as an annex to a Spanish monastery. There he spent the two remaining years of his life in offering gratuitous advice to his son Philip, performing religious devotions, strolling in his gardens, and in the rather unusual activity of rehearsing his own funeral. He died in 1558, strong in the Faith; his will provided that thirty thousand masses should be said for the repose of his soul.

THE WARS OF RELIGION IN FRANCE

Successive kings of France had wasted much blood and treasure in their long and futile effort to win dominion over Italy. More than anything else the nation needed peace and unity of purpose to recuperate. Instead, an even more costly and far more damaging civil war nearly destroyed France. Towns, villages, even families, split and fought one another, and assassinations, wanton destruction, and armed raids became part of everyday life in some areas. Eight separate civil wars, the first beginning in 1562 and the last ending in 1593, can be viewed as one war that lasted for thirty years broken by short periods of truce.

The enmity between Catholic and Protestant bore the largest share of responsibility for the war, and religious fanaticism explained the special ferocity of the combatants. Despite harsh persecutions, including torture and burning, many Frenchmen were attracted by the doctrines of their countryman Jean Calvin. By 1559 the Calvinists felt strong enough to convene a synod in Paris, at which seventy-two individual congregations were said to have been represented. They drew up the *Confession of Faith of the Reformed Churches of France*. The rapid diffusion of the new creed astonished contemporaries, including even Calvin, who followed events in his homeland closely and sent a stream of counsel from his stronghold across the border in Geneva. The Calvinists were very much in the minority. Out of a population of 16 million they numbered only about 1.2 million; the rest were Catholic. Calvinism, however, won many converts from the nobility: between 40 and 50 per cent of the French nobility were at one time Protestant. The movement drew its rank-and-file membership from among the urban merchant and artisan classes, making it strong in the towns. For these reasons the sect had a strength out of proportion to its numbers.

More than religion was at stake in the conflict. The still ambitious feudal nobility saw the opportunity to use religious controversy as a vehicle to win back its old dominance. The wars of religion were also wars of political factions headed by powerful noble families. If strong and wise kings had led France during those years, the country might have escaped its long agony. Instead, three of the weakest kings in French history followed one another on the throne during the thirty years from 1559 to 1589. They were the sons of Henry II (1547–1559) and Catherine de' Medici. For years Henry, infatuated with his mistress, Diane de Poitiers, had neglected his wife, a daughter of the Florentine Medici family whom he had married for her money. When Henry died as a result of a jousting accident in 1559, Catherine as queen mother came into her own, for her sons were incapable of ruling. The eldest, Francis II, was a youthful invalid who soon died; the second, Charles IX (1560–1574), was more than half-demented; the third, Henry III (1574–1589), was an effeminate degenerate. Catherine, who held the real power, was an ambitious and scheming woman. Unfortunately for France her talent for intrigue, cruelty, and duplicity far exceeded her not inconsiderable statesmanship.

Three aristocratic factions vied for control of the state. The Catholic party was headed by the duke of Guise, first Francis and then Henry. Members of the family held great stretches of land, were related to kings, and considered themselves on a par with royalty. The Huguenot party was led by Bourbon princes, one of whom was king of Navarre (on the French-Spanish border) and another the duke of Condé. The Bourbons were a junior branch of the French royal family. Ultimately a third party developed, whose partisans believed that the political unity of France was more important than its religion and wanted to end the senseless civil war by having the state tolerate both religions. They were called the *politiques.*

Open warfare began in 1562 when soldiers of the duke of Guise massacred a Huguenot congregation of three hundred at Vassy. In 1570 the Huguenot forces, led by Admiral Gaspard de Coligny, defeated the royal troops, and Queen Catherine had to promise freedom of worship to the Huguenots and turn over four important fortified towns to them for two years as a guarantee that she would fulfill her promises. To seal the agreement Catherine gave her daughter Margaret in marriage to the youthful Protestant leader, Henry Bourbon, king of Navarre.

Catherine soon regretted her concessions and arranged to have Coligny assassinated. The attempt failed. She decided to try again and this time to include as victims the many Huguenot nobles who flocked to Paris for the wedding of Henry of Navarre and Margaret, thereby obliterating the Protestant leadership with one savage blow. Early in the morning of St. Bartholomew's Day, August 24, 1572, armed Catholic bands under Guise leadership fell on the sleeping Huguenots and murdered them. The massacre quickly spread from Paris to other cities. Before the slaughter ended, ten thousand Huguenots had been killed, including a number of the cause's ablest leaders. Coligny's head was sent to the pope, who had a special medal struck to commemorate the massacre and commissioned the artist Vasari to paint the scenes in Paris when the Protestants fell. The unsmiling Philip II of Spain is said to have laughed aloud when he heard the news and ordered a *Te Deum,* the triumphant hymn of thanks to God for victory.

To avenge the St. Bartholomew's Day Massacre the Huguenots renewed the civil war. The Catholic party, led now by Henry, duke of Guise, formed the Catholic League. Supported by Spain, the league became the dominant power in the government. Henry III, the last of Catherine de' Medici's sons, sought to escape from its domination by ordering the assassination of Henry of Guise in 1588. When the league rose in fury against the king, Henry allied himself with the Protestant leader, Henry of Navarre, and together they besieged Paris, the stronghold of the league. Henry III's murder in 1589 by a Dominican friar ended the Valois line. Henry of Navarre became king of France as Henry IV, first monarch of the Bourbon dynasty.

Five years passed before Henry could win sufficient recognition of his title from his subjects to take possession of his capital, Paris. He had to abjure Protestantism and become a Catholic before the majority of his subjects would accept him. Henry did not find that too great a sacrifice; he is supposed to have said "Paris is worth a mass." Henry was a *politique.* "We are born not only for ourselves," he said, "but above all to serve our country." Conversion was a small price to pay for the restoration of peace to the realm.

Henry realized that the Huguenots had to be placated if internal order was to be maintained. Compromise offered the only way out of religious stalemate. Henry, with wisdom and tolerance, and after long and difficult negotiations with religious and political leaders, issued the Edict of Nantes in 1598. This decree granted Huguenots liberty of conscience and freedom to worship in two places in every district except large towns, where they had to hold their services outside the walls. It gave them civil and legal rights equal to those of Catholics, set up mixed tribunals of Catholic and Protestant judges to hear cases in which Protestants were involved, and turned two hundred fortified towns over to Huguenot governors and garrisons so that they could protect themselves if the need arose.

This famous edict stands as a landmark in the history of religious toleration. For the first time the government of a major European state recognized that two religions could coexist without destroying the state. On the other hand, the edict created a potentially dangerous political situation. By allowing the Huguenots to control fortified places, Henry created a "state within the state" that could become a serious threat to the supremacy of the central government.

THE SPANISH PREDOMINANCE

When Charles V, who had been born in the Netherlands, came to Spain for the first time twenty months after he had inherited its throne, he did not like his new subjects, and they returned his antipathy with interest. The youthful Fleming who could not speak their language and who gave high offices in the Spanish government and church to fellow Flemings was not to their taste. In 1520 open rebellion against his rule broke out and was put down only with difficulty. After this bad beginning Charles and the Spaniards began to be drawn to one another. The devoutly Catholic Spaniards admired his staunch defense of Catholicism and were proud of his vast dominions and imperial title. Charles, for his part, surrounded himself henceforth with Spanish grandees, appointed Spaniards to high office, and learned the language. He flattered all Spaniards when he remarked that Italian was the proper language to use when speaking with women, German with enemies, French with friends, and Spanish with God. More important, he made Spain the fulcrum of his empire, the "fortress, strength, treasure, and sword," as he himself put it, of his effort to defeat the enemies of Catholic Christendom, whether Turk or Lutheran.

He passed on the concept of Spain as the bulwark of Catholicism to his son Philip II (1556–1598). Under Philip's rule this idea was fused with a nationalistic fervor. The Spanish began to feel that God had given Spain the mission to save Catholicism in the Old World and to spread it in the New. This sense of messianic mission, buttressed by the vast resources Philip had at his command, made Spain the greatest world power in the second half of the sixteenth century.

The new king was Spanish to the core. Although his realm stretched far beyond the Spanish frontiers, he never left his homeland after 1559. He was a cold, reserved, and cruelly arrogant man. He lived in the Escorial, a magnificent but gloomy palace that he built near Madrid, separated from contact with human reality by the grotesquely elaborate court ceremonial that he himself devised. His policies and personality made him highly unpopular with most Europeans, and historians have often depicted him as a morose, fanatical tyrant. Spaniards, however, admired him, and today they count him as one of their greatest rulers — the one who led them to the highest pinnacle of power in their entire history.

"THE MOST CATHOLIC KING"

Philip, like his predecessors Ferdinand and Isabella and Charles V, identified the interest of Spain with the interest of Catholicism and bore with pride the traditional title of the Spanish monarch, "The Most Catholic King." He was an especially devout man and consciously tried to adjust his own policies and actions to the teachings of his church. In his determination to maintain the supremacy of Catholicism he allowed harsh persecution of non-Catholics and gave a free hand to the Inquisition. Nevertheless, when Spanish national interests or political necessity clashed with religious concerns, the former always triumphed; Philip rationalized the conflict by persuading himself that what was best for Spain was best for Catholicism. For instance, as long as the pope agreed with his policies, Philip was loyal and submissive, but when the pope disagreed with him, he did not hesitate to show his anger and oppose him. Indeed, Philip's actions made him seem in some ways almost as antipapal as Henry VIII of England. He all but extinguished Rome's jurisdiction in ecclesiastical disputes in Spain, forbade the publication of papal decrees without prior approval of Spanish officials, disregarded the decrees that did not suit him (such as the one excommunicating anyone who took part in a bullfight), and deprived the pope of any voice in church appointments. He regarded the Spanish church as an arm of his government, demanding that it assist him both politically and financially at any time. The papacy paid a price for Spain's orthodoxy.

Like other rulers of his time, Philip viewed as a threat to his power the existence in his state of any religion other than his own. The Inquisition ruthlessly ferreted out the members of the small Spanish Protestant community. After a number had been burned alive and others had been meted out less horrible punishments, the movement collapsed.

The Moriscos, or converted Moors, offered a more serious problem. When in 1502 the Moors of Granada had been offered the choice of conversion or exile, most had chosen conversion. The Moriscos, however, retained their own language, dress, and customs, and many of them were suspected of being secret Moslems. Their nonconformity was intolerable to the government and the Catholic Church, which subjected them to constant harassment. In 1567 Philip issued a decree outlawing their distinctive practices and the Moriscos rose in revolt in 1569. Government forces triumphed in 1570 after a conflict marked by atrocities on both sides. The government then moved the entire Morisco population to other parts of Spain and repopulated Granada with Spaniards of old Catholic stock. A series of decrees issued between 1609 and 1614 by Philip's successor ordered the Morisco's expulsion from Spain. Many of them evaded these orders and remained in Spain, shielded by large landowners who found them more docile farm workers than the Spanish peasants.

Photograph from FPG

View of the Escorial

> *"The Escorial engrossed the leisure of more than thirty years of [Philip II's]
> life: it reflects in a peculiar manner his tastes, and the austere character of his
> mind. . . . The traveller who gazes on its long lines of cold gray stone, scarcely
> broken by any ornament, feels a dreary sensation creeping over him. . . . But
> he may read in this the true expression of the founder's character. Philip did
> not aim at the beautiful, much less at the festive and cheerful. The feelings
> which he desired to raise in the spectator were of that solemn, indeed sombre
> complexion, which corresponded best with his own religious faith."* W. H.
> Prescott, HISTORY OF THE REIGN OF PHILIP THE SECOND (Boston, 1858).

TRIUMPH OVER THE TURKS

The Ottomans, who had given so much trouble to Philip's father, continued their westward push in the Mediterranean. By 1560 they had expelled the Christians from most of their outposts in northern Africa, and
in 1570 they took the Venetian island of Cyprus, the easternmost Christian possession in the Mediterranean. At the pope's urging, Spain and
Venice joined naval forces to stop the Turks. On October 7, 1571, Don
John of Austria, Philip's half-brother, commanding an allied fleet at

Lepanto in the Gulf of Corinth in Greece destroyed 80 and captured 130 Turkish galleys, killed or captured thousands of the enemy, and freed 10,000 Christian galley slaves.

Christian Europe went wild with joy at the news of the great victory. But excess caution and dissension among the allies prevented a follow up of their victory with further action against the enemy; they failed even to recover Cyprus. Though the Turks quickly built a new fleet and continued to ravage the coasts of the western Mediterannean, Lepanto ended the threat of Turkish domination over the Mediterranean. The Turks had suffered an overwhelming defeat at the hands of Europeans, and the Christian world began to lose some of the terror long inspired by the Ottomans. Philip could turn his full attention northward, where serious trouble had broken out in the Netherlands.

THE REVOLT OF THE NETHERLANDS, 1568–1609

The seventeen provinces that made up the Netherlands or Low Countries, corresponding roughly to modern Holland, Belgium, and Luxembourg, formed Europe's wealthiest area. For centuries the southern provinces had prospered by trade, finance, and industry. The northern provinces first amassed wealth through fishing and then shifted to commerce and shipping. The tenor of life was predominantly urban, and though the cities of the Low Countries were not independent city-states as in Italy, they were the centers of economic and political power. The provinces had no special ties with one another, and there was no unified system of central administration. Each province had its own special privileges that dated back to medieval times, its own nobility, its own law courts, and its own parliamentary estates. The only bond that held them all together was their common sovereign.

Charles V had been a Low Countryman and was considered one of their own, although he had begun policies of repression in the Low Countries that would provoke revolt under Philip II, of Spain, who was a foreigner and could speak neither Dutch nor French. He never visited the Low Countries after 1559, levied heavy taxes, kept Spanish troops in the provinces, and used Spaniards as his officials. In addition, Calvinism had won many converts in the Low Countries and when Philip ordered strict enforcement of the laws designed to repress the new faith, he incurred the hatred of the growing number of Protestants. He antagonized the nobility by excluding them from his administration or giving them only minor posts. The nobles feared, with reason, that Philip planned to make himself absolute ruler and deprive the Low Countries of their special political and legal privileges. Several hundred nobles banded together to resist this development. A Spanish official's contemptuous reference to them as "beggars" coined the proud nickname for all Low Countrymen who opposed Philip.

Matters reached a crisis in 1566 when Calvinist tradesmen and crafts-men, who had been stirred up by preachers, descended upon Catholic churches and monasteries in a frenzy of destruction. In their hatred of the symbols of "popery" they smashed images and stained glass windows and defaced paintings and tapestries. Though the noble "beggars" did not approve of the rioting of the common people, they were powerless to halt it and soon accepted the inevitable popularization of the insur-rection. The disturbances confirmed Philip's determination to root out Protestantism in the Low Countries, break the power of the nobility, and make himself absolute ruler. He sent an army of ten thousand under the duke of Alva to carry out these aims. Alva's brutality united nearly all Netherlanders in a common effort against the Spanish oppressor. In a land that until then had known no sentiment of national unity a new feeling of national consciousness arose. In 1568 there was an open revolt.

Hatred for the Spanish reached a peak in 1576 when long-unpaid Span-ish troops stationed in and around the great southern trade city, Ant-werp, sacked the city with dreadful ferocity. After this "Spanish Fury," Antwerp, formerly the chief business center of the Low Countries, never recovered its eminence. Infuriated Catholics and Protestants joined to-gether in 1576 in an agreement called the Pacification of Ghent to drive out the Spaniards. But religious suspicions, Spanish arms, and a shrewd assurance by a new Spanish general of the old political freedoms for the southern provinces soon broke up the alliance. Calvinists in the southern provinces sought refuge in the north (modern Holland), which strength-ened Protestantism there and left the southern provinces (modern Bel-gium) largely in the hands of the Catholics.

In 1579 the ten southern provinces, under Spanish auspices, formed the League of Arras to defend Catholicism. The seven northern prov-inces, where the rebels had established their control, countered with the Union of Utrecht in which they bound themselves in a common effort against Spain. In 1581 the United Provinces, as the seven northern provinces were called, declared their independence from Spain in the Act of Abjuration, whose words foreshadowed later declarations of inde-pendence in other lands. The document asserted that the ruler of a nation existed for the welfare of his subjects, rather than the people ex-isting only to serve his purposes, and declared that a ruler who destroyed the liberties of his subjects could lawfully be deposed.

The new state chose William of Orange to occupy the office of chief executive of the United Provinces. William, a Protestant noble, had won the nickname of "the Silent" (*le Taciturne*) as a young man because of his reserve in diplomatic negotiations with the French, though actually he was an eloquent and affable person. He had led the rebels from the beginning and emerged during the struggle as one of the great leaders of the age. His patience, tolerance, determination, concern for his people, and belief in government by consent held the Dutch together and kept alive their spirit of revolt. The seven provinces retained much autonomy and the States-General, the representative body — and William's master — required adroit handling to be sustained in revolutionary ardor over long years of war on land and at sea. Philip recognized William's unique importance by offering the huge bounty of 25,000 gold crowns for his assassination, in the hope that the revolt would collapse with William's death. After several unsuccessful attempts had been made on his life, William fell in 1584 before the bullets of a young Catholic fanatic.

Although the revolt faltered, new leaders quickly took over in the persons of William's son, and successor, Maurice of Nassau, who proved himself a skilled military tactician, and Jan van Oldenbarneveldt, who handled political and diplomatic affairs. The rebels continued to fight after 1584 with the aid of English troops and subsidies. After Philip's death in 1598 peace negotiations started, ending in 1609, when the weary combatants agreed upon a truce of twelve years. For all practical purposes the seven United Provinces of the north, and the territory of Drenthe commonly called the Dutch Republic or Holland (from its largest province), had won independence, though the Spanish refused to acknowledge the fact for another forty years. The ten southern provinces, henceforth called the Spanish Netherlands, remained under Spanish rule.

THE ANNEXATION OF PORTUGAL

Spain gained temporary compensation for the setbacks in the Netherlands by Philip's acquisition of Portugal. In 1580 the Portuguese ruling line died out. Philip claimed the throne through his mother, eldest daughter of King Manuel (1495–1521). Although others had better claims, Philip used diplomacy and threats to gain official approval for his succession. The Portuguese people, who harbored a traditional enmity for Spain, took up arms in support of another candidate, but Spanish troops easily put down the rising and Philip took the crown. He thereby united the Iberian peninsula under one scepter for the first time in nine centuries and acquired the vast Portuguese overseas possessions in South America, Africa, and Asia. Sixty years later in 1640 the Spanish would lose these gains when the Portuguese won back their independence.

THE ANGLO-SPANISH RIVALRY

The open aid that England gave to the rebellious United Provinces after prolonged surreptitious assistance was one more in a long series of provocations that Spain suffered from the island kingdom. During the reign of Mary Tudor (1553–1558), the second of Philip's four wives, England had been in the Spanish camp. When Elizabeth came to the throne in 1558, she retained the Spanish alliance, though soon relations between the two nations became strained. English ships boldly traded with the

Spanish colonies in the New World despite Spanish efforts to keep foreigners out of the trade. English pirates and adventurous "sea dogs," such as Sir John Hawkins and Sir Francis Drake, preyed on Spanish shipping, made daring raids on coastal towns in Spanish America, and carried slaves from Africa to the Spanish colonies in the New World.

Philip had to endure these aggravations because of his involvement in the Netherlands and because his lack of sea power made it impossible for him to invade England. He encouraged intrigues to make Mary Stuart, former Queen of Scots and a Catholic, the ruler of England in place of Elizabeth, and thereby reestablish Catholicism and (hopefully) amity with Spain. Mary, whose great-grandfather was Henry VII, was heir presumptive to the unmarried Elizabeth. She had inherited the throne of Scotland from her father and had also reigned as queen of France for a year before the premature death of her husband, Francis II (1560). Her religion, her politics, and her immoral personal life enraged her subjects, and a noble faction urged on by the fiery Calvinist rhetoric of John Knox forced her to abdicate in 1567 in favor of her infant son, James VI. She fled to England, where Elizabeth decided that prison was the safest place for an exile who was a Catholic rival for the English throne.

Since the reign of Henry VII, England had been sensitive to the presence of a major power in the Low Countries since a Spanish victory over the Dutch rebels would open an invasion route into England. When the murder of William the Silent weakened the rebels, Elizabeth sent six thousand English soldiers to help them. Then in 1587, a new Catholic plot to assassinate Elizabeth and give the throne to Mary Stuart was uncovered. Elizabeth reluctantly sent Mary to the block. Mary's execution persuaded Philip that he had to invade England to win it for Catholicism and for himself. He declared himself a claimant to England's throne. Indeed, Mary's death freed him from the anxiety that if she had become queen of England, France might have benefited more than Spain, since Mary, whose mother was a Guise and who had herself been raised in France, had strong ties with that land.

In 1587 Philip began assembling an "Invincible Armada" of 130 ships to carry 19,000 troops to England, establish a beachhead, and escort a further 30,000 troops from the Netherlands under the able duke of Parma to invade, take, and re-Catholicize England. A papal blessing went with the Armada as it sailed in May, 1588, but neither it nor Philip's careful plans and heavy investment were proof against the ineptitude of the Spanish commanders, the seamanship and gunnery of the English, and the vagaries of the weather in the English Channel. In July and August, 1588, a running battle between the smaller English fleet (with Dutch assistance) and the large lumbering ships of the Armada destroyed the Spanish formations and ships. Hopelessly beaten, the remnants of the

Armada sailed for home around the north of Britain, only to lose more ships in violent gales off the Scottish and Irish coasts. One-third of the Armada never returned; virtually all surviving vessels had sustained damages and heavy casualties. The English did not lose a ship and suffered only 60 dead.

The rout of the Armada did not end the war. The conflict dragged on until 1604. Neither side could claim victory. The battle did not mark the decline of Spanish naval power and the beginning of English supremacy, as sometimes claimed. English sea power had surpassed that of Spain for some time; in fact, the Spanish strengthened their navy and increased their sea power after the Armada's defeat. The English were never able to blockade Spain or to cut off the well-convoyed Spanish treasure fleets from the New World. Between 1588 and 1603 the treasure fleets brought more American gold and silver into Spain than during any other fifteen-year period in Spanish history. Contrary to popular myths about the capture of vast amounts of Spanish treasure, significant portions of the treasure were taken only twice: by the Dutch in 1628 and by the British in 1656.

The English triumph greatly encouraged Protestants everywhere. Spain, the wealthiest and strongest power in the world, was not invincible, and though Spain dominated Europe for another generation, other nations no longer stood in quite the same awe of it. In England the story of the Armada became part of the national legend, a symbol of the victory of free men over tyranny and of youthful vigor and daring over cautious and bumbling old age. It also served to obscure the vacillation and meagerness of so much of Queen Elizabeth's diplomacy and war policy.

Philip tried to regain prestige by intervention in the religious wars of France in the hope that he could establish domination of that country. He sent troops to aid the Catholic League. His plans came to nothing when Henry of Navarre became a Catholic, for it was no longer possible for Philip to claim that he was in France to defend it from Protestantism and he had to withdraw. Once again, Philip's retreat redounded to Elizabeth's advantage, for she had supported Henry with a modest force and a modest subsidy.

FINANCIAL TROUBLES AND BANKRUPTCY

Vast sums poured into Spain each year from the seemingly inexhaustible gold and silver mines of Mexico and Peru. Yet there never seemed to be enough to cover the costs of Philip's wars and domestic expenditures. He started his reign under the handicap of an enormous debt inherited from Charles V, and within little more than a year he had to make a declaration of bankruptcy. The brutal milking of old tax sources, oppressive and economically destructive new taxes, the sale of titles, offices, and monopolies on important commodities, forced contributions exacted from the clergy, and heavy borrowing at exorbitant interest rates were all expedients that failed to bring solvency. In 1575 the government again declared it could not pay its creditors. A composition of the debts by which the creditors suffered heavy losses was agreed upon, but brought only temporary relief. The tremendous expenditures on the Armada once more brought hopeless financial difficulties. Finally in 1596 the bankers refused to lend any more money, and for the third time Philip declared his state bankrupt. When he died in 1598, he left his successor an enormous and unpayable debt.

During Philip's long reign Spain reached the peak of its power and greatness — and also began the descent from its high point. Philip tried to do too much at one time, attempting simultaneously to develop, colonize, and protect a world empire, fight the Turks, retain mastery over the Netherlands, dominate Italy, France, and England, and always and everywhere defend Catholicism and crush Protestantism. This impossible program impoverished his country and earned it a host of enemies. The wonder is not that Philip failed to reach his goals but that he accomplished as much as he did.

ELIZABETHAN ENGLAND

The nemesis of Philip's Spain was Elizabeth's England. English money, arms, and men sustained the Dutch rebels, supported Henry of Navarre and helped turn the tide against the Catholic cause in France and dash Philip's hopes to put his daughter on the French throne; English captains raided New Spain and shipped slaves to her colonies; and England's navy served Philip his most humiliating, costly, and damaging defeat in 1588. Philip's instinct had been sound in 1559 when, within months of his wife Mary's death, he had made marital overtures to her half-sister and successor. Had Elizabeth consented, the history of both Spain and England would have been different. Instead, Philip married the daughter of Henry II of France in 1560, by which he would claim the French crown for his daughter. Elizabeth never married, and her dynasty died with her, the last Tudor.

ELIZABETH I

Elizabeth (1558–1603) was born in 1533, the daughter of Ann Boleyn and Henry VIII. In the womb, Henry's joyous hope, in the cradle, his woeful disappointment, she was not the long-awaited male heir. Her mother was mercilessly destroyed a few years later on trumped up charges of adultery, and Elizabeth was bastardized by act of Parliament. During the reign of Mary she stood in deadly peril as a potential Protestant claimant to the throne. Elizabeth adored her father (an unrequited love) and she consciously patterned her statecraft and even her personal style

Elizabeth I, attributed to Gheeraert

"She must not indeed . . . yield much to a young girl at sixteen. She has a very dignified, serious, and royal look, and rules her kingdom with great discretion, in desirable peace, felicitously, and in the fear of God. She has, by God's help and assistance, known well how to meet her enemies hitherto." Comment by Frederick, duke of Würtemberg, in William Brenchley Rye, ed., ENGLAND AS SEEN BY FOREIGNERS IN THE DAYS OF ELIZABETH AND JAMES THE FIRST (New York, 1967).

on Henry VIII. She was worthy of him in all respects save one: Henry, the uncompromising dynast, would never have approved of a Virgin Queen who would die without heir-of-the-body. Though she continued to negotiate marriage alliances for diplomatic advantage into her fifties, she never intended to marry. Comely, vivacious to a degree, and youthful at her accession, she had virtually free choice of foreign princes or native noblemen. Speculation by historians that she might have been physically incapable of consummating marriage misses the point. She had no intention of being the victim of a consort, as Mary had been Philip's victim, deserted and unloved, or a mistress to any master in her own house or realm. She conceived of her unusual role, a ruling queen, in appropriately masculine terms, and like her father referred to herself as "the prince." This was more than mere style. As the years passed it might be said of her "nihil muliebre praeter corpus gerens" (nothing of a woman about her but her body) for she became increasingly self-identified with her kingly role. Contemporaries noted that her tears and flattering femininity were carefully staged public performances; her male intimates accepted her as one of themselves, hard, capable, and proud. She was successful among men in a man's world despite her gender, not because of it.

Elizabeth's outstanding qualities were her singleness of purpose, her ability to accept compromise without inviting defeat, and her good sense in choice of advisers. Her application to affairs was prodigious, her involvement in government continuous, and the objects of policy were always hers and not those of others. She determined the direction of her government, and while she met considerable opposition, both domestic and foreign, she seldom yielded more in compromise than the means, continuing to seek the ends. Her shrewdness in choice of ministers was exemplified in the indefatigable and balanced William Cecil, Lord Burghley, her most efficient minister and closest adviser for forty years. Her favorites — the earl of Leicester (perhaps for a brief spring her lover) and in her last years the impetuous young earl of Essex — were given honors and titles but few offices and fewer significant responsibilities, except in military leadership in which they were both less than successful.

There was little of the innovator in Elizabeth. Almost all of the institutions of civil government that she used for forty-five years were already in existence at her accession. The Privy Council dated from about 1530; under Elizabeth it was a manageably small coterie of her principal ministers, meeting regularly, advising the queen, overseeing the central administration and local government, implementing the law and keeping order, serving as the focal point for intelligence, and heavily dependent on the agency of the queen's secretary of state (first Burghley, and later Burghley's son, Robert Cecil). The traditional financial body, the Exchequer, was reformed at the outset of Mary's reign, incorporating new machinery and new practices established by Thomas Cromwell in the 1530's to administer the financial windfall from the break with Rome and the dissolution of the monasteries. The courts of law, no least the extraordinary criminal jurisdiction of the Privy Council in the Star Chamber, were established in function and responsibility by 1558, though their jurisdictions expanded rapidly under Elizabeth, primarily in response to the demands of litigants rather than regal will. The local justices of the peace, responsible for enforcing the criminal law and the administration of the counties of England and Wales, already enjoyed a virtual monopoly of local government, and under Elizabeth received more duties and more power to be exercised under the oversight of the regularly visiting judges of assize from the capital and the constant prying, pressuring, and prodding from the Privy Council. Even the modernization of the militia, England's sole army, began with Mary and was entrusted to an officer first appointed by Henry VIII, the lord lieutenant. Henry VIII founded the royal navy; Elizabeth expanded it. Elizabethan government, strict and relatively effective though it was, was effected primarily by the revitalization of existing institutions.

There was only one area open for the exercise of the Queen's creativity: the church. This was from necessity not choice. Mary's uncompromising and archaic Catholic orthodoxy from 1553 to 1558, combined with her disastrous subserviency to Philip II of Spain and his interests determined that England under Elizabeth would be avowedly Protestant and blatantly anti-Spanish.

THE ELIZABETHAN SETTLEMENT

To describe Elizabeth's "settlement in religion" as an attempt at a middle way between Catholicism and Protestantism (for so it has been characterized traditionally) is misleading both with respect to her intentions and the eventual results of the settlement. Elizabeth and her new archbishop of Canterbury, Matthew Parker, and the almost entirely new bench of bishops appointed by them, sought to make the Anglican Church a moderately reformed Protestant church within the framework of episcopal control under the monarch as Supreme Governor, with a learned clergy desirous of preaching the Word of God, and a laity regularly attending the local parish church to worship by a uniform liturgy. Traditional Catholic practices in worship were abolished, wooden communion tables were substituted for the stone altars of the Middle Ages, and the liturgy was to be basically that of the most reformed period of the Edwardian Reformation, the Prayer Book of 1552. Comprehensiveness, the object of the settlement, demanded a lack of doctrinal definition, insofar as the plethora of competing Protestant doctrines were concerned. In 1563 the queen and her bishops promulgated Thirty-Nine Articles of Religion, each a gem of studied ambiguity. Every major (and some minor) doctrines of the Protestant reformation — justification by faith, predestination and election, the sole authority of the Bible — received commendation without being made mandatory or exclusive. Lutheran, Calvinist, or Zwinglian, a Protestant could be comfortable, provided he did not look for one truth only. A Catholic could find no comfort. The Thirty-Nine Articles were a credo for a reformed Protestant church, which was to be allowed to develop by the interpretations of the bishops under the Supreme Governor.

Within a few years the settlement was under attack. The demand for a more thoroughgoing reform along the lines of Calvin's Geneva was mounted by some of the clergy who, in exile during Mary's reign, had embraced the doctrinal certainty of Reformed Protestantism in the Rhineland and Geneva. Attacks on "Popish remnants" in the Anglican Church's practice in the 1560's grew by the 1570's into an attack on the authority of bishops to discipline Christian men. Those who sought a "purer" reformed church — already they were called "Puritans" — concluded that such could only be obtained by the creation of Calvin's presbyteries of clergymen and laymen. Since the Anglican Church had been established by the queen in Parliament, the Puritans in the 1570's became a vociferous and annoyingly persistent minority claque in the House of Commons pressing (unsuccessfully) the queen and her ministers to further reform of the church. Puritan laymen and clerical sympathizers set up local meetings, called "classes," for preaching and exhortation and the imposition of congregational discipline on the members. The classes developed the laity's consciousness of Calvin's doctrine of predestination and election and gave the participants the sense of their own "election" to salvation with God's mission to reform the Anglican Church. Those few who came to believe the church was unreformable became separatists, forming those tiny, hardy congregations of which the Pilgrims of 1620 were one. A new archbishop of Canterbury, John Whitgift, during the last two decades of Elizabeth's reign made effective legal and ecclesiastical war on the Puritans. By 1603 the Puritan movement was contained, its radical leaders ejected from the ministry and its more responsible clergy persuaded to quietism. The "elect" were not, however, finished. They awaited another day and another monarch.

THE CATHOLIC SPECTER

Until 1570 those Catholics who would not accept the settlement attended surreptitious masses in the houses of gentlemen of the Old Faith and occasionally attended the local Anglican church to avoid the light fines for non-worship there. In 1570, Pope Pius IV took the momentous step of declaring Elizabeth "a heretic and favorer of heretics," a person excommunicated and thus deprived of her title as queen, and calling upon her subjects to disobey her and her laws. This was tantamount to being outlawed, and fanatic Catholics concluded that Elizabeth's murder would be the execution of Christian justice. A rising of northern Catholics under the duke of Norfolk that the papal bull of 1570 was intended to assist, though quickly suppressed, raised the specter of Catholic disloyalty and rebellion that remained in English Protestant consciousness for two centuries. The laws against non-attendance at the established church were stiffened to the point of confiscation of property and in the next fifteen years almost all activity in furtherance of Catholicism was made a capital crime. Rome had no choice but to consider England a missionary field. From 1577 a growing stream of young priests travelled from Catholic house to Catholic house in civilian clothes to minister the sacraments to small groups of the faithful. These priests were idealistic young Englishmen trained at English seminaries on the Continent established by exiles. Armed with the faith of the Roman Catholic Church reformed by the Council of Trent, many of them Jesuits, the priests and their lay supporters produced almost 200 martyrs. Devoted, dauntless, and resourceful, the priests managed to keep Catholicism alive. Yet even watered with their blood, the Old Faith could not grow. The harshness of the laws and their effective execution and the identification of Catholicism with assassination of the queen, rebellion, and Spanish invasion undid their ministry.

Assassination plots swirled around Elizabeth's cousin, guest, and prisoner, the deposed Mary, Queen of Scots, Elizabeth's heir presumptive. The plots were continuous; increasingly Mary was privy to their planning. The underground priests were seen as the agents of sedition and conspiracy, and though they stoutly (and usually honestly) denied any political purpose, the erosion of the religious allegiance of her subjects could only be taken by Elizabeth as a direct political threat. After a particularly dangerous plot in which Mary's complicity was clear, she was executed in 1587. Catholicism's hopes then rested entirely with Philip's Armada. In the parlous days of 1588 the overwhelming majority of English Catholics stood with the queen and nation, a fact not lost on Elizabeth. While popular anti-Catholicism mounted, the tempo of official persecution of Catholics slowed. Indeed, in the last years of the reign, the Catholics were involved in a rancorous dispute between the secular priests and the Jesuits over jurisdiction and tactics that crippled the missionary effort. By 1603 the Catholic specter was only a ghost.

THE EXPANSION OF ELIZABETHAN ENGLAND

The most striking feature of this second-class European state, Elizabethan England, was the self-assurance of its pretense to greatness, its sense of a destiny bound to surpass the reality of its future. Its accomplishments were amazing. England's survival in the face of external and internal threats and the success of its foreign policy in the Low Countries and France were feats. Its sea dogs expanded the trade and the consciousness of Englishmen beyond Europe and took the first steps towards the creation of an immense empire. Its cultural expansion was no less marked; Shakespeare crowned a splendid galaxy of men of letters. A revolution in education sent the sons of the gentry, the clergy, and substantial merchants to Oxford and Cambridge and the law schools in London for a modest acquaintance with learning and manners. A cruder education for cruder men was furnished by the Bible, a strong spur to literacy and an invitation to religious — and hence, political — activism. A century after its invention, printing attained its potential in a broad range of books for widened tastes and varied interests.

Underlying the expanded horizons and the cultural growth of the age was rapid economic expansion. Prosperity grew with a rising population that increased demand and with mounting foreign trade that brought in gold and silver and drove up prices. Economic optimism attracted capital and in turn increased production and prices. Behind the legislation in 1563 that attempted to regulate the labor force by requiring apprenticeship for all trades and providing for the fixing of maximum wages was an increasing demand for goods. This law was virtually unenforceable, and the era was a heyday for the handcraftsman, with or without apprenticeship. The housing of England improved markedly, the amount and elegance of personal possessions increased, and nutrition improved, not only for the upper classes but also for many of the common folk. Indeed, by the end of the era the landed aristocracy, dependent upon relatively fixed rents for income, benefited least by the prosperity built on a rise in prices. Even for the marginally employed, the unemployed, and vagrants (probably over one-third of the population) comprehensive laws of 1598 and 1601 provided for at least a measure of relief paid for by local taxes.

Despite its constant meddling in the economy, as in all spheres of life, the Elizabethan government had less effect on economic growth than appears by its activity. The government gave a push to a few industries by the sale of monopoly rights, but the attention monopolies have received because they became a major political grievance has exaggerated their economic impact. Government encouragement for joint-stock companies to venture into new trade areas, which over the reign opened regular trade with Russia, the Baltic, the Mediterranean, and ultimately the East Indies, did less than new sources of capital in increasing commerce. The best contribution of government was in assisting the development of the new coal industry (critically important as the forests shrank), the iron industry, glassmaking, salt extraction by evaporation, gunpowder manufacture, and shipbuilding. The great traditional industry, the manufacture of woolen cloth, suffered from government restrictions as much as from closed markets, and developed more sophisticated organization and new sources for capital despite the government. Doubtless, Elizabeth's principal contribution to the economy was the currency reform of her early years. Yet, there can be no discounting the very optimism and bravado of "Elizabethan" Englishmen, which was a cause as well as an effect of prosperity and cannot be divorced from the almost universal adulation of the queen.

FIN DE SIECLE

Elizabeth's last years witnessed a dilution of the sincerity of the adulation, a cynicism in the use of hyperbole for personal ends that tarnished the substance, though not the surface, of the queen's image. Parliamentary opposition (to monopolies and taxation) reached crisis proportions, the interminable war with Spain and a quicksand-war against elusive Irish rebels sapped confidence in English arms, and a feud in the queen's councils attending the meteoric rise of her unstable young favorite, the earl of Essex, .was a subject of tavern gossip. Impatience and frustration with an old lady and her aging counsellors felt by a new generation whose idol was Essex erupted in his attempted *coup d'etat* to make himself king in 1601. Essex went to the block; more profoundly important, his generation disappeared to their country houses, disgruntled, suspect by government, politically neutral, and disengaged. Elizabeth leaned, almost pathetically, on the prematurely aged reincarnation of her trusty Burghley his second son, Robert Cecil. The succession remained unsettled, despite Cecil's discreet negotiations with James VI of Scotland, the son of Mary, Queen of Scots.

A cold March day in 1603 saw the end of an era, a dynasty, and a monarch. Two years before, Elizabeth had soothed an outraged Parliament with the words, "This I count the glory of my crown, that I have reigned with your loves." In 1603 that love was dimmed, not least by a large measure of relief that James VI had succeeded peacefully and that Queen Elizabeth, great though she had been, was no more.

THE BORDERLANDS
OF EUROPE
CHAPTER SEVEN

So far we have dealt almost exclusively with the countries of western Europe — Italy, Spain, France, England, Germany, and the Netherlands. These countries occupy a relatively small area; it is only 800 miles from Rome to Amsterdam, and 650 miles from London to Prague. Yet they formed the heartland of Western civilization. Most of the institutions, ideas, and techniques that characterize Western society and that have spread to all parts of the globe had their origins in these countries.

On the north this heartland was bordered by the Scandinavian kingdoms and on the east by the Slavic lands and the Ottoman Empire. At one time or another through the centuries each of these borderlands played an important part in the general course of Western history. The Ottoman Turks during the fifteenth and sixteenth centuries were the most feared people of Europe. In the sixteenth century Poland, then far larger than it is today, seemed destined to become a great power. Russia emerged as the chief Slavic state in the seventeenth century, though its time of greatest power and influence has come only recently. In the sixteenth and seventeenth centuries Denmark and Sweden became important powers.

THE CREATION OF THE RUSSIAN STATE

First place among the royal statemakers of Europe belongs to the men who ruled over Muscovy in the fifteenth and sixteenth centuries. No other European monarch equaled their success in establishing absolute rule over their subjects. The process started with Ivan III, called the Great (1462–1505), who transformed the grand duchy of Moscow into an all-Russian national state. His autocratic, centralizing policies and the pomp and ceremony with which he surrounded himself set the pattern for the men who followed him on the Russian throne.

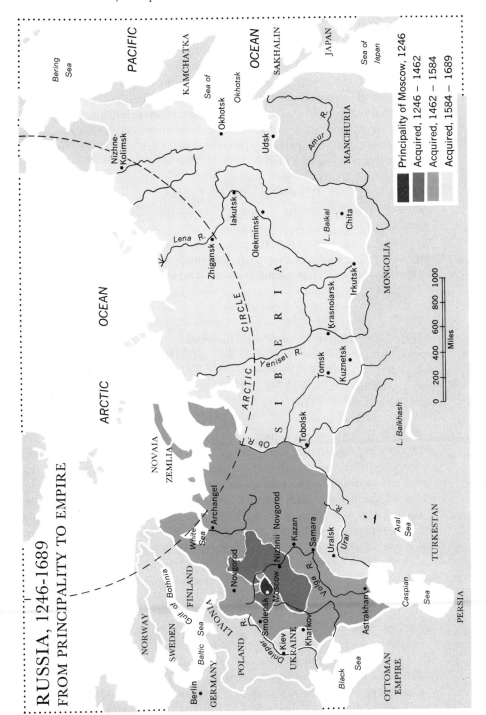

RUSSIA, 1246-1689
FROM PRINCIPALITY TO EMPIRE

Principality of Moscow, 1246
Acquired, 1246 – 1462
Acquired, 1462 – 1584
Acquired, 1584 – 1689

Many of the high nobility, especially the princes who had once ruled over lands absorbed by Muscovy and the descendants of the former rulers, resented the efforts of the Muscovite grand dukes to establish themselves as absolute monarchs. The princes had to accept unification under the leadership of the grand duchy, but they wanted to share in the rule of the new state. Ivan III and his son and successor, Vasilii III (1505–1533), did everything possible to curb their power and privileges. They were allowed to enter Muscovy's service but were not used as chief officials or advisers. When the princes protested, they were exiled, forced to become monks, or even executed.

Vasilii's death in 1533 gave the aristocracy its chance to seize power, for Vasilii's heir, Ivan IV, was an infant of three. Instead of uniting in a common cause against the throne, the great princely families vied with one another for control of the state, resorted to violence and murder, and threw the country into anarchy. In public the great nobles showed respect for the youthful monarch, but inside the Kremlin they treated him with contempt, looted his treasury, and committed acts of violence in his presence.

IVAN IV

Ivan suffered these affronts with the resolve that when he grew up, he would show the aristocrats that he was indeed their master. He took his first step at the age of thirteen when he suddenly ordered the arrest of a prince who had offended him and had him strangled and thrown to the dogs in the kennels. Three years later he announced that he would hold his coronation and take a wife. He had himself crowned with the title of tsar in 1547 and assumed personal rule of the country. He chose his tsaritsa from more than a thousand girls who were said to have appeared in answer to his summons to the Russian aristocracy to present their daughters to him. He picked the daughter of a noble family, against the wishes of the princes, who wanted him to marry into a princely family.

During the first thirteen years of his personal rule Ivan instituted a series of administrative and military reforms of major importance. A new law code modernized court procedure and improved administrative practices. Local government was reorganized to allow greater power to locally elected officials. A manual for the Church was drawn up that dealt with Church administration as well as religious and moral questions. In 1556 he established a ratio between the amount of land that a noble held and the number of soldiers that the noble had to provide for the tsar's army. Failure to meet this quota, or to pay a cash sum in lieu of soldiers, was punishable by loss of land. The noble himself had to serve in the tsar's forces from the age of fifteen until death, or until illness or old age incapacitated him. Ivan's record of domestic accomplishment was paralleled by his accomplishments in foreign affairs. Military campaigns against the Tatars of Kazan and Astrakhan brought the entire basin of the Volga River down to the Caspian Sea under his rule. This fertile territory of thousands of square miles was opened up to Russian colonization, and the Volga itself became a chief artery of expanding Russian commerce.

Friction grew between Ivan and the great aristocrats, although until the 1560's he remained on good terms with them and chose his closest friends and advisers from their number. Then he turned on them, arresting, exiling, or executing high nobles and their families on the slightest pretext. In 1564 he embarked on a policy designed to end forever the power of the aristocracy. He suddenly left Moscow with a great retinue and threatened to abdicate because of what he called the treasonous conduct of the aristocracy and clergy. He remained away until his subjects invited him back on his own conditions, which involved the division of the realm into two segments. The existing governmental machinery continued to operate and the landowners remained undisturbed in one segment. In the other, called the *Oprichnina,* a new administrative organization was set up and the tsar confiscated all private property. Ivan revealed his purpose by choosing to include in the Oprichnina that part of the realm containing the properties of the princes and the old high nobility. He kept about one-fourth of the confiscated lands for himself and gave the rest to the *oprichniki,* the men of the Oprichnina organization, who held the lands they received on condition of military service to Ivan. He executed many of the former proprietors (estimates of the number executed run from 400 to 10,000); the rest he settled on the frontiers, far from their old homes, on service tenure, transforming them from private proprietors to men who held their land in return for military service to the tsar.

The ostensible purpose of the Oprichnina was to root out treason. It was symbolized by the oprichniki's black uniforms, black horses, and the dog's head and broom attached to their saddles. Actually, Ivan used the oprichniki to terrorize his subjects into accepting his will without question. The oprichniki murdered, tortured, and pillaged not only the aristocracy but also the plain people. In 1570, when a rumor reached him that citizens of Novgorod planned to put their city under Polish rule, Ivan, without bothering to check the story, ordered the oprichniki to sack the city and harry the entire region. In Novgorod itself the slaughter of more than 60,000 people irreparably destroyed the city's prosperity and prestige. Similar episodes, though not as bloody, took place in other parts of the realm. Ivan disbanded the Oprichnina in 1572, deciding that it had accomplished its purpose. The power of the aristocracy had been smashed and everyone in the realm had been forced to recognize that "the great and the small live by the favor of the sovereign." But the violence of the Oprichnina upset social and economic life and left a legacy of suffering and discontent that was not erased for many years.

The damage done to the Russian social fabric by the Oprichnina was compounded by the long and unsuccessful Livonian War, which dragged on from 1558 to 1583. The conflict began when Ivan invaded neighboring Livonia (comprising present-day Estonia and parts of Latvia). He hoped to gain access to the Baltic by taking Livonia from the Knights of the Teutonic Order, military monks who had held it since the Middle Ages. The knights turned for help to their other neighbors, and Russia soon found itself fighting against Lithuania, Poland, and Sweden. The war brought much sacrifice and suffering to the Russian people, and in the end Ivan had to relinquish his ambitions for Livonian territory and also lost some of his own realm to Sweden.

The rebuff to Russian ambitions of expansion in the west was balanced by successes in the east. During the sixteenth century Russian merchants, especially the Stroganov family, penetrated into Siberia in search of furs, other forest products, and metals. Sponsored by the Stroganovs, in 1583 a band of nearly a thousand Cossacks from the steppes of southern Russia conquered western Siberia for the tsar.

Even as a child Ivan IV had evidenced the extremes of cruelty that marked him as a man. As he grew older his name became a byword for savagery and bloodlust. His subjects, who stood in dread and awe of him, dubbed him Ivan the Terrible. In one of his fits of ungovernable rage he killed his eldest son with a blow of his staff. Periods of vice-ridden dissipation alternated with seizures of remorse, when the frantically religious Ivan would prostrate himself with wild fervor before his icons. He kept lists of the people murdered at his command and paid priests to pray for their souls. He held the unshakable conviction that his sovereign power came from God, that he represented God on earth, and that those who resisted his power resisted God. By the time of his death in 1584, Ivan had established unchallenged authority in a vast realm that reached from the Polish frontiers far into Asia and from the Arctic Ocean to the Caspian Sea, but his subjects paid a heavy price in human suffering and degradation during and for many years after his reign.

THE TIME OF TROUBLES

On Ivan's death his eldest surviving son, Fedor, became tsar. Weak in mind and body, Fedor gladly allowed his wife's brother, Boris Godunov, to run the country. Boris was a keen, vigorous man of noble but not princely birth. He followed Ivan's centralizing and autocratic policies without the use of terror and established himself so securely that, when Fedor died childless in 1598, he easily gained the throne for himself. He soon encountered grave troubles. A series of crop failures brought on famine, brigandage, and widespread unrest; the peasantry, who formed the great mass of the population, resisted the new authority over them that had been given to the lords; and nobles and princes who were Boris's social equals or superiors considered him a usurper and intrigued against him. Boris's difficulties reached their climax when a pretender to the throne claiming to be Dmitrii, a son of Ivan IV who had died as a child, invaded Russia in 1604 with Polish aid and won a large following. His appearance ushered in the decade known as the Time of Troubles, during which the country was torn by civil war, social disorder, brigandage, and foreign invasion.

The unsettled state of the country following Boris's death and the murder of his son and successor by the false Dmitrii in 1605 gave the aristocrats a chance to realize their old ambition. A group led by Prince Vasilii Shuiskii murdered Dmitrii and proclaimed Shuiskii tsar. Widespread opposition to the new tsar, open rebellion, a new false Dmitrii, and invasion by Polish troops brought about the collapse of the Shuiskii regime in 1610. The nobles of Moscow offered the throne to the Roman Catholic son of the king of Poland on the condition that he govern with the aid of the nobles.

The Catholic Polish occupation of Moscow evoked a national liberation movement led by Orthodox priests and a meat dealer named Kuzma Minin. A militia of 100,000, composed mainly of lesser nobles and city people came into being; joined by Cossack forces, it drove out the Poles in 1612. The victors summoned a national assembly to meet in the city of Moscow in January, 1613, to elect a new tsar. The assembly's choice, after heated debate and much behind-the-scenes negotiation, fell on Michael Romanov, sixteen-year-old scion of a noble family. The assembly made Michael the absolute ruler of Russia with all the powers that Ivan IV had exercised.

The election of Michael marked the end of the Time of Troubles. The state that emerged from those difficult years was unlike any Western state, and far more absolute. It was a service state, in which every subject from the greatest noble to the humblest peasant had to perform specific functions designed to preserve and aggrandize the powers of the state. In return for the right to hold land and rule over their peasants, the nobles had to serve in the tsar's army and bureaucracy. In turn, the peasants had to work for their lords and pay them dues in cash and kind, so that the lords had the means to perform their state service.

THE RUSSIAN CHURCH

In their drive to gain autocratic power the Muscovite rulers had an invaluable ally in the Russian Church. Following the example set by the Church in the defunct Byzantine Empire, the Orthodox Church considered itself subservient to the political ruler. It preached submission to the throne and glorified the ruler's absolutism by declaring he had Godlike powers. In support of the claims of the throne to autocratic power, theologians advanced the theory that the City of Moscow was the "third Rome." According to this theory, the first Rome, in Italy, and the second Rome, Constantinople, had both fallen for their sins; Moscow succeeded Constantinople as the center of the true faith and the capital of the Christian world.

A serious threat to the power of the Church — and thus of the tsar — was raised in the sixteenth century by a group of churchmen who held that the acquisition of material goods undermined the ascetic ideals of monastic life. They urged that the monasteries rid themselves of wealth and land. The reformers had the support of secular landlords who, as in other European lands, yearned to acquire Church property. The throne finally confirmed the monasteries' right to keep their riches and to add to them. The support given to the throne's claim of absolutism by the Church leaders opposing monastic reform doubtless helped persuade the throne to decide against the reformers. By the second half of the sixteenth century certain monasteries owned huge complexes of property and, after the tsar, were the greatest landlords of Muscovy.

ECONOMIC CHANGES

In the latter part of the fifteenth and for much of the sixteenth century, while the rulers of Muscovy laid the foundations of absolutism, Russia experienced an era of economic growth. Money came increasingly into use, much new land was taken under the plow, population grew, internal trade flourished, and cities grew in size and took on new importance as centers of trade and industry and markets for farm goods. Foreign trade increased with both the East and the West. Trade with the West received an important stimulus when English seamen, in search of a northeast passage to the Indies, sailed above Scandinavia into the White Sea and in 1553 landed on the shores of northern Russia. Although the route was open for only three summer months (ice and storms made it unnavigable for the rest of the year), a lively trade sprang up with England and then with the Netherlands.

The economic upswing continued until the last third of the sixteenth century, when a catastrophic depression swept the country. A mass flight of population from the most populous and economically important parts of Russia, especially the Moscow region and the northwest, reached its height in the 1570's and 1580's. In some districts as many as 97 per cent of the farm homesteads were empty, and great expanses of land lay untilled. Most of the migrants fled east and south into the regions that Ivan IV's conquests had opened up to Russian settlement. A much smaller number went into the far less hospitable districts of northern Russia. Still others fled into the untamed steppe, the no-man's land beyond Russia's southern frontiers, to join the Cossack bands that roamed its open plains.

The great depopulation of the economic centers had serious repercussions on economic life. Agriculture, by far the chief industry of the country, suffered from the withdrawal of so much land from cultivation and the flight of so many farm workers. Trade and industry suffered from the sharp decline in both supply and demand.

The most important cause of the mass flight seems to have been the series of natural and man-made calamities that engulfed the most populous parts of the country in the latter half of Ivan IV's reign: the long Livonian War bringing heavy taxation and enemy invasion in the northwest; devastating Tatar raids; at least two plague epidemics and several years of famine; above all, the Oprichnina, with its violence, plundering, and heavy exactions. Recovery began in the late 1580's. People drifted back to their old homes, deserted land was once more cultivated, and agricultural production increased. The recovery continued until the beginning of the next century when a series of crop failures brought on famine and unrest, which was aggravated by the other miseries of the Time of Troubles. Once again, thousands fled their homes and economic life came to a standstill.

THE ENSERFMENT OF THE PEASANTRY

At the insistence of landlords in the fifteenth century, rulers began to impose restrictions on the right of peasants to move freely from one place to another and permitted lords to have legal jurisdiction over their peasant tenants. Until the economic upswing of the late fifteenth and sixteenth centuries, however, the landlords usually demanded only payments in cash and kind from their peasant renters and only exceptionally required the peasants to work for them. The economic expansion provided an opportunity for the lords to profit from producing for the market on their own account. To get the necessary labor, they increased their demands for labor rent from the peasants. The lords also raised the money rents, for they needed more money to meet the costs of the service the government now required of them and to cover the rise in living costs accompanying the economic expansion. In addition to the increased demands of their lords, the peasants' taxes rose, for the government needed more money to pay for its policies of war and expansion.

In order to meet these financial demands, many peasants borrowed from their lords at extortionate rates of interest. The loan agreement required the peasant to pay the interest by working full-time for the lord, and the law forbade the peasant to leave until he had paid his debt. Since the peasant was unable to amass enough cash to pay the principal of the loan, he became a permanent peon of the lord, bound by his indebtedness. The economic downturn in the latter part of the sixteenth century forced more of the peasantry into debt servitude. Even those who managed to stay out of debt lost their freedom: the labor shortage caused by the mass migrations impelled the lords to persuade the government to issue laws in the 1580's and 1590's forbidding peasants to move and compelling those who had moved to come back. Thus, the peasant lost his right of freedom of movement and became legally bound to the lord on whose land he lived. Not all the peasants who fled during the great migration returned home, but even they did not escape the new restrictions (except the small number who went north or joined the Cossacks), for the lands on which they settled belonged to nobles and the laws bound them to their new lords.

The peasants' resentment of these restrictions set off peasant uprisings in every part of Russia, but their efforts came to nothing. They had lost their freedom of movement and were subject to the will of their lord, having to work for him, make him payments in cash and kind, hold land at his pleasure, and accept his legal jurisdiction over them. In other words, by the seventeenth century the once-free Russian peasant had become a serf.

THE ROMANOVS, 1613–1682

Michael, the first tsar of the Romanov dynasty, which ruled Russia for the next three hundred years, was a weak and self-effacing man. First his mother and her greedy kinsmen dominated the state, then his father, Philaret, whom Michael had made patriarch (head) of the Russian Church, made himself co-ruler and ran the state until his death in 1633. On Michael's death in 1645 his sixteen-year-old son Alexis succeeded. Like his father, Alexis lacked qualities of leadership and allowed a succession of royal favorites to run the state for their personal gain. Alexis was succeeded in 1676 by his son Feodor, a sickly lad of fourteen, whose reign of six years was also dominated by grasping favorites.

Under these inept rulers Russia's economic structure recovered only slowly from the severe blows it had received. In the 1620's a very gradual upturn began. During the succeeding decades new crises, new wars, new uprisings, and misgovernment acted as brakes to economic improvement, but by the end of the seventeenth century the Russian economy had made up most of the ground it had lost.

Nearly all the great aristocratic families who had been so important in preceding centuries had been wiped out by the policy of extermination mounted by Ivan IV and by the disorders of the Time of Troubles. The few families that survived still kept some of their prestige, either because they were kinsmen of the Romanovs or had proved their loyalty to the new dynasty. The lesser nobility had also suffered in former times, especially during the Time of Troubles. Many had been killed; others had lost everything and sunk into the peasantry. Yet, as a class, they triumphed. They had been loyal partisans of the tsars in their struggle in the sixteenth century against the great nobility, leaders in the national revival of the Time of Troubles, and electors of Michael. They were rewarded by becoming the ruling class in place of the old aristocracy. They received land grants, serfs, and high posts in the government from their grateful sovereign, in return for service in the army and the bureaucracy.

During the second half of the seventeenth century the status of the serfs deteriorated. In the absence of government restrictions the serf owners bought and sold peasants like so many cattle. They even killed them without fear of punishment. The least oppressed were the 10 per cent or so of the peasantry who were not serfs but who lived on land that belonged to the state, mainly in the infertile regions of northern Russia. These people, who were supposed to pay taxes and quitrents to the state, were theoretically restricted in their ability to move about, but were in practice relatively free. Other peasants fled from the settled regions to join Cossack bands that roamed the Black Sea steppes. In the course of time the Cossack bands had formed loose, semimilitary, autonomous federations along the chief rivers of the southern steppes — the Dnieper, the Don, and the Volga. Hardened by their rough lives, they included in their ranks cutthroats capable of barbaric atrocities. The Cossacks won a reputation for military prowess in the service of both Russia and Poland.

The increased restrictions on personal liberty, the misrule by favorites, the wars that filled thirty of the seventy years between Michael's accession and Feodor's death, the heavy tax burden resulting from these conflicts, and the harsh punishments meted out to those who tried to escape their military or tax obligations — all served to stir up discontent and unrest among the masses. A number of uprisings in the chief cities were harshly repressed. In rural areas the peasants usually expressed their discontent by running away. Sometimes they turned to violence, bursting into disorganized local outbreaks. In 1670 there was a mass rural uprising that for a few months threatened the survival of the government. Stenka Razin, a Cossack who had won notoriety as a freebooter along the shores of the Caspian, led his gang along the Volga, burning, looting, and killing as they moved northward. He urged the peasants to turn against their masters and free themselves. Thousands heeded his call, and within a few months he had control of 800 miles along the Volga. In August, 1670, he was defeated by the tsar's troops, his revolt collapsed, and Razin himself (betrayed by some of his fellow Cossacks) was executed after excruciating tortures. His name lived on among the peasantry, long celebrated in their poems and songs as a champion of freedom.

Religious controversy added to the discontent of the people. Although the Russians were deeply attached to Christianity, many identified true religion with a superstitious veneration of external forms and the repetition of traditional prayers. The liturgy and sacred writings of the Russian

Church had come from the Greek Church, and when learned priests tried to correct errors in the liturgy or mistranslations in the writings, they were bitterly resisted. In 1652 a reforming priest named Nikon, who had won the favor of Tsar Alexis, was elected patriarch. He ordered corrections in the religious manuals and liturgies to bring them into line with the original Greek practices. Many of the changes seem petty, such as directing that the priests make the sign of the cross with three fingers instead of two, but the innovations raised violent opposition from clergy and people alike. Nikon, who was politically ambitious and offended the tsar by his pretensions, was deposed as patriarch in 1666, but his reform movement was upheld by Church and state, and its opponents were labeled heretics.

The dissenters formed a schismatic group called the Old Believers. They won a wide following among the masses, who were always ready to believe the worst of their rulers and saw the reform movement as a diabolical plot to deprive them of a chance for eternal salvation. Viciously persecuted by the authorities, thousands of Old Believers burned themselves alive in mass holocausts to save themselves from forced conversion to the abominated new practices. The extreme fanaticism subsided in the 1690's when the government's persecution became less violent, but the Old Believers retained their separate identity. Strongest in the backwoods of the north and northeast and in the southern steppe frontier, where they gained many adherents among the Cossacks, they often joined revolts against the government. Like so many other persecuted minorities, they also distinguished themselves by their industrious habits, and in the eighteenth and nineteenth centuries many became leaders in Russian economic life.

POLAND TO 1660

Poland in the first centuries of the modern era included large parts of today's Russia and Germany, stretching from the Baltic to the Black Sea. Much of this territory was Lithuanian, but after 1386 Poland and Lithuania had the same king. The two countries maintained separate governments until they were merged by the Union of Lublin in 1569. Under the union each partner kept its own administration and laws but had a common diet, currency, and system of land tenure.

The king of this vast realm was elected by the noblemen, though from 1386 to 1572 they always chose a member of the Polish-Lithuanian house of Jagiello. To win and hold the throne, the Jagiellos made many concessions to the nobility: the nobility formed the army, filled most government offices, comprised the national and provincial diets, and helped the king to rule by means of representatives. They used their political power to transform the once-free peasantry into serfs and to pass legislation in the interests of the landowners that crippled the economy of the towns and thereby prevented the development of a prosperous middle class. The nobles, extremely proud of their privileges, successfully resisted all efforts by the throne to centralize the state. Although they constituted less than 10 per cent of the population, they considered themselves "the nation," referred to their country as a Republic of Noblemen, and looked upon the king they elected as merely the titular head of their republic.

THE GOLDEN AGE

In time this semianarchic political arrangement led to the disappearance of the Polish state. For a few decades in the sixteenth century, however, during the reigns of Sigismund I (1508–1548) and Sigismund II (1548–1572), Poland seemed about to become a major European power. During this golden age of Poland's history, the country achieved relative political stability and made important territorial acquisitions. It also made significant cultural advances, stimulated in large part by Queen Bona, a Sforza of Milan and wife of Sigismund I. Bona made the Polish court a center of Italian Renaissance culture.

The Protestant Reformation made great headway in Poland, and for a time it looked as if Protestantism might establish itself permanently. The lure of Church property and the chance to assert the power and privileges of their class against the authority of the Catholic Church and the throne attracted many noblemen to Protestantism. Sigismund II, whose wife was a Calvinist, showed much sympathy for Protestant teachings. In 1555 he granted freedom of worship to all Protestants, and in 1573 the national diet, in which Protestants held a majority, passed the Compact of Warsaw, which affirmed the principle of religious liberty. Protestantism, however, lacked roots among the masses, and the many Protestant sects opposed one another as vigorously as they opposed Catholicism. When in the latter part of the sixteenth century the Jesuits led a determined counteroffensive, Catholicism was easily reestablished and Protestantism suppressed.

THE BEGINNING OF THE DECLINE

Sigismund II's death in 1572 ended the Jagiello dynasty that had been continuously in power since 1386. The field was open and foreign princes eagerly sought election, handing out bribes and favors to win support. Fifty thousand nobles met outside Warsaw and chose as their monarch the French candidate, Henry of Anjou, degenerate younger brother of King Charles IX of France. The noble electors required him to accept certain provisions (called the Henrician Articles), which all kings after Henry had to accept. The articles, a written summation of the privileges of the nobility, required the king to summon the national diet every two years, forbade him to marry without the diet's approval, allowed him no voice in the designation of his successor, prohibited him from leading his troops across the frontier without the diet's consent or for more than three months at a time, required him to accept the Compact of Warsaw guaranteeing religious freedom, and established a council of sixteen nobles who, in relays of four, resided at the court for six months to advise the king. The monarch's failure to carry out any part of the articles released his subjects from their oath of allegiance to him.

When Henry inherited the French crown after only a few months on the Polish throne, he returned home with alacrity. His successor, Stephen Bathory, prince of Transylvania, was elected after near civil war and proved himself one of Poland's ablest kings. Unfortunately, his achievements were cancelled out during the long reign of his successor, the Swedish Sigismund III (1587–1632). Because Sigismund was heir to the Swedish throne, Polish leaders hoped that the union of Sweden and Poland under one ruler would create a great new power that would dominate eastern Europe. But Sigismund's Catholicism cost him the Swedish throne, while in Poland his ineptness, bigotry, endless machinations to win the Swedish throne, and intervention in Russia during the Time of Troubles brought his country continuous war and much domestic suffering and discontent.

The recovery of Russia and the growth of Swedish power produced increased external pressures on Poland. The country's internal weaknesses prevented it from defending its vast territories from greedy neighbors, nor was it able to preserve internal order. Beginning in 1648, a series of catastrophes called the Deluge by Polish historians overwhelmed the country. During the previous decades there had been frequent risings of the bitterly oppressed serfs against their masters, and the Cossacks, who lived in the Ukraine (on Poland's southeastern frontier) and who resented the efforts of Polish nobles to settle there and impose serfdom and Roman Catholicism on them, had risen frequently in protest. In 1648 the current of revolt came to a climax in a great rising under Bohdan Khmelnitskii, who proclaimed himself *hetman* (leader) of the Cossacks. In 1654 Khmelnitskii induced Russia to go to war against Poland for possession of the Ukraine. In the next year Sweden took advantage of Poland's troubles by invading. Only the wave of religious zeal and patriotic ardor that swept Poland saved it from partition between Lutheran Sweden and Orthodox Russia. Peace with Sweden in 1660 cost Poland Livonia, and peace with Russia in 1667 cost it the eastern Ukraine and Smolensk. Although Poland had survived the deluge, her only hope for the future depended upon the nobility agreeing to constitutional reforms to limit their power. Instead, they became even more selfish and irresponsible, and a little over a century later, independent Poland disappeared.

POLISH JEWRY

By the mid-seventeenth century Poland, with about a half-million Jews, had the largest Jewish community in Europe. Most of the Jews earned their living from small trades and crafts. A few became wealthy and served the government as fiscal agents or tax farmers; others were employed by rich nobles to manage their property or run the inns and distilleries on their estates. A much smaller number were moneylenders, and a few became doctors and apothecaries. Polish Jews spoke a German dialect that they had brought with them into Poland, called Yiddish (from the German word *jüdisch*, Jewish). It was written with Hebrew characters and contained many words from Hebrew and other languages.

The Polish government in the sixteenth century allowed the Jews a remarkable degree of self-government. They had their own courts, where they were judged according to Jewish law based upon the Bible and rabbinical commentaries. A council made up of twenty-four Jewish laymen and six rabbis acted as an overall supervisory agency for Polish Jewry. It assisted in enforcing government edicts, acted as a court of appeal for disputes among Jews, passed laws concerning dress and social life, supervised education, and apportioned taxation.

In the seventeenth century calamities overwhelmed Polish Jewry. The Cossacks who rose under Khmelnitskii made the Jews their special target. Between 1648 and 1658 they massacred 100,000 Polish Jews. In the years that followed continued waves of anti-Semitic violence engulfed the country. Some Polish Jews, in search of a haven, began to move westward to new Jewish communities in the countries from which their ancestors had fled.

SCANDINAVIA TO 1660

In Scandinavia, as in Russia, and most of the rest of Europe, the struggle for supremacy between throne and nobility dominated the course of events during the first two centuries of the modern era. In the Scandinavian lands the nobles held an important advantage in the conflict because the throne remained an elective office, not a hereditary one. The nobles demanded increased privileges as the price for their vote and continued support.

DENMARK

Until the fifteenth century any Dane could become a noble, and be exempt from taxes, simply by equipping himself at his own expense for military service. Then, in order to make itself an exclusive caste, the nobility arranged that no one could claim nobility unless he showed that his ancestors for three generations had been exempted from taxes. When

SCANDINAVIA, 1523-1660

old noble families died out they could not be replaced by new ones and, as a result, the nobility was almost halved between the fifteenth and mid-seventeenth centuries. The nobility expanded their powers over the peasants, who made up the greatest part of the population, and by the end of the fifteenth century most of the peasants had been reduced to serfdom. The nobility also broke the legal monopoly held by town merchants on foreign trade by selling their produce directly to foreign buyers instead of through the middlemen of the cities.

For a few years during the early sixteenth century it seemed as if the throne might succeed in gaining the upper hand over the nobility. Christian II, who was elected king in 1513, tried to follow the model of the New Monarchs of France, England, and Spain and establish royal supremacy. With the support of the townspeople he attempted to reduce the power of the nobility and great churchmen, protect the rights of the merchants, abolish the worst abuses of serfdom, and make the crown hereditary. The nobility rose in revolt and in 1523 drove Christian from the throne and elected his uncle to succeed him. The power of the nobility stood at its zenith. They ruled the state in alliance with the king, exercised still greater control over the peasants, gained a monopoly of all high government posts, and were exempted from tithes to the Church. They profited even more in 1536 when Lutheranism was adopted as the state religion, for the king confiscated the property of the Catholic Church and divided it between himself and the nobility.

As a result of the power vacuum left by the decline of the Hanseatic League, Denmark and Sweden frequently engaged in furious wars that centered on the control of the Baltic during the sixteenth century. Although Denmark never succeeded in decisively defeating Sweden, it managed to establish its hegemony in the Baltic, increasing Denmark's international prestige and bringing new wealth by trade. The upswing in his country's fortunes persuaded King Christian IV (1588–1648) that he could make Denmark the chief power of northern Europe. He badly overestimated the strength of his country. He was soundly defeated in the Thirty Years' War (see Chapter Nine) and in a war with Sweden in the 1640's. When he died in 1648, whatever ascendancy and prestige Denmark had once enjoyed had disappeared.

SWEDEN

During the fifteenth and early sixteenth century the Danes engaged in endless intrigues and wars to reestablish the domination over Sweden that they had held briefly after the Union of Kalmar in 1937. In 1520 Christian II of Denmark had himself crowned in Stockholm as king of Sweden, but soon a revolt led by Gustavus Eriksson drove out the Danes. In 1523 a national assembly (*Riksdag*) of the four estates — nobility, clergy, townspeople, and peasantry — chose Gustavus as their monarch.

The new king, who ruled as Gustavus Vasa, faced a difficult task. Sweden was poor and thinly populated, an unruly nobility and the powerful Church posed threats to internal order, and the country was surrounded by foreign enemies. Gustavus proved equal to the problems. His technique of rule resembled that of the Tudors of England; like them he carefully cultivated good relations with the Riksdag. In 1527 he summoned the Riksdag in order to take possession of Church property, counting on the nobles' envy of Church wealth (the Church owned more land than all the nobles put together) and the growing religious discontent with Catholicism. A sizable proportion of the confiscated land went to the nobility. In the succeeding years under Gustavus's guidance Lutheranism became Sweden's state religion, with the Church firmly under the control of the king.

Gustavus extended his power over local government by replacing noble provincial governors with his own appointees. He introduced reforms into government administration and personally supervised all government activities, built up a strong army and navy, regulated and encouraged trade and industry, and operated a profitable business in goods he received as taxes or produced on his own properties. In 1544 the Riksdag, at his suggestion, repealed the old law that made the throne elective and declared it hereditary in Gustavus's line.

After Gustavus's death in 1560 the nobles made gains at the expense of his weak successors. Then in 1599 Charles IX, Gustavus's youngest son, took the throne. The new king, supported by the middle class and the peasantry, repressed the nobility and reestablished the supremacy of the royal power. During these years Sweden took the first steps in the creation of a Baltic empire for itself. Sweden entered the Livonian War between Russia and the Teutonic Order and made large territorial gains. Early in the seventeenth century Charles IX saw an opportunity to gain more power and land at the expense of Russia, then going through the Time of Troubles, and he invaded that country. He also became involved in wars with Poland and Denmark. When he died in 1611, he passed on all three wars to his sixteen-year-old son and successor, Gustavus Adolphus.

The new king proved to be the greatest ruler in Swedish history. At thirteen he was negotiating with ambassadors from foreign lands, and his proud father used him as an assistant in matters of state. Despite his early education in statecraft, the three unfinished wars that he inherited from his father placed him in a desperate position. The nobles took advantage of his difficulties and his youth to renew their demands for more power.

Gustavus Adolphus's personality, unusual intellectual abilities, and great military skill enabled him quickly to establish himself as leader of the country and to undermine concessions that he had earlier made to the nobles. He maintained control over the aristocrats by converting them into a service nobility whose task was to serve the state as government bureaucrats and army officers, and he placated them by creating a House of the Nobility as the upper house of the Riksdag and by giving them large tax exemptions. He reorganized the government by adopting the collegial method of administration, by which each government department was run by a board or college of officials. He improved the military administration and built up an exceptionally strong army, based originally on conscripts, though later reinforced by mercenaries. He converted the noble-dominated Council of State into a cabinet of heads of his administrative departments. In these and other reforms he had the invaluable assistance of Axel Oxenstierna, chief minister throughout his reign.

Gustavus Adolphus owed his international fame to his prowess as a war leader. The Lion of the North, as he came to be called, fought many wars and lost only one — the conflict with Denmark that he inherited from his father. His many victories, and above all his successful intervention in the Thirty Years' War, raised Sweden to the status of a great power and won it much new territory and domination over the Baltic. His last victory, at Lützen in 1632, cost him his life. (See pp. 222–223.)

Gustavus Adolphus left his throne to his only child, a six-year-old girl named Christina. A regency council headed by Oxenstierna and made up of the heads of the chief government departments, all of whom were noblemen, ruled the country. The nobility took advantage of the situation to win extensions of its privileges and to gain additional property for itself at the expense of lands belonging to the crown. Christina took over personal rule in 1644 but failed to reassert the supremacy of the throne. A person of much learning, she lacked the ability to rule, squandered money on a luxurious court, and gave away or sold great stretches of crown land. The country's internal political and economic situation began to deteriorate, and unrest appeared among the peasantry and townspeople. Weary of her duties and attracted to Catholicism, Christina abdicated in 1654 in favor of her cousin, who ruled as Charles X. A few days after her abdication Christina left Sweden dressed as a man, became a Catholic, and spent most of the rest of her life in Rome, supported by the charity of the pope.

The new king was able to restore some of the damage done to the throne's prestige during Christina's reign by persuading the nobility to return a large proportion of the crown lands she had given them and to accept taxation on one-fourth of their property. Noble opposition to these measures was stilled by the outbreak of a new war brought on by Charles's ambition to win territory at the expense of Poland. In the First Northern War, which lasted from 1655 to 1660, Sweden faced Poland, Russia, Denmark, Brandenburg, and Holland. If all of these states had cooperated, Sweden would have faced certain defeat; fortunately for Sweden, its enemies could not agree among themselves. Charles died before the war ended, but a council of regency took over for his infant son and successor and succeeded in making a peace by which Sweden gained more territory and retained its leading position in northern Europe.

THE OTTOMAN EMPIRE TO 1656

The Ottoman Turks stood at the zenith of their fortunes in the century after the fall of Constantinople, especially during the long reign of Sultan Suleiman the Magnificent (1520–1566). They continued their conquests until their empire extended to the Persian Gulf, across North Africa almost to the Atlantic, and deep into central Europe. Approximately 50 million people of many nationalities, languages, and religions lived within their sprawling realm.

SLAVES IN THE GOVERNMENT

In the course of their amazing ascent from obscurity during the thirteenth century the Turks developed a system of administration unlike that of any other major state. Its most striking feature was the part played by slaves who belonged to the sultan. They were members of the

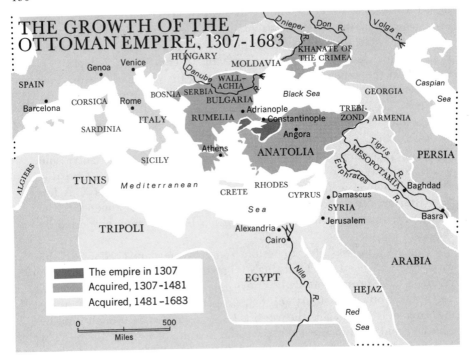

THE GROWTH OF THE
OTTOMAN EMPIRE, 1307-1683

- The empire in 1307
- Acquired, 1307-1481
- Acquired, 1481-1683

0 _____ 500
          Miles

ruling elite of the empire, holding high office in the government, in the sultan's court, and in the army. No social opprobrium was attached to slavery, and many of the most powerful and wealthiest men of the empire were slaves. The sultan himself was born of a slave mother, for all the women in his father's harem were slaves. The use of slaves in government did not originate with the Ottomans. From ancient times despots had preferred to be served by men who owed everything to them, including their lives, but the Ottomans developed the practice to a point never reached before or since.

In the mid-sixteenth century the sultan owned about eighty thousand slaves. The law entitled him to take one-fifth of all prisoners of war as bondsmen; his agents carefully selected the captives who best suited his purposes. He acquired others by purchase and by a periodic levy of male children between the ages of ten and twenty in the Christian provinces of the empire. Taken from their homes, screened for their abilities, converted to Islam, and given intensive training for the posts for which they seemed best suited, the young slaves began their careers at a low level. Advancement depended upon ability; they could rise to the highest offices in the empire, including that of grand vizier. The use of merit as the criterion for promotion stood in sharp contrast to Christian Europe, where theoretically birth, not ability, determined advancement. Since Islamic law prohibited the enslavement of born Moslems, the Ottoman

Empire, hated foe of Christendom, depended heavily upon men of Christian origin for its administrators and soldiers.

Many Christian parents dreaded the conscription, and to avoid it they sometimes married off their sons as children, for married boys were ineligible for the child tribute. On the other hand, the system was not without its compensations. The boy who became a slave of the sultan had a chance to acquire wealth and power far beyond what he could hope for if he stayed in his native village, and some ambitious Christian parents sought to have their sons chosen, while Moslem parents sometimes paid Christian families to take their sons and pass them off as their own in the hope that they would be taken into the sultan's service.

A special group of slave soldiers, the Janissaries, formed the elite corps of the Sultan's standing army, numbering about twelve thousand in the early sixteenth century. In peace as well as in war they lived in barracks under rigorous discipline, and until the late sixteenth century they were forbidden to marry. They were the sultan's shock troops and personal bodyguard.

The reigning sultan named his own successor from among the many sons born to him by his harem women. To prevent civil war among rival sons, it became customary for the designated heir to have all his brothers killed. This brutal practice became law in the late fifteenth century and continued for the next hundred years.

MOSLEM PARTICIPATION IN GOVERNMENT

The sultan had unlimited power over his slaves. In contrast, his power over his free subjects was limited by the sacred law of Islam, based upon the Koran and the teachings of Mohammed and applicable to secular as well as to religious matters. The sultan could not alter the Mohammedan law, for it was believed to be of divine origin. In order to adapt it to changed circumstances brought about by time, he could supplement it by issuing new regulations or interpretations, called *kanuns*. Since the chief religious and legal leaders of the Moslem population had to approve the kanuns before they became effective, there was a check on the absolutism of the sultan.

The men who passed on the sultan's decrees were part of a hierarchy of consultants, judges, and teachers known as the *ulema* (learned ones). They controlled the legal, religious, and educational systems of the empire. Rank in the ulema depended upon education (which was nearly free) and ability. The most important members were the *muftis*. Each major administrative division of the empire and each large city had a mufti assigned to it to hear appeals under Islamic law and to provide expert opinions on all legal and religious problems. The mufti of Constantinople, whom the sultan himself consulted, was known as the *Sheikh-ul-Islam*, the Elder of Islam. He was the empire's chief religious and legal authority. In this sense he stood over the sultan, for he could pass judgment on the sultan's actions or legislation, declare them illegal under the sacred law, and even call upon the people to depose the sultan.

THE TREATMENT OF MINORITIES

The Christians of the West considered the Turks cruel and uncultured barbarians who tyrannized the peoples they conquered. Actually, Turkish atrocities were no worse than the horrors perpetrated by Christians on fellow Christians, such as the Sack of Rome in 1527, the holocaust loosed by Ivan IV in Novgorod in 1570, or the St. Bartholomew's Day massacre in France in 1572. Moreover, Turkish culture compared favorably with that of the contemporary West. Although their religion forbade representations of the human form in painting and sculpture, the Turks stood at a high level of achievement in architecture, poetry, and decorative design. Most important, far from oppressing the peoples that they conquered, they allowed them a degree of freedom and toleration unparalleled in the Christian world of that day. In the Ottoman Empire no one suffered because of his religion or nationality. Each non-Moslem group was given official status, had its own ecclesiastical hierarchy, practiced its faith without molestation, provided its own education, and settled civil law disputes by its own religion and customs. Turkish courts exercised jurisdiction only in criminal matters.

Most of the Christian peasants of the Balkans enjoyed under the Ottomans a degree of peace and security that they had not known before. They were not taxed beyond their capacity to pay, and they were not brought under the yoke of serfdom that weighed so heavily on peasants in central and eastern Europe. Thousands of persecuted Jews streamed into the empire, where they could live and work without fear. When Ferdinand, who had a reputation for political wisdom, expelled the Jews from Spain in 1492 and they emigrated to the empire, the sultan is supposed to have said, "How can you call this Ferdinand wise — he who has impoverished his dominions to enrich mine?"

BEGINNING OF THE OTTOMAN DECLINE

The reign of Suleiman the Magnificent marked the end of a long, uninterrupted record of Ottoman victories and expansion. After his death in 1566 the empire began a gradual decline, punctuated by brief periods of recovery, which continued for centuries. The decline was attributable in large part to internal decay and demoralization. The first great setback came in 1571 when the Spanish-Venetian fleet defeated the Turkish navy at Lepanto. Thereafter the Turks were on the defensive although the Thirty Years' War, which preoccupied the European powers, gave them a respite from Western aggression during the first half of the seventeenth century.

SOCIAL, INTELLECTUAL, AND CULTURAL DYNAMISM, 1500–1660
CHAPTER EIGHT

The first one and one-half centuries of modern Europe were characterized by ferment in areas other than politics and religion, though all the developments were closely linked. Nowhere was the ferment more apparent than in the social structure, where classes were regrouping; in science, where new, empirically oriented methods were beginning to attain preponderance; and in the arts, where the baroque expressed a new extravagance and passion in the wake of the troubles of the sixteenth century.

SOCIETY AND SOCIAL DYNAMICS

Princes, popes, protestors, politicians, and painters have commanded much of our attention so far. Though their dominance makes the historian's task easier, it tends to obscure the mass of people whose lives they ordered but of whose existence they were aware only in a general way. It also obscures the unquestioned survival of the medieval hierarchic order of society long after its ideals and institutions had been undermined or destroyed outright. The elite conceived of the masses as their servants at best and as a police problem at worst. Yet in the sixteenth and early seventeenth centuries forces were at work in Europe that were rapidly smudging the neat medieval picture and creating new dynamics with which statesmen and theorists in the late seventeenth and eighteenth centuries would have to grapple. Some of the results of these forces have already been described: the decline of the feudal nobility, the destruction of the authority of the universal Church, and the unleashing of new religious aspirations by men who saw no necessity for a hierarchy between themselves and God. Other forces varied greatly in their incidence in any one part of Europe, but one or more of them were increasingly evident everywhere.

THE TRADITIONAL ORDER

The prince exalted above all his subjects, whose majesty does not admit of any division, represents the principle of unity, from which all the rest derive their force and cohesion. Below him are the three estates. . . . The estate of the clergy is placed first because of its dignity in ministering to religion. It includes both nobles [bishops] and commoners [priests]. Next comes the military estate, which also includes nobles and commoners [mere soldiers]. Last there is the third estate of scholars, merchants, craftsmen, and peasants.

JEAN BODIN (French, 1576)

Shepherds of people had need know the calendars of tempests in state, which are commonly greatest when things grow to equality. . . .

FRANCIS BACON (English, *c.* 1610)

These two quotations, though not wholly representative and wrenched from context, sum up the traditional notion of social order. The estates were the major groupings of society, and Bodin arranged them in hierarchic order under the prince. He made clear the functional distinctions that determined the groupings: the cure of souls, the defense of society, and the remaining — inferior — occupations. Any twelfth-century commentator could have written this, although he might not have spoken of the prince in such terms and he would not have included "mere soldiers." Bacon reflected the contemporary horror of equality and its supposed connection with civil disorder. The hint of social dynamics in Bacon's words was also in Bodin's words and is a clue to the necessity felt by both men to reassert vehemently the validity of the old order. In their countries, as elsewhere in Europe, there was a great deal of social movement within the existing framework — so much that the whole order seemed threatened by the dilution of the distinctive characteristics of each social group and the blurring of the lines between them. Neither man was arguing that movement should not occur, but only that the individual who had gone up (or down) the social ladder should accept the fact of his status. What worried them deeply was the possibility that the various levels in the hierarchy were becoming reversed, particularly the chance that the lowest estate was advancing at the expense of the second estate. Their anxiety was not unfounded.

For the clergy in western and central Europe, Catholic and Protestant, the era of the Reformation was socially damaging and sometimes disastrous. In some countries Protestantism's fundamental anticlericalism largely wiped out the privileged status of clergymen and eliminated the monastic clergy. The seizure of Church lands undermined the economic independence of the clergy. In England, where the Reformation was most conservative, the clergy retained more privileges, but symptomatic of their downgrading was the fact that they were no longer accorded the old honorific title "Sir." Ecclesiastical predominance in the House of Lords was ended when the dissolution of the monasteries removed the abbots from that assembly and left only the bishops. In the Catholic countries of France and Spain, the monarchs had already subverted the clerical establishments to their own ends, although in general the clergy remained more influential than in Protestant states. With the exception of the papal state, nowhere in western Europe in the seventeenth century was the Church the means to wealth and power that it had been in the sixteenth. The secularization of bureaucracy was nearly complete, even in France, where the two most prominent chief ministers of the early seventeenth century were cardinals. Indeed, in the Catholic Church itself after the Council of Trent the bishops were subjected to almost total papal control in areas where they were not firmly subject to monarchic power.

Almost everywhere the old nobility suffered a loss of power, if not of prestige, in the sixteenth and early seventeenth centuries. Their titles of honor remained as long as the families survived, but their status was diluted by the rise of the new nobility — those who had been ennobled for service to the monarch. The new nobility often lived sumptuously, as befitted noblemen; they gained the wherewithal to do so from service to the monarch or from fortunes made initially in commerce. The sale of offices was common practice in most of the states of Europe, and merchants and lawyers found it relatively easy to purchase office and nobility. Nobility everywhere had the right either to exemption from taxation or to some control over the assessment of taxes. The mark of the nobleman was a landed estate, and the return to the land of the new nobility in an era when prices rose faster than rents meant that the nobility had to increase rents, improve production, or both in order to survive. In the seventeenth century the economically least viable element of the landed nobility became increasingly impoverished, and the poverty-stricken *hidalgos* of Spain, *hobereaux* of France, lesser gentry of England, and petty nobles of Poland and Russia formed pockets of discontent.

THE DYNAMICS OF CHANGE

In 1500 Europe had perhaps 60 to 70 million people; by 1600 it had about 100 million. Every country apparently experienced the increase in population. Few people had yet migrated from Europe, although the population increase stimulated internal migration. Since more food was needed, people brought new areas of farmland into cultivation. Others were drawn to the cities by the increased demand for labor to produce goods and services; urban population, though still a small proportion of the total population, rose steadily. The volume and value of commerce and manufacturing within Europe grew enormously, and overseas expansion brought in goods from every quarter of the world. Although the total amount of imports from other continents was tiny in comparison with imports today, Europe's role — or more precisely northern Europe's role — as the organizer and center of a world-wide economy had begun.

By the mid-seventeenth century the long wave of economic expansion that had begun in the latter part of the fifteenth century came to its end in most of Europe. International trade declined. Imports of bullion from America fell steadily and by 1660 had shrunk to a fraction of what they were a century before. Prices dropped and the profits of business declined. The overseas expansion of Europe slowed up, a number of overseas trading companies collapsed, and efforts to establish new ones often proved unsuccessful. Despite this retardation, the gains that had been made during the sixteenth-century expansion were retained. The European economy in 1660 was greatly advanced over what it had been two hundred years before.

BUSINESSMEN

The expansion of economic activity that began in the late fifteenth century provided a literally golden opportunity for a relatively few clever and enterprising men to build up large fortunes. Most of these outstandingly successful capitalistic entrepreneurs came from the middle class, although some belonged to the nobility or gentry and others rose from the ranks of the peasantry or the urban working class. Usually they did not restrict themselves to one line of business but operated simultaneously in a number of fields; often they took an important part in politics. The Fuggers of Augsburg, Germany, had widespread textile and mining interests as well as their banking house, which had branches and agents throughout Europe and had made Jacob Fugger (1459–1529) the creditor of emperors, popes, and princes. The Russian Stroganovs dealt in salt, iron, furs, fish, grain, and other metals that were produced in their lands on the border of Siberia. They traded throughout Muscovy and had much to do with Russian expansion into Siberia. Thomas Gresham (1519–1579), member of a wealthy English family of merchants and landowners, dealt in English woolen cloth, iron, paper, and finance. Financial agent to Queen Elizabeth and an important political figure, he founded the Royal Exchange in London as an arena for business transactions between merchants and bankers, modeling it on the bourse of Antwerp, the most commercially advanced city of the century.

Not many businessmen amassed large fortunes. In business, as in every other field of human activity, only a few people had the imagination, ability, persistence, and luck needed to become outstandingly successful. Most businessmen were small merchants, shopkeepers, and peddlers. Many benefited from the price rise and the economic expansion, but only on a modest scale.

WAGE EARNERS AND PEASANTS

The great mass of Europeans did not share even moderately in the material benefits of the economic expansion. The increase in population produced a labor surplus, so that despite the growth in economic activity employers could hire workers at low wages. The scanty data on the wages of labor show that although wages went up, their increase lagged behind the increase in prices. As a result, the purchasing power of the workers' wages (their "real" wages) declined; workers could buy less with the amount of money they earned. Their standard of living fell. Money wages, however, did not represent the wage earner's entire income. Many — perhaps most — workers were fed by their employers during working hours or received a cash allowance to buy food. In addition, many laborers had a small plot of land or a garden that furnished them with part of their food needs. The data on prices show that the prices of a number of items bought by workers, such as low-quality textile wares and certain other manufactured goods, did not go up as steeply as food prices; in fact, the price of certain of these manufactured commodities did not increase as much as wages and the worker could therefore buy more of these wares. Nonetheless, it seems probable that the worker's standard of living did decline.

The economic position of many of Europe's peasants deteriorated during these years. A minority who owned their holdings and had enough land to produce a surplus for sale benefited from the economic expansion, as did those who held their land on permanent tenure or on long-term leases at low rents. These fortunate peasants profited as prices rose, while the nobles who owned the land had to content themselves with a fixed rental income, which fell drastically in buying power. Most peasants, however, did not share this good fortune. Those who held their land on short-term leases found that their rent went up with each renewal, often rising even more than the general price level. The increase in population worked against the welfare of the peasants, too, for it meant greater pressure on the land and therefore smaller holdings. Many of the holdings now were not large enough to support the larger families, and some peasants had to take part-time employment as laborers for neighboring lords, or other wealthier peasants. Those who had no land had to find work as full-time laborers either in the towns or in the countryside.

The increase in the number of laborers held down agricultural wages. Meanwhile, large landowners, recognizing the opportunity that farming now offered for profit-making, acquired more land, which they either operated on their own account or else rented on short-term leases. In eastern and east-central Europe the new interest of nobles in agriculture led directly to the final reduction of the peasantry to the cruelties and exploitation of serfdom. The once free peasants became tied to the will of their lords and were scarcely distinguishable, so far as rights were concerned, from the horses and cattle that also belonged to their masters. In Spain the peasants remained free but had little else for which to be thankful. Besides the increased demands made on them by their landlords they suffered from the special privileges held by a great gild of sheep raisers called the *Mesta*. The Spanish crown granted the Mesta the right to graze its flocks, totalling several million sheep, over a large part of Spain, allowed it to take over private pastures for grazing, and forbade the planting of crops in lands through which the sheep of the Mesta passed. Spanish agriculture decayed and the poverty-stricken Spanish peasants barely managed to keep alive.

The peasant's obligations did not end with the payments in cash, kind, and labor that he made to the landowner. He also had to support both state and church through taxes and tithes. In most of Europe the nobility paid no taxes even though they owned nearly all of the wealth. The tax burden rose nearly everywhere to pay for the expansion in governmental activities and for the many wars of the era. Ironically, the peasants suffered more from these destructive wars than did any other group in the population because the armies lived off the land, and friend and foe alike plundered the peasants.

Literally thousands of peasants (both farmers and rural craftsmen) found themselves unable to make a living in the face of all these hardships and were forced to roam the roads and cities and fields of Europe, living as best they could by begging and stealing. Contemporary accounts pointed to the alarming increase in vagrants and paupers, and many ordinances designed to handle the problem appeared in law books.

It is scarcely surprising that peasant unrest and peasant revolts became frequent occurrences everywhere in Europe during the sixteenth and the first half of the seventeenth centuries. Nor is it surprising that often the peasants were joined by wage-earners of the towns in blind — and always unsuccessful — attacks upon the society that had driven them to desperation.

TECHNOLOGY AND INNOVATION

It may seem paradoxical that impoverishment of the masses should have accompanied economic expansion. In our industrial age the long-term upward movement of economic growth has produced a higher, rather than a lower, standard of living. The reason that this did not happen in the economic upswing of the sixteenth century lay primarily in the failure of technology, above all in agriculture, to keep pace with the increase in population, so that the amount of goods produced was not enough to feed, clothe, and house adequately the growing number of people. Most Europeans lived on the margin of subsistence, and when crops failed, as they did with terrible frequency, famines swept the country and thousands died of starvation or, weakened by undernourishment, fell easy prey to disease. In a few regions of Europe, particularly in the Low Countries, farmers began to employ more intensive methods of civilization. They planted clover and turnips, which restored fertility to the soil and ,at the same time provided food for animals, and they used fertilizer. Nearly everywhere else farmers continued to use the traditional methods of tillage.

Although some technical innovations were made in industry, particularly in certain aspects of textile and metal manufacturing, new techniques remained very much the exception. Important changes did take place, however, in manufacturing organization. In preceding centuries the artisan gilds in the towns had usually controlled the manufacture, and even the sale, of many wares. As trade grew, merchants and gild members who had become discontented with the restrictive practices of the gilds distributed raw materials or semifinished goods to peasants in the countryside, in the so-called domestic or putting-out system. The peasants worked on these goods in their own homes at piece rates, usually performing just one stage in the manufacturing process.

In contrast to the dispersion of industry represented by the domestic system, centralized large-scale factories were also being established in this era, especially in England, where some of the new plants employed hundreds of workers. The factories did not use the special kinds of power-driven machinery that we associate with factory industry today. Factory workers used the same hand methods and simple tools and machines that small producers used in their shops and homes. The factories did offer important advantages in that the activities of the workers could be organized and coordinated to increase output per worker.

The leveling-off of economic expansion in the early seventeenth century coincided with the growth of the business form known as the joint-stock company, in which a group of merchants, each with limited capital, pooled their resources, invited investment, and usually obtained a royal charter of monopoly for a prescribed area of trade. The consequences of this development were most pronounced in England, where landed proprietors often invested in the companies, and in Holland.

THE SCIENTIFIC REVOLUTION

Greek science, particularly Aristotelian science, accepted as valid for nearly two thousand years, presupposed that nature works in an orderly fashion according to laws that are discoverable by reason alone. Experimentation and observation had little place in this process. Significantly, the Greek scientist was not so much concerned with how nature works as with why it works, raising questions more moral and aesthetic than mechanical. Those who first achieved radical breakthroughs in science in the sixteenth century did not reject Greek science, but they asked new questions of the Greek material. In the late sixteenth and early seventeenth centuries there was a shift toward gathering new data — data derived from observation and finally experimentation. The latter development was the beginning of empiricism. From that point the scientist's major question became not why but how nature works. The sum total of the scientific achievements in this century and a half comprised the Scientific Revolution.

THE OLD COSMOLOGY

The most dramatic and revolutionary scientific advances were made in the study of physics and astronomy. For centuries Western man had accepted the Greek view of the cosmos, which was in agreement with appearances. Men could plainly see the celestial bodies move each day in a circular path around the earth; consequently, they constructed a geocentric cosmology. The earth stood unmoving at the center of a series of hollow transparent spheres that daily rotated around the earth. Each of the crystalline spheres had imbedded in it one of the heavenly bodies — the sun, the moon, and the five known planets (Mercury, Venus, Mars, Jupiter, Saturn). Next came the sphere of the fixed stars, holding the stars that move about the earth but seem to be motionless with respect to one another. Finally there was an outermost sphere, the *primum mobile* or first mover, which provided spin to the spheres nested within it. Beyond lay the empyrean, where God dwelt. The heavenly bodies, glowing like great luminous jewels in their marvelously clear spheres, were thought to be made of a pure immortal substance, entirely different from the corrupt and mortal matter that made up the earth. Men believed, too, that they followed natural laws different from those of earthly phenomena.

This tidy arrangement of the cosmos satisfied everyone but the astronomers, who had difficulties with it from the very outset. The planets (from the Greek word for wanderer) presented an especially difficult problem. Instead of moving steadily in one direction from east to west, they seemed at times to stop briefly, then move in a backward or retrograde path for a while. They appeared brighter at some times than at others, and they did not seem to move at a uniform rate of speed. Yet astronomers assumed axiomatically that the planets follow circular orbits, for since ancient times the circle had been considered the perfect form of motion.

Claudius Ptolemy, the Alexandrian Greek astronomer and geographer of the second century A.D., modified the geocentric system so that the earth was not exactly in the center. The celestial bodies moved along an eccentric path with reference to the earth. This provided an explanation for the change in brightness of the planets: at certain parts of their

GREEK MODEL
OF THE UNIVERSE

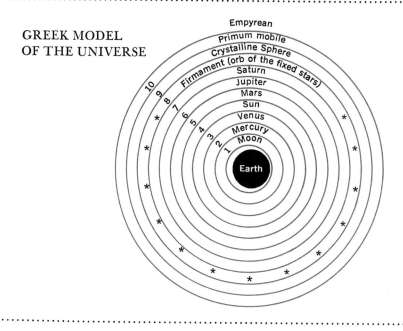

eccentric orbit they were farther from the earth than at other times. Ptolemy also created a system of epicycles to explain the retrograde motion of the planets. The heavenly bodies were said to move in a small circle whose center in turn moved in a large circle around the earth. He explained the apparent lack of uniformity in the planets' speed of movement by demonstrating geometrically that the motion was uniform with respect to one point, called the equant, and circular with respect to another point. Ptolemy's work was translated into Arabic and honored by the Moslems with the title *Almagest* (a contraction of "the greatest books"). It was transmitted to the West through translation from the Arabic in the twelfth century and became the fountainhead of Western astronomical science. It was supported by common sense, reason, and superficial observation. Moreover, the system worked well enough, and even today navigation is predicated on the earth standing still at the center of the constantly revolving heavens.

The growth of data on celestial movements, however, entailed constant modifications of the Ptolemaic model. By the middle of the sixteenth century over seventy simultaneous circular motions were required to explain the motions of the heavenly bodies. Astronomers, beset by the discrepancies between the theory and their own observations, found that they could not accurately predict the future positions of the planets. Imbued with the humanist spirit of the Renaissance, they turned to Ptolemy in

DIAGRAM SHOWING ECCENTRIC
AND EPICYCLIC MOTION

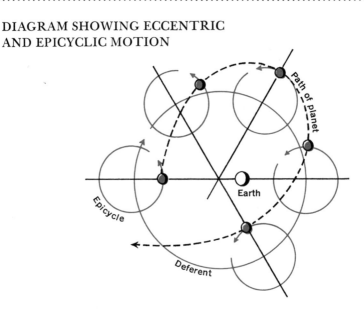

the original Greek in the thought that perhaps errors and inaccuracies had accumulated in the process of translation from Greek to Arabic to Latin. They did find errors of translation, but these did not alter the basic theory. In search of further guidance they studied the works of Ptolemy's predecessors in Greece. There they found the inspiration to create an entirely new concept of the universe, marking the start of the scientific revolution.

COPERNICUS AND THE HELIOCENTRIC THEORY

The book with which the revolution began appeared in 1543. Written in Latin, it was entitled *Six Books Concerning the Revolution of the Heavenly Spheres*. Its author was a Pole named Mikolaj Kopernik (Nicolaus Copernicus in Latin), born in Thorn in 1473. After study at the University of Cracow he spent ten years at Italian universities, where he immersed himself in humanist and medical studies. Through an uncle who was a bishop, he received an appointment as a canon of the cathedral at Frauenburg, a provincial town in East Prussia. There he spent the rest of his life busily occupied in church administration, the practice of medicine, and the study of the classics and astronomy.

Copernicus, who was not an outstanding observer of the celestial bodies, relied upon the recorded observations of others. He was drawn

COPERNICUS' MODEL
OF THE UNIVERSE

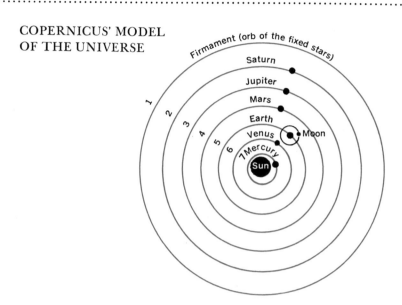

to the study of astronomy by a feeling of concern about the discrepancies in the Ptolemaic system. In addition, he had a curiously conservative — even reactionary — reason: his conviction that the ancient Greeks had been right in their belief that the planets follow perfect circular orbits at uniform velocities. The intellect, he wrote, "recoils in horror" from the thought that any other form of motion is possible for the heavenly bodies; "it would be unworthy to suppose such a thing in a universe constituted in the best possible way."

A well-trained humanist, Copernicus decided to study all the ancient writings he could find in order to work out "a more reasonable arrangement of circles." He found that ancient Greek scientists had suggested that the sun, not the earth, stands immobile at the center of the cosmos, and that the earth and the other planets rotate about the sun in concentric circles. Inspired by this discovery, he showed by brilliant calculations that the motions of the heavenly bodies can all be explained by assuming a sun-centered or heliocentric universe.

Copernicus's model of the universe had many shortcomings. Like Ptolemy he had to use epicycles to explain planetary orbits, although he did reduce their number from 80 to 34. He did not need Ptolemy's equant, but he had to use the eccentric path of motion, for the common center of the concentric circles of his system fell a little to one side of the sun. He retained the old belief that the planets were firmly imbedded in crystalline spheres. His insistence upon perfect circular motion proved wrong, and his explanation for the rotation of the earth and the other planets — that "rotation is natural to a sphere and by that very act is its shape expressed" — begged the question.

Copernicus belonged more to ancient than to modern science, yet his work had enormous consequences. His rearrangement of the solar system provided the stimulus for later scientists to complete the demolition of the old cosmology. By removing the earth from the center of the cosmos and placing it among the other planets, he struck the first great blow at the ancient belief in the distinction between base earth and pure celestial bodies. Earth and its companion planets were found to follow the same physical laws.

Catholic and Protestant religious leaders alike denounced Copernicus's book as being opposed to Holy Scripture. Scientists were less vehement, but it took over a century for them finally to give up the earth-centered cosmology. Even Tycho Brahe (1546–1601), the Danish scientist who was the ablest astronomer in the generation after Copernicus, did not accept the heliocentric theory. He developed an hypothesis in which the earth remained immobile at the center of the cosmos with the sun and moon revolving about it, but with the other five planets revolving about the sun. His theory appealed to many astronomers, for it had the simplicity of the Copernican system without its assertion of an orbiting and rotating earth, which was so contradictory to human experience and common sense. The traditional belief in the revolving crystalline spheres was shaken in 1577 when a new comet appeared in the upper sky and raced straight through what were supposed to be the impenetrable spheres. Although Tycho could offer no substitute for the spheres to explain how the planets stay in their orbits, most astronomers followed him in rejecting their existence.

Tycho's skill in astronomical observation won him the patronage of the king of Denmark. He was given a small island that lay between Sweden and Denmark, where he built a fantastic castle-observatory called Uraniborg, the Castle of Heaven. He designed measuring instruments of great size rigidly mounted on solid foundations to gain the highest possible accuracy for the unaided human eye. He was the first man since the Greeks to introduce major improvements into astronomical observation, and he attained an accuracy of measurement far beyond that of any previous astronomer.

KEPLER, "LEGISLATOR OF THE SKY"

In his last years Tycho quarreled with the king and lived for a time in Prague. There he engaged a young German assistant named Johannes Kepler (1571–1630). Tycho recognized that Kepler had great intellectual

Johannes Kepler, by Jan van der Heyden

"His life work was possible only when he succeeded in freeing himself to a large extent from the spiritual tradition in which he was born. . . . He had to free himself from an animistic, teleologically oriented manner of thinking in scientific research. He had to realize clearly that logical-mathematical theorizing, no matter how lucid, could not guarantee truth by itself; that the most beautiful logical theory means nothing in natural science without comparison with the exactest experience. Without this philosophic attitude, his work would not have been possible." From Albert Einstein's introduction to C. Baumgardt, JOHANNES KEPLER: LIFE AND LETTERS (New York, 1951).

---

powers and gave him access to his vast collection of observations in the hope that the younger man would firmly establish the truth of Tycho's geocentric theory. Instead, Kepler used Tycho's data to support the Copernican system.

More than any other astronomer up to his time Kepler insisted on the closest possible agreement between theory and observation. After four years of computations on the orbit of Mars he found a small discrepancy

KEPLER'S FIRST TWO LAWS

The planet follows an elliptical orbit (actually, the orbit is much closer to a circle than is shown here) with the sun at one focus of the ellipse. The planet sweeps out the shaded areas in equal times.

(not more than one-fourth of 1 per cent) between Tycho's observations, which he knew to be accurate, and the uniform and circular orbit required by Copernicus's theory. Other scientists might have explained away this seemingly insignificant discrepancy by making convenient assumptions. Kepler, with the integrity characteristic of great scientists, was not content, and back he went to his computations. After more years of work he reached the epochal conclusion that each planet moves not in a circular but in a slightly elliptical orbit, with the sun at one of the two foci of the ellipse. This was Kepler's first law, the law of elliptical motion. He also determined that the planets do not move at a uniform velocity, as men had always thought. They move faster as they near the sun and slow down at they go away from it. This rule, Kepler's second law, the law of equal areas, stated that a line joining the sun to a planet sweeps out equal areas in equal times.

All the data of observation fitted the new theory. The epicycles and eccentrics were gone forever. Gone, too, was the obsession of astronomers since Grecian times with the circle as the basis of cosmic order. Still, Kepler, who had published his first two laws in 1609, remained unsatisfied. His belief in the simplicity and harmony of nature — a conviction that has run through the entire history of science — persuaded him that an overall relationship of order and regularity exists among the motions of the different planets. After more years of seemingly endless calculations, in 1619 he announced with enormous and justified pride his third great principle, the harmonic law of planetary motion. It declared that the time a planet takes to orbit around the sun varies proportionately with its distance from the sun: the square of the time is proportional to the cube of the distance.

Astronomical observations made since Kepler's time have borne out the accuracy of his laws. In addition, modern physicists have found that they can use his laws to describe the motions of electrons around nuclei under the action of electrical forces. Kepler's contributions, however, went beyond astronomy and physics. He demonstrated to scientists the supreme importance of precise data. His use of mathematical relationships to explain planetary motion helped to establish the mathematical equation as the means of expressing laws of physical science. Above all, he was the first to seek a universal physical law to explain the motions of the universe in quantitative detail. Earlier astronomers had either held that the celestial bodies followed their orbits because of their special or even divine qualities or, like Copernicus, had maintained that it was the nature of a sphere to go in circles. Kepler set out to prove, as he wrote in a letter in 1605, "that the celestial machine is to be likened not to a divine organism but rather to a clockwork," with all its motions caused by a single force, just as a simple weight causes all the motions of a clock.

Kepler hit on what he thought was the all-powerful single force after reading a book called *De Magnete* (On the Magnet), published in 1600 by William Gilbert, an English physician. After much experimentation with compasses and lodestones, Gilbert had arrived at the conclusion that the interior of the earth was a huge magnet. This theory led Kepler to decide that a magnetic force emanating from the sun drove the planets in their courses. It was an imaginative answer to the question of what was the physical cause of planetary motion, but it was wrong. Before the right answer could be found, scientists had to gain a greater understanding of the laws governing the mechanics of motion. That understanding came through the work of the Italian scientist Galileo Galilei (1564–1642).

GALILEO

Before Galileo even the boldest scientists had not broken completely with the old Greek ways of thought. They still looked for meaning in natural phenomena, and they considered it their obligation to seek out final causes. Galileo concentrated on describing how natural phenomena operated and expressing his descriptions and observations in mathematical terms. He believed that the scientist could describe all natural phenomena mathematically. Science, he wrote, "is written in that great book which ever lies before our eyes — I mean the universe — but we cannot understand it if we do not learn the language and grasp the symbols in which it is written." His insistence on observation, on quantification, and on mathematics as the best methods for ordering and understanding nature made his work the watershed between the old and

The Rape of the Daughters of Leucippus, by Peter Paul Rubens

"In the 'Rape of the Daughters of Leucippus,' the two female figures form an almost uniform mass of light exactly in the lower centre of the picture, round which the rest is disposed like a cloud. . . . . But it can further be seen that the two magnificently developed female figures are precisely complementary, that the one presents exactly the view not presented by the other, and that the artist has isolated them from each other by an intervening space so that they nowhere overlap. And all this is fused with the incredible fire of the moment. No other artist, at any time or of any other school, could have created just this." Jakob Burckhardt, RECOLLECTIONS OF RUBENS (New York, 1950).

---

the new in science. Since his day science has been pointed in the direction he defined and away from the metaphysical speculations about first causes that had formerly preoccupied scientists. Galileo well merits the title of father of modern physical science.

Although Kepler had discovered the mathematical laws for the movement of the planets, Galileo found the laws for the movement of bodies on earth. Since the days of Aristotle it had been accepted that a heavier body falls more rapidly than a light one. A few men had questioned the maxim, but Galileo was the first to test and disprove it experimentally. The famous story that he simultaneously dropped two iron balls from the Leaning Tower of Pisa is now regarded as a legend, but he did prove that bodies of different weight fall at the same rate of speed (when allowance is made for wind resistance owing to difference in size and shape). Since the timing mechanisms available to him were not accurate enough to measure the speed of freely falling bodies, Galileo experimented with balls that were rolled down inclined boards. He thereby discovered the principle of uniform acceleration, by which the velocity of a freely falling body increases at a uniform rate. Continued researches led him in his last years to the monumental discovery of the law of inertia, by which a moving body will continue forever in a straight line and at the same speed unless acted upon by an outside force. A modern astronomer has written that this discovery was "one for which the world had waited two thousand years. From now on the science of dynamics could make progress at breakneck speed."

In 1609 Galileo heard that lens makers in the Netherlands had recently constructed a practical telescope. Inspired by this report and aided by his own knowledge of optics, Galileo built himself a telescope that magnified objects by thirty diameters. He turned his instrument heavenward, becoming the first man to so employ the telescope. His observations dispelled the widely accepted belief in the unblemished and unchanging nature of celestial bodies. He saw that the sun has spots, that Saturn bulges instead of being perfectly spherical, that Venus goes through phases like the moon, and that the moon itself has a rough surface with mountains, valleys, and plains like the earth and, like earth, reflects the light of the sun. Most surprisingly he discovered that Jupiter has moons revolving around it (he saw four of the twelve known satellites).

Galileo, who had long been convinced of the accuracy of Copernicus's cosmology, believed that his own observations supported the accuracy of that theory. He published his first findings in 1610 in a book called *The Sidereal Messenger.* He soon discovered, however, that scholars, philosophers, and churchmen who opposed the Copernican system because they felt that it flew in the face of theology and common sense not only refused to accept his findings, but would not even look through his telescope to see what he saw. Undaunted, Galileo continued to lecture and write in defense of the heliocentric theory until 1616, when the Catholic Church declared that it was contrary to the teachings of the Bible and ordered him neither to hold nor to defend it.

With the election in 1623 of Pope Urban VIII, who was reputed to be a humanist, Galileo felt encouraged to write again about the heliocentric theory. The pope agreed that he could write a comprehensive treatise on cosmology, provided he treated the Copernican system as an hypothesis and not as a proven fact. In 1632 Galileo published the *Dialogue on the Two Chief Systems of the World,* which purported to be an impartial discussion among three men of the relative merits of the Aristotelian-Ptolemaic and Copernican systems. In reality, it ardently defended the latter hypothesis, with the anti-Copernican defeated at every turn. Outraged, the pope ordered Galileo to come to Rome, where the Inquisition tried him and in 1633 ordered him to make a formal renunciation of the Copernican theory. Galileo complied. His book was placed on the Index of Prohibited Books where it remained until 1835. A sentence of imprisonment was immediately commuted to house arrest, which lasted for the remaining eight years of his life.

The trial of Galileo is one of the most famous episodes in the long struggle between freedom of thought and authoritarianism. In his case freedom won, for despite the Church's efforts Galileo's influence made itself felt throughout Europe. Even in Catholic lands scholars and churchmen read and accepted his arguments for the Copernican system. It was impossible for a serious scientist to continue to support the geocentric theory.

Instead of choosing martyrdom Galileo continued his researches in the years after his trial. One of his contemporaries, Giordano Bruno (1548–1600), made a different choice. Bruno had asserted that the stars were like the sun and were at an enormous distance from earth, and that space was infinite and the universe eternal, without beginning or end. These startlingly modern views brought him to trial for heresy. Bruno refused to renounce his beliefs, and after years of confinement in a dungeon he was burned at the stake in Rome in 1600 as a martyr not to religion but to a new cosmology which the old faith could not yet reconcile with its traditional order.

THE LIFE SCIENCES

The core of the scientific revolution was physics and astronomy. In other branches of science progress was less spectacular. The discovery of mathematics as a language of explanation of physical phenomena — not so readily applicable to the life sciences — probably contributed most to the discrepancy between physics and physiology.

Vesalius's pioneering work in anatomy in the early sixteenth century established the University of Padua as the center of medical study. Vesalius changed the basis of anatomy by exposing Galen's errors, but he continued to accept Galen's physiology, which maintained that air passes directly from the lungs to the heart and that the blood flows to the heart from the liver and passes from one side of the heart to the other through invisible pores in the thick tissue dividing the heart. These theories became increasingly suspect, and in 1628 William Harvey, a Padua-trained English physician, published his *Essay on the Motion of the Heart and the Blood,* which established that the heart is a pump circulating the blood through veins, lungs, and arteries. It remained for Marcello Malpighi, an Italian, to discover in 1661 (with the aid of the newly invented microscope) that tiny capillaries connect the arteries and the veins.

SCIENTIFIC METHOD

Seventeenth-century scientists had not yet broken with the mysticism and metaphysics that had surrounded the study of nature since Grecian times. They continued to seek the final causes of phenomena and believed that their discoveries showed that everything in nature fitted into a divine and harmonious plan. A few men, however, began to argue for the separation of the study of nature from metaphysical preoccupations. They saw no need to search for final causes and felt that empirical observation and mathematical measurement were all that were necessary in scientific investigation. They attacked the deductive method, in which for centuries scientists had deduced natural phenomena by reasoning from the general to the particular or from the abstract to the concrete, as when Copernicus said that the earth rotates because it is the nature of a sphere to rotate. They urged the use of the inductive method, in which one proceeds from the particular to the general and from the concrete to the abstract, so that theoretical propositions are derived by observing and comparing large amounts of data. Two men stand out as the prophets of this scientific method: Francis Bacon and René Descartes.

FRANCIS BACON

Francis Bacon (1561–1626), not a scientist but a distinguished English lawyer and statesman, was a man of sweeping philosophical interests. He planned to write a great work covering all knowledge, to be called the *Instauratio Magna* (The Great Renewal), but he published only two parts of the projected study — *The New Organon* and *The Advancement of Learning*. In *The New Organon* he argued that the inductive method should replace the deductive logic that had been taught in the original *Organon*, written many centuries before by Aristotle. He urged men to put aside false beliefs and prejudices, to which he gave the Platonic name of "idols." The "idols of the tribe" are the fallacies common to human nature and shared by all men. The "idols of the cave" are fallacies peculiar to an individual, since each man dwells in his own cave. The "idols of the market place" represent errors that arise from the imprecise use of words when men consort with one another. The "idols of the theater" are faulty philosophical dogmas, which are as unrepresentative of reality as a stage play.

In *The Advancement of Learning* Bacon offered a detailed criticism of medieval science, tried to classify the sciences in a logical order, and called for larger expenditures on science and increased educational and research facilities. Making no distinction between pure science and applied science or technology, he argued that all science should be applied to raising the material welfare of mankind. "Knowledge itself is power," he wrote, and should be sought not for understanding but for use.

Bacon's ideas made a lasting impression. His vision of scientific knowledge as the means to material improvement was the forefather of the idea of progress that has played so great a role in modern history. His emphasis on the importance of experiment gave wider currency to empiricism. His insistence upon the importance of precise terminology has become a characteristic of the scientist. Nevertheless, Bacon himself had only a limited understanding of science and made no contribution to actual scientific investigation. His advice to abandon old dogmas had much merit, but his overemphasis on the collection of data was inimical to generalization and the use of intuition and imagination, which are as important as data in the scientific process. Most of all, he failed to recognize the supreme importance of mathematics as a scientific tool. The abstractness of mathematics and the use of deduction in mathematical manipulations did not fit into his notion of experimentation.

CARTESIANISM

René Descartes (1596–1650) appreciated the importance of mathematics. He was one of the greatest figures in the development of that branch of learning, besides making important contributions to astronomy and physics. His invention of analytical or coordinate geometry united algebra and geometry. He showed that a curve in space can be expressed as an algebraic formula and can thus be handled mathematically. The application of algebra to spatial relationships proved an enormously valuable tool for scientific research, particularly in the study of motion.

Descartes's work in mathematics and other branches of science was part of his plan to construct a systematic scientific philosophy that could be applied everywhere and that would enable man to achieve certainty in his knowledge of the universe. In 1637 he published a number of scientific essays, including the *Discourse on Method,* to illustrate what he considered the successful application of his system of analysis. The *Discourse,* written in the form of an intellectual autobiography, contained the essentials of his philosophy and explained how he arrived at it. He said that he began by doubting the truth of everything in order to rid himself of erroneous philosophical beliefs. One fact alone remained beyond doubt — his own existence. His explanation was, "I think, therefore I exist" *(cogito ergo sum).* From this fundamental axiom he set out to deduce a system of universal philosophy predicated upon four rules: (1) to accept as true nothing that is not self-evident; (2) to break each problem into as many parts as possible; (3) to reason always from the simple to the complex; and (4) to make exhaustive notes of all the data to make sure that nothing is omitted.

The old metaphysical concern was not dead in Descartes. The fact that he could conceive of God as a perfect being seemed to him to prove the existence of God, for he did not know how else man could have gotten the idea of perfection, since man himself is imperfect. "God necessarily exists," he argued, "as the origin of the idea I have of him." As he proceeded further, he developed the theory, famed as Cartesian dualism, according to which there are two forms of reality, mind and matter, with God as the creator of both forms and the connecting medium between them. Mind and matter have separate existences; mind, the "thinking substance," exists in ourselves as our own self-consciousness, whereas matter, the "extended substance," occupies a portion of space.

Much of Descartes's scientific speculation turned out to be wrong, in great part because he failed to practice the scientific method that he preached. He succumbed to the seductions of deductive reasoning, starting from principles that he considered to be self-evident. He did not bother to make experimental verifications of his conclusions. His philosophy, however, made a profound and enduring impact, and the *Discourse on Method* stands out as one of the most influential books in Western intellectual history. Descartes's effort to prove that the universe is a perfect mechanism that runs according to mechanical laws, his conviction that mathematics provides the key to the operations of nature, and his belief that all knowledge can be unified into a single universal science influenced not only scientists but all of literate society. His faith in reason and his insistence upon clarity and simplicity were guides for the rationalists who dominated Western thought during the period of the Enlightenment in the eighteenth century.

Most important, Cartesianism proved of decisive importance in completing the break between ancient and modern thought. By urging men to doubt all old authorities and to use their reason to arrive at truth, Descartes made it seem natural for those who followed him to appeal to reason, that is, to use their own independent judgment, instead of appealing to some traditional, external authority. By demonstrating that man can start with the single premise of his own existence and, by unaided reason, work out the nature of the universe and the existence of God, Descartes fostered a new feeling of man's dignity and importance and an unlimited confidence in the possibilities open to human reason.

THE BAROQUE

The Renaissance exhausted itself in Italy by the second quarter of the sixteenth century. Other lands took over leadership in the arts, but they continued to look to Italy for instruction and inspiration. Many of their artists studied in Italy, and the Italian influence showed strongly in the works that they produced. New forces, however, such as the Protestant and Catholic Reformations, economic changes, and the emergence of the centralized national states, produced a society that differed in many ways from the society of Renaissance Italy. Artists sought to express the temper of the changed times, and their efforts brought on a new era in art history.

THE NEW STYLE

The transition from the Renaissance style took place gradually. Art historians generally agree that in their movement away from the Renaissance, artists first developed a style called mannerism. The mannerists rejected the Renaissance canons of proportion, perspective, and harmony. They painted subjective pictures, portraying scenes and people as they saw them in their inner vision rather than as they saw them with the eye, so that their paintings have abnormal perspectives and distorted figures. For example, the Spanish painter El Greco, the greatest of the mannerists, is said to have refused to go out into the streets of the city of Toledo when he was painting it because that would have dispelled his inner vision of the way Toledo looked.

Mannerism was too subjective to win wide acceptance. Artists in revolt against its principles developed a new style, the baroque. The word was coined by art critics of the eighteenth century who considered the style in bad taste; thus, the word came to mean extravagant or bizarre. The baroque emerged around the middle of the sixteenth century and reached its height around 1660. The new style was a general European phenomenon, but it was strongest in Catholic countries, from southern Germany to Italy and Spain. In fact, some have termed it the art of the Catholic Reformation because it expressed the religious ideas of the Council of Trent; Jesuits and other churchmen who had attended the council were responsible for spreading it through Catholic Europe. Yet the baroque style also found its way into Protestant lands. Moreover, not all baroque art was religious art; much of it was worldly and sensuous.

Baroque is difficult to define. One art historian has said that a single baroque style does not exist, and that the very diversity of styles was one of the distinguishing features of the seventeenth century. It is possible, however, to describe the essential characteristics or common denominators of baroque art. It aimed at grandeur, extravagance, and decorativeness. Baroque artists wanted to make things seem larger than life; they used elaborate theatrical effects to magnify the impressiveness of their work. Baroque art has been called "a grandiose make-believe." At the same time baroque painters rejected the fantasies and strange proportions and perspectives of mannerism. They believed that the artist should paint things as they really are. "Imitate natural things well," was the way one of the greatest baroque painters put it. Many artists had a passion for representations of everyday life, and landscapes and still-lifes became more important and more common than ever before. Space and light held a special fascination. Painters tried to give the illusion of boundless space, to convey a sense of the infinite to the viewer. Renaissance artists had learned how to give the illusion of depth. Baroque artists managed to give the illusion of infinite prolongation of the space confined within the canvas by means of lines reaching out from the front of the picture, by devices such as mirrors in the painting that reflected things not shown in the painting itself, or by including passageways that led to the end of the painting. They used light for this purpose, too; for example, they painted light coming into the picture from a source not shown in the picture.

The Flemish artist Peter Paul Rubens (1577–1640) has been called the most representative of the baroque style. He filled his pictures with a ferment of vitality, richness, excitement, dynamism, and sheer joy of life. They have an extravagance and grandiosity that seems to transcend reality. The people appear as demigods. Although he modeled his lusty, bulging nudes after the Flamandes (Flemish women) that he knew, they have been justly termed "cosmic Flamandes."

Baroque architects built lavishly ornamented churches and other buildings, replete with cherubs and angels, gilt and colored marbles, intricate designs, curved lines, and twisted and bent columns. Their buildings have a theatrical quality; they seem almost like scenery for the stage. They give the impression of tension and of a great mass in movement. Most of the important works were animated by a strong moral, religious, or political purpose. For example, the magnificent plaza in front of St. Peter's in Rome, designed by Giovanni Bernini (1598–1680) with two great semicircles of colonnades, presents a magnificently theatrical setting for the vast church, and overwhelms the viewer with the realization that he stands at the center of a great and powerful world religion.

In music, the baroque era ended the longest musical tradition in the West. Polyphony had originated in the twelfth century. It was the structuring of music from equal and independent parallel elements so that no one strand of music was significantly more important than another. In contrast, baroque music was characterized by a single element, the melody, supported by harmony. The human voice dominated polyphony; a significant development in the baroque change from polyphony to harmony was the beginning of instrumental dominance. Giovanni Palestrina (c. 1525–1594) represented the high point of polyphony with his mastery of an intricate vocal web of choral patterns. The Italian composer Claudio Monteverdi (1567–1643) represented the new departure into harmony and instrumental accompaniment. He and his disciples found in opera the perfect expression for the baroque passion for pageantry and exaggerated emotion.

Baroque characteristics also marked the work of many of the writers of western and central Europe during the years from the mid-sixteenth to the mid-seventeenth centuries. Like their fellow artists in other fields of creative activity, the writers of the baroque age took delight in exaggeration and overemphasis. They used ornate language, rich in adjectives and exclamatory expressions, and they piled up similes and metaphors. Their writing was filled with tension, struggle, and movement. They cherished the dramatic and theatrical, and they tried to achieve contrast and surprise. Violence attracted them; they were inclined to linger over scenes of horror and carnage. Above all, they tried to capture in their prose and poetry the deepest human emotions and to convey a sense of the supernatural forces that they believed control the destinies of men.

THE DYNAMISM OF THE AGE

Newly risen noblemen, aspiring merchants, astronomers, physicists, baroque writers and artists had in common a sense of dynamism, of power in motion. The depiction of supernatural forces sought by the baroque was most often cast in religious form, but its abiding attribute was its dynamism. Dynamism was no less the abiding attribute of Kepler's laws of motion, Galileo's postulates of terrestrial bodies in motion, Harvey's pumping heart coursing blood through the circulatory system, and Descartes's brilliant construct of the dynamic act of thought as the proof of existence. Society itself was dynamic in a way that it had not been before, as the old social order gave way before the new.

Yet European man's new sense of dynamism had about it a strange quality of fear and foreboding, almost as if they had opened a door on terrors that in the centuries before had been locked up. The wars and insurrections, the violence, destruction, and hard times of the first six decades of the seventeenth century justified this fear and foreboding.

AGE OF CRISIS, 1600–1660:
ABSOLUTIST SOLUTION
CHAPTER NINE

The first six decades of the seventeenth century have no universally recognized label, such as the Renaissance or the Reformation. It was an age of crisis, filled with uncertainty, confusion, civil conflict, and seemingly endless war. Economic difficulties multiplied, the vigorous demographic expansion of the sixteenth century leveled off and in some areas population actually declined, trade fell off, unemployment was widespread, periodic visits of the plague were particularly virulent, and crop failures occurred with destructive regularity. Above all, it was a time of crisis in relations between monarchs and their subjects, particularly the nobility, and revolutions against monarchic authority broke out in France, the Netherlands, Spain, Portugal, Naples, Savoy, England, Scotland, Poland, Sweden, and Russia.

It was also an articulate age, filled with theoretical controversy about the nature of government and the role of the sovereign. Participants in the debate ranged from monarchs, leading statesmen, and high churchmen down to humble cobblers and tailors. Missing from the controversial literature of the age was the Rennaissance's boundless enthusiasm for the "new man." Men were disturbed by what seemed to be the forces of evil and the conditions of decay surrounding them, and their sense of foreboding was articulated in violence, both verbal and physical.

The outlets were as various as men: masses and mysticism, the baroque yearning for cosmic unity in Catholic countries, the assurance of the salvation of the faithful or the elect in Protestant countries in passionate, interminable sermons, and everywhere the fearful and implacable pursuit of heterodoxy, witches, heretics, sinners. Astrology served for the more pagan spirits — the young imperial freebooter, Wallenstein, had his horoscope cast by Kepler. The solace of cynicism seemed to transcend faith and unfaith alike. War was almost a palliative to the lower orders when to stay at home might just as well mean starvation, beggary, or death of the plague.

The three greatest political developments on the Continent in this age — the Thirty Years' War, the decline of Spain, the reconstruction of France — were all intimately linked, and they were ingredients of the common crisis. The emergence of absolutism, which was both a cause and the ultimate effect of the crisis, seemed to most Europeans the only way out, the only escape from uncertainty, confusion, civil conflict, and hard times.

THE THIRTY YEARS' WAR

The Religious Peace of Augsburg had established a precarious religious and political balance between Catholics and Lutherans in the Holy Roman Empire. The men who had made that peace in 1555 had not foreseen the new disruptive forces loosed by the Catholic Reformation on the one hand and Calvinism on the other. The Catholic Church, inspired with a new fervor, refused any compromise with Protestantism. The Calvinists, who had taken the initiative from the Lutherans in the struggle against the militancy of the Catholic Reformation, easily matched their Catholic opponents in both zeal and intolerance. Conversion to Protestantism was spurred by the excuse it gave rulers to seize the property of the Catholic Church, a temptation that a number of German princelings, including some bishops, could not resist. Finally, both Catholic and Protestant rulers feared, with good reason, that the emperor would use the pretext of the defense of Catholicism to extend imperial control over Germany.

By the early seventeenth century tensions had so built up that a relatively minor incident in the Bavarian town of Donauwörth in 1607 led first to intervention by the emperor and then to the creation in 1608 of the Protestant Union, an alliance of Protestant German rulers. A year later the Catholic princes formed a Catholic League. The establishment of these two opposing alliances only served to heighten the tension. In 1609 the two groups nearly clashed in a dispute over the succession to the duchies of Jülich and Cleves. After five years of negotiations the dispute was resolved by assigning one duchy to a Catholic prince and the other to a Protestant. Each side knew that an armed clash was inevitable. The spark that set off the conflict could come from any part of the empire. It happened to come from Bohemia.

Bohemia had long been an elective monarchy in name. The estates, assembled in a diet, chose the monarch, but for nearly a century they had always found it politically expedient to elect a member of the Hapsburg family. Most Bohemians were Protestant and all were proud of their nation's past glories and independence. Increasingly, they feared the efforts of the Hapsburgs to expand the power of the central government and strengthen the position of the Catholic Church in Bohemia. Their fears reached a peak in 1617 when the childless Emperor Mathias had his cousin Ferdinand elected king of Bohemia and designated as successor to the imperial crown. Ferdinand had a reputation for extreme piety and intolerance. When he became king of Bohemia he swore to uphold the right of the Bohemian Protestants to practice their religion, but his actions soon belied his words. In 1618 a group of Protestant Bohemian nobles rebelled.

The first overt act of rebellion came in Prague on a bright day in May, 1618. A mob of Bohemian Protestants burst into a room high up in Hradschin Castle and threw three Catholic officials out of the window. The trio dropped nearly fifty feet but only one suffered injuries. Catholics claimed that angels had supported the men in their descent to save them from bodily harm, but Protestants noted that the three had landed in a pile of manure under the window. Whether miracle or comic accident, the event, known by the imposing name of the Defenestration of Prague, signaled the beginning of a war that lasted thirty years, in which nearly every European state became involved and which brought horror and misery to many of the common people of Germany and Bohemia.

THE HAPSBURG ASCENDANCY, 1618–1629

The Bohemian estates announced the deposition of Ferdinand and offered the crown to the youthful Frederick, imperial elector of the Rhineland Palatinate in western Germany, a staunch Calvinist, and leader of the Protestant Union of German princes. When Frederick and his wife, the daughter of King James I of England, came to Prague for his coronation late in 1619, the Jesuits mockingly prophesied, "He will be a winter king. When summer comes he will be driven from the field." Events soon proved them correct. Frederick failed to obtain hoped-for aid from his English father-in-law, the Dutch, and his fellow princes of the Protestant Union. At the same time Spain rallied to the aid of Ferdinand (who in 1619 succeeded Mathias as emperor), the pope sent him money and, most important, the ruler of Bavaria, who was head of the Catholic League of German princes, sent an army under the command of Count Tilly. In November 1620 at the Battle of White Mountain not far from Prague, Frederick's army was crushed and the "winter king" fled with his wife to Holland.

Emperor Ferdinand followed up his victory with ruthless repression and established an Austrian and Catholic domination of Bohemia that lasted for three hundred years. The Jesuits vigorously forced Catholicism upon the people; those who tried to keep their Protestant faith had to pay special heavy taxes and have soldiers quartered in their homes. An estimated 150,000 people fled the country, among whom were most of Bohemia's leading intellectuals. Ferdinand confiscated all or part of the lands of the rebel nobles and gained possession of half of Bohemia. He sold or gave away the confiscated lands to Catholics, many of whom came from other parts of the empire or abroad. In this manner the old Bohemian Protestant nobility was largely supplanted by a Catholic nobility who had no sentimental or historical attachments to Bohemia and who owed their position and their loyalty to the Hapsburg emperor.

The imperial forces followed up their easy victory over the Bohemians with the conquest of the Palatinate and the deposition of Frederick. Other Protestant princes in Germany, fearing that a similar fate would befall them, sought a leader. In 1625 Christian IV of Denmark, who as duke of Holstein was also a prince of the empire, decided to champion the Protestant cause. Concern about the fate of Lutheranism in Germany doubtless helped to inspire Christian's intervention, but the main impetus came from his desire to maintain and increase the German possessions of his dynasty. England offered to subsidize him heavily to help cover the cost of his campaign in the hope that he might restore Frederick in the Palatinate and harry Spain, England's prime enemy.

In search of additional military support, Emperor Ferdinand accepted an unusual offer from Albert von Wallenstein, duke of Friedland, to provide and lead an army of twenty thousand at no cost to the emperor. Wallenstein, a Catholic Bohemian landowner, was a lonely and sinister man, loving no one and loved by no one, driven by unfathomable ambition, believing in nothing except astrology and his own destiny. Through skillful management he greatly increased the fortune left him by his wealthy wife. When the Bohemian revolt broke out, he led local levies against the rebels and lent large sums to the emperor. After White Mountain he bought many of the confiscated lands of the Bohemian nobility at bargain prices. By the time he made the offer to the emperor, he owned one-quarter of all the land in Bohemia.

In his campaigns against the Danes Wallenstein showed himself to be a consummate general. By 1629 Christian had acknowledged defeat and had withdrawn from battle, ending the first phase of the war. Hapsburg power stood at its zenith, while the Protestant cause in Germany was apparently doomed. In the elation of victory the emperor issued the Edict of Restitution in 1629, decreeing the return to the Catholic Church of all lands taken from it by Protestants since 1552. The edict enraged Protestant rulers and convinced them that the emperor intended to destroy both Protestantism and princely independence. Catholic princes also became anxious when the emperor named his relatives to recovered bishoprics and when the Jesuits, who were so close to the emperor, took over some of the recovered monasteries. It seemed that Ferdinand planned to use the victory they had helped him win to increase Hapsburg control over Germany. They also feared Wallenstein, who with his own army and his great wealth appeared to be the emperor's tool in establishing imperial control over Germany as well as an unscrupulous adventurer carving out a new kingdom for himself at their expense. Filled with suspicions, leading Catholic princes refused to name Ferdinand's son "King of the Romans" (traditional title of the heir-apparent of the emperor) and demanded the dismissal of Wallenstein and the dissolution of his army. Ferdinand gave in, albeit unwillingly.

SWEDEN AND THE RESTORATION OF PROTESTANTISM, 1631–1635

Ferdinand received a much harder blow to his plans when King Gustavus Adolphus of Sweden invaded Germany in 1631. Gustavus — statesman, military genius, and devout Lutheran — entered the war to save German Protestantism, but like Christian of Denmark he had ulterior motives. The "Lion of the North" feared that too much power for the Hapsburgs in Germany would endanger Sweden and interfere with Swedish trade on the Baltic. He also had ambitions for territorial acquisitions on Germany's Baltic coast.

Part of the money that Gustavus Adolphus needed for his crusade to save Protestantism came from a Catholic country and a cardinal of the Church. The French government, under the guidance of Cardinal Richelieu, was alarmed at the growing power of the Hapsburgs, its traditional enemy. Already ringed by Spain, the southern Netherlands, and Italy, all under Hapsburg control, France wanted to prevent the Hapsburgs from closing the circle by gaining domination of Germany. "If Germany is lost," said Cardinal Richelieu, "France cannot exist." In 1631 France agreed to subsidize the Swedish fight against the Hapsburgs in the cause of Protestantism. In return, Gustavus Adolphus promised not to interfere with the practice of the Catholic religion in the regions that his armies freed from Hapsburg control.

In a series of brilliant campaigns over less than two years Gustavus Adolphus reversed the fortunes of the two faiths in Germany and placed the Protestant princes in the ascendancy. In desperation Emperor Ferdinand turned to Wallenstein for help. Before that irascible genius would consent to raise an army he demanded many concessions, including full charge of the army and large financial guarantees.

Wallenstein's enormous prestige and good pay attracted men to his regiments. In September, 1632, he faced Gustavus Adolphus for the first time with a powerful force, and the Swede tasted his first defeat on German soil. The two titans met again a few weeks later at Lützen, near Leipzig. Although the Protestants routed the imperial army, the Protestant cause suffered the irreparable loss of Gustavus Adolphus, who was killed in action. There is a story that as Gustavus lay dying on the battlefield, the enemy soldiers around him asked his name. "I am the

King of Sweden," he replied, "who do seal the religion and liberty of the German nation with my blood." His intervention had indeed saved Protestantism in Germany from the annihilation that it suffered in Bohemia, and he had frustrated the Hapsburg attempt to establish imperial supremacy.

The war continued as even more of a struggle for political power. Wallenstein intrigued with Protestant leaders and Cardinal Richelieu, apparently planning to seize political power and perhaps make himself dictator of Germany or king of Bohemia. When the emperor and his counselors decided to relieve him of command, Wallenstein ordered his army to desert to the enemy but only a thousand followed him. While in flight, he and four of his closest associates were murdered by officers loyal to the emperor and anxious for reward.

THE LAST PHASE, 1635–1648

Although in 1635 the German combatants negotiated a settlement, Cardinal Richelieu decided that France should actively enter the war on the Protestant side to smash the Hapsburg power. The French intervention prolonged the conflict another thirteen years. The war lost nearly all connection with religious issues and became a dynastic struggle between Bourbon France on the one side and Hapsburg Austria and Spain on the other. Superior resources and the brilliant leadership of two young generals, Condé and Turenne, turned the tide in France's favor after earlier defeats. Peace negotiations began in 1641. Three years later the representatives of the warring powers met in the towns of Münster and Osnabrück in Westphalia, northwest Germany, in the first peace congress of modern history. The delegates took four more years to agree on terms.

The terrible war reduced large parts of Germany to destitution. The competing armies lived off the land, and the soldiers, most of whom were mercenaries, had no pity on those they looted: civilians were considered legitimate prey. Soldiers stripped the countryside, brutally sacked the cities, and for amusement raped, burned, and tortured. In many regions farming came to a standstill. Germany's population, racked by famine and disease as well as war, fell drastically. Impoverished and torn by these disasters, the country suffered a severe economic setback. Another crippling effect of the war was the stimulation that it gave to princely particularism, preventing the cooperation of German states. The war did not destroy Germany, because there was no national entity to destroy, but it did fix on Germany the atomization into many independent sovereignties that was the enemy of German unity.

THE PEACE OF WESTPHALIA, 1648

The collective treaties negotiated in Westphalia, the Peace of Westphalia, ending the war in Germany represented a victory for German

The Peace of Westphalia

This contemporary print celebrates the signing of the Peace of Westphalia on October 24, 1648. The central figures are the boy king Louis XIV, Emperor Ferdinand III, and Queen Christina of Sweden. All three succeeded their fathers who had reigned at the beginning of the war. Kneeling are clergy and laity (D), a Catholic bishop to the left, a Protestant minister to the right. Peace (A) is seated on her throne and before her stands figures representing Fear of God (F) and Penance (G). On the right stands War (I) faced by a general (L) and a cavalier (M). An angel (H) praises Peace, and another angel (K) bearing a tattered flag and broken sword warns War to leave Germany. E. A. Beller, PROPAGANDA IN GERMANY DURING THE THIRTY YEARS' WAR *(Princeton, 1940).*

Protestantism and the sovereignty of German princes and a defeat for the Catholic Reformation and the imperial ambitions of the Hapsburgs in Germany. It confirmed the Religious Peace of Augsburg, which had given each German prince the right to determine the religion of his subjects, and it placed Calvinism on a par with Lutheranism and Catholicism. It allowed the Protestants to keep the lands they had taken from the Catholic Church after 1624. It gave recognition to each German state as a sovereign power with the right to govern itself and conduct its own foreign affairs. It directed that the emperor obtain the consent of the diet of the empire, formed of representatives of the 350 princedoms, bishoprics, and free cities of Germany, before he could issue laws, levy taxes, recruit soldiers, or make war or peace in the name of the empire. Since the ambitions, jealousies, and pettinesses of the many German rulers made agreement on such matters impossible, these provisions ended any possibility of imperial control over Germany and doomed German unification. As signatories of the treaties, France and Sweden became guarantors of the peace terms, which meant they could legally intervene in German affairs as protectors of the provisions of the treaty. France used this pretext time and again during the next 150 years to keep Germany disunited.

The territorial arrangements of the peace confirmed the disintegration of the empire. France received three bishoprics in Lorraine and extensive rights in Alsace. Sweden gained western Pomerania on the Baltic shores and the bishopric of Bremen, thereby winning control of the mouths of the Weser, Elbe, and Oder rivers, the three most important commercial water routes of northern Germany. The emperor recognized the independence of the Swiss, which had actually been won long before. Spain agreed to recognize Dutch independence and to end its war with the United Provinces.

Neither Spain nor France, however, was ready to end its war with the other. Spain foolishly hoped to recoup some of its losses, and France dared not pass up the opportunity to complete the ruin of its old foe. The war continued until 1659, when Spain had to accept defeat. In the Peace of the Pyrenees, signed that year, Spain recognized French conquests on the Spanish-French frontier that made the Pyrenees France's southern boundary, ceded some land to France in the Netherlands and, to seal the treaty, agreed to a marriage between the youthful French king, Louis XIV, and the daughter of the Spanish king.

The Peace of Westphalia settled religious and political issues that had long kept Europe in turmoil. Catholic and Protestant finally realized that neither was strong enough to destroy the other and that they must learn to live together. Out of the forced compromise a spirit of toleration slowly grew.

In politics the peace confirmed the end of Hapsburg dreams of domination in Germany, and also marked the end of Hapsburg supremacy in Europe. The once-powerful Hapsburg family alliance — the Madrid-Vienna axis — went down in defeat. The Austrian Hapsburgs turned their attention to the construction of a new domain in southeastern Europe. Hapsburg Spain, which had dwindled in power, was replaced by France as Europe's greatest power. In rejecting the old imperial idea, the Peace of Westphalia recognized a Europe organized into a system of independent sovereign states, each unabashedly following its own interests. The concept of a supranational unity based upon religion or politics vanished.

THE DECLINE OF SPAIN, 1598–1665

Shortly before his death in 1598, Philip II of Spain remarked sadly, "God, who has given me so many kingdoms, has not given me a son able to govern them." Philip III (1598–1621), known as the Pious, inherited the religious ardor of his father but none of his other qualities. Lazy, pleasure-loving, and unbelievably extravagant, he gave control of the government to ill-chosen favorites who used their power to enrich themselves and their families. Court and government were shot through with corruption and graft.

ECONOMIC DETERIORATION

The misrule of Philip's reign hastened the economic as well as the political decay of Spain. During the sixteenth century economic life had advanced in Spain, albeit less rapidly than in England, France, or the Netherlands. Toward the end of the reign of Philip II the trend turned markedly downward. The economic crisis was above all a crisis for Castile, the central kingdom under the Spanish crown. Castile supported the Spanish economy in the sixteenth century with its agricultural production, mercantile activities, and territories in the New World. From Castile came the bulk of the government's revenue and most of the manpower for the armies: approximately 80 per cent of the population of the Iberian peninsula was Castilian, and nearly one-half of the Castilians were located in the plateau country of central Castile within a one-hundred-mile radius of Madrid.

In the middle of the sixteenth century the expansion of the Castilian economy stopped. Foreign goods displaced Spanish-made wares, and Castile's trade and industry declined. Castilian manufactures were increasingly luxury goods, for which there was no mass market. The privileges of the Mesta (see p. 198) held back the raising of crops, drove up food prices and made Spain dependent upon northern and eastern Europe for grain. The agrarian depression in Castile caused extensive depopulation. Castile became less and less able to supply the men and the money upon which Spanish power rested.

To the crisis in the internal economy was added a crisis in the colonial economy. As long as silver imports were maintained at a high level, the effects of the Castilian economic crisis were moderated. After 1600 the flow of silver from America began to taper off, and by 1660 it had dropped to less than one-tenth of its amount in 1600. Exhaustion of mines, smuggling of bullion, and increasing shipments of precious metals from Spanish America to Asia were the chief causes of the silver decline.

The Spanish government had long depended upon the stream of bullion from the New World to subsidize its power; the diminution in this stream after 1600 signaled the decline of Spain in general.

A large measure of responsibility for the economic deterioration belonged to the inordinate ambitions and misguided policies of the government. The heavy cost of war, the crushing burden of taxation, the drain of the king's ornate court, and the inefficiency and corruption of the bureaucracy, placed heavy demands upon the economy and stifled economic advance. In particular, the government's credit policy had ill effects on the economy. To raise money for war the government borrowed at such high rates of interest that private investment in economically productive areas was discouraged. The government encouraged foreign merchants in return for their advance of credit to the government, resulting in a drain of bullion from Spain and increasing foreign encroachments on the colonial market. Finally, the government turned to a dangerous fiscal device which has been used by other hard-pressed governments: it cheapened the value of money to make it easier to pay its debts. The government debased its coinage by substituting copper for silver. Inevitably prices rose sharply. The overall rise in prices served to reduce the purchasing power of taxes, which added to the government's fiscal problems.

THE COUNT-DUKE OLIVARES

Philip IV (1621–1665), who was only sixteen when he succeeded his father, turned the rule of the country over to the Count-Duke Olivares. The new chief minister had for years intrigued to reach this eminence; when at last he attained his ambition, he exulted, "All is mine!" He was no more reluctant than his predecessors to use his power for selfish ends, but unlike them, he had loftier goals. He meant to return his country to the glorious days of Philip II, when it had been the colossus of the world. What Olivares did not sufficiently appreciate was that Spain could not recapture its past glory without an economic revival. More than anything else Spain needed a long period of peace and retrenchment. Instead, Olivares involved his country in disastrous wars.

The renewal of the war with the Dutch in 1621 and the precipitate intervention in the Thirty Years' War, which after 1635 meant war with France, postponed his proposed renewal of the economy. The heavy exactions of men and money that were imposed to continue the war effort deepened the economic crisis and met with resistance. In 1640 open revolt broke out, first in Catalonia and then in Portugal. The Catalans established a republic and put themselves under French protection. They held out until 1652, when a domestic crisis in France compelled the French to reduce their support and enabled Spain to reconquer the province. The Portuguese, who had been ruled by Spain since 1580, took advantage of the Catalan revolt to declare their independence. In a rising that lasted only three hours they overthrew the Spanish government in Lisbon. The Portuguese gave the crown to the duke of Braganza, who ruled as John IV and founded a dynasty that reigned until 1910. In 1647 a wild and bloody revolt flared in Naples, which had been a Spanish dependency since 1504. The revolt continued for over six months before the Spanish reestablished their control.

Failure to defeat the Dutch and the French, the revolts of 1640, and the heavy attrition of war cost Olivares his office in 1643 and ended Spain's hope of regaining its former position. In the war with the Dutch, which lasted until 1648, Dutch naval victories destroyed Spanish sea power and enabled the Dutch to consolidate their dominance in the East Indies and make extensive inroads in Brazil. The war with France dragged on until 1659, ending with the humiliating Peace of the Pyrenees. The final result of the long years of war was defeat on every front, economic ruin, and the fall of Spain to the status of a second-class power.

THE GOLDEN AGE OF SPANISH CULTURE

Spain entered its greatest period of artistic creativity in the latter part of the sixteenth century. Painting and literature were the glories of this golden age of culture, although other branches of the arts also flourished. All aspects of creativity were informed by the manneristic or baroque styles.

Among the painters of Spain three names stand out: El Greco, Velasquez, and Murillo. El Greco (*c.* 1547–1614), whose real name was Domenico Theotocopoulos, came from Crete; the Spaniards called him "the Greek." He had studied in Venice with the great Renaissance artists Titian and Tintoretto, from whom he derived a manneristic use of light and color. He settled in Toledo, where he painted the pictures that have won him immortality. He developed a distinctive style by which he conveyed to the viewer mystical and visionary experiences. Although a foreigner, he instinctively assimilated the spirit and psychology of Catholic Spain and became completely Spanish, like that other famous foreigner, Charles V.

Velasquez (1599–1660), who also studied in Italy and greatly admired El Greco's work, painted in a very different style. He was interested in bringing out personalities rather than expressing ideas and mystical experiences. He penetrated to the essentials of what he saw, leaving out details, so that his paintings are impressionistic rather than photographic; the French impressionists of the late nineteenth century hailed him as one of their precursors. His portraits are psychological studies: when Pope Innocent X saw the one that Velasquez had done of him, he winced and said, "Too true!"

Velasquez painted relatively few religious works, in contrast to Murillo

(1617–1682), who specialized in religious paintings. Murillo's pictures, although filled with warmth and gentleness, are sentimental and sometimes saccharine. He specialized in idealized portraits of saints with their eyes turned heavenward. He enjoyed great popularity during the eighteenth and nineteenth centuries, when he was regarded as one of the world's foremost masters.

In Spanish literature the great names are Cervantes, Lope de Vega, and Calderón. Cervantes (1547–1616) wrote many works, but he owes his fame to the prose epic *Don Quixote*. Some critics have called it the greatest novel ever written. Quixote, a simple country gentleman who reads so many stories about the days of chivalry that his brain becomes addled, rides forth on his old nag to do battle against injustice, defend the innocent and virtuous, and conquer a realm. He is loyally attended by Sancho Panza, an illiterate peasant with much common sense, who shares his madcap adventures. Sancho realizes that his master is mad but comes to love and admire him — as does the reader of the book — for Quixote, despite his folly, is a man of saintly character and full of courage, sincerity, and goodness. Above all, the tale is an allegory of the conflict between mystical idealism, exemplified by Quixote, and common-sense realism, exemplified by Sancho.

Lope de Vega (1562–1635), probably the most prolific writer of all times, was a dramatist and poet. In his later years he became the arbiter of Spanish letters and a national idol. Like Shakespeare, his contemporary, he was distinguished for ingenious plots of intrigue, patriotic and historical subject matter, archetypal characterization, and imaginative staging. Only a few of his many hundreds of plays and poems have great power, for he wrote too much and generally with too slight an intent.

Calderón (1600–1681) demonstrated both the strengths and the weaknesses of baroque drama in the many secular plays that he wrote in the first three decades of his career. They were dramatically effective, ingenious, and mystical, yet often shallow, precious, and stilted. It was in the short allegorical dramas on the sacrament of the eucharist, following his ordination to the priesthood at the age of fifty-one, that he wrote most movingly and originally. His devotional fervor reflected both the passion and the abiding religiosity that ennobled so much of the baroque style in the golden age of Spanish culture.

THE RECONSTRUCTION OF FRANCE

The history of France in the seventeenth century presents a striking contrast to the story of Spain's decay. An upward surge after the dissolution of the Wars of Religion carried France by mid-century to the position of European leadership that Spain had occupied in the sixteenth century.

ACHIEVEMENTS OF HENRY IV

France's recovery began with the reign of Henry IV (1589–1610), first king of the Bourbon dynasty. When Henry ascended the throne, France was in a sad state after many years of civil war. Whole districts had been devastated, fields lay untilled, roads and bridges were destroyed, navigable rivers had become silted, and economic life had suffered a severe setback. The kingdom was still plagued by political dissensions and religious hatreds, the throne had lost most of its prestige and was in danger of losing its power, and morale was at a dangerously low level. Henry was undaunted by the enormous task of reconstruction that faced him. By persuasion, bribes, pressure, and force he reestablished royal authority over the great feudal lords, the parlements, and the governors of the provinces. He quieted religious discontent by becoming a Catholic himself, while issuing the Edict of Nantes to placate the Huguenots. He worked hard to improve the well-being of his people; when he became king, he said in a typically warm and homely manner, "I hope to make France so prosperous that every peasant will have chicken in his pot on Sunday." His interest in the people's welfare stemmed not only from genuine love but from a realization that the prosperity of the country would strengthen the monarchy.

In his work of reconstruction, especially of economic life, Henry had the invaluable assistance of the duke of Sully, an austere and methodical Calvinist. Sully introduced economies into the government, reduced corruption and inefficiency, and encouraged economic growth to increase tax revenues. When he took control of the finances, he found a debt of 300 million livres; when he left office in 1610, the treasury had a reserve of 13 million livres. He was responsible for the repair and construction of roads, canals, and bridges, the dredging of rivers, and improvements in the postal service, and he encouraged agriculture in the belief that it was the only true form of wealth.

Another of Henry's Protestant aides, Barthélemy de Laffemas, headed a Commission of Commerce to stimulate the growth of all aspects of French economic life. The commission encouraged the development of old industries and introduced new ones, including the culture of silkworms and the manufacture of silk. Several government-sponsored efforts to found overseas trading companies modeled after the highly successful Dutch and English ventures failed, but in 1608 Quebec, the first successful French overseas colony, was established by Samuel de Champlain.

Under Henry's leadership France regained much lost ground, but at a price. The carefully hoarded reserve in the treasury deprived the country of capital badly needed for reconstruction and recovery. Taxes remained only a little less heavy than they had been during the civil wars. The burden of the *taille,* the principal tax, fell with increasing weight on the peasants, for nobles did not have to pay it and growing numbers of the bourgeoisie managed to evade it either legally or illegally. Henry was still far from providing the chicken on Sunday for the peasant's pot when in 1610 a religious fanatic named Ravaillac, who was obsessed with the idea that Henry was the archenemy of Catholicism, leaped on the king's coach in a narrow Parisian street and plunged a dagger into Henry's heart.

LOUIS XIII AND MARIE DE' MEDICI

Henry's son and successor, Louis XIII (1610–1643), was only nine at his accession, and his mother, Marie de' Medici (whom Henry had married for her money in 1600 after divorcing his first wife, Margaret of Valois) became regent. Lazy and slow-witted, she allowed Italian favorites to take power and enrich themselves, while Henry's wise, trusted, and disapproving counselors were turned out of office. Discontent, even civil commotion, again threatened France. In an effort to quiet the unrest the queen convened the Estates-General. The three orders — clergy, nobility, and commoners or Third Estate — met in 1614. They exchanged recriminations, accomplished nothing, and discredited the Estates-General as a representative assembly. Marie, tired of the harangues, dismissed the meeting. One hundred and seventy-five years passed before the Estates-General met again.

The discord mounted until a palace revolution in 1617 drove the queen from the court, killed her chief Italian favorite, and gave power to the young king. Nothing really changed, however, for Louis was weak and uncertain and new favorites took over. Revolts broke out among feudal lords and among Protestants, who feared new oppression by the Catholic Church. The situation continued to deteriorate until 1624, when the king named Cardinal Richelieu as his chief minister.

RICHELIEU AND THE REVIVAL OF FRANCE

The new minister had been born in 1585 in an old noble family. Through family influence he became a bishop at the age of twenty-two but politics, and not religion, became his consuming interest. His outstanding abilities won him the admiration of Louis XIII, who made Richelieu his chief minister in 1624. From then until his death in 1642 Richelieu ruled France. Throughout his long tenure he pursued one supreme goal with inflexible determination — the increase of the power and glory of the French throne at home and abroad. To that end he undertook three programs: the suppression of the political and military privileges of the Huguenots, the reduction of the power and prerogatives of the nobility, and the defeat of the Hapsburgs. He met with complete success in the first and third objectives, and almost complete success in the second.

Cardinal Richelieu, by Philippe de Champaigne

> *"Cardinal de Richelieu was a man of his word, unless great interests swayed him*
> *to the contrary, and in such cases he was very artful to preserve all the*
> *appearances of good faith. . . . He was more ambitious than was consistent with*
> *the rules of morality. . . . He distinguished more judiciously than any man in*
> *the world between bad and worse, good and better, which is a great qualification*
> *in a minister. . . . He had religion enough for this world. His own good sense,*
> *or else his inclination, always led him to the practice of virtue if his self-interest*
> *did not bias him to evil, which whenever he committed it he did so knowingly."*
> Cardinal de Retz (1613–1679), in his MEMOIRS (London, 1896).

Richelieu's hostility to the Huguenots did not come from any fanatical opposition to their religion. He considered the Huguenots a threat to the absolute power of the king and the security of the realm because of the special privileges and fortified places guaranteed to them by the Edict of Nantes. That the most eminent of their leaders were noblemen increased his concern. The difficulties they made in the years of unrest following Henry IV's death persuaded Richelieu that their power had to be reduced. In 1627–1628, after the Huguenots had once again risen against the government, royal forces besieged La Rochelle, their chief stronghold, and forced it to surrender. Soon other Protestant citadels capitulated. In 1629 in the Peace of Alais the government abolished the Huguenots' special military and political privileges but allowed them to keep their religious and civil freedom. Thereafter the Huguenots became loyal subjects, while Richelieu scrupulously respected their rights and exhibited no animosity toward them.

The cardinal moved with equal determination against the nobility, who had taken advantage of the disturbed times to resume many of their independent ways. The nobles resented his policies and constantly plotted his downfall. Richelieu, with spies everywhere, managed to outwit his enemies and to persuade the king to punish them severely. He sent a score of the highest aristocracy to the scaffold and drove others into exile. To reduce the nobles' power to wage local wars or terrorize the people of a rural district, he ordered the dismantling of all fortified castles except those on the frontiers. He sought to abolish dueling, the last vestige of the nobility's practice of waging private wars. Moreover, too many nobles were perishing in "affairs of honor"; in 1607, for example, four thousand nobles were said to have been killed in duels. Henry IV had tried without success to abolish the custom. Although Richelieu's efforts were more effective, they did not stop dueling altogether: in the twenty years following his death nine hundred nobles perished for the sake of their honor.

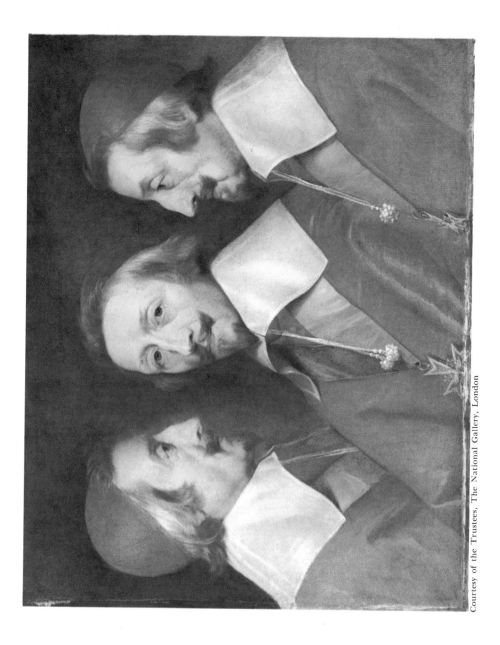

233

By completing the evolution of a sophisticated bureaucracy, Richelieu was able further to exclude the nobility from central government and to reduce their provincial power. Under him councils became the principal instruments of royal authority. Derived from the single council of the king in the Middle Ages, the councils permitted specialization and division of labor within the administration. The hierarchic and overlapping arrangement of responsibilities among the councils allowed for constant and effective control from the top. The High Council of State, presided over by the king and comprising his ministers of state, determined top-level policy in domestic and foreign affairs and supervised the other councils. The Council of Dispatches, including members of the High Council plus second-ranking officials, was an administrative body with oversight of police matters, power to imprison indefinitely by means of warrants called *lettres de cachet,* and responsibility for instructions to the *intendants,* the government's agents in the provinces. The Council of Finance, which was less august in membership, was responsible for fiscal policy and controlled the accounts. The Privy Council was the largest of the councils, in effect comprising the membership of all the other councils. It was essentially a court of justice with a wide appellate jurisdiction and the power to review criminal judgments. In 1632 the councils were empowered to revoke any judicial decrees that contradicted royal authority, threatened the public interest, or abridged the king's rights.

There were twelve parlements; the oldest and most important one was at Paris. Their members, who inherited their posts, formed a special class among the nobility. In addition to serving as trial and appellate courts, the parlements had the responsibility of recording royal legislation. Although the king alone legislated, the process of recording his acts gave the parlements the opportunity to petition for changes or to remonstrate against the royal legislation. The judicial autonomy of the parlements was severely limited by the 1632 edict empowering the councils to revoke judicial decrees. In 1641 their rights of protest when recording acts were drastically curtailed. With the Estates-General no longer convened, Richelieu was shutting off the last avenue of protest open to the nobility.

The intendants were the most effective means for reducing the provincial power of the nobility. Henry IV had begun the practice of sending out agents of the central government to attend to many of the duties of local administration. Richelieu developed the system, giving the administrators the titles of *intendant* (commissioner) of justice, police, and finance. Their powers involved inspection and supervision at the very minimum and could be instantly increased to meet any emergency. They became the chief administrative instruments for absolutist centralization.

Although certain places on the major councils were reserved for the nobility, Richelieu's policy was to staff the bureaucracy as much as possible from the middle rank of society, especially with lawyers. Intendants came from this rank. In this way Richelieu depleted the power of the old nobility and furthered the growth of the "nobility of the robe." (See pp. 275–276.) The new nobility's commitment to absolute monarchy was considered the safest counterpoise to the power of the old nobility.

In foreign policy Richelieu worked ceaselessly for the downfall of Hapsburg power in Spain, the Netherlands, and Germany in order to win security and international prestige for France. Although the cardinal died before the Thirty Years' War ended, his intervention was successful, for the House of Hapsburg was humbled and France stood supreme.

The French paid a heavy price for Richelieu's successes. Unlike Henry IV, he had no concern for the welfare of the people. He taxed mercilessly. More than once the peasants in different parts of the country were driven to armed insurrections, which were put down with a cruel hand. The week of mourning decreed by the king when Richelieu died in 1642 was in some places lit by bonfires to celebrate his passing.

MAZARIN AND THE FRONDE

Louis XIII died a few months after his great minister. Since the new king, Louis XIV, was only four, his mother, Anne of Austria, ruled as regent. The reins of power rested in the hands of an Italian-born cardinal named Jules Mazarin. The new chief minister had come to France as a papal legate, attracted the attention of Richelieu, become a French subject, and entered the king's service. Louis XIII had him elevated to the cardinalate (although he had never been ordained a priest) and, when Richelieu died, made him chief minister. Under the regent Mazarin's power greatly increased, for Anne conceived a strong affection for him and may even have secretly married him.

Mazarin, who came from a humble background, was an avaricious and grasping man. He used his high position to gain enormous wealth for himself and the numerous relatives he brought to France, as well as to marry his nieces into the greatest families of the kingdom. He also had enormous ability and tried to continue Richelieu's policies, but he found it difficult to hold in check the forces that opposed those policies. The old nobility resented the effrontery of the foreign parvenu who dared to carry himself as their equal. The middle classes and the nobility of the robe were alarmed at his financial excesses, rapacity, and the increased taxation, which was even being exacted from the formerly tax-exempt new nobility.

In June, 1648, the discontent erupted into an open revolt led by the parlement of Paris and joined by many of the old nobility. This was the first of two risings known collectively as the *Fronde* (taken from the word for the slingshot used by Parisian boys at play, since some of the nobles gave the impression of merely playing at revolt). Amid much talk

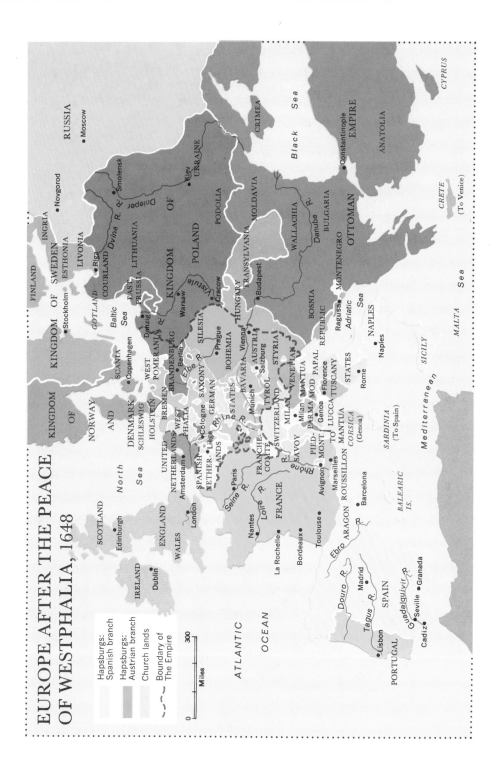

EUROPE AFTER THE PEACE
OF WESTPHALIA, 1648

Hapsburgs:
Spanish branch

Hapsburgs:
Austrian branch

Church lands

Boundary of
The Empire

0   300
Miles

of constitutionalism, a great deal of selfish power politics took place among the *Frondeurs*, especially the old nobility who were fighting to preserve their archaic privileges. The first revolt quickly collapsed. In 1650 a new Fronde broke out, led by the old nobility and their private armies and involving a number of the nobility of the parlements as well. Devoid of any unifying principle beyond individual ambitions, the nobles shifted allegiance rapidly and conducted a series of private wars rather than a concerted campaign. By 1653 the movement had died out, after bloody skirmishes and a great deal of looting and devastation of the common people.

Mazarin weathered the storm by astute withdrawals at critical moments and the foresight not to wreak vengeance upon his enemies. He remained in power until his death in 1661. He passed on to his former charge, the young King Louis XIV, a country in which the nobility had been tamed and the parlements discredited, a position in international affairs that was second to none, and a people who were ready to support a strong, absolute monarch as the apparent alternative to feudal anarchy.

THE EMERGENCE OF ABSOLUTISM

In the late Middle Ages the king ruled with the estates in a mixed monarchy in which the power of the king was shared with representatives of the clergy, the nobility, and the commoners — the orders or ranks of society that were privileged by law. Whether the institutional form of representation was called the Estates-General (France), Parliament (England), Riksdag (Sweden), Cortès (Spain), States (Netherlands), or Stati (Italy); whether the representatives met in one, two, or three chambers; whether the privileged orders excluded one or two of the ranks mentioned — whatever the differences in the extent of power and authority of the representatives, such mixed monarchy limited the exercise of royal power. The king and the estates were conceived of as separate but cooperating entities in a dualistic government.

In the second half of the fifteenth century strong kings emerged who were able to increase the power of the throne at the expense of the privileged orders. Monarchic power grew rapidly in the sixteenth century but was not yet able to eclipse completely the traditional institutions of the privileged orders. The climax of this royal struggle for freedom from the restrictions of mixed monarchy came in the first half of the seventeenth century. The crisis of that period was above all a crisis in the relations between monarchs and their privileged subjects, especially the nobility. It was a confrontation between the monarch who claimed to be the sole representative of the state and the traditional constitutional entities, the estates.

THEORETICAL FOUNDATIONS OF ABSOLUTISM

Mixed monarchy usually is regarded as the national counterpart of the supranational church-state dualism of the middle Ages. Therefore, it is argued, the destruction of the latter entailed the decline of mixed monarchy, a proposition that eludes proof. The Reformation did serve in two demonstrable ways to undermine mixed monarchy. First, it gave enormous vogue to Machiavelli's postulate of the preservation of the state as the transcendant morality in politics, for in the conflict with the Church the justification of the secular authority depended upon the moral primacy of the state. Second, striving to justify either the expulsion of papal authority or its reduction within their realms, princes made high claims to be under no sovereign power on earth: "this realm of England is an empire, and so hath been accepted in the world, governed by one supreme head and king." It was put thus in the preamble to an act of Henry VIII's Reformation Parliament in 1533 abolishing ecclesiastical court appeals to Rome. This kind of argument was easily domesticated into a weapon against the estates. It also slipped readily into an argument that the king ruled by divine right, as God's agent on earth, an argument that contradicted accepted medieval theory only in that it left out the pope as God's agent on earth in matters spiritual and the superiority of things spiritual to things secular. With the notion of the preservation of the state as the transcendant morality in politics and the divine right of kings, two essential ingredients of absolutist theory are already present.

Political theory in the late sixteenth and seventeenth centuries was concerned principally with sovereignty and where it was to be found: who has ultimate authority within the state? The quest for sovereignty strengthened the absolutist tendency in political theory, for in mixed monarchy by definition sovereignty was either dispersed and shared or else did not exist at all. The wars of religion and the crisis-ridden atmosphere of the early seventeenth century made men thirst for certainty, for a definition of the precise place where authority rested. Sovereignty came of age as a central concern in political theory with Jean Bodin (1530–1596), the French politique with whom we are already familiar and whose words we now repeat: "The prince exalted above all his subjects, whose majesty does not admit of any division, represents the principle of unity from which all the rest derive their force and cohesion." (See p. 194.) The vital phrase is that concerning the indivisibility of majesty. Bodin did not deny that sovereignty could rest in the people or an oligarchy, but his own predilection was for sovereignty vested in the monarch. The title to Book VI, chapter 4, of his *Six Books of the Commonwealth* (1576) is, significantly, "A comparison of three legitimate types of commonwealth, popular, aristocratic, and monarchial, concluding in favor of monarchy." Monarchy was preferable because there must be some "head of state in whom sovereign power is vested, who can unite all the rest." It required greater perspicacity and a more noble view of human nature than men of those troubled times could afford to have in order to conceive of unity coming from any source other than the will of one man.

The great emphasis on "reason of state," implicit in Machiavelli and first treated systematically by the Italian Jesuit, Giovanni Botero (1540–1617), made its contribution to absolutist theory by inducing men to define the state, the actions of which depended upon the justification of "reason of state." In *Of the Reason of State* (1598), Botero argued that the state is an ethical entity which though it might use unethical means to attain its ends must never divest those ends of their ethical content. It was difficult to conceive of a conglomeration of persons — an estate — as one ethical entity, but not at all difficult to conceive of a single person — the monarch — as the personification of the ethical state.

There was no theoretical opposition to monarchic absolutism comparable in weight to absolutism's proponents in the early seventeenth century. The German theorist, Johannes Althusius (1557–1638), an orthodox Calvinist, attacked absolutism on behalf of theocracy, whose end, if not technically absolutism could be a tyranny that would make monarchic absolutism seem tame in comparison. The Jesuit polemicists and theoreticians, Cardinal Robert Bellarmine (1542–1621) and Father Francisco Suarez (1548–1617), assailed the divine right of monarchs in defense of the divine right of the pope. They were, in one sense, merely exalting one absolutism to the detriment of many absolutisms. Thus the only theoretical opposition to monarchic absolutism came from the extremes of the Reformation and were directed in essence at the "blasphemous" nature of divine right monarchy.

THE NATURE OF ABSOLUTISM

Absolutism was monarchy with the restraining limitation of the estates removed; that is, it was unmixed monarchy, since one of the entities in the old dualism had disappeared. The king's authority was unbound by any higher authority on earth, particularly by any body of popular representation. Absolutism was not totalitarianism, for in the absolutist state vast areas of national life were practically, if not theoretically, outside the monarch's purview. The tendency in more recent times for government to expand its activities to the point of totalitarianism, beyond the traditional activities of preserving order, assuring defense, and conducting foreign relations, had little to do with absolutism in the seventeenth century. Neither was absolutism naked tyranny. It conceded limitations on power if not on sovereign authority; specifically, it recognized that the law of God and the law of nature limited the absolute monarch's power.

Though the absolute monarch could make law to govern his subjects, he could not change God's law or nature's law. In practice these unchangeable higher laws provided no guarantees to the subject, but they did remind the absolute monarch, as he recognized in his coronation oath, that his power was limited if uncontrolled. James I of England, the most articulate absolute monarch (and one of the least successful) put the case for absolutism as follows:

Kings sit in the throne of God and they are called gods. Therefore they must imitate God and His Christ in justice and righteousness, David and Solomon in godliness and wisdom — wisdom to discern godliness as the fountain from which wisdom floweth. Justice without righteousness were to no purpose. It must come from a clear heart, not for private ends. From this imitation all commonwealths, especially monarchies, are settled.

Clearly the king had to serve God's ends in his exercise of power; he had to approach as closely as possible the justice and righteousness of God. In the first sentence James struck the note of justification for absolutism: the divine right of kings. All seventeenth-century absolutists, with the significant exception of the Englishman Thomas Hobbes, founded absolutism on divine right.

THOMAS HOBBES

Thomas Hobbes (1588–1679) was over forty when he became fascinated by the new natural science and immersed himself in its study. He was convinced that social relationships could be described with as much precision and accuracy as the relationships among physical phenomena, and he adopted a materialistic view of the universe, believing that man himself is nothing more than a machine in motion. He had planned to develop his theories in three long treatises but political unrest in England interfered with his plans. Because of the civil disruption in England in the 1640's, he fled to the Continent, where he had lived from 1640 to 1651. While abroad he wrote several treatises in support of absolutist government, including *Leviathan,* his masterpiece, published in 1651. He chose the name because he compared the sovereign power of the state to the great sea monster mentioned in the Book of Job of which the Bible said "Upon earth there is not his like."

In *Leviathan* Hobbes argued that all men possess instinctive feelings of fear and self-preservation. These instincts, he said, provide the underlying motivation for social organization. Human life in the "state of nature," that is, in the absence of all government and with all men equal, was unendurable. There was a "war of all against all," constant fear reigned, and life was "solitary, poor, nasty, brutish, and short." Hobbes, like Machiavelli, held a low opinion of the human race. Driven by the instinct of self-preservation, men decided to leave the state of nature and made a contract with each other by which they agreed to transfer all their rights to a sovereign, to whom they gave unlimited power. The only rights they retained were those allowed them by the sovereign, who used his unlimited power to enforce obedience and unity. The government — the sovereign power — did not have to be a monarchy, but Hobbes favored kingship as the form of rule best suited to absolutism.

Hobbes's political theory based its demand for the total subjugation of the individual to the sovereign on enlightened self-interest. The assertion that absolute power came initially from the consent of the governed offended those who held that royal power came from God and also raised the question as to what would happen if the governed took back their consent. Hobbes said that this was impossible because the contract, once entered into, was unbreakable. In a society whose legal system enshrined the contract as a reciprocal agreement, the argument was feeble, for if the sovereign did not deliver his part of the bargain (security and peace of mind), the subjects might justly argue that they could take back their part (absolute obedience). Hobbes not only failed to satisfy the absolutists with his contract, but he could not win the adherence of their opponents, who saw his argument as a bulwark for absolutism. His materialism cost him all religious support. Consequently, his influence was limited in his own time, but *Leviathan* became the classic theoretical statement of absolutism and served as the starting point for much of later political theory.

THE TRIUMPH OF ABSOLUTISM

By 1660, absolute monarchs held sway over most of Europe, the principal exceptions being England and the Dutch Republic. Absolutism had received its theoretical framework and had been given ample justification. As a matter of political practice, absolutism still placed a heavy reliance on the loyalty and commitment of the monarch's ministers. The first half of the seventeenth century was the age of the great ministers: Richelieu and Mazarin in France, Olivares in Spain, Laud and Strafford in England, Oxenstierna in Sweden. Although these men advanced the programs of their monarchs, the attributes of absolutism were in their hands. Such men of power were potentially as great a threat to absolute monarchs as were the feudal nobility — greater even, because they controlled states that had already routed the feudal nobility. This threat was not unrecognized. Louis XIV of France, whose youth had been spent in the shadow of Mazarin, was alive to the danger. His final contribution to the fashioning of absolutism was to rule from 1661 until his death in 1715 without a minister able to challenge his absolute authority.

ABSOLUTISM VERSUS OLIGARCHY: ENGLAND AND THE DUTCH REPUBLIC
CHAPTER TEN

Absolutism's pattern of success was broken only in England and the Dutch Republic during the first half of the seventeenth century. The Wars of the Roses in the fifteenth century had so decimated the ranks of the English feudal nobility that Henry VII was able to build a more absolutist monarchy by 1500 than the French king was able to construct for another century. The chief beneficiaries of the decline of the old nobility, in addition to the king, were the people of middle rank, particularly the landed gentry. Because of the peculiar development of the medieval Parliament in England and the Tudors' own confidence that Parliament was a tool of monarchy, the House of Commons, the estate of the middle rank in England, was not destroyed and could serve as a stage from which to attack absolutism. As long as Tudor absolutism seemed the only alternative to chaos, the gentry cooperated with it, especially since the Tudors reciprocated by being solicitous of their interests. When Stuart absolutism threatened their interests, they had in Parliament the means to stem and ultimately to destroy absolutism.

The late sixteenth-century revolt against Spain in the northern Netherlands, enfeebled the old nobility by placing the preponderance of power in the middle class oligarchy of Holland, who alone could finance the war of independence and who never lost control of the conduct of the war. The same oligarchy enfeebled the potentially strong monarchy of the House of Orange in the seventeenth century.

To other European states in the seventeenth century, England and the Dutch Republic were simply "the Protestant powers" or, between 1649 and 1660, "the Protestant republics." Contemporaries noted that parliamentary institutions remained vital and vigorous only in these two countries. They were also the rising colonial and naval powers, building commercial empires at the expense of the Spanish and in collision with each other. Trade and finance bound Amsterdam and London in the tightest economic web of northern Europe. They commanded both sides of the narrow seas linking the North Sea with the Atlantic. At critical moments — whether they opposed Spain or France — the safety of one depended upon the survival of the other. Relations between the two countries were always complex: sometimes hostile, seldom affectionate, always respectful. They were more continuously and intimately involved with each other than with any other power. Once England intervened significantly in Dutch internal politics; once the Dutch intervened in English internal politics; and the two countries fought three wars with each other, largely because of commercial rivalry.

ENGLAND'S CONSTITUTIONAL CRISIS, 1603–1640

"When I came into this land, though I were an old king (having governed a kingdom since I was twelve years old), yet I came a stranger hither in government though not in blood." Thus did James I of England sum up his unfamiliarity with English institutions, laws, and customs, and the fact that he was the great-great-grandson of Henry VII and a cousin to Queen Elizabeth, whom he succeeded. He had reigned for thirty-six years on the throne of Scotland as James VI before coming to England in 1603. He continued as king of Scotland, uniting the two crowns, although each country remained independent of the other.

James's background and personal qualities went far in explaining his lack of success as the first Stuart monarch of England. His fixed ideas on almost every aspect of government had been born in the long struggle to curb the power of the nobility in Scotland and to establish his independence from the theoretically oriented Calvinism of Scottish churchmen. His ideas bore but slight relevance to the country that he was to rule until his death in 1625. He was a learned man. Like most monarchs of the day he believed in the divine right of kings; he even wrote a theoretical treatise called *The Trew Law of Free Monarchies* (1598) to explain and justify his conviction. Unfortunately he overestimated his abilities, was an extremely bad judge of men and political possibilities, and never understood the traditions or the obstinacy of the people he ruled.

James inherited from Elizabeth a war with Spain, a rebellion in Ireland, a sizable debt amounting to more than one year's revenue, an able chief minister in Robert Cecil, a somewhat antiquated bureaucracy (though as sound as any in Europe), an overwhelmingly Protestant populace, and a pattern of relatively frequent convocations of Parliament. By the end of 1605 James had ended the war with Spain, settled the Irish turmoil, and nearly doubled the debt by his courtly extravagance. He had also fallen afoul of the growing current for further reform of Protestantism in the Anglican Church and had come into head-on collision with Parliament.

PURITANISM

In 1603 puritanism was a perfectly respectable, repressed, minority movement within the established Church of England, desirous of clarifying the ambiguous Elizabethan settlement in more rigidly Protestant terms and ending what the Puritans considered vestiges of Roman Catholic practice in the Anglican Church. Two things puritanism was not: it was not separatist, that is, it had no intention of leaving the established church; and it did not differ significantly in doctrine from the conservative majority group in control of the church. The Puritans parted company with the episcopate, the bishops, in the latter's refusal to draw certain logical conclusions from its doctrinal position. For instance, the Puritans felt that the sacramental forms of worship laid down in the Book of Common Prayer were irrelevant, and that clerical garments, the use of the ring in marriage, and bowing the knee at the name of Jesus were mere "popish remnants." The bishops feared that if these established forms were discarded, the whole order of state and church would be in jeopardy. They especially feared the possibility of the replacement of episcopacy as the governing institution of the church by presbyteries, assemblies of ministers and lay elders of the various congregations.

Shortly after his accession James was presented with a petition — called the Millenary Petition because it supposedly represented the views of nearly a thousand Puritan ministers — requesting in restrained language certain changes in church practices. The petition induced James to call a conference at Hampton Court Palace in 1604 between the bishops and some of the Puritan clergy, with the king presiding. The bishops attacked the Puritans, pushing them into a more extreme position than they meant to take. James, who had experienced presbyterianism in Scotland, angrily told the Puritans that presbyteries "agreeth as well with a monarchy as God and the Devil," delivered the maxim "no bishop no king" to express his conviction that episcopacy and monarchy were interdependent, and threatened that if the Puritans did not conform, he would "harry them out of the land, or else do worse." Soon after the conference, canons compelling greater conformity to established church practices were promulgated, resulting in the expulsion of over two hundred Puritan ministers from their parishes. Puritanism began to take on a more radical hue, assuming more extreme positions against the worship of the church and against episcopacy as the governing institution of the church. The Hampton Court Conference had a happier result as well: James authorized a new translation of the Bible. Completed in 1611, the King James Version took its place as one of the greatest works of English prose.

PARLIAMENT

Every Tudor monarch had used Parliament to undertake major pro-grams of change: Henry VII to establish civil order, Henry VIII to accomplish the break with Rome, Edward VI to establish Protestantism, Mary to dismantle it, Elizabeth to reconstruct it. During the latter years of Elizabeth's reign there had been considerable continuity in the mem-bership of the House of Commons, more frequent sessions to obtain par-liamentary revenue for the war with Spain, and growing assertiveness by the Commons. The Spanish war dampened opposition during the 1590's, but in 1601 the old queen had to go personally to Parliament, concede to the vehement demand of the Commons for the suppression of royal monopolies, and smooth frayed tempers with her last great dulcet song of affection. Many members of the 1601 Parliament returned to sit in James's first Parliament in March, 1604.

The House of Commons was composed mostly of the landed gentry of England and Wales. There were approximately five hundred members: two representatives from each English county; one from each Welsh county; and two representatives each from towns that happened to have sent mem-bers in the late Middle Ages or that had been enfranchised by the Tu-dors. The county members were elected on a fairly broad franchise that included most substantial farmers as well as the gentry, although election rigging was common practice. With few exceptions the town members were elected by the town merchant oligarchies. Only London and a few other major economic centers, however, consistently returned merchant members. Increasingly during the sixteenth century the towns returned neighboring gentlemen, often at the behest of a powerful patron — a councillor of the king, a nobleman, or a major gentleman of the county. Many lawyers, who by status and inclination were as one with the gentry, were elected. Noblemen sat in the House of Lords, a body that could stop positive action taken by the Commons but could not prevent negative action taken by the Commons to impede the course of legisla-tion or financial proposals.

The gentry who sat in the House of Commons were the masters of their counties. They held the reins of local administration as justices of the peace, sheriffs, and commanders of the militia, the only military force in England. Their economic dominance was built on the lands of the monasteries dissolved by Henry VIII and was constantly reinforced by wealth from trade, law, and royal service brought by new recruits to the class. They were educated well above the average of the period anywhere in Europe. They were jealous of their social position at home and as-sertive of their "privileges" as members of the House of Commons: im-munity from arrest except for serious crimes during sessions of Parliament, the right to settle disputed elections, and the right to debate freely with-out fear of reprisal.

If James I and Charles I (1625–1649) had been able to live within the limitations of the ordinary royal revenue, they would not have needed to summon Parliament. Indeed, twice (from 1614 to 1621 and from 1629 to 1640) they attempted to get along without Parliament for long periods. Rising prices, extravagance, unforeseen circumstances (especially wars), and the inability to reorganize the bureaucratic structure to gain greater yield from existing sources of ordinary revenue compelled James and Charles to use extraordinary means to raise revenue and ultimately to fall back on Parliament. This gave Parliament the initiative and the House of Commons demanded the righting of "grievances" — including the abolition of extraordinary means of raising revenue — before it granted money. The king, unable to manage the Commons, either had to consent to the abridgement of his power by eliminating the grievances or had to dissolve Parliament without obtaining the money needed. This dilemma arose time after time between 1604 and 1640, and in such a war of attrition the king was at a serious disadvantage.

THE GRIEVANCES, 1604–1621

In James's first Parliament the broader constitutional issues of grievances were joined with the Puritan desire for reform — a combination that became increasingly disruptive of relations between king and Parliament. The first grievances concerned the Commons' privileges of settling disputed elections and freedom from arrest. In both issues James acceded. Then the Commons, in an unprecedented document called the Apology of 1604, justified all its privileges and informed the king that it would no longer disregard the incursions on its privileges that it had allowed during Elizabeth's reign out of respect for her age and sex. During the course of this first Parliament, the Commons raised again the issue of monopolies (which Elizabeth had barely managed to quiet in 1601), attacked the ancient right of the king to levy a sum of money for provisions for the royal household, attacked increased custom duties, and threw out legislation proposed by James to unite his two realms, England and Scotland. Most significantly, it complained of the court of High Commission, the major ecclesiastical court, which was particularly zealous in making Puritans conform to the established order in the church.

An untoward incident during this first Parliament gave fresh impetus to an old fear. The number of Roman Catholics had decreased sharply during the last two decades of Elizabeth's reign. Unrelenting persecution by the government produced frustrations that found expression in extremism. In November, 1605, a handful of Catholic terrorists plotted to blow up king and Parliament in one blast of gunpowder hidden in the cellars of the Parliament building. The plot was foiled just in time. The Gunpowder Plot excited an almost psychotic fear of Catholicism, which gave the Puritans an opportunity to revive the specter of "popery" as the sole alternative to further reform of the English church.

Although it did not sit continuously, James's first Parliament remained in existence for seven years. It was dissolved in 1610. It had evidenced the complete breakdown of the king's ability to control the Commons by the presence of royal councillors exercising initiative in debate, the secret of Tudor parliamentary management. In the vacuum left, the Commons had instituted a sophisticated system of committees, making the House more manageable by the leaders of the opposition. After three years of foundering with extraparliamentary financial expedients, James summoned a Parliament in 1614. Opposition of members to the king's demands led to its quick dissolution, and four members were imprisoned in direct defiance of the Commons' claim to freedom of speech in debate. Six more years of financial expedients followed during which James initiated a foreign policy that seemed to threaten the future of Protestantism in England and to lend support to the Catholic Hapsburgs, who in 1618 had opened war against Protestantism on the Continent and whose first victim was James's own son-in-law, the Protestant king of Bohemia. James sought to marry his son and heir apparent, Charles, to the daughter of the king of Spain. Hatred of Spain and Catholicism made the "Spanish match" the prime grievance of the Parliament of 1621.

The Parliament began in a conciliatory mood. Money was granted readily on the understanding that the king would help his son-in-law and the Protestant cause on the Continent. Nonetheless, the old grievance against monopolies was raised immediately, and the Commons revived its long-disused power to impeach, that is, to put on trial before the House of Lords a person suspected of high crimes. The weapon was turned against two monopolists and two judges suspected of taking bribes, one of whom was no less a person than the Lord Chancellor, Francis Bacon. Convicted by the Lords, the defendants were heavily fined and dismissed from office. Then the Commons turned to the Spanish marriage, petitioning the king to extirpate Catholicism in England and marry his son to a Protestant princess. James replied that foreign policy was his prerogative, not to be discussed without his leave. The Commons' remonstrance was torn from the record by the king's own hand, Parliament was dissolved, and the chief leaders of the opposition were sent to prison.

The Parliament of 1621 was the turning point in the constitutional confrontation. The Spanish marriage proposal raised the specter of Catholicism as could no domestic issue. The impeachment of the monopolists and Bacon produced a weapon that could be used against any of the king's ministers in the future. The opposition organization in the Commons had reached maturity, and able leaders stepped forward to lead it.

THE CONSTITUTIONAL CONFRONTATION, 1624–1628

When James convoked his last Parliament in 1624, the Spanish marriage proposal had broken down; Prince Charles and James's young favorite, the duke of Buckingham, had visited the prospective bride in Madrid and found neither the lady nor her countrymen to their liking. Parliament convened in high hopes of a war to retrieve Protestant fortunes on the Continent. It was not disappointed. James, having denied the Commons' competency to discuss foreign affairs in 1621, now gave over to it the direction of his foreign policy, entreating it to give "your good and sound advice." James declared war on Spain, and the Commons gave him greater support than at any other time in his reign. James died just at the outbreak of hostilities, with his sincerely pacifist policy of the previous twenty years in ruins and the political initiative in the hands of Parliament.

Charles I, a youth of twenty-five, was as wholly under the influence of the duke of Buckingham as had been his father. Buckingham was a capable but erratic, power-hungry, and arrogant man. In the last five years of James's reign he had built up a system of patronage that put every aspect of administration and policy into his hands. He thirsted for military glory, and the war offered him his chance.

The war went badly from the onset. A naval expedition to Cádiz was wholly mismanaged. The Commons impeached Buckingham, and except for Charles's timely dissolution of Parliament in 1626, his beloved lieutenant would have fallen. The dissolution left a shortage of money to carry on the war. In 1626 and 1627 Charles sent out writs to selected wealthy people, ordering them to lend money to the government. This forced loan met with stout resistance, and a number of wealthy men were arrested for their refusal to lend. Troops were forcibly billeted on poorer subjects. Meanwhile, despite his marriage to the sister of King Louis XIII of France in 1625, Charles had drifted into war with France in 1627. Buckingham commanded an expedition to help the French Huguenots at La Rochelle. His utter defeat set the stage for the summoning of Parliament in 1628 to finance the woefully bungled war.

THE PETITION OF RIGHT

The new Parliament directed an attack against the king's prerogative, those powers which the king alone might exercise and for which he was not answerable to either Parliament or the law. Charles held that those who refused to pay the forced loan could be imprisoned by order of his council without cause being shown and that such imprisonment and the loan itself were justified by his prerogative. He also maintained that troops might be billeted on individuals in time of emergency for the defense of the realm. The Commons countered that these practices were against the liberties of the subject, which were assured by law. The issue was a constitutional one in which both sides based their arguments on unclear history, ambiguous law, and arbitrarily chosen precedents. The issue was compromised when the king assented to a petition of the Par-

Courtesy of The Louvre

Charles I of England, by H. G. Pot

"His kingly virtues had some mixture and alloy, that hindered them from shining in full lustre, and from producing those fruits they should have been attended with. . . . He was very fearless in his person, but not very enterprising. He had an excellent understanding, but was not confident enough of it; which made him oftentimes change his opinion for the worse, and follow the advice of men who did not judge so well as himself. This made him more irresolute than the conjuncture of his affairs would admit: if he had been of a rougher and more imperious nature he would have found more respect and duty." Earl of Clarendon (1609–1674), HISTORY OF THE GREAT REBELLION (London, 1888).

liament asking that the subject's liberties be confirmed — specifically, that no one be compelled to make a gift or loan without the consent of Parliament, that no man be imprisoned without cause being shown, and that troops not be billeted upon individuals against their will. The Petition of Right, as this was called, proved a landmark in assuring the liberties of Englishmen, although it was hardly honored by Charles in the next decade.

LAUDIANISM

Buckingham's assassination in 1628 by an officer whom he had failed to promote removed the most awkward grievance of the Commons, but a new one quickly took its place. It, too, was personified by an individual, William Laud (1573–1645), bishop of London. Laud represented a new generation of Elizabethan churchmen who had been born in the 1570's and 1580's. These men had attended Oxford and Cambridge just as the Puritan tide in each university was turned by vigorous repression from Elizabeth's last archbishop of Canterbury, John Whitgift. Their idea of church order was derived from a comprehensive theological treatise published in the 1590's by Richard Hooker, an Oxford theologian. He wrote, "And that kings should be in such sort supreme commanders over all men, we hold it requisite as well for the ordering of spiritual as civil affairs." The Puritans' presbyterianism seemed to these men to threaten the king's supremacy; the Puritans' three-hour sermons, stark severity of dress, lack of church ornamentation, and distaste for the liturgical grandeur of the Book of Common Prayer did not reflect the "hidden dignity and glory" of the church in heaven.

To the Puritans it seemed that Laud and his adherents were bringing the Anglican Church back to Rome. Nothing was further from the Laudians' intention, but in the superheated atmosphere of virulent anti-Catholicism in early seventeenth-century England guilt by association stuck. Laudianism lacked the local roots that were the strength of puritanism and had few clerical adherents outside the church hierarchy and the universities. Laudians controlled the church organization, however, and could count on royal support and the assistance of the machinery of the state in their determination to break puritanism once and for all.

PERSONAL RULE, 1629–1640

In the second session of the 1628 Parliament the Puritan opposition to Laudianism was inextricably wedded to the constitutionalist opposition to unparliamentary financial exactions, inflation of the king's prerogative, and incursions on the Commons' privileges. A full-scale attack was mounted against both the Laudian bishops and the king's levying of customs duties without parliamentary consent. Charles dissolved the Parliament, but not before the opposition leaders had held the speaker of the

Commons in the chair while the house in an uproar resolved that the Laudians and those who counseled such duties were "capital enemies to the kingdom and commonwealth." The opposition leaders went to prison, where the most outspoken of them, Sir John Eliot, died three years later. Charles resolved never to call another Parliament and to rule by prerogative alone. The next eleven years were the period of his personal rule.

Charles managed to end the wars with Spain and France, which had been the largest drain on his resources. In Laud (whom he made archbishop of Canterbury in 1633) he had a prelate who was able to break the leadership of puritanism by means of the courts of High Commission and Star Chamber, and who repressed puritanism with enough vigor to people Massachusetts with its exiles. In Thomas Wentworth, later earl of Strafford, Charles possessed an adviser who, having been one of the leaders of the opposition in the Commons in the 1620's, had an insider's knowledge of the opposition. Laud and Strafford worked in close harmony, strove for a thoroughgoing reassertion of royal authority, and managed to finance personal rule as long as peace lasted. Their ambition was considerable: the tightening of royal control of local government in England and the extortion of every possible revenue from England and Ireland. The former they accomplished through vigorous surveillance of the justices of the peace by the king's council and its agents, the circuit judges of assize. The latter they managed by exploiting every source of finance available through the king's prerogative. These included customs duties, ship money (a tax on the counties of England to support the navy), the sale of offices, honors, monopolies, and immunities, heavy fines in Star Chamber for all kinds of derelictions or payments to avoid punishment there, and large loans floated through the city of London. By 1637 the personal rule seemed secure.

In that year Charles and Laud attempted to impose the Anglican Book of Common Prayer on the Presbyterian Church in Scotland. The reaction was a national rebellion. Charles was forced to raise the militia in England to reassert royal authority in Scotland. In 1639 he suffered a humiliating defeat at the hands of the Scots and was forced to make concessions that required heavy financing. Laud and Strafford urged him to summon Parliament; there was no other way to raise the money needed.

"ANOTHER PROTESTANT REPUBLIC"

In April Charles convened Parliament, only to be assailed by John Pym, leader of the opposition in Commons, for every act both secular and religious of his personal rule; the king dissolved Parliament after just three weeks. Charles's renewal of the attack against the Scots in the summer precipitated the disintegration of personal rule and European statesmen feared that England was about to become "another Protestant republic." The English militia was in mutiny, revenue was uncollectable, and sedition and civil commotion were rife. After the Scots had occupied the north of England and had only been halted by Charles's promise to buy them off, Charles convened his fifth (and last) Parliament in November. The Long Parliament (it did not formally dissolve until 1660) had Charles firmly in its grip, for if he could not get the money to pay the Scots, a Scottish Presbyterian army might make common cause with the English Puritans and overthrow him altogether.

THE LONG PARLIAMENT

Between November, 1640, and September, 1641, under the able leadership of Pym the Long Parliament unanimously dismantled the personal rule. Strafford was executed, Laud imprisoned for four years and then executed, other ministers driven into exile, the bishops reduced to obedience, the judges subdued, and Puritan prisoners of the previous decade released from jail. Ship money was declared illegal. The courts of High Commission and Star Chamber were abolished, and the king's power to commit persons to prison was made judicially reviewable. Statutes were passed requiring that Parliament be summoned at least every three years and that the existing Parliament not be dismissed without its consent. To all of this Charles assented; he had no choice.

The unanimity with which the members of the House of Commons carried through these measures continued until the late summer of 1641. Until then Pym had managed to curb the question of further reform of the Church, but he finally felt obliged to give in to a radical Puritan element in the Commons that sought to abolish episcopacy. An equally sizable element defended episcopacy. Those who believed that the king had conceded enough to safeguard the liberty of the subject attached themselves to this group. In November a massive catalog of the government's misdeeds coupled with a demand for remedies that would clearly abridge the king's prerogative was adopted by the Commons by a majority of only eleven votes.

The initiative still rested with Pym. Rightly distrusting Charles's sincerity, he sought further safeguards in the coming months. An armed attempt by the king personally to arrest Pym and four other leaders in the Commons failed. Pym attempted to push through legislation that would transfer command of the militia — the nation's only army — from the king to Parliament. Charles refused to give his consent, retired to the north, and in August, 1642, called upon his loyal subjects to join him in suppression of the Parliament. Nearly half the Commons rallied to his standard. The civil war had begun.

CIVIL WAR, 1642–1648

Most of those who chose sides in this conflict did so on the basis of political and religious scruples. Nevertheless, certain patterns appeared in the choice of allegiances in the conflict. There was no clear class distinction between the leaders of the Royalists and the Parliamentarians: they were all substantial landed gentlemen. Age and locale appear to have affected the commitment of the individual gentleman more than his wealth or social status. The gentlemen in the king's camp were by and large younger than those in Parliament's. Younger men were more susceptible to the color and dignity of the Laudian-influenced church, in reaction to the severity of their elders' puritanism. The majority of the Royalists came from the west and north, while those of the Parliamentarian cause came principally from the south and east, where puritanism had always been stronger. The people of the south and east were also more active in trade, industry, and finance, although this fact does not justify the frequently drawn inference that the Parliamentarians were the economically predominant element foreclosing on a bankrupt monarchy. Economic factors played a more important role in the choice of allegiances further down the social scale. The lesser gentry, those on the lower economic rungs, were jealous of the dominance of the greater gentry and saw a chance of increased power in the cause of Parliament. The nobility was overwhelmingly Royalist. The merchants (numerically many times greater than the nobility) were overwhelmingly Parliamentarian; most of the larger towns went Parliamentarian, even in areas that were Royalist. The rank and file of the two armies evidenced wide social differences. The king's army depended heavily on farmers and agrarian laborers; the Parliamentarian army included a large artisan element, which provided it with capable noncommissioned officers. The mass of the population preferred neutrality, but this luxury was not long allowed them, for as the war dragged on and on, both sides began conscripting troops.

The center of Parliamentarian power was London. The king's headquarters were in Oxford, sixty miles northwest of the metropolis. The navy went Parliamentarian at once and blocked assistance to Charles from Holland and France. The first two years of the war saw a great deal of skirmishing, culminating in a sizable advance by the king's forces toward London and the Parliamentarian perimeter in late 1643. To meet this threat the Parliamentarians mounted a bold new force, the New Model Army, drawn from the militia of the eastern counties. It was well disciplined, highly puritan in ideology, and ably officered. The second-in-command was a masterful strategist, member of Parliament, and landed gentleman named Oliver Cromwell. In a series of bitter engagements in 1644 and 1645 the New Model Army crushed the Royalists, forcing Charles to retreat northward. In 1646 Charles surrendered to the Scottish army. The Scots had come in on Parliament's side when Parliament agreed in the Solemn League and Covenant in 1643 to establish presbyterianism in England.

The victor was Cromwell and the New Model Army more than it was

Parliament and the Scottish allies. The New Model Army had a strongly radical political and religious complexion. Some noncommissioned officers and enlisted men demanded a broader franchise that would in effect extend the vote to handicraftsmen and small farmers (that is, to themselves). This won them the name Levellers. Others, called Independents, demanded congregationalism, that is, the autonomy of each church congregation. They opposed the presbyterian system supported by the majority in Parliament in which individual congregations were grouped together and governed by elected courts or presbyteries made up of clerics and laymen. Cromwell and most of the officers of the army favored congregationalism, although they were more conservative than most of the rank and file.

After two years of negotiations with the Scots, Charles won them to his cause by promising to establish presbyterianism in England and he started the war again. A rapid defeat of the Scots by the New Model Army resulted in the end of the presbyterian majority in the Commons — and the end of the monarchy. In December, 1648, a detachment of New Model troops led by Colonel Pride barred the presbyterian members from the Commons. The "Rump" — what was left of the Commons after "Pride's Purge" — tried Charles on the ground that he was an enemy of the people. In January, 1649, he was publicly beheaded, monarchy was abolished, and "another Protestant republic" was indeed established, called by its founders the Commonwealth.

THE COMMONWEALTH, 1649–1653

The government of the Commonwealth consisted of the fewer than one hundred members remaining in the Commons and a council of state elected by them. The House of Lords was dissolved. There was no clear authority except in the army, where Cromwell was leader. The all-important question of church organization was settled by having the church remain subject to the authority of the state — a far cry from Calvinist theocracy. Control over the church was in the hands of county committees, who also controlled local government. To destroy royalism and episcopalianism, many Royalists' lands were seized and the lands of the former church hierarchy were confiscated. Royalists who wished to save their lands from confiscation had to pay heavy fines, and in order to pay the fines, they often had to sell much of their estate. The beneficiaries of the land grab were merchants, lawyers, speculators, army officers, bureaucrats, and lesser gentry. A new landowning element came into existence, and despite partial restitution of lands to their former owners when the monarchy was restored in 1660, this new landowning element remained.

There was little enthusiasm outside the ruling group for the new government. Radical agitation continued to disturb the army. In addition, the government had to put down revolts in Ireland and Scotland.

During the reigns of James and Charles unrest had developed in Ireland over English efforts to convert the Catholic Irish to Protestantism, the settlement of English and Scottish Protestants in northern Ireland on land confiscated from Catholic Irish rebels, and the generally harsh rule of the English. Open revolt broke out in 1641, but neither the king nor Parliament could spare the soldiers to put down the rebellion. After the death of Charles, the Irish proclaimed his son, Charles II, their king. Late in 1649 Cromwell led an army across the Irish Channel and defeated the rebels. The savagery of his troops, who hated the Catholic Irish, and the extreme harshness of his settlement, by which thousands of rebels had to give up their lands to English and Scottish settlers, left a legacy of bitterness and hatred for England that has not yet disappeared. In 1651 Cromwell defeated a Scottish invasion that was also aimed at putting Charles II on the throne.

Meanwhile, Parliament was tied up in incessant wrangling over various constitutional proposals and reforms. Its strong civilian bias threatened the continued domination of the army. In April, 1653, Cromwell led soldiers into the Commons and drove out the members. Later that year he summoned a hand-picked Parliament of "godly men," derisively called the Barebones Parliament from one of its members who bore the name of Praisegod Barebones, but this assembly wanted more radical religious changes than suited the conservative leadership in the army. Cromwell's fellow officers convinced him to dismiss it and accept a new constitution called the Instrument of Government drawn up by them.

THE PROTECTORATE, 1653–1660

The new constitution of December, 1653, represented a form of quasi-monarchy. Cromwell was designated Lord Protector, ruling with a council and a Parliament composed of an Other House (similar to the old House of Lords) and a House of Commons, with which the Lord Protector was to share legislative power and the control of the army and navy. The franchise for election of members of the Commons was more restrictive than the old franchise. The Instrument, the first written constitution of the English-speaking peoples, was an attempt at legitimacy on Cromwell's part, but Parliament and Protector quickly found that they could not get along with one another. To suppress growing unrest, Cromwell imposed military rule on England. He purged the army of its more extremist elements and purged Parliament of the members who opposed him. Those who remained in the Commons offered to make him king. He refused the crown but accepted their offer to make the protectorship hereditary. The move cost him the allegiance of republicans. His support of religious toleration lost him the religious extremists. Burdensome taxes alienated everyone. He was forced to rely upon the army for the power to preserve order. As long as he lived, Cromwell never lost control of the army.

Courtesy of the National
Portrait Gallery, London

Oliver Cromwell, after S. Cooper

An Enemy Pays Tribute to Cromwell: *"He was one of those men whose enemies cannot curse him without at the same time praising him; for he could never have done half that mischief without great parts of courage and industry and judgement. And he must have had a wonderful understanding in the natures and humours of men, and as great a dexterity in applying them, who from a private and obscure birth (though of a good family), without interest of estate, alliance or friendships, could raise himself to such a height. . . . Wickedness as great as his could never have accomplished those trophies without the assistance of a great spirit, and admirable circumspection and sagacity, and a most magnanimous resolution."* Earl of Clarendon (1609–1674), HISTORY OF THE GREAT REBELLION (London, 1888).

When Cromwell died in 1658, his son Richard succeeded to the Lord Protectorship. By 1659 Richard had lost control of the army. Political chaos resulted. The man who stepped forward to end it was George Monk, an ex-Royalist but loyal Cromwellian general. Resisting the temptation to establish a military dictatorship, he sought stability by recalling the Long Parliament just as it had been prior to the purge of the presbyterians in 1648. Behind Monk stood the navy, most of the army, the city of London, legitimists, presbyterians, and Anglicans — in short, all those who had tasted too much of political instability and feared military dictatorship.

Charles II, who had been in exile on the Continent, issued a conciliatory statement at Breda, a town in the Netherlands, expressing his willingness to accept parliamentary government. Reassured by the Declaration of Breda, Parliament invited Charles to take the throne. He returned unconditionally, leaving to Parliament the terms of the amnesty to be extended to his former opponents (except those who had signed his father's death warrant), the religious settlement by which to restore the Church of England, and the question of the disposal of confiscated lands. Parliament settled these questions with considerable moderation and substantial justice. All the acts that had been passed in the Long Parliament from 1640 to 1642 and received Charles I's assent were held to be legally valid. The later ordinances of the Long Parliament and of the republican period were held to be null and void. Legally, it was as if the previous eighteen years had never occurred.

In other respects the previous years were not so easily eradicated. A king had been destroyed — not by covert murder following deposition, not on the field of battle, not by a mob, but by due process of law, even if the tribunal was illegal. In the last weeks of the king's life the House of Commons had declared "that the people are, under God, the original of all just power." Men could forget neither the action nor the words, and if in 1660 almost every Englishman viewed with horror the possible repetition of the execution of the king, the fact that institutionalized opposition had brought down a monarch in the name of the people made monarchy anything but absolute in England.

THE RISE OF THE DUTCH REPUBLIC

Although in 1609 Spain agreed to a twelve-year truce with the States-General of the seven northern provinces of the Netherlands (see p. 161), it refused to recognize the legal independence of the rebel provinces. The truce left Spain in control of the ten southern provinces. The boundary between north and south did not correspond with the linguistic, cultural, or religious boundaries of the Low Countries. After the truce the ten southern Spanish-controlled provinces were thoroughly re-Catholicized

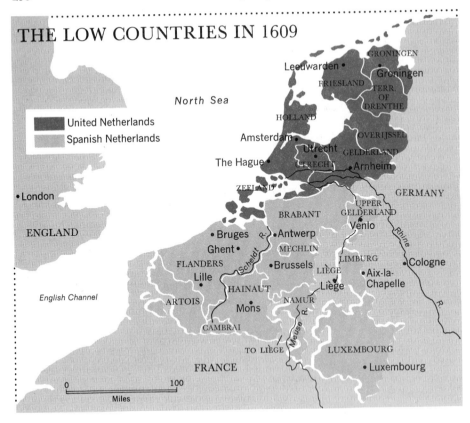

THE LOW COUNTRIES IN 1609

United Netherlands
Spanish Netherlands

North Sea

London

ENGLAND

English Channel

GERMANY

FRANCE

Leeuwarden • GRONINGEN
Groningen
FRIESLAND TERR. OF DRENTHE

HOLLAND

Amsterdam • OVERIJSSEL
Utrecht GELDERLAND
The Hague • UTRECHT Arnheim

ZEELAND

UPPER GELDERLAND
BRABANT
Venlo
• Bruges • Antwerp
Ghent • MECHLIN
FLANDERS • Brussels LIMBURG • Cologne
Lille LIÈGE
HAINAUT • Aix-la-Chapelle
ARTOIS NAMUR Liège
Mons
CAMBRAI
TO LIÈGE LUXEMBOURG
• Luxembourg

Rhine R.
Scheldt R.
Meuse R.

0   100
Miles

by Spanish Jesuits. The United Provinces or Dutch Republic to the north stood independent.

Dutch independence cut two ways. Each of the seven provinces retained a large measure of independence from the others. The Union of Utrecht of 1579 had established a loose confederation of the provinces with a national assembly, the States-General, composed of delegates from the provincial assembly or States of each province. The provincial assemblies were institutions of medieval origin representing the nobility and the various towns of the province. Each provincial States elected its own chief minister or stadholder. The States-General had jurisdiction over foreign affairs and defense. Traditionally it chose as its executive officer or captain general the stadholder of the province of Holland, who was also stadholder of four other provinces. In this complex arrangement of authority sovereignty was ill-defined. The history of the Dutch Republic between 1609 and 1660 is above all the history of the struggle between the proponents of provincial sovereignty, seeking to preserve the loose confederation and almost fanatically opposed to centralizing tendencies, and the adherents of the captain general, seeking to create a tighter federal union responsive to his authority.

PROVINCIAL DOMINANCE UNDER OLDENBARNEVELDT

Political and economic preeminence within the republic belonged to the province of Holland. It was the second largest, the most populous, and geographically the most commanding of the seven provinces. It was also the seat of government, and it contained Amsterdam, economic heart of the country. The States of Holland was led by Jan van Oldenbarneveldt (1547–1619). As holder of the appointive office of advocate, Oldenbarneveldt was nominally the servant of the States, but through his outstanding abilities and power of persuasion he became the commanding figure in the assembly. He headed the delegation of Holland to the States-General, and as chief representative of the most important province he dominated the States-General. For all practical purposes he determined the policies of the United Provinces. He overshadowed Maurice of Nassau (1587–1625), William the Silent's son and successor as captain general and stadholder of Holland. It was Oldenbarneveldt who had the political finesse to unite the seven provinces behind Maurice's brilliant war effort against the Spanish. It was also he who arranged the truce of 1609 against the will of Maurice.

Oldenbarneveldt's tenure marked one of the two periods of provincial dominance in the republic in the seventeenth century. The growing conflict between him and Maurice illustrates the conflict of sovereignty in the new republic between the provinces and the central government, represented by the captain general. The clash centered around a dispute between strict Calvinists and the Arminians, who were followers of Jacobus Arminius (1560–1609), a liberal Dutch theologian. Arminius challenged the rigid doctrine of predestination. He argued that by the exercise of will a man could condition his chance for eternal salvation or damnation. Oldenbarneveldt's sympathies were with the Arminians, while for political reasons Maurice declared himself a supporter of the strict Calvinists.

Oldenbarneveldt had also alienated some of the merchants of Amsterdam, who controlled the purse strings of the country. These men wanted to form a company that would challenge the lucrative monopoly of the Dutch East India Company, founded in 1602. Oldenbarneveldt, who was a key official of the East India Company, successfully opposed their plans, and the indignant merchants sided with Maurice and the orthodox Calvinists.

Continued religious disputes brought on civil disorders and a threatened break between the States-General and the province of Holland. The States of Holland raised a small army and took steps toward a declaration of independence from the States-General. Maurice and the States-General took up the challenge, and in 1618 Maurice marched into the province of Holland at the head of a body of troops. Not a hand was raised against him in defense of the position of the States of Holland, and Maurice took over undisputed control. Oldenbarneveldt was arrested, and after a trial before a special court without legal jurisdiction, nearly all of whose members were his personal enemies, he was executed in 1619.

STADHOLDER VERSUS STATES-GENERAL

Maurice's victory allowed him to tighten the loose confederation into a closer union that was increasingly dependent upon the captain general. His brother and successor, Frederick Henry of Orange (1625–1647), sought to centralize power still further. Persuaded by his brilliant generalship in the war with Spain that began in 1621, the States of the five provinces of which he was stadholder agreed to settle the succession on his sons. This was a clear break with the elective principle of the stadholdership.

Frederick Henry made himself a monarch in all but name. At the Hague he maintained a court that rivaled the courts of kings in its splendor. By marrying William, his son and heir apparent, to the eldest daughter of Charles I of England, he added luster to his upstart dynasty. He played power politics in the grand manner, allying the republic to Richelieu's France in the 1630's. He staffed the council of state with his own nominees, had ambassadors abroad correspond directly with him, and in 1634 obtained the support of the States-General for establishing a standing committee of that body, called the Secret Council, under his control.

Frederick Henry's dynastic alliance with the Stuart monarchy in England was a major ingredient in the downfall of his ambitions. His involvement on the side of Charles I brought him into serious conflict with the Calvinist merchants of Holland, whose economic interests, religious predilections, and political views put them in complete sympathy with

---

Two Women with a Child Learning to Walk,
by Rembrandt van Rijn

> *"Light removes in Rembrandt's works all restraints of studio-convention and manneristic formalism. The world of historical imagination became for him a world he had experienced in real life. He got his imagination out of observation of real life. That is Rembrandt's quite personal creative power, which enabled him to revolutionize the old academic convention. . . .*
> *This manner of acquiring imagination through life experience is a constructive element in Rembrandt's art. In the mirror of reality, he perceived his mental world. This world shows his own features."* Otto Benesch,
> REMBRANDT AS A DRAUGHTSMAN (Garden City, N.Y., 1960).

Courtesy of the Rijksmuseum

the English Parliamentarians. His alliance with France worked against him, too. In 1646 the Dutch discovered that Spain and France, who were at war with each other, were considering a deal by which France was to gain the neighboring Spanish Netherlands. Since France was considered a greater threat to Dutch independence than Spain, Frederick Henry was forced to begin peace negotiations with Spain. William II, who succeeded his father in 1647, wanted to continue the war, but Holland and the States-General wanted it to end. The latter prevailed and the Treaty of Münster was signed in 1648.

William, who was blocked at every move by the supporters of provincial rights, planned a coup against the States of Holland, but he died in 1650 before he could carry through his plan. His only child was not yet born. The States of Holland, the only effective authority remaining, found itself in command of the republic. A great national assembly was convened in 1651 to reestablish the old provincial autonomy. In 1653 the States-General delivered such powers as Oldenbarneveldt had formerly held into the capable hands of Jan De Witt, the chief executive or grand pensionary of Holland. The second golden age of Dutch republicanism began. It lasted until the return to power of the Orange dynasty in the person of William III as stadholder in 1672.

THE FIRST ANGLO-DUTCH WAR

It is ironical that just as republicanism reasserted itself in the Netherlands upon the death of William II and triumphed in England with the execution of Charles I in 1649, the two Protestant republics drifted into war with one another. Behind the first Anglo-Dutch war of 1652 to 1654 was a long commercial rivalry that had seen a number of tense and bloody confrontations in the East Indies, North America, and the West Indies. In what is today Indonesia, the English East India Company (founded in 1600) challenged its Dutch counterpart. In 1651 the English Parliament passed the Navigation Act, aimed at destroying the near-complete monopoly of the English carrying trade by Dutch shipping. The English demand to search Dutch ships suspected of carrying French goods (England and France were engaged in an undeclared maritime war) was resisted by the Dutch and triggered the war.

It was a maritime war of incredible feats of seamanship and valor on both sides. The Dutch admiral Tromp and the English admiral Blake were almost evenly matched as masters of naval tactics. England triumphed because of greater resources and a larger fleet of more heavily armed warships, built up during the civil war, whereas the Dutch relied mainly on armed merchantmen. The death of Tromp in action in July, 1653, while he was attempting to break the English blockade of the Dutch ports, helped to decide the outcome. The Dutch made peace overtures to Cromwell, who was in complete command of England. His reservations about war with a sister Protestant republic and hopes for a political union between the two induced him to meet the Dutch halfway. The treaty stipulated the expulsion of the exiled Stuarts from Holland and in a secret clause carried an ambiguous guarantee by the Dutch to exclude the house of Orange from the captain-generalship of the Dutch republic. This guarantee was meant to prevent assistance to the Stuarts from their Orange in-laws; it was repudiated on the restoration of the Stuart dynasty in England in 1660. The treaty was not harsh and did not seriously weaken the Dutch commercial dominance. Nevertheless, in two ways the war was decisive: it laid the foundation for English naval preponderance, which after 1688 was as much a bulwark to Dutch independence as before it had been a threat; and it determined the tactics of naval warfare for a century to come.

DUTCH DIVERSITY

To stress the political, religious, and constitutional struggles of the Dutch republic, its foreign entanglements, and its commercial dominance is to do less than justice to a nation whose diversity, like its resoluteness, was out of all proportion to its size. Nowhere else in Christian Europe was there such a large measure of toleration in religion in the early seventeenth century. Despite orthodox Calvinism's triumph within the state church after Oldenbarneveldt's death in 1619, there was little persecution of Roman Catholicism. A synagogue of Spanish Jews was publicly dedicated in Amsterdam in 1598, where Jews were readily accepted in the following years. The Dutch example persuaded Denmark, Savoy, Modena, and England under Cromwell to invite Jewish settlement. It was an Amsterdam Jew, Baruch Spinoza (1632–1677), who carried Cartesianism to its ultimate theological end by equating God and nature. It was an Arminian, Hugo Grotius (1583–1645), who laid the foundation for the rational and peaceable ordering of man's affairs on a global scale in the first systematic treatise on international law.

THE FLOWERING OF DUTCH CULTURE

The first half of the seventeenth century was the great period of Dutch art. The arts expressed the diversity of Dutch society as well as the exhilarating sense of integrity that came from newly won independence. Commercial wealth created a patron class that supported and encouraged the arts.

The impact of diversity was most evident in the differences between Dutch architecture and painting. Architecture in the Netherlands (north and south) in the late sixteenth century was manneristic in the extreme. Flamboyant strapwork decoration overpowered the classical lines of the structure itself. In the seventeenth century the manneristic style remained highly favored in the republic, while it was replaced in the Spanish Netherlands by the baroque. Under the stadholdership of Frederick Henry the Dutch Republic experienced a new elegance, in which the houses of the richer merchants and nobility expressed an absolutely correct and simple classicism.

In painting, on the other hand, Dutch artists created their own style. Their patrons were municipal councils, townsmen's clubs, and substantial merchants — but not the Calvinist Church, which called art "popish idolatry." Dutch patrons demanded portraits that depicted their own solid virtues and serenity, town scenes, seascapes, landscapes, animal pictures, and still lifes. The artists tried to capture quiet scenes of everyday life and objects that appealed to the material instincts of an affluent and comfortable people. Each town, especially in Holland, produced coteries of artists supported locally. Specialization was rife: a patron might turn to three different artists for a portrait, a canal scene, and a still life of oysters on a pewter platter.

Dutch painting was by and large sober, unspectacular, patient, detailed, and soft in color. The artists were extremely sensitive to light and shade, which they used to achieve visual unity — unlike the baroque artists, who used light to create startling dramatic effects. Out of the very rich run of Dutch painters, three can be selected for special mention. Frans Hals of Mechlin (1580–1666) specialized in group portraiture. He was more successful in grouping and capturing the dynamics of individual figures in a mass than in portraying personal character. Jan Vermeer of Delft (1632–1675) was a master of the home scene, immortalizing the prosaic of life in incredibly still, hushed tones. Although his technique was extraordinary, his most compelling characteristic was his complete detachment from the scene. Under his flawless brushwork mirrors and musical instruments and even people were transformed into a still life.

Rembrandt van Rijn of Amsterdam (1606–1669) towered over all other Dutch painters. He dealt with the common stuff of his countrymen, seeking an unsmiling sobriety and somberness. He cannot be called baroque because his passion was internalized, unlike Rubens's. Yet he was as intense and masterful as Rubens. He brought enormous psychological insight to his portraits and religious scenes. Working from the restricted horizon of Dutch painters, he came close to expressing the full range of human experience. No human emotion was outside his grasp, except joy; he repressed gaiety for serenity. This one flaw, reflecting the solid virtues of republican Holland and the moral overtones of a Calvinist environment, robbed him of unquestioned supremacy in the European art of his century.

ENGLAND AND HOLLAND — A BACKWARD GLANCE

During the two generations when the dominant tide in the principal powers of Europe was toward royal absolutism, in England and Holland alone the flood tide was turned to ebb. There were certain common causes for the reversal. In both countries the challenge to the authority of the state inherent in Calvinism was a potent solvent of absolutist ideas and sentiments. Unified moneyed interests centered in London and Amsterdam provided counterpoises to the power of the state. If Frederick Henry had been able to subvert Amsterdam's oligarchy or Charles I had been able to take London, the history of the two countries might have been different. The continuing vitality of representative institutions provided a platform for opposition to absolutism in both nations. The representative institutions also determined the conservative cast of mind of the opposition. Those who struggled against absolutism in Holland and England based their opposition on backward-looking principles, such as the preservation of "provincial sovereignty" or the "liberties of the subject." Although this circumstance grew from their basic commitment to historical representative institutions, it was fortuitous that the two men who wielded greatest power were not subverted by triumph. Jan de Witt and Oliver Cromwell, unlike many liberators who have entered a revolutionary matrix only to leave the mold as despots, were men of rare moderation. Above all, they were children of the States and Parliament.

ABSOLUTISM, ENLIGHTENMENT, AND REVOLUTION (1660-1815)
PART TWO

INTRODUCTION: ERA OF TRANSFORMATION

The period from the mid-seventeenth to the early nineteenth century was one of the great creative epochs in western history. Scientific breakthroughs made by men of genius in the later seventeenth century firmly established the mechanistic interpretation of the physical universe. Their discoveries also provided the intellectual movement of the eighteenth century that was called the Enlightenment with its belief in the power of reason to uncover universal natural laws that govern social behavior, just as the great natural scientists had found out the laws that govern physical matter. Transformations in economic life increased man's efficiency in the production of goods, manufactured and grown, and launched the European world on industrial and agricultural expansion that soon took on revolutionary proportions. During this epoch the political framework of our own times was established by the final triumph of the secular nation-state. The religious struggle that had kept Europe in turmoil for more than a century ended, and with it went the last hopes for a united Western Christendom. Religious disputes continued to disturb the internal peace of some countries and to affect relationships between nations, but religion no longer exercised the influence it once had in European affairs.

ABSOLUTISM, OLD AND NEW

By 1660 the absolutist solution to the continuing problem posed by the efforts of the nobility to increase its power at the expense of the sovereign and to the problem of creating the modern nation-state had won wide acceptance. The personal rule of Louis XIV of France brought absolutism in that country to its pinnacle, provided it with enough momentum to last three-quarters of a century after his death, and spawned imitators all over Europe. Russia emerged as a European power under the rule of Peter the Great, whose conscious imitation of the practices of Western absolutist monarchs was a kind of technological borrowing no less important than the technicians and artisans he imported into Russia in his program of "europeanization." In the eighteenth century a new brand of absolutism known as enlightened despotism evolved. It used the doctrines of the Enlightenment to justify absolutism, as theorists had used divine right in the sixteenth and seventeenth centuries. In three states absolutism was successfully resisted by oligarchies that won over princely pretensions: England, the Dutch Republic, and Poland. Of these three, Poland did not survive the eighteenth century, the Dutch Republic declined economically and militarily, and England alone emerged as a first-rank power able to seize an empire and retain unimpaired its representative institutions.

Absolutism, though it differed from state to state, invariably comprised governmental centralization, both legal and administrative, and a consequent growth of a bureaucracy dependent upon the absolute monarch; subjugation of the church within the monarch's domain and enforcement of religious uniformity as a facet of political loyalty; a standing army subject to the monarch's discipline; and an amalgam of economic policies aimed at building a strong national economy to make the state as self-sufficient as possible and thereby increase its capacity to wage successful wars. In the absolutisms of western Europe the nobility's power was eroded by the decline in the power of its traditional representative institutions, the process of centralization, and the rise through service to the monarch of a new nobility dependent upon the ruler's favor. In central and eastern Europe the absolutist monarch subjugated the nobility to his will by drawing them into state service and by allowing them greater privileges over their peasants. The object of absolutism everywhere was not domestic order and public welfare so much as the aggrandizement of the territory, the power, and the glory of the monarch and of his dynasty. Marriage alliances contracted between royal dynasties and wars were the accepted means to these ends. With the added dimension of the colonial dependencies of the powers, dynastic wars became in fact world wars.

REVOLUTION

In the last quarter of the eighteenth century the outbreak of revolution in the New World and the Old announced the end of absolutism and the dawn of a new democratic age. During the French Revolution wars were fought for the first time by mass mobilization of citizens in the defense and furtherance of a secular ideology. And for the first time — though unhappily not the last — the European world witnessed the facility with which democratic ideology could be turned to serve the ambitions of a dictator and support the apparatus of a despotic state bent upon conquest abroad.

THE PINNACLE OF
FRENCH ABSOLUTISM
CHAPTER ELEVEN

Absolutism reached its apogee during the long reign of Louis XIV. His France was consciously and sometimes slavishly imitated by monarchs of other lands in statecraft, bureaucracy, military organization, and the more ostentatious features of culture. There was certainly no more glittering model to follow. When Louis began his personal rule in 1661 his kingdom was the strongest in Europe. Spain was a defeated second-class power; the English king had just regained the throne; the Hapsburg emperor's hegemony in Germany was shattered and he was struggling against the Turks on the eastern frontiers. Within France a discredited nobility, having had its fling in the Fronde, was softened for the servility offered by Louis. The French administrative structure was the most highly developed in Europe. The Church, the middle ranks of society, and the corporate towns of France were solidly behind the throne. Richelieu and Mazarin, who had run France for almost four decades, had done their work well.

"I AM THE STATE"

Louis's parents, Louis XIII and Anne of Austria, detested one another; they had been married for twenty-three years before Louis, their first child, was born in 1638. So surprised were the French at the unexpected event that they hailed the infant "Louis the Godgiven." Five years later Louis XIII died and the child became Louis XIV, the third Bourbon king of France. As a youth, Louis gave little promise that he was to become one of the most renowned rulers of all time. The direction of his education was entrusted to Cardinal Mazarin. Apparently the tutors appointed by the cardinal did only a mediocre job in instructing their royal pupil in the usual academic subjects, but to judge from his later career, his tutelage under the masterful cardinal provided a matchless training in the art of absolutist kingship.

Louis XIV of France, by Hyacinthe Rigaud

*"He was born prudent, temperate, discreet, master of his emotions and his
tongue; can it be believed? he was born good and just, and God had endowed
him with sufficient to become a good king and perhaps even a rather great one
. . . Glory was to him a weakness rather than an ambition. . . Submissiveness,
servility, an air of admiration combined with sycophancy, and above all, an air
of being nothing without him, were the only ways to win his favor. If a man
strayed from this path ever so little there was no return for him."*
MÉMOIRES DE SAINT-SIMON (1675–1755) (Paris, 1916), Vol. XVIII.

When Cardinal Mazarin died in 1661, Frenchmen expected a new first minister to conduct the affairs of state while the handsome twenty-three-year-old king continued to content himself with the semblance of power. Instead, Louis called together his counselors and told them that he intended to be his own first minister and would run the state himself. Louis thus recaptured personal oversight of a bureaucracy that in its very complexity and efficiency threatened to serve its own interests rather than the king's. Louis believed himself to be by God's will the personification of the state and therefore the person best able to decide on the needs and interests of the realm. According to him, whatever aggrandized his own power and glory and that of his dynasty, aggrandized the power and glory of France. Although he never actually spoke the words "L'état, c'est moi" (I am the State), which are almost universally attributed to him, he certainly reflected the sentiment that they expressed.

THE MAN

Louis, who set so high a value upon his person and opinions, was actually of little more than average intelligence and abilities, but he was supremely self-confident. He had a majestic appearance and great personal charm; in fact, he was courtliness personified. He was also blessed with robust good health. Always in complete control of himself, he never for a moment forgot his own place nor that of any of his subjects. Short on imagination but long on common sense, he knew how to conceal his true feelings and intentions, and he trusted no one. He worked methodically and unceasingly, spent six to nine hours each day on the affairs of state, and permitted nothing to interfere with his daily work routine. He was not a great man, but he possessed a rare combination of talents and qualities that enabled him to play to perfection the role he assigned himself. He well merited the title sometimes given him, the Grand Monarch.

Louis's marriage in 1660 to Maria Theresa, his first cousin and daughter of Philip IV of Spain, was a state marriage for purely dynastic ends. He never loved her, and indeed he had earlier fallen in love with and hoped to marry Marie Mancini, Cardinal Mazarin's niece. Within a year of his marriage to Maria Theresa he took his first mistress, Louise de La Vallière. Royal mistresses had never been rare in European courts, but in the late seventeenth century they were kept more openly. They were, in effect, an institution of state, providing the monarch such companionship and loving solace as a wife married for reasons of state could not provide. Mistresses were generally reliable and at least initially grateful; queens were too often neither. La Vallière loved Louis, and her affection was requited until 1667, when she was forced to share the Grand Monarch with a haughty lady-in-waiting to the queen, the marquise de Montespan. In 1674 La Vallière retired to a nunnery and the marquise held the field alone.

In 1669 the widow of the poet Paul Scarron had become the governess of the children of Louis and the marquise de Montespan. Madame Scarron, who was then thirty-four, came from a famous Huguenot family but had herself become a Catholic, and a particularly devout one. Her new post brought her to the constant attention of the king, who found himself attracted by her intellectual and physical qualities as well as her piety and correctness of manner. In 1678 he created her marquise de Maintenon. When the marquise de Montespan's involvement with a notorious sorceress and purveyor of love potions and poisons became public knowledge in 1680, Louis dropped his old mistress and installed the ex-governess in her place. In July, 1683, Queen Maria Theresa died (she once said that in all her married life she had only twenty days of happiness). She bore Louis six children, only one of whom survived — Louis the Dauphin (heir apparent). Shortly after her death Louis wed the marquise de Maintenon in a private ceremony, but because of her nonroyal birth and previous marriage Louis never officially recognized her as queen. The marriage proved a turning point in his career. He abandoned his love affairs, settled down to a life of almost middle-class respectability and quickened piety, and found domestic happiness.

"NONE HIS EQUAL"

There was no power in the France of Louis XIV to challenge his unique authority within the state. His emblem was the sun, the center of the universe; because of this he was sometimes called the Sun King. His motto was *Nec pluribus impar,* None his equal. He liked to think — and panegyrists like Bossuet never tired of telling him — that the rays of glory and power descended from him to all his inferiors.

Louis made it a principle of administration to exclude men of high birth from the most important government offices. He chose his ministers from humbler backgrounds, so that they would owe their prominence to him alone. At first his chief counselors, whom he inherited from Mazarin, were Michel Le Tellier, secretary of state for war; Hugues de Lionne, in charge of foreign affairs; and Nicholas Fouquet, superintendent of finances. All three were from families of bourgeois origin. Fouquet quickly came under the suspicion of the young king as being overly ambitious, and in September, 1661, he was arrested on charges of high treason. His trial lasted three years; he was finally condemned to life imprisonment. His place was taken by Jean Baptiste Colbert, son of a merchant of Rheims who had entered government service under Mazarin.

SUBJUGATION OF THE NOBILITY

Louis's exclusion of the old aristocracy from the innermost ruling circle was part of a deliberate plan to destroy once and for all the threat that the nobles as a class presented to the power of the monarch and to reduce them as individuals to a condition of subservience to him. He never convened the Estates-General of the kingdom, and his officials kept close scrutiny upon the provincial estates. Early in the reign he sent out special courts to hear complaints against nobles and to deal out punishments to those who abused their powers and mistreated their peasants. The most famous tribunal sat in the province of Auvergne in 1665 and 1666, where it condemned several nobles to death. Although personal influence saved most of these men from the block, the nobility of France realized that the king was determined to make his law and his will supreme over the old feudal privileges.

Louis further diminished the status of the nobility by selling patents of nobility to wealthy commoners as a way of raising money and as a reward for faithful service. Although earlier monarchs had done the same, the traffic in titles reached a new peak in Louis's reign. He further cheapened the value of a title by revoking all new grants of nobility nine times during his reign and then compelling the nobles to purchase them over again. He broke with precedent by imposing taxes on the nobility. Immunity from ordinary taxes had long been one of the most prized privileges of the aristocracy; their contribution was supposedly in the form of military and other governmental services of feudal origin. The great wars of the last half of Louis's reign created such a need for money that in 1695 the king decided to levy a head tax on the nobles as well as all his other subjects, and in 1710 he ordered them to pay an income tax of 10 per cent, called the *dixième* or tenth.

Louis struck the most damaging blow at the nobility by making attendance at court and adulation of his person the price of favor. Those who would not live at court he would not favor: "He is a man I never see; I do not know him." If a noble wanted a pension or some ceremonial but lucrative post, if he wanted to maintain his standing among his peers, if he wanted his children to marry well — he had to live at court. The harshest punishment he could receive was to be banished from the king's presence. As a courtier once said to Louis, "Sire, away from Your Majesty one is not only miserable but ridiculous."

VERSAILLES AND THE COURT

When Louis began his reign, the court was at the Louvre in Paris. Louis disliked the city because it was the center of the Fronde and because the public came and went as it pleased at the Louvre, allowing the king little privacy. He knew that if he wanted to win and hold the awe of the masses he could not live too close to them. He decided to build a new residence that would surpass in splendor all the other palaces of the world. He selected Versailles, a few miles from Paris and already the site of a modest palace that had long been one of Louis's favorite rural retreats. In 1668 work began on new buildings. The court moved to Ver-

Palace of Versailles

> *"Your Majesty knows that apart from brilliant exploits in war nothing testifies
> more to the grandeur and the character of princes than buildings; and all
> posterity measures them by the scale provided by the magnificent palaces they
> built during their lifetime."* Colbert to Louis XIV, September 28, 1665, reprinted
> in LETTRES, INSTRUCTIONS ET MÉMOIRES (Paris, 1868), Vol. V.

---

sailles in 1682, although the buildings were not all completed until 1710.
In addition to Versailles, which was for the court, the king built two
other palaces nearby: the Trianon for himself and his ladies, and Marly
(destroyed during the French Revolution) for himself and his most favored friends. An elegant blend of architecture with magnificent formal
landscaping, Versailles conveys the grandeur that Louis intended. It was
imitated by monarchs of other lands who sought a monumental expression of power.

Under Louis the royal court became far more numerous and luxurious
than it had ever been. There were several thousand noble courtiers and
over four thousand servants, not including the military guards. The up-
keep of the huge establishment was one of the chief expenses of the state.
Life at court was regulated with fantastic precision, for Louis had a great
fondness for ceremony and lavish display. The center around which
everything orbited was the Sun King himself. The nobles were reduced
to the level of minor actors and onlookers in a continuing pageant.

The court's day began when the king arose, and ended when he retired. These two events, known as the *lever* and the *coucher,* were public

occasions. In between, the courtiers' time was occupied by attendance upon the king as he passed from one carefully planned activity to the next. About five thousand courtiers lived in apartments in the palace at Versailles and another five thousand lived nearby. They spent their lives in hunts, masquerades, concerts, plays, receptions, gambling, licentiousness, and above all, gossip. Boredom reigned supreme, and flattery and hypocrisy were the keys to success. It was inevitable that people who lived in such an artificial atmosphere and had no chance to occupy themselves in useful tasks should become demoralized. Louis indeed triumphed in his plan to reduce the nobility to impotency.

THE DECLINE OF THE NOBILITY AS A CLASS

The 10,000 who lived at or near Versailles were the pick of the aristocracy. Numerically they formed only a small part of the nobility. In 1715 an estimated 200,000 of France's 20,000,000 people were nobles. In France, as in other continental lands, all the children of a noble were themselves noble. The nobility ranged from the great lords who surrounded the king, through provincial nobles who lived comfortable if undistinguished lives, down to the minor nobility who owned tiny scraps of land and whose standard of living was hardly distinguishable from that of the more prosperous peasants. The impoverished squires were called *hobereaux,* small hawks, by their contemptuous fellow nobles.

Financial difficulties were not restricted to the *hobereaux.* One of the most striking phenomena of French social history during the age of Louis XIV was the impoverishment of the nobility as a class. There was a general economic decline in France in the last decades of the seventeenth and first decades of the eighteenth centuries, so that the income of all the nobility fell. Matters were made worse for the great aristocrats by the high cost of court life. They resorted to various expedients, such as marrying into wealthy bourgeois or recently ennobled families, but they found that the easiest way to solve their money problems was by the sinecures and pensions that the king gave them in return for their constant attendance upon him. Economic pressure had much to do with transforming the once turbulent and independent French aristocracy into a parasitic court nobility.

Besides the economic differences among them, the nobles were stratified according to rank. At the top were the princes of the blood, who were the king's relatives outside of his immediate family; then came the select group of great lords called peers, who were honored by the appellation of "king's cousins"; last came the nobles of various other titles down to baron. Nobles were also divided according to origin. Those who traced their noble lineage back through many generations or who had won their titles through military service were called the *noblesse d'épée,* nobility of the sword. They considered themselves socially superior to nobles who acquired their titles by purchase or by inheritance of certain offices. The latter were known as the *noblesse de robe,* nobility of the robe, from the gown worn by lawyers.

PERFECTING THE ABSOLUTIST MACHINERY

Despite the centralizing activities of one and a half centuries, in 1661 France still comprised some three hundred political and administrative areas, each with a measure of autonomy in functions and institutions. The provinces had distinctive legal and administrative institutions. Cities enjoyed special corporate privileges. There were hundreds of internal tariffs and tools. Louis was determined to supplant particularism with his own centralized administration in order that his will might penetrate into every corner of the kingdom.

Louis's approach to the problem of government represented a quest for orderliness and rationality that had spread from science and philosophy into the mainstream of political life. In some ways Louis was a good Cartesian, believing that he could create administrative machinery that would automatically produce security, the welfare of his subjects, and the perpetuation of his own power. Although he fell short of his goal, he came as near to perfecting the machinery of absolutism as any monarch of the age.

Louis completed the sophistication of the numerous councils of Richelieu's day, adding new ones but reducing the initiative of all of them. Except in the most routine functions, each council had to wait upon the will of the king. Since many of his officials held office by hereditary or traditional right, he was not in a position to get rid of them wholesale. Instead, he reduced the scope of their power and played one official against another, one administrative organ against another. He used special *ad hoc* commissions for particularly important and delicate matters that before would have been handled routinely by a council. The councils were relegated to the status of purely bureaucratic tools. Policy emanated from the king.

Intendancy was given its final form. Besides the duties that they had performed under Richelieu, intendants under Louis took over complete control of provincial and municipal government in time of war or crisis. In time of peace they performed a supervisory function in local government that greatly reduced the responsibility and power of the regular local officials. The provincial governors, who were drawn from the old nobility, became figureheads. The intendants were the eyes and ears of the central government, and upon their reports, surveys, and statistical tabulations the king based the decisions that moved the realm.

Louis completed the reduction of the parlements to impotency. In 1673 he decreed that the parlements were to record his laws at once and in their original form; objections to a law could be heard only once and only after it had been recorded. No longer could the parlements debate constitutional questions or take part in the formulation of general policy.

In all these changes Louis did no more than complete the bureaucratic developments that had been started in earnest under Henry IV and been advanced by Richelieu. Louis's main contribution was the orderly arrangement of governmental organs that previously had overlapped in jurisdiction and functions. The overlapping had been one means of control by which one group of officials watched another, but Louis meant to watch all by himself. The overlapping had created blind spots in which the administration could escape the surveillance of the king. Louis made the bureaucracy like the famous Hall of Mirrors at Versailles — a long chamber into every nook and cranny of which the king might see from a position of absolute centrality. As the mirrors reflected the sun throughout the hall, so the radiance of the Sun King was reflected everywhere in the administration.

Louis XIV came as close to erecting a police state as the limitations of communication and transportation in the period allowed. His political police were the intendants, spies, and other agents who sniffed out sedition and treason. The Bastille awaited the mighty or the humble. Men were seized by *lettres de cachet* and imprisoned indefinitely without recourse to trial or the possibility of acquittal. A standing army was ready at hand for the suppression of insurrection. Louis seldom sought to twist the processes of justice; he merely circumvented the whole system in cases of political crime, real or supposed.

ABSOLUTISM IN ECONOMICS AND RELIGION

Louis's own abilities would not have sufficed to undertake single-handedly the fiscal and economic reforms he envisaged. Although he trusted no man with the plentitude of his power, he permitted Jean Baptiste Colbert (1619–1683) a larger measure of responsible autonomy than any other minister. Colbert was a brilliant administrator with an enormous capacity for hard work. Though not a personable man (he was nicknamed The North because, like the north wind, he was cold and surly), he was entirely devoted to the king and to making France great. Louis appreciated him and entrusted him with the direction of industry, commerce, agriculture, colonies, maritime affairs, art, and finances.

Louis's ambitious projects demanded vast amounts of money. The bulk of the state's revenues came from taxes levied on the king's poorest subjects. Nobles and clergymen, who owned most of the wealth, were exempted from virtually all government levies until years after Colbert's death. Colbert was unable to change this system, but he did introduce order into the financial administration by decreasing the direct taxes paid by the common people, increasing the indirect levies that everyone paid, and eliminating much graft. Under his able management revenues tripled, and for a few years receipts actually exceeded expenses. Louis's ever-increasing expenditures in peace and war, however, made it impossible to maintain a balanced budget. After the beginning of the Dutch War in 1672, outgo regularly exceeded income and was often twice as large. The government went deeper and deeper into debt.

COLBERT AND MERCANTILISM

Like the rulers and ministers of many other European states, Louis and Colbert believed that the state should rule in economic as well as in political matters, and they also believed that the interests of the ruler were paramount to those of the individuals who engaged in economic activity. The economic policies that these rulers followed had a dual purpose: to build up the state's economic power and thereby strengthen the state, and to use the power of the state to promote economic growth and thereby enrich the state. These two aims and the measures which states took to achieve them are customarily lumped together under the label mercantilism, a word coined in the latter part of the eighteenth century by the Scottish economist Adam Smith. In the pursuit of the dual objective of power and prosperity each state had to deal with the conflicting ambitions of rival states with whom they aggressively competed for trade and territory. Thus, economic policies aggravated the antagonisms engendered by the political rivalries of the rulers of Europe.

Colbert's economic policies became the classical example of mercantilism in action; indeed, Colbertism is sometimes used as a synonym for mercantilism. Like the typical mercantilist that he was, Colbert considered gold and silver essential to national economic well-being. Since France lacked deposits of these metals it could increase its stocks of these precious metals only by increasing the value of its exports and decreasing the value of its imports so that it would have a favorable balance of trade. Then foreigners would owe money to France which they would have to pay in the form of gold and silver.

Colbert believed that the total volume of world trade and the total number of ships engaged in that trade were more or less fixed. He once calculated that all the trade of Europe was carried by twenty thousand ships, of which more than three-fourths belonged to the Dutch. Colbert argued that France could increase its share only by decreasing that of the Dutch, an objective for which he was prepared to go to war. He devoted much effort to promoting export trade, and he stressed the importance of colonies as sources of raw materials and potential markets for finished goods. His ambitions in this connection outran his capacities, however. Between 1664 and 1670 he granted chartered monopolies and other privileges to four companies to undertake French trade with the East Indies, West Indies, northern Europe, and the Levant. He hoped

Courtesy of the Metropolitan Museum of Art,
Gift of the Wildenstein Foundation, Inc., 1951

Jean Baptiste Colbert, by Philippe de Champaigne

*"It is necessary to re-establish or create all the industries, even of luxury; to
establish the protectionist system through the customs; to organize the producers
and merchants into corporations; to lighten the fiscal burdens harmful to the
people; to restore to France the transport of its commodities; to develop the
colonies and attach them commercially to France; to suppress all the
intermediaries between France and the Indies; to develop the navy to protect the
merchant marine."* Memorandum of Colbert quoted in J. E. King, science and
rationalism in the government of louis xiv (Baltimore, 1949).

that the companies would revive France's moribund oceanic commerce, break the monopolies of the English and Dutch companies, exploit the colonies France already had, and help in adding new ones. The companies were supervised by the government, or more precisely by Colbert. Since neither he nor the other government officials had any practical experience in foreign trade, the companies soon foundered and in a few years were liquidated. Yet they were not complete failures, for they served to revive French overseas trade and to train French seamen and merchants in the ways of oceanic commerce.

Colbert undertook an expansion of domestic commerce through improved communications, including the betterment of road and river networks and the construction of canals, and through the reform of internal tariffs. The system of internal tariffs forced up the prices of goods and impeded interregional trade. France had long been divided into two parts: the Five Great Farms (so called because the collection of tariffs had once been farmed out to private contractors under five separate contracts), which covered the northern half of France, and the rest of the country. Although there were no tariffs within the Five Great Farms, goods passing between the Farms and the other provinces paid heavy duties, varying according to the place where the goods crossed the line. In addition, shipments from certain provinces that had been recently acquired by France paid duties on entering any other part of the kingdom. Colbert could not abolish the division, principally because the tariffs were an important source of royal revenue, but in 1664 he issued a new schedule of tariffs between the farms and the rest of France that simplified and somewhat reduced the rates.

The great minister spent much time and effort in trying to build up industry so that France would become as nearly self-sufficient as possible. Subsidies, monopolies, tax reductions, loans without interest, and a host of other aids were extended to manufacturers to stimulate productivity. He arranged for the immigration of hundreds of skilled foreign workers and forbade the emigration of French artisans. He established new industries with government aid, particularly in fields where there was little or no French production. In return for assistance the manufacturers had to submit to close governmental regulation. Though French industry had always been subjected to outside control by government, church, town, and gild officials, intervention reached a new peak under Colbert. His instruments of control were the once independent craft gilds. He drew up new gild regulations in consultation with gild officials. Manufacturers were compelled to join the gilds. In 1666 and 1670 he issued regulations standardizing the quality and size of all sorts of goods, especially cloth. A corps of state inspectors was established to see that the regulations were obeyed, and severe punishments were ordered for those who disregarded them.

Colbert's purpose was to raise French goods to such a high and uniform quality that Frenchmen and foreigners alike would prefer French merchandise, but he was never able to enforce his system completely. He did not have enough inspectors and, more important, both manufacturers and consumers resisted his efforts at standardization. The manufacturers preferred their old ways, and the consumers often wanted goods of sizes and qualities different from the standards set by law. The regulations acted as an obstacle to experimentation and innovation on the part of producers and placed undue emphasis on the production of luxury goods, in which the gilds had traditionally dealt.

In addition to all these activities Colbert attempted to introduce improvements in agricultural production, and he promoted land reclamation and forestry. To build up a large and industrious population, he had the government forbid emigration, give tax exemptions to families with ten or more children, put difficulties in the way of people who wished to become nuns and priests, reduce the number of Church holidays from forty-one to twenty-four, and try to force vagabonds, beggars, and gypsies to find work by threatening them with the poorhouse or service in the Mediterranean galley fleet of the French navy.

Colbert accomplished much in his twenty-two years in power. On balance, however, the long-term results of his policies proved disappointing, for they failed to raise the level of the French economy. Although the wars and extravagances of Louis XIV were the chief causes for the failure to achieve economic growth, Colbert must share in the blame. The excessive paternalism of his system tended to stifle initiative without obtaining the advantage of planning. Planning was impossible because it assumed a greater capacity for control of the economy than either the physical power of the state or contemporary knowledge of economics allowed.

GALLICANISM

In his efforts to centralize and unify his realm the Sun King inevitably clashed with the papacy. From his forebears Louis had inherited the tradition of Gallicanism — control of the church in France by the throne — and he stoutly defended it. He had the unwavering support of most of the French clergy. Very early in his reign quarrels broke out between Paris and Rome. The most serious occurred in 1673, when Louis demanded that he receive the *régale,* the income from vacant bishoprics until they were filled by a new bishop. In 1682 the dispute came before an assembly of bishops in Paris under the leadership of Bishop Bossuet, who was noted as a defender of Gallicanism as well as of the divine right of kings. The prelates drew up a statement known as the Four Gallican Articles that reaffirmed the temporal supremacy of the king and restated the old claim that the doctrinal authority of the pope could be overruled by a church council. The adamant posture of both sides raised the possibility that the French church might break completely with Rome. The danger passed in 1693 when Louis, faced by a coalition of hostile Protestant powers and desirous of papal support, agreed to a compromise by which he retained the *régale* but agreed not to insist upon the application of the Four Gallican Articles of 1682.

Although Louis did not hesitate to disagree with the pope in matters pertaining to church-state relations, he felt himself at one with Rome in matters of faith. He was always a devout Catholic, and as he grew older his piety increased and rigidified, accentuated by the influence of the deeply religious Madame de Maintenon. Any position that departed from a narrow Catholic orthodoxy was anathema to him. He believed, too, that in the interests of national unity and strength all his subjects should be of the same faith. His mixed religious-political motives explain his campaigns against the Jansenists within the Catholic Church and against the Huguenots outside it.

JANSENISM

The Jansenists owed their name and doctrines to Cornelius Jansen (1585–1638), a Flemish bishop. The kernel of their belief was that man attains eternal salvation only if God predestines him to it, and that God's gift of grace is irrespective of any good works that man may do. Predestinarianism and rejection of free will brought the Jansenists close to the doctrinal position of John Calvin; their enemies called them "warmed-over Calvinists." The Jansenists, however, considered themselves loyal members of the Catholic Church who wanted to increase the personal holiness of priests and laymen and who opposed the Church's secular power. They complained that the pope misunderstood their position. They particularly condemned some of the Jesuits whom they called "Laxists" for too readily granting absolution of sins upon confession. The Jansenists held that such laxness made penance too easy and encouraged immorality. They themselves led puritanical lives and scorned the luxury and licentiousness that was then fashionable.

The movement had two centers, the monasteries of Port-Royal in Paris and Port-Royal des Champs near Versailles. A group of clerics and laymen attracted by the Jansenist doctrines settled near Port-Royal des Champs and dedicated themselves to a life of the mind and spirit. Among them was Blaise Pascal (1623–1662), scientist and philosopher. While living at Port-Royal, he wrote *Provincial Letters* (1657), a scathing attack upon the Jesuits.

During the first decades of Louis's reign the Jansenist teachings attracted a number of important people. The king was alarmed by this development. He believed that the movement endangered both church and state. He was also repelled by the Jansenist emphasis upon asceticism, which he took as a rebuke on his own style of life. His reactions were reinforced by the Jesuit priests who were his personal confessors. Louis urged that the movement be outlawed by the Pope, but for a time the Jansenists enjoyed the protection of two successive popes who disliked the Jesuit order. The next pope, Clement XI, was more obliging; in bulls issued in 1706 and 1713 he condemned the Jansenist teachings. The leaders fled to Holland. Although the movement was heavily persecuted in France, it managed to live on there until the nineteenth century.

SUPPRESSION OF THE HUGUENOTS

The Huguenots had been destroyed as a separate political force in Richelieu's day. They were allowed, however, to keep the religious and civil freedoms that had been guaranteed them by the Edict of Nantes in 1598. There were about two million of these French Protestants, among whom were many men of unusual energy and ability. Usually excluded from important positions in public life, they became leaders in trade, industry, banking, and the professions. Their economic success was envied by the Catholic majority, who already despised them as heretics. The autonomy enjoyed by the Huguenot religious communities made them appear a dangerous republican influence. The Catholic majority looked upon the Edict of Nantes as a temporary political expedient and believed that one day all Frenchmen must be Catholics.

Louis shared these feelings. He was outraged that any of his subjects should be of a religion different from that of their sovereign and starting in 1679 he embarked upon a program of undermining the Edict of Nantes. He permitted the destruction of three-quarters of the Protestant churches (or temples as the Huguenots called them), placed restrictions on the subjects that could be taught in the Huguenots' schools, suppressed their special courts, billeted troops in their homes with orders to be as unpleasant as possible, and harassed them at every turn. Simultaneously he sponsored a vigorous campaign to convert Huguenots, offering them money, exemption from the dreaded billeting, and other privileges.

The Edict of Nantes was practically a dead letter by the time Louis officially revoked it in October, 1685. He claimed that so many Huguenots had become Catholics as a result of his conversion campaign that the edict was superfluous. The remaining Protestant churches were destroyed, Protestant religious services and schools were banned, torture and brutality were freely used to compel conversion, and refugees caught trying to leave the country were sentenced to the galleys. About 200,000 Huguenots, among whom were many of the wealthiest and most industrious, managed with the aid of friendly Catholics at home and fellow Protestants abroad to escape to England, Holland, Brandenburg-Prussia, and British America. A number of exiles made important contributions to the economic development of their havens and strengthened France's enemies. Their departure undoubtedly weakened certain sectors of the French economy, but recent study has shown that it was less disastrous than hitherto supposed. Many of those who remained in France practiced their religion in secret, and after Louis's death in 1715 persecution abated.

FRENCH PREDOMINANCE

The principal aim of the foreign policy of Louis XIV was to make France the arbiter of Europe, exercising the primacy that had once belonged to the house of Hapsburg. Second, Louis sought to extend the boundaries of the realm to what would later be called the natural frontiers of France: the Rhine, the Alps, and the Pyrenees. His policy could only mean conflict with Spain — a conflict that put the seal to French predominance.

THE WAR MACHINE

Louis laid the foundations for his foreign policy by constructing with customary thoroughness the finest war machine in Europe. He was inalterably opposed to the traditional method of raising an army of semi-independent military chiefs and their private troops when the occasion demanded. Instead, he created the first great national army in Europe. It was directly under royal command. In 1667 the French army had 72,000 men; within ten years it had nearly quadrupled. Two men of extraordinary capacity — Louvois and Vauban — were the craftsmen of the new military force.

Michel Le Tellier, Marquis de Louvois and son of the minister of the same name who had earlier served Louis, succeeded his father as secretary of state for war in 1666 and served until his death in 1691. Louvois fashioned a close-knit fighting force of extraordinary discipline, high morale, and formidable power. A table of organization assigned the duties of every officer from ensign to marshal, with a rigid chain of command based on rank and, within each rank, on seniority. It remedied the worst aspects of the old system, by which officers had been recruited by purchase from a narrow social base. Pay scales for all ranks were fixed. Uniforms were widely adopted to improve morale and establish divisional distinctions within the army. Orders of merit and medals were instituted as rewards for valor and service. Military hospitals were built, and a pension plan was created for disabled veterans. Weapons were standardized. In 1687 a way was devised of fixing a bayonet to a gun so that the weapon could be fired with the bayonet attached; this allowed infantrymen to fire and then charge and thus made pikemen unnecessary. An effective force of dragoons or mounted infantry gave increased mobility to the army. Much of the artillery corps was integrated with the regular army

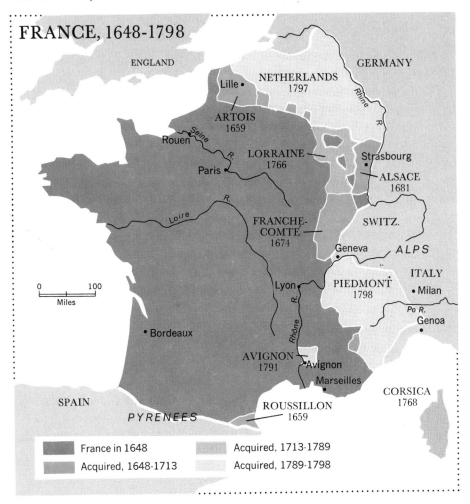

FRANCE, 1648-1798

establishment. A complex logistical system was devised, with permanent arsenals and supply depots linked to permanent barracks located strategically throughout France. The militia was completely reorganized to provide a reserve of reinforcements for the line. In 1668 the inspector general's office was created to inspect troops and equipment, enforce discipline, ensure training, and report on the merits of line officers for command. The name of the first inspector general of infantry, Colonel Martinet, is still a synonym for a rigid disciplinarian.

Marshal Vauban (1633–1707) was undoubtedly the greatest military engineer of his age. He was a master of fortification in an era when strategy entailed the taking of strong points rather than fighting pitched battles. He directed more than fifty sieges and devised parallel trenches, earthworks, and temporary fortifications to enable the army to besiege and reduce enemy forts with a minimal loss of troops. His own fortresses, ringing France and commanding the wilderness of Canada, were the epitome of scientific planning. Salients that projected out from the fortresses permitted a raking gunfire and made frontal attack suicidal.

Colbert was responsible for the birth of the French navy with Louis's grudging acquiescence. In 1661 the navy had 30 ships; in 1677 it had 199. Through technological advances and a system of shipyards and fleet staging ports, Colbert provided France with an effective sea force that might have established the maritime supremacy of France in the 1690's if Louis had not cut its budget after Colbert's death. Instead, England gained command of the sea, a fatal blow to French ambitions for over a century to come.

THE WAR OF DEVOLUTION, 1667–1668

Louis's first bid for martial glory in the quest for international power came in May, 1667, when his armies invaded the Spanish territories of Franche-Comté and the Spanish Netherlands. He explained his aggression by claiming that the territories belonged to his wife, Maria Theresa, because of an inheritance custom in those territories called the law of devolution, by which children of a first marriage inherited private property in preference to children of a second marriage. Maria Theresa was the eldest daughter of the first marriage of Philip IV of Spain, who had recently died.

This labored justification for Louis's attack did not prevent his troops from winning immediate and sweeping victories. His triumphs alarmed the Dutch. Although they were long-time allies of France against the Spanish Hapsburgs, they did not relish Louis as a next-door neighbor. When Louis struck, they were at war with England. They speedily ended that conflict and in 1668 made an alliance with England and Sweden against France. The French realized that the balance of power was against them, and on May 2, 1668, they ended the war by the peace treaty of Aix-la-Chapelle. France returned Franche-Compté to Spain but retained some of its Flemish conquests.

THE DUTCH WAR, 1672–1679

Despite the gains that France had made in the short War of Devolution, Louis was furious with the Dutch for having dared to oppose him. He called them a "nation of fishwives and merchants." Moreover, Holland was France's chief commercial rival. Louis decided that the Dutch Republic must be conquered. He made careful diplomatic preparations to isolate the enemy. By the judicious use of subsidies he obtained promises of neutrality from some of his fellow monarchs and promises of military aid from others. In 1672 a French army of 120,000 men marched into the United Provinces. The Dutch were greatly outnumbered, but led by the twenty-two-year-old Prince William of Orange, great-grandson of William the Silent, they managed to stall the French advances. Meanwhile they sued for peace, offering territorial concessions. Louis demanded more than they were willing to give. Other nations awoke to the danger of a French conquest in the Netherlands and combined against Louis to try to maintain the balance of power and prevent the French from establishing hegemony over Europe. A number of countries in the French camp switched over to the Dutch. Louis sought desperately for new allies but managed to hold only Sweden on his side.

Despite these odds, the French armies under the command of Marshal Turenne and Prince Condé, Louis's great generals, continued to win victories. In July, 1675, Turenne was killed in action, and soon thereafter Condé retired. The fortunes of war turned against the French and a stalemate developed. Peace negotiations began late in 1676. Louis decided to end the war when the Dutch leader, William of Orange, married Mary Stuart, niece of the king of England, and the English joined the Dutch against him. In the latter part of 1678 and early 1679 he signed a series of peace treaties with his opponents at Nijmegen in Holland. While giving up the Dutch conquests, he gained Franche-Comté from Spain and a line of fortified places in the Spanish Netherlands. The Peace of Nijmegen represented the peak of success for Louis's foreign ambitions. Although he had failed to destroy the Dutch, his armies had won general recognition as Europe's best, his new navy had given a good account of itself, he had strengthened his frontiers and added new territory, and he was acknowledged to be the most powerful monarch of Europe.

THE WAR OF THE LEAGUE OF AUGSBURG, 1688–1697

Louis was still not satisfied. Immediately after the end of the Dutch War he hit upon a new scheme to annex land on France's northern and eastern borders. His plan was to take advantage of loose wording in the articles of the Treaty of Westphalia, which had given France certain lands "with their dependencies." It was unclear which territories were dependencies and which were not, and Louis arranged for the creation of special courts, called Chambers of Reunion, to settle the question. He took care to pack the courts with people who would decide in his favor. By this unscrupulous procedure he annexed all of Alsace and other territories, and he was able to occupy them quickly because he had kept a large number of men under arms after the close of the Dutch War.

Once again Louis overplayed his hand. The other powers feared that unless they checked Louis's ambitions, he would reduce them to satellites or, to use their phrase, he would establish a "universal monarchy." In 1686 Holland, Sweden, the German Protestant princes, Austria, and Spain formed an alliance against him called the League of Augsburg.

England joined in 1689 after a revolution had placed Louis's implacable enemy, William of Orange, on the English throne as William III.

Knowing that war was certain to come, Louis decided to gain the advantage by taking the offensive. In 1688 he declared war on Austria and quickly gained several victories. When the other powers entered the conflict the French were put on the defensive. For a time they managed well enough, but by the end of 1693 Louis knew that he could not win and sued for peace. The allies spurned his offers and the war dragged on until 1697. By then the allies were becoming exhausted and peace was agreed upon at Ryswick in Holland. The terms of the treaty provided that Louis relinquish all territory he had acquired since the Peace of Nijmegen except Strasbourg. He had to make major commercial concessions to the Dutch and he also had to recognize William of Orange as rightful king of England and promise not to aid the deposed Stuart line in any future effort to regain the English throne.

THE WAR OF THE SPANISH SUCCESSION, 1701–1714

The Treaty of Ryswick marked a setback for the ambitions of Louis XIV. His expansionism had been effectively checked by the operation of the balance of power both on the battlefield and at the peace table. The Sun King's last war, beginning only four years after Ryswick, resulted from Louis's taking advantage of the last opportunity left him for extension of his power in Europe: to place his grandson on the Spanish throne.

The succession to the Spanish throne was the type of dynastic issue certain to provoke an international crisis. Charles II of Spain was a childless invalid, so that the Spanish Hapsburg line faced certain extinction. In anticipation of this event Louis XIV had long plotted to make the throne of Spain part of the Bourbon patrimony, claiming it for his family through his mother and his wife, both of whom were daughters of Spanish kings. He was not the only claimant. Both the mother and the first wife of Emperor Leopold of Austria were also daughters of Spanish kings, and Leopold demanded that Spain become part of the patrimony of his house, the Austrian Hapsburgs.

The dispute became the subject of diplomatic negotiations and treaties proposing the partition of the empire among the Bourbon and Hapsburg claimants. Charles refused to consider splitting up his realm, and in 1698 he named Emperor Leopold's grandson, the seven-year-old Electoral Prince Joseph Ferdinand of Bavaria, as his sole heir. A few months later the boy died, and new intrigues and new plans for partition got under way. Driven to distraction, Charles in October, 1700, signed a new will naming Philip of Anjou, second grandson of Louis XIV, to succeed him. Soon thereafter Charles died.

The news of the choice of a Bourbon heir aroused great excitement and talk of war in the courts of Europe. Not since the time of Charles V had the political balance of Europe been in such grave peril. Europe faced the prospect of French influence stretching from the North Sea to the Straits of Gibraltar and reaching around the world through the vast Spanish Empire. Louis hastened to give assurances that the thrones of Spain and France would never be held by the same person, and it seemed as if war could be averted. Then by a series of diplomatic blunders Louis destroyed the hopes for peace. He declared that Philip of Anjou, now Philip V of Spain, and his descendants still had rights to the succession to the French crown, sent French troops into the Spanish possessions in the Netherlands and Italy, and broke a promise he had given in the Treaty of Ryswick by recognizing the son of the deposed James II of England as rightful king of England. These acts were too much for the other powers. On May 15, 1702, England, Holland, and Austria declared war on France and Spain; the allies were eventually joined by Prussia and other German states, Portugal, Denmark, and Savoy.

The troops and ships of the allies far outnumbered those of Louis, and in Prince Eugene of Savoy, commander of the Austrian forces, and John Churchill, first duke of Marlborough (and ancestor of Winston Churchill), they had two of the greatest generals of modern times. After a bad start the allies rolled up a series of major victories — Blenheim (1704), Ramillies and Turin (1706), Oudenarde (1708), and Malplaquet (1709). They pushed into Spain, drove out Philip, and put Charles, second son of Emperor Leopold, on the throne.

The principal front of the war was the Spanish Netherlands and Germany. There was only one major sea fight. The English and Dutch fleets kept French and Spanish shipping off the seas while they freely transported their own troops and supplies. The allies' invasion of France in 1708 moved Louis to sue for peace. His overtures were spurned by his opponents, who were intent upon humbling the Grand Monarch. Louis seemed ready to yield, when in an incredible outburst of national pride and cohesiveness his subjects rallied around him and reinvigorated the French war effort. In 1712 the army of this seemingly defeated nation won its one great victory of the war at Denain in northern France. In Spain, too, the people had taken up the cause of the French, and aided by French troops, they restored the Spanish throne to the Bourbons.

These amazing reversals made the allies view the peace proposals with more interest. Negotiations were resumed, and after long parleys France signed separate peace treaties with all her enemies except Austria on March 31, 1713, at Utrecht, and with Austria on March 6, 1714, at Rastadt. The chief provisions of the agreements were: (1) Philip of Anjou was recognized as king of Spain, but the separation of the thrones of France and Spain was declared to be inviolable law; (2) Spain ceded Naples, Milan, Sardinia, and the Spanish Netherlands (henceforth the

Austrian Netherlands) to Austria, and Gibraltar and Minorca to England; (3) France ceded the Hudson's Bay territory, mainland Nova Scotia, Newfoundland, and St. Kitt's in the West Indies to England; and (4) Spain gave the English the exclusive right for the next thirty years to import up to 4,800 slaves a year into Spanish America and to send one trading ship a year with 500 tons of merchandise (later increased to 650 tons). The English agreed to give the Spanish king one-fourth of their profits on the slave trade. This slaving privilege, called the *Asiento* (contract), had been held by the Genoese until 1702 and then by the French.

France came out of the great war much better than it had reason to hope. Louis had succeeded in placing a Bourbon on the throne of Spain and he managed to retain the border territories he had gained in earlier wars. France had to give up some of her overseas possessions, but Spain had provided the victorious allies with most of the spoils of victory. Louis had not been able to carry through to completion the ambitious plans that had persuaded him to wage wars for over half a century. The long struggle had indeed extended France's frontiers and had made Louis the most powerful monarch in Europe. The new frontiers, however, invited trouble from those who had lost these lands to Louis. Despite all of France's land might, Britain dominated the seas around Europe, and the wars had produced poverty, misery and ever-increasing criticism of the government among Louis's subjects and a revival of noble opposition to the claims of the throne.

THE CULTURAL GLORY OF FRANCE

Louis's reign coincided with one of the greatest ages in the history of French literature and art. Although several of the outstanding figures in the outburst of genius had already produced their masterpieces before 1660, a good deal of credit for the flowering of culture belonged to the Sun King, who had a genuine taste for art and letters. He delighted in honoring creative artists, and he was a generous patron. He saw the artist and writer as instruments to glorify himself and to spread the fame of France.

ABSOLUTISM IN THE ARTS

As a result of his passion for control and regulation, Louis sought to impose central direction upon the creative arts. Colbert was entrusted with carrying out his aims. The conscientious minister applied as much energy and thought to the assignment as he did to fiscal and economic matters, and in the long run he was far more successful. The instruments he used to carry out his master's wishes were the academies. He took over the direction of the Académie Française, founded by Richelieu, and the Academy of Painting and Sculpture, and he established five other academies — of the dance, letters, science, music, and architecture. The academies formulated standards for their respective branches of art and learning, trained students, and performed services for the state, such as preparing designs, decorations, and inscriptions for public buildings and monuments. In a sense their members were royal officials, receiving pensions and awards for their services. Art and architecture were in many ways as much a part of the whole structure of Louis XIV's absolutism as Colbert's mercantilism and Louvois's army.

Early in Louis's reign major French architecture was almost the personal domain of François Mansart (1598–1666), whose work was classical and restrained. His most serious challenger was Louis Le Vau (1612–1670), a master of the baroque splendor that Mansart found disagreeable. Both men were still free of the standards set by the academies. Jules Hardouin-Mansart (1646–1708) was not. As official architect to the king, he was the principal bureaucrat-architect responsible for the buildings at Versailles. The landscaping of the magnificent formal gardens was done by André Le Nôtre (1613–1700).

Until the end of the seventeenth century French painting was dominated by classicism. Classicism was embedded in the standards of the academy and given expression in the works of Charles Le Brun (1619–1690), decorator of Versailles, Louis's official art counselor, and director of the state-owned Gobelin tapestry works. During the last years of Louis's reign France produced a court painter of insight and subtlety in Antoine Watteau (1684–1721). He attained pictorial depth by masterful design and color, and artistic depth by an implicitly critical depiction of the elegant inanity of court life and the transitory glory of the Grand Monarch and his noble herd. Under Watteau's hand the polished veneer of Versailles appeared wafer-thin.

Literature, particularly drama, was the chief cultural glory of Louis's reign. The dramatists, of whom the greatest were Corneille and Racine, achieved a clarity and elegance of expression that have rarely been equaled. They drew much of their inspiration from classical antiquity, imitating the measure, discipline, and dignity of the Greek and Roman authors and choosing many of their subjects from classical history and mythology. The greatest of the French writers, like their classical models, presented what they thought to be universal principles of human behavior, applicable to all men in all times. This approach characterized French literature from the end of the sixteenth to the early eighteenth century. The period, known as the classical age of French letters, received its fullest expression during the years 1660–1690.

In comedy Molière (1622–1673) was supreme. With sardonic humor he exposed the hypocrisy and affectation he saw about him. In *Tartuffe* he unmasked a pious fraud, in *Le Bourgeois Gentilhomme* he cruelly mocked the social climber, in *L'Avare* his pen speared the miser, in *Le Misan-*

thrope he lampooned the conformist — and so on through a whole gallery of social types. He also founded the Comédie Française, France's first state theater.

Among the prose writers La Fontaine (1621–1695) is best remembered for his *Fables.* They are vignettes drawn from his observations of society and nature and are universal and timeless in their quality. He portrayed people of all classes and held their failings up to gentle ridicule. The *Maximes* of la Rochefoucauld (1613–1680) is another work of the period that has had undying fame. In the five hundred or so pithy sentences that make up the book la Rochefoucauld cynically analyzed the motives of human behavior to show that man rarely acts on the basis of unalloyed altruism.

HOW GRAND WAS THE GRAND MONARCH?

The impact of Louis XIV on contemporary Europe was nowhere more manifest than in culture. Imitations of Versailles sprang up all over Europe. French etiquette, cuisine, dress, and coiffure enjoyed an enormous vogue among Europe's elite. The styles of the French court painters and the literary techniques of the French dramatists and essayists were widely copied. Both mighty and puny princes made Europe a firmament of sun kings, each with its orbiting noble satellites. Taste meant French; French meant Louis XIV. The French language, fashioned by the authors of the classical age into an elegant and dramatic tongue capable of the most subtle gradations of meaning, became in the eighteenth century the language of polite society from the Atlantic to the Urals. Imitation was no less marked in the more mundane areas of life. Armies were reorganized on Louvois's model; Vauban's designs for fortifications were copied faithfully on every known continent. Monarchs aspired to, although they seldom attained, the administrative precision of the French bureaucracy. Imitation is one measure of grandeur, and since this imitation was explicitly of Louis XIV, it is a measure of the grandeur of the Grand Monarch.

What of contemporary French opinion? The paeans of praise from the court panegyrists, the harsh condemnation of La Mothe-Fénelon in 1694 — "This is sufficient, Sire, to demonstrate that you have passed your entire life apart from the way of truth and justice" — and the vitriolic characterization of Louis in the famed memoirs of Saint-Simon are a spectrum of opinion, every color determined as much by the personal prejudice of the writer as by the objective truth about the king. It was the price paid by an institution of state, which in its personification obliterated the person; there was no Louis as an objectively graspable personality. The answer to the question, how grand the Grand Monarch? lies neither in the degree of acceptance by the rest of Europe of the patterns he set nor in contemporary French reaction to him. It lies in the assessment of the success or failure of Louis XIV as the state.

Louis's reign divided naturally into two parts in the year 1685. Until that date he was continuously and increasingly successful; after that date he at best held his own in domestic political and foreign affairs, and he lost ground rapidly economically. Death claimed his ablest counselors and the men with whom he replaced them were not their equals in either ability or devotion. Married to de Maintenon and infected with a new piety, Louis turned upon the Huguenots, forfeiting the contributions of many of his most competent subjects. The nations of Europe banded against him. Literally surrounded, Louis never again held the diplomatic or military advantage after 1685. The result was almost continuous war on four fronts — the Low Countries, Germany, the high seas, North America — from 1688 until the year before Louis's death in 1715. The drain on the economic strength of France was enormous.

Louis's early victories entailed neither the financial expenditure nor the human misery with which he purchased the diplomatic and military stalemates of his last quarter-century. The end of his reign was destructive of all the promising vigor of his early personal rule. The Sun King was a pathetic figure in his old age. Saint-Simon, who knew Louis well, summed up the king's last years as "so little his, so continually and successively those of some others . . . pulled down under the weight of a fatal war, relieved by no one because of the incapacity of his ministers and his generals." Louis had outlived his children and his grandchildren when he died on September 1, 1715, after a long and painful illness. He had reigned for seventy-two years, ruled for fifty-four years, and they had all been *his* years. Yet for all the splendor and all the grandeur, the Grand Monarch tasted remorse before he died. His charge to his five-year-old great-grandson and heir, Louis XV, is the most authoritative word on his reign: "Do not imitate me in the liking I had for buildings, nor the taste I had for war. Try rather to preserve peace with your neighbors. . . . Always follow good advice. Try to help your people, which I unfortunately have been unable to do myself." In indicting so much of his life and ambitions, Louis made a striking confession: he had chosen the wrong paths to the glory and greatness of the state.

ABSOLUTISM IN AUSTRIA, SPAIN, AND PRUSSIA
CHAPTER TWELVE

During the latter half of the seventeenth and first half of the eighteenth centuries three dynasties, the Hapsburgs in Austria, the Hohenzollerns in Prussia, and the Bourbons in Spain, established themselves as the absolutist rulers of their respective realms. The Austrian Hapsburgs and the Spanish Bourbons sought to revitalize their states; the Hohenzollerns intended to make Prussia a great power. With Louis XIV's France as their explicit model each of these dynasties adapted to its own ends and circumstances the basic tools of absolutism: bureaucratic centralization, a standing army subject to the orders of the monarch, mercantilistic economic policies designed to maximize the wealth and power of the state, and above all else, the subjugation of the nobility.

ABSOLUTISM AND THE NOBILITY

The submission of the nobility to the royal will was nowhere an abject surrender. Rather, it was a compromise. The nobility, like all other classes in the state, had bowed before the absolute monarch. It had been forced to surrender its independence and most of its political rights. In return, however, the monarch had been compelled to allow the nobility to retain valuable privileges. Society in the eighteenth century, even more than in the seventeenth century, was dominated by the nobility. In the absolutist monarchies of the eighteenth century the high offices in government and in the military and diplomatic services were filled almost exclusively by members of the nobility. Nobles served as the counsellors of the absolute monarchs and had an important, and sometimes determining, role in making their state's foreign and domestic policies. The nobility remained everywhere the social elite. In eastern and northern Europe nobles lived like absolute monarchs on their estates with great powers over the peasants who were their serfs and who paid them dues in cash and kind and labor. In central and western Europe peasants had long ago won their freedom and many of them owned their own land. Yet they still had to pay certain dues to nobles in recognition of the ancient feudal rights of lordship that the nobles had over the land. In many parts of eastern Europe only nobles could own rural land, and in most of the states of both the east and the west nobles paid no taxes. Special law codes protected the nobility, and when they were charged with a misdeed they were tried in special courts before special judges.

Nor had the nobility lost all of its political power. It still had strength enough to act as a brake on the monarch's efforts to increase his authority. It sometimes succeeded in frustrating royal policies that ran sharply counter to the interests of the nobility, such as the repeated efforts by rulers to reduce the power nobles had over their peasants. The fact of the matter was that the privileges and power of the nobility acted as a limitation on the authority of the absolute monarch.

THE AUSTRIAN HAPSBURGS

This interaction and conflict between absolute monarchs and privileged nobility provided a major theme in the history of absolutism in Austria. The Thirty Years' War left the empire weaker than ever before. The Hapsburg ruler retained merely the shadow title of Holy Roman Emperor in Germany.

Disappointed in their long-cherished hope of building a strong empire in Germany, the Hapsburgs decided to base their power upon lands in central and southeastern Europe over which they had sovereignty. The new empire that they built was called Austria, or the Austrian Empire or the Hapsburg Monarchy; it had no official name down to its disintegration during the First World War. It comprised the provinces of Austria, called the hereditary provinces, as well as the kingdom of Bohemia and the kingdom of Hungary, both of which were acquired by the Hapsburgs in 1526. The three regions differed markedly from one another in language, culture, and traditions, and their distinctiveness was further complicated by the existence within each of minority ethnic cultures, mostly Slavic-speaking. Their one important geographic feature was contiguity; they formed a single, large mass in central and southeastern Europe. No other bond united them except their recognition of a common sovereign who ruled from Vienna. The ability of the Hapsburgs to hold together this nameless agglomeration for over 250 years, and to impose a certain unity upon it and neighboring territories that were annexed in the course of time without destroying the unique integrity of its parts, was a tribute to their skill as rulers.

THE ABSOLUTISM OF LEOPOLD I, 1657–1705

The shift from German imperial ambitions to Austria-centered concerns had already been evidenced by the Hapsburgs during the Thirty Years' War. The new trend became the dominant theme of Hapsburg policy during the long reign of Leopold I (1657–1705). Leopold, the second son of Ferdinand III, had been educated for the priesthood. He remained deeply religious throughout his life, and the papal nuncio at Vienna once remarked that he was too pious for an emperor. He was a quiet, reserved man who loved books and music, whose private life was a model of propriety, and who hated to make decisions. He did not welcome his accession to the throne; it seemed to be an obligation imposed by God and wholly lacking in personal enjoyment. Scrawny and ugly, with the large pendulous lip of the Hapsburg men, he teetered on spindly legs. Unheroic and almost ridiculous, he appeared the antithesis of his glamorous cousin and lifelong opponent, Louis XIV. Yet he was no less conscious of his own dignity and had as great a sense of the mission of his dynasty. Throughout his reign three immense tasks preoccupied him: unification of the state; maintenance of the European balance of power against France; and defense of the realm against the Turks. He went far toward attaining his goals.

In 1657 the fortunes of his house were at a low ebb. War-torn Bohemia was exhausted and depopulated. The Turks held over two-thirds of Hungary. The principality of Transylvania, supposedly a dependency of the Hungarian crown, had become independent. In the western part of Hungary that was still under Hapsburg rule the Magyar magnates seriously restricted the sovereign's power. In all the Hapsburg possessions finances and administration were in confusion.

Each province of the monarchy had its own estates or representative assemblies, dominated by the provincial nobility and having extensive powers, including the veto of imperial taxes. Leopold began to infiltrate the nobility and the high administration of the provinces with men of his own choice. The new nobility, who were usually not natives of their province and were often of foreign origin, owed their property and their eminence to the emperor. They voted accordingly, so that in time Leopold transformed the estates from law-making bodies to law-accepting bodies — rubber stamps for his will.

Building on foundations laid by his predecessors, Leopold superimposed imperial administrative councils on the provincial political institutions. Although they did not displace local organs of government, the imperial agencies directed and controlled the provincial governments, administering the entire realm in the interests of the emperor. They were the principal instruments of monarchic centralization. Leopold modeled his court at Vienna on Versailles, but unlike Louis XIV he used the court aristocracy in important posts, tying them yet closer to the throne.

The Hapsburg standing army had come into being during the reign of Leopold's father, Ferdinand III. Leopold strengthened it so that it became one of Europe's largest. Until 1715 all the troops came only from the German-speaking provinces, while the officers, like the civil bureaucrats, were drawn from all parts of the monarchy and from abroad. Thus, the leadership of the army was supranational, owing its first allegiance to the emperor.

The imposition of religious uniformity was an essential part of Leopold's policies. By the end of the Thirty Years' War Protestantism had been rooted out from among the nobles and townspeople of the German provinces and Bohemia. It persisted among many of the peasantry who, ostensibly Catholic, practiced their religion in secret. Persecution by church and state forced them to give up their faith or drove them out of their homelands. Despite his personal piety, however, Leopold did not tolerate interference by the Catholic Church in affairs of state and steadily increased his own power over the church.

As a result of his policies of unification and centralization, the Hapsburg Monarchy by the end of the seventeenth century had advanced far in the direction of monarchic absolutism. It lagged behind the France of Louis XIV in the degree of centralization and the extent to which it had subordinated particularism, but the task of unification that confronted Leopold was much more difficult than the task facing his Bourbon cousin.

HAPSBURG VERSUS BOURBON

The struggle against French domination of Europe was the second of Leopold's three chief preoccupations. Louis XIV's ambitions to expand his kingdom to the Rhine and the Alps would have been enough to raise the Hapsburgs against him, for they would have fought to keep him out of Germany, but the ancient Hapsburg-French rivalry was heightened by Louis's claim to the Spanish throne. The Austrians were handicapped in their efforts to restrain Louis by having to fight the Turks and by the reluctance of the German princes, who were traditionally suspicious of Hapsburg ambitions in Germany, to offer assistance. After Louis's conquests in the second war against the Dutch, with whom Austria was allied, Leopold had to acquiesce to the French conquests at the Peace of Nijmegen, 1678–1679. At the height of his power Louis was so contemptuous of his Hapsburg enemy that he boldly seized parts of the Holy Roman Empire through the Chambers of Reunion and ringed the Austrian Monarchy by alliances with Brandenburg, Bavaria, Cologne, Sweden, Turkey, and Poland.

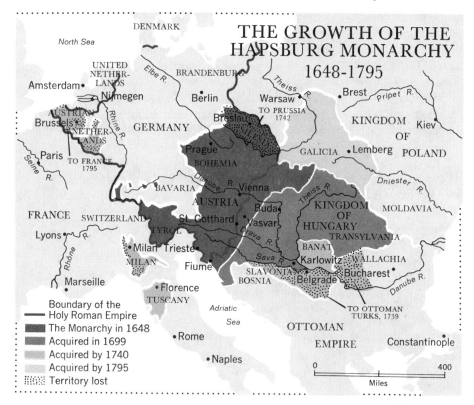

THE GROWTH OF THE HAPSBURG MONARCHY 1648-1795

Boundary of the
Holy Roman Empire
The Monarchy in 1648
Acquired in 1699
Acquired by 1740
Acquired by 1795
Territory lost

The Peace of Nijmegen was not without its advantages for Austria. It allowed Leopold to direct his full energies against the Turks. Victories over that old foe much enhanced Austria's power and prestige and enabled it to resume its anti-French activities. The Hapsburgs' leading part in the War of the Spanish Succession was rewarded at the Peace of Utrecht in 1713 with the cession to Austria of the Spanish possessions in Italy and the southern Netherlands.

EXPULSION OF THE TURKS

In 1663 a large Turkish army marched up the Danube to make new conquests for the sultan. The Christian powers, under papal auspices, combined in a Holy League to stop the threat and in 1664 vanquished the Turks and compelled them to agree to a twenty-year truce with Austria that gave part of Turkish-held Hungary to the Hapsburgs. Many Hungarians who found themselves under Austrian rule preferred Turkish hegemony, under which they had enjoyed considerable autonomy and religious toleration. For forty years after the truce they were in frequent revolt against Vienna, knowing that Hapsburg centralization would infringe upon their traditional liberties and that force would be used to coerce the many Protestants into becoming Catholics. Not unexpectedly, their rebellion received underground assistance from Louis XIV.

The Turks used the truce to consolidate gains they had made in the Mediterranean and to prepare for another invasion of the Hapsburg realm. Early in the 1680's they moved. The leaders of the Hungarian resistance offered themselves as allies and Louis XIV sent assurances that he would not come to Leopold's aid. By mid-July, 1683, the invading army of 250,000 Turks and Hungarians stood at the gates of Vienna. The city had but 14,000 soldiers to defend it. Pope Innocent XI's call for a crusade was ignored by Louis XIV, but Saxony, Bavaria, and Poland answered the summons. In a brilliant victory under John III Sobieski, king of Poland, the siege of Vienna was lifted in September. Europe hailed the Polish king with a line from the Gospel of St. John, "There was a man sent from God whose name was John."

Disagreements among the allies and Leopold's envy of the acclaim given Sobieski distracted the victors from immediate pursuit of the Turks. In 1684 a new Holy League mounted a vigorous campaign against the Turks by land and sea.[1] By 1697 the Hapsburgs had won nearly all of Hungary and Transylvania and part of Slavonia. By the Peace of Karlowitz, 1699, the Turks recognized these conquests and in addition ceded territory in southeastern Europe to Russia, Poland, and Venice. The Peace of Karlowitz proved one of the great turning points in European history. It marked the end of the centuries-long Turkish menace to Europe, and it established Austria as the foremost power of central and southeastern Europe.

SUBJUGATION OF HUNGARY

Bureaucrats and priests followed the Austrian armies into Hungary. They used stern repression and terrorism to break the resistance of the Hungarians. Although the Magyar nobles were left in possession of their lands and peasants and were permitted to retain their provincial assemblies and national diet, they were forced in 1687 to renounce the traditional rights to elect their own king and to bear arms against the monarch if they thought he had infringed their privileges. They agreed to make the Hungarian crown hereditary in the male Hapsburg line. Leopold further weakened Hungarian resistance by making grants of empty land in the newly won territories to non-Magyar nobles and by promoting the settlement there of German and Slavic peasants. Hence-

[1] During the war the Athenian Parthenon, used by the Turks as a munitions magazine, was reduced to the present ruins when Venetian ships bombarded Athens in 1687.

forth, imperial bureaucrats in Vienna administered Hungary. The Hungarians did not take easily to the new order. A rebellion, led by Francis Rakoczy, prince of Transylvania, and aided by France, broke out during the War of the Spanish Succession. After initial successes the rebellion was put down by Hapsburg troops in 1711.

The defeat of the Turks and the conquest of Hungary rounded out the work of Leopold. During his reign he had more than doubled the size of his dynastic patrimony, built up an administrative organization that held his polyglot Danubian realm together, and raised the monarchy to great-power status in Europe. Although he was not a Grand Monarch, he was an effective absolutist.

CHARLES VI, 1711–1740

Joseph, Leopold's son and heir, ruled only six years and died without children in 1711. The crown went to his brother Charles. The new empéror made a secret agreement in 1713 with the members of his family to guarantee the undivided inheritance of his dominions to his eldest son or, lacking a son, his eldest daughter. In 1719 he ordered the publication of this agreement, called the Pragmatic Sanction, in order to ensure the succession of Maria Theresa, his daughter and sole heir apparent, who had been born in 1717. He sought domestic and international consent for the sanction to forestall claimants after his death. The provincial estates of his own realm agreed readily enough, but foreign powers exacted diplomatic and commercial advantages in return for recognition of the sanction as inviolable fundamental law. By 1739 Charles had obtained the consent of all the powers except Bavaria and the Palatinate. In October, 1740, Charles VI died. Less than two months later Frederick II of Prussia invaded Austria, laying claim to part of Maria Theresa's inheritance despite Prussia's adherence to the Pragmatic Sanction. In touching off the War of the Austrian Succession, he undid Charles's carefully spun diplomatic web.

FISCAL PROBLEMS AND THE PEASANTRY

Military expenditures, the drain of wars, court expenses, and fiscal mis-management kept government finances in an unending state of crisis during the reigns of Leopold and his sons. Early in the eighteenth century the government made a determined effort to put its financial affairs in order, and for a few years conditions improved. Then Charles VI's heavy expenditures on his court and army once more brought a decline, so that when he died the state was near bankruptcy.

In its effort to increase revenues the government levied many new taxes, debased the currency, established monopolies, and borrowed money on lands that belonged to the monarch. Fiscal problems impelled the state to interfere in the relationship between nobles and the peasants who lived on their lands. Most of the monarchy's peasants were serfs of the nobles or hereditary subjects, as they were called in Austria. The serfs owed many obligations in cash, kind, and labor to their lords. They also paid taxes to the state for the land that they tilled for their own use. These taxes were the chief source of the government's income. The land that the peasants worked for their lords, the demesne land, was not taxed.

In Leopold's reign the government discovered that landowners were increasing their demesnes at the expense of serf land, thereby reducing the state's tax revenues. Moreover, the increase in demesnes forced the demesne peasants to spend more time in unpaid work for their lords, which reduced the amount of money they earned and consequently their taxes. Spurred on by peasant unrest as well as by loss of revenue, the government decided that in its own interests it should intervene to protect the peasants. Between 1680 and 1738 imperial decrees were issued to limit the lords' demands upon their serfs and to end the reduction in area of taxable land. Lacking adequate means of enforcement these laws were disregarded by the noble landowners, and the tax-paying capacity of the peasantry continued to decline.

The government sought to increase revenue by mercantilist devices. The central European variety of mercantilism was called cameralism, from *Kammeramt,* the German word for treasury, because its primary purpose was to increase the sovereign's revenues. New industries were introduced and old ones expanded in hopes of stimulating economic growth, increasing tax income, and meeting domestic demands for goods that would otherwise have to be imported. The government attempted to promote commerce by road improvements and, during Charles VI's reign, by developing the Adriatic ports of Trieste and Fiume. Despite these efforts, economic development lagged. Many of the new enterprises failed, and most of the others barely managed to survive.

THE SPANISH BOURBONS

After the long and brutal War of the Spanish Succession the powers involved in the Treaty of Utrecht recognized Philip of Anjou, grandson of Louis XIV, as Philip V of Spain. The first of the Spanish Bourbon monarchs found his new kingdom in a state of nearly total collapse. For almost a century Spain had been declining economically and its population had fallen from approximately seven million to less than five million. It suffered from chronic unemployment. Much land lay untilled. Taxes had increased without bringing government solvency. Steady devaluation of the copper currency resulted in an alarming inflation. The volume of shipping between Spain and its overseas empire had fallen to one-quarter of what it had been a century before. Industry stagnated and many trades disappeared. The power of the central government had declined, while the power of the nobility and the church increased. During the seventeenth century the number of clergy and religious orders had approximately doubled, comprising an economically unproductive burden on the weakened country. Once noted for its prowess, the army had been reduced to a rabble of twenty thousand men; the fleet had dwindled to twenty rotten ships. Intellectual life had stagnated, and the clergy, who were formerly leaders of thought, had become notorious for ignorance and sloth. The Treaty of Utrecht had stripped Spain of its Italian possessions, of the Spanish Netherlands, and of Gibraltar and Minorca; Spain was clearly the major loser in the war. The future of the country appeared bleak.

The new Bourbon regime embarked upon a program designed to reverse the country's decline. Under its guidance much progress was made during the eighteenth century: population increased and economic activity revived. Spain once again became an important power, although it never achieved the dominant position it had occupied in the sixteenth century. The instrument that the government used to achieve its goal was monarchic absolutism. The Spanish brand of absolutism was less dynamic and less creative than absolutism elsewhere, and its impact upon the traditional ways of life and administration was much less than that of other absolute monarchies. The personalities of Philip V (1700–1746) and his son Ferdinand VI (1746–1759), the first two Bourbon kings, had much to do with the relative timidity of Spanish absolutism, for absolutism reflected the strengths and weaknesses of the man at the head of state. In view of the personal qualities of Philip and Ferdinand, it was remarkable that so much was accomplished.

Philip was indolent, guilt-ridden, superstitious, hypochondriac, and dirty. His incompetence was relieved by the capacity of his second wife, Elizabeth Farnese, stepdaughter of the duke of Parma, whom he married in 1714 and upon whom he depended for the rest of his life. Energetic and ambitious, Elizabeth acquired skill in the practice of ruling the state. Philip's successor, Ferdinand VI, seemed no stronger a man than his father. Yet he recognized his own lack of ability and was content to follow the domestic policies laid down in the preceding reign and to let more able men run the government for him.

Credit for the achievements of the reigns of the first two Spanish Bourbons belonged more to their ministers, supported by Elizabeth Farnese, than to the monarchs themselves. Philip arrived in Spain with a corps of French advisers who were trained in the methods of French absolutism. They immediately instituted a series of internal reforms designed to strengthen the state and increase the central power. Their work was continued in later years by a succession of competent ministers, among whom the most able was Cardinal Giulio Alberoni, who came to Spain from Italy with Elizabeth Farnese in 1714.

CENTRALIZATION

The Hapsburgs had not united Spain; they had merely imposed a central authority of king's councils upon the constitutions and laws of the feudal kingdoms comprising Spain. As long as the monarchs were capable, the council system worked effectively. From Philip III through Charles II — through the entire seventeenth century — the monarchs grew progressively weaker while the forces of particularism grew stronger. The Bourbon regime retained the councils but established an administrative organization to run them. Patterned after the French model, it had six ministries: foreign, navy, war, justice, finance, and the Indies. Each minister was to have full authority in his sphere and was to deal directly with the king.

The Bourbons also established direct control over provincial and district administration. In imitation of the French system, intendants were made responsible for the main burden of government at the provincial level. The districts, into which the provinces were divided, continued to be administered by *corregidors,* as they had been under the Hapsburgs. The corregidors exercised a wide variety of functions and for the mass of the Spaniards were the embodiment of centralized power.

When Philip V came to the throne, two-thirds of the appointments to the multitudinous church offices in Spain were made by the papacy, which gained a large income from vacant church posts and from fees paid by Spaniards in church courts. After the War of the Spanish Succession — during which the papacy supported the Austrian claims — the Bourbon government entered into long diplomatic negotiations with Rome which finally produced the Concordat of 1753. This agreement gave the king the right of appointment held by the pope and the income from ecclesiastical vacancies, and it allowed him to tax church land. A victory for royal absolutism, the Concordat did not end the resistance of important sections of the clergy, especially the Jesuits, to these extensions of royal power.

Philip's French administrators introduced changes in tax collection and made economies in administrative operations. Later ministers tried to encourage the growth of trade and industry by reducing or abolishing oppressive taxes that were inimical to development, introducing new industries, attracting skilled foreign workers, building roads, raising tariffs against imports, building up the merchant marine and navy, and enforcing regulations against smugglers who cut in on Spanish trade with her American possessions. As a result, the government achieved solvency and could carry out its domestic and foreign policies.

FOREIGN AFFAIRS

Under Bourbon rule Spain once again played an active role in European power politics. Philip's reign, born in war, saw Spain in almost constant conflict with other powers over Spanish claims to parts of Italy (he won Naples and Sicily for his younger son, Charles, in 1735), attempts to gain the crown of France, and diplomatic intrigues to recover Gibraltar from Britain. The last of Philip's struggles grew out of British smuggling activities in Spanish America. The clause in the Treaty of Utrecht allowing the British to import a limited number of slaves each year enabled the British to smuggle in more than the quota and to engage in commerce in other contraband. When they seized smugglers' vessels, Spanish coast guards manhandled British crews. In 1738 an unsavory British seaman, Captain Jenkins, presented before a bellicose Parliament his severed ear, claiming that it had been cut off by a Spanish coast guard, and Britain went to war against Spain. The War of Jenkins's Ear, undertaken for commercial ends rather than the vindication of Captain Jenkins, merged into the general European conflict of the War of the Austrian Succession in 1742. Spain stood with Prussia and France against Britain and Austria. Spain's contributions were appreciable and costly,.but they were poorly rewarded. By the treaty ending the war in 1748 Spain regained for the younger brother of the king merely the Italian duchies of Parma and Piacenza. Ferdinand VI fought no more wars, even though Spain had made a remarkable comeback in the arena of dynastic power politics.

Compared to other absolutist monarchies, the achievements of the reigns of Philip V and Ferdinand VI were modest. Yet they placed Spain in the new current transforming the governmental structures of most European nations. They also prepared the way for more incisive changes under Ferdinand's successor, Charles III. (See pp. 450–451.)

HOHENZOLLERN PRUSSIA

At the end of the Thirty Years' War Germany was atomized into about 360 separate states. In addition, nearly 2,500 imperial knights held sovereign right as rulers of their own estates, although their properties averaged only about 100 acres each. None of the rulers conceived of a unified German state; atomization suited their individual purposes and ambitions. They followed independent courses to increase whatever power and wealth they possessed. Theoretically all were part of the Holy Roman Empire, and each sent representatives to the Imperial Diet, but the empire was no longer a viable political entity. Although the diet sat continuously at Ratisbon (Regensburg) from 1663 to the dissolution of the empire in 1806, its delegates spent their time in endless debate over singularly unimportant issues.

Among the many states, one was destined to unify Germany. The Electorate of Brandenburg had been ruled since 1415 by the Hohenzollern dynasty. During the first half of the seventeenth century the Hohenzol-

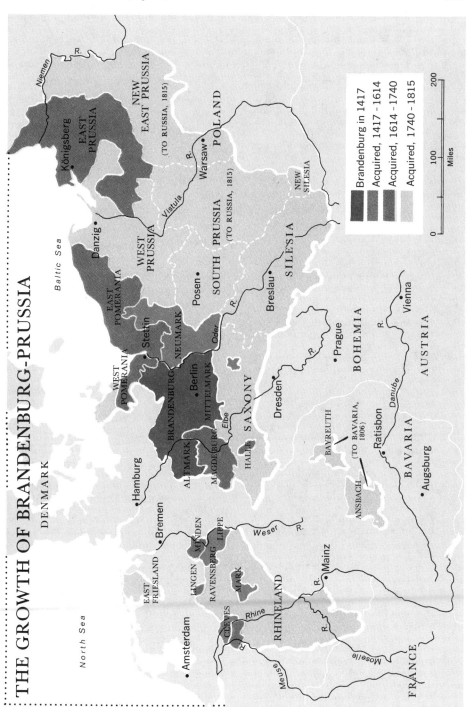

THE GROWTH OF BRANDENBURG-PRUSSIA

North Sea

Baltic Sea

DENMARK

• Amsterdam

• Bremen

• Hamburg

EAST FRIESLAND

LINGEN

MINDEN

RAVENSBERG

LIPPE

MARK

CLEVES

Rhine

RHINELAND

Meuse

Moselle

• Mainz

R.

FRANCE

Weser R.

ALTMARK

MAGDEBURG

MITTELMARK

Elbe

BRANDENBURG

• Berlin

HALLE

SAXONY

• Dresden

NEUMARK

Oder

WEST POMERANIA

• Stettin

EAST POMERANIA

WEST PRUSSIA

• Danzig

Vistula

EAST PRUSSIA

• Königsberg

Niemen R.

NEW EAST PRUSSIA

(TO RUSSIA, 1815)

POLAND

• Warsaw

R.

SOUTH PRUSSIA

(TO RUSSIA, 1815)

• Posen

NEW SILESIA

SILESIA

• Breslau

• Prague

BOHEMIA

R.

BAYREUTH

(TO BAVARIA, 1806)

ANSBACH

• Ratisbon

Danube

BAVARIA

• Augsburg

• Vienna

AUSTRIA

Brandenburg in 1417

Acquired, 1417 - 1614

Acquired, 1614 - 1740

Acquired, 1740 - 1815

0   100   200

Miles

lerns increased their holdings by inheritance and by the provisions of the Treaty of Westphalia to the extent that their realm became the largest of the German princedoms. Their possessions were scattered across northern Germany from the Polish to the Dutch frontiers. Each territory had its own government and laws, and like the Hapsburg domains the only common entity was the ruler, known by many titles, such as elector of Brandenburg, duke of Prussia, duke of Cleves, count of Mark and Ravensburg, and so on. There was not a single name for the realm until 1807, when it officially became the Kingdom of Prussia. The estates (representative assemblies) of each territory passed on all legislation and taxation and, similar to the States of the Dutch provinces, they had independent fiscal, judicial, and administrative powers. The limitations on royal authority were particularly strong in the eastern provinces, where a numerous and assertive landed gentry, the Junkers, dominated the estates.

The Hohenzollern dominions were particularly hard hit by the Thirty Years' War. Brandenburg, the home territory, was occupied by foreign troops from 1627 to 1643, and other parts of the realm were held and fought over by rival armies. A number of cities and large stretches of the country-side lost many inhabitants. Organized economic life was almost completely disrupted. Even the most astute political observer of the mid-seventeenth century would have been reluctant to prophesy that within a century a unified, absolutist state would be formed out of this scattered and impoverished agglomeration of territories.

Three circumstances worked to that end. The first and most important was that over four successive generations the Hohenzollern dynasty produced one ruler of genius, two others of extraordinary capacity, and one of better than average abilities. All four were infected with the ambition to be absolute within their territories and to be a power in Europe. The second circumstance was the accident that their territories were scattered from the Vistula to the Rhine rivers, providing bases for diplomatic and military operations throughout Germany. The third circumstance was one common to monarchies of the age: absolutism seemed the only guarantee of order and prosperity, both considerations made more pressing in Germany by the destruction and dislocation of the Thirty Years' War and the jungle-like power politics of dynastic statecraft.

THE GREAT ELECTOR, 1640–1688

Frederick William of Brandenburg, known to history as the Great Elector, was the first of the creators of Prussian absolutism. Born in the early years of the Thirty Years' War, he grew up in troubled times. He received an excellent primary education and at fourteen went to Holland, where he studied for four years at the University of Leyden. He traveled much in the Netherlands, and from the practical Dutch he learned lessons about statecraft, economics, and religious toleration that proved useful in later years. He succeeded his father in 1640 at the age of twenty. Heavyset and above average in height, Frederick William was a man of seemingly inexhaustible energy. Strong-willed, imaginative, and daring, he feared nothing and refused to let failures discourage him.

He showed his mettle from the very start. Most of his possessions were held by foreign troops; he had no available revenues; and he could not depend upon his army. He immediately began to conciliate his domestic and foreign enemies, built up a small but efficient army, and managed to gain new territory in the Treaty of Westphalia. After the war he set out to weld his possessions into an absolute monarchy. Like his fellow absolutists in other lands, he accomplished this end by subjugation of the nobility, bureaucratic centralization, and the establishment of a standing army under his control.

By gradual steps he deprived the provincial estates of most of their power. He persuaded the nobles to accept reductions in the power of the provincial estates by making them substantial concessions in other areas. For example, he ratified enactments that the Junkers had extorted from his predecessors giving them greater power over their peasants. He legalized the conversion of the Junkers' landed estates from fiefs, held in return for service to the crown, into properties held in full ownership. He recognized the Junkers as the only class that was allowed to own rural property and confirmed their exemption from payment of taxes and import-export duties.

In the administration of local government Frederick William replaced the nobility with his own bureaucrats and thereby laid the foundation for the Prussian civil service. A governor and a staff of agents and commissioners of the central government ran each province. The towns were permitted to keep the appearance of self-government and to elect their own officials, but Frederick William's commissioners told them whom to choose. The entire civil service was directed from Berlin by the Privy Council of Brandenburg. The Privy Council had been established in 1604 when a previous elector appointed a small group of men to serve as his private advisers. In 1651 Frederick William transformed the council into a ministry in which each privy councilor was responsible for the supervision of a province. The elector dominated the council and established the administrative policy that it carried out. He chose the councilors from all parts of the realm and from abroad. Initially most of them were nobles, but after 1660 bureaucrats of middle-class origins became increasingly important in the council.

The army was the most important instrument that Frederick William used to achieve the goal of a powerful, unified state. The army, plagued by unruly and disloyal troops before 1640, was purged and brought directly under the monarch's control. The independent authority of regimental commanders was reduced, and their power to commission junior officers was removed. A rudimentary general staff was organized to exercise centralized control over the units. Frederick William undertook to train, equip, and discipline a relatively small army (during his reign it never numbered more than thirty thousand) that was recognized by both his allies and his enemies as one of the most effective in Europe. The army's major role in unification was simply its presence: it represented the monarch's power in every one of his far-flung territories. By the end of the reign it had also begun to serve as the tax-collecting agency of the state as well as its police force.

ECONOMIC POLICY

Frederick William's prime domestic concern was to maintain the army. Over half of the state's revenues went to this purpose. He enforced strict mercantilist policies — high tariffs, external trade restrictions, subsidies and monopolies to manufacturers to stimulate domestic industry — in order to enrich the realm and increase its population. Roads, canals, and harbor improvements were major state concerns, and an efficient postal system was established. Attempts were made to found overseas colonies and create overseas trading companies. Frederick William invited people from other parts of Germany and other countries to settle in Brandenburg and East Prussia; he offered them exemption from taxes for a period of years and gave them farm tools, seed, and cattle to get started. He welcomed religious minorities that were persecuted by other absolutist monarchs, particularly the Huguenots in France under Louis XIV. The exiles brought in new techniques and industries and assumed important roles in economic life. The nobles among them applied their talents to becoming officers in the army.

In common with all the mercantilist absolutist monarchs, Frederick William enjoyed only partial success in his economic ambitions. Population increased from about 600,000 in 1640 to about 1,000,000 in 1688, but the country, still struggling to overcome the devastation of the Thirty Years' War, remained so poor that there was little excess capital available for investment in new enterprise. The urban middle class, so vital to economic development in other lands, demonstrated little vitality and remained content with stagnant economic conditions and meager incomes. Economic growth lagged. Although he increased taxes, Frederick William was unable to raise enough money and he was forced to depend upon subsidies from abroad and upon income from the crown domain. The crown domain comprised the estates and other productive enterprises that were the personal property of the Hohenzollern rulers. It was scattered throughout the territories and constituted a sizable aggregate. By careful economizing he increased its yield until by his death it produced over half of the state's total revenue. Such a feat of economy was achieved nowhere else in seventeenth-century Europe.

FOREIGN POLICY

Frederick William's foreign policy was undertaken for prestige as much as for the defense of his scattered possessions. Few others matched his skill in forming alliances; at one time or another he was the ally of nearly every power. As a price for his support he exacted subsidies for the maintenance of the army. Most of the time he was in the anti-French camp, although for short periods he aligned himself with Louis XIV.

His principal achievement in foreign affairs was to win full control over East Prussia, long held by the Hohenzollerns as a fief from the king of Poland. In 1656 he allied Brandenburg-Prussia with Sweden against Poland, then adroitly changed sides when Russia, Denmark, and Austria came to Poland's aid. By the end of the war he had managed to gain the allies' recognition of his sovereignty over East Prussia. Since the new territory was not part of the empire, by this act he raised his dynasty above the other German princes. As sovereign duke of Prussia, he became one of the crowned heads of Europe.

Frederick William's long reign was a record of extraordinary success. He transformed a devastated and disjointed collection of territories into a centrally directed, albeit superficially united, state. He elevated his dynasty above the rest of the German ruling families. He created an army and a military tradition that remained the bulwark of Hohenzollern absolutism. Finally, he made his state a power to be reckoned with in Europe.

FREDERICK I, 1688–1713

The Great Elector's son and heir, Frederick I, was a timid and sensitive cripple, lacking his father's energy and drive. He sought to compensate for his defects by imitating the splendors of the court of Louis XIV. He surrounded himself with courtiers, musicians, artists, and servants. He built the luxurious palace and gardens of Charlottenburg on the model of Versailles. He founded the University of Halle in 1694, the Royal Academy of Arts in 1696, and the Berlin Academy of Sciences in 1700, all of which were destined to play an important part in Prussian intellectual life. Unlike his hero — and unlike his father — he did not exercise autocratic control over the government, and inefficiency and corruption appeared in the highest levels of the bureaucracy.

He shared his father's faith in military might as the source of power and built up the army to 40,000. His faith was vindicated in 1701 when the hardpressed Emperor Leopold requested his assistance in the War of the Spanish Succession. In return for 8,000 men Leopold reluctantly agreed to recognize Frederick, his Brandenburg vassal, as king *in* Prussia, by virtue of his sovereignty over East Prussia. To placate the king of Poland, ruler of West Prussia, the "in" euphemism was used. Not until seventy years later, when Frederick's grandson annexed West Prussia, did the king *in* Prussia become king *of* Prussia.

FREDERICK WILLIAM I, DRILLMASTER, 1713–1740

In 1713 Frederick was succeeded by his twenty-five-year-old son, Frederick William I. The new king was uncontrollably violent in temper, vulgar in speech and manner, scornful of education and culture, and so deeply pious that he considered theaters "temples of Satan" and closed them when he became king, although later he allowed comedies to be presented in Berlin under strict censorship. He made a fetish of personal cleanliness, washing and grooming himself many times each day. He was so miserly that his own mother described him as avaricious. He had a mania about tall soldiers (he himself was only five feet five inches in height) and often judged the merits of his officers by their size, passing over able men for promotion because they were too short. He built up a 3,000-man personal guard, called the Potsdam Giant Regiment of grenadiers, recruited from all over Europe. Each guard was six to eight feet tall. The regiment was under his personal command and he delighted in drilling it for hours.

This royal neurotic was the most remarkable administrative reformer of his dynasty. He not only completed the work of centralization and despotic absolutism started by the Great Elector, but was the real father of Prussian militarism and Prussian bureaucratic efficiency. He called the army the "basis of his earthly bliss" and stated that upon it depended his "true interests, security, glory, and prestige." By spending four or five times as much annually on the army as on all other state activities, he increased its size from 40,000 to 83,000. It was the fourth largest army in Europe (after France, Russia, and Austria), although his state ranked only tenth in size and twelfth in population.

Previously the Prussian army had depended for manpower upon voluntary enlistment, impressment, recruitment in neighboring states, mercenaries and, in times of emergency, local militias. The king's harsh discipline encouraged desertion: between 1713 and 1740 over 30,000 soldiers fled the army. A new method of recruitment was obviously necessary, and in 1732 and 1733 decrees established the cantonal system of recruitment. Each regiment had a specific district or canton assigned to it. All young men in the district were enrolled upon the regimental recruiting list, and when the regiment could not fill its ranks from volunteers it drafted men from the list. All males were subject to call, but the bourgeoisie and upper stratum of the artisan class were generally exempted in the interests of promoting trade and industry. The conscripts came almost entirely from the least prosperous sections of the population, especially the poorest elements of the peasantry.

To promote efficiency and immediate obedience to orders the king introduced cruel discipline. Common soldiers were brutally whipped for the smallest offense. In 1714 Frederick William himself wrote the Infantry Regulations, governing every phase of the soldier's life in the garrison and in the field. The endless drilling and maneuvers that he prescribed made his troops the best trained in Europe.

THE OFFICER CORPS

An equally important innovation was to make the officer corps the monopoly of the landed nobility. Frederick William's grandfather had favored nobles for commissions, but he had allowed men of humble birth and foreigners to become officers and rise to high rank. At least three of the Great Elector's generals were sons of peasants, and in 1688 one-quarter of the officer corps were French Huguenots. Frederick William believed that Prussian nobles, accustomed to ordering about their serfs, would make the best commanders of the rustics who comprised the bulk of the army. He also had political reasons for drawing his officers exclusively from the landed nobility. Resistance to Hohenzollern absolutism persisted among the Junkers, and Frederick William was determined to stamp it out; his goal was to make the nobility "acknowledge no master but God and the King in Prussia." He made it illegal for nobles to enter the service of other monarchs. Lists were drawn up of all high-born youths between twelve and eighteen, and he personally selected boys from these lists for the cadet corps in Berlin, where they were trained for lifetime careers as army officers. By 1724 there were few noble families in all his possessions that did not have sons in the officer corps.

At the same time he provided solid advantages to service in the corps to hold the loyalty of the officers. To sons of families of small means he offered an education, a standard of living higher than any they could expect at home, and a social position second to none. The officer corps was the gateway to honor and prestige. The officer caste was a closed society and a superior one. At the same time there was complete social equality within it: everyone wore the same uniform (including the king, who always wore military dress), and only generals bore designations of rank. The nobility came to regard military service as its natural profession, and the officer corps became the chief supporter of absolutism. Its members thought of themselves not as Brandenburgers or Pomeranians but as soldiers of the Hohenzollerns. The nobility, once so jealous of its independence, had become a service nobility identifying its interests with those of the monarch.

The army and military life loomed so large in Frederick William's state that his son and successor, Frederick II, called it the "Sparta of the North." Yet for all the importance attached to the army, Frederick William used it little. He blustered and threatened, but when armed conflict seemed imminent, he withdrew. Perhaps he loved his soldiers too much to see them killed, or perhaps he was at heart a coward and feared to risk his power on the field of battle. Only twice did his regiments march to war. In 1714 he helped the Danes against the Swedes, and in the War of Polish Succession (1733–1735) he sent 10,000 men to aid the imperial forces, but peace was concluded before his troops saw action.

THE BUREAUCRACY COMPLETED

Frederick William carried his military scale of values over to the civil bureaucracy. It became as disciplined a machine as the army. He replaced the rule of councils that his grandfather had established with his own personal and direct rule. He set up a General Directory, headed by four ministers, as chief administrative agent of the central government and supervisor of the bureaucracy. Special bodies called Boards of War and Domain were established for each part of the realm. Their functions were similar in many ways to those of the French intendants. At the local level, tax commissioners were the agents of the central government in the towns, where all self-government had disappeared, while noble commissioners represented the state in the country districts.

The king managed his officials with an iron hand. Minutely detailed regulations and disciplinary rules were issued to guide the bureaucrats. Waste, slothfulness, corruption, deception, and disobedience were severely punished, sometimes even with death. Not only criticism of orders but initiative and self-reliance were considered acts of insubordination. Like the army, the civil bureaucracy became a special kind of organization with its own code, in which the supreme values were unswerving obedience, stern self-discipline, and hard work. Officials took a special pride in their jobs, saw service to the king as the highest duty and honor, and considered themselves superior to the people they governed.

"AN ARMY WITH A COUNTRY"

His army was so large and expensive that Frederick William had to mobilize the full resources of the country to support it. Years later a former Prussian general said of the Hohenzollern realm that it was "not a country with an army, but an army with a country that served as its headquarters and food supplier." Frederick William inherited a treasury that had been nearly emptied by his father's extravagances. By drastic reduction of non-military expenditures, efficient levying and collection of taxes, and skillful management of the crown domain, he doubled the state's revenues. He encouraged immigration to thinly populated territories (especially East Prussia), protected industry and agriculture with tariff barriers, and promoted industries that produced war materials, such as armaments or wool cloth for uniforms. Severe penalties were laid on people who did nothing gainful. When he met idlers on his walks through Berlin, he berated them and thrashed them with his cane. He even decreed that Berlin market women should spin, knit, or sew while waiting for customers or else lose their concessions.

Religion did not escape his surveillance. The pulpit became a loud-speaker to inculcate the duties of a citizen, particularly the prompt payment of taxes. Though Frederick William was an ardent Protestant and detested Catholicism he allowed his Catholic subjects religious freedom because he did not want them to emigrate and thereby decrease the population. He was less tolerant of Jews (there were about six thousand in his possessions), but he permitted them much economic freedom because he considered them useful in stimulating economic growth.

Frederick William's accomplishments were overshadowed by those of his more famous son, Frederick II, called the Great. Yet to the father belongs the dubious credit for founding Prussian militarism and despotism. It is little wonder that the Nazis considered him a great man and that a Nazi writer said, "Frederick William I speaks through Adolf Hitler."

FREDERICK THE GREAT, 1740-1786

Frederick II won the appellation "the Great" by virtue of his military prowess, his success in establishing Prussia as a great power, and his intellectual capacity. His admirers hailed him as the colossus of the age. He spawned imitators in the age of enlightened despotism as Louis XIV had in the age of divine right absolutism. Yet his detractors saw him as an evil genius — hypocritical, capable of any treachery, hungry for power and territory. He was, in truth, something less than a colossus and neither more nor less treacherous and power-hungry than most other monarchs of the age. He was simply more efficient and purposeful, while other absolutists succumbed to inertia. He was also calculating, bold, resilient, unceasingly industrious, cynical, and increasingly misanthropic as he aged. Above all, he commanded a state that was a military machine. It was not his creation, but he perfected it; its purpose was not his to choose, but he fulfilled it. The genius of Frederick II was to accept the Prussian military machine and the Hohenzollern goal of power and territorial aggrandizement and, with consummate skill and unswerving application, to use the one as the means to advance the other. His was a limited genius.

As a youth, Frederick was miserably unhappy in the barracks-room court of his father because he had a genuine love of music, art, and philosophy. He proved the most difficult cadet his father ever had, but the drillmaster king made a soldier of him. He burned the lad's books, broke his flutes, and thrashed him publicly. When the prince reached eighteen, he could take no more of the harsh discipline that caused peasants to desert the army in droves and was magnified many times over by his own sensitivity and his father's neurotic love-hate. He attempted to "desert" to France. Frederick was caught and forced to witness the beheading of his accomplice and best friend, a young officer named von Katte. He was even led to the scaffold himself in the belief that he, too, would die. After a spell in prison, Frederick bowed to discipline, took the wife his father chose, and accepted the life his father ordained. During his last illness in 1740 Frederick William said with a drill sergeant's pride, "I die contented since I leave such a worthy son and successor."

The reconciliation with his father was more than superficial. Although Frederick retained the serious intellectual and cultural interests of his youth — indeed, his reputation as an enlightened despot grew principally from such pursuits — culture was secondary to his furtherance of the traditional absolutist policies. They were his life's work. Though his commitment was as strong as his father's, his courage was greater. He was not simply a drillmaster. In 1740 within months of his accession at the age of twenty-eight he marched his army onto the field of battle. About one-quarter of his forty-six years on the throne were spent at war.

TUNING THE WAR MACHINE

Frederick changed no essential features of Prussian government, resting content to build on the foundations laid by the Great Elector and Frederick William I. At his accession he found the state administration and the army in excellent condition; he also found a huge cash reserve hoarded in casks in the cellar of the royal castle. He intervened far more frequently in the routine business of government than had his father, and he allowed his ministers less freedom of action. He made himself the single pivot for the whole government, the sole creator of policy. This herculean task was executed almost entirely by letter, since he rarely saw his ministers in person.

Frederick made personal tours of his territory to keep a close watch over the bureaucrats. In his snuff-stained, threadbare uniform "Old Fritz" (as he was called in his later years, not with much affection) was a familiar but awe-inspiring figure throughout his dominions to the end of his life. He used special agents, "Fiscals," and spies to sniff out corruption in the bureaucracy. On the whole, the civil servants performed their tasks efficiently, and they were well rewarded. Entrance into the service was gained by examination except for the top posts, for which nobles were favored. Promotion depended on merit.

Frederick's strong bias toward the nobility grew out of his belief that they alone possessed the superior natural qualities needed to lead and that they alone were moved by a sense of honor, enabling them to face danger and death unflinchingly and to serve without expectation of material reward. He scorned the bourgeoisie as money grubbers, incapable of

Brown Brothers

Frederick the Great of Prussia

"This is what I think as to politics. *I understand . . . that we are ever to try to cheat others. It is the way to have the advantage, or, at least, to be on a footing with the rest of mankind. For you may rest persuaded that all the states of the world run on the same career. . . . Never be ashamed of making alliances, and of being yourself the only party that draws advantage from them."* Heinrich von Treitschke, THE CONFESSIONS OF FREDERICK THE GREAT AND THE LIFE OF FREDERICK THE GREAT, ed. Douglas Sladen (New York, 1945).

self-sacrifice. If a bourgeois officer left the army in disgrace he turned to another career; a noble in the same straits chose suicide as the only honorable course. Frederick used bourgeois officers only in the exigencies of war, dismissing them or demoting them when opportunity allowed. Since the Junkers had been transformed into a state nobility they no longer posed a threat to the absolutist state. They enjoyed the largesse due to the loyal, receiving advances of money as either gifts or low-interest loans. Frederick encouraged the establishment of mortgage loan banks, where estate owners could borrow at low interest against their property; the banks were the first formally organized agricultural credit institutions in Europe.

Frederick extended to the Junkers the strong assurance that the state would not interfere in the administration of their estates or the control of their serfs. However, a major grievance of the peasantry had been the expropriation of their holdings by landlords who transferred the dispossessed peasants to their own demesne land as laborers. Frederick prohibited this practice in order to ensure that the peasants would have enough land to raise a family and provide the state with more taxpayers and army recruits. It was his only major agrarian reform, and it was only partially successful: many nobles continued to dispossess their peasants. On the king's own domain, forming about one-third of the kingdom, Frederick limited the labor services of the crown serfs and in 1777 provided assurance of inheritance of peasant holdings.

Frederick, no less than his predecessors, subverted the country to the maintenance of the army. He retained the cantonal system of recruitment but increased the proportion of foreign mercenary soldiers from one-third to.two-thirds of the total enlisted strength, because he judged that his subjects were more useful to the army as taxpayers and producers than as cannon fodder. He imposed rigorous and continual training on officers and discouraged marriage as inimical to devotion to duty. The largely bachelor officer corps provided an added dividend in reducing expenditures on pensions to widows. Constant drill and inspection, an improved supply system, and regular maneuvers kept the army on a constant war footing. A master tactician, Frederick emphasized mobility, fast deployment of troops, flanking attack, and integrated artillery as an infantry-support weapon. Its discipline, training, and tactics made the Prussian army the terror of far larger enemies with greater resources.

STRATEGIST AND STATESMAN

Frederick II's wars belonged to the mainstream of eighteenth-century power politics and will be treated later. It is only necessary here to describe briefly the genius that won him so many victories. Frederick was first and foremost a strategist, and his statecraft turned on strategical considerations. His actions were always conditioned by one overwhelming defensive concern: some part or another of his extended realm was immediately vulnerable to every major power in Europe except Spain. Such vulnerability put a premium not only on military might but also on careful diplomatic arrangements to protect home base while the army was in the field. Frederick's plan of aggression was to engage in short, sharp, surprise actions against a power that was diplomatically off balance, if only momentarily so, and to seize and hold its territory with a minimum of troops. This pattern of aggression marked his first three campaigns and paid rich dividends on the first two occasions. Only on the third occasion did Frederick get in deeper than he had expected.

His first attack, on Austrian Silesia in the late autumn of 1740, touched off the War of the Austrian Succession. It was a surprise move, made in defiance of the Pragmatic Sanction but in the certainty that most of the major powers would come in against Austria. The mobility of the attack assured rapid victory and in 1742 Austrian peace overtures were accepted by Frederick, Silesia was ceded to him, and he left the war. The general war continued and when the tide turned in Austria's favor against the rest of the powers, Frederick renewed war on Austria to safeguard his gains. In 1744 he made a sudden attack into Bohemia. He quickly accepted Austrian peace proposals after inflicting a stunning defeat on Saxony, Austria's ally, in December, 1745, and again withdrew from the war. In his third campaign in 1756 Frederick undertook a preventive war, because Austria, Russia, and France had concluded alliances that were clearly directed against him. The preventive war escalated into the Seven Years' War. (See pp. 395–397.) Though he won spectacular victories Frederick was on the verge of utter defeat three times. He gained no territory at the peace in 1763 and was thankful to receive confirmation of his Silesian conquest of twenty years before.

The Seven Years' War had a chastening effect on Frederick. For the rest of his reign, he tried to avoid war. In the almost bloodless War of the Bavarian Succession, 1778 to 1779, astute maneuvering of his army and a personal correspondence between Frederick and the empress kept Bavaria out of Austrian hands. In 1772 Frederick engineered the first partition of Poland in order to prevent a general war from growing out of the Austrian and Russian confrontation over Poland. His share was West Prussia. In the last year of his life he organized the League of the German Princes to prevent Austria from acquiring Bavaria.

ECONOMIC REVITALIZATION

The Seven Years' War, which ended midway in Frederick's reign, exhausted the Prussian economy. For the remaining twenty-three years of his reign Frederick tried to achieve the economic revitalization of Prussia. Silesia, his greatest conquest, proved invaluable. Rich in iron, coal, and lead, and possessing a highly developed textile industry, Silesia increased the Prussian population by half and provided a large area contiguous to the homeland of Brandenburg. After 1763 Silesia was fully exploited economically.

Better farming techniques and the introduction of new crops (especially the potato), land reclamation by marsh drainage along the eastern rivers, and repopulation that drew in about 300,000 settlers, principally from other German states, resuscitated Prussian agriculture. Mercantile practices such as subsidies, monopolies, tariffs, export restrictions, and abolition of internal tolls stimulated industry and domestic trade, although they discouraged foreign commerce. The state assumed a number of sales monopolies, engaged in mining and lumbering, and by virtue of the royal domain became the largest grain producer. A state bank was established at Berlin in 1765 with branches elsewhere. It stimulated investment by extending credit, controlled the currency by issuing paper money, and made a profit for the state.

By the end of the reign Prussia had a fairly diversified economy. Heavy taxation, made heavier in the last decade, prevented the economic recovery from being reflected in the standard of living of the masses and the army of 200,000 rather than the masses lived off such fat as the land of Prussia produced.

REQUIEM

In 1786 the dying Frederick could look back upon a reign of extraordinary accomplishments. Following the course set by his predecessors, he had added imagination and daring to their ambitions. He audaciously gambled everything in two great wars, which he himself started and fought with incredible skill, and he won universal recognition of Prussia as a great power. He purchased victory by the purposeful and ruthless application of his will to every obstacle — foreign and domestic, friend and enemy. His achievements seized the imagination of all Germans and stimulated the awakening of German nationalism. According to the eighteenth-century poet Goethe, the giant of German literature, Frederick was "the polar star, who seemed to turn about himself Germany, Europe, nay the whole world." Friedrich Meinecke, a modern German historian, wrote of Frederick that for the first time "cold and hard *raison d'état* took human form among us Germans." He excused Frederick's wars of aggression with the words, "He laid the foundations of Prussia's greatness and thus his action is justified by history." On March 21, 1933, Adolf Hitler chose Frederick's tomb as a suitable place to announce the official birth of the Nazi Third Reich.

ABSOLUTISM AND OLIGARCHY IN THE NORTH AND EAST
CHAPTER THIRTEEN

Absolutism gained a foothold on the northern and eastern peripheries of Europe, although the pattern of statecraft was not so monotonously absolutist as in the west. The Russian monarchy, initially far more despotic than western monarchies, was made absolutist in the western manner but with significant differences by Peter the Great (1682–1725). Denmark accepted absolutism without a murmur. Sweden's Charles XI (1660–1697) initiated an absolutism that was the principal model for Russia and Prussia. Yet it was in the north and east that absolutism suffered some of its earliest reverses. Poland (like the Dutch Republic and England) never developed a successful absolute monarchy. The Swedish aristocracy took advantage of a defeat in war and a succession crisis to reverse absolutism in favor of a highly traditional variety of noble oligarchy. The Ottoman Empire, where a thoroughgoing Eastern despotism precluded Western absolutism, became increasingly atomistic in political and social structure at the expense of the sultanate. Even in Russia the era of weak tsars from 1725 to 1762 enabled the nobility to condition Russian absolutism in a way that was highly favorable to themselves. European absolutism was, in fact, far more uniformly potent in the continental homeland than on the peripheries, east, north, or west.

RUSSIA BECOMES A GREAT POWER

The death in 1682 of the childless Tsar Fedor III precipitated a power struggle that threatened a new Time of Troubles. (See pp. 176–177.) In 1696, after years of turmoil during which the throne was occupied jointly by Fedor's brother Ivan, a half-blind mental defective, and his half-brother Peter, Ivan died and left Peter as the sole ruler. Peter's reign marked a major turning point in Russian history. Largely through his efforts Russia made its debut as a great power. At the same time, the blame for worsening many of the ills that plagued Russia must also be laid to him. More than most of his contemporary absolutist monarchs, Peter put the welfare of his subjects last.

PETER THE GREAT, 1696–1725

Peter had the crudeness and ferocity of a savage. He was coarse in manner and speech and contemptuous of ordinary decency, took a special delight in torture, had a violent and uncontrollable temper, and reveled in obscene and blasphemous drunken orgies. He married a nobleman's daughter when he was sixteen, forced her into a nunnery when he tired of her, and after a series of casual liaisons with women of the lower class married a Livonian peasant girl who became Empress Catherine.

This uncouth giant — he was six feet nine inches tall — possessed great ability as a ruler. He dealt decisively with problems and had vast energy and drive. Despite the toll taken by dissipation, he had an almost incredible capacity for hard work. He personally drafted almost all of the many legislative acts of his reign and handled much of the diplomatic correspondence. Most important, he had a vision of what he wanted his empire to be — a great power with himself as its absolute master — and he never lost sight of that dream.

Peter sought to realize his dream by borrowing ideas and methods from the more advanced societies of the West. The first tsar to travel abroad, he made a number of trips to the West to observe and learn at first hand and he induced hundreds of foreign technicians and artisans to come to Russia. His admiration for things Western was as excessive as all his other passions. With the exception of priests and peasants, his subjects were ordered to wear Western-style clothing and to shave their beards; those who would not shave were taxed in proportion to their wealth. He promoted the use of tobacco, hitherto condemned in Russia as sinful. He brought the Russian calendar into agreement with the European one — the Russians had formerly counted the years from what they believed was the date of the creation of the earth, September 1, 5508 B.C.

The most striking symbol of Peter's Western orientation was his new capital of St. Petersburg. Moscow was too Russian and too set in its ways to suit him. In 1703 he chose a site in the far northwestern corner of the realm that had been recently won in battle from the Swedes. He could get no closer to the West and still be on Russian soil. There, in bleak malarial marshes, a new city rose at immense cost in lives and money. Unlike Versailles, St. Petersburg was not a monument to regal glory. It was a window on the West through which Peter wanted his people to look in order to be drawn from their traditional ways. St. Petersburg also testified to the tsar's ambition to make Russia a naval power, for it looked out over the Gulf of Finland to the Baltic Sea.

Courtesy of the Rijksmuseum

Peter the Great, by A. de Gelder

"As a ruler, Peter knew neither moral nor political restraints, and lacked the most elementary political and social principles. His lack of judgment and his personal instability, combined with great talent and wide technical skill, astonished all foreigners. . . . In spite of the facts, that Peter's early moral guidance had been bad, that he had ruined his health, that his manners and way of life were uncouth, and that he had been unbalanced by the terrible experiences of his childhood, he remained sensitive, receptive, and extremely energetic. . . . He sacrificed everything to his sense of duty, but never succeeded in changing his personal habits." Vasili Klyuchevsky, PETER THE GREAT, tr. Liliana Archibald (London, 1958).

THE WARS OF PETER I

From 1690 to 1724 Russia was at war continuously except for thirteen months. Nearly all the wars were of Peter's own making, undertaken to expand his territories and to gain ports on the Baltic and the Black seas that would be open all year (Archangel, Russia's only seaport, lay on the White Sea and its harbor was frozen for nine months of the year). Above all, the wars were meant to demonstrate Russia's might.

Although Peter warred against the Turks, his greatest enemies were the Swedes, who held Finland, Karelia, and Livonia and dominated the eastern Baltic. Peter allied Russia with Poland and Denmark to partition the Swedish possessions and in 1700 hostilities began. The Great Northern War, 1700 to 1721, was contemporaneous with the War of the Spanish Succession; it was the northern theater of the general war that raged through Europe in the first decades of the eighteenth century.

The allies' expectation of an easy victory reckoned without the military genius of the youthful Swedish king, Charles XII. A few months after the war began, with just 8,000 troops Charles smashed a Russian army of 40,000 at Narva, a Swedish fortress on the Gulf of Finland. Peter fled in terror from the battlefield and for a time was ready to sue for peace, but fortune reprieved him when Charles turned his attention to Poland for the next few years. Peter rebuilt and rearmed his shattered army and constructed a formidable fleet. In 1707 Charles invaded Russia in force. Peter's armies, reorganized and trained, fell back before the advancing Swedes, drawing them ever farther into the vast Russian plain. Like the later invaders Napoleon and Hitler, Charles encountered Russia's most potent ally, winter. The winter of 1708–1709 turned out to be the worst in Europe for a hundred years and the Swedish troops suffered terrible losses. In June, 1709, weakened by their experiences, they met Peter's army in southern Russia at Poltava. The Swedes were routed and Charles fled; the victory resounded throughout Europe.

Peter's demand that Turkey give up Charles, who had taken refuge there, was refused. In the ensuing war Turkish victories forced Peter in 1711 to surrender some of his recent territorial acquisitions. Humiliated, the Russians turned to the northwest, where they had better fortune, conquering most of the Swedish Empire by 1719 and invading Sweden itself. By the Treaty of Nystadt in 1721 Peter gained Livonia and Estonia on the Baltic and Ingria and Karelia on the Gulf of Finland. Russia emerged as a major power, to be increasingly involved in European affairs. To celebrate his victory, Peter gave himself the titles Father of the Country, Emperor, and the Great. As if to confirm his self-esteem, within a year of the Peace of Nystadt he led an army into the Caucasus and wrested territories on the shores of the Caspian Sea from the shah of Persia.

THE PETRINE REFORMS

Peter's wars were responsible for many of the innovations and reforms to which he owes his fame. His need for men, money, and matériel dictated the establishment of a more efficient government and one completely under his control. He introduced a series of administrative innovations aimed at ending the chaos into which the governmental structure had disintegrated. He divided Russia into provinces (eight in 1707, increased to twelve in 1720), each subdivided into counties and districts, and all staffed by bureaucrats of the central government, in imitation of Western organization. The reform of the central administration began in 1711 when Peter set up a body of nine members, called the Governing Senate, as the principal administrative and judicial authority of the empire. Although it sometimes had a limited legislative role, its primary function, as Peter described it, was "to collect money, as much as possible, for money is the artery of war." To this end the senate exercised control over the fiscal system. When it became evident that the senate alone could not perform all the functions of a central administration, Peter established nine bureaus to run each of the major branches of government, based on the Swedish system. Like their Swedish models, the bureaus were headed not by one man but by a board or college of eleven men who made decisions by majority vote. Peter brought in a large number of foreign experts to act as advisers to these boards. Originally independent of the senate, the colleges were put under the supervision of that body in 1721.

Peter drew his administrators and army officers from the nobility. Unlike Prussia, where the Hohenzollerns had to tame the nobility, the Russian nobles had a tradition of state service. Peter's mushrooming bureaucracy and his almost perpetual wars made him demand much more of them than had his predecessors. To reduce evasion of state service, a bureau registered all nobles and kept records of their service. The noble entered service at fifteen and remained till death or disability ended his usefulness. No more than a third of the males of a family could be in the civil bureaucracy; the rest had to be in military service. Young nobles began their army service as ordinary recruits in line regiments or, if they came from important families, in the three special guards regiments organized by Peter. After a suitable period of training they received commissions.

Convinced that the demands of the state outweighed all other considerations, including lineage, Peter established the principle that social distinction rose from state service and not from ancestry. In 1722 he introduced a Table of Ranks that created fourteen parallel grades in the military and civil services. Every bureaucrat and officer was supposed to begin his service at the lowest rank and work his way up. A commoner became a noble when he won a commission as second lieutenant or ensign, lowest of the fourteen military ranks, or was promoted to the eighth rank (collegiate assessor) in the civil service. This system made the nobility heavily dependent on the favor of the tsar. It remained in effect, with some modifications, until the 1917 revolution. Although persons with wealth or connections rose more rapidly than others and filled most of the higher posts, a career in governmental service proved to be the road to nobility and fame for many persons of humble origin, and in this way the reform served to democratize the nobility.

To systematize and simplify the fiscal and military obligations that he demanded of his subjects, Peter introduced two major reforms: the poll tax and conscription. His military expenses, which sometimes amounted to 80 per cent of the government's total expenditures, kept him in a perpetual financial crisis. His counselors had long advised the replacement of the tax on households (hearth tax), the chief source of revenue, by a poll tax on every male. In 1719 Peter ordered a census of every male, including infants but excluding the nobility and clergy. The estimated military expenditures were divided by the total number of males, and the quotient was the poll tax rate. The yield was not as high as expected because some peasants were unable to pay the tax or managed to evade it, but enough came in to allow Peter for the first time to solve his financial difficulties. An incidental effect of the poll tax was that it wiped out the last legal distinction between serfs and slaves. Slaves had not been subject to taxation because they were not considered legal persons. Now they were entered in the tax rolls as serfs.

A new system of conscription proved as effective in meeting the demand for soldiers as the poll tax was in satisfying fiscal needs. Peter's predecessors had maintained a small standing army. After his defeat by the Swedes at Narva, Peter raised the army's size by drafting peasants and townsmen. The quota for each village or town was at first proportionate to the number of homesteads, but after the census of 1719 the quota was proportionate to the number of males in the community. The conscripts, who were between twenty and twenty-five when drafted, served for life. The system enabled Peter to increase his army from 35,000 to 40,000 in 1700 to over 200,000 at the end of his reign, reinforced by about 100,000 Cossacks and an undetermined number of troops from the non-Slavic peoples of the eastern frontiers. The system became a permanent part of Russian life, although the term of active service was reduced in later years.

In addition to increasing the army Peter created the Russian navy. He established shipyards, set aside forest tracts for ship timber, compelled state peasants to cut and prepare the timber, and set up factories for sails and naval stores. By the end of his reign he had 800 vessels and 28,000 sailors in the Baltic fleet — a force that played a large part in the victory over Sweden. After Peter's death the navy was neglected, and by the 1730's there were only about 15 seaworthy armed vessels under the Russian flag. The navy was later rebuilt, but Russia never became the sea power that Peter had hoped to make it.

Russian producers could not meet Peter's demands for military goods, and his depleted treasury made it impossible to buy the goods abroad. To build up the country's manufactures and increase the prosperity and therefore the taxpaying capacity of his subjects, Peter instituted a program similar to the mercantilist policies of his fellow monarchs in other lands. He established state-owned mines, foundries, arsenals, cloth factories, and other enterprises to make goods for the army and navy, imported foreign experts to run the plants and train native workmen, and sent young Russians abroad to learn new skills. Subsidies, monopolies, exemptions from taxes and military service, high tariff protection, and free importation of materials and equipment encouraged private entrepreneurs. Peter later turned over a number of state-owned enterprises to the new entrepreneurs. Thousands of state peasants were compelled to work at low wages in both state-owned and private enterprises. Despite extensive inefficiency and failure in the new industries, Peter's efforts established large-scale factory enterprise, which before had scarcely existed in Russia, as an integral part of the Russian economy. Especially successful was the development of iron and copper production in the Ural Mountains.

In order to promote internal commerce Peter embarked on an ambitious canal-building program designed to link the chief rivers of Russia. He made St. Petersburg the empire's center of foreign trade by ordering that a number of rich merchants settle there, that certain products (hides, hemp, caviar, tar, and potash) that were important in Russian export trade be shipped only from there, and that dock charges be less there than in Archangel, which was previously the chief Russian port.

THE CHURCH, CULTURE, AND EDUCATION

The Russian Orthodox Church's autonomy and great wealth posed a threat to Peter's ambitions for absolute power, and he resented the opposition of churchmen to his efforts to introduce Western ways into Russian life. When in 1700 the patriarch of the church died, Peter left the office vacant and appointed a priest who was subservient to him as "keeper and administrator of the patriarchal see." The keeper handed over the administration of church property to a government bureau, which gave the clergy only a part of the income from their properties and put the rest in the tsar's coffers. In 1721 Peter abolished the office of patriarch and placed the direction of the church under the Most Holy Synod, a committee of clergymen presided over by the Procurator, a layman chosen by the tsar. The church thereby became a part of the central administration and whatever independent political influence it had once possessed disappeared. The Holy Synod survived until 1917.

Peter's reforming zeal extended to cultural matters. Through his efforts printing became much more common. Until the end of the eighteenth century all presses in Russia belonged to the state or the church. Translations were made of European works, with the tsar himself supervising the choice of foreign books and personally editing the translations. Most of the books dealt with technical subjects, reflecting Peter's own interests, but historical and legal works were also published. In 1703 he established the first Russian newspaper. The Russian alphabet was simplified; the old alphabet was used only in church texts. In 1702 he introduced the public theater into Russia when he imported a company of German actors. He established the first hospital and the first museum in his country. He was the founder of the Russian Academy of Sciences, which combined scientific research and teaching. In the beginning it was composed of seventeen scientists and eight students who were all of German origin, for Russia lacked both scientists and advanced students.

The low level of education in Russia disturbed Peter. At his accession the only schools were a few poorly attended theological seminaries. Since his military plans required trained officers he organized several military academies whose students came almost exclusively from the nobility, although the schools were open to members of other classes. In 1714 he ordered the establishment of two technical schools in each province, but this effort to increase educational facilities proved a nearly total failure. Later a system of schools under church supervision was established; by 1727 these schools had a total of about 3,000 students, most of whom were sons of priests training for the priesthood.

THE SUCCESSION

Peter despised his son Alexis, who was born of his first wife. Those who opposed Peter looked upon Alexis as the symbol of their discontent and as their potential leader. Although Alexis renounced his right of succession after Peter had a son by Catherine, his father still persecuted him and Alexis fled Russia. In 1718 he was lured back by promises of the tsar's forgiveness, only to be imprisoned and, with his father and other dignitaries watching, tortured to death. On the day before he was buried his father celebrated his demise with a particularly brilliant court ball.

The murder of Alexis availed Peter nothing, for his infant son by Catherine soon died. His sole direct heir was the son of Alexis. Determined that this boy should not succeed him, Peter decreed in 1722 that the tsar could name his own successor. Peter himself never got around to naming one, with the result that as he lay dying in 1725 at the age of fifty-two, his once-powerful constitution ravaged by dissipation, a new succession crisis threatened. At the last moment a palace coup by high officials and guards officers succeeded in having Catherine accepted as his successor. The peasant wench and one-time camp follower became Catherine I, Empress of All the Russias.

PETER IN RETROSPECT

Peter's fame survived the Communist Revolution. Indeed, he is as commanding a hero to the Bolsheviks, who see many parallels between their efforts and his to equal and surpass the West, as he was to the tsarists. They consider his reforms necessary to the creation of a powerful Russian state and praise him as the man who led the nation toward progress and enlightenment.

Although all that Peter did had been foreshadowed by his predecessors of the previous two centuries, the fact remains that he made Russia a European power, established her on the Baltic Sea, remedied the organizational shortcomings that had made previous regimes inefficient, and forced the people out of their intellectual isolation by his sponsorship of Western culture. The Russians paid heavily for Peter's achievements, more heavily perhaps than the subjects of any other absolutist monarch of the age. The suffering, deprivation, and sacrifice caused by war was only a small part of the price. State service kept the nobility from the countryside, alienating them from the mass of the people and creating new and irreconcilable social antagonisms. The westernized nobility with their new ways, new dress, and clean-shaven faces were set still further apart from the masses. New and onerous burdens were imposed on the peasantry by the state and by the lords, and millions who had been free were forced into serfdom or the less onerous but still unfree category of state peasant.

The oppressions of Peter were not accepted passively. Peasant revolts punctuated his reign, and thousands fled to the still unsettled frontiers. Feared and hated by his subjects, Peter seemed to them to fulfill the prophecy of the Scriptures, as interpreted by the Old Believers, and they saw him as the Antichrist incarnate. In retrospect, he was something less than that, though some of his influence was nearly as malignant.

THE RULERS, 1725–1762

From Peter's death in 1725 until the accession of Catherine II in 1762 the history of the tsars is a fantastic tale of depraved monarchs, corrupt favorites, and palace revolutions. Much of the blame was Peter's. In decreeing that the tsar could name his own successor, he had destroyed the principle of fixed succession, leaving the way open for intriguing adventurers to gain power by backing a successful candidate for the throne.

Catherine I was the first in a line of six bizarre creatures who held the throne until 1762. She was succeeded in 1727 by the son of the murdered Alexis, the eleven-year-old Peter II, who reigned just three years. Anna, daughter of Ivan V (Peter the Great's co-tsar) who reigned from 1730 to 1740, gave over the government to a group of German adventurers headed by her lover and whiled away her hours with extravagance and the collection of freaks, both animal and human. Her two-month-old grand-nephew, Ivan VI, who was named her successor on her deathbed, reigned thirteen months until overthrown by a palace revolution that put Elizabeth, the thirty-two-year-old daughter of Peter the Great and Catherine, on the throne. Poor Ivan spent the rest of his life in confinement, reduced to idiocy by his long imprisonment and ill-treatment and finally murdered in 1764 at the command of the ruler when an attempt was made to free him.

Elizabeth (1741–1762) possessed all the vices and none of the capacities of her parents. She took a succession of lovers, delighted in an immense wardrobe (including men's clothes), and left the government to favorites. Her successor was her nephew Peter, duke of Holstein, whom she brought from Germany to Russia and married to a young German princess named Sophia, who was rechristened Catherine upon her conversion to Russian Orthodoxy for the marriage.

Peter III became tsar early in 1762 and reigned for a mere six months. Much of what is known of him comes from his wife — and usurper — and her adherents, and probably less than justice has been done him in most accounts. He was certainly peculiar, childish, and arrogant. In seeking reforms, he showed utter contempt for things Russian and idolized Frederick the Great of Prussia. A threat he made to secularize church property cost him the support of the clergy; another threat to take away the special privileges of the guards regiments contributed to the loss of his throne. His wife Catherine and her lover Orlov won over the guards and seized the throne in June, 1762. Crowned Empress Catherine II, she assented to, if she did not order, the murder of Peter a few days after the coup.

PATTERNS OF CHANGE, 1725–1762

If attention is focused only on the tsars, Russian history from 1725 to 1762 seems a preposterous parade of lewd and deranged sovereigns, corrupt favorites, and rebellious officers of the palace guard. When other facets of Russian life are examined, meaningful patterns appear. A new class cohesiveness developed among the nobles who won their freedom from the restrictions imposed upon them by Peter I and became the real masters of Russia. The condition of the peasantry worsened, and Russia became increasingly involved in international affairs.

Peter I had welded the nobles into a single class held together by common interests and common class privileges. After his death the feeling of cohesiveness continued to grow. Despite strata within the nobility, ranging from fabulously wealthy aristocrats to petty landowners who were almost indistinguishable from peasants, noblemen stood together in their

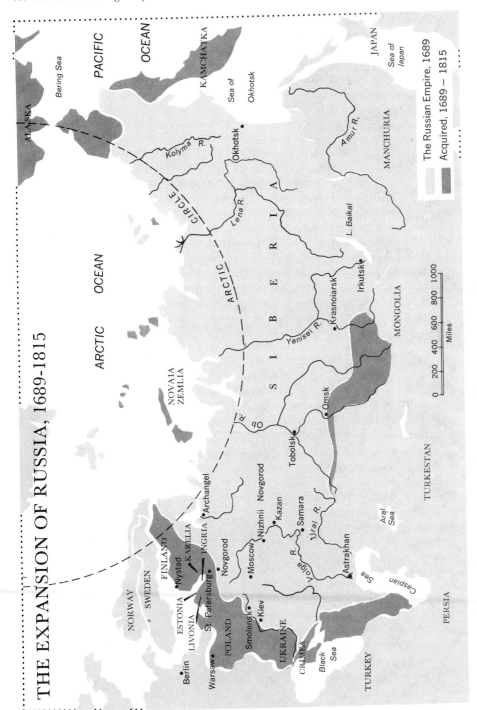

THE EXPANSION OF RUSSIA, 1689-1815

demands for greater privileges. The absence of a stable principle of succession to the throne and the character of the monarchs afforded the opportunity to attain their goals. The dependence of the sovereigns upon the nobility, particularly upon the predominantly noble guards regiments, to get and keep the throne enabled the nobles to exact increased privileges. Their most spectacular gain was the abolition of the hated requirement of service in the army or the bureaucracy. Gradual reduction of this obligation culminated in the abolition of all compulsory service for nobles in Peter III's reign.

The partial monopoly of the right to own land and serfs, won by the nobility in the seventeenth century, was made complete, although a few men of other classes continued to own serfs illegally. The police and judicial powers of the nobles over their serfs were so greatly expanded that the serfs were more than ever at the mercy of their lords. Many serfs fled to the unsettled frontiers to escape oppression. Others rose in rebellion. Peasant risings, sometimes of a handful of men and sometimes of thousands, were endemic. They were invariably crushed, sometimes with inhuman cruelty, but repression seemed only to encourage others to strike out against their oppressors.

In international affairs Russia played the great-power role that Peter had won for it, but government ineptitude limited Russian gains. In alliance with Austria Russia fought successfully to have the Russian candidate recognized as king of Poland in the War of the Polish Succession from 1733 to 1735. War against Turkey from 1735 to 1739 went badly, despite Austrian assistance after 1737, with no gains and heavy losses of men and money. War with Sweden from 1741 to 1743 saw easy victories by Russian troops and the occupation of most of Finland, but the concluding treaty brought only small territorial acquisitions. Russia stayed out of the War of the Austrian Succession until the last minute, entering only when a large annual cash subsidy from England persuaded her to send troops against France. The war was over before the Russians saw action, however, and Russia was not invited to the peace conference.

As the fear of Frederick II's expansionist ambitions grew in the 1750's, Russian policy became markedly anti-Prussian. An Anglo-Russian agreement in 1756 aimed at Prussia was abruptly terminated in the same year when Britain allied herself with Prussia and Russia joined Austria and France in the Seven Years' War. (See p. 394.) On the death of Empress Elizabeth in 1762 her successor, Peter III, switched sides and ordered his troops to fight alongside those of his idol, Frederick II. The thousands of lives and millions of rubles that Russia had spent to defeat Frederick had gone for nothing because of the whim of the tsar. When Catherine became empress, she withdrew her troops from the war, so that Russia was not represented at the peace conference in 1763 and gained nothing.

CATHERINE II, 1762–1796

The accession of Catherine II restored the Russian throne to a centrality in Russian life that it had not had since the death of Peter I. Catherine, who was far superior to the grotesque rulers who preceded her, bears comparison with the outstanding rulers of the time. Nevertheless she was not without personal aberrations, her most renowned being the inconstancy of her affections. Most of her twenty-one known lovers held her devotion for only a brief time, but all of them were rewarded with rich gifts, and three of them had much influence in government. Gregory Orlov was all-powerful during the first decade of Catherine's reign; Gregory Potemkin exercised great influence from 1771 to 1791, long after Catherine had broken her romantic attachment with him; and Platon Zubov, in his twenties, was entrusted with great power by the infatuated sixty-year-old empress.

Catherine developed an interest in the writings of the Enlightenment in the early years of her marriage, and for the rest of her life she kept up with the latest intellectual and literary movements. She corresponded regularly with Voltaire, Diderot, d'Alembert, and other foreign intellectuals and expressed sympathy with many of the ideas that they supported. She also wrote plays and essays in French and Russian.

The empress's enthusiasm for the new ideas was only partly motivated by genuine intellectual interest. Realizing that the French philosophes were the opinion-makers of the day, she deliberately curried favor with them so that they would create an image of her as an enlightened ruler. It not only pleased her vanity but also served Russia's political interests. In her letters she discussed Russian developments, always in the best light. Her correspondents, flattered to receive imperial confidences, talked about them in influential circles (as Catherine knew they would) and created a favorable foreign opinion of her. Catherine's self-advertising campaign was strikingly successful. She owed her reputation for enlightenment to Western intellectuals, not to her record as a ruler. Catherine's true importance for Russian history lay not in her philosophical views but in her pro-noble and anti-serf policies, her economic and fiscal measures, and her foreign policy.

CATHERINE AND THE NOBILITY

In striking contrast to the absolutists, including Peter the Great, who tried to restrict the privileges of the nobility, Catherine increased their privileges. Her reign turned out to be the golden age of the Russian nobility. She identified herself completely with the nobility and acquiesced in its demands even more than had her weak predecessors. She allowed the lords greater powers over their serfs and gave hundreds of thousands of state peasant families and their land to nobles, thereby converting the

Catherine the Great, by G. B. Lampi

*"Her actions like false pearls had more eclat but less value than the genuine
ones. There are some Russians who are sensible of this truth; but as flattery and
blind submission is become, for the greatest number, the only road to riches,
power and credit, these are even more zealous in applauding everything that comes
out of the Imperial Palace, than those who are sincere in their praises. . . . To
see Herself admired by everybody has increased Her vanity to such a degree,
that she begins to think of Herself above the rest of mankind."* Henry Shirley
(the English ambassador) to Lord Weymouth, St. Petersburg, February 28, 1768,
SBORNIK RUSSKAGO ISTORICHESKAGO OBSHCHESTVA (St. Petersburg, 1873), Vol. XII.

peasants into serfs. She established special banks to lend government funds to nobles and did not press them for repayment. Her pro-noble policy culminated in the Charter of the Nobility, which she issued in 1785. This long document confirmed the privileges that the nobles had already won, such as freedom from the service requirement, and exempted them from personal taxes, corporal punishment, and trial by judges other than those of birth equal to their own. The nobles of each province were organized into assemblies and given control over most of the governmental functions of the province, either directly or through officials they had chosen from among themselves. Thus Russian nobles were granted the right to form provincial estates entrusted with governmental functions at the very time when in other parts of Europe privileged noble assemblies were under heavy attack or no longer existent.

Catherine did not show the same regard for the Orthodox Church. Tsars had long struggled with the problem of controlling the great wealth of the church. In 1764 Catherine ordered the secularization of church property. All of its lands and serfs were turned over to a government bureau, many monasteries were closed, and henceforth the church was supported by government funds.

The growth in the privileges of the nobility was accompanied by a steady deterioration in the condition of the peasantry. Serfdom reached its nadir during Catherine's reign. Both the lords and the state increased their demands, serfdom was introduced into the Ukraine (the southeastern region annexed by Russia in the seventeenth century), the sale of serfs without land was legalized, and hundreds of thousands of state peasants were compelled to work at low wages in privately owned factories and mines. During the first decades of Catherine's reign there was an ominous increase in peasant unrest and violence, culminating in a great uprising in 1773. A Don Cossack adventurer named Emilian Pugachev, who claimed to be Peter III and to have miraculously escaped assassination, vowed to right old wrongs of the people and promised land and freedom to his followers and death to their oppressors. Thousands of state peasants and serfs enlisted under his banner. Soon he was in control of much of the Volga valley. The government had to launch a full-scale campaign to crush the rebellion and capture and execute Pugachev. Terrible reprisals were visited on the rebellious districts. Official attempts to stamp out every memory of the rising, however, were less than successful, and the peasants made a folk hero out of Pugachev as their defender against oppression. The rulers of Russia did not forget him either: from his time on they were haunted by the fear of a new Pugachev.

ECONOMIC REFORM

Catherine's economic policies proved to be the most progressive part of her program. In 1775 she abolished monopolistic privileges in trading and manufacturing and decreed that anyone could go into any kind of business, except distilling, which for some time had been an exclusive right of nobles. Nobles were the chief beneficiaries of the new policy; many of them established factories on their estates and used the serfs as unpaid laborers. Some peasants benefited, too, for many of them became active in cottage industry, and a few built up large enterprises.

This reform, combined with a general upswing in economic activity, was responsible for a remarkable growth of industry. The incomplete data available indicate that there were about 650 factories in Russia when Catherine began her reign and around 2,000 factories when she died. The most striking development was in iron production in the Urals. For a brief period in the last part of the century, that region was the world's chief producer of pig iron. The Russian plants, however, failed to adopt the new techniques developed in the West, and Russian production soon fell far behind that of Western iron-producing nations.

Catherine's government was active in bringing in colonists to settle uninhabited parts of the realm. The program, unsuccessfully attempted during Elizabeth's reign, was revived when Catherine ascended the throne. Most of the immigrants came from Germany. The government gave them land, loans, and subsidies to get started. Many of the colonists settled along the lower Volga, where their descendants retained the language, traditions, and culture of Germany until World War II, when their collaboration with the Nazi invaders persuaded the Soviet government to disperse them.

Much of the benefit of Catherine's economic policies was canceled by her disastrous fiscal activities. When she came to the throne the gross mismanagement of government finances and the heavy cost of the war against Prussia had brought the state to the edge of bankruptcy. Catherine's fantastic extravagances, notably in gifts to her favorites, and the costs of her wars made matters worse. To cover the deficit the government in 1769 began to issue paper money, at first in limited quantities then in increasing amounts, producing serious inflation. The government borrowed abroad, contracting a huge foreign debt in addition to the many millions of rubles owed to Russian creditors, and increased the tax burden two and one-half times during Catherine's reign.

FOREIGN POLICY

Catherine's dream in foreign policy was to expand her realm at the expense of Poland and Turkey in order to make Russia the prime power of Europe. She remarked to a friend, "If I could live for two hundred years all of Europe would be brought under Russian rule." She did not achieve all her ambitions, but she added 213,000 square miles — an area as large as France — and 12 million people to the Russian Empire, and Russia's international prestige reached new heights.

The opening gambit in her drive for conquest came in 1764 when

Catherine arranged to have a former lover, Stanislas Poniatowski, elected king of Poland after he promised not to oppose any of her policies in Poland. In 1768 this arrangement brought on war with the Turks who feared that Russian control of Poland would threaten the Ottoman Empire. The Austrians were also worried by Russian victories, not wanting Russian troops on their eastern flank, and they made an alliance with Turkey and prepared for intervention. The threat of a Russo-Austrian war was averted through the diplomacy of Frederick II of Prussia. Although he had allied with Catherine in 1767 against Austria, Frederick had no wish to fight to guarantee Russian annexations in Turkey. In 1772 he suggested the partition of part of Poland among Austria, Russia, and Prussia, in return for Russia's giving up its Turkish conquests. Fearful of war with Austria, Catherine agreed.

The Turkish war was ended in 1774 by a treaty signed in the Bulgarian village of Kuchuk Kainarji. As the Treaty of Nystadt in 1721 had given Russia access to the Baltic Sea, the Treaty of Kuchuk Kainarji gave Russia access to the Black Sea. Turkey ceded the northern Black Sea coast from the Dnieper to the Bug estuaries, opened the sea to Russian shipping, allowed Russian merchants passage through the straits into the Mediterranean, and recognized the Crimea as an independent Tatar state (making it susceptible to Russian conquest). A vaguely worded concession by the Turks permitted Russia to represent Christian subjects of the Ottomans if they were not fairly treated; it was used in later years as the excuse for repeated Russian intervention in Turkish domestic affairs.

With Russian prestige at its height, Catherine could indulge in her dream of completely expelling the Turks from Europe and establishing a new Byzantine empire in the Balkans. Her second grandson, born in 1779, was christened Constantine in anticipation of his becoming sovereign of the new empire centered in Constantinople. The Danubian areas were to be made into a separate kingdom under her favorite, Potemkin, as king. This ambitious "Greek Project," as it was called, received uneasy acceptance from Emperor Joseph II of Austria; a promise of territory in the Balkans to go to Austria helped persuade him to enter into a defensive alliance with Russia in 1781. Catherine annexed the Crimea and attempted to stir up rebellion against the Turks in the Balkans. In 1787 a showy river trip by Catherine, the Austrian emperor, and Western diplomats down the Dnieper into the Crimea, replete with signs along the river banks pointing "This way to Byzantium" and military and naval demonstrations, capped a series of provocations that moved the Turks to declare war on Russia. Austria joined Russia in 1788, but withdrew three years later after heavy losses. In 1792 the Treaty of Jassy recognized a Russian victory, and the Turks ceded the rest of the north shore of the Black Sea to Russia. Austria's defection, however, caused Catherine to abandon the Greek project.

Catherine's attention then turned to Poland. Following an invasion by

Russian troops in 1793, Russia and Prussia annexed more Polish territory in the second partition of that hapless country. Two years later Russia, Prussia, and Austria divided all that was left of Poland among themselves.

Intense russification and administrative unification of newly acquired territories were features of Catherine's expansion program. The new territories were divided into provinces and made subject to Russian law, institutions, and economic organization. Serfdom was introduced into regions taken from Turkey. In time many of the conquered peoples reconciled themselves to Russian domination. Others never ceased the struggle to regain independence.

THE BRIEF REIGN OF TSAR PAUL

Catherine was succeeded in 1796 by her son Paul, whom she despised and to whom she had never given any responsibility. Although Paul was clearly unbalanced mentally, he applied himself to needed reforms during his short reign. Among other things he established a fixed line of succession to the throne, thereby ending the uncertainties and schemings that had troubled the Russian succession since Peter's time. He began reforms in the central government in the interests of efficiency. He sought to help the serfs by recommending that they work no more than three days a week for their lords and by ordering the construction of granaries in every village to store food for emergencies.

His mistake was to try to lessen the privileges of the nobility. He did not reestablish the service requirement but he did make it clear that he expected nobles to spend their lives in government service. He taxed noble land, abolished the provincial assemblies of the nobility, and imposed new disciplinary regulations on army officers. Discontent and disaffection spread among the nobility, and in March, 1801, a band of officers of the elite guards murdered him. His son and heir, Alexander I, knew about the plot to drive Paul from the throne, but it is not known whether he was aware that it involved his father's assassination. In any event, he did not punish the murderers. One of his first acts as sovereign was to restore to the nobility all the privileges that Paul had taken away.

THE DECLINE AND DISAPPEARANCE
OF POLAND

In 1772 Poland was the third largest state in Europe in area, after Russia and Sweden, and stood fourth in population, after France, Russia, and Austria. By 1795 Poland had disappeared as an independent state. Its tale of decay and disappearance is the strange story of a nation that committed suicide. Ultimate responsibility for Poland's obliteration lay with the Polish nobility, who ran the country and whose selfishness and perversity made Poland defenseless against aggression.

NOBLE OLIGARCHY

The nobility elected the Polish king and in return for their votes exacted the assurance that the man elected would be nothing but a figurehead. The nobility, some 700,000 to 800,000 strong (approximately 8 per cent of the population), were predominantly petty country squires. Sixteen or seventeen families possessed enormous wealth, but the majority of the noblemen were miserably poor, half of them were all but landless, and many were barely distinguishable from the peasantry. Most of them were retainers of the wealthy lords and exercised their voice in politics according to the wishes of their patrons. The great lords struggled ceaselessly among themselves to attain political power, not hesitating to call in foreign troops or sell themselves for foreign subsidies.

Noble political power was concentrated in some fifty provincial assemblies, which were representative only of the nobility, unlike most other estates in Europe. The assemblies had ultimate power over national legislation, collected taxes, of which they turned over to the central government as much as they wished, and maintained their own armies. The assemblies elected the representatives to the diet, the only national authority other than the figurehead king. By the use of the *liberum veto* — merely rising and saying, "I object" — any noble deputy could force the dissolution of the diet, "explode" it, as it was called. The *liberum veto* not only dissolved the diet but nullified all measures previously adopted by that diet. Of the fifty-five diets convened between 1653 and 1764, forty-eight were exploded, their work undone. The one way to get around the *liberum veto* was by the use of the "confederation." Armed noblemen could with complete legality confederate and use force upon their opponents to push through legislation. The cure — "legally organized revolution" in theory, chaos in practice — was obviously as bad as the disease. Poland was, in effect, a loose federation of fifty or so little noble oligarchies without any effective central authority.

The nobility used its political power to free itself from compulsory military service and most taxes and to give itself a monopoly of land ownership, unlimited power over peasants who lived on noble land, and a monopoly of all higher offices in church and state. Three-quarters of the population were serfs, reduced to misery and unable to appeal to any higher authority for protection against their masters. The townsmen were excluded from all political participation, and the towns, most of them little larger than villages, were firmly under noble control. Town life and the portion of the economy dependent upon it steadily declined. The Polish nobles boasted of their "golden liberty" and scorned the nobility of other lands as the "slaves of despots," but in reality they were ineffectual petty tyrants presiding over a nation in decay, bereft of the institutions or the economy requisite to defend itself against the effective despotisms of Russia, Austria, and Prussia.

Polish disunity went deeper than politics. Only about one-half of the population was Polish, one-third was Ukrainian and White Russian, and the rest was a mixed bag of Germans, Lithuanians, Armenians, and Tatars. The Poles and Lithuanians were universally Catholic, the Ukranians and White Russians were Orthodox, the Germans were Protestant, and there were about one million Jews. During the Reformation, Poland had been among the most tolerant of nations, but in the later seventeenth and eighteenth centuries there was much oppression by the Roman Catholic Church, the official state religion. Many Orthodox peasants were forced to become Catholics, and other non-Catholics were deprived of their rights, restricted in the exercise of their religion, and on occasion victimized by mobs. Intolerance not only produced divisive discontent but also served Poland's neighbors, particularly Russia, as an excuse for intervention on behalf of coreligionists.

THE ROAD TO PARTITION

Poland's weakness became apparent during the reign of John Casimir (1648–1668). Invaded by Ukranian Cossacks, Russians, and Swedes, the country managed to survive these onslaughts but had to cede Livonia to Sweden in 1660 and the eastern Ukraine and part of White Russia to Russia in 1667. Poland's neighbors began to discuss the division of all of Poland among themselves. The succeeding years brought new wars and invasions, foreign intervention in Polish affairs, and heightened interest in the possible partition of Poland.

The question of what was going to happen to Poland and, if it broke up, who was going to get the pieces was a problem of major importance for the international balance of power. France saw Poland as a buffer state against Russia. Austria saw Poland as a buffer against Russia and Prussia. The Prussians wanted Polish territory so that they could unite East Prussia with Pomerania and Silesia; since the mid-seventeenth century they had been pushing the idea of partition at every opportunity. The Russians of that day, like the Russians of today, felt that they had to dominate Poland because if that country was truly independent or under the domination of another power Russia's own security would be endangered. The Russians and Poles were ancient enemies, but by the eighteenth century Poland had become a Russian satellite. With Poland under their domination the Russians had no special interest in splitting it up and therefore frustrated proposals for partition.

PARTITION

Russian opposition to partition changed under Catherine II. Her support of Stanislas Poniatowski for the throne of Poland precipitated the chain of events that led in 1772 to the partition of part of Poland among Russia, Prussia, and Austria. Poland lost almost one-third of its area

THE DISAPPEARANCE OF POLAND

Partition of 1772
Partition of 1793
Partition of 1795

RIGA
COURLAND
RUSSIA
Memel
Dvina R.
Kovno
POMERANIA
Danzig EAST PRUSSIA
Vilna
Dnieper R.
Smolensk
LITHUA-NIA
Minsk
WHITE RUSSIA
PRUSSIA
TO
Niemen R.
PRUSSIA
TO
Warsaw Bug R.
Brest-Litovsk
Pripet R.
Oder R.
TO
Prague
RUSSIA
Kiev
Kharkov
AUSTRIA
Cracow GALICIA
Lemberg
UKRAINE
Dnieper R.
AUSTRIA
Vienna
Danube R.
Dniester R.
HUNGARY
Budapest
MOLDAVIA
Jassy
0   100   200
Miles

and over a third of its people. Russia took the largest but least prosperous share, Prussia took the wealthiest, and Austria took the most populous.

Partition shocked many Poles into a new political awareness. They realized that the only way they could save what was left of Poland was by a radical change in their form of government. This realization was stimulated by an intellectual revival, connected with the translation of writers of the Enlightenment like Montesquieu, Rousseau, and Adam Smith. Periodicals were founded and books and articles appeared that questioned such basic institutions of Polish life as serfdom, the election of kings, and the *liberum veto*. In 1788 the Poles summoned a diet whose members agreed to prohibit the *liberum veto* at its sessions. In 1792 after long deliberations the diet made the throne hereditary, gave the king substantial powers, provided for a council of ministers and an efficient organization of the central administration, established representation of the towns in the diet, and allowed townsmen to purchase rural property (previously a monopoly of the nobility) and hold high government offices.

The reforms, which won the acclaim of liberals in western Europe, spurred a number of reactionary Polish lords to rebel against the new order. Catherine of Russia sent 100,000 soldiers to aid them on the pretext of "restoring Polish liberties," and soon Prussia sent troops to help the rebels. The Poles were compelled to abolish all the reforms and restore the anarchy that made them such easy prey. In 1793 Russia and Prussia agreed to a second partition of Poland. This time Poland lost about half of its remaining area and population. In 1794 a group of nobles again raised the banner of revolt, led by Thaddeus Kosciusko, who twenty years earlier had crossed the ocean to fight for American independence. Kosciusko assumed dictatorial powers and promised freedom to the serfs to win their support. Dissensions among the leaders, large Russian reinforcements, and the entrance of Prussian troops doomed the rebellion to failure. In 1795 Russia, Prussia, and Austria swallowed up the rest of Poland.

Poland had disappeared because its nobles, in pursuit of divergent and selfish interests, had awakened too late to the realization that responsibility is the price of privilege. Had they allowed Poland to develop a strong central government and thus be able to protect itself, the history of their country and of Europe would have been very different. The Polish problem did not disappear with the annihilation of the Polish state. The Polish people never gave up the resolution to regain their national identity, and the domination of Polish territory continued to be a source of contention among the great powers.

SCANDINAVIA

ABSOLUTISM IN DENMARK

The defeat of Denmark in the First Northern War, 1655–1660, afforded Frederick III (1648–1670) the opportunity to break once and for all the nobles' domination of Denmark. The Danish nobility, comprising 500 to 600 families, controlled the central government through the king's Council of the Realm. They also controlled local government, monopolized the chief offices in state and church, owned half the country, paid no taxes, evaded military service, and had the greatest voice in the election of the king. Frederick, who was a national hero by virtue of his brilliant though hardly successful leadership against Sweden in the war, won the support of the clergy and townsmen of Copenhagen for a bold and bloodless coup d'état in October, 1660, by which he forced the nobility to concur in making him hereditary king of Denmark.

The coup established a limited hereditary monarchy. Frederick, however, took advantage of the confusion of his opponents to make himself an absolute ruler. In 1665 he promulgated a document called the *Kongelov*, the King's Law, which accorded the monarch sweeping powers and declared him to be above the law as well as the sole maker of laws. In only five years Denmark had been transformed from a state dominated by a noble oligarchy into the most perfect example of absolute monarchy in all of Europe.

Frederick was succeeded in 1670 by Christian V, but the real ruler of the country was a man named Peter Schumacher, son of a wine merchant. Schumacher, later ennobled as Count Griffenfeld, had been the chief draftsman of the *Kongelov*. During his tenure of power he further developed the authority of the monarch. Griffenfeld was toppled from high office in 1676, but the policies he followed were pursued by his successors and accepted by the people. Not until 1848 was absolutism successfully challenged in Denmark.

In the seventeenth and eighteenth centuries Denmark was a much larger state than it is today. The royal possessions included Norway and the southern part of the Danish peninsula, now part of Germany. The realm included less than a million people, but its small population did not prevent Denmark from taking an active role in European affairs in the seventeenth century. In the eighteenth century it played only a small part in international politics, preferring to follow a policy of semi-isolation. In home affairs the old nobility declined in wealth and influence, while the royal bureaucracy gained in importance and status. Many of the bureaucrats were foreigners, chiefly from Germany. They owed their eminence to the king and were therefore loyal to him. The kings were an undistinguished, dreary lot, and under their uninspired leadership once-vigorous Denmark was turned into a backwater.

ABSOLUTISM IN SWEDEN

Once Charles XI of Sweden (1660–1697) had attained his majority and retrieved Sweden's fortunes from reverses suffered by its involvement in the Franco-Dutch War of 1672 to 1679 (see p. 287), he, too, turned to the creation of an absolute monarchy. In 1680 he ordered an investigation of the abuses of the regents or great landed aristocrats who had ruled during his minority. With the acquiescence of the Riksdag (the estates) he punished the regents by excessively heavy fines. Another commission was appointed to reclaim crown lands and revenues given to the nobility by former monarchs. The reduction, as the policy was called, was done with absolutist thoroughness. In 1652 almost three-quarters of the land in Sweden was in noble hands; in 1700 only a third was held by noblemen, and a third by the king, and a third by the peasantry. The economic foundations of noble dominance were shattered, and the seizure of the lands enabled the monarch to attain fiscal solvency. Charles XI enjoyed the wholehearted cooperation of the clergy and the townsmen as well as the peasantry, who had been threatened with enserfment when the nobility dominated the state.

Bureaucratization was thoroughgoing. The new corps of civil servants was drawn from the minor nobility and professional classes and was totally dependent on the king. The collegial system of administration that became the model for absolutist government in Russia and Prussia was Charles XI's creation. A large standing army was maintained by grants of crown land to officers and appropriation of part of the peasants' holdings in each district to support the volunteer enlisted men. The navy was built up to sufficient power to preserve communications in the far-flung reaches of the Baltic empire. The state Lutheran church was brought firmly under monarchic control. Mercantilist policies were initiated to promote economic growth.

CHARLES XII OF SWEDEN

In 1697 Charles XII, aged fifteen, succeeded his father. Sweden's natural enemies Denmark, Russia, and Poland saw his youth as an opportunity to carve up the Swedish Empire. Their concerted attack touched off the Great Northern War of 1700 to 1721. They underestimated their prey. Intelligent, courageous, and bellicose, Charles was a military genius. He fought a brilliant defense-offense against the forces allied against him in the first seven years of the war and brought Poland, Denmark, and Saxony to defeat. His disastrous invasion of Russia in 1707 ended in the Swedish rout at Poltava in 1709 and his exile in Turkey from 1709 to 1714, when he made a triumphant return to Sweden. Four more years of bitter warfare against the old enemies reinforced by Prussia and Hanover was a struggle against overwhelming odds. By the time he was killed in action in 1718, Charles was as worn out by the effort of war as was his land, which had lost almost a generation of its male youth and had consumed its prosperity in war. The peace treaties of 1720 and 1721 ended Sweden's hegemony in the north and her status as a major power: Livonia, Estonia, Ingria, and Karelia went to Russia, and all but a small part of her German territories went to Prussia and Hanover.

OLIGARCHY IN SWEDEN

Defeat and exhaustion in the Great Northern War and Charles's death without a direct heir (he never married) destroyed absolutism in Sweden. The nobility reestablished its power by making the succession of Charles's sister Ulrica and her German husband conditional upon a new constitution that gave the Riksdag almost supreme political power, recreating noble oligarchic rule in Sweden. The Age of Freedom, as its noble beneficiaries termed it, lasted from 1718 to 1772. Peace was the policy followed by Count Arvid Horn, the cautious and conservative noble oligarch whose twenty-year tenure in office enabled Sweden to regain much of her economic vitality. His fall in 1738, engineered by the war party intent on regaining Swedish glory, plunged Sweden into

Courtesy of Nationalmuseum, Stockholm

Charles XII of Sweden

"Charles XII, king of Sweden, dead at the age of thirty-six years and a half, after having experienced all the grandeur of prosperity, and all the hardships of adversity, without being either softened by the one, or the least disturbed by the other. . . . He carried all the virtues of the hero to such an excess as rendered them no less dangerous than the opposite vices. . . Severe to himself as well as to others, he too little regarded either his own life and labors, or those of his subjects; an extraordinary rather than a great man, and more worthy to be admired than imitated." Voltaire, HISTORY OF CHARLES XII (Boston, 1887).

a war with Russia from 1741 to 1743, which cost it more territory in Finland. Until 1766 the war party retained power, disastrously allying Sweden with France and subverting Swedish interests to the French.

Corruption, misrule, and economic distress produced a reaction in favor of a strong monarchy. In 1772 Gustavus III (1771–1792) forced the

Riksdag to assent to a new constitution under which the king enjoyed the command of the armed forces, the power to convene, terminate, and limit discussion in the Riksdag, and the sole responsibility for foreign affairs. The constitution contained significant limitations on the king's power: the Riksdag had to consent to legislation, the declaration of war, and amendments to the constitution, and it levied taxes and controlled the state bank. The old absolutism was not reestablished, but the Age of Freedom or noble oligarchy was ended.

THE OTTOMAN EMPIRE, 1656–1792

In the seventeenth and eighteenth centuries the Ottoman Empire plummeted from the pinnacle represented by the reign of Sultan Suleiman the Magnificent (1520–1566). Degeneracy, corruption, political strife, economic decline, and ethnic and religious antagonisms disrupted the internal life of the empire and cost it the external strength that had made it the most feared power in the sixteenth century.

The sultans were almost without exception weak and degenerate men, products of the incredible environment in which the royal princes were raised. The old practice of murdering all but one of the sons of the sultan (see p. 191) was replaced in the late sixteenth century by locking up all the sons with a harem and a few eunuchs in a separate part of the palace, called the Cage. One of the sons emerged to become sultan; the rest stayed until death, safely removed from power. Not unexpectedly, the chosen prince was often a puppet of oligarchic factions who were vying for power. The dominant figure was sometimes the grand vizier or a harem favorite such as the beautiful and ambitious Baffo, daughter of a Venetian nobleman, who was kidnapped and sold into Turkish slavery. She ruled for almost three decades during the reigns of her husband, Murad III, and her son, Mohammed III, in the late sixteenth century.

The lower levels of government reflected the decay at the top. Corruption and incompetence were endemic. The merit system was replaced by the purchase of offices and bribery to gain promotion. Tax collection was sold to the highest bidder and yielded a decreasing return as the taxes got heavier, since the profits went to the collector. The Janissaries, who were ostensibly the warrior backbone of Ottoman power and had been originally recruited from Christian boys to serve as the sultan's celibate slaves, were allowed to marry, to engage in trade and industry, and to enroll their sons in the Janissary corps. Increasingly recruited from the Moslem population, they became an unruly militia of merchants and artisans, only a fraction of whom were trained soldiers. By inciting mob violence they sometimes unseated the ruling faction and even overthrew sultans.

THE ADVENT OF NATIONALISM

The Ottoman Empire never became a nation-state. It remained an ag-glomeration of different ethnic groups and religions loyal to a community or a faith. Nationalist sentiment made its appearance in the Balkans, where the Christian peasantry in the heyday of the empire had been pro-tected by strict sultanic regulations from arbitrary incursions by their lords, the Moslem cavalrymen (*spahis*), who held the land from the sultan by military-service tenure. In the era of decline the spahis took advantage of the government's weakness to disregard the regulations, convert the fiefs into hereditary possessions, and exploit the Christian peas-ants. The peasants lost their hereditary right to their holdings, and extor-tionate rents and taxes placed them in perpetual indebtedness to the spahis, ending their freedom of movement and reducing them to near-serfdom. The peasants erupted periodically into insurrection or fled to the mountains and forests to form outlaw bands that robbed Turks and raided rich Christian monasteries. The bandits (called *haiduks* in Serbia and *klephts* in Greece) had no ideological commitment, but they created a Robin Hood-like romantic tradition of defiance to Ottoman authority that nurtured nationalistic consciousness.

In the late eighteenth century nationalist movements developed in the Balkans under the leadership of the Christian middle class, whose trade contacts with the West enabled them to judge the backwardness of the Ottoman Empire. They imported Western books, sent their sons to study abroad, and established schools free from control of the Orthodox Church, which was tainted by its collaboration with the Turks. The French Revolution awakened in the Balkan minorities, who were already influenced by the Enlightenment, the same passions that moved Western men: national determination and liberty.

EXTERNAL IMPOTENCE AND TERRITORIAL DECLINE

The Thirty Years' War gave the Ottomans a breathing spell from foreign embroilments, since their European enemies were at one another's throats. In the second half of the seventeenth century the Turks engaged in a series of wars with Christian powers and in 1683 pushed westward as far as Vienna. (See p. 299.) The Treaty of Karlowitz in 1699, ending the war between Turkey and the Holy Alliance, cost the Ottomans much of their territory and freed Christian Europe from the old threat of Turkish aggression, but it also presented a new problem. Was the Otto-man Empire to be carved up, and if it was, which powers were to get what pieces? This issue, labeled the Eastern Question by nineteenth-century statesmen, was to haunt European international affairs until the dis-solution of the Ottoman Empire in 1918.

Despite several wars, for sixty years after Karlowitz the Turks managed

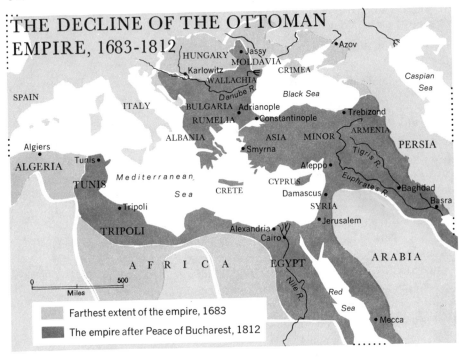

THE DECLINE OF THE OTTOMAN EMPIRE, 1683-1812

Farthest extent of the empire, 1683

The empire after Peace of Bucharest, 1812

to avoid serious territorial losses. Then the accession of Catherine II in Russia threatened to be as disastrous for Turkey as it was for Poland, since Russian aggression engendered a new string of wars. The first partition of Poland saved Turkey from partition, but the Ottomans had to cede a great segment of territory to the Russians in the treaties of Kuchuk Kainarji (1774) and Jassy (1792). Had Catherine been able to carry out her Greek Project the Balkan peninsula would have been divided between Russia and Austria. Instead, it remained under Ottoman rule until the nineteenth century, when, one after another, the Balkan peoples won precarious national independence with the assistance of the Christian powers, whose interests were anything but altruistic.

CONSTITUTIONALISM
AND OLIGARCHY
IN THE WEST
CHAPTER FOURTEEN

Two nations in western Europe swam against the tide of absolutism in the seventeenth century: the Dutch Republic and England. By the end of the century, when Louis XIV's France had become the model for absolutism, as his Versailles had become for the absolute monarch's palace, these two nations stood alone as oligarchies of wealth in which the oligarchs' ultimate power was constitutionally bulwarked against a strong executive. Both oligarchies had been tried in contest, and both had triumphed. It is difficult to assign common causes for their victories. Both states were Protestant, and both were colonial and commercial sea powers with their vital economies in the hands of strong and cohesive urban middle classes — although there were wide differences between their policies, economies, and social structures. Perhaps the most significant similarity was the survival and continued vitality of their representative institutions: the provincial States in the Dutch Republic and Parliament in England. Their survival depended in turn upon revolutions in both countries at a time when monarchy was not able to repress the representative institutions: in the Dutch struggle for independence from Spain in the late sixteenth century and in the English civil wars of the mid-seventeenth century. These revolutions, spawned by specific grievances originating in monarchic policies, strengthened the representative institutions at the expense of the executive.

THE DUTCH OLIGARCHY, 1660–1766

The high point of the Dutch oligarchy came in 1660. Since the death of Stadholder William II in 1650 no member of the House of Orange had held the highest national and provincial offices in the republic, and since 1653 Jan De Witt, the oligarchy's chosen leader as grand pensionary of

Holland, had directed the affairs of state with singular ability and great restraint. It was the golden age of Dutch republicanism. True, a war with England in 1652–1654 had given the more cautious merchant-oligarchs pause, for English sea power coupled with England's ambition to cut into the Dutch carrying trade in ocean commerce raised a disturbing prospect. But Spain, the traditional enemy, had recognized Dutch independence in 1648 and was obviously a declining power. Portugal appeared a greater threat to Dutch interests after it regained control over the territories in Brazil into which the Dutch had made deep inroads. Successful intervention by the Dutch in a Swedish-Danish war from 1657 to 1660 prevented Sweden from controlling the Baltic trade, a mainstay of Dutch commercial strength. Amsterdam was at the height of its vitality as the financial heart of the world; it and the other great Dutch commercial cities had triumphed at the expense of Antwerp in the Spanish Netherlands. Everywhere — Brazil alone excepted — Dutch colonies flourished, and the Dutch primacy in the carrying trade was not yet in question. Never had the nation been more prosperous, and the then current comparisons of the republic with Venice in its heyday and even with republican Rome were not so fanciful.

REGENT OLIGARCHY

From the beginning the republic was a loose confederation of seven provinces, each governed by its own representative assembly or States, and each States sending a delegation to the States-General, which was responsible for the conduct of foreign affairs and defense but little else. The territory of Drenthe was not represented in the States-General. The province of Holland was pre-eminent in the republic. Its States comprised the representatives of the eighteen towns of the province, each town with one vote, and the representative of the old nobility, with one vote. Sober, dignified, responsible, moderate, and God-fearing (though seldom preacher-fearing), the urban oligarchs of Holland or regents, as they were known, ruled for the general welfare but without respect for the general will. There was no democracy in the republic. The regents, in whose persons were joined political power and wealth, held all the major offices, executive and judicial. They controlled the town governments, the States, and the States-General.

The regent oligarchy was a closed society. Closely connected by marriage and common economic interests as well as by shared responsibilities of government, the regent group was virtually hereditary and self-perpetuating. This urban upper middle class had wholly eclipsed the old nobility in the provinces of Holland and Zeeland, and in the other five provinces it dominated the nobility. Although the lower middle class was politically conscious, it was excluded for the most part from political life, and its only organized political bodies, the craft guilds and civic guard (local militia), were closely controlled by the regents. The regents were not immune to popular pressure, but they were adroit in channeling and generally withstanding it. Because of their unchallenged preeminence, they could afford to allow a remarkable freedom of expression and criticism and extensive religious toleration. The most serious threat of disruption came not from the old nobility nor the lower middle class but from the firebrand ministers of the staunchly Calvinist Reformed Church, the established church of the republic, though only a minority of the population belonged to it. Popular pressure became dangerous only when the more fanatical ministers could fix upon an issue and use it to challenge the religious orthodoxy of the regents. In such circumstances the regents had to give up momentarily their accustomed tolerance and moderation if they were to turn off the clerical attack.

Two basic divisions within the republic threatened the primacy of the oligarchy and even the life of the republic. The first was the geographical distinction between the two "seaward" provinces (Holland and Zeeland) and the five "landward" ones (Friesland, Groningen, Overijssel, Gelderland, and Utrecht) with the territory of Drenthe. The dominant maritime and commercial interests of the first two sometimes conflicted with the agrarian concerns of the latter. Though all the provinces were supposed to contribute to the maintenance of the navy and the protection of the merchant marine, Holland and Zeeland shouldered the principal expense and the landward provinces were constantly in arrears for their agreed proportion of the navy's cost.

The second division was the fundamental political division between the Orangists and the Statists. The former sought greater unity under the leadership of the stadholder-captain-general of the House of Orange, while the latter were determined to preserve provincial autonomy, the sovereignty of the provincial States, and thus the oligarchic preeminence. The Orange dynasty had provided the young republic with a symbolic personification of its independence and integrity. The heroism of William the Silent, stadholder from 1579 to 1584, had been the birth glory of the nation, and his successors, Maurice of Nassau (1587–1625) and Frederick Henry (1625–1647), had been indomitable, brilliant warriors. As servants of the provincial sovereignty that effectively limited their urge for power, they won the admiration of all Dutchmen, even those who adamantly opposed any accretion of authority by the dynasty at the expense of provincial sovereignty. The Statists did not reject the leadership of the Orange stadholder, but only his predilection for centralization and his dynastic ambitions. In turn, the Orangists respected the Statists' rejection of anything approaching a centralized monarchy, and at its most extreme their demand was merely for a stronger federal system under Orange auspices. The independence of the Holland oligarchy and the fact that Holland and Zeeland provided most of the wealth, almost all of the sea power, and the largest number of men for the defense of the republic, discouraged any other Orangist ambitions. The political realism of both Orangists and Statists, their mutual respect, and common necessity, resulted in a marked lack of destructive political antagonism between them. Nevertheless, Dutch politics could be brutal and occasionally disruptive of unity, even in the face of an external enemy. This was never more evident than in the golden age of republicanism when there was no stadholder.

JAN DE WITT

Jan De Witt (1625–1672) was the epitome of the Holland oligarch. In a period of fast-shifting foreign relations when new alignments of the European powers were under way, De Witt, leader of the republic from 1653 to 1672, faced challenges comparable to any faced by stadholders since William the Silent. His leadership in war — with England from 1652 to 1654, with Portugal over Brazil from 1657 to 1661, with Sweden over the Baltic from 1657 to 1660, with England again from 1665 to 1672, and finally with France in 1672 — was never less than competent, often brilliant, and always courageous. His statesmanship was of a high order. He recognized that the interests of the republic could only be served by a tenacious defense of Dutch commercial and colonial activity. He built up Dutch finances after every war, rearmed the reluctant nation, and often provided direct military leadership. Though forced out of office abruptly in 1672 when French armies cut deep into Dutch territory, De Witt was far less responsible for that disaster than the oligarchs, who had countered his attempt to build Dutch power as vigorously as they had countered those of the Orange dynasty. Like Oldenbarneveldt before him (see p. 260), he was requited for his decades of service to the republic and to Dutch independence and prosperity by death — torn to pieces by a howling mob.

The French invasion was the immediate cause of De Witt's fall and also of the decline in dominance of the regent oligarchy. William III of Orange was called to the stadholdership of Holland on July 4, 1672, and four days later he was made captain and admiral-general of the States-General. It was not simply the Orangists who called upon him; it was also a beleaguered nation, which traditionally turned to Orange for leadership in times of trouble. The more profound causes of the decline of the oligarchs stemmed from the inherent divisions within Dutch politics. The Holland and Zeeland oligarchs had neglected the army. Maritime-oriented, they were reluctant to admit the threat of French invasion overland, and they had a traditional class distaste for the noble-officered army. In a period of supposed security on land and war at sea vitally affecting their commercial and colonial interests they had maintained only the navy. Religious antagonism had also broken out with increased virulence because of a new demand by militant Calvinist Reformed ministers in

The Bettmann Archive

Jan De Witt, from a picture by Netscher

"The supporters of the Prince of Orange and also many good patriots whom God has not armed with any remarkable steadfastness of purpose or courage are doing their utmost and are openly haranguing that . . . there is no choice but either to fall a prey to France and utterly to go under, or to throw ourselves into the arms of England. . . . I frankly admit that I believe the remedy to be worse than the evil itself." De Witt to Pieter de Groot, December 10, 1671, quoted in P. Geyl, THE NETHERLANDS IN THE SEVENTEENTH CENTURY (New York, 1964).

the 1660's for a greater voice in affairs of state in order to repress Catholicism and the non-Reformed Protestant sects. Characteristically, De Witt had withstood the demand. The militant Reformed, with an increasingly large following among the urban lower middle class, saw Orange as the natural counterpoise to the regents. Finally, the basic cause of the oligarchs' decline was the very weakness of the union and the autonomy of the provinces, which permitted the decline of the army for want of support and bred factionalism among the regents. Regent oligarchy was workable only so long as confidence in the regents was widespread. When that confidence cracked, there was no practical alternative to a prince of Orange as the champion of the nation and the bridge over divisions and factionalism.

WILLIAM III

William III directed the fortunes of the republic for thirty hazardous years. For the last thirteen of those years he was also king of England. His accession to the stadholdership in 1672 at the age of twenty-one came at the republic's darkest hour in a century. He was the architect of its brilliant resistance to Louis XIV's aggression, and after six years of hard fighting he brought peace in 1678 without loss of territory. For the rest of his life William had one consuming passion: the containment and destruction of the aggressive ambitions of Louis XIV of France. After he became England's king in 1689, he used English wealth and power in this struggle.

William's singleness of purpose accounted in part for his unwillingness in 1672 to grasp the opportunity to rout the Statists, reduce the power of the regents, and establish a more cohesive union under an Orange executive who would have been constitutionally more powerful than the stadholder and captain-general. In 1672 emissaries of his uncle, Charles II of England, in league with Louis XIV, offered the young captain-general the assistance of the two monarchs in making him king of the Dutch nation in return for small cessions of territory and his receiving the crown from them. William's answer was a more vigorous prosecution of the war against France and England. He rested satisfied with turning out De Witt's supporters in the town governments, the provincial States, and the States-General and replacing them with more pliant Orangist adherents. He did not attempt an organic reorganization of the cumbrous machinery of the republic, for he did not want to jeopardize the unity of the nation when it was beset by Louis XIV. When William died in 1702 without a direct heir, the regent oligarchy took control once again in the longest, the last, and the least successful of the periods without a stadholder, from 1702 to 1747.

THE REPUBLIC, 1702–1766

For the Dutch the eighteenth century marked a period of economic decline, costly and relatively unsuccessful involvement in far-flung wars, and an end to the vitality of the regent regime. The barrier towns ceded to the Dutch by the Peace of Utrecht in 1713 as protection along the

THE NETHERLANDS, 1660-1766

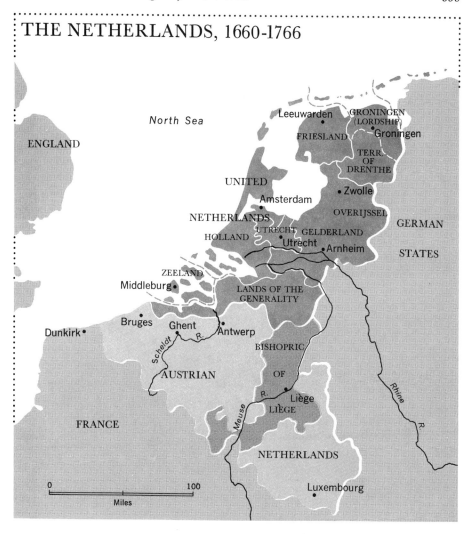

republic's southern border perpetuated the landward orientation of Dutch policy at the expense of the traditional maritime defense. The decline of the Dutch navy led to neglect of the republic's overseas interests. Moreover, war on the scale it was fought in the eighteenth century was such a heavy drain on the resources of the small nation that it could not afford to remain a competitor of Britain and France. It became dependent upon its British ally for protection landward and, increasingly, seaward. The price exacted by the ally was the encroachment of British merchants upon the Latin American trade, once the preserve of the Dutch.

During this period the regent oligarchy lost its sense of responsibility and cohesiveness. It became increasingly smaller in relation to the total population: since 1600 the population of the republic had almost doubled, but the oligarchy had remained the same closed group of families, jealously guarding its political and economic dominance. Luxury became the way of life of the oligarchs, whose sobriety and sensibleness had once been their hallmark. Interest in country estates replaced their former urban preoccupation and many of them aped the ways of the nobility. Factionalism, corruption, and self-satisfaction enervated the oligarchy, which had no other claim to leadership and power than its energy and success. Half-hearted attempts to strengthen the Dutch union foundered on oligarchic exclusiveness and town rivalries, and only served to make more rigid the jealous guarding of provincial sovereignty. In 1747 an invasion by France during the War of the Austrian Succession produced the familiar historical phenomenon — a call to William IV of Orange-Nassau (1711–1751). He was invested with a hereditary stadholdership of all seven provinces and the captain-generalship. He died after only four years of rule. Since his son, William V (1748–1806), was only three a regency was established that lasted until 1766.

THE TRIUMPH OF THE ENGLISH OLIGARCHY, 1660–1689

In 1660, after eleven years of exile on the Continent and one unsuccessful attempt to gain his throne, Charles II returned to England and the crown at the invitation of the reconstituted Parliament. Almost twenty years before, that same Parliament had taken up arms against his father, Charles I, and set in train two civil wars, ending with Charles I's execution in 1649. After that England had passed through a republican experience based on the notion "that the people are, under God, the original of all just power." The experiment in republicanism had two casualties: republicanism itself, bankrupted by its failure to find a legitimate foundation for power; and absolutism. If monarchy was vindicated in 1660, absolutist monarchy was not, and it was clear that Charles I's rule without Parliament could never be repeated. Absolutism was not a viable goal of monarchy in a nation in which men of property had made war upon and destroyed a king. The cynical, thirty-year-old Charles II recognized this prime fact of monarchic life in England and, as he flippantly remarked, had no intention of going upon his travels again.

THE POLITICAL SETTLEMENT OF 1660

In the settlement of 1660 there was no attempt to deal with the broad issues that had precipitated revolution, destroyed a monarch, and established a republic. No attempt was made at a fundamental restatement of the relations between king and Parliament. The settlement was political rather than constitutional. All acts that had passed the Long Parliament from 1640 to 1642 and received Charles I's assent were held to be legally valid; all other enactments were ignored. Consequently the settlement confirmed the abolition of ship money and other nonparliamentary revenues levied by the king's prerogative during Charles I's "personal rule" in the 1630's; abolition of the Privy Council's domestic criminal jurisdiction in the Star Chamber and of the High Commission court, which had enforced conformity to the state Church of England; and reduction of the king's power to imprison without trial — all enacted in 1641 and assented to by Charles I. It also confirmed the statute of 1641 requiring that Parliament be summoned at least every three years. Although the monarchy was reestablished without a definition of the limits of its authority, it could not be absolutist.

The restoration of Charles II had been possible only because the landed aristocracy — nobility and gentry — had made common cause with the upper-middle-class urban merchants to protect their property and preserve order — an order that in the confused months following Oliver Cromwell's death in 1658 had been rapidly dissolving. These were the oligarchs, and although they differed over specific political issues in the next three decades, they were always prepared to coalesce in defense of property and Protestantism.

The land settlement of the Restoration returned to the king, the church, and the royalists all lands confiscated from them. Nevertheless, a great many who had acquired such lands during the revolutionary decades retained possession. Lands sold by royalists to pay the heavy fines levied on them by the victorious Parliamentarians in the 1640's and 1650's remained with the purchasers. Those who had bought crown lands generally managed to keep them on long-term leases at low rents. Thus men of property had a special stake in avoiding a revival of monarchic pretensions.

THE RELIGIOUS SETTLEMENT OF 1660

By avoiding basic issues, the political settlement of 1660 held out promise of a successful new beginning for English political life. The settlement in religion was less auspicious. In the Declaration of Breda in 1659, presenting the terms on which he would return to the throne, Charles had made a faint promise of religious toleration to Protestants who could not accept the tenets of the Church of England, such as the Presbyterians, Congregationalists, Baptists, and Quakers. These were the heirs of Puritanism who would henceforth be called Dissenters. After the Restoration an attempt at reunification under the Anglican Church failed. As a result of the election of a new Parliament in 1661 with a staunchly Anglican and royalist majority, called the Cavalier Parliament, a series of repressive measures against the Dissenters were enacted between 1661 and 1665. Inappropriately called the Clarendon Code after Charles's chief minister, the earl of Clarendon, who in fact opposed several of the measures, the new legislation excluded all but Anglicans from national or local government, prohibited Dissenting religious services with more than five people present except in a private household, and forbade Dissenting clergymen to come within five miles of the place where they had been ministers.

Charles was interested less in toleration for Protestant Dissenters than in toleration for Roman Catholics. His own brother and heir presumptive James, duke of York, was a Roman Catholic, and Charles himself, in secret provisions in the Treaty of Dover with Louis XIV in 1670, promised to declare himself a Catholic at an opportune moment in return for a large subsidy from France. In 1673, just as Charles was taking England to war in alliance with France against the Dutch, he issued a Declaration of Indulgence suspending the laws against both Roman Catholics and Dissenters. Parliament, attacking this use of the royal prerogative to block legal proceedings, passed the Test Act, banning Catholics and Dissenters from civil or military office. Charles, at war and in need of parliamentary revenue, could not afford to veto the Test Act. Its first victim was his brother James, who had to resign his admiralship of the navy.

THE CATHOLIC SPECTER

The 1670's were dominated by Charles's pro-French policy and by the growing fear of a revival of Catholicism. The two were intimately connected, for when the secret terms of the treaty of 1670 leaked out, the pro-French policy was seen as a league with the "Romish anti-Christ." The presence of the Catholic James a heartbeat away from the throne heightened the fear. French subsidies enabled Charles to survive without long parliamentary sessions, and the old suspicions of personal rule began to revive. The marriage of James's eldest daughter Mary to the Dutch stadholder William III in 1677 as a sop to Protestant sensibilities did little to allay fears. In 1678 a wave of anti-Catholicism broke out in the wake of a far-fetched report of a "Popish Plot," fabricated by a charlatan named Titus Oates, claiming that the Catholics planned to murder the king, massacre Protestants, and bring about a French invasion of Ireland. Anti-Catholicism gained new strength in Parliament, and only by the dissolution in January, 1679, of the Parliament which had sat since 1661 did Charles prevent a move to exclude James from the succession.

The unresolved conflict over religion had precipitated a falling-out between king and Parliament that now took on constitutional proportions. During its long life the Parliament of 1661 to 1679 had become less vociferously Anglican and Royalist as by-elections to fill vacancies brought in younger men with less vivid recollections of the horrors of the civil wars and the republican experiment. An opposition had grown up in Parliament that lacked the ideological frame of the opposition of 1640 to 1642 but had a similar suspicion of the king's sincerity and a whole-hearted detestation of the likelihood of a Catholic ruler. Effectively led by a former minister of Charles II, the earl of Shaftesbury, the new opposition rallied all who feared a Catholic conspiracy, including some staunch Anglicans. Merchants, artisans, Dissenters, and a great many substantial farmers supported the opposition, as well as men of landed property whose fortunes had been made in the 1650's. The few remaining republicans and ex-Levellers (see p. 254) also made common cause with the opposition.

Between March, 1679, and March, 1681, three Parliaments of short duration wrestled with the exclusion of James from the succession, and except for the reluctance of the House of Lords, Parliament would have passed such a bill. The elections to each Parliament returned a larger proportion of the opposition. Yet after Charles had dissolved the last of these three Exclusion Parliaments, he was able to rule for the remaining four years of his life without another Parliament. This strictly illegal action was possible only because increased prosperity had brought a greater yield from taxes already granted him and because French subsidies had made him independent of new parliamentary appropriations. Charles recognized that the opposition was creating its own reaction, especially among Anglican landowners who were fearful of its Dissenter tone and its republican element. To these men exclusion of a lawful successor, even if Catholic, carried reminders of the revolution of the 1640's. They believed in passive obedience to the will of the monarch, as the church and tradition instructed them.

THE REACTION

In 1682 Charles felt strong enough to move legally against the opposition. Shaftesbury was accused of treason, and though he was acquitted by a highly favorable London jury he was forced to flee to Holland, where he died shortly afterward. In the next year the uncovering of the Rye House Plot by republican extremists to kidnap the king and the execution for treason of two leaders of the opposition for alleged complicity in plans for a revolt, discredited the opposition and enabled Charles to establish his ascendancy.

Charles's victory was not a triumph of personal rule so much as a triumph for the coalition of king and Anglican landowners. The opposition, derisively nicknamed Whigs after Presbyterian guerrilla fighters in the west of Scotland, still possessed an organization. The Anglican landowners, called by their opponents Tories after Irish Catholic bandits who preyed on Protestants, were less well organized, and their continued adherence depended on the king protecting the Church of England.

Charles II died in February, 1685. His Catholic brother succeeded as James II. A staunchly Tory Parliament voted James an ample life income. In June a Protestant rebellion in Scotland led by the duke of Argyll and an invasion of the southwest of England by Charles II's illegitimate son, the duke of Monmouth (whom Charles had exiled to Holland in 1683), and a handful of exiled radical Whigs were put down with severity, and both Argyll and Monmouth were executed. James, encouraged by the loyal enthusiasm with which his success was greeted, demanded the repeal of the Test Act and the acts of the Clarendon Code that barred Catholics from office. The rebellions had also given James an excuse to keep an army encamped on the outskirts of London. Parliament, even with its Tory majority, protested the presence of the troops and refused to repeal the Test Act, which moved James to adjourn it in November, 1685. It was never reconvened. James then embarked upon a policy of naming Catholics to posts in the government, local governments, army, navy, universities, and even the Church of England. Early in 1687 a Declaration of Indulgence suspending all laws that excluded Catholics and Protestant Dissenters from office thoroughly alienated the Tories while it won few Dissenters (most of whom were Whigs). James's actions seemed to forebode Catholic absolutism, for which the only model was the France of Louis XIV. When in 1688 the archbishop of Canterbury and six other bishops, after refusing to read a second Declaration of Indulgence from their pulpits, were tried for sedition and acquitted by juries, it was evident that the Tory adherence to James was at an end.

"THE GLORIOUS REVOLUTION"

The birth of a son to James and his Catholic queen in June, 1688, coalesced Whig and Tory into revolutionary action. They invited Dutch stadholder William III and his wife Mary, Protestant daughter of James II by his first wife, to assist them in protecting the Protestant religion in England. In November, 1688, William and a small expeditionary force landed in England and moved slowly toward London, gathering support from landowners and towns on the way. In panic, James and the royal family fled for France, only to be captured and returned to London. This embarrassment was rectified by allowing them to escape again. Literally without a shot fired a dynasty had fallen and a revolution had taken place, a revolution more superficial in the event but more profound in result than that of forty years before. This time the oligarchy — Whig and Tory, landed and mercantile — was firmly in control, and republicanism and Leveller radicalism were nowhere evident. Not the continuance of monarchy but only the person of the monarch was at issue.

A Convention (it could not legally be called a Parliament since no king had summoned it) was convened in January, 1689, to settle the question of the crown. It agonized over the precise legal formula to justify an act of usurpation by invitation. It found the justification in James's flight, which was tantamount to abdication. The Convention offered the crown to William and Mary as joint sovereigns, "whom it hath pleased Almighty God to make the glorious instrument of delivering this kingdom from popery and arbitrary power." Accompanying the offer, though not a condition of it, was a Declaration of Rights. Accepted by the new sovereigns and enacted into law by Parliament as a Bill of Rights, it guaranteed the right of petitioning the king, of bearing arms (Protestants only), of freedom of election to and debate in Parliament, of frequent meetings of Parliament, and of reasonable bail and jury trial. It also declared illegal the suspending of laws by the king and the levying of revenue and the keeping of a standing army in peacetime without Parliament's consent. Rather less than its illustrious American derivative of a century later, the Bill of Rights was a guarantee of the individual rights of Englishmen. More definitely it was a charter of independence for Parliament. A limited liberty of conscience was granted to Protestant Dissenters by the Toleration Act, in recognition of the Dissenters' opposition to James. Though the Toleration Act preserved the exclusion of Dissenters from office, it permitted them considerable freedom of worship.

JOHN LOCKE AND OLIGARCHY

The "Glorious Revolution of 1688" — as Whigs would honor it for centuries to come — found its prophet, its apologist, and its theoretician in John Locke (1632–1704). Confidant and assistant for fifteen years to the earl of Shaftesbury, the leader of the opposition to James, Locke lived in exile in Holland from 1684 until the advent of William III early in 1689. His political philosophy undergirded the political theories of the French philosophes of the Enlightenment, furnished the framework for the American Declaration of Independence in 1776, and dominates English political theory to this day. In 1690 Locke published his *Two Treatises of Government,* written between 1679 and 1683 as an unpublished contribution to the exclusion controversy. Upon its publication, the *Two Treatises* provided a persuasive rationale for the events of 1688–1689.

Locke rejected the accepted way of justifying a political position by appealing to history in general and to legal precedent in particular. Instead, he sought justification in an older tradition, appealing to fundamental natural law revealed not by history but by the use of reason. Like Thomas Hobbes and other predecessors, Locke used a "state of nature" — the absence of government — as a starting point for theory and as a device to invoke natural law to buttress immediate political arguments. Locke argued that men are created with equal rights to life, liberty, and property. No man can exercise authority over another. All men are governed by natural law, and since all men are essentially rational, they can

John Locke, by M. Dahl

"Whatever form the commonwealth is under, the ruling power ought to govern by declared and received laws, and not by extemporary dictates and undetermined resolutions. For then mankind will be in a far worse condition than in the state of nature. . . . For all the power the government has, being only for the good of the society, as it ought not to be arbitrary and at pleasure, so it ought to be exercised by established and promulgated laws; that both the people may know their duty and be safe and secure within the limits of the law; and the rulers too kept within their due bounds, and not be tempted by the power they have in their hands to employ it to such purposes, and by such measures as they would not have known, and own not willingly." John Locke,
AN ESSAY CONCERNING THE TRUE ORIGINAL, EXTENT AND END OF CIVIL
GOVERNMENT (1690).

discover and apply natural law. Political institutions did not exist in the state of nature. In this way Locke laid the natural law foundations for the existence of equality before the advent of government. When government came into being it was by an agreement, a contract among men in the state of nature, by which they gave the political authority the responsibility to preserve and protect their property.

Such a contract could have engendered a thoroughly egalitarian democracy (and this construction has been put upon Locke's intentions by later political philosophers). Democracy did not result, however, because two other developments occurred in the state of nature before the contract brought government into existence. First, inequality of property grew out of an agreement among men in the state of nature to translate not only their labor and the fruits of the earth but the land itself into money with which men might further increase their property by purchase. Second, natural law gave man the right to dispose freely of his own property, including the property of his own labor. Men sold their labor to other men and became employees, their labor becoming part of the employer's property. In his later studies, *Some Considerations of the Consequences of Lowering of Interest and Raising the Value of Money* (1691) and *The Reasonableness of Christianity* (1695), Locke observed that from these two developments came both the differences in property and, significantly, the differences in the rational capacity of men in contemporary society. When in the process of a money economy a few men had appropriated the greatest part of the property (including the labor of other men), those without property, who had to spend their lives in merely sustaining themselves, could not raise their thoughts to higher things, could not have the leisure to reflect upon nature and its laws, could not use their rationality to the full. Even before government was formed by agreement among men in the state of nature, then, the majority of men had been relegated to a status that would not enable them to participate in political life.

After the advent of government all citizens were protected in their right to life, liberty, and property, but those few who had gained the greatest part of the property alone controlled government. All men tacitly agreed to obey the laws of the government, but only those with a substantial amount of property contracted explicitly to form a government. If the government broke the contract they could change the government. The government broke the contract if it failed to protect property or if it attacked property itself. The propertied class determined by majority decision when the contract had been broken. Thus in 1688 men of property changed the government from James II to William III and Mary because James threatened property. This was the triumphant justification accorded the Revolution of 1688 by Locke's theory.

Locke did not set out to protect individual rights. Such a reading of

Locke was peculiarly American and intimately connected with the development of the American Constitution. Locke sought to protect the rights of property owners, not only against government tyranny but also against the propertyless. His theory did battle for the oligarchy against both these foes during the century and a half of the oligarchy's dominance.

THE AUGUSTAN AGE OF THE ENGLISH OLIGARCHY, 1689–1760

> A pleasing Form; a firm, yet cautious Mind;
> Sincere, though prudent; constant, yet resign'd:
> Honour unchang'd, a Principle profest,
> Fix'd to one side, but mod'rate to the rest:
> An honest Courtier, yet a Patriot too;
> Just to his Prince, and to his Country true:
> Fill'd with the Sense of Age, the Fire of Youth,
> A Scorn of Wrangling, yet a Zeal for Truth;
> A gen'rous Faith, from Superstition free;
> A Love to Peace, and Hate of Tyranny;
> Such this Man was; who now, from earth remov'd,
> At length enjoys that Liberty he lov'd.

Thus the poet Alexander Pope eulogized his friend Sir William Trumbull, attributing to him all the virtues of the eighteenth-century oligarch. Trumbull, a good Whig in the third generation of a family of officials, had faithfully served Charles II, James II, and William III in embassies and high office. Pope's elegant excessiveness was like that of the age, which in its manners and mores sought the simplicity of republican Rome, but in its thrust and ambition reflected the imperial glory of the Rome of Emperor Augustus.

THE OLIGARCHY

In 1696 Gregory King, a statistician, calculated that eight years earlier there had been 1,360,586 families in England. Of these, (1) 160 were headed by noblemen, (2) 26 by bishops, (3) 16,400 by landed gentlemen, (4) 10,000 by officeholders, (5) 10,000 by merchants, (6) 10,000 by lawyers, (7) 10,000 by clergymen, (8) 16,000 by persons in sciences and the liberal arts, and (9) 9,000 by army and navy officers. By the broadest interpretation the oligarchy of England comprised these 81,586 families or 6 per cent of the families in the nation. By the narrowest interpretation the oligarchy consisted of the first six categories, totaling 46,586 families or about 3 per cent of the families in the nation. In the broadest interpretation, status is the determinant; in the narrowest, wealth and political power are the determinants. Either way, the oligarchy formed only a fraction of the nation.

From it were drawn those who sat in Parliament and those who controlled election to the House of Commons. They comprised the bureaucrats who ran the state, the officers who directed its military might, and the lawyers who staffed the law courts and determined precisely the "undoubted rights and liberties" of Englishmen. The landed gentry filled the important local offices in the counties, such as justice of the peace and deputy-lieutenant in control of the militia. The merchants governed the towns, in which increasing numbers of Englishmen were coming to live. The clergy held the pulpits and monopolized education from the village school to the two universities, Oxford and Cambridge. In the hands of these oligarchs rested by far the largest part of the nation's acreage and its commerce and burgeoning industry.

Not unnaturally, in an age in which oligarchy had triumphed and stood unchallenged, these fortunate few had a livelier sense of what divided them among themselves than of what united them against the monarch above and the masses below. Social status was a horizontal divider; the duke of Devonshire would have been extremely annoyed had he been mentioned in the same paragraph with a Bristol tobacco importer. The nobility comprised a traditional and legally defined elite, little debased by their steady increase in number throughout the eighteenth century. They, together with the twenty-six bishops and, after 1707, sixteen Scottish peers, sat in the House of Lords, the upper house of Parliament. The landed gentry covered four degrees of rank (gentleman, esquire, knight, and baronet) and a wide range of wealth. They were the supreme local powers in the counties and the largest element elected to the House of Commons. The officeholders were socially indistinguishable from the gentry, being of the same ranks, but were functionally distinct and congregated principally in London. The army and navy officers were drawn almost exclusively from the gentry, and those who survived the service generally died on modest landed estates.

Physicians, academics, and artists were gentlemen by courtesy and never enjoyed higher status or prosperity than in the eighteenth century. The clergy (not including Dissenters) were generally university graduates, many of them younger sons of gentlemen and noblemen, and were dependent upon the landed aristocracy for their livings. The alliance between the gentleman's manor house and the parson's vicarage was never stronger than in the eighteenth century, and the upper ranks of the clergy were highly acceptable socially. Poverty among the clergy, of which there was a good deal, at least was genteel.

The merchants varied widely in wealth and political power. The greatest were almost merchant princes, allied with the landed aristocracy by marriage and economic interdependence. The great merchants of London were financiers, the creditors of kings, nobility, and gentry, who could expect office, honors, and even nobility. The successful merchant, whether in London or in the provincial towns, could establish himself on the land and his progeny in the gentry. Merchant control of town government meant control over most of the seats in the House of Commons although even the most independent towns sometimes elected gentry to Parliament and the merchants in some towns were subservient to local landed aristocrats. The generally rising economic prosperity of the eighteenth century, intimately connected with colonial trade and Britain's growing sea power, tied the merchants closely to politics.

The oligarchy was also divided vertically, between those whose lives were passed in the counties and those who congregated in London. This division was more meaningful than any other in the first half of the eighteenth century, and it reflected a political change completed by 1688–1689. Before the labels Whig and Tory came into being, those opposed to monarchic policies were called the Country party and those supporting the king were called the Court party. Thus, before 1688 Whig-Country and Tory-Court were the identifications. Although both invited William III to assume the throne, it was the Whigs rather than the Tories who enjoyed William's confidence. The Tories had been too closely allied with Charles II and too supine toward James II to reap the benefits of their defection from the doctrine of passive obedience to the monarch. The defection caused a crisis of conscience among the Tories, some of them becoming politically neutral, others becoming Jacobites, favoring the return of James II (Jacobus is the Latin name for James). The commercial connections of the Whigs made them readier supporters than the Tories of William's wars against France. Neither were the Tories in favor of the limited toleration accorded Dissenters.

Under Anne, William's successor, the Tories had a brief period in office from 1711 to 1714; but after Anne's death an abortive Jacobite rising in 1715 against the succession of the elector of Hanover as George I discredited Toryism, even those Tories who were not Jacobites. The Tories then became the Country party and the Whigs the Court party — the former in opposition, the latter in office. The Court party comprised the great landowners, including a growing number of peers and many of the upper gentry, officeholders, lawyers, bishops and higher clergy, and the merchants. The Country party comprised the country gentry, those with no more ambition than to dominate their county society and with a new-found distaste for London, and the country parsons. These designations were more realistic than the labels Whigs and Tories, which continued in political currency though with decreasing relevance to political positions in 1688 as the memories of that year grew fainter.

London was the heart of the Court oligarchy. It was the site of the king, Parliament, the hierarchy of the church, the bureaucracy, and the courts of law, as well as the commercial center of Britain. London's four points of power and wealth were its business houses, its coffeehouses (one,

Courtesy of Derbyshire Countryside Limited

Chatsworth

"The scene is one of peculiar beauty; the verdant carpet of Nature and the darker foliage of her draperies are so delightfully relieved and contrasted with the beautiful pale yellow masonry, — the chaste Grecian architecture, — white statuary, — sparkling fountains, — and the majestic river, — that for a moment imagination luxuriates within the ideal realms of Fairyland, or in one of the gorgeous valleys of the sunny South, rather than in northern climes, and amid the healthy mountains of the Peak." A DAY IN THE PEAK (Bakewell, Eng., 1868).

Mr. Lloyd's, became the insurance exchange of London and is still a household word: Lloyd's of London), its fashionable mansions, and above all its most exclusive club, Parliament. A remarkably free press supplemented gossip and debate in keeping the oligarchy alive to events. Coarse, slummy, filthy, foul from coal smoke, disease-ridden, a horror to 95 per cent of its half-million inhabitants, to the 5 per cent in positions of power in eighteenth-century Britain London was the universe.

PARLIAMENT AND KING

Glorious '88 was above all the victory of Parliament. Little in the settlement trenched specifically on royal power, but no monarch ever after could forget that William III and Mary had received their crowns from Parliament, or that George I (1714–1727) had been placed on the throne by an act of Parliament in 1701 that passed over fifty-seven Roman Catholics with a better hereditary claim in order to ensure a Protestant succession. Parliament, holding the purse strings and having the last word in keeping a standing army in being, continuously and routinely participated in affairs of state.

The House of Lords, which had about 200 members, could in fact seldom turn out more than 50 for its meetings. Its prestige was not lessened, but its power had been eroded in the period from 1660 to 1688 by the assumption of control by the House of Commons over granting parliamentary revenue. In the Augustan age of oligarchy the Lords did indeed manage the Commons, but did so through the great peers of the Court party who exercised control over elections to the lower house. There were 513 members in the Commons for England and Wales; after the union of Scotland with England to form Great Britain in 1707, there were 45 members for Scotland. Members from England's 40 counties, returning 82 MPs, were elected by all owners of land that produced an income of at least 40 shillings a year. The bulk of the members were elected by towns, however. All enfranchised towns returned two MPs. The narrowest franchise was that of the rotten borough of Old Sarum, whose two MPs were returned by no more than three electors, and the broadest was Westminster, adjacent to London, with almost universal male suffrage. Out of the total English and Welsh population of between 6 and 7 million only 250,000 had the suffrage.

The extent of the franchise was important only as it affected the price paid by an aristocratic patron to buy the election of an adherent. The most venal constituencies were the pocket boroughs, whose right of representation was controlled or virtually owned by an individual. Other boroughs held out for high prices, and a few followed a fairly independent line. The county constituencies were thoroughly controlled by the country gentry and comprised the bulwark of the Country party. Every attempt was made to avoid an election contest, for it was likely to cost both sides heavily in beer and tobacco, pensions and jobs. It was the expense of an election, whether contested or determined by agreement (usually by giving one seat of the constituency to the man promoted by one faction and the other to his opponent) that put the Commons in the hands of the wealthy noble patrons, the Whig oligarchs.

Party as such in Parliament did not exist, and the Whig and Tory labels are of no use in analysis. Three broad divisions were discernible: (1) the members of Parliament who were officeholders and pensioners and who always supported the government, no matter who controlled it; (2) the independent country gentlemen at the other extreme; (3) the political factions in the center, contending for power, but in fact composed of groups held together by common interests following one or another of the political leaders who contested for power.

From the accession of George I in 1714 to the accession of George III in 1760 three major administrations held office by skillfully manipulating and balancing the competing interests of the members of Parliament. From 1721 to 1742 Sir Robert Walpole as chief minister led Britain in a period of peace and commercial expansion. From 1743 to 1754 Henry Pelham, supported by the patronage manipulations of his brother the duke of Newcastle, fought the War of the Austrian Succession and weathered a final Jacobite rising in 1745 in Scotland in favor of Prince Charles, grandson of James II. From 1757 to 1761 William Pitt, sustained by Newcastle's patronage though heartily disliked by both that politician and King George II, fought a victorious war for colonies and commerce with France that ended in 1763 with the loss of France's empire in North America and the triumph of English hegemony in India. (See p. 396.) Although these three administrations were based on venality, each in its time represented the best interests of the oligarchy of great noble land-owners and London merchant princes.

The king did not remain neutral while Parliament was guarding the oligarchy's interests. William III, an executive by training and by the necessities of war, intimately and continuously directed his own administration. His successors were Anne (1702–1714), a woman of modest attainments; George I (1714–1727), a German prince who knew no English and preferred his native Hanover; and George II (1727–1760), who though Hanoverian understood the English situation and relied heavily on Walpole, Pelham, and Pitt. These three monarchs were circumspect and realistic. Entrusting their affairs to ministers who were competent politicians, they used royal patronage increasingly to build up a king's interest in Parliament. No ministry could survive without the votes of the king's interest, that is, without the king's confidence. This situation produced a stability in relations between the throne and Parliament that had been absent before 1688. Anne was the last monarch to veto a bill passed by Parliament (in 1707). This indicated not so much the erosion of royal power as the weightiness of the royal influence in Parliament and the identification of successive monarchs with the oligarchy's aspirations. What would happen if either king or Parliament upset the balance remained to be seen.

AGRICULTURAL INNOVATION

The interest of English landed aristocrats in amassing profits can easily be overlooked if one fails to realize how interested in money-making many of them were, and how closely land and trade were linked,

Constitutionalism and Oligarchy in the West

Courtesy of the National
Portrait Gallery, London

George I of England, by Sir Godfrey Kneller

*"The King's character may be comprised in very few words. In private life
he would have been called an honest blockhead. . . . No man was ever more
free from ambition; he loved money, but loved to keep his own, without being
rapacious of other men's. . . . [H]e was more properly dull than lazy, and
would have been so well contented to have remained in his little town of
Hanover, that if the ambition of those about him had not been greater than his
own, we should never have seen him in England. . . . Our customs and laws
were all mysteries to him, which he neither tried to understand, nor was capable
of understanding if he had endeavoured it."* Lady Mary Wortley Montagu
(1689–1762), in ENGLISH HISTORICAL DOCUMENTS (London, 1957), Vol. X.

despite high-sounding titles and aristocratic pomp and circumstance. Capitalism was not confined to the countinghouses of London. The "improving landlord" who ran his estate for profit became increasingly common.

An awakened interest in the improvement of agriculture to make it more profitable had evidenced itself around the middle of the seventeenth century with the introduction into English farming of new techniques and new crops that increased farm yields. In the succeeding decades these improvements gained wide acceptance. The improvements — most of them brought over from the Low Countries — owed their introduction and propagation chiefly to the initiative of the great landowners, whose estates grew in size and number in the latter part of the seventeenth and during the eighteenth centuries.

Improvement also meant consolidating the strips scattered through the open fields into individual farms enclosed by hedges or fences, and dividing the common pastures and wastelands of the village among those who had property rights to them. Enclosure was not a new phenomenon; it had been going on since medieval times and by 1700 around 40 per cent of the cultivated land in England lay in consolidated fields, though some regions had much more enclosed land than did others. Enclosure created more economical farming units and made easier the introduction of the new techniques and new crops that increased yields and profits. These considerations prompted a rapid increase in the number of enclosures in the eighteenth century. Until the middle of that century enclosure had been carried out by private agreements among the landowners concerned. Then it became the practice to obtain an act of Parliament to authorize an enclosure, making it easier for landowners to reach agreement among themselves and also providing safeguards that protected the smaller landowners. By 1820 nearly all of England's agricultural land had been enclosed.

Scholars long believed that the increase in enclosures during the second half of the eighteenth century had emptied the countryside by driving dispossessed peasants into the towns, and had reduced to pauperism most of those who somehow managed to remain on the land. Detailed local studies made in recent years indicate that these effects of enclosure have been exaggerated. Rural population rather than declining rose almost as rapidly as town population. The increase in urban population came primarily from natural increase rather than from migration from the countryside, and the number of small peasant owners and tenants actually went up rather than declined.

Those peasants who had no land, or who had only a hut with a vegetable garden, or who lived as cottagers on common or waste land, and who earned their livings as farm laborers, did suffer from enclosure because it deprived them of the chance they once had to graze the cow they might own on the common fields and to gather firewood in the common woods. The enclosures, however, did not throw them out of work and compel them to seek employment in the towns. The new, more intensive techniques of farming actually demanded more labor than did the old methods. The larger amount of farm goods now produced required more hands to plow, till, and harvest — labor-saving farm machinery was many decades away. More labor was needed to take care of the larger herds, to drain fields, and to build and maintain the hedges and fences that enclosed the fields. The growth of agriculture created a demand for more rural craftsmen such as wheelwrights and smiths, and the increased farm output made new jobs for carters and drovers to transport the products of the farm to market.

An earlier view of historians, that the pace of agricultural change was so great during the second half of the eighteenth century that those years deserved to be called the age of the Agricultural Revolution, is no longer accepted. The changes came at a much slower rate, reaching back to the mid-seventeenth century and perhaps earlier. But whether gradual or cataclysmic, the progress that was made enabled English agriculture to feed the people of England during a period of great population growth with little assistance — and that only beginning in the last years of the eighteenth century — in the form of imported foodstuffs.

DUTCH AND BRITISH OLIGARCHY BESET, 1760–1790

By 1760 the constitutionalist oligarchies of the Dutch Republic and Great Britain for over half a century had had things pretty much their own way. For both oligarchies the mid-eighteenth century represented a turning point in their fortunes: in the Netherlands the regent oligarchy was attacked from below, and in Britain the landed and commercial oligarchy was pressed from above and threatened from below.

WILLIAM V OF THE NETHERLANDS AND THE PATRIOTS

William V, the hereditary stadholder who had been subject to a regency since his father's death in 1751, came of age in 1766. An ineffectual ruler, he was backward-looking and unimaginative. His viewpoint, traditionally Orangist and pro-English, was reinforced because his mother was the daughter of George II of England. He confessed himself to be "no friend to novelties"; he was to see many of them.

Much against William's will, the Statist regents of Holland seized on the American Revolution as a chance to engage in trade and investment at British expense. British attempts to cut off that trade forced them into war with Britain in 1780. The war revived the old Statist-Orangist rivalry and added a new third force in Dutch politics, the Patriots, who were encouraged by the example of the American Revolution. The Patriots were a strange amalgam of landward nobles, Roman Catholics and non-Reformed Protestant sectaries, middle class burghers not of the regent oligarchy, and lower-middle-class craftsmen. Anti-Orangist because of a strong republican bent and anti-Statist because they meant to dismantle the regent monopoly of Dutch political life, the Patriots at first made common cause with the regents against the Orangists. In the province of Holland from 1782 to 1783 they agitated successfully for a reduction of the stadholder's influence in appointments to town governments. In Utrecht the movement took on a more radical complexion: lower-middle-class burghers, led by Peter Ondaatje, a redoubtable student orator, forced the town council to accept overseers from the lower middle class to sit with the regents' council. The humiliating peace concluded with Britain in 1784 swelled the ranks of the Patriots, and by 1786 they had gained control of Holland, Groningen, and Overijssel. The movement became increasingly insistent upon the introduction of full democracy in the republic. Its influence crested in 1786 when the States of Holland deposed William V as stadholder of that province and the Utrecht town council was reconstituted by popular election.

The Patriots' radical wing, a paramilitary force called the Free Corps, in 1787 clashed with William V's troops and threatened civil war. Yet within a matter of months the movement collapsed, and some thousand Patriots fled in exile abroad, mostly to France. The Patriots fell not before internal reaction but before external force. The French had armed and actively supported the movement because of its anti-British sentiments. The British grasped the opportunity afforded by imminent civil war to promote an expeditionary force of Prussian troops — William V's wife was the sister of Frederick William II of Prussia — and the show of force scattered the Patriots. A mild repression followed in which the regent oligarchy excluded from power all those suspected of Patriot sympathies and heavily censored the press. The Orangists' and regents' relief at being spared was relatively short-lived, however. The Patriot movement continued underground, and when French Republican armies invaded the Netherlands during the French Revolution, the Patriots in hiding and those returning with the French army deposed William V in 1795 and established a more representative government than any proposed by the Patriots a decade earlier.

BRITAIN'S "PATRIOT KING": GEORGE III

"Born and educated in England, I glory in the name of Britain, and the peculiar happiness of my life will ever consist in promoting the welfare of a people, whose loyalty and warm affection to me, I consider the greatest and most permanent security of my throne." Thus George III (1760–1820), aged twenty-two, pronounced his patriotism in his first speech to Parliament. These words were the death knell of the administration of the great William Pitt, for George meant to be his own chief minister, to regain the reins of administration, to arrest the tendency of ministers to stand humbler before the Commons than before the king, and to be the "Patriot King" and leader of his people. He had no intention of being an absolute monarch, for he took pride in what he once called "the beauty, excellence, and perfection of the British Constitution"; but his assertion of royal power would end the free-wheeling oligarchism that had been the habit of English politics for over half a century. Moral, courageous, and industrious, George III had a high sense of duty but too little flexibility. His collision with the oligarchy did not bring the settlement of 1688 into question, but it weakened king and oligarchy in the face of new pressures from below.

Pitt was dismissed in 1761, and the earl of Bute, pompous tutor of George, replaced him. By a more venal use of patronage than any the age had seen, Bute built up an expanded king's interest in Parliament. A dreary succession of ministers, alter egos of George-who-would-be-king, dominated the 1760's. The new Tory ministers were a sad lot — incompetent, inexperienced, and unimaginative. They must take the responsibility for failing to cope with the sentiment for independence manifested in the American colonies. However, neither they nor the king can be blamed entirely for the end of the Augustan age of oligarchy. By 1760 there was already a ground swell of resentment that would have major future political implications. The attack was mounted from two divergent quarters, both rooted in the urban middle class, which had become disenchanted with the elegance and dominance of the oligarchy.

JOHN WESLEY AND JOHN WILKES

In the religious reform movement called Methodism, John Wesley (1703–1791) created the tightest-knit organization and most formidable body of opinion in Britain in the last half of the eighteenth century. Methodism was overtly a two-pronged attack on oligarchy against the luxurious indifference to the work of God on earth exhibited by the Anglican Church, of which Wesley lived and died an ordained minister, and against the luxurious elegance and moral depravity of those of wealth and position who dominated society. Yet Methodism never questioned the validity of the Anglican Church, and it never mounted a political attack on oligarchy or the established institutions of government. Its message to the poor of Britain was to offer them hope for a better life in the next world, not hope for much improvement in this. In this respect Methodism proved a bulwark of the old order. The greater impact of Methodism, however, was destructive of oligarchic monopoly. Wesley's major appeal was directed to the thrifty, hard-working lower middle class, who by force of will and drudgery were fashioning new lives for themselves in the burgeoning industrial economy of Britain. Methodism's anti-intellectualism, mystical message, Biblical fundamentalism, and stress on the sinfulness of the flesh afforded its hundreds of thousands of converts pride and integrity which, while immunizing them to the blandishments of radical politics, gave them a new cohesiveness and identification.

John Wilkes (1727–1797), rake and rogue, was the antithesis of John Wesley. Many in the lower middle class whom Wesley did not move, Wilkes did. Following an attack on the king in 1763 in his scurrilous weekly *The North Briton*, Wilkes was forced to flee from criminal prosecution because George III had him expelled from the House of Commons and thus deprived him of his legal immunity as a member of Parliament. In 1768 he returned, ran for Parliament from Westminster, and was elected, only to be expelled again. Elected twice more by the craftsmen and little shopkeepers in that constituency, the only one in Britain with nearly universal male suffrage, Wilkes became the champion of the lower middle class, challenging king and Parliament. Finally, with the never-quiescent London mob marching through the streets shouting "Wilkes and Liberty" and the metropolis on the verge of revolt, he was seated in 1774. Though no paragon of virtue, in his long battle to uphold liberty he exposed parliamentary venality and monarchic influence in the Commons, forced Parliament to allow reporting of its debates, secured legal recognition of the right of the individual not to be arrested on unspecified charges, and awakened a popular concern with the "undoubted rights and liberties of Englishmen" which proved a powerful solvent of oligarchy.

THE WAVE OF REFORM

Wesley demonstrated the moral shortcomings of Augustan elegance, and Wilkes revealed its political depravity. Wesley inspired a reform movement within the Anglican Church, Evangelicalism, which through its spokesman in Parliament, William Wilberforce (1759–1833), pressed for legislation abolishing the slave trade and for more humane treatment of the natives in Britain's empire. Wilkes inspired a radical political movement of Dissenters who, excluded from office by the Test Act, agitated for universal manhood suffrage and wholesale reform of Parliament. Richard Price, Joseph Priestley (who won fame as a chemist), and John Cartwright were the fathers of British lower-middle-class radicalism, which in the 1780's moved the more perceptive of the oligarchs to attempt modest reforms in order to stave off unrest and possible rebellion.

The American Revolution was a powerful persuader in the direction of reform. Edmund Burke (1729–1797), a political theorist and practical politician who had sought a settlement of American grievances, later argued for reform of the most glaring inequalities and abuses in the election of members of Parliament. It was an uphill fight, made more difficult by the occupation of London by a mob during a week of anti-Catholic rioting in 1780 (the Gordon riots), an episode hardly likely to inspire confidence in the political stability of the masses. The unrest in Ireland that followed the American Revolution brought home to the oligarchy as nothing else could have the necessity for change. Burke, who was himself an Irishman, urged concessions to Irish demands and the most sweeping reforms, including allowing Irish Catholics to vote and hold office. In 1782 Burke and the parliamentary faction of Lord Rockingham, of which he was a leading member, had their opportunity when George III reluctantly called Rockingham to form a ministry to end the war with America.

In three short months in office, ending with Rockingham's death, this reform administration made a just and honorable peace with the American colonies and introduced and drove through Parliament legislation barring government contractors from Parliament and reforming the worst abuses of the patronage system. Concessions to Ireland were made, culminating in an act making the Irish Parliament autonomous and independent from the direct royal control that had subverted its authority for three centuries.

WILLIAM PITT THE YOUNGER

With Rockingham's death in July, 1782, George managed to pull down his ministry. He could not, however, replace it with another inept, rubber-stamp ministry to enable himself to play prime minister. In December, 1783, after a series of coalition ministries he called William Pitt, twenty-four-year-old son of the great William Pitt, to form a ministry. Ambitious but honest, adroit, and courageous, young Pitt enjoyed the king's support and the good will of the trading interests of London. He slowly but surely fashioned a following in the Commons by prodigal use of patronage and swamped the old landed aristocracy in the Lords by persuading the king to create almost a hundred new peers, many of them London businessmen. Determined upon economic and fiscal reform, Pitt reduced tariffs, introduced modern budgetary practices into government finance, and began a reduction of the public debt. He encouraged trade with the United States and reorganized the East India Company's government of India, preserving the company's power but purging its administration of the abundant invitations to corruption that marred its government in the previous decades. Pitt made a half-hearted stab at parliamentary reform and the abolition of the slave trade, in which he assumed the mantle of Burke and Wilberforce while lacking their commitment and zeal. William Pitt was not a reformer; he was an astute politician who intended to remain in power while introducing sound administrative practices, encouraging commercial prosperity, and making government fiscally solvent.

Pitt's first ministry lasted from 1783 to 1801 — the longest since Walpole's. His major domestic accomplishments were almost wholly confined to the first decade of the ministry; the second decade was dominated by the French Revolution and the war against France, in which Pitt and Britain played a major role in the coalition of European powers to check the spreading contagion of republicanism. The French Revolution's repercussions in Britain were immediate and disquieting. Tom Paine's *Rights of Man,* published in 1791 and 1792, appealed to the British to overthrow monarchy and organize a republic, striking a responsive note in the radical underground. Pitt took strong repressive measures against radical agitation, although there were, in fact, few radicals; Wesley's political conservatism proved more influential among the loom operators, weavers, miners, and cobblers. Burke's attack in 1790 on the Revolution, with its grim prophecy of violence, helped to disabuse intellectuals who had been inclined to greet the Revolution as the dawn of a new day for representative government and political liberty.

The French Revolution's excesses, manifest by 1792, discredited reform in Britain. The oligarchy was given a respite. Pitt's two decades in office at a critical juncture in the challenge to the old order by the still inchoate new order can be superficially seen as a reactionary resistance to change. In fact, however, Pitt made a notable contribution to the transformation. He reestablished the good name of Parliament, which had fallen into odium during George III's essay into parliamentary leadership. He trained an extraordinarily able group of young ministers who in the next generation would effect reforms that he himself could not accept. He forged groups of disparate interests in Parliament into something like a party and thereby pointed the way to the parliamentary practice of the nineteenth century. His commitment to good government, sound financing, and a burgeoning economy brought a new spirit to government that helped to make nineteenth-century administration more honest and more effective than any the nation had known before. Above all, by conditioning the oligarchy to face change and by diluting the oligarchy with new money and new men, William Pitt contributed to the stability with which English constitutionalism would accommodate the press for democracy in the nineteenth century.

WEALTH, WAR,
AND EMPIRE
CHAPTER FIFTEEN

In *Leviathan* Thomas Hobbes described the conduct of nations toward each other in these words: "Kings, and persons of sovereign authority, because of their independency, are in continual jealousies, and in the state and posture of gladiators; having their weapons pointing, and their eyes fixed on one another; that is, their forts, garrisons, and guns upon the frontiers of their kingdoms; and continual spies upon their neighbours; which is the posture of war." Each state utilized all the means at its disposal — diplomatic, military, and economic — in pursuit of survival and aggrandizement. Economic rivalry increasingly became a cause of international tension, much as religious disputes had earlier been in Europe. During times of peace nations thought of trade as unarmed warfare between rivals, and they did not hesitate to resort to armed conflict in order to strengthen their own trading position or to cripple and destroy that of their competitors.

THE EUROPEAN ECONOMY

During the first half of the seventeenth century the long upswing in economic activity that had started in the late fifteenth century gradually gave way to stagnation and decline. In some lands the downturn came earlier and was more severe than in others, often because of misgovernment or the effects of war. Spain, the Spanish Netherlands, Italy, parts of Germany, and parts of the Hapsburg empire were especially hard hit. France, Holland, and England were more fortunate, though the period from the mid-seventeenth to the mid-eighteenth century was for them at best a time of slow growth, often interrupted by years of stagnation and recession.

A levelling off, and in many regions a decline, in population accompanied the downturn in economic life. Epidemics, famines, and wars seemed to come more often and with more deadly effects. Until the first years of the eighteenth century the bubonic plague regularly swept across Europe and carried away many thousands. Long years of unusually bad weather brought on repeated crop failures and famines, some of them among the worst in all of Europe's recorded history. In addition to the many who died of starvation countless others, weakened by inadequate diets, easily succumbed to illness. The frequent and bloody wars brought death to many in battle, and far more fell victim to the disease and devastation that followed.

Traditional techniques of agricultural production remained unchanged in most of Europe. In a few areas in England and in northern Europe enterprising landlords and ambitious peasants introduced new crops and more efficient techniques, but these pioneers were still too few in number to affect European agriculture as a whole.

Most of Europe's commerce was generated within Europe itself, but overseas trade increased steadily though slowly, with the expansion of European colonizing and commercial activities in the Americas, Asia, and Africa. Monopolistic trading companies chartered by the state dominated the overseas trade. Many of these companies met with serious financial difficulties and ultimate failure because of mismanagement, competition from the trading companies of other states, and the competition of individual merchants trading illegally, or interloping, in the overseas area in which the company had a supposed monopoly.

Manufacturing made increased use of the domestic or putting-out system in which merchants turned over raw materials or semi-processed goods to peasants who, working in their own homes, converted these materials into finished products. Often, however, the peasant workers themselves turned out unfinished goods, which the merchant then took to skilled artisans in the towns to be finished. There were few large-scale manufacturing enterprises, and most of these were either state-owned, such as arsenals and shipyards, or state-subsidized, such as the metallurgical plants in the Russian Urals.

Signs of economic revival became evident in the second quarter of the eighteenth century. By the 1740's a new era of economic expansion had clearly started. Agricultural productivity increased as more and more farmers adopted improved techniques of cultivation. Commerce expanded enormously. Industry gained a new momentum with the first applications of the technological changes which were to culminate in the great Industrial Revolution of the late eighteenth and the nineteenth centuries.

Population increased, too, at a hitherto unmatched rate: for example, between 1740 and the end of the eighteenth century France's population rose by 50 per cent, from 20 to 30 million; the population of England and Wales also rose by 50 per cent, from 6 to 9 million and the population

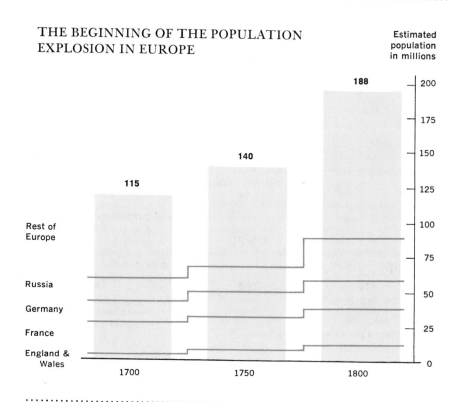

THE BEGINNING OF THE POPULATION
EXPLOSION IN EUROPE

Estimated
population
in millions

of Brandenburg-Prussia, not including population in new territories won
by Prussia, increased by 80 per cent, from 3.2 to 5.7 million. Population
rose apparently not because of an increase in the birth rate but because
of a fall in the death rate — people lived longer than they had in the
preceding era.

THE POLICIES OF ECONOMIC NATIONALISM

In good times and in bad the governments of Europe continued to
apply the narrowly nationalistic economic policies of mercantilism,
which they believed would promote economic growth and thereby increase both the power of the state and the prosperity of its people. (See
p. 279.) They engaged in aggressive competition with one another for
extension of territory and control of overseas possessions and trade. They
did so partly to make their countries self-sufficient in war, although
the very attempt to gain more territory or trade at the expense of other
states often led to war.

Despite similarities, each state had distinctive economic policies derived from peculiarities of local and national tradition, geographic circumstance, and possibly most important, the character of the state itself. Advocates of economic nationalism claimed that their policies were designed to benefit the state. But what was the state? It varied in character from the absolute monarchies of Louis XIV and most other continental powers to the burgher republics of the Dutch, the Swiss, and the Hanseatic cities. In no case did all or even a majority of the inhabitants participate in the process of government. Since the nationalism of the early nation-states rested on a class, not a mass, basis, the key to national differences in economic policy should be sought in the differing composition of the ruling classes.

In France and other absolute monarchies the wishes of the sovereign were paramount. Although few absolute monarchs had much understanding or appreciation of economic matters, they were accustomed to having their orders obeyed. The day-to-day administration of affairs was carried out by ministers and lesser officials, who were hardly more familiar than the monarchs with the problems of industrial technology and commercial enterprise and reflected the values and attitudes of their master. Elaborate regulations for the conduct of industry and trade added to the cost and frustration of doing business and encouraged evasion. According to legend, after one of Colbert's successors had outlined a program of new and expanded trade regulations to a delegation of influential French merchants, he asked what more he might do for them. They replied "Laissez nous faire" (let us alone). On large issues absolute monarchs often sacrificed both the economic welfare of their subjects and the economic foundations of their own power as a result of their ignorance and lack of concern. Thus, in spite of its great empire the government of Spain continually overspent its income, hamstrung its merchants, and steadily declined in power. Even France under Louis XIV, the most populous and powerful nation in Europe, could not easily support the continued drain of its wealth for the prosecution of Louis's territorial ambitions and the maintenance of his court. When he died, France hovered on the verge of national bankruptcy.

The United Netherlands, governed by and for the wealthy merchants who controlled the principal cities, followed a more informed economic policy. Living principally by trade, it could not afford the restrictive, protectionist policies of its larger neighbors. It established free trade at home, welcoming to its ports and markets the merchants of all nations. On the other hand, in the Dutch empire the monopoly of the Dutch traders was absolute.

England lay somewhere near the center of the spectrum. The landed aristocracy had been recruited primarily from recently risen merchants and mercantile-connected lawyers and officials, and great merchants had

The Royal Exchange, London, by J. Chapman

> *"Nor is trade itself in England, as it generally is in other countries, the meanest thing men can turn their hand to; but, on the contrary, trade is the readiest way for men to raise their fortunes and families. . . . [A]n estate's a pond, but trade's a spring: the first, if it keeps full . . . it is well, and it is all that is expected; but the other is an inexhausted current, which not only fills the pond and keeps it full, but is continually running over, and fills all the lower ponds and places about it."* Daniel Defoe, THE COMPLETE ENGLISH TRADESMAN (1745), reprinted in THE NOVELS AND MISCELLANEOUS WORKS OF DEFOE (Oxford, 1841), Vol. XVII.

long taken a prominent part in government and politics. After the revolution of 1688 their representatives in Parliament held ultimate power in the state. The laws and regulations that they made concerning the economy reflected a balance of interests, benefiting the landowners while simultaneously encouraging domestic manufactures and assisting shipping and trading interests. The most distinctive feature of England's economic policy was the relative freedom from restrictive legislation enjoyed by its merchants and manufacturers.

EUROPE OVERSEAS: COLONIES AND COMMERCE

During their overseas expansion Europeans possessed two advantages that facilitated their conquest and subjugation of alien peoples. They had a superior technology — ships and navigational techniques, gunpowder and firearms, tools and techniques of production, all of which enabled them to reproduce in strange and sometimes hostile environments the material features of European life. Psychologically they had the advantage of believing firmly in their own moral superiority because of their Christian faith. Whether Protestant or Catholic, they felt that God had given them license to conquer, to massacre if necessary, to destroy civilizations, and to subject whole races to slavery.

The Europeans also knew what they wanted. They were purposeful and prepared in the fashion of a businessman or an engineer, whereas the peoples with whom they came into contact were for the most part psychologically unprepared, organizationally weak, and subject to divided counsels. Among the world's great cultures only the Chinese and Japanese, who themselves had strong feelings of moral superiority, were able to withstand the European onslaught. In short, Europeans brought to the task of conquering and exploiting the world the zeal of the crusader, the rapacity of the warrior, and the shrewdness of the merchant.

THE SPANISH AND PORTUGUESE EMPIRES

The way in which colonies were governed differed from country to country. The Spanish regarded their empire essentially as a source of precious metals and as an extension of Spain. Spanish institutions, such as the latifundia or great estates that had existed in Spain from Roman times, were transplanted to the New World. The Inquisition was also carried overseas. The Spanish followed a very restrictive colonial policy, controlling immigration (for example, no heretics or non-Catholics were allowed to immigrate) and regulating trade minutely. Little intracolonial trade was allowed, and practically no trade was permitted between the colonies and foreign powers. Trade between Spain and its empire became the monopoly of a privileged group of merchants enjoying royal favor. Spain and its colonies did not progress economically in the seventeenth and eighteenth centuries, as did its rivals.

The Portuguese Empire in the East was at first exploited as a royal monopoly for the benefit of the king and his favorites. In the years from 1580 to 1640, when Portugal was under Spanish rule, the Portuguese lost the greater part of their overseas possessions to the Dutch. After winning back their independence, the Portuguese regained their Brazilian empire and reestablished control over colonial trade in a manner similar to Spain's; and like Spain, Portugal and its empire failed to progress economically.

THE DUTCH

Spain and Portugal had seized the most lucrative and attractive overseas dominions early in the sixteenth century and excluded other Europeans by force of arms. Adventurers from other lands sought new routes to the Orient through Arctic seas, hoping to discover a northeast or northwest passage to China or Japan, but their efforts proved fruitless. The Dutch, however, had little reason to complain, for the Netherlands held a privileged position in the Spanish Empire. The Dutch and the neighboring Flemings reaped a large share of the profits of colonial trade by supplying Spanish and Portuguese colonial merchants with manufactured goods and distributing colonial produce in northern Europe.

The Dutch war for independence in the late sixteenth century interrupted commercial relations between the northern Netherlands and Spain. The Dutch continued to trade with the Portuguese Empire via Lisbon, but in 1592 after an abortive Portuguese revolt against Spain the Spanish authorities closed the port of Lisbon to Dutch ships. Heavily dependent upon maritime commerce, the Dutch immediately began building ocean-going ships capable of the months-long voyage around South Africa to the Indian Ocean. So successful were these early voyages that in 1602 the government of the United Provinces, the city of Amsterdam, and several private trading companies formed the Dutch East India Company with a legal monopoly of trade between the Indies and the Netherlands.

Taking advantage of the weakness of Portugal under Spanish rule, the Dutch East India Company expelled both the Portuguese and English interlopers from the fabulous Spice Islands and Ceylon. The Dutch had too few people to undertake large-scale colonization, so they set up strongly fortified trading posts, made treaties with the native rulers, and strictly controlled the export of spices to Europe. From their bases in the East Indies and Ceylon they carried on trade with Japan, Formosa, the China coast, and India and settled a few colonists at the Cape of Good Hope to maintain a victualing station. The Dutch in the Indies followed a policy of monopoly and strict exclusion of both foreigners and Dutch traders who were not members of the East India Company. The company was a government within a government with nearly unlimited sovereignty in the Indies.

In the Western Hemisphere Brazil, a possession of the Portuguese crown, tempted Dutch adventurers. Again taking advantage of the weakness of Portugal, the Dutch established colonies on the Brazilian coast in 1624 and attempted to take control of the entire area. They failed to reckon with the Portuguese colonists in Brazil itself, who were resentful of Dutch intrusion and expelled the new settlers from all but one province in the north (Surinam or Dutch Guiana) and a few islands in the Caribbean.

In the same year in which the Dutch inaugurated their attempt to colonize Brazil another group of Dutch settlers founded the city of New Amsterdam on the southern tip of Manhattan Island. Dutch claims in the area dated from the voyages of Henry Hudson, an Englishman sailing under Dutch auspices at the beginning of the seventeenth century. The Dutch laid claim to the entire Hudson Valley and surrounding areas, founded Fort Orange (Albany), and gave out land under the patroon system of ownership to families such as the Rensselaers and Roosevelts who were destined to play a great role in the history of the United States.

ORIGINS OF THE FRENCH EMPIRE

At the beginning of the sixteenth century the French took an active interest in the exploration of North America, especially in the vicinity of the St. Lawrence River, which they hoped would prove to be the long-sought northwest passage to the Orient. Early attempts at settlement in the area failed, and in the second half of the century religious warfare and dynastic strife inhibited further efforts. After the reestablishment of strong government under Henry IV and Richelieu the French embarked on an ambitious program of conquest and colonization. Almost simultaneously they undertook trading expeditions to India, participated in the Dutch attempt to take over Brazil, seized West Indian islands from Spain, and made extensive explorations and some settlements in North America. In 1608 they established their first permanent base in North America at Quebec and named the surrounding area New France. They explored the entire basin of the Great Lakes and in the second half of the century extended their explorations to the Mississippi Valley.

In spite of their great effort and many substantial achievements, French colonial enterprise made little progress in the seventeenth century. The French colonies suffered simultaneously from excessive paternalism and inadequate support, the latter due in part to the magnitude of the French effort, but even more to the government's preoccupation with continental affairs. As late as 1660, half a century after the first settlement, all Canada contained only 2,500 colonists, a fraction of the number of Frenchmen in the few sugar islands of the West Indies.

BEGINNINGS OF THE ENGLISH COLONIAL EMPIRE

The English made an early attempt at exploration and discovery under the Cabots at the end of the fifteenth century, but the results of the mission were not promising for its mercantile supporters. What little overseas expansion the English undertook was for trade rather than for empire, and in the first half of the sixteenth century they were preoccu-

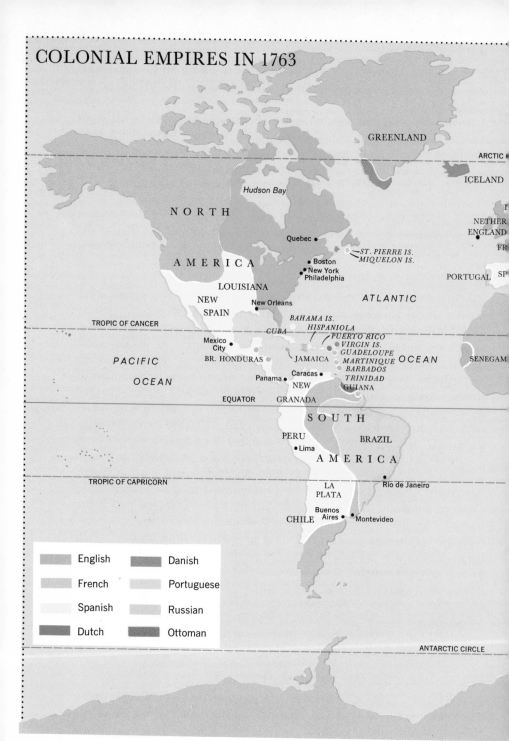

COLONIAL EMPIRES IN 1763

GREENLAND

ARCTIC

ICELAND

Hudson Bay

NORTH

NETHER
ENGLAND

FR

Quebec •

ST. PIERRE IS.
MIQUELON IS.

• Boston
• New York
Philadelphia

PORTUGAL   SP

AMERICA

LOUISIANA

NEW
SPAIN

New Orleans

ATLANTIC

TROPIC OF CANCER

BAHAMA IS.
HISPANIOLA

CUBA

Mexico •
City

PUERTO RICO
VIRGIN IS.
GUADELOUPE

PACIFIC

BR. HONDURAS

JAMAICA

MARTINIQUE OCEAN
BARBADOS

SENEGAM

OCEAN

Panama •

Caracas •

TRINIDAD

NEW

GUIANA

EQUATOR

GRANADA

SOUTH

PERU

BRAZIL

• Lima

AMERICA

TROPIC OF CAPRICORN

LA
PLATA

Rio de Janeiro

Buenos
CHILE   Aires • • Montevideo

English   Danish

French   Portuguese

Spanish   Russian

Dutch   Ottoman

ANTARCTIC CIRCLE

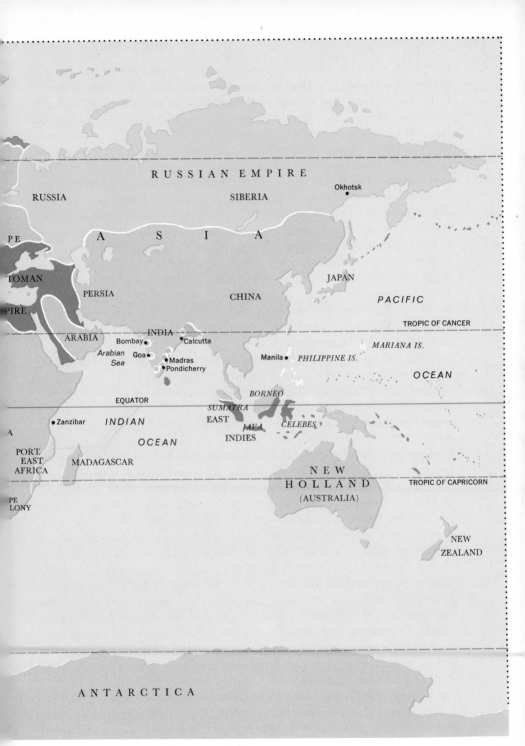

RUSSIAN EMPIRE

RUSSIA

SIBERIA

Okhotsk

P E

A   S   I   A

TOMAN

PERSIA

CHINA

JAPAN

PACIFIC

PIRE

ARABIA

INDIA

Bombay

Calcutta

TROPIC OF CANCER

Arabian Sea

Goa

Madras

Pondicherry

Manila

PHILIPPINE IS.

MARIANA IS.

OCEAN

BORNEO

EQUATOR

A

Zanzibar

INDIAN

SUMATRA

EAST

JAVA

INDIES

CELEBES

OCEAN

PORT.
EAST
AFRICA

MADAGASCAR

N E W
H O L L A N D
(AUSTRALIA)

TROPIC OF CAPRICORN

PE
LONY

NEW
ZEALAND

ANTARCTICA

pied with dynastic, diplomatic, and domestic problems. In the second half of that century interest in overseas trade and settlement revived, heightened in the last decade of the century by the publicist Richard Hakluyt's stirring accounts of voyages of exploration. The voyage of Richard Chancellor and Hugh Willoughby in 1553 through Arctic waters into the White Sea was a failure as far as discovering a northeast passage to the Orient was concerned (as were subsequent attempts to find a northwest passage), but it resulted in the establishment of trade relations with the growing Russian Empire and, through it, with the Middle East. The experience led to the formation of large chartered companies, each endowed with a legal monopoly of trade with a particular area, such as the Muscovy Company, the Levant Company, and the East India Company. Under Elizabeth I daring sea captains made privateering raids on Spanish ships and colonies in the New World. One of these captains, Sir Francis Drake, after raiding Spanish colonies on the west coast of South America sailed up the coast of California, crossed the Pacific, and returned to England in 1580 by way of the Indian and Atlantic Oceans, the second circumnavigation of the globe.

Two brief attempts by Englishmen to found colonies in North America during the reign of Elizabeth ended in failure, but in the first half of the seventeenth century England established successful colonies in Virginia (1607), New England (1620), and Maryland (1632), as well as on islands in the West Indies. The English colonies differed from those of other countries in that they were founded primarily under private rather than governmental auspices, although in most cases the founders obtained governmental authorization. They also originated from a variety of motives. The Virginia settlement, for example, was promoted by a company of London merchants and financiers as a commercial enterprise. After the settlers failed to discover gold or other readily exportable commodities, the settlement's future looked bleak until the introduction of tobacco cultivation in 1612. The Pilgrims were separatist Puritans who, after a brief sojourn in Holland, where they sought religious freedom, emigrated to America in 1620 in order to preserve both their English nationality and their religious independence. Boston was settled by Puritans in 1630 and grew rapidly as a result of Archbishop Laud's persecution of Puritans in England during the 1630's. Maryland represented a blend of religious and economic motives: the Calvert family obtained a royal grant for pecuniary gain but also used the colony as a haven for their Catholic coreligionists.

Although the English-speaking population of North America was no greater than 100,000 in 1660, important traditions, which exerted a profound influence on the subsequent history of the continent, had already been established. One of the most important was religious pluralism. Another was a strong desire for individual liberty and the wide latitude

PLACE OF ORIGIN AND DESTINATION
OF BRITISH FOREIGN TRADE, 1772–1773

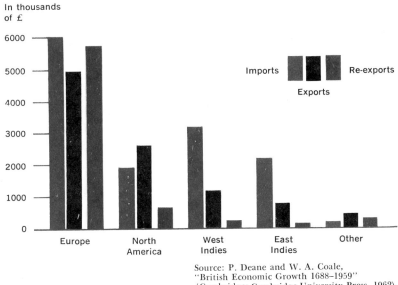

In thousands
of £

Imports   Re-exports

Exports

Europe   North   West   East   Other
America Indies Indies

Source: P. Deane and W. A. Coale,
"British Economic Growth 1688–1959"
(Cambridge: Cambridge University Press, 1962),
table 22.

permitted individual initiative and enterprise, tempered by the necessity
for collective agreement and action. In 1619 the first representative assembly in the Western Hemisphere met in Jamestown, Virginia, establishing a precedent that has contributed vitally to both the moral and
material strength of America. In the same year another, less happy precedent was established in the same colony: the introduction of the first
Negro slaves.

DYNASTIC AND IMPERIAL STATECRAFT, 1700–1763

Dynasticism was the escalation into national policy of the tendency of
an absolute monarch to consider his realm as the patrimony or hereditary
endowment of his dynasty, and to view his dynasty's interests as distinct
from and paramount to the interests of his subjects. According to this
view, the monarch's kingdom and his subjects served merely to increase the power and glory of his family. Narrow considerations of dynastic interest often gave form and content to relations among the states of

Europe. Marriage alliances between the royal houses and treaties and agreements establishing rights of succession were the staple of diplomatic activity and the fountain of war. War was primarily a means to assert a claim to territory based upon rights of marriage or succession. A marriage between two houses would in an instant ally two powers; the birth of an heir to such a marriage might result in the eventual union of the two powers. Either situation could provide a sudden, enormous accretion of wealth, territory, and population to an aggressive monarch. Almost in a matter of days the whole power structure of Europe might be drastically changed.

The fluidity created in international relations by dynasticism provoked a form of reaction: the balance of power. European monarchs could hardly question the universally recognized legal rights and benefits of marriage and succession. They could and did demand that the exercise of those rights and the settling of those benefits not result in so large and sudden an accretion of power to any one monarch that the power structure of Europe was unrecognizably changed and the balance of the powers upset. They formed coalitions strong enough militarily to outweigh any monarch who threatened to become too powerful. Two avenues for redressing the balance were open to a coalition: it might compel assurances that a marriage and potential succession would never result in the union of two crowns, or it might exact a cession of territory to another less formidable power in return for international recognition of the territory acquired by dynastic policy. The inherent difficulties of forming a coalition in the face of a threat meant that the balance of power seldom worked effectively until the aggressor had made considerable headway. The creation of a coalition always depended upon the intervention of one or two major powers whose concern stemmed less from a commitment to the balance of power than from their own dynastic ambitions.

PATTERNS OF WAR, 1651–1697

War was the logical extension of dynastic diplomacy. It served as the instrument both of aggression and of the balance of power summoned to contain it. The balance of power was not intended to preserve peace so much as to make war only moderately profitable to the victor and not crushing to the vanquished. In the late seventeenth and first half of the eighteenth centuries war involved almost all European powers; it was fought on many fronts (including the colonies); it demanded heavier expenditures on more ornate fortifications, increased fire power, improved supplies, larger armies of better-paid troops, bigger fleets of grander ships, and more guns; and destruction of enemy commerce was accepted as a prime strategy of maritime belligerents.

The wars of western European powers in the second half of the seventeenth century were usually three-cornered affairs, involving the Dutch,

French, and English, with incidental participation by other powers. The conflict between the English and Dutch in the mid-seventeenth century was the first almost wholly commercial war. In 1651 the English Parliament passed a navigation act forbidding the importation into England of any goods except those transported in English ships or ships of the nation producing the goods. Aimed directly at the Dutch carrying trade, the law provoked a maritime war that lasted two years. (See p. 262.) The war gave such an impulse to English commercial expansion that in the next few years England took the first steps toward becoming a Mediterranean naval power, became a commercial rival to the Dutch in the Baltic, and emerged as a commercial carrier of the first rank. The challenge of England's expansion coupled with the failure of the Dutch to regain a foothold in Brazil in the war with Portugal from 1657 to 1661 signaled the approaching end of Dutch commercial primacy and assured the loss of the most important of their colonies in the Western Hemisphere. In 1664 the English seized New Amsterdam from the Dutch, named it New York, and inaugurated the second Anglo-Dutch War (1665–1667).

The War of the League of Augsburg from 1688 to 1697 was transitional from the seventeenth-century pattern of war to that of the eighteenth century. The war had a new dimension in that it combined operations — maritime and military, continental and colonial — which foreshadowed all eighteenth-century dynastic and imperial warfare. French sea power enabled the deposed James II of England and a French army to open a front in Ireland against William III, newly crowned king of England. English naval power prevented further French troops from reaching Ireland, however, and at the Battle of the Boyne in 1690 William led his troops to victory over James's army. An Anglo-Dutch naval victory off La Hogue, France, in 1692 ended a projected invasion of England and swept the French fleet from the sea. In North America French Canadian colonists and New Englanders fought one another in what they called King William's War, marked by attacks on frontier strong points and raids by Indian allies of the French on isolated towns and farms in Maine and Massachusetts. The cockpit of the war was the Spanish Netherlands and the Rhineland; the battles at sea and the skirmishes in the colonies were peripheral. Yet the periphery was already assuming an importance that would increase, not diminish, in the future.

The wars of the last half of the seventeenth century left the Dutch Republic a second-class power with a shrinking empire and a shrinking economy. England, in contrast, experienced a burst of economic enterprise, enlarged its navy and merchant marine, created an effective standing army, added to its colonial possessions, created the Bank of England in 1694 as the financial resource for further colonial and commercial expansion and the reservoir to finance war, and entered the eighteenth century as Europe's foremost maritime power and leading contender for empire. France's dominance on the Continent was shaken but not cracked, and France remained a power of the first rank. In the rivalry between the two great Western powers England held an advantage because England's navy had grown as France's had diminished; and unlike France, which had been drained by three decades of costly land wars, England had the economic wherewithal to meet the price of war on three fronts — the Continent, the colonies, and the sea.

WESTERN EUROPE AFTER UTRECHT

The last and the most costly of Louis XIV's wars, the War of the Spanish Succession (see pp. 288–290), was brought to its close by the treaties of Utrecht (1713) and Rastadt (1714). The peace treaties brought a welcome end to nearly three decades of general war in western Europe. Coincidentally death made a clean sweep of the generation of kings and statesmen who had been the architects of the wars. New men and a new interest in stabilization held sway. In France Louis XIV's death in 1715 brought his five-year-old great-grandson Louis XV to the throne under a regency. The succession in 1714 of George I of the German house of Hanover brought a change of dynasty to England. Frederick I of Prussia was succeeded in 1713 by Frederick William I, who, though a renowned militarist, displayed a life-long reluctance to use his troops for more than playing soldiers. In Austria Charles VI became emperor in 1711 and found his new eminence more than adequate consolation for the loss of the Spanish throne that he had held so briefly. In Holland the death in 1720 of the grand pensionary Antonius Heinsius, who had controlled Dutch policy since 1702, made an effective break with the wartime past. Only Philip V, the new Bourbon king of Spain, smarting from the loss of Spanish possessions and spurred on by his second wife Elizabeth Farnese to find an Italian crown for their son Don Carlos, wanted war. In 1717 and 1718 Philip seized Sardinia and then Sicily, only to be forced in 1720 by British naval and French army action to give up his conquests and promise to abandon his Italian claims. The powers did not want a general war.

Peace was assured for a time by a remarkable alliance between Great Britain and France to preserve the balance of power. The alliance was joined by the Dutch in 1717 and by Austria in 1718, after which it was called the Quadruple Alliance. Until 1733 the alliance worked effectively, owing in part to the willingness of the powers to cooperate in settling crises arising from Elizabeth Farnese's continual machinations on behalf of Don Carlos, and in part to the interest of the British chief minister Robert Walpole (1721–1742) and his French counterpart Cardinal Fleury (1726–1743) in keeping the peace.

A war in 1733–1735 between France, Spain, and Savoy on the one hand and Austria on the other over the Polish succession did not become general, primarily because Britain remained neutral. The outbreak of war between Britain and Spain in 1739 was more ominous. In a burst of bellicosity the Whigs in Parliament took England into the War of Jenkins's Ear. (See p. 304.) This merged into the general struggle precipitated in 1740 by the attack of Frederick II of Prussia on the Silesian territory of Austria in defiance of the Pragmatic Sanction that guaranteed the claims of Empress Maria Theresa to all the Austrian possessions.

THE WAR OF THE AUSTRIAN SUCCESSION, 1740–1748

Had Frederick not invaded Austria, war would doubtless have broken out anyway. There were three claimants to the Austrian inheritance: Philip V of Spain, Charles Albert of Bavaria, and Augustus III of Saxony. A disputed succession in a major state could result only in a general war. The French — who even before Frederick's attack had decided to intervene on Spain's side in the War of Jenkins's Ear — formed a coalition with Prussia, Spain, Bavaria, and Saxony against Austria, while Britain and Holland allied themselves with beleaguered Austria. The coalition fell apart when in 1742 Frederick concluded a separate peace with Austria in return for Maria Theresa's recognition of his possession of Silesia. When Austria then began to win battles, Frederick, fearing that Maria Theresa would regain Silesia, re-entered the war, forced Austria to reconfirm his right to Silesia, then in 1745 again withdrew.

Britain gave financial aid to Austria but, lacking adequate land forces, was not of much help in the fighting in Europe. However, British military and naval action in the New World and on the high seas offset the reverses in Europe and balanced the scales of war. The fighting in King George's War, the name given the North American phase of the conflict, was significantly fiercer than earlier colonial struggles. French attacks on Nova Scotia and Massachusetts from the citadel of Louisburg on Cape Breton Island provoked a counterattack by English troops and Massachusetts militia in 1745 in which they captured Louisburg and so commanded the mouth of the St. Lawrence River. The British fleet was thus afforded unhampered access to the seaway and threatened the very existence of French Canada.

For the first time India became a theater of a European war, albeit a secondary one. The French and English East India companies, which had full political powers within their factories or trading stations and were in effect states, fought with one another. It was a purely commercial warfare, for which each side received only limited governmental assistance. The success of a small British fleet in disrupting French trade in the Indian Ocean moved the French company's governor, Dupleix, to take the English trading station at Madras in 1746.

As a result of naval victories by the British admirals Anson and Hawke in the West Indies in 1745, the lucrative French trade with her sugar islands was almost strangled. French privateering (quasi-official commerce raiding) in the Atlantic and Indian oceans could not balance the heavy commercial losses suffered by France from the British naval blockade and destruction of French shipping. Because these losses raised the possibility of the loss of her colonies, they moved France to agree to peace in 1748. Considerations of colonies and commerce had come to dominate the Anglo-French rivalry and even to dictate the Continental policy of France.

The Peace of Aix-la-Chapelle in 1748 was first agreed upon secretly by France, Britain, Spain, and Holland and then reluctantly accepted by Austria. The peacemakers made an effort to return Europe to the balance of power that had been established at the end of the War of the Spanish Succession. They decided on the restitution of all conquests in Europe and overseas, except for Prussia's annexation of Silesia. Maria Theresa and her advisers would have been far happier if the treaty had allowed her to regain Silesia and to give up the Austrian Netherlands, which had been occupied by the French during the war, but her English and Dutch allies demanded that she keep the Austrian Netherlands in the interests of a balance of power. Her right to the Hapsburg patrimony was recognized, although she had to cede three Italian duchies to a Spanish Bourbon prince. The right of the house of Hanover to retain the succession in both its German lands and Great Britain was confirmed.

Aix-la-Chapelle witnessed the emergence of a new great power — Prussia. Frederick's annexation of Silesia doubled Prussia's population and added greatly to its economic resources, while his skill on the battlefield won him the respect of the other powers. The Hapsburgs once again had survived an effort to drive them from their high position and to partition their empire. Now, however, they were faced with a new rival for the domination of Germany. Maria Theresa knew that in order to crush Prussia, she had to win back Silesia; and Frederick was resolved to hold it. Because of the Peace of Aix-la-Chapelle, war in central Europe was unavoidable. Nor did the peace settle anything for France or Britain except to establish a resolve on either side that the struggle for colonies and commerce must have another, and perhaps final, round.

THE "COLD WAR" OF 1748–1754

Neither the French nor the British governments yet recognized the full implications of their imperial rivalry. But at least one Frenchman and one Englishman did. Joseph François Dupleix, governor of the French East India Company, was in conflict with the company's purely commercial policies and sought to make the French trading stations militarily self-sufficient by raising revenues within the native states and leaguing with the native rulers. From the principal French base at Pondicherry he extended French influence over Indian rulers along much of the southeastern coast of India by supplying his clients with arms and modern military training and unleashing them on neighboring princes who were friendly to the British East India Company. From 1750 until Dupleix's recall to France in 1754 for defiance of company policy, the French and English companies fought each other behind the façade of native rivalries. Dupleix's nemesis, a young official of the English company named Robert Clive, wisely copied Dupleix's strategy and built up a system of clientage among the native princes while Dupleix's successor dismantled the French system.

Along the West African coast cold war incidents between French and English slavers were commonplace. In the West Indies French occupation of neutral islands used as bases by English smugglers resulted in a tense naval confrontation. Far more serious was the French decision to contain the British in Nova Scotia and to close the Ohio country to English settlers pushing westward from Pennsylvania and Virginia. French troops were poured into the Ohio Territory and an arch of forts was constructed from the St. Lawrence to central Illinois. The keystone of the arch was completed in 1754 with the construction of Fort Duquesne at the head of the Ohio River, where Pittsburgh now stands.

The governor of Virginia, the colony that claimed what is now western Pennsylvania and Ohio, dispatched a young Virginia militia colonel to warn off the French at Duquesne. He was rebuffed. On the trek homeward, Colonel George Washington's party met a French patrol, a volley of shots was exchanged, and the French officer in charge was killed. Washington constructed a rude wooden palisade — aptly dubbed Fort Necessity — and stood off a larger French force for some days before surrendering on July 4, 1754. This border incident started the colonial conflict called the French and Indian War, from which in two years would stem the greater European conflict that raged for nearly seven years.

The Anglo-French war was fought in a desultory fashion from 1754 to 1757. Formal British infantry tactics in North America were suicidal in the face of French and Indian ambushes, such as that which killed General Braddock in 1755 and routed his forces on their way to attack Fort Duquesne. The British managed only to break the French grip on the perimeter of Nova Scotia, and British naval action proved abortive. Yet the French, fighting defensively, scored only one victory — the capture of the prime Mediterranean base of Minorca.

THE DIPLOMATIC REVOLUTION

The chancelleries of Europe, certain that war would come again soon, busied themselves in diplomatic preparations for the expected conflict. The emergence of Prussia as a great power had upset the old balance and a new strategy had to be adopted to fit the changed circumstances. The efforts to seek a new balance led to a reversal of traditional alliances known as the Diplomatic Revolution of 1756. Until then France and Austria had been traditional enemies — the Bourbon-Hapsburg rivalry had been a constant in European international relations for a long time. The rivalry between England and France was even more venerable, and the English had allied with Austria against their common, traditional foe. France, in search of an ally, had turned to Prussia.

Prince Kaunitz, chancellor and foreign minister of Austria and the most astute diplomat of his time, recognized that these traditional ties no longer suited the best interests of his sovereign, Empress Maria Theresa. The continued existence of Prussia as a major power threatened Hapsburg domination of central Europe. Kaunitz decided to defy tradition, seek an alliance with France, and thereby deprive Frederick of his chief ally. He used every diplomatic wile at his command to persuade the French of the advantages of an Austrian alliance, promised support for French territorial ambitions, and hinted that Frederick was treacherously engaged in secret negotiations with France's oldest enemy, Great Britain.

Despite his best efforts, which included the use of the French king's mistress, Madame de Pompadour, as a go-between, Kaunitz made little progress in his scheme until Great Britain unwittingly came to his aid. The British, troubled by reports of diplomatic overtures between Austria and France, and faced with the problem of protecting Hanover (the German princedom that belonged to England's royal house), early in 1756 made an agreement with Frederick, called the Convention of Westminster, jointly to oppose the entry into or passage through Germany of any foreign troops. The French and the Austrians were outraged by what they considered a betrayal by their respective allies and joined in an alliance — to the great delight of Kaunitz. Russia, too, felt betrayed. Late in 1755, just a few short months before the signing of the Convention of Westminster, the British had signed a treaty with Russia, a sworn enemy of Frederick, to protect Hanover against possible Prussian attack. The Russians agreed to maintain a large force on the Russian-Prussian border, ready to march into Germany should Prussia move against Hanover, in return for a large British cash subsidy. Now, Britain had agreed with Prussia to keep foreign troops out of Germany. Filled with justified indignation the Russians allied with Austria to partition Prussia and reduce it to an insignificant German princedom.

THE SEVEN YEARS' WAR, 1756–1763

Frederick, well informed of all these supposedly secret negotiations, decided in August, 1756, to surprise his enemies and attack Austria's ally Saxony. His aggression plunged Europe into seven years of war in which France, Austria, Russia, Saxony, and Sweden were ranged against Prussia, Great Britain, and Hanover.

The war in Europe was a part of the world-wide struggle between France and Great Britain for colonial and commercial supremacy. The campaigns in Europe proved of decisive importance in determining the outcome of that struggle because they compelled France to divert men, arms, money, and attention from its overseas concerns, making it easier for the British to win an empire for themselves.

When the war began the odds were overwhelmingly against Frederick. He had to fight on three fronts. His state's population of about 4 million was one-third that of Austria, one-fifth that of France, and one-fifth that of Russia. His realm was poor and scattered. East Prussia was separated from the rest of his kingdom by northern Poland; a narrow corridor connected Silesia, which he had taken from the Austrians, with the main part of the realm; and other German states lay between Prussia and Frederick's possessions in western Germany. He could count on England for money but not for troops, though the Hanoverian army did protect his flank from French infiltration. In the face of what seemed certain and quick defeat only Frederick's military genius and unrelenting persistence allowed him to hold off his enemies.

He was confident that he could defeat any one of his foes alone although together they would overpower him. He had to keep the enemy armies apart by swift maneuvers and by avoiding battle against their united forces. When he did not succeed in this strategy he suffered terrible reverses, but he was always saved from final defeat by the ineptitude of the allies' commanders and the mutual suspicions and fears that kept dividing his adversaries. Yet, despite the shortcomings of his foes and his own military skills, the strain on Prussia became intolerable and the state seemed close to annihilation. At the end of 1761 Frederick wrote that his defeat was certain unless some unforeseen stroke of fortune delivered him.

That was precisely what happened. Empress Elizabeth of Russia, relentless foe of Frederick, died in January, 1762, and her successor, the mentally unbalanced Peter III, who idolized Frederick, issued immediate orders for an armistice. A peace treaty, drafted by Frederick himself at Peter's request, gave back to Prussia all of its territories occupied by Russian troops. A few weeks later Peter agreed to provide Frederick with troops to use against Austria, Russia's recent ally. Peter's assassination in June, 1762, ended that agreement; his successor, Catherine II, had no wish to continue the war. Meanwhile, Sweden had withdrawn from the conflict shortly after the Russians made peace with Frederick.

Though Frederick, besieged by seemingly superior forces, appeared time and again about to collapse, his British allies never allowed themselves to be deflected from that they considered their most vital interest — supremacy as a maritime and commercial power — and they poured subsidies into Germany to keep Frederick fighting the enemy there. William Pitt, brilliant war-time leader of Britain, called it "conquering

America in Germany." The stripping of the French empire began soon after the war started on the Continent. In 1758 the fortified port of Louisburg in Nova Scotia, Fort Duquesne (renamed Fort Pitt), and French slaving nations in Africa fell to the British. The next year brought still greater triumphs; the British called it the year of miracles. Britain won great naval victories off Lagos on the coast of West Africa and in Brittany's Quiberon Bay. In one of the great battles of history, fought on the Plain of Abraham outside Quebec, a British army led by General Wolfe defeated a French force under General Montcalm in a battle that cost the lives of the two commanders. Canada lay open to British conquest. In the West Indies the British took all but one of France's island possessions.

When the war broke out the French had more than double the number of troops and held more territory than the British in India. These initial advantages were cancelled by a combination of Robert Clive's military skills and British sea power. The troops commanded by Clive repulsed attacks and out-maneuvered the French, while British warships cut off French supplies and reinforcements. In 1761 France had to surrender its last foothold in India.

By the time the new king, George III, sacked Pitt (see p. 372) victory for Britain had been assured. France sued for peace; Austria, too, wanted the long war to end. After drawn-out negotiations separate peace treaties were signed in February, 1763. The Treaty of Hubertusburg among Prussia, Austria, and Saxony reflected the stalemate reached in the war on the Continent. The treaty ordered the return to conditions as they had existed before the war: the *status quo ante bellum* as the diplomats put it. Austria accepted Prussia's continued ownership of Silesia, and Prussia agreed to give up Saxony, which it had occupied during the war.

France did far better than her performance in the war warranted in the Treaty of Paris with Great Britain thanks to the negotiating skill of the duke of Choiseul, France's chief minister, and the inexperience and blunders of the men who represented England, now that Pitt had fallen from office. Nonetheless, the terms of the treaty crushed France's imperial ambitions. It lost all its North American possessions except two islands off Newfoundland. Spain, which had allied with France late in the war, ceded Florida to Britain. Britain returned to France all but one of its West Indian islands. Despite the return of its trading posts in India, France's power there was destroyed; and in Africa it lost its major slaving stations to the British.

The settlements arrived at in 1763 made that year one of the most memorable in European history. The continued existence of Prussia as a great power had been confirmed, and Austria had to accept continued Prussian rivalry for supremacy in central Europe. France had suffered severe losses, not only in overseas possessions but in international prestige, and its already weak finances had been badly shaken by the heavy costs of the war. Though the British failed to take full advantage of the victory they had won, they decisively established themselves as the world's strongest colonial power, and their control of the seas guaranteed safe passage to British shipping in war as well as peace. Yet in the triumph were sown many of the bitter seeds that in twenty years would cost Britain a large part of its empire, lost not to a foreign power but to British colonists.

THE AMERICAN REVOLUTION, 1763–1783

The revolt of Britain's American colonies was intimately connected with Britain's victory over the French. The colonists had contributed little either in money or in men to the victory. The war had been won by British troops and paid for by British taxes. When it was over the government in London decided that the colonies should bear a larger share of the costs of their government and defense. The efforts of the British to impose taxes on the colonists and systematically collect them met with stubborn resistance and led finally to the widespread belief that the colonies had come of age and should free themselves of their motherland.

THE AMERICAN COLONIES

By 1763 the white population of the colonies was over 1.5 million and was growing rapidly from continuous immigration and a high birth rate. It was still principally of English extraction, but more recent waves of immigration had brought large numbers of German Protestants and Scotch-Irish (Scottish settlers in northern Ireland). Protestantism — Congregational, Presbyterian, Anglican, Quaker, Reformed, and Lutheran — was the majority faith. Literacy was high, newspapers were numerous and avidly read, and the colonies boasted nine colleges of higher learning that produced clergymen, lawyers, physicians, and teachers. The colonial assemblies had grown in importance and power since their beginnings in Virginia in 1619. Compared with other eighteenth-century legislatures, they were broadly based. Although the franchise was limited to property holders, property holding was widespread, especially in the small-farm regions of New England, Pennsylvania, and North Carolina. All but one of the colonies had fairly well-established aristocracies, but they were founded on wealth, not birth or title. The aristocracy of merchant wealth dominated the major urban centers of the colonies: Boston, New York, Philadelphia, Charleston. The landed aristocracy had grown wealthy at the expense of small farmers, but the latter had pushed westward to new soil. There was no tenant peasantry except in New York, although in the southern colonies there were 175,000 Negro slaves.

No other bond among the colonies was so impressive as that of their economy. In the first half of the eighteenth century the colonial economy had burgeoned. The iron industry throughout the northern two-thirds of the colonies; shipbuilding in New England; naval stores (spars and masts in New England, pitch, tar, and turpentine in the Carolinas); tobacco, rice, and indigo in the South; and livestock and market produce in the Middle Atlantic colonies and southern New England could compete with the same industries elsewhere in the world in both quality and quantity. A sizable portion of the empire's carrying trade was in the hands of colonial shippers. There was little to hamper trade among the colonies, and the specialization among regions in production and commerce was so complementary that it created an integral colonial economy. For example, the southern plantation colonies depended on the ships of New England to transport their cash crops and to bring in the slaves to produce them, and also on the rum of New England (distilled from West Indian molasses) to purchase slaves in Africa. The colonies were separate political entities, but they were closely united economically.

The colonies also had a common legal tradition, common political institutions, and a common language. The common law of England was the heritage of all the colonies. The abundant litigation of the colonists in scores of courts great and small pressed the law into every man's consciousness, and service on the magisterial bench and jury duty were schools for statecraft and government. The common law provided the framework of the colonial assembly, the political institution common to all the colonies. By virtue of the assembly's power of the purse, it was independent of the governor, who represented the imperial government's interests. The colonists spoke the same language, and they also spoke the same jargon — the language of law, with its notions of "right," "property," and "liberty" and their embodiments in an independent judiciary, trial by jury, and a representative legislature.

On the surface these bonds seemed to count for little. Jealousies among the colonies were many, not the least of which was antagonism over boundaries, especially in the west. Indifference to the problems of neighboring colonies was widespread. The colonies had sprung from different origins, and poor land communications created intense localism. Each colony conceived of its tie with the mother country, three thousand miles away, as more potent and meaningful than its tie with a neighboring colony across a river or a parallel of latitude. To the colonists the mother country was a tolerant or indifferent, basically beneficent, seat of power, imposing commercial laws ostensibly for the benefit of all (readily broken by individuals when it was to their profit), providing protected markets and subsidies for colonial products (though the colonial merchants had no qualms about selling to the highest bidder, even to the enemy in wartime), and affording naval protection (at no cost to the colonies and a good profit to the producers of ships and naval stores). Colonists took pride in the vast British Empire and in the representative

Parliament in England that ruled lightly in the interests of an oligarchy with whom the colonial oligarchs had close business ties. There was pride among the colonists because of their identification with Englishmen in the overthrow of despotism in 1688. In 1763, therefore, beyond the routine friction engendered by commercial laws and their haphazard enforcement, the occasional veto of colonial legislation by the Privy Council in England, and the carping of colonial governors about the colonies' unconcern with the pressing problems of empire, there was nothing to hint at the division that would soon separate the colonies from the mother country. The most apparent safeguard to the imperial tie of each colony was the absence of any sense of common cause with other colonies.

THE PROVOCATIONS

The years from 1759 to 1766 changed all this. A series of provocative actions by the home government seemed to threaten the practical autonomy of the colonies. The actions stemmed from a desire by the government both to discourage the widespread illicit trade of the Americans with France, which had gone on in war and peace, and to shift the burden of the defense of the colonies to the colonies themselves. In 1759 the Privy Council's power to veto Virginian colonial legislation was made more effective by suspending such legislation until the council had passed upon it. The independence of the judiciary in New York and New Jersey was restricted in 1761, apparently in the hope that more pliant judges would deal more effectively with smugglers. In the same year broad powers of search were given to customs officers in Massachusetts. In 1763 the home government under George Grenville moved to enforce all the commerce laws by sending warships into American waters to assist the customs service. In the next year the American Act imposed new restrictions on colonial trade and levied taxes in the colonies to support a standing army in America. A newly established admiralty court in Nova Scotia with jurisdiction in sea commerce cases seemed to threaten a basic liberty, since trials for smuggling in that court would be without jury. Feelings were further aroused by the schemes of the established Church of England to proselytize in New England, the jealously guarded preserve of the Puritans' descendants. Boston Congregationalist minister Jonathan Mayhew spoke for many: "Is it not enough, that they persecuted us out of the old world? Will they pursue us into the new to convert us here?"

The Stamp Act of 1765 provoked almost open rebellion in the colonies. The tax, a levy on every printed paper and legal document, raised the thorny question of the authority of the British Parliament to tax colonies. The colonists argued that since they were not represented by members in Parliament, that body could not take away their property by taxation. The London government replied that the colonies were "virtually represented" in Parliament because every member represented the whole empire, not just the constituents who elected him. Collectors of the tax in the colonies were attacked by angry mobs, English goods were boycotted, and unstamped newspapers and legal documents were used without respect for the law. Most significant, nine of the colonies sent delegates to a congress in New York to draw up resolutions denying Parliament's power to tax them. What the threat of the French and Indians had never been able to do, the provocation of Parliament had done, at least temporarily — unite the colonies in common cause.

Although the Stamp Act was repealed in 1766, within a year another affront occurred when the home government ordered colonial legislatures to maintain British troops billeted in the colonies. The colonies' recalcitrance resulted in the imposition of duties on tea, glass, paper, and other items by the chancellor of the exchequer, Charles Townshend, and a tightening of the customs service. This led to another convention of colonial representatives in 1768 and the brawl in Boston known as the Boston Massacre in 1770, in which British troops shot down five rioters. After 1770, when the Townshend duties were repealed on all items but tea, an uneasy truce prevailed until a rash of incidents in 1772 resulted in the creation in Boston of the Committee of Correspondence, a resistance organization headed by the volatile Sam Adams. It found its first issue in the granting of a government monopoly to the East India Company to import tea into the colonies. The colonial reaction was the Boston Tea Party in December, 1773, which moved the imperial government to close the port of Boston, to alter the constitution of Massachusetts and strictly limit the town meetings (the heart of Massachusetts government), and to billet troops in Boston to enforce order. Boston, unrepentant, encouraged the creation of similar bodies in other colonies through its Committee of Correspondence.

The Quebec Act of 1774, which established representative government in that former French colony, gave broad privileges to the Roman Catholic Church, and closed off immigration from New York, Pennsylvania, and Virginia into the Ohio country, made those colonies receptive to the complaints of Massachusetts. In September, 1774, the first Continental Congress met in Philadelphia to resolve that the "English colonists . . . are entitled to a free and exclusive power of legislation in their several provincial legislatures" — a challenge to Parliament's supremacy. Shortly before the scheduled convention of the second Continental Congress, a clash of arms between the Massachusetts militia and British regulars at Lexington Green and Concord Bridge on April 19, 1775, began the War of Independence.

THE WAR

Contrary to almost universal expectations, the revolutionary movement did not collapse. In their challenge to Parliament the colonists had taken the first step toward both the equality of man and republicanism. These

Courtesy of Yale University Art Gallery

The Declaration of Independence, by John Trumbull

"What then is the American, this new man? . . . He is an American, who, leaving behind him all his ancient prejudices and manners, receives new ones from the new mode of life he has embraced, the new government he obeys, and the new rank he holds. . . . Here individuals of all nations are melted into a new race of men, whose labors and posterity will one day cause great changes in the world. . . . The American is a new man, who acts upon new principles; he must therefore entertain new ideas, and form new opinions. From involuntary idleness, servile dependence, penury, and useless labor, he has passed to toils of a very different nature, rewarded by ample subsistence. This is an American."
J. H. St. John de Crèvecoeur, LETTERS FROM AN AMERICAN FARMER (1782).

notions were merged with the Lockean defense of property and the right to preserve it by rebellion against tyranny in that charter of freedom, the Declaration of Independence, the promise and inspiration of Americans in search of independence.

The war was long and hard. Colonial particularism hampered the war effort. Washington's Continental Army relied upon the unreliable colonial militias, and the bold attacks of John Paul Jones's frigates in British waters did not constitute a navy in action. Hit-and-run warfare on land and sea was the only possible strategy for the Americans; formal battles were almost always won by the British, and only the mediocrity of British field commanders prevented disaster for the American cause. The turning point came with the surrender of Britain's General Burgoyne and his army at Saratoga in 1777. Britain lost her sole chance to cut the colonies in two, and the victory convinced the French to come in on the American side the next year. From that point the old Anglo-French struggle resumed. The French, joined by Spain in 1779, supplied a fleet sufficient to prevent regular supplies from flowing to the British armies, and a sizable force of French regulars and some able field officers gave real substance to the Continental Army. At Yorktown, Virginia, on October 17, 1781, the surrender of Britain's largest American army all but ended the war in the colonies. For the remaining two years of the war Britain effectively defended the rest of her empire against France and Spain.

THE "GREAT EXPERIMENT"

By the Treaty of Paris in 1783 Britain recognized American independence. The new nation's boundaries were drawn at the Canadian border, the Mississippi, and the Florida border, a settlement productive of disputes with both Britain and Spain in years to come. A new nation began its "great experiment," not yet prepared for the union that alone could preserve it, watched wonderingly by the European world, not quite sure of what it had spawned in this first rebellion of European colonists against a mother country. One realization stuck: liberty and the equality of man were no longer mere philosophic abstractions. Frenchmen — both those who like the Marquis de Lafayette and the Comte de Rochambeau had fought in America and the French *philosophes* who were spellbound by Benjamin Franklin in the salons of Paris — saw the great experiment as having direct applicability to France's own political malaise. In January, 1789, a bare six months before the outbreak of the French Revolution, Thomas Jefferson wrote from Paris to an English friend: "Though celebrated writers of this [France] and other countries had already sketched good principles on the subject of government, yet the American War seems first to have awakened the thinking part of this nation in general from the sleep of despotism in which they were sunk." The new world had stepped in, not to "redress the balance of the old" but to help upset it.

SCIENCE: THE SEARCH
FOR ORDER
CHAPTER SIXTEEN

The seventeenth century was born in dissonance and disorder, in the clamor of competing faiths, in the continuing confrontation of the most divisive forces the European world had yet unleashed. The Reformation, wars of religion, and the Dutch revolt dominated the late sixteenth century and spilled over into the next. The first half of the seventeenth century sustained its birthright. The Thirty Years' War was a complex of dynastic rivalries, religious hatreds, and power collisions, accompanied or followed by revolutions throughout Europe. By mid-century there was a discernible sentiment to achieve harmony and end disorder. It found many outlets during the succeeding decades. The ready acceptance of absolutism in France, Spain, the Hapsburg Empire, many of the German states, Scandinavia, and Italy was an acceptance of order. Although the restoration of Charles II in England was not a triumph of absolutism, it was a victory of the landed and commercial oligarchs whose aim was order. The balance of power was a device of order in the international relations of states. Even in the clashes of arms — and there were many in the latter half of the seventeenth century — order manifested itself in the new naval tactics of the line formation, in the disciplined troops massed in serried ranks, in the splendidly symmetrical designs of Vauban's forts, and in the measured pace of siege warfare.

Nowhere was the search for order more apparent, and nowhere did it leave a richer heritage, than in the realm of the intellect, above all in the labor of scientists during the decades between 1650 and 1720. The word scientist should not be taken in the narrow modern sense of a physical scientist, for the scholars of that day comprised a readily identifiable community of intellectuals with interests ranging over the three areas known today as the natural sciences, social sciences, and humanities.

They had a profound impact on their own age and an even more profound impact on the next, the Age of the Enlightenment.

THE SCIENTIFIC COMMUNITY OF INTELLECT

The great breakthrough in science had taken place in the century between the publication in 1543 of Nicolaus Copernicus's *Six Books Concerning the Revolution of the Heavenly Spheres* and in 1632 of Galileo Galilei's *Dialogue on the Two Chief Systems of the World*. The next stage in the evolution of modern science produced some men of equal genius and many more of lesser talent. It also provided improved technical apparatus for the experimentation that Sir Francis Bacon had so strongly urged. It saw the growth of official interest in science because of the technological benefits that might be derived from it. For example, much of the stimulus for astronomical and optical investigation stemmed from a desire to make a science of the art of navigation in an age committed to sea power. In the late seventeenth century science captured the interest and imagination of all who considered themselves learned, becoming an integral part of erudition even though it was not yet accepted in the universities, still dominated by the formal, Aristotelian curricula of medieval scholasticism larded over with Renaissance classicism. Men of learning formed an international community of the intellect, which became a distinctive feature of scientific endeavor of the period.

Each of the European world's earlier communities of intellect — the monasteries of the early Middle Ages, the universities of the late Middle Ages, and the academies of the Renaissance — had its own fundamental concepts, methodology, philosophical system, and sense of corporate identification. The new scientific community was no exception. Its fundamental concepts were the reasonableness of nature and the capacity of man to comprehend the rational order of nature by observation and the use of reason. These fundamentals, the methodology to use them, and the resulting philosophical system were in great part fashioned by two illustrious men of the previous generation: the Italian Galileo Galilei and the Frenchman René Descartes.

Galileo had shown that to understand the physical world man would have to use empirical analysis and would have to express that analysis mathematically. Implicit in his discoveries and method was the jettisoning of the speculative Aristotelian metaphysics that had hitherto dominated explanations of the physical world. Descartes had postulated a universe the mechanics of which could be discovered and expressed mathematically, and he had provided a method for the scientist to follow. The natural assumption of his mechanical universe was that the universe was one of order not chaos, was rational not accidental, and was consequently a universe operating by universally applicable physical laws. It was the clarity of this vision that made all of the scientists after Descartes Cartesians in some measure.

THE VIRTUOSI

The scientists of the generation after Descartes, who died in 1650, did not confine their search for universal laws of nature to the heavens or physical bodies on earth; they took a general interest in the arts and sciences. The breadth of their interests was a measure of their fervency and their confidence in the new scientific method. The age had a name for them: *virtuosi*. It was an apt name, smacking of the manliness of the Renaissance's *virtù*, of the masterfulness of an accomplished mind, a sure hand, and a restless spirit. These men spread themselves broadly over the realm of knowledge, but they were not dilettantes. Their achievements in the brief compass of three-quarters of a century represented a brilliant outburst of intellectual vigor rarely matched in any other epoch of so short a duration in the history of the Western world.

Cooperation and communication were the keynotes of the intellectual community of the virtuosi. They formed academies or societies in which they congregated regularly, read papers, conducted demonstrations, disputed, and conversed. The earliest societies, in Rome and Florence, were short-lived, as were a number of local societies in France, Germany, and England; but the Royal Society of London for Improving Natural Knowledge, chartered in 1662, and the Academy of Sciences in Paris, founded in 1666, still exist. The academies often began more scientific projects than they could complete, and scientists soon learned that science's technical capabilities fell far short of its speculative ambitions. Ample royal and noble patronage provided support for experiments beyond the means of individual scientists. The secretaries of the academies were voluminous correspondents and able propagandists of the new science, though with few exceptions — such as Robert Hooke of the Royal Society — they themselves were not creative scientists. They furnished the web of cooperation and communication that made the new science truly international, and they carried its gospel to the educated of Europe, giving science a great vogue among Europe's elite.

The communities of virtuosi were remarkably open for an age still hierarchically stratified. Bishop Thomas Sprat (1635–1713), a founder-member and historian of the Royal Society, boasted of the society: "It is to be noted that they have freely admitted Men of different Religions, Countries, and Professions of Life. . . . For they openly profess, not to lay the Foundation of an English, Scotch, Irish, Popish, or Protestant Philosophy; but a Philosophy of Mankind." The Royal Society was almost as open as Sprat claimed, and probably the only test for admittance was the implicit one that its members not be atheists. A number of clergymen were among its luminaries, and all its members were vociferous in their commitment to the proposition that there was no conflict between science and religion. Despite the sometimes profound differences of background, accomplishments, interests, and scientific opinions, despite some very virulent personal antagonisms, virtuosi sought each other's company for the mutual intellectual stimulation the community provided. Physicists, astronomers, philosophers, naturalists, architects, physicians, political economists, and political theorists met on the common ground of curiosity about the universe, man, and his society.

THE PHYSICAL WORLD

The commanding genius of the scientific community was Sir Isaac Newton (1642–1727). In his early twenties, while staying at his mother's farm at Woolsthorpe for eighteen months (from 1665 to 1667) to escape an epidemic that had forced a mass exodus from Cambridge University, he formulated in his mind three supremely important scientific discoveries. He arrived at the fundamental notion that particles of matter attract each other or gravitate toward each other; he perfected a new mathematical method, the calculus; and he reached tentative conclusions about the composition of light. There is no parallel in all recorded history to such intellectual creativity in so short a span of time.

THE NEWTONIAN SYNTHESIS

Newton's prodigious achievement was to bring together Kepler's explanation of planetary motion and Galileo's of terrestrial motion into a unified theory. Kepler had shown that the heavenly mechanism runs according to three rules: the law of elliptical motion, the law of equal areas, and the harmonic law of planetary motion. (See pp. 206–207.) Galileo's experiments with earthly objects had shown that there are two forces working on a body in motion, one horizontal and the other vertical. Consequently, the body's trajectory or path is a parabola, in which the body describes equal distances horizontally in equal times but accelerates vertically downward, so that in each successive time interval it travels a greater distance than before. Galileo had also demonstrated that the downward acceleration of a body in motion is independent of the weight of the body. Clearly, something else besides weight was necessary to explain the uniform acceleration of a falling body. It was for Newton to postulate gravity and to demonstrate that it is a single universal force acting on both Kepler's heavenly bodies and Galileo's earthly bodies, accounting for the elliptical orbits of the former and the parabolic trajectories of the latter.

Newton postulated that all bodies attract one another with a gravitational force that varies directly with the product of the masses of the two bodies and inversely with the square of the distance between them.

Courtesy of the National Portrait Gallery, London

Sir Isaac Newton, attributed to Vanderbank

"It was Sir Isaac Newton's peculiar happiness, to enjoy the reward of his merit in his life-time . . . . All the learned Men of a Nation, which produces so many, placed Sir Isaac at their head by a kind of unanimous applause, they acknowledged him for their Chief and their Master: not so much as one opposer durst appear, nay they would not even have admitted of a moderate admirer. His Philosophy hath been adopted throughout England, it prevails in the Royal Society, and in all the excellent performances which have come from thence; as if it had been already made sacred by the respect of a long series of ages. In short He was reverenced to so great a degree that death could not procure him new honours, and he himself saw his own apotheosis." Monsieur Fontenelle, THE ELOGIUM OF SIR ISAAC NEWTON (London, 1728), 23–24, in I. Bernard Cohen, ed., ISAAC NEWTON'S PAPERS AND LETTERS ON NATURAL PHILOSOPHY AND RELATED DOCUMENTS (Cambridge, 1958).

Newton's proof of the theory turned on his demonstration that the rate at which the moon is falling toward the earth is the same as that of a falling terrestrial body: sixteen feet per second. To determine the distance between the centers of the moon and the earth, it was necessary to calculate the exact radius of the earth. In the 1660's Newton used the accepted calculation of the earth's radius, which had come from ancient times, and found his calculations to be in error by about 15 per cent. He abandoned his theory as untenable. The fault, however, lay not in the theory but in the mistaken calculation of the earth's radius. In 1670 the French scientist Jean Picard (1620–1682) provided the figures for an accurate measurement of the earth's radius. In 1684 at the urging of Edmund Halley, a fellow member of the Royal Society who had been discussing the possibility of a force such as gravity with two other members, Christopher Wren and Robert Hooke, Newton recomputed his proof, this time using the correct radius of the earth. The new calculations banished the 15 per cent error of his earlier calculations, and the ideas which he had turned over in his mind since the days at Woolsthorpe fell into place. In 1687 he published in Latin the massive treatise *Philosophiae Naturalis Principia Mathematicae* (Mathematical Principles of Natural Philosophy).

The *Principia* incorporated Newton's demonstration of the law of gravity to explain the motion of the planets and their satellites. It also cast a wider net. On Galileo's foundations Newton constructed the science of mechanics, defining force, momentum, and inertia with the precision of mathematics. He disposed of Descartes's theory that the planets were held in an invisible fluid that filled all space and whirled around the sun, by showing with precise calculations that the motions of a body carried in a vortex would not follow Kepler's laws. After postulating the law of gravity he demonstrated that the pull of the sun and the moon cause the tides, that comets are under the influence of the sun's attraction and their orbits can therefore be calculated, and that the earth and the other planets are flattened at their poles. He showed that the sun's gravitational pull on the earth's slight bulge at the equator produces a slight twisting force that explains the phenomenon known as the precession of the equinoxes — the very slow change over the years in the position of the sun with respect to the fixed stars at the spring and autumn equinoxes. Newton had indeed ordered the universe.

The *Principia* was a difficult book even for skilled mathematicians, in part because Newton chose to use the theorems of classical geometry for his demonstrations instead of the calculus, although he must have used the calculus to work out and test the theorems. He did so presumably because he admired the mathematical methods of the ancients and because he wanted to make his book as abstruse as possible so as to avoid the criticisms of those whom he called "little smatterers in mathematics."

It took the scientific community nearly half a century to grasp all the implications of Newton's achievements. Once understood, the *Principia* became the classical textbook of physics until the first part of the present century. Only with twentieth-century physics and its improved apparatus has the dominance of Newtonian mechanics been reduced in the light of its inapplicability to much of the phenomena of the atom and the farthest reaches of space.

THE CALCULUS AND THE COMPOSITION OF LIGHT

The calculation of Newton's mechanics had depended upon Newton's discovery of the calculus, the mathematics of infinity, of variables and probables. The early seventeenth century had been remarkably productive of mathematical innovation. The Scot John Napier had invented logarithms and pioneered the use of decimals. Descartes's analytical geometry was the most commanding step forward before the calculus. Men of such opposed ideological views as the French Jansenist, Blaise Pascal, the Italian Jesuit, Bonaventura Cavalieri, and Newton's countrymen, the Puritan Parliamentarian, John Wallis, and the High Anglican Royalist, Isaac Barrow, all contributed elements to the mathematical study of infinity which Newton incorporated in his calculus. Newton did not so much invent as perfect differential calculus when, during those eighteen months at Woolsthorpe, he used it for the initial calculations of the theory of gravity. He did not tell any of his fellow mathematicians about his findings for several years and would not allow them to be published for thirty years. Meanwhile the German mathematician and philosopher Gottfried Wilhelm von Leibniz (1646–1716), ignorant of Newton's work, independently developed the method of the calculus and published his results in 1675. A rancorous controversy that arose over who was to be honored as the first discoverer for decades robbed English mathematicians of the benefits of the Continental improvements in the calculus, based on the more general and simply notated calculus of Leibniz.

The science of optics developed rapidly in the century following Galileo's improvement of Dutch telescopes in 1609. True to its origins in the technical side of instrument-making, optics provided the starting point for the study of the composition of light. The best lens of the day tended to color the image seen in it, a phenomenon apparent in the prism, which in refracting light breaks it up into the color spectrum. When Newton began to experiment with prisms it had already been established that white light was an amalgam of all the colors of the spectrum. Newton resynthesized white light from colored light by means of a lens to give final proof of the composite quality of white light. From these experiments Newton developed the reflecting telescope, which is still used for the largest optical telescopes. He also developed a theory of light that is still applicable. With Robert Hooke and Christian Huygens (1629–1695), the great Dutch optical technician, astronomer, and physicist, Newton agreed that light moves in waves. He proved the periodicity, or wave lengths, of light waves, and he went further than either of them in advancing the theory that light consisted of streams of particles emitted sporadically from the light source.

BOYLE AND THE FOUNDATIONS OF CHEMISTRY

The inquiring mind of Galileo had encompassed the study of gases as well as mechanics, optics, and astronomy. He invented the parent instrument of the thermometer and the barometer and first weighed air. In 1643 his secretary Evangelista Torricelli (1608–1647) invented the mercury barometer, which clearly proved that a vacuum could exist (contrary to Aristotle's dictum that "nature abhors a vacuum"), and suggested that variation in the weight of the outside air caused the mercury to rise or fall in the barometer. Three years later Blaise Pascal tested the principle and demonstrated that on top of a mountain the mercury would fall, from which he surmised that the weight of the outside air was less than at a lower altitude. By 1650 Otto von Guericke (1602–1686) made the first air pumps. With his "Magdeburg hemispheres," from which he pumped as much air as he could, he showed that teams of mules could not pull the hemispheres apart because of atmospheric pressure, that in a vacuum life and combustion are extinguished and the passage of sound is halted, but that light is not stopped in its passage.

Robert Boyle (1627–1691), youngest son of the earl of Cork, had been drawn to science while he was a student at Oxford. He became an inveterate experimenter, recording his findings in minute detail. Although he lacked mathematics, his industry, ingenuity, and patience gave a new respectability to experimentation, which previously had been considered chiefly as a method of demonstration rather than inquiry. In experiments in 1659 Boyle dealt with the physical problems of air but his conclusions were those of a chemist. Torricelli and Pascal had held that the weight of air causes the movement of mercury in the barometer's column. Boyle theorized that it is in fact the pressure of air that accounts for the phenomenon. He established that air is a gas, with a definite pressure, and he postulated the law, named for him, that the pressure of a gas varies inversely with its volume. His other physical experiments on the function of air in propagating sound, the expansion of water in freezing, and specific gravities and hydrostatics were valuable. But his greatest contribution rested in framing the science of chemistry.

Boyle conceived of chemistry as the study of the composition of substances, and he had the notion that elements are the irreducible constituents of material bodies. He analyzed the ingredients of chemical mixtures and compounds and furthered knowledge of specific substances. In common with most scientists of his day he held that matter is composed of atoms. Unlike them, he ascribed to atoms most of the chemical and physical phenomena he studied: "I look upon the phenomena of nature to be caused by the local motion of one part of matter hitting against another." This notion had important consequences, although an atomic theory as a usable facet of physics and chemistry was still far distant. The immediate result of Boyle's chemical investigations was to take the study of chemistry away from the alchemists and to exalt it above the pharmacological concerns of medicine. In Boyle's work originated the branch of science that a century later would flourish in the genius of Lavoisier.

PHYSIOLOGY

With William Harvey's (1578–1657) discovery of the circulation of blood the study of the human body passed from the realm of mere anatomy (the structure of the body) to physiology (the functioning of the body). The change here, as elsewhere, owed something to Descartes: his conception of the human body as a machine put a premium on physiology rather than anatomy. The increasing technical refinement of optical instruments made possible tremendous advances in physiology in the late seventeenth century. The construction of magnifying lenses by Dutch craftsmen launched microscopy. Jan Swammerdam (1637–1680) discovered red corpuscles in the blood and the valves of the lymph glands, and he made a major contribution to biology by dissecting insects and classifying them according to their development. When in 1660 the Italian Marcello Malpighi (1628–1694) dissected and microscopically studied the frog, he supplied the missing link in Harvey's circulatory system: the capillaries connecting arteries and veins. He also described the structure of the human lung, the brain, the spinal cord, and cell tissue, and he founded embryology with his investigations into the development of the fetal chick. The Dutchman Anton van Leeuwenhoek (1632–1723) discovered bacteria and spermatozoa, described the lens of the eye, and distinguished between voluntary and involuntary muscles. These men were observers and collectors of data, not theoreticians fashioning new explanations of the microscopic universe opened to them. It would be a century and a half before such rich discoveries spawned a sufficient conceptual structure in biology to begin to explain adequately the generation of life, the working of the nervous system, the particular functions of principal bodily organs, and the nature of cell tissue in plants and animals. For the moment the prime effect of these investigations was to add greatly to the pitifully small corpus of knowledge about the workings of the living organism.

THE NATURALISTS

Significantly, neither biology nor geology produced a Newton or a Boyle in the period 1650 to 1725. The virtuosi who engaged in biological

and geological investigations are best called naturalists: those who observe and describe but do not attempt to make the scientific inferences
that lead to general scientific truths. Few of them suspected how ancient
the earth is — how old life upon it is. In the seventeenth century, though
fossils and earth stratification had long been noticed by miners, the world
was still supposed to have been created about 4000 B.C. Ingenious explanations were advanced to dismiss fossils: they were seeds that had
grown into the rocks rather than out of the ground, or they were put by
God into rocks to test man's faith in the biblical account of the Creation.
By the end of the seventeenth century naturalists admitted that fossils
had indeed once been organic but claimed that they had been killed by
the Flood in Noah's time, which by their reckoning came well after 4000
B.C. There was nothing in the scientific revolution in mechanics and
astronomy, or in its postulate of a mechanical universe that apparently
had always existed, to point to a historical process —an evolution — involving the earth and life upon it.

The most important naturalist (and perhaps the most attractive of the
virtuosi) was the Englishman John Ray (1627–1705). Modest, open to
new ideas, and utterly honest, Ray argued persuasively for the organic
origin of fossils and perceived that the earth is much older than men
thought. His extraordinary methodicalness and acute powers of observation, married to abundant zeal, allowed him to produce between 1686
and 1710 an impressive series of volumes describing and classifying plants,
animals, birds, fishes, and insects.

The difference between a genius who posited the laws of a mechanical
universe and a man of more modest talents laboriously classifying thousands of creatures may be disappointing. But postulating laws of a mechanical universe required a slighter break with the metaphysical past and
a lesser challenge to accepted religious authority than postulating laws
of biological origin. A Newton was possible in the seventeenth century;
a Darwin was not.

THE PSYCHIC WORLD

The very discrepancy of achievement between the physical sciences and
the life sciences in the seventeenth century had one important result. The
virtuosi who turned to the world of man's mind, the psychic world,
brought to it mechanistic preconceptions derived from the brilliant
achievements in physics. To the planets in the heavens and the moving
bodies on earth they added man as an intricate particle of matter obey-
ing mechanical laws. They nevertheless knew less about him — less of
how he functioned and how he came to be as a species or an individual —
than they knew about the universe. Physics proved to be a poor foundation for the study of man's psyche, and the embryonic stage of the life
sciences could not provide an alternative to the mechanical analogy in

an age when the aspiration of man to know everything, and his unbounded confidence that he could, far outran his knowledge of himself.

Descartes's conception of man as a machine was fundamental to the investigation of the psychic world during these decades. The physical actions of the human body, he wrote, are mechanically explicable: "I say, that you consider that all these functions follow naturally in this machine simply from the arrangement of its parts, no more and no less than do the movements of a clock." He argued that the human body is occupied by a rational, immaterial soul or mind, however, and that this soul is married to the material body by the pineal gland in the brain. He attempted to give a crude physiological explanation of the way in which the pineal gland transmits the soul's perceptions to the body's actions. Since what the soul perceives is transmitted to it by the senses and since the soul is given only a replica of the external object, it follows that the transmission mechanism might distort reality. Hence "I think, therefore I am" — Descartes's great single certainty — is the one clear truth that man can rely upon, for the tree in front of him, apprehended in his mind, exists for him only in its replica state.

LOCKEAN ENVIRONMENTALISM

In *An Essay Concerning Human Understanding* (1690), John Locke sought to determine what knowledge is, how it is acquired, and how far it extends. He started with a simple premise that man's mind at birth is a blank page. "Let us then suppose the mind to be, as we say white paper, void of all characters, without any ideas — how comes it to be furnished?" His answer was that ideas are furnished by the perception of our senses and reflection on these perceptions. Thus, all man's ideas depend upon both experience and reason.

Locke took pains to point out that the certainty of knowledge is extremely limited, though the precise limits of certainty are more or less dependent upon the kind of knowledge. He described four kinds of knowledge: (1) analytical knowledge — ideas springing from the comparison of ideas; (2) mathematical and ethical knowledge; (3) scientific knowledge of the physical world; and (4) knowledge of the existence of one's self, the world, and God. Knowledge of the physical world is the most limited, for when the external object is no longer within range of the senses its continued existence can only be presumed — a sad thought for the virtuosi, but Locke reassured them that despite its limits, knowledge of the physical world derived from experience and fashioned by reason is enough to enable man to carry on bravely in this life, to be more than merely a chip on an ocean of infinite unknowingness.

Locke's emphasis on experience and reason made a tremendous impression on thinkers for three-quarters of a century. By the use of reason man might condition his environment, which is the source of human experience. A changed environment would in turn result in changed experience. Locke had denied the existence of innate ideas in the mind of man, but implicit in his philosophy of knowledge was an invitation to man to change his environment to make innate in it experiences which would scribble on the "white paper" of minds yet unborn.

LEIBNIZ'S INNATISM

Locke had conceived of a thing as having two qualities: a "primary" quality (its physically expressible attributes such as size, shape, motion, or number), and a "secondary" quality (its derived properties such as beauty, luster, taste, or color). He argued that although secondary qualities depend on somebody to perceive them, primary qualities exist whether there is someone to perceive them or not. The German virtuoso Leibniz undertook a critique of Locke's *Essay* that turned on this question of primary and secondary qualities. Leibniz made no distinction between the two. Both primary and secondary qualities are equally certain, for what the mind perceives is a perfect reflection of reality. Leibniz argued that knowledge is perceived not at all by the senses but is a creation of the mind. All ideas are innate, to be worked up into knowledge by the rational operation of the mind. Leibniz had no need to slide over the relationship between body and mind, as Locke had done, since there is no connection between body and mind; both work separately from each other but in perfect harmony because they obey the same laws of nature. Neither was he compelled, as Locke was, to argue that God is a demonstrable truth, for faith and reason, like body and mind, are harmonious though separate, and God must be the origin of such harmony.

THE SOCIAL WORLD

The virtuosi found it easier to postulate mechanistic laws for the functioning of men's minds than for their collective behavior in society. Too little was known about the mind, and far too much about society, even if knowledge of society was not very systematic. Social theory bore somewhat the same relationship to psychology that biology bore to physics: abundant data, readily observed, tended to defy arrangement, not least because the conceptual framework by which something might be made of the data was extremely rudimentary.

For two centuries theorists had been dismantling the medieval view of social structure, even though in practice much of that structure still remained as the bulwark of monarchic absolutism. Men had become aware of other ways of conceiving of society than the traditional hierarchic one. The intellectual ferment of the seventeenth century provided new strength to their reassessments. If the virtuosi who turned their attention to society were not Newtons or Lockes, their efforts were nonetheless productive of basic and bold new departures in man's view of his social world.

The best economic minds of the era often receive too little credit for providing the foundation of modern economics; that credit is usually given to the eighteenth-century French physiocrats and Adam Smith. Although the earlier economists remained within the context of mercantilist thought they nevertheless asked more penetrating questions than their predecessors had about such basic matters as price and value, and they formulated more sophisticated answers. The most important of these economists was the English virtuoso Sir William Petty (1623–1687), physician, wealthy landowner, and one of the first fellows of the Royal Society. Possessed of a breadth of vision that freed him from the shackles of orthodox mercantilist thought, he achieved a level of analysis not surpassed for a hundred years. No less an authority than Karl Marx labeled him the founder of political economy.

Petty made notable contributions to both the theory of economics and its methodology. He postulated the labor theory of value, in which labor was the source of wealth and the measure of value — a doctrine that the classical economists of the early nineteenth century and Karl Marx would raise to a Newtonian-like axiom of economics. He understood the advantages of the division of labor in reducing the price and raising the quality of a product. Although his views on foreign trade were colored by mercantilist notions, he recognized that restrictions on the export of gold and silver hampered economic growth, and he realized, too, that not only a deficiency of money but also an excess of it could damage a nation's economy.

Petty can rightly claim to be the founder of comparative social statistics as a science. While serving as a physician to Cromwell's troops in Ireland in the 1650's he saw how inefficiently the lands granted to soldiers there were surveyed. He produced a far more accurate survey, which took account not only of acreage and declared value, but of the quality of the land, population, and crafts as well. His motives were not wholly altruistic: he carved out a huge estate for himself in Ireland, upon which he set up model iron works, quarries, lead mines, and fisheries.

The statistical methods introduced by Petty were utilized by two of his countrymen, Charles Davenant (1656–1714) and Gregory King (1648–1712). In 1696 King made such an accurate estimate of English population on the basis of tax returns that the results have not been seriously questioned since. Both Davenant and King divided the population into those who increase the nation's wealth and those who diminish it, based on whether they were a contribution to or a drain on capital investment. They both mirrored a concern about overpopulation and poverty that was characteristic of western Europe during the seventeenth century. Since the mid-sixteenth century England, the Low Countries, and France had undertaken exceptional efforts to cope with pauperism by government action. It fell to an English virtuoso of the Royal Society and a chief justice of England, Sir Matthew Hale (1609–1676), to fix poverty clearly as a social evil resulting from economic causes, not from the moral depravity of the poor. In *Discourse Touching Provision for the Poor,* published in 1683, he argued that crime could be reduced by solving the problem of poverty through economic improvement.

Petty's Dutch counterpart was Pieter de la Court (1618–1685), a Leyden clothier, whose *True Interest and Political Maxims of Holland,* written in the 1600's, made a comprehensive and searching sweep of the political, social, and economic aspects of the Dutch Republic and attempted to establish guidelines for sound policy by subjecting old assumptions of government to the light of reason. Like Petty, he regarded the restriction on the export of bullion as inimical to Dutch commerce.

Jean-Baptiste Colbert, Louis XIV's minister, ranks with the other leading political economists of the age. Founder of the French Academy of Sciences and a patron of the new science, he sought to implement a coherent, organized economic policy. He left behind no corpus of written work, and his strong protectionist mercantilism obscured the novelty of many of his theories of domestic economy, but his papers indicate a Cartesian-like, mechanistic approach to economics. In Marshal Vauban (1633–1707) France produced not only a new-model soldier but also a new-model economist. In *Project for a Royal Tithe* (1707), suppressed by royal mandate as subversive, he urged the uniform application of a 10 per cent tax on all Frenchmen, ending the privileged exemption of the nobility. To Vauban, tax privilege was economic suicide for France, for it placed an intolerable tax burden upon the peasantry, whose labor he considered to be the mainstay of France's wealth.

THE HISTORIANS

The treatment of the past in the Middle Ages had been an adjunct to philosophy, with Divine Providence as the determining force in human affairs. The Renaissance humanists, inspired by both their reverence for antiquity and their contempt for medieval culture, began to conceive of the story of the past as a distinct branch of knowledge that would provide the model of classical society for European man's imitation. They put their historical accounts into a secular framework, sought causation in human motives and decisions rather than in the workings of Providence, and concerned themselves with the basic problems of history — the relevance of the past to the present and how the present grew out of the past. The religious controversies of the Reformation stimulated the study and writing of history, since Catholics and Protestants alike turned to the record of the past to establish the rightness of their own positions and to attack the claims of their opponents.

In the sixteenth and seventeenth centuries the conscious mining of the past for the purpose of polemics developed into a fine art. Increasingly the focus shifted from religious to political questions. The origins of this shift lay in the work of legal scholars attempting to use history to justify the growing monarchic power. The polemics were supplied both by those who exalted this power and by those who attempted to restrict it.

The historical endeavors of the century laid the foundation for historical method and provided much factual material. In England historian-polemicists began the serious study of the English medieval past that was to bloom in the nineteenth century. Anglo-Saxon language and literature, feudalism, medieval institutions, monastic history, and the origins of English common law received attention. In the Dutch Republic and Germany historians created national histories in defense of Dutch merchant oligarchs and German princes against monarchic pretensions. Leibniz undertook a monumental history of the dynasty of his patron, the house of Brunswick, beginning in 768; when he died, he had only reached 1005. In France a group of Jesuits who were called Bollandists in honor of one of their more eminent members, Jean Bolland, sought to establish the lives of the saints on historically sound grounds by collecting and editing masses of texts. The Maurists, monks in the Benedictine Congregation of St. Maur in Paris, led by Jean Mabillon, created methods of textual criticism and the study of the internal structure of historical documents that remain to this day the basic tool of ancient and medieval historians. Charles Du Cange, a French goverment official, compiled the first and still the greatest dictionary of early medieval Latin. Scholars authenticated old manuscripts and weeded out forgeries, studied ancient coins and established the science of numismatics, and made critical analyses of old inscriptions. The chronology of human history came under intensive examination, primarily because new knowledge about the ancient empires of China and Egypt had thrown doubt on the traditional chronology based on the Bible. By the end of the century the assurance with which historians had once accepted that chronology had vanished.

REASON VERSUS HISTORY

To a virtuoso committed to the pure light of reason, history was merely another form of challengeable authority, no better than metaphysics and perhaps more insidious. More specifically, Locke, in the *Essay on Human Understanding*, pointed the way explicitly to understanding man, implicitly to improving his condition. Reason founded on experience was the only path; authority, historical or otherwise, was irrelevant. Above all, in the Lockean scheme of knowledge experience could only be personal, never collective, and hence history (collective experience) was an impossibility.

The 1690's witnessed more than Locke's blow at the usefulness of history. In 1697, Pierre Bayle's *Historical and Critical Dictionary* dealt an almost mortal blow to history. Bayle (1647–1706), a Huguenot converted to Roman Catholicism by the Jesuits and reconverted to Calvinism, an exile in Holland from persecution in France for his Calvinism, removed from his chair in the Calvinist university of Rotterdam for his skepticism, was a walking pincushion of persecution. By patent ridicule, subtle irony, and murderous criticism in the light of reason, the *Dictionary* stripped all the history, secular and especially ecclesiastical, upon which Bayle could lay his hands, of its factualness and its authority. In a different atmosphere and within a different framework of knowledge than that afforded by Locke, Bayle's brilliant work might only have served to exorcise error from history. In his generation, Bayle's criticism consumed history. If history was to be reborn from the destructive onslaught of Bayle's criticism and its obsolescence through Locke's psychology, it would have to be structured on rational laws, and experience would have to be conceived of as collective (societal), not merely individual (psychic).

VICO AND THE SCIENCE OF HISTORY

A Roman lawyer holding a professorship of rhetoric in Naples, the intellectual backwater of the age, undertook to be the Newton of history, the discoverer of the laws of man's collective behavior in the operation of man's past. Giambattista Vico (1668–1744) is today claimed as a founding father by both sociologists and historians. Three strains merged in him: the vital historical activity of Roman lawyers in political polemics during the previous two centuries, the philological studies which were a feature of seventeenth-century letters, and the new science of mechanical laws and reason fashioned from experience. The richness of this patrimony, unique among the virtuosi, enables him to escape categorization as a Cartesian or a Lockean. His was a highly original mind, and more in intention than in the specifics of his endeavor he stood with the other virtuosi.

The title of Vico's masterpiece is almost a statement of his thesis: *Principles of the New Science of Giambattista Vico Concerning the Common Nature of the Nations* (1725, much revised 1730). Vico posited a "natural law" of peoples, common to all peoples, that explained the growth of human societies ("nations") and their institutions from the moment when brutish creatures became men. The first stage of civilization was born in the foundation of the institutions of religion and marriage when a fearsome thunderclap drove male and female, hitherto breeding promiscuously, into caves to become lifelong mates. This first stage was the age of gods, in which men communicated by signs and simple words related to physical objects, for observance of religious rituals was more important than discussion. The second stage was the age of heroes, in which men spoke in images and metaphors, wisdom being poetic. The third stage was the age of men, in which men communicated in words of commonly agreed and specific meaning, wisdom being conscious and rational. A distinct form of government and jurisprudence corresponded to each stage of civilization. History moved in cycles, the change from one stage to the next being accomplished by a process both of growth and decay.

Vico's contemporaries found his work strange, indeed ominous. His theory of historical cycles seemed to deny the never-ending progress of man which, by 1725, was already an article of faith of most intellectuals. He appeared to make a historical reality of a state of nature, which in Hobbes had been a philosophical presupposition and in Locke a symbolic convenience. Vico demanded a sophistication in dealing with past reality which was foreign to a generation that had consigned history to the rubbish heap along with irrational metaphysics. Yet Vico had demonstrated even to the satisfaction of the most skeptical of his contemporaries that experience could be collective. His rigid intellectual honesty in introducing complications into the clean, neat world of unending progress through reason, cost him his audience in the Enlightenment of the eighteenth century. Vico's day came when the Enlightenment had run its course and German historians in the early nineteenth century took up the serious task of writing scientific universal history.

RETROSPECT

The scientific achievements of the decades from 1650 to 1720 are not easily explained. They depended in part on the accident of genius. They were founded on the decisive breakthrough in understanding the physical world during the previous century and on the development of procedures of empiricism and mathematics. They owed a great deal to the more material attributes of the seventeenth century, that is, the patronage attracted by the prospects of technical advance through science. In no small part they can be traced to the extraordinary community of intellect that provided companionship of the mind, a sounding board for ideas, and an exhilarating sense of common destiny on new frontiers of knowledge.

Science, represented in the accomplishments of the virtuosi, had by the second decade of the eighteenth century become the new order of the European intellect, and in so becoming had effectively established itself in place of the old order it had destroyed. By 1720 the virtuosi had furnished their successors (and imitators), the *philosophes* of the Enlightenment, with a matchless patrimony: their methodology, their intellectual substance, their means, and indeed many of their ends.

THE ENLIGHTENMENT
CHAPTER SEVENTEEN

The new intellectual order that grew out of the scientific achievements of the seventeenth century was above all one of certainty — certainty in the value of experience, certainty in the ability of reason to solve all problems, certainty that the real world is indeed as man perceives it. Impressed by the success of the natural scientists of the seventeenth century in discovering the laws of the physical universe, the men of the eighteenth-century Enlightenment believed that they could uncover the laws governing human institutions and human behavior. They faced the future with optimism, thinking that the laws of human society, once determined, could be used to increase man's welfare and happiness and to guarantee unending progress in the human condition. "Enlightenment," said one of them, "is man's emergence from his self-imposed immaturity." Not everyone shared their new faith, and even among those who did there was no rigorous uniformity of outlook. Nevertheless, certainty, optimism, and a belief in progress were the trinity that furnished most intellectuals with their creed. The Enlightenment was an era when men tended to see everything in the pure light of reason. For over three-quarters of a century faith in reason dominated the intellectual life of Europe.

INTELLECTUAL ROOTS OF THE ENLIGHTENMENT

The men of the Age of Reason modified, sometimes clarified, and popularized the ideas they inherited from the seventeenth century. A process of selection was involved. The rules laid down by René Descartes in the *Discourse on Method* (see p. 213) were generally acceptable. On the other hand, Descartes's conception of the operation of the universe gave way around the 1730's to Newton's mechanics, though in France national pride delayed the final abandonment of Cartesian cosmology until after the middle of the century. The men of the Enlightenment also rejected Descartes's theory of knowledge, that the mind at birth possesses certain innate ideas from which by deduction we arrive at true knowledge about the world, in favor of the environmentalism of John Locke. Locke's doctrine, with its implicit premise that man could improve himself by a better environment and education, offered a theoretical justification for the Enlightenment's belief that man and society could be reshaped in accordance with natural law.

The ethical concerns that motivated the rational endeavors of the Enlightenment were derived from the best aspirations in the Christian tradition. However, the dogmatic, metaphysical, and mystical qualities of orthodox Christianity had been culled out during the seventeenth century, leaving only the ethics. Deism, the religion of reason that had been developed during the seventeenth century, became the new orthodoxy of the Enlightenment.

RELIGIOUS SKEPTICISM

Traditional religion was shaken by the new awareness of reason and fact of the seventeenth century. The contrast between the mechanical, predictable workings of nature and the miracles related in the Bible was disturbing, and belief in the historical accuracy of the Bible was shaken by the textual criticisms of such scholars as Thomas Hobbes, the English philosopher; Baruch Spinoza, a Dutch Jew; and Richard Simon, a French priest. Their studies showed that many parts of the Bible were actually written much later than biblical times, that the text had undergone numerous alterations and additions and contained obvious contradictions, and that biblical chronology did not agree with the chronology derived from ancient secular sources.

The increasing knowledge of non-European cultures intensified the questioning of orthodox Christianity. Travelers told of peoples who had never heard of Christianity and who had their own systems of religious and moral values that they believed were the only true ones sanctioned by God. The religions of the Far East especially, and the cultures built upon them, seemed hardly inferior to European culture. Some intellectuals began to adopt a relativistic attitude toward religion, maintaining that the doctrines of Christianity were not necessarily superior to those of any other creed.

This skeptical attitude toward Christianity was not a new phenomenon. Renaissance humanists, inspired by their study of classical writings, had counseled men to abandon rigid doctrines and opinions. The religious wars and persecutions of the sixteenth and seventeenth centuries had moved some thoughtful men to doubt the certainties claimed by the opposing creeds. Appalled at the horrors perpetrated in the name of religion, they urged toleration and recognition of the impossibility of proving the superiority of any one creed. Michel de Montaigne (1533–1592) was one of the first to react in this way. Custom, he said, dictates our religion just as it dictates the style of our clothes. Each religion uses the same arguments to prove that it alone is the only true faith. There is no way for man to know which one is right.

PASCAL AND SPINOZA

Most intellectuals of the seventeenth century viewed the conflict between the new knowledge and traditional religion with equanimity; to others it brought anguish of heart and mind. Blaise Pascal (1623–1662), the seventeenth-century French mathematician and philosopher, voiced the dilemma most clearly. He wrote that he felt himself "engulfed in the infinite immensity of space whereof I know nothing, and which knows nothing of me. The eternal silence of those infinite spaces terrifies me." Using the method of Cartesian doubt, he tried to convince himself that God exists by doubting all traditional doctrine and evidence. He concluded that reason could not persuade man to believe in God; he must accept that belief on faith alone. "The heart has its reason," he wrote, "which the mind does not know . . . and this is the essence of faith, that God is known to the heart and not to the reason." In a famous passage known as "Pascal's wager" he said, "We can say 'Either God is, or is not.' . . . What will you wager? You can argue reasonably in favor of either." He felt that the odds stood heavily against God's existence, yet he urged men to bet that God does exist. For if there is a God, the believer gains eternal life; if God does not exist, man loses nothing.

Pascal's despair was not shared by his contemporary Baruch Spinoza (1632–1677). Born in Amsterdam of a Portuguese Jewish family and educated in both religious and secular lore, Spinoza earned his living as a lens grinder. He adopted the mathematical method of Descartes for his own thinking because it allowed him to describe phenomena objectively, without ascribing cause or purpose, but he rejected the chasm between the material world and the immaterial mind postulated in Cartesian dualism. (See p. 213.) He argued that matter and mind are both aspects of God and have no existence apart from him. God is the only reality in the universe and is immanent in all matter and thought. Spinoza rejected the validity of orthodox religious concepts of God and denied the divine inspiration of the Bible. God is not the personal, loving Deity who heeds men's prayers and who causes everything. God is everything. Spinoza's philosophy, called pantheism, was branded atheism by Christian and Jew alike, and his teachings were denounced. Some who read Spinoza, however, found solace in his words, for he seemed to have closed the gap between the mechanism of the new science and the old belief in God.

DEISM

Spinoza's pantheism did not satisfy most of those who felt that orthodox religious dogma could not be reconciled with reason and fact. For these men satisfaction was found in a new kind of religion called natural religion or deism. By the late seventeenth century natural religion had become the vogue among the virtuosi. Newton, Boyle, Locke, and many lesser minds wrestled with the definition of the exact nature of God, producing theological works as voluminous as their scientific treatises. They believed that both reason and nature reveal the existence of God, of a natural order of morality that shows man the difference between good and evil, and of a life after death with reward or punishment for man's deeds. Vehement in their denunciation of atheism, they conveniently accepted the doctrines of Christianity that coincided with what they believed were natural principles and rejected the rest as being the products of superstition. They compared the universe to a precisely made machine, such as a watch, and placed God in the role of the watchmaker. He had made the universe and set the laws by which it operated. Once it was started He had no need to concern Himself with its workings, for as His creation it ran perfectly.

THE CIRCLES OF ENLIGHTENMENT

Although the Enlightenment was an international movement its center was in France, and since the center of France was Paris, so the center of the Enlightenment was Paris. France had already established its cultural supremacy along with its military might under Louis XIV, and though its military might diminished, its cultural supremacy increased. Courtiers and scholars in Berlin, Warsaw, and St. Petersburg spoke and wrote in the elegant French of Molière, scorning their native tongues as uncultured. Paris became the Mecca of the philosophers, writers, and artists of all Europe, who visited and studied there and returned home to spread French influences. French intellectuals and artists were much in demand at the royal courts and cultural centers of other lands.

Great Britain also played a leading part in the movement. In addition to the fundamental contributions of Newton and Locke to the thought of the Enlightenment, the English political structure, with its limitations on royal power and its system of representation, fascinated Frenchmen. Many studied it at first hand, returning home filled with enthusiasm for the system and usually with a good deal of misunderstanding about how it actually operated.

THE NEW READING PUBLIC

A remarkable expansion in the reading public during the eighteenth century helped to bring about a wide diffusion of the ideas of the Enlightenment. For the first time in history a mass reading public appeared, made up chiefly of members of the growing educated middle class, but also including many nobles, some city artisans, and a small number of country people. Private libraries in the homes of the well-to-do became more common. Books, pamphlets, and magazines poured from the presses. The number of newspapers multiplied, most of them journals of opinion more than of news. The coffee houses, cafés, clubs, and reading rooms that became so popular in western Europe subscribed to newspapers and magazines for their patrons to read. In 1720 Paris had over three hundred cafés, each with its own clientele, drawn mainly from the middle class, who came regularly to read the journals and talk about the ideas discussed in them. A coffee house in the provincial city of Strasbourg in Alsace in the 1780's received eighty-six periodicals in four languages.

In England, the Dutch Republic, and British North America the press was either free or subject only to a mild censorship. Censorship in other lands varied in severity, and enforcement was generally sporadic. To escape the censor's ban books and newspapers were often published clandestinely, smuggled in from abroad, or laboriously copied by hand and passed from reader to reader. Their illegality increased their attractiveness, so that censorship actually helped propagate the new ideas.

SOCIETIES AND SALONS

Learned societies patterned on the societies of the virtuosi were founded across the Western world from St. Petersburg, where Peter I established the Russian Imperial Academy of Sciences in 1724, to Philadelphia, where under Benjamin Franklin's leadership the American Philosophical Society came into existence in 1743. Such societies sponsored experiments, lectures, publications, libraries, and museums. They enjoyed such high prestige that their sponsorship of a new social or scientific theory did much to make it popular among the educated classes.

Salons became fashionable in Paris, and to a lesser extent in other cities. They were usually conducted in the homes of gifted women of wealth, where writers, clergymen, bankers, businessmen, and aristocrats met regularly for conversation, intellectual stimulation, or just to be seen. Much of the talk was little more than idle chatter; elegance of expression, malicious wit, and clever epigrams were more valued than profundity. Nonetheless, the salons brought together as equals men of different ideas and social origins, and inevitably they influenced one another. Aristocrats were persuaded to adopt liberal social and political views that ran counter to their own class interests. Writers, many from relatively humble backgrounds, gained a polish, self-confidence, and sophistication that made them more effective propagandists.

The international secret order of Freemasons provided an especially effective medium for transmission of the ideas of the Enlightenment. It had originated in the Middle Ages, when stone masons joined together into lodges to preserve their professional secrets. The order persisted in England into the eighteenth century, by which time it was composed entirely of professional architects, nobles, and intellectuals. After the union of four lodges into a Grand Lodge in London in 1717 all pretense of craftsmanship was abandoned, although the old symbols and rites that supposedly originated with King Solomon, the mythical founder of the order, were preserved. The English Freemasons dedicated themselves to the religion of reason, the creation of a moral and social order based upon the principles of reason, and the establishment of liberty and equality.

Through the initiative of merchants, diplomats, soldiers, and even prisoners of war, Freemasonry spread with remarkable speed to nearly every European land, to British North America, and even to India. It linked men of like views throughout Western society and acquainted them with the principles of the Enlightenment. Washington, Franklin, Jefferson, and many other leading Americans were Masons. In Europe even royalty belonged: Emperor Francis I of Austria was a member, and Frederick II of Prussia became master of a lodge in Berlin.

THE PHILOSOPHES

In the seventeenth century many of Europe's intellectual leaders had been mathematicians and scientists. In the eighteenth century the leaders of intellectual life were those who called themselves *philosophes,* philosophers. It was a misnomer. They did not concern themselves primarily with technical philosophical speculations, and with a few notable exceptions they were not creative thinkers. They were popularizers and propagandists of the ideas developed by the virtuosi. They were less enamored with advancing knowledge for its own sake than with using knowledge to refashion ethics and to reconstruct society according to reason and natural law. In pursuit of that goal they turned out histories, plays, novels, scientific treatises, political pamphlets, and literary and art criticism, as well as philosophical tracts. Seeking to reach as wide an audience as possible, they wrote in the vernacular rather than in Latin. They deliberately cultivated a limpid, easy style to attract the average educated reader. Many of them earned their living with their pens, unlike intellectuals of preceding eras, who had been men of wealth and leisure, clergymen, or professors, or had been supported by wealthy patrons.

Beyond a faith in reason the philosophes did not share a common program of action; indeed, they often plunged into rancorous disputes with each other. Their doctrines ranged through many shadings of liberal and radical thought. Yet almost without exception their views suited the needs and demands of the growing middle classes from which most of

Philosophes Dining, engraving after Hubert

Voltaire (1) presiding, Le Pere Adam (2), L'Abbe Mauri (3),
d'Alembert (4), Condorcet (5), Diderot (6), Laharpe (7).

> *"Reason is to the* philosophe *what grace is to the Christian. Grace causes*
> *the Christian to act; reason causes the* philosophe *to act. . . . Truth is not for*
> *the* philosophe *a mistress who corrupts his imagination. . . . He does not*
> *confuse it with the probable. . . . Civil society is, so to speak, an earthly deity*
> *to him; he burns incense to it, he honors it by his integrity, by his rigorous*
> *attention to his duties, and by a sincere desire not to be a useless or embarrassing*
> *member of it. . . . The* philosophe, *then, is an honest man who is guided in*
> *everything by reason."* ENCYCLOPÉDIE (Neufchâtel, 1775), Vol. XII.

them came. They were not conscious supporters of middle-class supremacy; they considered themselves defenders of the rights and liberties of
all men, not those of one particular group, and their ideas attracted
aristocrats and even kings. Nevertheless, they found their most numerous
and ardent supporters among the bourgeoisie, who had long suffered
under arbitrary rule and aristocratic domination. When in the nineteenth century the middle classes finally gained social and political equality, they appropriated many of the principles advocated by the philosophes for the foundation of their new order.

DOCTRINES OF THE PHILOSOPHES

In assuming that they could provide the same sort of orderly, mechanical explanation for the workings of society that the natural scientists had provided for the planetary system, the philosophes failed to recognize the all-important qualitative differences between the methods of Newton and their own. Newton contented himself with explaining how nature operates and did not inquire into the intent of nature or concern himself with ethical considerations. Neither was Newton particularly interested in the utility or the practical application of his findings. In contrast, the philosophes began with certain ethical premises and with the utilitarian conviction that knowledge must serve to improve material welfare. They assumed that existing social and political institutions were contrary to man's best interests and were therefore contrary to nature. Because their own tenets were based entirely upon reason, they assumed that these tenets were in accord with natural law and so were ethical and useful to mankind.

Most philosophes had a firm faith in the inevitability and uninterrupted continuity of human progress. Each generation benefits from the advances made by its predecessors. The idea of inevitable progress, like so much else in the Enlightenment, had been implicit in seventeenth-century thought. There had even been a literary feud in France and England in the seventeenth century known as the quarrel of the Ancients and the Moderns which had centered around the comparative merits of the classical age and their own time, with the Moderns asserting that the present was better because it could build on all the achievements of the past.

The optimism of the philosophes reached its climax in the work of the Marquis de Condorcet (1743–1794). In *The Progress of the Human Mind,* published in 1793 during the French Revolution, Condorcet prophesied that man was destined for unceasing improvement in all his faculties since he had found the sure method of reaching truth through reason and had adopted enlightened policies in government. "No bounds have been set to limit the improvement of the human race; the perfectibility of man is in reality indefinite," said Condorcet. Ironically, he was hiding from political enemies during the Reign of Terror when he wrote these words. Soon after his capture he died in prison — perhaps by his own hand.

The philosophes' critical attitude toward the European society of their own time led them to idealize societies in remote, non-Christian parts of the globe, though they often knew little about these regions. They assumed that distant peoples had far more natural morality and virtue than Europeans did. The Chinese sage became an especially favored stereotype of wisdom and cultivation. Later in the century some philosophes portrayed the American Indian as a "noble savage," the unspoiled child of nature whose simplicity and natural morality put the corrupt civilization of Europe to shame.

THE GREATEST OF THE PHILOSOPHES

Voltaire (1694–1778) has been well described as "the spirit incarnate of the Enlightenment, with all its virtues and all its faults." Born in Paris into a prosperous bourgeois family called Arouet, he early assumed the pseudonym Voltaire. At seventeen he wrote his first work; by the time of his death at eighty-four his published writings filled more than seventy volumes. Plays, novels, histories, poems, political pamphlets, treatises, and thousands of letters poured with equal ease from his pen, all stamped with a lucid style, incisive logic, irony, and never-failing wit. "In Voltaire's fingers," said Anatole France, "the pen runs and laughs." His literary skill, his learning, his wit, and his thirst for controversy made him Europe's best-known man of letters and the idol of intellectuals everywhere.

During his twenties Voltaire was twice imprisoned in the Bastille for disrespect to high aristocrats. Outraged by this injustice, he went into self-imposed exile in England for three years, immersing himself in English culture and becoming its great admirer. In 1733 after his return to Paris he published *Philosophical Letters on the English,* in which he compared the freedom of the press, speech, and religion, equality before the law, and equal taxation he felt existed in England with the injustices and inequities of caste-ridden France. The French government condemned the book, and Voltaire escaped another imprisonment only by again leaving Paris to live on France's eastern frontier. While in England Voltaire had acquired an enthusiasm for the works of Newton and Locke, and he became the leading popularizer of their ideas in France and Europe. His passion for physics even moved him to dabble in experiments in a laboratory set up in his home.

In 1749 Voltaire accepted the repeated invitations of Frederick II of Prussia, who fancied himself a philosopher-king, to live at his court. Voltaire sojourned at Potsdam for two years, but the clash of these two strong personalities produced an impossible situation and the Frenchman left. Since his writings, pensions from wealthy patrons, and shrewd investments had brought him a fortune, he decided to buy an estate at Ferney, then in Switzerland near the French border, where he lived for the rest of his life.

At Ferney, safe from molestation by the French government, Voltaire turned his attention increasingly to philosophical and political matters. He produced a stream of pamphlets, many aimed against the irrationality of Christian dogma and the bigotry of the clergy. An avid disciple of Pierre Bayle (see p. 418), Voltaire used material from the *Historical and*

Critical Dictionary in his own campaign against religious intolerance and persecution — a campaign that has been described as probably the greatest contribution ever made by one man to the freedom of conscience. He took as his war cry the phrase *Écrasez l'infâme,* "Crush the infamous thing," meaning the Roman Catholic Church.

The most famous of his battles for human freedom concerned a Protestant family in Toulouse named Calas. The father had been tortured and executed on the false charge of murdering one of his sons to prevent his conversion to Catholicism, and his two daughters had been immured in convents. The youngest son managed to escape and went to Ferney to seek Voltaire's help. The philosophe's outrage at Calas's condemnation for what he believed and not for any crime he had committed set him on a campaign to right the injustice. It lasted three years, during which time he said he never permitted himself to smile. He wrote pamphlets, sent letters to important people, and collected a defense fund, to which Empress Catherine II of Russia, George III of England, and the king of Poland contributed. His unrelenting pressure finally compelled the courts to declare Calas innocent. The chief judge responsible for the miscarriage of justice was dismissed, and Calas's daughters were released. In another case he spent nine years clearing the family of a Protestant named Servas, who had also been unjustly accused of murdering his daughter because she was about to become a Catholic.

THE RELIGION OF REASON

Voltaire, like most of his fellow philosophes, was a deist. Reason told man that God exists, for there had to be a First Cause. "If God did not exist, it would be necessary to invent him," said Voltaire. The Supreme Being, as the deists preferred to call God, had created a harmonious, ordered universe that ran according to eternal physical and moral laws. A school of thought called Optimism maintained that the world was not perfect, for only God could be perfect, but that it was the best of all possible worlds as far as humans could hope to understand it. Voltaire was an Optimist until the great Lisbon earthquake of 1755 and the outbreak of the Seven Years' War in 1756 compelled him to abandon Optimism because he could not reconcile the senseless suffering in those two disasters — one natural and one man-made — with the belief that this was the best of all possible worlds. He summed up his changed viewpoint in *Candide,* the immortal novel written in just three days in 1759. Candide, educated in his sheltered youth in the philosophy of Optimism, after exposure to the ways of the world defined Optimism as "the mania for pretending that all is well when all is ill."

Although relatively few people subscribed to the religion of reason, their influence far exceeded their number. The devotees of deism included some of the most important people of the time, including rulers and ministers of state. In America such leaders as Thomas Jefferson, Benjamin Franklin, and John Adams adopted reason as their guide to religious faith. Yet deism did not survive the era of the Enlightenment. Too cold and abstract for the masses, who much preferred the color, symbolism, and personal God of orthodox Christianity, it also lost its hold on the intellectuals. They came to realize that the arguments used by deists against Christianity could be turned with equal deadliness against the religion of reason itself. This realization persuaded some to retreat to skepticism or agnosticism. The more advanced skeptics went beyond agnosticism to complete materialism and atheism, holding God to be an unnecessary hypothesis. They maintained that the universe has always existed and that matter, by its nature, has the capacity for motion, sensation, and even thought. Baron d'Holbach (1723–1789), a German nobleman who became a French philosophe, was the best-known defender of this doctrine.

Although deism did not survive the Enlightenment, its attacks on traditional religion helped weaken the established churches during the eighteenth century. Some churchmen, including persons of high ecclesiastical rank, became supporters of the religious views of the Enlightenment, and in many areas their attitude adversely affected the morale of the lower clergy. The Church lost intellectual prestige, for now intellectuals held traditional religious philosophies in low esteem. Corresponding with the decline of religion's influence was a decline in the Church's political influence.

TOLERATION AND HUMANITARIANISM

The philosophes linked their attack on religion with a demand for toleration. They pointed out that it is irrational and immoral to force a man to believe what his conscience will not let him believe. Intolerance is not only incompatible with religious precepts of charity and love; it is also uncivilized. Religion, they held, is a matter of individual conscience, over which the state should have no control. Many who advocated toleration, however, sometimes proved unwilling to extend it to everyone — atheists and Moslems were still anathema, and the traditional Catholic-Protestant rivalry still made zealots of men who had no use for the theology of either.

Faith in reason led also to a demand for humanitarian reforms. It seemed barbaric to rationalists that in the enlightened eighteenth century the law still permitted cruelty and inhumanity. Slavery and the horrors of the slave trade aroused indignation and pressure for reform. Inhuman treatment of the insane and criminals came under attack, and the first steps were taken to improve conditions in asylums and jails. In an *Essay on Crimes and Punishments* (1764) the Italian philosophe Cesare Beccaria argued for the application of reason to the administration of justice. Laws, he said, should be invariable, fair, and clearly stated. The aim of punishment should be not vengeance but the deterrence of further crime. The penalty should fit the crime; justice should be swift; torture and capital punishment should be abolished as useless and contrary to natural right. The state should by education and rewards for good deeds try to prevent crime. Beccaria's book won great acclaim, was quickly translated into other languages, and stimulated penal reform movements in France, England, and Russia.

POLITICAL THEORY

The majority of political theorists among the philosophes spun their webs of theory from unproven assumptions. They generally believed that human nature is everywhere the same so that differences among nations and societies arise not from differences in human nature but from irrational customs and traditions. The principles or natural laws underlying human behavior and institutions can be determined by the use of man's reason. They assumed that man is by nature rational, basically good, and educable, and that he will accept the natural laws once they are discovered and follow them to construct societies that will maximize human welfare. Oppressive social, economic, and political institutions were merely the creation of rulers and the Church. Such views explain why most of the philosophes paid slight attention to the historical development of social and political institutions and grossly underestimated the extent to which history determines the structure of social relations.

The philosophes shared a basic conviction that society should be organized for the good of all its members, not just for the benefit of a ruling elite, and that natural laws provide the guidelines to reach this goal. Although they thought in terms of national states, their belief in natural law and man's rationality produced a cosmopolitan outlook. With the triumph of the principles of reason would emerge first a united and uniform European civilization, and ultimately a world civilization in which all nations would participate equally and in which wars would disappear.

Following the pattern set by earlier political theorists, especially John Locke, the political theorists assumed that governments and organized societies started when men formed contracts with one another to protect their rights. They argued that one of man's rights is to revolt against the government if it fails to protect his other rights. Few of the political theorists, however, supported democratic or representative forms of government. They favored absolute rule by an enlightened despot, assisted by an elite of educated men, who would follow the dictates of reason and introduce necessary administrative reforms, establish freedom of thought and religion, and promote material, technical, and educational progress. Voltaire, who abhorred the idea of government by the people, wrote, "No government can be in any manner effective unless it possesses absolute power."

MONTESQUIEU AND CONSTITUTIONAL GOVERNMENT

Charles de Secondat, baron de Montesquieu (1689–1755), was the most sophisticated of the Enlightenment's political theorists. Unlike the majority of his brethren, he was no fancier of enlightened despotism, and he was unwilling to make the assumption that human nature was everywhere basically the same. As a wealthy member of the French *noblesse de la robe,* Montesquieu opposed the absolutism of the French throne, as much for its ineffectiveness as for its repressiveness. He was, however, far more than a spokesman for special class interests, and he deservedly occupies a high place among the architects of modern constitutional government.

Montesquieu's first work, *Persian Letters* (1721), used the device of an imaginary correspondence between two Persian travelers in Europe to satirize the institutions and customs of his own society. Encouraged by the book's success to devote himself to scholarship and writing, Montesquieu in 1726 sold his seat in the *parlement* of Bordeaux and set out on a long European tour to find out at first hand about conditions in other lands. The trip included a stay of eighteen months in England, where he acquired a lifelong admiration for the English political system that deeply influenced his thought. After his return home he spent nearly two decades studying and writing, and in 1748 he published his masterpiece, *The Spirit of Laws.*

Montesquieu employed a comparative method to examine a number of political systems, ancient and modern, and to discover the fundamental principles upon which they rested. Dividing governments into republics, monarchies, and despotisms, he concluded that the form of government differed among nations according to their natural environment, their history, and their social and economic conditions. Republics depended upon the public spirit or civic virtue of the people, monarchies depended upon honor in the sense of distinctions awarded outstanding subjects by the monarchs, and despotism depended upon the fear in which the people held the despot. His researches convinced him that republics flourished only in small countries or city-states, monarchies worked best in nations of moderate size in temperate zones, and despotism was most suited for large empires in hot climates.

He urged France to follow the English pattern of the separation of powers as the best guarantee for the preservation of individual rights. In England, he said, the executive, legislative, and judicial authorities were independent of each other and balanced and checked one another, thereby preserving individual liberty. He did not recommend that France duplicate the English system in every detail, proposing instead that governmental power be divided among the king and such traditional "intermediate bodies" as the organized nobility, the *parlements,* the provincial estates, and the chartered towns. Actually, Montesquieu erred in his analysis of the course of English constitutional development, for the revolutionary settlement of 1689 had assured the supremacy of Parliament, so that even when Montesquieu wrote, the English system of government was moving toward the concentration in the hands of Parliament of the executive and legislative powers, rather than their separation. Nonetheless, Montesquieu's exposition did much to make the tripartite division of ruling power the model for liberals who wanted to protect the freedom of the individual citizen. It had a potent influence on the drafters of the American Constitution in 1787 and the drafters of many other constitutions during the nineteenth century.

THE ENCYCLOPEDISTS AND THE PROGRESS OF SCIENCE

In no other facet of the Enlightenment were the philosophes' ideas, outlook, and interests better epitomized than in the great cooperative work of the *Encyclopédie.* Its publisher originally intended it to be a simple translation of a two-volume English encyclopedia, but the plans changed when a hitherto obscure philosophe named Denis Diderot (1713–1784) took over the editorship. Diderot saw in the project the opportunity to create a reference work that would instruct its readers in the rational, scientific, and utilitarian spirit of the Age of Reason. Although many of the articles were written by second-raters, some of the most important philosophes, including Voltaire, were among the contributors, and the eminent mathematician Jean d'Alembert agreed to serve as Diderot's associate in editing the volumes. The word encyclopedist, used to describe the contributors, became synonymous with philosophe.

The *Encyclopédie* comprised seventeen volumes of text and eleven volumes of plates. The first volume appeared in 1751, and the last in 1772. Later five supplementary volumes appeared, but they were not edited by Diderot. Although the set was expensive, the *Encyclopédie* was a great success. Over 4,300 people subscribed to the first edition, and it rapidly went through six more editions. Its articles reflected the philosophes' faith in reason and science and their deep interest in technology and material progress. The *Encyclopédie's* subtitle was *An Analytical Dictionary of the Sciences, Arts, and Trades,* and long articles and carefully engraved illustrations provided detailed information about many manufacturing processes.

The Catholic Church denounced the *Encyclopédie* as the "gospel of Satan," and the French government twice revoked the license to publish the work. D'Alembert, alarmed by the second revocation, withdrew from

Agriculture in Eighteenth-Century France

This engraving from the Encyclopédie *typifies the didactic purpose of Diderot and his collaborators. It shows how tillage should be done, rather than how it was actually done. The plow (fig. 1), modeled after the type designed by Jethro Tull, the English agriculturist, the seeder (fig. 4), the spike harrow (fig. 6), and the roller (fig. 7) were all improved or new farm implements that were still almost unknown in French agricultural practices. Notice, too, the use of horses as draught animals, rather than the slower and less efficient oxen.*
C. C. Gillispie, ed., A DIDEROT PICTORIAL ENCYCLOPEDIA OF TRADES AND
INDUSTRY (New York, 1959).

---

collaboration, but the undaunted Diderot managed to overcome these difficulties and carried the work through to completion. The dangers of censorship and suppression, however, forced the encyclopedists to use innuendo and indirectness in the articles. They inserted political and religious criticism in unlikely places. The article on the goddess Juno cast doubts on the biblical account of the Virgin Mary; the article on salt recounted the injustice to the poor of taxes levied on necessities, including the hated salt tax; and the article of Geneva contained indirect criticism of the French government.

NATURAL SCIENCES

The men of the Enlightenment took special pride in the accomplishments of the natural scientists. Academies, public lectures, journals, and popular books spread a knowledge of science among educated laymen.

Science became fashionable, experiments were performed in salons, and prominent people dabbled in it, including monarchs. Benjamin Franklin's electrical experiments thrilled the powdered beauties of the Parisian salons. The overall accomplishments of eighteenth-century science, however, lagged behind the work of the giants of the seventeenth century. In the main the physicists, astronomers, and mathematicians of the Enlightenment devoted themselves to consolidating the discoveries of the preceding century, and their work was derivative rather than fundamental. The French mathematicians d'Alembert, Laplace, and Lagrange gave Newtonian mathematics a more precise expression. Better methods for teaching were introduced. Marked improvements in scientific instruments such as the thermometer, barometer, balance, and lenses facilitated experimentation.

Important advances were made in understanding the forms of energy. Research on the properties of heat, chiefly by the Scottish professor Joseph Black (1729–1799), provided a precise quantitative and conceptual foundation for its study. The serious investigation of electricity began and became the most progressive branch of eighteenth-century physics. Outstanding work in this field was done by the Italians Luigi Galvani (1737–1798) and Alessandro Volta (1745–1827), the second of whom invented the battery, the first usable source of electricity; Benjamin Franklin (1706–1790), who contributed the concept of positive and negative charges and studies of conduction; and the Frenchman Charles Coulomb (1736–1806), who began the quantitative study of electricity. The leading contribution to biology was the system of classification perfected by the Swedish botanist Carolus Linnaeus (1707–1778). The next step was suggested by Jean Baptiste Lamarck (1744–1829), curator of the Jardin des Plantes in Paris, who advanced a theory of evolution that explained changes in species as a result of adaptation to changing environment. Near the end of the Enlightenment several chemists — notably the Frenchman Antoine Lavoisier (1743–1794), whose experiments showed the importance of precise quantitative techniques — began a revolution in the concepts and methods of chemistry that was to bear brilliant fruit in the nineteenth century.

THE STUDY OF HISTORY

Montesquieu alone among the principal philosophes took into account historical factors in explaining the nature of contemporary society. Other philosophes, however, were not loath to use history to persuade people of the truth of the doctrines of reason. History was "philosophy teaching by example." A number of philosophes turned their talents to the writing of historical syntheses to illustrate the workings of reason in mankind. Voltaire wrote histories of European civilization from the time of Charlemagne to the eighteenth century in which he tried to demonstrate how reason had evidenced itself in historical evolution. Turgot in *Discourses on Universal History* took as his purpose the discovery of the laws of social development. Condorcet's *Outline for a Historical Presentation of the Progress of the Human Mind* portrayed the steady progress of mankind through the ages. The pre-eminent historian of the eighteenth century, the Englishman Edward Gibbon, in *The History of the Decline and Fall of the Roman Empire* blamed the collapse of Imperial Rome on the rise of the anti-rational Christian faith.

THE COUNTER-ENLIGHTENMENT

Reaction against the ideas of the Enlightenment came from men who were within the mainstream of eighteenth century intellectual endeavor and from men who stood apart from it. Both groups, for different reasons, rejected the conviction that the unaided human reason could propound the explanation of the universe and man.

RELIGIOUS REVIVAL

Enthusiasm for the religion of reason, as indeed for all the ideas of the Enlightenment, was confined mainly to the minority of the cultured in the upper strata of society. It held little appeal for ordinary people, nor did it satisfy some religiously inclined members of the educated upper classes. In addition, the inroads made by rationalism and religious liberalism among the clergy of the traditional churches disturbed people of deep religious feeling. They wanted a "religion of the heart" rather than a religion of reason. In their search for a more emotionally satisfying religious experience many of them joined mystical or semimystical sects that arose in the eighteenth century.

In Germany a rebirth of pietism emphasized the importance of inner religious experience, a spiritual awakening, and a "second birth" in conversion. Count von Zinzendorf (1700–1760), leader of the movement, drew on the mystical doctrines of seventeenth century Pietists to preach a personal and emotional faith to his followers. Zinzendorf's sect, called the Moravian Brethren, was founded early in the 1730's and established settlements in North America centering around Bethlehem, Pennsylvania. A similar movement, Methodism, grew up within the Church of England, led by the Anglican minister John Wesley (1703–1791), and in the 1790's it broke away to form an independent church. (See pp. 372–373.) In North America a revivalist movement known as the Great Awakening swept through the British colonies in the 1730's and 1740's, led initially by the redoubtable New England Congregationalist Jonathan Edwards (1703–1758). All three of these Protestant pietist movements were closely connected: Wesley's relations with Zinzendorf and his followers led to Wesley's mystical conversion in 1738, and Edwards's rustic revival in the

1730's prepared the way for the first successful Methodist mission to the colonies in 1740.

In the intellectually isolated Jewish communities of eastern Europe a revivalist movement called Hasidism, from the Hebrew word for pious, won thousands of adherents. Founded in Poland in the late 1730's by Israel ben Eliezer (1700–1760), a simple laborer whose followers called him Master of the Good Name, Hasidism taught that joyous religious fervor brought man into direct communion with God and was superior to the theology expounded by the rabbis. Mysticism even made inroads into Freemasonry, the bastion of rationalism. Mystical ideas and ceremonies, inspired by the desire for spiritual regeneration through direct supernatural contact with God, appeared among Masons in Germany, Russia, and France.

PHILOSOPHIC REACTION

Since the religious revival deliberately rejected science and formal philosophy, it hardly touched the intellectuals. They were reached by men of their own kind, who questioned the fundamental assumptions of rationalist philosophy in philosophic circles.

The skepticism of the Scottish philosopher David Hume (1711–1776) struck a hard blow at faith in natural law as well as religion. Hume insisted that man can accept as true only those things for which he has the evidence of factual observation. The philosophes lacked such indisputable evidence for their belief in a perfect Creator or in the existence of natural law and natural morality. Such assumptions may be true, said Hume, but we have no way of finding out and never will have, nor are we able to disprove completely the opposite assumption. "A total suspense of judgment," he concluded, "is our only reasonable resource." Faith in reason cannot be maintained either. According to Hume, man's nature is the product of habit and custom, and most of his opinions are the result of his early education and environment. Human nature, therefore, can never be explained by reason or reduced to universal natural laws.

Hume belonged to the Enlightenment, although he questioned its fundamental assumptions. A more damaging assault was made by Immanuel Kant (1724–1804), particularly in *Critique of Pure Reason* (1781). Kant was a professor of philosophy at the Prussian University of Königsberg. Educated as a Pietist, he sought to ally rationalism and Pietist religious sensibility. Kant agreed with Hume that science and reason do not provide man with indisputable explanations of such problems as the existence of God, moral law, and immortality. Science, according to Kant, can describe the phenomena of the material world but cannot provide a guide for morality. There are, however, certain human experiences or feelings, such as conscience, religious emotion, and awareness of beauty, whose reality cannot be doubted even though science cannot explain them. These intuitive instincts, implanted by God, make man aware of the difference between good and evil. Kant called this awareness the "categorical imperative." It cannot be denied; it compels man to make a choice between right and wrong. By his insistence that science is limited in scope and that science and morality are separate branches of knowledge, Kant opened the way to new views of man's role and destiny that refuted the rationalism of the Enlightenment. His philosophy became the point of departure for nearly all nineteenth-century philosophical speculation.

JEAN JACQUES ROUSSEAU

Even though he is counted among the greatest of the philosophes, Jean Jacques Rousseau (1712–1778) was the seminal figure in the reaction against rationalism. The new movement called romanticism, which was destined to supplant rationalism as Europe's dominant philosophy, sprang principally from his writings.

Born in Geneva into a lower-middle-class Protestant family, Rousseau had a neglected and unhappy childhood, ran away at sixteen, and never afterward found a place in which he felt completely at home or friends in whom he had full confidence. For years he earned a precarious living. After he became famous, he lived mainly on the generosity of friends or the patronage of important people, and he usually repaid his benefactors with ingratitude and incivility. In spite of universal recognition, throughout his life he felt insecure and alienated from society.

His unhappy life had much to do with shaping his thought. He believed that man in the state of nature, without civilization, is fundamentally good. Nature gives man warmth of feeling, sincerity and simplicity of heart, and love and sympathy for his fellow man. Civilization corrupts him; the progress in the arts and sciences in which the men of the Enlightenment took such pride actually debased man. Rousseau found the origin of society's ills in the introduction long ago of private property. This had given rise to inequality, avarice, envy, wickedness, class struggle, war, and not the least in the catalog of woes, government itself, established by man to protect his property.

Rousseau maintained that the natural, good qualities in man stem from his emotions, while the evil qualities come from his reason. Man should therefore rely on his heart and not his head. In contrast to his fellow philosophes, Rousseau believed that intuition and emotion provide far better guides to action than reason and philosophy. Such simple natural joys as family life, humble toil, and above all a feeling of community with our fellow men give meaning and value to life. Religious reverence and belief in God belong among the natural emotions, too, though Rousseau himself did not subscribe to any formal religion.

Rousseau admitted that his description of the state of nature and the origin of civilization were not historically true. He explained that he

Jean Jacques Rousseau

*"Myself alone! I know the feelings of my heart, and I know men. I am not made
like any of those I have seen; I venture to believe that I am not made like any
of those who are in existence. If I am not better, at least I am different.
Whether Nature has acted rightly or wrongly in destroying the world in which she
cast me, can only be decided after I have been read."* Jean Jacques Rousseau,
THE CONFESSIONS OF JEAN JACQUES ROUSSEAU (Paris, 1784).

employed these concepts as hypothetical arguments "to throw light on the
nature of things, rather than to show their true origins." He recognized
that man could not slough off civilization and return to his primitive
state. Nevertheless, in his influential novels, *La Nouvelle Héloïse* (1761)
and *Émile* (1762), he tried to fashion a program of reform in education

and environment (he was a good son of the Enlightenment in his environmentalism) that would enable man to preserve uncorrupted his innate
feelings for justice and virtue. Rousseau urged a return to nature as far as
possible. He was no fraudulent nature-lover; his large collection of pressed
flowers, neatly classified, can still be seen in the Jardin des Plantes in
Paris.

In *The Social Contract* (1762) Rousseau addressed himself to the more
serious problem of devising a government that would preserve, as much
as possible in modern society, the natural equality of man. In so doing, he
contradicted his earlier arguments favoring unlimited individual freedom. *The Social Contract* proposed a system of government in which
each individual would surrender all his natural freedoms to everyone else
in his society. Rousseau argued that when men left the state of nature
they made a contract with each other to subject themselves to what he
called the "general will." This general will is more than a decision of
the majority, which he called the "will of all." The general will represents
the real will of each individual in the society, even though the individual
himself might not realize it. The general will is always in the best interests of everyone. It aims at both the well-being of the entire society and
that of each person within the society. True freedom consists in giving
complete obedience to the general will, since each person's best interests
are contained in it. If individuals place what they mistakenly consider
to be their own best interest above the general will, inequalities, injustices, and impairment of freedom will result. Anyone who tries to do
this must be compelled to follow the general will. As Rousseau put it, "he
must be forced to be free." Rousseau provided no machinery for the discovery of the general will, though he thought that the will of all would
sometimes coincide with the general will. Nor did he realize that to coerce
a person to accept a pattern of behavior that somehow had been defined
as the general will could lead to the negation of individual freedom and
the tyranny of the strongest.

During Rousseau's lifetime *The Social Contract* was little read and
poorly understood. Two decades after his death, much better understood,
it became the ostensible model for Robespierre's Republic of Virtue in
revolutionary France. It has since enjoyed a long vogue, drawn upon by
theorists of both democracy and authoritarianism. All who have sought
to use it either for theory or in practice have had to make their peace
with its essential, inescapable conclusion — that society's corporate will
dominating the will of its members makes all men equal but equally unfree.

RETROSPECT

In retrospect, the Age of Reason takes on a peculiarly unreal tinge. The
eighteenth century ended in the convulsions of riots and revolution,

massacres and mass executions, the establishment of the first genuine hegemony over the breadth of Europe since the Roman Empire, and a world war of gigantic proportions lasting over two decades. Much of the slaughter, rapine, and conquest were done in the name of the principles that had been the articles of faith of the philosophes.

In his near classic *The Heavenly City of the Eighteenth Century Philosophers* (1932) the American historian Carl Becker argued that the Age of Reason was in reality an age of faith. The philosophes replaced traditional religion with a new faith in science and reason, and they looked forward to a better world with as much confidence as the theologians of the thirteenth century had looked forward to perfect happiness in life after death. Actually, there was a wide variety of views among the philosophes and there were many who did not share a wholly optimistic faith in progress, in the natural goodness of man, or even in reason.

For all of the philosophes' naiveté and ultimate ineffectualness, the Western world owes much to them. Tolerance, a decline in superstition, belief in the dignity and inherent rights of the individual, freedom of thought and expression, liberal political ideas, a conviction that governments should rule for the benefit of the governed, humanitarianism, and enthusiasm for education — in one guise or another all are our heritage from the Enlightenment.

THE CRISIS
OF ABSOLUTISM
CHAPTER EIGHTEEN

Absolutism in the mid-eighteenth century looked different from that epitomized in Louis XIV; indeed, contemporaries viewed it as a new variety of absolutism, which came to be called enlightened despotism. With hardly an exception men of the eighteenth century compared the old absolutism unfavorably with the new. Monarchs who were not considered enlightened were disapproved; those who were enlightened were applauded. What most contemporaries failed to see was how fragile absolutism — enlightened or otherwise — was by the mid-eighteenth century, and how little time it had left.

ENLIGHTENED DESPOTISM

Enlightened despotism was the attempt of rulers or their ministers to apply the political tenets of the philosophes to the practice of absolutism. To justify their claims to absolute power, enlightened despots appealed to reason and to a secular and utilitarian concept of monarchy rather than to divine right or dynastic prerogatives. Thomas Hobbes in *Leviathan* had provided their fundamental argument: reason demonstrates that government functions best when it is headed by an autocratic ruler, and that the alternative to absolutism is anarchy. Reason also demands that the monarch accept as his objectives the increased prosperity of his subjects and their uninterrupted progress, and that he incorporate the principles of the Enlightenment into his government to reach these objectives.

It should not be assumed, however, that the enlightened despots were altruistic philosopher-kings. They believed that their own interests could best be served by reforms inspired by the philosophy of reason. Greater prosperity that increased the wealth and number of their subjects

442

also provided the royal treasury with more tax revenues and the royal army with more soldiers. Rational reforms of administration strengthened the central government and increased its efficiency. The political and dynastic considerations that had moved the absolute monarchs of preceding generations had not vanished. They were only muted, and they always prevailed when they came into conflict with the doctrines of the philosophes.

Enlightened despots sat on the thrones of Prussia, Austria, Spain, Portugal, Sweden, Denmark, and a number of small German and Italian states. There was one notable impostor, Catherine II of Russia, whose enlightenment was a pose, not a practice; few governments have been less enlightened than her regime. Significantly, no French monarch's name can be added to the list, though not for want of trying by a few of their abler ministers.

The enlightened despots followed similar patterns of reform and innovation. They all sought to increase the level of agricultural productivity by sponsoring improved techniques, and often they tried to improve the economic and legal status of the peasants, who were by far the most numerous of their subjects. They reformed judicial procedures, codified and simplified laws, abolished or limited torture and inhumane sentences, and promoted better public health, hospitals, and asylums. They supported scientific, technical, and literary activities and attempted to raise the level of popular education. In religious matters they were strongly secular and, almost without exception, more tolerant than their predecessors. In Catholic states this secularism manifested itself in restrictions on papal influence over the Church. In several countries the Jesuits were expelled, and finally in 1773 the pope was persuaded to suppress the order. It was not reestablished until 1814, by which time the doctrines of the Enlightenment had fallen into disrepute among monarchs.

PRUSSIA

Frederick II of Prussia (1740–1786), the first monarch to proclaim himself a disciple of the Enlightenment, once told a philosophe, "Philosophes such as you teach what ought to be, and kings are there to carry out that which you have conceived." Actually, Frederick's enlightened despotism was raised on the solid and wholly unphilosophical foundations laid by his drillmaster father, Frederick William I. Little in the practice of his regime can be ascribed specifically to the Enlightenment. It was his style of rule and his intellectual predilections more than the introduction of enlightened reforms in government that admitted Frederick to the ranks of the enlightened despots.

He read widely and wrote long treatises on history and government, besides many poems and essays, which gained him the reputation of being a minor philosophe. His contemporaries always remembered him as the young Prometheus bound, desirous of giving himself to philosophy but frustrated by his father's boorishness and brutality. His first published treatise on politics, appearing in 1740 and called *Anti-Machiavel,* assailed the principles of Machiavelli as immoral. A few months later, however, Frederick launched an unprovoked attack on Austrian Silesia; from the very start of his reign he was not one to permit the humanitarian and pacific ideals of the philosophes to stand in the way of his political ambitions. He wrote and spoke only in French, for he said that German was "unmanageable and lacking in grace." He looked to French thinkers for intellectual inspiration and took much pleasure in the friendship and correspondence of French philosophes.

Convinced that government could be reduced to a science, Frederick held that the state was the supreme authority, with all persons, including the king, subordinate to its interests. The king was simply the chief official or, as Frederick put it, "the first servant" of the state, whose function was to promote the welfare of his people. To do so he must have absolute power, for "the prince is to the society what the head is to the body." (Frederick's analogy was not particularly original; William Harvey, discoverer of the circulation of the blood, had made the same point a century earlier in a political essay addressed to Charles I.)

Frederick's reform of the judicial system made Prussian justice the most incorruptible and efficient in all Europe. He laid the foundation for reform and codification of Prussian law and abolished the use of torture except on charges of treason and murder. He won special acclaim for introducing limited freedom of speech and the press. He was himself indifferent to religious faith and urged tolerance on his subjects. His own tolerance, however, did not extend to Jews, whom he excluded from the civil service, the professions, agriculture, and most trades, and from whom he extorted large sums of money through special taxes.

AUSTRIA: MARIA THERESA

The first victim of Frederick's aggression was Maria Theresa of Austria (1740–1780), who was not counted among the enlightened. She was less fortunate in her inheritance than was her Prussian arch rival, for a defeated army, an empty treasury, and a state on the brink of dissolution constituted her patrimony in 1740. The first eight years of her reign were given over to the desperate defense of her realm following Frederick's invasion of Silesia. As soon as hostilities were ended Maria Theresa dedicated herself to remedying the frailties that had brought her monarchy so close to dissolution. Her motives were simple: to assure that she would not lose another war with Frederick, and to regain Silesia. The latter was not accomplished, but under her leadership Austria did become far stronger and more unified. Maria Theresa's rivalry with Frederick,

Courtesy of the Kunsthistorisches Museum

Maria Theresa with her Family, by M. Meytens

"On the accession of Maria Theresa the monarchy had neither external influence nor internal vigor; for ability there was no emulation and no encouragement; the state of agriculture was miserable, trade small, the finances badly managed, and credit bad. At her death, she left to her successor a kingdom improved by her many reforms, and placed in that rank which its size and fertility and the intelligence of its inhabitants ought always to enable it to maintain." Joseph von Sonnenfels (1733–1817) quoted in L. Leger, A HISTORY OF AUSTRO-HUNGARY (London, 1889).

rather than the tenets of the Enlightenment, moved her to transform Austria.

Beautiful, gay, devoutly Catholic, and wholly without pretence of intellectuality, Maria Theresa bore no visible signs of greatness. Yet she had a strong sense of duty, was resourceful and courageous, sensible and intelligent, and was masterful in turning her feminine charm to get her way. Never loosening the reins of personal control, she readily accepted the services of ministers who were more creative and intellectual than she was. Prince Wenzel von Kaunitz, in effect a coruler, Count Ludwig Haugwitz, an administrator of extraordinary talent, Count Rudolph Chotek, an able financier, and many lesser officials, were sympathetic to the Enlightenment. The interplay between their more advanced views and the Empress's innate conservatism and pragmatic good sense produced a workable amalgam of reform for Austria.

The state's most pressing need was a reorganization of the central administration, for all other reforms depended upon its efficiency. Through Haugwitz's efforts the administrative system was rebuilt along the Prussian pattern. A central bureau, the Directorium, modeled after the Prussian General Directory, was established to exercise overall supervision. A Council of State, created to serve as the empress's advisory board, examined all projects of reform and made appropriate recommendations to the sovereign. To carry through this program of centralization it was necessary to reduce drastically the traditional privileges of the provincial estates. These bodies persisted, but their legislative and administrative functions were taken over almost entirely by agencies of the central government, staffed by German Austrians, under the control of the Directorium. A High Court of Justice was set up for the entire state, provincial law codes were recast, and a new criminal code was promulgated. Reform was instituted in the army, too, including establishment of a system of conscription, adoption of the Prussian tactics of swift deployment and rapid fire, creation of a military academy to train officers (all of whom were nobles), and standardization of uniforms.

Recognizing the need for improvements in the condition of the peasantry, the chief source of revenue and recruits, the government set out on a program of agrarian reform. Most of the empire's peasants were serfs, and the government's aim was to improve the condition of their servitude, not free them from it. Beginning in the 1760's codes were issued for each province regulating the relationship between lord and peasant, fixing the amount of dues and services the peasant had to pay his lord, protecting the peasant's rights in the land he tilled, allowing him more personal freedom of movement, and reducing the lord's police and judicial authority over the peasant. Special governmental agencies were established in each province to enforce the provisions of the codes. In the last years of Maria Theresa's reign a step was taken in the direction of abolishing serfdom. Peasants who lived on estates owned by the crown were freed of their servile obligations and became renters of the land they worked. The government's hope that private landowners would follow its example was in vain, for only a handful of proprietors adopted the system.

In addition to limiting the power of the lords over their peasants, the government subjected the nobles for the first time to a property tax on their demesne land — land that was tilled for them by their peasants. Although the tax rate was not as high as that paid by the peasants on the land they tilled for themselves, it established the principle of the tax liability of all subjects, regardless of class.

The empress and her advisers realized the value of education in making good citizens. Influenced by Gerhard van Swieten, a Dutch doctor who served as both Maria Theresa's physician and her adviser on educational matters, the empress promulgated a decree in 1774 establishing elementary schools supported by local and national funds, to be attended by all children between six and thirteen. Technical and classical high schools and teacher training schools were founded, and major reforms toward modernization were made in the curriculum of the University of Vienna.

Maria Theresa's reforms applied almost without exception only to the German and Bohemian parts of her realm. Hungary, Belgium, and Lombardy, all parts of the Hapsburg patrimony, were maintained as separate states with their own institutions. The empress and her advisers realized that attempts to extend the reforms to these regions could well lead to serious political difficulties and even revolt. The Hungarians especially resented Austrian rule and had bitter memories of the Hapsburg conquest. Maria Theresa changed all this when in 1741 she appeared personally before the Hungarian estates, with her infant son in her arms, to implore aid against Prussia. Her beauty, courage, and glowing words captured the minds and hearts of the Magyar aristocrats, who with shouts of enthusiasm promised her 100,000 men. It was the turning point in the history of Austro-Hungarian relations; from then onward the Hungarian nobility counted itself among the strongest supporters of the House of Hapsburg. Maria Theresa wisely rewarded them with high offices, titles, and land, lured them to Vienna, and educated their sons with her own in a private academy, suitably named the Theresianum. While Hungarian affairs were increasingly handled in Vienna and the chief officials of Hungary became functionaries of the crown rather than of the Diet, the empress was careful to retain Hungary's status as a separate part of her realm, to exempt it from nearly all her reforms, and to treat the Magyar nobles with special consideration.

In 1765 when Maria Theresa's husband died, their eldest son, Joseph, succeeded his father as Holy Roman Emperor and became coruler with his mother. Headstrong and infatuated with the ideas of the Enlightenment, Joseph had no patience with his mother's pragmatic and cautious method of government. There were many harsh words between them, but as the junior partner, Joseph had to yield. His chance finally came when the empress died in 1780.

AUSTRIA: JOSEPH II

Events were to prove that the son was not as capable a ruler as the mother had been. His doctrinaire implementation of the tenets of the philosophes was so extreme that his reign turned out to be one of revolution from above and failure. Like Frederick, he described himself as "the first servant of his people." All that the state did was to be done for the people, but nothing was to be done by the people. He, the enlightened despot, knew what was best for them. Concentrating administration in his own hands, he attempted to reorganize the entire empire into a uniformly rational pattern. Indifferent to the marked regionalism of the realm, he divided it into thirteen large districts, subdivided each into smaller units, staffed the new administrations with his own bureaucrats, and made German the only official language except in the Austrian Netherlands and Lombardy. He created a secret police whose task was to maintain rigid surveillance of the bureaucrats and of the political opinions of his subjects. He simplified the court system, establishing equal punishment for the same offenses regardless of the culprit's social standing, and he drew up law codes in which, among other things, the death penalty was abolished for many offenses for which it had hitherto been imposed.

Joseph's enlightened views made him a defender of religious toleration. One of his first acts was to make Protestants, Eastern Orthodox, and Jews equal with Roman Catholics before the law and allow them to hold public office and have their own schools, churches, and seminaries. He sought to increase state control over the Church at the expense of Rome, dissolving over seven hundred of more than two thousand monasteries on the grounds that the monks and nuns were unproductive. The income from these confiscated properties went to support schools, charitable institutions, hospitals, parish priests, and the ex-monks themselves. Education was freed of Church control, and marriage was made a civil contract. Bishops were made to swear allegiance to the state, and new bishoprics were created in which Joseph installed men of his own choosing. Rome's protests, even the pope's personal visit to Vienna, were of no avail. In modifying but not abolishing state censorship, Joseph let loose a stream of books and pamphlets, many of them attacking the Catholic Church and supporting the doctrines of the Enlightenment.

Although Joseph never completely abandoned the prevailing mercantilist views and, in fact, raised the already high tariffs, he was strongly influenced by the theories of economic freedom popular among some

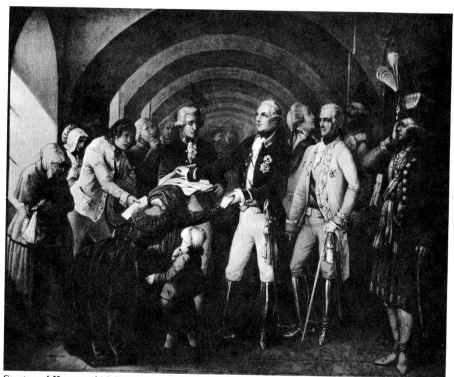

Courtesy of Heeresgeschichtliches Museum, Austria

Joseph II Grants an Audience to a Subject, drawing by
Ritter von Perger, lithograph by S. Bauer

"Since the good can only be of one kind, namely that which serves all, or at least the greatest number . . . and since equally all provinces in the monarchy must constitute only one whole, all jealousy, all prejudice, which until now has existed frequenty among nationalities must cease. . . .

"He who wishes to serve the state must think of himself last. . . . Only one intention can guide his action, the greatest good and usefulness for the greatest number." From Joseph II's Instructions to His Bureaucracy (1783), reprinted in E. M. Link, THE EMANCIPATION OF THE AUSTRIAN PEASANT 1740–1798 (New York, 1949).

men of the Enlightenment. The government began to relax its regulation of trade and manufacturing, and to reduce its subsidies to private enterprises. The contrast between the conservatism of Maria Theresa and the revolutionary fervor of her son was nowhere more clear than in their respective handling of the agrarian question. In 1781 he issued a decree giving peasants their personal liberty. Serfdom was abolished, although if the peasant remained on the lord's estate, he still had to pay him certain obligations in labor, kind, and cash. Other decrees in succeeding years protected the peasant from eviction from his holding and gave him the right to pass it on to his children. Finally in 1789 Joseph ordered that all the dues and services paid by more prosperous peasants to their landlords be converted into money rent. By the same law he equalized the land tax rates of the peasantry and the nobility.

A few months after the promulgation of this decree Joseph died, a broken man of forty-nine. Almost without exception his reforms had failed. Hungary and Belgium were in revolt against centralization. The nobility were outraged and on the verge of rebellion against the agrarian reforms and the loss of class advantages. Even the peasants were in revolt because the opposition of the nobles had compelled Joseph to suspend implementation of the agrarian reforms of 1789 and because these reforms extended only to the wealthier peasants. The war with Turkey into which Austria had been drawn in 1788 was going badly, and economic depression heightened Joseph's sense of failure. Bitter and disillusioned, he repealed some of the reforms shortly before his death in 1790 and was said to have been on the point of repealing them all. He summed up his career in the epitaph he wrote for himself: "Here lies a prince whose intentions were pure, but who had the misfortune to see all his plans miscarry." Joseph tried to go too fast and too far — Frederick II said of him that he always took the second step before he took the first. He was a revolutionary without a party to support him and without public opinion behind him.

He was succeeded by his brother Leopold II, who as grand duke of Tuscany had been one of Europe's most enlightened and most successful rulers. Leopold saw his mission as the restoration of internal unity to the empire. In his brief two-year reign he repealed most of Joseph's revolutionary legislation, although he refused to be cowed into utter reaction. Above all, he refused to give in to demands of nobles that he abolish the agrarian reforms of Joseph and those of Maria Theresa as well. He repealed Joseph's never-enforced agrarian law of 1789, but the peasants retained their freedom to choose their own occupations, to move about as they wished, to marry whom they pleased, and to occupy permanently their holdings.

SPAIN

In contrast to its fiasco in Austria, enlightened despotism in Spain under Charles III (1759–1788) piled up a record of achievements. King of Naples before succeeding to the Spanish throne, Charles was a man of average intelligence but of much experience in ruling, who was possessed of a desire to better the well-being of his subjects. Aware of his own intellectual limitations, he leaned heavily on able ministers who were deeply affected by the ideas of the Enlightenment.

Charles continued the policy of administrative centralization initiated by his Bourbon predecessors, revised the tax structure, ended many oppressive levies, and arranged for a more equitable distribution of the tax burden by a kind of graduated income tax. Though a devout Catholic, he completed the subordination of the church to the state. In 1767 he expelled the Jesuits, the chief opponents of the state domination of the church, and curtailed the powers of the Inquisition, which the Jesuits had controlled. Concerned by the ignorance and superstition of many priests, he attempted reforms in clerical education, issued regulations tightening monastic discipline, and appointed able men to bishoprics. He freed those of Jewish descent from the legal handicaps that barred them from military service and from many trades, although practicing Jews were still excluded from the country. He tried without success to end begging, a perennial problem in Spain, by establishing workhouses and asylums and by sending mendicants into the army, but the practice was too widespread and the state's resources too limited. Humanitarian legislation was issued to protect Negro slaves in Spanish America. Charles's educational reforms were especially ambitious. He promoted primary and vocational schools, strengthened university faculties, and introduced new curricula, including courses in science, despite protests from conservative academics that Newtonian physics did not help a student become a good metaphysician.

Charles was particularly concerned with economic problems. His government introduced measures to increase farm output by reclaiming land, bringing in foreign colonists, flood control, irrigation, and reforestation. It also adopted measures designed to increase peasant proprietorship and to decrease large-scale land ownership by absentee landlords. The privileges of the Mesta (see p. 198), the association of sheep raisers were greatly reduced, notably the right to graze its flocks on common land and to prevent enclosures. Measures directed at stimulating industry included the importation of foreign artisans, the opening of government-owned factories in new industries, construction of roads and canals, standardization of weights, measures, and coinage, a postal system, and drastic revision of internal tariffs. Royal support given to some seventy private societies throughout Spain called *Amigos de País* (Friends of the Country), composed of leaders in economic and intellectual life, promoted technical schools, new industries, and model farms. These public and private activities stimulated a marked increase in Spanish industrial and agricultural production.

The promise of continued development held out to Spain by Charles's reign was not fulfilled. He was succeeded in 1788 by his dull-witted and pleasure-loving son, Charles IV. The new king had no interest in following his father's policies; the old groups regained power, misrule and immorality became the order of the day, and the fortunes of Spain descended to a new low.

PORTUGAL

The decay of Portugal was momentarily halted during the reign of Joseph I (1750–1777). The marquis de Pombal, one of Joseph's ministers, so distinguished himself in directing the reconstruction of Lisbon after an earthquake and tidal wave in 1755 leveled the city and killed nearly thirty thousand people that the king gave him his unlimited trust. Pombal, infected with the ideas of the Enlightenment, believed that only absolute monarchy could save Portugal. He set out to crush the coalition of wealthy nobles and churchmen, particularly the Jesuits, who shared power with the throne. In 1758 the uncovering of a plot against the crown gave him his opportunity. He ordered the execution or imprisonment of leaders of the aristocracy and in 1759 succeeded in having the Jesuits expelled from the country.

Now able to carry out a reform program without interference, Pombal overhauled the administrative machinery of the state, sacked a host of useless officials, ended the nobility's monopoly of government posts, introduced the merit system into the civil service, reformed tax collection, and reduced corruption so that the government's revenues rose sharply. Tackling the problems of economic growth, he established trading companies, stimulated new lines of production, abolished internal tolls, and ended tariffs between Portugal and her colonies. Full civil liberties were extended to persons of Jewish ancestry, slavery was abolished, and a national educational system was created. Legal codification was projected. At the same time Pombal was a ruthless man whose spies were everywhere and who filled the prisons with those who disagreed with him. When Joseph died in 1777, Pombal's foes at court had him dismissed, his reforms languished, and Portugal soon fell back into its old torpor.

SCANDINAVIA

In Sweden and Denmark enlightened despotism was short-lived and demoniacally violent in its end. In Sweden Gustavus III (1771–1792) ended noble domination by a coup in 1772. Initially popular, nearly absolute in authority, and a devotee of the Enlightenment, Gustavus instituted a series of reforms that included tax revision, judicial reform and the abolition of torture, the lifting of internal tariffs, religious toleration, a free press, and educational reform. In the second decade of his reign the old conflict with the nobility broke out again, fired by the king's heavy military expenditures and reverses in war. Supported by the middle and lower classes, Gustavus triumphed briefly in a second coup d'état in 1789 and won still greater powers for himself, only to be shot in the back at a masquerade ball by a group of nobles in black masks.

In Denmark King Christian VII (1766–1808) suffered from insanity. In 1768 he engaged a new German physician, the young and handsome

Johann Friedrich Struensee, ardent disciple of the Enlightenment. The new doctor quickly managed to make himself chief adviser of the king and lover of the queen. By 1770 he ruled Denmark in all but name, and in two whirlwind years he introduced almost all the reforms associated with enlightened despotism. In 1772 a palace revolution, supported by the king's mother and brother, overthrew him, and he was executed. Many of his reforms were undone, yet his innovations paved the way for progressive measures in later years.

THE CRISIS OF ABSOLUTISM

Enlightened despotism hardly worked wonders anywhere. If undertaken in the pure light of reason without the political wisdom and energy of a Frederick II, Maria Theresa, or Charles III of Spain, it worked not at all. Everywhere in Europe in the middle years of the eighteenth century despots — both enlightened and unenlightened — confronted a dangerous new phenomenon. The nobilities of Europe, no longer content to remain satellites in the galaxies of sun kings, began to reassert themselves from the islands of privilege left to them by the absolutist state. Enlightened despotism tended more to aggravate the monarch's position than to improve it, for the reform programs impinged on the vested interests of the nobility and provided the nobility with a tangible target for attack. Some absolutist monarchs effectively met the challenge, principally in eastern Europe; those in Western Europe were seldom able to contain noble assertiveness so easily. Nowhere was this plainer than in the state that had set the pace for absolutism in all of Europe, that had provided the first and greatest sun king — France.

THE FAILURE TO RENOVATE FRANCE

LOUIS XV

Over a century ago the French historian Alexis de Tocqueville wrote of Louis XV, king of France from 1715 to 1774, great-grandson and successor of Louis XIV: "Had there been on the throne a ruler of the calibre and temperament of Frederick the Great, he certainly would have carried out many of the great changes in social conditions and in the government that were made by the Revolution, and not only would have kept his crown but would have greatly increased his power."

The invidious comparison of Louis XV with Frederick II of Prussia was apt. The comparison had to do not with enlightened despotism, but with the characters of men. Louis had few of the qualities of leadership that characterized the great Prussian. He was intelligent, able, and quick, but he lacked strength of character, application, and all those other capacities which absolutism demanded of kingship and which Frederick possessed. Louis XV preferred the continual diversions provided by hunting and by such famous charmers as the marquise de Pompadour and the countess du Barry. Although not unique failings for the age, the absolute sovereign of a great state could ill afford to spend so much time in these pursuits. Louis XV was a perpetual adolescent called to do a man's job.

Louis was five at his accession, and the first eleven years of his reign were passed under a regency filled with strife, intrigue, and indecision, presided over by two successive regents, the duke of Orleans (1715–1723) and the duke of Bourbon (1723–1726). Neither was particularly competent, and both were intent upon keeping their young charge as irresponsible as possible. By the time he had tired of Bourbon's intrigue and banished him in 1726, Louis had developed a fine taste for indolence and a suitably bored expression to go with it. For almost two decades he had the good sense to leave government to his capable, cautious, and honest old tutor Cardinal Fleury while he prolonged his youthful insouciance.

FLEURY'S ADMINISTRATION

Fleury's regime, lasting from 1726 until his death in 1743, was the sole extended period of political stability and peace that France knew in the eighteenth century, and Fleury was primarily responsible for it. He was the only chief minister of Louis XV who was not dismissed from office. He was a shrewd diplomatist, bent on peace and the containment of peripheral brushfire wars that might have set off a general war. With hardly a shot fired, he raised France's international prestige to a level it had not held since 1690, when the system of coalitions against Louis XIV had been perfected. He was a capable and steady administrator, summoning the best talent available. A number of the major ministers under Fleury were former intendants, men who had learned administration from the bottom up and retained a sharp sense of how policy made at Versailles might look different at Marseilles, Toulouse, Bordeaux, Tours, Rouen, or Strasbourg. There was nothing particularly brilliant about their administration; they were orthodox, methodical, honest, and effective. These qualities alone made them unique in eighteenth-century France. Some modest steps forward were taken. The codification of France's chaotic complex of laws and jurisdictions begun under Colbert was continued and the mounting assertiveness of the nobility in the parlements was contained, for the last time.

With peace and an honest administration France began to recuperate from the loss of men, money, and matériel suffered in Louis XIV's wars. French commerce revived, to the alarm of the English, and France's increasing fleet of merchant ships began to mount a challenge in the carrying trade of both slaves and general cargo. Fleury's diplomatic success with the Turks once more opened up the Levant trade for France.

Cardinal Fleury, by E. Harding

"Yesterday a foreign statesman said to me that when Cardinal Fleury dies France will lose an attractive gentleness and moderation which had done more for France than anyone realized; that in the midst of the greatest French undertakings the Cardinal had always made peaceful proposals and presented a peaceful and moderate front which was worth more to France than two armies, and that is the truth." Entry of November 26, 1741, JOURNAL ET MÉMOIRES DU MARQUIS D'ARGENSON (Paris, 1861), Vol. III.

The growth of French ports, on both the Atlantic and the Mediterranean, reflected commercial advance. Industries connected with colonial trade flourished, particularly distilling, sugar refining, cotton cloth manufacturing, and shipbuilding. The systematic improvement of roads undertaken by Fleury with the forced labor of the peasantry gave France a justifiably famous system of roads.

Events proved that the half-century from about 1725 to 1775 constituted the French monarchy's last opportunity to stave off disaster. It was a period in which the alternatives were a thoroughgoing renovation of France's governmental financial structure, or continued decay encouraging an assertion of the nobility's privilege and ultimately rebellion against absolutist monarchy.

THE DEAD HAND OF COLBERT

Fleury was content to allow the French economy to proceed on its own within the traditional system of governmental surveillance and interference. It was the last time that the system of Louis XIV's Colbert, built on foundations dating back to Henry IV's Sully, worked moderately well. Colbert had fastened on France an elaborate system of *inspecteurs, controlleurs,* corporations of craftsmen, high-tariffs and subsidization of luxury industries that was intended to prevent the ravages of unbridled domestic competition and to protect French industry from foreign competition. These measures turned out to be principally a means to raise revenue and to remunerate officeholders. They were an impediment to the growth of large industry, the introduction of technical improvements, and the development of a progressive market economy.

Colbert's reforms in government finance had been bold for the 1670's, but within half a century they had become insufficient to ensure the government's solvency even in peacetime, and they had fixed a rigidity on the fiscal structure that discouraged improvement. Colbert had been unwilling to tamper with the direct taxes from which most of the nobility and all of the clergy were exempt (the clergy paid the state a ridiculously small sum called a "free gift"), and had preferred to tighten up the collection of taxes and to increase indirect taxes, such as tolls, customs, and the hated salt tax. All efforts at increasing direct taxation were either defeated or watered down and the burden of taxation continued to be borne by the peasantry and townspeople. At the same time the exempted class of nobility was growing as successful merchants, lawyers, and bureaucrats bought themselves or their sons into the nob lity. While the nobility was prepared to shift any new tax likely to fal upon them onto the peasantry, they also resisted any attempt to incr ase taxes on the peasantry because that reduced the nobility's chief s urce of income, rents from their peasants. To make up the difference bel veen tax revenues and expenditures the government was thrown back on the sale of offices and honors, payments from private industry to escape inspection and control, and the floating of loans. These expedients were the equivalent of foregoing future profits for immediate gains, since the sale of offices and honors exempted that many more people from taxes, and the loans necessitated the payment of interest at increasingly stiff rates as the government's credit declined, especially in wartime.

LAW'S PANACEA

One notable attempt to stir up the stagnant waters and provide greater revenue for the state was the scheme of the mercurial Scottish financier, John Law (1671–1729). Son of an Edinburgh goldsmith, he was a student of mathematics and political economy and a prodigious gambler. While living in exile in France during the last years of Louis XIV's reign, he became an intimate of the duke of Orleans over the gambling tables. When Orleans became regent in 1715, Law settled in Paris.

Law's scheme was not unsound. The crux of it was to spur economic expansion by increasing the amount of money in circulation in France. The regent was impressed. In 1716 Law received a charter for a joint-stock bank in Paris with the right to issue notes acceptable as money. Two years later the government bought out the stockholders and Law's bank became the royal bank under Law's direction. By 1720 it had issued twice as much in paper notes as there had been currency in circulation when it was established. In 1717 Law founded the Company of the West, a trading company known popularly as the Mississippi Company, to which the government awarded the monopoly of trade with France's Louisiana territory. Two years later the company absorbed other French overseas trade monopolies, and the name was changed to the Company of the Indies. Law's enterprise now held the monopoly of all French colonial trade. In addition, it purchased the right to collect indirect taxes in France, to mint money, and to service the government debt. In 1720 it merged with the royal bank. In that same year the Scottish adventurer, who had recently adopted French citizenship and the Catholic faith, was appointed controller general of finance, the principal fiscal post in the government. France's economy was in Law's hands.

Law's plans for economic and fiscal reform were all-encompassing. They included a revival of Vauban's 10 per cent tax to be applied to everyone, uniform tax collection, dissolution of unnecessary offices, capital loans to manufacturers at reasonable rates to encourage industry, and a government program of public works. His plans were never put into operation. Law had financed the Company of the Indies by selling its stock on easy terms and paying high dividends, while his bank flooded the country with new paper currency so that people had much more money to spend and to invest. By overselling the potential of his commercial enterprise and by inflating the currency he produced a fever of speculation that he could not control. In the spring of 1720 investors realized that the stock of the company was fantastically overpriced and began to sell. The price slipped, panic swept the market, and the price plummeted. Law tried desperately to stave off collapse, but by October, 1720, he and his scheme were bankrupt. The royal bank closed, and Law fled France. The company lost most of its privileges but managed to survive as a modestly successful enterprise for several more decades.

This strange episode, called the Mississippi Bubble, had lasting effects on the French economy. A few, including some wealthy financiers, made great fortunes by selling out early. Thousands of others were ruined. The disaster marked the end to Law's proposed reforms of government finance as well as to the already fragile public confidence in the government's credit and solvency. Frenchmen acquired a distrust of central banks, paper money, and stock companies that was not dispelled for many years.

THE REGAL INTERREGNUM

Fleury died in 1743 in the midst of the War of the Austrian Succession. Instead of appointing another first minister, the thirty-three-year-old Louis, in an unsustained burst of application to affairs of state, set out to rule himself. For two decades France's government was that of a caretaker, with the owner of the house playing caretaker. It was a government of secret diplomacy known only to the king (who hardly kept the threads of it straight in his own mind), of palace intrigue, of playing one faction off against another, of inaction, drift, and contradiction. Madame de Pompadour, the king's mistress, was not, as legend has maintained, the real ruler of France, but she might as well have been. Ministers came and went — only the king remained. Every minister was under constant barrage from his enemies and ultimately fell afoul of Louis.

The ablest was Machault d'Arnouville, a former intendant, who as controller general from 1745 to 1754 managed to finance the War of the Austrian Succession in spite of the archaic fiscal system. He had the temerity to attempt the imposition of a uniform 5 per cent income tax on everybody, including nobility and clergy. The bold attempt failed in a howl of opposition from the parlements and the church, and Machault's fall from power was brought about by the customary intrigue.

Defeat in the Seven Years' War compelled Louis to choose a chief minister who was a not unworthy successor to Fleury. The Duke of Choiseul salvaged some of France's fortunes at the Peace of 1763. He also retired Louis to his pleasures and provided something like consistency in administration from 1758 to 1770. The one task he did not tackle was financial reform. Quietism was his policy, and his tacit alliance with the nobility in their reassertion of power in the parlements assured the preservation of the existing feeble fiscal structure.

THE PHYSIOCRATS

By the time of Choiseul's administration a theoretical basis for the renovation of the economy was not wanting in France. A distinctive group of philosophes had emerged, enthusiastic for economic engineering on the premises of the Enlightenment: rationality, mechanical laws, and progress. Called physiocrats, these men suggested practical solutions for the economic problems of all of France, and not least for those of the state.

The originator of the physiocratic school was François Quesnay (1694–1774), Louis XV's physician. A contributor to Diderot's *Encyclopedia,* Quesnay based his economic theories upon the concept of a natural order that was universal and without flaw. He and his followers maintained that the basis of the natural order in economic life was the right of private property, and that it was the state's obligation to protect that right but not to interfere with it through regulations and restrictions. They condemned the regulatory policies of Colbert as harmful to economic progress and coined the antimercantilist battle cry, "laissez faire, laissez passer." With a few earlier English economists, notably Sir William Petty, they shared the merit of discarding the mercantilist belief that trade and commerce were the only means of enriching a nation. Instead, they transferred the power of creating wealth to the realm of production — above all, to agricultural production.

They argued that only land (including natural resources) produced a surplus or "net product," as they called it, over the amount expended in working it. In contrast, the manufacturer and trader were "sterile" as far as producing wealth was concerned: the manufacturer only gave new form to the materials produced by the earth, and the trader only transferred these materials from one person to another. Neither produced a "net product" or added to the wealth of the country. It followed that everything possible should be done to encourage the development and prosperity of agriculture, including an improvement of the means of transportation and the removal of tariffs and tolls that impeded the free circulation of agricultural products both within France and to other lands.

The physiocrats' analysis of the central role of the land in economic life provided them with a solution to the perpetual crisis in French government finances. They proposed that the existing complicated, inequitable, and inadequate tax structure be replaced by a single tax, the *impôt unique,* to be levied on the net product produced by the land. This tax, which should not exceed one-third of the surplus gained from the land, would be easy to levy once the productive capacity of all the land in the kingdom had been determined by government survey, would be simple to collect, and would be levied on those best able to bear taxation. Most important, the taxpayer would pay the *impôt unique* out of clear, net gain, so that the government would not be siphoning off money that should be reinvested to create new wealth. The economy would then prosper, the net product would increase, and the resulting income from the single tax would provide the state with all the revenue it needed.

In a work entitled the *Tableau économique,* printed at the palace at Versailles in 1758, Quesnay analyzed the movement of the net product among the different economic groups in society. Inspired by the analogy of the circulation of blood through the body, Quesnay tried to show that wealth will freely circulate if an economy is unobstructed by barriers raised by government regulation. The *Tableau* rested upon arbitrary and unreal assumptions, such as that of constant prices, an unchanging net product, arbitrary assignments of the amount of goods that each class was expected to purchase from the others, and of course the fundamental fallacy that only land produces wealth. It nevertheless represented the first comprehensive attempt to trace the relationships of economic groups. Contemporaries hailed it as a triumph of science and reason. One true believer compared it with the invention of money and writing as one of the most important discoveries of the human mind.

Agricultural progress and fiscal reform were not the only parts of the physiocrats' program. For the economy to grow, the natural order required that the individual have freedom to buy and sell as he pleased, that guilds be abolished, that restraints on freedom of competition be barred, and that men and goods be able to move freely within France with a minimum of restriction. These material rights would be of no avail unless they were reinforced with freedom of speech, press, and conscience. Despite their defense of individual freedom, most of the physiocrats strongly supported enlightened despotism, which they called "legal despotism," as the best form of government. Only under a single, absolute authority, guided by the counsel of men infused with the doctrines of the Age of Reason, could the natural order triumph. They failed to realize that such a despot would have to be singularly enlightened and singularly self-restrained, for the role assigned to him by the physiocrats was little more than that of a policeman enforcing the "natural and essential laws" of society.

The physiocrats did not all share Quesnay's doctrinaire repudiation of the productive importance of commerce and industry. Vincent de Gournay (1712–1759), one of the earliest and most important members of the school, accorded larger significance to those sectors of the society. Another, Anne Robert Jacques Turgot (1727–1781), could never quite accept the idea that only land produced a net product or that all classes except that which worked the land were "sterile producers." Turgot eventually was given the opportunity to try to renovate France's economy and government finances through physiocracy — and failed, though not because of much fault in himself or in physiocracy.

THE PARLEMENTS AND THE NOBLE ASSERTION

To understand what did destroy the opportunity for reform presented by Turgot's tenure as controller-general (1774–1776), the history of the parlements after the death of Louis XIV must be outlined. The Sun King, following a policy inherited from Richelieu, had whittled away at these traditional courts in Paris and the provinces because they were instruments of noble political ambitions and preserves of noble privilege. He had abolished their veto of legislation by royal decree. The parlements were awed by Louis XIV and remained acquiescent. The weakness of the central government under Louis XV, however, encouraged the parlements to reassert themselves against royal authority. The king had almost no control over their composition, and although they had no ultimate power over legislation, they could still force the king to override their stand against unpopular legislation and they could still act as sounding boards for dissidence and opposition.

The first serious clash with the parlements came over Machault's attempt to impose a uniform 5 per cent income tax. The parlements objected vociferously, and the Paris parlement declared the tax illegal. Since the levy would touch the clergy, the parlements rallied the church, and together they forced Machault to abandon the tax. For the next two decades king and ministers alike moved warily in dealing with the parlements.

In 1766 the parlements threw down a challenge to royal authority that Louis could not ignore. The crisis began in Brittany, where the provincial parlement, in company with the Breton estates, fell into a bitter quarrel with the central government over charges that the royal power had disregarded provincial rights in the construction of roads in Brittany for military defense during the Seven Years' War. The dispute reached a climax when the leader of the parlement was arrested for his violent speeches against the military commander of the region. Other parlements joined the Bretons in denouncing the central government. They made such extreme assertions of their own power that they threatened the sovereignty of the throne and Louis could no longer tolerate the subservience of his chief minister, Choiseul, to the parlements.

Effective power in internal affairs passed to René Maupeou, a lawyer and a bitter opponent of the parlements. Maupeou skillfully provoked the Paris parlement into overt opposition to the king's authority, then early in 1771 he had the leading magistrates arrested, abolished the Paris parlement and set up six new courts for Paris (derisively called "Maupeou parlements"), with judges named by the king. In the wake of this shattering victory Maupeou set on foot wholesale changes in the law in order to curb noble privilege. His colleague Abbé Terray, controller-general of finance, began a fiscal reform aimed, like Machault's income tax, at a more equitable distribution of taxes, attempted to have more accurate assessments made of taxable income from land, and introduced other measures to increase state revenues. Maupeou's and Terray's work had only begun when Louis XV died of smallpox in 1774. Louis XVI, his grandson and successor, wanted above all to be mindful of the needs and wishes of his subjects and to disassociate his reign from that of his arbitrary and now discredited grandfather. Heeding the protests of the members of the parlements who had organized demonstrations to try to show wide public support for their demands, Louis dismissed Maupeou and restored the old parlements.

FRANCE ON THE EVE OF REVOLUTION

The new king, twenty years old, was devout, shy, kind, and moral, a skillful locksmith, and an adoring husband. He was also dull, poorly read, and no more capable of application to the labor of an absolutist monarch than was his recently deceased grandfather. He was destined to die not for his vices (the worst of which was his irresolution, which could only appear to his enemies as duplicity) but for his absence of kingly virtues. His wife Marie Antoinette, daughter of Empress Maria Theresa, cut a sharp contrast. Quick, charming, frivolous, extravagant, and haughty, she enjoyed an ascendency over her slow husband that no mistress had ever exercised over Louis XV. Although her extravagance was not, as once believed, responsible for the monarchy's bankruptcy, it epitomized to an increasingly hostile nation all that was decadent in absolutism.

TURGOT, NECKER, AND CALONNE

Shortly after Louis's accession his chief adviser, Jean Maurepas, decided that for "public relations" the government needed a known reformer in high office. The physiocrat Turgot was summoned to the controllership of finance. Turgot had served for twelve years as intendant of the city of Limoges in central France, where he had distinguished himself by his energetic and imaginative leadership. Among his achievements were founding the Limoges pottery works, using paid labor to build roads and bridges instead of the compulsory corvée of peasants who received no wages for their work, equalizing the collection of taxes as far as he was able, and financing public works at low rates of interest. Turgot's experience in administration and reputation as a physiocrat awakened hopes that he would be the great innovator and reformer that the government needed so badly.

His first fiscal reforms were cautious, though promising, including reduction in court expenses and in pensions paid by the government to

Louis XVI, engraving by Curtis after Bozè

"He had not a wish but for the good of the nation; and for that object, no personal sacrifice would ever have cost him a moment's regret; but his mind was weakness itself, his constitution timid, his judgment null, and without sufficient firmness to stand by the faith of his word." THE WRITINGS OF THOMAS JEFFERSON (Washington, D.C., 1903), Vol. I.

favored persons, simplification of the system of tax collection, and moves to bring the finances of other ministries (notably the ministry of war) under the surveillance of the controller-general. Turgot mounted his greatest offensive in the sphere of government control of the economy. His spearhead was the physiocratic doctrine of freer internal trade. He loosened the restrictions on grain movement after the bad harvest of 1774 in an attempt to cope with the grain scarcity and supply Paris with bread. Despite his caution, there was much opposition. Undeterred, early in 1776 he submitted to the king six edicts for reform that included extending earlier laws allowing for freer trade in grain, abolishing offices for enforcing restrictions on trade in agricultural produce, establishing a general tax on all proprietors of land for the maintenance of roads, and abolishing the corporations of craftsmen established by Colbert. The outcry was enormous. Clergy, nobility, financiers, colleagues in the ministry, and the craft corporations united in common cause. The opposition coalesced in the reinstituted parlement of Paris. Turgot persuaded Louis XVI to ram the six edicts through over the parlement's objections, but he was dismissed shortly afterward, and his reforms were quietly dismantled. With them ended the last great hope for the renovation of France. As ominous as his defeat was, more ominous was the means: the revolt of the nobility in the parlement reinforced by a broad and powerful segment of French opinion.

Jacques Necker, a Swiss banker and Turgot's successor in charge of finance from 1776 to 1781, played at reform. With an uncanny gift for self-advertisement he mounted a massive campaign to prove that the state's finances were never better. In fact, they were never worse. The government was in debt beyond repayment. Yet Necker's fall in 1781 was not owing to this deception but the result of his ambitious demands for more power.

In 1783 Charles Calonne, another former intendant, was made controller-general. Masterful and energetic, Calonne determined upon a plan of reorganization of the state's finances that owed much to the ideas of Turgot. He urged a new tax on landed income to be paid by all landowners, whether clergy, noble, or commoner; pressed for the abolition of restrictions on economic initiative; and proposed to gain the cooperation and understanding of the nation by presenting his program to provincial assemblies elected by all taxpayers, in which no distinction would be made among social classes. The king gave his support to these proposals. In February, 1787, at Calonne's behest he summoned an Assembly of Notables — a selected group of prelates and great noblemen — on the assumption that the parlements could not be persuaded to accept Calonne's tax but that the Notables could. Calonne's failure to persuade them sealed his dismissal.

His successor, Loménie de Brienne, the enlightened archbishop of

The Bettmann Archive

The Peasantry Bearing the Priesthood
and the Nobility on Its Back

eighteenth-century cartoon

"*Oct. 17, 1787. . . . Dined today with a party, whose conversation was entirely political. . . . One opinion pervaded the whole company, that they are on the eve of some great revolution in the government; . . . no minister existing . . . to promise any other remedy than palliative ones; a prince on the throne, with excellent dispositions, but without the resources of a mind that could govern in such a moment without ministers; a court buried in pleasure and dissipation . . . a great ferment amongst all ranks of men, who are eager for some change, without knowing what to look for, or to hope for; and a strong leaven of liberty, increasing every hour since the American Revolution.*"
Arthur Young, TRAVELS IN FRANCE DURING THE YEARS 1787, 1788, & 1789 (Cambridge, 1929) .

Toulouse, faced the parlements with Calonne's proposals. The parlement of Paris, warmly supported by the provincial parlements, rejected the proposals and called for the summoning of the Estates-General of France, which had last met in 1614 and 1615. The convening of the Estates-General, with its preponderance of the clergy and the nobility, could only have spelled disaster to Louis XVI. He had reached the same point that Louis XV had reached in 1771 when his authority was challenged by the parlements, and he chose the same course of action. He first banished the parlement of Paris in 1787, recalled it shortly afterward, was harassed by it for the next six months, and finally adopted the "Maupeou solution." In May, 1788, all the parlements of France were suspended, and new courts were established to take their places.

It was too late. The parlements resisted, supported by the nobility, the clergy, and the bourgeoisie. Riots in a half-dozen provinces and resistance everywhere forced Louis's capitulation. In August, 1788, the suspension of the parlements was rescinded, Brienne was dismissed, and Necker was returned to power. On September 23 the parlement of Paris returned to the metropolis amidst tumultuous celebrations to register a decree summoning the Estates-General to meet on May 1, 1789. The rebellion of the aristocracy had triumphed; the king had been defeated; and privilege, it seemed, had been confirmed.

THE ARISTOCRATIC REBELLION

The aims of the nobility as voiced in the parlements — such as the aggrandizement of their political power and the preservation of their privileges, especially exemption from taxation — were no more striking than the words in which they were expressed. In the years after Louis XIV's death when they were trying to revive their old privileges, the parlements had used the traditional historical arguments that they were the "sovereign courts" descended from the medieval king's council. Then around 1750 the notions of the Enlightenment began to creep into their arguments. The constitutionalism of Montesquieu enjoyed an extended vogue. Locke's idea of a contract between king and people was developed into a full-blown theory, replete with allusions to the "nation," "free consent," "liberties," and "the general will." All this smacked of self-delusion and even fraud, for the parlements, claiming that they were defending the "liberties of Frenchmen," conceived of those "liberties" as no broader than their own vested privileges. Nevertheless, the claim elicited the support of all those hostile to absolutism.

THE FRENCH REVOLUTION
CHAPTER NINETEEN

The French Revolution ranks with the Reformation as one of two great watersheds in the history of the European world. Into it virtually all of the past flowed; from it virtually all of the present has come. Every revolution since has been a variation on the theme of the French Revolution. In the streets of Budapest in 1848, 1918, and 1956, Hungarians sang the "Marseillaise." The Russian revolutions of 1917 — both Kerensky's and Lenin's — paid homage to the epoch of revolutions inaugurated at the Place de la Bastille on July 14, 1789. Much of the French Revolution survives only in form — Lenin was neither a Robespierre nor a Babeuf. Yet the change of substance into form is the way the past is preserved to influence the future. It is the translation of the "what was" into the "what will always be" in history, which has made all of us children of the French Revolution.

THE COMING OF THE REVOLUTION, 1788–1791

Between the end of September, 1788, when the decree to summon the Estates-General was issued, to its convocation in early May, 1789, the great topic of dispute was the composition of the Estates-General. Historically it consisted of three houses representing the three estates: the First Estate or the clergy, the Second Estate or the nobility, and the Third Estate or the commonalty. Each met and voted separately. The will of the Estates-General was expressed by either the unanimity of all three houses or a majority of two. The dispute in 1788–1789 stemmed from a realization that the interests of the clergy and the nobility in preserving their privileges were likely to coincide to the detriment of the commonalty, so that the First and Second Estates might consistently thwart the desires of the Third. Such a possibility had not been questioned before; now it was a stormy issue.

In the seven months before the convocation of the Estates-General hundreds of pamphlets poured out on both sides of the question. The two consistent positions of those advocating change were that the representation of the Third Estate should be doubled and that voting should be by head, each deputy of all three estates having one vote and the will of the whole Estates-General being a simple majority of the voting deputies. Necker in December, 1788, persuaded the king to double the representation of the Third Estate.

THE THIRD ESTATE

"What is the Third Estate?" asked the Abbé Sieyès rhetorically in a pamphlet of that title published early in 1789. "The Third Estate is a complete nation," he answered. Sieyès was one of a group of clergy and nobility who felt that the salvation of France from both absolutist monarchy and noble and clerical privileges lay in the Third Estate. Although the Third Estate was something less than a nation, it was the greatest segment of the society. It was also the most complex of the three social orders, comprising the peasantry, the bourgeoisie, the professionals, and the urban workers.

The peasantry constituted about 85 per cent of France's 25 or 26 million people. Many peasants owned all or part of their holdings and over one-third of France's soil was their property. Most of their holdings were too small to support them, however, and only by renting additional land or working part-time for a larger landowner or in trade could they survive. They also had to pay obligations to the nobles to whom their land had once belonged, which varied from place to place but usually included fees for using the village mill, bakery, or wine press and an annual small payment in cash or produce. These obligations were remnants of the feudal past, when the lords had exercised the powers of government over the peasants on their property. In addition, the peasants paid both a tithe to the church and direct taxes. Peasants who owned no land either rented a holding from a landowner for a money rent or a share of the crop, or hired themselves out as farm laborers. Serfdom had nearly disappeared. Estimates of the number of peasants who were serfs — and their serfdom entailed little more than the payment of certain special dues to their lords — run from 140,000 to 1,000,000, most of whom were in the eastern provinces of Franche-Comté and Lorraine, only recently annexed to France.

Even well-to-do peasants often lived humbly in order to avoid increased taxes. The available evidence indicates that after a half-century of gradual improvement the economic position of the peasantry worsened in the decade immediately preceding the Revolution. Poor harvests, a general rise in prices, and the nobility's reassertion of its privileges brought about the decline. The nobility, pressed by the price rise and determined to maintain the higher standard of living afforded by the general economic advance of the era, collected feudal dues more rigorously, revived forgotten obligations, and increased the rents of their peasant leaseholders and sharecroppers. The peasantry had long grumbled at the obligations due their lords, for which they received no services in return. With increased dues the customary discontent took on dangerous proportions.

The Third Estate lived in cities and towns. Most of them were craftsmen and hired workers. The workers were concentrated in a few centers, notably Paris, Marseilles, Rouen, and Bordeaux, and some were organized into embryonic unions to better wages and working conditions. Like the workers, the craftsmen or lower segment of the bourgeoisie were particularly hurt by the increase in food prices brought on by the succession of poor harvests. The upper segments of urban society, the middle and higher bourgeoisie, were jealous of preserving the social distinctions between themselves and the smaller bourgeoisie and workers. Always conscious of their social inferiority to the nobility, they began openly to resent their privileges. The nobility's increasing monopoly of office and the reassertion of noble privilege in the parlements intensified the hostility. The nobility's arrogance was made even less bearable by their obvious new power.

It was the Third Estate, more particularly the bourgeoisie, for whom the Enlightenment had the greatest meaning. By virtue of its utilitarian motivation, its appeal to rationality, its emphasis on material well-being, and its defense of individual rights, the Enlightenment was absorbed by the middle-class merchants, manufacturers, lawyers, physicians, teachers, and journalists, whereas it only softened the veneer of some of the nobility. The burden of the philosophes' message was an attack on privilege — noble and ecclesiastical explicitly, monarchic implicitly. Religious toleration, humanitarianism, freedom of the individual, and reforms to free economic endeavor from injurious restrictions were all facets of a way of life that the old order — the *ancien régime* — in state and church could not accept, though the philosophes had never given up hope that the absolutist monarch might be converted to their faith and work the reforms they sought. Above all, the philosophes called men to scrutinize existing social and political institutions in the pure light of reason. Many among the bourgeoisie had done so, and the France they saw in 1789 was a ramshackle edifice compared to the philosophes' blueprints. Few of the philosophes had urged revolution; few of the Third Estate had planned revolution in 1789. The Revolution issued from the spontaneous reactions to events of men interested in change rather than from a massive conspiracy to effect a new order. But the goals of change would have to bear some resemblance to the programs of the philosophes, the justification of events after the act would have to be couched in language furnished by the Enlightenment, because in eighteenth-century France there were no ideological alternatives to the Enlightenment to mold the new order.

....

THE ANCIEN RÉGIME: CLASSES IN FRANCE IN 1789

approximate numbers

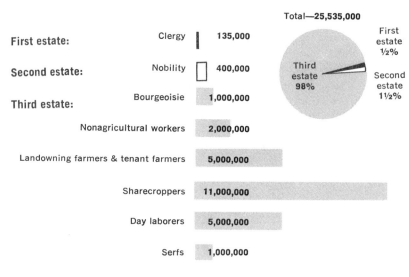

		Total—25,535,000	
First estate:	Clergy	135,000	First estate ½%
Second estate:	Nobility	400,000	Third estate 98%
Third estate:	Bourgeoisie	1,000,000	Second estate 1½%
	Nonagricultural workers	2,000,000	
	Landowning farmers & tenant farmers	5,000,000	
	Sharecroppers	11,000,000	
	Day laborers	5,000,000	
	Serfs	1,000,000	

Source: J. M. Thompson, "The French Revolution"
(New York: The Oxford University Press, 1945), p. 93.

....

THE FIRST AND SECOND ESTATES

The nobles in the Second Estate were divided into nine principal ranks, ranging downward from the great aristocracy through the nobility of the parlements to the tattered petty nobles in the provinces who eked out a meager living on a few ancestral acres. They were united only in their determination to preserve their privileges and expand their power, at the expense of both the monarchy and the bourgeoisie and to the deprivation of the peasantry. The successors of Louis XIV had assisted the nobles by failing to choke off the demands of the parlements. The bureaucracy, which under Louis XIV and his immediate predecessors had been drawn largely from the bourgeoisie, was increasingly recruited from the nobility.

The divisions and contrasts within the First Estate or the clergy were almost as marked as those within the Third. At the top was the hierarchy of archbishops, bishops, and heads of monastic houses, almost all of whom had noble origins. The cathedral clergy and priests charged with administrative responsibilities were between the top hierarchy and the rest of the clergy, who were about equally divided between monks and friars of religious orders and parish priests. The church was wealthy. It was the largest landed proprietor in France and derived large revenues from tithes, endowments, and gifts. The hierarchy and administrative clergy lived in opulence, and most monasteries were not characterized by sackcloth and ashes. Yet many of the parish clergy lived in extreme and parasitical poverty. The tithes intended for their support were siphoned off to the greater clergy, so that they were forced to wring from the peasantry every fee they could. The parish priest's discontent found an outlet in demands for a more democratic structure of church government. If voting in the Estates-General were by head, a fair proportion of the representatives of the clergy could be expected to align themselves with the Third Estate against the nobility and their own ecclesiastical overlords.

THE ESTATES-GENERAL

Besides doubling the representation of the Third Estate, Necker introduced other far-reaching innovations in the instructions attached to the summons to the Estates. Each estate was to elect its deputies. In the past those sitting in the Estates-General held their seats by personal right, appointment, or right of office. Although Necker's order was hedged with procedures for the indirect election of deputies from the Third Estate by electors chosen by the voters, it was tantamount to universal manhood suffrage. Each of the forty thousand local meetings convened to choose electors was also instructed to draw up a *cahier* or list of grievances, to be incorporated into a general cahier for the district, which would serve as instructions for the district's delegates to the Estates-General. The cahiers touched on all matters of concern, local and national, and though respectful in tone, were a terrible indictment of the France of that day.

In the elections in the early spring of 1789, 300 clerical deputies, mostly from the lower clergy, were returned to the First Estate; 300 noble deputies, primarily country rather than court nobles, were returned to the Second Estate; and 648 commoner deputies, most of whom were bourgeois and over half of whom were lawyers, with only a handful of peasants and workers, were returned to the Third Estate.

The Estates-General convened at Versailles on May 4, 1789. The representatives of the Third Estate insisted that the three estates meet as a single body and that the representatives vote as individuals, a procedure that would assure the Third Estate's dominance, since with its doubled membership and the support of some clergy in the Second Estate it could outvote the rest of the Second and the First Estates. When the government refused to accede to this demand a deadlock ensued that lasted for six weeks. Finally, on June 17 the Third Estate, joined by a few supporters from the clergy, declared itself a National Assembly and the only true representative of the nation. This was revolution. Three days later a gathering of the self-styled National Assembly found the doors of their

Oath of the Tennis Court (June 20, 1789), by Jacques Louis David

> *"The National Assembly, considering that it has been summoned to establish the
> constitution of the kingdom, to effect the regeneration of public order, and to
> maintain the true principles of monarchy . . . decrees that all members of this
> Assembly shall immediately take a solemn oath not to separate, and to reassemble
> wherever circumstances require, until the constitution of the kingdom is
> established and consolidated upon firm foundations; and that, the said oath
> taken, all members and each one of them individually shall ratify this steadfast
> resolution by signature."* Reprinted in J. H. Stewart, A DOCUMENTARY SURVEY
> OF THE FRENCH REVOLUTION (New York, 1951).

chamber locked. Unaware that this was merely to allow for the preparations for a joint session at which the king was to speak, and angry at
what appeared to be a lock-out, the deputies withdrew to a large indoor
tennis court nearby and solemnly swore not to disband until they had
drawn up a constitution limiting the powers of monarchy.

The Tennis Court Oath cemented an alliance between the king and
the nobility that had begun to form earlier in the face of the demands
of the Third Estate. At the royal session on June 23 the king's long-
awaited plan for reform proved to be a capitulation to the demands of
the nobility. Louis directed the estates to meet separately. Two days later
170 of the clerical deputies and 50 of the nobles joined the meeting of

the Third Estate to show their opposition to the king's order, and on June 27 Louis revoked his order and directed the estates to meet together and vote by head. At the same time, influenced by the most reactionary of the court nobility, Louis called 18,000 troops to Versailles to "maintain order." On July 11 he dismissed Necker, who had been hailed by the Third Estate and its allies when the three estates had met together for the first time on June 30.

EMERGENCE OF THE PARIS MOB

The monarch's and nobility's fear of popular support for the Third Estate was manifest in the dispatch of troops to Versailles. They would have proved more useful in Paris. A worsening economic situation had coincided with the political upheavals of the past two years. The decline of the French economy since 1778 was quickened by a commercial treaty with Britain in 1786 that flooded the French market with cheaper British wares and caused a business recession and unemployment. A bad harvest in 1788 brought a sharp increase in the price of food in the early spring of 1789. The sufferings of the urban workers, the smaller craftsmen, and the small peasants who could not profit by the scarcity, burst out in bread and grain riots in the spring and early summer. In July, 1789, the price of bread was higher than at any time in the previous three-quarters of a century. Hunger and unemployment stood behind the emergence of the Paris mob.

The emergence of the Paris mob was the first manifestation of political violence in the Revolution and an event of enormous consequences. Workers and craftsmen, aroused by agitators and alarmed by the concentration of troops at Versailles, ransacked public buildings and arsenals in search of weapons to arm themselves. On July 14 they attempted to storm the Bastille, an old fortress used as a prison and supposed to be filled with political prisoners. The small contingent of guards fired into the mob, killing nearly a hundred. After a promise of safe-conduct had brought out the guards, they were slaughtered by the frenzied crowd and the cells were thrown open to disgorge a total of seven prisoners — four counterfeiters, two lunatics, and a dissipated young noble. The mob began to tear down the Bastille but, finding the task wearisome, moved toward the city hall with the head of the Bastille's governor on a pike. Another mob at the city hall was already in action, and the head of the chief of city administration was soon hoisted aloft on another pike. In the next few days slaughter was random, and the bourgeois leaders of Paris, thoroughly frightened, appointed as mayor Jean Sylvain Bailly, astronomer and prominent deputy to the Third Estate, and established a National Guard to protect life and property under the command of the Marquis de Lafayette.

With Paris lost and a mob on the rampage, Louis tried to placate the

THE SOCIAL ORIGINS OF THE ÉMIGRÉS*

Social class	Total — 97,545
Clergy	24,596
Nobility	16,431
Upper middle class	10,792
Lower middle class	6,012
Working class	13,953
Peasants	18,910
No class given	6,851

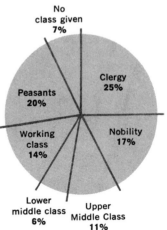

*78% of the total number of émigrés are included here; the social status of the remaining 22% is not known.

Source: D. Greer, "The Incidence of the Emigration during the French Revolution" (Cambridge: Harvard Univ. Press, 1951), pp. 64, 127.

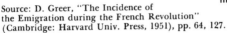

people by sending the troops away from Versailles, recalling Necker, and accepting the new city government of Paris. On July 17 Louis XVI, king of France, went to the city hall of Paris to receive from Bailly a blue, white, and red cockade, the revolutionary emblem: blue and red for the city of Paris, significantly surrounding white, the color of the house of Bourbon.

THE GREAT FEAR

In the countryside wild rumors of brigands in the pay of nobles who looted and burned the homes and fields of honest folk roused the peasantry into an outburst of collective mania known as the Great Fear. The rumors were groundless, and peasants found no brigands, yet in their inflamed mood they decided to move against their old oppressors, the lords. The Great Fear became a general, nationwide, agrarian insurrection, and the peasants swarmed into manor houses and demanded the destruction of records listing the obligations they owed the lords. Some of the noblemen and their agents who resisted were murdered and their houses burned.

The deputies to the National Assembly were now as fearful of insurrection as the king himself and realized that only swift capitulation could pacify the peasantry. At a dramatic night session on August 4, 1789, the assembly ordered the abolition of all feudal dues and privileges, ended tithes, and emancipated France's serfs. That same night the assembly approved the principle of equal taxation for all classes, ordered the end of the sale of public offices, and decreed that every citizen was eligible for any civil, military, or church office.

THE RIGHTS OF MAN AND THE RELUCTANT KING

The assembly then turned its attention to drafting a constitution. As a prelude, the assembly on August 26, 1789, issued a Declaration of the Rights of Man and Citizen. This great document owed its tone and content to the ideas of the Enlightenment and to the American Declaration of Independence and the Virginia Bill of Rights of 1776. It asserted as its first principle that all men were born and should remain free and equal in rights. Guaranteeing freedom of speech, press, and worship, and freedom from arbitrary arrest and punishment, it declared that the only sovereign was the nation itself. Posted all over France, it was quickly translated and broadcast throughout Europe to help spark the aspiration for liberty and equality everywhere.

The king withheld approval of the decrees of August 4 and the Declaration of the Rights of Man. He also refused to accept the proposed articles for the new constitution that provided for a unicameral legislature and limitation of his power to veto assembly legislation. His recalcitrance fed the suspicion that he planned to use force to overthrow the revolution, and suspicion turned to certainty when his brother, the Count of Artois, and other court aristocrats left France. These émigrés, the first of thousands to flee France, sought to stir up the other governments of Europe against the Revolution.

Despite Bailly's and Lafayette's efforts to control the Paris mob, it was being skillfully incited by golden-voiced agitators. Stirred by the threat of counterrevolution and driven by hunger, the Paris populace's radical elements were easy prey to the call for direct action. It came on October 5, 1789, when a mob of market women, housewives, and the ever-present agitators walked to Versailles — the "March of the Women" — followed by a contingent of the bourgeois National Guard. The women went first to the National Assembly, where they demanded that the price of bread be lowered, then forced their way into the king's residence and surrounded Louis. To restore order, Louis agreed to go to Paris with his family to live. The victorious women marched back to the city with the royal carriage in their midst, bearing Louis, Marie Antoinette, and their son, or as the women called them, "the baker, the baker's wife, and the baker's little boy." The royal family never saw Versailles again. They were prisoners of the people of Paris and pawns to the fortunes of the Revolution. A few weeks later the assembly moved to Paris, exposing itself to popular and radical pressures, for its galleries were filled daily with raucous crowds whose applause or hisses influenced the deputies.

Conservative deputies, fearing that the assembly would give in completely to the pressures, began to drop out; some emigrated.

THE CONSTITUENT ASSEMBLY

The National Assembly, now called the Constituent Assembly because it was preparing a constitution, promulgated a series of sweeping reforms that revealed the bourgeois concerns of the deputies. It preserved the hereditary monarchy but sharply curtailed the powers of the king. In the interest of more efficient administration it scrapped the old administrative divisions and divided the country into eighty-three departments, each subdivided into districts, cantons, and communes, with all local offices elective. The right to pass laws, levy taxes, override the king's veto, and control government expenditures was to be exercised by a unicameral legislature called the Legislative Assembly, comprised of elected deputies. Despite the guarantees of the Declaration of the Rights of Man and Citizen, suffrage was limited to so-called active citizens — men who paid a certain minimum in taxes. Moreover, the active citizens voted only for electors, who then chose the deputies to the Legislative Assembly as well as local officials. The tax qualification for an elector was so high that in all France only fifty thousand men could qualify. Some nobles and a few wealthy peasants were in the high tax bracket, but most of the fifty thousand were members of the bourgeoisie. In the *ancien régime* political power had followed ancestry; now it followed wealth.

The Constituent Assembly's solution for the state's financial problem was a simple and thoroughgoing attack on the old order. In November, 1789, the Constituent Assembly confiscated all church property and the estates of the nobles who had fled France. It then paid off the government's creditors, most of whom were bourgeois financiers, with special financial notes called *assignats*. These notes could be used to buy the confiscated lands, which were sold to the highest bidder. In this way much of this property went into the hands of the bourgeoisie, who either kept it or sold it at a profit to speculators or to peasants.

The bourgeoisie adhered to the physiocratic tradition of opposing restrictions on trade and industry and favoring free enterprise. The Constituent Assembly abolished the craft corporations on the ground that they were monopolies, and it threw open all trades and businesses to everyone. Characteristically the Constituent Assembly also outlawed *compagnonnages,* the clandestine trade unions organized by workers long before the Revolution, and decreed that wages should be determined individually between each worker and his employer.

THE CIVIL CONSTITUTION OF THE CLERGY

The confiscation of church property and the abolition of tithes deprived the clergy of its means of support. To maintain the clergy and ensure the church's complete subordination to the state, the Constituent Assembly promulgated the Civil Constitution of the Clergy in July, 1790. Bishops and priests were to be chosen by the same electors who chose the delegates to the Legislative Assembly and the local officials, and they were to be paid by the state. Archbishoprics were abolished, and the number of bishoprics was reduced from 130 to 83 — one for each department. When the constitution was submitted to Pope Pius VI for his approval, he not only rejected it but denounced all the works of the assembly, including the Declaration of the Rights of Man and Citizen. The assembly countered by ordering all French clergymen to swear allegiance to the Civil Constitution of the Clergy. Half refused. Called nonjuring or refractory priests, they condemned the constitutional clergy (those who swore allegiance) for being disloyal to the Roman Catholic Church, and they became bitter foes of the Revolution. Since they were numerous and popular, especially with the peasants, the government had no choice but to tolerate them. They remained islands of reaction and potential leaders of counterrevolution.

THE CONSTITUTIONAL MONARCHY, 1791–1792

The Constituent Assembly incorporated the reforms in a national constitution proclaimed in September, 1791. It then disbanded, having in little more than two years transformed France into a limited monarchy, swept away the remnants of feudalism, instituted equality before the law, reorganized the national and local administrations, established free enterprise, and made the clergy officials of the state. Satisfied that the Revolution was over, the deputies did not suspect that the regime they had fashioned would last barely ten months — and that the Revolution had only begun.

The first blow to the durability of the new regime came even before the promulgation of the constitution. Louis XVI, dismayed at the course of events and strongly influenced by Marie Antoinette, decided to flee France and appeal to his fellow monarchs for help. On the night of June 20, 1791, the disguised royal family bundled into a coach with a few servants and headed for the eastern frontier. Recognized when the coach stopped next morning to change horses, Louis was arrested at the village of Varennes and taken back with his family to Paris. The "Flight to Varennes" and a note denouncing the Revolution, which Louis had left behind when he fled, made it clear that he had joined the counterrevolutionaries. Obviously a constitutional monarchy headed by a king opposed to its principles had slight chance of success, and radicals demanded the establishment of a republic. The majority, however, still wanted a king, and after making a show of penitence, Louis was reinstated. The institution of monarchy had been badly shaken.

EXTERNAL REACTION

Another blow came from outside France. Absolutist monarchs elsewhere recognized that the doctrines of the French Revolution endangered their own regimes. The Declaration of the Rights of Man and Citizen had spread its message. Unrest and demands for reform by bourgeoisie and peasants appeared in Germany, Italy, the United Netherlands, and Britain. French aristocratic émigrés pressed unceasingly for war against the Revolution. Reluctant to start such a conflict, the monarchs nevertheless felt that something had to be done. In August, 1791, Leopold II of Austria, uncle of Marie Antoinette, and Frederick William II of Prussia met at Pillnitz in Saxony and issued a joint declaration pledging the use of force to help Louis restore absolutism and order in France if the other major powers would join them. Leopold knew that Pitt, the British prime minister, opposed intervention because war would make it impossible to carry through his domestic program. The Declaration of Pillnitz, therefore, was an empty gesture. It had an enormous impact in France, however, for it seemed to prove that Louis was in league with foreign monarchs and émigrés to overthrow the Revolution.

Pillnitz widened the gap between those who favored the constitutional monarchy and the more extreme revolutionaries. The division was apparent in the personnel of the new Legislative Assembly that met in October, 1791 — the Constituent Assembly had by its own decree excluded its members from standing for election to the Legislative Assembly. Of the new assembly's 745 members, 264 supported the constitutional monarchy and 136 opposed it; the remainder were uncommitted. In the Legislative Assembly's sessions the supporters of the monarchy chose to sit on the speaker's right, the radicals on his left, and the uncommitted between the two extremes. This was the origin of the expressions Right, Left, and Center that are part of our modern vocabulary of political reference.

THE CLUBS

Outside the Legislative Assembly the delegates grouped themselves into political clubs. The club called Friends of the Constitution (later changed to Friends of Equality and Liberty), and popularly known as the Jacobin Club because it met in a former Jacobin (Dominican) monastery, emerged as the most important of these organizations. Originally including many moderates, the Jacobin Club soon fell under the control of the radicals and with the resignation of the moderates it became the chief leftist organization. Despite its radicalism, the club's members were from the middle class, and some were from the upper bourgeoisie. Affiliated Jacobin clubs formed all over France, with the Paris club as their central chapter. In the assembly itself the Left was dominated by a faction of the Jacobin Club called the Girondists, so called because its leaders represented the department of the Gironde around Bordeaux.

Continuing economic difficulties and ceaseless agitation against the Revolution by both nonjuring priests inside France and émigrés outside France played into the hands of the extremists. Convinced that the Revolution would not be safe until its ideas had triumphed in other lands, they urged an international revolution led by the French that would overthrow kings and set up republics. Their desire for war was supported by conservatives who hoped that a military effort would unite the country behind the king and the constitutional monarchy. The war party's arguments were given point by the formation of an alliance between Austria and Prussia, which included proposed annexations of French territory. The accession of Francis II to the Austrian throne in 1792 helped to strengthen the fear of enemy invasion, for Francis was known to be much more conservative than his father, Leopold II. On April 20, 1792, the Legislative Assembly declared war on Austria, with whom Prussia and Sardinia soon allied themselves.

WAR AND THE END OF THE MONARCHY

The French army was poorly trained and equipped and lacked experienced leaders because so many of its officers had become émigrés. It suffered a string of reverses, and within weeks enemy troops led by the duke of Brunswick were on French soil. There was turmoil in Paris. On June 20 a mob poured into the palace of the Tuileries, where the king now lived, mocked him, and made him put on the red liberty cap that had become the symbol of the Revolution. When the duke of Brunswick learned of the insult he issued a manifesto on July 25 threatening to level Paris if the royal family was molested and inviting all Frenchmen to unite with him against the Revolution. The manifesto served only to raise patriotic fervor to fever pitch. Bands of volunteers streamed into Paris on their way to the front, and among them was a contingent from Marseilles singing a stirring march, since become the national anthem of republican France, the "Marseillaise." Its words caught the spirit of the moment:

> Arise ye children of the Fatherland,
> The day of glory has arrived . . .

The Brunswick Manifesto went far toward sealing the fate of the constitution and its monarch. It gave the radicals a lever of public opinion to topple the constitution. The Paris mob had been relatively restrained since July of the previous year, when Bailly, Lafayette, and the National Guard had repressed with gunfire a mass demonstration against the monarchy at the Champs de Mars. Now the mob was brought into action again by the extremists. The enemy's close approach to Paris provided an opportunity for Georges Jacques Danton and other Jacobin extremists to rise in revolt against the government. Provincial troops on their way to the front and Parisians stormed the Tuileries and butchered the king's guard.

Louis and the royal family had already fled to the Legislative Assembly for protection. They found none. The assembly, cowed by the rising of which they were as much the intended victims as the king, deposed Louis XVI, imprisoned him and his family, and ordered the election of a National Convention by universal male suffrage to draw up a new constitution. The events of August 10 and the continued advance of the enemy gave an excuse for the mob to vent its hatred in an orgy of bloodshed. Declaring that the enemy within must be destroyed before the invader could be repulsed, mobs stormed the jails in early September and murdered over a thousand prisoners, both men and women, whom they claimed were counterrevolutionaries. With these September Massacres as a backdrop, the hastily elected National Convention held its first session on September 20, 1792. On that same day French troops at Valmy halted the enemy advance. On September 21 the convention abolished monarchy, and the next day it proclaimed the Republic.

THE REPUBLIC OF VIRTUE, 1792–1794

Republics were a rarity in absolutist Europe. There were only Genoa, Venice, the Dutch Republic, and the Swiss Confederation. Of these four, Genoa and Venice had long since decayed, the Dutch Republic was in decline with its Orange stadholder well on the way to monarchy, and the Swiss Confederation was stagnant, with its young men still entering foreign service as mercenary soldiers (the guards butchered by the mob at the Tuileries on August 20 were Swiss). One republic of ex-Europeans in North America was just beginning to perfect a "more perfect union." The very word republican reeked of radicalism. With the greatest state of Europe now a republic and breathing a revolution of liberty and equality, Europe seemed to be standing on a precipice. France, in fact, was, for the most terrible days of revolution stretched just ahead.

Although the majority of the delegates to the convention were moderates, its leaders, among whom Danton was the most prominent, were all Jacobins. The Jacobins were now badly divided. The violence of the events of August and September had repelled the Girondists, who stood for a moderate bourgeois republic and opposed domination by Paris and the mob, and who comprised the Right in the convention. The radical Jacobins were the Left. They sat in the highest seats in the amphitheater in which the Convention met and were aptly named the Mountain.

"CITIZEN CAPET"

The Girondists and the Mountain split irrevocably on the king's fate. Both agreed to his treason, but the Girondists desired to delay his trial by the convention. Outvoted, they sought clemency for him, recognizing that his execution would have unfavorable repercussions abroad, but the

Mountain demanded his death. After long debate the Mountain won by a small majority, and on January 21, 1793, "Citizen Louis Capet," as Louis XVI was now called, went to his death under the guillotine.

Prior to Louis's execution French armies had occupied Belgium, the Rhineland, and Savoy. Flushed with triumph, the convention announced to the world in November, 1792, that the French Republic would come to the aid of people everywhere who wished "to recover their liberty." European powers that had until then remained neutral laid plans for action. The convention anticipated them by declaring war on England and Holland in February, 1793. A month later Spain joined the anti-French alliance. This was the first of many coalitions against France. It put almost all of Europe at war with her. The military pressure was enormous, but luckily for France the allies were suspicious of one another, and the attention of the Austrian and Prussian governments was diverted by their anxiety over getting as much as possible in the last partition of Poland.

Internal troubles added to the problems France faced. The execution of the king and military recruiting stirred up rebellion among the devoutly Catholic and royalist peasants of the Vendée in western France. Prices continued to rise as a result of serious food shortages. A group of extreme radicals, called the *Enragés,* agitated for price controls and rationing. In the convention the chasm widened between the Girondists and the Mountain. In May, 1793, the Paris mob once again seized the initiative on behalf of the most radical faction. It invaded the convention and demanded the expulsion of the leading Girondists. Those not arrested fled into hiding.

ROBESPIERRE AND THE TERROR

The Mountain was supreme. As its first move it drafted a new constitution that among other democratic features included an end to property qualifications for the suffrage. The constitution never went into effect. The military and domestic troubles that had brought the country to the edge of collapse gave the Mountain an excuse for dictatorship, and the Convention declared that the government would be "revolutionary until the peace." It established an emergency government with almost unlimited powers to direct the nation until the dangers were overcome; only then would the new constitution be implemented. A Committee of Public Safety, composed of nine (later twelve) deputies chosen by the convention, became the supreme administrative and policy-making authority. The convention itself became a rubber stamp. Maximilien Robespierre (1758–1794), provincial lawyer from Arras, disciple of Rousseau, incorruptible champion of democracy, idealist, and fanatic, emerged as the dominant member of the committee. A Committee of General Security, named by the Committee of Public Safety, held supreme police power,

··

THE SOCIAL ORIGINS OF
THE VICTIMS OF THE TERROR*

Social class	Total — 14,080
Clergy	980
Nobility	1158
Upper middle class	1964
Lower middle class	1488
Working class	4389
Peasants	3961
No class given	200

*This includes most of the victims condemned to death by the courts of the Terror; many thousands more were killed without trial or died in prison.

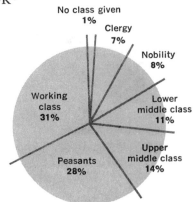

Source: D. Greer, "The Incidence of the Terror" (Cambridge: Harvard Univ. Press), pp. 137, 163; table VI.

··

and a Revolutionary Tribunal tried counterrevolutionaries with utter disdain for legal niceties.

This was the machinery of government that in September, 1793, instituted the Terror. In the name of saving the Revolution from its internal enemies hundreds of thousands were at one time or another imprisoned, and some twenty to forty thousand heads rolled. More than two-thirds of those executed were peasants, workers, and small craftsmen. Although legend has it that those who suffered most were from the First and Second Estates, only 8 per cent of the victims were noblemen and only 7 per cent were clergy. The dead included all sorts and conditions of men, from dissipated young noblemen and obscure peasants and artisans to the brilliant chemist Lavoisier, whose epitaph, spoken by his friend and fellow scientist Joseph Lagrange, can stand for all those of talent who died in the Terror: "It required but a moment for this head to fall and a hundred years perhaps will not suffice to produce the like." The dead ranged over the entire political spectrum, from Marie Antoinette through the Girondists to the *Enragés* on the left. The vivacious Madame Roland, in whose *salon* the Girondists had congregated, spoke history's judgment of the Terror a moment before she died: "O Liberty, what crimes are committed in your name!"

The Committee of Public Safety well recognized that the real threat to the Revolution came less from the poor wretches on their last ride to the guillotine than from the armies massing on France's borders. Under universal conscription, the *levée en masse*, almost all able-bodied, unmarried men between eighteen and twenty-five were mobilized, and by the spring of 1794 France's army stood at 800,000, the greatest in Europe's history. Mobilization of the entire French economy for war was another innovation. Some economic controls, such as ceilings on prices and wages, rationing, and prohibitions against hoarding, proved difficult to enforce. The overall effort, however, was highly successful. By October, 1793, the armies of the First Coalition had been repulsed, and French troops reached what Danton referred to as the "natural frontiers" of France — the Rhine, the Alps, the Pyrenees, and the Atlantic. The army of the Revolution had accomplished what Louis XIV could not accomplish. The newly won territories were either incorporated into France or turned into satellite states.

VIRTUE TRIUMPHANT

With its domestic enemies disappearing under the scourge of the Terror and its foreign enemies in retreat, the revolutionary government sought to reshape France's institutions and the tenor of French life. With the zest of the pure and righteous who have struck down privilege the radicals established a "Republic of Virtue." Christianity was equated with counterrevolution, and a program of de-Christianization raised the "Cult of Reason" in its place. Several thousand churches became "Temples of Reason"; the Virgin and other saints gave way before such "Revolutionary saints" as Rousseau and Voltaire. As a shrewd politician, Robespierre recognized that the Cult of Reason would alienate many from the Republic, but as a deist he believed that the "Supreme Being" had led France into becoming the Republic of Virtue and that credit should be given where it was due. Therefore in June, 1794, he introduced the "Worship of the Supreme Being" at a formal pageant, a parody of the Catholic liturgy done in utter seriousness.

A new calendar was introduced that did away with Sunday and all Church holidays, destroying the old Christian associations for calculation of time, and reduced the number of holidays — hard work became an attribute of patriotic virtue. September 22, 1792, the day on which the Republic had been proclaimed, was designated as the beginning of Year I. The year was divided into twelve months of thirty days each, and the months were named after the appropriate seasonal characteristics: for example, the autumn months were *Vendémiaire,* grape harvest; *Brumaire,* misty; and *Frimaire,* frosty. Each month comprised three periods of ten days, the tenth day being given to rest. The five or six days remaining at the end of the year to adjust the new calendar to the solar year were made national holidays to celebrate the Revolution. The new calendar lasted until 1806, when Napoleon abandoned it, to no one's regret.

Prisoners Arriving at Jail during the Reign of Terror, by Polignac

"It has been said that terror is the means by which a despotic government rules. . . . When despots rule because their subjects are terrified, the despots are justified — as despots. You put down all the enemies of freedom by means of terror, and you are justified — as founders of the Republic. The government of the Revolution is the despotism of liberty against tyranny. Must might be used only in order to protect crime?" Robespierre justifies the Terror in a speech of February 5, 1794, reprinted in SPEECHES OF MAXIMILIEN ROBESPIERRE (New York, 1927).

Virtue had no place for inequality or any remnant of the ancien régime. *Monsieur* and *Madame,* the old forms of address, were replaced by *Citoyen* and *Citoyenne* (citizen). The knee breeches (*culottes*) of pre-Revolutionary fashion disappeared, and good Republicans wore the trousers of the Parisian working class, the *sansculottes* (without breeches). Republican Rome was taken as a model. Women wore loose robes, sandals, and flowing natural hair, rather than the wigs of the court ladies. Simple classical furniture replaced the studied ornateness of the style of Louis XVI. The theater and the press became instruments of republican propaganda. Even playing cards were purified of the base remnants of monarchy: the King, the Queen, and the Jack of Spades went the way of Louis XVI, Marie Antoinette, and the counts of France. The new cards depicted soldiers, workers, La Belle Liberté, Rousseau, and figures of classical republican antiquity such as Brutus and Cato.

For all this excess, one lasting, substantial reform was undertaken. A commission under the scientist Joseph Lagrange fashioned the metric system of weights and measures, a rational and standardized decimal system. This improvement over chaotic local variations was adopted all over Europe and has survived to this day, with only the English-speaking peoples resisting its virtues.

VIRTUE DETHRONED

In his ruthless drive to save the Revolution as he conceived it, Robespierre antagonized and alienated the extreme radicals of Paris, called Hébertists. He ended their control of the Paris city government and then guillotined Jacques Hébert, their leader, and others. A few days later he turned on Danton and his followers, accused them of treason because they favored relaxing the Terror, and had them guillotined. Robespierre's own colleagues on the Committee of Public Safety suspected that they might be next. Continued French military success undermined whatever necessity might have justified the Terror. The fears of those who suspected that they would soon become Robespierre's victims seemed confirmed by a speech he made to the convention denouncing the delegates who opposed him. The next day, 9 Thermidor in the Republican calendar (July 27, 1794), these delegates rose to denounce Robespierre and stampeded their fellow members into ordering his arrest. The Paris city government, staffed by Robespierre's supporters, tried unsuccessfully to rouse the people of Paris on his behalf; it was the first time the Paris mob failed to respond to a radical call to arms. On July 28 the dictator, half-dead from a pistol wound in his jaw that may have been self-inflicted, was guillotined along with several scores of his followers. The Republic of Virtue died with them.

REACTION AND IRRESOLUTION, 1794–1799

THERMIDOREAN REACTION

The happenings of 9 Thermidor provoked an unexpected change in the attitude of the public — a change so pronounced that the period has become known as the Thermidorean Reaction. Public opinion, hitherto repressed by fear of the Revolutionary Tribunal, clearly favored a relaxation of tension. The end of the Republic of Virtue was greeted with enthusiasm. Amusements and luxuries that had been frowned upon as unrepublican and decadent reappeared overnight. Knee breeches came back into style, and women turned away from severe, classical fashions to revealing and luxurious dresses. Vulgar ostentation became the vogue. Gangs of young fops, *jeunesse dorée* (gilded youth), wandered the streets of Paris beating up *sansculottes*. In the provinces gangs of royalists call-ing themselves Companies of Jesus began their own "white terror" against the former Jacobin terrorists. Many Catholic churches reopened, and numerous nonjuring priests returned to Paris.

One-time firebrands in the convention hastened to abandon their revo-lutionary ardor. The powers of the Committee of Public Safety were cur-tailed. The Revolutionary Tribunal was restricted in its activities and, in 1795, abolished. The Jacobins were completely discredited, their pro-vincial branches died out, and in November, 1794, the headquarters in Paris was closed. Jacobins who had played leading roles in the Terror were punished, and many of those whom they had imprisoned were released. Thousands of émigrés returned home. The repeal of price con-trols and other economic regulations encouraged speculators and profi-teers. The resulting inflation hit the poor hard, and there were food riots and small insurrections. The lowly and the exploited, now lacking lead-ership, were easily repressed.

The demand for a return to normal conditions included a desire to end the war. Peace was made with Holland, where a satellite republic had been established after the French invasion. Peace was also made with Prussia, three small German states, and Spain. France won recognition of her conquest of the left bank of the Rhine and the Spanish part of the island of San Domingo in the West Indies. Austria, England, and Sardinia remained at war with the Republic.

THE CONSTITUTION OF THE YEAR III

Despite talk about a restoration of the monarchy, the bourgeoisie were determined to keep France under the rule of the middle class. Since they were in control of the convention their wishes prevailed in the new con-stitution, the Constitution of the Year III, which went into effect late in 1795. It was the third since 1791, supplanting the never-implemented constitution of 1793. Suffrage depended upon a property qualification, literacy, and having a trade or profession. The voters chose electors, who selected officials and members of the legislature. The property qualifica-tion for electors was so high that only about twenty thousand men were eligible in all France — less than the fifty thousand potential electors under the 1791 constitution establishing constitutional monarchy. The legislature consisted of a Council of Five Hundred that initiated legisla-tion and a Council of Elders, with 250 members, that approved or dis-approved the legislation proposed by the Council of Five Hundred. The Elders appointed an Executive Directory of five men from nominees sub-mitted by the Five Hundred, to serve for five years.

Conservative as these new arrangements were, they still offended right-ists and royalists. To prevent the Right from gaining control of the new government — which would have brought revenge down upon the heads of all who had voted for the death of Louis XVI — the bourgeois convention decreed that two-thirds of the members of the two new councils must be members of the outgoing convention. This brazen self-interest outraged the rightists of Paris, and on 13 Vendémiaire (October 5, 1795) thousands of them rose in insurrection. The government turned its defense over to Napoleon Bonaparte, a twenty-six-year-old brigadier general of artillery who chanced to be in Paris without a command. He ordered his cannon outside the Tuileries to fire point-blank into the advancing mob. That legendary "whiff of grapeshot" broke the insurgents' ranks, and they fled, leaving their dead and wounded in the streets.

THE DIRECTORY

The new regime, called the Directory, inherited massive problems, and the Directors were not equal to their task. Beset by internal disorder, enemies on both the right and the left, economic troubles, and the need to continue the war, the Directors failed to respond quickly and effectively to crisis. The Vendée revolt broke out again, and elsewhere bandits terrorized the countryside. The royalists were in touch with Louis XVI's brother, the count of Provence, whom they called Louis XVIII (Louis XVI's young son, the Dauphin, had died in prison). In 1795 he issued a declaration from his exile in Italy, announcing that when he regained the throne he would restore the ancien régime and punish those prominent in the Revolution. This threat shored up popular opinion behind the Directory and confirmed its resolve to prevent the reestablishment of the monarchy.

On the left, radical working-class leaders hatched secret plots to overthrow the regime. François Émile Babeuf, self-styled Gracchus in commemoration of the ancient Roman popular leaders of that name, formed the Society of Equals. Advocating the abolition of private property and parliamentary government and the introduction of a planned socialist economy, the society recruited about two thousand active members and nearly twenty thousand supporters. Babeuf, a journalist, and the other leaders were middle-class intellectuals, but their followers came mainly from the working class, especially poor craftsmen in Paris. In the spring of 1796 the Babeuvists plotted rebellion. Betrayed and captured, Babeuf was guillotined, the other leaders were executed or deported, and the movement collapsed. This minor, tragic episode has gained historical fame because Babeuf's doctrines foreshadowed some of the socialist programs of the nineteenth and twentieth centuries.

THE EMERGENCE OF BONAPARTE

In March, 1796, General Napoleon Bonaparte, savior of the Directory, was given command of the French army in Italy. He defeated the armies of Austria and Sardinia, set up the Cisalpine Republic in the valley of the Po and the Ligurian Republic in the old Republic of Genoa, making them French satellites, and pushed to within seventy-five miles of Vienna. The Austrians sued for peace, and in the Treaty of Campo Formio in October, 1797, they recognized the French annexation of Belgium, the left bank of the Rhine, and the Ionian Islands. As compensation, Austria was allowed to annex the Republic of Venice, thereby ending the thousand-year independence of that ancient state. Bonaparte was the talk of France.

Elections had been held in March, 1797, for the two councils, and the royalists had gained majorities. The dismayed republicans asked Bonaparte for help. On 18 Fructidor (September 4, 1797) the councils, protected by a military force commanded by an aide of Bonaparte, annulled most of the elections of the royalists. Having by this coup d'état forfeited its claim to be a constitutional government, the Directory henceforth clung to power only by such illegal acts as purges and quashed elections.

The conclusion of peace with Austria left Britain alone at war with France. General Bonaparte took command of an army supposed to invade England. He decided, instead, to strike at British economic supremacy by invading Egypt and thereby cutting off Britain's eastern and Mediterranean trade. He enjoyed some initial successes against the Turks who controlled Egypt, until a British fleet under Admiral Horatio Nelson defeated French naval forces in Abukir Bay at the mouth of the Nile in August, 1798, and isolated Bonaparte and his army in Egypt. It was Napoleon Bonaparte's first major defeat.

The fear of French expansion in the Mediterranean, awakened by Bonaparte's invasion of Egypt, persuaded England, Austria, Russia, Turkey, Naples, Portugal, and the papacy to form the Second Coalition against France early in 1799. Russian and Austrian troops commanded by Marshal Alexander Suvorov drove the French out of Italy. Other allied forces invaded Switzerland and the Netherlands. These military reverses bred still more discontent with the Directory. In 1799 the opposition made such great electoral gains that the Directory was afraid to invalidate them. Bonaparte, who was still in Egypt, saw these developments as an opportunity to win greater prominence for himself. Leaving his army to its fate, he managed to slip through the British fleet with a handful of men and returned to France, where he was greeted with great enthusiasm. He offered himself to those seeking to overthrow the Directory. On 18 Brumaire (November 9, 1799) the plotters moved. The next day troops invaded the meeting of the Council of Five Hundred and overthrew the Directory. A provisional government headed by three consuls took control, with Bonaparte as First Consul. The rebels carefully retained the republican form of government — but only the form. The coup d'état of 18 Brumaire in fact marked the end of the First French Republic.

THE IMPACT OF THE FRENCH REVOLUTION

In the context of Western history, the French Revolution emerges as part of a democratic surge felt throughout much of the Western world in the last four decades of the eighteenth century. Although the French Revolution was the most spectacular manifestation of the surge, demands for the abolition of special privilege and for political equality were not unique to France. They had been voiced by people of other nations well before 1789, not least in the American colonies of Britain.

Nonetheless, the French Revolution accomplished the rapid spread of democratic ideas. Its doctrines were highly exportable, for they spelled out the rights of man everywhere. The news of the great happenings in Paris inspired democratic-minded men in other lands and converted the timid. The news of absolutism and privilege overthrown struck terror into the hearts of rulers and statesmen and moved them to adopt repressive measures against the threat of popular government.

THE BRITISH ISLES

In Britain the events of the French Revolution encouraged men of the lower-middle and working classes to form clubs and societies demanding the principles the French were preaching. Many of these organizations entered into correspondence with members of the National Assembly in France and with various Jacobin clubs. The Revolution was hailed in artistic and literary circles, which thought the French had inaugurated a new age in which man was freed from the shackles of the past. Their reaction was summed up by the poet William Wordsworth, who many years later wrote:

> Bliss was it in that dawn to be alive,
> But to be young was very heaven!

Others, however, spoke out strongly against the Revolution. The greatest was Edmund Burke. His *Reflections on the Revolution in France* (1790) attacked the principles of the Revolution as abstract and dangerous, argued that a nation cannot break with its own traditions and character, and prophesied that the Revolution would lead not to the ideal society promised by its partisans but to violence and dictatorship. Many pamphlets appeared to rebut his arguments, the most successful being *The Rights of Man* by Thomas Paine, but events proved Burke's prediction correct.

The popularity of the Revolution — Paine's pamphlet sold tens of thousands of copies — alarmed many of the ruling class. Alarm turned into active repression when the French abolished the monarchy and offered aid to all people in the struggle against their rulers. Despite a trial of British radical leaders for treason and severe penalties handed out to them, the agitation and meetings continued. In 1795 and 1799 Prime Minister William Pitt put through Parliament stringent legislation making it treason to speak or write against the government and prohibiting large public meetings. In 1799 the Combination Acts forbade workmen to unite in clubs and societies for the purpose of improving their wages or working conditions; in short, labor unions were declared illegal. This wiped out centers of revolutionary propaganda and also provided employers with a powerful weapon against labor. Thus in Great Britain conservatism and reaction were strengthened for a time as a result of the French Revolution.

In Ireland young patriots, detesting Britain's rule, hailed the Revolution. In 1791 Wolfe Tone (1763–1798) organized the Society of the United Irishmen. It soon abandoned its original purpose, parliamentary reform, in favor of establishing an Irish republic. After the Franco-British war had begun in 1793, James Napper Tandy (1740–1803) and other United Irish leaders conspired with the French to send troops to free Ireland from English rule. The French invasion attempts were repelled, and a number of the Irish leaders were taken by the British. Tone committed suicide before execution, and his brethren were sentenced to be hanged, but with them had been born nineteenth-century Irish nationalism.

CONTINENTAL EUROPE

In Germany the events of 1789 elated many intellectuals, but they lost their enthusiasm after the September massacres and the execution of the king. German rulers met the threat of the Revolution by making their regimes more repressive in order to throttle at the outset any radical tendency. In Italy, intellectuals greeted the Revolution joyously, and revolutionary clubs were organized. Bonaparte's conquests in northern Italy and the establishment of the Cisalpine and Ligurian Republics caught the imagination of the people, and Italians began to dream of a free, united Italy.

In the Austrian Netherlands (Belgium) a group of liberal bourgeois intellectuals called Vonckists (after their leader J. F. Vonck) had cooperated with conservative groups in the rising against the reforms of Emperor Joseph II, only to be turned on by their conservative allies when they proposed moderate liberal reforms to broaden representation in the estates. Priests assailed the Vonckists as disciples of Voltaire, and there was a mass rising against them. Hundreds fled for their lives to France. Later, when they were able to return home, they agitated for a republic on the French model. The Belgian masses under reactionary clerical leadership opposed these revolutionary ideas, and in 1795 after the French had annexed Belgium and introduced republican reforms, there were popular risings and unrest, which were as much nationalist as antire-publican.

Following the abortive rising of the Patriots in the United Nether-lands, suppressed in 1787 (see p. 371), some of the leaders took refuge in France. They were enthusiastic supporters of the Revolution, and when France declared war on the United Netherlands in 1793, two thousand Patriots entered the French forces to serve in the Netherlands. With the French conquest northward these refugees came into their own. Under the French aegis and with the support of resident Dutchmen who had already embraced the Revolution's tenets in their societies and literary clubs, they established the Batavian Republic (Batavia was the Roman name for the Netherlands). Its constitution and laws were modeled on the French, and the Batavian Republic was a satellite of France. In 1798 a radical minority staged a coup d'état with the help of the French troops stationed there and established a unitary state by abolishing the old provincial sovereignty. Within five months the regime met its Thermi-dorean Reaction and was replaced by a more moderate government.

The return home of the exiled Dutch Patriots in French uniforms to fashion a satellite state for France bore witness to how deeply the ideas of the French Revolution had affected some men. Imbued with fervor for the rights of man, they were prepared to serve a traditional enemy and subject themselves and their nation to foreign domination. When Napoleon Bonaparte in his limitless ambition embarked on a Europe-wide conquest, one of his most potent allies was this fervor. Coming as a liberator and the instrument of the rights of man, Bonaparte had already half-defeated his opponents. The irony was that the very nationalism that had summoned Frenchmen to save the fatherland when "the day of glory had arrived" would manifest itself among France's satellites to help en-sure Bonaparte's ultimate defeat.

THE NAPOLEONIC ERA
CHAPTER TWENTY

NAPOLEON BONAPARTE

First Consul Napoleon Bonaparte, despite his short stature, was striking in physical appearance, with a large head, swarthy complexion,
sharply cut features, and brilliant steel-blue eyes. Born in 1769 on the
island of Corsica (annexed to France from Genoa the year before his
birth), he was the second of five surviving sons of a noble but impoverished family of Italian origin. At the age of ten Buonaparte — as he
spelled his surname before frenchifying it in 1796 — entered a French
provincial military school as a scholarship student. Discipline was lax, the
studies were general and pointless, and the lad applied himself with zeal
only to mathematics and Roman history. In 1784 he was accepted at the
military academy in Paris, where he began a year of hard, creditable
study in artillery, which won him a cadetship in the army in 1785 and a
commission the next year.

On frequent furloughs home between 1786 and 1793 Napoleon engaged
in the Corsican independence movement, in which his older brother
Joseph was prominent. An ardent Corsican patriot and avid reader of
Rousseau, young Napoleon resolved to free Corsica from "French
tyranny." The National Assembly's declaration of November 30, 1789,
extending to Corsica the rights and liberties of all Frenchmen and the
reforms of the Revolution, dampened his insular patriotism and caused
him to embrace the Revolution. He became increasingly republican, and
when in 1793 the ruling faction in Corsica repudiated the Revolution,
he and his family were forced to flee. Henceforth Napoleon Bonaparte's
fortunes were irrevocably linked to France — and shortly France's would
be linked to him.

THE MAN

The tendency in dealing with Napoleon is to paint him either in the
gigantic proportions of a superman or in the smudged lines of an enigma.
He was neither. Although he spent the last years of his life fashioning his

own legend, he could not cover the tracks he had left in his passage. Courage, resourcefulness, keenness, and decision — these soldierly qualities distinguished this superb leader of men who was an inspiring field commander, master tactician, and bold strategist. In later years, even in defeat, he never forfeited the admiration of his generals, the devotion of his staff, and the love of his soldiers. Personal magnetism marked his relations with almost all who came into contact with him. Whether charming and gay, angry, maniacal, or morose, he dominated everyone in his presence. An overbearing egotism was both a pose and the very substance of his being. He was capable of continuous, slavish toil on any task he set himself. Precision and orderliness, a passion for arrangement and symmetry, were dominant motifs in his chamber, his chancellery, and his camp. For a man so formidable and ambitious he was remarkably immune to rancor. For a man so devoted to his kinsmen, he was peculiarly lacking in sensitivity to suffering and in the capacity to love.

It is doubtful that Bonaparte possessed a shred of religious faith or ideology. He was a materialist, suspicious of the insubstantial, the ideal, the intangible. He had an unquenchable thirst for the factual and the knowable — for objective reality. Yet the visionary and subjective cast of his mind, distorting reality, was no less marked. That which distinguished him until near the end of his career was an intuitive capacity to reconcile objective reality and subjective vision and to wring advantage from both.

As a demagogue in an era sick of demagoguery, he was masterful. Egotism, magnetism, and the evocation of a vision planned down to the last objective detail constituted a formula for leadership so successful that he was never seriously threatened with the loss of French allegiance. Unlike other demagogues, Napoleon never deluded himself that his pronouncements represented the whole truth, but in his egotism he was unmoved by the prospect that the whole truth might catch up with him.

The most revealing personal quality of the man who would master Europe was devotion to his family. It moved him to almost boundless generosity in titles and wealth to his mother (his father died in 1785), four brothers, and three sisters. At its height about 1810 the Grand Empire of Napoleon was run like a family chain store enterprise: holding thrones in Napoleon's satellite states were Joseph (Spain), Louis (Holland), Jerome (Westphalia), Maria (Tuscany), and Caroline and her husband Marshal Murat (Naples). Only his brother Lucien, of whose marriage Napoleon did not approve, received no more than ambassadorships. He endowed his mother Letitia, called Madame Mother, with great wealth, much of which she thriftily hoarded, saying, "When it is all over, you will be glad of my savings." His uncle Joseph Fesch, who during the Revolution had temporarily given up his clerical calling for the more remunerative business of army contracts, became a cardinal and a chief religious figure of the empire.

Napoleon performed his first notable service to the Republic in 1793 as a captain of artillery. Royalists, aided by British and Spanish troops, had seized the major French naval base of Toulon on the Mediterranean, and the Republican army laid seige to it. Bonaparte used with deadly effect the concentrated artillery fire that he was to perfect as a prime tactic in his campaigns. He was in the van of the storming column that took the enemy's main position and forced the retreat of the British and Spaniards. Promoted to brigadier general by the Committee of Public Safety, he became chief of artillery in the Italian campaign launched in 1794. Robespierre's fall put him under suspicion, and he was arrested. He was soon released, but the Italian campaign had been shelved. In 1795, after refusing a command on grounds of ill health, he was struck from the list of general officers, and it seemed that his military career was finished.

Then came the opportunity offered by the Vendémiaire Royalist uprising in Paris in October, 1795, in which Napoleon dispersed the mob by firing a "whiff of grapeshot." A grateful Directory approved his new plan for the conquest of Italy in January, 1796, where he covered himself with glory. Next came his expedition to conquer Egypt, then his return to France where he participated in the coup d'état of 18 Brumaire (November 19, 1799) that overthrew the Directory and established the Consulate with Bonaparte as first consul.

DOMESTIC REFORMER

On December 15, 1799, the first consul, speaking for himself and his two fellow consuls, Abbé Sieyès and Roger Ducos, proclaimed the end of the French Revolution with the words, "Citizens, the Revolution is established upon the principles which began it. It is ended." Bonaparte did not propose to delude anyone when he said the Revolution was ended. It was. However, he intended to salvage from the Revolution substantial, material reforms, derived both from the Enlightenment's teachings and the Revolution's unfulfilled intentions.

The first task of the government was to draw up the Constitution of the Year VII (1799) — the fourth constitution in nine years. Drafted according to Bonaparte's wishes and heralded as based on the "true principles" of the Revolutionary past, the constitution established a thoroughgoing dictatorship in the guise of a democratic republic. It did not contain a declaration of the rights of citizens, nor did it guarantee freedom of speech and press. Bonaparte, as first consul, was made chief executive for ten years, aided by two other consuls and by a Council of State chosen by him. A bicameral legislature lacked any real power. All men over twenty-one could vote, but only for electors and by a procedure guaranteed to filter out the voters' will. In each commune the voters were to select one-tenth of their number as a communal list; members of all the communal lists in a department chose one-tenth of their number for a departmental list; those in the departmental lists then selected one-tenth of their number for the national list. The men in the national list, called the Notables of France, numbered about ten thousand — considerably fewer qualified electors than under the constitutions of 1791 (about fifty thousand) and 1793 (about twenty thousand). The members of the two legislative bodies, the chief judges, and the higher government officials were all selected from the Notables.

The new constitution was a mockery of both the democratic process and the principles of the Revolution. Yet when it was submitted to the people for their approval in December, 1799, 3,001,007 voted for it, and only 1,526 voted against it. Having voted away its freedom, France received for a time the most efficient, honest, and vigorous government in its history. Dominated by Bonaparte, who in the years of the Consulate was at the height of his creative powers, the new regime restored internal order and created or reshaped institutions that long survived Bonaparte's fall.

RELIGIOUS, FISCAL, AND ADMINISTRATIVE REFORMS

The most pressing need was to restore order. Within months Bonaparte suppressed the Royalist rebellion that had been raging in the Vendée since 1793, and wiped out the bands of brigands that had terrorized many parts of France. More significant, he ended the constant threat to internal order that the Catholic clergy's discontent with the Civil Constitution of the Clergy had posed. For this purpose, and also to obtain the papacy's good will preparatory to conquering Catholic states, he reached a settlement with Pope Pius VII on terms highly favorable to the French government. By the Concordat of 1801 the Pope agreed to give up all claims to Church property confiscated in the Revolution and to confirm French bishops nominated by Napoleon. The bishops were to name the lower clergy, subject to approval by the government; and the clergy, to be paid by the state, were to swear allegiance to the state. Bonaparte agreed to papal deposition of French bishops who fell under papal disapproval, reopening of the seminaries, and public Catholic worship, such as street processions. The Concordat of 1801 remained in force for over a century. If Pius VII had hoped that it would return France, "the eldest daughter of the Church," fully to the fold, he was soon disabused. Clerical privilege was not reestablished, and to show that Catholicism was not the only recognized religion in France, Bonaparte subsidized Protestant sects and in 1809 after conferences with Jewish leaders devised a scheme of local government for Jewish communities.

The Consulate remedied the state's financial feebleness, which had precipitated the Revolution and had continued during the 1790's. The Bank of France, established in 1800 for the purpose of lending money to the government, freed the state from reliance on private financiers and the necessity to float loans at extortionate interest rates. Bonaparte did what perhaps only the travail of the previous decade could have permitted anyone to do: he reorganized the entire fiscal structure. Tax collection was systematized and its efficiency increased enormously. Strict auditing of collectors' accounts reduced corruption and embezzlement. For the first time in over a century the French government rested on a sound financial base.

At the local administrative level elected officials were replaced by appointees of the central government, from prefects in charge of each department down to mayors and town councils. Thus Bonaparte completed the work of administrative centralization begun long before by Richelieu. Much of his system of local government still persists in France.

CODE NAPOLÉON

Bonaparte's most important domestic accomplishment was the codification of the law. Successive monarchs since the fifteenth century had talked of codification, and during the 1790's the revolutionary governments had taken the first steps in this direction. Although the actual codification was done by a committee of legal experts, Bonaparte took a deep personal interest in the work. Comprising five codes that were compact enough to fit in one volume, the *Code Napoléon* was a fusion and refinement of Roman law, the remnants of the numerous customary laws of France, and the legislation of the Revolution. The first of the five, the civil code, governed marital and familial relations and went into effect in March, 1804. It was followed by the code of civil procedure and the commercial code in 1807, the code of criminal procedure in 1808, and the penal code in 1810. The great merits of the Code Napoléon were its clarity, comprehensiveness (even though it lacked precision in detail), equitableness, and applicability to a bourgeois and secular social order. The code remains in force in France today, its original frame still discernible through the mass of subsequent additions and amendments that have enabled it to keep pace with industrialism and the modern state. Its merits were recognized elsewhere, and it was either adopted as, or greatly influenced, the codes of Belgium, Holland, Luxemburg, Italy, Spain, Portugal, Switzerland, Germany, Rumania, Egypt, a number of Latin American states, and Japan. It was deservedly the pride of Bonaparte among his domestic achievements.

EDUCATIONAL REFORM

Napoleon's reform of French education was a mixed blessing. Although it laid the foundation for a system of uniform excellence, it put French education in a straitjacket from which it is only now beginning to emerge. Successive revolutionary governments had planned a national educational system but had never implemented the plans. Bonaparte appropriated a large amount of money for public education,.and in 1802 he made provision for a network of primary and secondary schools and institutions of higher learning maintained at public expense. It was the first full-scale public school system in Europe. He left the primary and some secondary schools under local control, but placed other secondary schools, called *lycées*, and the higher institutions under the supervision of the central government. This centralizing tendency culminated in 1808 with the creation of the University of France, which was not a teaching institution but an administrative and supervisory organization for controlling all French educational institutions. It persists to this day.

Another creation of the First Consul that has survived is the Order of the Legion of Honor. All titles of nobility had been abolished in 1790, but Bonaparte recognized the deep appeal of special distinctions and honors. In 1802, over the strong protests of the legislature, who feared a restoration of special privileges, he established the Legion with himself as Supreme Commander. Persons who distinguished themselves in any field might be appointed to it. Initially limited to six thousand, within a few years its membership grew to over thirty thousand, and today its recipients are, indeed, legion.

The Legion of Honor represented one pole of the system of incentives that Napoleon introduced to replace the Republic's egalitarianism; merit brought its reward, and honors were generously showered upon the capable and the loyal. Demerit brought its deserts, too, and the other pole of Napoleonic incentives was represented by the efficient, inexorable, and harsh secret police headed by Joseph Fouché. Equality before the law meant equal application of censorship to the press, equal repression of dissent in speech, equal punishment for acts against the state, and equal surveillance by Fouché's agents. It was a society of equality, but it was not a free society.

EMPIRE BUILDER

Domestic achievement was not Napoleon· Bonaparte's commanding ambition. He had read too much Roman history — not of Republican but of Imperial Rome — at school and on lonely garrison duty as a young lieutenant; he had seen too much of the world at the head of columns of French Republican soldiers; he had tasted too often the sweetness of victory. In his passion for the concrete and the tangible he found gratification not only in reshaping France. He found it, too, in the shattering destruction of salvo after salvo of well-aimed cannonade, in marching long columns of disciplined troops to the farthest reaches of a continent, in redrawing the boundaries of states and modeling new nations as if the terrain of Europe were potter's clay.

THE FIRST STEPS

He began his quest for imperial glory with a brilliant maneuver. French reverses at the hands of the Second Coalition (Britain, Russia, Austria, and Turkey) had contributed to the destruction of the Directory. The First Consul bowed to France's desire for an end to the war, which had been going on since 1792. With a characteristic flourish on Christmas Day, 1799, he wrote a personal letter to the king of England and the emperor of Austria (Russia had quarreled with her allies and withdrawn from active participation in the war) indicating his desire for peace. He knew that neither power would accept his offer so long as France controlled Belgium and the Rhine and threatened Italy, but he convinced Frenchmen that he wanted to end the war and that the enemy was responsible for its continuation.

After the British and Austrians had reacted as he expected, Bonaparte led his troops into Italy through the St. Bernard Pass while it was still under snow and smashed the Austrian army at Marengo in June, 1800. His victory aroused tremendous enthusiasm in France and thwarted opponents there who had plotted a Bourbon restoration in the event of his defeat. In December the French invaded Austria, and Emperor Francis sued for peace. The Treaty of Lunéville in 1801 confirmed the provisions of Campo Formio (1797), and France regained the territories lost during the war with the Second Coalition.

With Austria retired, Bonaparte turned to Great Britain. Of all the powers, he most detested and most feared Britain. For a brief while he thought he could persuade Russia to join him against the hated island kingdom, for Tsar Paul had become violently anti-British. Paul's murder in March, 1801, the accession of Alexander I, who favored England, and the British ambassador's judicious bribing of Alexander's advisers, closed this avenue. A few months later the French army in Egypt surrendered to the British. The war was at a stalemate, with France dominant on the Continent and Britain in control of the seas. In March, 1802, the two powers signed the Peace of Amiens. It was highly favorable to France, for Britain recognized nearly all French conquests in Europe and overseas. In return Britain gained little, for Bonaparte refused to reopen to British trade continental countries controlled by France.

For the first and only time between 1792 and 1814 France was at peace with the other European powers. It was a brief interlude. The powers knew that Bonaparte would seek further conquests. Britain was especially apprehensive. French control of Belgium was "a pistol pointed at the heart of England." Bonaparte had never hidden his appetite for British territory in the Western Hemisphere, the Near East, and India. Deeply resentful of the exclusion of British commerce from French-controlled lands, British merchants feared that unless Bonaparte was checked, their trade losses would become still greater.

The disappointment of the British with the Treaty of Amiens contrasted with the joy with which the French greeted it. Peace had come at last, and with it victory. Bonaparte gave the French a chance to show their gratitude by arranging a plebiscite in May, 1802, to make him sole consul for life. The vote was 3,568,885 for him, 8,374 against him.

THE NEW CAESAR

The overwhelming vote of confidence told Bonaparte that he need stop at nothing. He made changes in the constitution to put almost all power in his hands. He assumed the trappings of royalty — using only his first name in official documents, holding court at the Tuileries, and minting coins with his portrait. France became an absolute monarchy in everything but name. A more dramatic stage set was required before he could declare himself emperor, and a royalist plot to assassinate him and restore the Bourbons supplied it. The conspirators implicated an unnamed member of the Bourbon family as the prime mover in the scheme. Napoleon's suspicions fell upon the youthful duke d'Enghien, a relative of the king, who had emigrated to Baden, close to the French border. In March, 1804, d'Enghien was kidnapped, brought to Paris, tried hastily by a military tribunal, and shot within four days of his arrest, although it was apparent at the trial that he was innocent.

The illegality and brutality of this incident awakened widespread revulsion, but it also made essential Bonaparte's survival and the continuation of his line if France was to be spared chaos. The simple — and popular — solution was the creation of a hereditary empire, so that if Napoleon was killed, his heir would be the recognized ruler. In May, 1804, the legislative bodies of the Consulate proclaimed Napoleon as hereditary emperor. Even then the fiction of a republic was preserved, for the Constitution of the Year XII commenced, "The government of the Republic is entrusted to an emperor, who takes the title Emperor of the French." Again Bonaparte asked the people to ratify his act; this time the vote was 3,572,329 in favor, and only 2,579 opposed.

Bonaparte turned to an ancient imperial tradition for his dramatic coronation on December 2, 1804. Pope Pius VII agreed to preside at the crowning of the new Charlemagne, whose dreams of ruling over the Latin and Teutonic peoples already had a semblance of reality. In the Cathedral of Notre Dame de Paris, amid imperial splendor, the pontiff raised an imperial crown, paused, and Bonaparte took it from his hands and crowned himself. The prearranged self-crowning went flawlessly, and the emperor of the French, though he might be said to rule under God, did not rule under God's vicar on earth. The pope's reward for his self-abnegation was France's abandonment of the Revolutionary calendar and return to the traditional one with its Sundays and religious holidays.

THE WAR OF THE THIRD COALITION

The Peace of Amiens of 1802 proved to be only a truce. Peaceful co-existence of Napoleonic France and the other powers was impossible, for the ambitions of Napoleon came into conflict everywhere with the interests of the other nations. In May, 1803, after little more than a year of peace, England declared war on France and its ally, Spain. In 1804 William Pitt became prime minister again after three years out of office. By offering large subsidies to powers that would join Britain, Pitt created another coalition in 1805, the third since 1792, comprising Britain, Austria, Russia, and Sweden. Spain, allied with France in the wars of the First and Second Coalitions, once more made common cause with the French.

In 1803 Napoleon assembled a large army on the French coast at Boulogne, ostensibly to invade England. For two years the expeditionary force waited for French naval mastery of the Channel so that it might cross. That mastery was never established. In 1805, as a result of Austria's and Russia's alliance with Britain, Napoleon suddenly marched the Boulogne army eastward to meet the Austrians. After a series of brilliant and lightning moves in Bavaria Napoleon encircled and shattered an Austrian army of eighty thousand at Ulm in October, 1805. The French captured nearly forty thousand prisoners, including eighteen generals, while French losses were insignificant. The Austrians fell back to join their Russian allies. In November Napoleon led his soldiers into Vienna and established headquarters in Schönbrunn, a palace of Emperor Francis.

In Vienna Napoleon learned that the day after his great victory at Ulm he had lost his last chance of wresting control of the seas from Britain. On October 21, 1805, the combined French-Spanish fleet under Admiral Villeneuve had been annihilated off Cape Trafalgar by a British fleet commanded by Admiral Horatio Nelson. After five hours of fighting marked by great courage on both sides, Villeneuve had lost twenty of his thirty-three ships, and the remaining thirteen were in full flight. The British had lost not a single one of their twenty-seven vessels. Their only major casualty was Nelson himself. Mortally wounded, he lived just long enough to know that his fleet had triumphed.

The sole official reference that Napoleon made to the French defeat at Trafalgar was in a speech in 1806: "Storms caused us to lose some ships of the line after unwisely engaging in a fight." That unwise fight off the Spanish coast was one of the most important naval battles in history. It shattered Napoleon's chances of invading England, brought to an end the long struggle between England and France for mastery of the seas, and established British naval supremacy for the next century. It compelled Napoleon to change his strategy from direct attack upon the British Isles to an attempt to strangle Britain by economic means — a change in strategy that led to Napoleon's downfall.

AUSTERLITZ

Upon receiving news of the defeat at Trafalgar, Napoleon attempted to open peace negotiations with Russia and Austria. His advances rebuffed, he marched from Vienna into the Austrian province of Moravia and on December 2, 1805, at the small town of Austerlitz crushed the combined Austrian and Russian armies. The battle was called the Battle of the Three Emperors, for the emperors of Austria and Russia commanded the armies that faced the troops of Emperor Napoleon. Bonaparte recognized it as his most brilliant victory — "the battle of Austerlitz is the most splendid of all I have fought."

On the very night of the battle Emperor Francis sued for peace. It was the third time that he had been humbled by Napoleon; the first two times were the Treaty of Campo Formio in 1797 and the Treaty of Lunéville in 1801. By the Treaty of Pressburg in December, 1805, Francis surrendered his remaining Italian possessions (Venetia, Istria, and Dalmatia) to Napoleon, recognized Napoleon as king of Italy, and surrendered his German possessions and the Austrian provinces of Tyrol and Vorarlberg to France's German allies — Baden, Bavaria, and Württemberg.

Before Austerlitz Prussia had been on the point of joining the alliance against France. Now Napoleon persuaded Frederick William III to sign a treaty agreeing to turn over some of Prussia's West German possessions to Bavaria and France and to keep British ships from the northwest coast of Germany. In return Napoleon gave Hanover, the ancestral home of Britain's kings, to Prussia. England stood firm, but William Pitt, broken in health and spirit by the collapse of the Third Coalition, died in January, 1806.

NAPOLEON'S PINNACLE

Napoleon then proceeded to reorganize his conquests according to his own wishes. He transformed the Batavian Republic into the Kingdom of Holland, with his brother Louis as king. He grouped together sixteen states in southern and central Germany into the Confederation of the Rhine (July, 1806), with himself as Protector — or dictator. The Confederation adopted the Code Napoléon and agreed to furnish sixty-three thousand soldiers for his army. Subsequently all German states except Prussia, Brunswick, and Hesse joined the Confederation, so that a large part of Germany was under Napoleon's scepter. Under French pressure further territorial consolidations were made, reducing still more the number of individual German states. Napoleon then announced that he no longer recognized the existence of the Holy Roman Empire. Emperor Francis accepted the inevitable and in 1806 gave up the title of Holy Roman Emperor that his family had held for centuries, and with it relinquished the Hapsburg claim to the domination of Germany. Thus perished the last reminder of the great but unfulfilled dream of a united Christendom, and the Corsican phoenix rising from its ashes might in truth claim to be the successor of Charlemagne.

Napoleon controlled the Continent from the English Channel to the Elbe River, from the North Sea to the Mediterranean. His domination did not go uncontested. Prussia, stung by the Napoleonic humiliations, declared war late in 1806 and was joined by Russia. Within a month Bonaparte had defeated Prussian forces in the dual victories of Jena and Auerstedt (October, 1807) and occupied Berlin. From there he marched into East Prussia. In February, 1807, at Eylau he fought a one-day draw against a combined Russian-Prussian army in one of the bloodiest battles in history: fifty thousand casualties, or one-third of the total number of troops engaged on both sides. Though even Napoleon was moved by the horrors of Eylau, he was not dissuaded from continuing the war. In June, 1807, at Friedland in East Prussia, the Russians went down to defeat and sued for peace.

The next month Napoleon, Tsar Alexander I, and King Frederick William III of Prussia came together at Tilsit on the Niemen River to discuss peace terms. Napoleon and Alexander got along famously, and the young tsar was mesmerized by the master of Europe. While the two conversed on a raft moored in the river between the two armies, the Prussian king paced along the bank in anxiety about what was being decided on the raft. His worries were well founded. The two emperors arranged a peace at Prussia's expense: Prussia's territory was halved, its ports were closed to British ships and goods, limitations were placed on the size of its army, a heavy war indemnity was levied, and maintenance of a French army of occupation was required until the indemnity was paid. Prussia's Polish possessions became the Grand Duchy of Warsaw, a French satellite under the king of Saxony. The western Prussian provinces, together with several West German states, were fused into a new Kingdom of Westphalia, with Napoleon's youngest brother Jerome as king. The tsar recognized all Napoleon's conquests and the new states he had created and consented to serve as mediator in bringing about peace between Britain and France. In secret articles Alexander agreed to ally with Napoleon if the British refused to make peace, and to aid Napoleon in compelling Austria, Denmark, Sweden, and Portugal to join them against England. In return Napoleon agreed to assist Alexander in his war against the Turks.

THE CONTINENTAL SYSTEM

Only Britain remained at war with France, and only Britain stood in the way of still greater conquests for Napoleon in the Near East and India. Britain had to be defeated. British naval supremacy made it impossible to invade the island kingdom, but there were other ways to humble the persistent foe. If Britain, heavily dependent on its export trade to the Continent, could be shut out of Europe, the ruin of its business community and resultant mass unemployment, discontent, and perhaps revolt against the government would so weaken it internally that it would have to sue for peace. Napoleon did not have the sea power to accomplish this end by a naval blockade of Great Britain, but he could use his military power to blockade the Continent. He would compel the continental nations to refuse to trade with England.

Economic warfare against England was not a new idea. The Revolutionary government had considered it in 1793, and it had been applied sporadically since then. Napoleon's domination of the Continent enabled him to apply the policy to a far greater area than had his predecessors, indeed, to so large an area that his strategy was named the Continental System. By excluding British goods he hoped to establish continental production of those goods and create an integrated economic system, revolving around France, which would make the Continent nearly self-sufficient.

In November, 1806, in a decree issued at Berlin Napoleon forbade the importation of British goods into states controlled by or allied with France. At Tilsit Russia and Prussia were bound to the Continental System, and subsequently other nations were compelled to join. The British replied in 1807 with orders in council (orders given by the king on the advice of his ministers) declaring that neutral vessels trading with continental ports must put in first at British ports, in the hope that the neutral ships would load with British goods and carry them to the Continent. Napoleon countered with the Milan Decree of December, 1807, threatening confiscation upon arrival on the Continent of any neutral ship that stopped in England or submitted to search at sea by British warships.

For Britain the most onerous result of the Continental System was a side effect. American shippers were caught in the cross fire of economic warfare; whichever course they chose, they risked capture and confiscation. President Thomas Jefferson attempted to steer a neutral course with the Embargo Act of 1807, forbidding all American exports to foreign nations, but it proved so harmful to the American economy that it was abandoned in 1810. America offered to resume trade with either France or England if either nation would annul its decrees against neutral shipping. Napoleon offered to do so if the United States would compel England to respect American rights on the high seas. Napoleon's offer appealed to expansionists in America who wanted to annex British territory in North America and who believed that Britian's involvement in war with France gave the United States that opportunity. In 1812 Congress declared war on England. Although Britain revoked the orders in council five days after the war began, the conflict dragged on for over two years, ending in a draw.

It was impossible to seal the Continent against smugglers, who brought in great quantities of English goods. Napoleon also had to grant licenses to import certain English products, such as wool cloth for army overcoats, and on occasion he allowed the export of grain and wine from the Continent to England. Britain more than balanced the trade losses to the Continent by increasing trade with non-European lands, particularly Latin America. Although the Continental System was awkward for the British economy, it never seriously threatened it. At the same time, the sea commerce of the continental states dwindled. British control of the coastal waters made it necessary to ship goods overland, and the cost of land transport pushed up prices. Most significant, the continental states were unwilling to make the sacrifices involved in excluding such imported wares as cane sugar and tobacco.

THE PENINSULAR WAR

The most dire consequence of the Continental System came as a result of Napoleon's unyielding determination to bludgeon the states of Europe into maintaining the embargo on British goods. The first step on the road to Napoleon's ruin was his invasion of Portugal in 1807; that country, faithful to its alliance with England, had rejected the Continental System. Next, a French army moved in to guard the Spanish coasts in 1808. Though allied with France since 1796, the Spanish had not enforced the Continental System. Napoleon forced the Bourbon king, Charles IV, to abdicate and transferred his brother Joseph from the throne of Naples to that of Spain; General Murat, Napoleon's brother-in-law, became king of Naples. A mass insurrection of Spaniards, led by aristocrats and inspired by priests, provoked the French to practice cruelties that only produced further resistance. Courageous and elusive Spanish guerrillas tied down an enormous French army. A small British force commanded by Arthur Wellesley, later duke of Wellington, landed in Portugal, forced the French to evacuate, and marched into Spain. From 1808 to 1814 Napoleon was engaged in a long and costly struggle known as the Peninsular War.

In his efforts to enforce the Continental System in Italy Napoleon occupied the Papal States in 1808. In the next year he annexed the states to France. When Pius VII excommunicated him, Napoleon arrested the pontiff and interned him away from Rome. Catholic Europe was shocked by this affront to the pope — a second Babylonian Captivity — and it heightened the resistance of the devout Spaniards.

The successes of the Spanish against the French persuaded the Austrians that Napoleon was not invincible. In April, 1809, they declared war. Rushing from Spain to take personal command, Napoleon in a swift and brilliant campaign defeated the Austrians at Wagram in July. For the fourth time Emperor Francis sued for peace. By the Treaty of Schönbrunn in October, 1809, Austria surrendered 32,000 square miles and 3,500,000 people to France and her allies and entered into an alliance with Napoleon.

The Continental System brought Napoleon into conflict with even his own brother. Louis Bonaparte, king of Holland since 1806, recognized that because his realm was primarily dependent on seaborne commerce, it would suffer too much from the system. He therefore did not enforce it. Napoleon, indignant at this disloyalty, annexed part of Holland to France in 1810 and sent French troops to guard Dutch harbors. Louis refused to remain king under these humiliating circumstances and abdicated. Holland was incorporated into France.

THE GRAND EMPIRE

In 1810 Napoleon's hegemony included all Europe. His own domain was the French Empire stretching from Rome to the North Sea. Subject to his command under a barely veiled dictatorship were the satellite states: the Kingdom of Italy, the Kingdom of Naples, the Kingdom of Spain, the Confederation of the Rhine, the Illyrian Provinces, and the Grand Duchy of Warsaw. These, together with the French Empire, made up the Grand Empire. Austria, Prussia, Russia, Denmark, and Sweden were still ruled by their old governments but were allied with Napoleon.

Napoleon sought to strengthen the Austrian alliance through marriage. In 1809 he had secured an annulment from his first wife, Josephine de Beauharnais, whom he had married in 1796, because she had not presented him with an heir. She struck a hard bargain for her consent to the annulment: a large income and retention of the title of empress. After considering the merits of eighteen eligible ladies, Napoleon married Marie Louise, daughter of Emperor Francis of Austria. The marriage was neither a great diplomatic nor a marital success, but she bore him a son in 1811, upon whom Napoleon bestowed the title of king of Rome.

As a thoroughgoing materialist who saw the benefits of the French Revolution in essentially utilitarian terms, Napoleon sought stability for the Grand Empire in the fundamental uniformity of social institutions. Equal rights, equal opportunity, abolition of privileges, abolition of serfdom, universal obligation to pay taxes, religious freedom, and the Code Napoléon were introduced into his subject lands. The curbing of the Roman Catholic Church was the corollary of the exaltation of the secular state. Napoleon summed up his program in a letter to his brother Jerome upon the latter's coronation as king of Westphalia in 1807: "What is above all desired in Germany is that you will grant to those who are not nobles but have ability an equal claim to offices, and that all vestiges of serfdom and of barriers between the sovereign and the lowest class of the people should be abolished. The benefits of the Code Napoléon, legal procedure in open court, the jury, these are the points by which your monarchy should be distinguished. . . . Your people must enjoy a liberty, an equality, a prosperity, unknown in the rest of Germany."

Italy was the most deeply influenced by Napoleon's governance. Although he plundered its museums and galleries, levied heavy taxes and military conscriptions, and mercilessly repressed resistance, to the Italians Bonaparte was looked upon as a fellow Italian whose exploits recreated the greatness of Imperial Rome. His achievements and reforms — driving out the old oppressive governments; introducing the Napoleonic law codes and civil equality; constructing badly needed roads, canals, bridges, and a school system; and improving the administration of taxes — became the starting point for the Italian nationalist movement or Risorgimento (revival), which led to the unification of Italy a half-century later. Bonaparte, however, was interested in only a partial unification of Italy, for a divided Italy was more easily dominated than a united one. In 1805 he changed the satellite Italian Republic (successor to the Cisalpine Republic) comprising the northern third of Italy, into the Kingdom of Italy with himself as king. The next year he packed off the Bourbon king of Naples and rather than annexing Naples to his northern kingdom placed his brother Joseph on the Neapolitan throne. The remaining Italian states, including Piedmont, Genoa, and the Papal States, were annexed to France between 1801 and 1810.

In Germany Napoleon's domination led to a territorial reconstruction of Germany that drastically reduced the number of states there. The Treaties of Campo Formio (1797) and of Lunéville (1801) had ordered that German hereditary rulers whose lands on the Rhine's west bank had been annexed to France should be compensated with German territory east of the Rhine that belonged to the Church, free imperial cities, and imperial knights. The arrangements for distribution of land among the hereditary princes took place in Paris, where the rulers and their emissaries flocked to beg Napoleon for concessions and to bribe and wheedle French officials. Talleyrand, Napoleon's foreign secretary, is said to have taken 10 million francs from the fawning Germans. The compensation program resulted in the disappearance of a myriad of small states. In 1815, after Napoleon's defeat, the statesmen of the victorious powers accepted his surgery by which the number of German states had been reduced from 360 to 39.

Despite his gigantic hegemony, rivaling Imperial Rome's, Napoleon's position had weakened measurably by 1810. The Peninsular War was a drain and the Continental System was a sieve. Tsar Alexander I no longer stood in sophomoric awe of the master of Europe. Fearful of Napoleon's unquenchable thirst for conquest and indignant at the harm done Russian trade by the Continental System, the tsar formally withdrew from the Continental System and in 1811 opened Russian ports to neutrals and levied a prohibitively high tariff on silks, wines and brandies, the chief exports of France to Russia.

Napoleon decided that he must invade Russia and crush the tsar. After extensive preparation he led a huge army, estimated at six to seven hundred thousand men into Alexander's empire in June, 1812. The Grand Army was probably the largest military force yet assembled under a single command. Only one-third was French, for Napoleon had drawn heavily on the troops of his allies and satellites. The Russians, whose forces totaled about 180,000 men, followed the strategy of avoiding pitched battles and drawing the invader ever deeper into the vast Russian plain. Only when he reached Borodino, seventy miles from Moscow, did he meet the Russians in force. He drove them back at a terrible cost to both sides and marched into Moscow in September, 1812. He found a deserted city, for most of its 300,000 people had fled. The day after the French entered the city caught fire, either by accident or design, and four days of raging flames destroyed three-quarters of Moscow. It was impossible for the French to remain without cover through a Moscow winter. Convinced that his occupation of Moscow had forced Russia to its knees, Napoleon three times offered to end the war. Alexander ignored his proposals. With winter approaching, Napoleon had no choice but retreat. Russian troops harassed the French columns as they moved westward. Winter set in unusually early. The retreat became a desperate rout. In December about 100,000 ragged and starving men crossed the Niemen River into the Grand Duchy of Warsaw. They were the entire remnant of the Grand Army; over 400,000 had perished, and 100,000 had been taken prisoner in the retreat.

THE WAR OF LIBERATION

The myth of Napoleonic invincibility, already shaken by French reverses in Spain, was shattered. In Prussia pressure from the Junker generals, smarting under the earlier defeats, and a popular rising compelled King Frederick William in 1813 to renounce his alliance with France and ally with Russia. A few months later Austria joined the coalition. The Swedes promised 30,000 troops, the Confederation of the Rhine began to disintegrate, anti-French riots broke out in Italy, and the duke of Wellington rolled back the French in Spain and led his soldiers across the Pyrenees into southern France. Britain poured a fortune into the Continent to subsidize the enemies of Napoleon: 32,000,000 pounds sterling between 1813 and 1815.

EUROPE IN 1810 AT THE HEIGHT OF NAPOLEON'S POWER

French Empire

Countries subject to Napoleon

Countries allied with Napoleon

Countries hostile to Napoleon

Independent states

* Battles

0   300
Miles

SCOTLAND

UNITED KINGDOM

OF GREAT BRITAIN AND IRELAND

Dublin•
IRELAND

ENGLAND

•London

English Channel

NOR

DEN

North Sea

Amsterda

•Brussels

Waterloo *
(1815)

Rhine

*Paris

FRANCE

Seine R.

Meuse R.

ATLANTIC

Loire   R.

Bay of
Biscay

OCEAN

•Bordeaux

Coruña

Garonne R.

Lyon• •Geneva

SV

Rhône R.

Marengo (18

Marseille
•

Oporto•

KINGDOM

Duero R.

Madrid   OF

Ebro R.

•Barcelona

COI

Lisbon•

Tagus   R.

SPAIN

K. OF PORTUGAL

BALEARIC IS.

KINGD
SAR

Seville
• •Bailen

Guadalquivir R.

Mediterranea

Cape Trafalgar (1805) * Strait of Gibraltar

FINLAND

L. Ladoga

St. Petersburg

RUSSIAN

Volga R.

Moscow

* Borodino (1812)

'EDEN

• Stockholm

• Riga

Baltic Sea

Dvina R.

• Smolensk

EMPIRE

'enhagen

• Tilsit

• Vilna

* Friedland (1807)

* Eylau (1807)

Don R.

PRUSSIA

GRAND DUCHY

• Posen   • Warsaw

Berlin

OF WARSAW

'pzig (1813)

Oder R.

Vistula R.

Kiev •

UKRAINE

Dnieper R.

(1806)

'rague

BOHEMIA

* Austerlitz (1805)

Aspern (1809) ** Wagram (1809)

Vienna •

'henlinden (1800)   Buda • Pest

EMPIRE OF THE

HAPSBURGS

BESSARABIA

MOLDAVIA

• Odessa

Sea of Azov

'LYRIAN

PROVINCES

Drave R.

HUNGARY

WALLACHIA

Bucharest •

Black   Sea

'M

Save R.

• Belgrade

Danube R.

.Y

OTTOMAN

MONTENEGRO

Adrianople •

• Constantinople

S

KINGDOM

OF

'Naples •   NAPLES

EMPIRE

Aegean

Sea

• Palermo

KINGDOM OF

SICILY

• Athens

CYPRUS

CRETE

The Prussians had been preparing for this War of Liberation ever since their calamitous defeat in 1807. Jena, Auerstedt, and Eylau, instead of crushing Prussia, had inspired an amazing revival of nationalist fervor. In spite of the French army of occupation the Prussians made ready for the struggle to throw off the Napoleonic yoke. Zealous government ministers carried through a broad program of reform to quicken the people's sense of loyalty and identification with the state. Under the guidance of Baron vom Stein and his successor Prince Hardenberg serfdom was abolished and the people were given a greater voice in local government. General Scharnhorst and Count Gneisenau revamped the army to make it an efficient fighting force. Baron K. W. von Humboldt reorganized the school system and in 1811 persuaded the king to establish the University of Berlin. Johann Gottlieb Fichte, professor of philosophy at the new university, held his youthful audiences spellbound as he spoke of the *Volksgeist,* the national spirit peculiar to the German people, finer than the *Volksgeist* of other peoples, and a precious heritage to be preserved from contamination by foreign influences. Moritz Arndt popularized nationalistic ideas in songs and poems. Friedrich Ludwig Jahn, or Father Jahn, as his devoted followers called him, organized young men into gymnastic societies, where he taught them the superiority of the Germans and hatred for foreigners and Jews while preparing them physically for war against the French. The Prussian renaissance awakened a new nationalistic spirit all over Germany. Thousands of new patriots, looking to Prussia for leadership in the struggle against French domination, formed Free Corps to aid Prussia in the war for liberation.

Napoleon — supremely self-confident, undaunted by his reversals, and contemptuous of the enemy — now carried through one of his greatest feats. In the first four months of 1813 he raised and equipped an army of 250,000 to replace the army he had lost in Russia. With his demagogic masterfulness he rallied the French people to his support, and with his energy and genius he organized and guided this great national endeavor.

The new troops were brave — and green. They were often poorly led as well, for Napoleon had lost many experienced officers. Napoleon himself seemed to have lost some of his own tactical skill, and his ambitions in the field outran his means. After a number of reverses, the allies defeated him in October, 1813, at Leipzig in a three-day battle, called by the Germans the Battle of the Nations. The French army, reduced to 80,000, retreated home. Once again Napoleon set about building up a new army, but the miracle could not be repeated. He could raise only 110,000 troops, many of them young boys. They fought a series of magnificently desperate actions, but the weight of enemy numbers overwhelmed him.

THE END OF THE EMPIRE

As the allies pushed the French westward they began a discussion of the peace settlement. By offers of large subsidies Viscount Castlereagh,

Courtesy of the Museum of Fine Arts, Boston

Napoleon at Bautzen, May 21, 1813, by Auguste Raffet

"Napoleon is the first and only man who could have provided Europe with the equilibrium for which she had sought in vain for many centuries, and which today is farther away than ever. . . . With this real equilibrium Napoleon could have given to the peoples of Europe an organization conforming to true moral law. . . . Napoleon could have done these things, but did not. If he had done them, gratitude would have raised statues to him everywhere. . . .
Instead . . . posterity will say of him: that man was gifted with a very great intellectual force; but he did not understand true glory. His moral force was too small or entirely lacking. He could not endure prosperity with moderation, nor misfortune with dignity; and it is because he lacked moral force that he brought about the ruin of Europe and of himself." Talleyrand, MÉMOIRES (Paris, 1891), Vol. VI.

---

the British foreign minister, persuaded Austria, Russia, and Prussia to join Britain in a security pact. The Treaty of Chaumont in March, 1814, bound the four powers to protect one another against France for the next twenty years, and each was to provide 150,000 men to enforce the peace terms. Three weeks later the allies marched into Paris, and Napoleon abdicated in favor of his infant son. The victors, however, gave the French throne to the count of Provence, brother of the executed Louis XVI, who acceded as King Louis XVIII.

In May, 1814, the allies signed the First Treaty of Paris with the restored Bourbon monarch. It reduced France to its pre-1792 boundaries. The victors were generous, demanding no indemnities, restoring some of

France's overseas possessions, and even permitting the French to keep the art treasures Napoleon had taken from the lands he conquered. Napoleon himself had already been sent into exile on the small island of Elba, lying between Italy and Corsica. The allies granted him Elba as his sovereign principality — eighty-six square miles — provided him with a sizable income, and allowed him to keep his title of emperor. His empress Marie Louise was also permitted to retain her title and received the duchies of Parma, Piacenza, and Guastalla, in Italy.

THE HUNDRED DAYS

With the war over, old suspicions and jealousies cropped up among the allies. Unable to agree on the distribution of the territories taken from Napoleon, they decided to meet in Vienna in the autumn and to postpone decisions until then. The Congress of Vienna was convened in September, 1814, and lasted until the following June. In the midst of its negotiations in rearranging the Napoleonic map the congress was stunned by the news that Napoleon had returned to France and received a tumultuous and frenzied display of affection and loyalty at every step of his trip to Paris. Frenchmen, not least the emperor's soldiers, who were used to the excitement and grandeur of Napoleon's time, had quickly tired of the colorless and cautious Louis XVIII; more important, they feared that the returning aristocrats and high churchmen would claim their old privileges. Napoleon hoped to capitalize on this discontent in France and by the shock of his return sunder the allies and reestablish himself. He landed in southern France on March 1, 1815, with about one thousand men from the small guard force allowed him in exile, and reached Paris on March 13. Louis had already fled to Belgium. Napoleon rallied Louis XVIII's army — his old soldiers — to his banner and was once more emperor of the French.

His reign lasted one hundred days. The news of his return ended the bickering at Vienna. A mighty army assembled under the supreme command of the Duke of Wellington. On June 18, 1815, near the Belgian village of Waterloo, a combined force of Germans, Dutchmen, and Englishmen crushed the new army that Napoleon had raised. The Hundred Days were over.

The final trip of the man who had crossed Europe at the head of armies was a voyage on a British warship carrying him as prisoner of war to the British-owned St. Helena, a bleak rock in the South Atlantic. There, 4,500 miles from Paris, Napoleon existed with a few faithful followers for six bitter years, fashioning his own legend for posterity by writing his memoirs. Although the Imperial Eagle chained to the rock lives on as the most brilliant man-myth of the European world, the man himself was mortal. On May 5, 1821, Napoleon died of cancer of the stomach. He was fifty-one.

THE NAPOLEONIC LEGACY

May 5, 1821, was the thirty-second anniversary of the convention of the Estates-General at Versailles. The man who died that day on St. Helena had been a subaltern on garrison duty in the old fortress town of Auxonne in eastern France that day thirty-two years before when the French Revolution began. He had ended the Revolution, but in two important ways it also reached out to finish him.

The British, who had had their revolution a century and a half before, saw Revolutionary France as the devil incarnate. Their implacable enmity to Napoleon Bonaparte had a bitter edge to it because he seemed to represent that Revolution on the march. More than any other factor, Britain's relentless pursuit of Napoleon undid him.

The other means by which the French Revolution finished Napoleon was the nationalism that it unleashed throughout continental Europe. Patriotic fervor was the most exportable article of the Revolutionary faith. Jacobinism, republicanism, even liberty and equality, varied in their relevancy to the conditions and aspirations of the Germans, Italians, Russians, Poles, Dutchmen, Belgians, Spaniards, and Portuguese. But patriotic nationalism had universal appeal. Germans from states that had been archrivals for centuries fought side by side at the Battle of the Nations, as Germans. Napoleon's foes, despots as well as democrats, rallied their countrymen to oppose and overthrow him by appeals to the national spirit.

Although it is impossible to disengage the French Revolution's impact from Napoleon's — he had, after all, used the Revolution's slogans and sometimes its doctrines as weapons of war and tools to build his empire — his contribution was clear and unique in four spheres. First, the Grand Empire had erected in Germany and Italy, if only for a few years, single entities out of the three-hundred-odd principalities of Germany and the dozen-odd states of Italy. Those historically divided peoples were granted a vision of unity that would in the future become a reality for both.

Second, Napoleon's armies, rather than native revolutionaries, overthrew privilege within the Grand Empire's reaches. For all its shallowness in practice, the conqueror's show of establishing representative government, equality before the law, individual liberty, and religious freedom provided peoples unused to them with a fleeting experience of a new and better order. Napoleon planted the seeds of aspiration for representative government and liberal constitutions, and he gave the middle classes of Europe a priceless moment of freedom from the arrogant repression of privilege.

Third, the Napoleonic era fixed upon France a legend of glory and grandeur that has affected French political life ever since. Although much of the legend was created by Napoleon in exile, its essentials were not; ephemeral though it was, the Grand Empire was not chimerical. Within a few years of his downfall Frenchmen forgot the heavy drain of men and wealth that were the price of his victories and remembered only the grandeur of his conquests.

Finally, Napoleon Bonaparte taught all authoritarian leaders who have followed him the essentials of dictatorship: propaganda, an effective and inexorable secret police forming a state within the state, the use of such democratic devices as the plebiscite to rally popular support behind the regime, state bureaucratization of the critical institutions of education and religion so that they might become instruments of indocrination, and the value of foreign adventures to make domestic repression bearable. Napoleon originated none of these tools of authoritarianism; his contribution was to weave them together into the instrument of the modern authoritarian state and to prove how effective internally that instrument can be.

The last word will be Napoleon Bonaparte's. In 1813 he summed up to Metternich his beginning and what he wished to be his end as a sovereign. Knowing well how uncertain was his future, and how slender his hold on the allegiance of his people, he told Metternich: "I shall know how to die, but never to yield an inch of territory. Your sovereigns who were born to the throne may get beaten twenty times and still return to their capitals. I cannot. For I rose to power through the camp."

THE NINETEENTH CENTURY: THE GOLDEN AGE OF THE EUROPEAN WORLD
PART THREE

INTRODUCTION: SOCIAL FORCES AND SOCIAL CHANGE

In spite of its recent revolutionary upheavals, the Europe of 1815 more nearly resembled the Europe of 1715 at the death of Louis XIV than it did the Europe of 1914 on the eve of the First World War. In 1815, as in the previous century, more than three-fourths of all Europeans lived in rural villages or isolated homesteads and gained their living directly from the soil. In 1914, on the other hand, the majority in western Europe lived in towns and cities and worked in factories, shops, and offices. In 1815 the average life expectancy at birth was no more than 25 or 30 years, little higher than a century before; in 1914 it exceeded 50 years in most of western Europe and was increasing rapidly. In 1815 only the children of the well-to-do obtained the privilege of a formal education; the majority could neither read nor write. By 1914 almost all European children could attend publicly supported elementary schools and acquire the elements of literacy. In 1815, as before the French Revolution, most governments of Europe were more or less absolutist and aristocratic; participation in the process of government by means of elections was a privilege conferred only on wealthy landowners in a few countries bordering the western seas. By 1914 almost all European countries had some form of representative, if not wholly democratic, government, and in most countries the suffrage extended to all adult males.

These are but a few of the more obvious differences that marked the beginning and the end of Europe's greatest century. How did the changes come about? A few of the broader, more pervasive social forces that provided the dynamics are briefly discussed below.

515

SCIENCE AND TECHNOLOGY

Among the most fundamental of all sources of social change is new knowledge. Two closely related areas in which new knowledge had a profound impact on Western society in the nineteenth century were the study of the physical universe, or science, and the study of the means of manipulating nature for the production of goods and services, or technology. Important developments in scientific knowledge laid the basis for an increasingly fruitful collaboration between scientists, on the one hand, and industrialists and agriculturists, on the other. Although the full fruits of their collaboration did not appear until the second half of the nineteenth century and later, when scientific theories provided the foundation for new industries and new processes, by the beginning of the century the methods of science were already being applied in technology with gratifying results.

The application of scientific methods to practical problems led to an increasing mastery of nature, but practical results were by no means the only objectives spurring scientific progress. What motivated most scientists was simple curiosity — the desire for a better understanding of nature. Many advances in pure science, such as the discovery of electromagnetism, had far-reaching practical consequences, but scientists frequently left the development and application of their discoveries to other men. Certain findings of science that did not have immediate practical application, such as the doctrine of organic evolution, affected society even more profoundly by questioning old beliefs and raising new philosophic problems.

DEMOGRAPHIC GROWTH
AND MATERIAL PROGRESS

Another factor responsible for important social changes was essentially biological. Just as the growth of a single individual from infancy to maturity produces changes in behavior and outlook, the growth of a population alters social institutions and attitudes. At the fall of Napoleon Europe contained approximately 200 million inhabitants, with another 20 or 25 million people of European stock overseas, out of a total world population of almost one billion. At the outbreak of World War I Europeans numbered more than 450 million, or about one-fourth of the world total, with an additional 150 million persons of European ancestry overseas. Peoples of European stock still formed a minority of the world's population, but possessed of a vastly superior technology for both production and destruction, the carriers of Western civilization at the beginning of the twentieth century enjoyed a preponderance of power on the world scene that had never before been witnessed.

The immense population increase could not have taken place without a proportionate increase in the production of the basic necessities of human existence — food, clothing, and shelter. This increase in production, together with the proliferation of commodities and services that were not necessities, actually surpassed the rate of growth of population. Therefore the standard of living rose simultaneously with the increase in population.

A part of the increase in production resulted from the opening of new lands and the tapping of new resources, but most of it resulted from the advance of technology. The increase in agricultural productivity lessened the need for peasants and farmers to be self-sufficient, and made them more able to exchange their surplus for cheaper machine- or factory-made goods. The increased supply of foodstuffs and raw materials also made it possible for a larger proportion of the laboring population to engage in nonagricultural production. Improvements in the technology of manufacturing and transportation were even more spectacular than those in agriculture. The invention of specialized, labor-saving machinery and the development of new forms of power, such as the steam engine, the electric dynamo, and the internal combustion engine, speeded up manufacture and transportation, lowered costs of production, and made possible new products and processes.

CLASS STRUCTURE AND CLASS STRUGGLES

The shift away from agriculture to the new forms of industry by the majority of Europeans led to the growth of cities, the rise of new social classes, the preponderance of new values and attitudes, and brought a host of new problems. It is readily apparent that an individual's place in the social hierarchy depends in part upon the way in which he gains a living, and that individuals in the same occupation are likely to share common values and a common outlook, different from and perhaps conflicting with the values and outlooks of those engaged in other occupations. During the nineteenth century bitter struggles between rival groups for social and political recognition or dominance sometimes occurred.

A close examination of nineteenth-century Europe reveals literally hundreds of identifiable social groups based upon differences in occupation and income, each with its own distinctive values and attitudes, yet each shading imperceptibly into the next along the social spectrum. It is possible to distinguish a few broad groups to which the more formal designation social class may be applied. The most commonly accepted classification distinguishes the landed aristocracy; a middle class of business and professional men (frequently subdivided into an upper middle class or *haute bourgeoisie,* including wealthy merchants, bankers, master manufacturers, and lawyers, and a lower middle class or *petite bourgeoi-*

sie, including retail tradesmen and handicraftsmen); an urban proletariat or working class; and the tillers of the soil or peasants.

At the beginning of the century the peasants formed by far the most
numerous class. At the end of the century they still constituted a majority
in Europe as a whole, but in the more industrialized areas their relative
numbers had drastically decreased. They stood near the bottom of the
social scale and rarely exercised effective political power. Isolated by poor
communications and bound by a traditionalist mentality, their greatest
desire was to obtain land. Their participation in broad social movements
was generally sporadic and limited to their immediate economic interests.

In the years immediately after Waterloo the landed aristocracy continued to enjoy a preponderance of social prestige and political power in
spite of the effects of the French Revolution. Its position of leadership
was sharply challenged, however, by the rapidly growing middle classes.
By the middle of the century the latter had succeeded in establishing
themselves in the seats of power in most of western Europe, and during
the second half of the century they made deep inroads into the exclusive
position of the aristocracy in central Europe.

At the beginning of the century the urban workers neither participated
in political life nor expected to participate in it. As their numbers grew
and the outlines of the new industrial system became clear, they gradually
developed a rudimentary class consciousness. At first their demands were
moderate, pertaining to improvements in material circumstances and a
more equitable distribution of income and wealth. Only later did they
seek a voice in government when they discovered the connection between
political power and economic reform. On the whole their attempts to
gain power by both peaceful and revolutionary means met with little
success until late in the nineteenth century, when the suffrage was gradually extended in western Europe and trade unions secured legal recognition.

NEW IDEOLOGIES

In the process of social change the aims of the various competing
groups became crystallized in doctrines that are sometimes called ideologies. The very word ideology is a creation of the early nineteenth century. It may be defined as a system of ideas concerned with a particular
social or political goal. Closely related to it is the suffix "-ism," whose
connection with specific doctrines or ideologies, as liberalism or socialism,
also dates from this period. The first half of the nineteenth century witnessed the introduction into our language of almost all the important
and highly charged "isms" of today, including both capitalism and communism. At that time, however, the most important were liberalism,
nationalism, and socialism.

An individual's social class did not always dictate his ideological convictions. Titled aristocrats sometimes took pride in calling themselves liberals or even socialists, and the majority of socialist leaders and intellectuals had middle-class backgrounds. On the other hand, many members of the lower and middle classes adhered to conservative views. Nevertheless, as a general rule individuals in the same social class tended to subscribe to the same ideology if they took any interest at all in political affairs. Liberalism was the credo of the middle classes, whereas socialism expressed the aspirations of the workers. Conservatism, though not always dignified (or derided) by the designation ideology, enshrined the ideals of those who wished to preserve the status quo; that is, the aristocracy. Nationalism did not belong to any social class as such. It was principally espoused by members of the educated middle classes, but it also reflected the aspirations of the divided peoples of Italy and Germany for a unified nation, and the aspirations of the subject nationalities in the Austrian, Russian, and Ottoman empires, the Belgian Netherlands, Norway, and Ireland for autonomy and freedom. Even the citizens of countries such as Britain, France, and Spain adopted fiercely patriotic attitudes when they thought that their nation's interests were threatened by a foreign power. The proponents of nationalism did not perceive its latent conflict with liberalism and socialism until the revolutions of 1848.

EAST AND WEST: THE WIDENING GAP

A complicating element in the study of the social changes of the nineteenth century is that economic and political developments proceeded at different rates in different parts of Europe. At the beginning of the century there was already a marked difference in the level of development between east and west in Europe, and the gap grew wider with each passing decade. In general, the development of commerce and industry and the ensuing social changes varied inversely with the distance from London, the focal point of capitalist economy. Thus, in the great revolutionary outbursts of 1848, the new middle class rulers of western Europe dealt with the demands of an urban proletariat, whereas the middle classes of central Europe struggled against the entrenched power of the aristocracy. The revolutions of 1848 caused hardly a ripple in Russia. More than half a century later middle classes and workers alike fought for elementary civil and political liberties in Russia, long after France had enacted universal manhood suffrage and at a time when German workers paid allegiance to the largest socialist party in existence.

ROMANTICISM AND REACTION
CHAPTER TWENTY-ONE

The great social changes of the nineteenth century did not sweep Europe all at once in 1815. Even after the cataclysm of the Revolution and the Napoleonic wars the vested interests of the Old Regime exhibited remarkable powers of revival and tenacity. In fact, during the decade following the Congress of Vienna the European scene was dominated by a twofold reaction to those driving forces of change. One was political, the other intellectual. The political reaction had for its aim the restoration of the Old Regime, and thus depended heavily on the doctrines of conservatism. The intellectual reaction, known as romanticism, is more difficult to categorize. Though in some areas, such as poetry and music, it seemed to follow an autonomous pattern of development, completely divorced from broader historical movements, in reality it did not.

So similar were the two reactions immediately after the Congress of Vienna that romanticism appeared to many to be no more than the literary adjunct of conservatism. The romantic temper could not be tied for long to a single political dogma, however. After 1820 a new generation of romantic writers and artists began to flout convention. Liberal and nationalist ideals permeated romantic art and literature, which in turn helped to shape the goals and content of the developing liberal and nationalist movements.

THE VIENNA SETTLEMENT AND THE CONCERT OF EUROPE

Even before the defeat and abdication of Napoleon in 1814 the allies had begun making plans for the reconstitution of Europe. The first Treaty of Paris between the allies and the government of the restored Bourbon Louis XVIII settled the status of France provisionally, but the

problems of a general European settlement presented so many complexities and conflicting interests that the victors decided to convene a diplomatic congress of all recognized European powers.

THE CONGRESS OF VIENNA

The Congress of Vienna, which gathered in September, 1814, and did
not complete its work until June, 1815, was one of the notable international assemblages of all times. It had a dual character, at once a lavish,
extravagant social spectacle of the crowned heads and highest aristocracy
of all Europe, and a serious meeting of statesmen and diplomats who
were to shape the political destiny of the Continent for more than a
generation. Actually, the full congress never assembled officially; the
important decisions were all made in secret session by representatives of
the great powers. The key personages in the drama were Prince Clemens
von Metternich, Austrian chancellor and foreign minister and archetype of
the conservative principle; the unpredictable Alexander I, tsar of Russia;
Lord Castlereagh, British foreign minister; and Prince Karl von Hardenberg, representative of the king of Prussia. Before the congress was over
the French foreign minister Talleyrand, a born aristocrat and consecrated bishop, who served with equal effectiveness the French Republic,
Napoleon, and the restored Bourbons, had insinuated himself into the
councils of the great powers at Vienna.

These men sought not merely to recreate a Europe congenial to the interests of their own classes and countries, but also to quell forever the
manifestations of revolutionary and Bonapartist sentiment and to restore
respect for the hierarchy and authority of the established order. In spite
of their common aims, they were not at all unanimous on the means of
accomplishing them. Divergences of interest arose to thwart their deliberations and delay decisions. By the beginning of 1815 Austria and Britain
were on the verge of war against Russia and Prussia as a result of the
latter's claims on Poland and Saxony, but Napoleon's return from Elba
persuaded them to overcome their differences and close ranks against the
common foe. While the armies of the allies gathered once more, the
diplomats brought their negotiations to a hurried conclusion and signed
the final act of the congress on June 8, 1815, ten days before the fateful
battle of Waterloo.

In the first Treaty of Paris the allies had willingly distinguished between France and its former ruler, but treated both with surprising
leniency. Napoleon was obliged to renounce the throne of France for
himself and his descendants, but in compensation he retained the title of
emperor, obtained the island of Elba as a sovereign principality, and received a guaranteed annual income for life. His wife, Marie Louise,
obtained the duchies of Parma, Piacenza, and Guastalla, which were to
pass on to their son at her death. France retained its boundaries of 1792,

larger than those of 1789, and regained its former colonies with the exception of a few strategic islands held by the British.

After the Hundred Days the allies could not overlook the enthusiasm with which the French people had responded to Napoleon; the terms imposed on France were accordingly harsher. The second Treaty of Paris (November 20, 1815) reduced France to its borders of 1790, exacted an indemnity of 700 million francs, required France to support an army of occupation for five years, and forced it to return the art treasures that the Revolutionary and Napoleonic armies had looted from all of Europe. Napoleon, banished to the island of St. Helena in the South Atlantic, died in 1821.

THE NEW MAP OF EUROPE

In redrawing the map of Europe, the diplomats at Vienna paid lip service to the principle of legitimacy, or the reestablishment of the pre-revolutionary situation, but in fact the settlement reflected expediency and compromise of the conflicting claims of the victors. The chief point of agreement was the desire to preserve peace through a balance of power. Specifically this meant holding France in check, although Britain and Austria also feared the expansion of Russian influence in Europe, and Austria kept a watchful eye on Prussian ambitions in Germany as well. (See map on p. 539.)

Russia had already acquired Finland from Sweden and Bessarabia from the Ottoman Empire, both of which it retained. Alexander asserted a claim to nearly the whole of Poland, but in the end he compromised by taking most of the former Grand Duchy of Warsaw, or about three-fifths of the Polish-speaking territory, on which he erected the Kingdom of Poland (the so-called Congress Poland) with himself as king. Austria obtained Polish Galicia, Prussia obtained Posen and Danzig, and Cracow became a free city under the joint protection of Austria, Prussia, and Russia. Prussia hoped to absorb all of Saxony, whose king had remained loyal to Napoleon, but this ambition ran counter to the interests of Austria. Although Prussia had to be content with receiving the northern two-fifths of Saxony, it accepted compensation (another catchword of the congress) in the form of a large extension of its prerevolutionary holdings in western Germany, including almost the entire German Rhineland, which provided a convenient bulwark against a renewal of French expansion.

At British urging the congress created another apparent bulwark in the same general area with the Kingdom of the United Netherlands. It was composed of the former Dutch Republic and Austrian Netherlands (modern-day Belgium) under the head of the House of Orange, King William I. The Kingdom of Sardinia (Piedmont) on the southeastern border of France was strengthened by the acquisition of the former repub-

lic of Genoa. Austria was "compensated" for giving up its outpost in the
Netherlands by the creation of a Lombardo-Venetian kingdom, including
the former duchy of Milan and Venetian republic, with the Austrian em-
peror as king. Austria further strengthened its hegemony in Italy with the
restoration of the other petty states to their former rulers, including the
States of the Church to the pope, under Austrian protection. Murat was
allowed to retain the throne of Naples as the price for his desertion of
Napoleon; but after rallying again to Bonaparte during the Hundred
Days he was shot as a traitor, and Naples and Sicily were reunited as the
Kingdom of the Two Sicilies under the restored Bourbon, Ferdinand I.
Another Bourbon, the archreactionary Ferdinand VII, likewise returned
to his throne in Spain. In the north Sweden received compensation for
the loss of Finland by being allowed to retain Norway, which it had previously won from Denmark, another late deserter of Napoleonic France.

One of the most difficult problems faced by the congress was the reorganization of Germany, complicated by the rivalry of Austria and
Prussia. Resurrection of the old Holy Roman Empire with its three
hundred petty states was unthinkable. Metternich blocked proposals for
a strong federal or unitary state for fear that Austria would lose its
influence in south Germany. The solution finally adopted was to create
the Germanic Confederation, a loose union of thirty-four sovereign states
and four free cities. The Diet, or parliament of the Confederation, which
met in the free city of Frankfurt, was in reality an assembly of ambassadors resembling the present General Assembly of the United Nations.
Since it had no effective executive authority and since the Diet was under
the permanent presidency of the Austrian delegate, the Confederation
served Austrian interests by blocking political and social reform. By
postponing the creation of a unified German state, however, it built up
a store of further difficulties.

Among the worthier and more lasting achievements of the congress was
the reestablishment of Switzerland as an independent confederation of
twenty-two cantons with an international guarantee of neutrality. The
congress inserted a provision for the international regulation of international waterways — the Rhine and Danube in particular. It also made a
pronouncement in favor of abolishing the slave trade but took no positive
action.

Britain, ultimately responsible for the final defeat of Napoleon, sought
no territorial gains on the Continent, although it retained control of the
Ionian Islands off Greece, Helgoland in the North Sea, and Malta
in the Mediterranean. Britain's main concern was to preserve the balance
of power on the Continent, which could be done more effectually without
territorial possessions there and by means of its position as the leading,
almost the only, seapower. During the wars the British navy had controlled the oceans and therefore the colonial empires of the other Eu-

ropean nations. After 1815 the empires were either returned or allowed to go their own course, except that Britain retained the Cape of Good Hope, Singapore, and Ceylon, taken from the Dutch, and several strategic islands in the Indian Ocean taken from France.

THE HOLY ALLIANCE

With the signing of the final act on June 8, 1815, the work of the congress was concluded, although the final settlement had to wait the outcome of the battle of Waterloo. In the fall of 1815 the leading sovereigns and diplomats transferred their activity to Paris to draw up a new treaty for the defeated French.

Meanwhile Alexander of Russia, who was given to mystical flights of imagination, had fallen under the influence of a female religious fanatic, Baroness von Krüdener, who persuaded him of the desirability of establishing the peace on a religious foundation. Accordingly, Alexander proposed to his fellow sovereigns a Holy Alliance, by which they were to regard one another as brothers and govern their conduct by the principles of the Christian religion. Such sentiments were by no means novel, but the document in which they were embodied was so full of empty rhetoric that it soon became a laughingstock. Nevertheless, to avoid offending Alexander, both Francis of Austria and Frederick William of Prussia signed. All the sovereigns of Europe followed suit, except the pope and the sultan — neither of whom had been invited — and the prince regent of Great Britain, whose foreign minister replied disingenuously that the British constitution prohibited him from acting upon "abstract and speculative principles." Although the Holy Alliance lacked operational effect it was regarded by liberals as a sanctimonious cloak to conceal a conspiracy of the signatories against all popular movements for liberalism and reform.

THE QUADRUPLE ALLIANCE AND
THE CONGRESS SYSTEM

Of more immediate practical significance was the Quadruple Alliance, to which Great Britain did adhere, along with Austria, Russia, and Prussia. Concluded on the same day as the second Treaty of Paris, it was mainly intended to protect the Vienna settlement and to ensure that France would not again disturb the peace of Europe. Of particular significance was the clause by which the contracting parties agreed "to renew their meetings at fixed periods . . . for the purpose of consulting upon their common interests, and for the consideration of those measures which at each of those periods shall be considered the most salutary for the repose and prosperity of nations, and for the maintenance of the peace of Europe." This clause inaugurated the congress system and the concert of Europe.

The first of the congresses held under the new system took place at Aix-la-Chapelle (Aachen) in 1818. Its principal business was to arrange for the liquidation of the French indemnity and the withdrawal of the army of occupation from French soil. In the three years that had elapsed since Waterloo the restored Bourbon dynasty had apparently entrenched itself in French political life, and France seemed truly reconciled to its new position. The business of the congress was conducted without disagreement. Not only was France relieved of the onus and embarrassment of the army of occupation, but it was admitted to the European concert on an equal footing by means of the new Quintuple Alliance. At the same time the other four took the precaution of renewing in secret the principal provisions of the older alliance to protect themselves against possible French aggression. The congress system thus got off to an apparently brilliant beginning — a success that was matched and complemented by contemporary intellectual developments.

ROMANTICISM IN LITERATURE AND THE ARTS

Romanticism is the word commonly applied to the characteristic intellectual and artistic values and attitudes of the first half of the nineteenth century. Like all such comprehensive terms it covers many diverse and even contradictory currents; it must therefore be used in an approximate rather than a precise sense. It is easier to describe what it was not, or what it was against, than its positive features. It was primarily a reaction against the formalism, mechanism, and rationalism of the Enlightenment. It was also a reaction to the French Revolution, especially to the Republic of Virtue of Robespierre and the tyranny of Napoleon. On its positive side it was essentially a mood, an attitude, a way of looking at and thinking about the world. It manifested itself in many areas — music, art, literature, religion, philosophy, and politics. It emphasized the emotional side of human nature and regarded the spiritual qualities of man as superior to his purely rational faculties. It stressed the unique, the individual, among men and nations instead of their common characteristics. It glorified nature and viewed the physical universe not as a mechanical system or a great cosmic machine but as a living, growing organism. Because it laid great stress on faith and tradition as determinants of and guides for human behavior and social policy, it reinforced the elements of mysticism and pietism in religion. Romanticism achieved its greatest successes in literature and the arts, with which it is most closely identified. Its emphasis on tradition and the glories of the past contributed to the study of history and jurisprudence. Its glorification of nature and opposition to mechanism created a favorable intellectual environment for the biological sciences and prepared the way for acceptance of the theory of organic evolution.

ORIGINS

Although romanticism came into its own in the first or second decades of the nineteenth century, it had its origins in the mid-eighteenth century during the very Age of Reason to which it was a reaction. Among the most important forerunners was Jean-Jacques Rousseau (1712–1778), whose writings contrasted the natural goodness of primitive man, or man in a state of nature, with the artificiality and acquired wickedness of civilized man. His *Confessions,* published in 1783 after his death, set the style for an introspective, intensely personal literature in which all the emotions of the author are bared to public view.

Johann Wolfgang von Goethe (1749–1832), regarded by many as the greatest of German writers, was another forerunner of romanticism, though he later turned against it. With Friedrich von Schiller (1759–1805) he led the *Sturm und Drang* (storm and stress) movement in German literature. The movement, which flourished in the 1780's, emphasized the turbulence of the human spirit — an emphasis that later became a hall-mark of romantic literature. Goethe's *Faust,* a long dramatic poem, is one of the literary masterpieces of all time. It is in essence the spiritual auto-biography of the author. Based on the old legend of the man who sold his soul to the devil, it portrays the futility of both the life of the mind and the experience of the flesh unless they are fused and ennobled by a generous spiritual compassion for the sufferings of humanity.

A major figure in the romantic movement — indeed, the one who christened it — was a woman, the Baroness de Staël-Holstein (1766–1817). Known to history as Madame de Staël, she was the archetype of the romantic heroine. Born Germaine Necker, daughter of the Swiss financier who became the principal minister of Louis XVI, she was raised in the fashionable Paris salon of her mother. There she was exposed to the wit and elegance of the most celebrated figures of the age. At the age of nineteen she married an obscure Swedish diplomat for whom she had no affection. Although she retained his name throughout her life she rarely lived with him and had several lovers, among them some of the most distinguished literary and political figures of the time, such as Talleyrand and Benjamin Constant. One year before her death she married a man twenty-two years her junior to whom she had already borne a child.

For the three decades from the eve of the French Revolution until her death Madame de Staël was the most talked about and probably the most talkative woman in Europe. She embodied all the diverse, contradic-tory elements of romantic literature. As a person she was strong-willed, passionate, and uninhibited. As a political figure she was a child of the Old Regime who first embraced the Revolution's program of constitu-tional monarchy, then turned against the Revolution and fled during the Reign of Terror. She spent much of the remainder of her life traveling in exile, both from the Revolution and from Napoleon, of whom she was an outspoken critic. As a literary figure she was a prolific if mediocre writer (her books are rarely read today), but the facility of her ideas, the force of her personality, and above all the range of her literary acquaintance enabled her to give a certain unity and focus to the romantic movement. In *De l'Allemagne* (On Germany) Madame de Staël first applied the name "romantic" to the new poetic literature of Germany, which was based on the chants of the troubadours and the legends of medieval chivalry that had been discovered by German folklorists. She contrasted this "modern" literature with the cold and formal "ancient" literature of the French classical writers of the seventeenth and eighteenth centuries. The distinguishing feature of romantic literature, she wrote, was "enthusiasm," which she defined as "the love of the beautiful, the elevation of the soul, the enjoyment of devotion, gathered together in the same sentiment which has both grandeur and calm. The meaning of the word according to the Greeks is its most noble definition: enthusiasm signifies *God in us*."

ROMANTIC POETRY

The romantic era was an age of poetry. Whatever else they wrote, most romantic writers also wrote poetry. Romantic poetry was distinguished by its lyrical qualities. In form it abandoned the stiff formalism of classical or Augustan poetry, and in content it expressed the personality of the poet. William Wordsworth (1770–1850), one of the foremost poets of the English language, exemplified one strand of romanticism. His poetry exudes a love of nature, simplicity, and the idyllic life.

> Therefore am I still
> A lover of the meadows and the woods,
> And mountains; and of all that we behold
> From this green earth;
>   well pleased to recognize
> In nature and the language of the sense,
> The author of my purest thoughts, the nurse,
> The guide, the guardian of my heart, and soul
> Of all my moral being.

Samuel Taylor Coleridge (1772–1834), Wordsworth's close friend, exhibited another tendency of romanticism in his fanciful poetic works "The Rime of the Ancient Mariner" and "Kubla Khan." In them he expressed a fascination with faraway places and exotic things. Three other English poets were romantics in their lives (and deaths) as well as in their literature. John Keats (1795–1821), whose father owned a livery stable, died of tuberculosis in Rome at the age of twenty-five. His friend Percy Bysshe Shelley (1792–1822) drowned the following year in a storm in the Mediterranean. Lord Byron (1788–1824) died two years later in Greece while fighting the Turks for Greek independence.

Outstanding among French romantic poets were Victor Hugo (1802–1885), a genius in every branch of literature; Alphonse de Lamartine (1790–1869), a sentimentalist; Alfred de Vigny (1797–1863), a philosopher in verse; and Alfred de Musset (1810–1857), a pessimistic, emotional egoist. The greatest German poet of the romantic era after Goethe was Heinrich Heine (1797–1856), a supreme lyricist. In northern Germany and the Scandinavian countries romantic poetry became fused with folklore, epic sagas, and fairy tales as in the poetry of Adam Oehlenschlager (1779–1850), Denmark's greatest poet, and even more in the works of Hans Christian Andersen (1805–1875) and the German brothers Wilhelm and Jacob Grimm (1786–1859, 1785–1863). German poets wrote many romantic *lieder* or tender lyrics, which were set to music by composers such as Franz Schubert (1797–1828) and Robert Schumann (1810–1856).

ROMANTIC FICTION

Novels were almost as popular as poetry as a literary form during the romantic period. In the early years of the movement novels stressed fantasy and imagination at the expense of verisimilitude. François René de Chateaubriand (1768–1848), accounted by some as the dominant figure in French literary history between Rousseau and Hugo, wrote voluptuous prose describing incredible events and sensations. Several of his novels were set in the wilds of North America and peopled with Indians or Eskimos. This device gave full scope to his ability to depict the savage beauty of nature, the primitive goodness of man, and the all-seeing benevolence of God. A vivid imagination, together with a cavalier disregard for ordinary fact and logic, frequently led him into hyperboles of fanciful exaggeration, such as this description of life among the Eskimos: "the iceberg balances on the waves, its peaks shining, its hollows ordered with snow; the sea wolves give themselves to the passion of love in its valleys. The whales follow its path over the ocean. The hardy savage in the shelter of his floating iceberg presses to his heart the woman whom God has given him and with her finds undreamt joys in this mixture of danger and passion."

Sir Walter Scott (1771–1832) was one of the most successful authors of historical romances. He thrilled readers throughout Europe and America with his stirring tales of medieval chivalry. The genre was continued with great success by the elder Alexandre Dumas (1802–1870). During the later years of the romantic era novelists created more plausible characters and dealt in believable fashion with real social or personal problems, whether they used historical or contemporary settings. The leading practitioners of the school of romantic realism were Stendhal (Henri Beyle, 1783–1842), Hugo, Charles Dickens (1812–1870), and above all Honoré de Balzac (1799–1850).

Across the Atlantic romanticism exercised a sway no less strong than in

Europe. The picturesque tales of James Fenimore Cooper, Washington Irving, and Nathaniel Hawthorne had an avid readership, not only in America but also in Europe. In poetry William Cullen Bryant's reverence for nature, Edgar Allan Poe's lyrical if undisciplined lines, and Walt Whitman's unique paeans of praise to individualism all mark them as true romantics. Henry David Thoreau, even more than Whitman, was a living romantic, intensely individualistic, seeking to live the life of man in the state of nature. Ralph Waldo Emerson's transcendentalism fully matched the idealism of German philosophy. In the United States romantic literature had an even longer vogue than in Europe, as may be seen in the poetry and tales of Henry Wadsworth Longfellow and James Russell Lowell.

HISTORY

History attained popularity as a literary form in the romantic era. In part its vogue resulted from the veneration for the past that was characteristic of the times; in part it arose because historians wrote for the literate general public, not just for other historians. History also had political uses, which helped it to popularity. Thomas Macaulay (1800–1859) wrote Whig history, glorifying England's progress and attributing it to the revolution of 1689; Thomas Carlyle (1795–1881) wrote Tory history, deploring the advance of industrialism and democracy. In France Adolphe Thiers (1797–1877) and François Guizot (1787–1874), both of whom were politicians as well as historians, wrote what might be called the Whig history of the French. Somewhat more radical, the popular historian Jules Michelet (1798–1874) wrote stirring imaginative history aimed at keeping alive the spirit and traditions of the revolution of 1789.

This same period witnessed the beginning of the movement for scientific history. In 1824 the young German historian Leopold von Ranke (1795–1886) published *Zur Kritik neuerer Geschichtschreiber,* which laid the basis for modern historical criticism. Ranke's aim was to write history "as it really happened," although he also professed to see "the hand of God" in history. Friedrich von Savigny (1778–1861), professor of law at the University of Berlin, established the discipline of historical jurisprudence, which maintained that the legal as well as the other institutions of each nation depended upon their own historical development. He opposed the so-called school of natural law, which held that deductive legal principles could be established for all times and places. Shortly afterward another group of German professors inaugurated the historical school of political economy in opposition to the classical or deductive school that flourished in England. The aspect of romanticism that extolled tradition and looked to the past thus proved to have a seminal influence in many areas of intellectual endeavor.

ART

The romantic mood affected the arts quite as much as literature and philosophy. Although sculpture did not flourish during the period, painting was quite distinctive. Artists were much more interested in a lavish use of color and in subject matter and imaginative elements than in the classical concerns of form and precision. As in literature, there were two distinctive tendencies in romantic art. One group of artists glorified the exotic and the heroic. They painted wild landscapes, exaggerated figures, and subjects that appealed to the imagination. Eugene Delacroix's (1798–1863) scenes of the Greek Revolution (although he had never set foot in Greece) are good examples. The other group of artists sought a return to simple, everyday, commonplace things. In the eighteenth century artists who had painted landscapes were regarded as second-rate, but English painters like John Constable (1776–1836) and J. M. W. Turner (1775–1851) restored the art of landscape paintings to its earlier prominence. Constable, for example, painted simple, idyllic rustic scenes that matched in spirit the poetry of Wordsworth. At the same time both groups had many things in common. Delacroix, who was perhaps the most famous of the romantic painters, freely acknowledged his indebtedness to Constable. What they had most in common was a revolt against the prevailing style and traditions of the classicists.

The transition from classical to romantic as the prevailing mode in painting came rather suddenly in the 1820's. During the first two decades of the century painting in Europe, especially in France, had been dominated by Jacques-Louis David (1748–1825), the great painter of the French Revolution and the Napoleonic era, and a confirmed classicist. The latent conflict between the old established doctrines and the new tendencies became public in 1819 with the exhibition of the "Raft of the Medusa" by Théodore Géricault (1791–1824). Classical critics accused romantic painters of "painting with a drunken broom." In reply, the more flamboyant romantic artists disdainfully turned up their coat collars whenever they stood in front of a classical painting "in order not to catch cold." By 1830 romanticism had won the struggle. It fitted better with the temper of the times, and it had greater appeal for the less cultivated artistic tastes of the new middle classes; classicism appealed principally to the older aristocratic values. Although some classical painters continued to work, romantic painting dominated the artistic scene until the advent of realism in the second half of the nineteenth century.

ARCHITECTURE

The romantic invasion of architecture, hinted at in a few buildings of the late eighteenth century, was delayed because of a classical revival stimulated by Thomas Jefferson in America and by Napoleon's admiration for the institutions of the Roman Republic and Empire. Outstanding examples of the classical revival in architecture are the rotunda of the University of Virginia, designed by Jefferson, and the Church of the Madeleine in Paris, which was begun in 1806 at the height of the Napoleonic Empire. Although the classical style continued in widespread use until the middle of the nineteenth century, by the 1830's and 1840's the romantic invasion had begun in earnest. It took the form of a so-called Gothic revival, which exemplified the romantic concern for the historic past — the Middle Ages in particular. It began with the restoration of many medieval castles and fortresses. In France, Viollet-le-Duc (1814–1879) restored the medieval walled city of Carcassonne and the beautiful and elegant Sainte Chapelle in Paris. During this period embellishments were added to a number of very old buildings. The cathedrals of Cologne and of Notre Dame in Paris, for example, had been built over several hundred years in the later Middle Ages, so that it was not too great a stretch of the romantic imagination for the architect to say, when he added a spire to Notre Dame in 1852, that he was "completing" the cathedral.

The rapid growth of cities in the nineteenth century and the no less rapid increase in wealth created a demand for many new buildings, public as well as private. Churches, schools, government buildings, and even railroad stations, gymnasiums, factories, and warehouses employed the Gothic revival style. In a few instances the results were strikingly beautiful and effective, as in the Houses of Parliament in London. Far more frequently, however, the Gothic revival structures were unsuited to the purpose for which they were built, were poorly proportioned and located, lacked adequate lighting and ventilation, and were encumbered by a superabundance of cheap ornamentation that detracted from their aesthetic effect. Much of the responsibility for this so-called Victorian Gothic can be attributed to the influence of the English author and art critic John Ruskin (1819–1900). Ruskin was in many ways a typical romantic, who sought to escape from the hated industrial system of the nineteenth century by encasing it in a medieval shell.

MUSIC

Romanticism registered some of its greatest creative achievements in music. Romantic music appealed to the emotions. Unlike the pure, almost mathematical forms of eighteenth-century music, much of romantic music was programmatic. Symphonies and concertos, as well as operas and songs, tried to tell a story or create a mood. Composers made a greater use of experimentation, innovation, and imagination; they felt less bound by formal rules. They used new instruments and larger orchestras to achieve effects. They drew their themes from ancient folk tales and sagas, as in the operas of Carl Maria von Weber (1786–1826), from nature, as in the great *Pastoral Symphony* of Beethoven, and from tales of heroism and love.

The transition from classicism to romanticism in music and the evolution of the latter is most evident in the works of the great German and Austrian composers from Haydn to Wagner. Ludwig van Beethoven (1770–1827) was the key figure. In the works of Haydn and Mozart the classical music of the eighteenth century had reached its highest peak. Although in the later works of Mozart and the first two symphonies of Beethoven innovations were made that indicated the future directions of music, the innovations remained within the traditions of eighteenth-century music. Not until the third symphony of Beethoven, appropriately called *Eroica* (Heroic), was there a definite break with tradition. Beethoven in music, like Goethe in literature, belonged to both the classic and the romantic periods and exemplified the best of both. Weber, Schubert, Schumann, and Brahms further developed the romantic style, which reached its ultimate development in the spectacular operas of Wagner.

In France the *Symphonie Fantastique* of Hector Berlioz (1803–1869), first performed in 1830, could be called a musical manifesto of the romantic movement. Berlioz acknowledged his indebtedness to Beethoven and asserted that he would realize through conscious discipleship the potentialities inherent in the innovations of Beethoven. In music, as in architecture, romanticism lingered on into the second half of the nineteenth and even into the twentieth century, strongly influencing composers of such widely differing temperaments as Tchaikovsky, Bizet, Dvořák, Grieg, and Sibelius.

ROMANTICISM IN PHILOSOPHY, POLITICS, AND RELIGION

Idealism in philosophy, closely related to romanticism, also flourished in the first half of the nineteenth century. Its most important forerunner was a German, Immanuel Kant (1724–1804). In *The Critique of Pure Reason* he reacted against the excessive rationalism of eighteenth-century philosophers and stressed spiritual qualities and phenomena that could not be grasped by human reason alone. In this respect his thinking accorded well with the temper of romanticism. Kantian idealism was further developed by Johann Fichte (1762–1814) and F. W. Schelling (1775–1854), but the outstanding figure in nineteenth-century idealism was Georg Wilhelm Friedrich Hegel (1770–1831), professor of philosophy at the University of Berlin.

HEGEL AND DIALECTICAL IDEALISM

For Hegel ideas were reality. Material objects and the events of history were mere reflections of ideas. Moreover, specific ideas were only imperfect pieces of a larger whole, an Absolute Idea. The one great reality was the Absolute Idea — "the Idea which thinks itself." One of Hegel's most important contributions to philosophy was the development of the dialectical method of reasoning. Dialectic was by no means new — it had been used at least as early as the time of Socrates — but Hegel made it into a formal logical method. According to the dialectical process, an idea, theme, or "thesis" is opposed by or gives rise to its opposite or contradiction, called the "antithesis." Out of the conflict of the thesis and the antithesis results a new idea or "synthesis," which is not a mere compromise of the old but is new and superior to both. The synthesis, in turn, becomes the new thesis, giving rise to its opposite and resulting in a new and higher synthesis. The process is never-ending. This was an accepted method of argument or reasoning in philosophy and science, but Hegel thought that the process could also be observed in the movement of history. According to him, history proceeds through the conflict of forces or, more precisely, through the conflict of ideas, since historical forces are merely manifestations of pure ideas.

One idea of great importance in Hegelian philosophy was the idea of the state. For Hegel the state was not simply a collection of individuals organized under a government. As an idea, the state was something antecedent to and superior to individuals. The state did not exist for the citizens; the citizens existed for the state. Hegel wrote in his *Philosophy of History,* "The State is the externally existing, genuinely moral life. . . . Truth is the unity of the universal and particular Will, and the universal is to be found in the State, in its laws, its universal and rational arrangements. The State is the Divine Idea as it exists on earth. . . . The State is the Idea of Spirit in the external manifestation of human Will and its Freedom." Such notions, drilled into generations of German schoolboys, had a profound effect on subsequent German history. Filtered through the philosophy of one of Hegel's self-proclaimed disciples, Karl Marx, they have exercised a great influence on the entire world.

According to Hegel, the Prussian state of the restoration period embodied the highest development that mankind had yet reached. He foresaw the further development of Prussia into a greater German nation; that is, the German nation would arise out of a dialectical process of struggle between the thesis of the Prussian state and various antithetical ideas. It would represent the *Volkgeist* or spirit of the German people. His philosophy struck a sympathetic note with the tendency in romanticism that exalted collective ideas and historical tradition, and it gave a profound impetus to nationalist movements, especially the pan-German movement.

Hegel's emphasis on the omnipotence of the state and on the element of conflict in the dialectical process had strong political overtones. As far as he was concerned, war served a moral purpose and was superior to peace, for it kept a people from becoming decadent and weak. The rules of private morality did not apply to states, which were laws unto themselves. Hegel even went so far as to suggest that there might be a few "world-historical" individuals who fitted into the same lawless category as the state.

Romanticism found another philosophical ally in Arthur Schopenhauer (1788–1860), a slightly younger contemporary of Hegel. Hegel's "world spirit" was rational, although it had certain affinities with the mystical anti-rationalism of some of the more extreme romantics. Schopenhauer replaced the spirit by the "will," which was expressly antirational. His influential and profoundly pessimistic book *The World as Will and Idea* prepared the way intellectually for the complete nihilism of certain late nineteenth-century philosophers, especially Friedrich Nietzsche. (See p. 804.)

ROMANTICISM AND RELIGION

Christianity appeared to be a dying force in Europe in the last years of the Old Regime. Under the influence of the Enlightenment even prelates of the Church expressed their skepticism openly, and during the French Revolution the adherents of the cult of reason made a frontal attack on traditional religion. But a religious revival had been foreshadowed in the eighteenth century by Pietism in Germany and Methodism in England. Romanticism greatly strengthened this development. Madame de Staël declared, "I do not know exactly what we must believe, but I believe that we must believe! The eighteenth century did nothing but deny. The human spirit lives by its beliefs. Acquire faith through Christianity, or through German philosophy, or merely through enthusiasm, but believe in something!"

Emotion, sentimentality, and enthusiasm — the hallmarks of romanticism and frequent components of religion — became the ties that bound the two together. Chateaubriand sought to justify Christianity on purely emotional and aesthetic grounds in his widely popular *Genius of Christianity, or Beauties of the Christian Religion* (1802). Fleeing from the "babble of science and reason," he claimed that the sheer beauty of Christianity is sufficient proof of its truth. The similarity between his sentiment and that expressed by Keats in the famous lines

> "Beauty is truth, truth beauty" — that is all
> Ye know on earth, and all ye need to know.

is indicative of the strong affinity between romanticism and the religious revival.

The emotionalism of evangelical preachers and reformers easily gave way to mysticism and fanaticism. In 1814 a Methodist prophetess in London promised to give birth to a Son of God at the age of sixty-five; she was no doubt mentally deranged, but many more or less normal individuals thought they saw visions, heard voices from the tomb, and could communicate with the spiritual world. The Baroness von Krüdener, whose eloquence reduced the Emperor of All the Russias to tears and persuaded him to undertake the Holy Alliance, held daily séances in her apartment in Paris in the fall of 1815. These bizarre gatherings, at which the hostess pretended to receive divine revelations, were attended by the tsar and other monarchs, as well as leaders of Parisian society. For most believers such frenzied experiences served as an emotional release from the cares and frustrations of the everyday world, but among the leaders of religious thought the "religion of the heart" reflected disillusionment with what they considered the "dry rot of rationalism" and the inability of human reason to solve the riddles of the universe. The influential German Protestant theologian Friedrich Schleiermacher (1768–1834) sought to reconcile science and religion by putting them on different planes. In *Addresses on Religion to the Educated Who Despise It* (1799) he explained that religion is not a system of thought but a mystical inner experience that places the individual in direct communion with God. Schleiermacher helped restore religion to respectability among the intellectuals, but many of his followers dropped his tolerance of science and the scientific spirit and went over wholeheartedly to mysticism and obscurantism.

The nineteenth-century religious revival occurred first among the Protestant sects, but it soon spread to Roman Catholicism, where it eventually had its greatest impact. In the 1830's the Oxford Movement tried to reintroduce Catholic doctrine and liturgy into the Church of England. Its leader, John Henry Newman, eventually left the Church of England for that of Rome, in which he became a cardinal. Many leaders of German romanticism became converts to Catholicism. Although this development was at first a personal and emotional reaction, it could not fail to have strong political overtones. With few exceptions its influence was heavily on the side of conservatism. Even the Methodists, most radical of the Protestant sects in religious doctrine, demanded loyalty and obedience to all established authorities. The Protestant state churches of northern Europe held the same view. The most striking religious development of the restoration period was the marked revival of the papacy's influence. Pope Pius VII (1800–1823) gained much sympathy — even in Protestant countries — as a result of Napoleon's persecution. In 1814 he regained temporal control of Rome and the States of the Church.

Most of the statesmen of the restoration regarded religion as a potential ally of great value in their attempt to restore the Old Regime and worked actively for the "union of throne and altar." Every European state had an established church that was supported financially by the state or by its own endowment of lands. Although disputes occasionally arose between the pope and the rulers of Roman Catholic countries over the appointment of bishops and similar matters, the normal situation was one of cooperation to preserve respect for traditional religious and political forms. Pius VII and his energetic secretary of state Cardinal Consalvi negotiated concordats with almost all of the Catholic countries and even made an agreement with Prussia for the regulation of Catholic matters in that Protestant country. The clergy organized societies of laymen, such as the Congregation of the Virgin in France, the San Fedists in Italy, and the Society of the Exterminating Angel in Spain, which were frequently used by aristocratic leaders as instruments for the persecution of liberals.

The belief in the absolute supremacy of the pope, known as ultramontanism, received strong intellectual support in the restoration period. Its greatest theorist was Count Joseph de Maistre, a nobleman who was expropriated by the French Revolution and returned to France in 1815 after many years of exile. In 1817 he published *Du pape* (Of the Pope), in which he argued that in questions of faith and morals the pope was infallible and that all Christian nations should recognize his supremacy as a cure for lawlessness, disorder, and revolution. Maistre did not, however, depend on moral authority alone as a correction for the ills of society: "All greatness, all power, all order," he wrote, "depend upon the executioner. He is the tie that binds society together. Take away this incomprehensible force and at that very moment order is suspended by chaos, thrones fall, and states disappear."

ROMANTICISM AND POLITICS

In politics romanticism is sometimes identified with conservatism because of their common opposition to the principles of the Enlightenment and the French Revolution. The close connection between romanticism and religion, especially the espousal of ultramontane doctrines by many romantic writers, also had much to do with its conservative tendencies. Chateaubriand served the restoration government of France as foreign minister, and many other leaders of romantic thought either took an active part in restoration politics or supported the principles of conservatism in their writings. Sir Walter Scott was an outspoken Tory. The Lake poets — Wordsworth, Coleridge, and Robert Southey (who became poet laureate in 1813) — had been favorable to the French Revolution in their youth, but by 1815 they had gone over to conservatism. The reaction went to even greater lengths among the German romantics.

At the same time, romanticism had no specific political content. It was not an ideology but a mood. If some romantics were conservative or even reactionary in their politics, at least as large a number went to the opposite extreme. The poets Byron and Shelley were flaming liberals, even radicals, in their day. Nor should it be forgotten that although romanticism stressed tradition and the glories of the past, it also gloried in the individual and in his right — indeed, his duty — to develop himself in his own way, according to his own unique experience and the dictates of his "inner voice" or conscience. After about 1820 many of the younger romantics who had not directly experienced the trauma of the French Revolution grew increasingly restive with the stodginess and restrictions of the restoration governments. In France Victor Hugo, who defined romanticism simply as "liberalism in literature," and the poet-politician Alphonse de Lamartine spread the doctrine of romanticism as a liberating force; Heinrich Heine did the same in Germany. Even Chateaubriand became disillusioned with the absolutist tendencies of his new sovereign, Charles X, and supported the Revolution of 1830. In addition, the force of nationalism, which in the first half of the nineteenth century was anything but conservative, drew heavily on the emotional reserves and historical penchant of romanticism.

RESTORATION POLITICS

METTERNICH AND THE CONSERVATIVE
REACTION IN GERMANY

The overarching purpose of the deliberations at Vienna and subsequently the congress system was the resurrection and preservation of the old established social order and the exorcism of the demons unleashed by the French Revolution — the demons of liberalism and nationalism in particular. No one could have been better fitted to supervise the task than Metternich. A West German (Rhineland) aristocrat by birth, whose ancestral domains had been swallowed by revolutionary land reform, he became foreign minister and eventually chancellor of the polyglot, multinational Austrian Empire. As Metternich saw it, the problem of Austria was the problem of Europe in microcosm: to preserve the vested interests of the antinational, antiliberal monarchy and aristocracy against the aspirations and encroachments of self-conscious nationalities and a rising middle class. The solution for both was identical, according to Metternich: divide and rule. The peace of Europe and the integrity of the Austrian Empire both demanded that all liberal and nationalist movements be squelched at their source. No means to this end were too reprehensible, nor did Metternich make a distinction between foreign and domestic policy except that of expediency. He suppressed the revolts in Italy and Germany with the same ruthlessness as he did those in Galicia and Lombardy; he intercepted the correspondence of and spied on the rulers of sovereign states as frequently as he did on the leaders of local secret societies. For Metternich, what was good for Austria was good for

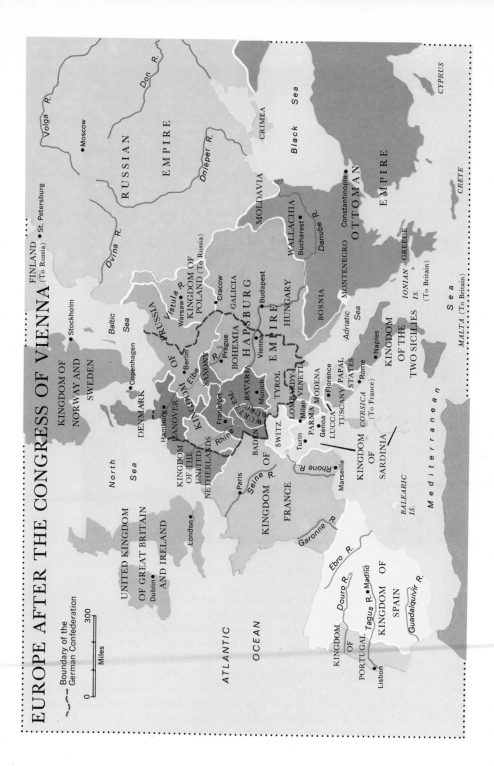

EUROPE AFTER THE CONGRESS OF VIENNA

‑ ‑ ‑ Boundary of the
German Confederation

0   300
Miles

ATLANTIC OCEAN

UNITED KINGDOM OF GREAT BRITAIN AND IRELAND

London●
Dublin●

North Sea

KINGDOM OF NORWAY AND SWEDEN

Stockholm●

Baltic Sea

Copenhagen●

DENMARK

Hamburg●

KINGDOM OF THE UNITED NETHERLANDS

Rhine

KINGDOM OF FRANCE

Paris●

Seine R.

Garonne R.

Ebro R.

Douro R.

KINGDOM OF PORTUGAL

Lisbon●

Tagus R.

Madrid●

KINGDOM OF SPAIN

Guadalquivir R.

BALEARIC IS.

FINLAND (To Russia)

St. Petersburg●

RUSSIAN EMPIRE

Moscow●

Volga R.

Don R.

Dnieper R.

Dvina R.

Vistula R.

Warsaw●

KINGDOM OF POLAND (To Russia)

PRUSSIA

Berlin●

Elbe

SAXONY

Prague●

BOHEMIA

KINGDOM OF HANOVER

Frankfort●

WÜRTEM BERG

BADEN

Munich●

BAVARIA

SWITZ.

TYROL

HAPSBURG EMPIRE

Vienna●

Cracow●

GALICIA

Budapest●

HUNGARY

LOMBARDY VENETIA

Milan●

Turin●

Genoa●

PARMA

MODENA

LUCCA

Florence●

TUSCANY

PAPAL STATES

Rome●

KINGDOM OF SARDINIA

CORSICA (To France)

Marseille●

Rhone R.

Naples●

KINGDOM OF THE TWO SICILIES

BOSNIA

MONTENEGRO

WALLACHIA

Bucharest●

Danube R.

MOLDAVIA

Black Sea

CRIMEA

OTTOMAN EMPIRE

Constantinople●

Adriatic Sea

IONIAN IS. (To Britain)

GREECE (To Britain)

Mediterranean Sea

MALTA (To Britain)

CRETE

CYPRUS

539

Clemens von Metternich, by Sir Thomas Lawrence

  *"It is necessary to point out in a more particular manner the evil which
threatens to deprive [society], at one blow, of the real blessings, the fruits of
genuine civilization. . . . This evil may be described in one word—presumption.
. . . It is principally the middle classes of society which this moral gangrene
has affected. . . . We see this intermediary class abandon itself with a blind
fury and animosity . . . to all the means which seem proper to assuage its thirst
for power, applying itself to the task of persuading kings that their rights
are confined to sitting upon a throne, while those of the people are to govern,
and to attack all that centuries have bequeathed as holy and worthy of man's
respect."* Secret Memorandum of Metternich to Emperor Alexander of
Russia, December 15, 1820, reprinted in MEMOIRS OF PRINCE METTERNICH
(New York, 1880–1882).

Europe; more pointedly, what threatened Europe in the form of revolution, wherever it took place and whatever its inspiration, threatened disaster for Austria.

In the wake of the Napoleonic wars liberal and nationalist aspirations were present throughout Europe, but especially in Metternich's own backyard, Germany. Both the French Revolution and the Napoleonic wars made a profound imprint upon Germany. The wars not only destroyed the antique Holy Roman Empire, the political framework of pre-Napoleonic Germany, but they also kindled a flame of patriotism for a German fatherland that had never been. The revolutionary reforms of the political, social, and economic orders in France led German liberals to believe that such reforms might equally well serve Germany. The Vienna settlement, as applied to Germany, failed to satisfy either the liberals or the nationalists. The weak Germanic Confederation disappointed the hopes of the latter for a unified German state, and the reactionary domestic policies of the rulers who were influenced by Metternich disappointed the liberal reformers. Prussia, in particular, disappointed both nationalists and liberals, who in 1815 had expected it to take the lead in creating a progressive German nation. Instead, reactionary elements in Prussia curbed the reforming zeal of Chancellor Hardenberg, while the king, Frederick William III, fell increasingly under the influence of Metternich and the Austrian emperor. In default of other leadership, university students strongly influenced by romanticism took over the liberal and nationalist movements. They organized student groups called *Burschenschaften* (the forerunners of American college fraternities) to agitate for liberal and patriotic goals. On the whole their methods were innocuous as their aims were idealistic, but occasionally the exuberance of youth led them into riotous demonstrations. For example, the Wartburg Festival of October, 1817, organized to celebrate two great patriotic events, the tercentenary of Luther's revolt from the Church and the fourth anniversary of the battle of Leipzig, climaxed in a bonfire episode in which various symbols of the old order were consigned to the flames. Metternich, whether personally alarmed or not, took advantage of such demonstrations to frighten the German rulers with specters of revolutionary conspiracy.

In 1819 the assassination of the reactionary journalist August von Kotzebue by a *Burschenschafter* from Jena gave Metternich the opportunity he needed to clamp controls on the universities and other centers of liberal ferment. He called representatives of the eight largest German states to Carlsbad in the summer of 1819 and persuaded them to adopt the Carlsbad Decrees, which he had ratified by the Federal Diet in Frankfurt the following September. The decrees contained three major provisions: (1) the appointment of political commissioners for all German universities, with powers of summary dismissal of both students and

542

"Colour Structure, Moon Burst," by J. M. W. Turner

"So great was Turner's output — his bequest to the nation comprised some two hundred and eighty pictures and between nineteen and twenty thousand water-colours and drawings — so vast his range and creative genius that one can say little more than this: what Michelangelo is in figure painting Turner is in landscape and seascape. Beginning as the assistant of Thomas Malton he advanced irresistibly, engulfing or comprehending all that had gone before him in landscape. . . . Having disposed of them he went his way, until he had created a new heaven of vision." C. H. Collins Baker, BRITISH PAINTING (London, 1933).

professors; (2) strict censorship of the press; (3) the creation of a special commission of inquiry — a sort of secular inquisition — to investigate and prosecute secret societies and others suspected of harboring subversive ideas. Although the rulers of some of the smaller states resented this inter-ference with their internal affairs, Metternich's system prevailed, rein-forced by a network of police spies and international agents. Except for a few brief and ineffectual episodes of agitation in the wake of the revolutions of 1830, his repression effectively stifled all manifestations of liberalism and nationalism in Germany until 1848.

THE BOURBON RESTORATION IN FRANCE

The government of the Bourbon Restoration in France rested on an uneasy compromise between the bourgeois liberalism surviving from the Revolution and the absolutist, so-called legitimist, aspirations of the monarchy and returned émigré nobility. This compromise, embodied in the Charter of 1814 and amended somewhat in 1830, served France as a constitution until 1848. The Charter, which Louis XVIII professed to grant voluntarily to his people, opened with a long preamble invoking Divine Providence and recalling the glories of the ancient monarchy, just barely omitting the phrase "divine right of kings." It continued with a series of twelve articles devoted to the "public rights of the French," a slightly modified restatement of the Declaration of the Rights of Man, and concluded with a brief and rather vague stipulation concerning the form of the government.

Executive power was vested in the king, to be exercised through his ministers. The Charter also provided for a bicameral legislature on the British model, with a Chamber of Peers appointed by the king — some hereditary, some for life — and a Chamber of Deputies indirectly elected by a franchise that was sharply restricted by age and property qualifica-tions. In effect, the vote was restricted to approximately one of every hundred adult males — that is, those who belonged to the landed aristocracy and the upper bourgeoisie. They were considered the legal nation or *pays légal.* Two provisions of the Charter — one deliberately vague, the other quite explicit — are especially notable because of their subsequent history. One stated tersely that the "King's ministers are responsible," without stating to whom — the king or the chambers. The other permitted the king to issue ordinances "necessary for the . . . safety of the State."

Hastily composed though it was, the Charter might have become the basis for an evolving constitutional monarchy of the British type if it had not been for the men who manipulated it. Although the compromise could not prevent the White Terror of 1815 and 1816, in which royalists wreaked vengeance on former revolutionaries and Bonapartists, the worldly, cynical Louis for a time succeeded in placating most segments of the French population. But in 1820 the assassination of the king's nephew, the duke de Berri, forced the king to countenance a reactionary policy inspired by the Ultras — the extreme rightists — surrounding his brother, the future Charles X. Charles succeeded to the throne in 1824. With the Villèle ministry, which lasted from 1821 to 1827, the Ultras made a determined attempt to restore as far as possible the position that they had held under the Old Regime.

TORY RULE IN BRITAIN

Great Britain emerged from the Napoleonic wars as the most powerful and resplendent nation of the time. Alone among the victorious allies, Britain had opposed France continuously since the outbreak of war in 1792 (except for the brief truce of Amiens, when all of Europe was at peace). British money financed the triumphant coalition, British industry supplied it, and at Waterloo British troops under the duke of Wellington led it to the final victory. The British navy ruled the seas, protecting an enlarged empire; it was the only remaining empire of any significance. At home the changes in agriculture and industry that were to revolutionize economic and social life in the course of the nineteenth century were already under way, creating new wealth and affluence.

Nevertheless, the victory was not achieved without sacrifice. Under the pressure of war many of the traditional liberties of Englishmen had been suspended or restricted, as in the hated Combination Acts of 1799 and 1800. The very changes in agriculture and industry that produced riches and victory also produced dislocation and distress. War-induced inflation redistributed income at the expense of the least well-to-do, and a long postwar depression, accompanied by unemployment and falling wages, created popular discontent and reinforced demands for political, social, and economic reform. These movements were led by men such as the radical journalist William Cobbett (1763–1835), the humanitarian philanthropist Robert Owen (1771–1858), the egotistical demagogue Henry

"Orator" Hunt (1773–1835), and the utilitarian philosopher Jeremy Bentham (1748–1832). The governing Tory party responded to them with a reactionary policy as severely repressive as that inspired on the Continent by Metternich.

The Tories had been in power almost continuously since 1783. Although generally their leaders came from the same social class as the Whigs — that is, the aristocracy — and did not differ greatly in matters of principle, they clung resolutely to their positions for reasons of personal interest. Lord Liverpool, prime minister from 1812 to 1827, was a man of upright character though mediocre intelligence, but many of his supporters were venal, corrupt, and reactionary. Their policies were facilitated by their victory over Napoleon and also by the upper-class fear of social revolution and by the weakened authority of the crown. The dissolute and unpopular Prince of Wales (who later became George IV) reigned as regent for his father George III, permanently insane from 1811 to his death in 1820.

The Tory response to the postwar depression took the form of the new Corn Law of 1815, which almost totally excluded imported grain, thereby raising prices and keeping up rents on the estates of the wealthy. The government abolished the income tax and imposed new excise taxes on commodities consumed by the populace. In answer to the demands for reform expressed in petitions, public meetings, demonstrations, and occasional riots, the government adopted the infamous Coercion Acts of 1817, which suspended the right of habeas corpus, extended the meaning of the expression "seditious and treasonable activities," and increased the severity of punishment for violations.

In 1819 in the midst of the postwar depression a crowd assembled on St. Peter's Field in Manchester to listen to "Orator" Hunt demand parliamentary reform and repeal of the Corn Laws. Although the gathering was peaceable in itself, the authorities took fright and ordered soldiers to arrest the speaker and disperse the mob. The ensuing melee, in which eleven persons were killed and more than four hundred injured, was dubbed the Peterloo Massacre. In addition to the use of force, the government resorted to stringent new legislation. The Six Acts of 1819 went further than the Coercion Acts, imposing restrictions on the press, the right of assembly, and the right to bear arms. In 1820 the government was further convinced that these measures were amply justified when it discovered and frustrated the Cato Street conspiracy, an extremist plot to assassinate the cabinet in one blow.

OTHER REACTIONARY REGIMES

Elsewhere the prospects for liberalism and reform fared no better. In Sweden the French marshal Bernadotte, who had been elected crown prince in 1810, succeeded to the throne as Charles XIV in 1818. He followed a sternly reactionary and absolutist policy in Sweden and also in Norway, which had been joined to the Swedish crown against the wishes of the Norwegians. The newly created Kingdom of the Netherlands had a moderately liberal constitution on the model of the French Charter, but the arbitrary and stubborn King William I, former Prince of Orange, frequently over-stepped his prerogatives and aroused the antagonism of his subjects. The Belgians in particular, who had not been consulted on the decision to unite them with the Dutch, resented the inferior position that they occupied in the union.

The situation was worse to the south. The Bourbon Ferdinand VII, restored to the throne of Spain in 1814, promised to retain the liberal constitution adopted by the Cortes in 1812 at the height of the Spanish opposition to Napoleon. He soon defaulted on his promise and unleashed an orgy of reaction, misrule, and persecution that alienated even the army, one of the pillars of his regime. Under the surveillance of Austria the petty despots of Italy willingly danced to the tune of Metternich. In Piedmont the restored Victor Emmanuel I hated the principles of the French Revolution so much that he abolished the French legal codes and other reforms and restored almost intact the old semifeudal regime. He even uprooted the French plants in his botanical garden. At Rome Pius VII reestablished the Jesuits on a worldwide basis; the order had been widely regarded as a friend of absolutism and had been officially dissolved in 1776. The pope also reinstituted both the Inquisition and the Index and created a wholly clerical government for the States of the Church. Even in decentralized, republican Switzerland most of the cantons followed a reactionary policy and, under pressure from the great powers, persecuted political refugees from neighboring countries. In eastern Europe Tsar Alexander I of Russia, regarded as somewhat liberal in his youth, became increasingly reactionary.

By the beginning of 1820 the revolutionary ardor that had disturbed the tranquillity of Europe for more than three decades seemed to have been quelled at last. Yet the appearance was deceiving. In the overseas outposts of Western civilization the fires of revolution burned brightly, and in Europe itself the embers smoldered beneath the ashes of reaction.

THE RISING TIDE
OF REVOLUTION
CHAPTER TWENTY-TWO

The antagonisms engendered by the oppressive policies of the restoration governments, together with powerful economic and social forces, gradually eroded and eventually overthrew the political and social system of the Vienna settlement. Revolutionary outbursts, at first weak and sporadic, grew in frequency and power throughout the first half of the century to culminate in the widespread and nearly simultaneous disorders of 1848. The revolutionists sought intellectual justification for their activities in the ideologies of liberalism and nationalism, sometimes strongly tinged with romanticism and occasionally with socialism. As long as both liberals and nationalists struggled against the same reactionary governments, it was easy for them to believe that they also struggled for the same objectives: liberty and self-determination. Not until 1848 did they discover the possibility of inherent conflict between the two.

REVOLUTIONARY CURRENTS:
LIBERALISM AND NATIONALISM

LIBERALISM

Liberalism has many definitions, but classical or nineteenth-century liberalism embodied a belief that human progress could best be achieved by means of individual liberty and free institutions. Liberals advocated constitutional government, freedom of the press and religion, free speech, and freedom for individuals to pursue their own economic interests. Liberalism did not, however, involve the idea of democracy in the first half of the nineteenth century, for democracy meant the rule of the people. Liberalism was the creed of the growing middle classes, who wished to curb the arbitrary power of absolute monarchs and the special privileges of the landed aristocracy but did not want rule by the unpropertied masses. With the passage of time the basic ideas of liberalism proved capable of great extension, and in some cases liberalism gradually blended into republicanism, socialism, or a faith in democracy.

The first use of the word liberal in a political sense occurred in the 1820's, and was intended as an epithet, in much the same way that a demagogue today might label his domestic political opponent a Socialist or Communist. The Spanish revolutionaries of 1820 called themselves *liberales.* Supporters of the conservative or reactionary governing parties in France and Britain promptly applied the label to their opponents, where it stuck, eventually to be worn with pride. English liberals liked to trace their origins back at least to Magna Carta. Whether or not that claim was legitimate, it is clear that the political experiences of the seventeenth century had much to do with shaping English liberalism. In particular, Locke's treatises on civil government served as a foundation for much of the best liberal theory in England as well as on the Continent and in North America. The outstanding contemporary philosopher of English liberalism was Jeremy Bentham (1748–1832).

BENTHAM AND UTILITARIANISM

Bentham, scion of generations of successful London lawyers, trained for the legal profession himself. From the outset of his career he took an interest in legal reform. In his first published work, *A Fragment on Government* (1776), the young radical attacked the great jurist Blackstone for the latter's praises of the British constitution, which Bentham believed to be exaggerated and unjustified. In 1789 he published his most influential book, *An Introduction to the Principles of Morals and Legislation.* He continued to agitate for reform and to write throughout his long life (his collected works fill more than a dozen large volumes), and he inspired a whole school of philosophers and reformers whose influence in the world today is very strong.

Unlike other liberal philosophers in the tradition of Locke and the Enlightenment (including the American and French revolutionaries), Bentham rejected the doctrine of natural rights as a basis of political philosophy, calling it in effect metaphysical nonsense. Bentham adopted what he thought was a more practical, realistic approach and attempted to root his philosophy in human nature and psychology. "Nature has placed mankind under the governance of two sovereign masters, *pain* and *pleasure. . . .* They govern us in all we do, in all we say, in all we think: every effort we can make to throw off our subjection, will serve but to demonstrate and confirm it." Human happiness, according to Bentham, consisted in the attainment of pleasure and the avoidance of pain. The quality or property of conferring happiness Bentham called "utility"; hence his philosophy is called utilitarianism. "By the principle of utility is meant that principle which approves or disapproves of every action whatsoever, according to the tendency which it appears to have

The Mansell Collection

Jeremy Bentham

"Bentham has been in this age and century the great questioner of things established. It is by the influence of the modes of thought with which his writings innoculated a considerable number of thinking men, that the yoke of authority has been broken, and innumerable opinions, formerly received upon tradition as incontestable, are put upon their defence and required to give an account of themselves. Who, before Bentham . . . dared to speak disrespectfully . . . of the British Constitution, or the English Law? He did so; and his arguments and his example together encouraged others. . . . Until he spoke out, those who found our institutions unsuited to them did not dare to say so, did not dare consciously to think so. Bentham broke the spell." John Stuart Mill, ESSAYS ON POLITICS AND CULTURE, ed. Gertrude Himmelfarb (Garden City, N.Y., 1962).

to augment or diminish the happiness of the party whose interest is in question." The object of government was to promote human happiness, which had been stated in the formula "the greatest good of the greatest number" by Beccaria, Bentham's Italian predecessor. Bentham and his followers, therefore, judged governments according to the manner in which their policies conformed to the principle of utility.

Bentham's followers included many distinguished intellects of the first half of the nineteenth century, including James Mill and his famous son, John Stuart Mill. The latter was a notable example of utilitarian education: he learned Greek at the age of three, digested David Ricardo's *Principles of Political Economy and Taxation* at thirteen, and had a nervous breakdown at twenty; but he recovered and went on to become one of England's foremost philosophers. The utilitarians were not overtly revolutionary; in their personal lives most of them were eminently respectable, even staid. Nevertheless, their ceaseless questioning and agitation for reform and a philosophy that was congenial to the British middle classes enabled them to carry out a series of silent revolutions, which were the more effectual in that they did not arouse undying, unregenerate opposition. In the words of John Stuart Mill, written in 1838, six years after Bentham's death, "The father of English innovation, both in doctrines and in institutions, is Bentham: he is the great *subversive*, or in the language of continental philosophers, the great *critical* thinker of his age and country."

CONTINENTAL LIBERALISM

French liberalism drew heavily on the writers of the Enlightenment and the ideals of the Revolution, but at the same time French liberals sought to dissociate themselves from Jacobinism and the excesses of the Revolution. As a result, whereas English liberalism was pragmatic, flexible, and evolutionary, French liberalism approached dogmatism. Indeed, one group of French liberals called themselves *doctrinaires*. They regarded the Charter of 1814 as a satisfactory instrument of government and were well content, on the whole, with the restoration government until it began to swing back toward royal absolutism under Charles X. Slightly to the left of the doctrinaires was a group that played a leading role in the revolution of 1830. It included the philosopher Benjamin Constant, the aging Marquis de Lafayette, and the fiery young journalist Adolphe Thiers. The greatest of the French liberal philosophers, Alexis de Tocqueville, belonged to no one school or party. Although he was an aristocrat, he foresaw the advent of democracy and sought to warn his countrymen and all mankind to make the most of its virtues without letting it result in mediocrity and mass tyranny. In his view the spirit of government was far more important than its outward forms.

Elsewhere on the Continent liberalism had few followers and fewer spokesmen, except in Belgium and Germany. Liberalism appealed especially to the middle classes of business and professional men. It flourished where they were most numerous and influential. In southern and eastern Europe liberalism became the creed of a few disaffected intellectuals who had little popular support. The smaller their prospects for success, the shriller became their pronouncements and the more violent their actions. Liberals in these areas of retarded economic and social development were eventually absorbed by the prevailing conservatism, or attracted to more radical ideologies.

NATIONALISM

The word nationalism refers to the awareness, sometimes reaching the intensity of a religious belief, of belonging to a distinct nationality. Although nation-states such as the Spanish, French, and English monarchies had arisen in the late Middle Ages, nationalism as a mass phenomenon developed only at the end of the eighteenth century. The first French Republic contributed to the development of popular nationalism with its patriotic symbols and *levée en masse* (military conscription). The revolutionary and Napoleonic wars helped spread it to much of the rest of Europe through emulation of or opposition to the conquering French. The Germans, who were divided and subject to foreign rule and oppression, were perhaps the foremost spokesmen of nationalist sentiments. Johann Gottfried Herder (1744–1803), a German clergyman and a forerunner of romanticism, first advanced a systematic theory of nationalism. His was a cultural nationalism, but under the impact of the Napoleonic wars nationalism became far more political. In "Addresses to the German Nation" Johann Fichte declared in 1808 that "to have character and to be German undoubtedly mean one and the same thing." When the War of Liberation began in 1813, he sent his students to fight against the French.

Nationalism continued to flourish and spread after the fall of Napoleon. National minorities in the polyglot Hapsburg and Russian empires and oppressed nationalities in Norway, Ireland, and the Belgian Netherlands sought to throw off alien rule. Politically divided nationalities — the Germans and Italians in particular — began to dream of unified national states. The current of nationalism even stirred the subject principalities of the Ottoman Empire in the Balkan peninsula. Romanticism played a part in this phase of the movement. The collectors of folk tales and folk songs, the philologists who sought to revive medieval Gaelic, Norwegian, or Slavonic languages, the poets and novelists who wrote of the heroic past, even the artists and musicians contributed to the development of national identities and patriotic sentiments. After 1815 the restoration governments pursued essentially cosmopolitan, antinational policies under the influence of Metternich, but they actually stimulated the growth of nationalism through their crude, inefficient attempts to repress it. Most of the youth groups and revolutionary secret societies that sprang up after 1815 — the *Burschenschaften* in Germany, the *Carbonari* in Italy, the *Hetairia Philike* in Greece, and others — were strongly nationalistic, as were the leaders of the revolutions in the New World.

REVOLUTION AND SELF-GOVERNMENT IN THE AMERICAS

The ideals of self-determination and self-government quickly took root in the Western Hemisphere after the successful revolt of Britain's American colonies. Not all who fought for American independence did so in the name of democracy, but the Declaration of Independence planted democratic seeds in virgin soil and the war itself fertilized them with the blood of patriots. Thereafter the growth of democracy could not be restrained. The example of the United States as a free, independent, and self-governing republic gave inspiration and courage to those both north and south of its borders who opposed the ineptitude and exploitation of their European rulers. After a series of constitutional struggles the inhabitants of Canada gained limited self-government within the framework of the British Empire. The colonies of Spain and Portugal achieved full independence, although difficulties of communication and the pronounced regionalism of some of the leaders of the former Spanish colonies resulted in the formation of many quarrelsome and unstable republics instead of one or a few large nations.

THE UNITED STATES: TERRITORIAL EXPANSION
AND THE RISE OF THE COMMON MAN, 1815–1850

At the time of adoption of the Constitution of 1789 electoral procedures in the United States were by no means democratic. The Constitution provided for indirect election of the President, the Vice President, and the Senate, and allowed each state to determine the manner of choosing its members of the House of Representatives. Most states had substantial property and other qualifications for the suffrage, which sharply limited the number of voters. As a result, for the first decade under the Constitution most state governments and the national government had a marked aristocratic character. The first notable change occurred with the election of Thomas Jefferson in 1800, sometimes called the Jeffersonian revolution because of Jefferson's forthright democratic philosophy. Thereafter the democratic tide rose rapidly, and by 1830 nearly all states had adopted white manhood suffrage. The new states west of the Alleghenies played a prominent part in the process of democratization. Their constitutions manifested the spirit of independence and egalitarianism of their inhabitants, who were mainly frontiersmen and small farmers. The triumph of democratic sentiment was symbolized by the presidential election of 1828, when Andrew Jackson of Tennessee became the first president from a state west of the Alleghenies.

The Constitution strengthened the central government at the expense of the states, but it did not reduce the latter to insignificance. Alexander Hamilton, Washington's principal adviser, sought to make the national government a more vigorous agency for the promotion of commerce and industry, but the Jeffersonians reversed the tendency. Although the exigencies of war in Europe and eventually in the United States required Jefferson and Madison temporarily to exert greater authority as presidents, with the end of the war they returned to their earlier doctrine of state sovereignty. In his last official act as president in 1817, Madison vetoed a bill that would have permitted the national government to undertake a substantial program of internal improvements (mainly road and canal construction). Until the Civil War his successors generally followed his precedent.

The limited powers exercised by the national government in the realm of internal affairs did not imply a negative role for government in general. State and local governments took an active part in promoting economic development and social welfare legislation in the first half of the nineteenth century. Their role differed from the role of governments in seventeenth- and eighteenth-century Europe, for instead of being imposed from above, their participation in the economic and social life of the citizenry sprang from the interests and wishes of the people themselves.

As a consequence of its rapid expansion the United States came into conflict with its neighbors, especially those to the south and west. In 1819 Spain ceded Florida to the United States after a series of border disturbances. Shortly afterward westward-bound Americans began to move into Texas, which had been part of Mexico since Mexico's successful revolt from Spain in 1821. By the 1830's Texas's population of Anglo-American stock surpassed that of Mexican ancestry. Texas declared and won its independence from Mexico in a brief war in 1836 and in 1845 the Republic of Texas petitioned for annexation to the United States. This action and other difficulties between the United States and Mexico led to war in 1846. By the Treaty of Guadalupe Hidalgo in 1848 Mexico gave up its claims to Texas, recognized the Rio Grande as the boundary between Mexico and the United States, and ceded the territories of New Mexico and California to the United States for the sum of $15,000,000. In 1846 the United States settled its dispute with Great Britain over the boundaries of the Oregon territory. These settlements, together with the Gadsden Purchase of land from Mexico in 1853, rounded out the limits of the continental United States.

BRITISH NORTH AMERICA: LIMITED
SELF-GOVERNMENT AND REBELLION

After the American Revolution thousands of British loyalists migrated from the United States to New Brunswick and the region north of lakes Erie and Ontario. To prevent difficulties with the French-speaking population, the British government in 1791 divided its territory into Upper Canada (later called Ontario and chiefly English) and Lower Canada (later Quebec, largely French). Each division had a royal governor, an appointed legislative council, and an elective assembly. These organs were given limited self-government, although Parliament retained the right to veto colonial legislation.

During the War of 1812 the United States attempted to conquer and annex Canada, but the Canadians remained loyal to the British crown and repulsed the invasion. Shortly after the war, however, trouble arose between the popularly elected assemblies and the imperial authority represented by the royal governors and legislative councils. After negotiations failed to solve the problems, the popular party led by William Lyon Mackenzie rose in an unsuccessful rebellion in 1837. Lord Durham, the new governor-general for all of British North America, treated the rebels with leniency and submitted a now famous report to London calling for colonial self-government. In 1840 Parliament passed the Union Act, which abolished the division between Upper and Lower Canada and introduced a number of administrative reforms. It did not fully meet the issue of responsible government, however, and the problem continued to plague British-Canadian relations until after the American Civil War.

REVOLT AND DISUNION IN LATIN AMERICA

During the Napoleonic wars, when the French drove Ferdinand VII of Spain from his throne and made Spain a French satellite, Spain's American colonies refused to acknowledge French sovereignty and began to experiment with self-government. The American and French revolutions had already implanted the idea of independence. When in 1814 Ferdinand indicated his intention to restore the old colonial system intact, the movement for independence gathered speed.

The Spanish colonies had ample cause for rebellion. Except for the ineffectual reforms of Charles III in the eighteenth century, the oppressive character of Spanish rule had changed little in almost three hundred years. The colonies enjoyed not the slightest measure of self-government. The viceroys and other high officials of both state and church came directly from Spain. The native-born inhabitants of Spanish ancestry, who were called creoles and controlled most of the domestic wealth, shared with the mestizos, those of mixed Spanish and Indian ancestry, a common hatred of their overlords. As for the Indians, they lived either in a tribal

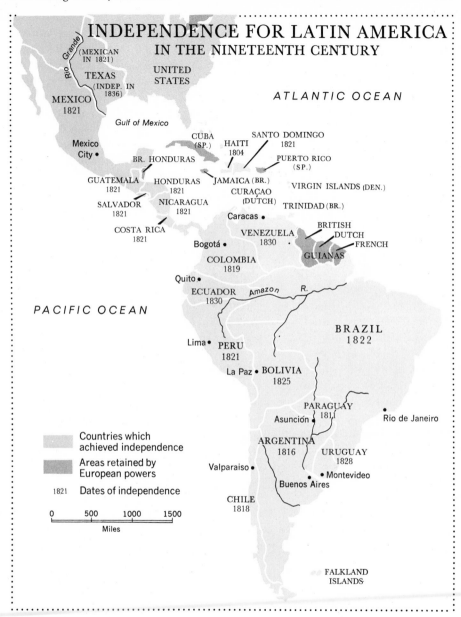

INDEPENDENCE FOR LATIN AMERICA IN THE NINETEENTH CENTURY

Rio Grande

(MEXICAN IN 1821)

TEXAS
(INDEP. IN 1836)

UNITED STATES

MEXICO
1821

ATLANTIC OCEAN

Gulf of Mexico

Mexico City •

CUBA (SP.)

SANTO DOMINGO
1821

HAITI
1804

PUERTO RICO
(SP.)

BR. HONDURAS

GUATEMALA
1821

HONDURAS
1821

JAMAICA (BR.)

CURAÇAO
(DUTCH)

VIRGIN ISLANDS (DEN.)

SALVADOR
1821

NICARAGUA
1821

TRINIDAD (BR.)

Caracas •

COSTA RICA
1821

Bogotá •

VENEZUELA
1830 •

BRITISH
DUTCH
FRENCH

GUIANAS

COLOMBIA
1819

Quito •

ECUADOR
1830

Amazon R.

PACIFIC OCEAN

BRAZIL
1822

Lima • PERU
1821

La Paz • BOLIVIA
1825

PARAGUAY
1811

Asunción •

Rio de Janeiro

ARGENTINA
1816

URUGUAY
1828

Valparaiso •

Montevideo

Buenos Aires

CHILE
1818

Countries which achieved independence

Areas retained by European powers

1821   Dates of independence

0   500   1000   1500
Miles

FALKLAND
ISLANDS

state or in a condition bordering on slavery. There was also a small number of Negro slaves.

The independence movement was hindered at first by the confused state of affairs in the mother country, the attitude of the local aristocrats, and poor communications. Only the United Provinces of La Plata (Argentina) and Paraguay had succeeded in establishing independence by 1816. Thereafter the movement developed rapidly. José de San Martín, one of the leaders of the Argentinian revolt, joined forces with Bernardo O'Higgins to liberate Chile in 1818. With the assistance of a British naval officer, Lord Cochrane, he then moved by sea against Peru, the center of Spanish power in South America, and proclaimed its independence in 1821. Simón Bolívar, another popular hero, led the independence movement in northern South America and created the state of Gran Colombia (comprising Colombia, Venezuela, Ecuador, and Panama). In Mexico the movement for liberation developed into a revolt of the lower classes against the native aristocracy, but when independence came in 1821, it took the form of a reactionary government dominated by aristocratic elements. Stimulated by the revolt in Mexico, the Central American provinces rebelled and in 1823 established the United Provinces of Central America. By 1825 Spain had been excluded from the Western Hemisphere except for the islands of Cuba and Puerto Rico.

Brazil arrived at the same point as the former Spanish colonies by a different route. The Portuguese king moved his seat of government to Brazil in 1808 when he was threatened by Napoleon, and he continued to reside there until 1821. During this period Brazil came to regard itself as an independent nation. When the king returned to Portugal he left his son, Dom Pedro, as regent in Brazil. The Brazilians declared their independence and persuaded Dom Pedro to remain at the head of the government as constitutional monarch of the Empire of Brazil.

Domestic revolutions in Spain and Portugal in 1820 and the favorable attitudes of Great Britain and the United States toward independence for the colonies materially assisted the movement. At the Congress of Aix-la-Chapelle in 1818 and again at Verona in 1822, Tsar Alexander of Russia proposed concerted intervention by European powers to restore Spain's colonial empire, but the British had developed strong commercial interests in Latin America and had no desire to see the colonies again placed under Spain's restrictive colonial regime. Inasmuch as Britain maintained undisputed mastery of the seas, the tsar's proposal came to naught. In 1823 George Canning, the British foreign minister, suggested that the United States and Great Britain issue a joint declaration warning other European powers not to interfere with Spain's former colonies, but John Quincy Adams, the American secretary of state, felt that the United States should not "come in as a cockboat in the wake of the British man-of-war." He preferred unilateral action. American officials were also concerned about the activities of Russian explorers and trappers along the Pacific coast. In December, 1823, President James Monroe stated the Monroe Doctrine in a message to Congress. Principally drafted by Adams, it declared "that the American Continents, by the free and independent condition which they have assumed and maintain, are henceforth not to be considered as subjects for future colonization by any European power."

The new nations of Latin America soon discovered that independence alone did not bring tranquility. A few idealists like Bolívar dreamed of a unified nation of all Spanish-speaking peoples in South America, and Mexico at one time attempted to incorporate all the states of Central America. Yet the sources of discord were too many and too great. The administrative divisions and isolation of the colonial period left a legacy of separatism and rudimentary nationalism that the ephemeral cooperation of the revolutionary period could not overcome. Poor communications and geographic and climatic differences also hindered attempts at permanent union and played into the hands of ambitious political leaders, each of whom wished to carve out his own personal domain. At the end of the wars of independence ten new nations emerged from the remnants of the old Spanish and Portuguese empires. Less than a generation later the number had grown to eighteen by a process of division and separation. Throughout the century border disputes and other conflicts proved to be the chronic state of affairs among these new nations.

Their domestic affairs were no more peaceful or happy than their interstate relations. Revolution, civil war, political instability, and other ailments of the body politic remained endemic. One of the most important difficulties was the fact that since most Latin Americans were illiterate, poverty-stricken, and completely inexperienced in managing their own affairs, they were unprepared for self-government. In addition, except for Brazil they all chose the most difficult form of government — the republican form. Because of the strong vested interests of the church and the resident aristocracy their history has been punctuated by revolution, palace revolt, and dictatorship. Liberals opposed conservatives, federalists fought centralists, anticlericals struggled against the clergy, and ambitious, scheming individuals sought positions of power, prestige, and wealth. The history of Latin America in the nineteenth century proved to be a dismally accurate preview of developments in the nations of Asia and Africa in the twentieth century when they were liberated from colonial rule.

ROMANTIC REVOLUTION, 1820–1829

Metternich's system survived its first test in Germany, but it soon faced greater strains elsewhere, leading to the ultimate disruption of the concert of Europe. The oppressive policies of restoration rulers in the Iberian and Italian peninsulas provoked popular uprisings which, although easily repressed by armed intervention of the great powers, caused a split between Great Britain and its continental allies. An eventually successful nationalist revolt in Greece produced a chain of repercussions that fur-

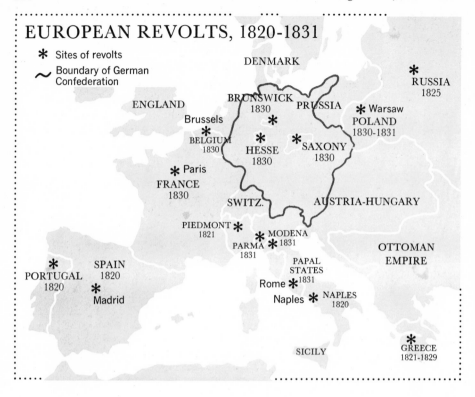

EUROPEAN REVOLTS, 1820-1831

✱ Sites of revolts

~ Boundary of German Confederation

DENMARK

ENGLAND

BRUNSWICK 1830

PRUSSIA

✱ RUSSIA 1825

Brussels ✱ BELGIUM 1830

✱ HESSE 1830

✱ SAXONY 1830

✱ Warsaw POLAND 1830-1831

✱ Paris FRANCE 1830

SWITZ.

AUSTRIA-HUNGARY

PIEDMONT ✱ 1821

✱ MODENA PARMA ✱ 1831 1831

✱ PORTUGAL 1820

SPAIN 1820

✱ Madrid

PAPAL STATES

Rome ✱ 1831

Naples ✱ NAPLES 1820

OTTOMAN EMPIRE

SICILY

✱ GREECE 1821-1829

ther weakened international cooperation. Finally, a liberal revolution in France broke the conservative monopoly of the reins of government and inaugurated a series of defections from the conservative camp.

SPAIN, 1820

The witless reaction of Ferdinand VII in Spain (see p. 546) led his government into increasing difficulties. In an effort to regain the American colonies, which had been a major source of government income, Ferdinand gathered a large army at Cadiz in preparation for embarkation. Demoralized by the incompetence of the government, the army mutinied and began to march on the capital. Spontaneous riots and demonstrations in support of the army broke out in Madrid, Barcelona, and other major urban centers, forcing Ferdinand to restore the liberal constitution of 1812.

At the first news of the revolt Alexander of Russia called for a congress to take concerted action to crush it. The British foreign minister, Castlereagh, responded that the Spanish revolution was a domestic affair; Britain was committed by treaty only to preventing the return of Napoleon and guaranteeing the territorial arrangements agreed upon at

Vienna. Castlereagh and Alexander had differed before on the question of the Spanish colonies at the Congress of Aix-la-Chapelle. Not only did Britain, as the world's greatest trading and industrial nation, stand to gain by the collapse of Spain's restrictive colonial system, but its interest in preserving a balance of power also required opposition to Russian intervention in the affairs of western Europe. Metternich, who also suspected Alexander's belated but overenthusiastic support for absolutism, had stood with Castlereagh in 1818 and was inclined to do so again, when events took an unexpected turn.

PORTUGAL AND ITALY, 1820

The revolution in Spain proved contagious. Within the year similar revolutions took place in Naples and Portugal, and during the following year in Piedmont and Greece. Metternich could ill afford to ignore the revolutions in Italy. In fact, Austria had a treaty with Naples prohibiting constitutional changes that had not also been agreed upon for the Austrian possessions in Italy. Alarmed by the outbursts, the great powers held a congress at Troppau, Austria. Russia, Austria, and Prussia signed an agreement, called the Troppau Protocol, providing for intervention by the powers to suppress domestic revolutions, which they labeled "a threat to the peace of Europe." Britain abstained but did not seek to prevent Austria from sending an expeditionary force to put down the risings in Italy. By the late spring of 1821 Austrian troops occupied Italy from tip to toe and the absolutist sovereigns had been restored in both Naples and Piedmont.

No decision concerning the revolution in Spain was reached at Troppau or at Laibach, to which the congress adjourned at the beginning of 1821. A new congress took place in Verona in 1822. Louis XVIII of France, seeking to bolster French prestige within the concert of Europe and to prevent Russian soldiers from crossing French soil on their way to Spain, applied to the congress for approval of his plan to restore Ferdinand and abolish the Spanish constitution. Britain opposed any joint action in Spain but could not prevent the French expedition, which after a brief campaign in the summer of 1823 defeated the revolutionary army and restored Ferdinand once again.

The revolution in Portugal contained elements of nationalism as well as liberalism, adding substance to its pronounced romantic coloring. During the Napoleonic wars the Portuguese king, John VI, had retired to Brazil, leaving the government of Portugal to a regency dominated by the British. After 1815 the anomalous situation continued until insurgents overthrew the regency, adopted a liberal constitution on the model of the Spanish constitution, and demanded that John return as constitutional monarch. Rather than lose his Portuguese throne altogether, John came back in 1822, but he soon began to intrigue against his liberal supporters. A civil war was in progress when John died in 1826. The country became further divided between the supporters of John's eldest son and heir, Dom Pedro, to whom he had earlier left the government of Brazil, and his younger son Dom Miguel, who was supported by the most reactionary factions. Dom Pedro complicated the situation by refusing to leave Brazil, whose independence from Portugal he had already declared. He abdicated the Portuguese throne in favor of his seven-year-old daughter Maria da Gloria, with the understanding that she would marry her uncle, Dom Miguel. Miguel, a personal friend and great admirer of Metternich, assented to this solution and even agreed to respect the constitution; but as soon as he arrived in Lisbon he deposed his young bride-to-be, abrogated the constitution, and ruled alone as absolute monarch.

GREECE, 1821–1829

The revolution in Greece had an even greater element of nationalism, strongly tinged with the romanticism of the Philhellenes, Western Europeans who regarded the modern Greeks as the direct descendants of the ancient Athenian democracy. After more than three hundred years of Turkish rule the Greeks had experienced a cultural and economic revival in the second half of the eighteenth century. Although the French Revolution did not affect Greece directly, it had contributed to the revival of Greek nationalism. Encouraged by the revolts in Spain and Italy, the Greeks finally rose against their Turkish masters in 1821. The revolt posed a delicate question for the diplomats of the great powers. On the one hand, the Greeks were Christian and European; the Turks were not. On the other hand, a revolution was still a revolution, regardless of the parties. Metternich's preferred solution was to let it burn itself out "beyond the pale of civilization," but it refused to do so. Paradoxically, Alexander wished to intervene on behalf of the revolutionaries, hoping to expand Russian influence in the Balkans at the expense of the Turks, long an aim of the Russians. Britain thereupon felt obliged to intervene in order to prevent Russian expansion.

While the great powers, including France, sparred with one another, the Greeks kept up the struggle against the Turks and even found time and energy to fight among themselves. The Turks, meanwhile, had been joined by the sultan's vassal, Mohammed Ali of Egypt. Eventually the Russians, British, and French, each with one eye upon the others, undertook semiconcerted action, with the Russians going so far as a formal declaration of war and an invasion of Turkey in 1828. The Treaty of Adrianople on September 14, 1829, ended the war and provided for an independent Greece. The Russians strengthened their protectorate over the principalities of Moldavia and Wallachia, still nominally within the Ottoman Empire, while those provinces gained greater autonomy for domestic affairs. Serbia, which had also been the scene of nationalist agitation, likewise obtained autonomy from Turkey.

THE DECEMBRIST REVOLT IN RUSSIA, 1825

Even Russia experienced a brief attempt at revolution. Until 1820 the changeable Alexander I had toyed with reform and plans for a constitution. When Russia acquired Finland from Sweden in 1809, Alexander organized that country as an autonomous grand duchy with himself as duke and allowed the Finns constitutional government. The Polish kingdom created at Vienna was also given a parliament and other constitutional forms, although Alexander as king frequently frustrated their operation and after 1820 increasingly opposed the aspirations of the nationalist Poles. Meanwhile, as Alexander's plans for reform in Russia never seemed to materialize and as he became more frankly reactionary and autocratic, army officers who had been infected with liberalism by contact with the West began to form secret societies to propagate their ideas.

When Alexander died on December 13, 1825, a brief interregnum resulted from his failure to stipulate clearly the line of succession. Since Alexander had no children, his brother Constantine would normally have succeeded him, but Constantine had renounced the succession in favor of his younger brother Nicholas — without informing Nicholas of the fact. For nearly three weeks Russia had no emperor. The leaders of one of the army's secret societies tried to take advantage of the situation by staging an ill-planned, half-hearted coup d'état. Nicholas immediately took charge, suppressed the uprising, summarily executed or exiled its leaders, and inaugurated a thirty-year reign of autocracy and repression. The ill-fated Decembrist Revolt became one of the legends of revolutionary liberalism, but Russia, like Spain and Portugal, did not in fact possess the social basis for a truly liberal movement.

LIBERAL REVOLUTION, 1830–1834

A dozen years after the Congress of Vienna the system it established had been tested in almost every spot. Liberal and nationalist demonstrations and revolts had been quelled in Germany, Italy, Spain, Portugal, and Russia. Reactionary domestic policies had hardly been challenged in the Austrian Empire and France. Only in Greece had a revolution succeeded, and that after several years of bitter struggle and with the support of some of the great powers. It seemed that Metternich's system of divide and conquer, repress and rule, had stood up well. Yet it was clear that a rift had taken place on the international scene and was growing wider, threatening to extend to domestic affairs as well. Although Britain was governed by a conservative majority, the Tories, its interests differed sharply from those of the landowning aristocracies and absolutist monarchies of central and eastern Europe. The growth of commercial and industrial middle classes, in France and the Low Countries as well as in Britain, strengthened the growing liberal movement and accentuated the differences between the constitutional governments of the west and the absolutist governments of the rest of Europe. The breakdown of the concert of Europe, presaged by the differences between Alexander and Britain on the question of the Spanish colonies as early as 1818, was accomplished by 1823. In the words of George Canning, who succeeded Castlereagh as British foreign minister in 1822, it was "every nation for itself and God for us all." Metternich's system had survived the first wave of revolutionary assaults but, weakened by the withdrawal of the British, it would be rudely shaken by the second.

THE REVOLUTION OF 1830 IN FRANCE

After the assassination of the duke de Berri in 1820 the French government became increasingly reactionary. It forced a new electoral law favorable to the old aristocracy at the expense of the middle class; enacted a stringent press law; turned education over even more completely to the church and in other ways facilitated the "union of throne and altar"; dissolved the National Guard, a stronghold of the middle class; and indemnified the nobility for their losses during the revolution at the expense of the bourgeois holders of government bonds.

These measures aroused opposition and resentment among the very people whose good will and cooperation was most necessary to the existence of the regime: the upper bourgeoisie and their journalistic and political henchmen. They included such men as banker Jacques Laffitte, industrialist Casimir Périer, journalist Adolphe Thiers, and wily, aging Talleyrand, who even in semiretirement could not break his lifelong habit of plotting against the regimes he had helped create. These men were liberals in politics, skeptics in religious matters, and ambitious in all things. Under the restricted franchise of the restoration monarchy they alone shared effective political power with the aristocracy; they were the cutting edge of the new social classes created by the revolutionary economic changes. Louis XVIII, for all his faults, had recognized the necessity of cultivating them and very nearly succeeded in attaching them permanently to the regime, at least as a "loyal opposition." To Charles X and his advisers, however, the wealth, ideas, and above all the social and political pretensions of these men were anathema.

Oblivious of the resentment his policies aroused, Charles in 1827 called for a new election to strengthen his majority in the Chamber of Deputies. Greatly to his chagrin the election returned a liberal majority. He was obliged to appoint a moderate ministry and rescind the most stringent provisions of the press and censorship law. In 1830 Charles again tired of the fetters of constitutionalism, dissolved the chamber, and called for

The Bettmann Archive

At the Barricades, July, 1830, by Georges Cain

"People of Paris, Charles X has ceased to reign over France! Unable to forget the origin of his authority, he has always considered himself as the enemy of our country and of its liberties which he was unable to comprehend. After attacking our institutions in an underhand manner by every means that hypocrisy and fraud offered him, when he felt himself strong enough to destroy them openly, he resolved to drown them in the blood of the French. Thanks to your heroism, an end has been put to the crimes of his power." Proclamation of the Municipal Commission of Paris, July 31, 1830, reprinted in J. B. Duvergier, COLLECTION COMPLÈTE DES LOIS, DÉCRETS, etc. (Paris, 1838), Vol. XXX.

a new election. Instead of giving him a majority, the election strengthened the opposition. Without convening the new chamber, Charles and his ministers began preparing a group of ordinances that had the effect of a royal coup d'état: they dissolved the chamber before it met, called for yet another election, amended the electoral law to reduce the electorate by three-fourths, and provided for strict censorship of the press.

These ordinances were published on July 25, 1830. Two days later Thiers and other journalists who had financial backing from the liberals defied the ordinances and distributed circulars calling on the people of

Paris to resist the king's violation of the Charter. Once again the French bourgeoisie asked the mobs of Paris to fight their revolution, and once again the barricades appeared. Revolutionary committees were quickly formed, arms appeared and were distributed to the street fighters, and elements of the disbanded National Guard redonned their uniforms. On July 28 the mobs seized the Hôtel de Ville (city hall) and raised the triumphant tricolor. After a dispirited attack on the crowds the regular troops revolted and fraternized with the people. Once again Paris had made a revolution — but this time with negligible bloodletting and almost before the provinces knew about it.

The revolution succeeded, but who was the victor? Two distinct elements participated in the victory: the liberal journalists and politicians who had fomented it, and the mobs of Paris, "the people," who had executed it. The former wanted a strictly limited constitutional monarchy dominated by the men of wealth, such as the one which had issued from the English revolution of 1689 and which the Charter had failed to give them. The Parisian street fighters were vaguely republican in sentiment but were less organized. On the morning of July 30 Paris awoke to find the city placarded with posters calling for Louis Philippe, duke of Orleans, to take the throne. He was a relative of the Bourbons but was well known for his bourgeois sentiments and interests. He had participated in the early stages of the great revolution of 1789, and his father, called Philippe Égalité because of his extreme devotion to the revolutionary cause, had even voted for the execution of Louis XVI. The next day, July 31, Louis Philippe traveled to the Hôtel de Ville where, draped in the tricolor, Lafayette presented him to the crowd and called for "a throne surrounded by republican institutions." Thus began the July Monarchy, so-called because of the date of its inauguration. After swearing to uphold the Charter, which had been amended by omission of both the monarchic preamble and provision for government by ordinance, Louis Philippe on August 9 was proclaimed "King of the French, by the grace of God and the will of the nation."

BELGIAN INDEPENDENCE

News of the revolution in France traveled fast. Within a month it triggered an uprising in Brussels, which, however, had more nationalist and fewer class characteristics. The Belgians had no voice at Vienna in the decision to place them under the rule of the Dutch king, who differed in language and religion (the Belgians spoke Flemish or French and were Catholic). The more numerous Belgians had a just pride in their own history and traditions and resented domination from The Hague. At first the revolutionaries demanded only a separate legislature and administration under a common king, but in the face of King William's stubborn opposition they soon declared for complete independence.

A number of international factors favored Belgian independence. The French, who were mindful of their own revolution and anxious for a revision of the Vienna settlement, were favorably disposed. Austria and Russia, who would have intervened by force, found themselves unable to do so because of similar nationalist uprisings in their own multinational empires. Most important, in Great Britain a new Whig ministry, with Viscount Palmerston as foreign secretary, had just taken over the reins of government. Britain had already split with the other great powers on the question of internal revolutions, and Palmerston in particular was favorable to national self-determination. He persuaded representatives of the other powers to accept Belgian independence and, when William attempted to regain his provinces by force, sanctioned British and French military and naval support to repel the Dutch invaders. William was forced to agree to an armistice but rejected a permanent peace settlement. Finally in 1838, under pressure from his own subjects as well as the great powers, he signed the treaty recognizing Belgium as an "independent and perpetually neutral state," whose neutrality was collectively guaranteed by all the great powers.

Meanwhile, under the benevolent protection of both France and Great Britain the Belgians had already created a national state — the first in Belgian history. As in France, the mobs in the streets were responsible for the success of the revolution, but middle-class business and professional men soon took over leadership of the movement. Of the various alternative forms of government they clearly preferred a strictly limited constitutional monarchy like that of France or England. Although the constitution they adopted was the most liberal in Europe at the time, it granted the right to vote to less than fifty thousand in a country with a total population of four million. Their first choice for a king was the duke de Nemours, second son of Louis Philippe; but the displeasure of Palmerston, who had no intention of seeing Belgium exchange a Dutch for a French king, persuaded Louis Philippe to veto the selection. The Belgians eventually settled on Prince Leopold of Saxe-Coburg-Gotha, a younger son of one of the oldest and most respected ruling houses of Germany. For the Belgians he had the additional advantage of having been "domesticated" by long residence and close connections in Britain, since he was the widower of Princess Charlotte of England and the uncle and trusted adviser of the future Queen Victoria. To enhance further his own prestige and that of Belgium, he shortly married the daughter of Louis Philippe.

REVOLUTION AND ANARCHY
IN THE IBERIAN PENINSULA

In Spain and Portugal the civil wars of the 1820's continued into the following decade. The coup d'état of 1828 by Dom Miguel of Portugal signaled a renewal of the struggle between absolutism and constitutionalism in that country. In 1832, with the assistance of Britain and France Maria da Gloria was restored to the Portuguese throne, and in 1836 she married Duke Ferdinand of Saxe-Coburg. The next quarter century was characterized by continued financial and political instability. Lacking fundamental legal reforms and the growth of a vigorous middle class, parliamentary liberalism maintained a precarious existence in Portugal, eventually to succumb to revolution and dictatorship.

After his second restoration to the throne of Spain in 1823, Ferdinand VII demonstrated his complete incapacity for learning from experience by resorting again to reaction and repression. After his death in 1833 his brother Don Carlos contested for the throne with the supporters of Ferdinand's infant daughter Isabella. Isabella's mother turned to the constitutionalists for support and, through them, to France and Britain. In 1834 Britain, France, Spain, and Portugal formed a Quadruple Alliance designed to protect the constitutional monarchs of the two latter countries. Although the alliance defeated the Carlists, the social and economic basis for enlightened self-government did not exist in Spain any more than in Portugal and the countries of eastern Europe. Corruption, instability, and civil war continued to characterize the government of Spain.

OTHER REVOLUTIONARY MOVEMENTS

The July Revolution in France had repercussions in other lands, but with few exceptions they accomplished little. In Italy secret revolutionary societies were formed by young liberals whose patriotism had been aroused during the Napoleonic era. Chief among them was the *Carbonari* (charcoal burners), which sought eventual unification in a single national Italian state. Early in 1831, encouraged by the success of the revolutions in France and Belgium and hoping for French intervention against the Austrians, they staged risings in Modena, Parma, and the States of the Church. Temporarily successful, the revolutionists were soon disappointed by the response of France, whose bourgeois government had no desire to jeopardize its own position by antagonizing the other great powers. The Italian revolts quickly succumbed to Austrian force.

Poland was another area in which patriotic and nationalist sentiments had been stirred by the Napoleonic reorganization and then left unrealized by the settlement at Vienna. In 1830 the Poles also revolted against their foreign overlord, the tsar. Led by secret societies of intellectuals, students, and aristocrats, the revolution at first scored a surprisingly quick success, but torn by factional disputes among their leaders and lacking the hoped-for assistance from the west, the revolutionaries fell in 1831 before the ferocious reprisals of the Russian army. Tsar Nicholas abolished the Polish constitution, closed the University of Warsaw, and initiated an intensive policy of russification of the Polish people. Most of the active revolutionists who escaped death, including the composer Chopin, fled to western European capitals, especially Paris, where they kept alive the hope of a Polish nation and contributed to the intellectual and cultural life of the West.

In central Europe the revolutions of 1830 had fewer repercussions. The subjects of the duke of Brunswick expelled their ruler, and the governments of some of the other smaller states made temporary liberal concessions, but Austria and Prussia stood firm. In 1832 Metternich persuaded the Diet of the Germanic Confederation to adopt the oppressive Six Acts, which renewed and extended the earlier Carlsbad Decrees. In 1833 the rulers of Austria, Prussia, and Russia signed a secret treaty in which each reaffirmed its absolutist policies and promised to aid the other in the event of revolution.

PARLIAMENTARY REFORM IN GREAT BRITAIN

Seasoned by centuries of evolving constitutional government, Great Britain narrowly avoided the kind of revolutionary upheaval that infected the Continent by a prudent if reluctant compromise on the part of the aristocracy with the new middle classes. In England the landowning aristocracy already had connections with the growing commercial and industrial movement. Nevertheless, in the immediate post-Napoleonic years the governing Tory party, frightened by demands for political, social, and economic reforms, pursued a reactionary domestic policy scarcely different from those on the Continent.

ORIGINS OF THE REFORM MOVEMENT

No sooner had the reactionary policies triumphed in England than a reaction to them developed. The government suffered a serious decline in prestige because of its unsuccessful attempt to force through a bill permitting the scandalous and dissolute George IV to divorce his wife, Caroline of Brunswick. The return of economic prosperity after 1821 caused a decline in radical demonstrations by the working classes, but at the same time it strengthened the self-confidence and ambition of the ever-growing middle classes.

In 1822 a series of cabinet changes following the suicide of Castlereagh introduced a number of younger men who, though they called themselves Tories, were more in step with the times than their predecessors. Until then the Whigs and Tories had not been political parties in the modern sense. The designations applied only to members of Parliament and their friends and supporters, all of whom in both parties belonged to the ruling elite. A man's allegiance within these loose alliances depended as much on personal ties and family tradition as on political principles. Party organization outside of Parliament was nonexistent, and party discipline within Parliament was lax. The reforms of the 1820's and 1830's did a great deal to bring the modern two-party system into being.

Among the outstanding new figures in the cabinet after 1822 was George Canning (1770–1827), who as head of the foreign office carried forward the independent, liberal-leaning foreign policies inaugurated by Castlereagh. William Huskisson (1770–1830), an economic and financial expert, simplified and reduced the maze of taxes and restrictions hampering the development of commerce and industry. Robert Peel (1788–1850), son of a wealthy manufacturer, became home secretary and revised the criminal and penal laws in a humanitarian direction. He obtained legislation reducing the number of capital offenses from over two hundred to about one hundred and created the Metropolitan Police Force, whose members were called bobbies or peelers, in derision at first, in affection later. In 1824 Parliament repealed the hated Combination Acts, which had been used to prevent the formation of trade unions. In all these reforms the influence of Jeremy Bentham and the utilitarians was very strong.

The next phase of the reform movement primarily concerned religious questions. The Test and Corporation acts, relics of the religious struggles of the seventeenth century, barred both Catholics and Nonconforming Protestants (dissenters from the established state church of England) from holding political office. Earlier attempts to repeal these obnoxious laws had been frustrated by the stubborn opposition of the Ultras, as the reactionary wing of the Tory party came to be called in the 1820's because of its similarity to the reactionary French aristocracy. In 1828 Lord John Russell, a Whig, introduced a bill exempting Nonconformists from the provisions of the acts. The duke of Wellington, who was himself an Ultra and who had just become prime minister, at first opposed the bill but then agreed to compromise in the hope of strengthening his support among the more liberal Tories and the Whigs. The bill passed with minor amendments. Immediately the reformers introduced a bill for Catholic emancipation. It passed the House of Commons by a narrow margin in spite of Wellington's opposition but was defeated in the House of Lords. In the following year Wellington, fearing a civil war in predominantly Catholic Ireland, reversed his stand and forced an emancipation bill through Parliament.

This action alienated Wellington's strongest supporters and weakened the Tory party, preparing the way for the first Whig government in almost half a century. In the summer of 1830, at nearly the same time as the July Revolution in France, George IV died and was succeeded by his brother, William IV. According to ancient custom, the change of monarchs required a new general election. The Whigs made a vigorous campaign in favor of reforming the House of Commons. Small groups of reformers had called for revision of the electoral system for many years, but reform had never before been a major issue in a general election. That the Whigs made it one in 1830 reflected as much their hunger for office and their desire to capitalize on the opportunities of the moment as it did their genuine interest in political and social change. The limited nature of the reforms that they proposed clearly indicated this fact.

THE STRUGGLE FOR REFORM

Without doubt, great need for reform existed. Apart from the high property and similar qualifications that limited the franchise to a small fraction of the population, the distribution of seats in Commons in no way reflected the true balance of either population or interests. Although boroughs (incorporated towns) and counties had representatives in Commons, the allocation of seats had been made centuries earlier, before the population shifts connected with the growth of manufacturing had occurred. Some boroughs were entirely under the control of one great landlord; they were called pocket boroughs. Others, the rotten boroughs, had such a small population that the voters could easily be bribed or intimidated. Many of the new manufacturing cities in the north had no representatives at all. In general, the older agricultural areas, dominated by the great aristocratic families, were greatly overrepresented at the expense of London and the new industrial areas.

The results of the election gave the Whigs a small majority, and the Wellington cabinet gave way to one headed by Earl Grey, the leader of the Whigs. His was a strange cabinet to bring about a popular reform, for it was composed almost entirely of aristocrats, a majority of whom were titled peers. But the Whigs had no intention of putting across a democratic reform. They differed from the aristocratic Tories only in that the latter felt that any "tampering" with the existing constitution would result in a national catastrophe, whereas the equally aristocratic Whigs believed that only a timely and judicious revision of the electoral system could prevent catastrophe. A radical journalist put the matter bluntly when he wrote, "The promoters of the Reform Bill projected it, not with a view to subvert, or even remodel our aristocratic institutions, but to consolidate them by a reinforcement of sub-aristocracy from the middle classes."

In spite of the moderate nature of the proposed reform and the electoral mandate in its favor, the Tories fought strenuously to prevent it. The First Reform Bill was introduced by Lord John Russell in March, 1831, and passed Commons with a majority of one in the largest vote ever recorded in Parliament, but it was thrown out on a technicality. Grey dissolved Parliament at once and called for a new election that became almost a referendum, since the Whigs campaigned for "the Bill, the whole Bill, and nothing but the Bill." Oddly enough, the electorate comprising the privileged few returned a majority favorable to the bill.

Culver Pictures, Inc.

The Reform Bill of 1832 Receiving the Royal Assent
in the House of Lords

*"The whole measure will add to the constituency of the Commons House
of Parliament about half a million persons, and these all connected with the
property of the country, having a valuable stake amongst us, and deeply interested
in our institutions. . . . I think that those measures will produce a farther
benefit to the people, by the great incitement which it will occasion to industry
and good conduct. For when a man finds, that by industrious exertion, and
by punctuality, he will entitle himself to a place in the list of voters, he will
have an additional motive to improve his circumstances, and to preserve his
character among his neighbors. I think, therefore, that in adding to the
constituency, we are providing for the moral as well as for the political
improvement of the country."* From Lord John Russell's speech introducing the
Parliamentary Reform Bill, March 1, 1831, HANSARD'S PARLIAMENTARY DEBATES,
3rd ser. (London, 1831), Vol. II.

The new Commons then passed the bill with more than one hundred votes to spare, but the House of Lords defeated it by a small majority.

By this time agitation throughout the country had reached a fever pitch. "Political unions" in the larger cities, especially Birmingham, held mass meetings and hinted at dire consequences if the House of Lords did not reconsider. Lawless mobs, composed of propertyless individuals who stood to gain nothing directly, rioted, rampaged, and even held the city of Bristol for two days. The reforming government put down the outbreaks and punished the offenders as severely as the Tories would have. At the same time the government threatened to force the king to create enough new peers to reverse the vote in the House of Lords if the latter did not accept the bill. In June, 1832, the House of Lords finally acquiesced and, with many abstentions by unrepentant Tories, passed a slightly amended bill.

THE NATURE AND SIGNIFICANCE OF THE REFORM

The immediate outcome little merited the tumult and excitement. Although the suffrage was extended by about 50 per cent, it was still restricted by formidable property qualifications. Less than 20 per cent of the adult male population (or approximately 750,000 in 1832) could vote after the reform. Only 143 seats of a total of more than 650 in the House of Commons were redistributed, with the counties and manufacturing cities of the north gaining slightly at the expense of the smaller towns. Pocket boroughs did not altogether disappear, for more than sixty members were still directly dependent on large landowners (mainly peers) for their seats. As before, the agricultural south remained overrepresented in comparison with the industrial north and, especially, London. Since the act contained no provision for a secret ballot, the voters in the smaller districts continued to be subject to bribery, influence, and coercion.

Nevertheless, the reform of 1832 did grant recognition to the growing middle classes and made them allies, not opponents, of the established order, as Grey intended. The mere fact of its passage marked a turning point in English constitutional history. The method of its passage — that is, appeal to the electorate, pressure on the king, and threatening the House of Lords — set precedents that were even more important than the reform itself. Although its immediate effects disappointed its more radical supporters, notably the working men who had demonstrated in its favor, it probably forestalled a violent political change and paved the way for eventual democratic evolution.

THE BALANCE SHEET OF REVOLUTION

The post-Napoleonic conservative reaction attained its apogee by 1820. Within a dozen years thereafter it had suffered severe setbacks throughout western Europe. The main challenge to the conservatism of crown, church, and aristocracy came from the liberalism of the growing middle classes. The latter groups achieved their greatest strength where the progress of commerce and industry was greatest; that is, in Britain, France, and Belgium. In central Europe the appeal of liberalism united with that of nationalism in the struggle against aristocratic, absolutist, antinational regimes, but they made little headway as long as commerce and industry remained small-scale and backward. In eastern Europe both liberalism and nationalism — faint breaths at best — were stifled beneath the heavy hand of absolutism. Thus, the ideological gap between east and west grew wider as the gap in material progress increased.

THE REVOLUTION IN
ECONOMIC LIFE
CHAPTER TWENTY-THREE

The revolutionary political changes of the first half of the nineteenth century cannot be fully understood without reference to the revolution in economic life. Indeed, the whole history of the European world in the nineteenth century and afterward may be seen as the story of the unfolding consequences and interconnections of two great revolutions that took place at the end of the eighteenth century: the political revolution in France and the revolution of agriculture and industry in Britain.

Some historians consider that revolution is a misnomer when applied to the changes in technology and business organization that constituted the core of the transformation of economic life. They point out that such changes had been taking place more or less continuously over many centuries — in fact, since paleolithic times — and that to call such a long drawn-out process a revolution is misleading. On the other hand, if we look at the consequences of those changes in the nineteenth century, the word revolution is appropriate. Until the end of the eighteenth century economic changes took place almost imperceptibly, too slowly to attract much attention or to modify significantly the traditional agrarian basis of society. Beginning in the 1780's, however, technical innovation in British industry remarkably stepped up the whole process of social change and by the middle of the nineteenth century had converted Great Britain into the first industrial society.

The diffusion of the new technology led other nations into industrialism: Belgium and France first, partly because of their proximity to Great Britain; then the United States, bound to Britain by cultural and economic ties. By the end of the nineteenth century Germany after an extremely rapid rise joined the others in the forefront of industrial nations. By that time other nations had begun industrial revolutions of their own: among them the Netherlands, Switzerland, the Scandinavian countries, northern Italy, Russia, and Japan. The twentieth century has seen the extension of industrial technology, sometimes with great political and social turmoil, to Latin America, Asia, and Africa, with almost every nation in the world attempting to acquire for itself the essentials of modern industry. The beginnings of the movement extended roughly from 1780 to about 1850 or 1860.

THE RISE OF MODERN INDUSTRY

The words industrialism and modern industry refer to the mode of production characterized by extensive use of mechanical power, heavy machinery, and other forms of expensive capital equipment. The most significant improvements in technology therefore involved the use of machinery and mechanical power to perform tasks that had been done far more slowly and laboriously by human and animal power, or that had not been done at all. To be sure, elementary machines like the wheel, the pulley, and the lever had been used from antiquity, and for centuries mankind had used a fraction of the inanimate powers of nature to propel sailing ships and actuate windmills and water wheels for rudimentary industrial processes. During the eighteenth century a notable increase in the use of water power occurred in such industries as grain milling, textiles, and metallurgy; and in recent times we have witnessed the proliferation of a wide variety of prime movers, from small electric motors operated on household current to huge nuclear reactors; but the most important developments in the application of power in the early stages of industrialization were those associated with the introduction of the steam engine and the spread of its use in both industry and transportation.

THE NATURE OF EARLY INDUSTRIALISM

Under the domestic system of manufacture the labor force had been dispersed throughout the countryside in close proximity to supplies of food, and although each worker was financially dependent upon his merchant employer, he was to some extent his own boss. On the other hand, water wheels and then steam engines required the concentration of operations and therefore of operatives at a single location. Buildings were needed to house both machinery and workers. Thus evolved the factory system. Originally factory meant an establishment for traders or their agents, called factors, carrying on business in a foreign country. It acquired its current meaning at the end of the eighteenth century, although before that time isolated examples of factories in the modern sense, with or without power machinery, could be found.

The use of mechanical power, especially steam engines, to drive machinery raised the further possibility of almost continuous and more or less automatic operation. The factory system thus revolutionized the

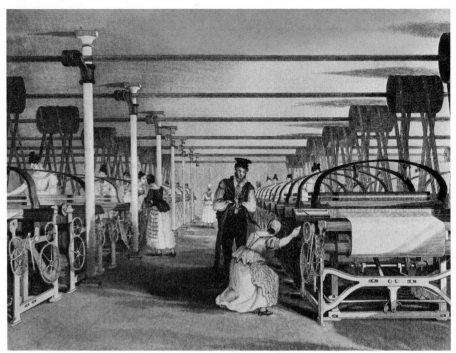

Radio Times Hulton Picture Library

Women Engaged in Power Loom Weaving,
from an engraving by Allom, c. 1840

"The industrial revolution is to be thought of as a movement, not as a period of time. . . . Its character and effects are fundamentally the same. Everywhere it is associated with a growth of population, with the application of science to industry, and with a more intensive and extensive use of capital. Everywhere there is a conversion of rural into urban communities and a rise of new social classes. But in each case the course of the movement has been affected by circumstances of time and place. Many of the social discomforts that have been attributed to the industrial revolution in Britain were, in fact, the result of forces which (for all we know) would still have operated if manufacture had remained undeveloped and there had been no change of economic form."
T. S. Ashton, THE INDUSTRIAL REVOLUTION; 1760–1830 (London, 1948).

habits and conditions as well as the results of human labor. The pace of industry, no longer governed by the rhythm of the seasons and frailties of the flesh, had to adjust to the throbbing pulse of engines and the tireless arms of iron. Before the development of more humane standards and the passage of protective labor legislation, the competition of unscrupulous or hard-pressed employers, struggling to pay the high fixed costs of the new equipment, stretched the length of the working day to twelve, fourteen, and even sixteen hours, with few if any breaks for meals or rest. Such hours, of course, were not unknown in the earlier domestic system or in agriculture, but those workers could set their own pace. Some factory owners failed to provide adequate health and safety facilities and paid their workers in truck (merchandise) instead of money.

Many laborers resented the new machinery, which they blamed for the loss of their skills, and objected to the monotonous routine of the factory. Labor discipline became a major concern. Employers frequently resorted to large-scale employment of women and children where it was made possible by automatic or semiautomatic machines, because they formed a more docile as well as a cheaper labor force. Another factor widening the gulf between employer and employee was the increasing size of enterprise. Under the handicraft system of production a master craftsman might employ a few apprentices, and perhaps a journeyman or two, all of whom might live under his roof. A merchant manufacturer might distribute his materials to a dozen domestic workers, or even as many as fifty, if his was a very large undertaking. The new factories employed hundreds, sometimes thousands, of workers. With such a labor force it became less and less usual for the employer to be personally acquainted with his workers or interested in them individually. The immediate adverse consequences of the technological and organizational changes, however, should not obscure the truly epoch-making benefits that resulted in the long run: the lighter burden and greatly increased productivity of human labor brought about by human ingenuity.

PREREQUISITES AND CONCOMITANTS OF INDUSTRIALISM

Before the factories, the machinery, and the new forms of power could take full effect, certain other changes had to take place. Among the most important were increased commercialization of economic life, the growth of banks and other financial institutions, and the improvement of transportation and communication facilities. Agrarian reform, although not a prerequisite in the strict sense, was an almost universal concomitant of industrialism.

Commerce — the exchange of one commodity or service for another, either directly in the form of barter or indirectly by means of money — is to be found in almost all forms of human society, from the most primitive to the most socialistic. In traditional agrarian societies such exchanges are restricted both geographically and in the volume and variety of goods and services exchanged. In modern industrial societies specialization and division of labor require a highly developed commercial or market system to facilitate exchange. There must be individuals who do not grow or otherwise produce goods directly but who make their living by serving as intermediaries or middlemen in the process of exchange.

Such a class of individuals had existed in western Europe for many centuries. They generally lived in the towns and were known as burghers or bourgeoisie. The geographical discoveries of the fifteenth and sixteenth centuries, which greatly extended the market area and the volume and variety of exchangeable goods, as well as stimulated the money economy by the influx of precious metals, caused their wealth to grow and strengthened their position in society. In the seventeenth and eighteenth centuries they were frequently able to influence the councils of state to adopt policies favorable to their mercantile interests, especially in the Dutch Netherlands and Britain. By the end of the eighteenth century organized commerce, domestic as well as international, occupied a significant segment of the population of western Europe and indirectly affected a far larger proportion.

As the commercialization of economic life increased, special institutions arose to provide credit and to finance trade and industry. The great public banks, such as the Bank of Amsterdam and the Bank of England, catered mainly to large-scale international commerce and the financial needs of governments. By the early nineteenth century most important financial centers had such public banks, which in time became central banks or bankers' banks, controlling the flow of credit throughout their national economies. For the smaller merchants and manufacturers numerous private bankers supplied the need for short-term credit to finance the turnover of trade and industry.

The movement of large quantities of bulky, low-value goods, such as grain from the fields to the growing urban markets, timber for building, coal and ores, required cheap dependable transportation. Prior to the railroad era water routes provided the most economical and efficient arteries of transport. Britain owed much of its early prosperity and its head start in modern industry to its island position. The long coastline, excellent natural harbors, and many navigable streams eliminated much of the need for overland transportation that hindered the growth of commerce and industry on the Continent. In the latter half of the eighteenth century the British extended their natural transport routes with hundreds of miles of canals and improved turnpikes. The greatest improvements in transportation and communication, however, such as railroads, steamships, the telegraph, and eventually automobiles, airplanes, and the wireless radio, developed out of the process of industrialization itself.

AGRARIAN CHANGE

Agrarian reform had several facets. The question of land tenure, how the land was owned or held, was perhaps the most fundamental. Feudal tenure did not recognize private property as such. Rights to the use of land were extremely diffuse, extending from the highest nobleman to the lowliest serf. The trend toward private ownership of property and individual responsibility worked itself out over a period of centuries and took various forms. The process of consolidation and enclosure in England eventually resulted in the creation of huge estates, sometimes of several thousand acres each, in the hands of a relatively small number of wealthy landlords. By the 1870's fewer than seven thousand individuals owned four-fifths of the land in the United Kingdom. The great estates were not generally cultivated as single units. Usually they were rented to capitalistic tenant farmers in farms of about one hundred acres.

In France the lands of the church (the largest landholder before the French Revolution) and the feudal aristocracy were expropriated during the revolution. In some instances peasants obtained legal title to the land that they cultivated, but much was taken by the government and sold to bourgeois speculators, who subsequently resold it to land-hungry peasants or returning aristocrats. In the end France became a nation of small peasant proprietors. In 1882, with over half the population engaged in agriculture, the average size of French farms was less than twenty-five acres. More than three-quarters of the peasant proprietors owned farms smaller than five hectares (12.5 acres), and two-thirds of these tiny farms were actually less than one hectare (2.5 acres) in size. These petty proprietors had to take jobs, frequently as hired hands on larger farms, to support themselves and their families.

The edict of emancipation of 1807 laid the basis for the liberation of the serfs in Prussia, the largest state in Germany. It was long believed that the Prussian reform resulted in the monopolization of most of the land by the aristocratic landowners (the Junkers), and that most of the peasants lost their holdings and were forced to become laborers on the farms of the Junkers, or, especially after 1850, moved to the burgeoning industrial areas to become factory workers. This view has been challenged by a modern German scholar who made a careful statistical analysis of the land records. He found that the number of large landowners did increase after the emancipation and that these men did dominate commercial production; but he also found that the number of small landowners increased as well, and at a much more rapid rate than the large landowners. These small proprietors acquired their land through the operations of the emancipation legislation, through the division of common pasture land and its conversion into plowland, and through the conversion into plowland of forests and of so-called wastelands that had hitherto been untilled. Some of these peasant proprietors had sizable and prosperous farms. By far the largest number, however, had holdings so small that, like their French counterparts, they had to find other employment, often as hired hands on the farms of the Junkers and the wealthier peasants, to make ends meet. In 1907, of the 2.6 million individual farms in the Prussian provinces, 63 per cent had only 5 acres or less.

Elsewhere in western and central Europe land reform followed either the French or the Prussian model. In much of eastern and southern Europe no effective reform took place until after the revolutionary upheavals in the twentieth century. Wherever it did occur, the usual consequence was increased productivity and the commercialization of agriculture.

The progress of agricultural technology was no less important than the reforms in land tenure. The latter were in part a means of achieving the former. So long as the land was cultivated in common, it was impossible for a single individual to introduce new crops and new methods of cultivation or to improve his livestock by selective breeding, and obedience to traditional routine prevented radical changes in technology by a whole village. When the consolidated and enclosed lands came into private hands, especially the hands of improving landlords or commercially-minded tenant farmers who had the wealth and the interest to experiment with new techniques, it became possible to discover and apply new and better methods.

THE INDUSTRIAL REVOLUTION IN BRITAIN

The expression industrial revolution has a long and controversial history. First used by Frenchmen in the 1820's to compare the economic changes with the great French Revolution of 1789, it gained currency at the end of the nineteenth century when it was used by British social reformers in interpreting the origins of contemporary social problems. The conventional dates assigned to the revolution were 1760 to 1830, although some scholars favored a longer period, such as 1750 to 1850, and others argued that the beginning date should be 1780 or 1785, with no fixed terminal date for the completion of the revolution. Still other authorities, stressing the continuity of industrial change, sought to prove that there was no such thing as an industrial revolution, or that at best it was but a special case of a more general process. Serious students of the subject have long since given up the cataclysmic interpretation, and most agree that the expression itself is meaningless except as a stylized, shorthand designation for a highly significant period in British economic and social history.

Whatever the dispute regarding the utility of the name, there is no doubt as to the importance of the process it describes. The two generations of Britons on either side of the year 1800 witnessed changes that have profoundly influenced the subsequent history not only of their island but of the entire world. But why Great Britain? Might not the industrial revolution have occurred elsewhere than in Britain? There is general agreement that the economic expansion of the second half of the eighteenth century, of which the industrial revolution was the culmination, was a general phenomenon affecting most of western Europe and North America as well. Had the British population been suddenly wiped out in 1750 by some mysterious plague that affected no other area, it is conceivable — even probable — that an industrial revolution would have occurred eventually either in western Europe or the United States. British primacy was due to a fortuitous combination of both dynamic and static factors. One such factor was its insular position at the crossroads of maritime traffic, both east and west and north and south; insularity not only lowered transport costs but also granted costless protection from the destruction and disruption of continental warfare. But insularity alone was not enough.

Commercialization of economic life had proceeded further in Great Britain than in any other nation except possibly the Netherlands. As early as the end of the seventeenth century British foreign trade per capita exceeded that of other nations, and London had developed a surprisingly sophisticated commercial and financial organization. Moreover, after 1689 the financial as well as the commercial policies of the government came into the hands of men experienced in private financial and commercial transactions.

Increased commercialization also interacted in dynamic fashion with that other great sector of economic activity, agriculture. Improvements in agricultural techniques introduced in the seventeenth century spread during the eighteenth century in response to the heightened demand brought on by the great increase in population. The result was a significant rise in agricultural productivity and agricultural income, making British agriculture a lucrative market for industrial products as well as a supplier of foodstuffs and raw materials for British industry.

The process of economic development was an immensely complicated one, involving social, political, and intellectual as well as economic changes. The dynamic central factor in the industrial revolution itself, however, was technical innovation in three strategic areas: cotton textiles, the iron industry, and the perfection of the steam engine.

The manufacture of cotton cloth was a relatively new industry in Great Britain. It grew up early in the eighteenth century after the woolen interests persuaded Parliament to adopt the Calico Acts of 1700 and 1720, prohibiting the importation of cotton goods from India. At first the industry employed the hand processes that were common in the other textile industries and frequently used a mixture of linen and cotton yarn in weaving. Because it was new, cotton manufacture was less subject than other industries to restrictive legislation and gild rules or to traditional practices that obstructed technical change. The popularity of gaily colored or printed cotton goods also led to a rapid increase in demand, which acted as a stimulus to technical innovation. Deliberate efforts to invent labor-saving machinery for spinning and weaving were made at least as early as 1730. The early spinning machines were not successful, but in 1733 a Lancashire mechanic, John Kay, invented the flying shuttle which enabled a single weaver to do the work of two, thereby increasing the pressure of demand for yarn. In 1760 the Society of Arts added to the incentive of the market by offering a prize for a successful spinning machine. Within a few years several devices for mechanical spinning were patented. The first was James Hargreaves's spinning jenny, invented in 1765 but not patented until 1770. The jenny was a relatively simple machine; in fact, it was little more than a spinning wheel with a battery of several spindles instead of one. It did not require mechanical power and could be operated in a spinner's cottage, but it allowed one man to do the work of several.

The water frame, a spinning machine patented by Richard Arkwright in 1769, had more general significance. Arkwright, a barber and wig maker by trade, probably did not invent the water frame himself, and his patent was subsequently voided; but of all the early textile innovators he was the most successful as a businessman. Because the water frame operated with water power and was heavy and expensive, it led directly to the factory system. The factories, however, were built most often by streams in the country or in small villages, so that they did not result in concentrations of workers in the cities.

The most important invention in spinning was Samuel Crompton's mule, so called because it combined elements of the jenny and the frame. Perfected between 1774 and 1779, the mule could spin finer, stronger yarn than any machine or hand spinner, and it could also be adapted for steam power. The steam engine was first applied to spinning in 1785 and soon became the almost inevitable concomitant of cotton manufacture.

The new spinning machines reversed the pressure of demand between spinning and weaving, and led to a more insistent search for a solution to the problems of mechanical weaving. In 1785 Edmund Cartwright took out a patent for a power loom. Cartwright, a clergyman without training or experience in either mechanics or textiles, solved the basic problem of mechanical weaving by the application of sheer intelligence. Many minor difficulties of a practical nature hindered the development of the power loom until the 1820's, however, when an improved version manufactured by the engineering firm of Sharp and Roberts in Manchester was widely adopted throughout the cotton districts.

A rapid increase in cotton consumption followed, creating a new bottleneck in the supply of raw cotton. India had supplied most of the imports of raw cotton, but its production did not expand rapidly enough to fill the growing demand. Cotton production began in the American South, but the high cost of separating seeds by hand from the short-staple American fibers discouraged it until 1793, when Eli Whitney, a New Englander visiting in the South, invented a mechanical gin. This machine answered the need so well that the southern United States quickly became the leading supplier of raw material to what soon became Britain's leading industry.

These inventions were the most important but by no means the only ones affecting the cotton industry. A host of minor improvements took place in all stages of production from the preparation of the fibers for spinning to bleaching, dyeing, and printing. Since Britain did not grow any cotton domestically, the import figures for raw cotton give a good indication of the pace at which the industry developed. From less than a million pounds at the beginning of the century, imports rose to about five million pounds in the 1770's, more than fifty million pounds in 1800, and more than a billion pounds in 1860. A large and growing percentage of the cotton manufacture was exported; by 1803 the value of cotton exports surpassed that of wool, which for centuries had been Britain's leading industry. As the cheap, machine-produced cottons went to markets all over the world, they spread enthusiasm for the new techniques of industry.

The second industry to be revolutionized was, unlike cotton, an ancient one in Britain. Iron had been produced there from the early Middle Ages, but it was primarily a rural occupation. Charcoal was used to smelt the iron ore; consequently, for reasons of economy, production took place on a small scale in forested areas far from the centers of population and industry. In the seventeenth century the increasing demand for iron, together with the high price of charcoal as a result of forest exhaustion, led to a search for a less expensive fuel. Coal, known to be plentiful in England, had long been used for some industrial purposes as well as domestic heating, but raw coal contained impurities that were injurious to the quality of iron produced with it. In the first half of the eighteenth century the Darby family, a father-and-son team of Quaker iron founders in the west of England, discovered through patient experiment that good quality iron could be made with coal if the coal were first coked (heated to high temperatures in closed ovens) to drive out the impurities. The process became public knowledge after 1750, and the output of both coal and iron increased rapidly.

The iron industry had not yet solved all of its problems. The product of the blast furnace, in which the ore is smelted, is not only hard but because of its carbon content is also brittle, and cannot be easily shaped or hammered. To remove the carbon and make wrought iron that is soft and pliable enough to be worked into useful shapes, the pig iron had to be refined. The traditional method required alternate heating and hammering of the pigs, or bars, to drive out all the carbon and other impurities. Even when done with the aid of huge trip hammers driven by water power, this was a slow and cumbersome process. Thus the use of coke in the blast furnace created an imbalance in the industry similar to that created in the cotton industry by the spinning machines. The solution was arrived at independently and almost simultaneously by two men, Peter Onions and Henry Cort, in 1783 and 1784. The puddling process of refining iron (so called because the molten iron was stirred in puddles)

Maudslay's Original Screw-Cutting Lathe (1797)

*"Modern industry had therefore itself to take in hand the machine, its
characteristic instrument of production, and to construct machines by
machines. . . . It was necessary to produce the geometrically accurate straight
lines, planes, circles, cones, and spheres, required in the detailed parts of
machines. This problem Henry Maudslay solved by the invention of the slide
rest, a tool that was soon made automatic. . . . This mechanical appliance
replaces, not some particular tool, but the hand itself, which produces a given
form by holding and guiding the cutting tool along the iron or other material
operated upon. Thus it becomes possible to produce the forms of the individual
parts of machinery with a degree of ease, accuracy, and speed, that no
accumulated experience of the hand of the most skilled workman could give."*
Karl Marx, CAPITAL (Chicago, 1906).

---

also used coke as a fuel, which freed the iron industry completely from
dependence on charcoal and concentrated it in larger units in the vicinity
of the coal fields. These regions became the new homes of the iron-using
industries as well. Cort also patented a rolling mill, in which white-hot
iron was squeezed between huge rollers to drive out impurities and to
impart desired shapes, such as sheets, rods, rails, and beams. Britain soon
changed from an iron-importing nation to the world's leading exporter of
iron and ironwares.

Without these developments in the iron and cotton industries there
would have been no industrial revolution, but the crowning technical

achievement of the eighteenth century was the perfection and utilization of the steam engine. Some of the properties of steam had been known in antiquity, but no serious attempts to utilize it for practical purposes occurred until the seventeenth century. At the beginning of the eighteenth century an English mechanic, Thomas Newcomen, built a crude engine capable of actuating a pump. Engines of this type were used for more than a century to pump water from coal mines, but their efficiency was too low to permit widespread application to other industrial processes. Between 1763 and 1782 James Watt, originally a builder of scientific instruments for the University of Glasgow, made a number of improvements that resulted in a far more efficient, economical engine. Watt's engine could convert the reciprocal movement of the piston into rotary motion, which made the engine adaptable for driving industrial machinery. Within a few years it had been applied to industries as diverse as mining, flour milling, pottery, brewing, and distilling, not to mention the two most important users, cotton manufacture and iron working.

In spite of the magnitude of these achievements, no single industry in Britain had completed its technical revolution as early as 1830, though iron and cotton had gone very far. By 1851, however, when Queen Victoria dedicated the Crystal Palace, a huge structure of iron and glass to house the world's first international industrial exhibition, workers in British industry outnumbered those in agriculture and Britain had become the "workshop of the world."

EARLY INDUSTRIALISM IN EUROPE AND AMERICA

Elements of the new technology began to be diffused almost immediately. In 1779, less than five years after completion of Watt's first successful engine in Britain, the Perier brothers set up an engine of the same type in France. In 1782 construction of the first continental blast furnace designed for coke began at Le Creusot in eastern France. French textile manufacturers had been in touch with the British industry even before the great inventions, and by 1790 there were approximately nine hundred spinning jennies in France. In the latter year Samuel Slater, an English mechanic who had worked in Arkwright's mills, emigrated to America, secured financial support from two wealthy merchants in Providence, and established a flourishing cotton industry in Rhode Island.

In spite of these early achievements, industrialism did not make rapid progress in either Europe or America. The manufacturers in Britain jealously guarded the secrets of their new industries. The government prohibited the exportation of machinery or the emigration of skilled artisans, for which it provided stiff penalties, including death. Although such laws were frequently circumvented, their existence discouraged widespread diffusion of the new technology. For example, Slater dared not bring either machines or drawings to America but memorized the designs and traveled incognito. The turmoil and dislocation brought on by the French Revolution and the revolutionary and Napoleonic wars, accentuated by Napoleon's Continental System and the British blockade, also hindered the diffusion of technology and the transition of continental industry to more modern methods. Perhaps most important, the prerequisites of industrialism had not been fully met either on the Continent or in America, much less in other lands, so that demand for the new methods was not as great as in Britain.

Effective industrialization began on the Continent only after 1815. Even then it was confined to a relatively small area and proceeded much more slowly than in Britain. Faced with the competition of their more advanced British counterparts, the new textile industries could not compete in international trade and had to rely on high tariffs to protect the more limited domestic markets. The iron industries of France and Belgium began the shift from charcoal to coke in the 1820's, but the transition was not completed until the 1850's. By the middle of the nineteenth century Belgium, favored by plentiful supplies of coal, an advantageous location, an industrious population, and wise legislation, had advanced further than any other continental nation on the road to industrialism. France ranked second, but it had more difficult problems of location and resources and was already beginning to manifest what became its typical schizophrenic attitude toward modern industry. The new techniques of industry had barely been implanted in western Germany, northern Italy, Bohemia, and in the immediate vicinity of Vienna. Elsewhere Europeans in 1850 were very far from even the beginnings of an industrial revolution.

The situation in the United States was slightly different. European travelers noted early the American passion for high productivity and their ingenuity in inventing labor-saving machinery. Eli Whitney, inventor of the cotton gin, made a still greater fortune by devising a system for the mass production of muskets with standardized, interchangeable parts. Many of the American labor-saving devices could be used on a relatively small scale, such as the mechanical reaper (1834) and the sewing machine (1846). This bent of American industrialism resulted from a number of factors: a chronic shortage of labor, especially labor having the traditional skills; the fluidity of American society; the abundant opportunities for individual advancement; and the wealth of natural resources. Yet in spite of its promising beginnings, America did not create an industrial society during the first half of the nineteenth century. The reasons that contributed to American inventive ingenuity also contributed to delaying the development of large-scale industry, especially abundance of land and resources and opportunities for individual achievement. Prior to the Civil War America was far more concerned with agriculture and the opening of the West than with industrialization.

RAILROADS

Inadequate transportation facilities constituted a major obstacle to industrialization in both continental Europe and the United States. Lacking Britain's endowment of natural waterways and handicapped by greater distances, continental and American industrialists found themselves pent up in local markets that offered little scope for extensive specialization and expensive capital equipment. The railroad and, to a lesser extent, the steamship changed this state of affairs. The railroads offered cheaper, faster, more dependable transportation, and also, during the period of their construction, which lasted roughly from 1830 until the end of the century, their demands for iron, coal, timber, and machinery proved a potent stimulus to the industries that supplied them.

German miners introduced wooden tracks for coal carts in the British coal industry as early as the sixteenth century. By the end of the eighteenth century British coal fields had many miles of railways on which wagons were propelled by gravity, horsepower, and human beings. Richard Trevithick operated the first steam locomotive on one of these tracks in 1804. Trevithick's engine and others like it were at first too heavy and inefficient to be commercially successful. After several improvements on both engines and tracks George Stephenson heralded the railway era in 1825 with a successful run over the tracks of the new Stockton and Darlington railroad, and inaugurated it in 1830 with the opening of the Liverpool and Manchester, the first railroad designed from the beginning for steam locomotion. Thereafter the British railroad network developed rapidly as each new line increased the demand for more. By 1850 Britain had more than a fourth of its eventual network, almost as much as the rest of Europe combined.

France, Austria, and the United States had short, horse-drawn railroads by 1830, but the United States outstripped Britain and rivaled all of Europe in the construction of railroads. It drew upon European capital and suppliers as well as upon the abundant enthusiasm of private promoters and federal, state, and local governments to span the vast distances of the country. Many of the railroads were cheaply constructed, however, and were built to widely varying standards.

Belgium made the best early showing of any continental country in railroad planning and construction. Rejoicing in its newly won independence, the middle-class government resolved to build a comprehensive network at state expense to facilitate the export of Belgian manufactures and win the transit trade of northwestern Europe. The first section, and the first wholly steam operated railroad on the Continent, opened in

1835. Ten years later the basic state-owned network was complete, after which the job of providing branch and secondary lines was turned over to private enterprise.

France and Germany were the only other continental nations to make significant railroad progress by mid-century. Germany achieved the most. Beginning with the Nürnberg-Fürth in 1835, construction took place at varying but generally rapid rates in several of the German states. Some followed a policy of state ownership and operation; others left railroads to private enterprise, usually with subsidies. Still others allowed both state and private enterprise. Although France had a centralized government and by 1842 a comprehensive railroad plan, it built more slowly. Parliamentary wrangling over the question of state or private enterprise and sectional conflicts over the location of the main lines held up the railroad era in France until the coming of the Second Empire. After 1852 railroad construction proceeded rapidly.

Table 1   *Railroad Mileage in Selected Countries, 1840–1870*

	1840	*1850*	*1870*
United States	2,800	9,000	53,000
Great Britain	1,800	6,600	15,600
German states	400	3,500	11,150
France	260	1,800	10,750
Austrian Empire	100	1,000	5,750
Russian Empire	25	400	7,000
Belgium	200	540	1,800
Netherlands	20	100	840
Switzerland	1	15	840
Spain	—	18	3,300
Italian states	12	240	3,700
Scandinavia	—	—	1,600

Table 2   *World Railroad Mileage, 1830–1870*

	1830	*1840*	*1850*	*1870*
Europe	60	2,800	14,000	65,000
North America	—	2,800	9,000	56,000
Asia	—	—	200	5,100
South America	—	—	—	1,800
Africa	—	—	—	1,100
Australia	—	—	—	1,000
World Total	60	5,600	23,200	130,000

STEAMSHIPS

The steamship, although developed earlier than the locomotive, played a less vital role in the expansion of commerce and industry. In fact, for ocean commerce the wooden sailing ship reached its peak development, both technically and in the tonnage of goods carried, after 1850. In the first half of the century steamers made their greatest contribution in the development of inland commerce. Credit for inventing the steamboat is usually given to the American Robert Fulton, whose ship the *Clermont* made its first successful run on the Hudson in 1807, though there are other earlier claimants for this distinction. Within a few years steamers appeared on the Great Lakes and the rivers of the Mississippi system as well as in coastal waters. Prior to 1850 steamboats probably contributed more than railroads to opening the trans-Allegheny West. In Europe they could be seen on such broad rivers as the Rhine, the Danube, the Rhone, and the Seine, as well as on the Mediterranean and Baltic seas and the English Channel. Steam came to the North Atlantic with the voyage of the auxiliary steamer *Savannah* in 1820, but regular transatlantic service began in 1838, when the *Sirius* and *Great Western* made simultaneous voyages from England to New York. Samuel Cunard, an Englishman, inaugurated his famous line in 1840, but soon ran into stiff competition from other companies. Until the end of the American Civil War ocean steamers carried chiefly mail, passengers, and expensive, lightweight cargo. The age of the ocean steamer did not arrive until the development of the compound engine and the opening of the Suez Canal in 1869.

COMMUNICATIONS

Perhaps no single invention of the nineteenth century compared with that of printing in the fifteenth century in its effect on the field of communications. Nevertheless, the cumulative effects of nineteenth-century innovations were comparable. Paper-making machinery, invented about 1800, and the cylindrical printing press, first used by the London *Times* in 1812, greatly reduced the cost of books and newspapers. Together with the reductions in stamp and excise taxes on paper and printing, they brought reading material within reach of the masses and contributed to their increasing literacy. By mid-century the penny press was a reality. The invention of lithography in 1819 and the development of photography after 1827 made possible the cheap reproduction and wide dissemination of visual images, with effects on the spread of culture and enlightenment that have been debated ever since.

One communications invention that won almost universal acclaim was the introduction of the penny post by Britain in 1840. Within a few years most Western countries had adopted a system of flat-rate, prepaid postal charges. Even more significant was the invention of the electric telegraph by the American Samuel Morse in 1832. Practical application of the telegraph did not begin until the 1840's, however, and the world did not feel its full effects until after mid-century.

SOCIAL ASPECTS OF EARLY INDUSTRIALISM

The revolutionary changes in technology and in the character of economic activity that took place with increasing rapidity throughout the nineteenth century cannot be fully appreciated without considering their impact on the people who experienced them. In fact, it is the human consequences that justify the use of the word revolution. These consequences varied widely from individual to individual, and from one social group to another, but there were certain broad social changes that affected the whole of Western civilization.

POPULATION GROWTH

One of the most spectacular results of industrialization was the enormous increase in population. In the middle of the seventeenth century the population of the world has been estimated at slightly more than 500 million people, of which about one-fifth lived in Europe. By the middle of the twentieth century world population approached 2.5 billion people, a five-fold increase in 300 years. All of the increase did not take place in Europe or areas of European settlement, which indicates that industrialization was not the only factor causing the growth; the correlation is close enough, however, to indicate that the two phenomena were associated.

The largest increase of people of European stock during this population explosion took place in the nineteenth century. Britain and Germany, the two most important industrial nations, had rates of growth averaging somewhat more than 1 per cent per year. (A constant rate of 1 per cent per year would result in a doubling of the population in about seventy years.) In the United States, where the growth of population was favored by wide expanses of cheap land, rich resources, free immigration, and a fluid social structure, population grew from about 5 million in 1800 to more than 75 million in 1900, for a growth rate in excess of 3 per cent. (At 3 per cent the population would double in less than twenty-five years.) Russia, which was one of the least industrialized countries in Europe but which possessed vast empty tracts of land, had one of the highest rates of population growth, from about 37 million to more than 100 million. France, which had the largest population in Europe in the early eighteenth century, lagged far behind the others in its rate of growth.

The growth in population was due principally to industrialization and the increase in agricultural productivity. The improvements in transpor-

Table 3   *The Growth of Population (millions)*

	1800	1850	1900	1950	
Europe	187.0	266.0	401.0	559.0	
United Kingdom	16.1	27.5	41.8	50.6	
Germany	24.6	35.9	56.4	69.0	
France	27.3	35.8	39.0	41.9	
Russia	37.0	60.2	111.0	193.0	(1946)
Spain	10.5	n.a.	16.6	28.3	
Italy	18.1	24.3	32.5	46.3	
Sweden	2.3	3.5	5.1	7.0	
Belgium	n.a.	4.3	6.7	8.6	
Netherlands	n.a.	3.1	5.1	10.1	
North America	16.0	39.0	106.0	217.0	
United States	5.3	23.2	76.0	151.7	
South America	9.0	20.0	38.0	111.0	
Asia	602.0	749.0	937.0	1,302.0	
Africa	90.0	95.0	120.0	198.0	
Oceania	2.0	2.0	6.0	13.0	
World Total	906.0	1,171.0	1,608.0	2,400.0	

n.a.: not available

tation and communication and in medical science and sanitation contributed to the growth of population even in areas that did not experience industrialization directly, sometimes with dire consequences.

URBANIZATION

Another striking characteristic of recent history, closely associated with industrialization and the growth of population, has been the growth of cities. Cities have existed from the beginnings of civilization, but until the industrial revolution the greater part of the population lived in small rural villages or the open countryside. At the beginning of the nineteenth century this proportion was 60 per cent in England and Wales, about 75 per cent in France, the Low Countries, western Germany, and Italy, and 90 per cent or more in most of the rest of the world. By 1850 half the English population lived in towns and cities, and by 1900 most other industrial nations had a simliar proportion of urban dwellers. This trend has continued to the present day.

The population of industrial countries not only lived in cities; it went by preference to the largest cities. For example, in England and Wales the proportion of the population living in small towns (2,000–20,000 inhabitants) has remained roughly constant at about 15 per cent from the beginning of the nineteenth century to the present day, whereas the proportion in large cities (over 20,000 inhabitants) has risen from 27 per cent to more than 70 per cent. In 1800 there were barely twenty cities

Table 4 *The Growth of Large Cities and Metropolitan Areas (thousands)*

	1800	1850	1900	1950a
London	959	2,681	6,581	10,200
Manchester	77	303	544	1,965
Liverpool	82	397	685	1,445
Birmingham	71	242	522	2,400
Glasgow	77	329	736	1,600
Paris	600	1,422	3,670	6,350
Marseilles	111	195	491	715
Lyons	90	177	459	740
Berlin	172	500	2,712	3,900
Hamburg	130	132	706	1,800
Cologne	50	97	373	1,125
Frankfurt	48	59	289	850
Essen	5	9	216	3,175
St. Petersburg (Leningrad)	220	485	1,150	3,250
Moscow	250	365	1,000	6,500
Kiev	20	61	275	925
Antwerp	62	88	277	630
Brussels	90	251	604	1,115
Amsterdam	201	224	511	1,125
Zurich	12	42	168	420
Copenhagen	101	130	469	1,215
Stockholm	76	93	301	985
Vienna	247	444	1,675	1,900
Prague	75	206	382	980
Budapest	54	178	732	1,670
Barcelona	115	175	533	1,550
Rome	153	175	463	1,625
Naples	350	449	564	1,230
Milan	134	200	491	1,575
New York	64	696	3,437	13,300
Chicago	0	30	1,699	5,325
Philadelphia	81	409	1,294	3,350
Detroit	1	21	286	3,275
Los Angeles	2	11	102	4,275

aMetropolitan area.

in Europe with a population of as much as 100,000, and none in the Western Hemisphere; by 1900 there were more than 150 such cities in Europe and North America, and by 1950 more than 600. In the mid-twentieth century there were more cities and supercities (called metropolitan areas) with a population in excess of 1 million (sometimes greatly in excess) than there were cities with a population of 100,000 in 1800.

There are many social and cultural reasons why people want to live in cities. Historically the chief limitation on the growth of cities has been economic: the impossibility of supplying large urban populations with the necessities of life. With the technological improvements of modern industry not only were these limitations relaxed, but in some cases economic considerations also required the growth of cities. In preindustrial societies even most of the nonagricultural population lived in rural areas. It was cheaper to carry the finished products of industry such as textiles and iron to distant markets than to carry food and raw materials to concentrations of workers. The introduction of steam power and the factory system, the transition from charcoal to coke as fuel for the iron industry, and the improvements in transportation and communication changed this situation. The rise of the factory system necessitated a concentration of the work force. Because of the new importance of coal some of the largest centers of industry arose on or near the sites of coal deposits — the Black Country of England, the Ruhr Valley in Germany, the area around Lille in northern France, and the Pittsburgh area in America.

As commerce expanded, the demand for specialized facilities for the movement and storage of goods and for various other commercial and financial services increased, adding to the importance of port cities and other transportation centers such as New York, Liverpool, Hamburg, Marseilles, and Cologne. Transportation factors also permitted the growth of commerce, industry, and population in the old established political, administrative, and cultural centers, such as London, Paris, and Berlin. As the industrial and commercial centers grew in size and importance, the service trades of butcher, baker, and barber, not to mention doctors, lawyers, firemen, hotel keepers, entertainers, and so on, gathered around to add their numbers.

The growth of cities was not an unmixed blessing. Living and working conditions in the earliest industrial cities were frequently as bad as or worse than anything that could be found in the preindustrial countryside. Cities were filled with huge ramshackle tenements or long rows of miserable cottages in which the families of the working classes crowded four, eight, even twelve or more persons to a room. The buildings were so badly constructed that sometimes whole blocks collapsed, as though struck by an earthquake. Sanitary facilities were generally nonexistent, and refuse of all kinds was disposed of by being thrown into the street. Where drainage facilities existed they usually took the form of open ditches in the middle of the streets, but more often than not rain, waste water, and refuse were left to stand in stagnant pools and rotting piles that filled the air with vile odors and served as breeding areas for cholera and other epidemic diseases. Swine and other animals ranged the streets and courtyards, rooting in the refuse heaps. The streets themselves were mostly narrow, crooked, unlighted, and unpaved. Over all hung a black pall of

The Houses of the Poor Are Not the Palaces of the Rich
engraving by Gustav Doré

"Every great city has one or more slums, where the working class is crowded together. . . . These slums are pretty equally arranged in all the great towns of England, the worst houses in the worst quarters of the towns; usually one or two-storied cottages in long rows, perhaps with cellars used as dwellings, almost always irregularly built. . . . The streets are generally unpaved, rough, dirty, filled with vegetable and animal refuse, without sewers or gutters, but supplied with foul, stagnant pools instead. . . . Further, the streets serve as drying grounds in fine weather; lines are stretched across from house to house, and hung with wet clothing." Friedrich Engels, THE CONDITION OF THE WORKING CLASS IN ENGLAND IN 1844 (London, 1892).

smoke and grit from factory smokestacks and household chimneys. Except for the greater quantities of smoke, conditions in the industrial areas did not differ greatly from those of earlier towns and cities, but their greater size and number made them more pernicious. That people consented to live in such conditions is evidence of the great economic pressures that drew them from the country into the factories.

In part, the deplorable conditions resulted from extremely rapid growth, inadequacy of the administrative machinery, lack of experience by local authorities, and the consequent absence of planning. For example, Manchester, the center of the cotton textile industry in Great Britain, grew from a "mere village" at the beginning of the eighteenth century to a town of 25,000 in 1770 on the eve of the industrial revolution. By 1800 it had a population of almost 100,000, and by 1850 more than 300,000. Yet it did not secure a charter of incorporation until 1838. The growth of other cities was even more rapid. Chicago, first settled in 1816, rose from 30,000 in 1850 to more than 500,000 in 1880 and more than 1 million in 1890.

Although there was a general if gradual improvement in conditions within the purview of public authorities throughout the nineteenth century, many of the worst conditions were beyond their competence until new laws were passed. The public authorities could pave the streets, install sewers and street lights, and issue regulations to provide for proper ventilation, but they could not except in the most general way ensure that buildings were properly designed and erected or prevent four families from living in a dwelling designed for one. The responsibility rested in part upon the greed or indifference of landlords and builders, but also upon the poverty and ignorance of the people themselves.

NEW SOCIAL CLASSES

A third major consequence of industrialization was the growth of new social classes that overshadowed or completely replaced those which had previously existed. The bourgeoisie, or middle class, had existed in limited numbers in preindustrial society in western Europe. As early as the seventeenth century in the more commercially advanced nations, such as Britain and Holland, the gentry and nobility had begun to form a loose, informal alliance with the upper middle classes, frequently by intermarriage. With the continued commercialization of society and the beginning of industrialization, the numbers and wealth of the middle classes grew, leading to an increase in their influence and especially their aspirations. In countries where the political and social structure was sufficiently flexible — Britain is the classic example — their aspirations were gradually translated into political power. The Great Reform of 1832 marked the triumph of this group and ensured middle-class dominance in British social and political life for almost a century. Where social and political institutions were not sufficiently flexible — and here the classic example is

France — the rising aspirations of the middle classes came into direct conflict with the interests of the older aristocracy, resulting in revolution. The great French Revolution of 1789 and the lesser revolution of 1830 were essentially bourgeois or middle-class revolutions.

A new class of industrial workers emerged with the industrial system and began to gain numerical superiority, especially in the cities. But to speak of "the" working class is misleading, for there were many gradations and differences within the laboring population. Factory workers proper (including many women and children), although among the objects of greatest attention for historians of the industrial revolution, were only one element of it. Moreover, within that one element there were many differences in attitude and circumstance, for instance, among textile workers, iron workers, pottery workers, and so on. Miners (also including some women and children in the earliest stages of industrialization), though they resembled factory workers in some respects, differed in many others. Domestic servants, artisans, and handicraftsmen had existed in large numbers before the industrial revolution. Many of the skilled workers sank to the status of the unskilled as machines replaced them in their work. Others, including carpenters, masons, machinists, and typesetters, found the demand for their services increasing with the growth of cities and industry. Casual laborers, such as dockers and porters, constituted another important group, as did transport workers, clerks, and so on. The common characteristic that enables us to treat these various groups as one for some purposes (although even it was not precise or universal) was the fact that the individuals composing them depended for a living upon the sale of their labor for a daily or weekly wage. Since wages were generally quite low, and since there were periodic seasons of slack work and industrial depression, the livelihood thus gained was skimpy and precarious. Bad as they were, the conditions of life and work of the industrial workers probably were better than they had been for the masses of the population before the industrial revolution.

ECONOMIC LIBERALISM, LAISSEZ FAIRE, AND FREE TRADE

The economic aspect of nineteenth-century liberalism was closely associated with the so-called classical school of political economy. The creators and leading spokesmen of this school were a kindly Scots philosopher, a parson of the Church of England, and a converted Jewish stockbroker of London.

CLASSICAL POLITICAL ECONOMY

Adam Smith (1723–1790), professor of moral philosophy in the University of Glasgow, was as much a product of the Enlightenment as was Thomas Jefferson or the Marquis de Condorcet. He was also thoroughly steeped in the British empirical tradition of philosophy (David Hume was a close personal friend), had traveled widely on the Continent, and had gained practical experience in business and government as a commissioner of customs (import taxes). His great work, *An Inquiry into the Nature and Causes of the Wealth of Nations,* was first published in 1776. In it Smith analyzed and vividly described the benefits of specialization and division of labor among individuals and geographical regions. Smith was thoroughly individualistic. Like Bentham and other liberals, he regarded the welfare of individuals as the ultimate goal of all human endeavor, and in common with other philosophers of the Enlightenment he had an optimistic view of the possibilities of human progress. Borrowing the concept of natural law from Newtonian physics, he thought he detected a "natural harmony" in the social universe, according to which an "invisible hand," the force of competition in free markets, led each individual to contribute to the interest of society while pursing his own self-interest. It followed that the government should interfere with individual economic activity as little as possible, apart from maintaining the basic conditions of order and justice: "According to the system of natural liberty, the sovereign has only three duties to attend to: . . . first, the duty of protecting society from the violence and invasion of other independent societies; secondly, the duty of protecting, as far as possible, every member of the society from the injustice or oppression of every other member of it, or the duty of establishing an exact administration of justice; and, thirdly, the duty of erecting and maintaining certain public works and certain public institutions." In short, *The Wealth of Nations* provided powerful arguments in favor of individual economic freedom and free international trade and against the cumbersome governmental restrictions on trade and enterprise that had grown up in preceding centuries.

The Reverend Thomas Robert Malthus (1766–1834) followed Smith on most points but radically reversed his optimistic view of the beneficent results of the economy operating in accordance with natural laws. In *An Essay on the Principle of Population* (1798) Malthus stated his view that population tends to grow more rapidly than food supply, except when it is checked by famine, disease, war, and other forms of misery and vice. Although Malthus later modified his theory to include "moral restraint" (voluntary limitation of births through celibacy and late marriage) as a "preventive check" on population growth, the implications of his theory were clear: the masses of mankind were forever destined to live in misery at a near-subsistence level of income.

When Malthus's gloomy conclusions were combined with the "iron law of wages" popularly associated with the name of David Ricardo, they led Thomas Carlyle to label political economy (or economics) the "dismal science." Ricardo (1772–1823), a stockbroker by profession, developed the "labor theory of value," which was implicit in the work of his predecessors Smith and John Locke and which later formed the basis of Marxian economics. According to Ricardo, the value of any commodity is proportional to the amount of labor necessary to produce it. Since labor itself resembles a commodity insofar as it is bought and sold, its value (the wage rate) varies with the price of food necessary for the subsistence of the laborer and his family. Ricardo argued that actual wages could not rise above a minimum subsistence level for any prolonged period, because the increase in population and in the price of foodstuffs would force them back to the "natural," or customary, level. Although this theory has long since been proven fallacious, it had great influence in the nineteenth century on the thought of orthodox economists and statesmen and of revolutionaries such as Karl Marx. It inspired the new Poor Law of 1834, which greatly simplified the administration of poor relief and contributed to the mobility of labor, but also imposed harsh "means tests" on applicants for relief and forced them into prisonlike workhouses as a condition for obtaining relief.

Classical economics received its ultimate statement from the pen of John Stuart Mill (1806–1873), who published his *Principles of Political Economy* in 1848. Mill added little of novelty but synthesized and systematized the contributions of his predecessors. Mill's authority was rarely questioned for more than a quarter of a century thereafter, and the general policy prescriptions of classical economics that he defined commanded wide adherence until well into the twentieth century. Nevertheless, criticism from without, from socialists and others, and new theoretical developments from within gradually eroded its theoretical basis. Mill himself in his later years began to question some of the principles that he had earlier taken for granted and he began to move in the direction of a vague humanitarian socialism. Meanwhile, the implementation of the classical doctrines in legislation and public policy marked a triumph rarely achieved by purely intellectual ideas. That triumph was best summed up in two phrases: free trade and laissez faire.

CORN LAW REPEAL AND FREE TRADE

The heart of the free trade movement in Great Britain was the drive to repeal the Corn Laws, which placed an almost prohibitive tax on the importation of wheat and other bread grains. Popular sentiment for the repeal resulted in 1839 in the creation of the Anti-Corn Law League under the leadership of Richard Cobden, a Manchester manufacturer and outspoken pacifist, and John Bright, a Quaker industrialist of Rochdale. The league mounted a strong and effective campaign to influence public opinion. It was supported in particular by the so-called Manchester School, which was not a school at all but a loose association of industrialists, humanitarian reformers, middle-class radicals, and intellectuals from London and other provincial cities as well as Manchester. The cir-

John Stuart Mill

"The rapid success of the Political Economy showed that the public wanted, and were prepared for such a book. Published early in 1848, an edition of a thousand copies was sold in less than a year. Another similar edition was published in the spring of 1849; and a third, of 1250 copies, early in 1852. It was, from the first, continually cited and referred to as an authority, because it was not a book merely of abstract science, but also of application, and treated Political Economy, not as a thing by itself, but as a fragment of a greater whole; a branch of Social Philosophy." AUTOBIOGRAPHY OF JOHN STUART MILL (New York, 1924).

cumstance that ensured the success of the movement was the disastrous potato famine of 1845–1846 in Ireland. The final vote in the House of Commons in May, 1846, found the Conservative prime minster, Sir Robert Peel, and about one hundred of his supporters joining with a majority of the Whigs in favor of repeal.

Peel's government had previously simplified customs procedures and had taken a few steps in the direction of freer trade. With the crumbling of the Corn Laws, the principal bastion of the protectionists, other legislative obstacles to complete free trade soon disappeared. In 1849 Parliament repealed the Navigation Acts, the foundation of the old colonial system, and by 1860 virtually complete free trade had been achieved.

LAISSEZ FAIRE

The free trade movement was one of the most conspicuous and successful aspects of a general tendency toward the relaxation of governmental controls over economic activity that characterized the middle decades of the nineteenth century, in Great Britain particularly. It derived its political and economic strength from the increasing power of the middle classes and its intellectual justification from the teachings of the classical economists. The principles underlying the tendency are sometimes referred to collectively by the French phrase *laissez faire,* which first appeared in English usage in 1825. The phrase is literally translated by the imperative "let do." The popular understanding of it was that individuals, especially businessmen, should be left free of all governmental restraint (except criminal laws) to pursue their own selfish interests. Carlyle satirized it as "anarchy plus a constable."

Laissez faire in practice, however, was by no means as heartless, as selfishly motivated, or as inexorable as extremist statements indicated. The main target of the classical economists and the new commercial and industrial classes was the old apparatus of mercantilist economic regulation, which in the name of national interest frequently erected pockets of special privilege and monopoly and in other ways irrationally interfered with individual liberty and the pursuit of wealth. In addition to the Corn Laws and the Navigation Acts, the means of mercantilist control included chartered companies with monopoly privileges, such as the East India Company and the Hudson's Bay Company, prohibitions on the export of machinery and the emigration of skilled artisans, the Combination Acts, the usury laws, and much similar legislation.

At the same time that Parliament was dismantling the old system of regulation and special privilege, however, it was enacting a new series of regulations concerned with the general welfare, especially of those least able to protect themselves. The measures included the Factory Acts, new health and sanitary laws, and the beginnings of public education. These measures were not the work of any one class or segment of the population. Humanitarian reformers of both aristocratic and middle-class backgrounds joined forces with leaders of the working classes to agitate for them, and they were voted for by Whigs and Tories as well as Radicals.

CONTINENTAL AND AMERICAN ECONOMIC POLICIES

Economic liberalism, though not confined to England, found its leading advocates and practitioners there. The French spokesmen of the classical school were J. B. Say, a follower of Adam Smith, and Frédéric Bastiat, who sought to popularize its doctrines in a series of "economic sophisms." While the majority of French businessmen paid lip service to the principles of individualism and laissez faire, at the same time they clamored for protection of their own economic interests. Instead of evolving in the direction of free trade, French commercial policy remained rigidly protectionist until after 1850. Industrialists and agriculturists alike sought subsidies and special favors for their own industries, while insisting on strict atomistic competition within the labor force. The hated *livrets* or workers' passbooks, requiring employer approval for a change of jobs, placed the workers at a great disadvantage in bargaining with their employers. Under the authoritarian regime of the Second Empire (see pp. 661–662), France at last took some hesitating steps in the direction of economic liberalism.

Middle-class rule in Belgium proved somewhat more dynamic and progressive than in France. The new government, favored by the cooperation of French and British capitalists and engineers, set out at once to add the benefits of material prosperity to the achievement of national independence. It established public and private credit on a sound basis and facilitated the formation of new industrial and commercial enterprises. As a result of such measures, its rich coal resources, and its favorable geographical location, Belgium soon became the most highly industrialized and one of the most prosperous nations on the Continent. It produced no great liberal economist of the stature of Adam Smith or J. B. Say, but it followed their teachings in practice with exemplary success.

In the interests of administrative efficiency and fiscal responsibility the government of Prussia reformed its tariff system and in 1834 took the lead in creating the Zollverein, a customs union or free trade area, which eventually included all German states except Austria. This promoted economic development and material prosperity and thereby strengthened the middle classes, but the Zollverein was also a political measure designed to strengthen Prussia at the expense of Austria. Prussia's leaders realized that a customs union from which Austria was excluded could be of great importance in a future struggle for supremacy in central Europe.

In general, in places where the middle classes had not yet succeeded in breaking the grip of aristocratic-autocratic rule, economic liberalism, like political liberalism, made little headway. The situation in Germany, where political liberalism had found an ally in nationalism, produced its own special variant of economic doctrine. Friedrich List (1789–1846), a forerunner of the historical school of political economy, and an ardent advocate of railroads and the Zollverein, published *The National System of Political Economy* in 1841. He argued that the doctrines of the classical economists did not have universal validity, though they were not wholly incorrect. According to him, the appropriate economic policy depended upon the specific conditions of time and place. Free trade and a minimal role for government suited England very well, where commerce and industry were already developed, but in a backward, divided nation like Germany the government should take a much more positive role in the development of the productive forces of the nation. List's argument had widespread influence, not only on Germany in the nineteenth century but also on the nations that tried to achieve national self-sufficiency between the two World Wars and on the former colonial dependencies that tried to develop their own national economies after World War II.

List lived for a number of years in the United States, where he obtained many ideas subsequently elaborated in his book. Americans in the first half of the century differed not so much on the role of the government in the economy as on which level of government should play the most active role. The classical economists had few purist adherents in the United States. Varied as actual economic policies were in the numerous burgeoning states, they achieved a pragmatic and workable compromise between the demands of individual liberty and the requirements of society. Owing to rival sectional interests and the triumph of the Jeffersonian and Jacksonian democrats, the federal government played the minimal role assigned by classical theory and until the Civil War followed a liberal or low tariff commercial policy. State and local governments on the other hand took an active role in promoting economic development and social welfare. The American System, as Henry Clay called it, regarded government as an agency to assist individuals and private enterprise and to hasten the development of the nation's material resources.

THE INDUSTRIAL REVOLUTION IN PERSPECTIVE

The industrial revolution, in the broadest sense of the term, cannot be assigned specific dates, nor was it confined to a single country or geographical area. Under a variety of labels, such as the automation movement in highly industrialized countries and programs of economic development in the poorer nations of the world, it is still going on today. In the long view of history, however, the industrial revolution in Britain appears as one of the great watersheds in the progress of civilization. For the first time in the annals of mankind a society surmounted the niggardliness of nature and broke out of the Malthusian trap. No longer were the masses destined to live out their earthly existence in endless backbreaking toil under the constant threat of death by starvation or disease.

In view of this achievement it is curious that so much of the historical controversy surrounding the industrial revolution has focussed on the question of whether it was good or bad. It is true that it involved displacement and the disruption of traditional behavior, along with much suffering on the part of many of those affected: any process of radical social change, no matter how beneficial in the long run, is bound to create hardship for those with a vested interest in the status quo. In arriving at a final assessment of the consequences of any historical event or movement, however, the historian must ask, What was the alternative? For the industrial revolution in Britain, the answer is provided by contemporaneous events in Ireland. (That the Irish were governed from London, although not unrelated to their fate, does not alter the significance of the example.) The Irish population increased from about 4 million in 1780 to more than 8 million in 1840 without significant industrialization or agrarian reform. The result was the disastrous potato famine of the 1840's, which through starvation and emigration reduced the population by more than 2 million in the space of ten years. Without the continued expansion of industry and the increase in agricultural productivity made possible by the industrial revolution, the whole of Europe might have shared Ireland's fate.

REVOLUTION AT FLOODTIDE
CHAPTER TWENTY-FOUR

Between 1832 and 1848 the middle classes in Great Britain, France, and Belgium, working in cooperation with the few liberal representatives of the old aristocratic elements, sought to consolidate their recently achieved preponderance of political power. Although they continued to make liberal reforms, liberalism in western Europe ceased to be a revolutionary force and became a defender of the new status quo in the face of growing demands by the urban working classes for more far-reaching democratic and social reforms. The rapidity of industrial development and the progress of reform in Britain and Belgium gradually reconciled the workers to liberalism. The slower pace of change in France, together with the narrow, short-sighted selfishness of French liberals, built up a store of tension and resentment in French society that suddenly overflowed in revolution. As on previous occasions, the revolution in France served to trigger a series of revolutionary outbursts throughout Europe, especially in central Europe, where liberal, national, democratic, republican, and socialist sentiments freely mingled in their common antagonism to the old order.

CONTRASTING LIBERALISMS IN THE WEST

THE VICTORIAN ERA IN BRITAIN

Parliamentary reform, in spite of its long-run significance, did not immediately introduce radical changes into the fabric of British life. It did accelerate the course of social and economic reform and inaugurated a gradual realignment of British politics and political parties. In the new alignment, which emerged gradually between 1832 and the second reform bill in 1867, party discipline was strengthened and both parties built extraparliamentary organizations to influence the electorate. The Tories

became the Conservative party, representing primarily the landed interests, the established church, and eventually the advocates of imperialism.
The Whigs became the Liberal party, spokesmen for the commercial and
manufacturing classes and advocates of reform. Paradoxically, Conservative governments carried two of the most important reforms of the century — the repeal of the Corn Laws in 1846 and the second reform bill or
Representation of the People Act of 1867, which extended the suffrage
to the majority of urban workers. These two reforms split party loyalties
and occasioned much delay in the emergence of the new system, but they
clarified the principles that divided the parties and laid the foundation
for subsequent party cohesion.

In the two preceding centuries the unpopularity, incapacity, and weakness of British monarchs had contributed greatly to strengthening the
evolving system of representative, parliamentary government. Under the
dissolute George IV (1820–1830) and the petty William IV (1830–1837)
the popularity of the monarchy reached a low ebb. When William died,
its future was uncertain. His successor on the throne was his niece Victoria, a girl of eighteen, who was scarcely prepared for the role she had to
assume. Under other circumstances her youth, inexperience, and sex
might have been fatal handicaps. As it happened, they suited almost perfectly the prevailing temper of the ruling bourgeoisie. She was prim,
almost prudish. She had a profound respect for the British constitution
and for her own place within it. She lacked imagination and a sense of
aesthetics, but she had a stern, puritanical devotion to duty and morality.
In 1840 she married Albert of Saxe-Coburg-Gotha, a serious, sensible man
who was her counterpart in almost every respect; she bore him nine children. Albert's encouragement of scientific, technological, and industrial
progress showed that he was in step with the times. Victoria's reign, the
longest in British history (1837–1901), coincided almost exactly with the
peak of British economic supremacy and political influence. It is hardly
to be wondered that her name became the symbol of an age.

THE PROGRESS OF REFORM

The victory of the Whigs in 1832 ensured the continuation of reform.
The reforms were of many types. Some of the major ones, such as the
electoral reform and the subsequent reorganization of local government,
reflected chiefly the interests of the middle classes. Administrative reforms, such as the New Poor Law of 1834 and the introduction of the
penny post in 1840, represented a triumph for the rationalism of the
exponents of Bentham's utilitarianism. Humanitarian measures such as
the abolition of slavery and factory legislation resulted from the reaction
of middle-class consciences to the exposure by utilitarian reformers of
grave social evils. John Stuart Mill put it well when he wrote in 1838,
"The changes which have been made, and the greater changes which will

be made, in our institutions, are not the work of philosophers, but of the interests and instincts of large portions of society recently grown into strength. But Bentham gave voice to those interests and instincts."

One of the first acts of the reformed Parliament in 1833 was the abolition of slavery throughout the empire. Trading in slaves had been illegal since 1807, but the institution of slavery itself still existed in the West Indies and other tropical colonies. To abolish slavery without violating the property rights of the slave owners, the British taxed themselves for 20 million pounds sterling to be paid as compensation to the owners.

A new Factory Act was passed in the same year with the aid of the Tories, who hoped to hit back at the newly enfranchised mill owners through their pocketbooks. It extended the scope of earlier laws dating back to 1802, which had prohibited the employment of children under the age of nine in cotton mills and limited the workday of children between nine and thirteen to twelve hours. The earlier legislation had covered only the cotton industry and failed to provide for effective enforcement. The act of 1833 extended the provisions to all textile factories, imposed a maximum eight-hour day on children from nine to thirteen, and a twelve-hour day on those from thirteen to eighteen, provided paid inspectors who were responsible to the Home Office in London, and insisted on two hours daily of compulsory schooling for working children.

The act of 1833 precipitated a campaign for the regulation of adult labor, which eventuated in the Ten Hours Bill of 1847. After shocking revelations of conditions in the mining industry, the Mines Act of 1842 extended regulation and inspection to coal mines and prohibited the employment of women and children underground. Another Factory Act in 1844 required safety devices on industrial machinery and imposed additional safeguards. In the next two decades more and more industries were brought within the scope of the factory acts, and the general principle of state regulation of working conditions was firmly established.

A major step that followed logically from the Reform Bill of 1832 was the Municipal Reform Act of 1835. It provided for town councils elected by the taxpayers and employing paid officials. Subsequent legislation further strengthened local self-government and at the same time provided for greater central coordination. For example, after a recurrence of cholera in 1848 sanitary reformer Edwin Chadwick secured the establishment of a central board of health with powers to create local boards. During the next two decades local authorities were compelled to provide a water supply, sewers, and waste disposal and to appoint professional sanitary inspectors.

THE JULY MONARCHY IN FRANCE

In France the Charter of 1814, as revised in 1830, was essentially a contract between the monarch and the upper bourgeoisie, who were its principal beneficiaries. The revisions abolished hereditary membership in the Chamber of Peers, dropped Catholicism as the state religion, restricted censorship of the press except against "radical agitation," and assured constitutional, parliamentary government. Control remained firmly in the hands of men of property. Amendments to the electoral law enlarged the suffrage from about 90,000 to about 170,000 but retained formidable property qualifications for office-holding and voting. An American, John Jay, had said, "The men who own the country ought to govern it"; no government more clearly exemplified that maxim than the July Monarchy in France.

The true political division of the country was tripartite, but two of the three major groups were excluded from the political process — one by choice, the other by legislation. On the extreme right were the ultramontanists and supporters of the defunct Bourbons, who began to call themselves legitimists. Although they were eligible to vote and hold office, the majority retired to their estates or town houses to await a counter-revolution that never came. On the extreme left were the republicans and socialists, most of whom were excluded from legal participation by the property qualifications. Concentrated in the cities, especially Paris, they agitated and conspired for a revolution, which, when it came, surprised even them. The middle-class parliamentary forces that occupied the center made a show of party politics with various sham divisions such as left center, or right center, but in fact they were firmly united in the belief that no more fundamental alterations in the social and political structure were desirable. Jacques Laffitte and Adolphe Thiers, leaders of the "party of movement," talked vaguely of extending the benefits of the regime to the less favored classes; but they did nothing about it in the few brief periods when they held the reins of government. Casimir Périer, first leader of the "party of resistance," defined his policy as that of the *juste milieu,* that is, the middle way between absolutism and clericalism on the one hand and republicanism and democracy on the other. He demonstrated his meaning in 1831 by suppressing with violence and brutality a rising of workers in Lyons, in which more than six hundred persons died. After his death in the cholera epidemic of 1832, his principal successor, François Guizot, piously proclaimed the government of the revised charter "the most perfect ever devised."

Much of the actual character of the July Monarchy derived from and was symbolized by its only monarch, Louis Philippe. Despite his noble birth, the new king had long associated with the men of wealth who put him on the throne. He shared their tastes and aspirations, their virtues and their vices. He was shrewd, sober, and industrious, prudent in conduct, inherently conservative in outlook. A wealthy man in his own right, he adored wealth for its own sake and admired the men who possessed it. In some respects a sort of male Victoria, he nevertheless harbored a secret desire to wield political power himself. He was able to gratify this desire after 1840 by means of Guizot, his principal minister and the other archetype of the July Monarchy.

Guizot was a Protestant who reflected well the spirit and outlook of the *haute bourgeoisie.* He had written a history of the English revolution of 1689 and found his ideal of society in the government and social order that resulted from that event. When he secured the king's confidence in 1840 after ten years of ministerial instability caused by conflicting personal ambitions of the supporters of the throne, he systematically consolidated support for his own ministry by means of wholesale bribery and corruption. Personally incorruptible, he did not scruple at preying on the moral weaknesses of others. In this way he contrived to impose on French government and society a superficial stability that lasted until 1848.

The notable difference between middle-class government in France and Britain was not the extent of corruption, for Britain had its share of that; it was the almost total absence of reform measures by the French. Not only did French ministers draw the line at further extensions of the suffrage, but they showed no interest in the administrative, judicial, and economic reforms that appealed to middle-class sentiment in Britain. Aside from an insignificant and ineffective child labor law, the one important piece of progressive legislation in the whole of the July Monarchy was Guizot's law of 1833 relating to elementary education. The principal purpose of the law was to establish at least one elementary school in each of France's 38,000 communes as the beginning of an attack on mass illiteracy. Although the objective was laudable, the law fell far short of its goal in execution. Moreover, the clergy received a large measure of control over the schools in order to ensure "safe doctrine" for the children of peasants and workers and to conciliate the Catholic Church, which had formerly been an object of attack by French liberals. All other demands for political, social, and economic reform Guizot countered with the self-satisfied admonition, "Make yourselves rich."

THE GROWTH OF SOCIAL PROTEST

While the middle classes of western Europe struggled to remake society according to their own ideas, the swelling urban working classes began to assert their claims as well. In the beginning their attempts took the form of futile riots and strikes against industrialism. Increasingly, however, the workers turned to the formation of labor or trade unions, which were often bitterly opposed and repressed by middle-class employers and governments. They sent petitions to the government for legislative or administrative remedy, formed friendly societies and cooperatives for mutual self-help, and resorted to outright revolutionary activity. The outbursts increased in intensity and frequency as the workers realized that the middle classes had no intention of sharing the gains that they had won with working-class support during the events of 1830 and 1832.

ROBERT OWEN

The first great spokesman for the workingman was not himself a member of the working classes, although he had risen from their ranks. Robert Owen (1771–1858), son of a Welsh artisan, left school at the age of nine to seek his fortune. After a variety of experiences he became at the age of twenty hired manager of a large Manchester cotton mill. Within a few years he became part owner and general manager of another mill in New Lanark, Scotland, which included a company town with schools, churches, and a hospital. It soon became a model of paternalistic endeavor.

A man of great humanitarian feeling, Owen early came to the conclusion that social environment exercised the greatest influence in the formation of individual character. By paying high wages, providing decent living and working conditions, and strictly limiting child labor, Owen created a contented labor force and also earned substantial profits. Beginning with the publication of *A New View of Society* in 1813, he sought to convince the aristocratic rulers of Europe and America to substitute his new "rational system of society," a system based on cooperation, for the existing organization. He campaigned ceaselessly for several years and built up a small but enthusiastic following among workingmen and a few radical reformers, but he made no lasting impression on the ruling classes. In 1824 he set off with a band of disciples to organize a cooperative commonwealth in the wilderness of America at New Harmony, Indiana. Quarrels and misfortune soon caused dissension, and it collapsed completely after Owen's return to England in 1828.

By then Owen had become the hero of the working classes. Many working-class organizations looked to him for leadership. Until 1832, however, he occupied himself in assisting passage of the Reform Bill, expecting that the reformed Parliament would extend the suffrage to workers. When it became evident that it would not, Owen turned for support to the working-class organizations. A number of trade unions had been formed after the repeal of the Combination Acts in 1824, and at the beginning of 1834 Owen organized most of them into "one big union," the Grand National Consolidated Trades Union, which soon enrolled more than half a million members.

The basic strategy of the organization was the general strike, a "Grand National Holiday," to force the government and employers to agree peaceably to the demands of the workers. The government took fright and in March, 1834, sentenced six Dorsetshire agricultural laborers, the famous Tolpuddle martyrs, to exile in the Australian penal colony for organizing a branch of the union. As a result of this example of government repression, as well as of the dissension among the leaders, the Grand

National broke up as quickly as it had formed. Although Owen continued to write and to agitate until the end of his long life, the leadership of working-class organizations soon passed to other hands.

CHARTISM

With the failure of their direct attempts to obtain redress of economic and social grievances, the leaders of the working classes returned to political action to secure it indirectly. In 1836 a group of politically conscious skilled workers created the London Working Men's Association to agitate for parliamentary reform, and in the following year the Birmingham Political Union, which had played an important role in the passage of the first Reform Bill, was reactivated. In 1838 these two groups, reinforced by delegates from the northern counties, met in Birmingham to adopt the People's Charter, a petition to Parliament for further political reform. The charter contained six points, all of which were related to the organization of Parliament. It called for (1) universal male suffrage, (2) annual parliaments, (3) a secret ballot, (4) equal electoral districts, (5) abolition of the property qualification for members of Parliament, and (6) payment of members.

Motions were introduced in the House of Commons to consider the charter in 1839 and 1842 after active campaigns and agitation throughout the country. On both occasions the motions were defeated by large majorities. Strikes, riots, and other popular disturbances followed, and each time the government took stern repressive measures. In 1840 more than five hundred Chartist leaders were in jail. Several, originally sentenced to death, had their sentences commuted to transportation to the Australian penal colony for life. In the face of such opposition the organization soon melted away. It revived briefly in the wake of the revolutions on the Continent in 1848, but the government took preventive measures, such as the recruiting of special constables from the middle classes, and a great demonstration planned for London broke up without even presenting its petition to Parliament.

In retrospect the demands of the Chartists appear reasonable. Within two generations all but annual parliaments had been achieved without special agitation. In the distressed period of the late 1830's and early 1840's, however, with its bad harvests, industrial depression, and popular unrest, Britain's new middle-class rulers felt too insecure to trust their fate to universal suffrage. A distinguished modern historian has stated that the failure of the Chartists demonstrated "not the weakness of the English working classes . . . but the strength of the middle classes." However that may be, the pace of industrial expansion, more rapid in Britain than in France, drained the pools of social unrest and sapped the basis of revolutionary discontent. As early as 1832 a witness before a parliamentary committee on manufactures was asked, "Do you think the

working classes . . . ever show political discontent so long as they are
doing well in their particular trade?" "Not at all," he replied.

FRENCH SOCIALISM

In France the number of urban workers rose spectacularly between
1830 and 1848. Paris had the largest concentration of industrial wage
earners of any city in Europe (London, the only city with a larger population, had fewer engaged in manufacturing and similar occupations).
Not all of them worked in factories; the majority, perhaps, toiled at
home or in small shops under less favorable circumstances than those of
the factory workers. Nevertheless, they all constituted a propertyless proletariat that proved to be fertile soil for radical reformers.

Paris also had the largest concentration of radical intellectuals of any
city in Europe. It served as the great gathering place of the dispossessed,
the disenchanted, and the exiled of all countries. Republicanism and socialism flourished in its intellectual climate, nourished by the traditions
of the French Revolution — Jacobinism and Babeuvism in particular —
as well as by the great and obvious contrast between rich and poor.

One of the first important socialist thinkers of modern times was the
quixotic philosopher Henri de Saint-Simon (1760–1825). Although of
noble birth, Saint-Simon fought against England during the American
Revolution, abdicated his heritage during the French Revolution, and
won and lost a fortune by speculation. For the last twenty-five years of
his life he settled down to serious study, meditation, and writing, frequently living off the charity of his friends. Saint-Simon criticized the
existing inequalities of wealth, but he criticized even more strongly the
social system that rewarded the unproductive or "parasitical" elements in
society, especially the aristocracy, while oppressing the workers or "industrialists." According to Saint-Simon, an *industriel* was anyone who produced a useful commodity or service; therefore farmers, common laborers,
artisans, merchants, engineers, and bankers were all industriels. He projected a hierarchic society governed by "wise men" — philosophers, scientists, and engineers — in which everyone would be obligated to work
according to his talents and would be rewarded in proportion to his contribution. Saint-Simon was no democrat, and many of his ideas were
wildly impractical, but his numerous writings provided a rich store of
inspiration for future reformers of all varieties, and some of the products
of his imagination proved strangely prophetic of the organization of later
societies, both democratic and totalitarian.

In his last years Saint-Simon attracted a small band of devoted disciples,
many of whom were young engineers, financiers, and intellectuals, who
created a school to propagate his ideas. They caught from him a vision
of the immense possibilities of science applied to industry and preached
the virtues of material advance. After the revolution of 1830 they thought

the time had come for social reorganization and undertook a vigorous missionary and propaganda campaign. The staid bourgeois monarchy of Louis Philippe had scant use for their bizarre customs and beliefs, especially after one of their leaders, Prosper Enfantin, converted their teachings into a mystical, half-pagan religion. Under legal prosecution the formal organization dissolved itself in 1832, but many of its members became wealthy and respectable businessmen, bankers, and engineers in capitalistic French society.

Some of the many socialists and other radicals who inhabited Paris under the July Monarchy devoted themselves to theorizing and constructing elaborate blueprints of ideal societies, others to organizing secret societies and working actively for the overthrow of the existing government. One of the most colorful of the latter was Auguste Blanqui (1805–1881). The son of a revolutionist of 1789, Blanqui joined the Carbonari at the age of sixteen. He participated in both the revolution of 1830, which inaugurated the July Monarchy, and in that of 1848, which overthrew it. In the intervening years he organized secret societies and participated in numerous plots and uprisings. Surely one of the longest-lived of all professional revolutionaries, he spent thirty-seven of his seventy-six years in prison, survived to take part in the overthrow of the Second Empire, and died while agitating against the Third Republic.

Two theorizers deserve special mention, more for the novelty than for the practical consequences of their ideas. Charles Fourier (1772–1837) devised a scheme whereby all mankind would be divided into groups of 1,620 individuals each, with equal numbers of men and women. They would be settled on great estates called *phalanstères,* where they would engage in both agricultural and industrial activities. Each phalanstery would have common facilities, such as kitchens, dining rooms, and nurseries. Individuals would not necessarily share equally in the produce, however. In fact, Fourier made special provision for capitalistic financing by means of stock issues and advertised in newspapers for backers, but no capitalist stepped forth to finance his socialist project.

Étienne Cabet (1788–1856), like Fourier, envisioned a utopia which he called Icaria, consisting of isolated, more or less self-contained communities; but unlike Fourier, Cabet required complete equality. In 1848 Cabet actually led a band of disciples to America, where they attempted to create such a community. Many similar communities were created in the American wilderness on the basis of Fourier's and Owen's ideas. Among the most famous of these "backwoods utopias" were Brook Farm, Massachusetts, and the Oneida Community in New York. The luster of the former was due chiefly to the literary celebrities who inhabited or patronized it, while the latter gained renown partly as a consequence of its commercially successful silver-plated tableware. The Mormons and other communitarian religious sects also borrowed from the

ideas of Owen, Fourier, and Cabet. Sooner or later they all broke up as
a result of economic failure or internal dissension, or they adjusted themselves to the society around them. None were ever established in Europe
itself.

Neither a system builder nor a conspirator, P. J. Proudhon (1809–
1865) gave birth to a new doctrine known as anarchism. Anarchism subsequently became identified with lawlessness, violence, and terrorism as
a result of the tactics of late nineteenth-century revolutionists who called
themselves anarchists. Such activities, however, had no place in the
thoughts or intentions of Proudhon, who was personally gentle and pacifist. Unlike most other radical thinkers, Proudhon was an authentic
product of the working classes, and began his career in the printing
trades. He read widely, educated himself, and became a prolific writer.
He opposed force and coercion in all forms and regarded the modern
state as the source of the greatest oppression. He held that state socialism
and communism were as antithetical to true liberty as capitalist or feudal
society. As the solution to social problems, he called for the voluntary
cooperation of free individuals organized in small communities under a
loose federalism.

Louis Blanc (1811–1882), one of the most influential of French socialists, played an active role in the provisional government of 1848. A
journalist and historian by profession, he published his most famous
book, *The Organization of Labor,* in 1838. In it he exposed what he
regarded as the evils of free, capitalistic competition, called on the government to guarantee the "right to work," and proposed the creation of
"social workshops" operated by the workers themselves. Blanc coined the
phrase, "From each according to his abilities, to each according to his
needs," in contrast to the Saint-Simonian doctrine, "From each according
to his abilities, to each according to his works." Unlike other early socialists who belittled politics and ignored or opposed the role of government, Blanc believed the government should assist in establishing the
social or national workshops. He did not regard revolution as inevitable
or even desirable; instead, he felt that the workshops, once established,
would beat the capitalists at their own game and ultimately drive them
out of business. Blanc was one of the most important forerunners of
modern democratic state socialism.

THE BIRTH OF MARXISM

Karl Marx (1818–1883), the most famous and influential of all socialist
theorists, and Friedrich Engels (1820–1895), his faithful friend and col-
laborator, were products of German bourgeois radicalism. Marx was sent
by his father, a Rhineland attorney, to study law at the University of
Bonn. He devoted his first year to romantic poetry and bacchanalian
brawls and was expelled for engaging in a duel. The next year he went

The Bettmann Archive

Karl Marx

"Marx was before all else a revolutionist. His real mission in life was to contribute, in one way or another, to the overthrow of capitalistic society and the state institutions which it had brought into being, to contribute to the liberation of the modern proletariat, which he was the first to make conscious of its own position and its needs, conscious of the contradictions of its emancipation. Fighting was his element. And he fought with a passion, a tenacity and a success such as few could rival." Friedrich Engels, "Speech at the Graveside of Karl Marx," in Karl Marx and Friedrich Engels, SELECTED WORKS (Moscow, 1955).

to the University of Berlin, where he fell under the spell of Hegelian philosophy and took a degree in philosophy. Prevented from teaching because he was an atheist, Marx edited a liberal bourgeois newspaper in Cologne for a time, but the paper was suppressed by the authorities in 1843 for criticizing the absolutist government of Russia. Marx then went to Paris, where he supported himself by writing while studying political economy and socialism. There he met Engels.

Engels, son of a wealthy Rhineland textile manufacturer, had earlier been sent to England to learn the cotton trade in his father's firm in Manchester. While there he wrote a book vilifying capitalism and describing in a somewhat exaggerated manner the condition of the English laboring classes. Although he charged the English capitalists with driving women and children into "wage slavery" and prostitution and destroying family life, he did not bother to marry the Irish factory girl whom he kept as a mistress for many years. On the other hand, Marx, far from living up to the stereotype of the wild-eyed revolutionary, was a conventional family man and a devoted husband and father.

In 1847 Marx moved to London at the invitation of Engels. They joined a small revolutionary group called the League of the Just, later renamed the Communist League, which Engels described as "not much more than the German branch of the French secret societies." Having been invited by the league to draw up a statement of principles, Marx and Engels published the *Communist Manifesto* in January, 1848, on the eve of the revolutions in Europe. The timing was purely coincidental, for the *Manifesto* had no influence at all in provoking or directing the course of the revolutions. Published in the German language in London, it was for many years known only to a small group of personal friends and acquaintances. Not until Marx had gained notoriety as a socialist with the publication of his *Critique of Political Economy* and above all of *Capital,* the first volume of which appeared in 1867, did the *Manifesto* assume a prominent place in socialist literature.

The *Manifesto* was intended primarily as a propaganda device to convince the workers of their own importance, call them to unity, and stir them to action. It began with a striking and wildly inaccurate introduction: "A spectre is haunting Europe — the spectre of Communism. All the powers of old Europe have entered into a holy alliance to exercise this spectre: Pope and Tsar, Metternich and Guizot, French Radicals and German police-spies." It concluded with an even more stirring call to action: "Let the ruling classes tremble at a Communist revolution. The proletarians have nothing to lose but their chains. They have a world to win. Working men of all countries, unite!"

Between these dramatic passages Marx and Engels set forth in drastically abbreviated form the substance of the historical and economic theory that Marx subsequently developed in his more scholarly publications. They developed the theory that "the history of all hitherto existing society is the history of class struggles." They cited the fact that feudal lords had replaced Roman patricians as the ruling class and serfs had replaced slaves as the exploited class of society. With the development of commerce in the late Middle Ages a new class, the bourgeoisie, developed to dispute control of society with the old feudal nobility. After many struggles the bourgeoisie eventually triumphed in the English revolutions of the seventeenth century and the French Revolution of 1789. Accordingly, the rest of Europe was now ripe for a bourgeois or liberal revolution. Meanwhile, the growth of the bourgeoisie as a social class had given rise to its antithesis, the proletariat. Society was becoming more divided as these two great antagonistic classes swallowed up all other classes. The stage was being set for the final clash of power between the proletariat and the bourgeoisie, in which the former would inevitably triumph in accordance with the laws of history.

The *Manifesto* also set forth the essence of Marxian economic theory, in which it was maintained that under capitalist society the proletarian class was being enlarged by the displacement of petty bourgeois elements and being driven to the margin of subsistence by the operation of capitalist wage slavery. Marx and Engels developed the idea that the Communists were the elite or "advance guard" of the proletarians, who would engineer the revolution against capitalist society. In a very general way they presented a program for the transition from capitalism to communism, involving measures such as the abolition of private property, enactment of a steep progressive income tax, centralization of credit in the hands of the state, and free public education. Finally they criticized the other socialist doctrines and tried to show that their own brand of socialism was the only one capable of resolving the "contradictions" of capitalist society.

It is important for an understanding of Marxism to know its sources, for little in Marxism was completely original. Marx's great contribution lay in his novel combination of a number of elements from various intellectual fields. From German philosophy, especially that of Hegel, Marx took the idea of the dialectical movement of history. Unlike Hegel, who regarded ideas as the dynamic forces, Marx acquired from the materialistic philosophers of the eighteenth century the notion that material conditions are the most important social forces: "What individuals are depends upon the material conditions of production. . . . The mode of production of the material subsistence conditions the social, political, and spiritual life-process in general. It is not the consciousness of men which determines their existence, but on the contrary it is their social existence which determines their consciousness."

English political economy, especially that of Ricardo, gave Marx the labor theory of value, which he carried to its logical conclusion: the goods produced by labor have a value greater than the subsistence wages paid to the workers. The "surplus value" is kept by the capitalist employers. For example, Marx estimated that a laborer working for six hours a day will produce enough to support himself and his family at a bare subsistence standard. The wage that he earns will be the equivalent of the cost of the commodities produced in those six hours. If, however, the laborer works for twelve hours, the employer will capture the surplus value produced by the additional six hours of labor. He will add it to capital in order to hire more labor and produce more commodities. Since the purchasing power of labor is insufficient to purchase all of the commodities created by capitalist production, the process results in overproduction and economic crises, which will become more and more severe until capitalist society itself finally disappears in depression and revolution.

From French socialism Marx acquired the idea of the necessity for common ownership of property or the means of production. After the final overthrow of capitalist society only one class will remain, the proletariat, which will own all property in common. With the abolition of private property no further antagonisms can arise to create a class struggle, and the socialist millennium will be inaugurated.

Marx and Engels had correctly predicted the outbreak of revolution on the Continent. In the spring of 1848 they returned to Germany to attempt to give the revolution a socialist direction, chiefly by publishing a newspaper in which they advocated the cause of the working classes against both the old absolutism and the new bourgeoisie. The revolution failed, partly because of the split between the bourgeoisie and the workers, and in 1849 Marx and Engels returned to England. Engels resumed his business career and used a part of the profits to subsidize his friend, while Marx took up the systematic study and elaboration of his doctrine.

THE REVOLUTION OF 1848 IN FRANCE

For almost twenty years French workers and radicals, who felt cheated by the sudden "change of ministries" of 1830, agitated and conspired for reform or revolution. Their opposition took the form of strikes, riots, urban insurrections, and assassination attempts against the king and his ministers. Most of their demonstrations had strong republican or socialist overtones. The authorities managed to keep them under control only by extreme repression. The rigidity and corruption of the regime under Guizot also led to demands for reform by the bourgeois or loyal opposition. Men like Thiers merely wanted a change of ministers that would return them to power. Others, such as the poet Lamartine, went so far as to suggest an abdication. Only a handful, including Louis Blanc and

Alexandre Ledru-Rollin, overtly proclaimed their republicanism, but even they did not openly advocate revolution.

Nevertheless, the course of events drifted steadily toward revolution. Humanitarian novelists like Victor Hugo, Georges Sand, and Eugène Sue depicted the plight of the common man in a form approaching an appeal for democracy and socialism. Jules Michelet, Lamartine, and Louis Blanc wrote histories of the Great Revolution suggesting its unfinished character, and Thiers recalled the glories of Napoleon in contrast to the timid, unglamourous foreign policy of Guizot. Poor harvests and a severe economic crisis in 1846–1847 increased working-class distress and led to a revival of protest meetings. Since the law forbade overt political gatherings, the meetings took the form of popular banquets at which the reformers addressed large assemblies of the lower middle and working classes. By the end of 1847 almost every city and town in France had staged at least one such banquet.

THE FEBRUARY DAYS

The leaders of the opposition planned to culminate their "campaign of banquets" with a huge gathering in Paris, right in the face of the government. First planned for February 20, 1848, it was postponed until February 22, then canceled altogether. The government ordered its cancellation and the moderate leaders willingly acquiesced, for they had become belatedly aware of the revolutionary temper of the common people in Paris and did not wish to give occasion for violence. But the people were not to be denied, and on the appointed day the streets of Paris filled with milling people. Groups of students and some of the more daring leaders resolved to carry out the banquet. The mobs alternately jeered and cheered the army troops and regiments of the National Guard that were called up to preserve order. Some of the guard even joined the people in calling for Guizot's dismissal. Stones were thrown, windows were broken, sporadic fighting broke out, and street barricades were erected in the working-class quarters of the city.

On February 23 Louis Philippe finally dismissed Guizot, but that evening soldiers guarding the ministry panicked and fired into the mob, killing several people. By morning the whole city was in an uproar. The troops were disorganized, and the National Guard refused to fire on the populace, demonstrating with it instead. On February 24 Louis Philippe abdicated in favor of his ten-year-old grandson and departed for England, but the Chamber of Deputies refused to accept his designated successor. While the duchess of Orleans was in the Chamber with her son, pleading with it to accept him as king and her as regent, the mobs invaded the Chamber and under the leadership of republican orators forced the deputies to name a provisional government. That evening at the Hôtel de

Ville the poet Lamartine, who had suddenly become converted to republicanism, announced the fall of the monarchy and proclaimed for the second time in French history a republican government.

THE PROVISIONAL GOVERNMENT

Once again the common people of Paris together with middle-class politicians had made a revolution with a minimum of bloodshed. Yet for a time it was uncertain what the outcome would be — whether the middle classes would reassert their predominance, or whether the workers would achieve their goal of a genuine social revolution. The Provisional Government was an amalgam of two groups: the moderate republicans, named in the chamber by the abdicating deputies (actually the list had been drawn up in the editorial offices of the moderate republican newspaper, the *National*), and the "social" republicans or socialists, named by the mobs at the Hôtel de Ville (their list had been drawn up in the offices of the radical newspaper, the *Réforme*). The outstanding figure was Lamartine, who took over Guizot's former post, the ministry of foreign affairs. The government also included the socialist Louis Blanc, the famous astronomer François Arago, a moderate republican, and a genuine proletarian called Albert (his last name was Martin but no one ever used it). Altogether there were eleven members of widely varying backgrounds, interests, and personalities.

Apart from its hasty formation and varied composition, the atmosphere in Paris made it difficult for the Provisional Government to pursue a straightforward policy. People still roamed the streets in a holiday mood, streaming through palaces and other public buildings and constantly sending delegations to call on the government. In the new democratic spirit of the times the government could not risk antagonizing them by failing to listen to their demands. Among a number of hastily decreed reforms it proclaimed universal suffrage, freedom of the press and of assembly, opening of the National Guard to all citizens, abolition of the death penalty, and many emergency measures to cope with the rapidly deteriorating economic situation.

Among the most famous of its actions was the creation of the National Workshops. Although they were ostensibly inspired by Louis Blanc's proposed "social workshops," they were far from the nationalized industries envisioned by him. The National Workshops were, in fact, mere open-air public works projects, which soon degenerated into simple ditch-digging and eventually into a straight dole for the unemployed workers. Instead of being placed under the supervision of Blanc himself, they were turned over to Alexandre Marie, minister of public works, who had little sympathy for the scheme. As a result of mounting unemployment throughout the country, workers streamed to Paris, where the workshops were concentrated. By June more than 120,000 had been enrolled, but another

Courtesy of Bibliothèque Nationale

The Mob Invades the Throne Room in the Tuileries Palace,
February 24, 1848, lithograph by Janet Lange

*"The blood of the people has flowed as in July [1830]; but this time this brave
people will not be deceived. It has won a national and popular government in
accord with the rights, progress and will of this great and noble people. . . .
The provisional government wants a republic, subject to the ratification of the
people, who will be immediately consulted. The unity of the nation, composed
henceforth of all the classes of citizens who compose it; the government of the
nation by itself; liberty, equality and fraternity as fundamentals; the people for
our emblem and watchword; this is the democratic government which France
owes itself and which our efforts will secure for it."* Proclamation of the
Provisional Government, February 29, 1848, reprinted in J. B. Duvergier,
COLLECTION COMPLÈTE DES LOIS, DÉCRETS, etc. (Paris, 1948).

50,000 had been turned away. The presence of these thousands of hungry, idle, sullen men, disquieting middle-class property owners with their talk of the "right to work," was an ominous portent for the future of the revolution.

In foreign affairs the policy of the Provisional Government exhibited the same indecision. News of the February revolution in Paris spread like wildfire throughout Europe, setting off other revolutionary outbursts and striking fear into the hearts of absolutist rulers and middle-class property

owners alike. Many Europeans expected revolutionary France to come to
the aid of revolutions elsewhere, as in 1792, and many Frenchmen advocated such a policy. But Lamartine, fearing defeat by a hostile coalition
and possibly the spread of radical revolution at home, equivocated. In a
"Manifesto to Europe," which violated established diplomatic protocol
by being addressed to peoples as well as to sovereigns, he declared that
France no longer felt bound by the treaties of 1815, but would abide by
them in fact; that it would "protect" legitimate national movements
abroad, but would not resort to arms. Such contradictory statements
made it not at all surprising that neither Frenchmen nor other European
governments knew what to expect from France.

THE CONSTITUENT ASSEMBLY

Meanwhile, the people of France prepared to give their answer to the
question: whither the revolution? The Provisional Government decreed
elections for a Constituent Assembly to be held under universal manhood
suffrage — the first time such a bold experiment in democracy had been
tried in Europe — although the more radical members of the government
wanted to postpone the elections in order to "educate" the rural voters.
Many peasants were illiterate; most had given no thought to politics.
Some feared expropriation of their property by the socialists. The majority, having no experience in elections or self-government and poorly
informed on the issues and the course of events in Paris, simply voted for
the local notables — attorneys, businessmen, and large landowners — who
had managed affairs under previous regimes. The result was a triumph of
the moderates, who gained about 500 of a total of almost 900 seats in the
assembly. The radicals and socialists together garnered fewer than 100.
It was even more disquieting for the future of the republic that avowed
monarchists, legitimists as well as Orleanists (partisans of Louis Philippe),
obtained more than a third of the total representation.

The Constituent Assembly had a dual task: to draw up a new constitution for the Second Republic and to govern it in the interim. It began
the latter task by dismissing the Provisional Government with a vote of
thanks that passed by only twelve votes. To replace it, the assembly
elected an executive commission of five men drawn from its own members. All of them had served in the Provisional Government, but none
were from the extreme left.

Unfortunately for France, the assembly and the Parisian workers at
once conceived an almost instinctive hostility for one another. The workers, most of whom were unemployed and hungry, demanded immediate
and far-reaching economic and social reforms, which the parliamentarians, as members of the propertied classes, had no intention of granting.
On May 15 a group of workers invaded the assembly, declared it dissolved, and named a new provisional government. This time the National
Guard, which had sided with the people against the government in Feb-

ruary, came to the aid of the assembly, dispersed the mob, and arrested its leaders.

THE JUNE DAYS

The social cleavage between the moderates and the workers now became more marked. The assembly immediately took steps to dissolve the National Workshops. The following month passed in growing tension as the workers, deprived of their most experienced leaders, retreated sullenly to their own districts in the city, while orators in the assembly demanded "order in ideas" as well as order in the streets. On June 22 Marie announced that the government would use force if necessary to disperse the men of the workshops. By morning of the next day the barricades were rising again in the streets, while the government prepared to carry out its threat.

The line of battle was clearly drawn: the bourgeoisie against the proletariat. The assembly named General Louis Cavaignac as military dictator. His favorite military tactic was to let the enemy dig into fortified positions, then blast it out with artillery. The first shot was fired shortly after noon on Friday, June 23. For three full days the streets of Paris flowed with blood and echoed to the sound of cannon and muskets as Frenchmen fought Frenchmen in the first clear-cut full-fledged class warfare in modern history. Unnumbered thousands of workers with their women and children participated in the defense of the barricades. They fought desperately and, for a time, effectively in the narrow, crooked streets and alleys; but the outcome was never in doubt. When quiet descended on the evening of June 26 (except for the sounds of firing squads summarily executing the leaders), fifteen hundred had been killed and thousands more wounded. Of some fifteen thousand prisoners, about two-thirds were imprisoned without trial for terms of one to ten years; thousands more were transported to Algeria.

Paris remained officially in a "state of siege" until October 19, with fifty thousand soldiers patrolling its streets. In this oppressive atmosphere most of the reforms decreed by the Provisional Government were revoked. Censorship of the press was reimposed and all political clubs forbidden. Imprisonment for debt and the death penalty for a variety of offenses were reintroduced. The assembly even scrapped the "right to work" clause, which had already been written into the first draft of the new constitution. Thus ended the first major attempt of the working classes to take the reorganization of society into their own hands.

OTHER REVOLUTIONARY MOVEMENTS

"When France sneezes, Europe catches cold." Metternich, to whom this witticism is attributed, did not take such a light view of the events that followed the February days in Paris, which drove even him into exile and

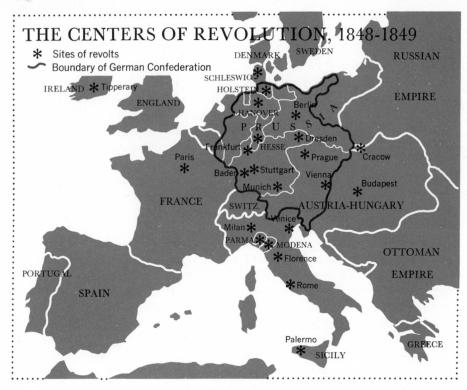

THE CENTERS OF REVOLUTION, 1848-1849

✻ Sites of revolts
⌒ Boundary of German Confederation

retirement. Revolutionary pressures had been building up in Europe for decades, and the poor harvests and commercial depression of the years immediately preceding 1848 brought them to the bursting point. Minor outbreaks of violence occurred in Switzerland and Italy even before the Paris insurrection. Before the year was over, every nation in Europe except Russia had felt the winds of change if not the full fury of the revolutionary storm.

In Belgium the liberals under Charles Rogier, a leader in the revolution of 1830, offered concessions before a revolution could erupt. A new electoral law doubled the number of eligible voters by lowering property qualifications, thus ensuring the allegiance of the lower middle classes. A public works program and liberalized poor relief sapped the revolutionary inclinations of the workers. Although a few riots and street demonstrations took place in the larger cities in the spring, a new election in June repudiated the radical party and vindicated the government's policy of compromise and reform.

The Netherlands's working class was not as large or important as that of Belgium, but the government was more absolutist. The middle classes pressed the king to accept a constitutional revision that introduced ministerial responsibility and substituted indirect election of members of the upper chamber for appointment by the king. In this way the Dutch avoided the violence that afflicted much of the rest of Europe, and paved the way for further peaceful democratic evolution.

In Denmark, Frederick VII ascended the throne in 1848 and immediately became involved in a war with the German states over the duchies of Schleswig and Holstein. At the conclusion of the war in the summer of 1849 Frederick granted a new constitution that provided for a bicameral legislature, a responsible ministry, and other features of limited monarchy on the British pattern.

Spain and Portugal had exhausted themselves in revolutionary struggles in preceding decades. The impotent middle classes and almost nonexistent industrial working classes offered but a slight base for the type of social revolution that took place elsewhere in western Europe. Attempted risings in Madrid and other cities barely got beyond the riot stage before being squelched by the authorities.

Britain averted class warfare during the revival of Chartist agitation, but in Ireland it faced a nationalist revolt by its Irish subjects. The famine of the "hungry forties" contributed to the growth of radicalism, and the leadership of Irish nationalism passed to the Young Ireland party, founded in 1840 by William S. O'Brien (1803–1864). A series of disturbances in 1847 and 1848 culminated in a full-fledged revolt at Tipperary in July, 1848. O'Brien had hoped for peasant support, but the peasants failed to rise, and the police quickly dispersed the rebels.

Except for the Irish outbreak, the revolutionary movement in western Europe exhibited a clear pattern of developing class consciousness brought about by the growth of modern industry. The propertied middle classes were able to curb the power of the monarchs and the aristocracy in proportion to their strength, while the growing working classes sought to share in the fruits of political reform. Although the possessors of special privileges naturally resisted efforts to dilute or abolish their privileges, the gradual peaceful evolution toward democracy in Britain, the Low Countries, and the Scandinavian nations showed that warfare between different social classes was not inevitable.

In central Europe another factor was added to these same elements of change: the force of nationalism, which was equally powerful and even more explosive. According to the German historian Friedrich Dahlmann, an active participant in the events of 1848, the Germans discovered then that their thirst for freedom was in fact a lust for power. John Stuart Mill commented sadly, "In the backward parts of Europe and even (where better things might have been expected) in Germany, the sentiment of nationality so far outweighs the love of liberty that the people are willing to abet their rulers in crushing the liberty and independence of any people not of their race and language." This powerful ideology, together with the greater economic and social backwardness of central Europe in comparison with the west, explains the greater violence and fewer lasting achievements of the revolutions there, as well as the slower and more difficult evolution of democracy.

THE GERMANIES

Within weeks of the abdication of Louis Philippe in France a series of popular demonstrations and constitutional changes took place throughout southern and western Germany. In Baden, Württemberg, Bavaria, Hesse-Cassel, Nassau, Brunswick, Thuringia, and the free cities of Frankfurt, Bremen, Hamburg, and Lübeck, the rulers bowed to demands for constitutions and responsible ministries where none existed, and liberalized them where they did. Preparations went forward for the convocation of an all-German constituent assembly. For the most part this activity was the work of middle-class liberals — the progressive business leaders and professional men of the thriving commercial centers of western Germany who had grown impatient with the restrictive and stuffy conservatism of existing governments. The nascent industrial working classes participated only slightly, and even then in support of the moderate demands of their employers. Few voices were raised on behalf of complete democracy, and almost none for socialism.

The changes came about peaceably, with few instances of violence. The rulers of the petty German states, along with everyone else, had been taken by surprise by the sudden collapse of the monarchy in France. When they discovered with relief that the reformers in their own bailiwicks would be satisfied with liberal reforms and did not demand republican government, they went along almost gladly.

The keys to the revolutions in central Europe rested in Vienna and Berlin. No one seriously believed that a revolution could succeed so long as Metternich stood firm and Frederick William of Prussia commanded an army. Great was the surprise, therefore, when on March 13, Metternich resigned and fled Austria. Three days later barricades went up in Berlin, mobs besieged the royal palace, and people fought with soldiers in the streets.

Frederick William, an emotional, dreamy, vacillating individual who eventually went insane, lacked all the qualities of greatness that the times required. From the beginning of his reign in 1840 he had made vague promises of reform that never seemed to materialize. As recently as 1847 he had convened a United Diet composed of representatives of the eight provincial diets of the Prussian kingdom, which he peremptorily dissolved when it failed to do his bidding. Now his "beloved Berliners" threatened him with bodily harm if he did not yield to their demands. After much hesitation and wavering the king decided on concessions.

As the crowds gathered on March 18 to hear his proclamation abolish-

Courtesy of Hamburger Kunsthalle

Cortege of the Victims of the March Revolution, 1848,
(detail) by Adolph Menzel

*"When the soldiery had marched off something happened that in dramatic force
and significance has never been surpassed in the history of revolutions. From all
parts of the city solemn and silent processions moved toward the royal palace.
They escorted the bodies of those of the people who had been killed in the
battle (with the royal troops); the corpses of the slain were carried aloft on
litters. . . . So the processions marched into the inner palace court, where the
litters were placed in rows in ghastly parade, and around them the multitude of
men with pallid faces, begrimed with blood and powder smoke, many of them
still carrying the weapons with which they had fought during the night."*
Carl Schurz (1829–1906), REMINISCENCES (New York, 1907–08).

ing censorship and reconvening the United Diet to prepare a constitution, fighting broke out between the soldiers and the people. For two
days the battle raged, until the king, sick at the sight of bloodshed and
at the thought of massacring his own people, had the troops withdrawn
and exposed himself to the mercies of the mob. His faith was not mis-
placed. Although he was obliged to salute the corpses of slain rebels and
parade through the streets in the newly adopted black, red, and gold
tricolor of united Germany, his subjects continued respectful and obedi-

ent. A new ministry took office, consisting mostly of middle-class liberals from the Prussian Rhineland, and the new Prussian Diet began to draw up a constitution. All went smoothly for a time. The king's weak behavior and lack of leadership lost him the support of some Germans who had expected him to take the lead in creating a German state, but there appeared no reason to doubt his commitment to reform. Attention shifted to Frankfurt, where delegates were assembled to debate the future of a united Germany.

The German National Assembly (*Nationalversammlung*) met for the first time in St. Paul's Church, Frankfurt, on May 18, 1848. More than two months previously a group of about fifty West German liberals had met in Heidelberg and issued a call for a preliminary parliament, which gathered in Frankfurt on March 31. This *Vorparlment* had no legal standing (only two Austrians attended, while seventy-two came from little Baden), but it took upon itself the task of arranging for the election of delegates to the National Assembly from all the German states. The resulting assembly was nearly six hundred strong. It included men of all ranks, from a Silesian peasant to a sovereign prince, but most came from upper middle-class occupations, and were lawyers, judges, bureaucrats, and professors. To give it a vestige of legality, the frightened Diet of the old Germanic Confederation had approved the elections, and after the Assembly met, the Diet actually dissolved itself.

All delegates agreed that Germany must be united, but the character of the union proved a thorny problem. A republic was out of the question, as well as any form of highly centralized state, because too many vested interests were involved, especially those of the ruling princes. Some sort of federal empire seemed to be indicated, in which the component parts would retain local autonomy. But in that case what states should be included, and who should be emperor? How could Austria, which was already an empire, be included in a larger empire? The *Grossdeutsch* (Great German) party favored including the German-speaking provinces of Austria (together with Bohemia), whereas the *Kleindeutsch* (Little German) group wanted to exclude Austria. While the dispute simmered, the assembly chose to involve itself in a more pressing matter, the war with Denmark.

Although the duchies of Schleswig and Holstein were for the most part German-speaking (in fact, the latter was a member state of the Germanic Confederation), they belonged to the king of Denmark. In the "springtime of nations" that followed the February revolution in Paris the duchies revolted against the new Danish king and declared their sympathy for the German parliament. When the Danish army occupied them, the assembly in Frankfurt commissioned Frederick William to send Prussian troops on its behalf to "liberate" their fellow Germans. Frederick William did so, but in August he succumbed to pressure from Britain and Russia to conclude an armistice and evacuate his troops.

By this time the German people were drunk with nationalism and regarded the armistice as a betrayal. The assembly at first refused to ratify it, but lacking an armed force or executive power, it eventually had to bow to the fait accompli and recognize the armistice. The mob in Frankfurt, harangued by nationalist demagogues, now turned on the delegates to the assembly as traitors and invaded their meeting place. The middle-class parliamentarians, thoroughly frightened by this view of the people, called on Austrian and Prussian soldiers to disperse the mob, which they did with their customary brutality. The results were disastrous for the prestige of the assembly. Alienated from the masses and embarrassed by their dependence on armed force against their own constituents, the delegates were vulnerable to the reaction that soon overtook them and their once-high hopes for a liberal, united Germany.

THE HAPSBURG MONARCHY

In Vienna the news of the revolution in Paris encouraged the opponents of Metternich's regime to press for liberal reforms. The reformers included persons from all social classes: business and professional men who resented economic controls and exclusion from political power, workers, peasants in the countryside, even a few aristocrats who were bored by the stuffiness and restrictions of the government. Students from the university, the sons of aristocracy and the upper middle classes, actually took the initiative in fomenting revolution. They paraded, fraternized with the workers from the factory suburbs, and clashed with soldiers guarding the imperial palace. Faced with the near-certainty of bloody street-fighting and unable to depend upon the loyalty of the troops, the 75-year-old Metternich resigned on March 13. Fully aware of his unpopularity, the champion of autocracy fled the country in disguise under cover of darkness to seek haven in that bastion of constitutionalism, England.

Without Metternich's iron will and wily mind, the government of the feeble-minded Emperor Ferdinand I floundered aimlessly. Within a few days it gave in to demands for the abolition of censorship, promised to convoke a constitutional convention, and permitted the formation of a volunteer National Guard. Flushed with their triumph over the aged chancellor, the students formed an "academic legion" and a "committee of safety" to keep watch on the government and prevent it from backsliding into reaction. In May the government attempted to reassert its authority but backed down when it met determined opposition. The imperial family fled to Innsbruck, leaving the city controlled by the students and middle-class guardsmen.

At the same time national minorities in the polyglot dominions of the emperor were raising the standard of revolt. The Hungarian Diet under the leadership of Louis Kossuth proclaimed a constitution that made Hungary entirely independent of Austria, retaining only the link of a common king-emperor. The Czechs of Bohemia and Moravia convened a Pan-Slavic Congress in Prague and demanded autonomy from Vienna. Lombardy and Venetia revolted, and most of the other subject nationalities — Croats, Slovaks, Serbs, Slovenes, Poles, Ruthenians, and others — demanded either autonomy or extensive reforms. So powerless was the government to resist that it appeared for a time that the ancient Hapsburg monarchy would simply evaporate.

The tide began to turn in June, when imperial armies in Bohemia and Lombardy scored victories over the rebellious subjects. Even more ominous for the national movements were their relations with one another. In spite of common grievances against the ruling German-speaking minority, they could not agree on joint action and mutual support. Although the Magyars of Hungary were insistent on independence for themselves, they tried to magyarize the predominantly Slavic peasant population and turned down requests for autonomy from the Croatians and other minorities within the boundaries of the kingdom of Hungary. The imperial government at last regained some of its customary composure and shrewdly took advantage of these differences by appointing Baron Jellachich, a Croatian, commander-in-chief of the imperial army in Hungary.

The imperial forces gradually regained control of the Austrian provinces of the empire and retook Vienna itself in October, but the battle raged back and forth in Hungary. In April, 1849, the Hungarians formally severed all ties with the old empire, proclaiming a republic with Kossuth as president. For a few months it appeared that they might succeed in winning their independence, but during the summer the Russian tsar, who was untroubled by revolutions of his own, sent his army to the aid of his fellow monarch. Kossuth resigned and fled in August. In the Hapsburg dominions, as in Germany proper, the conflicting objectives of liberalism and nationalism defeated one another.

ITALY

Divided and oppressed, Italy had fallen far from the position of leadership it once held in the arts of civilization and reached its nadir in the first half of the nineteenth century. More than three-fourths of the Italian population eked out a bare subsistence in agriculture. A large, ill-trained, and parasitic clergy, totaling in some areas a tenth of the population, weighed heavily on the country. Poverty, ignorance, and superstition were rife throughout the peninsula, each feeding on the other. Except in Piedmont and the States of the Church, the ruling classes were identified directly or indirectly with a foreign power. As a result, the revolutionary movement in Italy was infected from the beginning with nationalism, and revolutionary outbreaks took on the characteristics of a war of liberation.

In 1846 the college of cardinals elected a liberal pope, Pius IX. For the next two years he dallied with the notion of uniting all Italy under the protective shield of the Holy See. Fearful of the secular and radical nature of Giuseppe Mazzini's "Young Italy" movement (see pp. 665–666), he had naive dreams of restoring the papacy to a primacy in Italy that it had never really had. His hope of influencing Catholic Austria to agree to his ambitions proved futile, for Metternich's opposition to liberalism and nationalism was absolute. Pius built up a modest following of liberals in Italy and persuaded some conservative elements to be receptive to change — though hardly to the changes that caught even Pius by surprise in 1848.

Sicily, long treated as a conquered province by the Bourbon Kingdom of the Two Sicilies with its capital in Naples, rose in revolt in January, 1848. The insurrection soon spread to Naples, where liberals forced the king to grant a constitution. In little more than a month the rulers of Tuscany and Piedmont and Pius himself had given in to similar pressures. In the midst of these developments news of the revolutions in Paris and Vienna reached Italy, bringing new hope and courage to the Italians, who expected assistance from revolutionary France against a weakened Austria.

The inhabitants of Milan revolted on March 18 and in five days of house-to-house combat drove out the Austrian army of General Radetzky. Stimulated by this event, the Venetians under Daniele Manin proclaimed a republic on March 22. On the same day King Charles Albert of Piedmont, under pressure from the liberals and patriots who had earlier compelled him to grant a constitution, declared war against the Austrians in support of the Milanese. In a matter of weeks contingents of soldiers and volunteers from all Italy, including the States of the Church, joined in the attack. Patriotic excitement reached a fever pitch, and for a few days it seemed that Italy would soon be free of foreign domination from the Alps to Sicily.

These bright hopes were doomed to quick extinction. Pius IX, who had earlier given his blessing to the papal volunteers, now disclaimed any intention of making war on Catholic Austria, cutting the ground from beneath those patriots who had looked to him to head an Italian confederation. In May a successful counterrevolution in Naples resulted in the withdrawal of Neapolitan troops. Finally, the Piedmontese failed to follow up their early successes in the field. The Austrian government had ordered Radetzky to seek an armistice and to cede Lombardy to Piedmont if necessary, but Radetzky ignored these orders, launched a counteroffensive, and on July 24 delivered a crushing defeat to Charles Albert at Custozza. Within ten days the Austrians again controlled all of Lombardy and were restrained from an invasion of Piedmont only by warnings from Britain and France.

Defeated and disappointed though they were, Italian patriots did not give up the struggle. The Venetians held out against an Austrian siege, and both Piedmont and Tuscany retained their constitutions and their hopes. In Rome the liberals grew critical of Pius IX for his failure to lead a united Italy, whereupon he became bitter and resentful. After the assassination of his prime minister by a radical democrat, Pius fled in November to the protection of the reactionary king of Naples. The people of the States of the Church reacted by electing a constituent assembly, which on February 9, 1849, proclaimed the Roman Republic and called Mazzini to be its leader. Giuseppe Garibaldi (1807–1882), a colorful patriot and soldier of fortune, now put his legion of volunteers (called Redshirts from the only vestige of uniform they wore) at the service of the Roman Republic. In March Charles Albert once more succumbed to liberal pressures and broke the armistice with Austria; once more the patriots took heart and dreamed of a free, united Italy. Yet in less than two weeks Radetzky delivered another and final humiliating defeat to Charles Albert, who abdicated his throne, went into exile, and shortly died.

THE FAILURE OF '48

The revolutionary wave that broke over Europe in 1848 had been building for many years. After its first major crest in the 1790's it had receded slightly, only to come back with renewed force. By the logic of the situation — a logic perceived by such disparate personalities as Karl Marx and Metternich — it should have overwhelmed all opposition in 1848. But it did not. Why? The answer can be given only tentatively, even after the lapse of more than a century. It would seem to be related to the disparate progress of modern industry, on the one hand, and to the idea of nationalism, on the other. The revolutions of 1848 were at once class struggles, provoked by the rise of industry, and nationalist wars of liberation. The forces of conservatism took advantage of the divided ambitions of their opponents to crush the movements utterly. The high tide of revolution came in the late spring of 1848; thereafter the revolutionists fought defensive, losing battles. After 1848 the worst was still to come. Liberalism and socialism went into eclipse, and although nationalism survived and flourished, it was a nationalism far different from the noble, generous movement of pre-1848. In the reaction of realism — the ebb tide of revolution — all tender ideals had to adjust to the new world of science and power, or perish.

THE REALIST REACTION
CHAPTER TWENTY-FIVE

Europe awoke on the morrow of revolution as a man awakes after an evening of debauchery. Europe was sadder, wiser, less glamorous, less idealistic. A new outlook dominated the scene that, for brevity, may be referred to as realism, though conventional definitions cannot fully convey the realist cast of mind. The word was first employed in 1850 to describe a new style of painting, and it spread rapidly to literature. Soon it became evident that the literary tendencies to which the name referred had earlier roots, and that these, in turn, owed much to the progress of science in the first half of the nineteenth century.

As scientific progress accelerated and as the findings of science became more widely disseminated, the realist point of view permeated every area of life, including politics, where it frequently took the base form of *Realpolitik*. (See p. 658.) In literature and the arts realism was a reaction to the fantasies of the late romantic movement; in philosophy and social thought, to the idealism of Kant and Hegel; in science, to unverifiable speculation; and in politics, to the idealism and romanticism of the revolutionary epoch. Realism pervaded the whole of Western culture from the failure of the revolutions of 1848 to the new outbursts of nationalistic and imperialistic fervor in the 1880's. The manner in which the revolutions were liquidated did much to set the tone of the period.

EBB TIDE OF REVOLUTION, 1848–1851

By the late summer of 1849 the revolutionary movement had been suppressed throughout Europe. Its last vestiges were the ephemeral republics of Venice and Hungary. A period of stark reaction set in everywhere. Apart from the moderate parliamentary and electoral reforms in the smaller states of western Europe and the paper constitutions of Prussia

and Austria, the only permanent political achievement of the revolutionary outbursts seemed to be the Second Republic in France. Even there the
appearance was deceptive, for the political and social character of the
republic was markedly conservative, and the republic itself was destined
for a short life.

THE REACTION IN FRANCE

The Provisional Government of February, 1848, had been replaced in
May by the executive commission of the Constituent Assembly, which in
turn gave way during the June Days to the military dictatorship of General Cavaignac. Under his protection the assembly continued its work
of drawing up a new constitution. As approved on November 4, 1848, the
document provided for a single-chamber Legislative Assembly and a president to wield executive power. Both the assembly and the president were
to be elected by universal male suffrage, the former for three years, the
latter for four.

In the presidential election announced for December 10, 1848, five
candidates presented themselves. Cavaignac, touted as the "savior of the
republic," had the support of the more conservative republicans. The
moderate and radical republicans split over three candidates. The fifth
contender was a political dark horse with a name known to all, Louis
Napoleon Bonaparte.

Louis Napoleon was ostensibly the nephew of the first Napoleon, although his legitimacy was doubtful and there was no positive proof of his
paternity. After 1815 he fell under the proscription imposed on all members of the Bonaparte family. Raised by his mother in exile, he set foot in
France only twice between 1815 and 1848, both times as a conspirator and
outlaw. In 1836 he tried to foment a rebellion in the garrison at Strasbourg but was ignominiously captured and returned to exile. In 1840
he landed at Boulogne with a small band of followers, again was
captured, and was imprisoned in the fortress of Ham from which he had
escaped as recently as 1846.

Louis Napoleon was an enigmatic mixture of visionary dreamer, romantic adventurer, benevolent despot, and shrewd practical politician.
His great rival of later years, Chancellor Bismarck of Prussia, referred to
him contemptuously as "a sphinx without a riddle" and "a great unrecognized incapacity," but opinions of later historians remain divided on his
motives, his ability, and even his achievements and failures. Nevertheless,
in addition to the prestige of his name, it was precisely because he seemed
to be all things to all men that he scored his notable electoral triumphs.
In the presidential election of 1848 he obtained more than three-fourths
of the total vote.

The Second Republic resembled an unwanted child, rejected by its
parents almost as soon as it was born. The new president indicated the

strength of his republican sentiments by appointing a cabinet composed chiefly of supporters of the ousted regime of Louis Philippe. Elections for the new assembly in the spring of 1849 resulted in a clear majority for the monarchists — legitimists as well as Orleanists. The radical republicans made a slight comeback, but the moderate republicans who had framed the constitution were almost completely eliminated. The spectacle of a republic with a Bonaparte executive and a monarchist legislature was strange indeed. Moreover, the constitution contained a serious defect in that it did not provide a method for settling disputes between the legislature and the executive.

For a time Louis Napoleon cooperated with the conservative and monarchist majority while he consolidated the bases of his own personal power. In order to win favor with Catholics, he dispatched French troops in the spring of 1849 to suppress the Roman Republic and restore the pope. The following year he acquiesced in the Falloux Law on education, which gave the clergy a large measure of control over the educational system. The propertied middle classes in France had a tradition of Voltairean skepticism, but the rise of socialism and the threat of social revolution led them to view the Church as a bulwark of the status quo and a defender of property rights. In this respect the revolutions of 1848 brought about a religious revival among the middle classes in much the same way that the revolution of 1789 did among the aristocracy. Louis Napoleon also signed assembly sponsored bills that deprived the majority of the urban working class, the stronghold of radicalism, of its right to vote, imposed greater censorship of the press, and in other ways restricted political freedom.

At the same time Louis Napoleon built up his own Bonapartist party. As early as October, 1849, he replaced his Orleanist ministry, much of which was drawn from the assembly, with a cabinet of personal admirers from outside the assembly. Increasingly he came into conflict with the monarchist majority in the assembly. The crux of the dispute was the provision of the constitution prohibiting the president from succeeding himself. When his proposal to amend the clause was defeated by more than one hundred votes in July, 1851, Louis Napoleon resolved on other means to obtain his object.

The president made a series of speaking tours of the provinces, gauging the temper of the populace and posing as the champion of the people against the assembly. He also reorganized the higher echelons of the army and the civil administration, replacing officers and officials suspected of either monarchist or republican leanings with those loyal to himself. In great secrecy he and a small group of his closest collaborators, including the count de Morny, his illegitimate half-brother, laid plans for a coup d'état. Early in the morning of December 2, following a magnificent presidential ball on the previous evening, soldiers placarded Paris with the news that the president had dissolved the assembly. Other soldiers arrested a number of deputies, prominent journalists, and other potential opposition leaders in their beds and occupied the meeting hall of the assembly. Thus far the coup had gone without violence or bloodshed. On the following day, however, a group of republican deputies organized a rising in the working-class quarters of Paris. Barricades went up in the streets in the usual manner, but the army moved against them promptly and crushed the rebellion with much bloodshed and thousands of arrests.

The same proclamation that announced the dissolution of the assembly also proclaimed the restoration of universal suffrage and called upon the people to ratify the president's actions and give him authority to draft a new constitution. A plebiscite on December 21 resulted in a majority of 92 per cent in favor of the regime. Although it was a managed election with no alternative provided in the event of a negative vote, it appears that most Frenchmen, weary of both street fighting and parliamentary wrangling, preferred the security of a benevolent dictatorship to the strife and uncertainties of self-government. Thus ended the last act of a drama that had begun with the overthrow of Louis Philippe in February, 1848.

THE REACTION IN THE HAPSBURG DOMINIONS

The reaction began early in the Austrian Empire. In June, 1848, the wife of the military commander in Prague, Prince Windischgrätz, was accidentally killed in the course of a popular demonstration in support of the revolution. For five days Windischgrätz mercilessly bombarded the city with artillery from surrounding fortifications. At the end of that time no sign of resistance remained, and Windischgrätz made himself military dictator of all Bohemia. Simultaneously General Radetzky took the offensive against the Piedmontese in northern Italy and won an overwhelming victory on July 24 at Custozza. To reestablish his control and authority in Lombardy and to revenge himself for Milan's "five glorious days" in March, he subjected Milan to the same treatment as Prague.

Next came the turn of Vienna. In October Windischgrätz and Jellachich, the military commander in Hungary, surrounded the city and subjected it to the same methodical, ruthless bombardment. After the city fell they summarily executed scores of radical leaders. When Windischgrätz marched on Budapest in January, 1849, the city took note of the fate of the others and surrendered without resistance. The proclamation of the Hungarian Republic in the spring of 1849 temporarily gave the revolutionaries new hope, and they drove the Austrians out of all Hungary. Soon afterward, however, Austria accepted the proffered aid of the tsar, and Russian troops in the summer of 1849 joined with those of General Haynau, "the Hyena," to overrun and subjugate the Hungarians. In spite of earlier promises of clemency, General Haynau brutally executed the Hungarian leaders.

Prince Felix Schwarzenberg, brother-in-law of Windischgrätz and political adviser to Radetsky, became Austrian prime minister after the fall of Vienna. In December, 1848, he persuaded both the weak-minded Emperor Ferdinand and his brother, the Archduke Franz Karl, to abdicate in favor of the latter's eighteen-year-old son, Franz Josef. The new monarch followed the counsel of Schwarzenberg and soon proved himself the prince's equal in determination to tolerate no liberal tendencies. In March, 1849, Schwarzenberg dissolved the newly elected Reichstag, discarded its draft constitution providing for a decentralized, federal form of government, and promulgated one of his own that provided for a highly centralized administration. The provisions for a representative diet and a responsible ministry never took effect; in 1851 the constitution itself was "suspended" — permanently.

Schwarzenberg died in 1852, but his policies were carried on by his minister of interior, Alexander Bach. The administrative system of Austria for the decade between the revolution and the War of 1859 became known as the Bach System. In addition to extreme centralization and bureaucratic rule, the system was characterized by a vigorous policy of germanization and the strict repression of all liberal symptoms.

THE REACTION IN ITALY

The reactionary denouement in Italy followed swiftly Radetzky's defeat of Charles Albert in March, 1849. The Austrians mopped up in northern Italy and restored the grand duke of Tuscany, while in the south Neapolitan troops reconquered Sicily. Most disheartening of all, Louis Napoleon Bonaparte, recently elected president of the French Republic, sent a French expeditionary force to put down the Roman Republic and restore Pius IX by force of arms. Garibaldi and the Romans put up an heroic defense, holding out for more than two months, but on July 2 Garibaldi withdrew from the city and led his partisans on an equally heroic but disastrous retreat. On August 28, 1849, when the Venetians, besieged by the Austrians without and by starvation and cholera within, finally capitulated, the last spark of revolutionary nationalism in Italy seemed to expire. Thus ended Italy's attempt to "make itself."

THE REACTION IN GERMANY

In Prussia, King Frederick William, encouraged by the success of the Austrian government in retaking Vienna, dissolved the Prussian Constituent Assembly in December, 1848, and promulgated a constitution on his own authority. The constitution provided for a bicameral legislature, the Diet, with the upper house (*Herrenhaus*) reserved for the privileged orders. The lower house, nominally elected by universal manhood suffrage, actually gave a preponderance of influence to the wealthy by means

Giuseppe Garibaldi

*"When the people see him they take fire. There is a magic in his look and in
his name. It is only Garibaldi they want. . . . Sometimes he seems more than
a living being or is he an archangel who spreads his wings and whirls his sword
like a sunray?"* Entries of May 14 and Aug. 20, 1860, in Giuseppe Cesare Abba,
THE DIARY OF ONE OF GARIBALDI'S THOUSAND, tr. E. R. Vincent (London, 1962).

of a complicated system of indirect election based on taxpaying ability. The ministers of the government did not form a cabinet responsible to the Diet but were individually responsible to and directly dependent upon the king. When the Diet was not in session, the king could rule by decree. In spite of some superficial concessions to parliamentarianism, the Prussian state retained its authoritarian and aristocratic character.

With its authority reestablished, the Prussian government undertook a frankly reactionary policy. It repealed earlier liberal legislation, such as that curtailing the privileged position of the nobility, and enacted new and repressive measures directed against freedom of the press, freedom of assembly, and other liberties that peoples with constitutional governments had come to regard as rights. The nobility and the Junker aristocracy of great landowners monopolized the posts of power and prestige in the court, the government, and the army. Not only the radicals but even those who regarded themselves as liberals were hounded out of the government and, in some cases, out of the country. Many chose exile and new careers in the United States.

The triumph of reaction in Austria and Prussia ensured the success of similar movements in other German states, which in some cases called on the larger states for military support in suppressing their still rebellious subjects. The last hope of German liberals rested on the Frankfurt Assembly, but this hope, too, faded. Having been deflected from their original purpose of providing a parliamentary constitution for a unified Germany by the Danish question, then bogged down in the dispute between the *Grossdeutsch* and *Kleindeutsch* parties, the delegates finally agreed on a compromise document in March, 1849. Since the Austrians ruled themselves out of any participation in the proposed federation, the delegates invited Frederick William of Prussia to accept the title "Emperor of the Germans," provided for in the constitution. Frederick William had wavered back and forth on the question of a united Germany, as he had on many other questions. Now he half-assented to the proposal from Frankfurt but insisted that the rulers of the other German states must also agree to have him as their sovereign. Three weeks passed, and a number of the smaller states accepted the new constitution, but at the same time the king's conservative advisers were urging him to resist the temptation of "a crown from the streets" as inconsistent with his "divine right" as king of Prussia. On April 21, he announced that under no circumstances would he accept the crown from an elected assembly.

This announcement shattered the last illusions of the Frankfurt Assembly. Prussia and Austria ordered their delegates to return home, and the delegates from other states soon followed. Only a small band of the most radical deputies remained. When driven from their meeting place by Austrian troops, they tried to continue their sessions in Stuttgart, but again the soldiers dispersed them, imprisoning some and driving others into exile. Thus ended, ingloriously, the convention that had been hailed as "the most distinguished constituent body in history." The liberal parliamentarians in Frankfurt had demonstrated great oratorical ability but little governing ability. Distracted from the pursuit of liberty by the pursuit of power and national glory, they lost all. With their failure Germany lost its opportunity for peaceful unification under a liberal constitution.

REALISM IN LITERATURE AND THE ARTS

The new temper of Europe received its most forceful literary and artistic expression in novels and paintings, but the reaction in the intellectual and artistic spheres was neither as abrupt nor as complete as the political reaction. Although the vogue of realism reached its peak in the 1850's, earlier work had clearly foreshadowed the movement and formed a bridge between the romantic and the realist eras. It is even more important to realize that realist art and literature did not completely dominate the period. In Britain and the United States, art and literature were blander, less critical, and more at peace with the world, except for a few self-conscious social critics. Finally, as a result of increasing wealth, population, and literacy, more and more people from the middle classes became interested in art and literature. Since the newly successful businessmen and their wives were not necessarily sophisticated judges, not all of the vast increase in literary and artistic production was of high quality. Most of it continued to exploit the proven demand for subjects and styles of the romantic.

THE REALIST NOVEL

Realist novels can be distinguished from their romantic predecessors by both subject matter and method of treatment. The typical romantic novel dealt with heroic figures in exotic settings, while the typical realist novel dealt with ordinary people in ordinary pursuits. Instead of employing exaggerated language and emotions, realist novelists devoted themselves to close observation and precise description. Usually they sought to convey an impression of matter-of-fact detachment and absence of sentimentality. They often dealt with social and psychological problems, but in doing so the best of them let the episodes and characters speak for themselves, rather than pontificating on the obvious.

Stendhal (pseudonym of Henri Beyle, 1783–1842), earliest precursor of the new tendency, chose conventional romantic themes for his novels *Le rouge et le noir* (1830) and *La chartreuse de Parme* (1839), but the deft irony with which he treated them set him apart from other romantic writers. Honoré de Balzac (1799–1850) was perhaps the greatest of the romantic realists. His style was still in the romantic tradition of unruly exaggeration, but his subjects were ordinary people and his intention was to portray them clearly as such. The long series entitled *La comédie humaine* (*The Human Comedy*) is an almost documentary account of life in France under the July Monarchy. The style of the English writer Charles Dickens (1812–1870) was similar in many respects to Balzac's. Victor Hugo (1802–1885) — novelist, dramatist, essayist, poet — spanned the romantic and realist eras in the same way that Goethe bridged the romantic era and the Enlightenment. Hugo's *Notre Dame de Paris* (1831) is one of the masterpieces of romantic literature, but in *Les misérables* (1862) and *Les travailleurs de la mer* (1866) he dealt with contemporary social problems in a realistic fashion with only minor lapses into pathos and overt sentimentality.

William Thackeray (1811–1863) wrote what might be called a manifesto of the realist novelist in *Vanity Fair* (1848). It carried the subtitle *A Novel without a Hero,* a contradiction in terms to the romantics. According to Thackeray, a novel should "convey as strongly as possible the sentiment of reality as opposed to a tragedy or poem, which may be heroical." Gustave Flaubert (1821–1880) brought the realist novel to its pinnacle of perfection. His most famous work, *Madame Bovary* (1857), is a candid, penetrating study of the narrow, barren, and sordid life in the provinces. In *L'éducation sentimentale* (1869), the title of which might have belonged to a romantic novel, he portrayed his own youth with graphic, restrained irony in a study in disenchantment. Flaubert's meticulous craftsmanship influenced many younger writers, even those who adopted different literary styles.

Romanticism had a longer vogue in Germany and the United States than in France and England. Not until the last quarter of the century did American writers take up realist themes and styles, as in the novels of Samuel Clemens (Mark Twain), William Dean Howells, and Stephen Crane. Gottfried Keller's *Der grüne Heinrich* (1854–1855, revised 1879) is a landmark in Swiss literature, but it is little known outside German-speaking countries. Russian authors made some of their greatest contributions in this period. Ivan Turgenev (1818–1883), author of *Fathers and Sons* (1862), and Feodor Dostoevski (1821–1881), author of *Crime and Punishment* (1866) and *The Brothers Karamazov* (1880), were masters of the psychological novel, gripping stories of inner conflict with great emotional impact. Leo Tolstoi's *War and Peace* (1865–1869), an epic of the Napoleonic wars, is regarded by some critics as the greatest novel of the nineteenth century, by others as the greatest novel of all time. Although all three authors clearly belonged to the category of realist novelists, they brought new insights and inspiration from their Russian environment.

It should be noted that the realist novelists in no sense formed a school with definite rules or objectives. Nor was realism in literature restricted, even approximately, to the third quarter of the nineteenth century. On

the contrary, realism is a more or less permanent component of literature, now waxing, now waning, but always present in some degree. What the major writers of this period had in common was a tendency to react against the earlier artistic excesses of romanticism. Their reaction was strongly influenced by the political watershed of 1848 and by the growing prestige of science. The influence of science was particularly marked in the major development within realism called naturalism.

Émile Zola (1840–1902), the founder and leading exponent of naturalism, lived until the twentieth century, but his enormous output clearly reflected the formative influences of his youth during the Second French Empire. The most important influences were the literary canons of Flaubert, the reformist zeal of Victor Hugo, and most important, materialistic science. Zola regarded himself as a kind of scientist-artist. Not content merely to describe life as he saw it, like the earlier realists, Zola insisted on dissecting and analyzing it as a biologist would analyze a living organism. He called his twenty-volume series on the Rougon-Macquart family "the natural and social history of a family under the Second Empire." Zola even wrote a treatise on the "experimental novel" in the manner of Claude Bernard's famous treatise on experimental medicine. In it he said: "The experimental novel is a consequence of the scientific evolution of the century; it continues and completes physiology, which itself leans for support on chemistry and medicine; it substitutes for the study of the abstract and metaphysical man the study of natural man, governed by physical and chemical laws, and modified by the influences of his surroundings; it is in one word the literature of our age, as the classical and romantic literature correspond to a scholastic and theological age." Zola's views represented the extreme development of the realist reaction in literature. By no means did all of his contemporaries agree with him; even as he penned his manifesto, *Le roman expéri-*

"The Young Bather," by Gustave Courbet

"In particular, the art of painting can consist only in the representation of objects visible and tangible to the painter. . . . I hold also that painting is an essentially concrete art, and can consist only of the representation of things both real and existing. It is an altogether physical language, which, for its words, makes use of all visible objects. An abstract object, invisible or nonexistent, does not belong to the domain of painting.

"Imagination in art consists in finding the most complete expression for an existing thing, but never in imagining or creating this object itself." Open letter from Courbet to a group of prospective students, Paris, 1861, reprinted in R. J. Goldwater and M. Treves, ARTISTS ON ART (New York, 1947).

mental (1880), the pendulum began to swing back in the opposite direction.

REALIST PAINTING

Just as novelists were influenced by science, mid-nineteenth-century painters were influenced by one of science's technical offshoots, the infant art of photography. Although in later years painters regarded the improved camera as an unfair competitor and moved on to different styles, in the 1850's and 1860's they strove to emulate the camera in capturing reality. Realist art, like realist literature, differed from its predecessors in both technique and choice of subjects. Realist paintings contained neither the exaggerated and exotic figures of the romantics nor the stylized and lifeless creatures of the classical school. Instead, painters took scenes from everyday life — peasants, workers, merchants and prostitutes, the ugly as well as the beautiful (with perhaps a slight bias in favor of the former) — and painted them as they saw them. Gustave Courbet (1819–1877), the outstanding artist of the realist school, wrote of one of his earliest and most famous paintings, "The Stonebreakers," "I have invented nothing. I saw the wretched people in this picture every day as I went on my walks."

The word realism was first applied to painting to describe one of Courbet's paintings in 1850. Courbet, an egotistical man, wore the label proudly. His personal stationery carried the heading, "Gustave Courbet, Master Painter, without ideals and without religion." He frequently boasted that he had no use for women (other than his models) except as vehicles for carnal satisfaction, and many of his paintings reflect that attitude. However deplorable his personal morals, his influence on art was great. The critic Sainte-Beuve wrote of Courbet that he looked on "vast railway stations as new churches for painting, to cover the big walls with a thousand subjects . . . picturesque, moral, industrial . . . in other words the saints and miracles of modern society."

In realist art, as in literature, France held unquestioned pre-eminence. Honoré Daumier (1808–1879) was even more famous for his social and political caricatures than for his vivid paintings of ordinary life. The lithographs of Paul Gaverni (1804–1866) captured the grit as well as the glitter of Parisian life. Jean-Francois Millet (1814–1875) devoted himself to scenes from rural life, though with perhaps a touch of sentimentality that was not characteristic of most realist painters. Théodore Rousseau (1812–1867) and his disciples in the Barbizon School contributed robust landscapes. At the same time, Adolf Menzel (1813–1900) of Germany deserves credit for being the first serious painter to take as a subject the interior of a factory.

Realist painting of the French school had little direct impact on British art. In England a group of painters known as the Pre-Raphaelites formed a "brotherhood" in 1848. They usually chose historical subjects and had close affinities with the romantics, but in one respect at least they resembled the realists. They strove to avoid all "exaggerated action . . . false sentiment, voluptuousness, poverty of invention." For inspiration they looked to the "purity" and "simplicity" of the Italian painters prior to Raphael, from whom they chose their name.

POETRY, DRAMA, AND MUSIC

The lyric and dramatic arts suffered in the era of realism. Railroads, factories, and scientific laboratories did not lend themselves as themes for dramatic or lyric treatment. In "The Song of the Shirt" Thomas Hood tried to make poetry an instrument of social criticism and reform, but he succeeded only in creating bathos. Romanticism continued supreme in all these art forms. Although some outstanding figures emerged, such as Brahms, Liszt, Tchaikovsky, and Wagner in music, for the most part the quality was not high. Tennyson and Browning in England and Longfellow in the United States achieved great popularity, but their work has not stood the test of time as well as that of some of their less well-known contemporaries.

Like realism in the novel and painting, the most significant development in poetry was a reaction to romanticism. It was also a reaction against the bourgeois philistinism that made Tennyson and his followers rich and famous. Théophile Gautier (1811–1872) first announced the doctrine of "Art for Art's Sake" in 1835, but the movement did not reach its peak until the later 1860's. It was called the Parnassian movement from *Le Parnasse contemporain,* the journal of poetry that served as its organ. Its outstanding representatives were Charles Baudelaire (1821–1867), whose *Fleurs du mal (Flowers of Evil),* published in 1857, caused a sensation and Baudelaire's conviction on a charge of "corrupting public morals"; Arthur Rimbaud (1854–1891), who gave up poetry in 1873 at the age of nineteen; and Paul Verlaine (1844–1896). The scandalous private lives of the poets, especially Rimbaud and Verlaine, brought the movement into disrepute with the general public. The Parnassians shared with the realists, especially Flaubert, a concern for technical perfection and the precisely correct word, phrase, or intonation. In other respects, such as their colorful evocation of exotic or pagan themes, they were far removed from the main course of life and literature. As precursors of the symbolist movement of the end of the century (see pp. 798–799), they exerted a greater influence on subsequent generations than on their own.

ARCHITECTURE AND SCULPTURE

The realist reaction made no imprint on architecture itself. The few structures that showed new designs and utilized new materials — the

London Crystal Palace of 1851, iron railroad bridges, the first skyscrapers in Chicago and New York, and the Eiffel Tower of 1887 — all were created by civil engineers, not architects. For architecture the nineteenth century, especially its middle decades, was an era of eclecticism. Churches, schools, universities, and even hospitals were made to look like medieval cathedrals or monasteries. Public buildings, banks, and railroad stations adopted the classical, baroque, or renaissance styles. Domestic architecture might have had any or all styles, or no style at all.

It is difficult to account for this "poverty of invention" in architecture unless one considers the tastes — or lack thereof — of the consuming public. Architects, unlike writers and artists, must work to the order of their customers. The successful businessmen on city councils, the boards of directors of banks and railroads, the trustees of schools, colleges, and charitable institutions, had neither the training nor the time to appreciate subtle distinctions of style, much less to assess the significance of possible new developments. If they could distinguish between a classical and a Gothic façade, they had reason for self-congratulation. As a result, they relied on the judgment of such self-appointed arbiters of public taste as John Ruskin, whose popular books of literary and artistic criticism pandered to the lowest common denominator of public taste. "Ornamentation is the principal part of architecture," wrote Ruskin; and Sir George Gilbert Scott (1811–1878), one of the most sought-after Victorian architects, agreed that "the great principle" of architecture is "to decorate construction." Architects became "designers of façades," adding more and more corners, cupolas, gewgaws, and bric-a-brac with no functional significance.

Sculpture suffered a similar fate. The rapid growth of cities and the new wealth that they created brought an unprecedented demand for decorative and monumental statuary. Unfortunately the canons of taste responsible for its selection were no better than those in architecture. Not one sculptor of the period has left his name among those of the great.

THE PROGRESS OF SCIENCE

Modern science influences our lives in a multitude of ways; indeed, its influence is almost omnipresent. Since the eighteenth century there has been an increasing interaction between science and technology, affecting industrial progress and economic organization as well as working conditions and living standards. No less important has been the intellectual influence of science, altering man's conception of himself and his place in the universe. So pervasive has been its influence in modern times that the principal intellectual characteristics of an entire era are sometimes denoted by reference to a single science or scientific genius. In the eighteenth century the Enlightenment or Age of Reason was also called the Age of Newton. Under the intellectual supremacy of physics, physical and mechanical analogies such as natural law, natural rights, separation of powers, checks and balances, and so on, were applied in political and social philosophy, art, literature, and even music.

At the beginning of the nineteenth century the intellectual atmosphere was essentially antiscientific. The anti-intellectualism of the romantic movement and the political and religious reactions did not accord scientists the same high esteem which they had held prior to the French Revolution, and which they were to enjoy again later in the century. Nevertheless, scientific work continued and produced a number of important discoveries. The most momentous advance took place in the science of biology. The theory of organic evolution advanced by Charles Darwin (1809–1882) and several others had no significant applications, such as the new sciences of electricity, organic chemistry, or bacteriology; but in its general intellectual influence it ranked without a doubt as the major scientific theory of the nineteenth century. Evolutionary ideas were in the air even before the publication in 1859 of Darwin's *On the Origin of Species;* afterwards evolutionary thinking permeated every aspect of intellectual life, notably social and political theory and philosophy.

THE METHODS AND INSTRUMENTS OF SCIENCE

Scientific method is sometimes regarded by admiring but innocent laymen as a rigorous, prescribed set of rules governing all research and discovery in the natural sciences, certain to produce the desired results. In fact, very little is known about what goes on in the minds of creative scientists; scientists themselves are frequently unable to give coherent explanations of the manner in which they obtain new theoretical ideas. Nevertheless, certain generally accepted procedures have been followed by most scientists since the time of Bacon, if not that of Aristotle. These procedures include observation, experimentation, and reasoning or logical (including mathematical) analysis, although they do not necessarily occur in that order. Intuition also plays an important role but by its very nature defies any attempt to formulate rules for it.

Within this general framework there is much room for individual variation. Darwin and Louis Pasteur (1822–1895) are examples. Contemporaries of one another and both biologists, they held first rank as scientists by virtue of their contributions; yet their contributions as well as their methods belonged to quite different orders. Pasteur conformed to the popular notion of the scientist as a man who works in a laboratory with test tubes and similar paraphernalia. He made one great theoretical contribution to biology, the germ theory of disease, but he also devised a host of practical applications of this theory, including specific cures for diseases affecting the wine-growing and silkworm industries, an inoculation against hydrophobia or rabies, and the process of sterilization through pasteurization. By contrast, Darwin rarely entered a laboratory. He arrived at his single daring and shocking hypothesis before he was thirty years old, and then spent more than twenty years patiently gathering and marshaling the evidence before he published it.

Most scientists did their work in a laboratory or its equivalent. At the beginning of the nineteenth century the laboratory method and experimental technique were already established as a result of the great prestige of Lavoisier and his followers. Laboratories, however, like professional scientists, were still quite rare. The majority of scientists, especially in Britain, were men of independent means. On the Continent conditions were somewhat better. The great scientific institutions of the French Revolution, the École Polytechnique and the École Normale Supérieure, which combined instruction with research at a very high level, were widely imitated in other countries, especially Germany. The science faculties of the moribund German universities were reorganized in the first half of the century on the lines of the École Polytechnique. In the United States, pure science, as opposed to ingenious tinkering, had few devotees until after the Civil War, when American universities were reorganized on the German pattern, which by that time had become supreme.

In the course of their work scientists found it necessary to devise many new instruments of research. At the beginning of the century laboratory equipment was simple, not to say primitive. It consisted principally of weights and balances, rules and calipers, and a few miscellaneous caldrons and similar containers. During the next fifty years or so scientists added new devices for heating, lighting, and measuring and invented several major instruments of research. The achromatic microscope (*c.* 1830) proved a boon to all branches of biology and medical science and was especially influential in the development of cell theory. The spectroscope, perfected in the 1850's, not only facilitated the detection and identification of elements on earth but also helped to ascertain the composition of the stars and measure their temperatures and motion. The first of the giant modern reflecting telescopes, with a 72-inch metallic mirror, was erected in Ireland in 1845. Before his death in 1867 Michael Faraday had begun to conduct experiments with vacuum tubes, the essential instrument of atomic and radiation physics in the twentieth century.

The use of mathematics and the development of new mathematical methods and theorems became increasingly important for almost all branches of science. Because of Newton, mathematical analysis was already well established in mechanics and optics, and Lavoisier had made limited use of it in chemistry. The development of the laws of probability by Laplace, Gauss, and others at the beginning of the century laid the foundations of mathematical statistics, which were of fundamental importance for research on the kinetic theory of gases and for Mendel's work on genetics and heredity in the 1860's. Mathematics helped to break down the barriers between the various branches of science. At the beginning of the century physics, chemistry, botany, zoology, and so forth were all regarded as independent pursuits. Successive discoveries more and more affirmed the essential unity of nature and hence of science.

FUNDAMENTAL PRINCIPLES AND BASIC SYNTHESES

The belief that atoms are the smallest particles of matter, "the building blocks of nature," may be found among the ancient Greeks and Romans, but atomic theory received its first systematic modern statement from the Englishman John Dalton in 1808. By 1830 the list of common elements was near completion. The Swedish chemist Jöns Berzelius then introduced the notational system of modern chemistry, compiled a table of atomic weights, and derived the formulas of many simple compounds. In the 1860's the Russian Dmitri Mendeleev classified all the elements then known according to their atomic weights and other characteristics, deduced that their properties were functions of their weights, and predicted the existence of other elements that were then unknown. The periodic law that he formulated was verified with striking success within his lifetime: three of the unknown elements were discovered, had the properties he predicted, and fitted into the appropriate gaps in his periodic table. Since then many other elements have been discovered — and some created — all in accordance with the periodic law.

Another puzzling problem for chemists was the nature of organic compounds and their relationship to inorganic ones. According to the vitalists, whose ranks included Pasteur and many other eminent scientists, life processes did not obey the same laws that governed inorganic matter but were directed by some unexplained and perhaps inexplicable "vital principle." The first major blow to this position came in 1828 when the German Friedrich Wöhler synthesized urea, an organic compound, in the laboratory. It was soon discovered that all organic compounds contained the element carbon in combination with a relatively small number of other elements, chiefly oxygen, hydrogen, and nitrogen. They were all among the most common elements to be found on the earth's surface and in the atmosphere. In succeeding years many other organic substances, including some not found in nature, were synthesized in laboratories. The vitalist controversy was finally resolved in the biological sciences. The development of cell theory in the 1830's, the studies of digestion, respiration, and metabolism by the Frenchman Claude Bernard in the 1840's and 1850's, and finally the germ theory of disease itself convinced most scientists that the "vital principle" was an unnecessary postulate.

The new offshoots of biology, such as bacteriology and microbiology, together with organic chemistry had many important applications in medicine and pharmacy as well as agriculture and industry. In 1844 an American dentist, Horace Wells, first used nitrous oxide as an anesthetic; it was followed by ether in 1846 and chloroform in 1847. In 1865 a Scottish physician, Joseph Lister, introduced antiseptic surgery with the liberal use of carbolic acid. The combination of anesthesia and antisepsis effected a revolution in medical technology and greatly reduced the death rate in childbirth and surgery. The revolution was not effected without opposition, however, from both within and without medical circles. Religious leaders objected to the use of anesthesia in childbirth on biblical grounds (Genesis 3:16) until Queen Victoria's doctor administered chloroform to her in 1853.

THERMODYNAMICS AND ELECTROMAGNETISM

Thermodynamics, the science dealing with thermal energy or heat, was in a surprisingly backward state in the first half of the nineteenth century. The steam engine, its foremost practical application, had reached a fairly advanced stage of development on the slenderest of theoretical foundations. Indeed, scientists learned far more from the steam engine than its inventors and perfectors learned from science. A French scientist, Sadi Carnot, published a memoir in 1824 on the pure theory of heat engines, which laid the basis for subsequent research. Further work in the 1840's by J. R. Meyer in Germany and James Joule in England on the energy equivalents of heat in other forms (mechanical, electrical, etc.) led to the statement in 1847 by the German Hermann von Helmholtz of the First Law of Thermodynamics, concerning the conservation of energy. This seemingly simple, even obvious principle had numerous practical applications and immense theoretical significance.

The science of electricity belongs almost wholly to the nineteenth century. Electrical phenomena had been observed in ancient times, but as late as the eighteenth century electricity was regarded simply as a curiosity. Toward the end of that century the researches of Benjamin Franklin in America and of the Italians Luigi Galvani and Alessandro Volta, who invented the voltaic pile or battery, raised it from the status of a parlor trick to a laboratory pursuit. In 1807 Sir Humphry Davy discovered electrolysis, the phenomenon by which an electric current decomposes the chemical elements in certain aqueous solutions, which gave rise to the electroplating industry. The next phase in the study of electricity was dominated by Davy's student Michael Faraday, the Danish physicist Hans Oersted, and the French mathematician André Ampère. In 1820 Oersted observed that an electric current produces a magnetic field around the conductors, which led Ampère to formulate a quantitative relationship between electricity and magnetism. Between 1821 and 1831 Faraday discovered the phenomenon of electromagnetic induction (the generation of an electrical current by revolving a magnet inside a coil of wire) and invented a primitive generator and electric motor.

Building on these discoveries, Samuel Morse developed the electric telegraph in America between 1832 and 1844, although the industrial utilization of electricity was held up until the 1870's by the difficulties involved in devising an economically efficient generator.

Faraday's experiments and discoveries were of fundamental importance, but they lacked a satisfactory theoretical basis. It was supplied in the 1860's by James Clerk Maxwell, who deduced mathematically a theoretical velocity for electromagnetic waves that was equivalent to the velocity of light. In fact, Maxwell regarded light as one of many electromagnetic waves and predicted the existence of still others. His prediction received spectacular confirmation in 1885, when Heinrich Hertz of Germany observed the existence of radio waves, which were developed practically by the Italian physicist Guglielmo Marconi after 1895.

ORGANIC EVOLUTION

The most important scientific event of the nineteenth century in its impact on the world was the publication in 1859 of Darwin's *On the Origin of Species*. The essential message of this book, as it reached the public, was that nature's creatures — including man — had not been created *de novo* by the hand of God, as taught in the Old Testament and generally accepted by Christians and non-Christians alike, but that each had evolved from earlier and simpler forms of life. The reaction to this message in both scientific and nonscientific circles was immediate, far-reaching, and clamorous. Most scientists granted it at least qualified acceptance, and some, such as T. H. Huxley, became enthusiastic Darwinians. Nonscientists, however, especially those in religious groups, greeted it with reactions ranging from stunned disbelief to violent opposition.

In retrospect, the furor occasioned by this careful, modestly written book seems surprising. Evolution was by no means a new idea in 1859. In the previous year both Darwin and Alfred Russell Wallace, another British naturalist who had arrived independently at similar views, had presented their ideas in memoirs to the Linnaean Society in London. Darwin had formulated his basic hypothesis more than twenty years before. As early as 1802 the French paleontologist J. B. Lamarck had advanced a theory of evolution that even included the inheritance of acquired characteristics. Lamarck's arguments were not as solidly based as Darwin's, nor did he reach as wide an audience, but Herbert Spencer and others had already accepted the gist of them and were working along similar lines well before 1859.

Abundant evidence existed in both biological and nonbiological sciences to prove that the earth and its creatures had not subsisted without change from the day of creation. Employing James Hutton's *Theory of the Earth* (1785) and Sir Charles Lyell's monumental three-volume *Principles of Geology* (1830–1833), geologists were busy demonstrating that

Thames & Hudson Archives, London

Cartoon of Charles Darwin, from *The Hornet,*
March 22, 1871

"Man is descended from some less highly organized form. . . . The grounds
upon which this conclusion rests will never be shaken, for the close similarity
between man and the lower animals in embryonic development, as well as in
innumerable points of structure and constitution, both of high and the most
trifling importance . . . are facts which cannot be disputed. . . . When viewed
by the light of our knowledge of the whole organic world, their meaning is
unmistakable. The great principle of evolution stands up clear and firm, when
these groups of facts are considered in connection with others, such as the
mutual affinities of the members of the same group, their geographical
distribution in past and present times, and their geological succession. It is
incredible that all these facts should speak falsely." Charles Darwin, THE DESCENT
OF MAN (New York, 1875).

the age of the earth was far greater than even the most liberal interpretations of the biblical accounts would allow. They also proved that far from remaining in its original state, the earth's surface had undergone tremendous upheavals in the past and was still in a constant process of transformation. Paleontologists pointed to the fossilized remains of creatures that were no longer extant to show that earlier forms of life had existed. For a very long time men had been engaged in the selective breeding of livestock and other animals on an empirical, nonscientific basis. Economists like Friedrich List had emphasized the evolutionary nature of social development through a series of stages. Historians like H. T. Buckle had emphasized the influence of environment on personal and national characters. From many angles — natural science, agricultural technology, social philosophy, and history — influences were converging on the notion of organic evolution. Darwin supplied the missing element: a conception of the mode of operation of the evolutionary process.

The Darwinian theory may be reduced by drastic oversimplification to three major points. The first point Darwin took from the Malthusian theory of population: in every species nature gives birth to more individuals than the means of subsistence will support. Second, this overpopulation results in a competition for survival, a struggle for existence. Finally, and most important, in the process of inheritance chance variations or mutations occur among individuals, making some more suitable and adaptable to the environment than others. Those that are "naturally selected" for survival continue to propagate their own kind. The others, the "unfit," are weeded out and do not propagate. In spite of the title of the book, it was not actually a theory of the origin of species but only of their survival. Darwin slurred over the crucial question of why mutation takes place on the assumption that it was a matter of random variation. For biologists this point proved to be the most controversial, but its subtlety escaped most laymen. For them the controversy lay in other realms.

THE WARFARE OF SCIENCE WITH THEOLOGY

Historically there has been a long conflict between materialistic science and supernatural religion. For most of modern history this conflict seethed below the surface, but in the latter half of the nineteenth century it broke out into full-fledged ideological warfare. In earlier days, when religion was dominant, scientists had tried to disavow the conflict. Galileo and others recanted their scientific beliefs when challenged by the Church. Newton, a pious man, felt that his discoveries about the nature of the universe only established the greater glory of the Creator. Even Darwin, an agnostic, tried to disarm his critics in advance by writing, "I see no good reason why the views given in the volume [*On the Origin of Species*] should shock the religious feelings of anyone. . . . There is grandeur in this view of life, with its several powers, having been originally breathed by the Creator into a few forms or into one; and that, whilst this planet has gone cycling on according to the fixed law of gravity, from so simple a being endless forms most beautiful and most wonderful have been, and are being evolved." Yet this bland reassurance could not calm the troubled spirits within and without the churches.

SCIENCE ON THE OFFENSE

Many elements of conflict existed between the findings of science and the traditional teachings of Christianity. Most fundamental was the fact that scientists disputed the literal interpretation of the Bible, especially biblical chronology and the stories of Genesis. For instance, a seventeenth-century bishop had worked out a systematic but most unscientific chronology that placed the origin of the earth in the year 4004 B.C. In no way could this account be reconciled with geological, paleontological, archaeological, and even historical evidence on the age of the earth. Scientific evidence tended to undermine belief in miracles, such as the virgin birth and bodily resurrection. Defenders of religion asserted that these events could not be understood scientifically because they were supernatural and therefore superscientific, but scientists refused to be convinced.

Religious defenses were further shaken when some biblical scholars adopted the canons of modern historical and literary criticism and subjected the Bible to historical and realistic reinterpretation. Such books as D. F. Strauss's *Das Leben Jesu* (1836) and Ernest Renan's *Vie de Jésus* (1863), which pictured Jesus naturalistically as a mortal, were profoundly disturbing to the faithful. Other scholars sought to strengthen Christian faith by freeing it from a dependence on obviously discredited dogmas, and replacing the literal interpretation of the Bible with an allegorical one, trying to interpret it as a dramatic story that illustrates great moral truths. Even this could not deflect scientists' criticism of the attribution to God of such human traits as benevolence and anger. In such an intellectual environment the arrival of Darwinian biology did not cause the "warfare of science with theology," as the struggle was called by the president of Cornell University, Andrew Dickson White; it merely precipitated the outbreak of overt hostilities.

THE THEOLOGICAL COUNTERATTACK

The various churches reacted to the scientific offensive in different ways. Liberal Protestant and Jewish theologians attempted to redefine religion so as to remove the elements of conflict and make religion compatible with science. Other Protestants adopted a fundamentalist attitude: whenever scientific findings conflicted with the fundamentals of their faith they denounced science as untrue and a work of the devil. Only the Roman Catholic Church returned the challenge with a deliberate and sustained counterattack.

As early as 1832 Pope Gregory XVI in the encyclical *Mirari vos* had condemned liberty of conscience and the press as well as revolts against established government. In 1854 Pope Pius IX promulgated the Dogma of the Immaculate Conception, which held that the Virgin Mary was conceived without the taint of original sin bestowed on all other mortals. The pope hoped to strengthen the Church in its struggle with materialism; instead, he hardened the lines of resistance and made the reconciliation of science and religion even more difficult to achieve. The high point of the Church's counterattack came ten years later in 1864, when Pius IX issued the encyclical *Quanta cura* and its appended *Syllabus of Errors*. By then the papacy had lost all its temporal domain to the new kingdom of Italy with the exception of the city of Rome and its immediate vicinity. (See pp. 669–670.) Not only was it in danger of losing Rome itself, but also its political relations with several other states were in a precarious position. Accordingly, the pope lashed out at science and other aspects of contemporary society that he associated with the Church's troubles.

The *Syllabus of Errors* consisted of eighty propositions which it labeled as contrary to the principles of the Christian religion. They included pantheism, naturalism, "absolute" and "moderate" rationalism, and most other contemporary "isms." The syllabus castigated the notions of religious toleration and freedom of conscience, upheld the necessity of temporal power for the Roman Catholic Church, rejected the separation of Church and state but insisted on the supremacy of the Church over civil law, and claimed for the Church complete control over education, science, philosophy, and intellectual and cultural affairs in general. It concluded with a ringing denunciation of the idea that "the Roman Pontiff can and should reconcile and align himself with progress, liberalism, and modern civilization."

The syllabus brought joy to the hearts of Ultramontane Catholics, but it aroused further the suspicions and hostility of non-Catholics — Protestants, Jews, and freethinkers alike — and cut the ground from under liberal Catholics who had been working to restore Catholic prestige and make their church an instrument of progress.

The final salvo of the Catholic Church's counterattack came from the Vatican Council, the first general council of the church in three centuries, which assembled in Rome in 1869. The original intent of the council was to restate and strengthen the position of the Church on Church-state relations, but the only positive action it took (on a proposition that had not appeared in the original agenda) was to proclaim the Dogma of Papal Infallibility: the dogma that the pope, when speaking *ex cathedra* on a question of faith and morals, speaks with the voice of God.

THE CHURCH ON THE DEFENSIVE

The counterattack failed, at least in its primary objective. Soon after the proclamation of papal infallibility Italian soldiers occupied Rome and Victor Emmanuel proclaimed the Eternal City as capital of the kingdom of Italy. The Vatican Council adjourned *sine die*. The Italian government offered the pope an annuity and guaranteed him the treatment due the head of a sovereign state, but the pope (who had already excommunicated Victor Emmanuel and several Italian statesmen) refused all offers of compromise, placed the ban of the Church on the king and his government, and regarded himself as "the prisoner in the Vatican."

The Roman Catholic Church had its difficulties elsewhere as well. Immediately after the proclamation of papal infallibility Austria annulled its concordat with the Church. Soon afterward the chancellor of the new German Empire inaugurated a policy of persecution of the Church known as the *Kulturkampf*, which led to a long struggle on the question of Church-state relations and alienated many members of the Church. (See p. 731.) Within the Church the victory of the reactionary party led to the excommunication of the liberal Catholics who refused to accept defeat. Dissension among Catholics themselves spread to Germany, Austria, Switzerland, and the Netherlands.

No less disturbing to the Catholic Church was its loosening hold over its rank-and-file members. In this situation it was not alone, for all Western religions experienced the same problem. Basically the decline was brought about by materialism in the broadest sense. Propagation of the discoveries of science together with the spread of education and literacy led to an undermining of faith in religious teachings. Material progress, relaxed political controls, crumbling social distinctions, and the consequent attempt of individuals of all social classes to better themselves economically steadily diverted their attention from religious activities and weakened the church hierarchy's control. The large-scale population shifts induced by industrialization and urbanization also loosened church ties. The slow reaction of all churches to the demoralizing living and working conditions in the large new industrial centers further alienated large masses of erstwhile believers. The opposition of most established churches to trade unions, socialism, and other attempts of the workers to improve their lot gave ample opportunity to the proponents of religious disbelief.

Pius IX died in 1878. His long regime, which had been hailed at its inception in 1846 as inaugurating a new era for the Roman Catholic Church, ended with that Church shaken to its foundations, holding only the shreds of its former power and prestige. The new pope, Leo XIII, was sixty-eight years old and in very frail health. Few people expected him to live longer than two or three years at most. He was regarded as a temporary pope; the Church would regroup its forces and elect a young and vigorous head. Instead, Leo lived for another twenty-five years and brought the papacy to a new peak of prestige.

MATERIALISM AND POSITIVISM

Materialism in the strict sense is the belief that all phenomena of the universe, including man, consist ultimately of matter and energy. It is closely related to realism in modern philosophy, which is defined as the belief that the physical universe has an objective existence independent of the observer. Both conceptions are antithetical not only to the supernatural and metaphysical principles of revealed religion but also to the various idealist philosophies, such as the Hegelian, which hold that ultimate reality consists only of ideas.

Nineteenth-century science gave powerful support to the advocates of realism and materialism. It strengthened the tendency that had been present in political and social philosophy at least from the time of Locke to look at natural science as a model for the analysis of social phenomena. The founders of modern economics, or political economy, borrowed heavily from Newtonian physics for both their concepts and their terminology. Increasingly they referred to their subject as a science. In the nineteenth century the predominant influence on political and social philosophy came from the biological sciences, which affected them in two ways: first, by providing analogies and terminology; second, by providing the principle of evolution.

SOCIAL DARWINISM

The expression Social Darwinism refers to the application of the principle of organic evolution as stated by Darwin to the phenomena of society. The most popular and influential exponent of Social Darwinism was Herbert Spencer (1820–1903), an English engineer and social philosopher, whose prolific but often superficial pen inundated the literate public during the entire second half of the nineteenth century. Spencer, who had already begun his evolutionary thinking before 1859, eagerly seized Darwin's theory and applied it directly if indiscriminately to society, making social change a mere continuation of biological evolution. The doctrine implicit in Darwinian biological theory — that conflict and strife are good and synonymous with progress — became explicit in Spencer's version. According to him, the competition of individuals, business firms, or nations ensures the "survival of the fittest" and the subjugation or elimination of the "unfit," unless it is hindered by "artificial" restraints on the "natural" process of selection. Social Darwinism reinforced the arguments of the classical economists against state interference with the economy, which accounted for Spencer's enormous popularity with successful businessmen. Andrew Carnegie's reaction after reading Darwin and Spencer was, "Not only had I got rid of theology and the supernatural, but I had found the truth of evolution. 'All is well since all grows better' became my motto, my true source of comfort." Paradoxically, the radical intellectual doctrine of evolution had become an argument for maintaining the status quo.

Not all Social Darwinists — the expression is sometimes used rather loosely — derived the same lesson from organic evolution as Spencer and Carnegie. When the liberal English economist and political philosopher Walter Bagehot (1826–1877) applied it by analogy to the study of the British constitution in *Physics and Politics* (which might more aptly have been called "Biology and Social Science"), he argued for a greater degree of political freedom and democracy. On the other hand, the American sociologist Lester Ward denied the direct applicability of Darwinism to society. "The fundamental principle of biology," he wrote, "is natural selection, that of sociology is artificial selection. The survival of the fittest is simply the survival of the strong, which implies and would better be called the destruction of the weak. If nature progresses through the destruction of the weak, man progresses through the protection of the weak." Darwinism also inspired the British Fabian socialists (see p. 711), and exerted a profound influence on the thought of Karl Marx. Marx even wished to dedicate the first volume of *Das Kapital* to Darwin, but the latter circumspectly declined the honor.

Darwinism gave an apparently scientific basis to the fallacious distinction between "superior" and "inferior" races. The invocation of biology in this case served merely as adornment for arguments that sprang from quite different sources. In 1853 J. A. de Gobineau (1816–1882), a French nobleman, laid the basis for much subsequent pseudoscientific writing on the subject of race in an *Essay on the Inequality of Human Races.* Houston Stewart Chamberlain (1855–1927), an Englishman who married Richard Wagner's daughter and became a German citizen, did much through his writings to establish the myth of a uniquely pure and therefore superior "Teutonic race." Malicious journalists published reams of pseudoscientific material intended to convince their readers of the mental or moral deficiencies of the Semitic, Slavic, or Latin "races." One disastrous result of this perversion of Darwinian biology was its application to non-European "races" in the outburst of imperialist sentiment at the end of the century. (See p. 797.)

AUGUSTE COMTE AND MODERN SOCIOLOGY

The most ambitious, systematic, and comprehensive attempt to apply the methods of science to the study of society was made by the French philosopher Auguste Comte (1798–1857). Comte's major work was *La philosophie positive (Positive Philosophy)*. It was the foundation stone of modern positivism, the system of philosophy that recognizes only observable phenomena and scientifically established fact. Comte interpreted the intellectual history of the world as passing through three great ages: the theological, metaphysical, and scientific. He thought that Europe in the nineteenth century was on the verge of the third and final age.

Comte classified all "positive" (verifiable) knowledge into a series of categories of increasing specificity and complexity, in which the "laws" of the more complex sciences rested upon those of the simpler and more abstract. Mathematics, with its self-evident axioms and abstract theorems, formed the base of his intellectual pyramid, surmounted by the physical sciences, the earth sciences, and the biological sciences. Capping the edifice was sociology, a comprehensive social science including economics, anthropology, history, and psychology. Comte therefore has a claim as the founder of modern sociology as well as positivism.

Comte's writing is sometimes both ponderous and pompous. Apart from his classifications, conceptions, and strictures on scientific and philosophic methods, he contributed little of substance to either sociology or social philosophy. The vogue of positivism lasted only a short time, and sociology did not become a recognized social science until the end of the nineteenth century, when it took a form different from that envisaged by Comte. Nevertheless, Comte was a major figure in the history of thought. His influence, both direct and indirect, was enormous on men of such varied temperaments and accomplishments as John Stuart Mill, Herbert Spencer, Ernest Renan, Hippolyte Taine, and the American pragmatic philosophers of the twentieth century. He was as responsible as any for the general acceptance of science as a special and authoritative branch of knowledge.

REALISM IN RETROSPECT

Realism, the prevailing intellectual temper of the third quarter of the nineteenth century, placed a high value upon action, power, success, material progress, and the exact representation of nature. It glorified struggle and conflict, from which manliness and progress were presumed to result. It cared little for sentimentality, scoffed at romanticism and idealism, and scorned mysticism and the supernatural. The firmness with which the revolutions of 1848 were suppressed, and the success of *Realpolitik* in unifying Italy and Germany, seemed to justify this attitude in practical politics. The achievements of science and the retreat of traditional religion increased its intellectual stature as well as its popularity, especially among the middle classes, who were the chief beneficiaries of the substantial technical and economic progress of the period. Artists and litterateurs as well as social philosophers took natural science as their model and guide. In spite of a certain crassness and callousness, realism was an optimist outlook. Its legacy to succeeding generations was beneficial, on the whole. Yet it contained certain unresolved — almost undetected — ethical and philosophical problems, which caused immediate anguish and suffering for many and in the long run overwhelmed the optimistic outlook itself.

THE POLITICS OF POWER, 1852–1871
CHAPTER TWENTY-SIX

The two decades from the coup d'état of Louis Napoleon to the proclamation of the German Empire witnessed fundamental changes in the structure of the European state system, in the nature of the political process, and in the character and the behavior of statesmen and politicians. The most striking changes were the unification of Germany and Italy into two powerful nations in central Europe. Yet the method of their unification was itself a manifestation of equally important if more subtle changes in the mentality of political leaders, the essence of which can be stated in a single phrase: the willingness to use force to achieve purely political goals. Although the domestic political struggles of the first half of the nineteenth century frequently erupted in revolution, their objective was an idealistic vision of a more nearly perfect society. After the failure of the revolutions of 1848, idealism was replaced by political realism or *Realpolitik,* in which practical interests and material advantage became the sole consideration of ambitious statesmen and politicians, who felt that any practical means were justified in order to gain their often ignoble ends.

This new outlook operated on the international no less than the national plane. In fact, the growth of constitutional and democratic sentiment forced even dictatorial rulers to cater somewhat to public opinion domestically, or at least to manipulate that opinion behind a façade of constitutionalism, but no similar constitutional check existed in international relations. Astute political leaders could manipulate the passions of inflamed nationalism to support their use of naked force. Between 1815 and 1853 the interests of the great powers and the efforts of statesmen were aimed at avoiding wars among the European states; revolutions there had been, numbers of them, but no major wars. Again from 1871 to 1914, except for peripheral conflicts such as the Balkan wars, no European nation fought another. In the two decades corresponding to the life of the Second French Empire, however, European nations fought five significant wars, involving all the great powers in one or another. They were brief, limited wars, but they were fought for political advantage. With the possible exception of the Crimean War, they were deliberately provoked by some person or persons for a definite political purpose. Although circumstances differed in the United States, there, too, North and South resorted to the use of force in a long and bloody civil war rather than settle their differences by peaceful negotiations.

NAPOLEON III AND THE SECOND FRENCH EMPIRE

The coup d'état of December 2, 1851, ushered in a period of frankly dictatorial government, to which the trappings of constitutionalism were soon added. The plebiscite that confirmed the coup d'état also authorized the prince-president (as he was now called) to draw up a new constitution. One of its provisions extended the term of the presidency to ten years, but no one seriously expected the term to expire in a normal manner. The progress of Louis Napoleon Bonaparte from constitutional official to dictatorial chief of state to emperor paralleled that of the first Napoleon, but it took less time because of the earlier precedent. The Bonapartists prepared an elaborate campaign to organize popular acceptance for a return to the empire. The prince-president made a speaking tour of the provinces, much in the manner of later American presidential campaigns, at which paid demonstrators and soldiers raised cries of "Vive Napoléon" and "Vive l'empire." In November, 1852, a new plebiscite duly ratified a return to the empire, which was proclaimed on December 2, exactly one year after the coup d'état and forty-eight years to the day after the proclamation of the First Empire.

THE "AUTHORITARIAN EMPIRE"

The Second Empire introduced no fundamental changes in the structure of government. With minor changes in wording, the constitution of January 14, 1852, served the empire as well as the dictatorial republic. The empire was simply the frosting on the Napoleonic cake. The new emperor chose the title Napoleon III to indicate that he regarded himself as the successor to the son of Napoleon I, who in fact had never been recognized as emperor. The constitution gave the chief of state almost unlimited authority: he commanded the armed forces, the police, and the civil service; he alone could initiate legislation, declare war, and conclude treaties; and at his will he could rule by decree. To assist him in the task of government, the constitution provided four bodies, two of them actual working groups, the other two chiefly for decoration. In fact, the constitution stated expressly that "the Emperor governs *by means of* the ministers, the Council of State, the Senate, and the Legislative Body."

The ministers had charge of the day-to-day operations of the executive departments but did not form a cabinet in the modern sense. They had no collective responsibility either to the legislature or to the emperor; they were individually appointed by and could be dismissed by the emperor alone. Selected primarily on the basis of personal loyalty and competence, they were simply the chief administrative assistants of the emperor. The Conseil d'État, likewise appointed by the emperor, had as its principal function the drafting of legislation. It was not, however, a legislative body in the ordinary sense. Composed of high-ranking civil servants and other technical experts, it merely ensured that the laws desired by the emperor were given the proper form.

The members of the Senate were appointed for life by the emperor from outstanding persons in all walks of life. They had very little to do other than to perform ceremonial functions and to ratify such changes as Napoleon wished to make in the constitution. The Corps Législatif preserved a semblance of representative government, but no more than that. Its members, the deputies, were elected by universal male suffrage for six-year terms; but they lacked the power to introduce or amend legislation and could only accept or reject what the emperor proposed. Their debates were not open to the public, nor were any records preserved. Moreover, at election time the government put up a slate of official candidates whose campaign expenses it paid and whom it favored in other ways. Under these circumstances it required a hardy individual to pose as an opposition candidate.

Immediately following the coup d'état the government was a military dictatorship, but within a few months the dictatorship began to take on a more benign aspect. The first eight years are sometimes called the period of personal rule or the "authoritarian empire." The government maintained strict control of the press, suppressed all overt manifestations of political hostility, and mainly followed its own interests. Yet it was not an oppressive dictatorship; it was on the whole a rather benevolent despotism. The government did not lack popular support in the country, and it continually sought to increase the bases of that support by means of individual and group favors and political bribes. The peasants, who were still the most numerous class, provided the government with its largest number of supporters, while the upper middle classes, the bourgeoisie of rich merchants, manufacturers, financiers, and professional men — most of whom had been Orleanist in their sympathies — occupied the highest posts and derived the most benefits from government favors. The aristocracy remained legitimist (pro-Bourbon) in its sympathies for the most part, while the urban workers, despite some weak attempts by the government to gain their favor, remained tinged with republicanism.

THE "LIBERAL EMPIRE"

During the 1860's an evolutionary process gradually modified the political institutions of the empire. The emperor himself had said early in his career, "Liberty will crown the edifice." In the Second Empire liberty was the reward of the people for obedience, and it came after, not before, the establishment of order and the development of the constitutional system. Liberal reforms, aimed chiefly at giving the Legislative Body a greater share in government, took place in 1860, 1862, 1867, and 1869. Finally in 1870 the Senate became the upper house of the legislature, and a responsible cabinet was introduced — that is, a cabinet responsible to the legislature instead of the emperor. Opposition deputies increased from eight in 1852 to more than 150 in 1869, which represented a majority of the Corps Législatif. These developments were clearly in the direction of a constitutional monarchy. The reforms were not entirely voluntary, however. The emperor gave in to public opinion and to political pressures that were exerted upon him chiefly as the result of embarrassments over his foreign policies. Nevertheless, he did so with good grace and appeared to have established a dynasty and a government that might give France political stability.

DOMESTIC POLICY

When setting the stage for the proclamation of the empire in 1852, the prince-president sought to undercut those who insinuated that a return to the empire would involve France in war. On the contrary, he said, "L'empire, c'est la paix" (The empire means peace). What he should have said was, "The empire means prosperity" — within two years France was involved in the Crimean War — for the era of the Second Empire was one of the most prosperous periods in all French history. Favorable international conditions partially accounted for the prosperity, for it was a period of general economic expansion throughout the world; but Napoleonic economic policies were also responsible.

Napoleon III's economic policy contrasted strongly with his political policy. Whereas the latter was one of restraint, control, and supervision, the former encouraged private initiative and enterprise. Stimulated by a lowering of tariffs in the 1850's and a network of trade treaties beginning with the Cobden-Chevalier Treaty of 1860, foreign commerce expanded by more than 5 per cent per year. New business firms multiplied, especially after the passage of laws permitting free incorporation with limited liability in 1863 and 1867. New types of financial institutions were created by private initiative but with government encouragement and support; the Crédit Foncier, a mortgage bank, and the Crédit Mobilier, an industrial credit institution, were both established in 1852. They contributed to prosperity in France and also were widely imitated abroad. Three of the four largest commercial banks in France, nationalized in 1945, date from the era of the Second Empire.

The railroad network was one of the major achievements in the area of economic policy. The Second Empire granted charters for more than one-half the eventual mileage and witnessed the completion of more than a third of it. The telegraph network expanded from two thousand to more than seventy thousand kilometers. In 1855 the Crédit Mobilier created with a government subsidy the steamship company that became the French Line. Stimulated by railroad construction and the general economic expansion, the iron industry completed its transition to coke smelting and adopted new methods for making cheap steel. While transforming and expanding the domestic economy, Frenchmen extended their economic interests abroad. Foreign investments rose from about two billion to more than twelve billion francs, while French businessmen, bankers, and engineers spread through Europe and much of the rest of the world building railroads, digging mines and canals, and creating banks and industrial establishments. The greatest single achievement of French enterprise, and possibly the greatest engineering feat of the nineteenth century, was the digging of the Suez Canal, carried out between 1854 and 1869 by a company headed by Ferdinand de Lesseps.

A project closely related to economic policy (for it was intended in part to give employment to the workers of Paris and wean them from socialism), but which had broader cultural and even political objectives as well, was the reconstruction and beautification of Paris. This work went on for many years and cost many millions of francs. It made Paris one of the most beautiful cities in the world, with wide boulevards, magnificent vistas, beautiful parks, lavish public monuments, and a modern sanitary system. Fortunately for future generations, the city planners of the Second Empire did not neglect aesthetic considerations in their striving for efficiency.

The reconstruction of Paris was only one aspect of a general effort to restore the nation to the position of prestige that it had maintained in times past and to cover the empire with glory. The major part of this effort was expended in the nation's foreign relations, but Napoleon III and his supporters did not neglect the cultivation of artistic, cultural, and scientific triumphs. The emperor set the social tone early in his reign by his marriage to Eugénie de Montijo, the daughter of a minor Spanish nobleman. Having been unsuccessful in his attempts to find a bride from one of the reigning dynasties, he reportedly "married for love" this obscure and impoverished but chaste and dignified young Spanish beauty. The marriage contributed greatly to his popularity in the early years of the empire. In time Eugénie's clerical inclinations and legitimist sympathies created political difficulties for the empire, but as a generous and impulsive sponsor of charities she contributed greatly to making the empire palatable and even popular among workers and peasants alike, and as a leader of fashion she made Paris once more the center of European high society.

Eugénie's devout Catholicism symbolized the regime's dilemma in religious policy, and also contributed to it. The emperor, a free thinker, could not afford to antagonize the large body of French believers. As president of the republic he had made several concessions to the Church. Under the empire he continued this policy, but at the same time certain features of his foreign policy — his encouragement of Italian nationalism, in particular — tended to alienate the clerical party in France.

FOREIGN POLICY: THE CRIMEAN WAR
AND THE CONGRESS OF PARIS

The principal objective of Napoleon's foreign policy was to restore France to its position of power, influence, and glory as the arbiter of Europe. The several glaring failures that eventually led to the downfall of his regime sometimes obscure his temporary success. The first major test came in a renewal of what is known as the Eastern question. In 1853 Russia and Turkey went to war, and France and Britain joined Turkey as allies early in the following year. From one point of view the war was only one in a long series of conflicts between Russia and Turkey, but the involvement of the Western powers made it a struggle of more general significance. The apparent cause for French participation was a dispute between France and Russia concerning the custody of Christian shrines in Palestine, which had been growing more intense since 1851. The Ottoman Turks, as nominal rulers, had allowed both governments certain rights of protection for Christian pilgrims. Napoleon inflated this dispute far beyond its true importance, hoping to curry favor with the clerical opposition by posing as protector of the Church, and at the same time hoping to regain for France and the empire some of its lost glory by scoring a diplomatic victory over Russia.

The actual fighting, confined primarily to the Crimean peninsula in the Black Sea, was almost inconsequential. None of the powers involved regarded the issues as important enough to justify a major effort, and commercial relationships through the Baltic Sea were hardly affected. The casualties from disease and inadequate medical care rivaled those resulting from poor planning and logistics and the incompetence of the generals. Florence Nightingale eventually provoked sweeping reforms in army medical care and public health nursing by exposing the atrocious medical and sanitary conditions of the British army. Following the death of the Russian Tsar Nicholas I and the threat of Austrian intervention on the side of the Western allies, Russia agreed to an armistice at the beginning of 1856.

A general settlement of the issues growing out of the war took place at the Paris Peace Congress in the spring of 1856. Although Napoleon III failed to secure a revision of the Vienna settlement, the effect of the war and the congress was to reestablish France as the most powerful nation on the Continent. The birth of an heir to the imperial throne while the congress was in session added to the luster of the occasion and appeared to ensure the success of the dynasty. The congress also produced the germ of Napoleon's next major foreign policy adventure — his participation in the unification of Italy.

THE RISORGIMENTO AND ITALIAN UNITY

Prior to 1860 Italy had never been a unified nation. In ancient times it formed part of the Roman Empire, but not as a nation. After the fall of Rome it broke up into several barbarian kingdoms, and the process of fragmentation continued throughout the early Middle Ages. In the later Middle Ages Italy again became the center of European civilization, but it remained politically divided into numerous small republics and principalities. With the rise of large nation-states in early modern times these tiny city-states became battlegrounds and objects of plunder and oppression by their larger neighbors, a situation that continued until after the middle of the nineteenth century. The word *risorgimento,* therefore, meaning resurrection or resurgence, is not strictly accurate when applied to the political movement for national unity in Italy in the nineteenth century. Nevertheless, it does convey a sense of the patriotic spirit and messianic fervor that characterized the leaders of the movement.

THE RISE OF NATIONAL CONSCIOUSNESS

The first stirrings of national consciousness took place in the eighteenth century, when some educated Italians began to speak of their homeland as Italy rather than Tuscany, Lombardy, or Romagna. The French Revolution and the period of French domination under Napoleon fanned the flames of nationalism in Italy, as elsewhere, but the illusion of unity and nationality that Napoleon created with his sham Kingdom of Italy was short-lived. Italians who had hoped for a unified national state were gravely disappointed with the settlement of the Congress of Vienna, which resurrected the numerous small states, almost all of them under foreign domination.

The 1815 settlement did not reproduce exactly the pre-Napoleonic situation. In the north, Lombardy and Venetia were incorporated directly into the Austrian Empire. Under the protection of Austria, Bourbons or Hapsburgs ruled in the tiny duchies of Modena, Parma, and Lucca, in the slightly larger Grand Duchy of Tuscany, and in the still larger Kingdom of the Two Sicilies, whose capital was Naples. Only the

States of the Church had a genuinely native Italian ruler, and he, too, was under Austrian protection. The Kingdom of Sardinia, the eventual leader of the movement for Italian unification, was a curious mélange, an artificial state composed of four major subdivisions differing in climate, resources, institutions, and even language: the island of Sardinia, whence the union got its name, languishing in the backwaters of feudalism; Savoy, which gave the kingdom and later Italy its ruling dynasty, geographically, economically, and culturally a part of France; Genoa, the former commercial republic added to the kingdom in 1815; and Piedmont, the real head and body of the country, containing not only the capital but about four-fifths of the total population.

In the three decades after the Congress of Vienna the Kingdom of Sardinia showed no sign that it would eventually take the lead in a liberal and national movement; on the contrary, its restored monarch outdid the Austrian rulers of Lombardy and Venetia in the vehemence of his attempts to undo the work of the French Revolution and return to the ancien régime. The oppressive atmosphere of the Metternichean reaction seemed to stifle temporarily all liberal and nationalist sentiment. The most daring and fanatic radicals, mainly young intellectuals and adventurers, formed secret revolutionary societies, such as the Carbonari. These groups instigated the insurrections of 1820 and 1821 and 1830 and 1832, doomed to failure by the ignorance and apathy of the peasants. (See pp. 559, 566.) The early insurrections were aimed simply at the overthrow of existing governments and the attainment of an idealized, romanticized, abstract liberty. Their failure subtly transformed their romantic liberalism into a liberal nationalism with the goal of a united, independent Italy.

ALTERNATIVE APPROACHES TO NATIONAL UNITY

Between the revolutions of 1830 and 1832 and those of 1848 three different approaches to the problem of unity were proposed. Giuseppe Mazzini (1805–1872), a young veteran of the Carbonari, was disappointed but not disillusioned by the failures of 1830 and 1832. He advocated a centralized democratic republic, to be achieved by a simultaneous mass uprising against all the existing governments. To further his ideas he founded a new organization called Young Italy, which was to enroll young patriots and inculcate in them Mazzini's ideas of liberty, democracy, and republicanism. Similar movements in other countries soon imitated Young Italy, and in 1834 Mazzini took the lead in founding a Young Europe. Mazzini was a gifted orator and idealistic writer, but his program had limited appeal for the illiterate masses and the timid middle class. He dissipated his energies and organization in ill-prepared and ineffective risings like those of the Carbonari. Although he played a leading role in the short-lived Roman Republic of 1849 and lived to witness the unification of

Italy in 1870, he died a broken man, his ideal of a democratic republic unfulfilled.

Vincenzo Gioberti (1801–1852), a Catholic priest, advocated a federation of Italian states under the presidency of the pope. The supporters of his proposal, known as the Neo-Guelphs from the name of the medieval papal party, took heart with the elevation to the papacy of Pius IX in 1846. The new pope was regarded as a liberal reformer, and his first actions seemed to support this view, but his experiences in the revolution of 1848 left him an embittered reactionary. Support for the Neo-Guelph position could still be found as late as 1859, but the events of the following year permanently alienated the papacy from the nationalist movement.

The final approach to the achievement of Italian unity, the one that ultimately triumphed, developed slowly and with less precisely defined methods. Championed by middle-class and aristocratic Piedmontese statesmen such as Cesare Balbo, Massimo d'Azeglio, and Camillo di Cavour, it regarded the Kingdom of Sardinia as the only really independent state in Italy and the one that would have to take the lead. For this to come about, several conditions had to be met. First, the government itself had to be turned into a progressive, constitutional monarchy. Second and even more important, Austria had to be expelled from Italy. Both of these conditions seemed to be far in the future until the dramatic changes of 1848.

THE REVOLUTIONS OF 1848

The revolutions of 1848 gave the supporters of all three proposed solutions an opportunity to achieve what they could. For a very brief interval the various partisans actually cooperated with one another. The results, mostly negative, revealed the military weakness and divided councils of the Italian states. The pope's reversion to absolutism and reaction disqualified him as a leader of the nationalist movement. The failure of the Roman and Venetian republics to obtain popular support throughout the country, despite their heroic resistance against overwhelming odds, eliminated republicanism as a catalyst of Italian nationalism. Only one bright spot remained: the almost accidental fashion in which Piedmont retained its liberal constitutional regime. The inexperience of Victor Emmanuel, the new king, together with the firmness of d'Azeglio and the constitutional party, resulted in the retention of the liberal *Statuto* (constitution) of 1848 with its bicameral legislature and responsible cabinet.

CAVOUR AND THE PROGRESS OF PIEDMONT

Of the three possible means to a united and independent Italy, only one remained. Even that one might have amounted to naught if it had not been for the remarkable ability of Camillo di Cavour (1810–1861). A nobleman with the outlook of a progressive bourgeois, Cavour pioneered scientific agriculture in Piedmont, promoted banks and railroads, and in 1847 founded the liberal newspaper *Il Risorgimento*. To practical experience he added years of study in history, politics, and economics. He traveled widely, admired the constitutional regimes of France and England, and was an enthusiastic if undogmatic exponent of the classical school of political economy. Although he remained in the background, he played an important role in projecting and retaining the *Statuto* in 1848 and 1849, and in 1850 he drafted the Siccardi laws, which drastically curbed the powers of the Church. Later in the same year he entered the cabinet as minister of agriculture and commerce, shortly taking on the portfolios of the navy and finance as well. In 1852 he became prime minister, a post that he held almost without interruption until his death in 1861.

From the beginning of his political career Cavour made it clear that he intended to make Piedmont economically progressive and politically liberal. He negotiated trade treaties, built railroads, introduced new industries, and carried out a comprehensive reform of the administrative and legal systems. Although these actions had little apparent connection with the movement for unification, Cavour stressed time and again that financial stability and economic progress were the two "indispensable conditions" if Piedmont was to assume the leadership of the Italian peninsula. To accomplish these goals he warmly welcomed French and British investors, entrepreneurs, and engineers, who contributed greatly to the remarkable economic progress of Piedmont in the 1850's.

Cavour had another reason for cultivating the friendship of France and Britain. He correctly read the lesson of 1848 and 1849, namely that Italy could never "make itself," according to the slogan of those years (*Italia farà da sé*), as long as Austria stood in the way. It is frequently stated that Cavour took Piedmont into the Crimean War in 1855 on the side of France and Britain for the express purpose of embarrassing Austria and raising the Italian question at the peace conference. Whether or not that was true, he certainly made the best of his opportunities, and although he did not succeed in placing Italy on the agenda of the conference itself, he did obtain a favorable hearing for the cause of Italian independence. Cavour would have liked to have had Britain as an ally in a military confrontation with Austria, but he realized that such an alliance was out of the question, not only because of the distance but also because Britain depended upon Austria to maintain the balance of power in central and eastern Europe. The most he could hope for from Britain was benevolent neutrality. For an active ally he had somehow to persuade the quixotic emperor of the French to come to his assistance.

Napoleon III was not adverse in principle to aiding Piedmont. As Corsicans, the Bonapartes had Italian blood in their veins. Napoleon I had catered to Italian nationalism, had created a mock kingdom of Italy, and had called his son the King of Rome. Napoleon III had carefully fostered the legend that his uncle was a champion of oppressed nationalities and, as a romantic revolutionary himself, had even been a Carbonaro and taken part in the Italian revolts of 1830 and 1831. Moreover, he felt that to overturn completely the hated settlement of 1815 he must humiliate Austria as he had already humiliated Russia. On the other hand, Napoleon recognized the risks involved. The French clerical party was certain to oppose any tampering with the temporal rule of the pope. Britain was likely to oppose a disturbance of the status quo. Defeat by Austria was at least a possibility. Prussia might come to the aid of Austria by invading across the Rhine. Finally, a strong, united Italy might not be satisfied with the role of client state to France.

At length, however, Cavour persuaded Napoleon. In July, 1858, the two statesmen met secretly like conspirators in the resort village of Plombières in eastern France. There they agreed provisionally upon the terms under which France would come to the aid of Piedmont. They set up a "defensive" military alliance, which was to drive the Austrians out of Italy if Austria could be provoked into attacking Piedmont. Lombardy and Venetia were to be added to the Kingdom of Sardinia; all the Italian states were to be grouped into a federation under the nominal suzerainty of the pope; and as the price of its participation, France was to receive Savoy and Nice. As a preliminary arrangement, Napoleon's aging, dissipated cousin, Prince Jerome Napoleon, was given the fifteen-year-old daughter of Victor Emmanuel, Clothilde, in marriage.

THE WAR OF 1859 AND THE ACHIEVEMENT
OF ITALIAN UNITY

By a combination of intrigues and Austrian blunders Cavour provoked Austria into invading Piedmont on April 29, 1859. The Austrian general delayed so long in pressing his attack that the French army, utilizing the recently completed railroads in France and Piedmont, had time to arrive on the scene. After a series of preliminary skirmishes, two bloody battles were fought at Magenta and Solferino in June and resulted in an Austrian retreat into the Quadrilateral, a group of fortresses in Venetia. At this point, on July 11, 1859, Napoleon III, who had personally led his troops into Italy, suddenly signed an armistice with the Austrian emperor at Villafranca without consulting his Italian allies. The terms of the armistice provided for Austria to cede Lombardy to France, which would then give it to Piedmont; Austria retained Venetia. It has been said that Napoleon negotiated the armistice because the carnage of battle had turned him against war. It is far more likely that his immediate motives were his fear that a prolonged siege of the Austrian forces might tempt Prussia to cause trouble on the Rhine, his increasing difficulties with the French

THE UNIFICATION OF ITALY

SWITZERLAND   AUSTRIAN EMPIRE

SAVOY

PIEDMONT • Milan   VENETIA
KINGDOM   LOMBARDY
OF   • Venice
SARDINIA   PARMA
                                              BOSNIA
TO FRANCE   Genoa • MODENA
IN 1860
         NICE   LUCCA

                                      MARCHES   HERZE-
                  Florence •   GOVINA
                  TUSCANY   PAPAL

                           UMBRIA
         CORSICA   STATES
         (TO FRANCE)   Rome •
            1768

                              • Naples

         SARDINIA
                              KINGDOM

                              OF

                              THE

Kingdom of   TWO
Sardinia, 1849   Palermo
                        •
United with Sardinia to   SICILIES
form Kingdom of Italy, 1861   SICILY

Added by 1870
                              0   150
                                   Miles

clerical party, and his fear of the growing force of Italian nationalism. In any event, Victor Emmanuel accepted the terms, but Cavour, who regarded Napoleon's action as a breach of trust, resigned his premiership in a rage.

Meanwhile events in central Italy had taken an unexpected turn beyond the control of the principal actors. Popular revolts broke out in Tuscany, Parma, Modena, and some of the States of the Church, where the insurgents drove out their former rulers and demanded union with Piedmont. In order to take advantage of this new development, Cavour returned as prime minister in January, 1860. In the Treaty of Turin on

March 24, 1860, he negotiated the annexation of the duchies, giving Napoleon Savoy and Nice as provided in the original agreement at Plombières. At this point another flamboyant character re-entered the scene. Garibaldi, who had played a prominent part in the military defense of the Roman Republic in 1849, began organizing his volunteer Red Shirt army in Genoa in order to take Nice, his birthplace, and hold it against the French. While formally denouncing Garibaldi, Cavour secretly persuaded him to move on Sicily instead, hoping to save himself embarrassment with the French and also to cause difficulty for the reactionary Francis II, king of Naples and Sicily.

Garibaldi landed in Sicily in May and succeeded beyond all expectation. Having no more than a thousand untrained volunteers but supported by popular uprisings against the hated Bourbons, he defeated an army of twenty thousand, conquered Sicily in less than three months, and crossed the Straits of Messina to the mainland south of Naples, which he took without a struggle. Garibaldi now planned to march on Rome and perhaps Venetia. At this Cavour became alarmed, fearing French intervention. He acted to head off this possibility by sending his own army across the remaining States of the Church, avoiding Rome itself, and thwarting Garibaldi's further progress. Plebiscites in Naples, Sicily, Umbria, and the Marches favored union with the north. On March 17, 1861, the first Italian parliament in history proclaimed the Kingdom of Italy, with Victor Emmanuel as king and a constitution based upon the Piedmontese *Statuto* of 1848.

Cavour, the architect and first prime minister of a united Italy, did not long enjoy his triumph. In June he died of exhaustion and overwork, leaving to his successors a host of unsolved problems. Prominent among them was the fate of Venetia, still governed by the Austrians, and the province of Rome, still ruled by the pope and occupied by the French. No less important were the financial and political problems of welding into a single nation the disparate parts of the Italian peninsula. Venetia fell to the Italians in 1866 in return for their participation in the Austro-Prussian War of that year. Rome was annexed after the defeat of Napoleon III in the Franco-Prussian War of 1870. The domestic political and financial problems, however, remained to plague succeeding governments in Italy throughout the remainder of the nineteenth and well into the twentieth century.

FOUNDATIONS OF GERMAN UNITY

Germany, like Italy, had not been a unified state in modern times. The Holy Roman Empire had grouped more than three hundred petty principalities into a loose confederation from the time of the Middle Ages, but the empire as such had no effective power. The French under Napoleon

The Italian Army Breaches the Walls of Rome, September 20, 1870
sketch from *The Illustrated London News*

"At 5 o'clock on the morning of the 20th instant, a cannonade was opened, two breaches were effected at half-past 8, and at 10 o'clock the Italian troops entered the city. . . . Those who reflect cannot but foresee that the establishment, in one and the same city, of a constitutional and excommunicated King by the side of an infallible Pope, of a Representative Parliament by the side of an absolute authority, of a liberty of the press and freedom of discussion by the side of the Inquisition . . . is giving a legal sanction to a state of things which can hardly be expected to work harmoniously, or, indeed, without creating very serious embarrassment, confusion, and misunderstandings." The British Representative in Rome to the Foreign Office, September 22, 1870, BRITISH AND FOREIGN STATE PAPERS, Vol. LXII.

overthrew the empire in 1806, incorporated the left bank of the Rhine and part of northwestern Germany into the French Empire, organized central Germany from the Baltic to the Alps as the Confederation of the Rhine under Napoleonic domination, pushed Austria to the east almost out of Germany, and left Prussia as a truncated buffer state in the shadow of Russia. Opposition to Napoleon and the French occasioned a national revival in Germany that in time focused on Prussia as the potential liberator of Germany. Many Germans hoped that the Congress of Vienna would create a unified German nation, but this aspiration ran counter to the interests of Austria and of Metternich, who feared a loss of Austrian influence in a unified Germany. Therefore the congress sanctioned the creation of the Germanic Confederation (*Deutscher Bund*) under the permanent presidency of Austria, which was composed of only thirty-eight in place of more than three hundred sovereign states but which in other respects was similar to the old Holy Roman Empire. (See p. 18.) The oppressive Metternichean system appeared to stifle German political development until 1848; but powerful forces were at work behind the drab façade.

INTELLECTUAL AND CULTURAL FOUNDATIONS

Romanticism greatly influenced German nationalism. Romantic poets, novelists, and composers stirred nationalist aspirations by evoking a heroic and largely nonexistent past and extolling the greatness of the German people — the *Volk*. Philosophers and literary critics attempted to show that Germanic culture was superior to others. Hegel sought to show by means of dialectical reasoning how unity might come out of disunity, how strength might result from weakness. Friedrich List emphasized the role of the state in economic affairs and tried to show that a unified nation could be created by appropriate economic policies.

Liberalism also influenced the idea of German nationalism. The west German bourgeoisie wanted both constitutional government and favorable economic policies. Since they had neither under the existing regime, they hoped for a unified national state that would provide both. Liberalism reached its height in the Frankfurt Assembly of 1848. The failure of that body to achieve unification or constitutional government resulted in a revulsion against liberalism, and many liberals turned in disillusion or frustration to the reactionary forces of militarism and power politics to achieve the goal of national unity.

ECONOMIC FOUNDATIONS

The German economy was poor and backward in the first half of the nineteenth century. Primarily agrarian, it had small concentrations of industry in the Rhineland, Saxony, Silesia, and the city of Berlin, but much of the industry was of the handicraft variety. Poor transportation and communications facilities held back economic development. Progress was further retarded by the numerous political divisions with their separate monetary systems, commercial systems, and other obstacles to commercial exchange. The revolutionary reforms introduced by the French under Napoleon, many of which were maintained after 1815, alleviated the situation, but they were insufficient in themselves and did not extend

THE UNIFICATION OF GERMANY

Legend:
- Prussia before 1865
- To Prussia after Austro-Prussian War, 1866
- States joining North German Confederation, 1866-1870
- Boundary of North German Confederation
- Included in German Empire in 1871

to the whole of Germany. Statesmen like Stein and Hardenberg, who came to power in Prussia after the disastrous defeat at Jena, recognized economic backwardness as one cause of their military and political weakness. They sought to reform Prussia as a means of strengthening the nation to resist the oppressor Napoleon. They abolished serfdom, relaxed restrictions on economic activity (of the Jews in particular), promoted freedom of occupational choice, and created so-called free trade in land by abolishing the distinctions between noble and non-noble land. These and other reforms promoted greater geographical and social mobility and led to a revival of economic activity.

The most important economic reform instigated by Prussian officials was the formation of the *Zollverein* (literally, tariff or customs union). They laid its foundations in 1818 by enacting a common tariff for all of Prussia, which after the Congress of Vienna had more internal tariff barriers than political subdivisions. Several smaller states, some of which were completely surrounded by Prussian territory, joined the Prussian tariff union, and in 1834 the adherence of the larger southern German states resulted in the creation of the Zollverein itself. Abolition of artificial restrictions on the movement of commodities by creation of a common German market, a forerunner of today's European Common Market, increased specialization and exchange and made a German economy possible before there was a German nation.

If the Zollverein made a unified economy possible, the railroads made it a fact. When railroads were introduced in the 1830's all the German states begain building them more or less simultaneously, some by means of private enterprise, others by state initiative. As a result, Germany made relatively rapid progress in railroad building — more so, for example, than France, which had a unified government but was divided over the question of state versus private enterprise. To construct the railroads also required the states to agree upon routes, rates, and other technical matters, resulting in greater interstate cooperation. The linking of east and west by the railroads facilitated an exchange of ideas as well as merchandise and broke down local loyalties in favor of a greater German nationalism.

Taking advantage of the favorable opportunities presented by the Zollverein and the railroads, German businessmen created a number of new banks and industrial enterprises, especially in the 1850's and 1860's. They engaged in Germany-wide as well as international activities. For example, the Darmstädter Bank was founded in 1853 in the sleepy provincial capital of the small state of Hesse-Darmstadt, just south of Frankfurt, because its founders could not secure a charter from either the free city of Frankfurt or the Prussian authorities in Cologne, the two economic centers of western Germany. Nevertheless, it operated on a much wider stage than the petty state from which it had received its charter. It raised money in Paris and promoted industry — iron and steel mills, coal mines, and railroads — throughout Germany. Other banks founded on its model did likewise. Their activities contributed to the establishment of economic unification well in advance of political unity.

PRUSSIAN POLICY AND THE RISE OF BISMARCK

By the middle of the nineteenth century the way had been prepared for the eventual unification of Germany. Two large questions remained: Who would bring it about? What form would it take? The questions were essentially political, and they had several possible solutions. The liberal solution called for a centralized, parliamentary government, which might be either republican or monarchic. It had been attempted by the Frankfurt Assembly of 1848 and 1849 but had been defeated by the resurgence of conservatism.

The Prussian king, who was unwilling to accept the crown from the Frankfurt Assembly, had his own ideas for uniting Germany under Prussian hegemony. His plan, which resembled the *Kleindeutsch* or little Germany proposal, called for a federal union of the German states (except

Austria) under his presidency as king of Prussia. This proposal was put forward in 1849, and a draft constitution was ratified by representatives of a number of the smaller states at Erfurt in March, 1850. Immediately it encountered opposition from Austria, which reconstituted the Diet of the old Germanic Confederation and vied for the adherence of the smaller states. War between Prussia and Austria appeared imminent. Since the south German states favored the looser confederation projected by Austria, and the Russian tsar was threatening to take the side of Austria, the Prussian king sent his principal minister to Olmütz in November, 1850, to negotiate a strategic withdrawal. At the so-called humiliation of Olmütz the Prussians agreed to dissolve the Erfurt Union and recognize the reestablished Germanic Confederation under the presidency of Austria. Thus the situation that had existed before 1848 was substantially reestablished, and the question of further unification seemed to be postponed indefinitely.

The general political reaction that took place throughout Europe after 1848 was particularly marked in Prussia. Although the Prussian king had granted an apparently democratic constitution to his subjects after the revolution of 1848, he continued to exercise a large measure of autocratic authority. Instead of evolving in a liberal sense, as did the authoritarian government of Napoleon III, the Prussian constitutional system actually became more reactionary.

In 1857 Frederick William IV, who had always been mentally unstable, went insane. His brother, Prince William, became regent in 1858 and ascended the throne in 1861. By training a professional soldier, William I had the military man's devotion to duty but also his lack of understanding of and impatience with the intricacies of politics and civilian government. Austria's defeat in the War of 1859 provided Prussia with an opportunity to take a larger role in German affairs, but it was not prepared either diplomatically or militarily to assert itself vigorously. To remedy the latter deficiency, William's newly appointed minister of war, General von Roon, and the chief of the general staff, General von Moltke, undertook to modernize and enlarge the Prussian army. In doing so, they ran into opposition from liberals in the *Landtag* (lower house of Parliament), who feared the army as an instrument of reaction and oppression and who had no desire to pay the increased taxes that the army reforms would require. For more than two years they held the government at an impasse, refusing to vote the needed credits. At length in 1862, when William was on the point of abdication, von Roon persuaded him to bring Otto von Bismarck into the government.

Bismarck was a Junker, one of the aristocratic landowners from the area east of the Elbe River who formed the backbone of the Prussian officer corps and civil service. During the Frankfurt Assembly of 1848 he conceived a strong dislike for the parliamentary maneuvering of the bourgeois liberals. From 1851 to 1859 he served as Prussia's representative at the Diet of the Germanic Confederation, where he took the measure of Austrian diplomacy. In 1859 he went to St. Petersburg as ambassador to the tsar, and in 1862 he served briefly as ambassador to France before being recalled to become minister-president (prime minister) of the Prussian cabinet. An outspoken conservative and a man of indomitable will, Bismarck was also a master practitioner of *Realpolitik,* the politics of realism; indeed, it was he who gave currency to the word. Speaking to a committee of the Prussian Diet, he furnished the key to his personality and policy: "The great questions of the day will not be decided by speeches and majority votes — that was the mistake of 1848 and 1849 — but by blood and iron." When the Diet again refused to vote the necessary taxes, Bismarck simply ignored it and proceeded to collect and spend the money in defiance of the parliamentarians.

Bismarck was not a conventional German nationalist but a Prussian patriot. Far from dreaming of a greater German fatherland, he merely wanted to enhance the prestige and power of Prussia. To do so, he realized that he would have to diminish the influence of Austria and win the support of the smaller German states. He therefore took every opportunity to prick Austrian sensibilities and at the same time shrewdly courted the favor of those (including many liberals) who desired a united Germany. A prize occasion for doing both was the revival of the Danish question, which had so disastrously disrupted the German liberal movement in 1848.

THE DANISH WAR OF 1864

The duchies of Schleswig and Holstein belonged to the king of Denmark as his personal hereditary possessions, although both were populated largely by Germans and Holstein was a member of the Germanic Confederation. An attempt by the Danish king to incorporate Schleswig with Denmark and to impose a new charter on Holstein aroused German nationalists and led to a call for intervention by the federal Diet. Bismarck did not feel strong enough to act alone and persuaded Austria to join Prussia in an invasion of the duchies. The war, which ended quickly in the complete defeat of Denmark, furthered Bismarck's aims in three main ways. First, it gave the reformed Prussian army a baptism of fire, in which it proved itself an efficient fighting force. Second, it enhanced the prestige of Prussia with German nationalists. Third, it provided abundant opportunities for Prussia to pick further quarrels with Austria. In the Treaty of Vienna of 1864 Denmark ceded the disputed duchies to Austria and Prussia jointly. Under the Convention of Gastein in the following year the two powers agreed to maintain joint sovereignty, but Prussia was to occupy and administer Schleswig, whereas Austria was to do the same with Holstein. Thus, Austria-dominated Holstein became virtually an enclave in Prussian territory, with Vienna hundreds of miles away.

Meanwhile, Bismarck had made sure of his international position. He won the friendship of the Russian tsar by supporting the latter's suppression of the Polish rebellion of 1863. In 1865 Bismarck visited Napoleon III and hinted at possible French territorial gains in the Rhineland in the event of a war between Prussia and Austria in which the former was victorious. Finally in April, 1866, Prussia concluded an alliance with Italy, to take effect in case of war with Austria within three months; the prize for Italy was to be the cession of Venetia. The stage was now set. All that remained was to provoke Austria into war.

THE AUSTRO-PRUSSIAN WAR OF 1866

The provocation was easily arranged as a result of the difficulties in Schleswig and Holstein. Bismarck ordered Prussian troops into Holstein, and Austria persuaded the Diet of Confederation to declare Prussia an aggressor. Bismarck thereupon announced that the federal constitution had been violated and declared the Confederation dissolved. Since most of the German states took the side of Austria, the odds appeared heavily weighted against Prussia. But Prussia was prepared, and the others were not. Prussia's modernized army used new breech-loading rifles, called needle guns because the firing pin had a long needlelike point, whereas Austrian troops still relied on old-fashioned muzzle-loading muskets. The German general staff made effective use of railroads and the telegraph for quick deployment of troops. The campaign, known as the Seven Weeks' War, was a forerunner of the German blitzkriegs (lightning wars) of World War II. The federal Diet voted condemnation of Prussia on June 14, 1866. Before the end of June Prussian troops had overrun Hanover, Austria's chief northern ally, and turned against the south German states. The major campaign took place in Bohemia between Austria and Prussia. Using the railroads, three separate Prussian armies converged on the main concentration of Austrian troops, and on July 3 at Königgrätz (Sadowa) they won a crushing victory.

This sudden outcome surprised all Europe. Napoleon, who had expected a long war from which France would benefit, offered his services as mediator, but Bismarck outmaneuvered him. Although William I and the Prussian general staff favored marching to Vienna, Bismarck insisted on a quick armistice and lenient treatment for Austria, both to forestall the possibility of French intervention and to soothe injured Austrian pride. Austria had to give up Venetia to Prussia's ally Italy (which ironically had been defeated on both land and sea) and pay an indemnity to Prussia, but otherwise it suffered no territorial losses. Prussia incorporated Hanover, Hesse-Cassel, Nassau, and Frankfurt in addition to Schleswig and Holstein, and received a free hand to reorganize the remainder of the north German states. These provisions were contained in the Treaty of Prague, August 23, 1866.

Triumph in the field vindicated Bismarck's policy on the domestic front. In a patriotic frenzy the Prussian Diet voted overwhelmingly to legalize the government's past expenditures on the army and to allow increased funds for the future. The action split the Prussian liberals for two generations, with the majority supporting Bismarck in the newly formed National Liberal party and condemning the minority of Progressives to increasingly ineffectual protest. German liberalism, a fragile flower at best, virtually withered on the stem.

THE CLASH OF POWER
IN NORTH AMERICA

The willingness to use force in the settlement of disputes did not pertain to Europe alone. The United States had led the way in its war of conquest against Mexico from 1846 to 1848. In 1854 the American ministers to the principal European nations met in Ostend, Belgium, and declared that if Spain refused to sell Cuba, the United States would be justified in taking it by force. The Ostend Manifesto startled Europeans and also many Americans, for slavery was practiced in Cuba as well as in the southern states, and most northerners had no wish to see slavery extended. This fact made the Ostend Manifesto meaningless, and foreshadowed the impending struggle between slave states and free states in the American Civil War.

CIVIL WAR IN THE UNITED STATES

The causes of the Civil War were manifold and complex. They were rooted in the divergent economic and social development of North and South. Slavery was doomed to extinction in the United States until Eli Whitney's invention of the cotton gin and the burgeoning cotton industry in England gave it new life. Southern plantation owners found a buoyant and expanding market for cotton overseas, and the spread of cotton culture in the Gulf coastal plain entailed the spread of slavery. The North, meanwhile, began to develop manufacturing industry based on free labor.

The settlement of the Ohio Valley and the Old Northwest, chiefly by migrants from the Northeast, did not involve the question of slavery. Expansion into the trans-Mississippi West, however, brought the rival social systems into direct competition. In the Missouri Compromise of 1820 Missouri was admitted without restrictions as to slavery, but thereafter all portions of the Louisiana Purchase north of latitude 36°30′ (the southern boundary of Missouri) were to be free of slavery. The acquisition of Texas and the New Mexico territory and the admission of California to the Union in 1850 again raised the question of the extension of slavery. The Kansas-Nebraska Act of 1854, which established the doctrine of popular sovereignty, and the decision of the Supreme Court in the Dred Scott case in 1857, which declared the Missouri Compromise unconstitutional, further inflamed the issue. It came to a head in the presidential election of 1860.

The Republicans nominated Abraham Lincoln and campaigned on a platform opposing the extension of slavery and favoring a homestead law and a protective tariff, all of which were anathema to the South. Lincoln did not obtain a single electoral vote in the slave-holding states; but since the Democratic party split into two factions, North and South, and the border states formed yet another party, the Constitutional Union party, a Republican victory was assured. South Carolina seceded from the Union immediately after the election. By the time Lincoln assumed office, a number of other southern states had also seceded and had joined in the Confederate States of America. When the commander of the federal garrison of Fort Sumter in the Charleston harbor refused to surrender it to South Carolina in April, 1861, a Confederate army bombarded it. The Civil War had begun.

The North had an enormous advantage over the South with more than twice the population, a more highly developed transportation system, flourishing manufacturing industries, organized military forces, and an established civil administration. Nevertheless, Northern expectations of a quick victory were disappointed by inadequate planning, military blunders, and determined Southern resistance. The South was fortunate in obtaining as commander in chief of its forces General Robert E. Lee, a Virginian who resigned his commission in the Union Army to accept the position. The North was plagued by a succession of incompetent or politically minded generals until 1864, when Lincoln selected Ulysses S. Grant as commander in chief on the basis of his brilliant campaigns in the Mississippi Valley. By this time the South was approaching complete exhaustion. The Union blockade cut off its exports of cotton and imports of war supplies, while campaigns in the West split off Texas, Louisiana, and Arkansas and hemmed in the remaining Southern states. Grant finally surrounded the main Confederate army in Virginia, and Lee surrendered at Appomattox Courthouse on April 9, 1865.

The assassination of Lincoln just five days after Lee's surrender and the disputes between Congress and Lincoln's successor, Andrew Johnson, cost the nation the opportunity for a rapid and equitable reconciliation of North and South. Lincoln had proclaimed the emancipation of slaves on January 1, 1863, which was subsequently ratified by the Thirteenth Amendment to the Constitution. Determined to press its advantage in controlling the future development of the nation, the radical Republican majority in Congress imposed harsh measures of reconstruction on the vanquished southern states, which poisoned relations between North and South and retarded the political, social, and economic development of the latter for many years.

Westward expansion continued during and after the war years. The first transcontinental railroad was chartered by Congress with liberal grants of federal land in 1862 and was completed in 1869. The rapid spread of settlement that ensued brought renewed conflicts with the Indians, who were subdued by federal troops and placed on reservations.

INTERVENTION IN MEXICO

Shortly before the American Civil War another civil war, the equivalent of a social revolution, broke out in Mexico. The liberal faction under Benito Juarez (1806–1872) overthrew the dictator Santa Anna and undertook a large program of political, social, and religious reform. Napoleon III, seeking clerical support at home, new glory for the empire, and reconciliation with Austria over its loss of Lombardy, sent a French expeditionary force to aid the conservative opponents of Juarez and induced Maximilian of Austria, former viceroy of the Lombard-Venetian kingdom, to accept the throne of a Mexican empire under French protection. After a prolonged campaign in 1863 French forces occupied Mexico City, where Maximilian took up residence in the following year. Although the French action clearly violated the Monroe Doctrine, the United States's involvement in its own civil war prevented any immediate active response. The United States had earlier recognized the Juarez government, however, and as soon as circumstances permitted, it began to make energetic protests to France. Because of his precarious position in Europe after the Austro-Prussian War, Napoleon decided to withdraw in 1867. Juarez captured and executed Maximilian shortly afterward, thus ending Europe's last serious attempt at armed intervention in the New World.

CONFEDERATION IN CANADA

The Union Act of 1840, which united Upper and Lower Canada (see p. 554), did not fully meet the need for self-government. Difficulties and disputes over border questions continued to flare between the French-speaking and British inhabitants of Canada, between Canada and Britain, between Canada and the United States, and between Britain and the United States. Fortunately they were all settled without recourse to arms. In 1867 the British North American Act gave complete self-government to Canada. It provided for a federation of the provinces of Quebec, Ontario, New Brunswick, and Nova Scotia in the Dominion of Canada. Each province retained its provincial government with certain specified rights. With the example of the United States before it, however, the act provided that all rights not specifically conferred upon the provinces remained with the Dominion government. The latter consisted of a bicameral parliament, a responsible cabinet, and a governor-general with only nominal powers as representative of the British crown. In 1869 the Dominion purchased the Northwest Territories from the Hudson's Bay Company, and in subsequent years it admitted new provinces on a basis of equality with the old. By achieving consolidation and expansion without resorting to force, Canada was an exception to the rule.

THE WATERSHED OF 1867–1871

The changes in the map and temper of Europe after 1848 seemed to have no clearly defined pattern or direction before 1866. Until then they were subject to reversal. The outcome of the Austro-Prussian War, however, had a definitive stamp. In the next four years further major changes fixed the framework of European politics and diplomacy until 1914.

One consequence of the Austro-Prussian War was a fundamental reorganization of the Austrian Empire, known thereafter as the Austro-Hungarian Empire or Dual Monarchy. Another was the creation of the North German Confederation, the forerunner of a larger German Empire, under the domination of Bismarck and Prussia. Italy, enlarged by the addition of Venetia, now needed only Rome to complete its unification. Bismarck's skillful diplomacy and Napoleon's own foreign policy blunders (such as the ill-advised campaign in Mexico) served to isolate France diplomatically. Although Britain held aloof from European affairs, it, too, witnessed important domestic changes in the direction of greater democratization. The smaller states also underwent changes, and some became pawns in the game of great power politics.

THE SPANISH REVOLUTION OF 1868

After the death of Ferdinand VII in 1833 the nominal Spanish ruler was his daughter, Isabella II. (See p. 566.) Actually, control of the government alternated between rival and shifting alliances of ambitious generals and corrupt politicians. Isabella's own behavior contributed to the scandalous reputation of the court and the discredit of the government. Although a few railroads were built after 1848 and commerce and industry picked up somewhat through the initiative of foreign entrepreneurs, the lot of the people remained as miserable as ever. At length, in 1868, a rising of disaffected army officers led by General Juan Prim won the support of the masses, and the queen fled the country. A provisional government established universal manhood suffrage, promulgated a liberal constitution, and began a long and futile search for a suitable constitutional monarch. In the process the Spanish inadvertently provided an incident that served as one of the causes of the Franco-Prussian War. At the end of 1870 the Spanish persuaded Amadeo I, younger son of

Victor Emmanuel of Italy, to accept the throne. After two years of well-intentioned but continually frustrated struggles, Amadeo abdicated in disgust and returned to Italy, leaving the Spanish situation more confused than ever. After a brief attempt at republican government, followed by further civil wars, a conservative coup d'état in 1874 reestablished the Bourbon monarchy in the person of Isabella's son, Alfonso XII.

THE NORTH GERMAN CONFEDERATION

Meanwhile Bismarck undertook his reorganization of northern Germany. Since Prussia had already absorbed the largest of the other north German states except Saxony, the task was relatively simple. The constitution of 1867, which later served as the basis of the constitution of the German Empire, provided that the presidency of the confederation should be hereditary with the king of Prussia. The only other constitutional official was the chancellor (Bismarck), responsible to the king alone. To give the new regime the trappings of democracy Bismarck allowed a legislature, the *Reichstag,* elected by universal suffrage but with strictly limited powers. As a further check on the popular will the constitution provided for a kind of upper chamber, the *Bundesrat,* composed of the personal representatives of the various sovereign princes, but with their representation arranged in such a way that Prussia could always command a majority. The twenty-two component states retained autonomy in domestic matters, but foreign relations and military affairs were the exclusive province of the king acting through his chancellor.

By this time Bismarck was determined to unify Germany completely — excluding Austria — under Prussian auspices. Constitutionally the incorporation of the four states south of the Main River seemed to be an easy matter, since the framework already existed, but politically it was necessary to overcome the antipathy of the Catholic populations of southern Germany to Protestant Prussia, and to balk Napoleon's certain opposition to a strong, united Germany. The Danish War, by putting Prussia in the role of protector of German interests, helped break down southern as well as northern provincialism. This work was continued by the rabidly patriotic *Nationalverein* (National Society). The Austrian War, by excluding Austria from participation in German affairs, forced the southern states into an unwilling alliance with Prussia and left them with no other champion but France. Bismarck realized that the final resolution of the question would depend upon a successful war with France.

BISMARCK AND NAPOLEON

Bismarck had already made use of Napoleon's susceptibility to flattery and vague promises at the time of the Austro-Prussian War, when he dropped hints about allowing France "compensation" in the form of an extension of the French borders in the Rhineland. The sudden conclusion of the war and Bismarck's skillful maneuvering deprived Napoleon of any gain. He subsequently sought to salve his own and France's injured pride by annexing Luxembourg and Belgium. In both cases his diplomatic blunders and Bismarck's skill resulted in further humiliation.

Napoleon no less than Bismarck now regarded war as inevitable. Feverishly he sought to build alliances, but to no avail. Austria was clearly in no position to take the field again so soon; in any case, the Hungarians, who now shared power in the empire, would hear none of it. Italy was equally beholden to France and Prussia for previous gains but the French alone stood in the way of complete unification by their continued occupation of Rome. Bismarck also assured himself of the good will of Russia, and by communicating word of Napoleon's designs on Belgium to Britain, he effectively forestalled any sympathy for France in that quarter.

At this point the vacant Spanish throne played a part in Franco-Prussian relations. Prince Leopold of Hohenzollern-Sigmaringen, a relative of King William of Prussia, had been offered the Spanish crown but refused it on William's advice in deference to the sensibilities of Napoleon. In the spring of 1870 Bismarck engineered a renewal of the offer for the express purpose of embarrassing France. When news of the offer leaked out, the new and inexperienced French cabinet of the parliamentary empire reacted violently and demanded an immediate withdrawal of the prince's candidacy. Not content with obtaining this, the French sought a formal letter of apology from the Prussian king to Napoleon. The French ambassador presented the request to King William at the resort town of Ems. The king refused politely but firmly and sent Bismarck in Berlin a telegram detailing the affair. Eager to provoke France, Bismarck edited the telegram so as to make it appear to be a new insult to France and leaked it to the press.

THE FRANCO-PRUSSIAN WAR

Immediately upon publication of the famous "Ems dispatch," the French government decided upon war. It made a formal declaration on July 19, 1870. Napoleon was beset by doubt and hesitation, but his cabinet and the French populace in general went to war almost joyfully, expecting an easy victory. They did not realize the extent of inefficiency and demoralization in the French high command, nor did they take account of the fact that the Prussian general staff, with the Danish and Austrian experience behind it, had been planning this war for almost three years.

Three German armies invaded France simultaneously over the northeastern frontier and quickly got behind the main French forces, cutting their supply lines. They besieged one large French army in the fortress of Metz and surrounded another at Sedan near the Belgian frontier. Napoleon, physically ill and emotionally disturbed, had nevertheless insisted

Radio Times Hulton Picture Library

The Proclamation of the Kaiser, by Anton von Werner
Versailles, January 18, 1871, after the defeat of France

> *"I was convinced that the gulf which in the course of history had opened between north and south in our country because of differences in ways of life and dynastic and tribal loyalties could not be more effectively bridged than through a common national war against the traditionally aggressive neighbor."*
> Bismarck quoted in O. Pflanze, BISMARCK AND THE DEVELOPMENT OF GERMANY (Princeton, 1963).

on leading personally the army at Sedan. On September 2, 1870, after two days of merciless bombardment, Napoleon capitulated with 100,000 men.

When news of the event reached Paris, mobs from the streets invaded the legislature and demanded the overthrow of the empire. In accordance with well-established ritual a provisional government was formed. It proclaimed the Third Republic at the Paris city hall on September 4, 1870. Called the "Government of National Defense," it fought valiantly but in a hopeless cause. Most of the standing army surrendered meekly, and the raw recruits and untrained officers who fought on were no match for the Prussian army. Paris itself, which had been besieged by two Prussian armies since mid-September, surrendered on January 28, 1871, by which time resistance in the provinces had also collapsed. The Treaty of Frankfurt of May 10, 1871, required the French to give up Alsace and a part of

Lorraine, pay an indemnity of five billion francs, and maintain a German army of occupation until the indemnity was acquitted.

In the meantime Bismarck had carried out his aim of making the Prussian king ruler of all Germany. The French declaration of war forced the southern German states to fight on the side of Prussia, and the success of German arms in the field stimulated a popular demand for the union of northern and southern Germany. Bismarck negotiated with the German princes for them to proclaim William I emperor of Germany on January 18, 1871. With a keen but ironic sense of history, Bismarck staged this performance in the famous Hall of Mirrors in the palace at Versailles, where in former times other German princes had paid court to Louis XIV of France.

THE TRIUMPH OF REALPOLITIK

In less than two decades the map of central Europe had been redrawn almost completely. In France an empire rose and fell, and as it fell, a new one arose in united Germany. Italy took advantage of the withdrawal of French troops from Rome to replace them with its own and make Rome the capital of united Italy. The Austrians, driven from Germany and forced to share their power with the proud Magyars of Hungary, looked southeastward to the Balkans for further expansion. All these changes had been achieved by Realpolitik and the naked use of force, aided by the inflamed passions of popular nationalism.

In some respects the new balance of power was better than the old. For more than forty years it maintained the peace (except for minor peripheral conflicts), the longest period of general peace in European history. It was a period of unparalleled economic prosperity and apparent social progress. Yet the foundations of the new era contained a fatal defect. It had been created by force, and it had to be maintained by force; it was the era of the "armed peace." Eventually the foundations cracked, and Europe experienced a new and greater holocaust.

THE SPREAD OF
MODERN INDUSTRY
CHAPTER TWENTY-SEVEN

A quarter century elapsed between the Crystal Palace Exhibition in London in 1851, the first international industrial fair, and the Philadelphia Centennial Exposition in 1876, America's first "world's fair." During that period several nations joined Britain in the ranks of industrial societies. The Philadelphia event constituted a sort of declaration of American industrial independence from Britain a century after political independence, although the United States continued to import British capital. French industrialization, which made slow progress before 1848, speeded up dramatically under the Second Empire. Belgium, which began its rapid industrialization in the 1830's soon after winning political independence, was by 1870 the most highly industrialized nation on the Continent. Germany, Switzerland, and the Netherlands had all begun the process of industrialization, and in a few other countries signs of strain in the traditional agrarian framework of society were beginning to show. Nevertheless, Britain remained far and away the world's leading industrial nation.

By the beginning of the twentieth century the picture had changed radically. The United States, Germany, and France had all risen to challenge and in some cases to surpass British supremacy. The smaller nations of western Europe — the Scandinavian countries as well as Switzerland and the Low Countries — had modern progressive industries. In eastern Europe even autocratic Russia entered upon a sort of industrial revolution under tsarist auspices. Everywhere in Europe the old traditional society was giving way to the new social forces unleashed by modern industry.

In most respects the process of industrialization in the second half of the nineteenth century represented an intensification and geographical diffusion of earlier tendencies and produced similar consequences. At the same time it had certain distinctive characteristics that have led some historians to call it the "new industrialism."

TECHNOLOGICAL BASES OF THE NEW INDUSTRIALISM

Industrialization before 1850 was confined chiefly to coal, iron, and textiles, with steam engines supplying the motive power. Factory methods and new technologies gradually penetrated to other industries, but even in Britain much so-called manufacturing still took place under the putting-out (domestic) system or in small workshops with little or no mechanical power. As technology became increasingly scientific in the second half of the century — that is, based upon the findings as well as the methods of science — the flow of technical innovations quickened dramatically. New industries arose, existing industries adopted new techniques, the factory system spread, and an ever-larger proportion of an increasing population became involved in the industrial system.

CHEAP STEEL

Among the most important if not most dramatic technological innovations of the second half of the century were new methods for making steel. Actually a special variety of iron, steel had been made for many centuries but in small quantities at high cost. As a result, its use was limited to such quality products as watch springs, surgical instruments, and fine cutlery. In 1856 Henry Bessemer, an English inventor, announced a new method for producing steel directly from molten iron, eliminating the puddling process and yielding a product harder and more durable than puddled iron. The output of Bessemer steel increased rapidly and soon displaced ordinary iron in a variety of uses. The Bessemer process did not always yield a uniformly high grade of steel, however, and could not be used with phosphorus-bearing iron ores. To remedy the former defect a father-and-son team of French metallurgists, Pierre and Émile Martin, and the Siemens brothers, Ernst in Germany and William in England, developed in the 1860's the "open hearth," or Siemens-Martin, furnace. In 1878 two English cousins, Thomas and Gilchrist, patented a process to permit the use of the plentiful phosphorus-bearing iron ores. As a result of these and other innovations, the annual world production of steel rose from less than half a million tons in 1865 to more than fifty million tons on the eve of World War I.

The expansion of the steel industry had a profound impact on other industries, both those that supplied the steel industry (such as coal) and those that used steel. Steel rails for railroads lasted longer and provided greater safety than iron ones. Steel plates for shipbuilding resulted in

H.M.S. *Dreadnaught*

> *"From a very early period I had become deeply impressed with the importance*
> *of the application of my new steel to shipbuilding, and my first impulse was*
> *naturally to try and force my own conviction on the British Admiralty, and*
> *induce them to employ it in the construction of ships of war. But the*
> *remembrance of my treatment at Woolich [army arsenal] came upon me as a*
> *warning. . . . This experience determined me not to be foiled a second time by*
> *attempting to convince the "How-not-to-do-it" Government official. I therefore*
> *preferred to await the more certain and reliable action of mercantile instinct.*
> *Private shipbuilders, I had no doubt, would soon find out the merits of steel,*
> *and feel a personal interest in its adoption."* SIR HENRY BESSEMER, F.R.S. AN
> AUTOBIOGRAPHY (London, 1905).

larger, lighter, faster ships and could also be used as heavy armor for
warships. The use of steel beams and girders made it possible to build
skyscrapers and a variety of other structures. Steel replaced iron and wood
in tools, toys, and hundreds of other products ranging from steam engines
to hairpins.

NEW ENERGY SOURCES AND PRIME MOVERS

Steam remained the major source of mechanical energy throughout the
nineteenth century, but new forms of power developed to supplement and

in some cases to replace it. The steam engine itself underwent further developments, which made it a more powerful and efficient prime mover. In 1884 Charles Parsons, a British engineer, patented the steam turbine, which found its principal uses in driving ocean liners and warships and in generating electricity. The early reciprocating steam engines built by James Watt developed between 10 and 25 horsepower; in the 1860's large compound marine engines produced more than 1,000 horsepower; in the early twentieth century huge steam turbines could generate more than 100,000 horsepower.

The steam turbine applied the expansive powers of steam to the principle of the hydraulic turbine, which had been perfected by French engineers in the 1820's and 1830's. The hydraulic turbine had first been used in various milling operations as a more efficient substitute for its ancestor, the old-fashioned water wheel. It soon came to have a more exalted use in the production of electricity. The possibility of generating electricity mechanically had been known since the decisive experiments of Faraday with electromagnetism in 1831 (see p. 648), but no economically feasible means of generating power in large quantities had been discovered. In 1873 a paper maker in southeastern France attached his turbine, which drew water from the Alps, to a dynamo for the production of electricity. This apparently simple innovation had important long-range consequences, for it enabled regions poor in coal but rich in waterpower to supply their own energy requirements. The invention of the Parsons steam turbine in the following decade freed the generation of electricity from waterpower sites and shifted the energy balance back toward coal and steam, which remain today the most important sources of electrical energy. Nevertheless, the development of hydroelectric power became tremendously important for countries previously in the backwaters of industrial development, such as Norway, Sweden, Switzerland, and Italy.

Contemporaneously a host of practical applications for electricity were developed. Electricity had been used in the new electroplating industry and in telegraphy from the 1840's. Lighthouses began to utilize electric arc lamps in the late 1850's, and by the 1870's they were being used in a number of factories, stores, theaters, and public buildings. The perfection of the incandescent electric lamp between 1878 and 1880 almost simultaneously by Joseph Swan in England and Thomas Edison in the United States made arc lighting obsolete and inaugurated a boom in the electrical industry. For several decades electricity competed hotly with two other recently perfected illuminants, coal gas and kerosene.

Electricity had many uses other than illumination. It is one of the most versatile sources of power available to man. In 1879, the same year that Edison patented his electric lamp, another of the Siemens brothers invented the electric streetcar, which had revolutionary consequences for mass transportation in the burgeoning metropolises of the time. Within a few years electric motors had found dozens of industrial applications, and inventors were even beginning to think of household appliances.

Petroleum is another major energy source that came into prominence in the second half of the nineteenth century. Although it was known and used earlier through accidental discoveries, its commercial exploitation began with the drilling of Drake's well at Titusville, Pennsylvania, in 1859. Like electricity, liquid petroleum and its byproduct, natural gas, were at first used primarily as illuminants. Concurrently with their growth in production, several French and German inventors perfected the internal combustion engine. By 1900 a variety of such engines were available, most of which used as fuel one of the several distillates of liquid petroleum, such as gasoline or diesel oil. By far the most important use for the internal combustion engine was in light transport facilities, such as automobiles, motor trucks, and busses, but it also had industrial applications and made possible the development of the airplane in the twentieth century. Apart from its use in engines, petroleum competed with traditional energy sources in household and industrial heating.

THE APPLICATION OF SCIENCE

All of these developments relied much more than earlier technological innovations on the application of science to industrial processes. The electrical industry in particular required a high degree of scientific knowledge and training. In other industries scientific advance became more and more the prerequisite of technological advance.

The science of chemistry proved especially prolific in giving birth to new products and processes. It had already created artificial soda, sulfuric acid, chlorine, and a number of other heavy chemicals of particular importance in the textile industry. While seeking a synthetic substitute for quinine in 1856, William Perkin, an English chemist, accidentally synthesized mauve, a highly prized purple dye. This was the beginning of the synthetic dyestuffs industry, which within two decades had practically driven natural dyestuffs off the market. Synthetic dyestuffs proved to be the opening wedge of a much larger complex of organic chemical industries, whose output included such diverse products as drugs and pharmaceuticals, explosives, photographic reagents, and synthetic fibers. Coal tar, a byproduct of the coking process previously regarded as a costly nuisance, served as the principal raw material for these industries, thus turning a bane into a blessing.

Chemistry also played a vital role in metallurgy. In the early nineteenth century the only economically important metals were those known from antiquity: iron, copper, lead, zinc, tin, mercury, gold, and silver. After the chemical revolution associated with Antoine Lavoisier, the great French chemist of the eighteenth century, many new metals including aluminum, nickel, magnesium, and chromium were discovered. In addition to discovering them, scientists and industrialists found uses for these new metals and devise economical methods of producing them. One major use was in making alloys, a mixture of two or more metals that has characteristics different from those of its components. Brass and bronze are examples of natural alloys (which occur in nature). Steel itself is actually an alloy of iron with a small amount of carbon and sometimes other metals. In the second half of the nineteenth century metallurgists devised many special "alloy steels" by adding small amounts of manganese, tungsten, vanadium, etc., to impart specially desired qualities to ordinary steel. They also developed a number of nonferrous alloys.

Chemistry likewise came to the aid of such old, established industries as food processing and preservation. Canning and artificial refrigeration produced a revolution in dietary habits and, by permitting the importation of otherwise perishable foodstuffs from the New World and Australia, allowed Europe's population to grow far beyond what its own agricultural resources would support. At the same time the scientific study of the soil that was initiated in Germany in the 1840's led to greatly improved agricultural practices and the introduction of artificial fertilizers. Scientific agriculture developed along with scientific industry.

THE REVOLUTION IN COMMUNICATIONS

The nineteenth century witnessed a marked acceleration in the tempo of human life resulting from major innovations in the field of communications. The railroad and steamship inaugurated the process. Their major contribution was the increased volume and reduced cost of transportation. The most important innovation affecting the speed of communications was the electric telegraph, developed to a practical stage in the 1840's. By 1850 most major cities of Europe had been linked by telegraph wires, and in 1851 the first successful submarine telegraph cable was laid under the English Channel. In 1866, after ten years of trying and several failures, Cyrus W. Field succeeded in laying a telegraph cable under the North Atlantic Ocean, providing nearly instantaneous communication between Europe and North America. The telephone, patented by Alexander Graham Bell in 1876, made distant communication even more personal, but its principal use was in facilitating local communications.

In the area of mass communications improvements in printing and typesetting culminated in the Linotype machine, invented by the German-American Ottmar Mergenthaler in 1885, further extending the influence of the daily newspaper. One of America's great inventive geniuses, Thomas Edison, invented both the phonograph (1877) and the motion picture camera (1887). The Italian inventor Guglielmo Marconi invented wireless telegraphy or radio in 1895. As early as 1901 a wireless message was transmitted across the Atlantic, and by the time of the *Titanic* disaster in 1912 radio had come to play a significant role in ocean navigation. With the exception of mechanical typesetting, however, these innovations did not achieve commercial importance until after World War I. Their true significance was more cultural than economic. In the field of business communications the invention of the typewriter (Scholes patent, 1868; "Model I Remington," 1874) and other rudimentary business machines helped busy executives keep up with and contribute to the increasing flow of information that their large-scale operations and worldwide activities made necessary.

BUSINESS ORGANIZATION AND THE WORLD MARKET SYSTEM

The technological innovations discussed above, in addition to increasing the productivity of human labor and the range of products available to consumers, brought about significant changes in the organization of production and trade and posed important problems of public policy. In order to take advantage of the new methods of steel-making, power production, and other innovations, industrial firms had to operate on a much larger scale. This, in turn, required new legal forms of business organization to attract the necessary capital and technical skills. The new large-scale units undermined the individualistic basis of the economy and threatened to establish a new hierarchic order of society.

At the same time, the search for new sources of raw materials and new outlets for the products of expanding industries brought the whole world into the market system of Western economy. This expansion, together with the nationalist spirit of the times, frequently led Western nations to the brink of conflict with one another and to the extension of direct or indirect political as well as economic control over non-Western areas.

CORPORATIONS, CARTELS, AND TRUSTS

The expression "business organization" is frequently used in two different senses: functional and legal. Manufacturing establishments may be classified functionally according to whether they adopt the domestic (putting-out) system, the handicraft workshop, or the factory system. Although the introduction of the factory system is sometimes regarded as synonymous with the industrial revolution, it by no means immediately displaced the earlier and simpler forms of organization. They continued to exist in many old, established industries, and even some new industries found them suitable. The majority of new industries, however, especially those with large capital requirements or those that catered to mass markets, found it necessary to adopt the factory system. Modern mining operations also resemble the factory system in organization and discipline, even though they are not housed in factories.

Legally, business firms are grouped into single proprietorships, partnerships, and joint-stock companies or corporations. In America the term corporation usually means a business firm in which the owners have the privilege of limited liability; that is, they cannot be sued personally for the debts of the firm. In Europe the word corporation refers most often to political, religious, and fraternal organizations. The English equivalent of the American corporation is a limited company (meaning limitation of liability) or, more generally, a joint-stock company, although the latter may or may not have the privilege of limited liability.

In the early days of the industrial revolution nearly all business firms were proprietorships or partnerships. Charters of incorporation could only be obtained by special acts of king or Parliament, who usually reserved such charters for companies with monopolistic privileges, such as the Bank of England or the East India Company. As long as new firms could begin on a relatively small scale and grow by the reinvestment of profits this was a satisfactory situation, and a strong tradition of individual initiative and responsibility grew up in such British industries as iron and textiles. When it became necessary to make large fixed-capital investments at the beginning of an enterprise on which profits might be realized only over a span of many years, however, the simpler legal forms no longer sufficed. Such conditions were first encountered generally in canal and railroad building. Since such undertakings were in the nature of public utilities, the authorities readily granted charters of incorporation with limited liability, and by the middle of the nineteenth century investors in Britain, France, and Belgium were accustomed to buying and selling railroad shares and bonds on their financial markets.

Legislatures occasionally granted charters of incorporation to new mining, metallurgical, and banking enterprises as well, especially in Belgium and the United States, but to get these charters required special lobbying expenses and provided occasions for corruption and abuse. Continental countries possessed an intermediate form of organization called the *société en commandite* or limited partnership, which provided limitation of liability for some investors without the necessity for a special charter. With the increasing scale of enterprise, demands arose for general or free incorporation laws, that is, laws permitting any group of individuals to obtain a corporate charter by fulfilling certain specified conditions. Because of their egalitarian sentiments and hostile attitudes toward special privilege, the American states were the first to enact such laws in the 1830's and 1840's. Britain enacted a series of laws between 1855 and 1862 granting general limited liability upon simple registration, and most continental countries followed suit in the 1860's and 1870's.

By the 1870's new problems of industrial organization began to emerge. Cost reductions as a result of technical innovations and the widening of markets by improvements in transportation, together with the possibility of free incorporation, greatly increased competition among firms and led to cutthroat price wars and lower profits. To eliminate such ruinous competition, industrialists resorted to various tactics. On the Continent they formed cartels, in which independent firms agreed to divide their markets, limit production, and maintain prices. In Britain and the United States (especially the latter), where the common law doctrine of conspiracy in restraint of trade limited such combinations, legal trusts were formed to bring formerly competing concerns under a single management. A notable example was the Standard Oil Trust, formed by John D. Rockefeller and his associates between 1879 and 1882. A wave of antitrust legislation designed to enforce competition eventually broke up these trusts in the United States, while the temptation to break agreements in order to obtain a larger share of the market made the European and international cartels notoriously unstable.

Industrialists, frequently with the aid of bankers, then undertook to gain direct control of markets by outright consolidation and combination. In several industries, such as transportation, mining, and metallurgy, substantial economies in production could be secured by either horizontal or vertical integration, that is, by combining many units at the same stage in the production process under one management (horizontal integration), or by combining several units in successive stages (vertical integration). A company owning coal and ore mines, blast furnaces, steel mills, and metal fabricating plants is a good example of vertical integration. Such huge aggregations of economic power could easily eliminate smaller competitors, either by buying them out or by driving them into bankruptcy through localized price wars. By monopolizing both production and the demand for particular types of labor, they could also maintain high prices and low wages, thus creating enormous fortunes for those in control. Through bribery and corruption as well as more subtle forms of influence the owners of these large concentrations of wealth could also affect government policy, both foreign and domestic, in ways favorable to themselves.

THE NETWORK OF WORLD TRADE

The unprecedented growth of population and production together with improvements in transportation and communications broke down regional and even natural barriers to the movement of people and commodities. Western European nations, no longer able to supply their burgeoning populations and industries with domestically produced foodstuffs and raw materials, relied increasingly on imports from overseas. To pay for these essential imports, they exported chiefly manufactured goods. The British cotton industry, for example, drew its raw material from the American South, India, Egypt, and Brazil and sold its yarn and cloth in every country of the world. In the late nineteenth century overseas sales accounted for about two-thirds of its total receipts. British industry as a whole exported between 25 and 30 per cent of its entire production.

British dependence on overseas trade was unusually large, just as the cotton industry was exceptional in drawing all of its raw material from abroad. Nevertheless, some of the smaller nations of the Continent depended even more than Britain on foreign trade (chiefly with their neighbors), and all nations participated in the intensification of international commerce. For the world as a whole the role of such commerce became more important than it was at any time prior to 1860 or subsequent to 1914.

Europe had long depended on imports of such exotic commodities as the fabulous spices that lured the early explorers into the search for new routes to the East. In the nineteenth century the range and quantity of these goods increased, their production (usually under European control) became more systematic, and the techniques of their distribution became more complex and more highly refined. Even the lowest paid European factory worker could begin the day with tea from China or Ceylon, coffee from Brazil, or cocoa from Africa. More important than the trade in these amenities, however, was trade in the staples in which Europe had once been self-sufficient.

Wheat from Russia and the United States occasionally came to western Europe in years of poor local harvest and high prices after 1815. The flow increased along with the population. After 1870 it became a torrent, as transcontinental railroads and farm machinery opened new and highly productive wheat regions in America, and improvements in steamships made it possible to transport bulky goods cheaply over long distances. By 1900 western Europe imported more than half of its grain supply. The United States, Canada, Argentina, India, and Australia were the largest overseas suppliers. Southern Russia contributed significantly through its Black Sea ports. Britain became by far the largest importer, but a number of smaller nations also depended heavily on imports. Denmark and the Netherlands gave up wheat growing almost entirely and specialized in livestock production and dairying by feeding their animals on cheap imported grain. France and Germany, with more and better grain land, resorted to tariff protection for agriculture and depended less on imports.

Similar developments took place in other important staples. As early as 1850 Australia supplied the British woolen industry with half its raw material; by 1900 the quantity of wool coming from Australia and New Zealand had increased more than tenfold, completely swamping European production. Germany and Spain, formerly important exporters of high quality wool, became net importers. South Africa, India, and South America also added to the pressure on European wool growers. The opening of China and Japan, both important producers of raw silk, subjected French and Italian silk growers to stiff competition. European livestock producers suffered similar competition after the development of artificial refrigeration in the 1870's. Steamships equipped with refrigeration machinery brought mutton from Australia and beef from Australia,

Argentina, and the United States. This development stimulated a boom in the range cattle industry of the American West and led to the formation of huge meat-packing industries in such cities as Chicago, Omaha, and Kansas City.

The exchange of manufactures for foodstuffs and raw materials characterized the economic relations between western Europe and the remainder of the world. There was also sizable trade among the industrial countries themselves. They were, in fact, one another's best customers. Although in some respects their economies were competitive, in others they were complementary. Each specialized in the production of certain commodities and obtained the others by trade.

FREE TRADE AND THE RETURN TO PROTECTION

Although improvements in transportation and communications eliminated the natural barriers to a freer international exchange of goods, the world trading system that developed in the second half of the nineteenth century would not have been possible without changes in national economic policies to eliminate or reduce the artificial barriers. The early movement for free trade achieved notable success with Corn Law repeal in Great Britain in 1846 and the Anglo-French Cobden-Chevalier trade treaty of 1860. Britain was by then committed to practically complete free trade and negotiated no more important treaties. France became the keystone of a treaty system that brought the world as close to complete free trade as it has ever been. It did so by negotiating a number of trade treaties providing for mutual reduction or elimination of tariff barriers. The treaties usually contained a "most favored nation" clause, by which each signatory promised to extend to the other the lowest tariff rate available to any nation. Since France's trading partners also made treaties with one another, this resulted in an almost automatic general tariff reduction each time a new treaty took effect.

The only important trading nation to hold aloof from the movement was the United States. Before the Civil War the United States had usually followed a low or moderate tariff policy in deference to the cotton-exporting states of the South. The pressures of war finance led the Union to increase tariffs as a means of raising revenue. After the war, with the South reduced to political impotence, Northern manufacturers succeeded in raising tariffs to ever higher levels in order to protect themselves from foreign competition. For the remainder of the century and well into the next, the United States was the outstanding protectionist nation. It did not long stand alone, however.

The flood of agricultural imports into Europe in the 1870's, as well as the increased competition in manufactured goods among the industrial nations, soon led to demands by both farmers and industrialists for protection for their special interests. In 1879 Bismarck gave in to their demands for domestic political reasons, and by 1880 Russia, Germany, and France had begun to denounce their trade treaties and enact higher tariffs. Although Britain and some of the smaller nations remained faithful to free trade principles, the majority joined in a general return to protection. Nevertheless, protectionist measures did not attain the fantastic extremes of earlier centuries, or of the neomercantilism of the 1930's. For the world as a whole the entire period from about 1850 to 1914 appears in retrospect as one of relatively free international trade.

INCREASING COMPLEXITY OF CAPITALIST INSTITUTIONS

One of the distinguishing features of capitalism as an economic system is that decision-making is decentralized. For the system to function it is necessary to coordinate in some fashion the varied activities of the countless individuals who compose it. The most important institution for coordination under capitalism is the market, defined technically as any place in which buyers and sellers may communicate with one another for the purpose of concluding a transaction. (In this sense the market may be a telegraphic wire or even a postal system.) As capitalism expanded geographically and socially, bringing a larger proportion of the population within its ambit, the system of markets necessarily became more ramified and complex. The Australian shepherd, the Scottish sailor, the London dock worker, the German weaver, and the Polish peasant who bought a woolen cloak all belonged to the same chain of production, distribution, and consumption. Similar chains were represented by the American Negro sharecropper, the Liverpool porter, the Manchester cotton spinner, and the Chinese coolie; or the Canadian wheat farmer, the Dutch miller, and the Swiss baker. The connecting links in these chains were supplied by a host of specialized factors and agents: importers and exporters, auctioneers and warehousemen, bankers and brokers, insurance underwriters, and many more. Each contributed in some fashion to the functioning of the worldwide market system.

Organized markets and intricate communications systems flashed the news of shortages and surpluses, as reflected in price fluctuations, to producers and consumers around the world, enabling them to alter their plans accordingly. Commercial banks provided the short-term credit that enabled commodities to move in local as well as international trade, while investment banks, insurance companies, and stock exchanges facilitated the flow of individual savings into long-term investments. Although similar institutions had existed earlier, the first modern stock exchange was founded in London in 1773 and incorporated in 1801. Others soon followed in other financial centers. At first they handled mainly government securities and the shares of the great chartered companies, then with the coming of the railroad age and the growth of joint-stock companies they added other securities as well. It became possible for small investors to purchase stocks or bonds in businesses that they had never seen. Though unscrupulous persons sometimes took advantage of the unwary, and professional speculators occasionally rigged or cornered a market, the overall advantages of the system were many.

By this means it was possible for a capitalist to invest abroad without stirring from his office or home. Such foreign investment not only provided the fixed capital necessary for the development of backward countries, but also served as a vehicle for the diffusion of technology and organizational skills from more advanced nations. In addition to earning profits for the investor, it contributed to the general welfare by opening new sources of supply and providing new markets. Foreign investment had its darker side as well, however. In many instances, especially those involving loans to governments, the capital was not used productively but was spent for armaments, warships, and the support of enlarged armies and corrupt political regimes. Sometimes foreign investments served as the vehicle or the excuse for imperialist control by Western nations over non-Western peoples. Finally, in the political and monetary chaos following wars, such as that after World War I, investors might lose everything, although such risks were not confined to foreign investment but characterized the entire interdependent capitalist economy.

INTERNATIONAL MIGRATION

The free international economy involved the export of people as well as commodities and capital. International travel did not normally require passports or visas until World War I, and change of citizenship was generally a simple matter of declaring one's intentions. Altogether, about 60 million people left Europe between 1815 and 1914. Of these, almost 35 million came to the United States, and an additional 5 million went to Canada. Some 12 or 15 million went to Latin America, chiefly Argentina and Brazil. Australia, New Zealand, and South Africa took most of the rest. The British Isles (including Ireland) supplied the largest number of emigrants — about 18 million. Large numbers also left Germany, the Scandinavian countries, and after about 1890, Italy, Austria-Hungary, and the Russian Empire (including Poland). Migration within Europe was also substantial, although in many cases it was only temporary. Large numbers of Poles and other Slavic and Jewish peoples moved west into Germany, France, and elsewhere. France attracted Italians, Spanish, Swiss, and Belgians, while England obtained immigrants from all of Europe. In the east the tsar settled about 1.5 million peasant families in Siberia between 1861 and 1914, in addition to many criminals and political deportees.

Except for the latter, the migrations were mostly voluntary. In a few cases the migrants fled from political persecution or oppression. The majority moved in response to economic pressure at home and opportunities for a better life abroad. In the eight years following the great famine of 1846, for example, more than 1,200,000 people left Ireland for the United States and many more crossed the Irish Sea to Britain. In spite of occasional hostile reactions in the receiving countries, the immigrants and their children made significant contributions to the economic, cultural, and political life of their adopted countries. New and nearly empty lands overseas, such as Australia and New Zealand, attracted a steady stream of immigrants, most of them from the British Isles. Many Britishers went to Canada, too. Relatively large numbers of Italians and Germans migrated to what became the economically most progressive countries of South America. In the United States the economic, scientific, literary, artistic, and political achievements of immigrants and their descendants are both noteworthy and obvious.

NATIONAL ECONOMIC STYLES

The industrial countries had many characteristics in common that differentiated them from their preindustrial neighbors, but each also developed certain distinctive traits of its own. As a result of differences of physical environment, historical tradition, and the timing of industrialization, each specialized in particular lines of industry and developed its own style of economic institutions and responses to world market conditions. Britain, France, and Belgium, the pioneers of industrial development, served as tutors and suppliers of capital for their less highly developed neighbors. They also paid a penalty for their precocity in the form of overcommitment to lines of industry that were already becoming obsolete by the end of the nineteenth century. The younger and more vigorous industrializing nations profited from the experience and capital of the pioneers and also proved more flexible in adopting new technologies.

BRITAIN, FRANCE, AND BELGIUM: THE DIFFUSION OF TECHNOLOGY AND THE EXPORT OF CAPITAL

British artisans and entrepreneurs helped implant the seeds of modern industry on the Continent and in North America almost as soon as they sprouted in Britain itself. (See pp. 584–588.) Soon after the Napoleonic wars British capitalists began to invest some of the accumulated profits of industry in foreign countries. At first the export of capital took the form of loans to foreign governments, and by the 1840's British railroad contractors using British capital had begun to assist in the construction of railroads all across the Continent. After mid-century the British turned increasingly to overseas investments, especially in the British Empire and the United States. By 1870 British foreign investments approximated 4 billion dollars, of which about 60 per cent was in loans to governments

Table 1   The Progress of Industrialization, 1870–1913

	1870	1913
United Kingdom		
Coal (millions of long tons)	110.0	287.0
Pig iron (millions of long tons)	6.0	10.3
Steel (millions of long tons)	0.2	7.7
Foreign trade[1] (millions of dollars)	3,186.0	6,837.0
Germany		
Coal and lignite (millions of metric tons)	34.0	277.3
Pig iron (millions of metric tons)	1.3	19.3
Steel (millions of metric tons)	0.17	18.3
Foreign trade[1] (millions of dollars)	1,433.0[2]	4,970.0
France		
Coal (millions of metric tons)	13.1	40.8
Pig iron (millions of metric tons)	1.2	5.2
Steel (millions of metric tons)	0.08	4.7
Foreign trade[1] (millions of dollars)	1,094.0	2,953.0
United States		
Coal (millions of long tons)	29.5	508.9
Pig iron (millions of long tons)	1.7	31.0
Steel (millions of long tons)	0.07	31.3
Foreign trade[1] (millions of dollars)	868.0	4,392.0

(long ton = 2,240 lbs.)
(metric ton = 2,204.6 lbs.)

[1] Imports plus exports; figures for United Kingdom and United States include re-exports.
[2] Figure for 1872.
Sources: E. Varga, *Mirovye Ekonomicheskie Krizisy 1848–1935* (Moscow, 1937), I, part III, app. III, tables 1, 2, 3, 4; foreign trade data from W. S. and E. S. Woytinsky, *World Commerce and Governments* (New York, 1955), pp. 48, 50.

and the remainder in railroads, banks, and other commercial and industrial enterprises.

The resources for these investments came chiefly from the earnings of British shippers, bankers, and insurance underwriters, for Britain had long imported more than it exported. It could do so with ease, and could even increase its foreign investments as a result of income received from earlier investments. By 1914 British foreign investments amounted to 19 billion dollars, or almost 40 per cent of total British wealth excluding land. Most of the investments still represented loans to governments, but they also took the form of sheep ranches in Australia, cattle ranches in the United States and Argentina, wheat farms in Canada, tea plantations in Ceylon, rubber plantations in Malaya, and gold mines in South Africa, as well as railroads, banks, mines, and port and dock facilities distributed throughout every inhabited continent and in almost every country of the world.

As early as the 1830's French engineers, entrepreneurs, and capitalists began to assist the industrial development of France's neighbors, especially Belgium, Germany, and Italy. After 1850 the French took the major role in the construction of railroads throughout southern and eastern Europe, dug canals (of which the most famous is Suez), built port and dock facilities, water and gas works, and so on. The French also invested heavily in government securities, especially those of its Latin neighbors and, after 1890, Russia. By 1914 French foreign investments totaled nearly 10 billion dollars (about 30 per cent of French national wealth excluding land) and, like the British, were distributed throughout the inhabited world. Belgium also invested a large proportion of its national wealth abroad, but because of its much smaller population the total was less impressive. Belgian engineers played a significant role in mining, metallurgy, and railroads in Europe and elsewhere. Toward the end of the century other industrializing nations of Europe, notably Germany, the Netherlands, and Switzerland, repaid their foreign borrowings and became net lenders. Collectively, however, their investments in 1914 amounted to less than those of France alone and only about half those of Britain.

Britain reached its peak of industrial supremacy in relation to other nations in the two decades between 1850 and 1870. In the latter year it accounted for more than 30 per cent of the world output of industrial products. France and Belgium also reached their relative peaks in the same period, although French industrial output accounted for little more than 10 per cent of the world total, and Belgium accounted for only 3 per cent. All three countries continued to make industrial progress thereafter, but at a slower rate than previously and much slower in relation to the progress of other nations. In 1913 the United States produced a staggering 35 per cent of the world's manufacturing output and Germany produced more than 15 per cent, whereas Britain fell to 14 per cent and France fell to less than 7 per cent.

Textiles, coal, iron, and engineering, the bases of Britain's early prosperity, remained its standbys. British industrialists were slow to adopt new technological innovations, even in industries in which they had long maintained superiority. In part, the backwardness of the British educational system may be blamed, for Britain was the last major nation to adopt universal public elementary schooling, and the few great British universities paid slight attention to scientific or engineering training. In part, the relative decline of British, French, and other Belgian industry was the inevitable result of industrialization in other lands. Much of the responsibility, however, belonged to the entrepreneurs. The sons or grandsons of the original founders of British enterprises did not exhibit the dynamism of their forebears. Frequently they adopted the life of leisured gentlemen and left the day-to-day operations of the firms to hired managers. In foreign markets they lost ground to more aggressive trade rivals, such as Germany and the United States, and suffered the humiliation of an invasion of their domestic market by cheaper and better foreign manufactures. In 1914 Britain had the highest standard of living of any European nation, but it had lost its secure position as the world's leading industrial nation.

In France, a land of small peasant proprietors, agriculture continued to occupy a larger proportion of the population than in other advanced industrial nations. French industry, which was more varied and catered especially to limited markets for quality products, developed fewer large-scale, mass-production manufacturing units. The slow growth of French population and the policy of tariff protection for both agriculture and industry, which insulated French entrepreneurs from the stimulus of the world market, also condemned France to slower industrial growth. Nevertheless, on the eve of World War I Frenchmen enjoyed the highest standard of living on the Continent, and in Europe were second only to Britain.

GERMAN INDUSTRY AND ECONOMIC EXPANSION

While the older industrial economies coasted along on their early superiority, German industry grew rapidly. The growth of population alone — from less than 25 million in 1815 (according to the boundaries of 1871) to more than 65 million in 1914 — was sufficient to cause grave concern to Germany's neighbors. Three other outstanding factors also contributed significantly to German industrial progress.

First, Germany possessed unusually large reserves of coal, especially in the famous Ruhr Valley, which supported important metallurgical, engineering, chemical, and electrical industries. Second, the German educational system, from the preprimary grades — *kindergarten* is a German word — through the numerous excellent universities, was not only the most comprehensive in the world but also the best suited to the needs of an industrial state. A series of reforms in Prussia during the Napoleonic wars laid the basis for the modern educational system of Germany and provided for universal and compulsory education of all children from the ages of six through fourteen. Besides the elementary schools, a variety of secondary schools prepared students for the universities or gave them manual or technical training appropriate to their stations. Throughout Germany the old universities were revitalized and several new ones were founded. Scientific training borrowed heavily from the curriculum and methods of the École Polytechnique, the noted French revolutionary school, but was made available to a far larger number of students than in the French system. A number of specialized technical schools, including engineering colleges and business schools at the university level, were founded. Thus, as science became more and more the foundation of industry, Germany stood ready to take advantage of the situation. When American educators in the 1870's began to be concerned with the need for remodeling their system of higher education, they turned to Germany rather than to France or England for a model.

Third, Germany developed a banking system that was uniquely adapted to the need for industrial development. Prior to 1848 German banking, like the German economy as a whole, was backward in comparison with other Western nations. Again Germany borrowed from and improved on French models. In the 1850's and 1860's German financiers founded a number of banks similar to the French Crédit Mobilier (see p. 661), expressly for the purpose of creating and nourishing new large-scale industries. In time most of these banks established networks of branches and affiliates throughout Germany and in foreign countries. In this way they not only economized on capital and catered to the needs of German industry but also facilitated the extension of Germany's foreign commerce by providing credit to exporters and foreign merchants. The consequences were spectacular, and alarming, to industrialists and statesmen of other countries.

German coal production rose more than sixfold between 1870 and 1914, pig iron production rose more than tenfold, and steel, a relatively new industry in 1870, rose almost one hundredfold. By 1895 Germany produced more steel than Britain and by 1914 it produced more than twice as much. During the same period German foreign commerce surpassed that of the United States and France, and though it still lagged slightly behind that of Britain, the gap was closing rapidly.

INDUSTRY IN AMERICA

On the eve of World War I Germany was the most powerful industrial nation in Europe, but the most spectacular example of rapid national growth was the United States. The first federal census of 1790 recorded fewer than 4 million inhabitants. In 1870, after the limits of continental expansion had been reached, the population had risen to almost 40 million, larger than that of any European nation except Russia. In 1915 the population surpassed 100 million. Although the United States received the bulk of emigration from Europe, the largest element of population growth resulted from an extremely high rate of natural increase. At no time did the foreign-born population surpass one-sixth of the total. Nevertheless, the American policy of almost unrestricted immigration until after World War I placed a definite stamp on national life, and America became known as the "melting pot" of Europe.

The numbers of immigrants entering annually rose rapidly though unsteadily from less than ten thousand in the 1820's to more than 1 million in the years immediately prior to the first World War. Until the 1890's by far the majority came from northwestern Europe, including Germany.

Immigrant stock from these countries continued to constitute the largest part of the foreign-born population. By 1900, however, new immigrants from Italy and eastern Europe dominated the listings. In 1910 the foreign-born population numbered 13,500,000, or about 15 per cent of the total population. Of these, about 17 per cent came from Germany; 10 per cent from Ireland; almost as many from Italy and the Austro-Hungarian monarchy; about 9 per cent each from Great Britain, Scandinavia, Canada, and Russia; almost 7 per cent each from Russian, Austrian, and German Poland; and a scattering from other countries.

Income and wealth grew even more rapidly than population. From colonial times the scarcity of labor in relation to land and other resources had meant higher wages and a higher average standard of living than in Europe. This fact, together with the related opportunities for individual achievement and the political liberties enjoyed by American citizens, drew the immigrants from Europe. Between the end of the Civil War and the outbreak of World War I the average income per capita roughly tripled. The primary sources of the enormous increase were the same as those operating in western Europe, the rapid progress of technology and increasing regional specialization. In addition, the continued scarcity and high cost of labor placed a premium on labor-saving machinery. In agriculture, for example, the best European practices yielded consistently higher returns per acre than in the United States, but American farmers using relatively inexpensive machinery (even before the introduction of the tractor) obtained far larger yields per worker. The large internal market, entirely free of artificial trade barriers, permitted an even greater degree of regional specialization than the regime of relatively free trade in Europe.

In spite of the rapid growth of large cities, the United States remained predominantly a rural nation. The urban population did not pull abreast of the rural population until World War I. The westward movement continued after the Civil War, encouraged by the Homestead Act and the opening of the trans-Mississippi West by means of the railroads. Until the 1890's American exports consisted principally of agricultural products. Foundations were being laid, nevertheless, for America's subsequent industrial prowess. The nonagricultural labor force surpassed workers in agriculture as early as 1870. In the 1880's the income from manufacturing exceeded that from agriculture. By 1900 the United States had become the world's foremost industrial nation.

The large domestic market might have meant little for large-scale industry in America had it not been for the relatively open and fluid character of American social classes. In spite of the ethnic and regional diversity of the American people, the absence of rigid class boundaries assured the development of relatively uniform tastes, creating a large homogeneous market for mass-produced manufactures. American industrialists were quick to take advantage of the opportunity. All the features of the new technology that encouraged large-scale industry acted with extra force in the United States, and in one industry after another — iron and steel, petroleum, sugar refining, tobacco processing, meat packing, and many others — huge integrated concerns emerged to serve national and international markets.

The so-called antitrust legislation actually encouraged the concentration of industry, for although it penalized collusion in the form of cartel and trust agreements, it did not penalize bigness as such. As a result, a large merger movement developed in the 1890's. The first billion dollar corporation in the world was the United States Steel Corporation, created in 1901. By 1904 more than 300 large industrial combinations controlled more than 40 per cent of the manufacturing capital of the nation and affected about four-fifths of the major American industries. Of the 92 largest combinations in 1904, 78 produced 50 per cent or more of the output of their industries; 57 produced 60 per cent or more; and 26 produced 80 per cent or more. These figures actually understate the degree of concentration, for by means of interlocking directorates, communities of interest, and the cooperation of important investment banking houses, such as that of J. P. Morgan, a relatively small number of individuals could wield enormous power and influence throughout the whole economy.

American political life in the period after the Civil War reflected the domination of the country by big business. At the beginning of the twentieth century public exposure of a number of flagrant examples of evil and corruption in business and government, as well as in the living and working conditions of the industrial population, stimulated a reform movement. It was dominated by middle-class leaders from the liberal professions. Known as Progressives, these socially conscious citizens gained influence in both political parties and restored a measure of decorum and direction to American life.

INDUSTRIALIZATION
IN OTHER LANDS

Industrialism barely affected the smaller nations of northwestern Europe, except Belgium, in the first half of the nineteenth century, but in the second half of the century they all made rapid strides. In spite of important individual differences, the Netherlands, Switzerland, and the Scandinavian countries generally followed the same path of economic progress. This began with legal, commercial, and educational reforms dating from the French Revolution but not carried to completion in every case until after 1848. All developed strong educational systems and a vigorous middle class. They participated in the commercial revival of the 1850's, chartered banks, and began the construction of railroad systems. In the 1860's they joined the free trade movement. Industrialization proper did not get underway in earnest until the 1870's, but then it proceeded apace. Native industrialists developed industries that utilized skilled labor and local resources. Switzerland, Sweden, and Norway, for example, made extensive use of hydroelectricity, whereas Denmark and the Netherlands concentrated chiefly on intensive agriculture and the processing of agricultural products. By the beginning of the twentieth century all could boast of prosperous, progressive industries and a standard of living comparable with any on the Continent.

Northern Italy, lower Austria (the region around Vienna), and Bohemia also began to industrialize. Bohemia in particular developed some mining activity, and they all engaged in the processing of metals; but their mainstays were the relatively low-skilled industries, such as textiles and leather working. Their efforts to industrialize were not notably successful, and they remained predominantly rural and agrarian.

For Russia the Crimean War revealed that numbers and size were no offset to economic backwardness. Immediately after the war the tsar undertook an ambitious program of railroad construction, utilizing foreign capital and technical personnel. After a number of false starts the program finally began to catch on in the 1870's. In 1892 the government began construction of the Trans-Siberian railroad, the first track of which was opened in 1905. In spite of great progress, the vast distances in Russia left many areas completely inaccessible by modern means of transportation. The emancipation of the serfs was carried out by the tsar in 1861 as a deliberate effort to modernize his country, but it did not immediately have the desired effects. In fact, during the generation or so after liberation the agrarian situation deteriorated.

The efforts of successive tsars to make Russia a powerful industrial nation finally began to bear fruit in the 1890's. Massive imports of foreign capital were lured into Russia by political alliances, government guarantees, protective tariffs, and state subsidies. Under the direction of foreign entrepreneurs and engineers, Russia obtained large-scale, relatively modern industries. In the last decade of the century production of coal increased by 131 per cent, petroleum by 132 per cent, and pig iron by 190 per cent. Russia also had a large textile industry, which on the eve of World War I ranked fourth in the world in size. The petroleum industry, which developed rapidly after 1870, accounted for about one-fourth of the world production and vied with that of the United States for first place. Nevertheless, apart from the petroleum industry, which was based on unusually rich deposits, was financed and managed by foreign capitalists and entrepreneurs, and competed in the world market, Russian industries existed only by virtue of state protection and subsidy, islands of modernity in a sea of backwardness. Elsewhere in eastern and southern Europe similar if smaller islands existed, but they were of minor importance, having little influence on the preindustrial economy that characterized the area.

ORGANIZED LABOR AND THE REVIVAL OF SOCIALISM

The history of socialism and of organized efforts to improve the conditions of the urban working classes before 1848 belongs as much to the history of ideas as to the history of social movements. The two decades after 1848 showed this characteristic clearly. In Britain the failure of the Chartist movement temporarily disillusioned the rank-and-file workingmen with grandiose schemes of universal regeneration, while the gradual improvement in wages and working conditions brought about by the advance of industry dulled the edge of criticism of the industrial system. In France, persecution and exile for the popular radical leaders of the 1840's, as well as strict police supervision and repression of any hint of mass action by the mobs of Paris and other industrial cities, effectively squelched incipient labor movements and reduced the urban population to an unusual state of docility. Elsewhere in Europe political oppression was even more severe than in France. Industrial workers were too few in number and too weak in organization to present a serious threat to the existing political and social order.

THE COOPERATIVE MOVEMENT

In localities where industrial workers were sufficiently numerous and inclined to collective action, they resorted to devices that would ameliorate their circumstances without arousing the hostility of the larger community. Britain became the home of the consumer cooperation movement with the formation of the first such cooperative at Rochdale in 1844. By mid-century more than one hundred similar cooperatives had been formed in northern England and Scotland, and by 1863 the movement was strong enough to establish a Cooperative Wholesale Society. In subsequent years the movement extended its activities into production, insurance, and banking. In France and other continental countries small-scale artisans formed producer cooperatives and mutual credit societies in an effort to stave off ruin from the competition of larger, more efficient industrial units, but only in agriculture did producer cooperatives achieve notable success. Denmark is an outstanding example of a nation in which, after the 1870's, agriculture was organized predominantly on cooperative lines. In the twentieth century a strong cooperative movement developed in Sweden, embracing both agricultural and producer cooperatives in the urban areas. Outside of Scandinavia, however, the cooperatives affected only a small fraction of the working population.

THE RISE OF TRADE UNIONS

Another form of working-class self-help, which in the long run amounted to much more than the cooperative movement, was the trade (or labor) union movement. Although trade unions have a long history, running back to the journeymen's associations of the later Middle Ages, the modern movement dates from the rise of modern industry. In the first half of the nineteenth century unions were weak, localized, and usually short-lived in the face of opposition by antagonistic employers and unfavorable or repressive legislation. Most Western nations have passed through at least three phases in their official attitudes toward trade unions. The first phase, that of outright prohibition or suppression, was typified by the Le Chapelier Law of 1791 in France, the Combination Laws of 1799 and 1800 in Britain, and similar legislation in other countries. In the second phase, marked in Britain by the repeal of the Combination Laws in 1824 and 1825, governments granted limited toleration to trade unions, allowing their formation but frequently prosecuting them for engaging in overt action such as strikes. A third phase, not achieved until the twentieth century in some countries and not achieved at all in others, accorded full legal rights to workingmen to organize and engage in collective activities. A fourth phase, resorted to by totalitarian countries after World War I, in effect regimented workers into trade unions that became instruments of the state.

In Britain nationwide trade-union organization fell off between 1834 and 1851. Then the Amalgamated Society of Engineers (machinists and mechanics) was formed, the first of the so-called New Model unions. The distinctive feature of the New Model union was that it organized skilled laborers only and on a craft basis, such as typographers, tailors, stonemasons, shipwrights, and carpenters; it represented the aristocracy of labor. Unskilled workers and workers in the new factory industries remained unorganized until near the end of the century. New Model unions aimed modestly at improving the wages and working conditions of their own members, who were already the best paid in British industry, by peaceful negotiations with employers and mutual self-help. They eschewed political activities and rarely resorted to strikes except in desperation. As a result, they grew in strength but membership remained low. Attempts to organize the large mass of semiskilled and unskilled workers resulted in successful strikes by the "match girls" (young female workers in the match industry) in 1888 and the London dock workers in 1889. By 1900 trade union membership surpassed 2 million, and in 1913 it reached 4 million, or more than one-fifth of the total work force.

On the Continent, trade unions made slower progress. From the beginning French unions were closely associated with socialism and similar political ideologies. The varying and mutually antagonistic forms taken by French socialism badly splintered the union movement, resulted in a fickle and fluctuating membership, and made it nearly impossible to agree on nationwide collective action. In 1895 French unions succeeded in forming a national nonpolitical General Confederation of Labor (C.G.T.), but even it did not include all active unions and frequently had difficulty in commanding local obedience to its directives. Like French political parties, the French labor movement remained decentralized, highly individualistic, and generally ineffective.

The German labor movement dated from the 1860's. Like the French, it was associated from the beginning with political parties and political action; unlike the French, it was more centralized and cohesive. There were three main divisions in the German labor movement: the Hirsch-Dunker or liberal trade unions, appealing mainly to skilled craftsmen; the socialist or free trade unions, having a far larger membership; and somewhat later the Catholic or Christian trade unions, founded with the blessing of the pope in opposition to the "godless" socialist unions. By 1914 the German trade union movement had 3 million members — five-sixths belonged to the socialist unions — and was the second largest in Europe.

In the economically backward countries of southern Europe, and to some extent in Latin America, French influence predominated in working-class organizations. Trade unions were fragmented and ideologically oriented. They were savagely repressed by employers and the state and were mostly without consequence. Trade unions in the Low Countries, Switzerland, and the Austro-Hungarian Empire followed the German model. They achieved moderate success at the local level, but religious and ethnic differences as well as opposition from government hindered their effectiveness as national movements. In the Scandinavian countries the labor movement developed its own distinctive traditions. It allied itself with the cooperative movement as well as with the Social Democratic political parties and by 1914 had done more than any other trade union movement to alleviate the living and working conditions of its membership. In Russia and elsewhere in eastern Europe trade unions remained illegal until after World War I.

Early attempts to form mass working-class organizations in the United States came to naught in the face of governmental and employer opposition and the difficulty in securing cooperation among workingmen of different skills, occupations, religions, and ethnic backgrounds. In the 1880's Samuel Gompers took the lead in organizing closely knit local unions of skilled workers only, and in 1886 he united them into the American Federation of Labor. Like the New Model unions of Britain, the A.F.L. followed "bread and butter" tactics by concentrating on the welfare of its own members, steering clear of ideological entanglements and avoiding overt political action. In consequence, it succeeded in achieving many of its limited goals but left the majority of American industrial workers unorganized. In the British dominions trade unions developed in traditional British form but with a greater commitment to socialist programs. The first Trades Union Congress in Australia took place in 1879, only eleven years after the first of its kind in Britain.

Throughout most of the nineteenth century the Roman Catholic hierarchy regarded with disfavor the formation of exclusively working-class organizations, such as trade unions, and tried to prohibit its members from participating in them. Its opposition contributed to the weakness of the union movement in France and other Catholic countries. Pope Leo XIII (1878–1903) reversed this attitude and encouraged the formation of specifically Christian, or Catholic trade unions as a means of combating the secularism of socialist unions and winning workers back to the Church. Catholic union movements developed in Belgium, Austria, Italy, and Germany, but they remained relatively small and unimportant.

SOCIALIST THOUGHT AND ORGANIZATION

Although the two decades after 1848 were relatively barren of socialist political activity, they witnessed the elaboration by Karl Marx of the foremost of all socialist theories. Marx dabbled briefly in socialist political organization in 1864 when he took the lead in forming the International Workingmen's Association (later called the First International). The association was the creation of political refugees like Marx, and its objective was to foster the spread of socialist doctrine in workers' organizations throughout the world. The delegates to its conferences spent most of their time and energy wrangling with one another over points of doctrine and contributed little to the actual spread of socialism. The bitterest division took place between Marx and Mikhail Bakunin (1814–1876), a Russian anarchist, and eventually led to the disruption of the organization. To prevent the organizational apparatus from falling into Bakunin's hands, Marx contrived in 1872 to move the headquarters to New York, where it became moribund and quietly expired in 1876.

More vigorous social movements were growing up on the Continent. In 1863 Ferdinand Lassalle formed the General German Workingman's Association, partly a trade union and partly a political party. Lassalle accepted much of the Marxian doctrine but believed that socialism could be established by political action without revolution. In 1875, after the death of Lassalle, his followers amalgamated with those of Marx to form the German Social Democratic party. Under the astute leadership of Wilhelm Liebknecht and August Bebel the party achieved such surprising success at the polls that even Bismarck took alarm, and in 1878 he persuaded the Reichstag to outlaw the Social Democrats. (See p. 732.) The antisocialist laws lapsed after Bismarck's retirement, however, and the party, which had gone underground in the interval, bounded back stronger than ever. It obtained one and a half million votes in 1890 and more than four million votes in the elections of 1912. By then it was the largest single party in the German Empire, having almost a third of the members of the Reichstag, but because it steadfastly refused to participate in coalition governments the combined opposition of the other parties sufficed to keep it out of office.

French socialists also made political gains, but their internal divisions prevented them from presenting a united front to the electorate or in the French parliament. Although France had a Marxist party, French workers found the anarchist and syndicalist doctrines more attractive. The outstanding leader of French socialism was Jean Jaurès, an Independent Socialist who looked to the French revolutionary tradition rather than to Marxism or anarchism for the justification of socialism. At the same time he worked unceasingly to achieve cooperation among the various socialist groups. He succeeded for a time after 1905, but the French socialists splintered again in 1910 when one of their number who had joined the government used the army to break a railroad strike. On the eve of World War I the various socialist parties constituted the second largest group in the French Chamber of Deputies.

British socialism developed piecemeal, with little systematic theoretical basis. Curiously, Marx did not attempt to create an organized following in the country of his adoption. The Fabian Society, an organization devoted to peaceful social reform and the gradual socialization of industry, did not engage in political action as such but employed publications and lectures to expose the inadequacies of the existing social system and to propose remedies and reforms. The Fabians owed more to Bentham than to Marx. Their emphasis on gradualism and peaceful evolution was distinctively British. Whereas the Fabians represented a middle-class, intellectual approach to socialism, the followers of J. Keir Hardie, a Scottish coal miner and trade union organizer, represented a working-class, political approach. Hardie took the lead in uniting the various socialist factions and the Trades Union Congress in support of the Labour Representation Committee, which became the Labour party in 1906. Although the Labour party did not commit itself definitely to a program of socialization until 1918, the influence of its socialist components moved it steadily in that direction.

Social Democratic parties on the German model were founded elsewhere in Europe: Belgium (1885), Austria (1889), Hungary (1890), Bulgaria (1891), Poland (1892), Rumania (1893), Holland (1894), Russia (1898), Finland (1903), and Serbia (1903). The anarchist and syndicalist movements dominated socialist action groups in Italy, Spain, and Portugal. Social Democratic parties also developed in Denmark (1878), Norway (1887), and Sweden (1889), but because they were in close alliance with the cooperative and trade union movements, they adopted a more gradual approach to socialism, closer to the British than to the German model. The Christian Socialist movement did not develop an effective political arm.

From its beginnings socialism stressed the common, collective interests of peoples regardless of national frontiers and sought to develop a sense of international solidarity among its adherents. The First International, formed in advance of the national socialist parties, clearly reflected this emphasis. After its demise representatives of the various socialist parties formed the Second International Workingmen's Association in Paris in 1889. Unlike its highly centralized predecessor, the Second International was a loose association of component national groups. It did not establish a permanent secretariat until 1900. The debates at its annual congresses did much to stimulate public awareness of socialism and exposed national differences within socialist groups. One major difference concerned the role of socialist parties in national political life and was closely connected with the doctrinal dispute over "revisionism." (See pp. 735–736.) In general, socialists from countries where more or less democratic political practices prevailed (such as Britain, France, and the Scandinavian countries) favored peaceful cooperation and even collaboration with nonsocialist reformers. Those from countries with less well developed parliamentary forms of government or with none at all advocated nonparticipation in bourgeois politics and continued revolutionary agitation.

An even more important issue concerned the role of socialist parties in wartime, and on this rock the international socialist movement finally shattered. Congresses at Stuttgart (1907) and Copenhagen (1910) passed resolutions demanding joint action by workers to prevent war but provided no effective machinery for it. When war broke out in 1914, minorities in every socialist party adopted a pacifist or neutral stance, but the majority in every case supported their national war effort. This failure of the socialists to abide by their principles not only disrupted socialism as an international movement but also seriously divided and weakened the various national socialist parties.

RADICALISM AND THE WORKERS

Karl Marx had prophesied that with the advance of modern industrialism and capitalism the laboring masses would sink deeper into poverty and destitution as they grew in numbers, until at last they would rise in revolt against their capitalist overlords. One would suppose that in line with this prediction labor organizations would exhibit the greatest radicalism and be most disposed to violence in those nations where capitalism and modern industry had made the greatest strides. In fact, the events of history revealed this prophecy to be the very opposite of the truth. Britain, the first industrial nation in the nineteenth century and the most capitalistic, did indeed have the largest trade union movement, but its workers quickly abandoned the goal of a radical reconstruction of society in favor of a policy of gradual, peaceful reform. In Germany, which was still industrially backward in the 1860's, the early trade union movement adopted a radical ideology, but as German industry progressed and trade unions grew in numbers, trade union tactics followed an increasingly peaceable approach. The divided French union movement, which was given to periodic outbursts of violence, mirrored the small-scale, relatively unprogressive character of French capitalism. Ironically for Marx, who despised the Russians, it was in Russia, the least capitalistic of all major powers and the only one in which trade unions were entirely illegal, that the workers resorted to violence most often and finally achieved a proletarian revolution.

DEMOCRATIC REFORM AND SOCIAL STRIFE, 1871-1914
CHAPTER TWENTY-EIGHT

Paralleling their continued technological and economic progress, the nations of western Europe experienced what may with qualification be called political progress. By the third quarter of the nineteenth century the governments of all western European countries were responsive to, though not necessarily controlled by, the needs and interests of the middle classes. The leaders of the working classes had made their bids for political consideration, as in the Chartist demonstrations in Britain and the revolutions of 1848 on the Continent. That these bids most often took the form of demands for the right to vote testifies to the extraordinary effectiveness of the propagandists of the liberal political theory of representative government. By the end of the nineteenth century most of the demands had been conceded; with minor qualifications universal manhood suffrage was the rule in most western European nations. It did not follow that workers controlled the governments, however.

In spite of the great importance of modern industry, industrial workers rarely constituted an actual majority of the labor force. Peasants with a traditionalist mentality and workers in the various service trades, many of whom shared the outlook of the middle classes, usually outnumbered industrial workers. Moreover, the latter were frequently slow to develop their own political organizations. Many of them demonstrated a marked indifference to or ignorance of the political process, and the politically conscious workers rarely approached unanimity on political goals. The upper and middle classes made use of their greater wealth, superior organization, and the power of government itself to frustrate the intention of working-class political leaders to gain control of the apparatus of government. Continuing social strife resulted in spite of acknowledged progress in the political sphere.

THE TRIUMPH OF DEMOCRACY IN BRITAIN

The British Parliament after 1832 legislated a number of important economic and social reforms, but Parliament itself was far from being a democratic body. Only one adult male in six could vote for members of the House of Commons in the early 1860's. Several proposals for the extension of the franchise had been made, but all had been defeated by the combined opposition of the Whigs and Tories. The aristocratic and upper-middle-class politicians who dominated Parliament had reached what has been called the Victorian Compromise, blurring party lines and delaying the emergence of the modern two-party system. One of the chief architects of the compromise was Lord Palmerston (1784–1865). After Palmerston's death the rivalry between the Liberals and Conservatives, as the parties then came to be known, grew more acute, and the issues that divided them became more sharply defined. In large measure this development resulted from the personal rivalry and political astuteness of two remarkable men.

DISRAELI AND GLADSTONE

Benjamin Disraeli (1804–1881), one of the most colorful personalities in the history of British politics, typified a new breed of man — the professional politician. The son of a Christianized Jew, Disraeli lacked the aristocratic birth, wealth, and family connections that were normally required for political leadership in Britain; but he possessed driving ambition, a gift for oratory, a fertile imagination, and a prolific pen (he supported himself outside of Parliament as a writer of popular novels). By dint of sheer skill and audacity he worked himself into the highest ranks of the Tory (Conservative) party and became the leading spokesman for the landed aristocracy, many of whom were unable to speak coherently for themselves. He first attracted public notice in the 1830's as one of the young Tory Radicals concerned with the plight of the growing urban working classes. In the next decade he split with his party leader, Robert Peel, and spoke for the protectionist interests in the Corn Law debates. He served as chancellor of the exchequer on three occasions after 1852, became leader of the House of Commons in 1867, and prime minister in 1868. Although his party was defeated in the election that year, he remained as leader of the opposition and served again as Conservative prime minister from 1874 until 1880.

William Ewart Gladstone (1809–1898) was Disraeli's counterpart and his great rival as leader and architect of the modern Liberal party. The son of a wealthy Liverpool merchant, Gladstone made his debut in politics with the Tories, but during the Corn Law controversy he seceded with the Peelites and became the financial expert of the Liberal party.

Benjamin Disraeli

*"In Disraeli's career there was the realisation in fact of the dream which has
floated before the eyes of many an ambitious youth. . . . And though it was
attained in this case, as in most others, 'by force,' it was in fair and open
Parliamentary fight, and, as regards the main struggle, in what looked at first
like a hopeless defiance hurled by a pigmy at a giant. . . . Not only was
Disraeli's political advantage won in fair fight. It was also uncontaminated by
any suspicion that he was in politics for pecuniary gain."* George Earle Buckle
and W. F. Monypenny, THE LIFE OF BENJAMIN DISRAELI, EARL OF BEACONSFIELD
(New York, 1913–20), Vol. VI.

He was twice chancellor of the exchequer between 1852 and 1866 and served as prime minister four times between 1868 and his retirement in 1894.

THE "LEAP IN THE DARK" AND
FURTHER POLITICAL REFORMS

The first major issue to face Disraeli and Gladstone after the death of Palmerston found them on the same side, though for different reasons. Gladstone introduced a bill in 1866 for an extension of the electorate, only to have it defeated by defections from his own Liberal party. Although the Conservatives (as well as many Liberals) traditionally had been opposed to extensions of the franchise, it became clear to Disraeli that further electoral reform could not be long postponed. He resolved to capture the credit for his own Conservative party and win the allegiance of the underprivileged classes. He thereupon introduced his own bill for electoral reform, which became law on August 15, 1867.

This "leap in the dark," as the measure was characterized by the Conservative prime minister, Lord Derby, enfranchised the majority of the urban working classes and roughly doubled the electorate, from about 1 million to about 2 million. Thereafter all householders who paid a certain low minimum in direct taxes could vote in elections for members of the Commons. The franchise in the country districts remained restricted to the more substantial proprietors and farmers, however, and in the cities there were many who were unaffected, including women, domestic servants, and the lowest strata of workers. In spite of some redistribution of seats in the Commons, electoral districts were far from equal, and the medieval distinction between borough and shire (roughly, city and country) was maintained. Nevertheless, a significant reform had been achieved. Disraeli crowed that he had "dished the Whigs" and expected the people to be properly grateful. Unhappily for him the new electorate favored the Liberals, and in the next general election in 1868 Gladstone's party swept to an overwhelming triumph.

The next major extension of the franchise took place under the auspices of the Liberals. The Third Reform Act of 1884 removed most of the remaining barriers to universal manhood suffrage by adding some 2 million agricultural laborers and rural artisans to the voting rolls. The companion Redistribution Act of 1885 abolished the distinction between borough and shire and divided the country into single-member parliamentary constituencies of roughly equal size. Two archaic practices did not disappear until 1948: special members for the universities of Oxford and Cambridge, and plural voting for individuals — mostly wealthy businessmen — who lived in one constituency and worked in another. The final steps to complete universal suffrage took place after World War I. An act of 1918 gave the vote to all males over the age of twenty-one and all women over the age of thirty; and in 1928 women were placed on the same basis as men.

Meanwhile a number of other important political reforms had been effected. In 1858 the property qualification for members of Parliament was abolished. In the same year Lionel Rothschild, a well-propertied individual, became the first professing Jew to enter the House of Commons, which had refused him a seat for ten years although he had been repeatedly re-elected by the City of London. The Ballot Act of 1872 introduced the secret ballot, eliminating much bribery and intimidation at the polls and incidentally making it easier for radicals to secure election. One radical was Charles Bradlaugh, an avowed atheist first elected to Parliament in 1880, who refused to take the oath of office because it included the words, "So help me God." The Commons refused to seat him until 1886 when, after several lawsuits and repeated re-election, Bradlaugh took his seat. In 1888 he secured the passage of a bill removing all religious tests for members of Parliament.

A final set of measures democratizing Parliament and the nation became law in 1911. In 1909 the House of Lords defeated the budget bill of David Lloyd George, the Liberals' fiery chancellor of the exchequer. After two general elections in 1910 showed that the mass of the electorate were behind the Liberals, they persuaded the king to threaten to create 250 Liberal peers unless the Lords gave up the right of veto on all money bills and limited themselves to a suspensive veto on other legislation. In the face of this threat — the same weapon used by the Whigs in 1832 — the Lords capitulated in 1911. The bill provided for general elections at least once every five years, and another law passed shortly afterward provided for payment of salaries to members of the House of Commons. Thus, with minor exceptions, all the demands posed by the Chartists and brusquely rejected more than three-quarters of a century earlier (see p. 609) had been enacted into law.

THE RISE OF THE LABOUR PARTY

A major objective of the Chartists had been to secure representation for workers in Parliament and to make the latter body more responsive to the will of the masses. Even before all their demands had been achieved, the workers succeeded in making their voices heard in Parliament. A few trade union officials won election to the House of Commons as early as the 1870's; they usually voted with the Liberals and were known somewhat derisively as Lib-Labs. J. Keir Hardie foreshadowed a new approach when he won election as an independent in 1892 and shocked the Commons by appearing in the House in a tweed jacket and cloth cap, escorted by a trumpeter. In the following year he formed the Independent Labour party. To strengthen the bases of his support, Hardie persuaded the Trades Union Congress, the Fabians, and other democratic groups to join with the I.L.P. in forming the Labour Representation Committee. In the election of 1900 the committee supported fifteen candidates and succeeded in electing two. It was a small beginning, but it laid the basis for labor representation in Parliament. In the next general election in 1906 the committee put up fifty candidates, elected twenty-nine, and promptly transformed itself into the Labour party.

The new party received a severe setback in 1909, when W. V. Osborne, a union member, won a legal decision in the House of Lords (the final court of appeal) invalidating the practice of trade union contributions to political parties. Since most of Labour's representatives were trade union officials and their campaigns were financed in part with trade union funds, this posed a serious and immediate threat to the future of the party. In 1911 the Liberals came to their aid (thereby contributing to their own demise) with a provision for payment of salaries to members of the House of Commons, but the larger issue was left unresolved. The trade unions began to take matters into their own hands. A wave of increasingly bitter strikes in 1911 and 1912 and the invasion of syndicalist ideas from the Continent persuaded the Liberals in 1913 to pass a new Trade Union Act permitting the unions to make political contributions from a special fund, subject to the consent of individual members. Thereafter the strength of the Labour party increased steadily. Although it divided on the issue of supporting the war effort, as did workers' parties in other countries, one of its members served in the coalition War Cabinet, and in 1922 it replaced the Liberals as the official opposition party.

SOCIAL REFORM

Political reform and the rise of the Labour party were closely connected with social reform and governmental reorganization. In spite of its reputation as a bastion of liberty and its remarkable economic progress, British society in the second half of the nineteenth century was in many respects curiously antiquated. Carrying devotion to laissez faire principles to an extreme, the government acknowledged slight responsibility for such matters as public health, welfare, or education. The structure of government itself was a ramshackle conglomerate of diverse administrations with little centralized direction or control. Nepotism and minor forms of corruption flourished in a situation in which government was regarded almost as a family affair, or at best as the concern of the propertied classes.

Overhaul of the administrative machinery of government constituted a major prerequisite for extensive social reform and modernization. Gladstone tackled the problem in his first administration, from 1868 to 1874, with measures making the civil service accessible by competitive examination, reorganizing the army (including abolition of the practice of purchasing commissions), and reforming the judiciary. In his turn Disraeli codified and extended the various measures dealing with public health and sanitation and made an initial though inadequate attack on the disgraceful conditions of urban housing. Another Conservative government in 1888 carried further the reform of local government.

In spite of its head start in modern industry, Great Britain lagged behind the Continent in measures dealing with the specific hazards of industrial society. The Employers' Liability Act of 1880 required employers to grant compensation to workers for injuries received on the job if the worker could prove that the injury did not result from his own or a coworker's negligence. In 1906 the law was extended and the emphasis was reversed to cover all injuries "except in cases of serious and willful misconduct." In 1909 Lloyd George inaugurated old-age pensions for retired workers whose annual income was less than $150. In 1911 Lloyd George and young Winston Churchill, who was then a Liberal, led the fight for a National Insurance Act, the most important welfare legislation in Britain to that date. Modeled on German precedents, the law codified earlier accident insurance provisions, extended them to other forms of disability such as sickness, and introduced a limited plan for unemployment compensation. Although Great Britain did not measure up to the advanced practices on the Continent, it preceded the United States in these matters by a quarter of a century.

Nowhere did Britain lag further behind other Western nations than in public support of education. Until 1870 the only schools available were those operated by private or religious foundations, most of which charged fees, except for the parish schools in Scotland. As a result, fully half of the population received no formal education at all. Only the well-to-do received more than the rudiments. This factor more than any other served to preserve Britain's archaic class structure in an age of otherwise rapid social change and contributed notably to the relative decline of Britain's industrial leadership. The Education Bill of 1870 provided state support for existing private and church-connected schools that met certain minimum standards. Not until 1891, however, did education become, even in principle, both free and universal up to the age of twelve. As late as the 1920's only one in eight of the eligible population attended a secondary school.

In higher education England also lagged behind the Continent and the United States. Until state scholarships were instituted in the twentieth century, Oxford and Cambridge were open only to the sons of the wealthy, mainly the aristocracy. By contrast, Scotland, with a much smaller population than England, had four ancient and flourishing universities open to all qualified applicants. London's University College, in existence from 1825, became the University of London in 1898 with the addition of more colleges. In 1880 Manchester became the first provincial city to obtain a new university. By the beginning of the twentieth century the movement to establish municipal universities in the larger cities finally got under way, but even after World War I only four persons per thousand in the appropriate age group were enrolled in a university.

Adult education of the self-help variety had long been popular in Britain, partly as an offset to the inadequate provision of formal educational opportunities. With the rise of labor-class consciousness the movement took on a social orientation. In 1899 Ruskin Hall was established at Oxford as a workingman's college. The Workers' Educational Association, formed in 1903 to reach workers without access to other educational facilities, played a prominent role in bringing culture to the masses and preparing them for a more responsible — and occasionally more aggressive — role in society.

THE IRISH QUESTION

One of the most troublesome problems to face successive British governments in the nineteenth century was that of Ireland. The British had traditionally treated the Irish as a conquered people, and the Irish had never made willing subjects. When Gladstone became prime minister for the first time in 1868, he declared it his "mission" to pacify Ireland. Although he sympathized with oppressed nationalities elsewhere, Gladstone regarded religion and land tenure as the main sources of Irish discontent. Most of the Irish, except in the northern province of Ulster, were Roman Catholics, yet they were taxed to support the established Church of Ireland, the Irish branch of the Church of England. One of Gladstone's first measures was a bill to disestablish the Irish church, which became law in 1869. The following year Parliament passed the Irish Land Act, giving some protection to tenants and facilitating peasant proprietorship. These measures did not, however, allay Irish discontent with English rule. One group of Irish nationalists making use of the recent extension of the franchise formed the Home Rule party to agitate in Parliament for a separate Irish legislature. Charles Parnell, paradoxically a Protestant of English descent, took over the leadership of this movement soon after his election to the House of Commons in 1875. Parnell regarded land reform as a mere palliative and promptly initiated a campaign to ostracize any tenants or landlords who took advantage of the new law. A certain Captain Boycott, the first victim of the campaign, thereby acquired the dubious distinction of having his name become a new word in the English language. The government imprisoned Parnell and several of his followers but released them after six months on their agreement to call off the "boycotts" and to cooperate with the Liberals for further reforms.

After the general election of 1885 Parnell's party held the balance of power in the House of Commons. Parnell first allowed a Conservative government to take office, but when it failed to give him satisfaction, he threw his support to the Liberals. Gladstone promptly introduced a bill to grant home rule, but defections within his own party defeated it. After long debates Gladstone's second home rule bill passed Commons with a small majority in 1893, only to go down to overwhelming defeat in the House of Lords. Gladstone wished to call for new elections, but his cabinet refused to support him. He thereupon retired from politics, an old and disillusioned man, his dream of Irish pacification unfulfilled.

For a time the Irish problem subsided. The Conservatives, who ruled from 1895 to 1905, described their policy as "killing home rule with kindness." In 1912 the Liberals introduced a third home rule bill. It aroused great opposition, not only in the Lords, many of whom were landowners in Ireland, but also among the Protestant inhabitants of Northern Ireland or Ulster, who would be submerged in a united Irish parliament. After long and bitter debates the bill reached its third reading in the Commons in May, 1914. Had it become law at once, civil war between volunteer groups of militiamen in Ulster and the south would certainly have taken place. This catastrophe was postponed by the greater catastrophe of World War I, which overshadowed all other political issues. In a hastily reached compromise the bill received royal assent in September, 1914, with a proviso that it would not take effect until the war was over and new amendments were made to deal with the problem of Ulster. In the event, it never took effect, but bequeathed a bitter legacy to the postwar generation.

THE THIRD FRENCH REPUBLIC

The capitulation of Napoleon III to the Germans at Sedan on September 2, 1870, and the quick reaction of the people of Paris in deposing him brought down the curtain on the Second Empire with a sudden thump. No one knew what the title would be when it rose on the next act in the drama of French politics. Even the names of the principal actors could not be foretold with certainty. *Entre acte,* the Government of National Defense provided a thrilling diversion with its heroic but hopeless attempt to continue the war. It even brought forward a new star in Léon Gambetta, a young radical republican who escaped from besieged Paris in a balloon to organize resistance forces in the provinces. By mid-January the futility of further armed resistance became apparent to all but Gambetta and a relatively small number of last-ditch radicals and socialists. When Paris capitulated on January 28, the armistice provided for the election of a representative assembly to determine whether or not the war should be continued and, if not, on what terms the peace should be concluded.

The hastily called election took place on February 8. Under the circumstances elaborate campaigns and even systematic party programs were impossible. The only issue was peace or war. There could be no doubt that most Frenchmen, war-weary, dispirited, and dismayed, favored peace. Since the radical republicans constituted the only important group prominently identified with a desire to continue the war, it was not surprising that the people voted overwhelmingly for conservatives. When the new National Assembly met for the first time in Bordeaux on February 13, it counted among its numbers more than four hundred monarchists and only about two hundred avowed republicans.

The assembly elected Adolphe Thiers, the most prominent remaining Orleanist politician, as chief executive of the provisional government and empowered him to negotiate a peace treaty with Bismarck. The Prussians imposed severe terms: the transfer of Alsace and part of Lorraine to the new German Empire; payment of a war indemnity of five billion francs (about one billion gold dollars); and a Prussian army of occupation until final payment of the indemnity. Over the heated objections of Gambetta and other radicals (including Louis Blanc, a figure out of the past, and Georges Clemenceau, a prefiguration of the future), the assembly unhappily accepted these terms by a majority of more than five to one. In early March it moved to Versailles to decide upon the definitive form of government. Before it could come to grips with this difficult problem, it found itself involved in a brief but bitter civil war.

THE PARIS COMMUNE

The main republican strength lay in the working classes of the large cities, especially Paris. They had held out longest against the besieging armies and regarded the provisional government's capitulation as a form of betrayal. They resented the monarchist domination of the new assembly as well as the latter's decision to make Versailles, reminiscent of the Old Regime, the capital instead of Paris. When Thiers canceled the wartime moratorium on the payment of debts and rents and cut off the dole to members of the National Guard, the resentment of the Parisians mounted; when on March 18 he ordered the seizure of their arms, it overflowed. The regular army at first refused to fire on the people, but angry mobs seized and murdered two of its generals. The government then ordered a new siege of Paris, this time by Frenchmen. These developments, plus the fact that wealthier residents had long since fled the city, gave control of the city to the most radical elements. They proclaimed a self-governing Commune on the model of 1792 and called on other cities to take similar steps and convert France into a decentralized federal republic. Sympathetic rebellions elsewhere in France soon fell before government forces, but the Communards (not to be confused with Communists) of Paris held out for more than two months.

The fighting was the bloodiest of its kind in history. In the final week alone (May 21–28) more than 15,000 died — many more than during the

Bulloz

Execution at the Cemetery of Père Lachaise, May 28, 1871
from the series "Crimes of the Commune"

Sunday, 28 May 1871.
"I rode in a cab along the Champs-Élysées. In the distance legs, legs running
in the direction of the great avenue. I leaned out of the cab window. The entire
avenue was filled with a confused mob, between two lines of troopers. I got out
of the cab and joined the people running to see what was happening. It was the
prisoners who had just been taken at Buttes-Chaumont, marching in ranks of
five, with a few women in their midst. 'There were six thousand of them,' a
trooper in the escort told me. 'Five hundred were shot on the spot.'"
Edmond de Goncourt, JOURNAL (Paris, 1956).

June Days of 1848. The Communards executed many hostages, including
the archbishop of Paris, and in their last hours set fire to several public
buildings, notably the Tuileries palace and the city hall. The attacking
forces shot on sight, and after the final collapse of the Commune they
executed thousands.

Such an orgy of blood-letting could not fail to have important long-run
consequences. Coming after similar episodes at the beginning of the two
previous French republics, it created an almost unbridgeable chasm between the affected social classes. The collective psychological scars that it
left have not fully healed after a century. Yet in one sense it worked to
the benefit of the Third Republic. After many of the most radical republican leaders had been executed, imprisoned, deported, or exiled, those

who remained either stayed in the background or took a more moderate line, thereby giving the moderate and conservative republicans an opportunity to win the majority of the French people away from monarchic leanings. A notable example of the transformation was Léon Gambetta, who in spite of his earlier intransigence took the view that a conservative republic was better than no republic at all.

THE ESTABLISHMENT OF THE REPUBLIC

For most of its first decade the Third Republic threatened to relapse into a monarchy at any moment. That it did not do so at once can be accounted for only by the divisions among the monarchists themselves. In the assembly they were split almost evenly between the supporters of the Legitimist (Bourbon) count of Chambord (Henry V, as he styled himself), grandson of Charles X, and the Orleanist count of Paris, grandson of Louis Philippe. Since Chambord had no direct heirs, the rival monarchist groups agreed that he should first accede to the throne but should name the count of Paris as his successor. Chambord, who had spent forty of his fifty years in exile, returned to France in July, 1871, to announce the terms on which he would accept the throne. They amounted to little less than an integral restoration of the Old Regime, symbolized by his insistence on replacing the French tricolor with the Bourbon fleur-de-lis. Such a restoration was not acceptable to many of Chambord's own supporters, much less acceptable to the Orleanists, whose ideal was a British type of constitutional monarchy, and anathema to the resurgent republicans. In the by-elections held shortly before Chambord's manifesto the republicans gained 99 out of 114 seats in the assembly.

To give themselves time to regroup and reformulate their strategy, the monarchists allowed Thiers to assume the title of president of the Republic in August, 1871. At the same time they declared their intention not to dissolve the assembly until it had given France a new constitution, which they intended should be monarchic. As time went by, the monarchists became increasingly suspicious of Thiers's connivance with the republicans for a maintenance of the status quo. Thiers ultimately declared that "the republic is the form of government which divides us least." In 1873, therefore, as soon as Thiers's government had paid the last installment of the indemnity to Prussia, the monarchist majority in the assembly forced him to resign and replaced him with Marshal MacMahon, an old soldier of monarchist predilections but little experience in politics. At the appropriate moment he was to give way to royalty.

The results of by-elections steadily whittled down the majority of the monarchists, who realized that they would have to act promptly to preserve the framework for a royalist restoration. They obtained the enactment of the so-called organic laws of 1875, which served France as a constitution for the entire life of the Third Republic. It is one of the ironies of French history that the only republican constitution that did not proclaim itself to be based on "eternal and immutable" principles — one, indeed, frankly regarded as provisional — should have given France its longest period of stable government in modern times. The laws provided for a bicameral legislature with an upper house, the Senate, elected indirectly for long and staggered terms; a lower house, the Chamber of Deputies; a cabinet and prime minister responsible to the legislature; and a figurehead president elected by the legislature. Although republican in name, such a constitution could easily be made to serve a constitutional monarchy as well. On the last day of 1875 the National Assembly that had been elected at the beginning of 1871 to decide on the question of peace or war dissolved itself to make way for the new constitutional system that it had designed.

THREATS TO THE REPUBLIC

The new Chamber of Deputies, elected by universal manhood suffrage, had a republican majority of more than two to one. This majority did not mean that the Republic was solidly established, however, for MacMahon's term as president had five years to run, and the new Senate was dominated, as intended, by conservatives inclined toward monarchy. The republicans themselves were divided into three broad groups: conservative republicans, mainly ex-Orleanists like Thiers; moderate or opportunist republicans; and the radicals led by Gambetta, egalitarian in spirit and Jacobin by tradition. In subsequent years this division accounted for the extreme instability of ministries, whose life expectancy averaged less than one year. As long as the monarchist-clerical coalition posed a serious threat to republican institutions, however, the various republican groups banded together in an uneasy alliance to meet the successive crises, of which there were several in the next twenty-five years.

The first overt crisis was the *seize mai* episode. On May 16, 1877, President MacMahon in a moment of impatience provoked the resignation of Jules Simon, the moderate republican prime minister. When the Chamber of Deputies refused to approve the prime minister designated by the president, MacMahon dissolved it and called a new election. Although the republicans lost a few seats, they still commanded a substantial majority and forced the president to accept a ministry in which they had confidence. Thereafter no president or prime minister of the Third Republic forced a dissolution of the Chamber. In January, 1879, partial elections to the Senate resulted in republican control of that body. This surprising outcome demonstrated that republican sentiment had infiltrated and conquered even the small towns and villages, which held the balance of power in indirect elections for the Senate. Faced with hostile majorities in both Chamber and Senate, President MacMahon resigned a year before his term expired.

With the Republic apparently safeguarded, the opportunists, who now occupied the center of the stage, proceeded to carry out their legislative program. Its overriding objective was to instill such strong republican sentiments in Frenchmen that no internal threat to the Republic could ever again arise. In order to win the allegiance of the working classes, the government amnestied the remaining veterans of the Commune and in 1884 legalized trade unions once again. Otherwise the government paid scant heed to the needs and desires of workingmen, with the result that anarchist and socialist doctrines retained a strong hold on French workers, and their loyalty to the bourgeois republic remained suspect.

The government took more positive action in the field of education and religion. In both instances the aim was to restrict the influence of the church and the clerical party, the strongest allies of the monarchists. A law in 1882 introduced compulsory public education between the ages of six and thirteen and ensured that it would be free of all religious training. A generation of dedicated schoolmasters drilled the youth of France with ideals of patriotism, republicanism, and secularism. In the process they reduced illiteracy from a third or more of the adult population to a negligible figure. The government once more legalized divorce (first legalized during the Revolution, then banned in 1816), thus striking another blow at the moral influence of the church.

Before these measures could produce their full effects, new threats to the regime arose. In 1886 General Georges Boulanger became minister of war for a brief period. He was a strikingly handsome and impressive man, given to frequent and elegant public appearances (usually on a white horse), who came to symbolize for many Frenchmen the desire and possibility of revenge against Germany. Although originally sponsored in politics by the radical republicans, he soon began to cultivate friendships on the extreme right as well. In either case he was a danger to the center parties, who quickly dropped him from office. In 1887 the government was weakened by revelations that the president's son-in-law had been peddling political favors and influence, while Boulanger's popularity continued to grow in spite of all the government could do to keep him out of the public view. In January, 1889, after a particularly impressive showing by Boulanger in a Paris by-election, conditions seemed ripe for a coup d'état. Although it probably would have been accepted by a majority of the people, Boulanger lost his nerve at the crucial moment and, instead of marching on the government, sought the solace of his mistress. Soon afterward he fled into exile in Belgium, where he committed suicide in 1891.

The most serious threat, not only to the government but to the whole fabric of French society, arose in the Dreyfus case. Evidence that secret documents of the French army had been transmitted to Germany led in 1894 to the trial and conviction by a court-martial of Captain Alfred Dreyfus, a Jewish officer on the general staff. Dreyfus was sentenced to life imprisonment on Devil's Island. It subsequently developed that he had been convicted on forged evidence and that the real culprit was still on active duty with the army, but the army acquitted the guilty man and refused to reopen the Dreyfus case. In 1898 the affair became a cause célèbre with the dramatic intervention of the novelist Émile Zola, who published an open letter (*J'accuse*) to the president accusing by name the high officers of the army responsible for railroading Dreyfus and shielding the guilty. Individual personalities were soon pushed into the background by the political, social, and religious overtones of the struggle. The Dreyfusards, or defenders of Dreyfus, regarded themselves as defenders of the Republic and of the "ideas of 1789," whereas in the opposite camp were ranged all those who had consistently opposed those ideas in the past — the diehard royalists and ultramontane Catholics, as well as the aristocratic officer corps and professional anti-Semites. All France took sides, sometimes in the form of open clashes in the streets. Even the socialists under the leadership of Jean Jaurès rallied to the defense of Dreyfus and the Republic. At length in 1906 Dreyfus was completely exonerated, decorated, and restored to the army with the rank of major.

For the nation at large the more important consequence of the Dreyfus affair was the victory of the Republic over its enemies, the resulting reform of the army, and the separation of church and state. As early as 1901 the government adopted a set of stringent laws directed principally at the monastic orders whose members had taken an active part in the anti-Dreyfusard agitation. Stronger measures followed, resulting in the suppression of some orders, the closure of Catholic schools, and the secularization of church property. Finally in 1905 France abrogated Napoleon's Concordat with the pope and declared a complete separation of church and state. In subsequent years the restrictions on monastic orders were relaxed, Catholic schools reopened, and the churches returned to the congregations; but separation of church and state remains today as much a principle of French as of American political life.

LA BELLE ÉPOQUE

In spite of the humiliation of 1870–71 and the numerous crises both foreign and domestic in which France was involved before 1914, many Frenchmen after World War I looked back on the prewar years as *la belle époque*, the good old days. Their attitude seems paradoxical, but it had a reasonable basis. The outlook for France had been bleak indeed in the 1870's, but the situation gradually improved until, in the last decade before World War I, Frenchmen not only enjoyed reasonable political stability but also military strength and greater prosperity than ever before. After a long depression from 1882 to 1897 the French economy recovered its vitality and exhibited a growth rate equal to that of any advanced industrial nation. By the early years of the twentieth century the French had forged a strong alliance with Russia and had even brought Great Britain out of its "splendid isolation" into an *entente cordiale.* (See pp. 833–834.) Frenchmen could once more hold up their heads with the proud nations of the world.

After the Dreyfus affair no major political crisis or scandal troubled the domestic scene until World War I. Cabinets continued to rise and fall with alarming frequency, but such ministerial instability was accepted by the French as one of the facts of political life. It was quite consistent with a fundamental political and social stability, for the ministers in successive cabinets usually came from the same coalition of political parties. In many instances an individual minister retained his post even though the cabinet itself changed. The professional and expert civil service provided a fundamental continuity of administration through all the surface changes of ministries. Thus, the fragmentation and apparent disorderliness of French political life, with its multiplicity of parties and ever-changing ministries, was superficial and somewhat illusory. Frenchmen themselves, who through sad experience had grown to distrust strong governments, seemed to prefer the situation.

THE SECOND GERMAN REICH

The first Germanic empire, founded by Charlemagne, existed (in form, at least) for a thousand years. The second empire or Reich, founded by Bismarck, lasted only from 1871 to 1918. The immediate cause of its downfall was defeat in World War I, but even if there had been no war, it is unlikely that it would have long endured in its original form. More than any other government in modern times, including even the Napoleonic empire, it was the creation of a single individual. As long as the creator remained in control, he succeeded by devious stratagems and abrupt changes of course in making its complicated machinery function remarkably well. Thereafter, in spite of a superficial semblance of harmonious, almost monolithic operation, the centrifugal tendencies of its parts created strains that sooner or later would have torn it asunder. Accordingly, the history of the Second Reich divides itself for purposes of narrative and analysis into two periods: that of Bismarck (1871–1890) and that of his successors (1890–1918).

THE STRUCTURE OF THE GOVERNMENT

The form of the government was itself a bundle of paradoxes and ambiguities: monarchic, federal, and democratic in appearance, but paternalistic and authoritarian in fact. The constitution, adopted on April 14, 1871, was simply a remodeled version of the constitution of the North German Confederation, which had also been a creation of Bismarck. The empire was composed of twenty-five formerly independent states (four kingdoms; eighteen duchies, grand duchies, and principalities; and three free cities) plus the "imperial territory" of Alsace-Lorraine. The component states conserved much autonomy for strictly local government matters, such as education, although even there they had to fight against the Prussianizing tendencies of the imperial government. The imperial government had principal responsibility for military and foreign affairs but also exerted its authority in economic, social, and religious matters. For the exercise of its functions it possessed a bicameral legislature and an imperial cabinet or chancellery. The office of emperor was hereditary in the person of the king of Prussia.

The Reichstag, the lower house of the Imperial Diet or legislature, gave the regime its semblance of democracy. Representatives were elected from single-member constituencies by universal manhood suffrage. The powers of the body were severely limited, however, especially in the matter of finances, the crucial element in representative government. In certain circumstances the imperial government could dispense with approval of the budget by the Reichstag. All legislation from the Reichstag had to be agreed to by the Bundesrat or federal council, which consisted of the personal representatives of the ruling princes and in which Prussia could always command a majority. The imperial chancellor, appointed by the emperor, served as president of the Bundesrat, but he was responsible neither to it nor to the Reichstag.

Under these conditions the Reichstag functioned mainly as a register of public opinion, which the government might follow or not. Bismarck, as chancellor, did not scruple to override public opinion on occasion, but as a shrewd politician, he sought more often to lead and manipulate it. This he did by working with the principal parties in the Reichstag. The Conservative party represented chiefly the East Elbian Junker aristocracy, Bismarck's own class. The National Liberal party represented the west German bourgeoisie of wealthy merchants, industrialists, and financiers. The Catholic Center party had its main strength in south Germany, but it also had representatives wherever Catholics were numerous, as among Rhenish workers and Silesian peasants. In addition to these major parties there were several minor ones: the Progressives, liberals who had opposed Bismarck in the past; the Social Democrats, representing the workers; and representatives of national minorities such as the Danes, the Poles, and the inhabitants of Alsace-Lorraine.

BISMARCKIAN POLITICS

Bismarck's policies appear at first sight curiously contradictory, as though he did not know what he wanted. First he favored free trade, then he became an ardent protectionist. He opposed colonial expansion, but laid the foundations of the German overseas empire. He persecuted the socialists, but enacted the first state-supported social insurance system in the world. In foreign affairs, he who had earlier deliberately provoked three wars devoted his efforts to preserving the peace. Yet underneath these apparent inconsistencies lay a determined and consistent purpose: to preserve the empire and his own place within it. The empire had been created by force, and it might be destroyed by force; therefore he must prevent war. If the socialists constituted a menace to the internal stability of the government, the workers must be weaned away from socialism. When the National Liberals' enthusiasm for free trade and his own leadership showed signs of slackening because of the industrial depression of the 1870's and increasing foreign competition, he put through the protective tariff law of 1879 in order to placate the manufacturers and also curry favor with the Conservatives. Similarly, his conversion to colonialism was no more than a strategic concession to the force of public opinion.

The first major domestic problem faced — or provoked — by the new government concerned its relations with the Roman Catholic Church. The issue was the supremacy of church or state in the areas where their interests overlapped, especially with respect to authority over the individual. The name given to the issue, *Kulturkampf,* meaning struggle for civilization, signified Bismarck's intention that there should be no divided loyalties within the empire. As recently as 1864 in the *Syllabus of Errors* the Church had declared it an "error" (hence a sin) to believe that the civil authority of the state should be superior to or separated from the Roman Catholic Church, and in 1870 the Church had laid down the doctrine of papal infallibility in questions of faith and morals. It was perhaps even more important from Bismarck's point of view that the traditionally Catholic south German states resented domination by Protestant Prussia, for political and cultural as well as religious reasons, and it was they who provided the strength and leadership of the Center party in opposition to Bismarck.

Between 1871 and 1875 Bismarck undertook a number of measures designed to harass, weaken, and even destroy the Catholic Church in Germany. Most of the measures applied only to Prussia, since the other states retained autonomy in religious, educational, and cultural affairs. Some, however, including the expulsion of the Jesuits, the severance of diplomatic relations with the Vatican, and the law making civil marriage compulsory, affected the entire empire. In spite of intense persecution, the Catholics showed no sign of wavering and in some respects actually throve on it. At length Bismarck realized the futility of his policy; when the more diplomatic and conciliatory Leo XIII succeeded Pius IX in 1878, Bismarck relaxed his campaign and eventually called it off altogether. By 1883 the *Kulturkampf* was at an end.

Some historians have speculated that the religious question was secondary in Bismarck's mind when he undertook the *Kulturkampf* and that what he really wanted was a convenient whipping boy to divert public attention from other problems and to arouse popular sentiment in favor of the empire. This interpretation gains credence from the next episode in Bismarck's domestic policies, the persecution of the socialists. In the elections of 1878 almost all the opposition parties made gains at the expense of the National Liberals. This development prompted Bismarck to "build a bridge" between the agrarian protectionists in the Conservative party and the industrialists in the National Liberal party, who had begun to demand protection for their own products, by effecting the protective tariff law of 1879. Simultaneously he initiated a campaign against the socialists, who were the weakest and most vulnerable of the opposition parties. His justification came from two recent attempts to assassinate the emperor. Although the socialists were in no way involved with either attempt, he used them as a pretext for outlawing the Social Democratic party. Although the Reichstag refused to unseat the socialist members, and several were re-elected as independents with trade union support, the party itself was forced underground, and many of its leaders were imprisoned or sought refuge abroad.

When it appeared likely that this policy, too, might backfire, Bismarck resolved to win the workers away from socialism with a carrot-and-stick technique. In 1883 he sponsored a compulsory sickness insurance plan for workers, followed in 1884 by an accident insurance plan, and in 1889 by a pension plan for the aged and permanently disabled. These measures were consolidated and extended by Bismarck's successors and gave

---

Dropping the Pilot, cartoon from *Punch*
March 29, 1890

> *"The Emperor related the whole story of his difference with Bismarck. He said that relations had become strained as early as December. The Emperor then desired that something should be done upon the question of the workmen. The Chancellor objected. . . . This friction had considerably disturbed the relations between Bismarck and the Emperor, and these were further strained by the question of the Cabinet Order of 1852. Bismarck had often advised the Emperor to grant the ministers access to himself and this was done. But when communications between the Emperor and his ministers became more frequent, Bismarck took offense, became jealous, and revived the Cabinet Order of 1852 in order to break communications between the Emperor and his ministers. . . . The last three weeks were occupied by unpleasant discussions between the Emperor and Bismarck. It was, as the Emperor expressed it, 'a stormy time,' and the question at issue was, as the Emperor went on to say, whether the Hohenzollern dynasty or the Bismarck dynasty should reign."* MEMOIRS OF PRINCE CHLODWIG OF HOHENLOHE-SCHILLINGSFURST (New York, 1906).

Germany the first and most comprehensive system of social insurance and labor protection dealing specifically with the new problems created by modern industrial society.

DROPPING THE PILOT

In 1888 the old emperor, William I, died. Frederick III, his son and successor, survived him by only three months. The new emperor, William II, grandson of Queen Victoria of Britain as well as of William I, was only twenty-nine at the time. Handsome and intelligent, he promised to bring an unaccustomed glamor to the throne. But he was also headstrong

Courtesy of *Punch* Magazine

and unpredictable and lost no time in coming into conflict with the venerable Bismarck, who for so long had had things his own way. The differences between the two were not merely differences of policy, or even of
personality, though these counted for much; fundamentally they were
differences between the generations. The immediate sources of friction involved both foreign and domestic policy. William objected to Bismarck's
conciliatory gestures to Russia. At the same time he favored the conciliation of the working-class population at home and allowed the antisocialist
laws to lapse. Even more revealing of their basic differences, William objected to Bismarck's practice of sitting in on interviews between the emperor and his other ministers. At the beginning of 1890 William suggested
to Bismarck that he should "ask permission to resign." Bismarck refused,
but William persisted and soon drove him from the chancellery. It was an
ironic turn of events. Bismarck, who had so carefully insulated the office
of chancellor from both popular and parliamentary opinion, now found
himself ejected by his own creation, the emperor.

Bismarck's departure had more serious consequences for international
affairs than for domestic politics. (See p. 832.) It was in foreign policy that
he had achieved his greatest success, and this was precisely the arena in
which his successors were least able and successful. In domestic policy
he had managed by intricate footwork to hold in check temporarily the
centrifugal tendencies of the nation. In the long run, however, his domestic policies contributed to widening and perpetuating the internal divisions of the German people.

BISMARCK'S SUCCESSORS

William's dismissal of Bismarck made it clear that he intended to serve
in effect as his own chancellor. To fill the office, he first selected General
George von Caprivi, a soldier and administrator without political experience. Caprivi's tenure (1890–1894) was notable chiefly for the negotiation
of a number of commercial treaties that aroused the fury of the great
landowners, the stalwarts of the Conservative party. Caprivi also managed
to antagonize the Catholics, the colonialists, and the militarists. These
misfortunes, together with the difficulty of working with the emperor,
who was given to making policy pronouncements in public without consulting his ministers, led to Caprivi's resignation.

The chancellorships of Caprivi's successors — Prince Hohenlohe-Schil-
lingsfürst (1894–1900), Count von Bülow (1900–1909), and Theobald von
Bethmann-Hollweg (1909–1917) — were increasingly dominated by military and foreign affairs in the march toward World War I. Under
Hohenlohe two projects that had been long in preparation reached completion. The opening of the Kiel Canal, joining the Baltic and North
seas, capped a period of significant improvement in Germany's internal
communications system and symbolized its advent as a sea power. The

codification of civil law, which had been in process since 1871, gave the German states a uniform, comprehensive legal system for the first time in their history. The new code went into effect January 1, 1900.

THE "REVISIONIST" CONTROVERSY

The empire experienced its only parliamentary crisis of the Western type in 1906 when the Center party, which had held the balance of power in the Reichstag since 1890 and derived great advantage from it, joined with the Social Democrats and other radical parties to defeat a government bill to strengthen Germany's colonial empire. Bülow dissolved the Reichstag and called on the electorate to repudiate the Catholics and socialists. In the election of 1907 the Center party held its ground, but the Social Democrats lost heavily in their only major setback between 1890 and 1914. This defeat played an important role in the reorientation of Social Democratic policies, which in turn had reverberations in the entire international socialist movement.

At the time of its formation the German Social Democratic party had adopted a party platform that represented a compromise between Marxian revolutionary socialism and Lassallean state socialism. Under Bismarck's persecution the ideology of the party steadily became more revolutionary, until in 1891 it adopted an almost pure Marxian platform, which remained official doctrine until 1918. During the period of persecution some of the party members went into foreign exile. One of the exiles, Eduard Bernstein, spent much time in England, where he observed the operation of the British parliamentary system and became acquainted with several of the Fabian leaders. After his return to Germany in the 1890's he advocated that Social Democratic parties should abandon their revolutionary ideologies and work within the established political order for peaceful social, economic, and political reform. He pointed out that contrary to Marx's prophecy, the masses were not growing poorer; their position was steadily improving. The bourgeois state was not approaching a final crisis; it was gaining in strength as it became more democratic. Hence, instead of trying to overthrow the state, the socialists should try to hasten its evolution in the direction of democracy and socialism. Bernstein's modifications of orthodox Marxist doctrine became known as revisionism and had a powerful impact on the socialist movement both in Germany and abroad.

The German Social Democratic party debated Bernstein's revisionism in party congresses in 1901 and 1903. In formal votes the congresses defeated Bernstein's proposals, but in actual practice the leadership conformed more and more to the tactics of gradualism. Although the party clung to its tradition of nonparticipation in bourgeois governments, it went so far as to help the Progressives organize the Reichstag after the latter obtained a plurality in the election of 1912.

On the eve of World War I Germany appeared to be a powerful, cohesive state. Powerful it was, both militarily and economically, but politically and socially it was a divided nation in spite of its semblance of unity. Apart from its federal structure and the continuing suspicion between Protestant Prussia and the Catholic south, the social divisions between the workers and the middle classes, and between the urban dwellers, the landed aristocracy, and the peasantry, were great and pervasive.

The artificial Bismarckian constitution, despite its increasingly anachronistic character, remained rigid in the mold of its maker. Although the patriotic enthusiasm generated by the outbreak of World War I temporarily submerged the political and social antagonisms, they lay just under the surface and sprang forth in still more virulent form in the wake of the wartime defeat.

THE LESSER STATES OF WESTERN EUROPE

In an era of international rivalries the very fact of great power status introduces a bias into the domestic political history of the great powers, a bias often exaggerated by historians. With the smaller states, on the other hand, we can abstract from the influences of international politics and observe the details of social, political, and economic forces at close range, as though in a laboratory. And, in some cases, we can observe the repercussions of great-power politics on nations whose vital interests may be involved but who, in the nature of the case, cannot take independent action. The results are not without general interest.

ITALY

Italy occupied an ambiguous position in the late nineteenth century. Its population entitled it to rank with the smaller of the great powers, and its political leaders definitely had great power aspirations. They built up an army and navy, entered alliances with the other great powers, and made a bid for colonial empire. Yet basically Italy was a poor country with grave internal problems, quite unsuited for the great power status it tried to maintain.

Italy had few natural resources and no coal at all. The population density was one of the highest in Europe, yet much of the country was mountainous and infertile. Well over half the population derived its meager subsistence from agriculture, conducted under essentially medieval conditions, especially in the south. A few regions in the north, such as Piedmont and Lombardy, had relatively progressive agriculture and even some modern industry, but this only accentuated the great disparity between north and south. The majority of Italians were illiterate in 1860. The state made no provision for public education until 1877, and even then it was largely ineffective, although some gains in literacy were achieved by 1914.

One of the most critical Italian political problems was the relationship of the state and the Catholic Church. The pope refused to accept the law of papal guarantees (see p. 654) and forbade Catholics to participate in national politics or government. For a country with a 99 per cent Catholic population this might have led to a paralysis of all political and governmental affairs except that many Italians, though nominal Catholics, were either nonbelievers or anticlerical. Yet the Church's ban did prevent devout Catholics from contributing constructively to political life. The Church partially relaxed its ban on political participation in 1904 and repealed it in 1919; but it did not come to terms with the Italian government until 1929, when it concluded the Lateran Treaty with Benito Mussolini.

Italian political parties grouped themselves in loose coalitions of Right and Left, although the names themselves were almost meaningless. *Transformismo* (opportunism) is the best description of their policies, the objective of which was to gain and retain office by whatever means they could. In 1876 the Left overthrew the Right, which had governed the country since the death of Cavour; and until after World War I various shifting coalitions of the Left dominated the cabinet. Agostino Depretis, Francesco Crispi, and Giovanni Giolitti were the outstanding names of the period, chiefly for the ingenious forms of corruption and pressure that they invented to remain in power. The parliament served as a bazaar for special interests and a sounding board for demagogic nationalist oratory, while the social and economic welfare of the population went unheeded. Less than 10 per cent of the population had the franchise until 1912, when all males over the age of thirty were permitted to vote. Socialist and anarchist sentiment made rapid headway among the workers after about 1890. In the absence of any machinery for making their grievances known in a legitimate fashion, the workers resorted to strikes, riots, and other forms of lawlessness, which became endemic and provided the seedbed for the rival totalitarian movements that sprouted after World War I.

SPAIN AND PORTUGAL

Spain differed from Italy primarily in its steady retreat from any claim to great power status. The restored Bourbon government of 1874 had the appearance of a constitutional monarchy but the substance of a seventeenth-century absolute monarchy. The king ruled with the assistance of a cabal of ministers, who easily dominated the hand-picked Cortes (parliament). The enactment of universal male suffrage in 1890 failed to change the situation, for the strong clerical influence throughout the country was favorable to the monarchy. Spain remained predominantly rural, and economic and social conditions in the rural areas had changed little since the sixteenth century. In the few large cities where modern industry took root, notably Barcelona, socialists and anarchists made converts among the disaffected workers, but calls to class war in the form of general strikes went unheeded in the country at large. A more serious menace to the government was the pronounced regionalism in some of the provinces, especially in Catalonia and the Basque country, which took the form of demands for local autonomy or even a federal form of government.

Spain lost most of the remnants of its colonial empire in the war with the United States in 1898, although it retained a few toeholds in Africa. The war revealed for both Spaniards and outside observers the full extent of Spanish backwardness and political demoralization. Urgent pleas by patriotic liberals for national regeneration evoked little response. Apathy ruled on the surface, while revolutionary pressures were building up below.

Economic and social conditions in Portugal resembled those in Spain, but the revolutionary ferment formed more quickly. The extravagance and licentiousness of Carlos I (1889–1908) in a country noted for its poverty, together with an extremely repressive and dictatorial regime, provoked the assassination of the king and his eldest son in 1908. Two years later an insurrection overthrew Manuel II, his successor, and a republic was proclaimed. The republican regime had an idealistic program of reform, which it initiated with an attack on the privileged position of the Church, the stronghold of royalism and reaction. The liberal republicans maintained their precarious position for a few years, but they had little chance of success. They were a tiny group surrounded by powerful, reactionary landlords and an illiterate, clerically dominated peasantry on the one side and disaffected, anarchist urban workers on the other. Portugal, like Spain and Italy, lacked both the economic and social prerequisites to make a democracy function effectively.

SWITZERLAND AND THE LOW COUNTRIES

The history of the small nations of northwestern Europe furnishes an illuminating contrast to that of the Mediterranean area. Although the natural endowments of Switzerland and the Low Countries were no greater, and they were plagued with religious and ethnic divisions as well, they all contrived to make democracy work.

The Swiss consist of a German-speaking majority, with four French cantons in the west and two Italian cantons south of the Alps; but at no time has a major political dispute flared along linguistic lines. Although in 1847 the Catholic central cantons leagued against the Protestant cantons in the west and north, since the settlement of 1848 religious strife has been equally absent. This remarkable record was in part the result of a desire to preserve Swiss neutrality and to prevent great power intervention in domestic affairs. The spirit of toleration and willingness to compromise developed into a national tradition. In 1874 the constitution of 1848 was revised to give the federal government still larger powers at the expense of the cantons, but it also contained the novel democratic safeguards of the initiative and referendum. It strengthened the already advanced educational system by requiring universal free elementary schooling under federal supervision. Because of the Swiss system of education and their tradition of fine craftsmanship, modern industry made steady progress. After 1880 hydroelectricity helped to offset the lack of other natural resources. In the 1890's Switzerland adopted a comprehensive program of social welfare legislation on the German model, and in 1898 it began to nationalize the railroads. By 1914 the Swiss enjoyed not only political democracy but also one of the highest standards of living in Europe.

The Belgians are divided between the French-speaking Walloons in the south and east and the Flemish in the north and west. Although the nation is Catholic on the whole, the Walloons had a tradition of anticlericalism which flourished in the Liberal and later the Labor parties, whereas the Catholic party drew its main strength from Flanders. The Liberal-Catholic coalition that ruled the country in the perilous years after the achievement of independence in 1830 broke up in 1847. The Liberals generally controlled the government until 1884. In 1879 they passed a law that prohibited religious education in state-supported schools and withdrew state aid from Church-related schools. That resulted in their defeat at the polls in the next election. The new Catholic government reversed the law of 1879, and in 1895 a new law made instruction in the Catholic religion compulsory, even in public schools.

Property qualifications for voting, even after the liberalization of 1848, limited the electorate to less than 5 per cent of the population. The majority of workingmen were effectively disfranchised. In 1855 trade unionists and socialists formed the Belgian Labor party and began to agitate for electoral reform. Under the threat of a general strike in 1893 the parliament introduced universal manhood suffrage, but modified it with a provision allowing plural voting for those with special property, educational, and other qualifications. Agitation broke out again during the following decade, and in 1913 another general strike resulted in a promise of electoral revision; but before it could be implemented, World War I intervened. Not until 1919 did Belgium achieve the ideal of "one man, one vote."

The Dutch had no significant ethnic problems, though the religious division of the country provided a full measure of political headaches. Under the restricted suffrage that prevailed until 1917 (in spite of minor extensions in 1887 and 1896) the anticlerical Liberal party, which drew its strength from the professional men and merchants of the cities, had the largest representation in parliament. They stood firmly for a system of free secular schools. In 1889, however, a rare Catholic-Calvinist coalition secured financial assistance for the church-related schools. Religious disputes continued to flare up, to which were joined demonstrations by workers in favor of political and social reform. None of these reached revolutionary proportions, and the Netherlands, like Belgium and Switzerland, evolved peacefully if slowly in the direction of full democracy.

SCANDINAVIA

The Scandinavian countries, especially Sweden, present an unusual example of a relatively rapid, complete, and successful transition to modern industrial conditions with a minimum of social friction and dislocation. In 1850 economic conditions had changed little from those that prevailed in the eighteenth century and earlier. In Sweden, 90 per cent of the population lived in rural areas, and 80 per cent gained their living directly from agriculture. As late as 1870 more than 72 per cent of the population still drew their sustenance from agriculture, and the rural population accounted for 87 per cent. During the 1850's and 1860's the first railroads and modern financial institutions made their appearance. Economic thought and policy veered away from the older mercantilist notions toward liberalism and free trade. The rising world demand for iron and timber, especially after the free trade treaties of the 1860's, imparted a new impulse to Swedish industry. The curve of industrial production turned sharply upward in the 1870's and reached peak rates in the 1890's and the first years of the twentieth century, when the value of output in manufacturing, mining, and handicraft industries first exceeded that of agricultural and subsidiary occupations, including forestry. New industries — pulp and paper, mechanical engineering, electrical products and power — swelled the volume of industrial production and created new demands for labor. By 1910 more than half the population and an even larger proportion of the labor force lived and worked in nonagricultural conditions and occupations. Equally rapid and extensive political and social changes accompanied the economic changes with surprising ease. From autocratic-aristocratic rule the government evolved through liberal parliamentary forms toward the social welfare state for which Sweden has subsequently become famous. In 1914 the Social Democratic party, unknown in 1890, won a third of the seats in the lower house of the Riksdag.

Since the Scandinavians were relatively homogeneous in race, religion, and culture, they had no significant religious or ethnic problems. They did, however, have a nationality problem. At the Congress of Vienna Norway had been placed under the Swedish crown, although it had its own Storting (parliament). The Norwegians were never happy over union with the Swedes. In the latter half of the century a strong national revival took place, expressed chiefly in literature and music and producing such eminent figures as Henrik Ibsen, Björnstjerne Björnson, and Edvard Grieg. Political agitation followed, and in 1905 the Storting declared the union with Sweden dissolved. Rather than resort to force (as the Swedish king had done in similar circumstances in 1814), the Swedish Riksdag acquiesced and approved a treaty of separation. Norway elected a Danish prince as king but retained and extended its highly democratic political system, perhaps the most advanced in Europe.

Many factors accounted for the success of the Scandinavian countries in achieving both political and economic progress. Three in particular stood out (shared to some extent by Switzerland and the Low Countries), in sharp contrast to the countries of the Mediterranean. In the first place, all had relatively good educational systems dating from the early nineteenth century. This created a more intelligent, adaptable population and facilitated economic and political change. Second, none of the countries was tempted to play the role of a great power. They not only avoided the economic strain of maintaining large standing armies and engaging in armaments races but were also spared the establishment of military elites, which in almost every other country proved to be fundamentally undemocratic. Third, whether or not this contributed in a positive fashion to political stability, all the countries had multiparty political systems. Anglo-Saxons are accustomed to regard the two-party traditions of the British Parliament and the American Congress as the best guarantee of political stability and orderly government, so that it is worth noting that other, equally democratic countries have managed very well with three or more parties. Perhaps the fundamental reason for success is that the Scandinavians simply wanted democracy.

THREE ARCHAIC EMPIRES
CHAPTER TWENTY-NINE

The optimism, confidence, and increasing rapport between the government and the governed that followed the spread of democratic reform in western Europe was not shared by the peoples who lived in the three great empires that made up eastern Europe. In Russia, the Hapsburg dominions, and the Ottoman Empire the always immense gulf between rulers and ruled widened in the century between 1815 and 1914. The rulers sought to prevent the social and political changes of western Europe from invading their domains. Failing that, they tried to contain the changes within the old order in such a way as to subtract as little as possible from their own power and to keep their people in continued subservience. Their efforts failed, in part because they lacked the vision and the courage to make needed fundamental reforms in the political and social structure, in part because they could not overcome the unsatisfied aspirations of the subject peoples. As a result, their empires lacked the inner strength and cohesion to withstand the catastrophes that rained upon them during World War I.

/

RUSSIA IN THE NINETEENTH CENTURY

Until 1906 Russia successfully withstood the new liberal and nationalist pressures of the nineteenth century. The tsars were able to retain absolute power because most Russians were peasants who held their ruler in almost religious awe. The urban middle class — the people who in the west took the lead in progressive reform — formed a small minority of Russia's population. Leadership in the movement for reform came from the intellectuals or intelligentsia, as the Russians called them. They were drawn at first almost entirely from the nobility and gentry and only later in the nineteenth century from the educated members of the middle class. They used every device they could think of, from literature to assassination and open revolt, to force change. They met with repeated failures until early in the twentieth century, when changes in the Russian social and economic structure provided the mass following that they needed to compel the government to make concessions.

ALEXANDER I

Much was expected of Alexander I when he succeeded to the throne of Russia in 1801. As a youth, he had been drilled in the ideals of the Enlightenment by his tutor, César La Harpe, a Swiss disciple of the *philosophes*. Alexander liked to talk about the rights of man and the obligations of a monarch to his subjects, but events proved that his liberalism was only a façade. An indecisive man, he was given to paradoxical behavior and sudden enthusiasms, supporting without restraint any idea that attracted him, then tiring of it and devoting himself with equal ardor to some other proposal. Although he ordered a number of minor reforms during his early years on the throne and met frequently with a so-called unofficial committee of liberals to discuss innovations such as emancipation of the peasantry and granting a constitution, Alexander refused to face squarely the central issues of serfdom and autocracy.

With the passing years Alexander increasingly concerned himself with foreign affairs. As he grew older, he also turned toward religious mysticism. The uncertainty and indecision that clouded his reign pursued him even after his death in 1825. For years a fanciful story persisted that he had feigned death and gone to Siberia, where he supposedly lived as a saintly monk until 1864.

THE REIGN OF NICHOLAS I

In contrast to the ambivalence of Alexander, Tsar Nicholas I (1825–1855) knew exactly how he wanted to govern. His philosophy of government found expression in the doctrine called Official Nationality, which was proclaimed in 1833 by his minister of education, Count Uvarov. Its three principles were orthodoxy, autocracy, and nationality; that is, adherence to the state religion, unquestioned supremacy of the tsar, and dedication to the regime. A conscientious, hard-working man, Nicholas loved military life and thought he could run Russia as if it were one vast army that would obey without hesitation his every command. He could not abide opinions that differed from his; and to stamp them out, he gave greater powers to the secret police, allowing it to arrest and deport people and confiscate property without legal process. That organization, reputed to have its agents everywhere, became the hated symbol of Nicholas's regime.

Despised though he was by liberals, Nicholas was not unaware of the need for reform. Continued peasant unrest and a frightening increase in acts of violence by serfs against their masters persuaded Nicholas that unless serfdom was abolished, the security of the state would be in danger. During his reign he appointed ten different secret committees to make recommendations, but he could not bring himself to make changes that would reduce the privileges of the nobles, the bulwark of tsarist autocracy. He did permit Count Paul Kiselev, the minister for state domains, to improve the condition of the state peasantry, who lived on state land and made up over half of Russia's 50 million peasants. He also intervened on the side of the serfs by limiting the authority of serf owners in the Russian-Polish frontier provinces, where the lords were Roman Catholic Poles and the peasants Orthodox Russians. Political and not humanitarian considerations inspired the action: the Polish nobility had risen against Russian rule in 1830–31, and Nicholas wanted to clip its power and win the support of the peasantry for the throne.

The efforts made by Nicholas's government to stifle independent thought and expressions of discontent could not suppress the spectacular intellectual outburst that made his reign and his successor's the golden age of Russian culture. Men of great creative ability appeared in many branches of art and learning, above all in literature. Within a few decades a constellation of geniuses that included the poet Pushkin and the novelists Gogol, Turgenev, Dostoevski, and Tolstoi, to name only those best known to Western readers, created one of the world's great literatures. Nearly all the important writers of the period were members of the nobility and gentry, as were most of their readers. In spite of their highborn origins, they often criticized Russian institutions, especially serfdom, autocracy, and bureaucracy.

In the 1820's groups or circles of young intellectuals began to meet to discuss new Western philosophies, in particular those of Schelling and Hegel. The circles became the centers of intellectual life and therefore of intellectual discontent with and alienation from the Russia of their day. The movement reached its height in the early 1840's, when two opposing schools of thought emerged, the Westernizers and the Slavophiles. Their debate became a central theme of Russian intellectual life, lasting into the twentieth century. The Westernizers maintained that the Slavic world was part of Western culture and that Russia should follow the same pattern of development as the nations of the West. The Slavophiles were romantic nationalists who held that Russian culture was superior to that of the decadent West. Russia, they said, contained within itself the seeds of its own regeneration and need not look abroad for guidance.

Nicholas, who was as determined to prevent change in other lands as he was to maintain the status quo in Russia, saw himself as the champion of legitimacy and the foe of revolution everywhere. In 1830 he was ready to send an army into western Europe to put down the revolutions. When in that same year Polish patriots rebelled against Russia, he moved

Culver Pictures, Inc.

Retreat of the Russians from the South Side
of Sevastopol, September 8, 1855

*"The army of Sevastopol, like the sea in a gloomy, billowing night, surging and
receding, and agitatedly quivering in all its mass, swaying near the bay, on the
bridge and on the northern side, moved slowly in the impenetrable darkness,
away from the place where it had left so many brave brothers — away from the
place which had been watered by its blood — from the place which for eleven
months had withstood an enemy twice as numerous, and which now it was to
abandon without a battle."* From Leo N. Tolstoi, SEVASTOPOL, reprinted in
THE COMPLETE WORKS OF COUNT TOLSTOY (Boston, 1904–05), Vol. II.

---

ruthlessly against them, ended what was left of Polish autonomy, and
introduced a vigorous program of russification. In 1848 he sent troops
to suppress the Rumanian nationalist movement against Turkey, Russia's
old enemy, lent money to Austria to aid in its fight against revolutionaries, and in the summer of 1849 ordered 200,000 troops into Hungary to
crush the revolt against the Hapsburgs.

In addition to these defenses of legitimacy, Nicholas's armies won easy
victories in short wars against Persia and Turkey. His record of success
gave the tsar inflated ideas about Russian military strength that led him
into the Crimean War. (See pp. 663–664.) That war not only resulted
in a military defeat but also created difficult financial problems for the
government and, far more serious, led to a great new wave of peasant un-

rest and violence. Nicholas died in December, 1855, and his son, Alexander II, quickly agreed to an armistice.

THE TSAR-LIBERATOR

The new tsar was by nature and conviction a conservative who admired his father's methods of government and shared his dread of change. The Crimean fiasco and the rural disorders, however, compelled him to realize that unless fundamental reforms were made the state might collapse, and that the abolition of serfdom was the most urgent reform. Most of the serf owners opposed the measure, warning of dire social and economic consequences, but Alexander made it clear that nothing would deter him. After several years of intensive preparation the law was ready for the tsar's signature in February, 1861. Its provisions fell far short of the hopes of Russia's peasants. It gave the serfs land and freedom, but the conditions worked hardship on them and favored their former masters. The peasants did not get land immediately; many of them had to wait as long as twenty years. The price the peasant paid his former master for the land was set by law at a figure well above the market price. The state paid the nobles for the redeemed land in government bonds bearing 5 per cent interest, and the peasants had to repay the state in annual instalments at 6 per cent interest over a period of forty-nine years. The peasants could get the land at no cost only if they were willing to take an allotment one-fourth the area of a full-sized holding.

The emancipation decree also placed severe restrictions on the peasant's individual freedom. Since the men who drafted the law believed that the freed serfs would not be ready to run their own lives, they put them under the control of the village communes. The commune, not the individual peasant, held title to the redeemed land and periodically redistributed it among the commune members, supervised farming operations, provided village government and police services, and arranged for tax and redemption payments, which were paid communally. A peasant had to get the commune's permission to leave the village, and even if he never returned he remained a member of the commune, responsible for his share of communal taxes and other obligations. The intention of the restrictions was to prepare the peasant for complete personal freedom, but as the years went by, this intention was forgotten. Many Russians, from the reactionary right to the radical agrarian left, acquired a mystical attitude toward the peasantry, holding that it made an irreplaceable moral and spiritual contribution to Russian life and must therefore continue to be given special protection and special treatment and to remain in the communes. Not until the revolution of 1905 did the government abolish most of the restrictions that barred the peasant from the personal freedom enjoyed by other subjects of the tsar.

Alexander II of Russia

"Alexander II was by no means insensible to the spirit of the time. He was well aware of the existing abuses, many of which had been partially concealed from his father, and he had seen how fruitless were the attempts to eradicate them by a mere repressive system of administration. . . . He had inherited from his father a strong dislike to sentimentalism and rhetoric of all kinds. This dislike, joined to a goodly portion of sober common sense, a limited confidence in his own judgment, and a consciousness of enormous responsibility, prevented him from being carried away by the prevailing excitement." D. Mackenzie Wallace, RUSSIA (London, 1877).

The shortcomings of the emancipation law laid the foundation for decades of rural poverty, discontent, and radical agitation. The peasants were burdened with heavy redemption payments or allotments of land too small to support them. Their poverty and the system of communal land redistribution discouraged individual initiative in the improvement of farming, so that productivity remained low. The former landowners, who had been heavily in debt before the emancipation (mainly to the government's mortgage banks), used most of the redemption money paid them by the government to settle old debts or spent it foolishly; they invested little in improving the land that they still had. Within two decades of the emancipation many of them were more heavily in debt than ever and had lost all or part of their land through foreclosure.

"THE GREAT REFORMS"

The emancipation decree was the first in the series of reforms carried through by Alexander II. In 1864 local government, which had been in the hands of aristocrats and crown officials, was reorganized with the establishment of district and provincial assemblies or *zemstvos*. The members of each district zemstvo were elected by a system that favored the nobility but gave the peasantry a voice; delegates to the provincial zemstvo were chosen by the district zemstvos of the province. The activities of the zemstvos were limited to such matters as schools, public health and welfare, roads and bridges, and the encouragement of local industry and agriculture. They met only once a year, and they had to depend upon the officials and police of the government to carry out their programs. The reform was introduced initially in only nineteen provinces and spread gradually to others. As the years went by, the increasingly reactionary government imposed additional restrictions on zemstvo activities. Despite these handicaps the zemstvos compiled an outstanding record of achievement, especially in providing schools and medical services for the peasantry. As a first step toward representative government, they whetted the appetites of many Russians for a greater voice in running the country. In 1870 municipal government was reformed by the introduction of arrangements much like those of the zemstvo system.

Shortly after passage of the zemstvo law in 1864 Alexander ordered the reconstruction of the judicial system on the Western model to replace Russia's archaic, corrupt, and unfair system of justice. The reform provided for equality before the law, simplification of the court system with lower and higher courts, public trials, juries for serious criminal cases, uniform judicial procedures, defense lawyers, and judges who were government employees but could not be removed except for misconduct in office. As with the zemstvo system, the judicial reform was introduced gradually and sometimes with important modifications. In Poland and certain other areas, for instance, trial by jury was not allowed and special courts were retained for the peasants and for ecclesiastical matters, including divorce. The government retained its power to punish without trial those whom it felt threatened public order, and it used pressure on judges. Nonetheless, the new system was greatly superior to the old one. Despite government interference the courts maintained a high degree of independence, and the practice of the law attracted many able and courageous men of progressive views who became leaders in movements for greater freedom.

The last of the "great reforms" in 1874 reorganized the army, whose conscripts had come exclusively from the lower classes, especially the peasantry. All males became eligible for the draft at the age of twenty. The term of active service, which had been reduced a few years earlier from twenty-five to fifteen years, was cut to six years, followed by nine years in the reserve and five more in the militia. The conditions of army life were improved somewhat, and elementary education was made available to draftees.

Alexander's reforms swept away antiquated institutions and practices and prepared Russia to take a place among the modern nations of Europe. The transition from old to new, however, was not easy. The reforms themselves, as well as their shortcomings, encouraged demands for more liberalization, while the government, fearing that more concessions would weaken its autocratic power, refused to go any further. Discontent grew, and radicals began to engage in underground activities. In 1863 revolution broke out again in Poland, where only the year before Alexander had restored much autonomy to the Poles. The rising was crushed and a harsh retribution was carried out, including an acceleration of the policy of russification. These developments played into the hands of the reactionary elements in the nobility and bureaucracy who had always opposed reform. When in 1866 a former university student tried to assassinate Alexander, reactionary influence once again became paramount in government. New controls were put on the universities, censorship was tightened, and new regulations began to dilute the impact of the zemstvo and judiciary reforms.

RADICALS AND REVOLUTIONARIES

The reaction strengthened the radical sentiment, especially among intellectuals, who more and more came from non-noble backgrounds; by 1880 over half of Russia's university students were from the middle and lower classes. Many intellectuals were attracted to the doctrines of populism, which maintained that the peasant communes and the artisans' cooperatives (artels), institutions peculiar to Russia, would enable Russia to pass directly into socialism without going through the capitalist stage of development. In the 1870's thousands of youthful populists called *Narodniki* (from *narod*, people) disguised themselves as peasants and in groups of two and three "went to the people," infiltrating the villages to preach their revolutionary creed. The peasants were bewildered and suspicious of the invaders; sometimes they aided the police in apprehending them. Other radicals adopted the extreme cult called nihilism — Turgenev coined the word in the novel *Fathers and Sons* in 1862 — which urged the renunciation of all traditional values and institutions as worthless. Still others were drawn to the revolutionary anarchism taught by Michael Bakunin, which condemned state and society and praised destruction. Nihilism and anarchism merged with terrorism when these idealistic but irresponsible young people began to work off their frustrations against the regime in deeds of senseless violence.

After the collapse of the "to the people" movement some populist leaders decided that if the masses could not be roused, intellectuals acting alone should try to overthrow the government. They became full-time revolutionaries. Police bungling that would be unbelievable if it were not documented enabled these people to move freely around the country, to penetrate the police apparatus with their own agents, to escape from prison, and when jailed to keep in touch with their confederates. Some of them decided that by assassinating government leaders they could produce chaos and revolution or at least frighten the government into making concessions. One group took Alexander II as its special target, and in 1881, after seven attempts, it succeeded at last in killing its quarry. Although the radicals won the sympathy of many people, the number who took an active part in the movement was always small. Their historical importance, however, far outweighed their small number, for they established the organized revolutionary movement that in one of its several forms eventually took over Russia and had an enormous effect on the course of world history.

THE LAST ROMANOV AUTOCRATS

Far from promoting the cause of freedom, the assassination of the tsar and other officials served to deepen the reactionary policies of the government. Alexander III (1881–1894) and Nicholas II (1894–1917), son and grandson of the murdered Alexander, were narrow-minded bigots of limited intelligence who surrounded themselves with extremely reactionary counselors. The government did its best to hobble the reforms of Alexander II, much preferring the despotism of Nicholas I. Under the guidance of Constantine Pobedonostsev, chief lay official of the Russian Orthodox Church, the state instituted a militant religious policy that identified loyalty to the state with loyalty to the church, saw the Orthodox Church as the bulwark protecting Russia from the corruption of Western liberal ideas, and discriminated against other religions.

The Jews, who after centuries of harsh treatment had received some concessions from Alexander II, became the victims of especially cruel persecution. The prominence that they had won in scholarship, business, the professions, and above all in the revolutionary movement persuaded the government to take extreme measures, such as disenfranchisement and restrictions on the number admitted to secondary schools and universities. It also tolerated and sometimes instigated bloody anti-Jewish riots, called pogroms, in cities in southwestern Russia. In its effort to impose uniformity and curb nationalistic sentiment among its other subject peoples, the government put new emphasis on russification, including the compulsory use of Russian as the language of instruction in schools and the abrogation of local privileges. This policy led the government in 1899 to take away the special provincial autonomy of the Finns, thereby transforming them from loyal subjects of the tsar into his bitter enemies.

LIBERALS AND MARXISTS

A liberal movement that favored a constitutional monarchy on the Western model emerged in the 1890's, drawing its chief support from men who were active in the zemstvos and the professions and who were repelled by the extremism of both the revolutionary radicals and the reactionary government. Braving official disapproval, they held conferences, issued resolutions, and published an illegal newspaper to spread their views. In 1905 they formed themselves into the Constitutional Democratic party, called Cadets from the initials (KD) of the party's name in Russian.

Meanwhile, radicalism, continuing to win new adherents from those who saw no hope for Russia save through a violent overturn, consolidated itself around the turn of the century into two main groups. The heirs of the populists called themselves Social Revolutionaries or SR's and continued to place their hopes in mass peasant rebellion and terrorism. Others, disenchanted with populism's reliance on the peasantry, turned to Marxism.

Marxism had first won adherents in Russia during the 1880's, and in 1898 nine representatives of Marxist groups met at Minsk to form the Social Democratic Labor party or SD's, the precursor of the Communist party of Soviet Russia. Subsequent party congresses were held abroad until 1917, since the party itself was proscribed and most of its members were living in exile. It was in London in 1903 that the fateful split occurred between the Bolsheviks (majority), led by Vladimir Ulyanov, better known as Lenin, and the Mensheviks (minority) over the question of party control. The Bolsheviks favored tight central control of the party and insisted that after the revolution a dictatorship of the proletariat must be imposed, in which there would be no collaboration with the liberal bourgeoisie. The Mensheviks looked forward to a transitional period during which liberals and socialists would cooperate and from which the socialist society would evolve. Efforts in later years to reconcile

the two groups failed, and in 1912 the Bolsheviks expelled the Mensheviks from the party, and so committed it to rigid central control and
noncooperation with other leftist movements.

ECONOMIC CHANGE

Between 1861 and 1914 Russia finally began to modernize its economy.
From the 1860's to the mid-1880's the economy moved forward slowly, in
part because it was a period of adjustment to the great reforms, in part
because the government had long been uninterested in promoting industrialization and in fact had feared it as a disruptive force. In the latter
part of the 1880's Russian industrial production began to advance at a
startling pace, growing during the 1890's at an estimated average annual
rate of 8 per cent.

A change in the government's attitude toward active sponsorship of industrialization played the determining role in bringing about the up-
surge. Credit for the reversal of policy mainly belonged to S. Y. Witte,
who in 1892 became minister of finance. Witte argued that the tsarist
autocracy could not survive and Russia could not remain a great power
unless the government sponsored and guided economic growth. He concentrated on railroad construction (between 1890 and 1900 nearly 15,000
miles of track were laid) and on the iron, steel, and machinery industries.
Lacking the capital needed for expansion, the government borrowed
abroad, especially from France, in order to import the necessary equipment. To pay the interest on its debts, the government imposed heavy
indirect taxes, which bore with special weight upon the peasantry. The
peasants had to sell more grain to raise the cash for the increased taxes,
which provided additional grain for export. In effect, the cost of the
forced industrialization of the 1890's was borne mainly by the peasants, as
it was again in the era of forced industrialization under Soviet Communism. The boom of the 1890's ended in 1900, and depresssed conditions persisted until 1906, when industrial production again rose sharply.
By then an entrepreneurial class had emerged that was able to take over
leadership in economic life from the government.

Industrialization brought with it a large increase in the industrial proletariat, although as late as 1914 there were only about 3 million factory
workers out of a population of 170 million. Most of the workers were
concentrated in a few industrial centers. Russian factories were typically
large establishments, since the government was not interested in sponsoring small factories; over half the industrial enterprises had more than five
hundred workers each. This concentration made it easier to propagandize
and organize the workers. Unrest developed early, strikes became frequent,
and the Marxists made many converts among the industrial workers.

The condition of the peasantry continued to deteriorate, aggravated by
the burden of taxes and redemption payments and by the great increase

in rural population, which produced a steady diminution in the size of the average family's holding. There was no compensating increase in agricultural productivity, for the peasants persisted in their traditional, inefficient farming methods. By 1900 an estimated 52 per cent were unable to support themselves from their shrunken holdings and had to find supplementary employment. Living as they did on the margin of subsistence, they fell easy prey to famine and disease; the death rate in Russia at the beginning of the twentieth century was nearly twice that of England.

THE RUSSO-JAPANESE WAR

The political degeneration of China and the construction by Russia between 1891 and 1903 of the Trans-Siberian railroad linking European Russia with the Pacific stirred Russian ambitions for territorial expansion in the Far East. Russia extended its sphere of influence to Manchuria, obtained a twenty-five year lease on the Liaotung peninsula with the city of Port Arthur, and started a military penetration of Korea under the guise of exploiting timberlands. These advances brought Russia into conflict with Japan, which had its own plans for expansion at China's expense. Like everyone else, the Russians underestimated the strength of the Japanese, who had only recently emerged from centuries of backwardness. In February, 1904, the Japanese attacked the Russian fleet at Port Arthur without warning, as they were to do thirty-seven years later against the American fleet at Pearl Harbor. In the war that followed, Russian forces were handicapped by grotesquely inadequate leadership and matériel and by the difficulties of supplying the war theater. They suffered defeat after defeat, culminating in the destruction in May, 1905, of the Russian Baltic fleet in the Tsushima Straits off Korea after it had sailed halfway around the world. At the peace conference arranged by President Theodore Roosevelt at Portsmouth, New Hampshire, in 1905 the Russians had to give up their recent acquisitions and accept a Japanese protectorate over Korea.

THE REVOLUTION OF 1905

The unrelieved series of military and naval defeats in what had been from the outset an unpopular war inflamed public opinion against the autocracy, and demands for political liberties and other reforms gained a massive following. In St. Petersburg a huge but orderly crowd of workers led by Father Gapon, a priest who was also a police agent, came to the Winter Palace to petition the tsar for reforms. Troops opened fire on the demonstrators, killing well over a hundred and wounding many more. Bloody Sunday, the name that was quickly attached to the massacre, spurred new demands and new unrest. Strikes erupted in many parts of the country; peasant unrest and open outbreaks spread. A council or *soviet* of workers' deputies, dominated by the radicals, was elected in St. Petersburg; soon similar soviets were formed in other cities. Sailors on the battleship *Potemkin* mutinied. The radicals stepped up their propaganda, and some of them renewed the terrorist tactic of assassinating high officials. The revolutionary wave culminated in October, 1905, in a general strike that paralyzed the empire.

The tsar and his advisers finally realized they must yield. Nicholas issued a manifesto providing for freedom of speech, press, and assembly, the election of a Duma or parliament by nearly universal manhood suffrage, and the promise that no law would be promulgated without the Duma's approval. The October Manifesto converted autocratic Russia into a constitutional monarchy. It satisfied the liberals, but not the radicals. Nor did it end worker and peasant unrest; the government had to use military action and arrests before order was restored at the end of 1905.

THE CONSTITUTIONAL MONARCHY

Just before the first Duma convened in 1906, the government, back firmly in control, issued the so-called Fundamental Laws that provided for the retention by the tsar of many of his autocratic powers. Dominated by anti-government parties, the Duma quickly came into conflict with the administration, and Nicholas dissolved it and ordered the election of a new Duma. The second Duma met for only three months before it, too, was dissolved by the tsar. To ensure cooperative Dumas in the future, the government changed the electoral laws to guarantee the domination of the landed gentry. The third and fourth Dumas each lasted the full term of five years.

With the Duma under control, the government under the leadership of Peter Stolypin, the chief minister, set out to eradicate the revolutionary movement. In 1906 and 1907 thirty-five hundred people, mostly government officials but also a significant number of innocent bystanders, had been assassinated by terrorists. Using extralegal means, the government's police agencies rounded up, imprisoned, and executed radicals, and for a while Russia enjoyed relative freedom from revolutionary agitation, although Stolypin himself was assassinated in 1911.

Stolypin did not rely on suppression alone to ward off revolution; he hoped to win mass support for the throne by a program whose central feature was an agrarian reform that abruptly reversed the government's peasant policy. A series of decrees known collectively as the Stolypin Reforms wiped out most of the restrictions on the personal liberty of the peasant, allowed him to sever his connection with the commune and become the owner of his own holding, permitted him to exchange the scattered strips of his communal allotment for a consolidated farm, arranged for the partition of common pastures and meadows among the new individual peasant proprietors, canceled the remaining redemption payments, and established a Peasant Land Bank to lend to peasants who wanted to buy more land. Stolypin called these measures "a wager, not on the wretched and drunken, but on the sound and strong," expecting that the industrious and ambitious peasants would take advantage of the law, prosper, and become the rural bulwarks of the regime. By the end of 1915 between one-quarter and one-half of the peasant households in European Russia had withdrawn from their communes to become private proprietors. Government pressure explained only part of the success of the reform; the peasants welcomed the opportunity to free themselves from communal restraints and at long last became their own masters.

WAR AND REVOLUTION

During the years of constitutional experiment Russia became more deeply involved in international power politics, climaxed by the outbreak of war in August, 1914. Russia's entry into that war at first met with a great patriotic outburst, but defeats in battle and privation at home soon turned the people against the government. In March, 1917, a revolution broke out that forced Nicholas from the throne and opened a new era in Russia's and the world's history. As those events recede into the past, the thesis that imperial Russia would have survived if it had not been for the shock of World War I gains supporters. They argue that the reforms introduced after 1905 gave Russia a viable constitutional form of government, that the economy was advancing, and that the spread of education produced growing numbers of forward-looking men who would have led their nation in continued progress. If fate had only given Russia time — if there had been no First World War — there would have been no Russian Revolution and no Soviet Union. Such is the view of one group of experts. Others believe that military defeat only hastened the decay that had been eating away at Russia for a long time. Had there been no war, revolution would still have come, though perhaps not in the extreme form of communism. According to this view, the war only speeded up the inevitable collapse.

AUSTRIA: THE MULTINATIONAL EMPIRE

The Hapsburg Monarchy was not a state in the modern sense of the word; it was the personal realm of the house of Hapsburg. Elsewhere monarchs dedicated themselves to welding the groups over whom they ruled into a common nationality. In contrast, the Hapsburg emperors rejected the national idea, spurning it so completely that they did not even have an official name for their realm: Austria and the Hapsburg Monarchy served only as names of convenience. The empire was an association of eleven nationalities — German, Magyar, Czech, Pole, Croat, Italian,

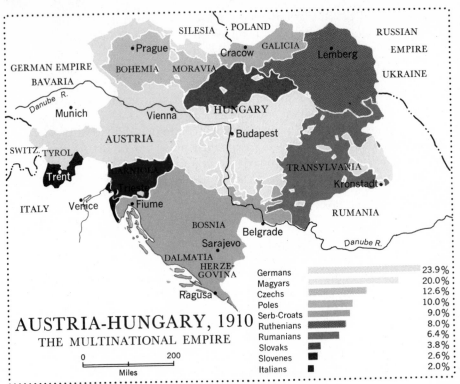

SILESIA :POLAND   RUSSIAN
•Prague   GALICIA   EMPIRE
Cracow   Lemberg
GERMAN EMPIRE   BOHEMIA   MORAVIA   UKRAINE
BAVARIA
Danube R.
Munich   Vienna   HUNGARY

AUSTRIA   •Budapest
SWITZ. TYROL
Trent   TRANSYLVANIA
Trieste   Kronstadt•
ITALY   Venice   •Fiume
RUMANIA
BOSNIA   Belgrade
Sarajevo   Danube R.
DALMATIA
HERZE-
GOVINA   Germans   23.9%
Magyars   20.0%
Ragusa•   Czechs   12.6%
Poles   10.0%
AUSTRIA-HUNGARY, 1910   Serb-Croats   9.0%
Ruthenians   8.0%
THE MULTINATIONAL EMPIRE   Rumanians   6.4%
Slovaks   3.8%
0   200   Slovenes   2.6%
Italians   2.0%
Miles

Ruthenian, Rumanian, Slovak, Serb, and Slovene — each with its own
language, culture, and traditions. The Germans and the Magyars were the
dominant nationalities, forming 23.9 per cent and 20 per cent respectively of the empire's population in 1910. Next came the Czechs with 12.6
per cent and the Poles with 10 per cent. The other ethnic groups ranged
from 9 per cent to 2 per cent of the total population. Most of the people
of each nationality lived in their historic homelands: the Germans in the
western provinces (modern Austria), the Magyars in Hungary, the Czechs
in Bohemia and Moravia, the Poles and Ruthenians in Galicia, and so on.
There had been much internal migration, however, so that different
national groups, especially the Germans, were scattered through the
realm.

The single most important reason why this strange empire stayed together was that its peoples shared a common loyalty to the Hapsburg
emperor. Although the intensity of the loyalty varied among the nationalities, the dynasty provided the supreme bond of union. The armed
forces and the bureaucracy, whose members were drawn from all nationalities, also served as important cohesive forces and symbols of the supranational character of the empire. The throne had close ties with the

Roman Catholic Church, to which three-quarters of the empire's people belonged, and Catholicism acted as another supranational unifying force. Similarly the aristocracy, with its close links to the throne and its monopoly on social, political, and military leadership, helped to hold the empire together. Economic factors had an important cohesive effect, the industrial districts of the German and Bohemian provinces exchanging their manufactured goods for the foodstuffs and raw materials of Hungary and Galicia. Most of the empire was linked by the Danube and eventually by the railroad network that reached out in every direction from Vienna.

These unifying forces created among the peoples of the empire feelings of common interest that were the foundations upon which the empire rested. Until 1916 many among even the most ardent nationalist leaders believed that the empire would survive. They wanted to gain a greater voice for their nationalities within the empire, not to destroy it. Their agitation, however, continually threatened the authority of the government. To deal with the threats, the rulers in Vienna tried a series of solutions, but none could satisfy all the conflicting desires. In the end, unsatisfied nationalist aspirations, aggravated by defeat in World War I, led to the empire's collapse in 1918.

CENTRALIZED ABSOLUTISM: THE BACH SYSTEM

The first attempted solution, a regime of centralization called the Bach System, was adopted after absolutism had re-emerged from the events of 1848 and 1849. Provincial privileges and autonomy were abolished, and an intensive policy of germanization was introduced, with German the only official language and the chief language of instruction in higher education. The government actively promoted economic development. In agrarian matters it provided emancipated serfs with sizable holdings of land at prices averaging one-third of the market value and required the peasants to pay only a third of that, with the central and provincial governments paying the other two-thirds. This policy stimulated farm production and made the peasants a major market for manufactured goods. Austrian industry and commerce also participated in the general prosperity of the 1850's.

Despite prosperity the government had trouble meeting the costs of its expanded program. When depression occurred in 1857, the government's fiscal position became critical. To make matters worse, during the Crimean War Austria had alienated both Russia and the western powers. Nationalist discontent with the policy of centralization reached alarming proportions, especially in Hungary. In 1859 Austria's difficulties persuaded Emperor Napoleon III of France and Prime Minister Camillo Cavour of Sardinia to strike at the Hapsburgs' Italian possessions. Defeat in that war reduced Austria's prestige still further, worsened its financial problems, and stirred up new troubles in Hungary. Emperor Franz Josef, always suspicious of abstract principles and long-range plans, preferred to handle problems as they arose. Deciding that it was time to abandon centralized absolutism for a new policy, he dismissed Bach and other ministers and inaugurated a new policy.

CONSTITUTIONAL ABSOLUTISM

Decrees of 1860 and 1861 established a constitutional system for the monarchy with an imperial diet (Reichsrat) and provincial diets, but the throne still held supreme power. The value of the reform was vitiated by an electoral system that assured German domination of the Reichsrat, by the extreme limitation of the powers of the provincial diets, and by the failure to provide for parliamentary control over legislation and finance.

The reform understandably did not satisfy non-German nationalists. Their passive resistance, including refusal to send representatives to the imperial diet, made it impossible for the government to function effectively. After 1864, with the war with Prussia approaching, the emperor decided to try a new tactic to hold the empire together. His ministers entered into negotiations with the Magyars, who were the second largest ethnic group in the empire and implacable foes of centralization. Francis Deak, leader of the Hungarian nationalists, proposed a compromise that would make the Magyars equal partners with the Germans in dominating the empire. Discussions were in progress when war broke out with Prussia. Austria's quick defeat played into the hands of the Magyars, for more than ever the Hapsburgs needed Hungary to prevent the dissolution of the empire and to regain status as a great power. The emperor agreed to Magyar proposals, and the famed Compromise (*Ausgleich*) of 1867 opened a new era in Hapsburg history that lasted until 1918.

DUALISM

The Ausgleich transformed the unitary Hapsburg empire into a dual monarchy of two equal states with one ruler, who was simultaneously emperor of Austria and king of Hungary, one army, and joint ministries charged with the conduct of foreign affairs, finance, and military matters. All the other nationalities were made subservient to the will and interests of the Germans in the Austrian part of the empire and to the Magyars in the Hungarian part. Each part had its own parliament, ministers responsible to the parliament, and civil service. Each parliament chose sixty-man delegations, who met to decide matters of common interest. Treaties between the two countries, renewable every ten years, regulated tariffs, currency, and similar matters.

Dualism worked well enough to enable the empire to hold together for another fifty years, but throughout that half-century the danger of collapse was never distant. The unsatisfied nationalist ambitions of the subject peoples grew in proportion to the efforts of the dominant Germans and Magyars to suppress them. Cultural and social organizations that emphasized ethnic traditions took on new vitality. Most of the nationalist leaders did not yet want independence, however, demanding instead a federal system in which they would be on an equal footing with the Germans and Magyars. The Magyars, meanwhile, gained an even greater influence in the army and the central administration.

The Czechs, third largest ethnic group in the empire, replaced the Magyars as the most vocal and discontented of the subject nationalities. To placate them, Franz Josef in 1871 offered them autonomy and agreed to be crowned king of Bohemia; but the determined opposition of the Magyars, who feared that concessions to the Czechs would stir up demands from the Slavs in Hungary, persuaded him to withdraw his offer. The disappointed Czechs showed their resentment by boycotting the imperial and provincial parliaments until 1878.

In 1879 the emperor broke with the German bourgeois liberals who dominated the Austrian parliament. The rupture worked to the benefit of the Czechs and other national groups. The German liberals had put through a series of progressive measures that included reform of court procedures, freedom of speech and press, the abolition of church control of the schools, and the establishment of compulsory elementary education. Franz Josef, who had never been happy with the liberals, lost his patience when they opposed Austrian occupation of the Turkish provinces of Bosnia and Herzegovina. He decided to appease the subject nationalities to gain their support against the German liberals. He appointed Count Edward Taafe as the new prime minister to carry out the program. Taafe, a master of political improvisation and compromise, persuaded the representatives of the Czechs and other nationalities to join with the German conservatives and clericals in a parliamentary bloc, known as the Iron Ring, to support the emperor's policies against the liberals. He rewarded them with a series of concessions to their nationalist ambitions. The Czech language was recognized as an official language along with German; changes in the electoral laws enabled the Czechs to win control of their provincial diet; and the University of Prague was split into two sections, one Czech and one German. Similar though less extensive concessions were made to the Poles and Slovenes.

NATIONALIST TENSIONS AND CONSTITUTIONAL CRISIS

Taafe's political skill gave the empire more than a decade of relative calm, a luxury it had not enjoyed for thirty years. It did not, however, stifle the nationalist strivings of the subject peoples. After his fall in 1893 nationalist agitation took on still more fervor with new and more aggressive organizations, such as the Young Czechs. The Pan-Slav movement, advocating a union of all Slavic peoples, gained strength, and some of its adherents talked of "liberation" by Russia, greatest of the Slavic states. Nationalist activity also assumed a new vitality among the Yugoslavs (South Slavs), as the Serbs, Croats, and Slovenes were called.

The increase in nationalist activities of the subject peoples stimulated increased opposition by the Magyars and Germans. The Magyars, who formed barely half the population of the Hungarian part of the empire, intensified their policy of holding the other ethnic groups in check. The Croats, who as a reward for loyalty to the Hapsburgs in 1848 had been allowed to retain much autonomy within the Hungarian kingdom, lost many of their privileges. They and other minorities were subjected to an unrelenting program of magyarization.

The Germans, frightened by the threat to their domination of Austria, turned in increasing numbers to new, stridently nationalist movements. A fanatic named Georg von Schönerer preached doctrines of German racial superiority, anti-Semitism, and pan-Germanism, pointing to Hohenzollern Germany as the leader of all Germans. Karl Lueger, mayor of Vienna from 1897 to 1907, formed the Christian Socialist party, whose platform combined clericalism, anticapitalism, and anti-Semitism. He drew wide support from urban shopkeepers and artisans, who felt threatened by the advances of capitalist industry and commerce. Peasants, who suffered from the competition of large estates and mechanized farming, were also attracted by the appeals of Christian Socialism. Such people were traditionally suspicious of the Jews and were easily convinced that the latter, who had become important in Austrian economic life, were responsible for their economic difficulties. Among those who found themselves in sympathy with Lueger's doctrines was a recent arrival in Vienna, a young drifter named Adolph Hitler.

During this period Viktor Adler, a one-time rabid pan-German, organized scattered Austrian Marxian groups into the Social Democratic party. Although the new organization at first accepted Marx's doctrine of inevitable revolution, it soon copied the revisionist outlook of the German Social Democrats, advocating social change by parliamentary means rather than violent overthrow. Reflecting the ethnic diversity of the empire, the socialists split their party and the trade unions they dominated into separate and virtually independent national sections united only in name.

As nationalist passions rose, debates in the Austrian parliament became so heated that physical attacks and raucous disturbances made it impossible for the legislature to carry on business. Since the emperor and his ministers were authorized by law to legislate when the parliament was not in session, they dissolved the parliament and summoned it only when the budget had to be passed. Constitutional parliamentary government broke down, and the empire stood on the verge of dissolution.

Franz Josef once again realized that changes had to be made. In 1907 he introduced universal manhood suffrage in the Austrian part of the empire, taking care to ensure adequate representation for the national minorities. The Social Democrats were the chief beneficiaries of the reform, becoming the largest party in the parliament. Yet the reform did not alter the pattern of the parliament's unruly behavior and ineffectiveness. Most of the ministries from 1907 to 1914 lacked a parliamentary majority, and the government had to resort frequently to its emergency powers. Universal suffrage had not been extended to Hungary, and Franz Josef used the threat of its introduction — and the diminution in Magyar power that it would produce — to beat down Magyar's demands for more independence from imperial control. By not introducing suffrage reform into Hungary, however, Franz Josef stirred up still more resentment among the subject peoples.

The emperor's only son, Rudolf, shot himself and his young mistress at Meyerling in 1889 in a tawdry tragedy that still inspires novelists and playwrights to endless romantic speculations. The Archduke Franz Ferdinand, nephew and now heir apparent of the aged Franz Josef, seems to have favored a vague form of federalism that would have increased the power of the subject nationalities and strengthened the power of the throne at the expense of the dominant Germans and Magyars. The emperor did not care for his nephew, however, and in any case Franz Ferdinand never had the opportunity to demonstrate his intentions.

In the years before 1914 Vienna won universal fame for its beauty, its aristocratic splendors, and the courtliness, gaiety, and sophistication of its people. It was a world center of art, letters, drama, music, education, and science. All the world danced to Viennese waltzes and hummed the melodies of Viennese operettas. Most of its people seemed unaffected by the crisis of the empire. Nevertheless, the crisis grew greater with each passing year. Austria's involvement in the Balkans, always a source of international tension, brought on a new threat of war in 1908 when the empire formally annexed Bosnia and Herzegovina. Relations with Russia and Serbia deteriorated, Slavic nationalist movements in the empire took on new strength, and new enthusiasm appeared for the cause of Pan-Slavism. Other national groups who had been relatively quiescent, such as the Italians in southern Austria, began to make trouble. In Hungary deputies rioted in parliament and at one session fired a shot at the prime minister. Fighting broke out in the streets, and young, rabidly nationalist Serbs and Croats decided to take matters into their own hands by resorting to terrorism and assassination. Such was the situation in June, 1914.

THE OTTOMAN EMPIRE

Like the realm of the Hapsburgs, the Ottoman Empire was torn by the nationalist aspirations of its subject peoples. It suffered other grave disabilities: extreme corruption and inefficiency in government and the constant intervention of the great powers in its affairs. Paradoxically, the latter handicap helped stay the disruptive force of nationalism, for each power was so fearful that a rival might gain from the dissolution of the empire that each thought its own best interest lay in keeping the empire alive.

By the beginning of the nineteenth century the disintegration of the central government proceeded so far that only a few districts remained under the direct control of the sultan. Although the empire stretched from Algeria to Persia and reached up into the Balkan peninsula of Europe, most of the provinces were governed by nominal vassals who paid only ceremonial tribute and allegiance to the sultan. In the course of the century foreign conquest and native rebellions gradually whittled away the provinces until on the eve of World War I the empire included only the region between the Mediterranean and the Tigris-Euphrates rivers and a small strip of Macedonia, in addition to its historic homeland in Anatolia.

In 1830 France began a long-drawn-out conquest of Algeria, and in 1881 it established a protectorate over Tunisia. In 1831 Mohammed Ali, an Albanian adventurer who had entered Ottoman military service and rose to become ruler of Egypt, challenged the sultan's control of Syria. After a decade of strife and confusion the government of the sultan regained Syria with the aid of Great Britain and other European powers, but in return he recognized Mohammed Ali as the hereditary ruler of Egypt. In 1878 Great Britain occupied the island of Cyprus and in 1882 established its control over Egypt. Italy completed the spoliation of the Turks' North African empire with the conquest of Tripoli in 1911–12.

THE "NEW NATIONS" OF
THE NINETEENTH CENTURY

The majority of the inhabitants of the Balkan territories of the Ottoman Empire were European in speech and Christian in religion. Increased commercial and intellectual contacts with western Europe introduced men of the middle classes to Western ideas of freedom and secularism, while continued Turkish oppression and corruption stirred up discontent among the peasantry. Inspired by the French Revolution, leaders began to urge rebellion and independence.

In 1804 the Serbs rose against their Turkish overlords. Led by George Petrovich, also known as Kara (black) George, a prosperous pig dealer, the Serbs enjoyed initial success, but by 1813 the Turks had regained control. In 1815 the Serbs rose again, led by Milosh Obrenovich, another pig dealer and a political rival of Kara George. In 1817 the sultan recognized Obrenovich as prince of Serbia, and in 1829 by the Treaty of Adrianople he granted Serbia a large measure of local autonomy, although it remained until 1878 as a province of the Ottoman Empire. The feud between the Obrenoviches and the Karageorgeviches, with the two dynasties alternating on the throne for more than a century, was symptomatic of the internal divisions within the other Balkan nationalities, which hindered their liberation from Turkish rule or condemned them to internal strife and political turmoil after achieving independence.

The initial Serbian risings attracted little international attention, unlike the reaction when the Greeks revolted in 1821. (See pp. 560–561.) When the great powers finally established Greece as an independent kingdom in 1830, they drew frontiers for the new state that left many Greeks outside its borders. That decision caused much trouble in later years.

The Treaty of Adrianople of 1829 granted Russia a protectorate over the principalities of Moldavia and Wallachia, although they remained nominally parts of the Ottoman Empire. After defeat in the Crimean War, Russia had to give up its protectorate, but reestablishment of direct Turkish rule was unthinkable. After several years of dispute among the powers over the disposition of the territories, the native inhabitants took matters into their own hands in 1859 by electing Alexander Cuza, a native landowner, as prince of both. Two years later they merged into a single state called Rumania. Cuza initiated a reform program that included freeing the peasants from forced labor for the landowners, confiscating monastic estates, and providing a constitution and universal manhood suffrage. Such radical reforms in a country that was still under the nominal sovereignty of the sultan alienated the dominant landowning classes. In 1866 they overthrew Alexander and replaced him with a Hohenzollern prince, whose dynasty ruled Rumania until 1944. The other new nations created by the gradual dissolution of the Ottoman Empire — Montenegro, Bulgaria, and Albania — had to await further international developments before achieving independence.

TURKISH ATTEMPTS AT REFORM

The Turkish rulers of the Ottoman Empire strove vainly to prevent the loss of their sovereignty. Internal divisions between those who wished to introduce Western reforms and those who wished to return to old-fashioned centralized despotism, as well as the vested interests of many semi-independent military, political, and religious leaders, repeatedly frustrated their attempts. Sultan Selim III (1789–1807) attempted to remodel the military establishment on European lines and to introduce other Western reforms, but the powerful janissary corps dethroned and murdered him. Mahmud II (1808–1839), his successor, was plagued by the revolts in Serbia and Greece and moved more slowly to consolidate power, but in 1826 he took advantage of a revolt by the janissaries to massacre the entire force and abolish it forever. Mahmud's last years were marred by the success of the revolt in Greece, defeat by Russia in 1829, and the encroachments of his vassal Mohammed Ali of Egypt, with the result that he failed to reestablish authority and power of the central government.

Abdul Mejid (1839–1861), Mahmud's successor, was a mere boy at the time of his accession. Under the influence of his principal minister, the Western-educated Reshid Pasha, he introduced a new era of reform in Turkey called the *Tanzimat*. A series of decrees introduced changes in many aspects of Ottoman administration and legal procedures with the aim of making the empire into a modern nation on the Western model. The alliance of Turkey with the Western powers in the Crimean War further strengthened the hand of the reformers, and in 1856 the sultan promised increased efforts to modernize the empire. The reformers could not, however, overcome the inefficiency and uncooperativeness of the bureaucracy or the opposition of vested interests to changes in the power structure. The reforms also proved costly in a pecuniary sense. The government borrowed in Great Britain and France to finance its role in the Crimean War, and the debt rose rapidly in succeeding years. Unable to meet the interest payments, the government defaulted in 1876 and had to submit to financial control by the great powers on behalf of its European creditors. This development, together with the renewed revolts in the Balkans, led to the overthrow of the reforming party and brought the *Tanzimat* to a close.

THE "SICK MAN OF EUROPE"

The reformers made one last effort to retrieve the situation in 1876 by staging a coup d'état and proclaiming a constitution of the Western type that called for the assembly of the first Turkish parliament. Abdul Hamid II (1876–1909), the new sultan, allowed the regime to function just long enough to prevent further intervention by the Western powers, then he prorogued the parliament, abolished the constitution, and restored the traditional despotism. In spite of the defeat by Russia in the war of 1877–78, which led to complete independence for Rumania, Serbia, and Montenegro, and autonomous status for Bulgaria under Russian protection (see p. 839), the "sick man of Europe," as Turkey became known in the Western press, exhibited remarkable powers of survival and recuperation.

During these years tensions were heightened within the empire and its former provinces by an intensification of Western interest which was part of the new age of imperialism. The major European states used their economic power to extend their political control over the economically backward countries of the Balkans and the Near East, building railroads and public works, organizing banks, and extending loans to governments in return for economic concessions and political alliances. Foreign economic penetration promoted the growth of capitalist techniques and institutions, which increasingly displaced traditional methods of production and exchange and brought more and more people into the market system. Taxes soared as governments tried to get money to repay foreign

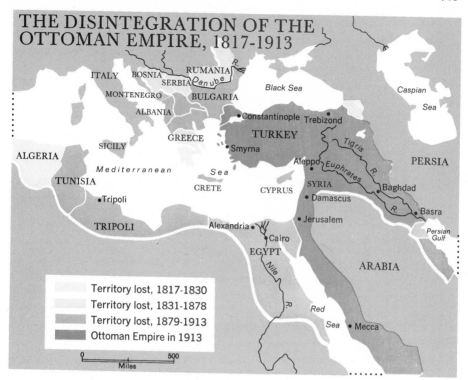

THE DISINTEGRATION OF THE OTTOMAN EMPIRE, 1817-1913

Territory lost, 1817-1830
Territory lost, 1831-1878
Territory lost, 1879-1913
Ottoman Empire in 1913

loans, and when not enough money could be raised, the governments had to agree to varying degrees of foreign control over state revenues to ensure repayment. The difficulties of economic life were worsened by a population increase that produced rural overpopulation; many peasants were left landless, and most of the others had plots too small to support a family adequately.

Increasing contacts with the West fostered a discontent with the traditional way of life and the traditional system of values that had earlier made the people accept their lot without complaint. Men of the new generation saw that it was possible to break free from the old restraints and rise to wealth and prominence. The expansion of educational facilities gave ambitious young men the opportunity to prepare themselves for leadership.

THE YOUNG TURK REVOLUTION

The new attitudes found political expression in increased nationalist activity and in the formation of underground revolutionary and terrorist societies with such names as the International Macedonian Revolutionary Organization (usually called IMRO), Union or Death, and the Black

Hand. The first successful revolution engineered by the new generation occurred in Turkey under the leadership of men who called themselves the Young Turks. In 1908 a secret organization of army officers threatened armed revolt unless Abdul Hamid, whose name had become an international byword for cruelty and misrule, restored the constitution of 1876. The sultan yielded, but the next year after an attempted counterrevolution, the Young Turks forced Abdul Hamid to abdicate and changed the constitution to make the cabinet responsible to the parliament rather than to the sultan.

The success of the Young Turk revolution awakened fears in the Balkan states, Austria, and Russia that Turkey might be on the verge of a revival that would lead to efforts to regain lost territory and lost prestige. Austria and Russia decided to move before that could happen. They agreed that Austria would annex Bosnia and Herzegovina and that Russia would have the right to send its warships through the straits of the Bosporus and Dardanelles. Austria quickly announced the annexation, but the Russians discovered that the other powers would not consent to the straits passage. Bitter charges and countercharges were exchanged, and for a time war seemed inevitable. The danger was overcome, but Russia, chagrined and furious with what it considered Austria's duplicity, planned revenge and worked to persuade the Balkan states to league together in defense against further Austrian territorial expansion in the Balkans. The danger of Turkish revival convinced the Balkan leaders that such a confederation was necessary. In 1912 Serbia, Greece, Bulgaria, and Montenegro formed the Balkan League, directed against Turkey. Thus the stage was set for the Balkan wars, which served as a prelude to World War I and the eventual demise of the "sick man of Europe."

THE REVIVAL OF
WESTERN IMPERIALISM
CHAPTER THIRTY

While the great land empires of eastern Europe were undergoing stress and change that eventually led to their downfall, the nations of western Europe embarked upon a disastrous race for overseas empires that held profound implications for the entire world. In fact, the period from 1870 to 1914 is sometimes referred to as the "age of imperialism," but this is misleading if not positively inaccurate. The main scramble of European nations for overseas territories did not get under way in earnest until the 1880's; nor did they begin to relinquish their colonies until forced to do so by circumstances during and after the Second World War. More fundamentally, imperialism was not a new phenomenon in either 1885 or 1870. Imperialism is as old as civilization itself. In the earliest civilizations of which we have any record, those of Egypt and Sumer, native populations were ruled and exploited by alien conquerors. A large part of recorded history deals with the rise and fall of empires. Vast, well-organized empires existed in Asia when half-naked savages still populated most of Europe. Empires existed in Africa and America after a fashion before the voyages of Columbus. Europeans themselves, however, have been among the most expansionist and imperialist of peoples, from the time of their Greek and Roman forebears right down to the twentieth century. In the Middle Ages they expanded throughout continental Europe. Between 1500 and 1800 they spread their civilization to North and South America and established beachheads around Africa and the Indian Ocean.

Imperialism was thus not new, but in spite of the ubiquity of earlier imperialisms, that of the late nineteenth century did have certain distinctive features. In the first place, the expansion was more rapid, better organized, and the penetration into alien societies was deeper than in previous imperialisms. Second, imperialist conquest was directed chiefly toward tropical or semitropical areas. Third, imperialism was not accompanied by large-scale migrations from Europe to the areas of imperial control. Emigration occurred, of course, on the largest scale in history; but the emigrants went chiefly to self-governing nations and territories such as the United States, Latin America, and the British dominions. Finally, the great burst of imperialist expansion after 1885 came after almost a century in which Europeans had generally manifested a striking lack of concern for imperial expansion, amounting in some cases to outright anti-imperialism.

THE SECOND BRITISH EMPIRE

The first or old British Empire attained its greatest extent in the decade following 1763. As a result of the Seven Years' War, Britain gained Canada, islands and trading posts in the West Indies and Africa, and a greatly enlarged sphere of influence in India. The American Revolution reduced substantially the extent of the empire, deprived it of its most flourishing colonies, and led to some fundamental changes in imperial policy. The Napoleonic wars represented the last of the great colonial struggles between France and Britain. The outcome completely eliminated France as a rival in the traditional areas of imperial conflict, brought some more or less fortuitous accretions to the British Empire, and left Britain the undisputed "mistress of the seas." Shortly afterward the revolt of the Spanish colonies in America and the separation of Brazil from Portugal reduced the formal hegemony of European powers in overseas areas to its smallest extent in three hundred years.

For two generations thereafter colonial and imperial questions receded in public interest. Continental countries focused their attention on domestic and European problems: reform and revolutions, national unification, industrialization, and power politics. With but few minor exceptions these left little energy for or interest in the creation of colonial empires. Britain, with its far-flung possessions and mastery of the sea lanes, was in a very different position. It could not afford to ignore questions of imperial policy, and it continued to make minor additions to its empire throughout the century. It has been said that Britain "acquired an empire in a fit of absence of mind." That is not literally true, of course, since each acquisition either had a specific objective or was a reaction to a specific situation; yet the statement does emphasize that there was no comprehensive design for imperial conquest.

AUSTRALIA, NEW ZEALAND, AND THE SOUTH PACIFIC

Europeans first became aware of Australia in the early decades of the seventeenth century as a result of the exploratory activity of the Dutch, who called it New Holland, although it may have been sighted by the

Portuguese a hundred years earlier. Its full extent and its character as an island-continent remained unknown for many years. Its inhospitable western and northern coasts and the lack of any obvious resources of value to Europeans did not encourage settlement. Not until the English explorer Captain James Cook discovered the more fertile east coast on his first Pacific voyage (1768–1771) did the British government take an interest. At first the government contemplated using it for the resettlement of loyalist refugees after the American Revolution but eventually decided on making it a penal colony to relieve the crowded British prisons. In January, 1788, the first convoy of convicts dropped anchor in Botany Bay near the site of the future city of Sydney.

The first years of the colony, named New South Wales, were difficult and turbulent. Convicted criminals did not make ideal settlers in a virgin land, even though many came from debtors' prisons or had been imprisoned for other minor offenses. Not until sheep raising was introduced in 1794 did the colony have the foundations of a viable economy. The first free settlers apart from soldiers arrived in 1793. By 1810 more than 3,000 free settlers had come, attracted by the offer of land grants. In 1816 the British government removed all legal restrictions on free emigration to Australia. Britain continued to use New South Wales as a penal colony until 1840, however, and convicts were sent to some other parts of Australia until 1867. Altogether, approximately 75,000 convicts were transported, but free settlers outnumbered both convicts and emancipists (those who had served their penal terms) long before the practice ceased. In the process of settlement the native inhabitants were almost exterminated before measures were taken to place them on reservations and protect them.

When first settling at Botany Bay, the British claimed only the eastern half of the continent. Until 1803 the belief persisted that New South Wales and New Holland (the western half) were separate islands. In 1829 the government extended its claim to the whole continent, and shortly afterward it founded or allowed settlements at Perth in Western Australia, Adelaide in South Australia, and Melbourne in what eventually became the province of Victoria. Settlements had been established in Tasmania as early as 1803. As penal colonies, the settlements were at first under the direct control of the crown, whose authority was exercised by a royal governor. Elements of representative government were introduced in the 1820's and broadened in subsequent years. In 1850 Parliament passed the Australian Colonies Government Act, which granted the colonies complete self-government for most practical purposes.

The discovery of gold in Victoria in 1851 stimulated the economy and brought an influx of new immigrants from all over the world. Although sheep raising remained the staple industry and the foundation of the Australian economy throughout the nineteenth century, its labor requirements were not large, so that most of the new arrivals settled in the coastal cities. Australia became a predominantly urban society at a relatively early date. In 1866 the parliament of Victoria enacted a protective tariff at the height of the free trade movement in Europe, and most other colonies followed suit. Australia also experienced a precocious development of trade unions, and before the end of the century several of the colonies, with Victoria again leading the way, had adopted remarkably advanced social legislation.

During the nineteenth century each of the colonies more or less went its own way under both royal and self-government. Until the 1880's all attempts to create some sort of federation or national government foundered on the mutual jealousies of the separate colonies. In 1898 agreement was reached on a draft constitution for a federal structure which borrowed many of its elements from the United States but retained the British system of responsible cabinet government. On January 1, 1901, the first day of the twentieth century, the Commonwealth of Australia came into existence.

New Zealand was discovered by the Dutch mariner Abel Tasman in 1642 and rediscovered by Captain Cook in 1769, but Europeans made no effective settlement there until well into the nineteenth century. The native inhabitants, Maoris of Polynesian origin, were far more advanced socially and culturally than the aborigines of Australia and made excellent warriors. In addition, both European missionaries and the British government opposed European settlement. Eventually the political pressure of colonization companies together with the depredations of unprincipled traders and illegal settlers persuaded the British government to proclaim sovereignty in 1840; the first formal settlement took place in the same year. The early years were marked by lawlessness and conflict with the natives, culminating in the first Maori War (1843–1848). The progress of the colony was rapid, however, and by 1852 the British settlers had achieved effective self-government.

As in Australia, pastoralism formed the basis of the New Zealand economy. Sheep raising was supplemented by cattle and dairy farming after the introduction of mechanical refrigeration in 1882. The New Zealanders also developed a strong labor movement and enacted progressive social legislation. In 1907 the British government granted New Zealand dominion status.

In the process of acquiring and settling Australia and New Zealand the British discovered and took possession of a number of islands in the South Pacific. The first British settlement on a Pacific island was strictly illegal: the settlers were mutineers from the famous ship *Bounty,* who landed on Pitcairn Island in 1790 and took wives among the native women. The British government annexed the island in 1838.

British activity in exploration and discovery in the South Pacific was paralleled by that of the Dutch and French. In 1828 the Dutch laid claim to the western half of New Guinea, and in 1842 the French initiated a deliberate policy of annexation in compensation for diplomatic rebuffs in Europe. The main rush to claim Pacific islands came after 1880, however, when France and Britain were joined by Germany and the United States.

SOUTH AFRICA

The British first established themselves in South Africa during the Napoleonic wars in order to prevent the Cape of Good Hope from falling into the hands of the French. Cape Colony had been settled by the Dutch in the mid-seventeenth century as a way station for ships of the Dutch East India Company. Utilizing slave labor, the colonists devoted themselves to agriculture and pastoral pursuits. By the middle of the eighteenth century they had pushed the limits of their settlement north to the Orange River. After the Napoleonic wars the British government encouraged immigrants to settle in Cape Colony, instituted new administrative and judicial systems, and substituted English as the official language. The abolition of slavery throughout the British Empire in 1834 (see p. 605) created labor problems and financial difficulties for the Boers or Afrikaners (as descendants of the Dutch colonists were called), who claimed they received insufficient compensation. The British attempts to ensure more humane treatment for the natives by granting them land and permitting them to move about freely also annoyed the Boers, who had pursued a policy of native repression. To escape this interference, the Boers in 1835 began their Great Trek to the north, creating new settlements in the region between the Orange and Vaal rivers (which became the Orange Free State), north of the Vaal River (the Transvaal, which became the South African Republic in 1856), and on the southeast coast (Natal).

In spite of the Boers' attempts to isolate themselves from the British, conflict continued to mark the history of the colonies throughout the century. In 1843 after a short war with the Boers the British annexed Natal, which contained British settlers. For a few years at mid-century the British claimed sovereignty over the entire area south of the Vaal River, but by a convention of 1854 they agreed to withdraw to the Orange River. In 1877, after a failure of efforts to create a South African federation, the British governor of Cape Colony forcibly annexed Transvaal. A revolt of the Boers in 1880–81 led Gladstone, who had again become prime minister, to recognize the independence of the South African Republic once more. In addition to the conflicts between the British and the Boers, both groups clashed frequently with the African tribes. The encounters ended sooner or later in defeat for the latter. Many of the tribes were practically exterminated as a result, and most of the remainder were reduced to a state of servitude not far from slavery, especially those under Boer rule.

The Boer and British settlements were at first primarily agrarian, but in 1867 the discovery of diamonds in Griqualand, a region formerly set aside for natives, led to a great influx of treasure seekers from all over the world. In 1886 gold was discovered in Transvaal. These events completely altered the economic basis of the colonies and intensified political rivalries. They also brought to the fore one of the most influential persons in African history, Cecil Rhodes (1853–1902).

Rhodes, an Englishman, came to Africa in 1870 at the age of seventeen and quickly made a fortune in the diamond fields. In 1880 he helped found the De Beers Mining Company, which by 1888 had acquired a practical monopoly of diamond mining. He also organized the Consolidated Goldfields Company, which achieved a similar position in the Witwatersrand, or 'Rand. In 1887 he organized the British South Africa Company, and in 1889 he secured a royal charter from the British government granting it extensive rights and governing powers over a vast territory north of Transvaal, subsequently called Rhodesia.

Not content with mere profits, Rhodes took an active role in politics and became an ardent spokesman for imperialist expansion. He entered the Cape Colony legislature in 1880 and became prime minister of the colony ten years later. One of his major ambitions was to build a railroad "from the Cape to Cairo" — and to build it all on British territory. President Kruger of the South African Republic, who not only would not join a South African union but also refused permission for the railroad to cross Transvaal, temporarily blocked his objective. Rhodes determined to squeeze Transvaal into submission between the vise of his South Africa Company in the north and Cape Colony in the south. He also encouraged the *Uitlanders* (Dutch for foreigners, mainly British) within the South African Republic in their plans to revolt against Kruger. The plan called for Dr. L. Starr Jameson, chief administrator of Rhodes's South Africa Company, to lead a force across the border in support of the rebels. Jameson jumped the gun, however, and the Boer government, which had discovered the plot, captured him and his army of five hundred on January 2, 1896, only four days after he had crossed the border.

The repercussions of the Jameson Raid were numerous and far-reaching. The British government denied any knowledge of the conspiracy, sentenced Jameson to prison, and forced Rhodes to resign as prime minister of Cape Colony because of his complicity. It genuinely desired to avoid war with the Boers, but extremists on both sides in South Africa pushed the issue to its fateful conclusion. In October, 1899, the South African or Boer War began. The British, who had only 25,000 soldiers in South Africa against 75,000 Boers, suffered a number of early defeats. With the arrival of reinforcements, numbering 300,000 by the end of the war, the British rallied and in less than a year completely overran both the Orange Free State and Transvaal. The Boers resorted to guerrilla warfare that dragged on for another year and a half before they finally yielded on May 31, 1902.

The British had introduced limited representation in the Cape Colony as early as 1825. In 1853 they introduced a representative assembly, and in 1872 they permitted fully responsible government. The Boer republics had also been self-governing, and soon after the Boer War the British in an extraordinary reversal changed their policy toward the Boers from one of repression to one of conciliation. Transvaal regained responsible government in 1906, and the Orange Free State in 1907. The movement for union with Cape Colony and Natal gathered momentum, and in 1910 the Union of South Africa joined Canada, Australia, and New Zealand as a fully self-governing dominion within the British Empire.

INDIA

Early British conquests in India had been made not by the British government but by the East India Company acting under a royal charter. After the Seven Years' War widespread corruption among company officials and brutal exploitation of the natives led to progressive government intervention. The Regulating Act of 1774 provided for the appointment of a governor-general by the crown and the limitation of the company's privileges. The India Act of 1784 placed the company under the control of the newly created India Office, thus providing a clumsy "dual government." A law in 1813 abolished the company's monopoly of trade between India and Britain, and another law in 1833 abolished its monopoly of trade with China.

The East India Company thus ceased to be a trading company almost completely. It obtained most of its revenue in the form of taxes from the provinces it governed. Some it administered directly, others indirectly by means of native rulers. By 1820 it had brought all of India under its control. Subsequently it added several outlying provinces, such as Kashmir, Punjab, and a part of Baluchistan. In a series of wars between 1825 and 1885, Burma was annexed bit by bit, and eventually was attached to British India. The British became involved in the Malay peninsula during the Napoleonic wars and gradually extended their control over it in the course of the century, and also took Ceylon from the Dutch.

Governing this vast conglomerate was no easy task. A great diversity of languages, religions, customs, and traditions existed side by side. Hindus and Moslems accounted for the major part of the population of some 200 million, but there were many lesser religious cults as well. Each great cultural tradition contained many different races, sects, and social castes. Such diversity and lack of national sentiment had facilitated the original conquest, but it complicated enormously the task of government.

Sepoys Dividing the Spoils

"We are in sad anxiety about India, which engrosses all our attention. Troops cannot be raised fast or largely enough. And the horrors committed on the poor ladies — women and children — are unknown in these ages, and make one's blood run cold. . . . There is not a family hardly who is not in sorrow and anxiety about their children, and in all ranks — India being the place where every one was anxious to place a son." From a letter of Queen Victoria to the king of the Belgians, September 2, 1857, in Arthur Christopher Benson and Viscount Esher, THE LETTERS OF QUEEN VICTORIA (London, 1908), Vol. III.

The company made a few attempts to introduce unified practices on the Western model, such as British courts and law codes, but native susceptibilities were easily offended. On the whole, the company found it easier to leave things as they were.

One example of the difficulties occurred in 1857 and brought about the final extinction of the East India Company. Four-fifths of its army consisted of natives — Moslems, Hindus, and others. A number of actions and rumors of actions by the officials of the company inflamed the religious ardor of the troops and aroused fears of forcible conversion to Christianity. In May three regiments of sepoys (native troops) mutinied and marched on Delhi. The revolt soon spread to other parts of India, and for a time it appeared that the British would be driven out entirely. Eventually they rallied and by July, 1858, had defeated the rebels and restored their power. The reaction in Britain was distinctly unfavorable to the company. In August Parliament passed a new India Act transferring the company's powers directly to the crown, which then introduced a number of reforms in the Indian administration. Although the changes were immediately provoked by the Sepoy Mutiny, they corresponded with a new attitude toward imperial and colonial affairs that had been gaining strength in Britain.

ANTI-IMPERIALISM AND THE REVIVAL
OF IMPERIAL SENTIMENT

India and the "settlement colonies" (those with large numbers of British settlers), which eventually became self-governing dominions, were not the only components of the British Empire in the mid-nineteenth century. The empire included a number of minor possessions in and around the Caribbean and trading posts on the West African coast, as well as a number of islands and other fortified strong points on sea lanes throughout the world, held chiefly for strategic reasons: Gibraltar, Malta, Aden, Singapore, the Falkland Islands, and others. The methods by which this disparate assemblage was governed were complex, confusing, and at times even chaotic. No single, simple system of colonial administration existed either in the colonies or in London. Each colony had its own unique legal system, which might include elements of French, Spanish, Dutch, or even Moslem or Hindu law, depending on its prior history. Both crown and Parliament claimed the right to regulate colonial affairs. In practice, Parliament usually left matters to the various government departments, but it never abdicated its right to legislate either for particular colonies or for the empire as a whole. In addition to the India Office, which had its own more or less clearly defined responsibilities, colonial affairs fell under the jurisdiction of the Colonial Office (attached to the War Office until 1854), the Board of Trade, the Treasury, and even the Home Office on occasion. Moreover, military and naval officers, governors-general, high commissioners, and other officials in the field frequently acted quite independently of superior authority, although nominally taking orders from London.

The generation after 1815 witnessed a growing wave of criticism of some of the pillars of the old colonial system: slavery, the penal system, the restriction of colonial trade, and the political restrictions imposed on the colonies by the government in London. Critics accused the colonial administration of extravagance and inefficiency. Political, religious, humanitarian, and economic arguments were advanced to buttress the criticism, which owed much to the growth of Benthamite liberalism. Three schools of thought gradually emerged on the subject of colonial reform. The first, which gained influence in the 1830's, paradoxically sought to cure the evils of the old colonial system by a new and more vigorous wave of colonial expansion — by the emigration of British settlers to unpopulated territories rather than by the conquest of existing societies. Led by Edward Gibbon Wakefield, the founder in 1830 of the Colonization Society, this group influenced settlement policy in Australia and was instrumental in securing the annexation of New Zealand in 1840. At the other extreme were those who wanted to see Britain shed its colonies altogether in the belief that it could gain the commercial advantages of trade without the expense and political risks of administration. They used as their prime example the rapid growth of commerce with the United States after the American Revolution. Called "little Englanders," they achieved their greatest influence, such as it was, in the 1850's and 1860's at the peak of the free trade movement. A third, intermediate, more pragmatic group stressed administrative simplification and efficiency, humanitarian reform, and the gradual extension of self-government. Although they were less vocal than the others, they succeeded in obtaining responsible and strategic positions in the government and in the long run were the most influential.

None of the colonial reformers had his way entirely. No matter how dedicated and hardworking, they were frustrated by the inertia of the political system, stymied by the resistance of vested interests, and overwhelmed by the march of events throughout the vast and far-flung territories that they administered. After 1870 major new developments completely altered the environment in which they labored. In the election of 1874 the Conservatives under Disraeli defeated Gladstone's Liberals on a platform of "giving the country a rest" from domestic reform measures. In 1875 on behalf of the British government Disraeli melodramatically purchased from the bankrupt khedive of Egypt his shares in the Suez Canal Company. In 1876 he bestowed on Queen Victoria the title "Empress of India." In these and other ways he rekindled popular enthusiasm for imperial expansion. No less important was the changing world situation, which brought other nations into the imperial picture. The creation of the German Empire, the Russo-Turkish War, and the depression that began in 1873 set the stage for a competitive scramble for colonies in which Britain, as the leading imperial nation, could hardly avoid involvement.

THE OPENING OF ASIA

Although parts of Asia had been open to European influence and conquest since the beginning of the sixteenth century, much of it remained in isolation. In the first half of the nineteenth century Britain controlled India and some of its surrounding territories, the Dutch held most of the islands of the East Indies, and Spain retained the Philippines. The French and Portuguese maintained small trading settlements on the Indian coasts. The vast and ancient empire of China, however, as well as Japan, Korea, and the principalities of Southeast Asia, attempted to remain aloof from Western civilization, which they regarded as inferior to their own. They refused to accept Western diplomatic representatives, excluded or persecuted Christian missionaries, and allowed only a trickle of commerce with the West.

RUSSIAN EXPANSION IN ASIA

Russian frontiersmen began to explore the vast wilderness of Siberia about the time of the first English settlements in North America. In 1637 they reached the Pacific coast, and by the end of the seventeenth century they were encroaching on the Chinese borders far to the south. Russian expansionism was relatively quiescent in the eighteenth century, although by the end of the century the Russians had established a claim on Alaska and in the early years of the nineteenth century set up trading posts on the coast of northern California. Siberia, a forbidding land at best, remained thinly populated and underdeveloped. The next main thrust of Russian expansion in Asia, which took place in the nineteenth century, was directed toward the warmer lands to the south and was closely connected with the desire to secure ice-free ports.

In a series of wars against the Ottoman Empire and Persia between 1800 and 1830 Russia gained control of the entire north coast of the Black Sea. In succeeding decades it pressed its advance into central Asia, annexing the trans-Caspian area in 1881 and Turkestan in 1884–85. These advances resulted in conflicts with Persia and Afghanistan and in tense diplomatic relations with the British. Britain had earlier fought minor wars with both Persia and Afghanistan to protect its passage to India and the Indian frontiers, and it had established a sort of informal protectorate over both countries. The Anglo-Russian tension in the Middle East continued throughout the final quarter of the nineteenth century, becoming especially acute after 1896. At length the Anglo-Russian Entente of 1907, occasioned by mutual fear of Germany (see p. 836), led to agreement and the relaxation of tension. Afghanistan remained a buffer state between Russian Turkestan and British India, with Russia recognizing predominant British interests in the control of its foreign relations. Without consulting the Persian government, the two great powers divided Persia into spheres of influence, north and south, with a neutral sphere between them. Thus, although both Persia and Afghanistan retained nominal independence, they were in fact narrowly circumscribed.

The Russians pursued aggressive policies in eastern Asia as well. In 1850 they established a settlement on the Amur River on the border of the Chinese Empire. Shortly afterward they extracted from the Chinese two treaties that extended Russian territory to the shores of the Sea of Japan. In 1860 they founded the city of Vladivostok. Toward the end of the century intervention in the Sino-Japanese War and in Korea, the lease of the Port Arthur naval base on the Yellow Sea, and the occupation of Manchuria brought them into conflict with the equally aggressive Japanese. Russian refusal to negotiate differences led directly to the outbreak of a disastrous war in 1904. (See p. 753.)

CHINA, THE PAPER DRAGON

The Chinese Empire in the nineteenth century was ruled by the Manchu dynasty, the last in a long succession of dynasties that had risen and fallen in China for more than three thousand years. The Manchu dynasty was about two hundred years old and had already begun to show signs of decrepitude before the Europeans intervened to hasten its demise.

British commercial interests provided the initial occasion for intervention. Chinese tea and silks found a ready market in Europe, but British traders could offer little in exchange that appealed to the Chinese until they discovered that the Chinese had a marked taste for opium. The Chinese government forbade its importation, but the trade flourished by means of smugglers and corrupt customs officials. When one honest official at Canton seized and burned a large shipment of opium in 1839, the British traders demanded retaliation. Lord Palmerston, the foreign secretary, informed them that the government could not intervene for the purpose of permitting British subjects to violate the laws of the country with which they traded, but the military and diplomatic representatives on the spot disregarded these instructions and took punitive action against the Chinese. Thus began the Opium War (1839–1842), which ended with the dictated Treaty of Nanking. Under it China ceded to Britain the island of Hongkong, agreed to open five more ports to trade under consular supervision, established a uniform 5 per cent import tariff, and paid a substantial indemnity. The opium trade continued.

The ease with which the British prevailed over the Chinese encouraged other nations to seek equally favorable treaties, which were accordingly granted. Such a show of weakness by the Chinese government provoked demonstrations that were both anti-government and anti-foreign and led to the Taiping Rebellion (1850–1864). Government forces eventually defeated the rebels, but in the meantime the general lawlessness gave Western powers another excuse for intervention. In 1857–58 a joint Anglo-French force occupied a number of principal cities and extorted further concessions, in which the United States and Russia also participated.

China's history for the remainder of the nineteenth century followed a depressingly similar pattern. Concessions to foreigners led to fresh outbreaks of anti-foreign violence and lawlessness, leading in turn to further reprisals and concessions. Recognizing the general weakness of China, still other nations joined in the scramble for concessions and special privileges: Germany, Portugal, and even Japan, which had resisted Western pressures while adopting Western ways. Japan went to war against China in 1894–95, forcing the latter to recognize the independence of Korea and to cede Formosa, the Pescadores Islands, and the Liaotung peninsula. Other nations were eager to participate in a general dismemberment of China but could not agree on the division of spoils. In the end, China avoided complete partition by the great powers only by virtue of great power rivalry. Instead of outright partition, Britain, France, Germany, Russia, the United States, and Japan contented themselves with special treaty ports, spheres of influence, and long-term leases of Chinese territory. At the initiative of the American secretary of state, John Hay, the great powers agreed in 1899 to follow an "open door" policy in China by not discriminating against the commerce of other nations in their own spheres of influence.

Continued humiliations resulted in a final desperate outburst of anti-foreign violence known as the Boxer Rebellion (1900–1901). Boxers was the popular name given to the members of a secret society called The Society of Harmonious Fists, whose aim was to drive all foreigners from China. In risings in several parts of the country they attacked Chinese converts to Christianity and murdered hundreds of missionaries, railroad workers, businessmen, and other foreigners, including the German minister to Peking. The first attempts of British and other military forces to occupy Peking were repulsed. A second and larger joint expedition took the capital, meted out severe reprisals, and exacted further indemnities and concessions. Thereafter the Chinese government was in a state of almost visible decay. It succumbed in 1912 to a revolution led by Dr. Sun Yat-sen, a Western-educated physician, whose program was "nationalism, democracy, and socialism." The Western powers did not attempt to interfere in the revolution, but neither were they perturbed. The Republic of China that resulted remained weak and divided, its hopes of reform and regeneration long postponed.

JAPAN REBUFFS THE WEST

In the first half of the nineteenth century Japan maintained its policy against foreign intrusion more effectively than any other Oriental nation. Gradually, under continuous Western pressure for diplomatic representation, missionary activity, and commercial intercourse, the pillars of resistance weakened. In 1853–54 they collapsed in the face of representations made by Commodore Matthew Perry, a United States naval commander, backed by the threat of force. Soon other Western nations obtained trading and diplomatic privileges similar to those gained by the United

States. As in China, anti-foreign rioting broke out, lives were lost, and property was destroyed. The Western navies began to take reprisals. It seemed as if Japan was destined to repeat the experience of the other victims of Western imperialism, perhaps even more rapidly. Then a remarkable change took place.

Prior to 1868 Japan was ruled not by the emperor but by the shogun, a powerful feudal lord; the nominal emperor's functions were chiefly religious. The anti-foreign sentiment provoked by the concessions of the shogun developed into a movement to restore the emperor to his rightful position as head of the government. The movement was fortuitously aided in 1867 by the accession of a vigorous, intelligent young emperor, Mutsuhito, almost simultaneously with the accession to the shogunate of a man who belonged to the emperor's party. In the following year the latter abdicated the shogunate, and the emperor began to rule in fact as well as in name. The event, marking the birth of modern Japan, is called the Meiji Restoration from the name Meiji, meaning Enlightened Government, which Mutsuhito chose to designate his reign, as was the custom in Japan. The Meiji period lasted from 1868 to the death of Mutsuhito in 1912.

Immediately upon coming to power, Mutsuhito changed the tone of the anti-foreign movement. Instead of attempting to expel the foreigners, Japan cooperated with them but kept them at a polite distance. Intelligent young men went abroad to study Western methods in politics and government, military science, industrial technology, trade, and finance, with the aim of adopting the most efficient methods. The old feudal system was abolished, almost in a single stroke, and replaced by a highly centralized bureaucratic administration modeled on the French system, with an army of the Prussian type and a navy of the British type. Industrial and financial methods came from every country, but especially from the United States. The results of this vigorous, forward-looking policy soon became apparent. Foreign commerce made spectacular gains, modern industries arose where none had been before, and Japanese military might soon won the incredulous respect of the Western world. In 1894–95 Japan quickly defeated China, its neighbor and former mentor, and joined the ranks of the imperialist nations by annexing Chinese territory and staking out a sphere of influence in China proper. Even more surprisingly, just ten years later Japan decisively defeated Russia.

The Russo-Japanese War resulted directly from the imperial rivalry of the two nations in China and Korea. Japan attempted to negotiate a settlement of disputed claims on several occasions, but the Russians, who regarded the Japanese as little different from the Chinese and Koreans, treated the proposals with disdain. Provoked by the affront to their national pride, the Japanese in February, 1904, bottled up the Russian Asiatic fleet in Port Arthur and two days later declared war. To Western observers it looked like an Oriental David attacking the Russian Goliath. The Japanese soon showed their mettle by inflicting a series of defeats on Russian armies along the Yalu River and in Manchuria. To regain control of the seas between Japan and the mainland, the Russians sent their Baltic fleet on a seven months' cruise around the tip of Africa, but no sooner had it arrived in Eastern waters in May, 1905, than the Japanese sank almost the entire fleet. This shattering and humiliating loss, together with the outbreak of domestic revolution, persuaded the Russians to accept President Roosevelt's offer of mediation. By the Treaty of Portsmouth in September, 1905, the Russians acknowledged Japanese predominance in Korea, transferred their lease on Port Arthur and the Liaotung peninsula to Japan, and ceded to Japan the southern half of Sakhalin. Thus did the Japanese prove that they could play the white man's game.

KOREA, INDOCHINA, AND THAILAND

Korea in the nineteenth century was a semi-autonomous kingdom under the nominal suzerainty of the Chinese, although the Japanese had long had claims there. Like China and Japan, Korea followed a rigid policy of exclusion. Shipwrecked foreign seamen were not allowed to leave the country, and the few missionaries who entered the country in one way or another, mainly French Catholics, were frequently persecuted. Western "gunboat diplomacy" gradually opened the country to foreign influence and commerce in the second half of the century, but the bitter rivalry of China and Japan for predominance as well as the general poverty of the country discouraged Western diplomats and traders. After increasing tension over a period of twenty years, war finally broke out between China and Japan in 1894. The Japanese won easily. Although Korea had been the principal cause of the war, the Treaty of 1895 ending it did not result in Japanese annexation. Japan remained content with China's recognition of Korean "independence." For the next ten years Russia replaced China as Japan's chief rival for hegemony in Korea, until the outcome of the Russo-Japanese war forced Russia to concede Japan's "preponderant interests." Finally, after a series of rebellions against Japanese-imposed puppets, Japan formally annexed Korea in 1910.

Indochina is the name frequently applied to the vast peninsula of Southeast Asia because the culture of the area is essentially an amalgam of classical Indian and Chinese civilization. Prior to the nineteenth century the rulers of the various principalities and kingdoms recognized a vague allegiance to the Chinese emperor. In the course of the century the British, operating from India, established control over Burma and the Malay States and eventually incorporated them into the empire. The eastern half of the peninsula, including the principalities of Tonkin, Laos, Cambodia, Cochin China, and Annam, was ruled by the emperor of Annam. French missionaries had been active in the region since the seventeenth century, but in the first half of the nineteenth century they were subjected increasingly to persecution, giving the French government an excuse for intervention. In 1858 a French expedition occupied the city of Saigon in Cochin China, and four years later France annexed Cochin China itself. Once established on the peninsula, the French found themselves involved in conflicts with the natives, which obliged them to extend their "protection" over ever larger areas. In the 1880's they organized Cochin China, Cambodia, Annam, and Tonkin into the Union of French Indochina, to which they added Laos in 1893.

Thailand (or Siam, as it was called by Europeans), between Burma on the west and French Indochina on the east, had the good fortune to remain an independent kingdom. It owed its independence to two principal factors: a series of able and enlightened kings, and its position as a buffer between French and British spheres of influence. Although it was opened to Western influence by gunboat treaties, like most of the rest of Asia, its rulers reacted with conciliatory gestures and at the same time strove to learn from the West and to modernize their kingdom. Even this might not have saved it from the fate of Burma and French Indochina had it not been for the Anglo-French rivalry. In 1893 it faced a grave threat from the French, but an Anglo-French agreement of 1896 gave it a joint guarantee of independence. Few other non-Western nations were so fortunate.

THE PARTITION OF AFRICA

Culturally, most of Africa in the nineteenth century was at the opposite extreme from Asia. Asia had very ancient, even decadent civilizations, while Africa south of the Sahara had none, or so it appeared to Europeans of that time, although results of recent research have shown that this view was incorrect. Islamic North Africa, on the other hand, resembled Asia. Asians had highly developed and refined religious traditions; the religions of black Africa were primitive and tribal. The tribe served as the basis of social and political organization, although tribes might occasionally be grouped into something resembling kingdoms and even empires.

Whatever the differences between Asians and Africans, their similarities are more important for an understanding of their vulnerability to Western imperialism. They were alike in three principal ways. In the first place, they were technologically backward. Second, they had weak, unstable governments, shifting political allegiances, and warring internal factions. A third similarity had no functional significance, yet it did have an important bearing on Western attitudes toward Asians and Africans: both had colored skins, in contrast to the predominantly fair-skinned Europeans.

Although the similarities explain much of the vulnerability of Asians and Africans to Western imperialism, they do not explain why Europeans wanted to create colonial empires, or why the revival of imperialism took place when it did. The precise timing of Western imperialism can be understood only in relation to intra-European diplomacy and power politics, inasmuch as imperial rivalries were mostly extensions of European great power rivalries. In the specific case of Africa the timing can be explained partly by the gradual dissolution of the Ottoman Empire in the north and by the mutual antagonism of two ethnic groups of European descent in the south, the Boers and the British.

The continuing conflict between the Boers and the British pushed the limit of European settlement and control north from the southern tip of Africa. In the process native Africans were overrun, outflanked, pushed aside, and sometimes brutally butchered as if they were animals in the path of the two antagonists. They were rarely the direct objects of the imperialist drive; rather they were its incidental victims. The Anglo-Boer conflict resulted in the settlement of Transvaal and the Orange Free State and also brought into the British Empire Basutoland (1868), Bechuanaland (1885), Swaziland (1902), and Rhodesia (1889).

ISLAMIC AFRICA

Prior to 1880 the only European possession in Africa, apart from British South Africa and a few coastal trading posts dating from the eighteenth century or earlier, was French Algeria. Charles X undertook to conquer Algeria in 1830 in a belated attempt to stir up popular support for his regime. The conquest came too late to save his throne and left a legacy of unfinished conquest to his successors. Not until 1879 did civil government replace the military authorities. By then the French had begun to expand from their settlements on the African west coast. By the end of the century they had conquered and annexed a huge, thinly populated territory (including most of the Sahara Desert), which they christened French West Africa. In 1881 they took advantage of border raids on Algeria by tribesmen from Tunisia to invade Tunisia and establish a protectorate. The French rounded out their North African empire in 1912 by establishing a protectorate over the larger part of Morocco (Spain claimed the small northern corner) after lengthy diplomatic struggles, especially with Germany.

More important events were taking place at the eastern end of Islamic Africa. The opening of the Suez Canal by a French company in 1869 revolutionized world commerce. It also endangered the British lifeline to India — or so it seemed to the British. Thereafter it became a cardinal tenet of British foreign policy to exert as much control as possible over the canal area and its approaches and to prevent them from falling into the hands of an unfriendly power at any cost. Their designs were fortuitously favored by the financial difficulties of the khedive (king) of Egypt. Although the khedives were nominally tributary to the sultan in Constantinople, they had long followed an independent policy, at times amounting to outright insubordination. In their effort to build Egypt up to the status of a great power they incurred enormous debts to Europeans (mainly the French and British) for such purposes as an abortive attempt at industrialization, the construction of the Suez Canal, and an attempted conquest of Sudan. This financial stringency enabled Disraeli to purchase the khedive's shares in the canal company. In an effort to bring some order into the finances of the country, the British and French governments appointed financial advisers who soon constituted the effective government. Egyptian resentment at foreign domination resulted in widespread riots in which many Europeans living in Egypt lost their lives. To restore order and protect the canal, the British in 1882 bombarded Alexandria and landed an expeditionary force. The occupation of Egypt had begun.

Gladstone, the British prime minister, assured the Egyptians and the other great powers (who had been invited to participate in the occupation but declined) that the occupation would be temporary, since its only purpose was the restoration of order and the preservation of European lives and property. Once in, however, the British found to their chagrin that they could not get out easily or gracefully. Besides continued nationalist agitation, which necessitated the presence of the army, the British inherited from the government of the khedive the latter's unfinished conquest of Sudan. In pursuing this objective, which seemed to be justified by the importance to the Egyptian economy of controlling the upper Nile, the British ran head-on into conflict with the French, who were expanding eastward from their West African possessions. At Fashoda in 1898 rival French and British forces faced one another with sabers drawn, but hasty negotiations in London and Paris prevented actual hostilities. At length the French withdrew, preparing the way for British rule in what became known as Anglo-Egyptian Sudan.

One by one the Turkish sultan's nominal vassal states along the North African coast had been plucked away until only Tripoli remained, a long stretch of barren coastline backed by an even more barren hinterland. Italy, its nearest European neighbor, was a late-comer both as a nation and as an imperialist. It had managed to pick up only a few narrow strips on the East African coast and had been ignominiously repulsed in an attempted conquest of Ethiopia in 1896. It watched with bitter, impotent envy while other nations picked imperial plums. In 1911, having carefully prepared a series of agreements with the other great powers in order to have a free hand, Italy picked a quarrel with Turkey, delivered an impossible ultimatum, and promptly invaded Tripoli. The war was something of a farce, with neither side vigorous enough to overcome the other. The threat of a new outbreak in the Balkans, however, persuaded the Turks to make peace in 1912. They ceded Tripoli to Italy, and the Italians renamed it Libya.

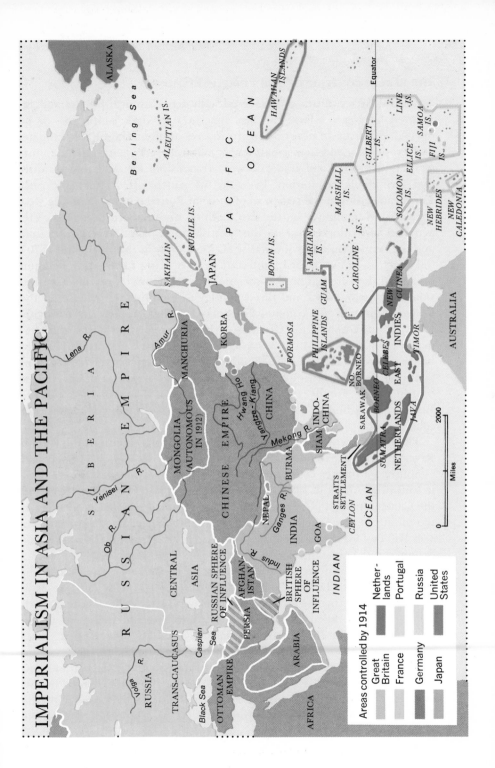

IMPERIALISM IN ASIA AND THE PACIFIC

ALASKA

Bering Sea

ALEUTIAN IS.

HAWAIIAN ISLANDS

Equator

PACIFIC OCEAN

LINE IS.

GILBERT IS.

ELLICE IS.

SAMOA IS.

FIJI IS.

MARSHALL IS.

SOLOMON IS.

NEW HEBRIDES

NEW CALEDONIA

MARIANA IS.

CAROLINE IS.

KURILE IS.

SAKHALIN

JAPAN

BONIN IS.

GUAM

NEW GUINEA

AUSTRALIA

Lena R.

SIBERIAN EMPIRE

MANCHURIA

KOREA

FORMOSA

PHILIPPINE ISLANDS

CELEBES

EAST INDIES

TIMOR

Amur R.

Yenisei R.

Ob R.

RUSSIAN EMPIRE

MONGOLIA (AUTONOMOUS IN 1912)

CHINESE EMPIRE

Hwang Ho

Yangtze-Kiang

CHINA

SIAM

INDO-CHINA

Mekong R.

NO. BORNEO

SARAWAK

BORNEO

NETHERLANDS

SUMATRA

JAVA

CENTRAL ASIA

RUSSIAN SPHERE OF INFLUENCE

AFGHAN-ISTAN

BURMA

Ganges R.

NEPAL

Indus R.

INDIA

GOA

STRAITS SETTLEMENT

CEYLON

BRITISH SPHERE OF INFLUENCE

TRANS-CAUCASUS

Volga R.

Caspian Sea

Black Sea

RUSSIA

PERSIA

OTTOMAN EMPIRE

ARABIA

AFRICA

INDIAN OCEAN

2000

Miles

0

Areas controlled by 1914

Great Britain	Nether-lands
France	Portugal
Germany	Russia
Japan	United States

THE BERLIN CONFERENCE AND FINAL PARTITIONS

Central Africa, much of it covered with dense tropical jungles and inhabited by Negroes, was the last area in the "dark continent" to be opened to European penetration. Its inaccessability, inhospitable climate, and exotic flora and fauna — all amply embroidered upon in the accounts of early explorers and traders — were responsible for Africa's sobriquet and formidable reputation. Prior to the nineteenth century the only European claims in the region were those of Portugal: Angola on the west coast and Mozambique on the east, both on the southern perimeter. The activities of explorers such as the Scottish missionary David Livingstone and the Anglo-American journalist H. M. Stanley in the 1860's and 1870's did much to arouse popular interest. In 1876 King Leopold of Belgium organized the International Association for the Exploration and Civilization of Central Africa and hired Stanley to establish settlements in the Congo. Agitation for colonial enterprise reached a peak in Germany with the formation of the German African Society in 1878 and the German Colonial Society in 1882. A reluctant Bismarck allowed himself to be converted to the cause of colonialism. The discovery of diamonds in South Africa stimulated exploration in the hope of similar discoveries in central Africa. Finally, the French occupation of Tunis in 1881 and the British occupation of Egypt in 1882 set off a scramble for claims and concessions.

The French, who had earlier staked a claim at the mouth of the Gabun River, hurriedly extended it to a large region north of the Congo and established a further claim to Dahomey. The Germans established a base in southwest Africa in 1883 and claimed protectorates over Togoland and the Cameroons in 1884. In the same year Portugal claimed both sides of the mouth of the Congo, and early in 1885 Spain claimed protectorates over Rio de Oro (Spanish Sahara) and Rio Muni (Spanish Guinea), while Britain did the same in Nigeria.

The sudden rush for territories naturally created frictions that might have led to war. To head off this possibility, and incidentally to balk British and Portuguese claims, Bismarck and Jules Ferry, the French prime minister, called an international conference on African affairs to meet in Berlin in 1884. Fourteen nations including the United States sent representatives. The conferees agreed on a number of pious resolutions, including one calling for the suppression of the slave trade and slavery, which was still a flourishing institution in Africa. More important, they recognized the Congo Free State headed by Leopold of the Belgians, an outgrowth of his International Association, and laid the ground rules for further annexations. The most important rule provided that a nation must effectively occupy a territory in order to have its claim recognized.

On the east coast of Africa much the same process of occupation took place. In 1882 the Italians occupied Assab at the mouth of the Red Sea and used it as a base for expansion into Eritrea and Italian Somaliland. Not to be outdone, the French and British soon afterward established protectorates on parts of the Somali coast. Farther south two chartered East Africa companies, one German and one British, staked large claims reaching inland to the eastern borders of the Congo Free State. The French, who had an old but ineffectual claim to the island of Madagascar, finally annexed it in 1896. One of the few regions of Africa left unclaimed by a European power was the Coptic Christian kingdom of Ethiopia, also known as Abyssinia. In 1895 the Italians decided to annex it to their coastal territories. They began a slow and difficult march to the interior. Early in the following year the Italian army of twenty thousand men was annihilated by barefoot Ethiopian tribesmen at Adowa. That humiliating defeat ended temporarily Italian designs on the "king of kings."

In this fashion was the dark continent carved up and made to see the light. Before the outbreak of World War I only Ethiopia and Liberia, established by emancipated American Negroes in the 1830's, retained their independence. Both were nominally Christian. Annexation was one thing, however, effective settlement and development were quite another. The African colonies would have to wait a long time before receiving the fruits, if any, of European tutelage. The process of partition frequently brought the nations of Europe to the brink of war, but somehow the diplomats averted full-scale fighting, except in the special case of the Boer War. Perhaps it was the existence of this open frontier that enabled the expansive Europeans to work off their mutual antagonisms without resorting to arms. In any case, soon after this safety valve was sealed the European boiler exploded.

INTERPRETATIONS AND PERSPECTIVES

Asia and Africa were not the only areas subject to imperial exploitation, nor were the nations of Europe the only ones to engage in it. Once Japan had adopted Western technology, it pursued imperialistic policies not unlike those of Europe. In spite of strong domestic criticism, the United States embarked on a policy of colonialism before the end of the century. Besides the purchase of Alaska in 1867 and the acquisition by lease of the Panama Canal Zone in 1903, the United States participated with Britain, France, and Germany in the division of the islands of the Pacific, taking Hawaii and part of Samoa as its portion. In the war with Spain in 1898 the United States won the Philippines and Guam in the Pacific as well as Puerto Rico in the Caribbean.

Some of the British dominions were far more aggressively imperialistic than the mother country itself. The expansion of South Africa, for example, took place mostly through South African initiative and frequently against the wishes and explicit instructions of the government in London.

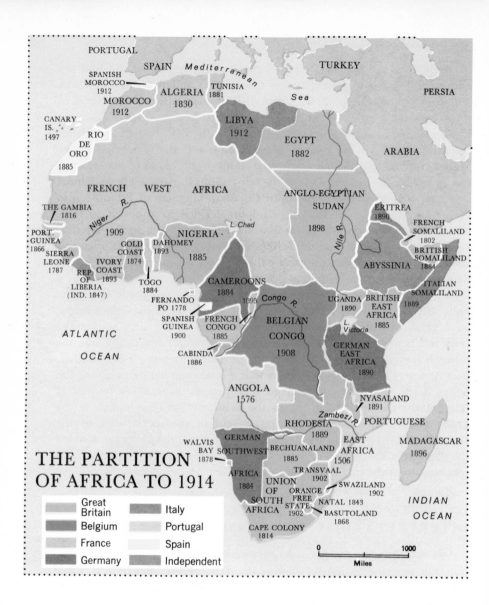

PORTUGAL

SPAIN *Mediterranean*

SPANISH
MOROCCO
1912
MOROCCO
1912

ALGERIA
1830

TUNISIA
1881

TURKEY

PERSIA

Sea

CANARY
IS.
1497

RIO
DE
ORO
1885

LIBYA
1912

EGYPT
1882

ARABIA

FRENCH   WEST   AFRICA

THE GAMBIA
1816

R.

Niger

L. Chad

PORT.
GUINEA
1866
SIERRA
LEONE
1787

1909

GOLD
COAST

IVORY
COAST

REP.
OF
LIBERIA
(IND. 1847)

1893

DAHOMEY
1893

NIGERIA
1885

ANGLO-EGYPTIAN
SUDAN

1898

Nile R.

ERITREA
1890

FRENCH
SOMALILAND
1802

BRITISH
SOMALILAND
1884

ABYSSINIA

ITALIAN
SOMALILAND

1889

TOGO
1884

FERNANDO
PO 1778

CAMEROONS
1884

1895 *Congo R.*

UGANDA
1890

BRITISH
EAST
AFRICA
1885

ATLANTIC

SPANISH
GUINEA
1900

FRENCH
CONGO
1885

BELGIAN
CONGO
1908

*L.
Victoria*

OCEAN

CABINDA
1886

GERMAN
EAST
AFRICA
1890

ANGOLA
1576

NYASALAND
1891

Zambezi R.

RHODESIA
1889

PORTUGUESE

THE PARTITION
OF AFRICA TO 1914

WALVIS
BAY
1878

GERMAN
SOUTHWEST
AFRICA
1884

BECHUANALAND
1885

TRANSVAAL
1902

EAST
AFRICA
1506

MADAGASCAR
1896

UNION
OF
SOUTH
AFRICA

SWAZILAND
1902

ORANGE
FREE
STATE
1902

NATAL 1843

INDIAN

BASUTOLAND
1868

OCEAN

CAPE COLONY
1814

	Great Britain		Italy
	Belgium		Portugal
	France		Spain
	Germany		Independent

0   1000
Miles

The British annexation of southeastern New Guinea in 1884 (after the Dutch had claimed the western half and the Germans the northeast) was directly due to the agitation of the Queensland government in Australia. A distinction is sometimes made between imperialism and colonialism. Thus, neither Russia nor Austria-Hungary had overseas colonies, but both were cleary empires in the sense that they ruled over alien peoples without the consent of the latter. The imperial powers did not as a rule establish colonies in China, yet China was clearly subject to imperial control. The countries of Latin America experienced no new attempts at conquest by outside powers, but it was frequently alleged that they constituted part of the informal empires of Britain and the United States as a result of economic dependence and financial control.

The causes of imperialism were many and complex. No single theory suffices to explain all cases. Nevertheless, it is worth reviewing some of the more important interpretations; whatever their validity, the interpretations themselves are a part of the intellectual history of the epoch.

THE HUMANITARIAN ARGUMENT

In the intellectual crosscurrents of the late nineteenth century confusion was bound to arise concerning the motives for imperial expansion. Although some proclaimed the expansion to be a necessity for the Western nations — for good or evil — others demanded the expansion on behalf of the colonial areas. Missionary activity, the desire to bring the comforts of Christianity to the "heathen races," and the belief of well-intentioned humanitarians that non-Europeans would benefit from Western legal institutions or technology, even if imposed by force, were advanced as reasons for dispatching expeditionary forces to distant lands. Rudyard Kipling (1865–1936), famed poet, wrote eloquently of "the white man's burden," and French apologists for imperialism spoke of their *mission civilisatrice*.

The evangelical zeal of both Catholic and Protestant missionaries is beyond dispute. For centuries before the nineteenth century they had carried their message far and wide to the most remote corners of the habitable world. In both Asia and Africa they usually preceded by many years the traders, diplomats, armies, and administrators. Normally they did not ask for military protection from their homelands, much less for territorial annexation. Theirs was a spiritual mission, quite unconnected with politics. When they were subjected to persecution, torture, and even death by the people they sought to convert — and this treatment was by no means rare — the demands for retaliation came most often from journalists, military men, and others, who had reasons of their own for desiring imperial conquest. In short, in the imperial game as it came to be played in the late nineteenth century, arguments based on religion were simply convenient excuses, and missionaries were pawns in the game.

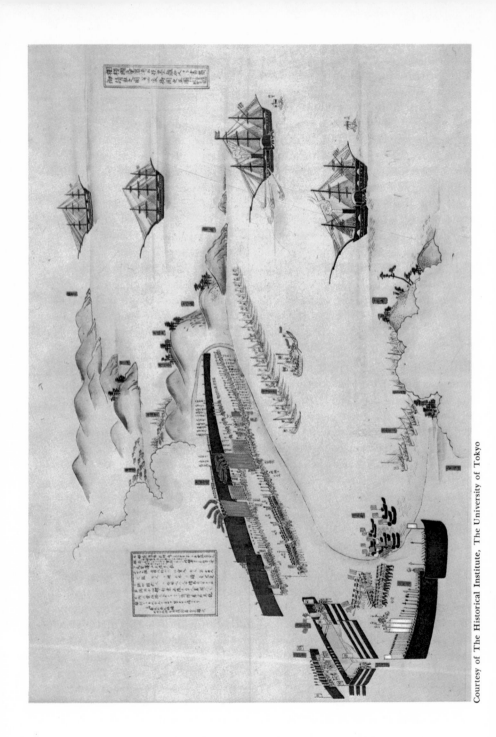

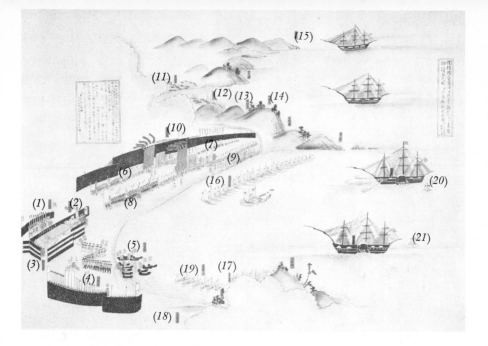

Scene of the Receipt of a Letter from the American [Commodore Perry] at Kurihama, Sagami, and a True Picture of the Four Clan Guard, Plus an Exposure from Kurihama Village

Two main vessels, steamer named Syusukuinna manned 350 and plain ship named Misushisufi manned 300. Strong vessel named fushikatto Furimouts manned 200 and the same named Saratoka m. 150 (k=g, f=p). The number of landing men at Kurihama: Geweer group composed of 284 men; officers 7 men; flute players 15 men; drummers 7 men; flags 6 piece, gong 1 piece, dog 1 head; head gunners 2 men, directors 8 men; boats names 'batteira.' Fourteen boats brought these people to the land, the officers and directors bear on waists six-ch'd revolvers; all the guns mentioned above are equipped with dondorof tubes. In the 6th mo. 6th yr. Kaei, at the camp in Miyata, by order of the master, painted by Kyūkisai Unrai (send.)

(1) *Additional force from Ogaki clan*
(2) *Camp of Gorr of Uraga*
(3) *Gur Kayama*
(4) *Kawagobe Clan Force*
(5) *boats named* batteira
(6) *gunners*
(7) *45 knights*
(8) *gunners*
(9) *60 knights*
(10) *Hikone Clan Force*
(11) *East Urga*

(12) *West Uraga*
(13) *Light House*
(14) *Hirame, Mtn.*
(15) *Kannon Saki*
(16) *Aizu Clan Force 1/10*
(17) *Sumiyoshi Shrine*
(18) *Kurihama Village*
(19) *Oshi Clan Force 1/10*
(20) *Uraga's*
(21) *Hikone's*

Courtesy of Henry T. Rockwell

The White (?) Man's Burden, cartoon from
Life, March 16, 1899

> *"History shows me one way, and one way only, in which a high state of
> civilization has been produced, namely the struggle of race with race, and the
> survival of the physically and mentally fitter race. . . . This dependence of
> progress on the survival of the fitter race, terribly black as it may seem to some
> of you, gives the struggle for existence its redeeming features; it is the fiery
> crucible out of which comes the finer metal."* Karl Pearson, NATIONAL LIFE FROM
> THE STANDPOINT OF SCIENCE. AN ADDRESS DELIVERED Nov. 19, 1900 (London, 1901).

In analyzing the broader argument of imperialism as a humanitarian movement, one can look at the results. It is true that some colonial areas benefited from the introduction of elementary law and order, of Western technology in the form of better medicine, of improved sanitary facilities, roads and railroads, and so on. Most of the improvements, however, were designed to benefit the colonial administration and to facilitate the economic or military exploitation of the colony on behalf of the imperial power. The benefits to the native populations were slight and indirect. After half a century or more of colonial development the average standard of living of the natives in most colonial areas was but little if at all above what it had been in the nineteenth century. This is telling evidence against the humanitarianism of imperialism, whatever the motives may have been.

THE ECONOMIC INTERPRETATION

One of the most popular explanations of modern imperialism concerns economic necessity. In fact, modern imperialism is often referred to as "economic imperialism," as if earlier forms of imperialism had no economic content. There is just enough empirical evidence in favor of these explanations to make them plausible.

One such explanation goes as follows: (1) competition in the capitalist world becomes more intense, resulting in the formation of large-scale enterprises and the elimination of small ones; (2) capital accumulates in the large enterprises more and more rapidly, and since the purchasing power of the masses is insufficient to purchase all the products of large-scale industry, the rate of profit declines; (3) as capital accumulates and the output of capitalist industries goes unsold, the capitalists resort to imperialism in order to gain political control over areas in which they can invest their surplus capital and sell their surplus products. Such is the essence of the Marxist theory of imperialism or, better, the Leninist theory, for Marx did not foresee the rapid development of imperialism even though he lived until 1883. Building on the foundation of Marxian theory and in some cases modifying it, Lenin published his theory in 1915 in the widely read pamphlet *Imperialism, the Highest Stage of Capitalism.*

Lenin was by no means the first person to advance an economic explanation of imperialism. He borrowed heavily from John A. Hobson, the liberal British critic of imperialism, who in turn adopted in revised form many of the arguments of the advocates of imperialism in capitalist countries. One such person was Captain A. T. Mahan, an American naval officer who strongly influenced Theodore Roosevelt, America's leading exponent of imperialism. Mahan's dictum was "Trade follows the flag." Still another capitalist advocate of imperialism was Jules Ferry, a French journalist and politician who twice became prime minister and was chiefly responsible for the largest colonial acquisitions of France. Interestingly, on both occasions his policy of colonial annexation cost him the premiership; but the French, like the British, found it difficult to withdraw once they had become committed to a particular conquest or annexation. It is equally interesting that Ferry did not utilize economic arguments in defending his actions before the French assembly; instead he stressed French prestige and military necessity. Only after he had permanently retired from office did he write books justifying his actions in which for the first time he emphasized the economic gains that France would supposedly realize from its colonial empire.

In many instances the advocates of imperialism were mere opportunists. Journalists sought to sell their books and articles; politicians sought election to office; military and naval officers sought larger appropriations of money for their armies and navies. They tried to achieve their ends by persuading the general public, as well as statesmen and bureaucrats, that imperialism would be good for the nation. The rise of new industrial nations and the massive imports of commodities from the Western Hemisphere and Australia had increased competitive pressures in both industry and agriculture. A severe depression beginning in 1873 inaugurated a long decline in general prices that lasted until 1896. These events precipitated the return to protective tariffs. Although tariffs went higher and higher in the last two decades of the century, they did not produce the desired results. Sales and profits increased for some industrialists and farmers, but decreased for others engaged in export industries. The masses — workers, salaried professionals, even the farmers themselves — paid the cost of this protection, which created social unrest and discontent and encouraged the growth of trade unions and socialist parties.

At this point the advocates of imperialism stepped in with their arguments for expansion. They argued that in addition to offering new markets and outlets for surplus capital, the colonies would provide new sources of raw materials and serve as outlets for the rapidly growing populations of the industrial nations. Many businessmen believed the arguments, and a few enriched themselves by taking advantage of privileged positions in the colonies. Others sanctioned imperialist adventures as a means of preventing unrest and possibly revolution by stirring up patriotic and nationalist sentiment and diverting attention from domestic political, social, and economic issues. It is therefore reasonably clear that belief in the necessity for economic expansion in colonial areas was important in motivating imperial policies. Whether or not that belief was justified is another question.

The argument that the colonies would serve as outlets for surplus population is easily seen to be fallacious. Most colonies were located in climates that Europeans found oppressive. Most emigrants preferred to

Table 1   *Trade with Empire as a Share of the Total Foreign Trade of European Colonial Powers, 1894–1913*

		Imports	Exports	Total
Great Britain	1894–1903	21.27%	30.42%	24.92%
	1904–1913	25.71%	34.75%	26.73%
France	1894–1903	9.86%	11.20%	10.49%
	1904–1913	10.58%	12.61%	11.53%
Germany	1894–1903	0.10%	0.35%	0.21%
	1904–1913	0.37%	0.62%	0.48%
Italy	1894–1903	0.04%	0.30%	0.16%
	1904–1913	0.21%	1.55%	0.75%

Source: *Essays on Unbalanced Growth*, Publications of the Institute of Social Studies, series maior, vol. X ('S-Gravenhage, 1962), p. 142.

go to independent countries, such as the United States and Argentina, or to the self-governing territories of the British Empire. It is true that colonies did in some cases furnish new sources of raw materials, but access to raw materials or to any purchasable commodity did not require political control. In fact, North and South America and the self-governing dominions of Australasia were the largest overseas suppliers of raw material for European industry.

The justification of colonies as markets for surplus manufactures was also fallacious. The colonies were neither needed for this purpose nor used for it after they were acquired. Prior to 1914 little more than 10 per cent of French exports went to French colonies. The colonies were too sparsely populated and too poor to serve as major markets. Moreover, as in the case of raw materials, political control was not required. India, "the brightest jewel in the British crown," was indeed a large market, for in spite of its poverty India purchased large quantities of European wares – but not from Britain alone. The Germans sold far more in India than in all their own colonies together. France sold more to India than to Algeria. Moreover, as important as India was for British manufacturers, the British sold far more to Australia, which had only a fraction of India's population. In spite of protective tariffs, the industrial, imperialist nations of Europe continued to trade predominantly with one another. The largest external market for German industry was Britain, and one of the largest markets for British industry was Germany. France was a major supplier and a major customer of both Britain and Germany. The United States was also a large customer and supplier of European countries.

Perhaps the most important argument for imperialism as an economic phenomenon concerned the investment of surplus capital, at least in

Marxist theory. Here again the facts do not substantiate the logic. Britain had the largest empire and the largest foreign investments (see p. 700); but over half of Britain's foreign investments were in independent countries, especially the United States, and in self-governing territories. The facts on France are even more surprising: less than 10 per cent of French foreign investments before 1914 went to French colonies. The French invested heavily in other European countries and in Latin America. Russia alone, itself an imperialist nation, took more than a fourth of French exported capital; and the French invested in Germany and Austria-Hungary, with whom they eventually went to war. German investments in German colonies were negligible. Some of the imperialist nations were actually net debtors; they included Russia, Italy, Spain, Portugal, and the United States.

Thus, the idea that imperialism was an economic necessity for the highly developed industrial nations is essentially fallacious, although it does contain some elements of truth and plausibility. The most crucial test for the validity of the economic argument is, did imperialism pay? And if so, to whom?

DID IMPERIALISM PAY?

This question has many aspects, and a complete answer would be very complex. Broadly, imperialism did not pay in a strictly pecuniary sense. With few exceptions, of which India was the most important, taxes collected in the colonies rarely sufficed to cover the costs of routine administration, much less those of conquest. It was argued, however, that the indirect benefits from increased trade made the venture worthwhile. Here the statistics are difficult to unravel and interpret. Colonial trade certainly did not bulk large in international trade; and in some cases, notably in France and Germany, the total value of trade with the colonies did not amount to as much as the expenditure incurred in taking and maintaining them.

It is indubitable that some individuals made enormous fortunes in colonial ventures — Cecil Rhodes is the outstanding example — and that many others earned a modest living; but the profits were by no means equally shared. Taxes had to be raised in the imperial nations to pay for the military and naval expeditions and garrisons and the officials who administered the colonies, as well as for whatever public works they constructed. Manpower had to be diverted from other uses to staff the armies, navies, and colonial services. Under the prevailing system of taxation in Europe, most of the tax money came from ordinary workers and farmers, who had no pecuniary interest, direct or indirect, in the colonies. In effect, income and wealth were redistributed by the process of taxation and expenditure; the masses paid the costs, the profits were garnered by a favored few. The ultimate costs, however, should be reckoned by the suffering and dislocation of the peoples subjected to Western imperialism, as well as the rivalries and frustrations generated in the race for colonial supremacy — rivalries that prepared Europe psychologically for war and themselves were factors leading to war. These costs are still being paid.

SOME FINAL REFLECTIONS

If neither the economic explanation, nor the belief in the validity of that explanation (which, it should be clear, are two different things), nor the humanitarian motive is sufficient to explain the burst of imperialism in the late nineteenth century, how can it be explained? Major responsibility must be assigned to sheer political opportunism, combined with growing aggressive nationalism. Disraeli's conversion to imperialism (he had been an anti-imperialist early in his career) was motivated principally by the need to find new issues with which to oppose the Liberal Gladstone. Bismarck encouraged French imperialism as a means of deflecting French campaigns for revenge on Germany, but at first rejected it for Germany itself. When at last he allowed himself to be persuaded, he did so to strengthen the bases of his own political support and deflect attention from the social question in Germany.

Power politics and military expediency also played an important role. Britain's imperial policy throughout the century was dictated primarily by the supposed necessity of protecting the Indian frontiers and lifeline. This explains the British conquest of Burma and Malaya, Baluchistan and Kashmir, as well as British involvement in the Near and Middle East. The occupation of Egypt, undertaken reluctantly by Gladstone with the promise of an early withdrawal, was deemed necessary to protect the Suez Canal. Other nations emulated the successful British, either in the hope of gaining similar advantages or simply for national prestige.

The intellectual climate of the late nineteenth century, strongly colored by Social Darwinism, likewise favored European expansion. Although Herbert Spencer, the foremost popularizer of Social Darwinism, was an outspoken anti-imperialist, others applied his arguments for the "survival of the fittest" to the imperial struggle. Theodore Roosevelt spoke grandly of "manifest destiny," and Kipling's phrase, "the lesser breeds without the law," reflected the typical European attitude toward the non-white races. The historical roots of European racism and ethnocentrism, however, reach far deeper than Darwinian biology. Christian missionary activity itself was an expression of old beliefs in European, or Western, moral and cultural superiority. Throughout their history — at least until the mid-twentieth century — Europeans and Christians have been expansionist and evangelical. In the final analysis, modern imperialism must be regarded as a psychological and cultural phenomenon as well as a political or economic one.

EUROPEAN CULTURE AND SOCIETY: THE END OF THE GOLDEN AGE
CHAPTER THIRTY-ONE

Along with the economic, social, and political changes of the last decades of the nineteenth century, novel intellectual currents filtered through the European world. The new streams of thought resulted in part from growing industrialization, urbanization, and democratization; in part they were reactions to these processes. Above all they reflected the issues raised by the continuing progress of science. For some thinkers, reconsideration of Darwinian biology and mechanistic physics converted earlier optimistic ideas of universal progress into philosophies profoundly pessimistic in their conclusions and implications. A parallel and related development in imaginative literature and the arts clearly indicated disenchantment with conventional nineteenth-century standards and heralded the pessimistic, abstract, and neo-realistic tendencies of twentieth century art and literature. By 1914 these currents of thought had not yet created a new intellectual ethos for Western civilization, but they had made deep inroads in the old philosophic, moral, and aesthetic standards and presuppositions, indicating that the temper of twentieth-century civilization would be immeasurably different from that of the nineteenth.

FIN-DE-SIÈCLE LITERATURE AND ART

The reaction against realism in literature was most pronounced in poetry, which in fact had never undergone a realist phase. By 1885 the new movement in poetry had been christened "symbolism." It soon became clear that the new departures were not limited to poetry, or even to imaginative literature in general. Similar changes were taking place under a variety of labels in the fine arts of music, painting, and sculpture, as well as in philosophy and other fields of scholarship. In 1890 a Frenchman coined a new expression to cover all these diverse manifestations; he called them simply fin de siècle (end of century).

Alternating fashions in literature and art — from classicism to romanticism, from romanticism to realism to symbolism and neo-romanticism and so forth — are sometimes likened to the swings of a pendulum. A biological metaphor would be more appropriate: each movement originated in the womb of its predecessor, inherited many of the latter's features, and broke into open revolt only after gaining full self-consciousness. In the case of the fin-de-siècle movements the attainment of self-consciousness was fostered by new discoveries and inventions in science and technology, and new questionings of the role of intellect in mass society.

POETRY

Although the term symbolism had affinities with other branches of literature and art, it applied chiefly to poetry, and even more specifically to French poetry. Stéphane Mallarmé (1842–1898), the central figure, unlike many of his friends and contemporaries, lived an uneventful life as a teacher of English in French secondary schools. His entire poetic output consisted of less than two thousand lines, but his most famous poem, *L'Après-midi d'un faune,* has been called "the most skillful poem" and "one of the purest jewels" of the French language. Symbolist poetry was usually esoteric and oblique, not to say opaque, and almost always experimental, with great freedom of style. The symbols from which it got its name were not the standard symbols of historic literature but *ad hoc,* even private symbols. Although it abandoned the lyricism of romantic poetry, it made a great effort to convey musical images, as well as those of color, by means of words. The relationship was reciprocal among the artists of the time. The original edition of Mallarmé's *L'Après-midi d'un faune* was illustrated by the artist Édouard Manet, and in 1894 Claude Debussy composed a tone poem of the same name to serve as a prelude.

The symbolist movement has influenced almost all major poets, directly or indirectly, since the 1890's. Its influence was especially noticeable in the early work of the Irish poet William Butler Yeats (1865–1939), the Anglo-American T. S. Eliot (1888–1965), and the German Stefan George (1868–1933). With the triumph of symbolism many poets ceased to write primarily for the general public and wrote increasingly for those versed in literature itself.

DRAMA

Drama, which had reached a low ebb in the middle decades of the century, staged a remarkable survival. Symbolism influenced the theater, notably in the work of the Belgian Maurice Maeterlinck (1862–1949). The most important fin-de-siècle influence on the theater came from the Norwegian Henrik Ibsen (1828–1906). Ibsen was a bitter critic of contemporary bourgeois morality and hypocrisy, and partly for this reason his work was slow in gaining public recognition. Although starkly realistic in portrayal, his dramas went beyond conventional realism in the depth of their psychological probing and symbolic content, revealing their relationship with other novel intellectual currents. Other playwrights eventually followed Ibsen's lead. Among the notable examples of plays in a similar style are *Miss Julia* (1888) by the Swedish dramatist August Strindberg, *The Weavers* (1892) by Gerhart Hauptmann, and *The Cherry Orchard* (1904) by Anton Chekhov.

The leading English-language playwrights of the prewar generation were the Anglo-Irishmen George Bernard Shaw (1856–1950) and Oscar Wilde (1854–1900). In his earlier role as literary and music critic Shaw had been instrumental in winning British acceptance of Ibsen's dramas and Wagner's operas. In his plays he, too, dealt with important social and psychological problems, but both he and Wilde adopted a far more light-hearted manner than other leading dramatists, forcing their audiences to laugh at their own foibles.

FICTION

Realism and naturalism retained their sway much longer in fiction than in other branches of literature. Even after they began to yield to the influence of psychological and symbolist thought, novelists such as Thomas Hardy (1840–1928) and Joseph Conrad (1857–1924), as well as Zola, continued to make use of typically realistic settings. Occasionally novelists such as Anatole France (1844–1924) broke over into fantasy bordering on symbolism, as in *Penguin Island* and *The Revolt of the Angels*. After 1900 symbolism and new discoveries in psychology exerted a strong effect on novelists such as Romain Rolland (1866–1944), André Gide (1869–1951), and James Joyce (1882–1941). The stream-of-consciousness technique, pioneered in fiction by Joyce in *Ulysses* (1915), owed much to the new knowledge of psychology.

PAINTING

The vogue of realism in painting lasted but a short while. For exact portrayals of nature and life painters could not compete with the camera; for conveying moods and interpreting nature and life, the camera could not compete with painters. This discovery was made as early as the 1860's by Édouard Manet (1832–1883), the forerunner of a group of painters who came to be called impressionists. Although impressionism eventually spread to all countries, its fountainhead, like that of symbolism, was France. Its greatest names were Claude Monet (1840–1926), Edgar Degas (1834–1917), and Auguste Renoir (1841–1919). Making use of new scientific knowledge of light, color, and optics, the impressionists portrayed the impression that they received from their subjects, although their themes and temperaments were different. Thus their paintings had hazy outlines and blurs of color. In the use of light and color and the choice of subject matter the impressionists showed a kinship with the writers of naturalistic fiction as well as with the symbolist poets. The expatriate American painter Whistler, who had much in common with the impressionists, painted symphonies and nocturnes in color, while some of his contemporaries created poems in color.

Toward the end of the century Paul Cézanne (1839–1906) and Paul Gauguin (1848–1903), two talented French painters, sought to restore more exact form to painting while preserving the light and color of the impressionists. They were the leaders of the postimpressionist school, which had an enormous influence on twentieth-century painting. Although the Dutchman Vincent Van Gogh (1853–1890), a close friend of Cézanne, is sometimes grouped with the postimpressionists, he preferred to think of himself as an expressionist. He tried to put his own feelings, his own personality even, on the canvas in great blobs of color. At the beginning of the twentieth century a group of young artistic rebels who adopted and developed Van Gogh's techniques became known as *les fauves* (wild beasts) because of the exuberance of their paintings.

In the last decade of the century an artistic bombshell burst in Europe. It was the style called *art nouveau*. It pertained not only to painting but also to print making, design, typography, home furnishings and decorations, and even to architecture. Although its popularity lasted less than two decades, it opened up new vistas of almost unlimited horizons in painting as well as in other plastic arts, by breaking completely with the traditions of the past. In the first decade of the twentieth century abstract and nonrepresentational art had already carved out their niche, well before World War I shattered what was left of traditional art themes in Western civilization. The latest vogue in painting before the cataclysm of war was cubism, the forerunner of surrealism and other postwar styles of nonrepresentational art.

ARCHITECTURE, DECORATION, AND SCULPTURE

The nineteenth century was at best undistinguished for originality in architecture. Near the end of the century, however, new and distinctly original influences began to make themselves felt. Although they developed first from a concern for decoration, the ideal of nineteenth-century architecture, they evolved subtly but rapidly into a concern for simplicity of design and eventually into a belief in the harmony of form and function known as functionalism. Paradoxically, the central figure in the artistic movement that formed the bridge between past and future was reactionary in at least one respect, as was the movement itself. William Morris (1834–1896), a gifted artist and designer, revolted against the ugliness of English industrial cities and the lack of taste in domestic architecture and furnishings. Politically his revolt led him to socialism, but aesthetically he advocated a return to the simplicity of an earlier age, in which every craft was also an art. His simple yet intricately beautiful designs were the products of a reaction against the machine, but — ironically — they proved admirably suited for machine reproduction. The associated art nouveau, which reduced the overly decorated furniture and bric-a-brac of the Victorian era to flamboyant but elegantly simple lines, proved to be the opening wedge in the distinctive architectural styles of the twentieth century. To borrow a phrase subsequently made famous in another context, art nouveau and the reactionism of Morris were steps taken backward in order to go forward. The first really forward steps in architecture were taken by the Americans Louis Sullivan (1856–1924) and his protégé, the young Frank Lloyd Wright (1869–1959). In Europe the leading exponent of the new ideas in architecture was the German Walter Gropius (1883–1969).

At the end of the nineteenth century sculpture, like drama, experienced a noteworthy revival as a serious art form — in contrast to its use in monumental decoration. The man mainly responsible for it was Auguste Rodin (1840–1917), an independent artist who rarely accepted commissions but developed a revolutionary style that set him apart from the conventional sculptors who worked to order. Rodin's greatest work, "The Thinker," is one of the most renowned statues of all time. Another eminent sculptor of the period was Gustav Vigeland of Norway, who succeeded in capturing in stone, bronze, and even wrought iron the full range of human emotions from radiant joy to deepest despair. A large park in Oslo is devoted entirely to exhibiting his work.

MUSIC

Music, like poetry, did not experience a realist phase. On the contrary, the romantic movement in music continued to flourish in the works of Brahms, Lizst, and above all the dramatic operas of Wagner at the very time that realism was riding high in fiction and painting. After the death of Wagner in 1883 musical composition branched off in two directions. One continued in the romantic tradition and allied that tradition even more closely to the growing popular nationalism. It is best represented in the works of such nationalist composers as Tchaikovsky, Grieg, Smetana, Sibelius, and Dvořák. The other allied itself with symbolism and impressionism and produced such compositions as the tone poems of Debussy and Richard Strauss. In time the composers in this tradition deliberately broke with the poetic imagery of romantic and late romantic music and attempted to write pure or absolute music. Igor Stravinsky, Gustav Mahler, Béla Bartók, and Arnold Schönberg led in this development, which even before World War I had begun to make use of atonality, the twelve tone scale, and other strange innovations that became typical of serious compositions in the mid-twentieth century.

POSITIVISM AND ITS CRITICS

At the beginning of the final quarter of the nineteenth century the dominant philosophical system in Europe was positivism. (See p. 657.) Hippolyte Taine pithily summed up the general philosophical import of positivism in 1870: "All human facts, moral as well as physical, being bound up with causes and subject to laws, it follows that all works of man — art, religion, philosophy, literature, moral, political or social phenomena — are but the results of general causes that must be determined scientifically." By the end of the century this confident philosophy, complacently maintained by comfortable philosophers, had been almost completely eclipsed among serious and original thinkers. The reasons for its decline, though many, can be conveniently grouped in two broad categories. In the first place, new discoveries in science itself cast doubt on simple cause-effect relationships and undermined the basis of belief in a naive scientific or materialistic determinism. Second, the relative neglect and shallowness of the treatment of ethical and aesthetic problems, especially by such popularizing proponents of positivism as Herbert Spencer, aroused the moral indignation of a younger generation of social and intellectual rebels who identified positivism with the middle-class cult of crass material progress.

New developments in philosophic, scientific, and social thought accompanying the decline of positivism took two general directions, corresponding to the nature of the attacks on positivism. The first, the work of scientifically minded individuals in many fields of learning, did not reject positivism altogether but sought to build on and go beyond it. It continued to emphasize the use of rationality and logic while recognizing the existence of nonrational elements in human behavior and inexplicable phenomena in the universe. On the other hand, the fomenters of the revolt against positivism consisted mainly of literary philosophers, writers, and artists. They pointed out the role of intuition as a component of knowledge, laid great stress on the existence of primordial subconscious drives in human personality, and emphasized the importance of myths and mysticism in human history. Some went so far as to glorify the irrational qualities in man and to approve social action based on instinctual and anti-intellectual behavior. The dividing line between the two groups of critics of positivism was not always clear, but the first group fell, by and large, in the tradition of the thinkers of the Enlightenment, whereas the second belonged to the tradition of romanticism.

PHILOSOPHIES OF VIOLENCE

The Second Law of Thermodynamics, formulated by Kelvin in 1852, implies that eventually — in some millions of years — the sun will burn itself out and the solar system will freeze up like a mill pond on a cold day in January. Darwin's theory not only placed man among the animals but also by implication denied him immortality. These seemingly alarming conclusions did not immediately disturb those who accepted the scientific validity of the theories; instead, they rejoiced in the knowledge of physical certainty and congratulated themselves on being a part of such an advanced stage of evolutionary progress. Few troubled to examine the other aspects of their faith in progress, which was so vitally affected by the new discoveries of science. One who did was the German philosopher and litterateur Friedrich Nietzsche (1844–1900). Given to fits of irrationality that drove him permanently insane in 1888, Nietzsche was one of the important thinkers of the nineteenth century — all the more so in that his ideas inspired or were used to justify some of the most brutal outrages against humanity of the following century. Influenced by Schopenhauer as well as Darwin, Nietzsche regarded human life as a profound tragedy; at the same time he accepted the evolutionary process, which he interpreted as an imperative challenge to struggle and combat. He regarded traditional Christian morality as a "slave morality," incompatible with the great life struggle, the aim of which should be to produce a new race of supermen. "What is good? All that heightens in man the feeling of power, the desire for power, power itself. What is bad? All that comes from weakness. What is happiness? The feeling that our strength grows, that an obstacle is overcome. Not contentment, but more power; not universal peace, but war; not virtue, but forcefulness. The weak and ineffective must go under; that is the first principle of *our* love for humanity." Such ideas, wedded to then fashionable pseudoscientific racial theories, were used by demagogic orators to infect popular nationalism and convert it from a constructive to a destructive force.

One of the people influenced by Nietzsche was Georges Sorel (1847–1922), who combined his influence with that of Marx. Sorel created the doctrine of syndicalism (from *syndicat,* the French word for trade union), which became influential in the labor unions of all Latin countries, including those of South America. Accepting the Marxian notion of class war and Nietzsche's espousal of violence as an end in itself, Sorel advocated "direct action" by trade unions to achieve their goal of a socialist society: strikes, sabotage, riots, and any other form of violence. In Sorel's thought even more than in Nietzsche's there was an acceptance of the irrational as a legitimate motive of human conduct. It was the same message taught in their own way by the symbolist poets. It soon received a semblance of scientific backing in Freudian psychology.

THE LOGIC OF SCIENCE

Adhering to a naive materialism, convinced positivists regarded nature as the mechanical interaction of particles of matter having definite locations in space and time, and they accounted materialistically for purely mental phenomena such as consciousness, memory, empathy, and intuition. The Austrian physicist and philosopher Ernst Mach (1838–1916) reversed this emphasis. He remained a positivist in method but discarded completely the materialist view. According to Mach, men could know the "real," external world only by means of the sensations it produced on them, which were physical or mental phenomena. Carrying his reasoning one step further, Mach concluded that the world as we know it consisted exclusively of sensation, and the "real" world was an illusion. Known as "phenomenalism," this doctrine played an important role in the development of modern psychology.

The French mathematician and physicist Henri Poincaré (1854–1912) expressed similar views. According to him, scientific theories were accepted not because they were "true," for ultimate truth was not within the comprehension of mortals, but because they were "convenient," that is, they produced results. The German Hans Vaihinger (1852–1933) went even further than Poincaré. In *The Philosophy of "As If"* he maintained that such scientific concepts as lines, points, and atoms were pure fictions, but *useful* fictions in that they allowed valid predictions to be made. In other words, nature behaved as if it were composed of atoms, molecules, and so forth.

The culmination of this stream of thought came in the new philosophy of pragmatism, the lineal descendant and successor of positivism. The American philosopher and psychologist William James (1842–1910) called pragmatism "a new name for some old ways of thinking." With Poincaré the pragmatists denied that mortals could attain absolute certainty, absolute exactitude, or absolute universality. Instead of seeking ultimate truth, they were more interested in the meaning of ideas, concepts, and propositions, as seen in their consequences for individual behavior and social action. "A true proposition is one the acceptance of which leads to success, a false proposition is one which produces failure and frustration." Pragmatism thus introduced into philosophy a relativistic concept of truth analogous to Einstein's theory in physics.

The pragmatic emphasis on activity, consequences, and success was especially congenial to the American temperament, and pragmatism as a philosophy scored some of its greatest successes in the United States. An outstanding proponent was John Dewey (1859–1952), who developed a variety of pragmatism called instrumentalism or experimentalism. Pragmatism also exerted an important influence on philosophic, scientific, and literary thought in Europe that coincided with the sudden emergence of American influence in other more mundane matters, such as international politics and economic affairs, and may be taken to mark the end of America's provincialism and the beginning of its role as an independent shaper of the European world.

THE SCIENCE OF SOCIETY

Auguste Comte, founder of positivism, envisioned sociology as a comprehensive social science forming the capstone of his pyramid of knowledge. Karl Marx, founder of "scientific" socialism, regarded his subject matter alternatively as a "science of society." The social sciences did in fact emerge as distinct academic disciplines in the latter part of the nineteenth century, and all owed something to both Comte and Marx; but their actual emergence, as well as the specific forms they took, depended greatly on concrete historical developments and on the contemporary debates respecting philosophy and scientific method.

In earlier times the subject matter of the social sciences had been dealt with under moral and political philosophy, much as physics and chemistry were regarded as branches of natural philosophy. Economics, it is true, had broken away as political economy even before Comte and Marx; but it, too, went through a period of methodological strife after 1870 as successors of the German historical school of political economy opposed their empirical, historical, and "realistic" methodology against the essentially deductive methods of classical economics. The result was the establishment of economics on a new, more scientific basis and the creation of a new discipline: economic history.

Herbert Spencer and other Social Darwinists, such as William Graham Sumner in the United States, viewed sociology as a continuation of Darwinian biology, a study of the struggle for survival in society. Their approach to the subject was radically modified in the generation before World War I. In the United States, where rapid urbanization, the growth of big business, and the influx of new immigrants created novel social problems that gave rise to the Progressive movement in politics, and where pragmatic philosophy gained an early following, sociology attracted numbers of reformers who were more interested in the alleviation of social ills than in the dispassionate study of society. In continental Europe, however, differing academic traditions and the lively methodological debates in science and philosophy gave sociology a more scientific character.

Early social scientists faced three major methodological problems, all closely related. One was to divest their subject matter of value-charged and metaphysical notions, to give it a positive, empirical orientation by making it the study of actual social structures and processes. Another problem was that of objectivity: since individual social scientists were themselves members of society, belonging to specific races, nations, and social classes, how could they get "outside themselves" and free themselves from bias and preconceived ideas? Finally, since science proceeded by the use of reason, it assumed a rationality or underlying logical order in nature that was capable of being comprehended by reason, but increasingly the existence of irrational and nonrational elements in human personality and social behavior was becoming evident. Was it possible to study and understand by rational methods that which was itself not rational? The pioneers of social science did not fully succeed in solving these problems, nor have they yet been satisfactorily solved. But the prewar generation at least recognized and faced up to the problems. That was its greatest contribution to subsequent generations of social scientists.

Émile Durkheim (1858–1917), who established sociology as an academic discipline in France, was a positivist in that he regarded social phenomena as subject to scientific investigation, but he discarded the biological and organic analogies employed by the Social Darwinists. For him the study of society was an empirical task requiring painstaking observation, factual description, and inductive theorizing about such concrete social phenomena as the division of labor, suicide, and religious behavior. The Italian Vilfredo Pareto (1848–1923), trained as an engineer, achieved eminence as one of the first great mathematical economists, but he was equally prominent for his contributions to sociological theory. Pareto labeled the conscious products of the human mind "derivations"; they were highly transitory and changeable. The true unvarying determinants of human conduct, which he called "residues," were essentially nonrational and beyond human comprehension. Pareto is also known for his social philosophy, a theory of elites, which some regard as a precursor of fascism and other totalitarian systems. Max Weber (1864–1920), the greatest name in German sociology, attempted to bridge the gap between the study of natural phenomena and social phenomena by the process of critical yet sympathetic understanding called *Verstehen*. According to Weber, the social scientist could get "outside himself" by getting "inside" the social phenomena that he was studying. Weber is known especially for his studies of religion; his most widely read book is *The Protestant Ethic and the Spirit of Capitalism.*

Another way in which early social scientists attempted to achieve objectivity was by the study of contemporary primitive peoples, such as the Australian bushmen, Trobriand islanders, and Eskimos. Not only could they detach themselves from their own environments, but they also thought that the fundamental determinants of social behavior — analogous to Pareto's residues — could be discovered when uncluttered by the complexities of modern society. Archaeologists studied extinct civilizations such as the ancient Egyptian, Sumerian, and Mayan by means of the remnants of their material culture. The combination of ethnology, archaeology, and human biology produced the modern discipline of anthropology.

Political science is at once one of the oldest and newest of the social sciences. It resulted from the combination of political philosophy with detailed descriptive and analytic studies of the actual functioning of governments. Gaetano Mosca (1858–1941), who had long experience as a practical politician in Italy, was one of the founders of the new discipline. He came to the conclusion that politics and government were essentially the functions of small, self-selected, and self-perpetuating cliques or elites. Robert Michels (1876–1936), born of a German father and a French mother, had personal experience in the socialist parties of several countries before becoming an Italian citizen. He became disillusioned with the lack of democratic procedures even in social democratic parties and formulated the "iron law of oligarchy": in every organized social group effective power eventually devolves upon a small self-selected group. Michels, Mosca, and Pareto, who shared many views, are sometimes referred to as neo-Machiavellians. More idealistic views were held by Woodrow Wilson, one of the first political scientists in the United States, who was a professor and president of Princeton University before entering active politics.

The writing of history was also affected by the emergence of the social sciences and debates on scientific method. Historians in the positivist tradition tried to assimilate historical methods with those of the new social sciences; others in the idealist-romantic tradition denied that the methods of science were appropriate to the study of human phenomena. The Germans Wilhelm Dilthey and Ernst Troeltsch and the Italian Benedetto Croce argued that since man possesses a spirit, his history and culture have to be studied by methods entirely different from those used on the subjects of natural science. Their efforts to recapture the spirit of an age as expressed in its art, literature, and other products of culture showed an affinity with the symbolists in literature, on the one hand, and with the methods of Max Weber, on the other. All were reinforced by new discoveries in psychology.

THE DISCOVERY OF THE SUBCONSCIOUS

In 1899 Sigmund Freud (1856–1939), a Viennese physician, published a book entitled *The Interpretation of Dreams*. It became the foundation of modern psychoanalysis. Experimental psychology first developed out of physiology, notably through the work of Wilhelm Wundt and William James. Because of its physiological base, it is not surprising that early psychologists regarded their subject as a natural science. The phenomenon of consciousness was almost banished from the field in the work of the Russian Ivan Pavlov (1849–1936) on conditioned reflexes and in the so-called behavioral school of the United States. As a practicing physician, Freud found their approach of little value in dealing with the mental illnesses of his patients. He detected that human beings react not only to physical stimuli (as the behaviorists said) and to conscious motives (as the rationalists said), but also to purely mental stimuli of which they are unaware. The latter source of motivation Freud labeled

Brown Brothers

Sigmund Freud

"The unconscious is the larger circle which includes the smaller circle of the conscious; everything conscious has a preliminary unconscious stage, whereas the unconscious can stop at this stage, and yet claim to be considered a full psychic function. The unconscious is the true psychic reality; in its inner nature it is just as much unknown to us as the reality of the external world, and it is just as imperfectly communicated to us by the data of consciousness as is the external world by the reports of our sense-organs." Sigmund Freud. THE INTERPRETATION OF DREAMS, 3rd English edition, rev. (London, 1937).

the "subconscious." He maintained that the major part of subconscious mental activity derives from infantile experiences — in particular, the repression or sublimation of infantile eroticism and sexuality. In his view the animal instinct in humans fosters such sexuality, but the demands of civilization require that it be controlled. A "healthy" individual is one who manages to sublimate his sexual drives into socially approved activities. A mentally ill person has merely repressed, not sublimated, his primitive drives. Freud's method of treatment, called psychoanalysis, consisted in having the patient recall from his subconscious the events that had caused inner conflict or distress; the "cure" resulted from an "understanding" of these causes.

Even before Freud's main work Henri Bergson (1859–1941), a French philosopher, thought he had divined in dreams the key to the understanding of man's personality. Bergson distinguished between consciousness, a "superficial psychic life," and a life in the "depths of consciousness" in which "the deep-seated self" follows a logic of its own that is not comprehensible by mortal reason. Bergson called this "deep-seated self" the *élan vital* (vital spirit, intuition, instinct), which he regarded as the mainspring of human progress. For Bergson, reality was not a state of being but a process of becoming. He called the process "creative evolution."

The affinity of the ideas of Bergson and Freud to those of Nietzsche and Sorel — and even to Schopenhauer's concept of the "will" — are obvious. Such ideas were common property among the avant-garde intellectuals at the turn of the century. Bergson, a Nobel prize winner, and Freud, a man of science, gave them philosophical and scientific justification and thus heightened their currency. Bergson's concept of creative evolution inspired George Bernard Shaw's plays *Man and Superman* and *Back to Methuselah,* and Freudian psychology has made itself felt throughout modern literature. Bergson's influence waned sharply after World War I, but Freud's has continued to grow.

THE NEW REVOLUTION IN SCIENCE

The generation maturing at the turn of the century witnessed a number of discoveries in natural science that led to a new era in the interpretation of nature. Although the full significance of the discoveries did not become apparent until the twentieth century was well advanced, for the knowledgeable they overthrew earlier certainties about the essential simplicity of the physical universe and cast doubt on the associated belief in materialistic determinism.

The claim of science as a special and authoritative brand of knowledge accessible to humans through the powers of reason, which had been gathering force from the time of Galileo and Newton, reached a crescendo in the work of James Clerk Maxwell. (See p. 649.) The mechanical equivalence of heat and electricity had already been demonstrated. Maxwell's mathematical theorems purported to show that electricity, magnetism, and even light are essentially identical. Near the end of the century the discovery of electromagnetic or radio waves by Heinrich Hertz (1857–1894), in fulfillment of Maxwell's prediction, climaxed the triumph of classical physics. A few years later a renowned scientist remarked that the secrets of the universe had been unraveled: all that remained for the physicists of the twentieth century was to refine the measurements of phenomena discovered by the scientists of the nineteenth. Even before he spoke, however, new discoveries growing out of the work of Maxwell, Hertz, and others had begun to undermine the theoretical structure in which he exhibited so much confidence.

RADIOACTIVITY AND RELATIVITY

The atomic theory of matter, which had been basic to the achievements of nineteenth-century physical science, was the first element of the classical edifice to undergo modification. According to John Dalton, atoms, the smallest particles of matter, resemble tiny billiard balls; they are infinitesimally small but hard and solid. The combination of atoms into molecules implied that they possessed some form of attractive force, but the nature of the force was not fully understood. The study of electricity and magnetism revealed that particles of matter contain positive and negative charges, or forces of attraction and repulsion, but the charges were believed to be properties of different types of atoms rather than distinct phenomena. As knowledge progressed, Dalton's concept came to be recognized as unsatisfactory, and in 1892 the Dutch physicist Hendrik Lorentz posited the existence of electrons, tiny particles of electrically charged matter separate from but related to atoms. Lorentz's formulation proved to be incorrect, but it led to intensive study of the structure of the atom and abandonment of the billiard ball concept.

Experimental verification of the complex structure of the atom soon followed and demonstrated that atoms are not necessarily stable or indivisible. In 1895 the German physicist Wilhelm Roentgen discovered X-rays, and in the following year Antoine Becquerel, a Frenchman, observed the radiation of uranium. Shortly afterward the Franco-Polish couple Pierre and Marie Curie isolated and identified the radioactive elements radium and polonium. Further experimentation by the Englishman J. J. Thomson and his student Ernest Rutherford, a New Zealander, revealed that atoms are composed of still smaller particles and emit a variety of mysterious rays. The different combinations and arrangements of the smaller particles determine the chemical properties of the atoms. In 1919 Rutherford succeeded in transforming nitrogen into hydrogen by bombarding nitrogen gas with alpha particles from the element radium. The goal of the ancient alchemists — the transmutation of one element into another — had been achieved.

In 1887 Albert Michelson and E. W. Morley in America devised a new and greatly improved experiment for measuring the velocity of light. They discovered that it is a constant regardless of the velocity of its source. This experimentally determined fact had important theoretical implications in that it contradicted the laws of inertial motion and cast doubt on belief in the existence of a "luminiferous ether," which supposedly filled all space and was the medium by which the light of distant stars (as well as other objects) was transmitted to earth. In 1900 the German Max Planck discovered that radiation takes place not continuously but in discrete units or "quanta." According to classical physics all nature consists of two fundamental substances, matter and force (or energy), each with its own laws of conservation. Matter was thought to exist in discrete units or particles and to have weight; force was thought to operate continuously and to be weightless. The new quantum theory, developed principally by Planck, Albert Einstein, and the Danish physicist Niels Bohr, cast doubt on this entire intellectual edifice. Energy, it seemed, also exists in particles that have weight, or mass. Moreover mass or matter itself represents bundles of energy. Instead of two fundamental substances — matter and force — and two laws of conservation, the new theory posited a single substance — mass-energy — and a single law of conservation.

Einstein's special theory of relativity in 1905 and his general theory in 1915 incorporated these notions. The theory of relativity marked the greatest advance in man's understanding of the universe since Newton propounded his laws of gravitation. It succeeded in explaining all phenomena accounted for by the Newtonian system as well as some others that Newton's laws could not satisfactorily explain. It turned out, in fact, that the Newtonian laws represented a special limiting case of the general theory of relativity. The new theory passed its most crucial empirical test in 1919, when during a total eclipse of the sun scientists on both sides of the Atlantic Ocean observed the bending of light rays in the gravitational field of the sun, as predicted by Einstein.

Although it was incomprehensible in its details to all but a few highly trained specialists, the theory of relativity exercised an important intellectual influence on the Western world. In addition to replacing the classical dichotomy of matter and force by the singular entity massenergy, the theory overturned the classical (and common-sense) dichotomy of absolute space and time. According to the theory of relativity, two events that are simultaneous for one observer may not be simultaneous for another. For example, with powerful telescopes we see now

Culver Pictures, Inc.

Albert Einstein

"*Galileo and Newton made the universe Euclidian simply because reason dictated it so. But pure reason cannot do anything but invent systems of methodical arrangement. . . . It is clearly not these systems, not pure reason, which resolve the nature of the real. On the contrary, reality selects from among these possible orders or schemes the one which has more affinity with itself. This is what the theory of relativity means. The rationalist past of four centuries is confronted by the genius of Einstein, who inverts the time-honored relation which used to exist between reason and observation. Reason ceases to be an imperative standard and is converted into an arsenal of instruments; observation tests these and decides which is the most convenient to use.*" J. Ortega y Gasset, THE MODERN THEME (New York, 1933).

events in outer space that took place millions of years ago, such as the explosion of galaxies. The theory of relativity replaced three-dimensional space and one-dimensional time by a single four-dimensional space-time continuum. In conjunction with the quantum theory, it replaced the earlier belief in inexorable natural laws that determine all events according to cause and effect by a system of thought in which events take place in accordance with the laws of statistical probability — that is, in more or less random fashion. The concepts of cause and effect, certainty, and the absolute, which underlay so much nineteenth-century thought, no longer appeared either certain or absolute.

GENETICS AND EUGENICS

According to Darwin the explanation of biological evolution lay in small individual variations transmitted cumulatively from generation to generation by means of natural selection. Biological experiments in the last two decades of the nineteenth century seemed to show that small variations of the type assumed by Darwin were incapable of producing the effects attributed to them. The same experiments revealed that larger, discontinuous variations, called mutations, occur from time to time and that these traits, too, are transmissible by heredity. In 1900 the biological fraternity discovered, or rediscovered, in the annals of a scientific society in Moravia the results of scientific experiments of great significance. Gregor Mendel, an Augustinian monk who became abbot of his monastery but died in 1884 without achieving other distinctions, had been a contemporary of Darwin. Experimenting with common garden peas, he discovered what appeared to be fixed proportions in the characteristics of successive generations of hybrid plants. In these fixed proportions lay the secret of the transmission of hereditary characteristics, and thus of biological evolution. Mendel's experiments were re-

---

"The Bay of Marseille Seen from the 'Estaque,' "
by Paul Cezanne

> "*His conception of space is modern. . . . By dint of paintin‚ rocks and trees, and merging them closely into another, by dint of seeing then ‚urely as solid figures, he finished by painting things at whose dimensions one cannot guess. One does not know whether one is looking at small rocks seen from very near, or big rocks seen from very far away; whether one is looking at shrubs an arm's length away or kilometres away. One devises some theory and the picture takes on certain characteristics; one devises another theory and the picture seems completely different. But after all, it is space that one sees in abstract pictures; the forms are near or far away, depending on what one imagines they could represent.*" Yvon Taillandier, P. CEZANNE, tr. Graham Snall (New York, 1961).

peated and confirmed with a variety of other plants and insects. The carriers of hereditary characteristics were identified as genes, submicroscopic elements present in the reproductive cells of all living beings. The combination of the genes of male and female parents determines the characteristics of the offspring. The study of the processes involved gave rise to the new science of genetics, the part of biology concerned with heredity.

Identification of the carriers of hereditary characteristics as discrete units, and the observation that biological change takes place by means of discontinuous jumps or mutations in place of the continuous variation of Darwinian evolution, introduced a quantum concept into biology that was analogous with the new view of atomic structure and radiation. In methods as well as concepts biology drew closer to physical science, producing the new hybrid disciplines of biochemistry and biophysics. Physical science already relied extensively on mathematical reasoning and made increasing use of the laws of statistical probability. Mendel was the first biologist to make significant use of mathematics in experiments. His successors in the science of genetics depended increasingly upon mathematics and statistical probability and made significant contributions to modern statistical theory as well as to biology.

Another new discipline stimulated by the progress of biology lay dangerously close to the uncertain border between science and pseudoscience. Eugenics was defined by Sir Francis Galton, its founder and a cousin of Darwin, as the study of the inherited characteristics of man and the application of that knowledge to the improvement of the human race. The more optimistic advocates of this new branch of knowledge believed that the physical and mental characteristics of the race could be improved by deliberate selective breeding in much the same way that agronomists and horticulturists produce new strains of livestock or fruit trees. William Bateson, a distinguished biologist, wrote in 1909: "The outcome of genetic research is to show that human society can, if it so please, control its composition more easily than was previously supposed possible. . . . Measures may be taken to eliminate strains regarded as unfit and undesirable elements in the population." Others took a more pessimistic view, pointing out that the declining birth rate of Europeans — of the upper income groups in particular — raised the possibility that the world would soon be overrun by "inferior" peoples. Even highly trained and qualified scientists encountered difficulties in maintaining scientific detachment and objectivity when they turned from their laboratories to the social implications of their findings. It is not surprising that less disciplined and more prejudiced minds made unwarranted and inappropriate use of the ideas of science. Social Darwinism and crude racialism continued to flourish long after their supposedly scientific bases had been shown to be incorrect or irrelevant.

TO THE ENDS OF THE EARTH: ARCTIC
AND ANTARCTIC EXPLORATION

Not all of the scientific research of the period took place in laboratories and libraries. As in earlier days, men learned much about nature from direct contact with it. By the final quarter of the nineteenth century most of the earth's surface had been charted if not thoroughly explored. The principal exceptions were the polar regions.

Efforts to discover northwest and northeast passages from the Atlantic to the Pacific dated from the early years of the sixteenth century. Three hundred years later they were still unsuccessful. It became obvious that such routes, even if discovered, would have no commercial value, but man's natural curiosity and restless spirit drove him on to new efforts. In 1818 the British government offered a prize of £20,000 (almost $100,000) for the discovery of a northwest passage, and an additional £5,000 for the first person to reach 89° north latitude, or within seventy miles of the North Pole. (Henry VIII awarded John Cabot £10 for his discoveries!) In the course of the nineteenth century more than fifty major expeditions penetrated the Arctic seas, but none collected the rewards. Explorers from almost every country in Europe, the United States, and Canada participated in the voyages, financed sometimes by governments, more often by private resources. Many lost their lives or suffered cruelly from the harsh environment. Still they came — for glory, adventure, or scientific curiosity. They tried to reach the imaginary North Pole by ship, on foot with sledges over the Arctic ice packs, and eventually by balloon, dirigible, and airplane. Rarely were the financial returns commensurate with the efforts and hardships, but they added significantly to the store of geographical and other scientific knowledge.

As early as 1831 James Ross of Britain located the north magnetic pole, which lay in the Boothia peninsula of northern Canada some 1,200 miles south of the true pole. In 1878 and 1879 the *Vega,* commanded by A. E. Nordenskiold, a Swedish professor, steamed, sailed, and drifted from the Atlantic to the Pacific above Siberia — the northeast passage — reaching the Bering Sea after nine months' imprisonment in the pack ice. Not until 1906 did the Norwegian Roald Amundsen first succeed in forcing the northwest passage after four years of continuous battle with the elements in Arctic seas. Between 1893 and 1896 another Norwegian expedition under the command of Dr. Fridtjof Nansen carried out a remarkable feat. Utilizing a specially designed ship, the *Fram,* Nansen deliberately sailed into the pack ice north of central Siberia and allowed the polar drift to carry him within 400 miles of the pole. At that point Nansen and a single companion left the ship and tried to reach the pole over the ice with dog team and sledge. They achieved a record northern latitude but fell short of the pole by about 200 miles. They

818

managed to survive on the ice, on foot, for a full year until they were picked up by a relief ship in the Franz Josef archipelago (or Fridtjof Nansen Land). Nansen and his companion reached Tromsö, Norway, only a few days after the *Fram* had put in at the same port. The climax of Arctic exploration came in 1909, when the American Robert E. Peary, accompanied by a Negro, Matthew Henson, and four Eskimos, reached the pole on foot after a journey of more than 300 miles from their base ship.

Until the twentieth century the south polar region attracted much less interest than the north. Since ancient times rumors had persisted of a great Terra Australis Incognita or unknown southern continent. As late as the sixteenth century some maps showed it extending to tropical latitudes, but the Antarctic continent was not actually sighted until 1820. Only after many years was its continental nature definitely established. Several expeditions penetrated the south polar seas between 1820 and 1850, mainly in connection with the lucrative whale fisheries of the adjacent islands, but not until 1895 did human beings set foot on the polar continent itself. In the same year the Sixth International Geographical Congress meeting in London called attention to the importance of Antarctic exploration. Expeditions were launched almost yearly thereafter. As with Arctic exploration, explorers of many nations participated, financed by both government and private sources. National pride and personal glory proved the most important motivating forces, and a dramatic race for the honor of planting the first flag at the pole ensued. It was won by the Norwegian Amundsen, who had been deflected from a similar race for the north pole by the news of Peary's triumph. His party of five reached the south pole in December, 1911, after a harrowing seven-week dash across the glacial plateau. Just a month later a British party led by Captain R. F. Scott reached the same destination, but perished of starvation and exposure on the return journey. Such were the incentives and rewards of scientific exploration.

Red House

"Red House, which Philip Webb and Morris built, boasted no exquisite or palatial beauties, but a beauty and a homeliness all its own. Unlike other houses of that period, it was built entirely of red brick and roofed with red tiles. The building was L-shaped, two stories in height, standing amidst a veritable forest of apple and cherry trees, so closely to them, in fact, that in after years some of the apples actually fell inside the windows, disturbing many a restless sleeper on hot August nights." Lloyd Wendell Eshleman, A VICTORIAN REBEL; THE LIFE OF WILLIAM MORRIS (New York, 1940).

EUROPEAN SOCIETY AT THE END
OF ITS GOLDEN AGE

Influential though they were, the artistic, literary, and scientific developments discussed above occupied the minds of only a small portion of the Western populace. For most people, untroubled by such complicated ideas, the last decade or so of the nineteenth century and the first few years of the twentieth century brought unprecedented material progress and intellectual complacency. The growth of wealth, the spread of literacy, the progress of democracy, the apparent obsolescence of warfare — all fitted well with the earlier optimistic predictions of Comte and Spencer, Hugo, Browning, and Walt Whitman.

CHANGING CONCEPTS OF SOCIAL CLASS

Rapid industrialization and urbanization, especially in northwestern Europe, brought about a major realignment of social classes. The traditional upper class, the landed aristocracy, found its importance greatly diminished by the large fortunes made in industry and commerce. The traditional middle class burgeoned to unprecedented proportions as its ranks were swelled by new professions and the growing class of salaried employees and executives. Historically the middle class had been identified with town dwellers to such an extent that middle class and bourgeoisie had become almost identical, but in an age when most of the population lived in cities, it was no longer realistic to identify the bourgeoisie exclusively with the middle class.

In place of the old designations based on the relationship of individuals to the land or the means of production, classes came to be defined chiefly according to income. There was still a close correlation between education, occupational status, and income. Those who worked primarily with their hands, whether in factories, workshops, or on farms, had the least education and lowest incomes. The middle classes included not only those who combined sedentary labor with the ownership of some property, such as small merchants and manufacturers, but also those whose investment in education or whose acquisition of special skills enabled them to earn a higher return from their labor. The expression upper class came to signify people of great wealth, whether inherited or earned, who could afford to live on the income from their property without being forced to work. Intellectuals and descendants of ancient titled families sometimes sneered at the social pretensions of the newly rich, but in Great Britain and other countries with monarchic institutions the device of newly created peerages made it possible to integrate into the upper classes people who had distinguished themselves in the art of making money as well as in other fields. In the United States no such devices were needed: wealth alone provided the key to social recognition.

Two changes that contributed to the increasing social mobility were the spread of public education and the growth of democracy. Between 1870 and 1900 almost every country in western Europe adopted or increased its facilities for public education. In most countries public education became compulsory (in principle, at least) for periods ranging from three to eight years. These were only small steps toward the goal of universally educated societies, but they were essential. They greatly increased the range of opportunities for young people. The spread of democracy created a new ladder of social mobility — professional politics — which together with business enterprise supplemented and partly replaced the old ladders of the army and the church.

POPULAR CULTURE AND RELIGION

Increased educational facilities produced a remarkable rise in literacy. During the 1860's in the countries of northwestern Europe between 50 and 60 per cent of the adult population was classed as literate. By 1900 approximately 90 per cent was so classified. The proportions were much less in southern and eastern Europe: about 66 per cent in Austria, 50 per cent in Italy and Hungary, 30 per cent in Spain and Portugal, and 20 per cent in Russia and the Balkans.

Literacy, however, means only the ability to read simple sentences and write one's name; it does not automatically create in one a desire for the world's great literature. The most popular living authors at the turn of the century were not Stéphane Mallarmé, the leader of the symbolists, or even Henry James or Thomas Hardy, much less Nietzsche or Sorel. They were such writers as Émile Zola, then at the height of his powers and a political figure as well; Rudyard Kipling, poet and novelist; Jules Verne and H. G. Wells, masters of the new art of science fiction; Arthur Conan Doyle, inventor of Sherlock Holmes and the detective novel; and the American adventure writer Jack London.

At a still lower level were the writers published in cheap magazines and newspapers. Between 1880 and 1900 the number of newspapers in Europe doubled from 6,000 to 12,000. By far the greater number were in the industrial countries of northwestern Europe. By 1900 several newspapers in the largest cities had daily circulations of more than a million copies, as compared with 50,000 for the London *Times* during the 1860's, the largest circulation of that period. Technical innovations in printing and publishing, such as typesetting machines, cheap paper made from wood pulp, and high-speed presses, as well as the larger market helped to reduce costs and increase the output of this branch of the information and entertainment industry. The 1890's witnessed still another innovation: "yellow" journalism or the featuring of lurid, scandalous, and often

sensational stories in order to increase circulation and advertising revenue. Its pioneers were William Randolph Hearst in the United States,
Alfred Harmsworth in Britain, and the Mosse family in Germany.

The most common forms of art enjoyed by the masses, apart from the
frequently lurid sketches in newspapers and magazines, were cheap reproductions of religious paintings in the homes of the devout. Even substantial middle-class homes were more likely to contain stylized imitations
of the old masters and mass-produced porcelain or plaster figurines
than the works of contemporary painters and sculptors. A similar situation characterized music. Only people of refined musical taste or social
pretention attended operas or concerts featuring the works of noted
composers. Even operettas such as those of Gilbert and Sullivan were
beyond the taste and pocketbook of the majority. Music entered their
lives, if at all, only through the church, spontaneous singing of folk
music and popular ballads, and the Sunday concerts of military bands
in garrison cities.

The separation of art from everyday life worked in both directions.
Many of the artists and writers who subsequently became famous led
miserable if rather flamboyant lives. As rebels against conventional
standards in life as well as art, they found themselves outcastes in society
— their works unsold, their very existence ignored by the more conventional and successful practitioners who catered to the popular taste. As
a result they developed a creed that went beyond the concept of "art
for art's sake." It can best be summarized as "the supremacy of art over
life." Not only was art an end in itself: it was the supreme end; nothing
else mattered. This aesthetic view was shared even by relatively successful writers, such as the American expatriate Henry James and the eccentric and tragic Oscar Wilde.

Analogous developments took place in theology and religion. Theological disputes became increasingly recondite and concerned with the
deeper issues of philosophy, whereas religion itself became increasingly
democratic. Official Protestantism put more emphasis on good works,
relatively less on personal piety. Catholics tended toward social Catholicism, and Pope Leo XIII, who did much to restore the prestige of the
papacy after Pius IX, encouraged the study of science by Catholics.
Protestant theologians inclined toward modernism, reconciling the
teachings of the Bible with modern advances in science. Intellectuals
within the churches inclined toward skepticism, but clergymen who had
closer contact with the rank and file went in the opposite direction. In all
countries where Protestantism flourished new splinter sects came into
being and fundamentalism — belief in the literal interpretation of the
Bible — opposed modernism both in the church and in everyday life.
Closely related were the temperance movements, which opposed the use
of alcoholic beverages in any form. They grew up in most countries with

large Protestant populations and achieved their greatest successes in Scandinavia and in the adoption of the Eighteenth Amendment (prohibition) to the United States Constitution in 1919.

IDEOLOGY AND LIFE

The various literary, artistic, and philosophical currents of thought at the turn of the century inevitably attracted the ubiquitous suffix "-ism," but they did not qualify for the more technical name of ideology. The ideologies that constituted focal points for mass followings at the end of the century were the same that had grown to prominence in its beginning, namely, liberalism, socialism, and nationalism.

Liberalism had to its credit a remarkable series of triumphs. In Great Britain it was accepted with much the same unquestioning faith — and much the same backsliding in practice — as the Christian religion. Even members of the Conservative party accepted the fundamental principles of liberalism as an ideology while contesting with the Liberal party for control of the government. Although liberalism never attained the same degree of acceptance on the Continent as in Britain, it was largely responsible for the introduction of parliamentary government and other liberal institutions in one country after another. Even its bitterest opponents, such as the tsar of Russia and the sultan of Turkey, were forced to come to terms with it. Paradoxically, however, liberalism was a dying force in Europe by the beginning of the twentieth century. In large measure its weakness stemmed from the very extent of its success. In Britain and other democratic countries many of its ideals had already been achieved. Its proponents faced the dilemma of standing pat on its accomplishments and running the risk of being labeled old-fashioned or conservative, or of borrowing programs and slogans from more advanced or radical ideologies. In either case it meant the demise of classical liberalism.

Socialism had a much larger following in 1898 than in 1848, but it also suffered a kind of internal crisis. The failure of society to develop in accordance with the Marxist prediction deprived socialism of some of its messianic appeal. The desertion of some of its leaders to the heresy of revisionism appeared to be a fatal concession to bourgeois liberalism, dividing the movement just when the weakness of its opponents promised success.

The one ideology that continued to strengthen itself was nationalism, because it did not rival but fed upon other ideologies as a parasite. A conservative liberal or a liberal socialist was a contradiction in terms, but no one quibbled about a national liberal or a conservative nationalist. They were the names of recognized political parties in Germany. Even the various socialist parties organized themselves within the framework of national states, although they were nominally committed to international solidarity. Increasing literacy (minimal though it was) contributed to the growing force of nationalism. During periods of increased international political tension mass-circulation newspapers inflamed popular nationalism by magnifying even a minor dispute to the proportions of a *casus belli*. Nationalism received stimuli from other sources as well, and as public opinion became more and more important in the formation of public policy because of the spread of democracy, diplomats and politicians sometimes found themselves committed to courses of action contrary to their wishes. The nationalism that at the beginning of the nineteenth century had been a hopeful, liberal, constructive force had become a potential threat to the very objects of nationalism: the nation-states themselves. Yet such considerations carried no weight with the general public. To the generation of Europeans that reached maturity at the opening of the twentieth century the era seemed a prelude to infinite, universal progress. In reality, it was the end of the golden age for Europe.

THE TWENTIETH CENTURY: FROM WESTERN CIVILIZATION TO WORLD CIVILIZATION PART FOUR

INTRODUCTION: FROM WESTERN CIVILIZATION TO WORLD CIVILIZATION

The world in the twentieth century is experiencing a process of millennial dimensions: the birth of a global civilization. What the mingling of classical and barbarian cultures in the European Dark Ages was for Western civilization, the mingling of Western and non-Western cultures is for the civilization of the future. As in the Dark Ages, the process is accompanied by violence and conflict. Just as Western civilization inherited characteristics from both its predecessors, so world civilization is taking on characteristics of both Western and non-Western cultures. Few of the participants, then or now, have been aware of the historic significance of their age; much less have they been able to predict the character of the emerging civilization. For all but a few, problems of personal and group survival in an uncertain but hostile environment discourage contemplation of the forces of historical change. A final resemblance is of particular interest for the last survivors of a uniquely Western civilization: just as the birth of Western civilization was preceded by the decadence, disintegration, and schism of classical civilization, so the birth of world civilization has been preceded by decadence, disintegration, and schism in the West.

THE DISINTEGRATION OF WESTERN CIVILIZATION

The distinguishing characteristics of Western civilization, especially as manifested in its final flowering in the nineteenth century, were a concern for freedom and rationality. In economic life these principles took the form of a rational, scientific technology and a worldwide organization of the economy based on free enterprise, free international trade, and free international migration. In political life they found expression in the proliferation of parliamentary institutions and the spread of democracy; in governments of laws, not of men; and in the guarantees of elementary civil and political liberties. They can be seen most clearly in the intellectual sphere in the almost unrestricted pursuit of science, the epitome of rationalism, and in the greater freedom of expression allowed artists and authors.

The triumph of rationality and freedom was not, of course, complete. The continuation of political absolutism in eastern Europe, the revival of economic restrictions and imperialism in the late nineteenth century, and the willingness of nations to resort to force in the settlement of international disputes reflected the least progressive aspects of the heritage of the past and accumulated a store of troubles for the future. New elements of irrationality and new restrictions on individual liberty crept in before the end of the century. But the most blatant defects in the character of Western civilization on the eve of its debacle resulted from the excesses of its virtues. Preoccupation with material goals and emphasis on pragmatic or realistic means together with a corresponding neglect of philosophic ends brought a near denial of the idealistic and humanitarian traditions of Western civilization. In a similar vein, excessive emphasis on individualism and liberty developed insensibly into crass egotism, the belief in the right of the individual to do as he pleased without regard for others, and the denial of the bonds of community and society. The development manifested itself in extreme versions of laissez faire economic policy and Social Darwinism, competition for empire and colonial exploitation, and the growth of militarism in Europe. The sudden, dramatic outbreak of World War I abruptly heralded the catastrophe of collapse; but the war itself was neither the beginning nor the end of the process of disintegration.

RIVAL PLANS FOR RECONSTRUCTION

When after two decades of continuing political, social, and economic crises it became apparent to all that a fundamental malaise afflicted Western civilization, blueprints for reconstruction proliferated in surprising numbers. Unfortunately most of them mistook the symptoms of disintegration for its causes, especially in the liberal plans for reconstruction. A further difficulty was that many of the schemes were mutually, even internally, contradictory.

As early as 1917 a scheme for total reconstruction based on an attempted fusion of Western rationality and Eastern despotism went into operation in Russia, which was itself an amalgam of Eastern and Western civilizations. Soon afterward, first in Italy, then in Germany and elsewhere in central Europe, new plans of reconstruction used rational means to achieve irrational ends and deny freedom. The dilatory and half-hearted attempts at reconstruction in western Europe and America allowed these denials of the basic values of Western civilization to gain headway.

THE FORGOTTEN TWO-THIRDS

The beneficiaries of Western civilization constituted a minority of the world's population. Most of them knew little and cared less about the rest of the world. Increasingly in modern times, however, non-Western cultures and civilizations have been affected by Western civilization. The contacts usually involved violence and coercion by the West, as well as more subtle forms of influence. The results were sometimes disastrous for the indigenous cultures, bringing them close to extinction. In all cases the West undermined the bases of traditional cultures and civilizations or modified their content. Frequently what non-Western peoples learned from the West through bitter experience reflected the worst, the most retrograde aspects of Western civilization. Insofar as they absorbed the progressive features, it was mainly in the sphere of material technology.

At the beginning of the twentieth century the power gap between the West and the rest of the world had never been wider or the extent of Western control greater. Both the disparity and the dominion seemed likely to grow indefinitely. Serious writers wrote about the eventual extinction of nonwhite races, while others wrote more vividly of the "Yellow Peril" and the necessity for prophylactic action. In 1914 it seemed unlikely that non-Western peoples would ever emancipate themselves from the tutelage of or bondage to the West. Yet fifty years later, although the disparity of material circumstances remained as great as ever, few non-Western peoples remained politically subservient to a Western nation. A comparison of membership in the League of Nations and the United Nations is revealing. In 1925, 48 of a total League membership of 55 were nations with a predominantly Western heritage (even without Germany, the Soviet Union, and the United States); 26 lay in Europe proper. In 1970, 74 of a total of 126 members of the United Nations were basically non-Western. If Latin America is excluded, only 31 nations within the European tradition belonged, and 10 of those were under Communist control.

This startling reversal resulted not from any increase in the physical strength of the rest of the world but solely from moral collapse and division within the West. World War I, which in spite of its name was essentially a civil war within Western civilization, inaugurated the process, although its consequences, a new global *Kulturkampf,* did not immediately become apparent. World War II, which more nearly lived up to its name even though it, too, began as a purely internal struggle within the West, delivered a hammer blow to Western pre-eminence. After the war Western material and technological superiority continued to increase, but the basic schism also increased, negating the claim of the West to moral leadership of the world as well as destroying its ability to lead. This was the paradox: as Western nations, divided into rival ideological camps, grew stronger, their own unique civilization became more diluted. The rising political power of non-Western nations reflected neither an increase in their material strength nor a reassertion of their traditional cultural traditions but the supersession of both Western and non-Western cultures by a new, global culture.

THE FIRST WORLD WAR
CHAPTER THIRTY-TWO

The end of the Franco-Prussian War left the newly founded German Empire the most powerful nation in Europe. France was not only defeated but isolated diplomatically. Although Great Britain was not indifferent to developments on the Continent, it was preoccupied with domestic reform and problems of empire. Russia, like Britain, devoted itself to domestic issues and its land empire in Asia. Austria-Hungary sought to unravel the problems of its dual monarchy; Italy, indebted to Prussia for the opportunity of acquiring Venetia and Rome, struggled for economic progress and social community to accompany its superficial political unity. The lesser states of Europe served only as pawns in the game of great power politics, and overseas the only nation that could pretend to great power status — the United States — was involved in the exploitation of its vast hinterland.

How different was the situation less than fifty years later at the end of World War I: Germany was prostrate, Austria-Hungary and the Ottoman Empire were dismembered; France was victorious, surrounded by its allies Britain, Italy, and the United States as well as several lesser nations. Russia, an erstwhile ally, was in the throes of revolution and civil war. Other allies and new powers on the international scene included Japan and the British dominions.

Developments on several fronts contributed to this startling reversal in international relations. The most important factor was the Franco-German rivalry. Other developments included the progressive collapse of the Ottoman Empire under constant Russian pressure and rising Balkan nationalism; the resulting Austro-Russian rivalry for dominance in the Balkans; the Russo-Japanese confrontation in eastern Asia and the rise of Japan as a great power; the German challenge to British naval supremacy and Britain's retreat from its "splendid isolation"; and American involvement in European power politics. The worldwide colonial rivalries influenced almost all aspects of international relations.

THE DIPLOMATIC PRELUDE, 1871-1914

The sentiment for revenge against Germany was high in France in the years following 1871. Although it abated or was deflected from time to time, the thought of Alsace-Lorraine under the German flag never let it die entirely. Frenchmen realized, however, that they could never again afford to go to war alone with Germany; they must have allies. The search for dependable allies was the constant preoccupation of the French foreign office. Bismarck — in Germany until 1890 only Bismarck's opinion mattered in foreign policy — having achieved his goal of German unification under Prussia, sought only to maintain the status quo. He realized that to do this he must prevent France from acquiring allies; the best way was to pre-empt all likely allies for Germany.

In effect, only five great powers existed in Europe in 1871; Italy was a dubious sixth. In order to ensure a balance of power in Germany's favor, Bismarck had to league at least two of them with Germany. "You forget," he once chided the Russian ambassador, "the importance of being a party of three on the European chessboard. . . . Nobody wishes to be in a minority. All politics reduce themselves to this formula: try to be *à trois* in a world governed by five powers." Such was Bismarck's dictum, and as long as he remained at the helm in Germany, he followed it with success.

BISMARCKIAN FOREIGN POLICY

Britain, France's traditional enemy, seemed safe enough from Germany's point of view as long as the British maintained their policy of nonalignment in European politics. This left Austria and Russia. Bismarck's greatest fear was a war on two fronts; at all costs he must prevent an alliance of France with either Austria or Russia. Although there appeared to be little likelihood of such an alliance in 1871, Bismarck took no chances. Foreseeing the possibility of Austro-Russian rivalry in the Balkans, he wanted to put himself in a position to mediate any possible dispute between them and thus to prevent one or the other from turning to France.

In 1872 Bismarck arranged for the three emperors — Franz Josef of Austria, Alexander II of Russia, and William I of Germany — to meet with their foreign ministers in Berlin. Under Bismarck's prodding both Austria and Russia agreed to try to maintain the status quo in the Balkans, at least temporarily. In the following year a series of bilateral military agreements among the three powers, by which each promised to aid the other in the event of an unprovoked attack on it, further strengthened their ties. Although the association of the three powers was not a formal alliance, it became known as the *Dreikaiserbund* (Three

Emperors' League). The association was further strengthened in the same year by a visit of King Victor Emmanuel of Italy to Vienna and Berlin to gain support in the event that France should try to restore Rome to the pope.

The Dreikaiserbund received its first test in 1875 and was found wanting. Clerical royalists had returned to power in France and, determined to pursue a policy of *revanche* (revenge), they began a campaign of rearmament and encouraged the German Roman Catholics in their Kulturkampf. (See p. 731.) Bismarck, hoping to frighten the French into backing down, inspired a press campaign in German newspapers hinting that war was again in sight. The French foreign minister at once declared to the other great powers that Germany was preparing a "preventive" war and must be restrained. Austria remained silent, winning Bismarck's gratitude, but Britain and Russia both protested to Berlin. They were not prepared to help France in an aggressive war on Germany, but neither were they willing to see German predominance strengthened further at French expense. Bismarck disavowed the whole episode, but he had discovered Germany's true friends.

The Congress of Berlin of 1878, which settled the Russo-Turkish War (see pp. 839–841), further strained Russo-German relations. Bismarck offered to serve as the "honest broker" in the settlement of the dispute, but Russia, nominal victor in the war, felt it gained less than Austria, which had not participated. Aware of Russian dissatisfaction, Bismarck decided to strengthen Germany's ties with Austria. In 1879 the two countries signed a treaty (the Dual Alliance), which remained in force until 1918. Its principal provision obligated either country to come to the aid of the other if attacked by Russia. Bismarck saw it as a purely defensive and precautionary alliance, but Austrian officials frequently regarded it as giving them a free hand to do what they liked in the Balkans without fear of Russian intervention.

The details of the Austro-German treaty remained secret, though the existence of such a treaty was well known. Fearing that it had a sinister implication for them, the Russians sought some assurance from Germany, preferably in the form of a treaty of mutual defense. The Russians also feared the possibility of a British fleet in the Black Sea as the result of their tense relations with Britain in the Middle East and elsewhere. Although Bismarck had temporarily deflected French *revanchisme* by encouraging the French conquest of Tunisia, he gladly accepted the opportunity of reestablishing friendly ties with Russia, but not precisely in the form requested. In 1881, after intensive persuasion on his part, he again brought Austria, Russia, and Germany together in a formal Dreikaiserbund. Whereas the earlier one had been no more than an informal understanding among the three monarchs, the new one was a formal commitment by the governments. In addition to guaranteeing to each at least the friendly neutrality of the others in the event of war with a fourth power, the treaty committed them to consultation and joint action if there were any changes in the status quo in the Ottoman Empire and the Balkans. Concluded originally for three years, the treaty was renewed for an additional three years in 1884.

Bismarck capped this achievement with yet another master stroke. The Italians, anxious for recognition as a great power, had planned to annex Tunisia, when France suddenly beat them to it. Humiliated and outraged, the Italians angrily turned to Bismarck for consolation; and in 1882 Austria, Germany, and Italy signed a treaty establishing the Triple Alliance, which endured until broken by Italy in 1915. In essence it guaranteed that Austria and Germany would support Italy if it were attacked by France, pledged Italy to support Germany under similar circumstances, and provided for Italian neutrality in the event of an Austro-Russian war.

The years 1882 to 1884 marked the high point in the success of Bismarck's policies. Soon after the formation of the Triple Alliance Britain occupied Egypt, much to the displeasure of France, and inaugurated twenty years of intense colonial rivalry between the two powers. As in the French occupation of Tunisia, Bismarck had secretly encouraged the British to take Egypt, but at the same time he secretly expressed his "sympathy" for France. This led to a temporary rapprochement with France, further strengthened by the Berlin Conference of 1884, called by Bismarck and Jules Ferry, in part to thwart British plans in Africa. Bismarck even boasted privately that he had reestablished Napoleon's Continental System with its center in Berlin.

The Franco-German entente did not last long. French nationalists and anti-imperialists engineered the fall of Ferry, while Bismarck came to terms with Britain on the colonies. Anti-German feeling reached a peak in France in 1886–87 during the meteoric rise of General Boulanger, but his even more rapid fall brought a reduction in temperatures and passions. Meanwhile the Three Emperors' League expired, and Russia refused to renew the treaty as a result of new disputes with Austria. Bismarck persuaded Russia to sign a secret three-year Russo-German Reinsurance Treaty guaranteeing the neutrality of one if the other became involved in war, except for an aggressive war by Russia against Austria or by Germany against France. Thus, in spite of increasing difficulties, Bismarck managed to keep France isolated and Russia in line.

THE FRANCO-RUSSIAN ALLIANCE

The headstrong young emperor William II peremptorily dismissed Bismarck on March 18, 1890. (See pp. 733–734.) On March 23 the German government decided against renewing the Reinsurance Treaty, due to expire on June 18. In a matter of days Bismarck's successors began to dismantle the structure that he had patiently built and maintained over twenty years.

The French quickly seized the opportunity presented by this un-expected turn of affairs. As early as 1886 private pressure groups in France and Russia had taken advantage of the anti-German feeling prevailing in both countries to urge a Franco-Russian alliance; but Russia, traditionally suspicious of and hostile to France — especially Republican France — had preferred to seek accommodation with Germany. Now there was nowhere else to turn. During a personal visit to Russia shortly after the expiration of the Reinsurance Treaty, William evaded the efforts of his kinsman the tsar to reach a new agreement. The Russians were further put off by obvious German moves to draw closer to Britain and by an early renewal of the Triple Alliance. In July, 1891, during a friendly visit by a French naval squadron to the Russian base of Kronstadt, the Emperor of All the Russias stood bare-headed while a marine band played the revolutionary anthem, the *Marseillaise*.

The French had hoped to obtain a definite treaty of alliance, but the Russians were still moving cautiously. The best the French could obtain in 1891 was an *entente cordiale* (cordial understanding) and an agreement for joint consultation in the event of any "threat to peace." The following year the chiefs of staff of the two armies agreed on a military convention which provided that each would come to the aid of the other if either were attacked by Germany, whether alone or in league with Austria or Italy. Significantly, the convention was to have "the same duration as the Triple Alliance." Although it was drawn up in 1892, political scandals and cabinet shake-ups in France delayed its ratification until the beginning of 1894.

These two agreements — the entente cordiale and the military convention — formed the basis of the Franco-Russian alliance. Their precise conditions remained secret, of course, and the two governments did not refer to them publicly until 1895; but during the twenty years after their ratification massive investments by Frenchmen in Russian government bonds and corporate securities demonstrated the popularity of the alliance with the French people. Frequent consultations and joint planning by the military authorities strengthened its fabric. The immediate effect of the alliance was to restore the balance of power to something like an equilibrium: neither France nor Germany, Austria nor Russia, had an obvious advantage over the other. For the future, however, Bismarck's nightmare came closer to reality: if war should come, Germany would be forced to fight on two fronts.

GERMAN NAVAL EXPANSION AND
THE END OF BRITISH ISOLATION

As long as Britain pursued its policy of nonalignment with European powers, Bismarck was content to let Anglo-German relations coast. William II began his independent direction of foreign policy with earnest attempts to formulate an Anglo-German alliance, but at the end of a dozen years he succeeded only in driving Britain into the arms of France. Maladroit German diplomacy, such as William's ill-advised telegram to President Kruger of the South African Republic congratulating him for squelching the Jameson raid and hinting at promises of German support, served to alienate the British government and public. More fundamental forces also acted to produce an estrangement between the British and German nations.

The rapid growth of the German economy and its expansion into overseas markets adversely affected British economic interests. German businessmen were both efficient and aggressive and made deep inroads in traditional British markets. They even penetrated the British home market. In 1887 Parliament passed the Merchandise Marks Act, requiring foreign merchandise sold in Britain to be labeled with the name of the country of origin in order to discourage the German invasion. By the end of the century, however, British consumers had come to regard the stamp "Made in Germany" as a guarantee of quality rather than the reverse.

Because of the extension of Germany's overseas commerce as well as its debut as a colonial power, the German Admiralty had little trouble in 1898 in persuading the Reichstag to grant funds for a naval building program. In 1900 the program was enlarged, and German naval strategists developed the theory of the "risk fleet." They did not expect to surpass Britain as a naval power, but they reasoned that if their fleet and the next largest were together larger than the British, Britain would be unwilling to go to war against Germany in support of a third power. As early as 1889, however, the British navy had become alarmed by the growth of French and Russian sea power and had adopted the so-called two-power standard. This implied that Britain must have a fleet equal to the combined fleets of the next two largest navies. Thus the German decision touched off a naval armaments race that theoretically had no limit.

The British grew increasingly anxious over this development. It seemed as though the world was closing in on them. They had been at odds with France ever since the occupation of Egypt, and for a few months in 1898 they were on the brink of war over the Fashoda crisis. They had opposed Russian expansion in the Ottoman Empire, Persia, and East Asia. In 1902 they departed from their traditional policy of "splendid isolation" and concluded an alliance with Japan against Russia. Two years later, after almost a year of preliminary negotiations, they concluded a far-reaching agreement with France that provided for a complete settlement of all outstanding colonial disputes between the two powers. The Anglo-French entente of 1904 in no way committed the two nations to a military alliance, but subsequent conversations and negotiations resulted in a close understanding on many questions and placed

Courtesy of the Museum of Fine Arts, Boston

The European Balance, by Honoré Daumier

*"History shows that the danger threatening the independence of this or that
nation has generally arisen, at least in part, out of the momentary predominance
of a neighboring State at once militarily powerful, economically efficient, and
ambitious to extend its frontiers or spread its influence. . . . The only check on
the abuse of political predominance derived from such a position has always
consisted in the opposition of an equally formidable rival, or of a combination of
several countries forming leagues of defense. The equilibrium established by
such a grouping of forces is technically known as the balance of power, and it
has become almost an historical truism to identify England's secular policy with
the maintenance of this balance."* Secret memorandum of Eyre Crowe of
the British Foreign Office, Jan. 1, 1907, BRITISH DOCUMENTS ON THE ORIGINS OF
THE WAR (London, 1928), Vol. III.

Britain under a "moral obligation" to come to the aid of France in the event of an unprovoked attack on it.

Although Britain still regarded Russia with grave distrust, the Russo-Japanese War revealed Russian weakness and put an end to the Russian danger in East Asia. Moreover, as a result of the British annexation of Cyprus in 1878 and its stronger position in Egypt, especially after the agreement with France, Britain had fewer fears of a Russian threat to Suez. Russia, for its part, was badly shaken by defeat and the revolution of 1905 and was anxious to resolve its differences with Britain. In 1907 the two countries reached agreement on spheres of influence in Persia and Afghanistan and settled other disputes. Although the agreement did not provide for positive military collaboration, it did make cooperation easier. With France serving as the pivot, the pincers were closing on Germany.

ITALIAN DUPLICITY

While this new and strange alignment of powers was emerging, Italy played a double-dealing game. It adhered to the Triple Alliance even though its traditional archenemy Austria was included, through fear of French retaliation for 1870 and in anger over the French seizure of Tunisia. In 1887 it joined Britain and Austria in a Mediterranean Agreement to thwart Russian designs on the Ottoman Empire. The other two signatories also undertook to support an Italian claim to Tripoli. In renewing the Triple Alliance in the same year, Germany agreed to far-reaching support of Italy in its North African rivalry with France. Ten years later Italy made a commercial treaty with France settling their long-drawn out tariff war, and in 1900 the two countries agreed to give one another a free hand in Tripoli and Morocco, respectively. In 1902 Italy went further and assured France that it would remain neutral if France became involved in war with a third power; it even asserted that this promise in no way violated its other "international obligations," although the promise flatly contradicted Italy's promises to Germany in the Triple Alliance, which was still in force. Italian duplicity reached a new peak in 1909 when Italy agreed to support Russian aims in the Dardanelles in exchange for Russian support of Italy's claim on Tripoli, in spite of Italy's obligations to Austria under the Agreements of 1887. Italy's behavior throughout this period can be explained in part by the amorality of its politicians. Equally important was the Italian desire for colonies, especially after the humiliations in Tunisia and Ethiopia; they were determined to avoid a similar reverse in Tripoli.

THE MOROCCAN CRISES

Tripoli and Morocco, the last two areas of Africa to come under European control, had far more significance for European diplomacy than their importance as colonial acquisitions would seem to warrant.

Morocco, a poverty-stricken, revolt-torn semidesert on the northwest corner of Africa, achieved importance mostly as a result of German intransigence and diplomatic blundering. Germany had no important interests in Morocco, economic or otherwise, whereas the French had common borders with Morocco in both Algeria and French West Africa. The frequent Moroccan tribal revolts occasionally spilled over into French territory. The French, therefore, made agreements with Italy, Spain, and Britain in the hope of establishing an eventual French protectorate over most of the country, with Spain having the northern tip. Germany, however, was determined to use Morocco to test the strength of the new Anglo-French Entente of 1904.

In the spring of 1905 William II visited Tangier and strongly indicated German support for Moroccan independence. His action created an uproar not only in Paris but also in London, where the government had already taken alarm at Germany's naval program. In January, 1906, an international conference including the United States and several smaller nations as well as the great powers met at Algeciras at the southern tip of Spain to deal with the Moroccan situation. In the showdown only Austria supported the German position – a clear indication of the new alignment of powers. The Act of Algeciras reaffirmed Moroccan "independence" but placed the police under French and Spanish tutelage and set up a state bank, in which France had a controlling interest, to deal with the country's disordered finances.

A new Moroccan crisis blew up in 1908 when French authorities forcibly seized three German deserters from the Foreign Legion who had taken refuge with a German consular official. The immediate issue was submitted to arbitration by the International Court in The Hague, but the more important result was a Franco-German agreement in 1909. Germany recognized France's "special political interests" in Morocco in return for French consideration of German economic interests.

The third and final Moroccan crisis occurred in 1911. As a result of anti-foreign demonstrations, the French occupied the city of Fez. The Germans, who had been dissatisfied with the operation of the agreement of 1909, dispatched the gunboat *Panther* to the coastal city of Agadir hoping to force a French withdrawal. Instead, the English rallied in support of the French. The result was that Germany gave France the free hand that it had so long been seeking in Morocco, in return for cession by the French of two strips of disputed territory in the Congo. In the following year France forced the sultan of Morocco to accept a French protectorate.

The true significance of the Moroccan crises for European power politics was that they converted the Anglo-French Entente of 1904 from a mere agreement to settle colonial disputes into an active military alliance. German strategy backfired completely, though not for the first nor the last time.

FROM THE EASTERN QUESTION
TO THE BALKAN WARS

It is not easy to understand why the murder of an Austrian archduke in a remote village of southeastern Europe by a fanatical member of a secret society should have precipitated a global war, yet that is what happened. The secret-treaty network of alliances helps to account for the chain of events expanding the war after the first declaration, but it fails to explain why the great powers attached so much importance to this backward, poverty-stricken corner of Europe. All of them had, or thought they had, or came to have, interests in the Balkans. Had it not been for the progressive atrophy of the Ottoman Empire, these interests might not have arisen or might have remained latent; but as nature abhors a physical vacuum, so politicians abhor a political vacuum.

The Russian interest was most obvious and persistent. For more than a century a fundamental theme of Russian policy had been the drive to secure ice-free ports. Closely related to this was the Russian wish to control the Dardanelles and Bosphorus in order to permit the egress of Russian warships into the Mediterranean and to prevent the entry of hostile vessels into the Black Sea. Russian territorial claims in the Balkans were secondary, and complementary, to these two points. Even before the construction of the Suez Canal, Britain had resisted the Russian drive on the Balkans as a danger to communications with India; after the completion of Suez, Britain regarded control of the eastern Mediterranean as absolutely vital. It followed that the Dardanelles must be kept closed, or opened only with British permission.

After Austria-Hungary had been expelled from the leadership of central Europe in 1866, it looked to the Balkans for territorial aggrandizement to bolster its injured pride. Its diplomats occasionally manufactured slogans about controlling the mouths of the Danube or keeping open the route to Salonika, but their really vital interest in the Balkans was the purely negative one of keeping out the Russians. The French had long had important commercial relations with the Ottoman Empire, to which they added substantial foreign investments after the Crimean War. Although protection of their economic interests did not require territorial control, they naturally wanted a voice in deciding upon any changes in the status quo. Although German interests, symbolized by the Berlin-to-Bagdad railroad (rather, the Anatolian railroad, conceded to a German syndicate in 1888) were of recent date and as much political as economic, they were no less vigorous for that. Italy had no direct interests in the Ottoman Empire as such, but obsessed with the notion of obtaining Tripoli, it could not abstain from any activity that promised to weaken further the grip of the Turks.

Underneath this jumbled mosaic of conflicting great power interests lay the aspirations and ambitions of the people whose homes were in the Balkans: Albanians, Bulgarians, Greeks, Macedonians, Rumanians, various South Slavs (Serbs, Croats, Bosnians, Slovenes, Montenegrins) — and Turks. Although the inhabitants of the area were frequently regarded by the great powers as so many cattle, in the final analysis their actions and reactions provided the dynamic element in the entire Eastern Question.

THE RUSSO-TURKISH WAR AND
THE CONGRESS OF BERLIN

In July, 1875, the inhabitants of Herzegovina and Bosnia rose in rebellion against their Turkish masters. Within a few months the revolt had spread to Macedonia and Bulgaria. In the following year Serbia and Montenegro declared war in sympathy with the rebels. In Constantinople, where the government had already defaulted on its foreign debt payments, a series of palace revolutions deposed two sultans in quick succession. It looked like the end of the Ottoman Empire. The powers hastily conferred but could reach no agreement on the disposition of the corpse of the "sick man of Europe."

Surprisingly, the sick man demonstrated unusual vitality, crushing the revolts with great brutality and driving the Serbs back into their homeland. The Serbs appealed to the powers for mediation. Under a threat from Russia the Turks agreed to an armistice and a conference of the great powers in Constantinople. Turkey outflanked Western demands for reform, however, by proclaiming a new constitution, which it promptly scrapped when the conference adjourned. Meanwhile, Russia had agreed with Austria to allow the latter a free hand in Bosnia and Herzegovina in return for a free hand for Russia in Rumania and Bulgaria, with independent Serbia as a buffer between them. In April, 1877, Russia declared war on Turkey.

The Serb, Montenegrin, Rumanian, and Bulgarian irregulars again went to war, joining with the Russians who were advancing south through the eastern Balkans. Again the Turks put up unexpectedly strong resistance, holding the Russians at the fortress of Plevna in Bulgaria for almost six months. At length the Russians broke through and in January, 1878, stumbled exhausted to the gates of Constantinople. Unable to do more and fearful of intervention by the other powers (Britain dispatched warships to Constantinople in February), the Russians hurriedly forced the Turks to sign the Treaty of San Stefano, which provided for a large autonomous state of Bulgaria under Russian protection.

As Russia feared and Turkey hoped, the other great powers would not accept the results of the Treaty of San Stefano. After preliminary bar-

THE CONGRESS OF BERLIN, 1878

Independent nations

Under Austrian occupation

Proposed "Greater Bulgaria"
Under Treaty of San Stefano

Boundary of Ottoman Empire, 1878

RUSSIA

BESSARABIA

MOLDAVIA

AUSTRIA-HUNGARY

TRANSYLVANIA

R U M A N I A   DOBRUJA

BOSNIA   Bucharest

Sarajevo   SERBIA   WALLACHIA

HERZE-   BULGARIA   Black
GOVINA   NOVI-   Autonomous, 1878   Sea
              BAZAR   Independent, 1908

MONTENEGRO

                                  EASTERN RUMELIA
                                    To Bulgaria, 1885

Adriatic   O T T
  Sea   O M   Bosporus
          Tirana   MACEDONIA   Adrianople Constantinople
ITALY   To Turkey after Congress   San Stefano
        ALBANIA   of Berlin Salonika   Sea of Marmara

                            Dardanelles

                                  Aegean
            GREECE   Sea   TURKEY

                Athens

0   200
     Miles

Mediterranean   Sea

gaining, representatives of the six great powers plus those of the Ottoman Empire met in Berlin at the invitation of Bismarck in the summer of 1878. The dispositions of the congress generally followed those of the Treaty of San Stefano except for the creation of Greater Bulgaria, which was divided into three parts: Bulgaria proper, north of the Balkan mountains, an autonomous principality within the Ottoman Empire;

Eastern Rumelia, south of the mountains (including the Black Sea coast), restored to the Turks but under a special administration; and Macedonia, returned outright to the Turks with promises of reform. Rumania achieved full independence and gained most of Dobrudja on the mouths of the Danube, but had to give up southern Bessarabia to Russia. Serbia and Montenegro also gained independence but within smaller boundaries than those provided at San Stefano. Austria occupied Bosnia and Herzegovina and stationed a garrison in the Sanjak (province) of Novi Bazar. Britain took over the administration of Cyprus, ensuring control of the Mediterranean approaches to Suez as well as to the Dardanelles. Apart from regaining Bessarabia, which it had lost in 1856, Russia obtained only a few towns in the Caucasus.

Hailed as a great peace-making achievement, the Congress of Berlin actually left most participants and beneficiaries less satisfied than before. It stifled the aspirations of Serbia, Bulgaria, and Greece. The Ottoman Empire lost most of its territory in Europe and was left with the remainder in a precarious, exposed condition, subject to both domestic agitation and foreign conquest. More ominous for the future of Europe, Russia, victorious in war, suffered humiliation in peace. Austria gained much at little cost, but incurred the hostility of the new Balkan states, whereas Russia earned their gratitude. Britain gained an important advantage, but it remained profoundly suspicious of the Russians. Finally, Bismarck, "the honest broker," incurred the enmity of the influential Russian nationalists and Pan-Slavists and found himself tied to Austrian ambitions in the Balkans.

BULGARIA AND SERBIA

The Bulgarians had the greatest reason of all to be dissatisfied with the Congress of Berlin. Their territory had been cut back to a fraction of its projected size, they still paid tribute to Constantinople, and their policies were decided in St. Petersburg. They received as their prince Alexander of Battenberg, a German who knew nothing of Bulgaria but was a favorite nephew of the Russian tsar. Nevertheless, when Eastern Rumelia revolted in 1885 and demanded annexation to Bulgaria, Alexander was forced to accept the leadership of the movement despite the protests of Russia, which in the meantime had turned against both him and the idea of a Greater Bulgaria. British pressure forced the sultan to recognize Alexander as governor of Eastern Rumelia and thereby accept the de facto union of the two provinces.

Although both Turkey and Russia had to accept the fait accompli of the enlargement of Bulgaria, the jealous Serbs, who regarded their country as "the Piedmont of the Balkans," did not. In 1885 Serbia declared war on Bulgaria with the aim of securing "compensation." Surprisingly, the Bulgarians defeated the Serbs so badly that the latter called on

Austria-Hungary, the oppressor of the South Slavs, for protection against their neighbor. Soon afterward the Bulgarians forced Alexander to abdicate and elected as his successor Prince Ferdinand of Saxe-Coburg. Since Ferdinand was even less acceptable to Russia than Alexander had come to be, Russia persuaded other nations to withhold recognition of his regime until 1896. Nevertheless, Ferdinand held on with the strong support of his adopted people.

Balkan politics, both domestic and international, appeared to many Western observers to have something of a comic opera aspect, despite the obvious suffering of the people. (George Bernard Shaw wrote a successful comedy based on the Serbo-Bulgarian war, *Arms and the Man,* which Oskar Straus converted into an even more successful muscial comedy, *The Chocolate Soldier.*) Serbians regarded Austria much as the Italians had in 1859, yet until 1903 the ruling dynasty of Serbia placed itself under Austrian protection. Russia had liberated Bulgaria from the Turks and treated it as a client state, yet the Bulgarians hated the Russians almost as much as they hated the Turks or the Serbs. In 1903 the Serbians overthrew the Obrenovich dynasty and recalled the Karageorgeviches, who had been banished some forty-five years previously. Thereafter Serbian hostility to Austria became more overt, while the Serbs looked increasingly to Russia as the protector of the South Slavs. Bulgaria, on the other hand, gradually grew closer to Austria in spite of improvement in its relations with Russia after 1896, and it eventually went to war against Russia as the ally not only of Austria and Germany, but also of Turkey.

THE POWDER KEG OF EUROPE

In 1908 the Young Turk revolution broke out within the Ottoman Empire. In the ensuing confusion Bulgaria declared its complete independence, and Austria-Hungary proclaimed the outright annexation of Bosnia and Herzegovina. Only the Turks objected to the former action, but the latter move aroused vigorous protests from Russia and Serbia as well as the Turks. The Russians demanded an international conference, and the Serbs were on the point of war with Austria. Both eventually backed down, but the episode left a further legacy of bitterness and distrust.

The next major disturbance in the Balkans resulted from the action of Italy, which in 1911 finally undertook its long-planned conquest of Tripoli. Unable to win a decisive victory, the Italians occupied the Dodecanese Islands off the coast of Turkey, and the war appeared to be heading for a stalemate. Taking advantage of the situation, Montenegro, Serbia, Bulgaria, and Greece patched up their mutual quarrels and in October, 1912, went to war with Turkey. The Balkan allies won a succession of victories and were on the point of overrunning Constantinople itself when the great powers intervened to save the remains of Turkey.

The Treaty of London on May 30, 1913, ended the first Balkan War. Turkey was obliged to give up the island of Crete and all but a small corner of its European territory. Since both Austria and Italy objected to the expansion of Serbia to the Adriatic, the new independent state of Albania was established.

The first Balkan War had just ended when the second erupted. Disappointed by the great powers in its claims on the spoils of war, Serbia demanded a larger share of Macedonia from Bulgaria. When the Bulgarians refused and launched a surprise attack, Serbia and Greece declared war on Bulgaria. They were shortly afterward joined by Rumania and Turkey. The second Balkan War lasted only a month, with Bulgaria quickly defeated under such heavy odds. By the Treaty of Bucharest on August 10, 1913, Rumania obtained southern Dobrudja; Greece and Serbia obtained the lion's share of Macedonia. In the separate Treaty of Constantinople on September 29 Turkey regained Adrianople.

The new nations of the Balkans had learned the lessons of *Realpolitik* only too well. No notions of enlightened self-interest, economic or otherwise, held back their expansionist tendencies. Their state finances were in deficit, their living standards were little above the subsistence level; still their leaders played the game of power politics with a reckless abandon that made even post-Bismarckian German diplomats shudder. Such was their exhilarating legacy of independence after more than four centuries of Turkish rule — plus the tutelage and example of the great powers.

THE WAR

The system of alliances erected by Bismarck was purely defensive. Its purpose was to prevent war, not provoke it. So, too, was the network of agreements worked out by France after 1890. Although many Frenchmen still harbored ideas of revenge on Germany, they feared the possibility of a German preventive war. In any case they would have been unable to persuade either Russia or Britain to go to war to restore Alsace-Lorraine. The system of alliances and ententes served its purpose up to a point. For more than forty years — the longest period in modern history — no major Western nation fought another despite the many rivalries and conflicts of interest. Nevertheless, it was in the nature of the alliance system that if war between two or more of the great powers should begin, no matter where it started or how trivial the cause, it would become a general war involving all.

SARAJEVO AND THE MARCH TO WAR

On June 28, 1914, a young Bosnian revolutionary shot and killed the Archduke Franz Ferdinand, heir to the Austro-Hungarian throne, and his wife in the course of the archduke's visit to Sarajevo, capital of the

Austrian province of Bosnia. Exactly one month later Austria declared war on Serbia. By the end of the following week general war had erupted.

Serbia, the focal point of Pan-Slavism in the Balkans, had long been a thorn in the flesh of Austria. Intent on creating a Greater Serbia incorporating all the Slavic peoples in the Balkans, the Serbian government made or tolerated anti-Austrian propaganda, gave haven to political refugees, and generally hampered Austrian efforts in the Balkans. The Austrian annexation of Bosnia and Herzegovina in 1908 particularly incensed the Serbs, who regarded the provinces as properly belonging to Greater Serbia. Austria's frustration of Serbia's plans to incorporate Albania at the end of the first Balkan War added fresh fuel to the fire of Serbian hatred. Austria long since would have squelched the Serbs if it had not been for the threat of Russian interference. Now the government resolved to do so in spite of the threat.

Franz Ferdinand was known to be more liberal than his aged uncle, the king-emperor. It was widely believed that on his accession to the throne he would give the Slavic inhabitants of the empire much greater autonomy, perhaps a position similar to that enjoyed by the Magyars, in a federal empire. Since that might postpone indefinitely the creation of a Greater Serbia, the Pan-Serbian secret society Union or Death, also known as the Black Hand, decided on his assassination.

The Austrians suspected the complicity of the Serbian government in the plot but could not prove it. During the month between the assassination and the declaration of war Austria conducted an intensive search for the proof that would forestall Russian intervention. Although they could not find the evidence, the Austrians decided to take over Serbia anyway. On July 23 they delivered an ultimatum to Serbia on the pretext of needing to carry on their search in Serbia itself. Had the Serbs accepted the ultimatum, it would have meant the end of Serbian independence. Acting on Russian advice, they replied in a conciliatory tone, indicating acquiescence on some of the Austrian points but evading the major issues.

Meanwhile the great powers had been engaged in frequent consultations. World public opinion was shocked by the assassination and viewed with favor Austrian efforts to punish the guilty parties; the French and Russians, however, suspected the Austrians of wishing to go further than mere punishment. The Russian government, in particular, had decided even before the episode at Sarajevo that its objectives could be achieved only as the result of a general war; hence, it was prepared for — even welcomed — a showdown in the Balkans. The German government also had reasons for allowing a showdown. Bethmann-Holweg, the chancellor, and many other Germans were obsessed by fears of Russian expansion and favored a preventive war. Convinced that a two-front war was inevitable and hoping that Britain would remain neutral, the German

General Staff had prepared a strategy as early as 1905, called the Schlieffen Plan, which demanded implementation before France and Russia became stronger. The German emperor, therefore, assured his confrere in Vienna of his support with the remark that he appreciated the necessity of "freeing your Serbian frontiers of their heavy pressure." The remark was interpreted by the Austrian government as the offer of a blank check from Germany. The French regarded it as simply another test of the strength of their alliances, similar to the Moroccan crises, and assured Russia of their support. Sir Edward Grey, the British foreign secretary, proposed an international conference, but Austria refused point-blank to submit "a question of national honor" to arbitration.

Immediately after the Austrian declaration of war on July 28, the German government pressured Austria into resuming direct negotiations with Russia while it tried to separate France from Russia and offered Britain a guarantee that it would not annex any part of France or Belgium in return for a British promise of neutrality. Neither France nor Britain would make a firm commitment, but Britain demanded that Germany respect the neutrality of Belgium, to which Germany would not commit itself. The Russian government, which had ordered a general mobilization of the army immediately on receipt of the news of the Austrian declaration, changed its order to limited mobilization against Austria when informed of the apparent German efforts to make peace. When the final Austro-Russian negotiations broke down, it again ordered general mobilization. The climax came on August 1. Almost simultaneously, Germany and France ordered general mobilization. That evening, having received no reply to a twelve-hour ultimatum to Russia to halt mobilization, Germany declared war on Russia.

The following day the German army had already moved into Luxembourg and requested permission of the Belgian government to cross Belgian territory. The Belgians refused, but the Germans invaded anyway, violating Belgian neutrality guaranteed by all the great powers by international treaty in 1839. On August 3 Germany declared war on France. The British cabinet was still struggling with its painful decision, but the invasion of Belgium settled the matter: on August 4 Britain declared war on Germany. By the end of the week all the great powers except Italy were involved, as well as Serbia, Montenegro, Luxembourg, and Belgium. Before the month was out, Japan declared war on Germany and Austria; and by the end of the year Turkey entered on the side of the latter two nations.

THE BALANCE OF FORCES

If it is the business of diplomats to prevent war, it is the business of generals to prepare for it. There is no question that in 1914 Germany was better prepared militarily than any other nation. The credit belonged principally to the German General Staff. The long tradition of Prussian militarism carried over into the German Empire, under whose peculiar constitution military leaders had enormous influence with only minor accountability to civilian authorities. When war broke out other nations required from one to three weeks to mobilize their forces; Germany was able to take the offensive immediately.

In a short war, which was all that anyone expected in August, 1914, Germany's modern industries, great production of coal and steel, dense, well-integrated rail network, and military preparedness would have given it the advantage. Its chief disadvantage, and Bismarck's nightmare, was the necessity of fighting on two fronts, even though its shorter supply lines and efficient transport system minimized that handicap in the short run. Moreover, Austria-Hungary, less modern and less efficient than Germany, bore the brunt of the fighting on the eastern front in the war's opening stages.

France had a smaller population, possessed fewer and smaller heavy industries, and lacked the military planning and preparedness of the Germans. Russia, in spite of a huge population, was backward both militarily and economically. As early as December, 1914, the Russian commander in chief informed his allies that he could no longer take the offensive for lack of military supplies. Russia's great distances and inadequate rail network hampered the movement of troops and supplies, while separation from its Western allies rendered negligible any hoped-for assistance from them. Although Britain controlled the sea lanes, it had only a small professional army and no system of compulsory military service. It could provide only marginal assistance to France at the war's outset.

Eventually Britain's sea power and overseas resources — including help from the self-governing dominions, who at once cast their lot with the mother country — proved decisive. In spite of a devastating German submarine campaign, the British fleet and merchant marine assured the supply of foodstuffs and war materials for the Western allies. The British naval blockade of the Central Powers (as Germany and its allies were called) imposed privations and hardships on the civilian population and military services alike and cut off supplies of many strategic materials, such as rubber, tin, and petroleum. Finally, the entry of the United States into the war at the very time that Russia was knocked out assured the Allied Powers of that superiority of men, machines, and materials essential to ultimate victory.

THE EARLY CAMPAIGNS

German strategy was based on a plan drawn up in 1905 by Count von Schlieffen, chief of the German General Staff from 1891 to 1906. It called for a defensive holding action against the Russians in the east while striving for an early defeat of France in the west. According to the military authorities, the capture of France would either keep Britain out of the war or prevent the landing of British troops. The Russians could then be dealt with easily.

On the western front the Schlieffen Plan envisaged another holding action on France's northeastern frontier, where heavily fortified and wooded hills were considered too dangerous to attack directly. The largest part of the army was to sweep through Holland, Belgium, and the level plain of northern France, cut off the Channel ports, and encircle Paris from the west. (That the plan called for the violation of Belgian neutrality showed the influence and independence of the German military authorities.) If any resistance then remained, it would be destroyed by a pincer movement hinged on the German fortress of Metz and closing in from both east and west.

The strategy nearly succeeded. The Germans began the invasion of Belgium on August 3, captured Brussels on August 20, and by the early days of September were within forty miles of Paris with a large area of northern France under their control. The French government hastily moved to Bordeaux. At that point, however, the Allied forces rallied and launched a strong counterattack along the Marne River northeast of Paris. The entire fleet of Paris taxis was pressed into service to carry soldiers to the front. After a week of heavy fighting (September 5–12) the German forces gradually retired to take a new stand on the Aisne River.

Apart from the strong resistance of the Allies on the Marne, several German tactical errors accounted for the failure of the Germans to carry out their original strategy. At the last minute before the war began, the German high command switched several divisions from the Belgian front to Lorraine to counter an expected French offensive. Instead of invading through Holland, they sent all their forces through the relatively narrow gap between the fortress of Liège and the Ardennes hills, incurring additional casualties and losing time in mopping up the Belgians. The unexpectedly early arrival of the British (between August 7 and 17) took the Germans by surprise. Instead of continuing on to the Channel coast to cut off new reinforcements, they headed directly for Paris but were pushed eastward by the defending French and British, making encirclement impossible. Perhaps most important, the German General Staff, believing the issue settled by the end of August, withdrew a number of divisions for use on the eastern front.

The Battle of the Marne marked the farthest German advance of the entire war. After the German retreat to the Aisne the two opposing armies settled in for months of exhausting, muddy, bloody trench warfare. The war of movement gave way to a war of position. In spite of numerous heavy attacks and counterattacks in which both sides suffered

Courtesy of Imperial War Museum, London

Trench Warfare

"The trench lines ran continuously from the Alps to the sea, and there was no
possibility of manoeuvre. . . . All the wars of the world could show nothing to
compare with the continuous front which had now been established. Ramparts
more than 350 miles long, ceaselessly guarded by millions of men, sustained by
thousands of cannon, stretched from the Swiss frontier to the North Sea. . . .
For the first time in recorded experience there were no flanks to turn. The turning
movement, the oldest manoeuvre in war, became impossible. Neutral territory or
salt water barred all further extensions of the Front, and the great armies lay
glaring at each other at close quarters without any true idea of what to do next."
Winston S. Churchill, THE WORLD CRISIS, 1915 (London, 1923).

hundreds of thousands of casualties, the line of battle did not change by
more than ten miles in the next three years.

The eastern front in the early months of the war was in reality two
fronts. On the Austro-Russian frontier the Russians took the offensive
and overran Austrian Galicia in the first six weeks before being stopped
at the Carpathian Mountains. Russia invaded East Prussia and made an
extensive advance before being turned back by a revitalized German

army under generals Hindenburg and Ludendorff, whose forces killed and captured approximately 250,000 Russian soldiers. By the end of 1914 the Russians had fallen back almost to Warsaw. During the winter of 1914–15 the fighting on the eastern front was inconclusive. The Germans and Austrians mounted a new offensive in 1915, capturing nearly all of Poland. In 1916 the Russians took the offensive for the last time. They achieved limited successes against the Austrians in Galicia but failed in their ultimate objective. From that time forward the Russians were not only on the defensive but in a state of progressive military and political collapse. The revolution in the spring of 1917, although it did not remove Russia from the war, effectively ended any possibility that the Russians could make a positive contribution to the eventual Allied victory.

In the Balkans neither Austria nor Serbia was strong enough to penetrate far into the other's territory. After seesaw fighting in the fall and winter of 1914–15 their positions stabilized along the lines of the prewar frontier, while Austria devoted its main resources to the Russian front and Serbia recuperated. Meanwhile the diplomats from both sides tried to entice Greece, Bulgaria, and Rumania into the war with lavish promises of territorial acquisition. In September, 1915, Bulgaria was the first to succumb to the blandishments of the Central Powers. A combined offensive by the Bulgarians in the east and an Austro-German force in the north soon overran the entire peninsula north of Greece. Russia persuaded Rumania (which had been allied since 1883 with Austria and Germany) to enter on the side of the Allies in August, 1916. The timing was singularly unfortunate, for it was then that the Russian offensive collapsed. Within six months almost the whole of Rumania was in the hands of the Central Powers. Greece became the unhappy victim of a tug of war between rival foreign and domestic factions. The Allies could not budge Greece from its position of neutrality, but a French and British expeditionary force landed anyway at Salonika in a belated attempt to succor the Serbs. After months of internal strife amounting to civil war, in 1917 the Allies finally forced King Constantine to abdicate and installed a government that dutifully declared war on the Central Powers.

With the entry of Turkey on the side of the Central Powers in November, 1914 (in accordance with a secret treaty between Turkey and Germany, signed August 1), the area of conflict broadened. Although the Turkish offensives came to nothing, the British had to keep large numbers of troops in the Near East to protect the Suez Canal. Turkey closed the Dardanelles and Bosporus to Allied shipping, cutting off Western supplies to Russia except by the expensive and unsatisfactory routes to the Arctic ports and Vladivostok. The attempt of a British expeditionary force in 1915 to land at Gallipoli and capture Constantinople resulted

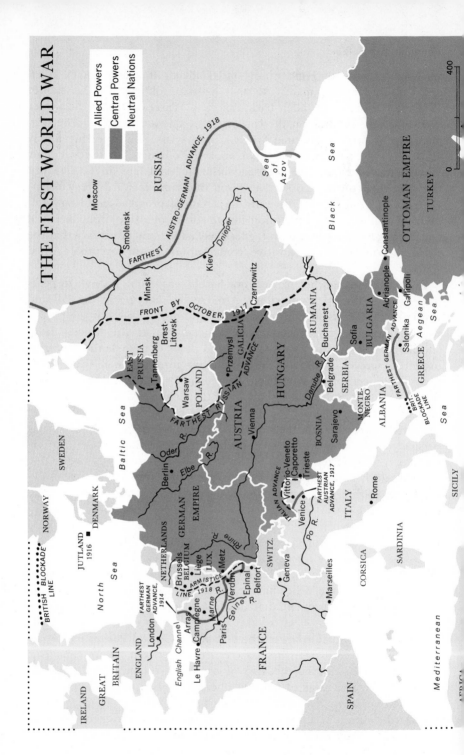

THE FIRST WORLD WAR

Allied Powers
Central Powers
Neutral Nations

IRELAND

GREAT BRITAIN

ENGLAND

London

English Channel

Le Havre

Arras

Campagne

Paris

Seine R.

FRANCE

Marseilles

SPAIN

NORWAY

SWEDEN

DENMARK

JUTLAND
1916

North Sea

BRITISH BLOCKADE LINE

Baltic Sea

NETHERLANDS

Brussels
BELGIUM
Liège
LUX.
Metz
Verdun
Epinal
Belfort
ARMISTICE LINE, 1918
Marne R.
FARTHEST GERMAN ADVANCE, 1914

Berlin

GERMAN EMPIRE

Oder R.

Elbe R.

Rhine R.

SWITZ.

Geneva

Po R.

Venice

Vittorio-Veneto
Caporetto
Trieste

ITALY

Rome

SARDINIA

CORSICA

SICILY

Mediterranean

Moscow

RUSSIA

Smolensk

FARTHEST AUSTRO-GERMAN ADVANCE, 1918

Minsk

Kiev

Dnieper R.

FRONT BY OCTOBER, 1917

Brest-
Litovsk

EAST PRUSSIA

Tannenberg

Warsaw

POLAND

GALICIA

Przemysl

FARTHEST RUSSIAN ADVANCE

Vienna

AUSTRIA

HUNGARY

Czernowitz

RUMANIA

Bucharest

Danube R.

Belgrade

SERBIA

BOSNIA

Sarajevo

MONTE-
NEGRO

ALBANIA

Sofia

BULGARIA

Adrianople
Constantinople

Gallipoli

Salonika

GREECE

Aegean Sea

BRIT.
BLOCKADE
LINE

FARTHEST GERMAN ADVANCE

OTTOMAN EMPIRE

TURKEY

Sea of Azov

Black Sea

ITALIAN ADVANCE

FARTHEST AUSTRIAN ADVANCE, 1917

0   400

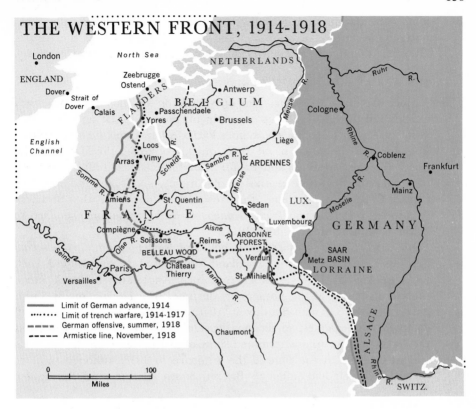

THE WESTERN FRONT, 1914-1918

London •   North Sea   NETHERLANDS

ENGLAND   Zeebrugge   Ostend   • Antwerp   Ruhr R.

Dover•   Strait of   Dover   •Calais   B E L G I U M   Cologne•

FLANDERS   •Passchendaele   •Ypres   •Brussels

English Channel   •Loos   Liège   Rhine   •Coblenz   Frankfurt•

Arras•   •Vimy   Scheldt R.   Sambre R.   ARDENNES   Mainz•

Somme R.   •Amiens   •St. Quentin   Meuse R.   Sedan•   LUX.   Moselle

F R A N C E   Luxembourg•   G E R M A N Y

Compiègne•   Aisne R.   ARGONNE FOREST

Seine R.   Oise R.   •Soissons   •Reims   SAAR

BELLEAU WOOD   Verdun•   Metz• BASIN

•Paris   •Château Thierry   Marne R.   •St. Mihiel   LORRAINE

Versailles•

——— Limit of German advance, 1914
•••••••• Limit of trench warfare, 1914-1917
– – – – German offensive, summer, 1918
– •– •– Armistice line, November, 1918

Chaumont•

ALSACE

Rhine R.

0   100
Miles

SWITZ.

in failure. Not until 1917 did British forces in the Near East under General Allenby (supported by desert Arabs led by the romantic figure T. E. Lawrence) make substantial gains against the Turks.

The final theater of the war in Europe was in Italy. Having deserted its partners in the Triple Alliance in favor of an ambiguous neutrality, Italy pursued some hard bargaining throughout the winter of 1914–15 to see which side would offer most for its services. The Central Powers were handicapped in the bargaining by Austrian resentment of Italian perfidy and by extravagant Italian claims on Austrian territory. The Western allies had no compunctions in the matter, and in the secret Treaty of London on April 7, 1915, granted Italy lavish promises of territorial acquisition, some of which flatly contradicted other commitments of the Allies. It proved a poor bargain. After two years of repeated attacks along a very narrow front on the Austrian frontier northeast of Venice, the Italians had advanced only ten miles. After mopping up in Serbia and Rumania, the Germans sent six divisions in in 1917 to reinforce the Austrians on the Italian front. On the first day of the attack they regained all that the Italians had won in two years. At the end of a month the Italians had fallen back to the Piave River, where they held until the last weeks of the war, when the visible collapse of the Austro-Hungarian monarchy made it possible to advance into Austrian territory.

THE WAR AT SEA AND IN THE COLONIES

Since Germany's colonies had only skeleton military garrisons, they quickly fell to the Allies. Japan's main purpose in declaring war in August, 1914, was to secure Germany's Pacific islands and Chinese concessions for itself. Japanese naval forces quickly occupied the Marianas, the Marshalls, the Carolines, and Palau; a combined sea and land operation took over the Shantung peninsula of China. A New Zealand force occupied German Samoa, and the Australians took over the Bismarck Archipelago and German New Guinea. All these operations were secure by the beginning of November, 1914.

In Africa the German garrisons held out longer, although the actual fighting was rarely severe. Togoland capitulated to an Anglo-French force in August, 1914. Another combined Anglo-French attack drove the Germans out of the Cameroons during 1915. The Union of South Africa invaded German Southwest Africa at the beginning of 1915 and completed its conquest in six months. Only in German East Africa did the Germans put up a determined show of resistance. Their troops were still in the field at the time of the armistice in 1918, although most of the colony itself had fallen to British, South African, and Portuguese forces.

With few exceptions, the war at sea was singularly uninteresting. The highly touted and expensive German High Seas Fleet remained in port throughout the war except for a single inconclusive sortie. The British Grand Fleet was not much more venturesome, taking refuge on the west coast of Scotland, though its cruisers patrolled the North Sea on the lookout for submarines and occasional German raiders. The beginning of the war found a number of isolated German battle cruisers in foreign ports. They immediately put to sea and did some damage to Allied shipping and shore stations in the Pacific and Indian Oceans, but most were destroyed in the first few months of the war.

The one major naval engagement of the war, the Battle of Jutland, took place in 1916 in the Skagerrak between Denmark and Norway. The German fleet had timidly put to sea and was discovered by a British cruiser squadron. The Germans tried to retreat, but the main body of the British fleet came up behind and cut across its line. In the ensuing battle each fleet lost six capital ships, but the British losses were more important. Although the Germans had shown themselves superior in marksmanship and maneuver against a larger British force, they retreated to their own harbors, where they remained until the end of the war. The risk fleet took no more risks.

The most important development in naval warfare was the widespread utilization of submarines, especially by Germany. At the beginning of the war it was not clear what could be expected of these craft, but they soon proved to be exceedingly effective. In the early months German submarines sank several outmoded British warships. Soon they began to concentrate on merchant shipping and even passenger liners. In February, 1915, the Germans announced a submarine blockade of Britain. The sinking of the Cunard liner *Lusitania* on May 7, 1915, with a loss of 1,200 lives (including many Americans) outraged the Western world and brought the United States to the brink of war with Germany. Germany eventually agreed not to sink passenger ships in the future without warning and without provision for rescuing the passengers, but submarine attacks against ordinary merchant ships continued at an accelerated pace.

By the beginning of 1917 Germany had more than one hundred submarines and announced that it would no longer respect the rights of neutrals or provide for passengers. In April it sank 875,000 tons of Allied and neutral shipping. Germany's unrestricted submarine warfare was the major factor in bringing the United States into the war. The German military planners took account of this possibility but decided they would be able to drive Britain out of the war by cutting off its supplies of food and raw material before the United States could make an effective contribution. At the insistence of civilian authorities, however, the British navy finally began the practice of convoying merchant ships and improved its techniques of antisubmarine warfare. By the end of 1917 the worst of the submarine danger had passed. The Allies were destroying German submarines faster than they could be built and building new shipping tonnage faster than it could be sunk.

ENTER THE UNITED STATES, EXIT RUSSIA

The American declaration of war on Germany on April 6, 1917, was preceded by several attempts to seek a negotiated peace. At the beginning of 1916 President Wilson sent Colonel House, his confidential adviser, to Europe for consultations with leading Allied statesmen. Colonel House let it be known that the president was prepared to mediate a peace settlement; moreover, if the Allies accepted his offer but the Germans did not, the United States would probably go to war against Germany. The Allies were still confident of victory in the coming spring offensives, so nothing came of the offer. Toward the end of the same year Germany requested that the United States inform the Allies that it was prepared to consider a negotiated peace. Again the Allies rejected the offer. A part of the difficulty lay in the fact that neither side had clearly formulated or announced its war aims.

After Allied rejection of the German peace overture, the German government fell more than ever under the influence of the generals, especially Ludendorff. In January, 1917, the German war council decided on the policy of unrestricted submarine warfare. As soon as this news reached the United States, President Wilson severed diplomatic relations with Germany; still he did not take the country into war.

From the beginning many Americans had been sympathetic to the Germans. Many more — undoubtedly a majority at the beginning of the war — adopted the attitude that the war was none of America's business. Only a relatively small group, chiefly in the East, felt that America should join the Allies early in the war. Gradually their number grew as Allied propaganda had its effect (because the British controlled the transatlantic cables, America rarely received news directly from Germany). Others became converted because of the submarine campaign. Still others — influential bankers and financiers in particular — became converted because of the large American loans to the Allied Powers. When German submarines torpedoed several American vessels in February and March of 1917, majority opinion swung sharply to a desire for intervention.

America entered the war with a very small standing army and no system of military conscription. To recruit, train, and transport soldiers to France in substantial numbers required more than a year. Thus, although the navy went into action at once in convoy and antisubmarine duty, American soldiers did not make an appreciable contribution to the Allied cause on land until the summer of 1918.

Simultaneously events in Russia were drawing to a climax. Recurrent military defeats, increasing civilian hardships, and the autocratic and inefficient character of the government brought domestic unrest to a new peak. In March, 1917, a palace revolution overthrew the monarchy and installed a provisional government. (See p. 861.) Liberal and republican in character, the new government attempted to continue the war, but the breakdown of the internal administrative machinery was complete. The armies suffered new defeats, and conditions in the cities approached famine proportions. Soon after the March Revolution the Germans transported Lenin and other Bolshevik leaders to Stockholm, whence they made their way to St. Petersburg and organized the workers into an antigovernment party. In November the Bolsheviks overthrew the provisional government and at once began to negotiate for an armistice with Germany.

The Germans made extensive demands on the new regime, which even the Bolshevik government felt it could not accept. For almost three months the negotiations dragged on while the Bolsheviks attempted to consolidate their power and the Germans grew impatient. Meanwhile the old tsarist empire was breaking up into its constituent parts. The provisional government had already recognized the independence of Poland. While negotiations with Germany were taking place, Finland, Estonia, Latvia, the Ukraine, and Bessarabia all declared their independence of Russia. To prevent further defections and to rally their forces to fight the civil war that had broken out within Russia, the new Soviet government at last signed the Treaty of Brest Litovsk on March 3, 1918. Although the treaty compelled Russia to make extensive concessions to Germany and the new states, it remained a dead letter because of the German capitulation to the Allies eight months later. The final determination of the new Russian boundaries and the nature of the regime awaited the outcome of the civil war.

THE FINAL CAMPAIGNS

At the end of 1916 the Central Powers controlled the entire Balkan peninsula north of Greece. Greece was still technically neutral but was occupied by a small Allied expeditionary force. By knocking Russia out of the war in 1917, the Germans secured their eastern frontiers and could divert the released manpower to the deadlocked western front. It had become clear that the unrestricted submarine campaign could not alone drive Britain out of the war. General Ludendorff, who had become a virtual military dictator of Germany, decided on a last gigantic effort to achieve a decision in the west before the Americans could reach the front in large numbers. He launched his great offensive in March, 1918, with an unprecedented artillery barrage and the extensive use of poison gas. Favored by a persistent heavy fog, he broke the British lines in northwestern France, then launched a savage attack against the main French positions northeast of Paris. By the end of May he had driven to the Marne, within striking distance of Paris. Once again, as it had so many times before, the German strategy almost succeeded. On this occasion the offensive stalled because of the exhaustion of the German soldiers and the arrival in the nick of time of fresh American troops at the beginning of June. In the second Battle of the Marne (July 15 to August 7, 1918) the Allied forces definitely turned back the German threat. Thereafter the offensive lay with the Allies, and in view of the steady reinforcement of American troops the outcome was only a matter of time. The Germans now fought a defensive action to keep Allied soldiers off German soil until an armistice could be arranged.

From other fronts the Germans received nothing but bad news. Bulgaria capitulated on September 30 in the face of a massive Allied offensive launched from Albania and Greece. In the following month the Turks surrendered. At the beginning of November the Serbs re-entered Belgrade and began to invade Hungary. By this time the Austro-Hungarian monarchy had reached an advanced state of decomposition, with wholesale desertions from the army, riots and popular demonstrations in the cities, and risings of subject nationalities against their German and Magyar rulers. The Allies earlier had recognized the claims of the Czechs, Yugoslavs, and Poles to independent nationhood and allowed national brigades of their soldiers to fight along with Allied armies. At the end of October the Italians won a major victory at Vittorio Veneto and pushed on to occupy Trieste and Fiume. On November 3 the Austro-Hungarian government sued for peace.

On October 4 a new government took over in Germany. It was headed by Prince Max of Baden, a well-known liberal, and had the support of the Center, Progressive, and Socialist parties in the Reichstag, to which it agreed to be responsible. Immediately the new government appealed directly to President Wilson to arrange an armistice, basing its plea on Wilson's famous Fourteen Points. (See p. 858.) Wilson did not act on this request at once but began an exchange of notes to determine the exact terms of the proposed armistice. In the interim the political situation deteriorated seriously in Germany, with widespread rioting and street disorders. On November 3, having been ordered to sea for a last-ditch raid after spending the war bottled up in port, the sailors of the German navy mutinied. On November 7 a full-fledged revolution broke out in Munich, and on November 9 the government announced the abdication of William II. Although the emperor had not given his consent, he followed the advice of his military leaders and fled into exile in the Netherlands. On November 8 the German armistice commission met with Allied military leaders in France and worked out the details of the armistice. The harsh Allied terms fell little short of unconditional surrender, but the Germans had no alternative. On November 11, 1918, at 11 A.M., the armistice took effect. All was quiet on the western front.

SPECIAL FEATURES OF THE WAR

Before it became known in history books as the World War (later the First World War), the war of 1914–18 was known to millions of Europeans who experienced it as the Great War. In retrospect it seems a tragic prelude to the war of 1939–45, but for the generation who lived before 1939 its emotional and psychological as well as physical impact clearly justified the name. For concentrated destructiveness it surpassed anything in human history until the mass air raids and atomic bombings of World War II. Human casualties numbered about 10 million killed and twice that many seriously wounded. The direct money cost has been estimated at more than 180 billion dollars (contemporary purchasing power), and the indirect money cost (through property damage and so forth) at more than 150 billion dollars; but such figures have little meaning. The true costs — the broken lives, the shattered societies, the residues of frustration, bitterness, and hate that led to still further outrages on civilization — cannot be measured.

Apart from the magnitude of the war, it presented a number of special features that set it apart from all previous wars, even those of the Napoleonic era. Although the concept of total war did not emerge until World War II, its foundations were clearly laid in World War I. Never had entire populations been so directly engaged in or affected by a war effort. Almost all the continental countries had had some form of compulsory military service before the war; Britain introduced it in 1916, the United States in 1917. All combatant nations resorted to rationing strategic materials and many consumer goods; to requisitions, price controls, labor controls and allocation; and to many other forms of economic planning. All nations imposed either formal or informal censorships and in other ways curtailed ordinary human activities. Even Britain, the historic haven of individual liberties, adopted the Defense of the Realm Act, which in effect imposed martial law on the country.

In the half-century preceding the war industrial technology became increasingly scientific. As would be expected, so did military technology. A number of new and destructive weapons developed from the new science and the new industrial technology. The most effective was the submarine. More portentous for the future were the tank and military aircraft, although they played a secondary role in the war itself. Heavy artillery, which had been used in the past, experienced a spectacular advance in range, accuracy, and explosive force, as the shelling of Paris from forty or fifty miles away demonstrated. At the other extreme the machine gun greatly increased the effectiveness of small arms fire, especially on defense. These two devices, together with the tardy and incomplete development of the tank and the airplane, accounted for the immobility as well as the terrible destructiveness of the fighting on the western front. Trench warfare became a way of life for millions of young men on both sides and left terrible psychological as well as physical scars on many of those who survived.

Chemistry played a spectacular part with the development of toxic gases, but was no less important in the invention of ersatz or artificial commodities to replace natural commodities in short supply. The Germans took the lead in this area, both because of their superior chemical industries and education and because of their greater need. The nitrogen fixation process, invented by the German scientist Fritz Haber on the eve of the war, played a major role in maintaining German food production when the British blockade shut off the supply of Chilean nitrates for German agriculture. The wireless radio, another prewar invention with fruitful peacetime uses in the postwar period, played a limited role in military operations, especially at sea.

Propaganda was another war weapon which, though scarcely new, reached a new peak of development. Each nation sought to convince its own people as well as those of neutral nations that it was right, that the opponents were not only wrong, but committed all sorts of atrocities. They sought to undermine the morale of enemy soldiers and civilians by spreading false rumors about the course and conduct of the war. On the whole, because of their control of international cables, the Allied nations were favored in this psychological battle, especially in spreading their message to neutral nations overseas.

Closely related to propaganda were the statements of war aims by the various national leaders, which were intended to bolster the morale of their own people and to weaken the will to resist of the enemy. America was far and away the champion in this form of making war. For the first three years of the war both the Allied and the Central Powers limited their statements to protestations of innocence with respect to the origins of the war; for them it was simply a matter of survival and self-defense. For the Americans, however, it was a "war to end war" and "to make the world safe for democracy." (Fortunately for the latter slogan, the autocratic government of Russia was overthrown just before America entered the war.)

The most resounding and influential of all statements of war aims was embodied in President Wilson's Fourteen Points, delivered in an address to the Senate in January, 1918. Among other things, he called for frank and open diplomacy ("open covenants openly arrived at"), the readjustment of frontiers "along clearly recognizable lines of nationality," the right of all nations (including Russia) to "the freest opportunity for autonomous development," the limitation of armaments, and the creation of an international organization to settle disputes and guarantee peace. Although President Wilson was undoubtedly sincere in making the statement, it was never adopted by the United States as a formal statement of war aims, much less accepted by the Allies. Nevertheless, it was regarded as such by the Germans and by many Americans during the final months of the war and the first few months of peace. Indirectly and unintentionally, therefore, it was responsible for much of the misunderstanding, confusion, and acrimony that followed the war and disturbed the peace.

DISINTEGRATION
AND COLLAPSE
CHAPTER THIRTY-THREE

The great crisis of Western civilization was a political, economic, social, and cultural crisis all in one. The first overt manifestation came with the breakdown in international relations culminating in the First World War, although the symptoms had been building for at least half a century and the aftereffects persist to the present day. The period of actual collapse lasted less than two decades, from 1914 to 1933.

The war disrupted normal social life and political relationships. It also resulted in a breakdown of the international economy and temporarily suspended the operation of free markets in most national economies. In Russia two successive revolutions, followed by a long and debilitating civil war, overturned the old order of society. Elsewhere in eastern and central Europe war-induced political collapse and social disorganization led to political demagoguery, organized banditry, mob violence, and mass hysteria. Instead of stabilizing the situation, the peace treaties concluding the war added new elements of tension.

Not realizing how extensively the foundations of society had been eroded, the people of western Europe and North America looked forward to a "return to normalcy." For them reconstruction meant primarily physical reconstruction and a return to the old way of life. Reconstruction, however, proved to be no simple matter. The difficulties experienced in all countries as a result of currency disorders and the first postwar depression in 1920–21 partially revealed the extent of the damage to the economic mechanism. Disastrous hyperinflations in Germany and elsewhere in central Europe provided further evidence and gave support to the critics of the peace treaties. By the beginning of 1925 the Western nations had succeeded in shoring up temporarily the economic mechanism and patching some of the more obvious rents in the social fabric. For a few years a precarious, almost frantic prosperity ensued. But the foundations had rotted, and the whole structure crashed in the worldwide depression from 1929 to 1933.

THE RUSSIAN REVOLUTION, 1917–1921

DISINTEGRATION, 1914–1917

The enthusiasm with which the Russian people greeted their country's entry into the First World War and their confidence in a quick victory soon disappeared when the old story of inept leadership at home and at the front led to crushing defeats and enormous casualties. The stupid and obstinate Tsar Nicholas relied increasingly for counsel on his hysterical wife and her adviser, the unordained monk Gregory Rasputin, an unwashed and illiterate Siberian peasant. Despite his openly immoral life, his bizarre behavior, and his blatant venality, Rasputin gained great power over the empress by his supposed ability to stop the hemophiliac bleeding of the youthful heir to the throne. In time she came to believe that God had sent him to guide Russia. When in 1915 the tsar left the capital to take personal command of the armies in the field, effective control of the government fell into the hands of the empress and Rasputin. Ministers came and went in confusing succession while corruption and inefficiency reached new heights. High aristocrats who feared for the survival of tsardom implored the tsar to dismiss Rasputin. When he refused, a small group of them assassinated the monk in December, 1916. Their act accomplished nothing, for Nicholas and his wife, resentful of the murder of their "Holy Friend," became ever more obstinate as the government approached complete paralysis.

The economic drain of the war, worsened by the mismanagement of the central government, brought severe stresses. Troop mobilization took manpower away from farming and industry: Russia raised an army of 15 million men. Much of the country's output went for military needs, while the imports of manufactured goods upon which Russia had depended heavily before 1914 dwindled. The costs of the war, the scarcity of goods, and the government's fiscal irresponsibility produced destructive inflation, so that by the beginning of 1917 the cost of living had risen approximately 700 per cent since 1914. During 1916 strikes and bread riots occurred with increasing frequency in the industrial centers of the empire.

THE FEBRUARY REVOLUTION

On February 23, 1917 — March 8 according to the Western calendar[1] — strikes and demonstrations broke out in Petrograd (the new name given to the capital to replace the German-sounding name of St. Peters-

[1] Imperial Russia used the old Julian calendar; the Soviet regime adopted the Gregorian calendar on January 31, 1918.

burg). At first no one expected that the disturbances would touch off a revolution, but the strike movement spread rapidly in succeeding days. Troops in Petrograd joined the demonstrators and gave them arms, while railroad workers prevented other troops from coming in to restore order. On March 12 and 13 leaders of the strikers and soldiers and representatives of socialist parties formed a Soviet (council) of Workers' and Soldiers' Deputies, as in the 1905 revolution, arrested the government's ministers, and took over control of the capital. On March 12 a committee of the Duma (parliament), which had previously been reluctant to join the developing revolution, decided to establish a provisional government. The new ministry headed by the liberal Prince George Lvov and dominated by members of the Constitutional Democratic party (Cadets) included only one socialist, Alexander Kerensky. On March 15 it obtained the tsar's abdication in favor of his brother Michael, who in turn abdicated the next day.

The long reign of the Romanovs had ended, terminated by a brief, leaderless, and nearly bloodless revolution. Many people both in Russia and abroad had long recognized the strong probability of the collapse of tsardom; but no one, not even the extreme radicals, had expected it to take place so quickly and easily.

THE PROVISIONAL GOVERNMENT

The new regime speedily introduced liberal political reforms, proclaimed freedom of speech, press, and religion, and announced plans for a far-reaching program of social reform and land distribution. It promised to summon a constitutional assembly to decide on Russia's permanent form of government. By vowing to continue the war against Germany it won recognition from the Western democracies, who held high hopes for it. In spite of its promising beginning, the provisional government lasted only eight months. Of the many factors that contributed to its early demise, two stand above the rest: its decision to continue the war, and its inability to establish control over the Petrograd Soviet of Workers' and Soldiers' Deputies.

The strength of the Petrograd Soviet lay in its close connection with the restless working class and its ability to marshal the masses for quick action. Until autumn of 1917 it was controlled by moderate socialists. They believed that Russia was not yet ready for socialism and were therefore willing to allow the provisional government to hold power until society had gone through the "bourgeois-democratic" stage of evolution. They supported the provisional government in the continuation of the war, claiming that now it was a democratic struggle against reactionary Germany and Austria. Soviets were formed elsewhere in the country, and in June hundreds of delegates met in Petrograd for the first All-Russian Congress of Soviets. Most of the representatives were

Socialist Revolutionaries (SR's) and Mensheviks. (See p. 751.) The Bolsheviks were very much in the minority.

The Bolsheviks had not been inactive, however. In April, 1917, V. I. Lenin, acknowledged leader of the Bolsheviks, returned from Swiss exile. The German government provided a special sealed train to take him across Germany to Stockholm, whence he reached Petrograd, in the hope that his agitation would disrupt the Russian war effort; but the Germans hardly expected that they would soon have to deal with him as head of the Russian government. Until Lenin's return the Bolsheviks could not decide whether to cooperate with the provisional government or not. Lenin had tried to direct policy by letter from Switzerland, but he had been unable to persuade the party to follow his advice. Once at the center of the revolution, he quickly assumed control. In his speeches and in a statement called the April Theses he announced his complete hostility to further cooperation with the provisional government. He declared that the revolution would soon pass through its bourgeois phase into a socialist dictatorship of the proletariat and insisted that "all power in the state from top to bottom, from the remotest village to the last street in the city of Petrograd, must belong to the soviets." He also urged Russia's immediate withdrawal from the war, capitalizing on the war weariness of the people and turning it into hostility to the provisional government.

The Bolsheviks had fewer than 30,000 members in February; by the end of April membership had increased to 76,000. The party's strength, however, lay not in numbers but in the ability and dedication of its members, in the appeal to the masses of its idyllic vision of a state run by the people, and in the skill and shrewdness of Lenin's leadership. He knew how to move quickly and surely in the uncertainties of the revolutionary situation, and unlike the leaders of other parties, whether bourgeois or socialist, he knew exactly in which direction he wanted the revolution to go.

Popular discontent arising from the continued hardships of the war compelled a series of cabinet reorganizations that brought more socialists into the provisional government. The general unrest erupted into civil violence in July when soldiers, sailors, and workers in Petrograd, inflamed by Bolshevik propaganda, attempted an insurrection. The Bolshevik Central Committee, the ruling body of the party, considered the rising premature and tried to curb it, but the government accused them of inspiring it. Loyal troops put down the insurrection, the government arrested several of the Bolshevik leaders claiming they were German agents, and forced the others into hiding. Lenin himself took refuge in Finland.

Soon after the July rising socialist pressure forced Prince Lvov to resign as head of the provisional government, and the moderate socialist

The Bettmann Archive

V. I. Lenin

"It was just 8:40 when a thundering wave of cheers announced the entrance of the presidium, with Lenin — great Lenin — among them. . . . Unimpressive, to be the idol of a mob, loved and revered as perhaps few leaders in history have been. A strange popular leader — a leader purely by virtue of intellect; colorless, humorless, uncompromising and detached, without picturesque idiosyncrasies — but with the power of explaining profound ideas in simple terms, of analysing a concrete situation. And combined with shrewdness, the greatest intellectual audacity. . . . Now Lenin, gripping the edge of the reading stand, letting his little winking eyes travel over the crowd as he stood there waiting, apparently oblivious to the long-rolling ovation, which lasted several minutes. When it finished, he said simply, 'We shall now proceed to construct the Socialist order!' " John Reed, TEN DAYS THAT SHOOK THE WORLD (New York, 1919).

Alexander Kerensky became prime minister. Constitutional Democrats, army circles, and other nonsocialist groups then formed a right-wing opposition that looked upon General Kornilov, newly appointed commander in chief of the army, as its leader. The rivalry between the Kerensky and Kornilov factions culminated in Kornilov's withdrawing his allegiance from the provisional government in September and ordering his troops to march on Petrograd. Kerensky turned to the Bolsheviks for help in meeting the threat to his regime; he freed the Bolshevik leaders from jail, armed their followers, and encouraged Bolshevik agitators to spread propaganda among Kornilov's advancing troops. Demoralized by the Red propaganda, poor leadership, and inadequate supplies, Kornilov's soldiers refused to fight. The general was arrested and his mutiny collapsed.

Several weeks of confusion followed, with charges and countercharges from both Right and Left. After nearly a month Kerensky formed a five-man directory with himself at its head. Meanwhile the Bolsheviks had gained a majority in the soviets of Petrograd and Moscow as well as in most of the provincial soviets. Lenin, who was still hiding in Finland, decided that the time had come for his party to seize power. He returned secretly to Petrograd and urged his followers to ready themselves for armed insurrection.

THE OCTOBER REVOLUTION AND WAR COMMUNISM

During the night of October 24 (November 6 in the Western calendar) armed workers called Red Guards and sympathetic regular troops occupied the railroad stations, post offices, power stations, and other strategic points in Petrograd. At noon the next day they stormed the Winter Palace, the seat of government, and arrested members of the government. Kerensky himself had already fled. In less than one day the Bolsheviks took over both Petrograd and the Russian government. The next day Lenin formed a new government called the Council of Peoples' Commissars. The Bolsheviks had come to power.

The Bolsheviks quickly discovered that it was more difficult to retain power than to seize it. Nearly four years of bitter suffering, civil strife, and war followed the October Revolution. In their effort to survive and stay in power the Bolsheviks introduced a drastic regime called War Communism. It included nationalization of the urban economy, confiscation of land and its distribution among the peasants, and a new legal system. Its outstanding characteristic was the deliberate adoption by the government of a single-party dictatorship and of what Lenin called "an unsparing mass terror." In December, 1917, the government established a special secret police to combat "counterrevolutionaries." It was called the Cheka from the first letters of its Russian name. The Cheka was destined under different names to become a permanent and dreaded part of Soviet life.

In the elections to the long-awaited constitutional assembly the Socialist Revolutionaries won a large majority of the seats. The assembly met in January, 1918, but Lenin sent troops to dissolve it after one session, branding the Socialist Revolutionaries and other opponents of the Bolsheviks as counterrevolutionaries. The middle classes were persecuted from the start of the October Revolution, and it was not long before the workers and peasants also lost their freedom. Under the pressure of events and of their own ambitions for power, the men who had promised a society with freedom for all created a terrorist police state.

Russia suffered heavy territorial losses. The provisional government had recognized Poland's independence, and immediately after the October Revolution the new government acceded to Finland's demand for independence. In the next few months Lithuania, Estonia, and Latvia won independence in spite of Bolshevik opposition. The treaty of peace with Germany cost Russia much territory. The disintegration of the Russian army left the government powerless to resist German advances deep into Russia, and Lenin, who had initiated peace negotiations immediately upon seizing power, eventually had to accept the harsh German demands despite the opposition of many Bolshevik leaders. In March, 1918, the Russians signed the peace treaty of Brest Litovsk, in which they agreed to give up large parts of the Ukraine, White Russia, and Transcaucasia. Russia lost over 60 million people and 1.3 million square miles, including a large part of its industry and natural resources.

CIVIL WAR AND INTERVENTION

The enemies of the Bolshevik revolution ranged from radical Socialist Revolutionaries to extreme reactionaries who wanted to restore tsarist absolutism. The Socialist Revolutionaries revived their traditional policy of assassination, picking Bolshevik leaders as their victims this time, and in August, 1918, succeeded in severely wounding Lenin. The Bolsheviks met this threat with an official reign of terror that wiped out many of their political opponents and maintained their control of the central government, located after March, 1918, in Moscow.

The government found it far more difficult to combat the military anticommunist movements that erupted on the borders of Russia. A so-called White Army was formed in the Cossack lands of the south. Another was organized in eastern Russia and Siberia, augmented by forty thousand Czechs whom the Russians had captured during their war with Austria and who wanted to fight on the side of the Allies. Early in 1919 two other White armies were organized, one in the north and the other in the northwest.

In 1918 the government was beset by a new threat: Allied intervention. Russia's withdrawal from the war released great numbers of German troops for action on the western front and gave the Germans an opportunity to seize the large stocks of war material supplied to Russia by the Allies. To prevent this from happening and to gain whatever advantage they could from the seemingly certain disintegration of Russia, Allied nations ordered troops into northern and southern Russia and into Siberia. Only Japan, with 60,000 men, sent a large contingent. The United States sent about 8,500, Great Britain about 1,500, and France about 1,000; the other nations involved were represented by even smaller contingents. Although the Allied troops engaged in skirmishes with the Red Army, the major importance of the intervention lay in providing military supplies to the Whites and in blockading the Russian coasts. The Allies withdrew their troops in 1920, except for the Japanese, who remained in western Siberia until 1922 and in the Russian part of the island of Sakhalin until 1925. In the end the intervention accomplished nothing except to make the Russians suspicious of other powers and to embitter their relations with them for many years.

If the anticommunist forces had been as strong in the summer of 1918 as they ultimately became in 1919, the Bolshevik regime might have been overthrown. Their early weakness gave the Reds the opportunity to build up their own army under the inspired leadership of Leon Trotsky, a long-time revolutionary who became War Commissar in March, 1918. Until the end of 1919 victory seemed within the Whites' grasp. Then the tide turned. By the end of 1920 the Reds had triumphed and the civil war ended.

THE POLISH WAR AND NATIONAL SEPARATISM

The victory over the Whites did not bring an end to war. Early in 1920 the Poles, aided by Ukrainian nationalists and the southern White Army under General Wrangel, invaded the western Ukraine and White Russia, claiming that these territories belonged to Poland. The fortunes of battle went back and forth until French aid in the form of supplies and military advice won the upper hand for the Poles. Wearied of fighting, the Bolsheviks asked for peace in October, 1920. In the Treaty of Riga of March, 1921, they gave in to Polish demands for territories east of the Polish-Russian ethnic frontier (the so-called Curzon line, suggested in 1919 at the Versailles Peace Conference as the proper boundary between the two countries). More than 4 million Russians lived in these lands, a factor that disturbed Russo-Polish relations until World War II.

The Russians were also confronted with national independence movements in the Ukraine, Transcaucasia, and other frontier regions. In theory the Bolsheviks were committed to national self-determination for such peoples. When faced with concrete demands for independence, however, they proved as unwilling as their tsarist predecessors to free their subject nations and used troops and local Bolsheviks to reestablish Russian control. The status of the non-Russian nationalities remained unclear for two years after their reconquest. Then in 1922 Lenin decided to make Russia a federation, at least in name, against the advice of his specialist on nationality problems, the russified Georgian Josef Stalin. On December 30, 1922, the Union of Socialist Soviet Republics (U.S.S.R.) came into being. It was composed of the Russian Soviet Federated Socialist Republic (R.S.F.S.R.), including most of European Russia and Siberia, and the republics of the Ukraine, White Russia, and Transcaucasia. Later in the 1920's three central Asian republics were added. The federation was dominated by the R.S.F.S.R., the giant of the new organization. The other republics were allowed to retain a large measure of cultural autonomy, but political authority was exercised by Moscow, where the same small group of men controlled the machinery of both the Communist party and the government.

THE PEACE OF PARIS AND ITS AFTERMATH

While civil war raged in Russia, the diplomats of the victorious Allies gathered in Paris in January, 1919, to decide the fate of Germany and its defeated partners. Representatives of twenty-seven nations took part in the proceedings, although most major decisions were made by the Big Four: President Wilson; David Lloyd George, prime minister of Great Britain; Georges Clemenceau, premier of France; and Vittorio Orlando, prime minister of Italy. Since the Italian delegates boycotted the conference for a few weeks to protest the nonrecognition of some of their claims, many important decisions were made by the Big Three. Russia was not invited to the conference, and delegates from the defeated nations were called in only to accept the terms laid down to them. From the beginning, therefore, the conference took on the appearance of a cabal of the victors intended to parcel out the spoils of war.

The Allied leaders were by no means unanimous on the treatment to be accorded to the vanquished. With Clemenceau and the French people generally, the desire for revenge was uppermost; they demanded not only territorial compensation for the humiliation of 1870–71 but also reparations for the heavy costs of the war and security against further German aggression. The Italians demanded large territorial acquisitions at the expense of the now defunct Austro-Hungarian and Ottoman empires, basing their claim on the secret treaty of 1915. Although Lloyd George was personally disposed to moderation, he found himself hampered by the success of his own wartime propaganda in stirring up the British people to hatred of the Germans; as recently as December, 1918, his coalition government had won a general election with promises to punish German leaders and make Germany pay for the war. The claims of the lesser Allies had also to be heeded. Belgium demanded reparation for war damage. Japan had already seized Germany's Chinese and Pacific

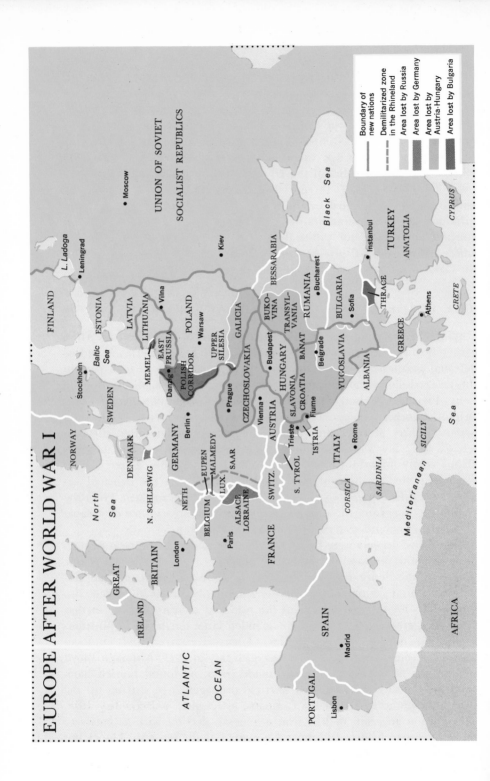

EUROPE AFTER WORLD WAR I

Boundary of
new nations

Demilitarized zone
in the Rhineland

Area lost by Russia

Area lost by Germany

Area lost by
Austria-Hungary

Area lost by Bulgaria

UNION OF SOVIET
SOCIALIST REPUBLICS

Moscow

L. Ladoga
Leningrad

FINLAND

ESTONIA

LATVIA

LITHUANIA

Vilna

Kiev

Black Sea

CYPRUS

TURKEY

Instanbul

ANATOLIA

CRETE

BESSARABIA

Bucharest

RUMANIA

BUKO-
VINA

TRANSYL-
VANIA

GALICIA

Warsaw

POLAND

UPPER
SILESIA

BULGARIA

Sofia

THRACE

Athens

GREECE

Baltic
Sea

Stockholm

SWEDEN

EAST
PRUSSIA

MEMEL

Danzig

POLISH
CORRIDOR

Prague

CZECHOSLOVAKIA

Budapest

HUNGARY

BANAT

Belgrade

YUGOSLAVIA

ALBANIA

NORWAY

DENMARK

N. SCHLESWIG

Berlin

GERMANY

EUPEN
MALMEDY

SAAR

Vienna

AUSTRIA

CROATIA

SLAVONIA

Fiume

Trieste

ISTRIA

ITALY

Rome

SARDINIA

SICILY

Sea

North
Sea

NETH.

BELGIUM

LUX.

SWITZ.

S. TYROL

ALSACE
LORRAINE

Paris

FRANCE

CORSICA

Mediterranean

GREAT
BRITAIN

London

IRELAND

ATLANTIC

OCEAN

SPAIN

Madrid

PORTUGAL

Lisbon

AFRICA

possessions. The successor states of the Austro-Hungarian Empire, who had been accorded de facto recognition by the Allies before the end of the war, began to squabble among themselves over disputed territory. The situation in Russia posed a grave threat to the stability of any attempted settlement in eastern Europe.

Only the United States made no territorial or financial claims on the defeated nations. President Wilson, the first American president to travel abroad during his term of office, received tumultuous popular ovations on his way to the conference. Wilson's personal popularity and the enthusiasm in Europe for the United States overshadowed temporarily the gulf between American and Allied war aims, but it did not alter the basic situation. Wilson's vision of the peace was based upon his Fourteen Points, above all on the provision for an international organization that would keep the peace. The Fourteen Points had been accepted by the Germans as the basis of the armistice, but neither Wilson nor the Germans reckoned sufficiently with the determination of the other Allies to press for a vindictive settlement. France and Britain had no great enthusiasm for Wilson's proposed "League of Nations" but used it as a bargaining counter to force concessions from Wilson on reparations and other matters of importance to them. The final form of the treaties, therefore, represented a series of compromises among the victors. The representatives of Germany and the other defeated nations had no option but to sign or face invasion and occupation.

The actual treaties received the names of the various suburbs of Paris in which they were signed. They were the Treaty of Versailles, with Germany (June 28, 1919); the Treaty of Saint-Germain, with Austria (September 10, 1919); the Treaty of Neuilly, with Bulgaria (November 27, 1919); the Treaty of the Trianon, with Hungary (June 4, 1920); and the Treaty of Sèvres, with Turkey (August 20, 1920).

THE TREATY OF VERSAILLES

The armistice of November 11, 1918, was dictated by the French military commander Marshal Foch and signed with only minor modifications by Matthias Erzberger, a German civilian and member of the new provisional government. It was designed to make it impossible for Germany to resume the war. It required the surrender of the entire German submarine fleet, most of the rest of the navy, 5,000 locomotives, 5,000 motor trucks, 150,000 freight cars, and large quantities of arms and munitions. It also provided for German evacuation and Allied occupation of the Rhineland and required that Germany renounce the treaties of Brest Litovsk and Bucharest. All these provisions of the armistice were incorporated in the Versailles Treaty, along with many others more severe.

The treaty deprived Germany of about one-tenth of its prewar territory and a corresponding proportion of its population. Alsace-Lorraine was

The "Big Four" at Versailles, 1919. Left to right: Lloyd George,
Vittorio Orlando, Georges Clemenceau, and Woodrow Wilson.

> *"Clemenceau (having seen with his own eyes the Palais de St. Cloud smoking
> across the flames of 1871) was, and with every justification, obsessed by the
> need of French security. Mr. Lloyd George . . . hoped to combine the vae victis
> which the British Public expected, with the more reasonable pacification which
> his own instincts desired. And Signor Orlando, exponent of sacred egoism,
> sincerely strove to provide his unstable country with those spoils by which
> alone (so he imagined) the demon of socialism could be exorcised. . . .
> President Wilson disagreed with almost everything his colleagues
> suggested."* Harold Nicolson, PEACEMAKING, 1919 (Boston, 1933).

returned to France. France occupied the coal-rich Saar Valley, where it
operated the coal mines for itself; the treaty provided for a plebiscite
after fifteen years to determine the wishes of the inhabitants. Belgium
received three small border communes. Wilson blocked a French proposal
for a separate buffer state in the Rhineland, but he agreed to its demili-
tarization and occupation by the Allies for fifteen years. A plebiscite in
Schleswig resulted in the northern part of that province returning to
Denmark. In the east, Germany gave up Posen and West Prussia to the
new state of Poland; West Prussia formed Poland's "corridor to the sea"
and separated East Prussia from the rest of Germany. The German-
speaking city of Danzig on the Baltic Sea became a free city within the
Polish customs frontier. Poland also secured the most valuable part of
Upper Silesia with its important mineral resources, although a plebiscite
yielded a German majority for the province as a whole. Germany re-

nounced claims on its former colonies, which had already been seized by the Allies.

The Allies sought to prevent future German aggression by rigid limitations on its war-making potential. In addition to Allied occupation of the Rhineland (with Germany bearing the costs) a belt thirty miles wide on the right (east) bank of the Rhine was demilitarized. The German army was to be limited to 100,000 men, and the General Staff was to be abolished. Germany might possess no tanks, no heavy artillery, no poison gas, no military aircraft, and no submarines. The navy was limited to six capital ships and a few supporting craft, and the naval base at Helgoland was razed. Finally, the emperor and the top military leaders were to be handed over for trial as "war criminals." Several of these provisions were never carried out effectively. The Dutch government refused to surrender the emperor, and charges were brought against only a few of the other leaders. In subsequent years the Germans found ways of circumventing the restrictions on their armed forces. The General Staff remained intact.

The Allies also imposed commercial restrictions on the Germans. They had to hand over all merchant ships of over 1,600 tons, half of those between 800 and 1,600 tons, and a quarter of the fishing fleet, as well as much coal and other raw materials. The German rivers were internationalized, and the Kiel canal was opened to the shipping of all nations. German property in Allied countries was confiscated and sold, and Germany's power to impose tariffs and other trade barriers was restricted.

The wisdom and expediency of these measures have often been debated. Many argued that they were not severe enough, especially Frenchmen. Others, the proponents of a "soft" peace, alleged that by so penalizing the Germans the peace treaty built up a store of bitterness and resentment that made a resumption of aggression inevitable. The validity of the arguments cannot be established, for the actual course of subsequent events was compatible with both. It is a fact that the treaty did not provide adequate means for enforcing all the penalties it imposed. In that sense it was unwise. Of far greater significance, however, were two additional provisions of the treaty.

WAR GUILT AND GERMAN REPARATIONS

Article 231 of the Treaty of Versailles read as follows: "The Allied and Associated Governments affirm and Germany accepts the responsibility of Germany and her allies for causing all the loss and damage to which the Allied and Associated Governments and their nationals have been subjected as a consequence of the war imposed upon them by the aggression of Germany and her allies." This statement was intended to justify Allied claims to German reparations, but at the same time it saddled Germany with the entire moral blame for the war, including the actions of its allies. In subsequent years it served to discredit the republic that accepted it and enabled the Germans to persuade themselves that the entire treaty lacked any moral force.

The question of reparations was itself a complex matter that excited angry passions on both sides. France and Britain demanded that Germany pay not only damages to civilians (reparations proper) but also the entire cost incurred by the Allied governments in prosecuting the war (an indemnity). Wilson made no claims for the United States and tried to dissuade the others from pressing theirs; but the American argument was not a strong one inasmuch as the United States insisted on repayment in full of the large loans it had made to the Allies to enable them to prosecute the war. A stronger but equally unheeded argument was put forward by the British economist John Maynard Keynes (1883–1946), who pointed out the literal impossibility of requiring Germany to pay the full costs of the war. According to him, even to force Germany to pay any sizable fraction would seriously derange the international economy and react adversely on the economic interests of the Allies themselves, as well as endanger the economic viability and political stability of Germany. His prediction proved to be all too accurate. The eventual compromise required Germany to pay as much as the Allies thought they could possibly extract, but in deference to Wilson the entire amount was called "reparations."

The method of assessing and collecting the reparations added further to German difficulties and exasperation. Since the Allied experts were unable to estimate the maximum bill before the treaty was signed, the treaty merely stated that the German government would be notified of the full amount it would have to pay "on or before May 1, 1921." In the meantime it would have to pay 5 billion dollars, against which offsets were allowed for confiscated German property and deliveries in kind. The sum ultimately imposed on April 27, 1921, was 33 billion dollars, an amount several times as large as Germany's total annual national income.

That German government that signed the onerous and humiliating *Diktat* of Versailles — as it was subsequently called in Germany, notably by Adolf Hitler — was not the government that fought the war. Immediately after the emperor's enforced abdication a new ministry formed by the Socialists, the Center party, and the Progressives (or Democrats, as they renamed themselves) proclaimed a republic and called for elections to a national assembly to draw up a new constitution. With the emperor in exile and the army in defeat, the chief opposition to the new republic came at first from the radical left wing of the old Social Democratic party, who now called themselves Spartacists. In January, 1919, they attempted a revolution of the Bolshevik type in Berlin. Although they were defeated by the provisional government with the aid of the remnants of the army, the revolt constituted a bad omen for the fledgling republic. In subsequent years the republic had to fend off domestic attacks from both Communists and the extreme Right as well as to struggle with the burdens laid on it by the Allies.

When the terms of the Treaty of Versailles became known, several ministers resigned rather than sign it. Their successors faced up to the inevitable, for Germany was in no position to resist. After futile attempts to have the war guilt clause removed, the government accepted the treaty rather than undergo indefinite occupation by Allied forces.

REDRAWING THE MAP OF EASTERN EUROPE

The minor treaties with Austria, Hungary, Bulgaria, and Turkey sought vainly to impress the seal of legitimacy on accomplished facts. The basic dispositions had already been made on the field of battle in the last weeks of the war, but continuing civil and international conflict kept the entire area of eastern Europe and the Near East in an unsettled state for several years after the conclusion of the treaties.

The breakup of the Austro-Hungarian Empire had been decided by the Congress of Oppressed Nationalities meeting at Rome in April, 1918, and by the action of various national councils of the subject nationalities. The emperor abdicated on November 11, 1918, and the proclamation of separate republics in Austria and Hungary soon followed. The Treaty of Saint-Germain ratified this situation but at the same time forced the new republic of Austria to pay reparations on behalf of the old empire. Austria recognized the independence of Czechoslovakia, Yugoslavia, Poland, and Hungary, and ceded the Trentino, South Tyrol, and Trieste to Italy. Formerly the center of an empire of 50 million, Austria was now a truncated state of less than 8 million whose economic viability was subject to great doubt. The Austrians themselves would have preferred to unite with Germany, but although this course was in accord with Wilson's principle of self-determination, it was specifically forbidden by both the Saint-Germain and the Versailles treaties.

Revolution, counterrevolution, and border wars delayed the separate treaty with Hungary until June 4, 1920. In March, 1919, a Communist revolt headed by Bela Kun overthrew the new republic and promptly went to war with Czechoslovakia and Rumania, who were destined under the peace treaty to receive large slices of Hungarian territory. The Rumanians were victorious. They overthrew the Communists and occupied Budapest from August, 1919, until February, 1920, when the great powers persuaded them to withdraw. In March, 1920, Admiral Nicholas Horthy proclaimed Hungary a monarchy with a vacant throne and named himself regent and chief of state. The counterrevolution in effect restored the old order. The Treaty of the Trianon, which in its territorial provisions merely confirmed decisions already made, sheared the historic kingdom of Hungary of almost three-fourths of its territory and two-thirds of its population. Yugoslavia took Croatia, Slavonia, and part of the Banat of Temesvar; Rumania took the rest of the Banat, Transylvania, and part of the Hungarian plain; Slovakia was joined to Bohemia in the new state of Czechoslovakia; and Austria received a portion of western Hungary near Vienna. All these cessions provoked constant irritation between Hungary and its neighbors over the next twenty years. To insure themselves against Hungarian attempts to regain lost territory, Czechoslovakia, Rumania, and Yugoslavia formed the so-called Little Entente.

The Treaty of Neuilly cut Bulgaria back to less than its 1913 territory. Bulgaria gave up its Aegean coastline to Greece and other small bits of territory to Rumania and Yugoslavia. Like Austria and Hungary, Bulgaria had to make reparations payments and suffer restrictions on its armed forces. Nevertheless, of all the former Central Powers Bulgaria received the mildest treatment.

In Turkey the situation was even more complicated and confused than in Hungary. During the war the Allies had made several secret treaties regarding the disposition of the old Ottoman Empire, envisioning among other things Russian occupation of Constantinople and Greek and Italian acquisitions on the mainland of Anatolia. After the Russian Revolution the Bolsheviks published these treaties to embarrass the Allies. President Wilson, who had not been a party to them, refused to recognize them as valid or binding. Nevertheless, the Greeks and Italians supported by other Allied forces made landings in Asia Minor. In August, 1920, the helpless government of the sultan was forced to sign the Treaty of Sèvres. By this treaty Turkey renounced all non-Turkish territory (principally the Arab states at the eastern end of the Mediterranean) and recognized the Greek and Italian claims on Anatolia.

Meanwhile, the Turkish Nationalist movement under the leadership of Mustapha Kemal (later called Kemal Atatürk — father of the Turks), who advocated a strictly Turkish nation following the modern Western model, had been gathering strength in inland centers since the end of the war. After the signing of the Treaty of Sèvres the Nationalist movement definitely broke with the government of the sultan and refused to recognize the treaty. Obtaining military supplies from Soviet Russia, Kemal's forces launched a counterattack against the Greeks and persuaded the Italians to withdraw. After routing the Greeks in 1922, they deposed the sultan and abolished the sultanate. In the following year Kemal's government signed the Treaty of Lausanne, which replaced the inoperative Treaty of Sèvres and became the definitive treaty of peace between Turkey and the Allies. Turkey abandoned all claims to non-Turkish territory but regained eastern Thrace, including the city of Adrianople. Greece retained most of the Aegean Islands, and Italy retained the Dodecanese, but both renounced claims on Anatolia, and Greece agreed to a large-scale compulsory exchange of populations. More than a million Greeks whose ancestors had lived in Asia Minor since ancient times were eventually repatriated to Greece, and a somewhat smaller number of Turks living in Greece took their places. Finally, Britain obtained formal possession of Cyprus, which it had occupied since 1878.

POSTWAR POLITICAL TURMOIL

The conclusion of the peace treaties did not mean the end of conflict in eastern Europe. Despite the pious pronouncements at Paris, it proved impossible to settle the boundaries "along clearly recognizable lines of nationality." In fact, the new frontiers left 3 million Germans inside the new state of Czechoslovakia, half a million both in Poland and Yugoslavia, and lesser numbers in the other countries. A million and a half Magyars lived under Rumanian control, 700,000 lived in Czechoslovakia, and 500,000 lived in Yugoslavia. Italy and Yugoslavia disputed the possession of Fiume and the Dalmatian coast until 1924, when Italy acquired Fiume in exchange for other coastal points. Yugoslavia was also torn by internal strife over the demands of the Croatians for a federal state in opposition to the Serbian desire for centralization. Italy and Greece resorted to warfare over the island of Corfu in 1923.

Greece, like most other Balkan countries, had its share of internal troubles. King Constantine, who had been deposed in 1917, was recalled in 1920 but deposed again in 1922. His son, George II, followed him into exile the following year. The Greeks proclaimed a republic in 1924, then recalled George in 1935. Meanwhile the country had been ruled by a succession of military juntas, one of which countenanced an invasion of Bulgaria in 1925. Bulgaria, for its part, engaged in border raids on Yugoslavia.

Austria and Hungary disputed the Burgenland, a small strip of land in historic Hungary only fifteen miles from Vienna and populated mainly by Germans. As a result of a plebiscite in 1921 most of it went to Austria. Because of its tense relations with its neighbors, Hungary's internal problems sometimes had international repercussions. On two occasions in 1921 ex-emperor Karl of Hapsburg returned to assume the royal dignity in Budapest, but on both occasions threats by Yugoslavia and Czechoslovakia to go to war forced the Hungarians to return him to exile. Hungary remained a monarchy without a king.

Poland proved to be one of the most troublesome countries of eastern Europe. It owed its resurrection in the first instance to rival attempts by Russians and Germans during the war to win Polish support with promises of independence. The Allies also promised independence, and the Treaty of Versailles fixed the western boundaries of the country, subject to slight subsequent alterations. A brief border war flared between Poland and Czechoslovakia in 1919–20 over the former Duchy of Teschen; Allied diplomats settled the matter by a division of the disputed area. In Upper Silesia the Poles refused to accept the results of a plebiscite in which the inhabitants voted overwhelmingly for reunion with Germany. A force of Polish irregulars occupied the area and with French support obtained a decision from the League of Nations granting the most important industrial areas to Poland.

The eastern boundary could not be settled in Paris owing to the absence of the Russians. British foreign minister Lord Curzon suggested a line drawn along the rather indistinct linguistic frontier that deprived the Poles of the city of Vilna. They occupied Vilna in defiance of the League of Nations and precipitated a long dispute with the new Baltic state of Lithuania. The Poles insisted on their historic boundaries of 1772, which included large areas of White Russia and the Ukraine and involved them in war with Russia. In 1921 the Polish borders were temporarily stabilized, but their long, exposed land frontiers populated by alien ethnic groups remained a constant temptation to the aggressive ambitions of resurgent Germany and Russia.

Russia for its part made a virtue of weakness while still in the midst of its own civil war. The Bolsheviks denounced imperialism and disclaimed any territorial ambitions beyond the historic frontiers of Russia proper. In 1920 they recognized the independence of Finland, Estonia, Latvia, and Lithuania. In 1921 they signed the Treaty of Riga with Poland and made treaties of friendship with Turkey, Persia (Iran), and Afghanistan. To Turkey and Persia they ceded small bits of disputed territory in the Caucasus area. In 1922, in the wake of an unsuccessful general European conference at Genoa, the two pariahs of Europe, Germany and the Soviet Union, concluded at Rapallo, Italy, a far-reaching agreement of friendship that contained provisions for mutual economic, technical, and military assistance. Although the Soviet-German understanding proved to be unstable, it enabled both countries to circumvent restrictions placed upon them by the victorious Western powers and cast a shadow of things to come.

THE GERMAN INFLATION

Germany's capacity to pay reparations depended ultimately on its ability to export more than it imported in order to gain the foreign currency or gold in which the payments had to be made. For a time it maintained a small surplus, but the other economic restrictions imposed by the treaty ensured that the surplus could never be large enough to meet the entire bill. Moreover, economic interests adversely affected by German competition persuaded Allied governments to raise new barriers against German exports, adding further to Germany's difficulties. In the late summer of 1922 the value of the German mark began to decline disastrously as a result of the heavy pressure of reparations payments. By the end of the year the pressure was so great that Germany ceased payments altogether.

French and Belgian troops promptly invaded the Ruhr in January, 1923, took over the coal mines and railroads, and attempted to force the German mine owners and workers to deliver coal. The Germans met the occupation with passive resistance: the miners, supported by both the mining companies and the government, refused to work. The government printed huge quantities of paper money to distribute as compensation payments to workers and employers, setting in motion a wave of uncontrolled inflation. The impasse lasted until the autumn of 1923, by which time the mark had depreciated to such an infinitesimal figure that it was worth less than the paper on which it was printed.

The adverse consequences of the inflation could not be confined to Germany. The French franc depreciated by one-fourth, and the international economy was confronted by a crisis much as Keynes had predicted. The French withdrew from the Ruhr, and a hastily convoked international commission under the chairmanship of Charles G. Dawes, an American investment banker, recommended a scaling down of annual reparations payments, the reorganization of the German Reichsbank, and a large international loan to Germany. Meanwhile a German financial expert, Hjalmar Schacht, initiated a plan to replace the depreciated and discredited German currency. As a result of these operations, especially the large loan to Germany (most of which was raised in the United States), the German economy revived and actually prospered with a continued inflow of American capital until the new and greater international economic crisis that lasted from 1929 to 1933.

The disastrous inflation left deep scars on German society. The unequal incidence of inflation on individuals resulted in drastic redistributions of income and wealth. While a few clever speculators gained enormous fortunes from the sudden and violent fluctuation of financial values, most citizens, especially the lower middle classes, saw their modest savings wiped out in a matter of months or even weeks. People whose money income was fixed (pensioners, bond holders, many salaried employees) suffered a sharp decline in their standard of living as a result of the lowered purchasing power of their fixed incomes. The inflation created personal hardship and social discontent, with many of those affected becoming converted to radical political programs of both the Right and the Left. Significantly, both Communists and Nationalists made large gains at the expense of the moderate democratic parties in the

Reichstag elections in the spring of 1924. In the following year retired Field Marshal von Hindenburg, candidate of the Rightist parties, became president, succeeding the Social Democrat Friedrich Ebert.

The Dawes Plan temporarily relieved but did not solve the problems created by reparations. In the summer of 1929 a new international commission headed by the American Owen D. Young reported a plan designed as a permanent solution. Before it could take effect the great crisis of 1929 again threw the international economy into a tailspin. As the financial crisis deepened President Hoover in 1931 proposed a one-year moratorium on all intergovernmental debts, including reparations and the inter-Allied war debts. In effect, the moratorium marked the end of reparations. Before normal financial relations could be resumed, Adolf Hitler came to power in Germany and proclaimed an end to "interest slavery."

ECONOMIC DISINTEGRATION AND COLLAPSE

Prior to 1914 the world economy had functioned freely and on the whole efficiently. In spite of some restrictions in the form of protective tariffs, private monopolies, and international cartels, the bulk of economic activity was regulated by free markets. The prices of commodities were determined not by governmental fiat but by supply and demand. A rise in the price of one commodity constituted a signal to the entire world that the commodity was in short supply in relation to demand, and the rise would accordingly stimulate an increase in production that tended to restore the price to equilibrium; conversely, a fall in price indicated an oversupply in relation to demand and was similarly self-adjusting. As a consequence, each area of the world tended to specialize in the production of goods for which it was best suited, taking into account its resources, the skills and education of its population, and other natural and acquired advantages.

Another feature of the prewar international economy was a general adherence to the gold standard. Most nations undertook to buy or sell their national currencies for a fixed weight of gold, which guaranteed stability of exchange rates (the rate at which one currency could be exchanged for another) and stimulated international trade and investment. These and other features made the world economy highly specialized and interdependent. Each nation depended on the others for goods that it did not produce and, in many cases, for capital as well. Such interdependence had the supreme advantage of greatly increasing productivity for the world as a whole, but it also had the disadvantage of making the economy extremely susceptible to outside shocks, of which war was the most damaging.

ECONOMIC CONSEQUENCES OF THE WAR

In addition to human casualties, direct war damage during World War I included the destruction of housing, industrial plants and equipment, livestock and farm equipment, transportation and communications facilities, and so forth. Most of the damage took place in northern France, Belgium, a small area of northeastern Italy, and the battlefields of eastern Europe. Ocean shipping also suffered greatly, primarily as a result of submarine warfare. The damage has been estimated at more than $150 billion, although such estimates are by their nature subject to wide margins of error. Not included are losses of production such as those occasioned by shortages of manpower and raw materials in industry or by overcropping and lack of fertilizer and draft animals in agriculture. In central and eastern Europe, which were cut off from economic relations with the rest of the world and further disrupted by the marching and countermarching of armies, the fall in agricultural output had reduced large areas to the point of mass starvation.

The war also occasioned indirect damage to the economic mechanism as a result of the disruption and dislocation of normal economic relations. Unlike the direct damage, the indirect damage did not cease with the war itself but continued to take its toll well into the postwar decade. In every belligerent nation the imposition of direct governmental controls on prices, production, and labor distorted the normal relationships of the economy, artificially stimulating some sectors and restricting others. The reestablishment of peacetime relationships after the removal of controls took place with difficulty. An immediate postwar boom in 1919–20, during which both consumers and producers sought to make up for wartime shortages, was followed in 1920–21 by a severe but relatively brief recession.

A more lasting dislocation resulted from the loss of foreign markets. During the war overseas nations undertook to manufacture for themselves or buy from other overseas nations goods that they had formerly purchased in Europe. Several Latin American and Asian nations established manufacturing industries which they protected after the war with high tariffs. The United States and Japan, which had already developed important manufactures before the war, expanded into overseas markets formerly regarded as the exclusive preserve of European manufacturers. Britain, highly dependent on overseas trade, was especially hard hit; Germany but slightly less so.

As had the loss of foreign markets, the loss of income from shipping and other services retarded the recovery of the European economy. Before the war Britain had by far the largest merchant fleet in the world; it carried goods not only to and from Britain, but also between foreign countries, thus adding substantially to Britain's overseas income. Britain emerged from the war with its fleet much diminished, while the United States had a greatly augmented merchant fleet and became a major competitor in international shipping for the first time since the American Civil War. Germany, which had to give up its merchant fleet in payment of reparations, also suffered. London and to a lesser extent other European financial centers likewise lost some of their income from banking, insurance, and other financial and commercial services, which had been transferred to New York and elsewhere (Switzerland, for example) during the war.

Before the war Britain, France, and Germany were the most important foreign investors. Since Britain and France in particular imported more than they exported, the income from foreign investments supplemented other invisible income (from banking and insurance, for instance) to close the gap left by the visible trade. Germany's investments in belligerent countries were confiscated during the war, and subsequently all were liquidated against reparations claims. Britain and France were both obliged to sell many of their investments to finance the purchase of urgently needed war materials. Other investments declined in value as a result of inflation and related currency difficulties. Still others suffered default or outright repudiation, notably the large French investments in Russia, which the Soviet government refused to recognize. Since Britain was the largest foreign investor as well as the most dependent on imported foodstuffs and raw materials, again it suffered most. The United States, on the other hand, converted itself from a net debtor into a net creditor as a result of its large loans to the Allies.

A fifth dislocation in both national and international economies resulted from inflation. The pressures of wartime finance forced all belligerents (and some nonbelligerents) except the United States off the gold standard. They all resorted to large-scale borrowing and the printing of paper money to finance the war. This caused prices to rise (which is the equivalent of a decline in the value of money), though they did not all rise in the same proportion. At the end of the war prices in the United States were on the average about 2.5 times as high as in 1914; in Britain, about 3 times; in France, about 5.5 times; in Germany, more than 15 times; and in Bulgaria, more than 20 times. The great disparity in prices and in the values of currency made the resumption of international trade difficult, and caused unfortunate social and political repercussions such as those in Germany.

ECONOMIC CONSEQUENCES OF THE PEACE

As though the wartime damage and dislocations were not enough, the peace settlement further exacerbated the difficulty of economic recovery and readjustment. The peacemakers did not intend this to happen (except in the treatment of Germany); they simply failed to take account of economic realities. Two major categories of economic difficulty resulted from the peace treaties: the growth of economic nationalism, and monetary and financial problems. In neither of them were the peace treaties solely to blame; yet in both the treaties added to the problems involved instead of attempting to solve them.

The prewar Austro-Hungarian Empire, however politically anachronistic, had performed a valuable economic function by providing a large free-trade area in the Danube basin. It encompassed manufacturing areas in Bohemia and the vicinity of Vienna and other large cities, as well as vast agricultural regions in the Hungarian and Slavic parts of the empire. The interchange of goods was mutually beneficial. The new nations that issued from the breakup of the empire were jealous of one another and fearful of great power domination. They therefore asserted their nationhood in the economic sphere by trying to become more or less self-sufficient in both agricultural and industrial production. Although complete self-sufficiency was a manifest impossibility because of their small size and generally backward economic condition, their efforts to achieve it hindered the economic recovery of the entire region and added to its instability. The height of absurdity came with the disruption of transportation. Before the war two large railroad companies had served the entire empire. Immediately after the war when borders were subject to dispute and border fighting continued, each country simply refused to allow the railroad locomotives and cars in its territory to leave. For a time trade came to an almost complete standstill. Eventually international agreements overcame such extremes of economic nationalism, but other types of restriction remained: in addition to protective tariffs, new devices in the form of physical quotas and discriminatory treatment of foreign merchandise.

Economic nationalism was not restricted to the new nations that emerged from the breakup of empires. During its civil war Russia simply disappeared from the international economy. When it re-emerged under the Soviet regime, its economic relations were conducted in a manner completely different from any previously experienced. The state became the sole buyer and seller in international trade. It bought and sold only what its political rulers regarded as strategically necessary or expedient.

In the West, countries that formerly had been highly dependent on international trade resorted to a variety of restrictions including protective tariffs and also more drastic curtailments on trade, such as import quotas and absolute prohibitions. At the same time they sought to stimulate their own exports by granting export subsidies or setting the foreign exchange value of their currencies at artificially low rates. Among the major European nations France was one of the worst offenders, but it was by no means alone. Great Britain, before the war the great champion of free international trade, had imposed tariffs during the war as a measure of war finance. They remained after the war, and in the 1920's new industries producing for the domestic market grew up beneath the umbrella of tariff protection. The United States, which already had relatively high tariffs before the war, raised them to unprecedented levels thereafter. The Emergency Tariff Act of 1921 placed an absolute embargo on imports of German dyestuffs. (The dyestuff industry had not even existed in the United States before the war; it began with the confiscation of German patent rights during the war.) The Fordney-McCumber Tariff Act of 1922 contained the highest rates in American tariff history, but even those were surpassed by the Smoot-Hawley Tariff of 1930.

The adverse economic consequences of this neomercantilism, as such policies were called, did not stop with the immediate application of the laws in question. Each new measure of restriction provoked retaliation by other nations whose interests were affected. Whereas total world trade had more than doubled in the two decades before the war, it rarely achieved the prewar level in the two decades that followed. During the same period the foreign trade of European countries, which had also doubled in the two prewar decades, equaled the prewar figure in but a single year — 1929. In 1932 and 1933 it was lower than it had been at the end of the nineteenth century. Such exaggerated economic nationalism delayed the return to normal economic intercourse between nations and contributed to the heightening of tension in international politics.

The monetary and financial disorders occasioned by the war and gravely aggravated by the peace treaties led eventually to a complete breakdown of the international economy. The problem of reparations was at the heart of these disorders, but the "reparations tangle" was in reality a complex problem involving the question of inter-Allied war debts and the whole mechanism of international finance. The insistence of Allied statesmen, especially Americans, in treating each question in isolation instead of recognizing their relationships was a major factor in the subsequent debacle.

Until the United States entered the war, Britain was the chief financier of the Allied war effort. By 1917 it had loaned almost 4 billion dollars to its allies. France had loaned 500 million, roughly equal to its borrowings from Britain. Over half of all these loans had gone to Russia and were repudiated by the Soviet regime at the end of the war. When the United States entered the war, it took over the role of financier from Britain, whose financial resources were almost exhausted. By the end of the war inter-Allied debts had reached almost 20 billion dollars, about one-half of which had been loaned by the United States government. Among the European allies the loans had been loans in name only;

actually they treated them as direct subsidies and expected to cancel the indebtedness at the end of the war. They naturally regarded the American loans in the same light, all the more in that the United States had been a latecomer to the war, had contributed less in both manpower and materials, and had suffered negligible war damage. The United States, however, regarded the loans as commercial propositions. Although it agreed after the war to lower the rate of interest and lengthen the period of repayment, it insisted on repayment of the principal in full.

The failure to link the question of war debts with that of reparations revealed the full extent of misunderstanding of the basic problem. The United States wanted the Allies to renounce reparations altogether, or at least hold them to a minimum, but at the same time insisted on repayment of the war debts. The French wanted the United States to cancel the war debts but insisted on collecting reparations. The British suggested the cancellation of both, but the Americans stubbornly refused to recognize any relationship between the two. The American attitude was summed up in a remark subsequently made by President Coolidge: "They hired the money, didn't they?"

In fact, given the weakened economies of the European countries and the precarious state of the international economy, France, Britain, and the other allies could repay the United States' loans only if they received an equivalent amount in the form of reparations. Germany and the other defeated powers could in fact pay reparations only if they exported far more than they imported, or if they in turn received unilateral transfers of funds from an outside power. The crisis of 1923 revealed the inadequacy of the arrangements. The system was temporarily saved by the Dawes Plan of 1924 with its provision of a large international loan, chiefly from the United States, to allow Germany to get on its feet and resume reparations payments. It was followed by a further flow of American capital to Germany in the form of private loans to German municipalities and business corporations, who borrowed extensively in the United States and used the proceeds for modernization. In the process the German government obtained the foreign exchange it needed to pay reparations.

For the five years from 1924 to 1929 it seemed that "normalcy" had returned. Reconstruction of physical damage had been largely achieved; the most urgent and immediate postwar problems had been solved; and under the newly formed League of Nations and the "spirit of Locarno" (see pp. 894–895) a new era in international relations apparently had dawned. Most countries, especially the United States, Germany, and France, experienced a period of prosperity. Yet the basis of the prosperity was fragile indeed, depending on the continued voluntary flow of funds from America to Germany.

THE GREAT DEPRESSION

Unlike Europe, the United States emerged from the war stronger than ever. In economic terms alone, it had converted itself from a net debtor to a net creditor, had won new markets from European producers both at home and abroad, and had established a highly favorable balance of trade. With its mass markets, growing population, and rapid technological advance it seemed to have found the key to perpetual prosperity. Although it experienced a sharp depression in 1920–21, the drop proved to be brief, and for almost a decade its growing economy felt only minor fluctuations. Social critics who insisted on revealing the disgraceful conditions in both urban and rural slums, or who pointed out that the new prosperity was shared most unequally between the urban middle classes on the one hand and factory workers and farmers on the other, were dismissed by the former as cranks who did not share the American dream. For them the "new era" had arrived.

In the summer of 1928 American banks and investors began to cut down their purchase of German bonds in order to invest their funds through the New York stock market, which accordingly began a spectacular rise. During the speculative boom of the "great bull market" many individuals with modest incomes were tempted to purchase stock on credit. By the late summer of 1929 European economies were already feeling the strain of the cessation of American investments abroad, but since stock prices were at an all-time high, American investors and officials paid scant heed. With European financial institutions strained to the utmost in the attempt to continue international payments, and with American credit resources locked up in stock market speculation, any small quiver in the financial system could set off a chain reaction that might bring down the whole system.

On October 24, 1929 — Black Thursday in American financial history — a wave of panic selling on the stock exchange caused stock prices to plummet and eliminated millions of dollars of fictitious paper values. By mid-November the index of stock prices stood at half the peak it had reached before the crash. Banks called in loans, forcing still more investors to throw their stocks on the market at whatever prices they would bring. Americans who had invested in Europe ceased to make new investments and sold existing assets there in order to repatriate the funds. Throughout 1930 the withdrawal of capital from Europe continued, placing an intolerable strain on the entire financial system. In May, 1931, the Austrian Creditanstalt, one of the largest and most important banks in central Europe, suspended payments. The panic spread from bank to bank, industry to industry, country to country. Millions of workers in all countries were thrown out of work, adding further to the deflationary cycle.

Table 1   *Economic Collapse, 1929–1932*

	1929	1932
United States		
Index of industrial production	119	64
(1923–1925 = 100)		
Unemployed (in 1,000's)	1,864	13,182
General wholesale price index	139	95
(1910–1914 = 100)		
Foreign trade[1] (millions of dollars)	9,788	2,967
United Kingdom		
Index of industrial production	110.6	84.9
(1924 = 100)		
Unemployed (in 1,000's)	994	2,273
General wholesale price index	141.1	94.1
(1913 = 100)		
Foreign trade[1] (millions of dollars)	8,956	3,555
Germany		
Index of industrial production	101	60
(1928 = 100)		
Unemployed (in 1,000's)	1,679	5,575
General wholesale price index	137.2	96.5
(1913 = 100)		
Foreign trade[1] (millions of dollars)	6,415	2,471
France		
Index of industrial production	127	96
(1913 = 100)		
Unemployed (in 1,000's)	9.7	305
General wholesale price index	143	94
(1901–1910 = 100)		
Foreign trade[1] (millions of dollars)	4,247	1,945

[1] Imports plus exports.
Sources: E. Varga, *Mirovye Ekonomicheskie Krizisy 1848–1935* (Moscow, 1937), I, part II, tables 41, 42, 43, 44 for index of industrial production and general wholesale price index; International Labor Office, *Year-Book of Labor Statistics, 1935–36* (Geneva, 1936), table 1, for unemployment statistics; W. S. and E. S. Woytinsky, *World Commerce and Governments* (New York, 1955), pp. 48, 50 for foreign trade statistics.

President Hoover, forced by circumstances to recognize the interdependence of the international economy, called for a one-year moratorium on all intergovernmental payments in the summer of 1931, but it was too late to stem the panic. In September Great Britain, which had returned to the gold standard with great difficulty in 1925, was again forced off, followed by many others. After a severe American banking crisis that included thousands of failures and led to the decree of a four-day "bank holiday" as an emergency measure by Franklin Roosevelt, the new president, the United States also abandoned the gold standard in the spring of 1933. The international monetary chaos was complete.

CRISIS OF THE SPIRIT

The twentieth century began in an atmosphere of optimism. Pessimists were in a minority and spoke in muted voices. For the multitude the age was one of universal progress. In the European world living standards were improving more rapidly than ever, democracy was spreading at an unprecedented rate, and large-scale war seemed a thing of the past. World War I, followed by economic collapse and the rise of totalitarian political systems, brought radical changes in outlook. As early as 1918 Oswald Spengler, a German philosopher of history, published his influential book *The Decline of the West,* in which he asserted that Western civilization was dying. For many the titles of two of T. S. Eliot's poems, *The Waste Land* (1922) and *The Hollow Men* (1925), symbolized the spirit of the times. The latter concludes with the mockingly bitter lines

> This is the way the world ends
> Not with a bang but a whimper.

By the 1930's the dominant mood was one of stark pessimism.

A noted literary critic of the 1890's referred to fin-de-siècle literature as a "decadent movement." Decadent or not, it proved to be the germ of much creative literature of the next century, and especially of the grim interwar decades. The stylistic features of fin-de-siècle literature and art — symbolism and free verse in poetry, stream of consciousness in fiction, greater abstraction and nonobjectivism in painting and sculpture — were increasingly exploited and subjected to further experimentation and innovation. Cubism and futurism, the last of the pre-World War I fads in art, were succeeded by dadaism and surrealism. They had in common subjects drawn from dreams and the subconscious mind and methods of execution that seemed to lack conscious design. The dadaists were deliberately absurd in their revolt against prevailing taste, morality, and behavior. One of them wrote of their creations, "These pictures are Realities in themselves, without meaning or cerebral intention. We rejected everything that was copy or description, and allowed the Elementary and Spontaneous to react in full freedom." The fad of dadaism soon passed, but surrealism, which took itself more seriously, continued to influence young artists for many years. The most renowned artists of the first half of the twentieth century belonged to no single school, although they greatly influenced surrealism and similar movements. Among them were Marc Chagall, Vasily Kandinsky, Paul Klee, and the most famous of all, Pablo Picasso.

The new departure in music dated from the publication in 1911 of Arnold Schönberg's *Theory of Harmony.* Schönberg abandoned traditional scales in favor of the twelve-tone scale. Igor Stravinsky and Paul

Hindemith achieved similar effects with atonality and polytonality. The world premiere of Stravinsky's *Sacre du Printemps* in Paris in 1913 ended in a riot that had to be quelled by police; the composer escaped from the angry crowd through a window backstage. One of the early advocates of futurism in music wrote: "The art of combining musical sounds reached its peak at the end of the nineteenth century. In the music of the future the sounds of our mechanical civilization — its machinery and crowded cities — will be subtly combined into an art of noises."

In spite of the mood of disillusion and despair that darkened the interwar years, the need for postwar reconstruction and continued urbanization stimulated the development of new architectural forms. One of the most creative centers of architectural thought and design was the school called the Bauhaus, founded in Germany by Walter Gropius in 1919. In the Bauhaus Gropius brought together not only architects but also interior decorators, furniture designers, and even painters; Kandinsky and Klee were two of its teachers. The style of architecture that Gropius favored was functionalism. Le Corbusier (the pseudonym of the Franco-Swiss Charles-Edouard Jenneret), at one time associated with Gropius and one of the leading exponents of the new architecture, defined a house as "a machine for living in." The triumph of the Nazis, traditionalists in art and architecture, halted the innovations in Germany, but indirectly led to their spread elsewhere as many famous architects, Gropius himself among them, fled abroad.

The stupidity of war, the wastefulness of economic depression, and the divergence between the ideals and realities of Western culture gave rise to a literature of social protest. H. G. Wells wrote novels frankly intended as tracts for social reform. Marcel Proust, perhaps the outstanding French novelist of the first half of the twentieth century, pictured society in a state of dissolution as a result of inner moral corruption in outwardly respectable people. Aldous Huxley revolted against the stifling conformity fostered by the modern industrial system; his most famous novel, *Brave New World* (1932), is a bitter satire of that system. American writers such as Sinclair Lewis, John Steinbeck, John Dos Passos, and Ernest Hemingway depicted the futility of war, criticized the existence of poverty in the midst of plenty, and satirized the hypocritical complacency of America's middle classes. Another American author, Pearl Buck, became the third American to win a Nobel Prize for literature (after Lewis and Eugene O'Neill) for her sensitive, dramatic story of ordinary peasants caught up in the Chinese civil war, *The Good Earth* (1932). Two of the most influential novels of the period were the posthumously published works of a driven man, Franz Kafka; in both *The Trial* (1925) and *The Castle* (1926) a semi-anonymous anti-hero finds himself involved in a living nightmare in which his efforts to understand lead only to further bewilderment and eventual destruction. "Kafkaesque" became a synonym for the predicament of modern man, and his novels gained a prophetic reputation after the revelation of Nazi torture chambers and Russian purge trials.

Freudian thought exerted an enormous influence on literature in the interwar period and afterward. D. H. Lawrence was one of the earliest authors consciously affected by Freud, but after World War I very few writers could avoid his influence altogether. The greater frequency of sexual themes and symbols and the more graphic description of sexual episodes, even by writers otherwise ignorant of the significance of Freudian psychology, testified to his influence. Although writers of the stature of Thomas Mann, one of Germany's greatest novelists, did not emphasize sexual matters, they acknowledged the importance of Freud's elucidation of the role of subconscious motives and irrational drives in human nature. Freud's influence was also heavy on Eugene O'Neill, possibly the most powerful dramatist in any language in the interwar period. One of his closest rivals for that distinction was the Italian Luigi Pirandello whose play *Six Characters in Search of an Author* seemed to symbolize the confusion and aimlessness of the interwar years.

LIBERAL ATTEMPTS
AT RECONSTRUCTION
CHAPTER THIRTY-FOUR

The twentieth-century inheritors of nineteenth-century liberalism little realized the extent of the damage the war caused society. They regarded the war as a great catastrophe, but failed to perceive either its origins in the nineteenth century or its full implications for the future. For them it was one of the unfortunate accidents of history, the responsibility of a relatively small number of willful, malicious men — militarists and autocratic rulers. At most, it was evidence that the liberal reforms of the nineteenth century had not proceeded far enough in eliminating archaic survivals from the past. Accordingly, their program for postwar reconstruction was appealingly simple and straightforward, involving above all the extension of liberal principles to all areas of life. It implied further democratic reforms in countries that already had representative governments (women received the vote for the first time in Britain, Germany, the United States, and several smaller democracies in the decade following the war); the establishment of compact nation-states with parliamentary governments in areas of eastern Europe previously dominated by autocratic, multinational empires; and on the international plane the creation of an organization by means of which the independent nation-states, without surrendering their sovereignty, might work in concert for the maintenance of peace and social progress.

President Wilson typified this view of the world and its problems. His Fourteen Points gave the most concise statement of the liberals' war aims and the liberal program for reconstruction. Although the actual settlement did not accord with Wilson's points in every detail, it did so in its main outlines. That it did not produce the desired results — this became increasingly evident throughout the interwar period — caused spreading dismay among liberal theorists and policy makers. Shaken, but still clinging to the notion that their analysis of the problem had been basically correct, they were reduced to emergency expedients in dealing with the mounting crises. It is not surprising, therefore, that after events had falsified their earlier diagnosis, their subsequent attempts at reconstruction should have been hesitant, confused, and contradictory.

THE LEAGUE OF NATIONS AND COLLECTIVE SECURITY

Wilson regarded the League of Nations as the most vital part of post-war rehabilitation. In order to secure the adhesion of France and Britain he compromised his principles on many other points, notably the question of reparations, in the belief that the League itself would be able to rectify any defects or inequities in the treaties. He emphasized this feature in his opening address to the peace conference on January 25, 1919. "Settlements may be temporary, but the actions of the nations in the interests of peace and justice must be permanent. We can set up permanent processes. We may not be able to set up permanent decisions." Ironically, it was Wilson's insistence that the Covenant of the League be inserted as an integral part of each of the peace treaties that hampered the use of the League as an instrument of revision and conciliation, for it was thereafter identified by victors and vanquished alike with the settlement itself.

The League in no way constituted a superstate or world government. It was not even a federation of nations but merely a voluntary association. The framers of the Covenant, among whom Wilson was foremost, made it quite clear that the League did not infringe the sovereignty of any nation. It had no independent powers of coercion, and members might withdraw simply by giving notice. The League thus represented a return to the old idea of the concert of Europe on an extended and more formal basis. Even the provision for mutual aid to prevent or punish aggression — the famous concept of collective security — did not mark a new departure, for in that respect the Covenant resembled a multilateral defense treaty depending upon the good faith of the signatories to make its decisions effective, as was the case in all such treaties. The League was simply an application of nineteenth-century liberal political theory to international relations. Although in the beginning it was widely regarded as the foundation of a new world order, it was in effect only the capstone of the old. Unperceived by the architects, the true foundations had been shaken beyond repair.

In accordance with the provisions of the treaties, the League formally came into existence on January 10, 1920, although its first meeting did not take place until the following autumn. It began with forty-one charter members, growing to fifty by 1924. More significant than the quantity of members was the importance of some of the nonmembers.

Both Germany and Russia were excluded, outcasts from the society of nations. No less important, the United States, whose elected leader was the father of the League, refused to join. Under the United States Constitution ratification of treaties and international agreements required the concurrence of at least two-thirds of the Senate. In the elections of 1918 the Republicans had gained control of both houses of Congress; in effect, Wilson had lost a vote of confidence just before leaving for the peace conference. Although the Senate contained several of Wilson's personal enemies, they opposed him not just for personal reasons or for the sake of opposition, but because a strong current of opinion in the country at large advocated a return to America's historic policy of diplomatic isolation and noninterference in European affairs. The League was, of course, primarily a European body. After long and bitter debates the Senate refused to ratify the Treaty of Versailles in March, 1920. Although the vote was actually against the League, it had the incidental effect of leaving the United States technically at war with Germany; this situation was not remedied until 1921.

ORGANIZATION

The League consisted of two principal deliberative bodies; the Council and the Assembly. The latter included the entire membership on the basis of one nation, one vote. With few exceptions, all major decisions had to receive unanimous approval in the Assembly in order to take effect. The most important exception prevented members who were party to a dispute from voting on that question. The Council acted as a sort of steering committee for the Assembly, deciding (also by the rule of unanimity) what matters might be discussed in the larger body. The initial draft of the Covenant provided for five permanent members of the Council (the United States, Britain, France, Italy, and Japan) and four rotating members elected by the Assembly. When the United States refused to join, the number of permanent members was reduced to four. The rotating membership was raised to six in 1922 and nine in 1926. Of the four permanent members of the Council, Japan and Italy withdrew from the League in 1933 and 1937, respectively, after being charged with aggression, and subsequently went to war against the others. Of all the great powers only Britain and France — neither of whom had been enthusiastic about the League at its beginning — belonged throughout the interwar period. This fact lent some substance to the charges that the real effect of the League, if not its original purpose, was simply to preserve the advantages that France and Britain had gained by the treaties.

In addition to the Council and Assembly the League maintained a permanent secretariat at its headquarters in Geneva and sponsored a number of specialized agencies. Among the more important of the latter were the Permanent Court of International Justice, set up in The Hague

Meeting of the Council of the League of Nations

> *"Ah, gentlemen, the cynics, the detractors of the League of Nations, those*
> *who take pleasure daily in putting its solidity in doubt and who periodically*
> *announce its disappearance, what are they thinking if they attend this session?*
> *Is it not a moving spectacle, especially edifying and comforting, that, only a*
> *few years after the most frightful war in history, with the battlefields almost*
> *still damp with blood, the same nations that fought one another so bitterly are*
> *here assembled peacefully and mutually affirm their common desire to collaborate*
> *in the work of universal peace."* Aristide Briand, speech on the admission of
> Germany to the League of Nations, September 10, 1926, from Aristide Briand,
> DISCOURS ET ÉCRITS DE POLITIQUE ÉTRANGÈRE, ed. Achille Elisha (Paris, 1965).

in 1922, and the International Labor Office with headquarters in Geneva.
The International Court supplemented but did not replace an earlier
Court of Arbitration, which had been set up by an international conference at The Hague in 1900; it rendered legal decisions (as distinct
from arbitration awards) on disputes between nations involving international law, but only if requested to do so by all parties to the dispute.
The ILO sought to achieve improved working conditions and uniform
labor standards in all countries. Both of these semi-independent agencies
survived World War II and the League itself.

FUNCTIONS

The primary function of the League was to provide the machinery for the settlement of international disputes without recourse to war. It also performed a number of lesser services, some well, some less well, which often escaped public attention. They included the elaboration of codes for the protection of women and children, the suppression of the slave trade and illicit traffic in drugs, and activities to protect public health and prevent disease. In the field of international administration the League's civil servants conducted plebiscites in disputed territories and provided a professional staff to administer the Saarland and the city of Danzig, both of which were placed under League control.

The former German colonies and the ex-dominions of the sultan in the Near East were also placed nominally under League control. The League did not attempt to administer them directly but turned them over as "mandated territories" to the powers that were already in effective occupation. The only obligations assumed by the mandatory powers were to abide by a few vague and pious rules set forth in the Covenant and to render an annual report to the Permanent Mandates Commission. In fact, mandated territories soon became indistinguishable from ordinary colonies. The Covenant did, nevertheless, distinguish between mandated territories on the basis of the degree of their development in the direction of self-government, granting some greater local autonomy than others. Thus the Arab countries at the eastern end of the Mediterranean became Class A mandates, divided between the French and British; those of central Africa became Class B mandates; and the former German Southwest Africa, which went to the Union of South Africa, and the Pacific islands became Class C mandates.

Recognizing the problems created by the boundaries in eastern Europe, the League Council created a permanent committee on national minorities. Theoretically all League members agreed to observe certain uniform standards concerning ethnic or national minorities within their territory. The committee could hear complaints from minorities who alleged violation of the standards, and it could publish reports on them, but it had no power to take direct action against an offending member, for minorities constituted "internal problems" and to interfere would be a violation of national sovereignty. Such action was no part of the League's program.

ACHIEVEMENTS AND FAILURE

Members of the League undertook, in the words of the Covenant, "to promote international cooperation and to achieve international peace and security: by the acceptance of obligations not to resort to war, by the prescription of open, just and honorable relations among nations, by the firm establishment of the understandings of international law as the actual rule of conduct among Governments, and by maintenance of justice and a scrupulous respect for all treaty obligations in the dealings of organized peoples with one another." Of the methods provided for the settlement of disputes, the most commonly used were arbitration, judicial settlement by the International Court, and reports by the Council itself. Utilization of the first two required the consent of the parties to the dispute; that of the last required a unanimous vote in the Council. All were difficult to achieve. Once a settlement was made, however, if a member (or even a nonmember) failed to abide by it, all the others might impose "sanctions" ranging in severity from a formal reprimand to a declaration of war. The crux of the matter was that effective enforcement depended upon both the willingness and the ability of the various states to take the indicated action; the League itself, as a separate organization, was powerless to impose sanctions.

In its early years the League scored some small successes in the settlement of disputes between Sweden and Finland (1921), Poland and Germany (1922), and a few others. In the same years, however, it failed to settle the bitter quarrel between Poland and Lithuania over the city of Vilna. Moreover, Mussolini refused to submit his disputes with Greece and Yugoslavia to League jurisdiction, and such major issues as French occupation of the Ruhr were not even raised in formal League discussion, which strengthened the view that the League was in reality a league of the large states against the small, of the victors against the vanquished.

After the settlement of the Ruhr crisis, the stabilization of the German monetary system, and the temporary return of prosperity, the tensions in international relations eased somewhat. In 1925 at the Swiss resort city of Locarno the foreign ministers of Britain, France, Germany, and several smaller states met to conclude a number of important agreements. Among other things they provided for an undertaking by Britain to guarantee the Franco-German and Belgian-German borders against aggression from either side, and a similar undertaking by France (Britain demurring) with respect to Germany's borders with Poland and Czechoslovakia. It was also agreed informally that Germany should be admitted to the League, an event that took place in 1926. Although the agreements contained a number of grave defects which subsequently became apparent, the mood of friendship and conciliation they engendered became known as "the spirit of Locarno." This balmy spirit prevailed so long as prosperity lasted and the men who created it remained in office; that is, about four years.

The Locarno spirit owed much to the personal characteristics of the foreign ministers of Germany, France, and Britain: Gustav Stresemann, the apostle of "fulfillment" of German treaty obligations; Aristide Briand, an old socialist and apostle of peace; and Austen Chamberlain,

Courtesy of *The Columbus* (Ohio) *Dispatch*

The Highest Point Ever Reached in Europe

cartoon by Ireland in The Columbus Dispatch

"The representatives of the German, Belgian, British, French, Italian, Polish and Czechoslovak Governments, who have met at Locarno, from the 5th to the 16th October, 1925, in order to seek by common agreement means for preserving their respective nations from the scourge of war and for providing for the peaceful settlement of disputes of every nature which might eventually arise between them, have given their approval to the draft treaties and conventions which respectively affect them and which, framed in the course of the present conference, are mutually interdependent." Final Protocol of the Locarno Conference, reprinted in W. H. Cook and E. P. Stickney, eds., READINGS IN EUROPEAN INTERNATIONAL RELATIONS (New York, 1931).

an urbane Englishman. In 1928, as a result of communications between Briand and American secretary of state Frank B. Kellogg, sixty-five nations signed the Pact of Paris or Kellogg-Briand Pact, which committed them to the "renunciation of war as an instrument of national policy." The pact was regarded as especially significant in that it included not only France and Germany but also the United States and the Soviet

Union, neither of whom were members of the League. The euphoria of
the moment (which earned Briand the Nobel Peace Prize) obscured the
fact that all nations already had made equivalent pronouncements and
undertakings and that the pact provided absolutely no means for enforcement.

Such easing of tensions as took place in the late 1920's was not brought
about directly by the League but rather by old-fashioned methods of
diplomacy. Nevertheless, the League continued with its work, primarily
in the cause of disarmament. Early in the 1920's Britain, the United
States, and Japan made several agreements outside the League proper for
the limitation of naval armaments, but overall disarmament proved
more difficult and elusive. In spite of many meetings and conferences
both in and outside the League, the nations were as far apart in 1933,
when they gave up the attempt altogether, as they had been in 1923.

The Locarno era ended abruptly in 1929 when both Chamberlain and
Briand lost office and Stresemann died, all within six months of one another and of the Wall Street crash. Although hopes remained that peace
might be preserved, the outlook grew darker and darker. In 1933 the
Japanese announced their withdrawal from the League over the Manchurian question. (See p. 948.) In the same fateful year Adolf Hitler
became master of Germany and soon withdrew it from the League. Although Soviet Russia then rushed to gain international respectability by
applying for membership, and was accepted, the League was weaker
than before. The Italian rebuff to the League in 1935 and the failure
of its members to take effective action (see p. 949) spelled its doom
as either a peace-making or peace-keeping body. It staggered on a few
years more, and in its weakness did what it had not dared to do in earlier
and balmier days when it might have helped; it expelled a member, the
Soviet Union, in 1939 for an attack on Finland. That proved to be its
dying gesture; World War II had already begun.

THE WEIMAR REPUBLIC IN GERMANY

Of all liberal attempts at reconstruction, none began more hopefully
nor ended more pathetically than the German republic. On paper — that
is, in its constitution — it appeared to be one of the most advanced democratic nations of the times, but almost from the beginning it encountered
die-hard opposition from both ends of the political spectrum. Its founders
carried the onus of having accepted the Versailles treaty with the
war guilt clause. It was overwhelmed by the worldwide depression, which
struck Germany with greater severity than almost any other nation. Fur-
thermore it failed to carry out any fundamental economic or social reforms. It did not break up the General Staff (as the Versailles treaty had
demanded) or the Junker estates of eastern Germany, which were the

economic base of the Prussian military caste. Finally, it did not attempt to break the power of big business in either economic or political life; in fact, it encouraged the formation of monopolies and cartels.

The republic got off to a bad start. The provisional government declared an immediate end to martial law and the reestablishment of traditional civil liberties and set about preparing for an election for a constituent assembly. Before the election could take place the Spartacist uprising in Berlin showed that the forces of democracy would be opposed on the Left as well as the Right. The government called on elements of the old imperial army to suppress the revolt and executed its leaders without trial, both of which were bad precedents for a new democracy. At the same time it went ahead with plans for the election, the freest and most democratic in Germany's history.

The election gave the Social Democrats 163 of a total of 423 delegates to the assembly. They were the largest party but fell far short of an absolute majority. The Catholic Center party and the Democrats, the two other moderate groups, had as many delegates combined, while the Nationalists and other right-wing groups and the left-wing Independent Socialists had many fewer. The three moderate parties formed a coalition both to govern the country and to frame a new constitution. The assembly elected Friedrich Ebert first president of the German republic, with Philipp Scheidemann, also a Social Democrat, serving as chancellor.

At the beginning of February, 1919, the constituent assembly convened in Weimar, the city of Goethe and Schiller, in order to avoid intimidation by the army and the mobs of Berlin, still in a state of anarchy. Although the seat of government remained in Berlin, and the assembly itself moved there after a few months, the short-lived democracy to which it gave birth will forever be known as the Weimar Republic.

THE STRUCTURE OF GOVERNMENT

The constitution borrowed freely from American, British, French, and Swiss precedent and practice, but all of these democratic shoots were grafted onto a solidly Germanic trunk. Although the republic was federal in form, the states were clearly subservient to the central government, which had greater power in principle if not in fact than it had under the Second Reich. There were also fewer component states than in the Second Reich as a result of amalgamation. The president, elected for a seven-year term, was similar to an elective constitutional monarch, as in contemporary France, rather than being an active head of government, as in the United States. He did, however, possess certain important emergency powers. The actual business of governing was confided to a chancellor and cabinet of ministers responsible to the legislature.

The legislature, bicameral in form, was unicameral in effect, as clearly indicated in the constitution itself. The Reichstag (the name lingered, even in a republic) voted all legislation and determined the fate of ministries. The Reichsrat, the second chamber, was composed of delegates from the state governments and had only a suspensory veto on legislation and no authority over ministries.

Although Social Democrats dominated the moderate coalition in the beginning, they were not strong enough to give the constitution a socialist character. The few references in it to economic organization specifically guaranteed "freedom of trade and industry," freedom of contract, and the right of private property. As a predominantly political document, the constitution incorporated the most advanced features of contemporary liberal political theory, including "universal, equal, direct and secret suffrage by all men and women over twenty years of age," proportional representation, a provision for referenda, and a broad range of civil rights and liberties. Ironically, Article 48 of the constitution provided that "if public safety and order . . . are materially disturbed or endangered," the president might suspend the constitution and "take the necessary measures to restore public safety and order . . . if necessary . . . by force of arms." The purpose of this article was to prevent either a communist or a monarchist *putsch* (coup d'état) against the republic, either of which appeared quite possible in the spring of 1919. In fact it was used in 1933 by Adolf Hitler, after he had acquired power by legal means, to dispose of the republic itself.

THREATS TO THE REPUBLIC

The republic was under constant pressure throughout its short life. Although it suppressed the Spartacist uprising in Berlin, further communist putsches were attempted in Berlin and other cities in subsequent months. A Soviet-style republic held Bavaria for a time in the spring of 1919, and the following year another revolt very nearly succeeded in the Ruhr. After the Treaty of Rapallo with the Soviet Union in 1922 the threat of Communist revolution subsided, but right-wing threats remained.

The government's use of free corps or volunteer armies of ex-servicemen to put down the Spartacist rising, together with its extremely broad interpretation of the constitutional provision for freedom of association, gave rise to the phenomenon of private armies, of which the Nazi Brownshirts or storm troopers became notorious. Lawlessness was rife and took such extreme forms as frequent assassinations of political leaders. Two of the outstanding leaders of the moderate coalition — Matthias Erzberger (who signed the armistice agreement of 1918) and Walter Rathenau — were assassinated within a year of one another in 1921 and 1922 by right-wing conspirators. The most serious of the attempted reactionary revolts was the Kapp putsch of 1920. Organized by Wolfgang Kapp, a minor politician, with the assistance of Generals von

Lüttwitz and Ludendorff, returning soldiers from the Baltic provinces who were destined to be demobilized by Allied command took Berlin, proclaimed the fall of the Weimar government, and installed Kapp as chancellor. The legal government escaped to the country and, in view of the passivity and outright sympathy for the revolt of many professional army officers, called for a general strike of workers. The strike proved effective, and the leaders of the putsch fled in fear and confusion within a week, but the experience revealed the reactionary spirit and doubtful loyalty of the officer corps.

If the Kapp putsch demonstrated the unreliability of the military, still dominated by East Elbian Junkers, it also showed that most workers were loyal to the democratic republic before the great inflation. The inflation constituted one of the two great watersheds of the Weimar republic. The other was the depression of 1929 to 1933, which brought the republic to an end. Although the almost miraculous economic recovery and prosperity that followed the inflation temporarily covered over the wounds it left in the body politic and social, they festered all the more for being hidden. Reactionary and nationalist sentiment, strong before the inflation, had been confined to social classes that were temporarily discredited by the war, including the officer corps itself and other Junker aristocrats. The war guilt clause of the Versailles treaty had been a bitter pill, but most Germans had swallowed it even though the Scheidemann cabinet resigned rather than sign it, and the great German sociologist Max Weber predicted, "We shall all be nationalists in ten years." The inflation, together with the accompanying French action in the Ruhr, cut the ground from under the moderates and overturned the political allegiances of the various social classes. The group that suffered most was the lower middle class of shopkeepers, clerks, and white-collar workers, who later formed the backbone of Nazi supporters. Both skilled and manual workers also suffered, and after being disillusioned by the weakness of socialism and democracy, they divided into hostile camps. The majority became increasingly enticed by communist blueprints of a workers' state, but many others worked off their frustrations and found emotional release in Nazi rituals and discipline and anti-Semitic demonstrations.

STRESEMANN, LOCARNO, AND "FULFILLMENT"

In the first elections to the Reichstag in June, 1920, the Social Democrats lost their dominant position, and after 1923 they participated in no further cabinets until 1928. The People's party, a resurrection of the old National Liberals dominated by big business interests, took their place in the moderate coalition, which thus moved a step to the Right. In the elections of 1924 Communists and Nationalists both gained at the expense of the moderate parties, and in 1925 a new cabinet included a

Photoworld

Unemployed Line Up for Free Soup

*"The situation deteriorated in 1930 more rapidly in Germany than in England
or the United States. . . . Total industrial production shrank, relatively, as
much or more than it did in this country. . . . The total number of unemployed
was about 3 millions during the first ten months and rose to nearly 4.4 in
December. There cannot be any doubt that . . . extra-economic factors . . . had
much to do with this. Superimposing themselves on what would in any case have
been a depression, they intensified it greatly."* J. A. Schumpeter, BUSINESS CYCLES
(New York, 1939), Vol. II.

Nationalist for the first time, marking yet another step to the Right. In
the presidential election soon afterward, Field Marshal von Hindenburg,
the Nationalist candidate, won with a mere plurality — not a majority —
as a result of Communist inroads on the moderate vote.

Meanwhile both the domestic economic picture and the international
diplomatic scene had changed radically for the better, if only temporarily. The inflation had come and gone, leaving a wreckage of broken
hopes, homes, and dreams, but also clearing the decks of debt and leaving
the enterprises and individuals who had survived it wide-open opportunities for economic expansion and prosperity under the new regime
of international loans. Large new vertical and horizontal combinations
took shape, such as the I. G. Farbenindustrie (chemicals, dyestuffs,

pharmaceuticals), and the Vereinigte Stahlwerke A. G. (steel, armaments, engineering). The rationalization movement, which sought both technical modernization and the elimination of unwanted competition through merger and amalgamation, made rapid headway.

The most significant development on the political and diplomatic front was the advent of Gustav Stresemann, a businessman and former ardent nationalist, who emerged as leader of the People's party. Stresemann served as chancellor for four months in 1923, long enough to preside over the liquidation of the inflationary upheaval and to inaugurate the new, stabilized currency. Although he lost the chancellorship thereafter, he remained as foreign minister in every succeeding cabinet until his death in 1929. His efforts at Locarno and afterward were dictated by the hard-headed businessman's respect for realities; they gained him a Nobel Peace Prize and won Germany's entry into the League of Nations as a member of the Council in 1926. His principles did not prevent him from renewing the Rapallo treaty of friendship and neutrality with the Soviet Union, also in 1926, under which the German army gained valuable experience with new developments in military technology in exchange for industrial and technical aid to Russia.

The gains for democracy, whatever they may have been, proved fleeting. Stresemann's death coincided with the onset of the great depression. The middle-class government, deathly afraid of a repetition of the collapse of the mark of 1923, pursued a deflationary policy in the midst of the worst deflation the world had experienced in over a hundred years. By the beginning of 1932 the number of unemployed in Germany had reached 6 million — more than one-fourth of the labor force. Conditions were ripe for the Nazi revolution.

ADOLF HITLER AND THE
DEATH THROES OF THE REPUBLIC

Adolf Hitler, son of a minor Austrian civil servant, showed signs of paranoia from early childhood. He rebelled against his strict, narrow-minded father, and after the latter's death took advantage of his over-indulgent mother. In the last years before the First World War he made a precarious living as a third-rate artist in Vienna, where his failures and frustrations crystallized into a bitter, burning anti-Semitism. Shortly before the war he drifted across the border into southern Germany, and after its outbreak he enlisted in the Bavarian army, where during four years of service he rose to the rank of corporal. War service provided an emotional release for his twisted yearnings, and he became an intense pan-German nationalist. He was in a military hospital recovering from gas poisoning when the armistice was signed; the effect of the event appears to have produced a kind of emotional crisis that strengthened his fanaticism and released his libido. After demobilization he returned to Munich, where in the turbulence and confusion of the first postwar year he became an informer for the army, checking up on communist sympathizers in the wake of the short-lived Bavarian Soviet Republic.

In this connection he first acquired knowledge of the German Workers' party, one of the hundreds of little political groups formed in the early months of the German republic. Although the name was suspect, he soon discovered that its small membership consisted principally of fanatical nationalists like himself. He joined the party in September, 1919, became a member of its executive committee, and the following year altered its name to the National Socialist German Workers' party (*National Sozialistische Deutsche Arbeiter Partei* or NSDAP), whose members received the nickname, at first derisive, of Nazis.

For several years the party remained small and ineffectual, although Hitler gained a local reputation for spellbinding demagogic oratory. In 1923 it achieved temporary national prominence when with the assistance of General Ludendorff it sought to overthrow the Bavarian state government in the Munich beer-hall putsch. This was one of the lesser of many such attempts by disaffected groups. The government easily put down the putsch and sentenced Hitler to five years in prison. As it had after the Kapp putsch, the government let Ludendorff off in deference to his services to the old Reich; such were the ambivalent feelings of Germans toward monarchy and democracy. Hitler was pardoned after only a year, during which time he had dictated to his faithful henchman Rudolf Hess, imprisoned with him, the book *Mein Kampf* (My Struggle), subsequently known as the bible of the Nazi party. Originally entitled "Four and a Half Years' Struggle against Lying, Stupidity, and Cowardice," it is a rambling, confused account of Hitler's early life and political activities to the time of his imprisonment, as well as a turgid exposition of his hates, prejudices, and visions of a Germany dominated by himself. Except for its seemingly prophetic passages and the insight it gives into its author's psychology, it is not worth reading today.

The Nazis remained insignificant throughout the Locarno period, but they hung on somehow. The depression provided them with their great opportunity. Unemployed workers joined the brown-shirted storm troopers, for which they received a pittance plus indoctrination in loyalty to their leaders and hate for "the others," whomever they might be: communists or capitalists, Jews or the beneficiaries of the Diktat of Versailles. In the election of September, 1930, the party's representation in the Reichstag jumped from twelve to more than one hundred. The Communists also increased to seventy-seven, while all the moderate parties except the Social Democrats lost heavily. During the next two and a half years parliamentary government ceased to function. Unable to form stable majorities out of the shifting coalitions of the Reichstag, successive chancellors resorted to ruling by decree under Article 48 of the constitution, with the consent of Hindenburg, while in the streets armed clashes between Nazi Brownshirts and Communists became increasingly frequent and destructive.

A new election in July, 1932, sent the Nazi representation up to 230, giving them the largest party in the Reichstag. After several futile attempts to form a stable government without the Nazis or to enlist their support for other parties, which Hitler refused except on his own terms, President Hindenburg named Hitler chancellor on January 30, 1933. Hitler immediately called for another election on March 5, using the combined powers of the government and his storm troopers to stir up popular support for the Nazis and to intimidate his opponents. Five days before the election a fire broke out in the Reichstag. Although the real arsonists (who may have been Nazis) were never apprehended, Hitler accused the Communists and used his emergency powers under Article 48 to outlaw the Communist party. In spite of this tactic the Communists won 81 seats, while the Nazis obtained 288. The Nazis still did not have a majority in the Reichstag, but with the aid of their Nationalist allies, the expulsion of the Communists, and the intimidation of the moderates, Hitler forced through the Reichstag on March 23 the crucial Enabling Act, which gave him emergency dictatorial powers for a period of four years. Thus he accomplished the Nazi revolution and put an end to Germany's liberal attempt at reconstruction.

THE DEMOCRACIES OF WESTERN EUROPE

Although victorious in war, Britain, France, and Belgium faced many of the same problems in peacetime as did their defeated enemy. They succeeded with difficulty in retaining their traditional attachment to political and civil liberty and parliamentary forms of government, but they were no more successful than Weimar Germany in solving the economic and social problems issuing from the collapse of Western civilization. Even the smaller Western democracies that had remained neutral in the great conflict — Switzerland, the Netherlands, and the Scandinavian countries — found themselves involved in the general collapse and disintegration. Traditional remedies availed little. Only in Scandinavia did the people and their political leaders respond creatively to the crisis and bring forth solutions both novel and effective.

BRITAIN, IMPOVERISHED EMPIRE

Economic problems loomed large in postwar Britain. Even before the war Britain's unusually great dependence on international trade and overcommitment to lines of industry that were rapidly becoming obsolete had guaranteed that the British would face a difficult period of adaptation to the twentieth century. During the war they lost foreign markets, foreign investments, a large part of their mercantile marine, and other sources of overseas income. Yet they depended as much as ever on imports of food and raw materials, and they found themselves with even greater worldwide responsibilities as the strongest of the victors in Europe and as the administrator of new territories overseas. Export they must, yet factories and mines lay idle while unemployment mounted. In 1921 more than 1 million men — about one-seventh of the industrial labor force — had no work; even in the relatively prosperous years of the 1920's the rate of unemployment rarely fell below 10 per cent, and in the worst years of the depression it mounted to 25 per cent or more.

The government's measures to deal with its economic problems were timid, unimaginative, and ineffective. Its only solution for unemployment was the dole, a system of relief payments that was entirely inadequate to support the families of the unemployed while placing a heavy burden on an already overstrained budget. For the rest, government economic policy consisted mainly in paring expenditures to the bone, thus depriving the nation of urgently needed expansion and modernization of its schools, hospitals, highways, and other public works. The single forthright initiative taken by the government in the economic sphere resulted in disaster. In 1925 the chancellor of the exchequer, Winston Churchill, who had earlier shifted his allegiance from the Liberal to the Conservative party, resolved to return Britain to the gold standard at the prewar gold parity. Because of the inflation that had occurred since 1914, this measure necessitated a substantial fall in prices, which while it restored the prewar purchasing power of fixed money incomes also produced a fall in wages averaging about 10 per cent. It also brought about a redistribution of income in favor of the rentier classes, adding to the discontent of the workers who were already suffering from unemployment and short time, or reduced working hours.

The coal industry was one of the most severely affected by the loss of foreign markets and higher costs. Coal miners were among the most radical of British workers; they had already staged several major strikes in the early postwar years. When faced with a wage cut as a result of the government's policy, the miners went out on strike on May 1, 1926, and persuaded many other trade unions to join them in what was intended to be a general strike. About 40 per cent of British trade union members joined in, mainly those in public utilities and similar industries, but the strike lasted only ten days and ended in a defeat for the unions. Middle-class volunteers manned essential services, and the trade union leaders gave up rather than risk civil war in the face of the government's strong and successful opposition. Brief as it was, the general strike left a bitter legacy of class division and hatred, which made concerted national action against both domestic and international problems even more difficult.

Lloyd George's handling of the wartime coalition government, which remained in office until 1922, resulted in disaster for his own Liberal party. The Labour party then emerged as the second largest party and replaced the Liberals as His Majesty's Loyal Opposition. For a few months in 1924 it actually formed a government, but this turned out to be a misfortune instead of an opportunity. Without an absolute majority in the House of Commons, it could not have carried out a program of reform even if it had had one — which it did not. A similar situation occurred in 1929, when it formed another minority government just on the eve of the depression. As the crisis deepened Prime Minister J. Ramsay Mac-Donald could offer no program but the conventional middle-class solution of budgetary retrenchment. His inadequacy cost him the support of his own party. MacDonald thereupon reformed his cabinet in 1931 as a coalition dominated by Conservatives. His own party expelled him and went into opposition once more, where it remained until World War II. Thus ended all attempts at socialist reform until 1945.

While domestic difficulties mounted Britain still had to fend for and contend with its empire, enlarged by the acquisition of the former German colonies and the mandated territories of Palestine, Transjordan, and Iraq. The sun still shown on the British Empire, but a hint of things to come shot forth like a shower of sparks from Ireland, "John Bull's other island." The Home Rule Bill of 1914, which was to have taken effect after the war, never did so. In April, 1916, the Sinn Fein (We ourselves) party of Irish Nationalists launched the Easter Rebellion, relying on German assistance which never arrived. Although the British easily suppressed the rebellion, the anti-British agitation continued and again broke out into general warfare in 1919–20. Suppression proved more difficult this time, despite the greater ferocity of the British counter-offensive. In 1920 the British Parliament passed a new home rule law, but the Sinn Fein refused to accept it, insisting on complete independence. After long negotiations the British in 1921 signed an agreement providing for dominion status for southern Ireland as the Irish Free State. Although a majority of the Irish accepted the solution, a militant minority of Irish republicans refused to do so and initiated a guerrilla civil war against their own Irish government.

One of the most militant leaders of the Irish Republicans was Eamon de Valera, born in New York of a Spanish father and an Irish mother. Sentenced to death for his part in the Easter Rebellion, he was reprieved because of his American nationality and in 1917 became the leader of the Sinn Fein movement. He broke with the majority of his party and refused to recognize the treaty of 1921, but in 1926 after imprisonment and release by his own former comrades he entered the politics of the Irish Free State on a more normal basis. In 1932 he became chief of the Irish government, a post that he occupied continuously until 1948 (and again from 1951 to 1954 and from 1957 to 1959), during which time he completely severed southern Ireland's ties with Britain, reorganizing it as the Irish Republic or Eire. The six northern counties in the Protestant province of Ulster had accepted special status in the United Kingdom of Great Britain and Northern Ireland under the act of 1920.

Although the self-governing dominions of Canada, Australia, New Zealand, and South Africa loyally joined Britain in the war, they showed increasing signs of restiveness with their position in the empire in the postwar period. In 1926 an imperial conference declared Great Britain and the dominions to be "autonomous communities within the British Empire, equal in status, in no way subordinate to one another in any aspect of their domestic or external affairs, though united by a common allegiance to the crown." In 1931 Parliament passed the Statute of Westminster, giving the force of law to that declaration and creating the British Commonwealth of Nations.

Other portions of the empire had to wait longer for independence. Britain formerly renounced its protectorate over Egypt in 1922 but maintained an army of occupation and advisers in Egypt until after World War II, with the result that it was continually embroiled in difficulties and disputes there. In India the British introduced a strictly limited degree of self-government in 1919 and extended it slightly in 1935. Not satisfied, the Indians under the moral leadership of Mohandas K. (Mahatma) Gandhi began a campaign of passive (nonviolent) resistance to British rule, which culminated in independence after World War II.

In Britain a long, slow, and incomplete recovery from the depression got under way in 1934. With a single notable exception, the nation's attention gradually shifted to foreign affairs in the march toward World War II. The exception was an interlude devoted to the royal family, more than ever an object of public concern and affection since the monarch had ceased to rule. George V died at the beginning of 1936 after a twenty-six-year reign, in which he set the style for modern constitutional monarchs. His son and successor Edward VIII was a bachelor, but rumor soon linked his name with that of Mrs. Wallis Warfield Simpson, an American whose second marriage was headed for the divorce courts. Edward indicated his intention of marrying Mrs. Simpson, but the government of the day, presided over by Stanley Baldwin, raised a constitutional issue and refused to proceed with the coronation ceremony. In December, 1936, Edward abdicated, having reigned uncrowned for less than a year, and assumed the title Duke of Windsor; he married Mrs. Simpson the following year. He was succeeded by his younger brother, who carried on the tradition set by their father. For the two years from the Silver Jubilee of George V in 1935 to the coronation of George VI in 1937 British newspapers devoted more space to the royal family than to either economic or foreign affairs. It was symptomatic of a concern for propriety at the expense of action.

FRANCE, THE FRIGHTENED VICTOR

No Western nation suffered more from the war than France. Most of the fighting on the western front had taken place in its richest area. More than half of France's prewar industrial production, including 60 per cent of its steel and 70 per cent of its coal, had been located in the war-devastated area, which was also among the most important agricultural regions. Most appalling was the loss of life: 1.5 million Frenchmen — one-half of the prewar male population of military age — had been killed, with half as many more permanently disabled. It is not surprising, therefore, that France demanded that Germany pay for the war, nor that Frenchmen sought security above all. Unhappily, whatever the justice or equity of the French demands, they could not easily be reconciled with the realities of the world situation. Attempts to attain them in spite of all difficulties contributed to weakening France still more.

Counting on German reparations to pay the cost, the French government undertook at once an extensive program of physical reconstruction of the war-damaged areas, which had the incidental effect of stimulating the economy to new production records. When German reparations failed to materialize in the expected amount, the ramshackle methods used to finance the reconstruction took their toll. The problem was compounded by the expensive and ineffective occupation of the Ruhr. The franc depreciated more in the first seven years of peace than during the war. Realizing at last that "the Boche" could not be made to pay, a coalition cabinet headed by Raymond Poincaré and containing six former premiers stabilized the franc in 1926 at about one-fifth of its prewar value by drastic economies and stiff increases in taxation. This solution was more satisfactory than either of the more extreme solutions utilized by Germany and Britain, but it alienated both the rentier class, which lost about four-fifths of its purchasing power in the inflation, and the working classes, which bore most of the burden of increased taxation. Thus, as in Germany, the inflation contributed to the growth of extremism on both Right and Left.

On the Left the Socialist party congress in 1920 voted by a three-to-one margin to join the Third International, directed from Moscow, and renamed itself the French Communist party. The minority led by Léon Blum walked out; they retained the name Socialist but gave up all else — the party newspaper, organizational apparatus, and most of the membership. The future of the non-Communist Left looked bleak indeed, but the astute leadership of Blum, plus the incompetence of the Communist party leaders and constant meddling from Moscow, revived the Socialist party in a most remarkable way. By 1932 the Socialists outnumbered the

Communists in the Chamber of Deputies by 100 to 10, and in 1936 Léon Blum became French premier as the head of the largest party in the Chamber.

On the extreme Right several shrill but small groups preached doctrines similar to facism. The most important was an organization called Action Française, led by the vitriolic writer Charles Maurras. It was rabidly nationalist and frankly reactionary, appealing for a return to the monarchy and clerical domination of the state. Although at first supported by the Catholic Church, it was repudiated by the Vatican in 1926 and its popular influence declined rapidly. Its intellectual influence lingered on, however, and flowered again in the Vichy regime during World War II.

In spite of the growth of radical and extremist movements, political control of France remained firmly in the hands of the moderate parties. The multiplicity of parties in the French Chamber of Deputies, already notable before the war, became even more striking with the adoption of proportional representation in 1919. More than thirty parties were represented, resulting in a succession of shifting coalitions and cabinet upsets. The moderate parties fell into two main groups; the right-center *Bloc National,* to which Clemenceau belonged and which was subsequently dominated by Poincaré and Briand; and the left-center *Cartel des Gauches,* dominated by Édouard Herriot, leader of the so-called Radical Socialist party (which was neither radical nor socialist).

French political parties united on only one objective: the desire to preserve French hegemony on the Continent. They hoped to accomplish it through the League with the aid of the United States and Britain. The United States Senate, however, not only refused to join the League but killed a tripartite treaty by which the United States and Britain would have guaranteed France assistance if attacked by Germany. Britain thereupon regarded its responsibilities under the treaty as abrogated. Britain also differed with France on reparations. This desertion by their allies, as Frenchmen regarded it, accounted for much of the stridency and go-it-alone attitude of France's foreign policy in the early 1920's, culminating in the occupation of the Ruhr. That fiasco tempered French intransigence so much that France did not again resort to unilateral action even when it might have been effective, as during the German remilitarization of the Rhineland in 1936. (See p. 951.) Instead, it speeded construction of the Maginot line, a vast network of interconnecting fortresses along the Franco-German border, and built a paper wall of treaties around Germany with Poland and Little Entente powers of Czechoslovakia, Rumania, and Yugoslavia. Realizing the weakness of these allies, Briand came to terms with Germany itself in the Locarno agreements. In 1935, after Hitler had announced German rearmament in defiance of Versailles, France even negotiated an alliance with Soviet Russia, which had been anathema to most Frenchmen ever since Lenin had repudiated the debts of the tsarist government. That treaty was no more effective than the others in protecting France from a resurgent Germany. Meanwhile the depression struck, later in France than elsewhere and perhaps less severely, but also longer lasting. The trough did not come till 1935 or 1936, and France was still floundering when war broke out in 1939. As it had in other countries, the depression spawned social protest and a new crop of extremist organizations. For a time in the winter of 1933–34 many Frenchmen expected a reactionary or fascist coup d'état, and open rioting broke out in February, 1934, ominously reminiscent of the Berlin street fighting in 1932. The political storm blew over, however, and the next political turning for France was to the Left.

To combat fascist tendencies, the Socialists overcame their dislike of the Communists and brought them together with the Radicals in a Popular Front. This step was made easier by the recent Franco-Soviet alliance. In the elections of 1936 the Socialists emerged as the largest party, the Radicals second, and the Communists made a surprising leap from ten to seventy-two seats in the Chamber of Deputies. Léon Blum became the Popular Front prime minister. Although held back by its Radical allies from outright socialization, the government enacted a number of reform measures, especially in the field of labor, including a legal forty-hour work week, compulsory arbitration of labor disputes, and paid vacations. As mild as these reform measures were, they aroused the hostility of the conservatives, and after the first blush of enthusiasm for reform had passed, Blum had to give way as prime minister in 1937 to a Radical colleague. In 1938 the Popular Front broke up after only two years as foreign affairs increasingly dominated the political scene. In France as in Britain liberalism proved too weak, too timid, too lacking in imagination to tackle the task of reconstruction of society as a whole.

THE SMALLER DEMOCRACIES

Even more than before World War I the fate of the smaller nations of Europe lay beyond their control, intimately associated with international affairs and the policies of the great powers. As a result two major features of the interwar period, the depression and the diplomatic trials and failures that eventually led to World War II, overshadowed the purely domestic histories of the smaller democracies. Only the Scandinavian countries managed to shield themselves from some of the ravages of the depression, and only Sweden and Switzerland remained neutral during the Second World War.

The problems of Belgium, the only one of the small nations of western Europe to be involved in the first war, resembled those of France. The response to those problems also resembled the French; that is, the Belgians followed strictly orthodox economic and financial policies in coping with successive crises until 1936, when the government of the day followed the French Popular Front in introducing very mild social and economic reforms. In foreign policy Belgium tied itself more closely to France, even participating in the occupation of the Ruhr. In 1936, however, in the face of growing German strength and obvious French weakness, the Belgians sought vainly to save themselves by denouncing their military alliance with France and reverting to their traditional neutrality. In internal affairs Belgium was troubled, as were all democratic countries in the 1930's, by the growth of domestic totalitarian movements. Calling themselves Rexists, the Belgian fascists reached the peak of their strength in 1936 when they won twenty-one seats in parliament; but by 1939 their influence had been reduced to insignificance. A more serious social conflict for Belgium was the old hostility between the French-speaking Walloons and the Flemish. A law in 1922 made both Flemish and French the official languages, as a concession to the Flemings, but after 1932 French was used only in the Walloon provinces, with Flemish the only official language in Flanders. The capital, Brussels, remained officially bilingual. In spite of such concessions, riots and other forms of conflict continued to mark the relations between the two ethnic groups.

The Netherlands, traditionally a free trade nation and heavily dependent on international commerce, suffered from both the depression and growing economic nationalism. The Dutch took the initiative in attempts to keep trade free with Belgium and Luxembourg, ultimately resulting in the Benelux customs union after World War II. They also played a prominent role in negotiating the Oslo Convention of 1932, intended to facilitate trade among the Low Countries and those of Scandinavia. A Dutch National Socialist party modeled on the German caused grave concern from 1934 to 1936, but as with the Rexists in Belgium, its strength had been spent by 1938.

Switzerland's overweening national interest throughout the interwar period lay, as always, in maintaining its historic neutrality. Its location and scenery made it a favorite spot for international conferences and the headquarters of international organizations (the International Red Cross was established at Geneva in 1864, the International Postal Union at Bern in 1874). This also had its drawbacks, however. After the diplomats in Paris chose Geneva as the seat of the League of Nations in 1919, it was a full year before the Swiss responded to the honor with a decision to enter the League, and then only after receiving assurances that they would not be called upon to go to war in support of League decisions. The national referendum by which the Swiss decided the issue gave the League a margin of only four to three. Significantly, Switzerland was the only independent nation that later chose to remain outside the United

Nations. The Swiss tried to avoid antagonizing Italy and Germany, although they refused to extend diplomatic recognition to the Soviet Union until after World War II. At the same time, by means of their unique system of universal military service and strong border fortifications they let it be known that they would not be willing victims of aggression.

By 1938 the only outpost of democracy in eastern Europe was Czechoslovakia. In spite of the absence of any tradition of self-government, the presence of hostile nations on all sides, and the existence of strong religious and ethnic divisions within the country itself, the literate and industrious Czechs had managed to establish and preserve parliamentary government as well as an elementary respect for basic civil and political liberties. Much of the credit belonged to Thomas Masaryk, who served as president from the creation of the provisional government in 1918 until 1935, and to his successor Eduard Beneš. Czechs, Slovaks, and Ruthenians made up the greater part of the population of the Czechoslovak state, but owing to decisions made in the peace conference, it also included several minority nationalities. The largest and most important of the minorities were the Germans, numbering more than 3 million, who lived principally in the Sudeten Mountains that ringed the western end of the long, lizard-shaped country. Although their inclusion in the new state was clearly a violation of Wilson's principle of nationality, it was justified by the diplomats — and acquiesced to by Wilson — on the grounds that the mountains provided the Czechs with their only natural defense against Germany. In any event, the Sudeten Germans provided fertile soil for the growth of irredentist agitation after the advent of National Socialism in Germany. The activities of the Nazi-inspired *Sudeten-deutsche Partei* of Konrad Henlein prepared the way for German dismemberment and absorption, which was carried out with the acquiescence of both France and Britain after the historic Munich conference of September, 1938. (See pp. 952–954.) Thus was democracy extinguished in eastern Europe. It has yet to be revived.

In the Scandinavian countries, on the other hand, democracy flourished as never before. One of the most heartening triumphs for democracy was the emergence of Finland, after more than a century of tsarist rule, as a democratic nation between the rival threats of local communist and fascist movements supported by the Soviet Union and Nazi Germany, respectively. All the Scandinavian countries had been fortunate in escaping the ravages of war. They were less fortunate in the depression, but owing to such relatively enlightened international cooperation as provided for in the Oslo Convention and to bold, imaginative antidepression policies, they suffered far less than most. Sweden was the most successful. Its political spectrum broke down into Conservatives, Agrarians, Liberals, and Socialists. The Socialists dominated the govern-

Brown Brothers

Dr. Thomas Masaryk

"We restored our State in the name of democratic freedom, and we shall only be able to preserve it through freedom increasingly protected. In home affairs as in foreign, democracy must be our aim. . . . Our position is not solely that our State must be democratic; it cannot be undemocratic. . . . In the past our democratic aims were negative, a negation of Austrian absolutism. Now they must be positive. What we took as our ideal must become reality — and it will not be easy." Dr. Thomas Garrigue Masaryk, THE MAKING OF A STATE, ed. Henry Wickham Steed (London, 1927).

ment for most of the interwar period, but almost always in coalition with at least one of the other parties. Partly for this reason but partly from temperament, their socialism was of a pragmatic, not dogmatic, variety. In the 1920's they enacted a wide range of progressive labor and social welfare legislation, and in the 1930's they encouraged cooperatives and municipal governments to undertake large-scale housing programs. As a result Sweden had the lowest rate of unemployment in western Europe and boasted the best-housed population and most attractive cities in the world. Norway, Denmark, and Finland had similar political line-ups and followed similar policies; but their economies, less evenly balanced than Sweden's, left them more exposed to the fluctuations of international markets.

THE UNITED STATES: NEW ERA AND NEW DEAL

In spite of the relatively brief and limited American involvement in World War I, the war introduced a number of significant changes into the tone and tempo of American life. Mobilization of the economy resulted in basic changes in the economic organization that persisted long after the last American doughboy had returned from Europe. The war hastened the process of social change and gave it new directions. Politically the war induced a revulsion against American involvement in European and world affairs. In the presidential election of 1920 Warren G. Harding, the Republican nominee, campaigned successfully on a platform calling for a "return to normalcy."

"NORMALCY" IN AMERICA

The most readily observed changes in American life occurred in the realm of fashions, manners, and social intercourse. With one exception, all these changes reinforced and accentuated the tendency toward greater personal freedom and informality. The single exception resulted in part from the wartime controls prohibiting the use of food products for making distilled beverages, in part from the popular belief that most breweries and distilleries were owned by Germans, and in part from the absence of large numbers of young men in Europe. All these factors facilitated the adoption in 1919 of the Eighteenth Amendment to the Constitution, banning the manufacture or sale of intoxicating beverages. Prohibition ensured that all hard drinking of the New Era would be strictly illegal, contributed directly to widespread disrespect for legal and moral standards, and made it possible for criminal elements engaged in illegal liquor traffic to exercise powerful political influence.

By providing new sources of income and employment the war hastened the emancipation of women, culminating in the adoption of the Nineteenth Amendment regarding women's suffrage in 1920. Woman's new role, together with increased urbanization, the faster pace of life made possible by the automobile and radio, and the prosperity of the 1920's, accounted for much of the tone of social life in the postwar decade. Jazz came to be regarded as a respectable popular art form, night clubs and movies replaced vaudeville and the traveling medicine show as popular entertainment, and Hollywood became a new symbol of American life. Americans, it seemed to the rest of the world, sought diversion and merriment as avidly and earnestly as they sought wealth. There may have been a connection between the two.

In more serious matters, the postwar decade witnessed a reversal of America's historic policy of free immigration. Organized labor (many of whose leaders were immigrants or sons of immigrants) campaigned for restriction in the mistaken belief that they could thereby obtain higher wages; misconceptions of Darwinian biological theory and popular notions of Social Darwinism convinced many Americans that the new immigrants were somehow undesirable; and the war itself made Americans more conscious of foreigners. The Immigration Act of 1921 limited the number of immigrants from each country annually to 3 per cent of the foreign-born persons of its nationality residing in the United States according to the census of 1910. A new law in 1924 further limited the numbers and discriminated against immigrants from southern and eastern Europe by restricting the annual quotas to 2 per cent of foreign nationals according to the census of 1890. It also provided for total exclusion of Japanese immigrants, thereby violating an unofficial agreement of the United States with Japan.

Political life was more completely dominated by big business than at any time since the end of the nineteenth century. One of President Coolidge's aphorisms, "The business of America is business," summed up the popular view. In the popular mythology small business was as important as big business, but this notion was belied by the statistics of corporate concentration and the influence in politics of a relatively small number of key industries. The petroleum industry, once the whipping boy of American politics (the Standard Oil Company had been broken up by court order as recently as 1911), wielded enormous behind-the-scenes influence and typified the new international outlook of big business. Primarily as a result of the oil industry's concern over the fate of oil fields in the Near East, the Harding administration reversed its policy of noninterference in European affairs and sent an observer to the Lausanne conference of 1923. The oil industry also involved the United States in bitter disputes with its neighbor Mexico. The famous Teapot Dome episode of 1924, the greatest political scandal of the 1920's, resulted from oil company bribes to the secretary of the interior, Albert Fall. Shrewder men discovered a more effective way of securing favorable government treatment than bribery. Andrew Mellon, head of a vast empire that included coal, steel, aluminum, and sulphur as well as oil, served as secretary of the treasury throughout the 1920's and was responsible, among other things, for the generous depletion allowances in the tax liability of oil producers and owners of other mineral resources.

The political influence of big business reflected changes in the structure and organization of American industry. Although the changes were inherent in the technological progress of the preceding fifty years, the wartime organization of the economy hastened them along. Underlying the organizational changes was a philosophy of both government and industry that held that government participation in the economy was desirable when its purpose was to assist and encourage private enterprise, but intolerable when it aimed at regulation and control. One of the leading exponents of this view was Herbert Hoover, a brilliant mining engineer with wide international contacts and experience who served as wartime food administrator, then as director of American famine relief in Europe. He became secretary of commerce under Presidents Harding and Coolidge and used the office effectively to promote greater rationalization and integration of the economy and to coordinate the activities of American business in foreign markets. Largely because of his success in that field the American people elected Hoover to the presidency in 1928.

Taking office at the peak of the boom, Hoover spoke for the many businessmen and business-oriented government officials who thought that they had discovered the key to perpetual prosperity. Great was their dismay when less than a year later the bottom dropped out of the stock market to signal the beginning of the worst depression in American history. The stock market crash was not identical with the depression, nor even the cause of it; but it was both symptomatic and symbolic. The people who lost money — in many cases borrowed money — in the Wall Street collapse had been the beneficiaries of the new prosperity: independent businessmen, corporation executives, professional men, and middle-class housewives, as well as wealthy rentiers. The depression, however, was by no means confined to them. The greatest suffering affected the millions of unemployed factory workers and the hundreds of thousands of farmers who lost their farms through debt foreclosure or were evicted for inability to pay their rentals. For the farmers, the depression had begun several years before, as farm prices fell steadily through the 1920's from their inflated wartime peaks. Factory workers, too, had failed to share in the prosperity of the twenties, for real wages rose hardly at all. Had the exponents of the new business system looked at the trend of real wages or at farm prices instead of corporate profits and stock prices before 1929, their optimistic forecasts might have been more guarded.

ROOSEVELT AND THE NEW DEAL

When Franklin Roosevelt took office as thirty-second president of the United States on a cold, blustery day in March, 1933, the nation lay in the grip of its worst crisis since the Civil War. With more than 15 million unemployed — almost 50 per cent of the industrial labor force — industry had virtually shut down and the banking system was on the verge of complete collapse. Nor was the crisis solely economic. An army of about 15,000 unemployed veterans marched on Washington in 1932, only to be dispersed by the regular army. In rural areas farmers sometimes took the law into their own hands to prevent the foreclosure of mortgages; and violence ruled in city streets. Membership in the American Communist party reached an all-time peak, and protofascist groups sprang up across the land. It was uncertain whether or not the United States would go the way of Italy and Germany.

In his campaign speeches Roosevelt had called for a "new deal" for America. In the famous hundred days that followed his inauguration a willing Congress did his bidding, turning out new legislation at an unprecedented rate. In fact, for the four years of his first term the volume of legislation surpassed that of any previous administration. It dealt mainly with economic recovery and social reform in the areas of agriculture, banking, the monetary system, the securities markets, labor, social security, health, housing, transportation, communications, natural resources — in fact, every aspect of the American economy and society.

Perhaps the most characteristic enactment of the entire period was the National Industrial Recovery Act. It created a National Recovery Administration to supervise the preparation of "codes of fair competition" for each industry by representatives of the industry itself. Although hailed at the time as a new departure in economic policy, it turned out to be very like the trade association movement that Hoover had promoted as secretary of commerce (without the element of coercion). It was even more like the wartime economic administration; a number of high government officials had, in fact, served in the wartime mobilization of the economy (including Roosevelt himself, as assistant secretary of the navy). The NRA also bore striking similarities to the fascist system of industrial organization in Italy, though without the brutality and police-state methods of the latter. In essence, it was a system of private economic planning ("industrial self-government"), with government supervision to protect the public interest and guarantee the right of labor to organize and bargain collectively.

In 1935 the Supreme Court declared the NRA unconstitutional. In other areas in which the Court struck down his initial legislation Roosevelt achieved his goals by new laws, but with respect to industry he altered his stand and initiated a campaign of "trust busting" (itself subsequently reversed with the approach of World War II). The industrial recovery had been disappointing, and in 1937 the economy suffered a new recession without having achieved full employment. The United States returned to war in 1941 with more than 6 million still unemployed. Although many of the New Deal reforms were valuable in themselves and continue to make a vital contribution to American life, the New Deal system as a whole was no more successful as an answer to the problems that beset Western civilization than contemporary programs in Europe.

THE NEW DEAL AND FOREIGN POLICY

The foreign relations of the New Deal were even more contradictory and confusing than its domestic policy. Roosevelt began by breaking up an international monetary conference called for the summer of 1933 in London in an attempt to secure agreement on international currency problems. In the following year Congress reiterated its condemnation of countries in default on intergovernmental indebtedness, but at the same time it passed the Reciprocal Trade Agreements Act which gave the president wide authority to reduce tariffs by agreement. In strictly political foreign relations Roosevelt respected the country's ingrained isolationist bias toward Europe but took the initiative in formulating a "good neighbor policy" for Latin America. Both the government and the country publicly deplored Japanese aggression in China (see pp. 948–949) but were not prepared to take positive action to deter it. As the war clouds gathered in Europe the president openly expressed his sympathies for the democracies, but he was so far from persuading the country of the desirability of intervention that in September, 1939, he officially proclaimed American neutrality in the "European" war.

AUTHORITARIAN ATTEMPTS
AT RECONSTRUCTION
CHAPTER THIRTY-FIVE

Liberal attempts at reconstruction were characterized by piecemeal, ad hoc measures to patch up the old order, to improve its virtues, and to eliminate its defects. Most authoritarian attempts aimed at a total reconstruction of society along radically different lines. The emphasis on the totality of the effort, extending to the means as well as the ends, resulted in the invention of a new word to describe such societies: totalitarian.

Totalitarianism covers all attempts at social organization in which all the resources of the society are devoted — by coercion if necessary — to the realization of one all-embracing goal. It applies to the conventional political Left, or communism, as well as to movements on the political Right, which go under a variety of names. In a sense it applies even to the organization of the war effort of the United States and the other Western allies in World War II, in which the single goal was total victory, implying total mobilization of the society for total war. The crucial difference is that the totalitarian effort of democratic nations was intended from the beginning to be temporary, ending with the achievement of victory, whereas in the totalitarian nations proper it is regarded as the permanent state of society.

Several other terms closely identified with totalitarianism need preliminary definition to avoid confusion. The most important is dictatorship, which refers simply to the authoritarian rule of a single individual or political party. Dictatorship is an ancient form of government, and historically it has been one of the most common. Although dictatorship is an essential ingredient of modern totalitarianism, it is only one ingredient of a concept that is much broader and more inclusive.

Another closely related word, sometimes regarded as synonymous with totalitarian dictatorship, is fascism. Originally applied to the doctrines of the Fascisti, a political party organized in 1919 by Benito Mussolini to take control of the government of Italy, it derives from the Italian *fascio,* meaning group or bundle, which in turn derives from the Latin *fasces,* a bundle of sticks or rods with an ax projecting from them used as a symbol of authority in ancient Rome. By extension, fascism came to be applied to any right-wing totalitarian movement.

Nazism refers more specifically to the totalitarian movement headed by Adolf Hitler in Germany. It derives from the German pronunciation of the first two syllables of National Sozialistische Deutsche Arbeiter Partei (NSDAP), the National Socialist German Workers' party (Arbeiter was subsequently dropped). This party took as its symbol the swastika, in ancient times a symbol of welfare or well-being but since the 1930's a symbol of hatred and cruelty because of its association with the Nazis. Other authoritarian movements took other names (the Falange in Spain, for example) and other symbols (the rising sun of the Japanese Empire or the hammer and sickle of Russian Communism), but all had common elements that set them off clearly from movements deriving from the liberal tradition of the nineteenth century. There were also important differences among authoritarian movements, especially between Communism on the extreme Left and the various authoritarian movements on the Right.

COMMUNISM IN RUSSIA, 1921-1938

Communism constituted the most comprehensive and systematic of all the attempts to reconstruct society in the period between the wars. To say that it was systematic, however, does not imply that its realization involved the implementation of a preconceived plan. The foremost aim of the Bolshevik leaders in 1917 was to seize power and after that to maintain themselves in power. They had formulated their other aims in only the most general way. The eventual form of the Soviet state and society evolved by a process of trial and error, pragmatic compromise, and internal rivalry and dispute over more than fifteen years.

THE STRUCTURE OF GOVERNMENT

Several constitutional changes have occurred in the history of the Soviet Union. The brief description here is based upon the most important common features of the constitutions of 1923 and 1936. Superficially the government of the Soviet Union (the Union of Soviet Socialist Republics) resembles that of certain Western democracies. It is a federation of nominally independent republics, of which the Russian Socialist Federal Soviet Republic is by far the most important.[1] It is democratic

---

[1] The number of constituent republics within the Soviet Union has fluctuated with internal political changes and external conquest. Just prior to World War II there were eleven: the Russian S.F.S.R., the Ukrainian S.S.R., the Byelorussian S.S.R., the Armenian S.S.R., the Georgian S.S.R., the Azerbaijan S.S.R., the Uzbek S.S.R., the Turkmen S.S.R., the Tadjik S.S.R., the Kazakh S.S.R., and the Kirghiz S.S.R. After the war several new republics were created in the conquered areas in the west.

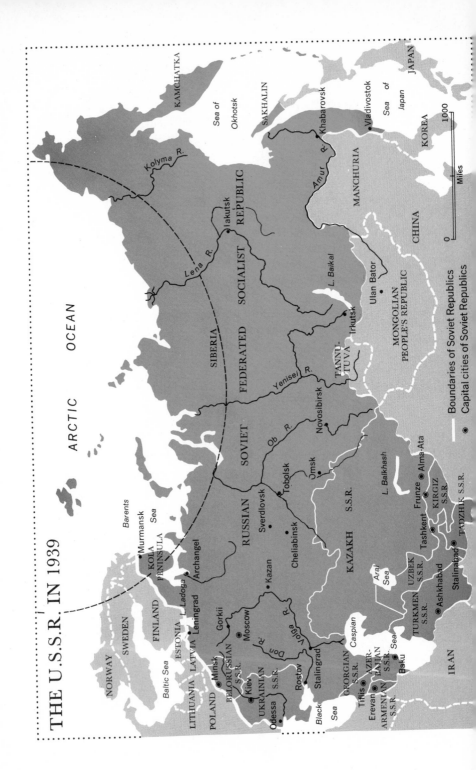

THE U.S.S.R. IN 1939

ARCTIC OCEAN

Barents Sea

NORWAY
SWEDEN
FINLAND
KOLA PENINSULA
ESTONIA
LITHUANIA LATVIA Leningrad
POLAND
Baltic Sea

Murmansk
Archangel
L. Ladoga

Minsk
BELORUSSIAN S.S.R.
Kiev
UKRAINIEN S.S.R.
Odessa
Black Sea

Gorkii
Moscow
Don
Volga R.
Rostov
Stalingrad
Kazan

GEORGIAN S.S.R.
Tiflis
Erevan
ARMENIAN S.S.R.
AZER-BAIJAN S.S.R.
Baku
Caspian Sea

IRAN

RUSSIAN
SOVIET
FEDERATED
SOCIALIST
REPUBLIC
SIBERIA

Sverdlovsk
Cheliabinsk
Tobolsk
Omsk
Ob R.
Novosibirsk
Yenisei R.
Lena R.
Iakutsk
Irkutsk
L. Baikal

Kolyma R.

Sea of Okhotsk
KAMCHATKA
SAKHALIN
Khabarovsk
Amur R.
Vladivostok
Sea of Japan
KOREA
JAPAN

MANCHURIA
CHINA
Ulan Bator
MONGOLIAN PEOPLE'S REPUBLIC
TANNU-TUVA

Aral Sea
L. Balkhash
Alma-Ata
Frunze
KIRGIZ S.S.R.
Tashkent
UZBEK S.S.R.
KAZAKH S.S.R.
TURKMEN S.S.R.
Ashkhabad
Stalinabad
TADZHIK S.S.R.

Boundaries of Soviet Republics
● Capital cities of Soviet Republics

0   1000
Miles

and parliamentary in form, with almost universal suffrage and a pyramidal structure of parliamentary institutions from the village councils at the base to the bicameral All-Union Congress of Soviets — later called the Supreme Soviet — at the apex. The Supreme Soviet rarely meets, however, and only to ratify the decisions of the real rulers of the country, who hold positions of power within still smaller bodies. Among the smaller bodies are the Presidium or central executive committee of the Supreme Soviet, whose president is nominal chief of state of the Soviet Union; and the Council of People's Commissars — later called the Council of Ministers — whose chairman functions as the prime minister. In addition, there are many administrative bodies.

Paralleling the formal organization of the government is the real ruling organ of the state, the Communist Party of the Soviet Union, as the Bolsheviks renamed themselves in 1918. It, too, has local, regional, national, and federal or all-union units of organization. The apex of the party organization is the All-Union Congress, corresponding to the Supreme Soviet, but as in the government, the most important decisions are made in smaller groups: the Central Committee of the All-Union Congress, corresponding to the Presidium; and the Politburo (Political Bureau), corresponding to the Council of Ministers. In practice, there is a large degree of overlap in the membership of the Central Committee and Politburo and their corresponding organs in the formal government structure. The most powerful position in the Soviet state is that of secretary of the Central Committee of the party, which Stalin held from 1922 until his death in 1953. Both Stalin and his successors have frequently held the office of chairman of the Council of Ministers (or premier) as well.

The Communist party is the only legal political party in the Soviet Union. It nominates all candidates for elective office. Although it may on occasion nominate a person who is not a member of the party, all nominees are carefully screened for their loyalty, not merely to the Soviet Union but also to the ruling clique within the party. As the "vanguard of the revolution," the party was and remains an elite group, constituting before World War II no more than 2 or 3 per cent of the adult population. Although the numbers fluctuated somewhat as the result of numerous purges as well as new additions, the membership in 1940 was about 3 million.

No account of the structure of Soviet government would be complete without mention of the secret police. Under different names at different periods (Cheka, OGPU, NKVD) the police — both secret and not-so-secret — have been of fundamental importance in enforcing both civic and party discipline, in engaging in espionage against enemies of the regime and of the ruling clique within the party, and in disposing of disaffected persons by legal or illegal means. Had it not been for the secret police, the government of the Soviet Union would be vastly different today; it is quite likely, in fact, that there would be no Soviet Union at all.

THE "NEW ECONOMIC POLICY"

When the Bolsheviks seized power in 1917 they had no immediate, concrete plans for taking over or operating the economy. Their immediate objective was to secure political control, and they expected to deal with economic questions after their control had been firmly established. Their first important measure in the economic field was a decree to legitimize and hasten the peasants' expropriation of the land, livestock, and equipment of the tsarist landowners. The Bolsheviks soon discovered, however, that they could not depend upon capitalist owners and managers of industrial enterprises, banks, etc., to continue producing for them. They were thus forced into a policy of hasty, widespread, and unplanned nationalization or confiscation. This so-called policy of War Communism lasted from 1918 to 1921. Although the new regime succeeded in winning the civil war and repulsing foreign intervention, the damage and dislocations of the wartime upheavals (before as well as after the revolution) and the lack of skilled technicians and managers resulted in a disastrous drop in production. By the end of 1920 over-all industrial production had fallen to about one-fifth of its prewar level.

Bolshevik agricultural policy produced no better results. Agricultural output fell to about half its prewar level. Worse than that, the peasants whose land seizures the Bolsheviks had legitimized refused to deliver grain and other products at the artificially low prices set by the government, preferring to consume it themselves, hoard it, or sell it illegally at inflated prices. As early as August, 1918, the government sent detachments of armed industrial workers into the countryside to force the peasants to sell their grain at the legally fixed price or, if the peasants refused, to confiscate it.

Faced with economic paralysis and the possibility of peasant revolts on a scale larger than any of the tsarist period, Lenin in the spring of 1921 decided on a radical reversal of the policy of War Communism. Called the New Economic Policy (NEP), it was a compromise with the capitalist principles of production based on private property and exchange in free markets. Lenin called it "a step backward in order to go forward." The new policy had three major features. (1) A special tax in kind on agricultural produce was substituted for compulsory requisitions; peasants were allowed to sell their surpluses at free market prices. (2) Internal free trade and free markets were reintroduced: small-scale industries (employing fewer than twenty workers) were returned to private ownership and allowed to produce for the market; some existing enterprises were leased to foreign entrepreneurs, and special concessions were granted to others to introduce new industries. (3) The so-called commanding heights of the economy remained under state ownership and operation; they included all large-scale industries, transport and communications, finance and banking, and foreign trade. Other features of the NEP period included a vigorous program of electrification of the country, the establishment of technical schools for the training of engineers and industrial managers, and the creation of a more systematic organization of planning and coordination for the state-owned and operated sectors of the economy.

The results of the New Economic Policy were much as Lenin had predicted. Despite some further difficulties with the peasants, output increased in both the agricultural and nonagricultural sectors. By 1926 or 1927 the prewar levels of output had been substantially regained. Meanwhile, crises of a different nature were taking place within the Communist party.

INTERNAL RIVALRIES

In May, 1922, Lenin suffered the first of three paralytic strokes. Although he returned to his office briefly in the autumn of 1922, he never completely regained his strength. He weakened steadily during 1923 and died on January 21, 1924. Prior to his illness Lenin had gained complete supremacy within the party. So great was his prestige that no other party official dared challenge him directly; even after his death any official who could plausibly argue that he was carrying out Lenin's wishes found strong support from the party faithful. In spite of his great position of strength, Lenin refrained from explicitly designating his successor. In fact, in a unique political will, read before the assembled Central Committee of the party shortly after his death, he pointed out both the strengths and the faults of all his close associates and possible successors.

The most popular figure in the party after Lenin was Leon Trotsky. As war commissar (minister of war), he had been the "organizer of victory" over the White armies during the civil war. He was also a gifted orator and had a large following both within and outside the Communist party. As a potential successor to Lenin, however, he suffered from his late conversion to the Bolshevik cause, having followed an independent policy within the party until the October Revolution. He was therefore suspect to the Old Bolsheviks, who also may have been jealous of his oratorical abilities and popularity.

Another possible successor of Lenin was Joseph Stalin, although he was not seriously considered as such in the years immediately following Lenin's illness and death. Stalin was one of the oldest of the Old Bolsheviks. He had been a faithful adherent of Lenin since the party split of 1903, and he had dutifully performed a variety of tasks within the party ever since. Just a month prior to Lenin's first stroke he had become general secretary of the Central Committee, a position he used effectively to build up his own strength within the party. In spite of his allegiance to Lenin, the latter's will accused him of "rudeness" and lack of scruples and warned the party against an overconcentration of power in his hands. Stalin managed to gloss over these criticisms, as well as other slights by Lenin, but he was not yet strong enough to take over unquestioned leadership. He had to rely on his political shrewdness to put together a network of shifting alliances with more prominent party members in order to dispose of his great rival, Trotsky.

Among the other leaders of the party at the time were Grigorii Zinoviev, chairman of the Leningrad Soviet and president of the Comintern (see p. 929); Leo Kamenev, chairman of the Moscow Soviet; Nikolai Bukharin, whom Lenin called the party's "greatest theorist"; Mikhail Tomsky, leader of the trade unions; and Aleksei Rykov, who succeeded Lenin as chairman of the Council of People's Commissars. Prior to Lenin's death Zinoviev, Kamenev, and Stalin had formed a sort of informal triumvirate with the purpose of isolating and eventually deposing Trotsky. They succeeded, partly because of Trotsky's own egotism and his penchant for making tactless statements about his colleagues. In January, 1925, the Central Committee removed Trotsky from the War Commissariat; in 1926 he was removed from the Politburo; and in the following year he was dismissed from the party. Soon afterward he was banished to Turkestan, then allowed to go into exile. After several years of wandering he eventually settled in Mexico, where he continued to try to organize opposition to Stalin within the party. For this reason Stalin engineered his assassination in 1940.

The internal party struggles arose not merely from clashes of personalities but also from fundamental issues of foreign and domestic policy. Whereas Trotsky advocated world revolution, Stalin's motto became "socialism in one country," namely, the Soviet Union. Trotsky's power had scarcely been broken before Stalin began to maneuver his erstwhile associates Zinoviev and Kamenev into the ranks of the "Left Deviationists," as he called them, for their criticisms of the NEP. He formed an alliance with Bukharin, Rykov, and Tomsky, all of whom were advocates of the NEP, and drove his former fellow triumvirs into disgrace. Then Stalin immediately turned on his new associates for their "Rightist Opposition" — that is, advocating too strongly the merits of the NEP! Stalin maintained that since prewar levels of production had been regained, it was imperative to move on to a new stage in the development of socialism by means of comprehensive economic planning. Stalin launched his attack on Bukharin and his associates in 1928; by 1930, when Stalin's henchman V. M. Molotov succeeded Rykov as chairman of the Council of People's Commissars, Stalin's control over the party and the country was almost complete.

SOVIET ECONOMIC PLANNING

Stalin had already initiated the most ambitious attempt in modern times to regiment an entire society. The basis of the attempt was comprehensive economic planning. So drastic and sweeping were the measures and their consequences for the Soviet people that the inauguration of the first five-year plan in 1928 has been referred to as the "second Bolshevik revolution."

The purpose of the five-year plans was not just to achieve socialism. Stalin and the other Soviet leaders, who had long since given up the hope of a worldwide communist revolution, decided that it was necessary for the survival of their regime in the face of a hostile world to industrialize the country and make it both self-sufficient and powerful. Economic planning was also a convenient device for increasing their control over the lives of their subjects, stifling dissatisfaction, and preventing attempts to overthrow the regime. Consequently the initiation of the five-year plans marks the real beginning of Soviet totalitarianism.

The decision to undertake comprehensive economic planning had several implications. Perhaps the most important was an all-out drive for industrialization, especially in heavy industries. Addressing a group of industrial managers in 1931, Stalin declared, "We are fifty to a hundred years behind the advanced countries. We must cover that distance in ten years. Either we do this or they will crush us." Nearly as important was the collectivization of agriculture, necessary for two reasons: first, in order to obtain the labor and other resources for industrialization; second, to break the peasants of their traditionalist orientation and convert them into an agricultural proletariat dependent upon the state for access to the means of production and livelihood. Finally, since collectivization and forced-draft industrialization involved heavy sacrifices in consumption and the free choice of occupations, they had to be undertaken against the wishes of the people. Economic planning thus involved the use of coercion and, on occasion, violence.

All resources of the Soviet government were directly or indirectly utilized in the effort. On the purely technical plane the State Planning Commission (Gosplan) was the over-all planning agency with the responsibility for formulating plans, setting output goals, and sending directives to various subsidiary agencies. The Gosplan was paralleled at regional and local levels by planning bureaus for areas and for special industries. Industries were organized in what the Russians called trusts, cartels, and syndicates, words with a familiar capitalist ring; in essence, what the Soviets did was to adapt the organizational devices of large-scale, concentrated capitalist industry to planning in a socialist country.

The trade unions were called upon to assist in the industrialization of the country. In totalitarian countries trade unions and other labor or-

Leaders of the Communist Party and the Soviet Government
on the Experimental Field of the Tractor and Automobile
Scientific Research Institute, by K. I. Finogenov

> *"The fundamental task of the five-year plan was to convert the U.S.S.R. from an*
> *agrarian and weak country, dependent upon the caprices of the capitalist*
> *countries, into an independent and powerful country, fully self-reliant and*
> *independent of the caprices of world capitalism. . . .*
>   *"What dictated this fundamental task of the five-year plan; what were the*
> *grounds for it? The necessity of putting an end to the technical and economic*
> *backwardness of the Soviet Union, which doomed it to an unenviable existence;*
> *the necessity of creating in the country the prerequisites that would enable it*
> *not only to overtake but in time to outstrip, technically and economically, the*
> *advanced capitalist countries."* Stalin to the Joint Plenum of the
> Communist Party, January 7, 1933, reprinted in J. V. STALIN, WORKS
> (Moscow, 1955), Vol. XIII.

---

ganizations perform functions very different from those of trade unions
in North America and western Europe. In place of representing workers
and protecting their interests, they preserve labor discipline, prevent
strikes and sabotage, encourage productivity, and in other ways facilitate
the attainment of state objectives. The ideal of "workers' control" of
industry, held by Tomsky and other trade union leaders before the final
triumph of Stalin, had no place under the five-year plans.

The collectivization of agriculture presented the Soviet government with one of its most difficult and persistent problems. During the NEP the peasants had been left almost entirely to their own devices. In addition to bringing output back to prewar levels in a relatively brief period, a few of them, called kulaks (village usurers) by the Communists, had become fairly prosperous. Almost all the peasants had strengthened their traditional attachment to their own plots of soil and livestock.

The government had two devices for collectivization: state farms and collective (cooperative) farms. It preferred the state farm. In it the state owned all the land, livestock, and equipment and appointed a professional manager; the peasants who worked it constituted a pure agricultural proletariat. Not surprisingly, the peasants resisted this kind of regimentation, in many instances burning their crops and slaughtering their livestock in order to prevent them from falling into the hands of the government. In the face of such determined resistance even Stalin backed off, though not until many peasants (especially the kulaks) had been killed outright or shipped off to prison or exile in Siberia and the far north. As a compromise with the peasants, the government allowed them to form collective farms, on which most of the land was tilled in common but with each household retaining small plots for its own use and even for the sale of its surplus on the free market. The state supplied technical advice and machinery to the collective farms from state-owned Machine-Tractor Stations, which could also be used for inspection, propaganda, and control.

The objectives of the first five-year plan were officially declared to have been achieved after only four and one-quarter years. In fact, the plan was far from a complete success. Although output in some lines of industry had grown prodigiously, most industries failed to make their quotas, which had been set at unrealistically high figures. In agriculture about 60 per cent of the peasants had been collectivized, but agricultural output had actually fallen and the number of livestock had declined to between one-half and two-thirds of the 1928 figure. The costs of the five-year plan were enormous, especially the human costs. In the collectivization of agriculture alone more than 5 million people lost their lives through starvation or execution.

In 1933 the government inaugurated a second five-year plan. The emphasis was supposed to be on consumer goods, but in fact the country continued to devote an extraordinary proportion of its resources to capital goods and military equipment. In spite of great increases in industrial production, which put the Soviet Union in the second or third rank in many lines of industry and even in the first rank in a few, the country remained predominantly agrarian, and agriculture was its weakest sector. A third five-year plan, launched in 1938, was interrupted by the German invasion in 1941.

ASPECTS OF SOVIET SOCIETY AND CULTURE

Although the Soviet population remained primarily rural at the outbreak of World War II, urban growth had made rapid gains with industrialization. In 1926 more than 80 per cent of the population lived in rural areas, almost as large a percentage as during the last years of the tsarist regime. A dozen years later the figure was less than 70 per cent. The bulk of the growth was concentrated in the largest cities. Moscow and Leningrad both doubled in population between 1926 and 1939. In the latter year there were twenty-eight cities with more than a quarter of a million people, as against only nine in 1926.

Most Russians were devoutly religious, a characteristic of a peasant society. Prior to World War I the Eastern Orthodox Church had been the state religion of the Russian Empire. There were also sizable groups of Moslems, Jews, and people of other religions among the 180 or so separate ethnic groups. Most leaders of the Communist party, however, were militant atheists and regarded traditional religion as an obstacle to be destroyed in achieving the new society. At first they proceeded cautiously; Lenin did not want to jeopardize his major goals over what, for him, was a trivial matter. After Stalin took over totalitarian control the campaign against the church stepped up, but even Stalin did not try to abolish it altogether. He worked through weak and willing tools within the church hierarchy itself to ensure that it did not seek to undermine his rule.

The Communists faced a similar problem in dealing with writers, artists, and other intellectuals. Under the old regime many of them had belonged to disaffected or radical groups and welcomed the revolution as a liberating movement. In the first years the new regime followed an ambivalent policy, striving to woo the intellectuals both within and outside Russia by means of honors, promises, and propaganda, but at the same time trying to coax, persuade, and at times coerce them into bridling their intellectual freedom in the interests of the party and the state. Stalin had no compunctions about artistic or intellectual freedom; for him the only test of a good writer, artist, or musician was whether or not he followed the party line. His own artistic tastes were rather primitive, betraying his peasant upbringing. He had no use for the modernism characteristic of the art, literature, and music of the 1920's. By strictly enforcing his own canons of taste, he stifled the development of many promising artists and writers.

The Soviet leaders realized that in order to build an industrial society they had to have trained scientists, technicians, and managers. At the time of the revolution over half the Russian people were illiterate. A system of universal education was established — compulsory to age twelve — that gave ample opportunity for advanced training to those who were intellectually and ideologically fitted. It reduced illiteracy to less than 20 per cent by 1939. At the same time the educational system was used for ideological indoctrination; the leaders had little hope of converting the majority of the prerevolutionary generation to a whole-hearted acceptance of socialism, but they expected to attain their goals with the new generations. For this reason they also set up youth organizations (Little Octobrists, Pioneers, Young Communists) as training grounds for future members of the Communist party.

The use of secret police, informers, brutality, and terrorism continued to be characteristic of the regime. Indeed, after the consolidation of Stalin's power they came to be its hallmark. Between 1934 and 1938 the "great purge" of the Communist party occurred, the causes and convolutions of which remain a mystery to the outside world to this day. More than 8 million people were arrested; many were executed, but the majority were merely deported to forced labor camps or left to languish in prison. The chief targets were the Old Bolsheviks of the former Right and Left opposition, although all of them had recanted their errors, sometimes more than once. All surviving members of the 1921 Politburo except Stalin were executed. In many instances Stalin's own henchmen were tried, or executed without trial — including the chief of the secret police who had been responsible for rounding up the Old Bolsheviks. The purge extended far down into the ranks of the Communist party and even into the mass of ordinary citizens, who had no idea of why they were arrested. One of the most mystifying elements was the series of mock trials at which prominent leaders of the party, the government, and the army confessed to political crimes they could not possibly have committed.

SOVIET FOREIGN POLICY

In the main, Soviet foreign policy followed the shifts in domestic policy. During the period of War Communism, when the Western Allies were lending assistance to the White armies and the Bolsheviks expected a proletarian revolution in the West momentarily, they did what little they could to effectuate it. Their principal instrument was the Third, or Communist, International (Comintern), which was supposed to be an international organization of working-class leaders similar to the First and Second Internationals. In fact, it was a collection of Communist conspirators organized, subsidized, and dominated by the Communist party of the Soviet Union. The Comintern continued to work for the overthrow of so-called bourgeois governments even after the Soviet Union had officially established friendly relations with them.

After the advent of the NEP the official Soviet policy toward the West changed to one of conciliation. Although the Soviet government refused to recognize the debts of the tsarist regime, it sought by other means to establish normal diplomatic relations with Western nations. When invited to the Genoa conference of 1922, it responded with alacrity. Although the conference failed to produce any notable results, it led to the Rapallo agreements between the Soviet Union and Germany. (See p. 900.) The Soviet Union also signed the Kellogg-Briand Peace Pact.

After the triumph of Stalin and the inauguration of the first five-year plan the Soviet Union relapsed into a sort of isolationism in international affairs. The major exception was its contradictory role toward Germany. On the one hand, it continued economic and military collaboration with the Weimar Republic in the spirit of Rapallo; on the other, it occasionally collaborated with the Nazis by means of the Comintern and the German Communist party in order to overthrow the republic. Stalin apparently expected that the seizure of power by the Nazis would unite the German people behind the Communist party. He realized his mistake too late. Not until 1934 did he definitely break off relations with the Nazis and begin to favor a popular front, an alliance with the socialists, in France, to which he had previously been hostile. After the withdrawal of Germany the Soviet Union was finally admitted to the League of Nations, but by that time the international situation had deteriorated too far for it to make any difference. After a brief intervention in the Spanish Civil War against the forces of Germany and Italy (see pp. 949–950), the Soviet Union withdrew once more from the world arena. When it re-emerged in 1939, it did so in a totally different guise.

FASCISM IN ITALY, 1922–1938

Postwar Italy proved a fertile breeding ground for diseases of the body politic. Although allied with the victors, Italy's contribution to the victory had been negligible. The refusal of the men of Versailles to give Italy a larger share of the spoils of war galled the more fervid nationalists among the Italians, of whom there were many. One of the most picturesque, the poet Gabriele D'Annunzio, gave vent to his feelings by leading a band of volunteer legionnaires against the Adriatic port of Fiume, which had been assigned to Yugoslavia. He seized and occupied it for several months in 1919–20 in defiance of both international opinion and his own government. The government demonstrated its own weakness by its unwillingness or inability to deal summarily with such open defiance of its authority.

The prewar coalitions of so-called Liberal splinter groups had been shaky enough; in the infinitely more trying times after the war they were beset on both Right and Left by rival political parties with few scruples and less respect for the existing system. Over all lay the pall of economic chaos. Poverty, endemic in Italy, had been made much worse by the economic dislocations of the war and the postwar depression. Italy suffered simultaneously from a heavy burden of debt and taxation, a yawning government deficit that produced rampant inflation, severe unemployment, and dire shortages of basic foodstuffs and essential raw materials for industry. The workers responded to these economic and political conditions by staging strikes and sabotaging factories; the employers resorted to lockouts of striking or unruly workers; the unemployed indulged in street riots and mob violence; the peasants seized large estates and destroyed property; and the deputies in parliament castigated one another's shortcomings — past, present, and future. The government did nothing.

MUSSOLINI AND THE ORIGINS OF FASCISM

Benito Mussolini (1883–1945), the future *Duce* (leader) of Italy, was the son of an anticlerical blacksmith. Dismissed from a Catholic seminary for allegedly putting a knife in one of his fellow seminarians, he led a gypsy existence for a number of years, skipping the country to avoid military service and then getting expelled from both Switzerland and Austria. Along the way he picked up a smattering of socialist doctrine and supported himself as a trade union organizer and radical journalist. He gained a certain amount of notoriety by opposing Italy's conquest of Libya and spent a few months in jail for the manner in which he expressed his opinion. In 1912, after his release, he became editor of the *Avanti* (Forward) of Milan, the leading socialist newspaper in Italy. Mussolini broke with his socialist comrades on the question of Italian intervention in World War I. They upheld international socialist solidarity and pacifism, while he became an ardent nationalist, using the curiously perverted Marxist argument that Italy, as a "proletarian" nation, must attack "capitalist" Austria. He became so carried away by his patriotism that he actually enlisted in the army, where he rose to the rank of corporal.

Clearly, Mussolini was neither a conventional socialist nor a conventional nationalist. Consistency was not one of his characteristics. As he later said of his doctrines, "The spirit of Fascism is will and action, not intellect." Yet he was not without ability: he was persuasive as both a journalist and an orator, had the shrewdness of a peasant, and above all had ambition, though at times his boldness was interspersed with indecision bordering on cowardice.

After the war Mussolini toyed with the notion of trying to regain his position within the socialist movement in order to make himself master of Italy, much as Lenin had done in Russia. His former comrades would have nothing to do with him. He therefore devoted himself to organizing an anti-socialist group called the *Fascio di combattimento*. Most of his followers were ex-soldiers and unemployed youths, but he also obtained financial support from wealthy industrialists who found his strong-arm bands useful for breaking strikes and intimidating workers. Mussolini dressed them in black shirts and subjected them to military discipline, with elaborate rituals and frequent parades. He had no specific positive program, but the conditions of the time favored his anti-Communist stand. The left wing of the Socialist party split off in 1920, becoming the Italian Communist party with strong Russian connections through the Comintern. Thereafter Mussolini's movement attracted wide support from frightened property owners, devout Catholics, and others terrified by the prospect of a Soviet Italy. Within a few years his Fascist party had 300,000 members, and in the election of 1921 it seated thirty-five members in the Chamber of Deputies.

THE MARCH ON ROME

Economic unrest and social disorder continued to mount until the late summer of 1922, when the Socialists declared a general strike. Preparations for the strike were badly made and it proved an immediate failure; nevertheless, it gave the Fascists a welcome opportunity to flex their muscles by attacking strikers, Socialist party headquarters, newspapers, and even Socialist-controlled city governments. When the national government did not interfere to prevent the Fascists from taking over the city governments by force, it consigned itself to oblivion. In October, 1922, the Fascists held a triumphant party congress in Naples, and Mussolini boasted to his uniformed followers that "the government will be given to us or we shall march on Rome." Preparations for the march were made, although Mussolini himself did not participate directly. Meanwhile, the Liberal prime minister demanded permission from King Victor Emmanuel III to declare martial law in order to deal with the situation. The king refused, and the cabinet resigned. The country was thus without a government in this crucial moment. The king, who had already been in contact with Fascist politicians, named Mussolini prime minister. Although he had resorted to threats and violence, Mussolini's accession to power was, in a technical sense, perfectly legal.

THE ORGANIZATION OF THE
FASCIST STATE AND PARTY

Mussolini's first action as prime minister was to demand and obtain from the cowed parliament a year's grant of dictatorial power. During this year he placed his followers in strategic spots throughout the government, brought the army into line, and enacted a new electoral law. After another campaign of terror and violence, the Fascists in a rigged election in April, 1924, obtained an overwhelming majority in the Chamber of Deputies. By the end of the year their domination of Italy was complete.

Brown Brothers

Mussolini and Hitler Review Troops

"I always enjoy meeting the Duce. He's a great personality. . . . Don't suppose that events in Italy had no influence on us. The brown shirt would probably not have existed without the black shirt. The march on Rome, in 1922, was one of the turning points of history. The mere fact that anything of the sort could be attempted, and could succeed, gave us an impetus. A few weeks after the march on Rome, I was received by the Minister Schweyer. That would never have happened otherwise." Hitler, July 21, 1941, in HITLER'S SECRET CONVERSATIONS, 1941–1944 (New York, 1953).

The Fascists still had no notable, positive program except the will to power. Mussolini was content to retain the forms of monarchy while Victor Emmanuel receded into the background as a barely visible figurehead. A series of constitutional changes reduced the parliament to a rubber stamp for the Fascist party; all other parties were outlawed. The Fascists exercised tight censorship of the press and controlled the other mass media directly. A secret police organization kept check on the activities of actual and potential enemies of the regime, while squads of Blackshirts, now full-fledged instruments of the state, awed the populace.

Membership in the party, which in its early days had attracted mainly roughnecks and hoodlums, became a position of prestige and power, attracting ambitious politicians, businessmen who wished favors from the state, and even remnants of the old aristocracy. Except for individuals who could be immediately useful to him, Mussolini prescribed a long period of apprenticeship and limited membership to about 5 per cent of the total adult population. In 1932 the party rolls carried the names of approximately 1,250,000 people, organized in a hierarchy of about 10,000 local and regional units. Presiding over all was the Fascist Grand Council, composed of about twenty of the most important leaders and dominated by Mussolini. The Grand Council was in effect a sort of supergovernment in that it named all candidates for political office, supervised regular government officials in the performance of their duties, and dictated the general policies of both government and party.

FASCIST IDEOLOGY AND THE CORPORATE STATE

In order to bolster the ideological underpinnings of his regime Mussolini employed the philosopher Giovanni Gentile, a former student of Benedetto Croce, to provide a rationalization of Fascism which was then widely publicized as Mussolini's own philosophy. What emerged was an amorphous blend of ideas from a variety of sources, including Hegel, Croce, Nietzsche, Sorel, Pareto, and other idealist and antirational writers. Fascism glorified the use of force, upheld war as the noblest human activity, denounced liberalism, democracy, socialism, and individualism, treated material well-being with disdain, and regarded human inequalities as not only inevitable but desirable. Above all, it deified the state as the supreme embodiment of the human spirit: "For us Fascists, the State is not merely a guardian, preoccupied solely with the duty of assuring the personal safety of the citizens; nor is it an organization with purely material aims, such as to guarantee a certain level of well-being and peaceful conditions of life. . . . The State, as conceived of and as created by Fascism, is a spiritual and moral fact in itself. . . . The State is not only a living reality of the present, it is also linked with the past and above all the future, and thus transcending the brief limits of individual life, it represents the immanent spirit of the nation." The government employed compulsory military service, Fascist youth groups, and similar devices in the largely unsuccessful attempt to inculcate these ideas into the populace.

As an attempted total reconstruction of society, Fascism had to have a distinctive form of economic organization. Mussolini developed the corporate state, one of the most publicized and least successful innovations of the Fascist regime. In principle, the corporate state was the antithesis of both capitalism and socialism. Although it permitted private ownership of property, the interests of both owners and workers were to be subordinated to the higher interests of society as a whole, as represented by the state. To accomplish this, all industries in the country were organized into twelve corporations — corresponding to an American trade association rather than to a business corporation. Workers, proprietors, and the state were represented, with party functionaries holding the important administrative posts. All previously existing labor unions were suppressed. The functions of the corporations included the regulation of prices, wages, and working conditions and the provision of social insurance. Later elaborations provided for the replacement of the Chamber of Deputies with a Chamber of Corporations. In practice, insofar as the corporations functioned at all, they acted mainly as capitalistic trade associations with the aim of increasing the income of businessmen and party administrators at the expense of laborers and consumers. Other aspects of Fascist economic policy were no more successful. In spite of a large public works and armaments program, Italy suffered severely from the depression; even the argument that "Mussolini made the trains run on time," sometimes used by American apologists for Fascism, was false.

THE LATERAN TREATY

One of the most successful of Mussolini's policies concerned his relations with the Catholic Church. Since the Italian occupation of Rome in 1870 no reigning pope had set foot outside Vatican City, a small enclave within the city of Rome, or received the ruler of Italy. The Lateran Treaty of 1929, named for the church in which it was signed, ended the long dispute between the Church and the Italian state and bestowed the pope's implicit moral approval on Mussolini's regime. In return for a promise by the pope not to interfere in politics and to obtain government approval of the appointment of bishops (who also had to swear loyalty to the state), Mussolini granted Pius XI recognition as sovereign over the "temporal domain" of Vatican City, promised financial support, and allowed the Church a large measure of control over education. Mussolini thereby not only disposed of a troublesome domestic political issue but also gained the approval of many Catholics and others outside Italy.

NAZISM IN GERMANY, 1933–1938

Although the election in Germany in March, 1933, was carried out under the coercive influence of the Nazi storm troopers in an atmosphere of near hysteria after the burning of the Reichstag, it did not result in a clear victory for the Nazis. More than half the electorate voted against the National Socialist party. With the aid of some fifty conservative Nationalists in the Reichstag, however, Hitler was able to form a new government. In spite of the tenuousness of his victory, he moved quickly to consolidate his power and eliminate the opposition.

THE CONSOLIDATION OF NAZI POWER

Immediately after the election Hitler arrested the leaders of the Communist party and expelled the Communist members from the Reichstag, using the Reichstag fire as the excuse. With the opposition thus reduced he introduced in the Reichstag the so-called Enabling Act to give the cabinet full legislative and budgetary powers for four years, allowing it to govern without check either from the Reichstag or the president. On March 23, 1933, with its temporary meeting place surrounded by storm troopers, the Reichstag considered the bill. Only the leader of the Social Democratic party spoke in opposition; only the Social Democrats voted against it. The bill passed by a vote of 441 to 84. The Reichstag had abdicated its power to Hitler.

The pace of Nazi ascension accelerated. Hitler reorganized the civil service, dismissing more than a quarter of its officials, especially those in the higher posts, and replaced them with his own trusted lieutenants. Hermann Goering — a World War I flying hero, president of the Reichstag, and one of Hitler's most trusted henchmen — took charge of the nation's police forces and at once organized a special secret police division, the Gestapo, with almost unlimited powers. Hitler ousted the elected officials of state and local government units and replaced them with men of his own choosing, usually local *Gauleiters* (district leaders) of the Nazi party. The judiciary and the universities were similarly reorganized and screened for loyalty, or at least obedience, to the Nazis. In January, 1934, Hitler completed the process of centralization by abolishing in form as well as in fact all local government divisions; for the first time in history Germany became a completely unified, centralized state.

Hitler tidied up the political scene by abolishing all other political parties. After the Communists had been outlawed, the turn of the Social Democrats came in June, 1933. Other parties were allowed to dissolve themselves voluntarily. On July 14, 1933, Hitler declared the Nazis the only legal party. The Nazis also moved against other voluntary organizations, subjecting them to party discipline or forcing them out of existence. On May Day, 1933, traditionally a labor holiday, the government declared a national holiday and cooperated with trade union leaders in staging a giant celebration. The following morning the trade union leaders returned to their offices to find them raided, their records confiscated, and themselves under arrest.

To facilitate the education of the German people in Nazi aims and ideology, the government took complete control of the radio. It already controlled the postal, telephone, and telegraph services, and did not hesitate to use them for espionage and surveillance. It established a heavy censorship of the press, cinema, and theater. Public meetings were forbidden, except those organized by the Nazis, and even the churches were subjected to surveillance. Joseph Goebbels, the Nazi minister for propaganda, organized huge mass meetings and other programs to inculcate positive loyalty to the regime. As in Italy and the Soviet Union, special youth groups indoctrinated children and young people in Nazi ideology and trained them to spy on others, including their parents, for signs of disloyalty to the regime.

Hitler sought to consolidate popular support for his regime by providing a scapegoat, "somebody to hate," in the persecution of whom the masses could work off the frustrations accumulated in ordinary life. An ideal vehicle for his purpose was the latent anti-Semitism of many Germans, which was amply attested by the popularity of *völkisch*, romantic, and racist literature from the nineteenth century. In *Mein Kampf* Hitler had fulminated against the Jews as the manipulators of both communism and "usurious capitalism." On April 1, 1933, the day the Enabling Act took effect legally, he unleashed an orgy of persecution against them. Persons of the Jewish faith or with Jewish ancestry were dismissed from the government and prohibited from practicing such professions as law and medicine. The police tolerated and even abetted the destruction of Jewish property and the physical molestation of Jewish shopkeepers and industrialists by organized gangs of roughnecks. In later years an even more terrible fate awaited the survivors of these pogroms.

Within less than a year after coming to power Hitler had succeeded in making himself almost complete master of the nation. Only two potential sources of opposition remained: the army and dissident elements within his own Nazi party. The way in which he used these two groups to neutralize one another and to ensure his own supremacy was indicative of his unscrupulous cunning and will to power. Many within the party felt that the Nazi revolution had not gone far enough and that the leaders were coming to terms with the old power structure and calling a halt to the revolution. They wanted more power and plunder for themselves. The ringleader of these radicals was Ernst Roehm, chief of staff of the storm troopers, whose desire was to become commander of all the armed forces of the nation.

The army, for its part, had generally remained aloof from the political maneuvering preceding and following Hitler's advent to power. The officer corps had survived intact both wartime defeat and the pacifism of the Weimar Republic; its members regarded themselves as the trustees and ultimate defenders of the nation's honor and traditions. Although

Photoworld

Adolf Hitler on the First Anniversary of His Government

"The Fuehrer combines in himself all of the sovereign authority of the state;
all public authority in the state . . . comes from the authority of the Fuehrer.
We must speak not of 'state authority' but of 'Fuehrer-authority' if we wish
to designate properly the political authority in the Reich. For it is not the
state as an impersonal entity that holds political authority, but this is entrusted
to the Fuehrer as the executor of the collective will of the Volk. *The authority*
of the Fuehrer is complete and total . . . extends to all areas of the life of
the Volk . . . *is not limited by spheres of privilege or individual rights, but is*
free and independent, exclusive and unlimited. However, it is not tyrannical
and it is not arbitrary, but carries its obligations within itself. It comes from
the Volk, *it is on behalf of the* Volk, *and it derives its justification from the*
Volk. *It is free of all external ties because in its innermost being it is*
inextricably tied to the fate, the welfare, the mission, and the honor of the
Volk. Ernst R. Huber, VERFASSUNGSRECHT DES GROSSDEUTSCHEN REICHES
(Hamburg, 1939).

they looked upon Hitler and his cronies with contempt as upstarts, they made no effort to prevent the Nazi seizure and consolidation of power so long as their own status was not challenged — and Hitler was careful to avoid that.

Roehm's aggressiveness, therefore, presented Hitler with a dilemma: he must either disavow a substantial element within his own party, or risk antagonizing the army, the only power in the nation that was strong enough to topple him. Events moved toward a showdown in the early summer of 1934. With the connivance of Goering and Heinrich Himmler, who were rivals and personal enemies of Roehm, Hitler secretly arranged for the sudden seizure and murder of Roehm and hundreds of his associates and sympathizers in the famous Blood Purge of June 30, 1934. As an excuse for this betrayal of his own supporters Hitler cited an alleged conspiracy to overthrow his government, but the conspiracy was mainly if not wholly of his own making. In any case, he not only silenced the potential opposition within the party but also won the approval of the General Staff. When the aged President Hindenburg died the following August, Hitler assumed the office of *Fuehrer und Reichskanzler* (leader and imperial chancellor) and received a personal oath of loyalty from the entire army. From that time forward he wielded absolute power in Germany.

NAZI IDEOLOGY

The Nazi seizure of power was facilitated by several more or less fortuitous occurrences — German defeat in World War I, the humiliations of the Versailles treaty, the disastrous economic and social consequences of the hyperinflation and the great depression, and the special features of the Weimar constitution — but the Nazis gained strength as a mass movement by appealing to certain intellectual and emotional tendencies long present in German history. Hitler's genius as a politician consisted in uniting his appeal to deep-seated ideological tendencies with an efficient organization, discipline, and a maniacal will to power. The temper of the German people in the interwar decades that allowed him to succeed has been called a "flight from reality." Hitler himself was one of its foremost examples.

Nazi ideology drew heavily on the romanticism of the early nineteenth century, on the racism of such writers as H. S. Chamberlain, and on the antirationalism and nihilism of some late nineteenth- and early twentieth-century philosophers. Like the romantics, the Nazis drew inspiration from legends of the heroic past of the Germanic people, clouded in the mists of obscurity but shining brightly in their purity and nobility. After 1933 the Bayreuth festival of Wagnerian opera became an official Nazi rite. The basic tenet of Nazi ideology was belief in the moral supremacy of the Aryan race, whom the Nazis identified with the Teutonic ancestors of the German Volk. According to Hitler, the whole of history was a cosmic struggle by this "master race" to dominate various "inferior" races, such as the Slavs, the Latins, and especially the Jews. The belief, whether real or feigned, that they were merely the executors of some grand design of Fate or Providence provided the Nazis with a convenient rationalization for their persecution of the Jews, for systematic terrorism, and for the grossest kind of barbaric, inhuman actions. Nazi racist policies attained their ultimate manifestation during World War II when thousands upon thousands of men, women, and children were executed in gas chambers and by firing squads for no other crime than that of being "non-Aryan."

The Nazi notion of a "master race" fitted well with Nietzsche's concept of a "superman" who was not bound by ordinary conventions of law and morality. So, too, did their emphasis on eternal struggle, violence, and power for its own sake. In some respects, however, the Nazis were quite conventional, even old-fashioned. Their viewpoint on the role of women in society was summed up in the slogan *Kinder, Kirche, Küche* (children, church, and kitchen). To indoctrinate the nation in their ideology, they made extensive use of mass rallies, great political spectacles with torchlight parades, military displays, and other devices that subordinated the individual personality to the "collective will." Their objective was to impress the populace with the Nazi notion of the individual's highest duty: service to the state.

NAZI ECONOMIC POLICY

The Nazis came to power in the midst of the greatest economic depression of modern times; indeed, the distress produced by that depression was one of the major factors that catapulted them to power. To counteract the depression Hitler introduced a gigantic public works program that melded gradually into a rearmament program. As a result Germany was the first nation to recover from the depression. In the process it developed the first modern highway system (the famed autobahns) and greatly strengthened and expanded its industries, which gave Germany a decided advantage over its enemies in the early years of World War II. From 6 million unemployed in 1933 the German economy reached the point in 1939 of having more jobs than workers to fill them.

In place of the voluntary trade unions, which were destroyed in 1933, the Nazis established compulsory membership in the National Labor Front under the leadership of Robert Ley. They abolished collective bargaining between workers and employers, substituting boards of labor trustees with full power to determine wages, hours, and conditions of work. Industrialists were persuaded to cooperate with the new industrial regime by the promise of an end to labor problems if they did and the threat of confiscation and imprisonment if they did not. Unlike the totalitarian regime in Russia, the Nazis did not resort to wholesale nationalization of the economy (although confiscated Jewish enterprises were frequently turned over to party members); they relied on persuasion and controls to achieve their objectives.

One of the principal economic objectives of the Nazis was to make the German economy completely self-sufficient in the event of war. They recalled the crippling effects of the Allied blockade in World War I and wished to be immune to such difficulties in the future. They directed their scientists to develop new *ersatz* or synthetic commodities, both consumer goods and military supplies, which could be manufactured from raw materials available in Germany. The policy of *Autarkie* (self-sufficiency) determined the character of German trade relations with other nations. Dr. Hjalmar Schacht, Hitler's economic adviser, devised numerous intricate new financial and monetary controls to prevent the flight of capital from Germany. He also negotiated trade agreements with Germany's neighbors in eastern Europe and the Balkans providing for the direct barter of German manufactured goods for raw materials and foodstuffs. Very few German goods were in fact shipped, but the policy successfully tied eastern Europe into the German war economy.

HITLER'S FOREIGN POLICY

In his propaganda campaign before achieving power Hitler had repeatedly hammered the theme of the immorality and injustice of the Diktat of Versailles. Soon after taking office he used the depression as an excuse to proclaim "an end of reparations," and in the autumn of 1933 he utilized the disarmament conference, then in session at Geneva under the sponsorship of the League of Nations, to discredit the Versailles treaty. Hitler demanded peremptorily that all other major nations reduce their armaments to the level imposed on Germany by the treaty. When the demand was refused, as Hitler had anticipated, he withdrew Germany from the League. This successful defiance of the League and of international opinion not only strengthened Hitler within Germany but also encouraged him in his aggressive foreign policy.

OTHER AUTHORITARIAN REGIMES

According to Woodrow Wilson, World War I had been fought to make the world safe for democracy. As factual description, such a statement was patently false; but in the first flush of Allied victory many people were carried away by Wilson's high-sounding phrases and idealism and actually believed that democracy would be universal. Disillusionment soon set in. By 1933, when the Weimar Republic succumbed to Hitler's Nazis, democracy was everywhere in retreat before the forces of authoritarianism. In Europe seventeen of the twenty-seven nations had one or another form of authoritarian government.

AUSTRIA

The Austrian republic, a "head without a body" after the dissolution of the Hapsburg monarchy, was now composed almost entirely of German-speaking citizens. Beset by currency disorders and widespread unemployment, it struggled desperately merely to exist. The country was sharply divided between two bitterly antagonistic political parties: the conservative Christian (Catholic) Socialists, who controlled the government but had their main strength outside Vienna, and the radical, Marxist-oriented Social Democrats, who controlled the municipal government of the capital. This division was further complicated by the rise of an Austrian Nazi party that took its orders from Hitler. To combat the Nazi menace after Hitler's accession to power, Austrian chancellor Engelbert Dollfuss created his own brand of fascism, a Christian Corporate State, and destroyed the Social Democrats as an organized body by armed force. In 1934 the Austrian Nazis attempted a coup d'état and assassinated Dollfuss, but the intervention of Mussolini and France prevented Hitler from taking advantage of the situation to absorb Austria. Kurt von Schuschnigg succeeded Dollfuss as chancellor and continued his policies; but with the Social Democrats out of the way the will to resist Hitler found few strong adherents in Austria, and Hitler had only to bide his time for a favorable moment to incorporate Austria into the German Fatherland.

EASTERN EUROPE

Except for Czechoslovakia and Finland, which hung onto democratic forms by the barest margin, eastern Europe capitulated entirely to authoritarian regimes. The Poles, whose nation had been resurrected in republican form at the end of the war, found it as difficult to agree among themselves as they had a century and a half before. To put an end to the wrangling of the political parties, Marshal Joseph Pilsudski staged a coup d'état in 1926 and established a military dictatorship. A similar development took place in Rumania in 1930 when King Carol II, who had been barred from the throne, deposed his infant son and assumed dictatorial powers. Hungary never tasted the fruits of democracy. After its short-lived Communist government at the end of the war, the old Magyar aristocracy regained power, and Admiral Nicholas Horthy governed in dictatorial fashion as regent for a nonexistent king. Yugoslavia was torn by continuing struggles among the various ethnic groups that composed the new nation. The struggles culminated in 1928 with the assassination of the opposition leaders in parliament. Shortly afterward King Alexander dissolved parliament, suspended the constitution, and governed as dictator. Alexander himself was assassinated on a trip to France in 1934, but the regency that governed in the name of his young son Peter II continued his policies. Greece and Bulgaria, both of which were nominally constitutional monarchies, experienced continual conflicts between dictatorial kings and reactionary military cliques. Albania and the new Baltic republics of Lithuania, Latavia, and Estonia also succumbed to dictatorial governments after brief experiments with democracy.

THE IBERIAN PENINSULA

Having avoided involvement in World War I, Spain escaped many of the dilemmas and problems that beset other European countries. Nevertheless, Spain was a poor and backward country, unprogressive politically as well as economically. It had never enjoyed democratic government, and during the premiership of Miguel Primo de Rivera from 1923 to 1930 the government became frankly dictatorial. Unrest mounted throughout the country. To save himself, King Alfonso XIII forced Primo de Rivera to resign; when that did not quell the discontent, the king himself fled to exile in the following year. Proclamation of a republic followed this bloodless revolution, and the democratic forces within Spain set out to create a progressive, enlightened commonwealth against the trend of the times.

Unhappily for Spain, neither its internal resources nor the external environment favored the experiment. The mass of the population, poverty stricken and illiterate, lacked both the experience and the ability — perhaps even the desire — for self-government. The government itself was a loose and refractory coalition of middle-class liberals, radical democrats, socialists, and even anarchists. In addition to its internal divisions, it soon encountered determined opposition from the conservative and reactionary elements who still controlled the bulk of the wealth of the country: the Church, the great landowners, and most of the higher army officers. In 1936 General Francisco Franco led a revolt against the government. The bloody, destructive civil war that followed invited foreign intervention and became a major milestone on the road to World War II. For Spain it resulted in the triumph of General Franco, who reorganized the Falange party, created by Primo de Rivera, on the model of Mussolini's Fascists and Hitler's Nazis, and proceeded to establish a reactionary authoritarianism that outlasted by far its models.

Portugal, like its neighbor, was a poor, benighted country. In spite of the revolution of 1911, which established a republican form of government, the country remained a prey to social strife and political unrest. In 1926 a military coup overthrew the elected government, and in 1932 Dr. Antonio Salazar, finance minister since 1928, became prime minister and in effect dictator. In the following year he introduced a new constitution which resembled in many respects that of Fascist Italy. Salazar retained his power for more than thirty-five years, outlasting even Stalin and setting a new record in modern times for one-man rule.

MILITARISM IN JAPAN

Authoritarian movements also arose in countries outside of Europe. They did not make much headway or constitute a serious menace to existing forms of government in the United States or the British dominions, but in Latin America, where democracy had never been effectively established, some form of dictatorship, however diluted, was the general rule. Most of Africa and much of Asia were ruled in the 1930's by the democratic countries of western Europe, though the method of rule was anything but democratic, with the result that democracy in those areas suffered a taint of hypocrisy which time has not yet erased. The independent or semi-independent countries of the Near East, the Middle East, and the Far East (East Asia, as it has come to be called) had no liberal or democratic traditions and continued to be ruled in the tradition of Oriental despotisms.

The one non-Western nation that had succeeded in adapting itself to Western ways followed the trend toward totalitarian dictatorship. During the 1920's Japan made progress in the extension of democratic practices and followed a policy of international cooperation in spite of the objections of Japanese militarists. The great depression cut short this peaceful evolution. Japan had a population of 65 million — half that of the United States — in an area smaller than the state of California. It was heavily dependent upon international trade, both for markets for its exports and for imports of food stuffs and raw materials. The shrinkage of international trade during the depression gave the militarists and other ultranationalists, including the great industrial dynasties, their opportunity to seize power. In 1931 they carried out the conquest of Manchuria despite the feeble protest of the League of Nations (see p. 948), and on the basis of this success they consolidated their domestic political power. The Japanese emperor, Hirohito, who had been a constitutional monarch, became a mere figurehead for the militarists and imperialists who used his prestige and attributes of divinity as a rallying point for ultranationalist sentiment. Making full use of the special advantages of Japanese tradition, they converted their nation to a brand of totalitarianism even more fanatical than those of Italy, Germany, and Russia.

THE COMMON ELEMENTS

In spite of differences, totalitarian and other dictatorial regimes possess many elements in common. The most obvious is the very fact of totalitarianism itself; that is, the subordination of all individual interests and objectives to one supreme goal. This feature is in marked contrast to the pluralism or multiplicity of recognized individual interests and objectives that characterizes liberal societies. The subordination of the individual implies the existence of only one political party to give voice to the prevailing official doctrine. Criticism and dissent are not tolerated. In a totalitarian country the very notion of a loyal opposition is a contradiction; any opposition to the regime or to official dogma is by definition disloyal.

For loyalty or disloyalty to exist there must be an object of loyalty. In the 1930's the focus of totalitarian loyalty was the national state. In fact, totalitarianism is sometimes referred to as "integral nationalism," an exaggerated, all-encompassing nationalism. Even in the Soviet Union, which is sometimes regarded as the fountainhead of international revolution, nationalism plays a large role. Nationalism, however, is not enough. The goals of the nation are determined by the party, and those of the party by its leader, whether he be *Il Duce, Der Führer,* or the People's Commissar. All power springs from the top. Such is the essence of totalitarian dictatorship.

The forms of dictatorship are many and varied. Consciously or unconsciously dictators follow the dictum of Machiavelli that tyranny is most easily achieved under familiar names. Thus, the Soviet Union takes the form of a federated republic; Fascist Italy was nominally a constitutional monarchy; and Nazi Germany at first took the guise of a republic, then in a strange anomaly became an empire without an emperor.

There are normally three stages in establishing a dictatorship. First is the stage of preparation, in which ideology is important as a device for attracting followers. The specific content of the ideology is of less significance than its mere existence. It should contain both positive inducements – a promise of reward – and poles of negative attraction – "somebody to hate." Even more important than ideology is the organization, the party. To achieve power and eliminate all other parties, the party must be extremely well disciplined. The second stage is investiture. It may or may not be achieved by legal means. In Soviet Russia and Spain it came about by means of revolution, but in Italy, Germany, and Japan it was achieved initially by legal processes. The third and in many respects the most crucial stage is consolidation. It involves the systematic elimination of all rival parties as well as all dissidence within the party. In Russia the former was achieved during the civil war, and the latter was effected by a long succession of intrigues ending with the great purge trials of the 1930's. Since in Italy and Germany the dictators had come to power in the first place by legal means, they were able to utilize the legal instruments of the state to eliminate the opposition, but they, too, were forced to resort to purges to purify their parties.

Once a dictatorship has established itself, it must strive by constant vigilance to maintain itself. For this it has many instruments. To discourage overt hostility to the regime, it utilizes force, violence, and terrorism: the armed forces, paramilitary forces, regular police, secret police, spies, and informers, to say nothing of prisons, concentration camps, torture, and death. To indicate positive loyalty, still other devices must be called into play — and it is in this area that modern totalitarian regimes have distinguished themselves from old-fashioned tyrannies. Propaganda is a major weapon. The use of propaganda for political purposes is by no means new, but modern mass communications and psychology make it infinitely more powerful and important than ever before. Closely related to propaganda are compulsory membership in patriotic organizations and the use of indoctrination and education for thought control. Censorship is resorted to as a matter of course in totalitarian societies, as are the teaching of special ideological subjects in schools and universities, political supervision of academic institutions, and loyalty oaths for both students and teachers. Academic freedom, like other freedoms, is a meaningless expression in such societies.

Dictatorships are established by force and maintained by force. The rulers must keep their subjects in a constant state of tension and anxiety to divert their attention from daily hardships and to provide a justification for the use of police-state methods. Fear can sometimes be aroused by alleging a threat of internal subversion. Even more effective is the pretense of an external threat to the nation, so that patriotism can be utilized to reinforce whatever loyalty the subjects may feel for the regime. Life in such a society becomes a constant state of war or preparation for war and is subject to the discipline of the barracks.

Finally, since dictatorships are created by force and maintained by force, they also perish by force. Napoleon, who is sometimes regarded as the first modern dictator, reputedly remarked that although bayonets were useful for many purposes, they could not be used as stools. Such is a dictator's paraphrase of the biblical injunction that those who live by the sword shall die by the sword.

THE SECOND WORLD WAR
CHAPTER THIRTY-SIX

The demoralization of the democracies in the wake of economic collapse and the failure of their liberal attempts at reconstruction enabled the dictatorships not only to consolidate their power internally but also to engage in external aggression. Repeatedly in the 1930's Japan, Italy, and Germany flouted international opinion, disregarded the League of Nations, and broke their treaty obligations. It seemed that the United States had permanently turned its back on the rest of the world in a retreat to isolation, and the feeble, half-hearted efforts of France and Britain to halt the aggressors merely annoyed the latter and stimulated them to further aggression. If, as Winston Churchill said, the Second World War was an "unnecessary" war in the sense that a vigorous and determined collective effort to halt aggression at any time prior to 1938 would have prevented it, thereafter the war became necessary for the survival of democracy.

In spite of the clear portents in the months and years preceding, the outbreak of the war in September, 1939, found the democracies tragically unprepared militarily, economically, and psychologically. The dictatorships, on the other hand, had for several years been engaged in a deliberate military and economic build-up, and the confidence engendered by their recent triumphs gave them a substantial psychological advantage. In the early years of the war Nazi Germany in particular went from success to spectacular success. After a series of disastrous defeats, Britain rallied in 1940 to fight off almost single-handedly a threatened invasion, while the United States gradually bestirred itself. In 1941 the aggressors made two fatal mistakes. Hitler suddenly and unexpectedly turned on the Soviet Union, his former partner-in-conquest, forcing it into an alliance with the Western powers; and with equal unexpectedness Japan attacked the United States, galvanizing American efforts in what at last became a common cause. For almost two more years the issue remained in doubt, but when the Allies finally mobilized their overwhelming resources, they gradually forced the Axis Powers back into their homelands. The war ended in Europe in May, 1945, with the complete and unconditional surrender of Germany, and in the Pacific in September with a similar surrender by Japan.

THE ORIGINS OF TOTALITARIAN AGGRESSION

Germany, Italy, and Japan, together with their satellites, eventually became allied as the Axis Powers, so-called from the Italo-German treaty of October, 1936, which established the Rome-Berlin "axis." Prior to 1936 each had pursued its aggressions independently and to some extent in opposition to one another.

JAPANESE EXPANSION IN ASIA AND THE PACIFIC

Japanese participation in World War I had been motivated principally by the desire of the Japanese to take over German possessions in the Pacific and German concessions in China. In this goal they were successful. They also utilized the Russian revolution to extend their interests in Manchuria, under the nominal suzerainty of China, by taking control of the South Manchurian Railway. In September, 1931, the Japanese troops guarding the railroad occupied Manchuria by force and shortly afterward set up a puppet regime, renaming the country Manchukuo. China appealed to the League of Nations for protection against the violation of its sovereignty; but France and Britain, in the midst of great economic difficulties, were reluctant to antagonize Japan, and the League proved powerless to act. A special commission took more than a year to produce a report, during which time the Japanese consolidated their position in Manchuria. Although the commission's report was critical of Japan, it recognized Japan's "special interest" in the area and recommended an "autonomous" government under Japanese tutelage. Even this solution did not satisfy the Japanese, who withdrew from the League in 1933 and defied its injunctions with impunity. Thus the first major test of the League's ability to prevent aggression tended to discredit it and encouraged other attempts to defy its authority.

Japan continued its pressure on China with the intention of forcing the Chinese into a position of subordination in what the Japanese rulers began to refer to as a "New Order" in Asia — a euphemism for a greatly enlarged Japanese Empire. The Chinese, much to the surprise of world opinion, overcame their internal divisions and under the leadership of a rejuvenated government put up a determined resistance. Despairing of gaining their objective without resort to force, the Japanese in 1937 provoked a military "incident" and began an all-out though still undeclared war on China. Japanese superiority in organization and equipment enabled them to capture the major cities and control the entire seacoast of China, but the Chinese fought on desperately and retreated slowly inland, refusing to surrender. The struggle had reached a stalemate when the outbreak of war in Europe gave the Japanese further opportunities for expansion elsewhere in Asia.

THE CONQUEST OF ETHIOPIA

Italy's Mussolini, eager for a foreign policy triumph and encouraged by the failure of the League to intervene effectively in the Manchurian dispute, resolved upon the conquest of Ethiopia, the one remaining independent native state in Africa. Ethiopia had galled the pride of nationalist Italians ever since the Ethiopians defeated an Italian army in 1896. In December, 1934, soldiers in Italian Somaliland provoked a border dispute as a pretext for an invasion. Frantic diplomatic negotiations ensued, but differences between France and Britain as to whether the Italians or the Germans constituted the greater menace prevented effective cooperation. Hoping to secure Italian support against the remilitarization of Germany, France in effect gave Italy a free hand. Britain concentrated a naval force in the Mediterranean, but lacking French support and adequate air power, it refrained from direct or provocative action. In September, 1935, Italian troops crossed the Ethiopian frontier and began the conquest of the country.

The League of Nations, which was in session at the time, immediately declared Italy the aggressor and voted sanctions in the form of a boycott of Italian exports and an embargo on exports to Italy. The embargo did not include petroleum; moreover, several nations that had just declared Italy an aggressor and voted for the sanctions refused to enforce them. Unwilling to risk an armed conflict, the British did not close the Suez Canal to Italian ships, although it was the only practical way for Italy to transfer troops and supplies to the battlefront. Utilizing modern weapons, including aircraft and poison gas, the Italians soon overcame the barefooted Ethiopian tribesmen and occupied the country. The actions of the League had no other effect than to antagonize Mussolini and push him closer to Hitler. In a vain attempt to prevent a rapprochement between Italy and Germany and to keep Italy in the League, the League formally voted to withdraw the sanctions against Italy, in effect recognizing the Italian conquest. The action completely discredited the League in the eyes of both friends and foes.

INTERVENTION AND NONINTERVENTION IN SPAIN

The furor over the Ethiopian crisis had barely subsided when civil war broke out in Spain. The Republican government, which had recently formed a Popular Front similar to that in France, immediately appealed to France and Britain for assistance; but those two countries, hoping to localize the conflict, called for an international agreement against intervention and banned the shipment of war materials to either side. Although Germany and Italy participated in the committee on non-intervention, they also supplied men ("volunteers"), munitions, and equipment to General Franco's insurgents. In the early part of the war the Soviet Union sent military advisers to assist the Loyalist forces, as well as driblets of equipment by means of merchant vessels, but distance and the difficulties of communication prohibited any large-scale aid to the Republican government. The United States maintained its now traditional posture of isolation and neutrality, but many idealistic young Americans, as well as antifascists from other lands, joined an International Brigade to fight for what they regarded as the cause of freedom and democracy. In this respect as well as in the sphere of military technology the Spanish civil war seemed to be a sort of rehearsal for World War II. The major German contribution took the form of dive bombers and other mechanized equipment, which proved to be the decisive factor in the triumph of the insurgent forces and gave the German General Staff valuable experience in the new techniques of warfare.

In spite of their disadvantages in trained manpower and modern equipment and supplies, the forces loyal to the Republican government fought on doggedly for almost three years. The struggle destroyed cities, ravaged the countryside, and left Spain both physically and morally exhausted. It took almost a million lives, including executions and civilian deaths from bombing and starvation, out of a population of approximately 25 million. In its international aspect it gave the forces of aggression further cause for self-congratulation and further sullied and demoralized the democracies.

THE ASCENDANCY OF NAZI GERMANY

Hitler's repudiation of the League of Nations within nine months of his accession to power clearly indicated the future trend of Nazi foreign policy. Although he received a minor setback in 1934 when Mussolini opposed his designs on Austria, it proved to be temporary. In January, 1935, the inhabitants of the Saarland on the border between France and Germany voted overwhelmingly for reunion with Germany in a plebiscite provided for by the Versailles treaty. On the strength of this triumph Hitler shortly afterward denounced the clauses of the treaty pertaining to the limitation on German armaments and reintroduced universal military service in Germany. Thoroughly alarmed, France convoked representatives of Britain and Mussolini's Italy at a conference in Stresa, Italy, and secured a condemnation of Germany by the League. The League, however, had no means of forcing German adherence, and Hitler cleverly divided his opponents by agreeing to a limitation on naval armaments with Britain. This agreement strained Franco-British relations, prevented effective cooperation in the Ethiopian crisis, and led France to seek an alliance with Soviet Russia. In the following year Hitler took advantage of Italy's involvement in the Ethiopian war with its international repercussions to denounce the Locarno agreements of 1925 and to remilitarize the Rhineland. France protested, but momentarily isolated diplomatically and embroiled in a domestic political crisis, it took no effective action.

Thus far only Mussolini had effectively opposed any of Hitler's moves in the international arena. After his African adventure, however, Mussolini himself began to feel the need for a friend on the international stage. The fact that both Germany and Italy were revisionist nations (in the sense that both wanted to revise the territorial provisions of the Treaty of Versailles), the similarity in their forms of government, and their common collaboration with the Spanish insurgents drew the two totalitarian dictatorships together. Only the Austrian question separated them. To remove this obstacle, Hitler in 1936 concluded a pact with the Austrian government wherein he promised to respect Austrian sovereignty; for its part, Austria agreed on the advice of Mussolini to conduct itself "as a German nation." With the path thus cleared, Hitler and Mussolini reached an accord in October, 1936, which resulted in the formation of the Rome-Berlin "axis." The following month Germany and Japan signed an "Anti-Comintern" treaty, ostensibly directed against the spread of international communism, to which Italy adhered in the following year. The Axis Powers of World War II had initiated their fateful alliance.

Hitler's early opinion of Mussolini had been one of exaggerated respect, whereas Mussolini had regarded Hitler as something of an upstart. Their opinions underwent a subtle transformation in the two years following the Italo-German accord. Hitler greatly impressed Mussolini with German efficiency and industrial and military power during an elaborately staged state visit in 1937, while Hitler cynically took the measure of his Italian ally. Hitler continued to go forward with his rearmament program in Germany and further established his ascendancy over both the army and the foreign office by replacing career officers in the highest positions by men who were personally loyal to him, such as Joachim von Ribbentrop as foreign minister.

THE ANNEXATION OF AUSTRIA

Hitler's first attempt at foreign aggrandizement had been directed against Austria in 1934. It was a natural, even a predictable move: Hitler was himself a native of Austria, and on the first page of *Mein Kampf* he had stated his belief in the desirability of uniting all German-speaking peoples in a "Greater Germany." His own weakness and Mussolini's opposition had stymied the first attempt, but the situation had changed greatly since then. Italy and Germany were now bound by a treaty of friendship and cooperation, and Italy was heavily involved in Mediterranean affairs. As for France and Britain, the only other powers able to interpose effective opposition, they had already shown their weaknesses.

In February, 1938, Hitler peremptorily summoned the Austrian Chancellor Kurt von Schuschnigg to his mountain retreat at Berchtesgaden in the Bavarian Alps. He stormed and ranted that the Austrian government was violating the agreement of 1936 by suppressing and persecuting the Austrian National Socialist party. Without giving Schuschnigg an opportunity to reply, Hitler demanded that all imprisoned Nazis in Austria be pardoned, that Nazis be allowed to engage in political activity, and that some of them be admitted to the Austrian cabinet. Hitler specifically demanded that Arthur Seyss-Inquart, the Austrian Nazi leader, be made minister of the interior with full control of the police. He added that neither France nor Britain, nor even Italy, would intervene on behalf of Austria, that Germany was invincible, and that he, Hitler, had become "perhaps the greatest German in history." Schuschnigg, who had traveled to Germany with but a single attendant, weakly agreed; but after returning to Austria, he sought to circumvent Hitler by calling for a national plebiscite. When Hitler learned of it, he went into one of his characteristic rages and immediately ordered the closure of the Austrian frontier and the mobilization of German troops along the border. At the same time he sent a personal messenger to Mussolini with a letter of explanation and reassurance. Greatly to his relief, Mussolini raised no objections — it was possibly the last time until the end of the war that Hitler entertained any doubts of his own infallibility — and Hitler put his plan in motion. With Goering giving the orders by telephone from Berlin, Seyss-Inquart forced Schuschnigg's resignation and seized power for himself. He then called on Germany to send in its army to preserve "law and order." On Saturday, March 12, 1938, German troops marched into Austria; the following day Hitler laid a wreath on the tomb of his parents in the little town of Braunau. The wayward son had returned.

On March 14 in Vienna Hitler formally proclaimed the *Anschluss* (union) of Austria and Germany. To legitimize his victory, he called for a plebiscite and new elections to the Reichstag. Under Nazi supervision, which was accompanied by unusually severe persecution of the Jews and other potential enemies of the regime, the Austrians responded with a 99.75 per cent favorable vote.

THE MUNICH CRISIS AND CZECHOSLOVAKIA

The ease with which Hitler achieved his objective in Austria tempted him to further conquests. Czechoslovakia was the next logical victim.

Hitler had come to hate the Czechs during his early days in Vienna. The multinational state, an artificial creation of the Treaty of St. Germain, projected into Germany like a drumstick in the mouth of a ravenous man. Its western fringes contained more than 3 million German-speaking citizens — the *Sudetendeutsch*. Aided by the local affiliate of the Nazi party led by Konrad Henlein, Hitler utilized the German minority to agitate first for self-determination for themselves and then, more boldly, for unification with the Third Reich. As in Austria, Hitler made full use of the slogans of Wilson during World War I. He prepared for an invasion in May, 1938; but an unexpectedly strong stand by France, which had defensive treaties with both Czechoslovakia and the Soviet Union, deterred him.

French belligerence did not last long. Deeply divided on domestic political and social questions as well as militarily weak, France was subject to a strong current of pessimism. This was known equally well to Hitler and to the French government. Hitler intensified his pressure on the Czechs, even stating his general intentions publicly at a Nazi party congress. Britain, for its part, was not only militarily unprepared but strongly influenced by pacifism. Many Britons, convinced of the mistakes of the Versailles treaty, sympathized with German desires to revise it and insisted on "peace at any price." British prime minister Neville Chamberlain, half-brother of the earlier British foreign minister Austen Chamberlain, shared their view, apparently believing that Hitler was no less sincere than Stresemann. In August, 1938, he sent his representative, Lord Runciman, to Prague to persuade the Czech leaders to conciliate Hitler. In September Chamberlain personally made three flying trips to Germany, an unprecedented action for a British prime minister, to confer with the German leader. On the final trip he was joined by Édouard Daladier, premier of France, and Hitler's ally Mussolini. On September 29–30 in Munich these four, acting without representatives of either Czechoslovakia or Russia, with whom both France and Czechoslovakia had alliances, agreed to the partition of Czechoslovakia. Chamberlain returned to Britain to the cheers of the multitude and with the slogan "Peace in our time." Subsequently, "Munich" and "appeasement" became almost synonymous with shortsightedness and cowardice.

The Munich agreement only provided for the cession of the Sudetenland to Germany. Although it was all that Hitler had demanded both in public and with Chamberlain, he secretly harbored the desire to eliminate Czecho-Slovakia (as it was spelled after Munich) altogether. He therefore encouraged both Poland and Hungary in their desires to chip off portions of the truncated country, and he supported the Slovaks and Ruthenians in their demands for autonomy from the Czechs. With the help of such internal disturbances it proved a simple matter in March, 1939, for Hitler to swallow completely the remains of Bohemia and

Delegates at Munich, 1938. Left to right: Neville Chamberlain,
Édouard Daladier, Adolf Hitler, Benito Mussolini

> *"[The people] should know that we have sustained a defeat without a war . . . ;*
> *they should know that we have passed an awful milestone in our history . . .*
> *and that the terrible words have for the time being been pronounced against*
> *the Western democracies: 'Thou art weighed in the balance and found wanting.'*
> *And do not suppose this is the end. This is only the beginning of the reckoning.*
> *This is only the first sip, the first foretaste of a bitter cup which will be proffered*
> *to us year by year unless, by a supreme recovery of moral health and martial*
> *vigor, we arise again and take our stand for freedom as in the olden time."*
> Speech by W. S. Churchill in the House of Commons, October 5, 1938, in
> W. S. Churchill, BLOOD, SWEAT, AND TEARS (New York, 1941).

Moravia, the homeland of the Czechs, and to make Slovakia a "protectorate" of Greater Germany. Hungary absorbed Ruthenia and thereby
gained a common frontier with Poland. These actions caught the democracies completely by surprise, for many had believed Hitler when he
stated that the reunion of the *Sudetendeutsch* with Germany fulfilled

his final international objective. Although this perfidy was carried out in circumstances that rendered the democracies powerless to act, it strengthened the hands of those in the West like Winston Churchill who had come to regard war with Hitler as inevitable.

BLITZKRIEG, 1939–1941

In one of his first actions in the field of foreign affairs Hitler had concluded a ten-year nonaggression pact with Poland in January, 1934. In the wake of the Munich agreement he encouraged the Poles in their demands on Czechoslovakia. Six months later, however, Hitler created a crisis in Polish-German relations by demanding cession of the Free City of Danzig to Germany and rights of extraterritoriality for Germans in the so-called Polish Corridor, the strip of Poland bordering the Baltic Sea, which separated East Prussia from the rest of Germany. The crisis was not entirely unexpected, for apart from historic Polish-German hatreds the Germans had never reconciled themselves to their loss of territory to resurrected Poland after World War I, and German Nazis in Danzig had been agitating for reunion with Germany for several years. Even before the rise of Hitler, Poland had sought to insure itself by concluding alliances and agreements with France, Rumania, Yugoslavia, and Czechoslovakia, as well as with another historic enemy of Polish independence — Russia. The Czechoslovakian debacle showed the worthlessness of the existing agreements and initiated a diplomatic scramble to preserve the existing situation in eastern Europe. Britain and France at once pledged assistance to Poland in the event of attack and began to negotiate with the Soviet Union for a common front against the Axis Powers.

In the 1920's, when both the Soviet Union and Germany were outcasts among the family of nations, they had engaged in clandestine cooperation. After the rise of Hitler with his blatant anti-communist program and pronouncements the Russians had sought alignments with the West. They entered the League of Nations, encouraged communists in France and elsewhere to enter Popular Fronts, and concluded alliances with France and Czechoslovakia directed against a renewal of German aggression. The weakness and vacillation of the Western powers in the face of repeated crises gave the Russians little confidence in their ability to withstand Hitler, however. Before Munich the Russians had publicly declared their willingness to support Czechoslovakia against Germany, but in spite of the joint Franco-Russian guarantee to the Czechs they were not even consulted during the Munich crisis. Although Chamberlain had called on Hitler three times in person, the British sent only a civil servant to negotiate in Moscow in the spring of 1939. The Russians therefore remained profoundly suspicious of the Western powers and took steps of their own to ensure their western borders by negotiating secretly with Hitler. On August 23, 1939, in a historic reversal of both Nazi and Soviet policy, Germany and the Soviet Union concluded a nonaggression pact that prepared the way for a new partition of Poland.

In spite of frantic diplomatic activity and last-minute appeals by President Roosevelt, Germany attacked Poland without a formal declaration of war on September 1, 1939. Fast-moving motorized columns streaked across the Polish plain, converging on Warsaw from East Prussia, Silesia, and Slovakia. In the air the new German *Luftwaffe* quickly knocked out the inadequate Polish air force, and German dive bombers added a new dimension of terror and destructiveness to warfare by mass bombardments of hapless civilians. The Germans called their new military techniques *Blitzkrieg* (lightning war). It proved devastatingly effective, breaking the backbone of Polish resistance in a matter of days. France and Britain formally declared war against Germany on September 3, but they were in no position to render immediate material aid to Poland.

SOVIET AGGRESSION

The rapidity of the German advance startled the Russians no less than the Western powers. A secret protocol to their treaty with Germany provided for a sharing of the spoils in eastern Europe. To make sure that they would obtain their share they launched a sudden invasion of Poland from the east on September 17, and two days later they joined up with the advancing German columns at Brest Litovsk, the scene of a previous historic German-Soviet encounter. On this occasion they met as cobelligerents. Before the month was out German and Russian troops completely subdued Poland and divided the country between them.

In the crisis leading up to the invasion of Poland the Baltic countries of Lithuania, Latvia, and Estonia had all signed treaties with Germany under thinly veiled threats of coercion. They now found themselves almost completely surrounded by the Soviet Union, except for the Baltic sea front and a short Lithuanian-Prussian border. Under similar threats from Russia they signed far-reaching agreements that made them virtual protectorates of the Soviet Union. In the following year they became component republics of the Union of Soviet Socialist Republics.

The Soviet Union made similar demands on Finland which the Finns rejected. On November 30, 1939, three Soviet armies invaded Finland to begin the Winter War. The Finns fought bravely and inflicted heavy losses on the numerically superior Russians, but in the absence of external aid the eventual outcome was never in doubt. In March, 1940, the Finns sued for peace. They ceded the Karelian Isthmus, an important naval base, several islands, and other pieces of territory to the Soviet Union, but they retained their autonomy. The heroic defense of their homeland by the Finns, though it ended in military defeat, constituted the only source of encouragement to the foes of aggression in a long year of disappointment and disaster.

NEW NAZI SURPRISES

Throughout the fall and winter of 1939–40 action on the western front had been minimal. The French dug in behind their supposedly impregnable Maginot Line, expecting World War II to be a replay of World War I, while German forces mopped up in Poland and then redeployed to the west. The British concentrated on building up their armaments and imposed a naval blockade on Germany. Cynical Western journalists, especially in the neutral United States, dubbed the war in the west a "Phony War" and a *Sitzkrieg*. Some faint-hearted souls even hoped that Germany and the Soviet Union would become embroiled with one another and give France and Britain an opportunity to withdraw. Hitler soon disabused them of the notion.

Before dawn on the morning of April 9, 1940, German armored columns crossed the border of Denmark, with which Germany had signed a nonaggression pact less than a year before, and German airborne troops parachuted down throughout the country. At the same time Germany launched an air and sea invasion against Norway. Caught defenseless and completely by surprise, the Danes surrendered to German occupation without formal resistance. The Norwegians, equally surprised but having more opportunity to organize resistance, fought fiercely for a time. A small Anglo-French expeditionary force was hurriedly sent to their assistance, only to withdraw with heavy casualties after two weeks. The conquest of Norway required less than a month. King Haakon VII and his government escaped to London in British naval vessels and remained a "government in exile" throughout the war. In both Denmark and Norway the German success was facilitated by local Nazi sympathizers. The name of one of them, Vidkun Quisling, who subsequently became head of the Germans' puppet regime in Norway, became synonymous with traitor.

Hitler's victorious legions gave the Allies no time to recover from their shock. On May 10 the *Wehrmacht* and the *Luftwaffe* struck simultaneously in the neutral Netherlands, Belgium, and Luxembourg with no more warning than before. A massive air attack using incendiary bombs practically wiped out the city of Rotterdam, inflicting enormous civilian casualties. The Dutch opened the dikes and flooded their low-lying country, but even that recourse could not slow the airborne conquerors. On May 14 the small Dutch army capitulated. The government and royal family followed the Norwegian precedent and fled to London.

The Belgians held out longer, supported by the French and a small British expeditionary force, until in a lightening drive across northern France to the Channel coast the Germans separated them from the main body of the French army. Short of supplies and faced with overwhelming odds, King Leopold ordered his troops to lay down their arms on May 26. The remaining French and British troops, along with some Belgians who refused to surrender, fell back on Dunkirk where they were trapped with their backs to the sea. Harassed by constant air attack and long-range bombardment, hundreds of British vessels — warships, fishing boats, even pleasure craft manned by civilian volunteers — miraculously evacuated more than 300,000 men (including 100,000 French and Belgians) from the Dunkirk beaches in the early days of June. The cost was enormous: more than 30,000 casualties and prisoners, and abandonment to the Germans of nearly all equipment and munitions.

THE FALL OF FRANCE

Dominated by the strategic thinking of World War I, the French high command had taken psychological as well as physical refuge behind the Maginot Line. In spite of the precedent of a German invasion through neutral Belgium in 1914, they had constructed only a light line of fortifications along the Belgian frontier. The German air force and armored divisions were greatly superior to the French in both quantity and quality. The French were therefore almost totally unprepared for the kind of warfare forced upon them by Hitler's *Panzer* (armored) divisions. The shock of realizing the extent of their unpreparedness shattered the morale of the French army and society — from the high command to the lowliest recruit, from cabinet ministers to kitchen help. The only notable resistance offered by the French army was a tank attack near Abbéville, brilliantly executed against overwhelming odds by a major general named Charles de Gaulle. The French received a further jolt on June 10 when Mussolini unexpectedly declared war and launched an invasion of southern France. Paris fell without a battle on June 14. The government fled to Bordeaux amid recrimination and dispute as to whether to fight on or to sue for peace. On June 16 Marshal Henri-Philippe Pétain, the "hero of Verdun" in World War I, replaced Paul Reynaud as premier and immediately requested an armistice.

The truce terms, dictated by Hitler personally at Compiègne in the same railroad carriage that had been the scene of the armistice of 1918, forced France to disband its armed forces, surrender all military equipment and munitions (including the navy), and submit to German occupation of more than half of its territory. The government of octogenarian Marshal Pétain moved to the health resort of Vichy in unoccupied France, where it became known as the Vichy regime. The dazed and frightened parliament voted dictatorial powers to Pétain, who formally abolished the Third Republic and set up an authoritarian government with himself as chief of state and Pierre Laval as prime minister.

THE EXPANSION OF GERMANY, 1935-1939

Dates of acquisition thus: Mar., 1938

Germany in 1933

Boundary of Germany, 1939

SWEDEN
DENMARK
Copenhagen
Baltic Sea
Hamburg
NETHER-LANDS
Elbe R.
GERMANY
Cologne
Berlin
Oder R.
RHINELAND RE-MILITARIZED, Mar., 1936
LUX.
Frankfurt
SAAR PLEBISCITE, Jan., 1935
Danube R.
FRANCE
Rhine R.
Munich
SWITZ.
Geneva
ITALY
Sept., 1938
SUDETENLAND
Prague
BOHEMIA
Mar., 1939
MORAVIA
CZECHO-SLOVAKIA
Berchtesgaden
Vienna
AUSTRIA
Mar., 1938
MEMEL
Mar., 1939
Danzig
Königsberg
E. PRUSSIA
Vistula R.
Warsaw
POLAND
TO POLAND, 1938
RUTHENIA
TO HUNGARY
Nov., 1938
TO HUNGARY
Mar., 1939
Budapest
HUNGARY
RUMANIA
LITHUANIA
Kaunas

0   150
Miles

Not all Frenchmen paid allegiance to the Vichy government. Thousands fled to North Africa, Britain, and elsewhere. Among them was Charles de Gaulle, who had been one of the few to recognize and decry the obsolescence of French military policy in the 1930's. He secured recognition from the British government as head of the French National Committee of Liberation (popularly known as the Free French or Fighting French). He organized the remnants of the French army in Britain (and later in North Africa) as an adjunct of the Allied forces and made stirring radio broadcasts from London to his countrymen in France. Many Frenchmen who remained in their homes and jobs joined the *Maquis* and other underground organizations of French patriots, and engaged in espionage and sabotage against the Germans.

THE BATTLE OF BRITAIN

Immediately after the German invasion of the Low Countries Winston Churchill replaced Neville Chamberlain as prime minister of a National (all-party) government in Great Britain. Churchill had been an articulate but little-heeded critic of both Hitler and British appeasement in the 1930's. His oratorical abilities now played a crucial role in stimulating British morale and weaning the United States from its isolationist mentality. With the fall of France Britain became the only active belligerent against the Axis Powers in Europe, although it was supported by the British dominions, which had all made common cause with Britain in 1939.

In September, 1940, Germany, Italy, and Japan (which was still at war with China) concluded a new and more far-reaching military and economic alliance. Hitler turned his attention to crushing his last rival in Western Europe. In order to do so, it would be necessary to invade Britain, but a cross-channel invasion required mastery of the air. The Battle of Britain was first and foremost an aerial battle. The *Luftwaffe* mounted massive attacks by both fighters and bombers in order to destroy British airpower, industrial capacity, and civilian morale. The losses inflicted were enormous. Thousands of civilians died in mass bombings, accentuated by the use of incendiary bombs. The automotive center of Coventry was reduced to rubble, as were large portions of many other industrial and port cities, including London. But the Royal Air Force, strengthened by contingents of volunteers from many lands and aided by a newly developed radar network, held its own and exacted an exhorbitant cost from the attackers. In the three months of most intense aerial warfare (from the beginning of August to the end of October, 1940) the RAF destroyed almost 2,500 enemy aircraft while losing less than 1,000 of its own. Churchill's eulogy is their most lasting monument: "Never in the field of human conflict was so much owed by so many to so few."

While Britain stood almost alone in actual combat, the United States extended increasing material aid. In response to a direct appeal from Churchill after Dunkirk the American War Department shipped large quantities of military supplies to Britain. In September, 1940, President Roosevelt exchanged fifty overage American destroyers for long-term leases on British military and naval bases in the Western Hemisphere. In March, 1941, he persuaded Congress to enact the Lend-Lease Bill, by which the United States supplied vast amounts of foodstuffs and military equipment to beleaguered Britain. The United States Navy also took an active part in antisubmarine patrols and convoy duty in the North Atlantic.

Had the Germans actually launched an invasion of Britain in the autumn of 1940, it is conceivable that they might have succeeded, even though Churchill promised that "we shall fight on the beaches . . . on the landing grounds . . . in the fields, and in the streets . . . we shall never surrender." Apparently the German high command overestimated the British reserves of supplies, equipment, and trained manpower, which were then at an all-time low. The General Staff was reluctant to undertake a cross-channel invasion, and it seems clear in retrospect that Hitler himself, who had overruled the timidity of his generals and admirals before, never really wanted or expected to invade Britain. He waited a month after the fall of France before unleashing his great air attacks in the expectation that Britain itself would ask for a truce, and he gave the preparatory orders for an invasion only after the British had declined to respond to a conciliatory speech he made in the Reichstag. In any event, the *Luftwaffe* never achieved the aerial superiority regarded as necessary even by Hitler, and with the approach of winter the Germans gradually abandoned their plans for an invasion of Britain in favor of further expansion in the east.

AFRICA AND THE BALKANS

Meanwhile Hitler's ally involved him in costly and annoying diversions in the south. Mussolini had piously proclaimed Italy's neutrality during the invasion of Poland and watched with envy Hitler's spectacular successes in Scandinavia and the Low Countries. Even crumbling France had held his armies at bay after having been defeated in the north. Hitler added to his humiliation by refusing to let Italian troops occupy the south of France and take over the French empire in Africa. To salve his wounded pride, Mussolini took advantage of Britain's preoccupation with the defense of its homeland to launch attacks from Ethiopia and Libya against British possessions in Africa. In October, 1940, he sprung an invasion of Greece from the Albanian protectorate which he had acquired almost unnoticed in the alarums of the spring of 1939.

At first his aggressive intentions succeeded. British forces evacuated British Somaliland and retreated in both Egypt and central Africa, and the Greeks recoiled in the face of his surprise attack. Within a few months, however, the situation reversed itself. In December British and Imperial forces under General Wavell counterattacked with spectacular success in Africa, and at the same time Greek units, supported by the scanty British garrison in Egypt, repulsed the Italians and invaded Albania.

Hitler, whom Mussolini had neither consulted nor forewarned, fumed and raged, but in order to protect the German flank he came to Mussolini's rescue. He had already imposed his will upon the governments of Hungary, Bulgaria, and Rumania in the fall of 1940, forcing Rumania to give up territory to the other two. In the spring of 1941 the Germans overran Yugoslavia and unleashed a massive ground and air attack on Greece, which succumbed in a matter of weeks. The British troops in Greece retreated first to Crete, then fled from an airborne invasion of that island to Cyprus and Egypt. Simultaneously German troops under the command of General Erwin Rommel, who had entered Africa by way of Italy, forced the British North African army back on Egypt. The Germans once more demonstrated their superior organization and tactics, but the dispersion of their forces prevented them from driving on to total victory in any single area.

THE INVASION OF RUSSIA

Notwithstanding his cynical pact of August, 1939, with the Soviet Union, Hitler never abandoned his plans for an eventual attack on Russia. His contempt for Slavic peoples was second only to his hatred of the Jews. His sudden onslaughts against Norway, Denmark, and the Low Countries and his rapid victory in France had been intended primarily to protect Germany from an attack from the west while it carried out its aggressive intentions in the east. He hoped and expected that Britain would sue for peace after the fall of France, and he undertook the Battle of Britain with reluctance. Even while that battle was at its height in the fall of 1940, he gave the order to prepare an invasion of Russia.

Hitler originally contemplated the invasion of Russia for the spring of 1941 in order that German airpower and mechanized equipment could be used to best advantage during a long summer campaign. The problems created by Mussolini's failures in the Balkans and North Africa forced a postponement of the invasion. Hitler's own failure to persuade General Franco to enter the war deprived him of the opportunity to take Gibraltar and nullify British power in the Mediterranean. Overruling his military advisers, who advised a decisive contest in the Mediterranean and North Africa, Hitler went forward with his long-nourished dream for the conquest of Russia.

Although taken by surprise in the matter of timing, the Soviet Union was not entirely unprepared for this act of perfidy. Its own adherence to the pact with Germany had taken place in full recognition of Hitler's ultimate intentions. It had fortified itself in the summer of 1940 by taking over the Baltic republics; subsequently it took over Bessarabia and northern Bukovina from Rumania. Hitler's occupation of the Balkans and a treaty with Finland giving German troops the right of access to that country had strengthened Stalin's suspicions. Militarily, however, the Soviet armies were no match for German power. The German invasion, supported by Rumanians, Hungarians, and Finns, began on June 22, 1941, across the entire length of the western frontier of the Soviet Union. Following the tactics that had proved so successful in the two previous years, the invaders quickly rolled back the Russian defenders.

Sovfoto

The Battle of Stalingrad

"The soldiers of the Red Army have sealed this German Army group within an unbreakable ring. All hopes of the rescue of your troops by a German offensive from the south or southwest have proved vain. The German units hastening to your assistance were defeated by the Red Army. . . .

"The German air transport fleet, which brought you a starvation ration of food, munitions and fuel, has been compelled . . . repeatedly to withdraw to airfields more distant from the encircled troops.

". . . The situation of your troops is desperate. They are suffering from hunger, sickness and cold. The cruel Russian winter has scarcely yet begun. Hard frosts, cold winds and blizzards still lie ahead." From the Russian demand for surrender, January 8, 1943, reprinted in D. Flower and J. Reeves, eds., THE WAR 1939–1945 (London, 1960).

History never repeats itself exactly; yet the parallels between Napoleon's invasion of Russia and that of Hitler are striking. Hitler, like Napoleon, invaded Russia after attempts to bring Britain to its knees had failed. Like Napoleon, Hitler had allies among several of the smaller states of Europe, whose rulers hated and despised the Russians but feared Hitler even more. In 1941–42, as in 1812, the invaders were better equipped and disciplined than the defending armies but did not take sufficiently into account the vast distances, the bitter winters, and the dogged resistance of the Russian people — civilians as well as soldiers. Finally, the crowning parallel was that the Russian invasions of both Napoleon and Hitler marked the peak of their power after several years of almost unbroken success: the checks and eventual defeats that they suffered in Russia proved the preludes to a sudden drastic shrinkage and then collapse of their respective empires.

Before the invasion Hitler confidently expected to conquer Russia in the course of the summer. He might well have done so had the invasion begun on schedule. As it was, the German armies completely encircled Leningrad, drove to the outskirts of Moscow, and occupied most of southern Russia before the onset of winter temporarily halted the German offensive. The winter punished the German troops severely and gave the Russians a much-needed respite to reorganize their defenses and begin receiving supplies from Britain and the United States, whose material contributions to the Allies increased enormously after it became directly involved in the war in December, 1941. The German offensive resumed in the summer of 1942, and although it failed to take either Leningrad or Moscow, it made further substantial gains in southern Russia, pushing deep into the Caucasus in an attempt to gain the Caspian oil fields. By September the invaders had penetrated to Stalingrad, a strategic point on the Volga River.

Stalingrad marked the high point of the German invasion. By that time the invading armies had greatly overextended both their supply lines and their battle lines. German industrial production suffered from increasingly heavy Allied aerial bombardment, and troops had to be diverted to meet Allied invasions in the Mediterranean area, while Russian equipment and munitions increased in both quantity and quality as a result of American aid. Again the winter set in. After a fierce battle that raged for four months, the Germans finally abandoned the attack on Stalingrad at the beginning of 1943 and began a long, slow, costly retreat. By mid-April the Russians had regained all the territory conquered by the Germans in their 1942 offensive. The war continued on Russian soil for more than a year, until August, 1944, but the invaders were gradually driven backward into their homeland. Hitler's bid for mastery of the Eurasian heartland had failed.

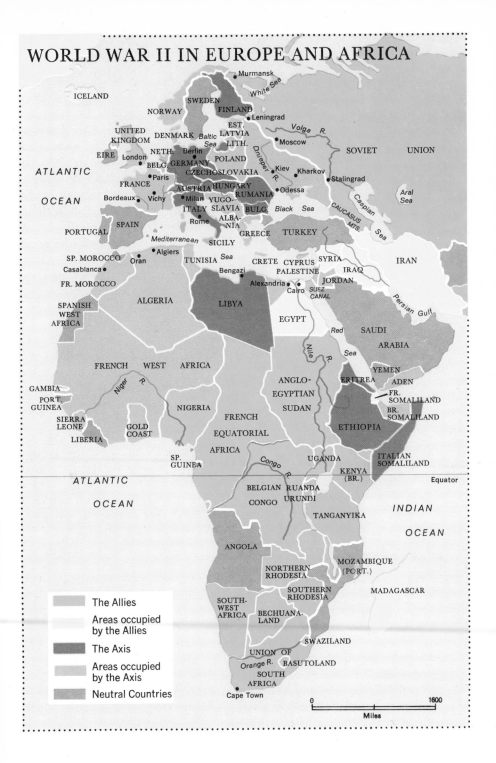

WORLD WAR II IN EUROPE AND AFRICA

The Allies

Areas occupied by the Allies

The Axis

Areas occupied by the Axis

Neutral Countries

0   1600

Miles

965

PEARL HARBOR AND THE
WAR IN THE PACIFIC

Japan took advantage of the war in Europe to enhance its power in Asia. Germany and Italy, who had no vital interests of their own in the Orient, sought to draw Japan into a closer alliance in order to embarrass France and Britain, who did have extensive interests there. Hoping to avoid harassment from the rear, the Soviet Union agreed to a settlement of outstanding differences with Japan concerning East Asian territory and even signed a treaty of neutrality in April, 1941. After the fall of France, Japan and Germany pressured the Vichy government into granting Japan a virtual protectorate over French Indochina. Hoping to avoid open hostilities with Japan, Britain withdrew its forces from China and halted the flow of supplies to the Chinese Nationalist armies over the Burma road. Japan began to speak boldly of a "Greater East Asian Co-prosperity Sphere," a more ambitious version of its "New Order."

In the United States President Roosevelt and other opponents of Axis aggression had been working to prepare the American public, still strongly isolationist in sentiment, for the possibility of eventual intervention in the war. The government relaxed its neutrality laws so as to favor the provision of war equipment to the Allies, strengthened its military and political ties with Latin American countries, built up its own army and navy (notably by introducing the first peacetime draft in American history), and issued various warnings to the Axis Powers. Throughout 1941 tension between the United States and Japan mounted. The Japanese, increasingly under the influence of militaristic leadership, regarded the United States as the only obstacle to their complete domination of the Orient. In the fall of 1941 they resorted to desperate measures to remove that obstacle.

THE JAPANESE OFFENSIVE

Early on the Sunday morning of December 7, 1941, Japanese carrier-based aircraft, operating thousands of miles from their home islands, made a daring strike against the main United States naval base in the Pacific at Pearl Harbor, Hawaii. Taken completely by surprise in spite of the recent build-up in diplomatic tension, the main body of the fleet lay at anchor in the harbor with boilers cold and only skeleton crews on actual duty. In the ensuing confusion the United States suffered more than 5,000 casualties and lost five battleships, three cruisers, and numbers of lesser craft, as well as 177 airplanes, most of which were destroyed on the ground. Other ships and military installations suffered serious damage. It was the worst military disaster to befall the United States in its history.

Photograph from U.S. Navy

U.S.S. *Shaw* Exploding During the
Japanese Raid on Pearl Harbor

*"Yesterday, December 7, 1941 — a date which will live in infamy — the United
States of America was suddenly and deliberately attacked by the naval and
air forces of the Empire of Japan.*

*"The United States was at peace with that Nation, and at the solicitation
of Japan, was still in conversation with its Government and its Emperor
looking toward the maintenance of peace in the Pacific. Indeed, one hour
after Japanese air squadrons had commenced bombing in Oahu, the Japanese
Ambassador to the United States and his colleague delivered to the Secretary
of State a formal reply to a recent American message. While this reply stated
that it seemed useless to continue the existing diplomatic negotiations, it
contained no threat or hint of war or armed attack."* Address of President
Roosevelt to the Congress, December 8, 1941, U.S. Department of State,
PEACE AND WAR: UNITED STATES FOREIGN POLICY, 1931–1941
(Washington, 1943).

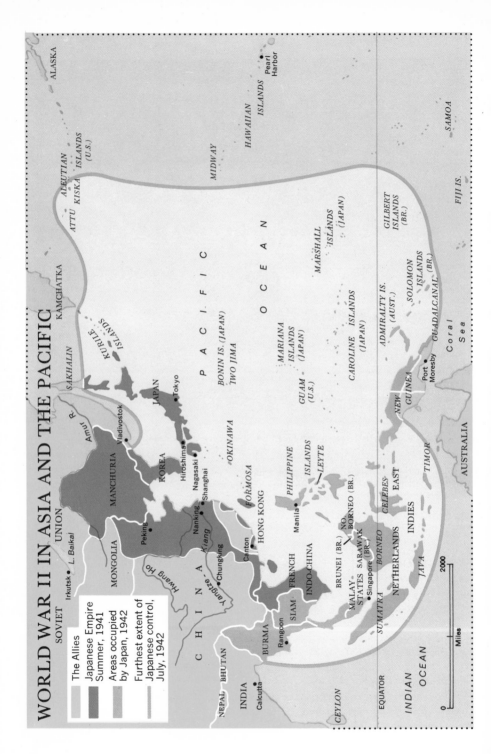

WORLD WAR II IN ASIA AND THE PACIFIC

The Allies

Japanese Empire Summer, 1941

Areas occupied by Japan, 1942

Furthest extent of Japanese control, July, 1942

SOVIET UNION

ALASKA

ALEUTIAN ISLANDS (U.S.)

ATTU KISKA ISLANDS

KAMCHATKA

Irkutsk • L. Baikal

MONGOLIA

SAKHALIN

Amur R.

Vladivostok

KURILE ISLANDS

JAPAN

Tokyo

KOREA

Hiroshima

Nagasaki

Shanghai

MANCHURIA

Peking •

Nanking

Kiang

Chungking

Yangtze

Hwang Ho

C H I N A

Canton

HONG KONG

FORMOSA

OKINAWA

BONIN IS. (JAPAN)

IWO JIMA

P A C I F I C   O C E A N

MIDWAY

HAWAIIAN ISLANDS

Pearl Harbor

SAMOA

FIJI IS.

GILBERT ISLANDS (BR.)

MARSHALL ISLANDS (JAPAN)

MARIANA ISLANDS (JAPAN)

GUAM (U.S.)

CAROLINE ISLANDS (JAPAN)

ADMIRALTY IS. (AUST.)

SOLOMON ISLANDS (BR.)

GUADALCANAL

Coral Sea

NEW GUINEA

Port Moresby

AUSTRALIA

TIMOR

EAST INDIES

CELEBES

NETHERLANDS

JAVA

SUMATRA

BORNEO

NO. BORNEO (BR.)

SARAWAK

BRUNEI (BR.)

MALAY STATES

Singapore (BR.)

FRENCH INDO-CHINA

SIAM

BURMA

Rangoon

NEPAL BHUTAN

INDIA

Calcutta

CEYLON

EQUATOR

INDIAN OCEAN

PHILIPPINE ISLANDS

LEYTE

Manila

2000

Miles

0

NANKING

Immediately following their success at Pearl Harbor Japanese forces struck other United States military installations in the Pacific. Guam capitulated within a week, Wake Island within two weeks. Early in January, Japanese forces captured Manila and the United States naval base at Cavite in the Philippines. The remaining American and Philippine forces entrenched themselves on the Bataan peninsula and the island of Corregidor in the entrance to Manila Bay. General Douglas MacArthur, the American commander in the Philippines, escaped to Australia on the command of President Roosevelt. After a valiant defense the remaining American forces under General Jonathan Wainwright finally capitulated in May, 1942.

Meanwhile the Japanese pursued their prime target: control of the sources of oil, rubber, tin, and other strategic supplies in Southeast Asia and Indonesia. Great Britain declared war on Japan immediately after the United States, and the Japanese responded by sinking two British battleships that had been dispatched to reinforce the major British base at Singapore. Japan concluded an alliance with Thailand and persuaded it to declare war on Britain and the United States. Operating from its newly acquired bases in Indochina, Japan captured Hongkong and launched invasions of Burma, the Malay peninsula, and Indonesia. Singapore, which was heavily fortified on its seaside but all but defenseless by land, fell to the Japanese from the rear in mid-February. At the end of the month the Japanese won an overwhelming naval victory over combined Allied naval forces in the Battle of Java Sea and forthwith occupied the Dutch East Indies. The British evacuated an untenable position in Rangoon, and Japan quickly overran and occupied Burma.

In less than six months after the attack on Pearl Harbor Japan had achieved mastery over all of Southeast Asia and the Southwest Pacific as far as New Guinea. The way lay open for the conquest of Australia — or so it seemed. On May 7 Allied air and naval forces intercepted a large Japanese fleet, including troopships, steaming southward through the Coral Sea and sank more than 100,000 tons of Japanese shipping. That defeat convinced the Japanese that they would have to complete what they had begun at Pearl Harbor but had failed to carry through: the destruction of United States naval power. They assembled a large armada and headed once more for Hawaii, while sending a decoy force to make landings in the Aleutian Islands. The United States had succeeded in breaking the Japanese radio code and did not fall for the decoy. It concentrated the remnants of its naval and air forces and intercepted the Japanese near Midway Island. There in early June a tremendous air and naval battle raged for four days. The United States suffered many losses, but the Japanese losses were heavier still, forcing them to withdraw and relieving the pressure on the United States Pacific defenses.

The early Japanese successes were facilitated by careful planning, the element of surprise, and the unpreparedness of the United States, which had not fully recovered from the great depression of the 1930's. The very enormity of the Japanese gains, however, required time for assimilation and organization, and strained Japanese manpower and resources to the utmost. The Battle of Midway marked the high tide of Japanese conquest and power. Thereafter their losses in both manpower and materiel accumulated more rapidly than military conscription and industry could replace them. In the United States, by contrast, the shock of Pearl Harbor settled the lingering dispute over isolation or intervention, unified the American people behind the war effort, and brought the full range of American industrial capacity and manpower into battle on the side of the Allies. While retaining private ownership and operation of industry for the most part, the American government initiated a far-reaching system of organization and control which resulted in an ever-increasing flow of airplanes, tanks, ships, munitions, and other war materials for the supply not only of the American army, navy, and air force but of its allies as well.

Allied forces had stemmed the Japanese advance in the great naval battles of Midway and the Coral Sea, but the danger was by no means ended. In August, 1942, United States forces invaded the Solomon Islands in order to protect communications with Australia, and after months of heavy fighting they finally dislodged the enemy. For the next year sporadic fighting took place in New Guinea and the adjacent islands, but neither side launched a major campaign. The Allies had agreed to concentrate their major efforts on winning the war in Europe first, and the Japanese were still engaged in consolidating their earlier gains and replacing their losses. In the summer of 1943 the Allies began a systematic campaign of "island hopping"; that is, instead of attempting to retake every Japanese-held island in the Pacific, they selected their targets strategically to knock out the major Japanese bases and cut the enemy's supply lines, leaving the remainder to "wither on the vine." Their strategy succeeded so well that within a year American forces had conquered the Mariana Islands, from which huge United States Air Force bombers could bomb the Japanese home islands. It marked the beginning of the end of the war in the Pacific.

THE GRAND ALLIANCE

Although American policy had been staunchly isolationist in the 1930's and many influential individuals and groups remained so until the tragedy of Pearl Harbor, it became increasingly clear to perceptive observers that the entry of the United States into the war on the side of Britain was only a matter of time. As early as November, 1939, Congress amended the Neutrality Act of 1937 to permit the export of arms and munitions to belligerents on a "cash and carry" basis; the act manifestly favored Britain and France, who had both foreign currency reserves and control of the oceans. Immediately after the fall of France the United States greatly stepped up its defense expenditures, began construction of a "two ocean navy" and a greatly enlarged air force, and initiated compulsory military service. The "destroyers for bases" deal of September, 1940, and the Lend-Lease Act of March, 1941, as well as the activities of the United States Navy in tracking German submarines and convoying merchant vessels, brought the United States closer to the status of an active belligerent. Well before the Japanese attack on Pearl Harbor the United States was, in effect, engaged in undeclared naval warfare with Germany.

ROOSEVELT AND CHURCHILL

In August, 1941, President Roosevelt and Prime Minister Churchill held a dramatic meeting on board a warship off the coast of Newfoundland to discuss problems of global strategy and logistics. At the conclusion of the meeting they issued a statement known as the Atlantic Charter. This document, the germ of the United Nations Charter, was an attempt to formulate war aims (even though the United States was still technically at peace) in such a way as to lay the basis for an enduring peace, and at the same time to influence public opinion in favor of an Anglo-American alliance. In the Charter the signatories declared that they had no territorial ambitions, promised that after the return of peace boundaries would be drawn and governments established in accordance with the principles of national self-determination, recognized the importance of "the fullest collaboration between all nations in the economic field," and re-emphasized the concept of the "Four Freedoms" that Roosevelt had earlier enunciated: freedom of speech and of worship, freedom from want and from fear. In many ways the Atlantic Charter resembled Wilson's Fourteen Points, but in spite of the unfortunate parallel fifteen governments — nine of them in exile — endorsed the Atlantic Charter within a few weeks.

Among the subjects discussed at this first conference between Roosevelt and Churchill was military aid to Russia, recently attacked by Nazi Germany. Britain and Russia had already agreed upon a mutual aid treaty, and after the United States formally entered the war the Soviet Union became one of the chief beneficiaries of Lend-Lease aid. In 1942 Churchill made trips to both Washington and Moscow to promote collaboration among the three major Allies, and in 1943 an even more important series of conferences took place between Roosevelt and Churchill:

in Casablanca, French West Africa (January), attended by General de Gaulle; in Quebec (August), attended by representatives of the British commonwealths; in Cairo, Egypt (November–December), attended by Chiang Kai-shek; and in Tehran, Iran (December–January, 1944), attended by Stalin. The last conference served as a prelude to the still more important conferences between the heads of the three major Allies at Yalta in February, 1945, and at Potsdam, Germany, in July, 1945.

NORTH AFRICA AND ITALY

Meanwhile the Allies had taken the offensive. In November, 1942, an Anglo-American amphibious force under General Dwight D. Eisenhower made landings in French Morocco and Algeria. After token resistance the representatives of Vichy France in North Africa capitulated and made common cause with the Allies. The German and Italian troops in North Africa were caught between the invaders and British and Imperial forces in Egypt. Fierce fighting ensued, but by the end of May, 1943, Axis forces had been eliminated and the Allies controlled the entire North African coast, freeing the Mediterranean for Allied shipping and exposing Italy to invasion.

The Allies invaded Sicily in July, 1943, and effected its conquest in less than six weeks. Meanwhile, dissident elements in Italy with the active assistance of the king had overthrown Mussolini and begun negotiations for an armistice with the Allies. A provisional government under Marshal Pietro Badoglio, conqueror of Ethiopia, surrendered on September 3, one day after Allied landings in southern Italy. German troops had already taken over the defense of Italy, however; they rescued Mussolini and installed him as puppet ruler of an Italian Fascist Republic with its capital in Milan. Fighting in southern Italy during the winter of 1943–44 was unusually severe and costly for the Allies. They did not take Rome until June, 1944, and did not expel the Germans from Italy until the final defeat of Germany in 1945. After the collapse of the Nazi-Fascist regime in Italy, Italian partisans (underground fighters) seized Mussolini as he was trying to escape to Switzerland with his mistress, assassinated both without trial, and hanged their corpses by the ankles in Milan. Such was the inglorious end of one totalitarian dictator.

THE LIBERATION OF FRANCE

Stalin had long been agitating for a second front in Europe. The relatively unsuccessful Italian campaign did not satisfy him. Allied military leaders also recognized that the ultimate battles would have to be fought in Germany itself. At length on D-Day, June 6, 1944, after a long build-up of air, sea, and ground forces in England, a huge Allied amphibious force under General Eisenhower, supreme Allied commander, landed on the Normandy peninsula of France. It was the most massive and, from a technical point of view, the most elaborately organized military campaign in history. For months Allied bombers had insistently pounded German cities, industrial establishments, troop concentrations, and communications centers. On D-Day great armadas of naval vessels joined the bombers in destroying the German defenses. Huge concrete piers and docks were floated across the channel from England to facilitate the landing of troops, who came in by airplane and parachute, amphibious ship, and troopship. The Germans put up a strong defense, but having lost mastery of the air their defeat was not in doubt. By the beginning of August Normandy was secured for the Allies, and on August 15 a second invasion in southern France added to the German debacle. Members of the French underground rose in Paris on August 24, and by the beginning of September the Germans had been effectively routed from France. A new provisional government under the leadership of General de Gaulle took charge.

THE COLLAPSE OF GERMANY

The Allies quickly followed up their success in France by liberating Belgium and beginning the invasion of Germany. Simultaneously Russian forces in the east cracked the spine of German resistance and began to roll back German armies across the broad plains of Poland. Nevertheless, in spite of enormous losses of manpower and crippling aerial bombardments, the German defense stiffened as it retreated into German territory. In December, 1944, the Germans launched a desperate counter-offensive against the Western Allies in Belgium and very nearly succeeded in breaking the Allied lines in the Battle of the Bulge. In the east the Germans fought off the Russians within thirty miles of Berlin for almost ten weeks. But the overwhelming might of the combined Allies eventually broke the German defense like a mighty nutcracker. At the end of April American and Russian troops joined forces on the Elbe River, and on April 30, 1945, Adolf Hitler, entrenched in an underground fortress in Berlin but unwilling to surrender, committed suicide in company with his mistress and a few faithful retainers. Thus ended the days of glory of the Thousand Year Reich.

THE JAPANESE SURRENDER

In the Pacific theater the war against Japan moved swiftly to a climax. In October, 1944, American forces invaded the Philippine Islands and with the help of Philippine underground fighters quickly drove out the Japanese. In the Battle of the Philippine Sea the Japanese navy lost forty ships and more than four hundred airplanes. It withdrew to its home waters and thereafter no longer seriously challenged American naval superiority. Nevertheless, the Japanese continued to resist desperately; the conquest of the strategic islands of Iwo Jima and Okinawa in the spring of 1945 cost many thousands of American casualties, and specially trained and indoctrinated *kamikaze* pilots flew suicide missions, ramming their explosive-packed planes directly into American warships in a futile attempt to turn the tide. The helplessness of the Japanese navy, the conquest of island airbases within a few hundred miles of Japan, and the surrender of Germany, depriving Japan of its last ally and releasing hundreds of American bombers for operation in the Pacific, led to increasingly frequent and damaging attacks on Japan itself. During the summer of 1945 the United States Air Force unleashed an aerial offensive against Japan greater even than the Allied bombardments of Germany.

The culmination of the offensive came on August 6, 1945, when an American bomber dropped the first operationally effective atomic bomb on the city of Hiroshima, with results both spectacular and disastrous. A single bomb flattened half of the large industrial city, killed over seventy thousand people, and maimed many thousands for life — perhaps for generations. Three days later the Americans dropped a second atomic bomb on the city of Nagasaki, with similar lethal effects.

The Soviet Union hastened to declare war on Japan on August 8 and began a massive invasion of Manchuria. Stalin had agreed at the Yalta Conference earlier in the year to bring the Soviet Union into the war against Japan within three months of the end of the war in Europe but had hoped to gain further political advantage, expecting that the invasion of Japan would be a long and costly operation. Faced by this new coalition and realizing their helplessness against further atomic attacks, the Japanese agreed to an "unconditional surrender" on August 14, 1945. (Japanese officials requested a single condition, which the Allies accepted: maintenance of the hereditary position of the emperor as nominal head of the government.) On September 2, 1945, General Douglas MacArthur accepted on behalf of the Allies the formal surrender of the Japanese authorities on board the U.S.S. *Missouri* in Tokyo Bay, bringing the Second World War to its end.

SPECIAL FEATURES OF THE WAR

The Second World War was by far the most massive and destructive of all wars in history. In some respects it represented merely an extension and intensification of features that had manifested themselves in World War I, such as increasing reliance on science as the basis of military technology, the extraordinary degree of regimentation and planning of the economy and society, and the refined and sophisticated use of propaganda both at home and abroad. In other respects it differed markedly from all previous wars.

Truly a global war, it involved directly or indirectly the populations of every continent and almost every country in the world. Unlike its predecessor, which had been primarily a war of position, it was a war of movement — on land, in the air, and at sea. Aerial warfare, an incidental feature of World War I, became a critical element in the Second World War. Naval operations, especially the use of carrier-based aircraft, became far more important. Science-based technology accounted for many of the special new weapons, both offensive and defensive, ranging from radar to rocket bombs, jet-propelled aircraft, and the atomic bomb. The economic and especially the industrial capacities of the belligerents acquired new importance. Mere numbers counted for less than ever before, even though size was still a factor in assessing the relative power of the opposing sides. In the final analysis the production line became as important as the firing line: the ultimate secret weapon of the victors was the enormous productive capacity of the American economy.

THE AFTERMATH OF WAR
CHAPTER THIRTY-SEVEN

At the end of the war Europe lay prostrate, almost paralyzed. All belligerent countries except Britain and the Soviet Union had suffered military defeat and enemy occupation. Large areas of the Soviet Union had been effectively occupied by the Germans and fought over foot by foot, twice or even more often. Although Britain had not been occupied (except by Americans), it suffered severe damage from aerial bombardment of its densely populated cities and from acute shortages of food and other necessities. Only the few European neutrals escaped direct damage, but even they suffered from many war-induced shortages.

Wartime casualties in Europe, exclusive of the Soviet Union, have been estimated at more than 15 million deaths: over 6 million soldiers and more than 8 million civilians, including 4.5 to perhaps 6 million murdered Jews. Military and civilian casualties in the Soviet Union may have added another 10 million deaths. These estimates do not include the millions more who were wounded or who suffered from near-starvation and disease. Whole populations were uprooted and displaced, first by the policies of Nazi Germany, then by the surge of warring armies and the flight of refugees. Political boundaries were almost obliterated by the tides of battle and the armies of occupation. Martial law and provisional regimes replaced normal political authorities.

The economy came to a near standstill. Warfare destroyed or damaged railroads, highways, bridges, and port facilities, gutted buildings and factories, collapsed and flooded mines, and leveled cities. Fields remained uncultivated for want of manpower; or if planted, in many instances they were ravaged by battle before the harvest. In the first year after the cessation of hostilities farm production lagged substantially behind that of the prewar years, not only because of the shortage of labor but also because yields had fallen drastically with the shortages of fertilizer and equipment.

Both land and aerial warfare took their toll of housing. In Germany approximately 10 million dwelling units — about 40 per cent of the prewar total — were either destroyed or rendered unfit for habitation. France lost between 20 and 25 per cent of its dwellings. In Rotterdam the whole center of the city was leveled, and many other cities suffered almost as much. Millions of buildings that escaped total destruction were severely damaged, and even those not directly affected by hostilities had deteriorated from inadequate maintenance during the war years.

Factories, which had been among the prime targets of aerial bombardment, survived surprisingly well. Although many were damaged, only about 10 per cent were knocked out completely. More serious was the poor condition of their equipment and especially the shortages of raw materials. In the industrial heartland of continental Europe — that is, in Germany, northern France, and Belgium — production fell by more than half.

A major reason for the shortages and dislocations in both industry and agriculture was the damaged transportation system. Of all sectors of the economy it suffered the greatest physical damage. Every bridge over the Loire and Seine rivers, which separate northern and southern France, and all but one bridge over the Rhine in Germany, were destroyed. Other railroad bridges, junctions, and dock and port facilities were hard hit. The stock of locomotives and other railroad equipment fell to less than half the prewar level in France, Germany, and some other areas. The destroyed bridges and other debris clogged rivers and canals, hindering navigation. Highways suffered similarly. Civilian automobile and motor truck production all but ceased during the war, while a large part of the existing stock of motor vehicles either was destroyed or deteriorated.

Besides direct damage and dislocations the war left other serious economic problems. The currencies of all countries, even neutral ones, had been greatly overissued, resulting in rampant but uneven price inflation. Attempts to impose direct price controls led to evasions and black markets, further intensifying shortages of goods. Germany reverted to an almost pure barter economy when the population deserted the legal currency and substituted such items as cigarettes, coffee, and chocolate as media of exchange.

Before the war Europe imported more than it exported, foodstuffs and raw materials in particular, and paid for the difference with the earnings of its foreign investments and shipping and financial services. After the war, with merchant marines destroyed, foreign investments liquidated, financial markets in disarray, and overseas markets for European manufacturers captured by American, Canadian, and newly arisen firms in formerly undeveloped countries, Europe faced a bleak prospect merely to supply its population with basic needs. Millions faced the threat of death from starvation, disease, and the lack of adequate clothing and shelter immediately after the war. Victor and vanquished were alike in their misery. The urgent need was for emergency relief and reconstruction.

EMERGENCY RELIEF AND RECONSTRUCTION

Relief came through two main channels, much of it originating in America. As the Allied armies advanced across western Europe in the winter and spring of 1944–45, they distributed emergency rations and medical supplies to the stricken civilian population, enemy as well as liberated. Because the Allies had committed themselves to a policy of unconditional surrender, after the cessation of hostilities they had to assume the burden of policing defeated Germany, which included the continuation of emergency rations for the helpless civilian population.

Even more impressive than the Allied military help was the emergency aid administered through UNRRA, the United Nations Relief and Rehabilitation Administration. A collective international agency, it performed its major tasks from 1944 through 1947. In 1945–46 it spent more than 1 billion dollars and distributed more than 20 million tons of food, clothing, blankets, and medical supplies. Most of it went to the liberated and former enemy countries of eastern Europe and to China. The United States bore about two-thirds of the cost, other United Nations members the remainder. After 1947 the work of UNRRA was continued by the International Refugee Organization, the World Health Organization, and other specialized agencies of the United Nations, as well as by voluntary and official national agencies.

EXHAUSTED VICTORS

One of the most urgent tasks facing the peoples of Europe after the satisfaction of their survival requirements was the restoration of normal law, order, and public administration. In Germany and its satellites Allied military governments assumed these functions pending peace settlements. Most of the countries that had been victims of Nazi aggression had formed governments in exile in London during the war. These governments returned to their homelands in the wake of the Allied armies and soon resumed their normal functions.

Their return, however, did not imply a mere "return to normalcy," the chimera of the 1920's. Memories of the economic distress of the 1930's lingered through the ordeal of war, and no one wanted a repetition of either experience, which almost all agreed were in some way related. On the Continent the leadership of the underground opposition to Nazi Germany played a large role in postwar politics, and the comradeship of those movements, in which Socialists and Communists had figured prominently, did much to overcome prewar class antagonisms and bring new men to positions of power. The wartime collaboration of the Soviet Union and the Western democracies facilitated the formation of popular front governments in which Communists collaborated with reformist political parties, such as Socialists and Christian (or Catholic) Democrats. In Britain the participation of the Labour party in Churchill's wartime coalition cabinet gave its leaders great prestige and influence. Finally, the very magnitude of the task of reconstruction indicated a much larger role for the state in economic and social life than had been characteristic in the prewar period.

In all countries the consequence of these various tendencies was widespread public demand for political, social, and economic reforms. The response to the demands took the form of nationalization of key sectors of the economy, such as transportation, power production, and parts of the banking structure; extension of social security and social services, including retirement pensions, family allowances, free or subsidized medical care, and improved educational opportunities; and assumption by governments of greater responsibilities for maintaining satisfactory levels of economic performance. Even the United States passed the Employment Act of 1946, which created the President's Council of Economic Advisers and pledged the federal government to maintain a high level of employment.

THE FOURTH REPUBLIC IN FRANCE

France had a government in exile headed by General de Gaulle, but he was not an elected representative of the French people. In spite of difficult personal relationships, Churchill and Roosevelt granted him half-hearted recognition and after the Normandy invasion allowed him to form a provisional government, which included representatives of the underground resistance to Nazi Germany. The provisional government set about at once to restore the damaged French economy. It nationalized the railroads, coal mines, gas and electricity companies, the armaments industry, the Bank of France, and a number of the largest commercial banks and insurance companies. Under Jean Monnet it instituted a novel form of economic planning that relied more on persuasion than on coercion. The provisional government also reorganized the army to participate in the final assault on and occupation of Germany, and it brought to trial as traitors the principal officials of the Vichy regime. Both Marshal Pétain and Pierre Laval received death sentences, but that of the former was commuted to life imprisonment in recognition of his earlier services to his country.

In October, 1945, de Gaulle called for the election of a National Constituent Assembly to draw up a new constitution for France. The Communist party polled the largest number of votes — almost a third. The Socialists and a new Christian Democratic party, the MRP (Popular

Republican Movement), also seated large groups of deputies. That leaders of all these parties had figured prominently in the resistance movement had an important bearing on their electoral success. The traditional center parties saw their representation cut drastically, and the prewar Right was eliminated almost entirely.

The new assembly elected de Gaulle provisional president of the republic in deference to his prestige, but it refused to follow his wishes in designing the new constitution. He favored a constitution providing for a strong executive. Opposition on this issue and harassment on others led de Gaulle to resign the presidency in January, 1946, and to campaign publicly for rejection of the draft constitution. Caught between Communists on the left and Gaullists on the right, the Socialists and Popular Republicans were maneuvered by the old center parties into supporting a bicameral legislature with a figurehead president and a prime minister and cabinet subject to the whims of the National Assembly. The Fourth Republic, therefore, bore a striking resemblance to the Third. The French electorate rejected the first draft constitution in a referendum in May, 1946, but in October it adopted a slightly revised version by a vote of about 9 million to 8 million — with almost 8 million abstentions. The Fourth Republic thus got off to a bad beginning and soon exhibited all the faults and weaknesses of its predecessor. It survived for only a dozen years.

SOCIALISM IN BRITAIN

In one of the most stunning electoral upsets in British history the voters in June, 1945, chose the Labour party and Clement Attlee over the Conservatives and Winston Churchill. Churchill, first elected to the House of Commons in 1900, had entered politics as a Conservative, deserted to the Liberals in 1903, then rejoined the Conservatives in 1924. During the 1930's he held aloof from all parties until the outbreak of war. As prime minister in the wartime coalition government he had given the most important posts concerning domestic matters to members of the Labour party. In the election Labour capitalized on its wartime record of "fair shares" and campaigned on a platform calling for the nationalization of several key industries and the broad extension of social services.

True to their campaign promises, the Labourites nationalized the railroads, the motor transport industry, the coal mines, the electricity industry, the Bank of England, and the steel industry. They instituted a comprehensive "cradle to the grave" social insurance system and a National Health Service providing free medical care. Unfortunately for Britain, however, not all of its economic difficulties could be solved by domestic reform. Britain was even more dependent than other European countries on international trade. Before the war it had imported two-thirds of its food supply and almost as large a proportion of the raw materials for industry. It had paid for much of the imports with earnings from its merchant marine, banks, insurance companies, and foreign investments. During the war it had been forced to liquidate its foreign investments; much of its merchant shipping had been sunk; and the bulk of international financial transactions had shifted from London to New York. Its manufacturing industries had emerged from the war with obsolete, damaged, or deteriorated equipment, while their overseas markets had been captured by other producers. To enable the country to live within its income, the Labour government found itself obliged to adopt a strict austerity program of high taxation, rationing of all essential commodities, and rigid controls on imports, foreign exchange, and foreign travel. The unpopularity of these measures, together with the failure of the socialized sector of the economy to perform as well as had been hoped, cost the Labour party much of its electoral support. It retained its majority in the House of Commons by a narrow margin in 1950, but it lost to Churchill and the Conservatives in a new election the following year.

THE SOVIET UNION

Russia suffered the greatest damage in an absolute sense of any nation engaged in the war, with 10 million killed and 25 million left homeless. Large areas of the most fertile agricultural land and some of the most heavily industrial regions had been devastated. The situation was not improved in 1946, the first full peacetime year, when drought caused widespread crop failures and desperate food shortages.

In spite of the sufferings of the Russian people, the Soviet Union emerged as one of the two super powers of the postwar world. Its vast territory, the largest in the world, and its population, the greatest of any European nation, as well as the tight control exercised by the government over the people, allowed it to play this role. To restore the devastated economy and boost output to new high levels, the government launched the fourth five-year plan in 1946. As previous plans had done, it emphasized heavy industry and military production, giving particular attention to atomic energy, which indicated that the Soviet leaders intended to maintain and strengthen their position in world affairs. The new plan made extensive use of physical reparations and tribute from the former Axis countries and Russia's new satellites.

Stalin, more powerful than ever, instituted a number of changes in the high offices of both government and the economy in the immediate postwar years. A constitutional revision in 1946 replaced the Council of People's Commissars by a Council of Ministers, in which Stalin assumed the position of chairman or prime minister. The ministries charged with supervision and control of industry and agriculture experienced drastic purges of personnel on grounds of incompetence and dishonesty. Other high officials of government and party were dismissed on similar grounds, although there is reason to believe that Stalin's real motive was distrust of their personal loyalty to him.

Stalin continued to insist upon complete ideological conformity. In 1948 the Central Committee of the Communist party accused such leading composers as Shostakovich, Prokofiev, and Khachaturian of betraying "bourgeois" influences in their music and obtained from them confessions of "guilt" and promises of reform. Shortly afterward the biologist T. D. Lysenko, who occupied a leading position in the Academy of Sciences, denounced classical or Mendelian genetics in favor of a theory harking back to the time of Lamarck, which stressed the inheritance of acquired characteristics. Scientists who refused to accept the party line on this subject were demoted and sent to remote outposts and even jailed. Because the insistence on conformity was carried to such lengths, Russia's intellectual and cultural life in the last years of Stalin's rule showed few signs of originality or creativity.

OTHER ALLIED NATIONS

The United States emerged from the war stronger both relatively and absolutely than when it had entered. To a lesser extent, so also did Canada, the other Commonwealth nations, and several countries of Latin America. Spared from direct war damage, their industries and agriculture benefited from the high wartime demand, which permitted full utilization of capacity, technological modernization, and expansion. The United States possessed the world's largest air force, navy, and merchant marine. Many American economists and government officials feared a severe depression after the war, but after the removal of price controls and rationing, which had held prices at artificially low levels during the war, the pent-up consumer demand for war-scarce commodities created a postwar inflation that doubled prices by 1948. In spite of the hardships that the inflation brought to people living on fixed incomes, it kept the wheels of industry turning and enabled the United States to extend needed economic aid for the rebuilding of Europe and other war-devastated and poverty-stricken lands.

DEFEATED ENEMIES

At the same time that they undertook the reconstruction and reconversion of their own shattered countries, the victorious Allies in Europe and North America had to face the problem of making peace with their former enemies. Most statesmen were well aware of the failures of the peace settlement after World War I and were determined not to repeat the mistakes of the Versailles treaty. They succeeded remarkably well in this objective. New difficulties arose in the form of disagreements among the victors, however, rendering the resulting settlements both tentative and fragile.

THE BIG THREE

Relations between Russia and the western Allies were clouded by what each regarded as the perfidious behavior of the other in the critical years from 1938 to 1940, as well as by still older animosities. Although Churchill had promised aid to Russia immediately after the Nazi attack in 1941 and the United States had granted Lend-Lease assistance even before it became formally involved in the war, Stalin had refused to travel far from his homeland to attend the earlier conferences of the wartime leaders. In part to overcome his suspicions, Roosevelt and Churchill agreed to meet with him on nearby neutral territory in Tehran in the winter of 1943–44. Their discussions focused mainly on the plans for a second front in Europe, although the Big Three also took up the question of a possible postwar international organization — the United Nations.

A year later with the end of the war in Europe in sight the Big Three met again at Yalta in the Russian Crimea. Three topics dominated the discussions: (1) final plans for the defeat and disposition of Germany and eastern Europe; (2) the date and agenda for a conference to establish the United Nations; and (3) participation of the Soviet Union in the war on Japan. With respect to the first, the Allies agreed not to try for an immediate settlement after the German surrender but to occupy Germany jointly until a final peace treaty could be decided. They agreed that a conference to draw up the charter of the United Nations should be convened in San Francisco on April 25, 1945 — by chance, on the same day that Russian and American troops met at the Elbe. The third topic was in many ways the most difficult. Although work on the atomic bomb was well advanced, it had not yet been tested, and there was no certainty that it would be successful. Roosevelt and Churchill were therefore anxious that the Soviet Union should join the war on Japan at the earliest possible moment in order to avoid, if possible, a long and costly invasion. To persuade Stalin, they made several concessions that subsequently caused dispute and bitterness between Russia and the West, as well as in American domestic politics.

The Big Three met once again in July, 1945, at Potsdam, Germany, in the wake of the German defeat. President Roosevelt had died shortly after his return from Yalta and had been succeeded by Harry S Truman. Midway through the Potsdam Conference the results of the British election called for Clement Attlee to replace Churchill. Stalin was thus the only one of the original Big Three to participate in the final deliberations. Few formal decisions were actually made at the conference, though in the long run its actions achieved a permanence not intended by its delegates. The decision to have a four-power occupation of Germany and to postpone a final settlement was reaffirmed and made more precise. A council of foreign ministers was charged with the responsibility for preparing peace treaties with Italy, Austria, Hungary, Bulgaria, Rumania, and Finland. In return for ceding a large part of its prewar territory to the Soviet Union, the Polish provisional government was granted "temporary administration" over most of East Prussia and that part of Germany east of the Oder and Neisse rivers. Finally, in return for a promise to enter the war on Japan at the earliest practical moment, the Soviet Union obtained a promise of substantial advantages in East Asia. In both the decisions arrived at and the matters left undecided the Potsdam Conference built up a store of troubles for the future of East-West relations.

THE PARTITION OF GERMANY

The initial decision for joint occupation of Germany was not meant as a permanent division of the country but was merely for temporary convenience. As events unfolded, the disagreements between Russia and the Western Allies led the latter to give greater and greater measures of autonomy to the Germans in their zones of occupation. The Soviet authorities responded with similar nominal concessions in the eastern zone, though they maintained firm control through their puppets and the presence of Soviet troops. The ultimate result was the division of Germany into two separate states: the German Federal Republic (West Germany) and the German Democratic Republic (East Germany).

The Soviet zone of occupation extended from the Oder-Neisse line in the east to the Elbe in the west. British troops occupied the northwest sector of the country, including the mouth of the Elbe and the lower Rhine. The United States took southern Germany as its zone, and France received two strips of territory adjacent to its borders. Although Berlin was deep inside the Soviet Zone, it, too, was divided into four sectors. In the absence of a German government the Allied Control Council served as the nominal supreme authority, although in fact each occupying power administered its zone independently.

The Potsdam Conference had condoned the dismantling of German armaments and other heavy industries, reparations to the victors and the victims of Nazi aggression, strict limitations on German productive capacity, and a vigorous program of denazification, including the trial of Nazi leaders as war criminals. In fact, only the last aim was realized as originally intended. In November, 1945, an Interallied Tribunal began the trials of twenty-two of the most important Nazi leaders at Nürnberg, the site of many Nazi party rallies. After almost a year in trial the tribunal acquitted three defendants and convicted the remainder with

DIVIDED GERMANY

sentences ranging from ten years' imprisonment to death. Lesser officials were also brought to trial. The United States conducted the last of its war crimes trials in 1949, then turned its responsibilities over to the new West German government, which continued to bring former Nazis to trial.

The Soviet authorities dismantled many German factories in their zone and carried them to Russia as reparations. After a brief attempt by the Western powers to collect physical reparations and to break up large industrial combines in their zones, they realized that the German economy would have to be kept intact not only to support the German people but also to assist in the economic recovery of western Europe. They reversed their policy and, instead of limiting German production, took steps to facilitate it. One means of doing this was to provide for economic reunification, a process initiated with the creation of Bizonia, a union of the American and British zones of occupation at the end of 1946, to which the French zone was subsequently added. Just as the Zollverein served as the precursor of the German Empire, the economic unification of the western zones of occupation delineated the future German Federal Republic, which was officially proclaimed in May, 1949. Not to be outdone, the Soviet authorities soon afterward set up the so-called German Democratic Republic. Thus, without a peace treaty ever having been signed or even seriously discussed, the rivalry of the former Allies resulted in the creation of two nominally independent Germanies from the rubble of a former common enemy.

THE RESTORATION OF ITALY

Italy occupied an ambiguous position in the immediate postwar period. Although it had been one of the original Axis aggressors, it was allowed to change sides after the overthrow of Mussolini. No separate peace treaty was signed, however, and it was treated as one of the defeated nations after 1945. Victor Emmanuel III had sought to preserve the monarchy for his dynasty by deserting Mussolini after the Allied invasion of 1943, then by abdicating in favor of his son Umberto in May, 1946. His efforts proved in vain, for the Italians in the next month voted in favor of a republic. Although the Italians were allowed the formality of maintaining an independent government, final authority was wielded by an Allied military government until the ratification of the peace treaty in 1947.

The treaty required Italy to give up its colonial empire, to cede the Dodecanese Islands to Greece, and to give Venezia Giulia to Yugoslavia. Trieste and its hinterland became a free territory under United Nations supervision until 1955, when an agreement between Italy and Yugoslavia gave Trieste itself to Italy and the surrounding territory to Yugoslavia. Italy had to pay reparations of $360 million, of which $100 million went to the Soviet Union and most of the remainder to Yugoslavia and France.

After resuming control of their own affairs in 1947, the Italians faced many difficult problems, including widespread poverty and unemployment, inflation, and government instability. The political spectrum in Italy was broader than that of most countries, ranging from monarchists and neo-Fascists on the right to the largest Communist party in western Europe on the left. To add to its troubles, the Italian Socialist party split into two factions, one a Marxist group usually allied with the Communists, the other favoring democratic socialism and aligned with moderate reformist parties. The most important of the moderate reform parties was the Christian Democratic party headed by Alcide de Gasperi. From 1947 until his retirement in 1953 he succeeded in maintaining a fluctuating but manageable coalition of center and left-center parties.

THE REHABILITATION OF JAPAN

As with Germany, the Allies did not quickly seek a peace treaty with Japan. They wished to maintain control for a considerable period in order to re-educate the Japanese and to establish democratic political institutions. For this purpose General Douglas MacArthur, Allied commander in the Pacific, became the supreme authority in Japan. The Japanese had to give up their colonial empire as part of the unconditional surrender, but MacArthur retained the existing governmental structure to facilitate the execution of his orders. In quick succession he abolished the trappings of Japan's militarist and imperialist past, including the compulsory state religion, leaving Shintoism as one of several competing sects; restored civil liberties; introduced universal suffrage; revised the educational curriculum; and encouraged the formation of labor unions. At MacArthur's instigation Emperor Hirohito in a New Year's message on January 1, 1946, disavowed the divinity attributed to him by the Shinto religion. An international military tribunal undertook the trial of Japan's wartime leaders and eventually sentenced General Hideki Tojo and six others to death. In 1947 MacArthur promulgated a new constitution for Japan, providing for a bicameral legislature, a responsible cabinet, a substantial degree of local self-government, and a broad range of civil rights and liberties.

The Japanese accepted these imposed reforms with alacrity. Vigorous democratic political activity developed quickly, and MacArthur came to occupy a position of prestige in Japanese opinion second only to that of the emperor. Japan's main problems were economic: how to maintain its large, dense population after the loss of its colonial empire and under the restrictions placed by Allied regulations on its industrial production and foreign trade. For a time the United States subsidized the Japanese while simultaneously insisting on the enforcement of the restrictive regulations. The definitive solution to Japanese economic problems came with the outbreak of the Korean War in 1950. Japan served as the staging area for American troops and benefited from an economic boom. The new alignment of powers on the international scene led the United States to press for a lenient peace settlement. In 1951 the United States and forty-seven other nations signed a treaty with Japan restoring the latter's sovereign powers. The Soviet Union and other Communist countries refused to recognize the treaty and did not end their formal state of war with Japan until 1956.

THE FATE OF EASTERN EUROPE

Although the Allies found it inexpedient at first and subsequently impossible to agree on the terms of a peace treaty with Germany, they did succeed in signing treaties with Germany's satellites and in agreeing on the treatment of the victims of Nazi aggression in eastern Europe. The general terms of the east European settlement had been foreshadowed in wartime conferences, notably the one at Yalta. They had envisaged a preponderant role for the Soviet Union, although Stalin had promised to allow free elections and "broadly representative governments" — a promise that proved to be meaningless. After a year and a half of postwar negotiations among the foreign ministers of the Big Three and other Allied nations, at which representatives of the defeated nations had the opportunity to plead their cases, treaties were signed in Paris with Rumania, Hungary, Bulgaria, and Finland, as well as Italy, in February, 1947.

THE LIBERATED NATIONS

The resurrection of Czechoslovakia and Albania was taken for granted. Since those countries had never been at war with the Allies — had, in fact, been among the first victims of Axis aggression — there was no problem in restoring their independence. The manner in which they were liberated, however, guaranteed that they would be within the Russian sphere of influence. Albanian partisans under Communist leadership took over the country in the wake of the retreating Axis forces, and the government that they formed received official diplomatic recognition in November, 1945. In January, 1946, a constituent assembly proclaimed the People's Republic of Albania.

Czechoslovakia was liberated by Soviet troops, and Eduard Beneš returned as president of the provisional government. In a relatively free election in May, 1946, the Communists polled a third of the votes and seated the largest delegation in the new constituent assembly. Klement Gottwald, the Communist leader, became prime minister, but the assembly unanimously re-elected Beneš as president. The country continued under a coalition government, with Beneš hoping to make Czechoslovakia a bridge between Russia and the West, until the Communists seized power in February, 1948.

During the war Churchill and Stalin, without consulting Roosevelt, agreed to exercise equal spheres of influence in Yugoslavia after the war. In fact, Yugoslav partisans led by Marshal Tito liberated the country with very little help from Russia and negligible aid from Britain, thus allowing the country a measure of independence. Elections in November, 1945, gave Tito's Communist-dominated National Liberation Front

Brown Brothers

Marshal Tito

"We study and take as an example the Soviet system, but we are developing Socialism in our country in somewhat different forms. In the present period under the specific conditions which exist in our country, in consideration of the international conditions which were created after the war of liberation, we are attempting to apply the best forms of work in the realization of Socialism. We do not do this in order to prove that our road is better than that taken by the Soviet Union, that we are inventing something new, but because this is forced upon us by our daily life." Letter from the Central Committee of the Communist Party of Yugoslavia to the Central Committee of the Communist Party of the Soviet Union, April 13, 1948, in Robert Bass and Elizabeth Marbury, THE SOVIET-YUGOSLAV CONTROVERSY, 1948–58: A DOCUMENTARY RECORD (New York, 1959).

a substantial majority in the new constituent assembly, which promptly overthrew the monarchy and proclaimed a Federal People's Republic. On paper the new constitution closely resembled that of the Soviet Union, and Tito governed the country in a manner similar to that of Stalin in Russia. He refused to accept dictation from the Soviet Union, however, and in 1948 publicly broke with the latter and its other Communist satellites.

The determination of Poland's postwar boundaries and form of government constituted one of the thorniest problems of peacemaking. In the closing phases of the war there had been two Polish provisional governments: the government in exile in London and the Soviet-sponsored Committee of National Liberation in the Russian-occupied part of Poland. At Russian insistence and with Western acquiescence the two groups merged to form a Provisional Government of National Unity, with a promise of early "free and unfettered elections." The coalition lasted until 1947, when the Communists ousted their partners and assumed complete control.

The territorial settlement agreed on provisionally at Potsdam in effect moved Poland three hundred miles to the west. The language of the agreement had provided only that Poland should have "temporary administration" of the area east of the Oder-Neisse line, or about one-fifth the area of prewar Germany, but the Poles with Soviet support regarded the settlement as definitive compensation for their cessions to the Soviet Union, which constituted almost half of prewar Poland. They forthwith expelled the millions of Germans who resided in the area to make room for other millions of Poles streaming in from the Russian-occupied zone. The enormous transfers of population, together with similar transfers in other parts of eastern Europe, including the movement of Germans from the Sudetenland, returned the ethnic boundaries to something resembling "the *status quo ante* 1200 A.D.," in the words of Arnold J. Toynbee.

THE SATELLITE STATES

The peace treaties with Rumania, Bulgaria, and Hungary — Germany's east European satellites — contained territorial provisions that fell into a well-established historical pattern. Rumania regained Transylvania from Hungary, but it had to return Bessarabia and Northern Bukovina to the Soviet Union and Southern Dobrudja to Bulgaria. Hungary lost the most, for it gained nothing and had to cede a small area to Czechoslovakia. All three defeated nations had to pay reparations: $300 million for Hungary and Rumania and $70 million for Bulgaria, the bulk of which went to Russia. Under the protection of Soviet troops the Moscow-trained Communists in their popular front governments had few difficulties in disposing of their Liberal, Socialist, and Agrarian collaborators and soon established people's democracies in the Soviet pattern. Finland lost some territory to Russia and had to pay $300 million in reparations, but it escaped the fate of other popular front governments on Russia's borders and maintained a precarious neutrality.

The peace treaties had nothing to say about the disappearance of the Baltic countries of Latvia, Lithuania, and Estonia. Part of the tsarist empire before 1917, they had been incorporated by the Soviet Union in 1939–40, then overrun by Germany in 1941. Reoccupied by the Red Army in 1944–45, they were quietly annexed to the Soviet Union as so-called autonomous republics. That they were not mentioned in the peace negotiations implied recognition that they again formed parts of the new Russian empire.

Austria was treated as a liberated territory rather than as a willing accomplice of Germany, but a treaty was necessary to formalize its independence. Until a treaty could be signed, it was subjected to four-power occupation. As in the case of Germany, its capital, Vienna, was located inside the Russian zone and was jointly occupied. Free elections held in 1945 resulted in a negligible vote for the Communists and sizable votes for the Catholic People's party and the Social Democrats, who formed a coalition government. The coalition enjoyed substantial domestic autonomy but remained subject to the Allied Control Commission. In numerous conferences the Soviet Union blocked the final signature of an Austrian treaty on one pretext after another until 1955 while drawing large reparations in the form of petroleum and machinery. The treaty of 1955 restored Austrian sovereignty, pledged it to perpetual neutrality guaranteed by the great powers, and forbade reunion with Germany.

THE UNITED NATIONS

The failure of the League of Nations to prevent World War II disillusioned many persons who had expected much from international organization and cooperation. For many others the experience seemed to call for a stronger, broader-based organization to preserve the peace. From the union of this belief and the wartime cooperation of the Allied Powers the United Nations was born.

The Atlantic Charter, agreed upon by Roosevelt and Churchill in the summer of 1941, contained the germ of the union. In December, 1941, soon after the Japanese attack on Pearl Harbor, Churchill visited Washington, and on January 1, 1942, the representatives of twenty-six nations, including the Soviet Union, proclaimed adherence to the principles of the Atlantic Charter. Roosevelt began to refer to the Allies as "the United Nations." Wartime discussions between the leaders and representatives of the Allies anticipated continued international cooperation after the war; and on April 25, 1945, a conference including representatives of fifty-one nations convened in San Francisco to draft a charter for the permanent structure of the United Nations. The resulting organization resembled the League in many respects, but it also differed in several important particulars.

ORGANIZATION

The principal resemblances occur in the formal structure of the two organizations. Like the League, the United Nations is a voluntary association of sovereign nations. As did the League, it consists of two main deliberative bodies: the General Assembly and the Security Council. The General Assembly includes all member nations on the basis of one nation, one vote. Unlike the League, it can decide most questions by majority vote. The Security Council, however, charged specifically with the maintenance of world peace, requires unanimity of at least its five permanent members except on procedural questions. These members are the United States, Great Britain, the Union of Socialist Soviet Republics, France, and China (China was named to the Security Council chiefly because of the insistence of the American delegates; the fall of the Nationalist government to the Communists in 1949 created grave problems for the entire organization). The Security Council also contains ten rotating members elected for two-year terms.

Like the League, the United Nations operates under the administrative direction of a permanent Secretariat and maintains a number of specialized bodies. Among the most important of these are the International Court of Justice, successor to the Permanent Court of International Justice established in The Hague, and the Economic and Social Council, which has several regional commissions. There are also numerous agencies related to the United Nations such as UNESCO (United Nations Educational, Scientific, and Cultural Organization), the World Health Organization (WHO), the International Labor Organization (ILO), the International Monetary Fund, and the World Bank.

The General Assembly annually elects a president, but the office is largely honorific. The first president was Paul Henri Spaak, a devoted internationalist from Belgium. In subsequent years presidents have frequently come from former colonial nations. A more permanent and important position is that of secretary general, the main administrative officer of the organization. As the chief international civil servant, the secretary general is supposed to be above both party factionalism and nationalism. Although formally separated from policy-making decisions, the secretary general is in a position to wield great influence because of his constant preoccupation with all affairs of the United Nations. The first person to hold the post was Trygve Lie of Norway. He resigned in 1953 after years of criticism and abuse by the Soviet Union. His successor was Dag Hammarskjöld from neutral Sweden, who was killed in a plane crash in 1961 while trying to bring peace to the strife-torn Congo. U

Thant, a former General Assembly president from Burma, succeeded Hammarskjöld. The Security Council, originally deemed the most powerful element in the United Nations, has no permanent officers. Each representative serves as chairman for a month at a time under a system of continual rotation.

The location of the headquarters of the United Nations posed a problem. Switzerland, disillusioned with the League, refused to join the United Nations. After lengthy investigations and debate the General Assembly accepted a gift of land on Manhattan's East Side from John D. Rockefeller, Jr., and built a large modern skyscraper and other buildings of advanced design to house its large staff. Although it is located physically within the United States, the United Nations is not within its legal jurisdiction. Delegates and staff members enjoy the same privileges that are accorded to diplomats in Washington.

FUNCTIONS

The primary purpose of the United Nations, as of the League, is to preserve international peace. Unlike the League, the United Nations has provided special peace-keeping military forces for selected world trouble spots, such as Palestine, Cyprus, and the Congo. It has no permanent or regular forces of its own but utilizes mixed contingents drawn from various members, usually the smaller and traditionally neutral nations, such as Sweden and Eire. Technically, all the troops engaged in these activities are under the banner of the United Nations.

The United Nations' record as a peace keeper has been spotty. Although no wars between the great powers have occurred during its existence, it cannot take major credit for this fortunate circumstance. Other factors, such as the general fear of the awesome destructiveness of an atomic or thermonuclear war, have been greater deterrents. The intervention of the United Nations in the Korean War resulted from the prompt action of President Truman and the temporary absence of the Soviet Union from the Security Council. The United Nations has had only limited success in preventing or halting even the minor wars between neighboring countries that have wracked the newly emerging (or re-emerging) nations, such as the Palestinian War of 1948–49 and the dispute between India and Pakistan over Kashmir. The prompt cessation of the 1956 invasion of Egypt by Israel with French and British support was due to threats and persuasion by the United States and the Soviet Union rather than to any action by the United Nations. The brevity of the Arab-Israeli war of 1967 resulted from the rapid success of the Israelis in achieving their limited objectives. The United Nations has not even attempted to intervene in certain potentially major disputes, such as those between China and India and between China and Russia.

There are several reasons for the relatively poor showing of the United

Nations as a peace keeper. One is that it has no independent source of revenue and is dependent upon the voluntary support of its member nations to finance its activities. Even more important, its charter forbids it to interfere in the internal affairs of sovereign nations. Several important wars, including the Algerian war for independence from France, the struggle of Egypt and Saudi Arabia in the Yemen, and above all the series of wars in Southeast Asia, have passed under the guise of domestic revolts and revolutions and have thus escaped the active involvement of the United Nations. The most important reason for the United Nations' inadequacy is the split that early developed between the Soviet Union and its satellites on the one hand, and the Western Allies on the other, which has tended to paralyze United Nations action in all disputes involving the great powers, such as the Berlin blockade of 1948. Nevertheless, by providing a regular, permanent forum in which all nations can express their views on important issues, and by furnishing facilities for immediate consultation and conciliation, the United Nations has made important indirect contributions to world peace.

DIVIDED ALLIES

In the rosy afterglow of Allied victory over the Axis Powers many people hoped and expected that the wartime cooperation of the great powers would continue in the postwar period and ensure the peaceful reconstruction and rehabilitation of a shattered world. In this spirit they hailed the charter of the United Nations. Others, less sanguine and possibly more realistic, predicted that the very achievement of the wartime goal — the defeat of their common enemies — would remove the incentive to cooperate and result in the reassertion of mutually antagonistic policies by Russia and its Western Allies. Without doubt, influential persons in both the Soviet Union and the nations of the West neither expected nor wanted continued cooperation. Some American military leaders even advocated a "preventive war" against the Soviet Union while the United States still had a monopoly of atomic weapons. Fortunately for the world, saner counsels prevailed within the highest echelons of government.

THE THREAT OF ATOMIC WARFARE

Control of atomic energy was one of the most vexing political problems of the postwar era, domestically as well as internationally. American military authorities wanted to retain exclusive jurisdiction over the production and disposition of fissionable material. After lengthy public discussions and congressional debates the Congress in 1946 enacted legislation to create an Atomic Energy Commission under civilian control, along with a watchdog Joint Congressional Committee on Atomic Energy. At about the same time the United Nations created its own Atomic Energy Commission to discuss ways and means of developing peaceful uses of atomic energy and preventing its use for aggressive or belligerent purposes. The United States government proposed to turn over both its fissionable material and its scientific formulas to the United Nations on condition that other nations should open themselves to inspection to prevent clandestine production of atomic weapons, but the delegates of the Soviet Union and its satellites argued that the control of atomic energy should be considered in the context of proposals for general disarmament. The United States objected, and the Soviet Union killed discussion of the American proposal in 1947 with a veto in the Security Council. One of the reasons for Russian intransigence on this issue became clear in 1949 when the Soviet Union exploded its own atomic bomb.

THE TRUMAN DOCTRINE AND
INCREASING TENSIONS, 1946–1947

President Roosevelt apparently believed that he would be able to win Stalin over to a policy of continued cooperation after the war. After Roosevelt's death President Truman and his advisers, frustrated by Russian attitudes on such matters as atomic energy and the German question, adopted a more cautious attitude. In the words of Secretary of State James F. Byrnes in September, 1946, dealing with the Russians required "patience and firmness." Six months later American policy veered around to one of "containment" of the expansionist attempts of the Soviet Union and international communism.

In 1946 Greece, which had been liberated and occupied by the British in the closing months of the war, became the scene of a civil war between the restored royalist government and guerrillas supplied by Communist-dominated governments in Bulgaria, Albania, and Yugoslavia. Early in 1947 the British, hard pressed by domestic difficulties as well as by worldwide commitments, served notice of their intention to withdraw their occupation forces. The following March President Truman requested that Congress authorize a program of far-reaching military and economic aid to Greece and Turkey and, by implication, to other nations threatened by communist subversion. This policy became known as the Truman Doctrine. Shortly afterward General George Marshall, who had become secretary of state, called on all European nations, including the Soviet Union and its satellites, to unite in a program of economic recovery with American assistance.

The leaders of international communism had been quietly tightening their grip on the nations of eastern Europe while continuing their policy of collaboration with popular front governments in western Europe. In accordance with classical Marxist doctrine, they believed that a final catastrophic economic collapse would overtake the capitalist nations in the postwar period and that they would succeed to positions of power either by legitimate means or by internal subversion. They discovered to their disappointment that instead of collapsing, the countries of western Europe were becoming stronger. In the spring of 1947, in a desperate attempt to paralyze and possibly overthrow the governments, Communist-dominated labor unions in France and several other countries resorted to strikes and fomented civil disorders. The democratic elements within the governments responded with stern measures. In France and Italy they expelled their Communist colleagues from the government in May; Belgium, the only other country of western Europe with Communist cabinet ministers, had taken the same step two months earlier. These actions marked the end of popular front collaboration in western Europe. In retaliation, the Communist-dominated governments of Bulgaria, Rumania, Hungary, and Poland, with the support of the Soviet armies of occupation, systematically purged all non-Communists from their governments in the summer of 1947.

THE MARSHALL PLAN AND THE "COUP DE PRAGUE"

In July, 1947, in response to Secretary of State Marshall's invitation, representatives of sixteen European nations met in Paris to draw up a joint request to the United States for financial aid to assist in their economic recovery. The following spring the United States Congress passed the Foreign Assistance Act, establishing the European Recovery Program or Marshall Plan, and authorized an initial sum of $5.3 billion to be distributed as loans and grants by the newly created Economic Cooperation Administration (ECA). The recipient nations formed the Organization for European Economic Cooperation (OEEC) to administer the aid in Europe and pledged themselves to a long-term program of mutual assistance and cooperation.

Under the law creating the ECA, recipients of American aid had to put up in their own currencies a sum of money equivalent to the amount received from the United States. These "counterpart funds" were then expended along with the original aid money according to plans drawn up by the OEEC and approved by the ECA. In the four years of its existence the ECA supervised the expenditure of more than $11 billion in American aid. Most of it went for "social overhead capital," such as improvements to railroads, highways, port facilities, and installations for power production, although some also took the form of loans to privately owned or nationalized industries to aid in the rehabilitation of mines and factories and to provide fertilizer and modern equipment for farms. The most populous nations received the largest share of the aid, with the largest absolute amounts going to France, Great Britain, Italy, and West Germany (admitted to the OEEC in 1949). All European nations outside the Soviet sphere of influence except Spain and the neutrals eventually participated in the European Recovery Program.

The Soviet Union and most of its satellites immediately branded the Marshall Plan a new instrument of "capitalist imperialism" and declined to attend the meeting that led to the OEEC. Czechoslovakia and Finland, however, the two countries in the Soviet sphere that still had democratic regimes, sought to participate until they were called to account by the Soviet Union. In the fall of 1947 representatives of Communist parties throughout the world met in Warsaw at the behest of the Soviet Union to establish the Communist Information Bureau (Cominform). In effect, it was a resurrection of the Comintern that had been dissolved in 1943. The purpose of the organization was to coordinate the activities of the various national Communist parties and to make them more amenable to control from Moscow.

In February, 1948, in a still more daring and brutal show of force than the purges of the summer of 1947, the Communists in Czechoslovakia expelled the democratic members of the government, murdered or brought about the suicide of Jan Masaryk, the internationally respected foreign minister, and forced the resignation of President Beneš, who died soon afterward. Called the *coup de Prague,* this action caused widespread revulsion in the West and rendered still more unlikely the possibility of further cooperation between the Soviet Union and its former allies. Largely as a result of events in Czechoslovakia, the Western Allies decided to go ahead with the economic and political reconstruction of West Germany.

THE BERLIN BLOCKADE

In June, 1948, the Western powers carried out a reform of the German currency as a measure to stimulate economic recovery. In retaliation, the Soviet authorities immediately instituted a blockade of West Berlin by closing off all rail and highway transportation from West Germany. The Soviet Union hoped to force a withdrawal of Western forces from Berlin, or at least to secure concessions on disputed points; instead, the Western Allies responded promptly with a large-scale air life of strategic supplies. In a tremendous operation lasting more than a year the United States Air Force and the RAF flew almost 300,000 flights into Berlin, transporting at its peak more than 8,000 tons of supplies daily. The air lift supplied not only Western troops but also the 3 million inhabitants of West Berlin.

In May, 1949, the Russians finally lifted the blockade. The outcome was a substantial victory for the Western powers, greatly strengthening their prestige among the Germans in particular. During the blockade the Allies worked out a plan for the transference of political authority in West Germany to a German government operating under the surveil-

Photoworld

Gatow Airport During Berlin Airlift

"I was down at Tempelhof airfield that first morning to see the planes arrive. They were wartime twin-engined C-47 transports — 'Gooney Birds,' the pilots called them with affectionate contempt. Old, tired, and patched, the planes had been hastily collected from military airfields in the Western zones of Germany and rushed into the Berlin service. Many veterans still wore their camouflage paint from North Africa. Each plane had brought in two and a half tons of flour in a two-hour flight from Frankfurt. . . .
"The airlift was a reality by the first week in July, acquiring strength with every succeeding day. That first month, we brought in fifty thousand tons of food for civil consumption, a fraction of what we were to achieve when the lift got into its stride, but enough to convince the Russians that we meant business and to prove to the Germans that, if they stood by us, we could feed them." General Frank Howley, BERLIN COMMAND (New York, 1950).

lance of an Allied High Commission. In 1949, shortly after the Russians lifted the blockade, the new German Federal Republic came into existence.

NATO AND COMECON

In the atmosphere engendered by the Marshall Plan the nations of western Europe undertook a number of other ventures entailing greater international cooperation. France and Britain had already signed a treaty of alliance in February, 1947, and in October Belgium, the Netherlands, and Luxembourg ratified an agreement for the Benelux customs union. In March, 1948, these five nations signed the Treaty of Brussels, providing for joint consultation and cooperation in economic, social, and military affairs. In the following year they were joined by Denmark, Norway, Sweden, Ireland, and Italy in the Council of Europe, with headquarters at Strasbourg, France. The Council consisted of a Consultative Assembly with representatives elected by the parliaments of the participating nations and an executive committee of foreign ministers. Its functions were mainly consultative and advisory. To be binding, decisions of the committee of ministers had to be unanimous. Many persons hoped that from this organization a United States of Europe would grow. Greece, Turkey, Iceland, Austria, Switzerland and West Germany were subsequently admitted, as well as Cyprus and Malta.

Simultaneously with the establishment of the Council of Europe most of its member nations plus Portugal signed a treaty with the United States and Canada (April 4, 1949) creating the North Atlantic Treaty Organization (NATO). The signatories pledged themselves to mutual assistance in the event of armed aggression against any one of them, and they undertook far-reaching military collaboration under the direction of the North Atlantic Council. In the following year West Germany was admitted to the Council of Europe, and plans were made for the inclusion of West German forces in a unified European command.

Between the promulgation of the Truman Doctrine in the spring of 1947 and the formation of NATO in the spring of 1949 the international communist movement suffered continual setbacks in its attempt to gain power in western Europe. The Soviet rulers and their puppets abroad reacted to the situation by severe measures to increase their control over eastern Europe and by new, more overt attempts to embarrass or overthrow the governments of western Europe. In January, 1949, following the initial success of the European Recovery Program, the Soviet Union created the Council for Mutual Economic Assistance (COMECON) in an attempt to mold the economies of eastern Europe into a more cohesive union. Thus the division of Europe into two rival ideological camps became more pronounced and apparently more nearly permanent than ever.

As early as March, 1946, Winston Churchill, speaking at Westminster College in Fulton, Missouri, under the approving eye of Harry S Truman, coined the phrase "an iron curtain" for the borders of the Russian sphere of influence, extending from Stettin on the Baltic to Trieste on the Adriatic. By 1949 the phrase was common parlance in the Western world, and a still newer phrase, "the Cold War," to define the East-West struggle, had entered Western vocabularies. In little more than a year the Cold War became uncomfortably warm.

Photograph from UPI

President Truman Presents Winston Churchill to
Westminster College Audience, Fulton, Missouri

*"From Stettin in the Baltic to Trieste in the Adriatic, an iron curtain has
descended across the Continent. Behind that line lie all the capitals of the
ancient states of Central and Eastern Europe. . . . These famous cities and
the populations around them lie in what I must call the Soviet sphere, and all
are subject . . . to a very high and, in many cases, increasing measure of*
control from Moscow. . . .
*"From what I have seen of our Russian friends and Allies during the war, I am
convinced that there is nothing they admire so much as strength, and there
is nothing for which they have less respect than for weakness, especially
military weakness. . . . If the Western Democracies . . . become divided or
falter in their duty and if these all-important years are allowed to slip away
then indeed catastrophe may overwhelm us all."* Speech of Churchill at
Fulton, Missouri, March 5, 1946, reprinted in W. S. Churchill,
THE SINEWS OF PEACE (Boston, 1949).

THE KOREAN WAR

The dramatic events taking place in Europe in the years following the war deflected the attention of Americans as well as Europeans from the no less dramatic and important events in Asia. After the government of Chiang Kai-shek had taken its place in the United Nations as a permanent member of the Security Council, a Chinese Communist revolution drove it into exile on the island of Formosa (Taiwan). In Korea after the defeat of Japan American and Soviet armies occupied the country jointly. Their zones were separated only by the thirty-eighth parallel of latitude. Efforts to unite the country under a single regime failed, and in 1948 Soviet and American authorities organized separate regimes in their respective zones of occupation and shortly afterward withdrew their armed forces. Difficulties soon arose between the Communist-dominated North Korean government and the somewhat autocratic regime of President Syngman Rhee in South Korea. On June 25, 1950, a well-equipped force of North Koreans launched an all-out attack on South Korea and soon overran Seoul, the nation's capital.

The United Nations, at the urging of the United States during a temporary boycott of the Security Council by the Soviet Union, branded North Korea an aggressor and demanded the withdrawal of North Korean troops, but to no avail. President Truman, with United Nations approval, quickly ordered American troops based in Japan to the defense of South Korea and called on other nations to do likewise. Before the United Nations forces could effectively organize themselves, the North Korean forces had driven them almost off the peninsula. After a determined holding action on the Pusan beachhead the United Nations forces under the command of General Douglas MacArthur launched a strong counterattack, and in two months they had driven the North Koreans almost to the border of China. At this point, at the end of November, 1950, large forces of so-called volunteers from Communist China intervened on the side of North Korea, and by the end of the year they had driven the United Nations armies back to the vicinity of the thirty-eighth parallel. There the fighting settled down to a long-drawn-out period of trench and siege warfare. After months of fruitless negotiations a truce was finally arrived at in 1953.

The Soviet Union did not participate directly in the Korean War, but North Korean and Chinese Communist armaments were almost all of Russian manufacture. Neither did the Soviet Union take any part in the truce negotiations. These facts further divided the Soviet Union from its former allies. Moreover, the intervention of the Chinese Communists signaled another important turn in world history: henceforth the struggle of Communists and anti-Communists would no longer be confined to Europe. It had become global in extent.

THE END OF
WESTERN HEGEMONY
CHAPTER THIRTY-EIGHT

In the four centuries and more between the voyages of Columbus and the outbreak of World War I the nations of European culture had come to dominate directly or indirectly virtually the whole of the inhabited world. The First World War resulted in some changes in the identity of the ruling powers with the breakup of the German and Ottoman empires. It also caused some changes in the legal forms of control when former colonies became mandates or trust territories under nominal League of Nations supervision. In many respects, however, the interwar years witnessed the apogee of European imperialism and colonialism, for under the impress of exaggerated political and economic nationalism the imperial powers sought to assimilate and integrate the economies of their colonial possessions with their own.

The Second World War dealt a death blow to European imperialism. The Philippines, the Dutch East Indies, French Indochina, and British Burma and Malaya fell under the temporary control of Japan. Elsewhere in Asia and Africa the defeat of France, Belgium, and Italy and the preoccupation of the British with the war effort left their colonial dependencies largely on their own. Some dependencies proclaimed their independencies at once; others witnessed the rise of independence parties that agitated against continued colonial rule. The wartime slogans of the Western Allies themselves, calling for liberty and democracy throughout the world, strengthened the appeal of the independence movements by highlighting the contrast between Western ideals and the realities of colonialism; they also undermined the willingness of the peoples of western Europe to tax themselves in order to dominate others. In the immediate postwar years the imperial powers regained control temporarily in most of their former colonies, but their own war-induced weaknesses, the growing strength of native independence movements, and the ambivalent position of the United States led to a gradual abandonment of imperialist controls. In a few cases colonial areas fought successful wars of independence against their former masters. Increasingly the imperial powers relinquished dominion voluntarily, if reluctantly, rather than experience the costs and hazards of war. By providing a forum for the expression of the sentiments of independent non-Western nations the United Nations likewise hastened the end of Western imperialism.

NEW NATIONALISMS

One of the many elements of Western culture that was absorbed, albeit imperfectly, by colonial peoples during their long years of tutelage was the idea of nationalism. Both African tribalism and pre-Western imperialism in Asia had been fundamentally nonnationalistic. The growth of nationalism amongst non-Western peoples was abetted by the example of the imperialist nations themselves and by the common experience of subordination to uniform colonial laws and controls. Frequently the nationalism of colonial peoples had no tangible basis other than the more or less arbitrary political divisions imposed by the imperial powers, although in some cases it was reinforced by common religions and languages.

ARAB NATIONALISM

Although the majority of the inhabitants of western Asia and North Africa speak the same Arabic language and pay allegiance to the same Moslem faith, the new nations that have come into being in these areas reflect the political divisions initially imposed by the Ottoman Empire for administrative convenience and subsequently maintained by the Western powers when they assumed control in the nineteenth and twentieth centuries.

After the fall of France in 1941 Lebanon and Syria declared independence, but the British and Free French occupied them to forestall German penetration. At the end of the war France attempted to reassert control, but because of widespread local opposition Britain and the United States persuaded France to recognize Syrian and Lebanese independence. Britain granted independence to Iraq in 1930 but maintained control of its military and foreign policy by treaty agreements. During the war British troops again occupied the country, where they remained until 1947. Britain granted independence to Transjordan in 1946, which soon renamed itself the Kingdom of Jordan. In both Iraq and Jordan, Britain tried to maintain influence by means of subsidies, military assistance, and technical advice, but both countries pursued policies that made them increasingly independent of Britain. In 1958 a revolution overthrew the ruling dynasty in Iraq and replaced it with a strongly nationalistic republic.

In Egypt Britain maintained control of military affairs and foreign policy after formally terminating its protectorate in 1922. During the war Egypt served as the main base of Allied military operations in Africa and western Asia. Nationalist agitation continued after the war, and in 1952 a military junta led by General Mohammed Naguib overthrew the British puppet King Farouk. The following year Naguib proclaimed a republic. Naguib in turn gave way to the still more strongly nationalistic Colonel Gamal Abdel Nasser. In 1955 Nasser's government forced the withdrawal of the last British troops, and in 1956 it nationalized the Suez Canal.

In 1945 the governments of Egypt, Iraq, Lebanon, Saudi Arabia, Syria, Jordan, and Yemen formed the Arab League in an attempt to speak with one voice for their thirty-five million Arabic-speaking subjects and their two hundred million coreligionists of the Islamic world. Libya, Sudan, Tunisia, Kuwait, Algeria, and Morocco joined the league soon after gaining independence. Cultural affinities of language and religion, however, could not overcome the nationalistic legacy of postimperial political divisions. On the political spectrum the members of the league ranged from strongly socialist republics to the absolute monarchy of Saudi Arabia. In 1958, after one of Syria's perennial military coups d'état, Syria joined Egypt in the United Arab Republic. Nasser hoped to expand the U.A.R. to include the entire Arab world; but he obtained no new recruits, and three years later after another coup Syria withdrew. In 1962 Egypt supported a revolution against the imam (ruler) of Yemen and came into conflict with royalist Saudi Arabia, which supported the imam. Similar differences prevented effective cooperation in military and economic affairs. The one subject on which all Arab nations agreed — although even there they could not achieve unanimity of action — was opposition to the new state of Israel.

THE REBIRTH OF ISRAEL

The world's Jews had been a homeless, persecuted minority since the Diaspora (dispersion) of Roman times. During the Dreyfus affair in France — a nation that had previously been regarded as the most urbane and tolerant of all — Theodor Herzl (1860–1904), an Austrian journalist of Jewish faith, had projected the idea that the Jews should have a "national homeland." A movement called Zionism developed in support of his idea. By no means did all Jews support Zionism, nor did all of those who became Zionists intend to move to the "national homeland" if one could be found. In 1917 in a move calculated to win Jewish support for British war aims Arthur Balfour, the British foreign secretary, pledged British government cooperation for the settlement of Jews in Palestine, their biblical home. At that time Palestine was nominally a province of the Ottoman Empire, inhabited chiefly by Arabs. Jews constituted less than one-tenth of the population, and they lagged far behind European Jews in wealth and culture. Nevertheless, when Britain gained Palestine as a League of Nations mandate after World War I, it facilitated the efforts of wealthy, philanthropic Jews in Europe and America to purchase land in Palestine as a haven for Jewish refugees. The refugees flooded in, especially after the accession of Hitler to power in Germany, in spite of the bitter opposition of Palestinian and other Arabs, who resorted to riots, terrorist activity, and boycotts of Jewish and British merchandise. By the outbreak of World War II the Jews amounted to one-fourth of the population in Palestine.

Interwar efforts to establish self-government in Palestine foundered on the undying hostility between Jews and Arabs. The British were forced to rule by executive decree and frequently by martial law. The postwar influx of Jewish refugees from central and eastern Europe, entering illegally in many instances, exacerbated not only the political problem but also the economic problem of how to support the thousands of new inhabitants in what was essentially a barren, crowded land. The United Nations had no better success than the British in finding a solution to Jewish-Arab conflicts, and in 1948 the hard-pressed British withdrew their forces and terminated the mandate, leaving Jews and Arabs to their own devices. The Jews at once proclaimed the state of Israel and made Chaim Weizmann, an internationally known chemist, president and David Ben-Gurion premier.

Open warfare immediately broke out between Jews and Arabs. The Jews, at first on the defensive, soon gained the upper hand as a result of superior organization and equipment. In 1949 a United Nations mediation commission arranged a fragile truce, which led to the de facto division of Palestine into a Jewish national state (with a substantial Arab minority) and the incorporation of the remainder of the country into the Kingdom of Jordan. Israel made good use of the accumulated skills and knowledge of its European settlers and, aided generously by European and American Zionist philanthropists, soon outstripped its Arab neighbors in wealth and industry. This intensified Arab hatred and did nothing to alleviate the latent antagonism between the European and Islamic worlds.

THE MODERNIZATION OF IRAN

The ancient kingdom of Persia, officially renamed Iran in 1935, became increasingly involved in European diplomacy, especially after the discovery of oil by European concessionaires in 1908. During World War II the country was jointly occupied by American, British, and Russian forces. After the war the Russians attempted to organize a separatist movement in the northern province of Azerbaijan, but the Iranians defeated the movement after intervention by the United Nations. In 1951 the strongly nationalist Mohammed Mossadegh became premier and sought to exterminate British influence, chiefly by nationalizing the Anglo-Iranian Oil Company. Mossadegh was overthrown and imprisoned in 1953, but the oil concessions were nationalized. In subsequent years Mohammed Reza Pahlavi, a shah (king) who ruled as a benevolent dictator, introduced a number of legal, economic, and social reforms with a view to modernizing his country.

INDIA AND PAKISTAN

Nationalist sentiment had been growing in Britain's vast Indian empire since the Sepoy Rebellion of 1857. Nationalism had many obstacles to overcome in India, however. With two major religions, each with numerous sects, several mutually unintelligible languages, and a variety of forms of government in the many provinces, India's millions had only common opposition to British rule to unite them. Eventually India's nationalism polarized around the two principal religious faiths, Hinduism and Islam, which were more antagonistic toward one another than toward Britain.

The first self-conscious organ of Indian nationalism was the Indian National Congress (a political party, not a legislative body), created in 1885. Because of its agitation Britain introduced a strictly limited degree of self-government in 1909. During World War I India remained loyal to Britain, but demands for self-government and independence increased. In 1919 the British Parliament enacted the Government of India Act, conferring a larger measure of self-government, but even this measure failed to satisfy most Indian nationalists. About that time a remarkable person arose to become the leader and symbol of Indian opposition to British rule.

Mohandas K. Gandhi (1869–1948), popularly called Mahatma (great-souled), a London-educated lawyer of aristocratic Indian birth, sought to revive both the spiritual and political greatness of ancient India. Although he might have lived a life of luxury, he identified with the common people of India, dressed simply (a loin cloth was his usual costume), ate simply in strict accordance with Hindu dietary laws, and fasted often. His most notable contribution to the techniques of political agitation was the doctrine of civil disobedience and passive resistance. He used it so effectively that the British imprisoned him on several occasions, but they always discovered to their dismay that his martyr-like incarceration caused them more trouble than his freedom. During the Second World War Gandhi adopted a pacifist position with respect to the war while continuing his campaign of passive resistance to the British.

Other nationalist leaders, including Gandhi's close friend Jawaharlal Nehru, felt that more would be gained for India's cause by supporting the British war effort. Britain had already offered to grant India domes-

Photoworld

Nehru and Lord Mountbatten, July, 1947

"After a generation of intense struggle with a great and powerful nation, we achieved success and perhaps the most significant part of that achievement for which credit is due to both parties was the manner of it. History hardly affords a parallel to the solution of such a conflict in a peaceful way followed by friendly and co-operative relations.

"It is astonishing how rapidly the bitterness and ill-will between the two nations have faded away giving place to co-operation and we in India have decided of our own free will to continue this co-operation as an independent nation." Address of Pandit Nehru at Columbia University, October 18, 1949, BEFORE AND AFTER INDEPENDENCE . . . SPEECHES DELIVERED BY JAWAHARLAL NEHRU (New Delhi, 1950).

---

tic autonomy with dominion status, but Gandhi and Nehru would settle for nothing less than complete independence. After the war Britain's Labour government finally agreed to their demands. At this point civil war broke out between Moslems and Hindus.

As independence drew near, it became clear that India would be dominated by the Hindu majority. In the 1930's the Moslem League under

Mohammed Ali Jinnah, its fiery leader, had begun to demand a separate Moslem state. Although Gandhi had earlier opposed partition, the clashes between Moslems and Hindus on the eve of independence persuaded him to accept it. When Britain at last withdrew from India on August 15, 1947, after almost two centuries of dominion, not one but two independent nations emerged: the Union of India and the Islamic state of Pakistan (Land of the Pure). Both retained dominion status within the Commonwealth.

Neither independence nor partition solved India's pressing problems. Both new nations were badly overpopulated and desperately poor. Pakistan was divided into two widely separated parts: West Pakistan (with the nation's capital, Karachi), which stretched on both sides of the Indus River, and East Pakistan across India on the Ganges River. In spite of partition and massive exchanges of population, both nations contained sizable minorities of the opposite faith. The most serious problem involved Kashmir, a mountainous province in the northwest, which both nations claimed and neither would relinquish. Efforts of the United Nations to mediate the dispute came to naught.

Nehru became the first prime minister of India, a post that he retained until his death in 1964. In 1948 a Hindu extremist assassinated Gandhi for his part in the partition. Nehru set the nation on a course of moderate, democratic socialism, and in 1949 he converted it into a federal republic while still retaining its ties with the Commonwealth. Pakistan followed suit a few years later. Ceylon, which had been governed as a part of India, did not participate in the internal Indian struggle for power, but it obtained a large measure of self-government in 1946. In 1948 it gained dominion status and full self-government.

BURMA AND MALAYSIA

Burma was another nation created in the mold of colonial rule. Burmese unity had been a tenuous thing prior to the British conquest, but resentment against colonial government provided a common focus for Burmese nationalism. Britain promised dominion status for Burma near the end of World War II, but the Burmese preferred complete independence. In 1948 they proclaimed a federal republic, the Union of Burma, free of all ties to the Commonwealth. As with India and Pakistan, independence not only failed to solve the nation's problems but added many new ones. Separatist movements developed in a number of the component states, and Communist agitation alienated large segments of the population from the central government.

After most other former British colonies in Asia had gained complete independence, either within or outside the Commonwealth, the Federation of Malaya remained dependent on Britain while gaining more self-government. For several years after the war Communist forces kept up a guerrilla war against British rule and the established local governments. In 1963 the former crown colonies of Singapore, Sarawak, and North Borneo joined the other Malayan states in the Federation of Malaysia, a fully self-governing dominion within the Commonwealth of Nations; but in 1965 Singapore withdrew.

THE REPUBLIC OF INDONESIA

The peoples of Java, Sumatra, Borneo, and the hundreds of other islands comprising the Dutch East Indies had long resented Dutch rule, but they did not succeed in establishing a cohesive independence movement until the Japanese occupation during World War II. Immediately after the withdrawal of the Japanese the Indonesian People's party under the leadership of Sukarno (like many Indonesians, he had only one name) proclaimed the independence of the Republic of Indonesia. The Dutch refused to recognize the new government and with the aid of the British defeated the Indonesian People's Army, but then agreed to the creation of a United States of Indonesia as an equal partner with the Netherlands under the Dutch crown. Both sides soon found fault with the agreement, and repeated violations of the truce occurred. In 1949, under pressure from both the United Nations and the United States, the Dutch agreed to full independence for Indonesia, which was admitted to the United Nations the following year.

The problems facing the new nation were formidable. It had a population of more than 70 million scattered over 3,000 islands within an area of hundreds of thousands of square miles. Population densities on some of the islands were among the highest in the world, while other islands consisted almost entirely of uninhabited tropical jungle. The Islamic Buddhist, Hindu, and Christian faiths intermingled, not always peacefully. Levels of living were among the lowest in the world. Dissident groups within the islands staged revolts against the central government, which sought to impose its authority as brutally as the Dutch had done in the colonial era. Instead of attacking its economic, political, and social problems directly, Sukarno, who governed in dictatorial fashion, indulged in the most pernicious excesses of nationalism, nationalizing all Dutch property in 1955, forcing the Dutch from West Irian (Dutch New Guinea) in 1962, and objecting to the creation of the Federation of Malaysia in 1963. In 1965 Indonesia became the first member to withdraw from the United Nations, in protest over the seating of Malaysia on the Security Council, and later that year the pro-Chinese Communist party with the tacit agreement of Sukarno tried to take complete control of the country. The army under General Suharto smashed the attempted coup, stripped Sukarno of his powers, and put the nation back on a friendlier course with the West. In 1966 Indonesia resumed membership in the United Nations.

Before World War II the French had granted only the barest nominal concessions of self-government to their possessions in Southeast Asia. During the war and the Japanese occupation the nationalist movement made considerable headway, but the new government of the Fourth Republic showed no signs of willingness to grant independence. Instead it organized its former colonies as partially self-governing "Associated States within the French Union." Fighting broke out in 1946 between the French and the strongly nationalist Viet Minh organization in Annam, the largest of the former French colonies. The independence movement received support from the Soviet Union and later from Communist China. In spite of military aid from the United States, the French suffered defeat at the hands of the Viet Minh in 1954, and accepted partition between North Vietnam, under Communist control, and South Vietnam. The truce agreement provided for a plebiscite to determine the form of government for the entire country, but in 1955 Ngo Dinh Diem, the pro-Western premier of the interim government of South Vietnam, proclaimed the southern zone a republic and made himself president. The plebiscite was never held. In the end France granted independence to all its former Asian colonies, including Laos and Cambodia.

In 1935 the Philippines, America's greatest colonial possession in the Asian Pacific area, obtained commonwealth status providing a substantial measure of self-government, and was promised eventual independence. World War II delayed the achievement of independence until July 4, 1946, when the Republic of the Philippines was formally established. Like all former colonial possessions, the Philippines faced difficult economic problems in adjusting to world markets. It also had to deal with the Communist-inspired guerrilla warfare of the Hukbalahap or Huks. The Huks finally called off their civil war in 1954, but the Philippines still faced the problems of dire poverty, backward social arrangements, and a burgeoning population.

THE CHINESE REVOLUTIONS

China underwent two revolutions in the space of a generation. The first, the Nationalist revolution, was incomplete at best. It never succeeded in unifying the country or in throwing off foreign domination. The second, the Communist revolution, not only overthrew the Nationalist government and established dominion over the whole of mainland China but also engaged in imperialist adventures of its own.

THE NATIONALIST REVOLUTION

Although the revolution of 1912 (see pp. 778–779) was apparently successful in that it overthrew the decadent Manchu dynasty, it fell prey to internal divisions. The first president of the Republic of China, a former official of the Manchu Empire, soon sought to restore the monarchy and to make himself emperor. He was defeated by the Kuomintang (National Peoples' party) of Dr. Sun Yat-sen, but rival warlords, military leaders who refused to recognize the sovereignty of the central government, ruled their individual provinces in dictatorial fashion.

China remained subject to foreign imperialism in the form of territorial concessions, financial controls and indemnities stemming from the Boxer Rebellion, and the rights of extraterritoriality for foreign citizens, which exempted them from the jurisdiction of Chinese courts. In 1915 the Japanese presented a humiliating set of "Twenty-One Demands," which made China a virtual protectorate of Japan. Partly in the hope of escaping from its ignominious position, China declared war on Germany in 1917, but it was allowed to contribute only labor battalions. The Versailles treaty disappointed Chinese nationalists in that it transferred Germany's concessions in China to Japan instead of returning them to China. China retaliated by refusing to sign the treaty and instituted an ineffective boycott against Japanese merchandise.

Failing to secure support for his movement in the capitals of Western nations, Dr. Sun turned to the Soviet Union for assistance in the drive for independence and unity. After Dr. Sun's death in 1925, General Chiang Kai-shek, who had received military training in both Japan and the Soviet Union, became de facto head of the Kuomintang. With the support of Russian technicians and advisers he launched a successful military campaign against the warlords in the north. As soon as he had achieved victory in 1927, Chiang broke with his Communist supporters. He established a single-party government with himself as president and, in effect, dictator. The organic law which served as a constitution made no provision for an elective legislature. Dr. Sun's goal of nationalism had apparently been achieved, but democracy was postponed, and socialism was abandoned altogether. Chiang's alliance with native Chinese capitalists, symbolized by his marriage in 1927 to a daughter of the wealthy Soong family, played a prominent role in succeeding developments.

The renewal of Japanese aggression in 1931 and its intensification in 1937 brought an unaccustomed unity to Chinese policy. Even the Chinese Communists, whom Chiang had disavowed and persecuted, supported him in his resistance to the Japanese. The Soviet Union began to supply him with military equipment as early as 1937, while the United States and other Western powers were still trying to effect a reconciliation with Japan.

THE CHINESE IN WORLD WAR II

Japan's undeclared war on China merged gradually into the greater conflict of World War II. The Kuomintang forces, poorly equipped and supplied, retreated to the west and established a capital at Chungking in the mountainous province of Szechwan. There they were cut off from communication with the Western powers by sea and received only a tiny driblet of supplies via the long and difficult Burma Road. After the Japanese attack on Pearl Harbor the United States and Britain granted direct military and financial aid to the Chungking government and sent the American General Joseph Stilwell as Allied commander of the China-Burma theater. Although the Allied forces, now including those of the Kuomintang, did not win any notable victories in China, they did keep large numbers of Japanese troops tied down on the mainland, and thus facilitated Allied victories in the Pacific. The suffering of the Chinese people was enormous. Already one of the poorest peoples in the world before the war, suffering frequent famines and natural disasters such as floods, they now had the added horrors of aerial bombardment of overcrowded, defenseless cities, the disruption of agriculture by military operations, and a drastic hyperinflation brought on by unlimited issues of paper money. The war prevented the Kuomintang government from carrying out its promised reforms, and the corruption, venality, and inefficiency of many of its officials turned the Chinese people against it even though they supported the war against Japan.

THE COMMUNIST REVOLUTION

During the war the Chinese Communists cooperated with Chiang in his resistance to the Japanese but maintained an independent army in northern China, supplied and equipped by the Soviet Union. As Japanese power on the mainland collapsed in the closing months of the war, both the Nationalists and the Communists rushed in to fill the vacuum, and as a consequence came into armed conflict with one another. Shortly after the end of the war President Truman sent General George C. Marshall to effect a conciliation between Communists and Nationalists. Although he once arranged a brief truce, his mission met with repeated frustrations because of the irreconcilable attitudes of reactionaries in the Kuomintang and radicals among the Communists. Marshall at length gave up the mission, reporting that "sincere efforts to achieve settlement have been frustrated time and again by extremist elements of both sides."

Nevertheless, the United States continued its military and financial aid to the Nationalist government, which came to depend upon it as almost its only support. The aid was badly used, and the government fell more and more into the hands of reactionary and corrupt elements.

Sovfoto

Chairman Mao Tse-Tung

"The contradiction between imperialism and the Chinese nation and the contradiction between feudalism and the great masses of the people are the basic contradictions in modern Chinese society. Of course, there are others, such as the contradiction between the bourgeoisie and the proletariat and the contradictions within the reactionary ruling classes themselves. But the contradiction between imperialism and the Chinese nation is the principal one. These contradictions and their identification must inevitably result in the incessant growth of revolutionary movements. The great revolutions in modern and contemporary China have emerged and grown on the basis of these basic contradictions." From "The Chinese Revolution and the Chinese Communist Party," December 1939, in SELECTED WORKS (Peking, 1965), Vol. II.

The inflation continued to unprecedented heights, and some Nationalist officials actually sold American arms and munitions to their Communist enemies for personal profit. The Communists, meanwhile, had won large numbers of supporters among the war-weary peasants. The Nationalists steadily lost ground to the Communists in 1948, and in the following year their retreat turned into a rout. On October 1, 1949, the Communists under Mao Tse-tung and Chou En-lai formally proclaimed the People's Republic of China with the capital in Peking. Chiang Kai-shek and his remaining supporters in the Kuomintang completed their evacuation to Formosa (Taiwan), which had been returned to China by Japan, and abandoned the mainland to Communist control.

CHINESE COMMUNIST IMPERIALISM

According to classical Marxist doctrine, China was even less prepared for communism than Russia had been in 1917. The Communists nevertheless began a wholesale reorganization of Chinese society, nationalizing factories and organizing peasant villages into rural communes. Although they achieved some success in increasing the production of steel and other heavy industrial products, their agricultural progress failed to keep pace with the rapid increase of population in the overpopulated country.

In spite of severe economic problems, the government did not hesitate to engage in political and military action beyond its frontiers. In 1950, just a year after its formal establishment, it sent legions of so-called volunteers to oppose the United Nations in Korea. The following year it scored a bloodless coup by taking control of Tibet and gaining a common frontier with India. This circumstance brought on sporadic armed clashes with India, a strong protagonist of neutralism in the struggle between communism and the Western democracies. China replaced the Soviet Union as the chief supporter of Communist revolutionary movements throughout Southeast Asia. As Soviet foreign policy began to swing back toward "peaceful coexistence" with the West, Chinese insistence on an ultimate war of annihilation led to increasing tensions and an eventual rupture between the two most powerful partners in the Communist bloc. Communist China's greatest technological and political triumph came in 1964, when it exploded an atomic bomb. Thus, in the space of half a century China had changed from a helpless decaying nation subject to imperialist exploitation to an aggressive, expansionist nation with imperialist intentions of its own.

THE EMERGENCE OF INDEPENDENT AFRICA

The political map of Africa at the end of World War II differed little from that of the interwar years. The great imperial powers of the past still ruled almost all the continent. British colonies included most of east central Africa — the Rhodesias, Nyasaland, Tanganyika, Kenya, and Uganda — and important areas in West Africa, such as Nigeria and the Gold Coast. Although Egypt was nominally independent, it remained subject to British military control, and Britain and Egypt exercised joint authority in the Sudan. The Union of South Africa, a member of the British Commonwealth governed by a white minority of European culture, ruled not only its own territory but some adjacent areas as well. The French Empire included most of West Africa, the North African littoral from Tunisia to Morocco, large parts of Central Africa, and the island of Madagascar. Belgium retained the huge Belgian Congo. Portugal controlled Angola, Mozambique, and a few smaller possessions. Spain retained its few colonial territories on the west coast. Superficially, the momentous events of the two previous decades appeared to have had little effect on Africa. Underneath the surface, however, powerful currents of change had been set in motion that in the next two decades completely altered the face of the continent.

A few changes that took place immediately after the war were indicative of the shape of things to come, but they were either so slight or so expected that they left the world unprepared for the magnitude of subsequent changes. Italy lost its African empire, of course. Ethiopia regained independence and formed a federation with Eritrea. Libya came under United Nations supervision with a promise of eventual independence. Italy retained temporary administration over the former Italian Somaliland, but with independence promised by 1960.

The French Empire underwent some changes. The constitution of the Fourth Republic, adopted in 1946, changed the status of the former colonies to that of "overseas territories and departments" within a "French Union," gave their inhabitants full rights of citizenship, and provided for representation in the French parliament, although not in proportion to population. On paper this represented a substantial improvement in the position of their subjects, and the new regime introduced a number of ameliorations in the fields of health, education, and economic affairs; actually, the realities of political control changed little. The British government also liberalized educational facilities for Africans and allowed them to enter the lower ranks of the civil service. The Belgians, however, continued their policy of paternalism in the Congo, and the Portuguese resisted all symptoms of change.

INDEPENDENCE FOR NORTH AFRICA

The former Italian colony of Libya became the first African nation to gain independence after the war. The United Nations made the decision as early as 1949, and the new state came into existence at the end of 1951 as a constitutional monarchy. With its sparse population, paucity of natural resources, and backward economy, the future of the new nation was far from promising, but Western subsidies, some of which took the form of payments by the United States Air Force for air base facilities, helped it to survive until the discovery of petroleum deposits strengthened its economic base. Although it retained ties with the Western powers, to whom it owed its independence (the Soviet Union had opposed and refused to recognize it until 1955), Libya also adhered to the Arab League. In 1969 a military coup ousted King Idris and installed an Arab Socialist regime.

Egypt, after gaining its independence, expressed a determination to retain control of the Sudan. The British, however, took measures to introduce self-government in the Sudan before their withdrawal. In a plebiscite in 1955 the Sudanese voted heavily in favor of independence under a republican form of government. The Sudan thus became the second new African nation to secure independence in the postwar period.

In contrast to the relative ease with which Libya and the Sudan obtained independence, the former French colony and protectorates of Algeria, Tunisia, and Morocco engaged in long, difficult, and costly struggles. Tunisia and Morocco had retained their traditional forms of government, which functioned under the direction of French authorities. Algeria, on the other hand, where the French had been established for more than one hundred years and which had more than a million inhabitants of European ancestry (about one-tenth of the population), was treated as part of France for some purposes. Strong nationalist and pan-Arab movements developed in all three countries after the war. The French government responded with nominal concessions to greater autonomy for Tunisia and Morocco but attempted to integrate Algeria more firmly with France. Neither policy worked. The nationalist parties in Tunisia and Morocco demanded complete independence, and in 1956, rather than engage in another war like that in Vietnam, the French granted them "independence within interdependence." Under this arrangement the former protectorates retained privileged positions in the French market and obtained economic aid in return for allowing French military bases on their territory. Both countries subsequently moved steadily in the direction of complete independence. In 1957 the Neo-Destour party in Tunisia overthrew the Bey of Tunis, a figurehead monarch, and proclaimed a republic under the presidency of Habib Bourguiba, strongest leader of the nationalist movement. In Morocco the former sultan became king, took a more active role in the movement for independence, and emerged as the actual as well as the nominal ruler of the country. After independence the governments of both Tunisia and Morocco engaged in vigorous efforts to modernize their countries and on the international scene tried to follow a policy of friendship but nonalignment with both East and West.

The success of the independence movements in Tunisia and Morocco stiffened the determination of some Frenchmen — notably the Algerian

THE NEW NATIONS IN AFRICA AND ASIA

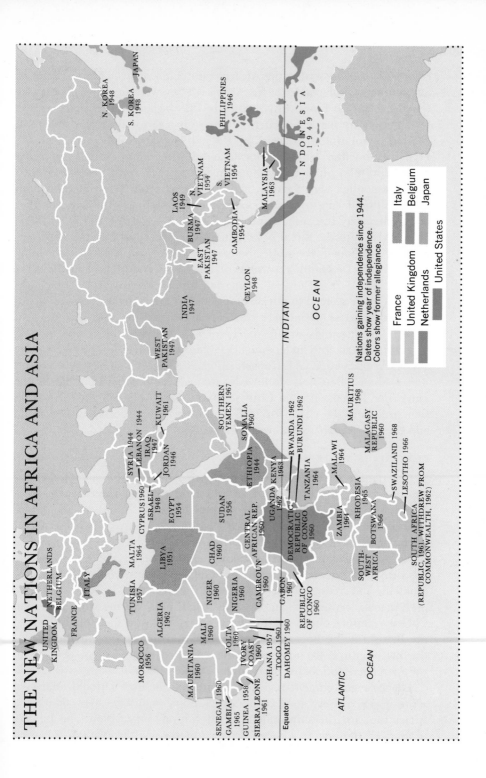

Nations gaining independence since 1944.
Dates show year of independence.
Colors show former allegiance.

France
Italy
United Kingdom
Belgium
Netherlands
Japan
United States

N. KOREA 1948
S. KOREA 1948
JAPAN
PHILIPPINES 1946
INDONESIA 1949
MALAYSIA 1963
N. VIETNAM 1954
S. VIETNAM 1954
CAMBODIA 1954
LAOS 1949
BURMA 1947
EAST PAKISTAN 1947
CEYLON 1948
INDIA 1947
WEST PAKISTAN 1947
SYRIA 1944
LEBANON 1944
IRAQ 1947
CYPRUS 1960
ISRAEL 1948
JORDAN 1946
KUWAIT 1961
SOUTHERN YEMEN 1967
SOMALIA 1960
ETHIOPIA 1944
SUDAN 1956
EGYPT 1954
LIBYA 1951
CHAD 1960
CENTRAL AFRICAN REP. 1960
UGANDA 1962
KENYA 1963
RWANDA 1962
BURUNDI 1962
TANZANIA 1964
MAURITIUS 1968
MALAGASY REPUBLIC 1960
MALAWI 1964
RHODESIA 1965
ZAMBIA 1964
SWAZILAND 1968
LESOTHO 1966
BOTSWANA 1966
DEMOCRATIC REPUBLIC OF CONGO 1960
REPUBLIC OF CONGO 1960
GABON 1960
CAMEROUN 1960
NIGERIA 1960
NIGER 1960
TUNISIA 1957
MALTA 1964
ALGERIA 1962
MOROCCO 1956
MALI 1960
VOLTA 1960
IVORY COAST 1960
GUINEA 1958
SIERRA LEONE 1961
GHANA 1957
TOGO 1960
DAHOMEY 1960
MAURITANIA 1960
SENEGAL 1960
GAMBIA 1965
SOUTH-WEST AFRICA
SOUTH AFRICA
(REPUBLIC, 1961, WITHDREW FROM COMMONWEALTH, 1962)

UNITED KINGDOM
NETHERLANDS
BELGIUM
FRANCE
ITALY

INDIAN OCEAN
ATLANTIC OCEAN
Equator

colons (European settlers in Algeria) and high army officers — to resist
any notion of independence for Algeria. They were opposed by the National Liberation Front (FLN) which in 1954 began an intensive guerrilla
war, frequently marked by acts of terrorism against both the European
civilian population of Algeria and the natives who collaborated with the
French authorities. Unable to locate and destroy the top leadership of the
movement, who often took refuge in other Arab countries, the French
Army responded with terrorist activities of its own. The government in
Paris followed confusing and sometimes contradictory policies, neither
giving the army full support nor exercising firm control over it. In May,
1958, faced with the threat of an army revolt and coup d'état, the government of the Fourth Republic abdicated its powers to General de Gaulle.
(See p. 1040.) De Gaulle returned to power with the support of the army
and the Algerian settlers, who expected him to keep Algeria French. At
first de Gaulle seemed intent on doing so, but after further years of bloodshed and fruitless attempts to reach an understanding with the Algerian
leaders for autonomy within the French Community, he agreed in 1962
to grant Algeria full independence. This decision was followed by the
wholesale evacuation of European *colons* to France. The new government
under Ahmed Ben Bella followed a strongly nationalist line, but at the
same time flirted with the Chinese Communists, who sought to increase
their influence in Africa. In 1965 a military coup overthrew Ben Bella
and the new leaders took a neutralist stance.

REACTION IN SOUTH AFRICA

The population of the Union of South Africa at the end of the war
was approximately 12 million, of whom more than three-fourths were
Negroes. The population also included sizable numbers of Asians
(mainly from India) and "colored" persons (mulattos). Inhabitants of
European descent constituted less than a fifth of the population, and of
those the Afrikaners (Dutch-speaking) outnumbered the English-speaking peoples by about three to two. The Europeans controlled the government and most of the wealth of the country. In spite of some
pro-German sentiment among the Afrikaners during the war, Jan
Christian Smuts, South Africa's great statesman who had fought against
the British in the Boer War, kept the nation in the war on the side of
the British. In 1948, however, Smuts's United party lost an election to
the Afrikaner Nationalist party under Daniel Malan.

The new government revealed its attitude in international affairs by
refusing to convert its League of Nations' mandate over Southwest
Africa into a trusteeship under United Nations supervision, and in 1949
it annexed the area in express defiance of the United Nations. Of even
greater significance for the future was the government's policy of *apartheid* or strict segregation of the races. The government enacted a series

of stringent laws depriving Negroes of elementary civil liberties and property rights; when the South African Supreme Court ruled some of the laws unconstitutional, the parliament passed a new law declaring itself to be the highest court on constitutional questions. The government's repressive policies resulted in domestic opposition and foreign criticism, especially from the new nations of Africa and Asia. In 1961 in a gesture of defiance to Great Britain the government reconstituted itself as a republic. The following year the Republic of South Africa withdrew from the Commonwealth. Meanwhile it intensified its oppression of the nonwhite population of the country, provoking them to strikes, riots, and the formation of underground and exiled revolutionary organizations.

THE EMANCIPATION OF BLACK AFRICA

In the early 1950's most observers expected that a generation or more would be required for the Negro peoples of Central and West Africa to obtain independence; yet within a decade more than a score of new nations had arisen from the former British, French, and Belgian colonial empires. The strength of native independence movements accounted for this striking development only in part. Equally important, domestic difficulties of the imperial powers made them unwilling to bear the high cost — economic, political, and moral — of continuing to rule alien peoples against their will. Once the process of emancipation had begun, it continued like a chain reaction, with each new day of independence hastening the next.

After the war the British government realized that it would have to do a better job of preparing its African wards for self-government if it was to avoid costly colonial wars and a total loss of the economic benefits of empire. It began by establishing more schools, creating universities, and opening the civil service to Africans. In 1951 the Gold Coast and Nigeria obtained constitutions granting them a measure of local autonomy. The British intended that, perhaps after several decades, they should acquire still greater rights of self-determination. In the Gold Coast, however, Kwame Nkrumah, a remarkable political leader, demanded immediate independence for his people and showed determination to win it even from his prison cell. Rather than risk a full-fledged revolt, the British agreed to most of Nkrumah's demands, and in 1957 the state of Ghana (so called from the medieval African empire of that name) emerged as the first black nation in the British Commonwealth. Ghana also became a member of the United Nations. With this precedent before it, Nigeria achieved independence in 1960 and other former British possessions in West Africa did the same in subsequent years.

Paradoxically, the first British colonies in Africa to achieve full in-

Kwame Nkrumah

"My . . . two recurrent themes. The first is freedom of the individual. The second is political independence, not just for Ghana or for West Africa, but for all Africa. I do not know how anyone can refuse to acknowledge the right of men to be free." Kwame Nkrumah, I SPEAK OF FREEDOM (London, 1961).

dependence were among the least advanced economically and politically. Because they were populated almost entirely by black Africans, there was no problem of white minorities. In East Africa and the Rhodesias, however, British settlers had acquired vast tracts of property and enjoyed substantial local self-government. Deprived of political rights and economic opportunity, the Africans constituted sullen, rebellious majorities who sometimes resorted to violence, such as the Mau Mau terrorism in Kenya during the 1950's. By 1965 Britain had granted independence to all its African colonies except Rhodesia. The exception resulted from the refusal of Rhodesia's white population to accord equality of status to their black fellow citizens, who greatly outnumbered the whites. In 1965 the white-dominated government of Premier Ian Smith made a unilateral declaration of independence — the first such occurrence in the British Empire since 1776. Britain attempted to apply economic sanctions to force Rhodesia to change its policy, but with some assistance from the Republic of South Africa Rhodesia successfully resisted the sanctions. Several years of negotiations between Britain and Rhodesia produced no results, but Britain was unwilling to employ military force, as advocated by some black African nations.

When promulgating the constitution of the Fifth Republic in 1958, France's de Gaulle offered the French colonies, except Algeria, the option of immediate independence or the position of autonomous states within the new French Community (a replacement for the defunct French Union) with the right to secede at any time. Although this remarkably liberal offer was occasioned in part by de Gaulle's recognition that it would probably be impossible to hold the colonies against their will, it nevertheless stands in marked contrast to the stubborn unrealism and blunders that had previously characterized French colonial policy. Of their fifteen colonies in black Africa (including Madagascar), only Guinea, under the leadership of Sekou Touré, chose independence. The others organized their own governments but allowed France to retain control of defense and foreign policy in return for economic and technical assistance. In 1960 a further constitutional change granted them full independence while permitting them to continue to enjoy special economic rights and privileges.

The sudden achievement of freedom by France's colonies stirred the formerly placid subjects of Belgium to rioting, pillage, and demands for similar treatment. The Belgians had made no provision for self-government in the Congo, much less for independence. The disturbance took them by surprise, but they promised in January, 1959, that a plan for independence would be worked out speedily. A year elapsed, but no plan materialized; political and social unrest mounted in the Congo, with new outbreaks of violence. Early in 1960 the Belgian government suddenly decreed that the Congo was to become independent on June 30. Elections were hastily arranged, a constitution was drawn up, and the largely illiterate Congolese, none of whom had ever voted before, were called upon to choose a complete set of government officials. When the day of independence arrived, many of them expected their standard of living to be magically transformed to the level enjoyed by their affluent former masters. In their disappointment they again resorted to pillage and wanton destruction. The Congolese army proved unable to maintain order and sometimes even contributed to the looting and violence. Rival political groups fell to attacking one another, and the mineral-rich province of Katanga tried to secede from the new nation. The central government called for assistance from the United Nations to restore order, but rebellion and wild outbursts of violence continued to occur sporadically.

THE REMNANTS AND LEGACY OF COLONIALISM

By the mid-1960's the former European colonial powers, with the exception of Portugal, had granted independence to almost all their African dependencies. South Africa faced the problem of enforcing its policy of apartheid without inflaming its victims to the point of open revolt or attracting the intervention of their African brethren. Portugal scornfully rejected all suggestions that it prepare its colonies for eventual liberation. In spite of these remnants of colonialism, the magnitude of the changes that had taken place in less than twenty years constituted one of the outstanding and most hopeful occurrences of the postwar period. The dark continent had found a place in the sun.

Although colonialism was dying if not dead, it left a rueful legacy. With few exceptions, and those confined to the areas of European settlement, African nations were desperately poor. In three-quarters of a century of colonialism the nations of Europe had extracted vast fortunes in minerals and other commodities but shared little of their wealth with the Africans. Only belatedly had some of the colonial powers made any effort to educate the Africans or to prepare them for a responsible role in government. When retribution came in the form of riots, civil wars, and terrorism accompanying the struggles for independence, it fell on the innocent and the guilty alike — and there were more of the former than of the latter.

In spite of their unhappy experiences at the hands of the democratic nations who had ruled them, most of the new African nations made at least a pretense of following democratic forms, and some made a valiant effort to achieve true democracy. As in some other parts of the world, however, the social and economic bases for stable, viable democracies did not exist. Because of this as well as the lingering irritant of the remnants of colonialism, Africa would long remain a continent in turmoil.

LATIN AMERICA IN FERMENT

Before World War II the Spanish- and Portuguese-speaking nations of the Western Hemisphere resembled in many respects the African and Asian colonies of Europe, although they were not subject to foreign political dominion. Most were very poor, with accompanying low levels of literacy, widespread unemployment or underemployment, and a high incidence of malnutrition and disease. In spite of their general poverty, great extremes of wealth existed between the relatively small landowning class and the masses. Their economies depended primarily on agriculture, much of it the subsistence variety with backward technology and low productivity. The few modern sectors were frequently owned by foreigners and produced mainly for export. Their extreme dependence on exports of one or a few primary products — coffee in Brazil, sugar in Cuba, meat, wheat, and hides in Argentina, copper and nitrates in Chile, tin in Bolivia — rendered them highly vulnerable to international economic fluctuations. All these factors contributed to social unrest and political instability. They had been particularly hard hit by the great depression of the 1930's, and this gave rise to a variety of political extremist movements of both Right and Left.

During and immediately after the war most Latin American nations benefited from strong demands and consequent high prices for their major exports. Some of them — notably Argentina, Brazil, Chile, and Mexico — took advantage of the wartime shortage of manufactured goods to begin new industries producing for their domestic markets. These embryonic industrial revolutions ran into difficulties in the 1950's with the recovery of the European and Japanese economies and the unfavorable price movements for their export products. They also suffered from the continuing wide gap between the very rich and very poor, which deprived them of mass purchasing power for the products of industry. The inefficiency of the governments allowed galloping inflations that contributed to dislocation, misery, and social unrest.

THE MEXICAN REVOLUTION

Mexico became the first Latin American nation to experience a social revolution. After the brief experiment with democracy under Juarez (see p. 680), Mexico relapsed into the long dictatorship of Porfirio Díaz (1876–1911). In 1911 a broadly-based revolutionary movement overthrew Díaz, but the revolutionary leaders soon became engaged in factional strife. A state of near anarchy ensued, complicated by armed intervention by the United States in 1914, 1916, and 1917. Paradoxically, the intervention helped to unify the revolutionary movement and to give it a strong nationalist and anti-imperialist character. In 1917 the Mexican Congress adopted a new constitution with many progressive social provisions, such as universal suffrage, agrarian reform, minimum wages and an eight-hour day for urban workers, and restrictions on the power and property of both the church and foreign property owners. The constitution of 1917 continued as the basis of Mexican government, but for almost three decades Mexico hovered on the verge of a relapse into dictatorship or anarchy. In 1946 Miguel Alemán became the first civilian to occupy the office of president, and since that time democracy and social reform, accompanied by rapid economic development, have continued to grow, giving Mexico one of the most stable and progressive governments in Latin America.

DICTATORSHIPS OF THE RIGHT

The military elite played a prominent political role in most Latin American countries. In the smaller, more unstable countries military juntas made and unmade presidents and prime ministers without benefit of elections; sometimes they held sham elections in which the outcome was never in doubt. One of the hardiest Latin American dictators was General Rafael Trujillo of the Dominican Republic, who wielded unchallenged authority in his small island domain from 1930 to 1962. He ruled the country as a personal fief and even renamed the capital city Ciudad Trujillo. Although petty despots in other countries had less time to entrench themselves, they often followed similar policies. Fulgencio Batista ruled Cuba as either president or president-maker from 1940 until he was overthrown by revolution in 1959.

Even the larger, more stable, and generally more democratic countries had their periods of dictatorial rule. In 1930 a depression-bred revolt in normally calm Brazil brought Getulio Vargas to the presidency. By a series of constitutional changes Vargas gradually tightened his control on the office and introduced a number of fascist economic and political organizations. When World War II broke out, however, he followed the lead of the United States, and Brazil became one of the first Latin American nations to declare war on the Axis Powers. In 1945 a combination of his opponents, including some of his former supporters, forced Vargas to resign, but he was elected again in 1950 and served until 1954. He was again confronted with demands for his resignation, and he committed suicide.

Argentina, another country with a better-than-average record for democracy and stability and with one of the best balanced, most prosperous economies in Latin America, contained a number of influential Axis sympathizers. It remained neutral until the very last weeks of World War II, when it made a token declaration of war against the Axis Powers. In 1946 the Argentinians elected Colonel Juan D. Perón president. Perón had a record of collaboration with Nazi Germany and soon showed his totalitarian bent with police state methods, including strict censorship of the press, regimentation of the economy, and the use of force against his opponents. Although re-elected for a six-year term in 1951, Perón succumbed to a junta of his former fellow officers in 1955 and went into exile in Europe. For the next decade Argentina was governed by a succession of weak presidents, but in 1966 a military coup overthrew the constitutional president and replaced him with a general. Both Vargas and

Perón relied heavily on the political support of organized labor, which further confused the conventional distinction between Left and Right in Latin America.

DICTATORSHIPS OF THE LEFT

Communists and other left-wing radicals found fertile ground for cultivation in the miserable living and working conditions of the lower classes in Latin America. At times they commanded substantial popular followings, but they rarely achieved the seats of power. In most countries Communist parties were outlawed, and their leaders had to resort to subversive activities. In a few cases, however, left-leaning governments did come to power. In both Bolivia and Guatemala revolutionary left-wing regimes gained power temporarily in the postwar period. In British Guiana the Communist-supported government of prime minister Cheddi Jagan, a native of India, frequently conflicted with both the large Negro population and the British Colonial Office until it was turned out in the election of 1964. The new government achieved full independence in 1966. Brazil's President João Goulart (1961–1964) seemed to be leading his country in the direction of Communist control until he was toppled by a military coup in April, 1964.

The only thoroughly Communist government to install itself in the Western Hemisphere was that of Fidel Castro in Cuba. Castro was one of many idealistic young Cubans who resented the corrupt and reactionary Batista regime. For more than two years before 1959 he led a romantic guerrilla war against the government in the mountainous Oriente Province of Cuba. In spite of military aid from the United States in the form of modern weapons and equipment, Batista's regime was unable to suppress the movement, which had the sympathy and active support of the peasants in the area. In the latter months of 1958 Castro's July 26 Movement gathered increasing popular support, while Batista's discredited regime visibly crumbled. Batista fled in December, and on January 8, 1959, Castro made a triumphal entry into Havana. At that time Castro was committed to a program of far-reaching social and economic reform but had not formally proclaimed allegiance to either Marxist principles or the Communist party. A series of diplomatic blunders by the United States, combined with pressure from some of his closest advisers, persuaded Castro to turn to communism and to an alliance with the Soviet Union.

HEMISPHERIC COOPERATION AND CONFLICT

The nations of Latin America have traditionally regarded the United States with a mixture of fear, envy, and respect. In the early years of the twentieth century American intervention in the internal affairs of Mexico and the Caribbean nations gave rise to impassioned anti-Ameri-

Fidel Castro

"I believe that we have arrived at a decisive moment in our history: tryanny is overthrown, and joy is immense everywhere. Nevertheless, there is much still to be done. . . . The first duty of every revolutionary is to speak the truth. To deceive the people, to delude them with false illusions would result in the worst consequences. That is why I say that we must be on guard against exaggerated optimism." From a speech on January 8, 1959, by Fidel Castro.

canism, but successive administrations since that of Herbert Hoover have striven to erase the impression that the United States was one of the imperialist nations. These efforts have taken the form of Roosevelt's Good Neighbor policy of the 1930's, wartime cooperation for the defense of the hemisphere, economic aid under the Truman and Eisenhower administrations, and the Alliance for Progress inaugurated by the Kennedy administration. The United States also encouraged the formation of hemispheric organizations, such as the Pan American Union, an information bureau dating from 1889, and the Organization of American States (OAS), created in 1948. Nevertheless, heavy handed American policies such as support for a projected invasion of Cuba in 1961 and direct armed intervention in the Dominican Republic in 1965 tinted the American image with hypocrisy in the eyes of many Latin Americans.

After decades of mutual bickering the nations of Latin America exhibited tendencies of a greater willingness to cooperate with one another in the postwar years. The small countries of Central America created a single customs union as the possible precursor of a more extensive economic union, and the Latin American Free Trade Association (LAFTA) promised to establish a single market for the entire continent, although its actual accomplishments were small. These efforts were manifestly intended to promote economic development as a means of reducing Latin America's dependence on the more advanced industrial nations and ending forever the stigma of colonialism.

THE WEST AND THE REST

The end of Western hegemony over the rest of the world marks a turning point in world history no less momentous than that brought about by the voyages of Columbus and Vasco da Gama at the end of the fifteenth century. Just as they inaugurated the era of Western predominance in the development of civilization, so the assertion of independence and the right of self-determination by peoples outside the Western tradition, or only marginally related to it, signals the advent of a truly global civilization. Whether or not the global civilization of the future will represent an improvement over its predecessors remains to be seen. One thing is certain: a great responsibility lies upon the principal carriers of the Western tradition, still the most powerful nations on earth, to preserve world peace and create a framework within which the civilization of the future can evolve.

THE STRUGGLE FOR A
NEW WORLD ORDER
CHAPTER THIRTY-NINE

By 1949 the worst ravages of the war in Europe had been repaired, and most of the sources of political confusion had been dissipated. The Soviet blockade of Berlin climaxed the growing tensions between the former Allies and radically altered the character of East-West relations. Instead of dealing with Germany as a defeated enemy, the Soviet Union and the Western Allies began to assist the economic and political recovery of their respective zones of occupation and to integrate them into their own regional power blocs. The Soviet bloc and the reconstructed Atlantic alliance settled down to what leaders of both sides expected to be a protracted rivalry for economic and military superiority and political domination. With the threat of atomic or nuclear destruction ever present, the welfare of mankind urgently required a new and more stable framework for international relations, but the national interests of the principal protagonists also demanded that they remain strong enough to resist potential aggression. In these circumstances the struggle for a new world order began.

RECOVERY AND REINTEGRATION IN WESTERN EUROPE

The economies of Western Europe had substantially recovered their prewar levels of production even before the Marshall Plan took full effect. The years just before the war, however, had been years of depression and stagnation. The levels of production of 1929 were not achieved until 1950 or 1952. In effect, the European economies had stagnated for an entire generation. In addition to having forfeited their potential increment of growth, they operated with obsolete equipment, lagged behind the United States in technological progress, and still suffered the handicaps of prewar and war-time restrictions and barriers to trade. Clearly, the economic health of Europe required more than mere recovery of prewar levels of production.

The Marshall Plan allowed the nations of Western Europe to maintain essential imports, especially foodstuffs and capital equipment, until they could achieve economic independence. Concurrently the OEEC conditioned statesmen and businessmen alike to new techniques of cooperation in the international sphere, laying the groundwork for further, more comprehensive programs of cooperation and integration. The results of the Marshall Plan were spectacular. In the three years from the end of 1947 to the end of 1950 physical output in the OEEC nations registered a 25 per cent increase. After the Korean War broke out, and with the regeneration of Western Europe's economy assured, the United States shifted the emphasis of foreign aid from economic to military assistance, renaming the Economic Cooperation Administration the Mutual Security Agency.

THE ECONOMIC MIRACLE

The rapid postwar economic growth of Western Europe continued throughout the 1950's and 1960's, making it the longest period of economic progress uninterrupted by slumps or depressions since the origins of the modern industrial system. By 1962 the total output of goods and services of the OEEC countries was double that of 1948 and the prewar years, and it was expected to double again by 1975. So remarkable was this performance — and so unexpected as late as 1952 — that it was described as an "economic miracle." The expression was first used with reference to West Germany, but it soon came to be applied to Western Europe generally. France and Italy in particular, two countries that had lagged behind the leaders in adopting modern industrial technology, had growth rates in the postwar era as high as that of Germany. Great Britain, on the other hand, fell behind, with a growth rate only about one-half that of Western Europe as a whole. The United States also grew more slowly than Western Europe, although at a very satisfactory rate in comparison with its record in the interwar years. Nevertheless, because of the high level of per capita income achieved by the British before the war and their smaller amount of war damage, they still had one of the highest standards of living in Europe. For the same reason per capita income in the United States remained far higher than that in Europe.

Unprecedented though it was, there was really nothing miraculous about Western Europe's economic resurgence. Many factors contributed, a few of which had primary importance. American aid played a crucial role in sparking the recovery. Thereafter Europeans kept it going with high levels of saving and investment. At times the competition between consumption and investment spending caused severe inflationary pres-

sures, but none were so disastrous as the hyperinflations after World War
I. Much of the investment went into equipment for new products and
processes. During the depression years and the war a backlog of technological innovations had built up which only awaited capital and skilled
manpower to be employed. Thus, technological modernization both
accompanied and was an important contributory factor to the so-called
economic miracle.

Another major factor was the attitude and role of governments. They
participated in economic life both directly and indirectly on a much
larger scale than previously. They nationalized some basic industries,
drew up economic plans, and provided a wide range of social services.
Nevertheless, private enterprise was responsible for by far the largest part
of economic activity. On the average, between one-fourth and one-third
of the national income in Western Europe originated in the government
sector. Though this proportion was much greater than it had been before
the war, it was less than half the contribution of the private sectors of
the economy. The economic systems of postwar Western Europe were
equally far from the stereotyped old style capitalism of the nineteenth
century and from the doctrinaire socialized economies of Eastern Europe.
In the mixed or welfare state economies that became characteristic of the
Western democracies, government assumed the tasks of providing over-all
stability, a climate favorable to growth, and minimal protection for the
economically weak and underprivileged, but it left the main task of producing the goods and services desired by the population to private enterprise. The postwar governments of Western Europe also took the initiative in dismantling the barriers to international economic cooperation
and competition erected by their predecessors.

THE DRIVE FOR UNIFICATION

The dream of a united Europe is as old as Europe itself. Charlemagne's
Holy Roman Empire closely approximated the boundaries of the present-
day European Economic Community plus Switzerland and Austria. Napoleon's French Empire and its satellites in the Continental System
encompassed almost all of continental Europe. The concert of Europe,
which grew out of the Vienna Congress of 1815, represented an attempt
to coordinate policy at the highest level of government. The League of
Nations was a concert of the European victors in World War I. Hitler
very nearly succeeded in creating a *Festung Europa* under Nazi domination. All such efforts failed, however, owing to the inability of the
would-be unifiers to maintain a monopoly of coercive power and the unwillingness of the members to submit voluntarily to their authority. In
earlier times the difficulties of communication contributed to the frac-
tionation of Europe. Then the idea of nationalism became so deeply entrenched in European thought, especially after the French Revolution,

Table 1 *The Economic Recovery of Western Europe, 1948–65*

	Index of general industrial production (1958 = 100)		Steel production (1,000's of metric tons)		Production of electrical energy (in million kilo-watt hours)		Manufacture of passenger cars and trucks (in 1,000's)		Foreign trade (imports plus exports; millions of dollars)	
	1948	1965	1948	1965	1948	1965	1948	1965	1948	1965
France	54	138	7,236	19,604	28,851	101,442	198.4	1,616.1	5,453	20,390
West Germany	27	157	6,790	36,821	32,836	168,762	59.6	2,971.4	2,270	35,374
Italy	44	176	2,125	12,660	22,694	79,228	59.4	1,175.5	2,616	14,535
United Kingdom	74	132	15,116	27,439	48,036	196,027	508.1	2,344.4	14,367	28,881
Belgium	78	148	3,920	9,169	8,236	21,706	–	–	3,736	12,758
Netherlands	53	163	334	3,138	5,577	25,010	–	–	2,895	13,865

Source: United Nations, *Statistical Yearbook, 1966* (New York, 1967).

that sovereignty — that is, supreme authority or dominion — and nation-hood became almost synonymous in the minds of Europeans. Prior to World War II modern nation-states zealously opposed all proposals or attempts to infringe upon or in any way diminish their sovereignty.

It is important to bear in mind the distinction between international and supranational organizations. International organizations depend upon the voluntary cooperation of their members and have no direct power of coercion. Supranational organizations require their members to surrender at least a portion of sovereignty and can compel compliance with their mandates. Both the League of Nations and the United Nations are examples of international organizations. Within Europe the OEEC and most other postwar organizations of nations have been inter-national rather than supranational. Continued successful cooperation may lead eventually to a pooling of sovereignties, which is the hope of the proponents of European unity. Proposals for some kind of supra-national organization in Europe have become increasingly frequent since 1945 and have issued from ever more influential sources.

The proposals spring from two separate but related motives — political and economic. The political motive, manifested somewhat tenuously in the Council of Europe, is rooted in the belief that only through supra-national organization can the threat of war between European powers be permanently eradicated. Some proponents of European political unity further believe that the compact nation-state of the past is now out-moded; if the nations of Europe are to resume their role in world affairs, they must be able to speak with one voice and have at their command resources and manpower comparable with those of superpowers such as the United States and the Soviet Union. The economic motive rests upon the argument that larger markets will promote greater specialization and increased competition, thus higher productivity and standards of living. The two motives merge in agreeing that economic strength is the basis of political and military power and that a fully integrated European economy would render intra-European wars less likely, if not impossible. Because of the deeply entrenched idea of national sovereignty, most of the practical proposals for a supranational organization have envisaged economic unification as a preliminary to political unification.

BENELUX

The Benelux Customs Union, which provided for the free movement of goods within Belgium, the Netherlands, and Luxembourg and for a common external tariff, grew out of the realization that under modern conditions of production and distribution the economies of the separate states were too small to permit them to enjoy the full benefits of mass production. Belgium and Luxembourg had, in fact, joined in an eco-nomic union as early as 1921, and the governments-in-exile of Belgium and the Netherlands had agreed in principle on the customs union during the war. Formal ratification of the treaty came in 1947. Statesmen of these countries have been the warmest advocates of a European common market and have continued to work for a closer economic integration of their own countries independently of broader European developments.

THE SCHUMAN PLAN

The OEEC and its subsidiary organizations such as the European Payments Union (EPU) resulted from American initiative and provided only for cooperation, not full integration. In 1950 French foreign minister Robert Schuman proposed the integration of the French and West German coal and steel industries and invited other nations to participate. Schuman's motives were as much political as economic. Coal and steel lay at the heart of modern industry — the armaments industries in particular — and all signs pointed to a revival of German industry. Schuman was desirous of propitiating German industrialists and at the same time keeping German industry under control or at least under surveillance. Anxious to be admitted to the new concert of Europe, West Germany responded with alacrity, as did the Benelux nations and Italy, afraid of being left behind if they did not participate. Great Britain, with nationalized steel and coal industries at the time, replied more cautiously and in the end did not participate. The treaty creating the European Coal and Steel Community (ECSC) was signed in 1951 and took effect early in 1952. The treaty provided for the elimination between signatory nations of tariffs and quotas on trade in iron ore, coal, coke, and steel, as well as a common external tariff on imports from other nations. To supervise its operations several bodies of a supranational character were established: a High Authority with executive powers, a Council of Ministers, a Common Assembly, a Court of Justice, and a Consultative Committee. The community was authorized to levy a tax on the output of enterprises within its province in order to finance its operations.

EUROPEAN DEFENSE COMMUNITY

Soon after the signing of the treaty creating the Coal and Steel Community the same nations attempted another giant step forward on the road to integration with a treaty for a European Defense Community. Developments such as the Korean War, the formation of the NATO alliance, and the rapid economic recovery of West Germany had demonstrated the importance of including German contingents in a Western European military force, but proposals to do this naturally aroused the suspicion and hostility of the nations that had recently been the victims of German aggression. One proposal to overcome their fears suggested including the German contingents in a unified military command. The EDC treaty made provisions accordingly, but after prolonged debates the French National Assembly finally rejected the treaty outright in August, 1954. This setback to the movement for unification demonstrated once again the difficulty of securing agreement on proposals for the limitation of national sovereignty. Other ways were found for Germany to make a contribution to the military defense of Western Europe. Meanwhile proponents of European unity resorted to more cautious tactics, once again in the area of economics.

THE COMMON MARKET AND EURATOM

In 1957 the participants in the Schuman Plan signed two more treaties in Rome, creating the European Atomic Energy Community (EURATOM) for the development of peaceful uses of atomic energy and, most important, the European Economic Community (EEC) or Common Market. The Common Market treaty provided for the gradual elimination of import duties and quantitative restrictions on all trade between member nations and the substitution of a common external tariff over a transitional period of twelve to fifteen years. Members of the community pledged themselves to implement common policies respecting transportation, agriculture, social insurance, and a number of other critical areas of economic policy and to permit the free movement of persons and capital within the boundaries of the community. One of the most important provisions of the treaty was that it could not be renounced unilaterally and that after a certain stage in the transitional period further decisions could be made by a qualified majority vote rather than by unanimous action. Both the Common Market and EURATOM treaties created high commissions to oversee their operations and merged other supranational bodies (councils of ministers, common assemblies, courts of justice, and consultative committees) with those of the ECSC. The Common Market treaty took effect on January 1, 1958, and within a few years it confounded the pessimists by shortening instead of lengthening the transitional period. In 1965 the high commissions of the three communities were merged, providing a more effective agency for eventual political unification. On July 1, 1968, all tariffs between member nations were completely eliminated, several years earlier than the date originally foreseen.

BRITAIN BETWEEN EFTA AND EEC

In the preliminaries to the treaties of Rome invitations were extended to other nations to join the Common Market. Britain objected to the surrender of sovereignty implied in the treaties and attempted to persuade the OEEC nations to create a free trade area instead. After signature of the Common Market treaty Britain, the Scandinavian nations, Switzerland, Austria, and Portugal joined in the European Free Trade Association (EFTA), the so-called outer seven, in opposition to the inner six of the Common Market. The EFTA treaty only provided for the elimination of tariffs on industrial products among the signatory nations. It did not extend to agricultural products, it did not provide for a common external tariff, and it could be abrogated by any member at any time. It was thus a much weaker union than that of the Common Market.

In 1961 Britain signified its willingness to enter the Common Market if certain conditions could be met. If effected, this move would have entailed the membership of most of the EFTA partners also. Lengthy negotiations over the terms of entry ensued, but in January, 1963, President de Gaulle of France in effect vetoed Britain's membership, an action he repeated in 1967 and 1969. After de Gaulle's retirement, however, the French government took a more moderate attitude on the question of British membership, which the other Common Market countries favored.

THE ATLANTIC ALLIANCE

Another development of the postwar era that was no less striking than the rapid economic progress and political cooperation of Western Europe was the acceptance by the United States of global responsibilities — a startling reversal of the isolationism of the interwar years. The two developments were intimately related. The Marshall Plan not only assisted the recovery of Europe but also sparked the cooperation that eventuated in the Common Market and other international and supranational ventures. The United States continued its policies of cooperation with and assistance to other nations of the so-called free world. It took a prominent part in the formation of the Organization of American States in 1948, the North Atlantic Treaty Organization in 1949, and the regional military alliances for Southeast Asia (SEATO) and the Middle East (the Bagdad Pact). It came to the assistance of Greece and Turkey in 1947 and of South Korea in 1950; it sent military advisory missions to Vietnam and several other world trouble spots. Hardly a day passed without producing newspaper headlines telling of American involvement in some remote or not-so-remote corner of the globe. In most instances United States policy makers justified their actions as a means of "containing communism" or "opposing Soviet aggression," although humanitarianism also lay behind American aid to underdeveloped nations. A brief review of some aspects of the domestic history of the United States since 1945 will help give an understanding of America's involvement in international affairs.

THE UNITED STATES IN
THE POSTWAR ERA

One notable feature of recent American history has been the continuity of basic policy through Democratic and Republican administrations. Harry S Truman, a Democrat, succeeded Roosevelt at the latter's death on the eve of victory over Germany and won an upset victory over Thomas E. Dewey in 1948, serving almost two full terms. Truman followed Roosevelt's major policies in both foreign and domestic affairs. Surprisingly, Dwight D. Eisenhower, former supreme commander of the Allied forces and the first Republican president in two decades, continued such fundamental features of American policy as military and economic aid to nations outside the Soviet bloc (including Fascist Spain and Communist Yugoslavia) and the extension of social security and other welfare state activities. John F. Kennedy, the first Catholic president and the youngest man ever elected to the presidency, won a closely contested race against Republican Vice President Richard Nixon in 1960. Kennedy studded his administration with intellectuals from the academic world and emphasized "new frontiers" to challenge the imagination and ingenuity of Americans, but in actual practice he did not depart radically from established policies. After his tragic assassination in 1963, Vice President Lyndon B. Johnson, a veteran legislator and able politician, generally followed and expanded the policies laid down by his predecessors. That these policies commended themselves to the American people received striking confirmation in 1964 in the overwhelming victory of Johnson over the conservative Senator Barry Goldwater, who offered the electorate the most clear-cut choice of programs in many years. Johnson's escalation of the war in Vietnam cost him so much support among the liberals in his own party, however, that he withdrew from the election of 1968, which Richard Nixon won by a narrow margin over Vice President Hubert Humphrey, who inherited the legacy of the Johnson administration.

Certain domestic problems had an important bearing on the image of the United States abroad and on its capacity for world leadership. One that commanded widespread attention abroad was the struggle for legal equality by American Negroes, known as the civil rights movement. Citizens of other lands, especially in Asia, Africa, and South America, viewed with interest the apparent divergence between American ideals and reality and the efforts made to repair it. In 1954 the Supreme Court issued a historic decision banning legalized segregation in public schools and followed it with several other decisions aimed at eliminating from all aspects of life segregation based on race or color. The decisions met with strong resistance in parts of the American South. At length Negroes took matters into their own hands, organizing massive campaigns reminiscent of the passive resistance movement inspired by Gandhi in India. In 1964 Congress passed a strong civil rights law. In the same year the Reverend Martin Luther King, one of the Negro leaders, became the second American Negro to win the Nobel Peace Prize for his part in organizing the movement. (Ralph Bunche had been the first for his role as United Nations mediator in the Arab-Israeli war of 1948–49.) King's assassination by a white racist in 1968 fueled the fires of a far more militant and violent campaign against white society that had begun winning converts among Negro youth as early as 1965.

A similar issue, of great interest abroad, concerned questions of patriotism, loyalty, and the role of dissent in a democratic society. The issue commanded greatest attention in the early 1950's when Senator Joseph McCarthy of Wisconsin made widely publicized but undocumented charges of disloyalty against government officials, university professors, and others. Playing on widespread fears of a Communist conspiracy and internal subversion, McCarthy and other demagogues wreaked havoc with the lives of innocent persons and brought the nation near to mass hysteria. McCarthy himself received a formal vote of censure from the Senate in 1954, which relegated him to obscurity even before his death in 1957; but the mischief he caused lived after him, notably in the attitude and behavior of young people.

The college students of the late 1940's, including many veterans of World War II continuing their education with federal assistance under the G.I. Bill, had maintained some of the idealism that had characterized young people in the 1930's and the war years. During the 1950's, however, under the baleful influence of McCarthyism and the general atmosphere of apprehension, college students and other youths imitated their elders and adopted an attitude of cautious noninvolvement in controversial questions that led them to be dubbed "the silent generation" and "the beat generation." The true beatniks, also called hippies in the 1960's, who wished to demonstrate indifference to social conventions but feared to participate in social controversy, resorted to wearing outlandish clothing, invented a special variety of slang, and made frequent public exhibitions of their unconventional morality, including widespread use of marijuana and more powerful drugs. In the 1960's much of youth regained its more normal activist mentality, as evidenced, on the one hand, by the notable participation of both white and Negro young people in the civil rights movement and, on the other, by their somewhat unaccustomed role of leadership in various conservative and reactionary movements. Such activism reached a peak in the protests against American policy toward Vietnam and in the related youthful revolts against the alleged hypocrisy of adult American society. The protests were directed at the universities in particular, and in a few instances threatened to disrupt the educational process completely.

NATO

The North Atlantic Treaty Organization, created in 1949, further demonstrated the willingness and determination of the United States to assume leadership of the non-Communist world in order to prevent the spread of Communist-controlled governments. The original members of the organization were the United States and Canada, Britain, France, the Benelux countries, Denmark, Norway, Iceland, Italy, and Portugal. Greece and Turkey adhered in 1951; West Germany became a member in 1955. The treaty creating the organization declared that "an armed attack against one or more" members of the organization "shall be considered an attack against them all." Coming after the *coup de Prague* and the Berlin blockade, the treaty meant in effect that the nations of Western Europe were determined to resist armed aggression by the Soviet Union and that the United States stood ready to assist them in this determination. The treaty provided for a ministerial body, the North Atlantic Council, to direct operations and for a unified military command. General Eisenhower, who had commanded the Allied invasion of Europe in World War II, was called back from retirement to serve as the first Supreme Commander, Allied Powers, Europe, from 1950 until his resignation to run for the presidency of the United States in 1952.

THE REHABILITATION OF WEST GERMANY

The economic miracle of West Germany has been frequently commented upon, but its economic recovery was no more miraculous than the creation of a genuinely democratic state in a nation long subject to authoritarian monarchy and dictatorship. The process began as early as 1946 when, in accordance with the Potsdam agreements, the Germans elected officials for new state (*Länder*) governments. In 1948 Britain, France, and the United States allowed a parliamentary council of the states within their zones of occupation to meet in the ancient university city of Bonn in the Rhineland. The council drew up a basic law which took effect the following year and continued to serve the German Federal Republic as a constitution. It was modeled on the constitution of the Weimar Republic, modified to remove such obvious defects as the emergency powers of the president. Much of the success of West Germany in regaining international prestige resulted from the political sagacity and skill of Konrad Adenauer, its first chancellor, who served from 1949 until his retirement in 1963 at the age of eighty-seven. Adenauer headed the Christian Democratic Union (CDU), the largest political party in West Germany, though it did not always command an absolute majority in the Bundestag (lower house of parliament). As a result, the CDU frequently formed coalitions with the Free Democratic party and smaller groups. The main opposition came from the Socialist party

(SPD) until 1966, when the SPD joined the CDU in a so-called grand coalition. In a turnabout after the election of 1969, the SPD formed a coalition with the Free Democrats.

West Berlin occupied an anomalous position that occasioned several international crises. Located well inside East Germany, it was not technically a part of the German Federal Republic. Nevertheless, the two entities maintained close relations, and Willy Brandt, the Socialist mayor of West Berlin, became foreign minister of the German Federal Republic in the coalition government of 1966, and chancellor in 1969. In spite of its tremendous concentration of population (over 3.5 million in 1970), its enormous wartime damage, and the difficulties imposed by its location, West Berlin enjoyed a booming prosperity and one of the highest standards of living in Europe. Expenditures of the Allied occupation forces and subsidies from West Germany helped. Another reason for the rapid growth and prosperity of West Berlin, particularly in the 1950's, was the enormous influx of refugees from East Germany. To put a stop to this embarrassment and the drain of skilled manpower, the East German authorities in 1961 built a high wall between East and West Berlin, making the separation more than merely symbolic.

The German Federal Republic faced many difficult problems in its early years, but it surmounted most of them successfully. At first the flood of refugees from East Germany and other Soviet-dominated areas, totaling more than 12.5 million persons, posed a serious problem because of the shortages of housing and jobs; as recovery persisted, they proved a blessing in disguise. Their skills and energies contributed to the rebuilding of West Germany and alleviated a severe labor shortage. Other major problems involved West Germany's relations with the Soviet bloc and the Western allies, the question of rearmament, and the even more ticklish question of reunification. With respect to the first two, Adenauer followed a policy of friendship and cooperation with the West, which resulted in the restoration of German sovereignty in 1955. This led in turn to the beginnings of rearmament under the auspices of NATO and to tacit recognition by the Soviet Union despite the lack of a formal peace treaty. Adenauer repeatedly postponed serious consideration of the reunification of East and West Germany without ever disavowing the possibility of eventual reunion. The continuing integration of West Germany in the Common Market and the North Atlantic Alliance has rendered reunification ever more unlikely, but as long as East and West Germany remain divided, the situation will present a strong temptation to ambitious demagogues.

"THE REPUBLIC IS DEAD; VIVE LA RÉPUBLIQUE!"

France under the Fourth Republic compiled an ambivalent record. Superficially all was chaos and instability. The constitution deliberately provided for a figurehead president and a cabinet dependent upon the National Assembly. The latter split into a number of volatile parties, no one of which could command a majority. The Communist party, usually the largest single party with about a fourth of the deputies, was the only one to maintain strict party discipline. The center parties formed coalition governments, sometimes with Socialist support or at least acquiescence, but their lack of party discipline resulted in their frequent overthrow. The average life of cabinets under the Fourth Republic was even shorter than under the Third. In other respects postwar France seemed to be tottering on the brink of a volcano. The labor movement, like the political parties, splintered into various rival groups, with the Communists commanding the largest membership. Strikes, often politically motivated, were more frequent than in almost any other country. Inflation remained a persistent problem. France's colonial empire engaged in a series of revolts and civil wars, nearly all of which went badly for France and drained it of manpower and wealth.

In spite of this apparently dismal record, the nation made substantial progress in several respects, proving that even in the twentieth century governments are not the sole determinants of a nation's welfare. After a century of slow, almost stagnant population growth, the birth rate rose at the end of the war and remained at a level comparable to that of other Western nations. As the age distribution shifted toward younger people, their greater vitality was reflected in the nation at large. After some transitional difficulties in the early postwar years, the French economy staged a spectacular revival and transformation. Industrial production rose 55 per cent between 1952 and 1958 — a greater percentage than in any other Western nation. Agricultural production increased substantially while the labor force employed in agriculture declined by half; by 1958 France was the only nation in Western Europe that was self-sufficient in agricultural production, and even had a surplus for export. Because of its modernized economy France enjoyed one of the highest standards of living of any of the former belligerents of Europe in World War II.

France took the initiative in many of the ventures in international cooperation. In spite of frequent cabinet shuffles, government personnel changed relatively little. Robert Schuman and Georges Bidault, both members of the same party, between them held the portfolio of foreign affairs throughout most of the life of the Fourth Republic. The French civil service, highly educated, competent, and relatively permanent, provided an important element of stability and continuity underneath the troubled surface.

The downfall of the Fourth Republic resulted from its failure to solve the problem of Algeria. Faced with the threat of an army coup d'état in May, 1958, the government called on General de Gaulle, who for some years had been writing his memoirs in semiretirement, to take over as prime minister. De Gaulle refused except on condition that he be granted almost dictatorial powers, including the power to remake the constitution. After some days of anxious negotiation the president and parliamentarians accepted most of de Gaulle's terms, and on June 1 he took over the reins of government. He went to work at once to revamp the constitution. In September the electorate, thoroughly wearied of the Fourth Republic, approved the constitution of the Fifth Republic in a popular referendum by a vote of four to one.

The new constitution greatly strengthened the presidency at the expense of parliament. The president appoints all ministers, including the prime minister, and personally presides over the cabinet or Council of Ministers. Through his ministers he proposes legislation, and if the National Assembly passes a vote of censure on the government, he may dissolve it and call for new elections. He may take proposals for constitutional amendments and other major questions directly to the people in a popular referendum, and in case of emergency he may govern by decree. The parliament, consisting of a National Assembly elected by universal suffrage in single-member constituencies and a Senate elected indirectly, has strictly limited powers. It may initiate legislation as well as approve or disapprove what is proposed by the government, but it no longer has the power, as under the Fourth Republic, to provoke ministerial crises of indeterminate length. The new constitution also provided for a number of administrative and judicial reforms aimed at modernizing and streamlining the governmental apparatus.

De Gaulle was elected first president of the Fifth Republic for a seven-year term by an overwhelming vote in December, 1958, and took office (in succession to himself as last premier of the Fourth Republic) the following January. Somewhat surprisingly he continued most of the policies of the discredited Fourth Republic, but with greater firmness and éclat. Assisted by a monetary reform at the beginning of 1960, the economy continued its upward march. De Gaulle respected France's commitments in the treaties creating the Common Market and other international obligations, and he brought about greater cooperation with Germany through his personal friendship with Chancellor Adenauer. He did, however, veto Britain's membership in the Common Market, and in general he favored a "Europe of fatherlands" rather than a United States of Europe. For this reason he persisted in making France the fourth nuclear power when the United States refused to share its atomic secrets, and acted independently of NATO in other respects. In 1966 he actually withdrew France from NATO's military command, and forced the latter to transfer its headquarters from France to Belgium. The most decisive and meaningful accomplishment of his regime was the liquidation of France's colonial empire, including Algeria. In the process he brought the army to heel and purged its top echelons of potential leaders of military juntas. In 1965 de Gaulle was re-elected for a new seven-year term. In the spring of 1968 a series of popular demonstrations that began as a student revolt in a university on the outskirts of Paris threatened to boil over into social revolution; and later that year a severe financial crisis threatened the value of the franc. De Gaulle stood fast on both occasions, but resigned the presidency the following year, as he had done in 1946, over a relatively minor issue. In the election of June, 1969, Georges Pompidou, a former Gaullist prime minister who had fallen from the general's favor, was elected president of France.

OTHER POLITICAL DEVELOPMENTS

In Great Britain a Conservative government was elected in 1951. It denationalized the steel industry and reopened the motor transport industry to private enterprise, but it did not interfere with the other nationalized industries and it maintained the social reforms of the Labour party with only minor modifications. The venerable Churchill resigned as prime minister in 1955 at the age of eighty-one but retained his seat in the House of Commons until 1964, the year before his death. Anthony Eden, who succeeded Churchill as prime minister, led the party to victory in the election of 1955 but was forced to resign in the aftermath of the Suez crisis of 1956. (See p. 1058.) Harold Macmillan, also a Conservative, served as prime minister from 1957 until 1963, having again won over the Labour party in the election of 1959. Labour at last won an election by a narrow margin in 1964, and Harold Wilson became prime minister.

After the death of Alcide de Gasperi in 1953, Italy was governed by a succession of unstable coalitions built around the Christian Democrats, who remained the largest single party. The Communists maintained their strength undiminished, commanding between 20 and 25 per cent of the vote in parliamentary elections; but the possibility of a Communist take-over, which appeared very strong in the immediate postwar years, receded as the alliance between the Communists and the left-wing Socialists crumbled. A brief revival of monarchist and neofascist activity in the 1950's amounted to little. In the early 1960's the center coalition created an "opening to the left," climaxed by the election of a Socialist as president, but the left-center coalition was no more durable than its predecessors. Italy's major problems have been economic and social — in particular, the continued great contrast between the backward, agrarian south and the industrially progressive north. Superficial political instability has not prevented Italy any more than France from making rapid economic gains, but it still has far to go to catch up with its more prosperous neighbors. Italy's coalition governments have steadfastly supported the Common Market, NATO, and other instruments of international cooperation and unification.

French Students During Paris Riots

"The March 22nd movement constitutes a tiny minority in the [French Student Association]. . . . We realized how sterile verbal differences were in relation to the possibilities of common action. . . . During the famous night of March 22, we tried to define.the framework in which it would be possible for all of the 'sects' to participate in a single political activity: the challenge to the university." French student leader on Radio Luxembourg, May 17, 1968.

EUROPE IN 1970

Members of the Free
Trade Association

Members of the European Economic
Community (Common Market)

The Communist Bloc

Members of the North Atlantic
Treaty Organization (N.A.T.O.)

Members of the Warsaw Pact

0 _____ 500
Miles

ICELAND

NORWAY

Bergen

Oslo

SCOTLAND
Glasgow
Edinburgh

UNITED KINGDOM
EIRE   Belfast
Dublin   OF GREAT BRITAIN
Cork
WALES
ENGLAND
London
Manchester
AND NO. IRELAND

North
Sea

DENMARK
Copenhagen

ATLANTIC

OCEAN

Amsterdam
NETHERLANDS   Bremen
Brussels
BELGIUM   Cologne
Le Havre   Rouen
Paris   LUX.   GERMANY
Loire   R.   R.   Strasbourg
FRANCE

Hamburg
EAST
Potsdam
WEST
GERMANY
Bonn
Nuremberg
Munich

Bay of Biscay
Bordeaux   Geneva   SWITZ.
Berne
AUS
Lyon
Toulouse   Milan   Venice
Turin   Po   R.   Tri

Oporto
SPAIN
Lisbon   PORTUGAL   Tagus   R.   Madrid
Guadalquivir   R.
Seville

ANDORRA
Marseille   Genoa
Florence

Ebro   R.
Barcelona   CORSICA   ITALY
Rome

SARDINIA
Naples

Strait of Gibraltar

AFRICA

*ALBANIA aligned with Communist China
*FINLAND aligned with Soviet Union by treaty
*YUGOSLAVIA Communist but independent of the Soviet Union

Palern
SICILY

Mediterran

White Sea

Archangel

N. Dvina R.

Tobolsk

U. S. S. R.

Perm

Chelyabinsk

L. Onega

L. Ladoga

Helsinki

Gulf of Finland • Leningrad

Tallinn

ckholm ESTONIAN
S.S.R.

RUSSIAN SOVIET FEDERATED

Kazan

Magnitogorsk

SOCIALIST REPUBLIC

LATVIAN

Riga • S.S.R.

Moscow •

LITHUANIAN

Kaliningrad S.S.R.

Dvina R.

• Smolensk

Ural R.

nsk

Vilna

• Minsk

BELORUSSIAN
S.S.R.

Don R.

KAZAKH S.S.R.

AND

Warsaw

Volgograd •

Volga R.

Vistula R.

Kiev •

Kharkov •

UKRAINIAN   S.S.R.

Lvov

Krivoi
Rog •

• Donetsk

Zhdanov • • Rostov

IA

dapest

MOLDAVIAN
S.S.R.

Dnieper R.

Sea of
Azov

Caspian

ARY

• Cluj

Odessa •

CRIMEA

Sea

RUMANIA

• Yalta

GEORGIAN
S.S.R.

AZER-
BAIJAN
S.S.R.

• Baku

rade

Bucharest •

Black   Sea

ARMENIAN
S.S.R. • Erevan

evo

Danube R.

LAVIA*   BULGARIA

Sofia

• Istanbul

IRAN

IA* • Salonika

• Ankara

GREECE

Izmir

TURKEY

Tigris R.

Athens

Adana •

• Aleppo

Euphrates R.

• Baghdad

Nicosia •

SYRIA

CRETE

CYPRUS

LEBANON

IRAQ

a

Greece and Turkey, although subject to mutual suspicion and jealousy over the fate of the island of Cyprus and other questions, were united in their fear of Soviet aggression and support of the Western alliance. Both joined NATO in 1951, and ten years later they became "associates" of the European Economic Community. Greece became a cause of anxiety within the alliance in 1967 when a military junta overthrew the legitimate government, established a dictatorship, and subsequently expelled the king. Spain and Portugal were gradually assimilated in the Western alliance in spite of their dictatorial forms of government. Portugal, in fact, participated as a charter member of NATO and in 1957 became associated with Britain and other nations in the European Free Trade Association. Spain was treated as an outcast among nations by both East and West after the war, but it gained formal recognition from the United States in 1953 and two years later under American sponsorship was admitted to the United Nations. Spain's participation in the military alliance depended upon its bilateral relationship with the United States, which maintained air bases in Spain. In 1959, however, the OEEC admitted it to membership in return for a promise to stabilize its economy and to permit a liberalization of its international exchanges. The harsher features of Spain's political system were moderated somewhat in anticipation of the replacement of General Franco, its elderly dictator, who in 1969 indicated Juan Carlos de Borbon, grandson of Alfonso XIII, as his eventual successor as head of state. All of the Mediterranean countries remained desperately poor, although each one made some progress in modernizing its economy after centuries of stagnation.

The Nordic countries differed in their approaches to international cooperation. All participated in the OEEC; Denmark, Norway, and Sweden also joined the Free Trade Association. Denmark, Norway, and Iceland became charter members of NATO, but Sweden held aloof, concerned for its traditional neutrality. Treading a fine line in the shadow of the Soviet Union, Finland could not afford wholesale cooperation with the West in either the political or the economic spheres, but it drew closer to the Scandinavian countries with trade and cultural agreements. Austria and Switzerland continued their policies of political and military neutrality but joined the Free Trade Association and indicated their willingness to become associated with the Common Market, though not as full members.

COMMUNISM AFTER STALIN

A new era opened for the Communist world when Joseph Stalin died in March, 1953. In the Soviet Union the Stalinist system of government, based upon fear and terrorist repression and marked by the imprisonment or execution of real or imagined opponents, evolved in the direction of more humane, if still harsh, methods of rule. Within the Soviet bloc of nations a gradual movement away from a monolithic character and toward greater diversity developed as each nation worked out its own variations of Communist ideology and institutions. The Soviet Union suffered reverses in dealing with other Communist nations, above all with Yugoslavia and China, as well as in its relations with the Western powers. Finally, the economic recovery of the Soviet bloc was far slower than that of the Western nations. There was no economic miracle on the other side of the iron curtain.

POLITICAL STRUGGLES WITHIN THE
RUSSIAN COMMUNIST PARTY

After Stalin's death leading political and army figures bargained for power among themselves until a triumvirate emerged. Georgi Malenkov, chairman of the Council of Ministers, held the leading position, with Lavrenti Beria, chief of the secret police, and V. M. Molotov, expert in foreign affairs, as his chief coadjutors. The new collective leadership was soon torn by internal dissension. In the struggle Beria lost. In July, 1953, he was arrested as an "enemy of the people" and secretly executed together with a number of his supporters. After Beria's death a little-known party figure named Nikita Khrushchev, who after Stalin's death had become first secretary of the Communist party, became a member of the triumvirate. Under Malenkov's leadership the government introduced a new emphasis on consumer goods and attempted to reorganize agricultural production. Malenkov's program failed, and in February, 1954, he was forced to resign as premier, although he remained in the Politburo for a time. Nikolai Bulganin became premier and nominal head of government, but it soon became obvious that Khrushchev was the dominant figure.

At the Twentieth Communist Party Congress in February, 1956, Khrushchev gave a long speech in which he denounced Stalin as a ruthless, morbid, almost insane tyrant who had ordered the execution of countless innocent people, whose egotism had led him to make mistakes for which all Russia suffered, who had caused the government to lose touch with the people, who had established the "cult of personality" to glorify himself. Khrushchev carefully pointed out, however, that Stalin's despotism represented an aberration from an essentially correct policy and claimed that the new collective leadership had returned to proper Leninist principles of government. Supposedly secret, Khrushchev's speech was allowed to leak out to the public. It caused much confusion and ferment among the peoples of the Communist countries and did serious damage to the cause of communism by its confirmation of the evils of Stalin's regime. The government began an official program of "de-Stalinization" that included the removal of Stalin's pictures and statues from public

Sovfoto

Molotov, Stalin, and Andreyev

*"Stalin acted not through persuasion, explanation, and patient co-operation
with people, but by imposing his concepts and demanding absolute submission to
his opinion. Whoever opposed this concept or tried to prove his viewpoint,
and the correctness of his position — was doomed to removal from the leading
collective and to subsequent moral and physical annihilation. . . . Arbitrary
behavior by one person encouraged and permitted arbitrariness in others. Mass
arrests and deportations of many thousands of people, execution without trial
and without normal investigation created conditions of insecurity, fear, and
even desperation. . . .*

*"The cult of the individual acquired such monstrous size chiefly because
Stalin himself, using all conceivable methods, supported the glorification of
his own person. . . . Was it without Stalin's knowledge that many of the
largest enterprises and towns were named after him? Was it without his
knowledge that Stalin monuments were erected in the whole country?"*
Speech of Khrushchev to the 20th Congress of the Communist Party,
U.S.S.R., February 25, 1956.

places, changes in the names of towns and schools that had been named for him, and the removal of his body from the famed Lenin Tomb in Moscow's Red Square. Changes bringing about a more relaxed social and political atmosphere were introduced, such as reforms in court procedure to provide more protection for accused persons, the release of thousands of political prisoners, and improvements in wages and pensions.

Risings in several of the satellite states and economic difficulties at home intensified the power struggle in the Kremlin. Khrushchev was blamed for these troubles and for weakening the regime by his disavowal of Stalin. In mid-1957 a bitter fight broke out in the innermost councils of the party aimed at forcing Khrushchev to resign. He managed to ride out the storm and forced his opponents from their high posts, branding them an "anti-party" group. In the spring of 1958 Bulganin, who had gone against Khrushchev, resigned as premier and Khrushchev took over his office. Officially he was both head of the party and leader of the government. The era of collective leadership seemed to have ended.

Khrushchev's difficulties were far from over, however. For a few years, it is true, he appeared to wield power almost as absolute as Stalin's and was on the verge of establishing a new cult of personality. But reverses in international affairs, economic difficulties at home, and the growth of diversity and discontent in countries of the Soviet bloc compelled him to adopt a defensive tone in some of his addresses. He publicly stated that owing to his advancing years — he became seventy in 1964 — he could not expect to remain in office much longer. He showed no willingness, however, to transfer any of his power to others. In October, 1964, that decision was made for him when without warning the government announced that he had been relieved of his duties for reasons of "age and deteriorating health." Leonid Brezhnev and Aleksi Kosygin were named to succeed him as head of the party and premier, respectively. Khrushchev had been overthrown by a revolt of men within the Kremlin who were dissatisfied with his leadership.

SOVIET INDUSTRY AND AGRICULTURE

Soviet industry continued to increase its output of heavy goods but still fell far short of the intention expressed by Soviet leaders to overtake and surpass the production of the United States. In 1955 the government announced the fulfillment of the goals of the fifth five-year plan, instituted in 1950, although high officials complained of widespread inefficiency, and Premier Bulganin stated publicly that one-third of Soviet industrial enterprises failed to meet their production targets. The production of consumer goods, always given a low priority in Soviet planning, continued to lag, so that the citizens were plagued by shortages and inferior goods.

Soviet agriculture remained in a condition of almost unrelieved crisis throughout the postwar period, despite massive efforts by the government to increase productivity. The collective farm system did not offer enough incentive for the peasants. Instead, they concentrated their energies on the small private plots of up to one-half hectare (1.2 acres) that they were allowed to cultivate, part of whose produce they could sell on the market. These plots formed little more than 3 per cent of Russia's cultivated land, but they produced as much as one-fifth of the country's milk and one-third of its meat. In 1954 Khrushchev, who had long been interested in agriculture, started a "virgin lands" project to bring great stretches of arid land in Soviet Asia into cultivation. The next year he launched a drive to increase the production of corn, and in 1957 he announced a campaign to overtake the United States by 1961 in the production of milk, butter, and meat per person. None of these programs came anywhere near their stated goal. Despite threats of dire punishment and wholesale dismissals of agricultural officials, Khrushchev and his planners could not overcome poor soil, bad weather, bureaucratic mismanagement, fertilizer shortages, and above all the peasants' lack of enthusiasm. Food shortages continued to characterize Soviet life, to the embarrassment and discomfort of the regime. In 1963 the situation became so bad that the government was compelled to buy for gold over 10 million tons of grain from Canada and Australia.

"THE THAW"

In 1955 Ilya Ehrenburg, a well-known Soviet author, published a story called "The Thaw." The title was widely believed to refer to the changes that had been taking place in Russia since Stalin's death, and it became the symbolic name for the new era that began in 1953. The Soviet Union remained a totalitarian state, but the dread of the secret police, of purges, and of forced labor camps that had haunted Soviet life during Stalin's rule lessened. The government relied more on persuasion than on coercion to gain popular support. Selected Russians were allowed to travel and even study abroad, and foreign visitors were welcomed. A lively cultural exchange developed between the Soviet Union and the non-Communist world. Writers and other intellectuals were allowed greater freedom of expression. They were constantly reminded, however, that if they criticized aspects of Soviet life, they had to point out that those and all other shortcomings of Soviet society were being successfully overcome by the Communist party, or else they could expect some form of censure or punishment. The world became aware of this harsh fact in 1957 when *Dr. Zhivago,* a novel by Boris Pasternak, sixty-seven-year-old

Soviet novelist and poet, appeared in translation in several Western countries but could not be published in Russia. Although the novel was imbued with a deep love of Russia and its people, it questioned certain values of Soviet society. Pasternak was denounced as an enemy of socialism and forced to decline the Nobel Prize for literature offered him in 1958. He had to plead with Khrushchev to be allowed to remain in his beloved Russia. After four decades the Soviet rulers were still so uncertain of their hold over the people that they feared a single voice of dissent.

THE SOVIET BLOC

When Stalin died in 1953 the Soviet bloc in Europe presented the appearance of monolithic unity. It included Albania, Bulgaria, Rumania, Hungary, Czechoslovakia, Poland, and East Germany. (China and North Korea also formed a part of the Communist world, but they stood on a somewhat different footing.) Each of the satellites was more or less a small-scale replica of the Soviet Union, and all danced to the same tune — called in Moscow. Nevertheless, divisive tendencies hid behind the façade of unity. When Yugoslavia had earlier broken away from the Soviet bloc, although remaining a Communist nation, numbers of people in the other satellites would have liked to have done the same. Almost every Communist party had included some "national Communists" who wanted their nation to follow independent policies, but after Tito's defection the Stalinists — those who faithfully followed the Moscow line — had dismissed them from positions of leadership with the assistance of Soviet troops and police and in some cases had imprisoned or executed them. Soon after Stalin's death a wave of restiveness swept over the satellite states. In Czechoslovakia strikes and other demonstrations reached such proportions that Soviet tanks had to be called in to quell them, and in June, 1953, a full-fledged revolt broke out in East Germany, requiring several days of bloody fighting to be repressed.

In an effort to hold the bloc together without such an overt use of force the Soviet Union developed its own versions of NATO and the Common Market. In May, 1955, shortly after West Germany had been admitted to NATO, the Soviet Union and its satellites signed the East European Mutual Assistance Treaty, commonly called the Warsaw Pact, a twenty-year agreement of friendship, military assistance, and collaboration in international affairs. At the same time Russia reinvigorated the East European Council of Mutual Economic Assistance, founded in 1949 as a counter to the Marshall Plan but inactive for some years. Known as COMECON, it was ostensibly intended to coordinate the economic development of the Communist countries and promote a more efficient division of production among them; actually, however, Russia hoped to use it to make the satellites economically dependent on the Soviet Union.

DE-STALINIZATION AND THE HUNGARIAN REVOLT

After Khrushchev's speech to the Twentieth Party Congress de-Stalinization began to take effect in the satellites as well as the Soviet Union. Many political prisoners and victims of earlier purges were released from prison — or honored posthumously — and a slight relaxation of police controls became evident. Liberalization did not proceed fast enough or far enough to suit most people, however, and a new wave of unrest rippled across Eastern Europe. In the summer of 1956 riots in Poznan, Poland, became so serious that the Soviet authorities had to use force to suppress them. They then decided to rehabilitate Wladyslaw Gomulka, a former party leader who had been imprisoned for Titoism in 1948, and make him a member of the government. Gomulka refused to join the government unless the Russians agreed to recall the Soviet marshal who served as Poland's minister of defense and to permit other reforms. In October the Russians consented. Gomulka calmed the people and obtained for Poland an unprecedented degree of freedom within the Soviet bloc. He even succeeded in getting aid from the United States.

Encouraged by the success of the Poles, the Hungarians also pressed for more and faster reforms. Imre Nagy, a "national Communist" who had earlier been dismissed from the party, was restored and on October 24, 1956, became prime minister. He promised widespread reforms, including free elections, and persuaded the Soviet authorities to withdraw their troops from Hungary. On October 31 the last Soviet troops left Budapest; meanwhile, however, the Soviet army had been massing on Hungary's northeast border, and detachments began to pour into the country and surround every large city and important military and industrial installation. Nagy announced that Hungary was withdrawing from the Warsaw Pact and requested that the United Nations guarantee the perpetual neutrality of Hungary on the same basis as Austria. Too late: on November 4 at 4 A.M. Soviet tanks and bombers began a synchronized attack, inflicting destruction at least as horrible as that of World War II. For ten days Hungarian workers and students fought heroically against overwhelming odds with weapons furnished by their own soldiers. Even after the Russians and a new puppet government under Janos Kadar regained control, many continued guerrilla activity in the hills, while more than 150,000 escaped across the open border to Austria and eventually sought refuge in the West. The Western powers expressed sympathy for the rebels but did nothing to aid them, in part because of the paralysis caused by the Suez crisis. (See p. 1058.) The Hungarian revolt showed plainly that even a de-Stalinized Russia was not prepared to give up its Communist empire.

Photograph from Keystone Press

Revolutionaries in Budapest

" *'We wanted freedom and not a good comfortable life,' an eighteen-year-old girl
student told the [United Nations] Committee. 'Even though we might lack bread
and other necessities of life, we wanted freedom. We, the young people, were
particularly hampered because we were brought up amidst lies. We continually
had to lie. We could not have a healthy idea because everything was choked in
us. We wanted freedom of thought. . . .'*
*"It seemed to the Committee that this young student's words expressed as
concisely as any the ideal which made possible a great uprising. The motives
which brought together so many sections of the population were essentially
simple. It seemed no accident that such clear expression should be given to them
by a student not as part of a set speech, but simply and spontaneously, in answer
to an unexpected question."* Foreign Office, THE HUNGARIAN UPRISING.
AN ABRIDGEMENT OF THE REPORT OF THE UNITED NATIONS SPECIAL COMMITTEE
ON THE PROBLEM OF HUNGARY (London, 1957).

RELATIONS WITH YUGOSLAVIA AND CHINA

The unity of the Communist world had first been breached in 1948
when Yugoslavia, under the leadership of Marshal Tito, broke with the
Soviet Union. Stalin's successors made peaceful overtures to Tito, and
by 1956 the two governments had become officially reconciled, with
Russia agreeing that Yugoslavia had the right to determine its "own road

to socialism." In succeeding years relations between the two countries fluctuated between friendship and cold formality. The Yugoslavs carefully retained their position of nonalignment, refusing to link themselves either to the Soviet bloc or to the West. This policy of neutrality, skillfully directed by Tito, placed Yugoslavia in the advantageous position of being courted with economic and military assistance by both the Soviet Union and the United States.

The next great rift occurred between China and the Soviet Union. The latter had provided Red China with a steady stream of economic aid, arms, advisers, and technicians. In 1955 Russia agreed to furnish China with equipment and experts for developing atomic power for industrial purposes and to train Chinese students in atomic physics. The leaders of the two countries vied in praise of one another and promises of eternal amity. The Chinese even included a statement of friendship with the Soviet Union in the preamble of the constitution adopted in 1954. As early as 1956, however, Chinese leaders made it clear that although they appreciated Soviet aid, they did not intend to be subordinate to Russia. By 1959 greater strains had appeared in Sino-Soviet relations, caused mainly by Chinese suspicion of Khrushchev's efforts to establish peaceful relations with the West. Fearful of a rapproachement between Russia and the United States, the Chinese began to praise Stalin for his unceasing enmity to the "imperialist" powers, violently attacked the United States as the arch-imperialist, and indirectly criticized Khrushchev's policy by condemning what they called "right-wing revisionism." They found supporters for their position in other Communist parties, notably that in Albania, the smallest and poorest state of the Soviet bloc. Russia, unwilling to assail China directly, turned on Albania. It withdrew its aid and technicians, forced Albania out of COMECON, and in 1962 broke off diplomatic relations. Albania turned to China for aid and protection. Relations soon deteriorated to the point where the Chinese and Russian leaders publicly denounced one another and resorted to other forms of harassment. The situation was complicated by the outbreak of the "great cultural revolution" in China, apparently the result of an internal power struggle within the Chinese Communist party from which Mao Tse-tung again emerged victorious. In 1969 Russian and Chinese soldiers actually fought one another in limited clashes along the Chinese-Siberian border.

ANOTHER OCCUPATION OF CZECHOSLOVAKIA

Meanwhile Russia's European satellites continued to agitate for greater independence and freedom. In 1965 Rumania adopted a new constitution that proclaimed it a Socialist rather than a People's Republic. The following year it threatened to withdraw from COMECON and the Warsaw Pact, but was restrained by Russian counterthreats.

Revolutionaries in Prague

*"The boy [an 18-year-old machine tool worker] said 'None of us are afraid of the
Russians. This is our country.' A young worker from Slovakia who also was present
last night said that the Russians did not dare disperse the students because this
would give the lie to their assertions that they were here as liberators. The
youths of Prague have many other ways, besides defying curfews, to express their
contempt for the Russians."* NEW YORK TIMES, August 26, 1968.

The movement for genuinely democratic socialism went furthest in Czechoslovakia. In January, 1968, the Czech Communist party under Alexander Dubcek dismissed the old-guard Stalinist leaders and instituted a far-reaching program of reforms that included a greater reliance on free markets in place of government-dictated prices, the relaxation of press censorship, and a considerable measure of personal freedom. The rulers in the Kremlin, annoyed by criticism of the Soviet Union in the Czech press and fearful that Czech attitudes and policies might spread to other countries in the Soviet bloc, held several conferences with Czech leaders to try to persuade them to return to orthodox Communist policies, but without success. At length, in August, 1968, the Soviet army and air force — with token contingents from Poland, Hungary, and East Germany — invaded Czechoslovakia and established martial law. Efforts to set up a puppet government at first failed in the face of the near-unanimous support given by the Czech people to their leaders. Young people taunted the Russian soldiers, and in a few instances engaged in violent demonstrations against them; but for the most part the Czechs accepted the occupation with passive resistance, hoping that international opinion would oblige the Russians to withdraw and permit a resumption of the program of liberalization. When this hope failed to materialize, a few passionate patriots resorted to dramatic actions, such as self-immolation, to demonstrate their opposition to the Russian occupation. In April, 1969, the Russians succeeded in forcing the Czech Communist Party to replaced Dubcek with Gustav Husak, a Slovak more amenable to Russian wishes. Once again, as in East Germany in 1953 and in Poland and Hungary in 1956, events proved that Russia's Communist empire could be held together only by force.

BIRTH PANGS OF WORLD CIVILIZATION

Although the emergence of world civilization in the second half of the twentieth century was facilitated by organizations such as the United Nations, new ideas of national and racial equality and justice, and the accelerating revolution in communications, it frequently threatened to abort in global conflict based on old ideas of power politics, national sovereignty, and religious or racial superiority. The history of international relations after about 1950 can be characterized by two main themes: the East-West split between the powerful industrial nations of the world, chiefly European; and the struggle of the emerging nations of Asia, Africa, and Latin America for political recognition and economic progress. Each of these struggles, in turn, was complicated by internal fissures within the protagonist groups.

The Soviet Union, leader of world communism, experienced increasing difficulty in keeping its minions in line — notably Red China, which came to play an independent role as the major power in Asia and challenged the Soviet Union for the leadership of the Communist movements in Africa and Latin America. Similarly, the United States, the heart and core of the Atlantic alliance (which also included Japan as a sort of associate member), was unable to secure the unswerving allegiance of its nominal allies — especially de Gaulle's France, which pursued a course not unlike that of Mao's China in the Soviet bloc. Finally, the emerging nations were tempted — and divided accordingly — by the blandishments of both great power blocs and their rival forms of government and economy.

KOREA TO VIETNAM: THE STRUGGLE IN THE EAST

The Korean War settled down to a desultory though destructive stalemate in 1951 during the protracted negotiations for a truce. When it was finally concluded in June, 1953, the armistice merely restored the status quo ante bellum. The cost in human suffering and material destruction had been enormous, considering the war's limited scope, yet the outcome left the situation in Korea fundamentally unchanged. What had changed was the balance of forces in Asia.

China emerged as an independent power on the world stage. Although it remained for a time in the Soviet orbit, it became the dynamic nucleus of Communist advance in Asia and the Pacific. It compensated for its poverty and industrial backwardness by sheer size and numbers and the ideological commitment of its rulers. At enormous cost to their subjects the rulers engaged in a gigantic effort, a "great leap forward," to industrialize their nation as the Soviet Union had done between the wars. The industrialization program broke down when Chinese agriculture failed to produce enough food to support the burgeoning population, and a great famine ensued, the traditional nemesis of Chinese despots. Even this did not deter the Chinese Communist leaders from their aggressive course.

They gave aid and encouragement to Communist-led movements throughout Southeast Asia. The Viet Minh expelled the French and set up a Communist-dominated government in North Vietnam. In Malaysia, Burma, Laos, Cambodia, and especially South Vietnam, Communist China supported local efforts to undermine or overthrow established governments. It supported Indonesia in that country's aggressive designs on Malaysia and in its decision early in 1965 to withdraw from the United Nations. Even India, a fervent advocate of neutralism in the struggle between East and West, fell victim to the aggressive tendencies of Chinese communism in a series of border conflicts provoked by China in 1962 and afterward.

The most overt, vicious, and costly struggle developed in South Vietnam. After the partition of Vietnam in 1954 the Communist-led

Viet Cong, an underground organization opposed to the Western-oriented government of South Vietnam, engaged in subversion and guerrilla warfare with the encouragement and assistance of North Vietnam and, ultimately, Communist China and the Soviet Union. The United States supplied military advisors and assistance to South Vietnam, but corruption in the government of the latter, bitter disputes between the country's Buddhist majority and Roman Catholic minority, and a series of coups d'état weakened the people's will and ability to resist. In 1964 the United States initiated a major military build-up, committed American forces to large-scale ground combat, and shortly after began to bomb military and industrial targets in North Vietnam to force that nation to cease its aid to the Viet Cong. While stepping up its military operations the United States announced its willingness to engage in "unconditional negotiations" for peace, but not until 1968, with many conditions imposed by all concerned, did negotiations actually get underway. Meanwhile the unpopularity of the war made it a major political issue in the United States, and it was largely responsible for President Johnson's decision not to seek re-election in 1968.

THE EXPLOSIVE NEAR EAST

Farther west but in an area of the world still regarded by people of European heritage as part of the "mysterious East," troubles of a somewhat different nature threatened the peace of the world. In 1956 the young state of Israel, surrounded by bitterly hostile Arab neighbors, learned of a projected holy war to destroy it. Taking advantage of its superior organization and intelligence network and hoping to capitalize on world preoccupation with the Hungarian revolt and American preoccupation with the presidential campaign, the Israelis in October launched a surprise attack against Egyptian forces in the Sinai Desert. Britain, angry with Nasser for having nationalized the Suez Canal in violation of Egypt's treaty obligations, and France, angry because of Egyptian assistance to the Algerian rebels, joined forces to launch a combined air attack against Egypt. The Israelis scored a spectacular success against greatly superior Egyptian forces, but Nasser appealed to the United Nations.

Both the United States and the Soviet Union demanded a cease-fire and withdrawal of all forces, and the General Assembly by an overwhelming vote branded the Israeli action as aggression. Faced with hostile criticism within their own countries as well as with adverse world opinion, the British and French governments withdrew. United Nations security forces moved into the Sinai Desert to serve as a buffer between Egypt and Israel. Israel gained its immediate objective, the destruction of Egypt's potential attacking force, but as a consequence Egypt closed the Suez Canal to ships coming from or destined for Israel's ports. In spite of the humiliation of defeat by Israel, Egypt gained prestige among its Arab neighbors by having successfully appealed to the United Nations against France and Britain. The French and British intervention irritated their relations with the United States and allowed the Soviet Union to offset the damage to its reputation from events in Hungary by appearing before the nations of Asia and Africa as their champion against the imperialist powers of old.

Neutral soldiers under the flag of the United Nations served as a buffer between Egypt and Israel along the Sinai-Negev border for more than ten years. Meanwhile Arab terrorists operating from Syria and Jordan continued to harass Israel, and border incidents were frequent. In May, 1967, President Nasser of Egypt, stung by taunts from fellow Arab rulers that he was hiding behind the U.N., demanded the withdrawal of United Nations troops. Secretary-General U Thant acceded reluctantly. Almost immediately Egyptian troops occupied the Gaza Strip and the heights overlooking the Strait of Tiran, through which shipping bound for the Israeli port of Elath had to pass. Shortly afterward Nasser declared the strait closed to Israeli shipping. Frantic activity at United Nations headquarters produced no tangible results, and both Israeli and Arab leaders issued increasingly bellicose statements. On June 5, 1967, after a round of artillery attacks from Jordan and Syria, Israel unleashed a stunning air attack that destroyed on the ground virtually the entire air forces of its three belligerent Arab neighbors. Concurrently Israeli ground forces sliced the Egyptian army in ribbons and occupied the whole of the Sinai peninsula, Jordanian territory on the west bank of the Jordan river (including the Old City of Jerusalem), and the Golan Heights in Syria.

The Security Council called for a cease fire on June 6, which both Arabs and Israelis accepted on June 10. The resulting truce remained extremely fragile, however. The Arab nations refused to enter into direct negotiations with Israel and declared that they would maintain a state of war as long as Israel occupied Arab territory. The Israelis, on the other hand, declared that they would not evacuate the conquered territory until the Arabs agreed to a peace settlement and recognized the right of Israel to exist. The United Nations again showed its powerlessness to achieve a peaceful settlement. Border incidents became almost daily occurrences, and the Israelis responded to Arab terrorist raids with devastating retaliation.

On the world stage the Five Days' War further polarized the East-West split. The Arab nations broke off diplomatic relations with the United States and Great Britain with the unfounded charge that their warplanes had aided the Israeli attack. The Soviet Union, for its part, severed diplomatic relations with Israel and promptly began to re-supply the Arab states with planes, tanks, rockets, and other military hardware, and military advisors as well. De Gaulle's France tried to adopt a neutral stance, but after Israeli forces attacked the Beirut (Lebanon) airport in retaliation for another terrorist attack, de Gaulle personally forbade the further sale or delivery of French military equipment (especially airplanes) to Israel, and confiscated funds that Israel had already paid to French manufacturers. The situation remained tenser than ever, as any new outbreak of hostilities might easily involve both the Soviet Union and the United States.

Another Near Eastern trouble spot was the island of Cyprus. Occupied by Britain since 1878, the island ceased to be of strategic importance after the withdrawal of British forces from Suez in 1955. The Greek-speaking majority of the island's population had long agitated for *enosis* (union) with Greece. Britain, fearing reprisals against the Turkish-speaking minority, arranged for the island to assume independence in 1959 under an arrangement prohibiting union with Greece. The Greek Cypriots accepted the arrangement, but in 1963 they renewed terrorist attacks on their Turkish compatriots. United Nations forces intervened to keep the peace, but the resulting tensions between Greece and Turkey threatened to undermine the unity of the NATO alliance in the eastern Mediterranean.

THE AFRO-ASIAN BLOC

The growing number of newly independent states with mutual economic problems and political grievances led them to attempt to concert their efforts in the world arena. In 1955 a meeting in Bandung, Indonesia, attracted delegates from twenty-nine nations of Asia and Africa. In 1957 the Asian-African People's Solidarity Conference at Cairo was attended by representatives of forty countries, including the Soviet Union. Such meetings produced unanimous votes on resolutions condemning colonialism and racism and favoring disarmament and economic assistance, but the interests of the members were too heterogeneous and sometimes too conflicting to enable them to take concrete positive action. Even in the United Nations, where they tended to vote as a bloc on issues concerned with colonialism or similar matters, they could rarely achieve unanimity on other questions.

As Africa moved rapidly toward independence, its political leaders sought to speak with one voice by forming the Conference of Independent African States, subsequently transformed into the Organization of African Unity. Representatives of only eight nations attended the first meeting in Accra, Ghana, in 1958; six years later its membership had grown to more than thirty-five. Increasing world recognition came to Africans when Chief Albert Lutuli, a leader of South Africa's persecuted Negroes, won a Nobel Peace Prize. In 1964 Sir Alex Quaison-Sackey of Ghana became the first black African to be elected president of the General Assembly of the United Nations.

Conflicting interests also divided the former colonial countries. Some of them succumbed to one-party governments, frequently influenced by Russian or Chinese Communists. Others remained loyal to the liberal parliamentary institutions inherited from their former colonial masters, in spite of great difficulties. Some, such as the Congo and Nigeria, fell victim to internal anarchy and civil war because of the feuds of rival tribes. At a meeting of African political leaders in Cairo in 1964 Premier Moise Tshombe of the Congo was forcibly detained by Egyptian police and prevented from attending because of his use of white mercenaries in fighting rebellious tribesmen. In 1967, after his government was overthrown by a coup d'état, he was kidnapped and held prisoner by the Algerian government, where he died under mysterious circumstances in 1969. The rivalry of interests in Africa, both among and within the countries, posed a threat to world peace by tempting outsiders — Communists or others — to exploit them in their own interests.

CUBAN CRISES

Other threats to world peace arose from the success of the Cuban revolution and the conversion of Fidel Castro to communism. In April, 1961, the new Kennedy administration, acting on plans devised by the Central Intelligence Agency under the Eisenhower administration, carried out an attempted invasion of Cuba, in which Cuban exiles supported by American sea and air forces were to regain control of the island. The invasion attempt resulted in a ludicrous fiasco, damaging the reputation of the United States throughout the world and giving the Soviet Union the opportunity to pose as Cuba's protector by threatening atomic war in the event of a renewal of the invasion effort. A year and a half later another Cuban crisis again brought the world to the brink of atomic war. Russian technicians and military advisers began installing rocket-launching bases in Cuba with Castro's consent and probably at his insistence. The United States detected the installations in aerial photographs, and President Kennedy in a dramatic television appearance warned the Soviet Union to withdraw its missiles or face the consequences of an American missile attack. For several days the world waited in suspense, but the Soviet leaders, unprepared to risk war over Cuba, withdrew their missiles and technicians.

SUMMITS AND SHADOWS

Khrushchev's ten-year rule as dictator produced many alternations in the Soviet Union's relations with the West. At times Khrushchev acted with all the ruthlessness of Stalin, as in the suppression of the Hungarian revolt and his bellicose pronouncements on the Suez and Cuban crises. More often he posed as a jovial rival, speaking eloquently of "peaceful coexistence" and friendly competition to raise the world's living standards. The two faces of Khrushchev received extraordinary exposure in two successive "meetings at the summit" or gatherings of the heads of state of the Big Four (the United States, Russia, Britain, and France) and several lesser powers. The first meeting took place in Geneva in 1955. The main item on the agenda was discussion of the reunification of Germany. No binding decisions were reached, but the atmosphere of the conference was so congenial that Khrushchev followed it up with a visit to the United States, where he visited with Iowa farmers and enjoyed the attractions of Southern California as well as conferring with President Eisenhower. The next summit conference, scheduled for 1960 in Geneva, ended in confusion and dismay. Khrushchev took advantage of the recent shooting down of a United States reconnaissance aircraft over Russia and the capture of its pilot to denounce the United States "espionage," and the conference broke up without even discussing the agenda. In 1961 President Kennedy confronted Khrushchev in Vienna, and in 1967 President Johnson and Premier Kosygin met in Glassboro, New Jersey, in the wake of the Arab-Israeli war; but none of these meetings resulted in the permanent settlement of differences between the two superpowers.

The threat of atomic warfare continued to hang over the world like a symbolic mushroom cloud. In 1952 the United States announced that its scientists had perfected a far more powerful hydrogen bomb, and stories leaked out about other deadly atomic weapons. Britain, France, and eventually Communist China succeeded in creating atomic and hydrogen bombs, and new fears were aroused that in time all nations would have atomic arsenals, increasing the likelihood of atomic war as the result of mischance or the action of an irresponsible leader in any one of a hundred or more nations. To reduce the possibility of an atomic accident triggering an all-out war, the American and Russian leaders agreed to establish a direct radio-telephone connection, the "hot line," from Washington to Moscow. Meanwhile discussions and negotiations to remove the possibility of a nuclear holocaust continued fitfully. In 1963, after many deadlocks and disappointments, the Soviet Union, the United States, and the United Kingdom signed a treaty banning atomic or nuclear testing and explosions in the atmosphere, underwater, or in outer space. Although it was a step toward reducing the threat of radioactive poisoning of the atmosphere, the treaty left intact the already formidable atomic arsenals of the two great powers, and it did not prohibit atomic testing underground. Even more ominous, both France and Communist China refused to sign the treaty. In 1968 the United States, the Soviet Union, and the United Kingdom agreed on a nuclear non-proliferation treaty (ratified by the United States Senate in 1969) to which many non-nuclear nations adhered; but again France and China, as well as several other nations, stood aloof. The world still lives in the shadow of the mushroom cloud.

TENDENCIES OF
TWENTIETH-CENTURY
CIVILIZATION
CHAPTER FORTY

SCIENCE, TECHNOLOGY, AND INDUSTRY

A list of the distinguishing features of twentieth-century civilization might include such factors as its increasingly global dimensions, the greater role of science, and man's enhanced ability to master his environment. One feature, however, pervades all others and seems to provide the key to understanding the distinctive character and special historical import of the twentieth century: the accelerated pace of change. In earlier ages the mark of success of human societies was their ability to adapt to their environments. In the modern world the mark of success is the ability to manipulate the environment and adapt it to the needs of society. The fundamental means of manipulation and adaptation is technology — more specifically, technology based on modern science. A major reason for the more rapid pace of social change in recent times is the marked acceleration of scientific and technological progress.

It sometimes appears that science and technology have pursued an independent course unaffected by the political, social, and economic dislocations to which they have contributed. It is no doubt true that both possess an internal dynamic whereby each scientific discovery, each new technological triumph, contributes to still further progress; it is also true that both the rate and direction of scientific and technological progress are profoundly influenced by political, social, and economic factors. Many new developments in the basic sciences of chemistry and biology have been stimulated by their commercial applications in agriculture, industry, and medicine. The requirements of war and national rivalry have led governments to devote huge resources to scientific research and development for military purposes. Military crash programs have resulted in the development of radar and other electronic communications devices, in the successful harnessing of atomic energy, and in experiments leading to the launching of space rockets and artificial satellites. Medical research has also been stimulated by military needs as well as by a heightened social consciousness of the possibility and desirability of mitigating human suffering. Whether or not scientific progress would have been as rapid in the absence of military demands and the political circumstances behind those demands is a moot question. Certainly it would have taken a different direction. Fortunately for mankind, however, even the most deadly developments of military technology have proved adaptable to constructive peacetime purposes.

THE ACCELERATION OF SCIENTIFIC PROGRESS

The recent history of transportation and communications provides a graphic example of the acceleration of scientific and technological progress. At the beginning of the nineteenth century the speed of travel had not changed appreciably since the Hellenistic era. By the beginning of the twentieth century men could travel at velocities of up to eighty miles per hour by means of the steam locomotive. The development of automobiles, airplanes, and space rockets dwarfed even that achievement in speed and also in range and flexibility. Until the invention of the electric telegraph, communication over appreciable distances was limited to the speed of human messengers. The telephone, radio, and television added immeasurably to the convenience, flexibility, and reliability of long-distance communication. Almost instantaneous communication with most inhabited portions of the world became commonplace. Each successive improvement in the means of transportation and communication depended increasingly on the application of basic science.

The ability of science and technology to grow rapidly depends upon a host of accessory developments, some of them stemming from the progress of science itself. A major example is the electronic computer, which performs thousands of complicated calculations in a fraction of a second. The first mechanical calculating machine beyond the simple abacus was invented in the 1830's and was powered by steam. By the beginning of the twentieth century a few rudimentary mechanical devices were employed, chiefly for commercial purposes, but the age of the electronic computer did not dawn until after World War II. Its progress since then has rivaled the rapidity with which it operates. Without it many other scientific advances, such as the exploration of outer space, would have been impossible.

Another requisite for scientific and technical advance is a sizable pool of educated manpower — or brainpower. At the beginning of the twentieth century more than half the population of the Western nations possessed at least rudimentary literacy. By mid-century almost all the

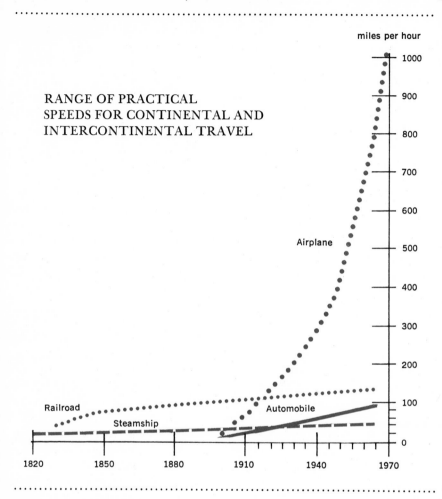

RANGE OF PRACTICAL
SPEEDS FOR CONTINENTAL AND
INTERCONTINENTAL TRAVEL

educable population had attained literacy, and the average number of years of schooling ranged from six to ten. The ability of individuals to participate fully and effectively in the new scientific-technological matrix of civilization, whether as scientists and technicians or in its commercial and bureaucratic superstructures, increasingly required advanced study at the college or university level and beyond.

There is little doubt that science generally is a paying proposition, but scientific research is also expensive and rarely can scientists or scientific institutions garner the pecuniary benefits directly. Subsidies for scientific research have increased enormously in the twentieth century, especially in recent decades. The largest sums come from governments, followed by private philanthropies and the industrial and commercial concerns that exploit the discoveries of science. There is a tendency for the rich nations to become richer in relation to the poor ones because they can afford the large initial expenditures required for basic research.

The widening technical gap between the developed and underdeveloped parts of the world is reflected in differences in educational levels as well as in differences in income. In many parts of Asia, Africa, and Latin America literacy rates in the mid-twentieth century averaged much less than 50 per cent — as low as 10 per cent in some nations. The proportion of university-trained people was much lower.

The demands of science affect the nature of education as well as the number of the educated. Russian scientific achievements, symbolized by the rapid development of atomic bombs and even more by the first space flight of Sputnik I in 1957, shocked the United States and other Western nations into recognizing inadequacies in their educational systems. Curricular reforms that had previously been proposed by some educators benefited from public support at a strategic moment and affected the teaching of science and mathematics and of other subjects as well, including history.

THE CONQUEST OF DISEASE

Although notable progress in medical science was made in the last half of the nineteenth century by Pasteur, Koch, Lister, and others, the general level of medical practice at the beginning of the twentieth century even in Western nations was still quite low. It is questionable whether doctors cured more patients than they killed. Tuberculosis, influenza, and pneumonia were major causes of death; such childhood diseases as measles, mumps, and diptheria were potent killers.

One reason for the low level of medical practice was the poor state of medical education. Practical medicine was still an art, lacking a scientific basis. Bacteriology, microbiology, and biochemistry, which provided the basis for the subsequent scientific practice of medicine, were still in their infancy. The Rockefeller Foundation and other philanthropic organizations led the way in the areas of medical research, education, public health, and preventive medicine. In the nineteenth century local governments in advanced countries assumed the responsibility for providing water and maintaining other sanitary facilities in large cities, but governmental activities in the area of health and medicine were narrowly restricted until the private organizations, including church-supported missionaries, demonstrated the possibility of effective action. The most spectacular successes were recorded in the prevention or control of hookworm, malaria, and yellow fever. Although they were among the most lethal and widespread of all diseases at the beginning of the century, by mid-century hookworm and yellow fever had been all but eradicated and the incidence of malaria had been greatly reduced. The successes of the private philanthropic organizations led to the establishment of public health services as integral parts of government in almost all nations, climaxed in 1948 by the creation of the World Health Organization under the auspices of the United Nations.

Laboratory scientists made progress in isolating and identifying the causes and carriers of many diseases and in developing immunization techniques. Within a few decades vaccines were developed for typhoid fever, typhus, tetanus, yellow fever, and cholera. In the 1950's, after a well-financed and highly publicized program against poliomyelitis spanning more than three decades, Dr. Jonas Salk and Dr. Albert Sabin succeeded in creating effective vaccines which came within reach of eradicating the disease within a few years. Their success was facilitated by the earlier discovery that polio and several other diseases, including influenza and the common cold, are caused by viruses, microorganisms smaller than bacteria. Research by biochemists discovered and identified vitamins and other food elements essential to growth and to disease prevention.

Although some of the most spectacular advances in medical science took place in the new field of preventive medicine, equally important discoveries were made in curative medicine. Early in the century new drugs were developed for the treatment of syphilis and diabetes. In the 1930's and 1940's a large family of sulfa drugs, derivatives of sulfanilamide, was developed with applications for many bacterial diseases. In 1940 medical researchers successfully applied penicillin, the first of many antibiotic drugs. Surgery, one of the oldest medical specialties, developed techniques for delicate operations on the brain, heart, and other vital organs, including transplantation of organs, that previously had been regarded as impossible. Psychiatry, the medical specialty dealing with diseases of the mind, absorbed much from the teachings of Sigmund Freud and became a flourishing branch of medical practice. Many of the traditional killing diseases have been brought under control, and the emphasis in medical research has shifted to diseases whose incidence is greatest in the later years of life — cancer and heart disease in particular.

NEW MODES OF PRODUCTION

The productivity of human labor, rapidly advanced by the application of scientific technology beginning in the nineteenth century, continued at an accelerated pace in the twentieth. Output per worker in agriculture — still the major source of supply for the majority of the world's foodstuffs and raw materials — has been increased greatly in Western nations by scientific techniques of fertilization, seed selection, and stock breeding, and by the use of mechanical power. Much progress has also been made in growing food in the seas, and important experiments now under way will sooner or later result in artificial photosynthesis, greatly increasing potential supplies of foodstuffs for the world's expanding population.

The rise in power production is even more remarkable. World power production increased more than forty-fold between 1900 and 1970. Most of the increase took place in areas of European culture and in forms that had been in their infancy at the beginning of the century. For example, the generation of electrical energy increased more than one hundred times. Petroleum and natural gas, which at the beginning of the century accounted for only a small fraction of the total energy consumption, have surpassed coal as a source of energy, approaching 50 per cent of the world's energy output. The growing importance of electricity and petroleum products has brought numerous social and economic changes. Electric energy is far cleaner, more efficient, and more flexible than most other forms of energy. It can be transmitted hundreds of miles at a fraction of the cost of transporting coal or petroleum. It can be used in massive concentrations to smelt metals or in tiny motors to operate delicate instruments, as well as to provide light. Its application to domestic appliances has helped to revolutionize patterns of family life, the status of women, and the employment of domestic servants.

The internal combustion engine, the most important consumer of petroleum, was an invention of the nineteenth century, but it produced a revolution only when applied to two of the most characteristic technological devices of the twentieth century; the automobile and the airplane. A few automobiles were built in the last years of the nineteenth century, but not until Henry Ford introduced the principle of mass production with a moving assembly line in 1907 did the automobile become more than a rich man's toy. Ford's techniques of production were soon imitated by other manufacturers in the United States and Europe, and the automobile industry became one of the largest employers of any manufacturing industry, as well as providing unprecedented opportunities for personal mobility. The techniques of assembly line production were adopted in other industries, including the aircraft industry in World War II. Social critics complained that they reduced workers to automatons, but the critics overlooked the additional fact that the assembly line saved labor and therefore resulted in higher wages and fewer working hours.

The scientific basis of modern industry resulted in hundreds of new products and materials. Beginning with the invention of rayon in 1898, dozens of artificial or synthetic textile fibers have been created. In relatively recent years plastic materials made from chemicals have replaced the more conventional wood, metals, earthenware, and paper in thousands of uses ranging from lightweight containers to high-speed drilling machines. The increasing use of electrical and mechanical power, the invention of hundreds of new labor-saving techniques, and the development of automatic instruments of control have brought about a revolution in the conditions of life and work more far-reaching than the classic industrial revolution in Britain. In an extreme instance, a single worker can oversee the operations of a huge petroleum refinery. These new developments in industry have created a role for human labor vastly different from anything previously experienced. Sheer strength counts for less than ever before; intelligence and training for far more. The cascading improvements in technology have made millions of unskilled laborers redundant, creating technological unemployment; but they also created a new demand for special skills and knowledge with remuneration proportional, not to the number of hours worked or human energy expended, but to the specialized talent of the employee.

THE RELEASE OF NUCLEAR ENERGY

No field of science has experienced more rapid or extensive changes in both pure and applied aspects than physics. The gradual understanding of the complex structure of the atom, beginning with the discovery of X-rays and the radioactive properties of certain elements, opened great theoretical possibilities. The work of Albert Einstein and others indicated that tremendous sources of energy lie locked within the atom. Beginning in the 1930's, huge cyclotrons and other atom smashers were used to transform the atoms of one element into those of another. In the process scientists discovered that they could create new elements heavier than those that occur in nature. Some of them, such as plutonium, were found to be especially susceptible to chain reactions that could generate enormous quantities of energy. In December, 1942, at the University of Chicago a group of physicists under the direction of the exiled Italian scientist Enrico Fermi set off the first controlled chain reaction of atomic energy. In July, 1945, another group led by J. Robert Oppenheimer exploded an experimental bomb on the proving grounds of Los Alamos, New Mexico. The following month the bombs dropped on Hiroshima and Nagasaki inaugurated a new age of terror.

Governments have responded to the possibilities for the peaceful use of atomic energy with markedly less alacrity than to its military potentialities. Some progress has been made, nevertheless. Medical science has found a number of important uses for radioactivity and associated phenomena. The most promising use for atomic energy is in the generation of electrical power. Several generating stations are at work in various parts of the world, and it is predicted that by the end of the century between one-third and one-half of the world's electricity will be generated by atomic energy. Other projects made possible by atomic energy include digging a new isthmian canal in Central America, reversing the flow of a river in Siberia, and changing the climate of the Libyan desert by means of a canal from the Mediterranean to a newly created artificial sea.

Astronaut Edwin "Buzz" Aldrin on the Moon, July 20, 1969

"That's one small step for a man, one giant leap for mankind." Astronaut Neil
Armstrong's comment as he became the first man to step on the moon.

THE EXPLORATION OF SPACE

As recently as the 1940's manned flight in space was chiefly a subject
for science fiction. While comic strips portrayed scantily clad men and
women of the twenty-fifth century flying through space with rockets
strapped to their shoulders, learned men made calculations that purported to prove that no vehicle could ever attain the velocity required
to leave the earth's gravitational field. During World War II scientists
gained much valuable experience as a result of their work with jet
engines and military rockets, but few people expected that it would
be possible for men to survive in outer space even if they could reach it.
New developments such as more powerful rocket engines, electronic
signaling and control devices, and computers for rapid calculation of
trajectories concurred to make space flight a real possibility. On October
4, 1957, scientists in the Soviet Union put a capsule into orbit around the
earth. The Space Age had begun.

Further progress took place rapidly, largely stimulated by national
rivalry. A second orbiting Russian rocket followed a month later, and
early in 1958 the United States placed a capsule in orbit. Within a few
years both nations rocketed men into space and successfully retrieved
them. Unmanned satellites were put into more or less permanent orbits to
relay scientific information back to earth by means of radio and television, and other rockets were sent to the moon, Venus, and Mars with
similar aims. In December, 1968, the United States put a space crew in
orbit around the moon, but outdid even that feat the following year.
On July 20, 1969, astronauts Neil Armstrong and Edwin Aldrin, supported by astronaut Michael Collins and a crew of thousands of scientists
and technicians on earth, became the first men to set foot on the moon.
Truly, mankind had created a new age. One measure of the difference
between that new age and all previous eras of human achievement lay in
the manner in which the event was publicized. When Columbus discovered the New World (which he mistook for the Indies), the event
was witnessed only by the actual participants, and it was months, even
years, before the news reached a large public. The first step of man on
the moon, in contrast, was witnessed by hundreds of millions all over the
earth by means of television relays — the largest audience, in fact, ever to
witness a single event.

NASA

While astronauts explored the nearby fringes of outer space, astronomers and astrophysicists continued their probes of the outermost reaches of space in the hope of discovering the secrets of the universe. Aided by powerful new reflector and radio telescopes, they made startling discoveries, but the secret of the origin and nature of the universe continued to elude them. As recently as 1930 they discovered Pluto, the outermost planet of the solar system. In 1965 astronomers using the huge 200-inch telescope on Mount Palomar in California discovered a group of quasars (for "quasi-stellar radio sources") more than 8 billion light years distant — excitingly close to the 13 billion years which some astronomers thought represented the age of the universe. Further discoveries of this kind may help settle the question of the origin of the universe: whether it originated in a "big bang" at some definite point in space and time billions of years ago, or whether it is infinite and eternal, as other astrophysicists maintain.

SOCIAL TRENDS

The spectacular growth of science and of a science-based technology is reflected in almost equally spectacular social changes. New industries have arisen on the basis of new technologies, creating new skills, new patterns of work and leisure, new standards of behavior — and new social problems. Among the most potent social foces are the advances in biological and medical science, which brought about a population explosion.

THE POPULATION EXPLOSION

In the two and one-half centuries between 1650 and 1900 the world's population increased threefold, rising from approximately 500,000,000

No. 160b (Improvisation 28), 1912, by Vasily Kandinsky

"The freer the abstract form, the purer and more primitive is its appeal. In a composition, therefore, where the material side may be more or less superfluous, it can be accordingly more or less omitted and replaced by non-objective forms or through abstractions of de-materialized objects. In any case of translation into the abstract or the employment of non-objective forms, the artist's sole judge, guide, and principal consideration should be his feeling. Finally, the more abstractions the artist employs the more at home will he feel in the realm of the non-objective. Likewise the observer, led by artistic attainment to better knowledge of the language of the abstracted, finally, becomes fully conversant." Kandinsky, ON THE SPIRITUAL IN ART
(New York, 1946).

to about 1,500,000,000. In the next two generations, from 1900 to 1960, the population doubled, attaining approximately 3 billion. At presently projected rates of increase the number of persons is expected to double again, surpassing 6 billion, by the end of the century. Such staggering rates of increase are without precedent in the history of the world.

Table 1   *World Population, 1930–1967*

	Population in millions (estimated)		Annual rate of increase (per cent)	Population per sq. km.
	1930	*1967*	*1960–1963*	*1963*
Africa	164	328	2.5	10
North America	134	220	1.5	10
Latin America	108	259	2.9	11
East Asia	591	877	1.5	71
South Asia	529	1030	2.4	58
Europe (without USSR)	355	452	0.9	89
USSR	179	236	1.7	10
Oceania	10	18	2.3	2
World	2070	3420	1.9	23

Source: United Nations, *Demographic Yearbook, 1967* (New York, 1968).

In earlier eras rises in population usually resulted from temporary increases in birth rates or equally temporary decreases in death rates. The dominant factor in population growth in the past century has been the apparently permanent decline in death rates. In large areas of the world famine has been eliminated as a cause of death, and the incidence of disease, especially in the early years of life, has been greatly reduced. In Ceylon the widespread use of DDT for mosquito (malaria) control

Ronchamp, by Le Corbusier

> "*Although the church, in its union of cavern with thrusting force, is an appropriate embodiment of the Virgin to whom it is dedicated . . . it is most of all an image of modern man, full of memories, with an ironic view of himself, no longer believing that he occupies the center of the world by right. He is under pressure in the interior of Ronchamp, which does not swell outward from him but presses in upon him. . . . he can only act, or gesture; and that act, like . . . the upward lifting prow of Ronchamp on its hilltop, has no defined boundary and is open-ended toward the ultimate reaches of space.*" Vincent Scully, Jr., MODERN ARCHITECTURE (New York, 1961)

resulted in a halving of the death rate between 1945 and 1960. With the birth rate almost unchanged, the resulting increase in population was little short of fantastic. The Japanese death rate fell by one-half in an even shorter period, from 1947 to 1955, but the birth rate also declined significantly.

The unequal incidence of changes in birth and death rates has resulted in changes in the relative geographic distribution of population. Voluntary limitation of births by means of contraception and other birth control measures began to reduce birth rates in Europe in the nineteenth century, but birth rates have remained high in many other areas of the world. In 1900 about 40 per cent of the world's people lived in Asia; by 1960 the proportion had grown to 50 per cent; and by the year 2000 an estimated 60 per cent of the world's population will be Asian. By that time at the present rates of increase there will be more people in China alone than there were in all the world in 1900.

Such alarming rates of population growth create pressing new problems — economic, social, political, and even moral. Any positive rate of population growth, if long continued, must eventually produce an unacceptably large population, in which the majority will live in misery and die of starvation, disease, or war. An equilibrium of births and deaths is essential if mankind is not to be overtaken by such Malthusian horrors.

NEW STYLES OF LIVING

The civilization of the twentieth century proved to be an increasingly urban culture, in underdeveloped no less than in developed areas. The changes in agriculture together with the rapid growth of population directed increasing streams of people into the cities. The swelling size of cities created pressures for new social services, including mass rapid transit. Tramways or streetcars, subway trains, and eventually automobiles worked a revolution in the design of cities. To accommodate the automobile, large areas of valuable land were taken for interurban express highways, urban expressways, and parking facilities. The relative importance of central cities declined, creating slums and breeding delinquency, crime, and alienation, whereas outlying suburbs mushroomed as new recruits to the ever-growing middle class sought to escape the disadvantages of city living while retaining its conveniences.

The great productivity made possible by modern technology created wealth in amounts and forms undreamed of by earlier generations. It also resulted in its more equitable distribution, especially in the industrial nations of the West. Greater economic equality fostered greater social equality by increasing social mobility and blurring the lines between social classes. In many instances workers in modern industries, though functionally members of the working class, enjoyed a standard of living that would have aroused the envy of the middle classes of an earlier generation. Socially the middle class expanded at both ends of the spectrum, encompassing a larger and larger proportion of the population, leaving only a small archaic upper class at one end and a somewhat larger but contracting group of unfortunates at the other.

Poverty by no means disappeared even in the wealthiest societies, but besides afflicting a smaller proportion of the population, it changed its forms. In earlier times and in poorer societies poverty was regarded as the more or less permanent state of the masses, both urban and rural. In the twentieth century in technologically progressive nations it afflicted certain rather well-defined groups. These include chiefly those who, for whatever reason, failed to secure a rudimentary education, older workers rendered obsolete by technological change, and persons isolated either by geographical barriers or by various kinds of discriminatory practices.

THE USES OF LEISURE

For those who benefited most from material progress the new technology opened a new era of comfort and convenience and also posed new moral and social problems. As income increased, the demand for leisure also increased. At the beginning of the twentieth century a sixty-hour work week was common in most employments. By mid-century the forty-hour week was standard, and in some occupations hours were even fewer. As leisure time increased, the question of how to use it became more pressing. The solutions of earlier, less complicated times — churches, voluntary social organizations, village or neighborhood taverns — no longer sufficed. Large new industries grew up for the sole purpose of providing entertainment and diversion on a commercial basis. The cinema and radio spurted to prominence in the interwar years; television placed them both in partial eclipse after World War II. Professional sporting events, assiduously promoted by profit-minded entrepreneurs, gained in popularity. Moralists and philosophers frequently deplored the stultifying effects of such uses of leisure, together with the opportunities they created for the unscrupulous manipulation of mass sentiment for pecuniary or political advantage. That these diversions did not satisfy completely the desire for the constructive use of leisure time was demonstrated by the increasing popularity of facilities for adult education, both private and public, and new efforts to overcome the work-leisure dichotomy. Some of the efforts took the form of do-it-yourself movements in which individuals who put in six or eight hours in a factory or office as specialized parts of huge impersonal organizations reverted at the end of the day to simple craftsmen, working in gardens or building and repairing their own furniture, boats, and even homes.

The challenge of leisure time affected young people in particular. Instead of being forced to earn their way from the age of ten or twelve, as in the past, child labor laws, compulsory school attendance, and changing social customs kept them out of permanent gainful employment until ever higher ages. For most of those fortunate or ambitious enough to pursue higher education the increased leisure presented few problems, but for many it created problems both for themselves and for society. With the natural energy and exuberance of youth liberated from the necessity of continual labor and not provided with alternative constructive social outlets, they sometimes turned to such antisocial activities as delinquency and vandalism, or to social and political agitation and revolution.

MANNERS AND MORALS

The status of women altered greatly in the first half of the twentieth century. In 1902 Australia became the first nation to grant women the right to vote. Elsewhere the woman's suffrage movement made little headway before World War I. In many nations, including some otherwise advanced in the arts of civilization, the law regarded women as little more than chattels in the hands of their fathers or husbands. World War I with its large demand for female labor to replace men called to arms acted as a powerful stimulus to the movement for female emancipation. Women secured the right to vote on equal terms with men in the United States in 1920, in Great Britain in 1928, and in several other nations in the same or following decades. In Latin nations female suffrage had to wait until after World War II; and in Switzerland, often praised as the world's oldest democracy, women still cannot vote.

The success of the woman's suffrage movement owed much to the increasing economic independence of women. Domestic service declined with increasing opportunities for higher-paying jobs in industry and commerce, while such household labor-saving devices as washing machines and vacuum cleaners lightened the burden of domestic chores. Paralleling women's political and economic progress was their greater social freedom. The number of divorces rose from less than 5 per cent of the total number of marriages in Western Europe (less than 1 per cent in Great Britain) at the beginning of the century to more than 10 per cent after World War II; in the United States approximately one marriage in four ended in divorce in the postwar period. The higher divorce rates both symbolized and contributed to greater sexual freedom, which was also facilitated by the invention of simple and inexpensive contraceptive devices.

Urbanization and the emancipation of women altered the character of family life. Falling birth rates reduced the average size of families. Whereas in rural environments children could begin to earn their keep as early as the age of six by helping in various farm operations, under the conditions of modern urban societies they remained financial burdens on the family until they attained adulthood. Residence, workplace, and school were often widely separated, adding to the dichotomy between work and leisure. Instead of working together or in close proximity throughout the day, modern families frequently came together only at bedtime — if then. (This change affected the middle classes primarily; working-class families were often separated in this way from the beginning of the nineteenth century.) Although children and young people remained economically dependent upon their parents longer, they, like women, gained more social freedom, manifested in greater informality in clothing and in relations between the sexes.

THE "AMERICANIZATION" OF SOCIETY

Before the First World War educated Europeans regarded Americans as country cousins — brash, uncultured, lacking in social refinement. The increasing influence of the United States in world affairs, notably in the two world wars and after 1945, required some modification of that view, especially when American methods and fashions began to be imitated in Europe. Many of the social changes of the twentieth century appeared first in the United States before spreading gradually to Europe. Most Europeans favor the importation of American technology, which they believe to be the foundation of American wealth and power, but many deplore what they feel is the growing influence of American social customs and patterns of behavior. Much of what they deplore is not in fact specifically American but the result of modern technology and the affluence it produces. The Americanization of society is in reality merely the operation upon society of fundamental technological and economic change.

THE ARTS IN TWENTIETH-CENTURY CIVILIZATION

The rapid pace of change observable in science, technology, and social mores had its counterpart in literature and the arts. Technological progress affected modes of artistic expression, and changes in themes and styles created an intellectual revolution as far-reaching as the theory of relativity in physics or the impact of Freud on psychology. Technological change made its most profound impression on music and drama. The invention of the cinema, phonograph, radio, and television created audiences of millions for forms of artistic expression that had earlier been limited to a select few.

SERIOUS ART VERSUS POPULAR ART

The growth of income and leisure time, the expansion of the middle class, and above all the proliferation of modern mass communications media made commercial exploitation of the fine arts possible. Music was most profoundly affected. In earlier times music had not been subjected to market forces. Folk music sprang spontaneously from the people; serious music was usually subsidized by the church, public authorities, or wealthy patrons. The commercialization of music offered composers and performing musicians an unaccustomed degree of economic independence and even affluence, but in some respects it was disastrous for the general level of musical taste. Tunesmiths whose creations made the hit parade and shaggy-headed, musically illiterate singers who tapped the teenage market became celebrities, while serious new compositions still subsidized by the universities, private philanthropies, and governments, became increasingly esoteric and remote. The influence of commercialization and the mass media was not, however, wholly bad. It enabled some forms of folk music, notably jazz, to acquire the status of serious art. More important, it permitted millions without access to operas or symphony concerts to become familiar with and enjoy the masterworks of music by means of electronic reproduction.

The cinema, radio, and television revolutionized the dramatic arts. The stage suffered a relative decline in popularity, although the intellectual influence of a few playwrights made itself felt far beyond the world of the theater. The new media — the cinema in particular — created new possibilities for the dramatic arts but also imposed new limitations on them. The extreme commercialization or state control to which they were subjected in most countries resulted in a generally low level of quality. Innovation was more apparent in technical aspects of production than in artistic conception. Many writers and producers deliberately sacrificed edification for cheap entertainment. A few, however, such as Ingmar Bergman of Sweden, exploited the artistic possibilities of the new media imaginatively and produced great modern dramas.

Commercialization similarly influenced painting, sculpture, and the graphic arts. The demand for illustrators and commercial artists, especially in the new profession of advertising, guaranteed large returns to technically proficient artists, but it produced no masterpieces of the human spirit. Serious artists who did not cater to the public taste — indeed, in many instances they seemed determined to outrage the public — nevertheless found themselves lionized by avant garde intellectuals. Private collectors, many of whom viewed their art purchases as investments, vied with one another in seeking to discover promising young artists whose creations might grace the museums of the future. Thousands of individuals found in amateur art a satisfying use for leisure time and relief from the tensions and frustrations of the workaday world. Probably not since the eighteenth century did art and artists hold such a prominent place in society as in the second half of the twentieth century. Whether the average quality of artistic production merited that status is a question beyond objective evaluation.

THEMES AND TENDENCIES

The main tendencies of twentieth-century art, music, and literature had already been indicated before the First World War. (See pp. 798–802.) In spite of great diversity, the various modern art forms shared certain common characteristics that clearly distinguished them from the art of earlier centuries. They exhibited a greater degree of abstraction, notably in painting and sculpture, greater freedom of expression in both themes and manner of execution, and a pronounced reaction against earlier aesthetic standards of order, harmony, and unity. The tone of many modern works was irrational, even antirational, and was frequently combined with a strong current of pessimism. Modern art reflected the rootlessness of modern urban culture, the rapidity of social change, the disillusion produced by modern warfare, and the challenge to traditional beliefs posed by the discoveries of science.

Abstract and nonobjective subjects dominated painting even more completely after World War II than in the interwar period. In the earlier period nonobjective artists were frequently the objects of ridicule and achieved recognition only with great difficulty, but the tables were turned after the war; then it was the representational artist who had to prove the relevance of his subject. Even the later works of Picasso, Matisse, and Chagall, who were still active in the postwar period and whose works occasionally contained recognizable objects, seemed almost conventional in comparison with the blobs and swatches of color (or black and white lines) of the dominant school of abstract expressionism. One artist, Josef Albers, devoted his whole life to painting "Homage to the Square" consisting of nothing but superimposed squares of various colors. The American Jackson Pollock was the pioneer of the school of action painting, which had many followers in Europe in the 1950's. Pollock literally threw himself into his work, dripping and dribbling paint on a canvas stretched out on the floor and working from all directions. Pollock commented on his technique, "When I am *in* my painting, I'm not aware of what I'm doing. It is only after a sort of 'get acquainted' period that I see what I've been about." Such tendencies led almost inevitably to the pop art and op art of the 1960's. More serious European and American artists studied and adopted motifs and styles from Oriental and African art, thus testifying to the universality of art in the twentieth century. African and other primitive art forms were especially influential in sculpture.

ARCHITECTURE AND MODERN DESIGN

Architecture, which for so long had been essentially imitative, became one of the most creative art forms of the twentieth century. Like modern art, it was bedeviled by false starts and encountered strong opposition on aesthetic and other grounds, but it eventually developed a distinctive twentieth-century style. Technological advance in the form of new materials and techniques of construction created new opportunities for architects and engineers. Concurrently, new ideas concerning the purpose and nature of architecture replaced the notions of the nineteenth century. The American Frank Lloyd Wright and his master Louis Sullivan had already broken new ground before World War I, and Wright's influence continued to grow throughout the century. A leading exponent of the so-called international style of architecture was Ludwig Mies van der Rohe, a disciple of Walter Gropius who came to the United States in 1937. He won fame primarily as a designer of large modern office buildings. Le Corbusier, who designed the new capital of India at Chandigarh, and Otto Niemeyer, a Brazilian of German extraction who designed the strikingly modern new capital of Brazil, also won many new converts to modern architecture. Finnish architects were among the most daring innovators, and the Japanese proved themselves expert, as usual, at combining the modern international style with their own traditions.

The chief characteristic of modern architecture is its functionalism. It makes extensive use of glass, reinforced and precast concrete, and new materials like aluminum. Many of its earlier structures appeared massive and ungainly, but gradually architects refined their designs to produce the impression of light and airy space. The architectural revolution primarily affected cities, which, under intense pressure for efficient land use, grew upward as well as outward.

Interior decoration and furniture design underwent a similar transformation. Scandinavian designers took the lead in this development, in which the key word was functionalism. In place of the overstuffed, heavy decorations of the Victorian era, modern furnishings have abstract, simple lines.

THE LIFE OF THE MIND
IN THE TWENTIETH CENTURY

The twentieth century witnessed the greatest increase in both population and in standards of material well-being of any equivalent period in human history. Yet this same period has been referred to as an "era of violence" and an "age of crisis." Is there a contradiction here?

The student of history should learn — as perhaps he has learned from this text — that every historical epoch has episodes of heroism and great achievement along with episodes of failure and despair, just as every human life has moments of both triumph and tragedy. The common man of the European world, whether peasant, carpenter, or clerk, has experienced the advantages of modern civilization: the higher living standards, greater longevity, mass education, and mass entertainment by radio, television, and similar media. Even the inhabitants of the non-

European world have participated at least marginally in the march of progress. Yet the verdict of thinking men on the progress of the twentieth-century civilization is one of guarded hopefulness at best, deep despair at worst.

IMAGINATIVE LITERATURE

Poets, dramatists, and novelists, have been called the consciences of humanity. It should not be surprising, therefore, that after the brutality of totalitarian regimes, the horrors of World War II, the fear of the atomic bomb, and the tensions of the cold war, a principal theme of imaginative literature should have been man's inhumanity to man or, in the words of a famous novel, "the human condition." Although some serious authors continued to deal with the problems of the inner man or the individual personality (perhaps mankind writ small?), the majority turned its attention to mankind in general. William Faulkner, one of America's greatest novelists who received the Nobel Prize for literature in 1949, stated the problem for many: "There are no longer problems of the spirit; there is only the question, *when will I be blown up?*" But Faulkner, an optimist in spite of himself, went on to say that men had been dominated by fear for so long that "by now we can even bear it."

Similar sentiments were expressed by France's existentialist novelist-poet-playwright-philosopher, Jean-Paul Sartre, who attracted a large following in the immediate postwar years. Another French novelist, also claimed by the existentialists, whose stories dealing with ordinary individuals may well outlast those of Sartre, was Albert Camus; his message was that life is what it is, but it must go on. A British novelist and essayist, George Orwell, who had been tempted by communism in his youth, dealt more directly with contemporary political questions. In *Animal Farm* (1945) he satirized the class structure of Soviet society ("all animals are equal, but some animals are more equal than others"); in *Nineteen Eighty Four* (1948) he evoked a Kafkaesque state of permanent warfare and totalitarianism that infected all regions of the earth.

In the second half of the twentieth century the theater continued to exert a primary influence on social thought in spite of the financial difficulties it encountered as a result of its competition with the cinema and television. Paradoxically, the competition itself insured its survival, since its most successful plays almost inevitably became the basis for even more successful screenplays. The German Marxist, Berthold Brecht, was one of the most fertile sources of inspiration, even though his productions were forbidden in both Nazi Germany and the German Federal Republic. Other dramatists in the Brechtian vein were Peter Weiss, whose *Persecution and Murder of Jean Paul Marat as Staged by the Inmates of the Asylum of Charenton under the Direction of the Marquis de Sade* achieved international success, and Rolf Hochhuth, who in

The Deputy blamed the papal legate in Germany, subsequently Pius XII, for failing to try to stop the Nazi persecution of the Jews. In Britain a group of "angry young men," mostly of working-class background, revolutionized the theater and had a notable impact on fiction as well. In the United States Tennessee Williams, Arthur Miller, and Edward Albee achieved international acclaim for their dramas of personal maladjustment. One of the leading dramatists writing in the French language was the Irishman Samuel Beckett, whose existentialist drama *Waiting for Godot* was one of the first experiments in what has been called the "theater of the absurd."

Poetry suffered an eclipse in the clouded, uncertain decades after Hiroshima, in spite of the gesture by young President John F. Kennedy in asking the venerable Robert Frost to read from his poems at the 1961 inauguration. The ebullient Welshman, Dylan Thomas, who died prematurely in 1953, made a valiant effort to restore lyricism to poetry. The contributions of non-Europeans to world literature began to receive recognition after World War II. In 1945 Gabriela Mistral, of Chile, became the first Latin American to receive a Nobel Prize for literature. Her left-leaning countryman, Pablo Neruda, also received international recognition for his verse. In 1968 a Japanese author, Yasunari Yawabata, became the first Oriental to receive a Nobel Prize for literature. The Anglo-Indian, Rabindranath Tagore, had received a Nobel Prize as early as 1913, but the Nobel Prize commission was slow to bestow its accolades on writers in non-European languages.

PHILOSOPHY IN AN AGE OF CRISIS

The philosophical outlook of any age usually reflects issues of vital concern to the public, especially in periods of political and social upheaval or crisis. In the twentieth century academic or professional philosophers, nominally engaged in the abstract pursuit of truth, beauty, and goodness, could not avoid dealing with the concrete issues of practical life. Moral and ethical questions fused with political, social, and economic problems. Even logic, the most abstract branch of philosophy, felt the impact of change in the external world. In addition to political and social turmoil, the new discoveries in science forced a reconsideration of accepted philosophical positions. Freudian psychology and the theory of relativity had already shaken the foundations of the rationalist, materialist philosophies of the nineteenth century. In 1927 the German physicist Werner Heisenberg added to the difficulties of those who still sought simple cause-effect relationships with his announcement of the principle of uncertainty, according to which it is impossible to determine simultaneously the position and velocity of a subatomic particle. It seemed that the world of nature was no more orderly or predictable than the world of man.

Two new philosophical movements grew up in response to the problems of the twentieth century. Logical positivism (later called logical empiricism to disassociate it from the positivism of the nineteenth century) was a radical form of empiricism that denied meaning to any proposition that was not subject to rigorous empirical verification. The logical positivists declared the whole of metaphysics and most of ethics and aesthetics to be meaningless. Their denial of meaning to large parts of human experience represented one form of the philosophy of despair.

The other form of the philosophy of despair was existentialism, which had certain affinities with logical positivism but reached fundamentally different conclusions. Existentialists did not possess a single coherent logical structure for their philosophy, but all agreed that man gains a knowledge of reality not by detached reason or reflection but by immediate experience, with the emphasis on the inner personal character of experience. Existentialism was thus fundamentally antirational, even anti-intellectual in some of its manifestations. It was symptomatic of the revolt against reason that characterized the first half of the twentieth century. The existentialists claimed as forerunners Nietzsche and the nineteenth-century Danish theologian Sören Kierkegaard. Among their outstanding exponents — who, however, did not in any sense form a school — in addition to Sartre, were Martin Heidegger of Germany, Nikolai Berdyaev, a Russian exile, and José Ortega y Gasset of Spain.

Not all philosophers reached such pessimistic conclusions. The rationalist, analytical philosophy of Bertrand Russell and the pragmatists occupied a middle ground between the extreme skepticism of the logical positivists, on the one hand, and the despair of the existentialists, on the other. The rationalism of St. Thomas Aquinas experienced a modern revival in the movement known as neo-Thomism. Étienne Gilson and Jacques Maritain, both French Catholic laymen, did much to restore metaphysics as a respectable branch of philosophy.

THEOLOGY AND THE CHURCHES

The new philosophical movements had important implications for theology. The logical positivists thought they had banished theology as a serious intellectual subject, but existentialism proved quite adaptable to theological ends, even though many of its exponents were avowed atheists. Kierkegaard, its putative founder, was a Protestant theologian; and Paul Tillich, also a Protestant theologian, proved to be one of its more lucid expositors. According to Tillich, Christ was the prototype of existential man who solved the dilemma of existence by obedience to God. Not all Protestant churches accept existentialism, however. Karl Barth, a Swiss and perhaps the most noted Protestant theologian of the twentieth century, preached a pessimistic neofundamentalism. According to Barth, God cannot be apprehended by reason or attained by human endeavor; men are miserable sinful creatures wholly at His mercy. Roman Catholicism eschewed modernism in philosophy but benefited from the revival of Thomist philosophy, which facilitated the reconciliation of Church dogma with modern science.

Organizational developments within the churches were at least as important as theological movements. At the beginning of the century the Roman Catholic Church was embroiled in difficulties with several countries over church-state relations. As the most international — or supranational — of Christian churches, it also found itself in a particularly difficult position during both World Wars. The pope made fitful attempts to play the role of peacemaker but without success. All denominations suffered from increasing urbanization and the anonymity of large cities. Church membership continued to grow, but it is doubtful that the number of active communicants kept pace with the growth of population. To counteract the demoralizing influence of cities, the churches instituted social action programs specifically aimed at urban workers, but their efforts were only moderately successful.

One of the most important developments in religious organization was the ecumenical movement. Several Protestant sects that had earlier splintered rejoined one another, and negotiations took place for the eventual merging of several of the larger denominations. In 1948 the World Council of Churches brought together representatives of the Anglican, Orthodox, and most Protestant churches in an organization to promote interfaith and international cooperation. The Roman Catholic Church at first held aloof from the ecumenical movement, but under Popes John XXIII (1958–1963) and his successor Paul VI it instituted a number of significant reforms. It invited other denominations to send observers to the Second Ecumenical Council of the Vatican (1962–1965), hailed as one of the most important gatherings of Roman Catholic prelates since the Council of Trent in the sixteenth century. The council streamlined the organization of the Roman Catholic Church, made it more democratic, and allowed the introduction of the language of the people into the liturgy in place of the traditional Latin. On the important subject of birth control, however, Pope Paul overruled the recommendation of his own commission to restudy the subject and reaffirmed the Church's traditional opposition to artificial contraception, thereby setting off a storm of opposition within the Church and criticism from outside.

SOCIAL AND POLITICAL THOUGHT

Most of the social sciences were still in their infancy at the beginning of the twentieth century. The most authoritative pronouncements on social questions came from statesmen, theologians, philosophers, journalists, and businessmen. Universities then began to give specialized professional training in the various social science disciplines. At first the training followed the pattern already established in history, philosophy, and other humanistic disciplines, but gradually it took on a more scientific character, including an emphasis on precise measurement, the testing of hypotheses, and the use of mathematics. Until the 1930's professional and social scientists found employment chiefly as university professors. After the brilliant career of John Maynard Keynes (1883–1946) and the so-called Keynesian Revolution, economists were increasingly called on to serve in government and business. During and after World War II extra-academic employment opened up for other social scientists in a variety of occupations. In the second half of the twentieth century the most authoritative pronouncements on social questions still came from statesmen (usually ghost-written by professional advisers) and occasionally from journalists and businessmen, but the theologians and philosophers were replaced by professional social scientists — although the general public sometimes had difficulty in distinguishing the categories.

The functions of government, with its manifold interferences in the lives of individuals, grew enormously in the twentieth century in democratic nations as well as in authoritarian ones. The twentieth century generally acknowledged that governments must accept responsibilities today that in the nineteenth century were left to private individuals. In this respect the nineteenth century appears to be an aberration; the twentieth is more in line with the practice of earlier centuries, but with the difference that in the past governments were looked upon as the masters of men, whereas now they are proclaimed on both sides of the Iron Curtain as their servants. For democratic nations this growth in the participation of government in everyday life posed several dilemmas. In view of the complexities of the modern world and the findings of social science concerning the role of irrationality in human behavior, is it really possible for men to govern themselves? Some political scientists maintain that the democratic process is a delusion, that in fact all key decisions are made by a relatively small group of individuals, not all of whom are visible to the public or subject to democratic control. Voters, they say, are manipulated by the techniques of social psychology and mass communications and are given only the illusion of choice. Even less cynical students of society are obliged to recognize that modern social science has eroded the foundations of the contract theory of government, just as the events of the twentieth century brought about the decline of classical liberalism. One of the most excruciating dilemmas of twentieth century democratic thought is the role of the individual in mass society. Is it possible to preserve individual liberty and freedom from the tyranny of mass conformity as well as from the tyranny of omnipotent government?

In the fifteenth and sixteenth centuries the greater power and resources of such nation-states as France, Spain, and England rendered the small medieval city-states obsolete. In the twentieth century the power and resources of such superstates as the United States, the Soviet Union, and potentially China and a possible "United States of Europe" have rendered the traditional nation-state obsolescent. The decline of the nation-states does not necessarily mean that they will cease to exist, for the ideology of nationalism is still so strong that the twentieth century has witnessed the proliferation of dozens of new nations. It does suggest, however, that new forms of international or supranational organization will have to be devised to overcome the limitations of existing national boundaries and to obtain the political, economic, and military advantages of superstates. A number of regional organizations, such as the European Economic Community, the Organization of African Unity, and the Organization of American States, are potential embryos of new superstates.

In a sense even the superstates are already obsolescent, because the development of weaponry since World War II has given the two existing superstates the ability to inflict irreparable damage on each other in the event of war, regardless of which struck first. For the time being this massive retaliatory power serves as a deterrent to all-out war, but as new superstates arise, the situation will not remain stable. World government is a conceivable alternative, although in the eighth decade of the twentieth century there are few visible signs that it is imminent. Nevertheless, any reasonably informed person can infer that the system of international relations that resulted from the breakdown of the nineteenth-century balance-of-power concept is transitory at best — calamitous at worst.

EPILOGUE: THE EMERGENCE OF WORLD CIVILIZATION

Although serious historians resist, with good reason, the temptation to prophesy the future, it is a part of their responsibility to identify the features of the past that have helped to shape the present and which, by implication, will also affect the future. In the final third of the twentieth century it is possible to identify at least some of the basic features of the world civilization that has begun to emerge during the last half-century.

To say that Western civilization is being superseded does not imply that Western nations or Western society will cease to exist. Not only will Western nations continue to exist, but many elements of their civilization will be incorporated in the new. For the peoples of the rest of the world the outstanding feature of Western civilization has been its technology; this is what destroyed their own civilizations, and this is what they have been able to absorb from the West. The technological basis of the civilization of the future will grow out of the technology of the West. Whether non-Western peoples will also be able to take over and absorb the rational spirit that underlay the development of that technology — indeed, whether the lineal heirs of the West will be able to retain that spirit — is questionable. Equally in doubt is the ability of the generations to come, Western and non-Western alike, to retain the belief in freedom, rooted in respect for the individual human personality, which has been one of the basic values of Western civilization. Although many non-Western nations have superficially adopted the political forms of the West it is still too soon to know if those forms, and the values they embody, will take root and grow.

The influence of non-Western traditions on global civilization lies chiefly in the field of nonmaterial culture. Oriental and African art forms have already had a significant influence on Western art, and it is likely that the art of the future will blend both traditions even more thoroughly as well as bring forth completely new themes and forms of expression. Oriental religions have influenced religious thought and expression in the contemporary West. Indeed, the two predominant religious traditions of the West, Judaism and Christianity, themselves originated in the Orient.

The creation of a new civilization is not a matter of decades or even generations. In the case of Western civilization fully five centuries elapsed after the collapse of classical civilization before the distinctive traditions of its successor became firmly established. Nor is civilization a static concept, as the history of the Western world in the last thousand years makes abundantly clear. Thus, time will be an essential ingredient in the emergence of a global civilization. It may be that modern technology, especially the technology of communications, which has speeded up every aspect of modern life, will also hasten the process of cultural assimilation and amalgamation. Yet modern technology, together with the social tensions and political strains that inevitably accompany cultural change, also poses a serious threat to the future of terrestrial civilization. The outcome cannot be predicted, but barring a nuclear holocaust that would reduce all the works of man to heaps of radioactive ashes, historians of the future will look back to the twentieth century for the origins of world civilization.

Chronology

Date*	Europe and Europe Overseas	Western Europe	Central Europe	Borderlands Europe	Arts, Letters, and Science
1450			Sforza despot of Milan (1450–66)		
1453		end of Hundred Years' War		fall of Constantinople	
1455		English Wars of the Roses (1455–85)			
1459					Platonic Academy founded in Florence
1460	death of Prince Henry the Navigator				
1461		Louis XI (1461–83)			
1462				Ivan III, the Great (1462–1505)	
1478		Spanish Inquisition established	Pazzi Conspiracy in Florence		
1479		Ferdinand and Isabella (1479–1516)			
1480				Tatar Yoke thrown off by Ivan III	
1485		Henry VIII (1485–1509)			
1486			Maximilian (1486–1519)		

* Dates after rulers indicate years of reign or term of office.

1487	Diaz rounds Cape of Good Hope			
1492	discovery of the New World	Spain expells Jews and conquers Granada	Pope Alexander VI (1492–1503)	
1494			French invade Italy; burning of Savonarola	
1498	Cabot's voyage to Nova Scotia			
1499	Da Gama returns from India		Swiss defeat the Emperor	Michaelangelo's "Pietà"
1501	second voyage of Amerigo Vespucci			
1503			Pope Julius II (1503–13)	
1508				Sigismund I (1508–48); University of Alcala founded
1509		Henry VIII (1509–47)		
1511			the Holy League	Erasmus's *Praise of Folly*
1512				Michaelangelo completes Sistine vault
1513	Portuguese reach Canton, China			Machiavelli's *Prince*
1514				
1515		Francis I (1515–47); Concordat of Bologna		
1516				More's *Utopia*
1517			Luther's Ninety-Five Theses	
1519	Magellan's circumnavigation (1519–22)		Charles V (1519–58)	
1520		Field of the Cloth of Gold	Diet of Worms	Suleiman II, the Magnificent (1520–66)
1521	Cortez conquers Mexico			

Date	Europe and Europe Overseas	Western Europe	Central Europe	Borderlands Europe	Arts, Letters, and Science
1523				Gustavus Vasa (1523–60)	
1524			Peasants' Revolt		
1526				battle of Mohács Denmark becomes Lutheran	
1527			Sack of Rome		
1528		Treaty of Cambrai			Castiglione's *Courtier*
1529			Augsburg Confession		
1532	Pizarro begins conquest of Peru				
1534		Act of Supremacy	Pope Paul III (1534–49)		
1535			Siege of Munster		
1536					Calvin's *Institutes*
1537		Pilgrimage of Grace			
1539		Act of the Six Articles			
1540	Society of Jesus (the Jesuits) founded				
1543					Copernicus's *Revolution of the Spheres*
1545	Council of Trent (1545–63)				
1546			Schmalkaldic War		
1547		Edward VI (1547–53) Henry II (1547–59)		Ivan IV, the Terrible (1547–84)	
1548				Sigismund II (1548–72)	
1552		Second English Prayer Book			
1553		Mary of England (Bloody Mary) (1553–58)			

1555	the Marian Persecution	Religious Peace of Augsburg division of Habsburg domain		
1556	Philip II (1556–98)			
1558	Elizabeth I (1558–1603)			
1559	Treaty of Cateau-Cambrésis			
1560	John Knox converts Scotland			
1562	Wars of Religion, France (1562–93)			
1563	Thirty-Nine Articles of Religion			
1565				Palestrina composer to papal chapel
1567	abdication of Mary Queen of Scots			
1568	revolt of the Netherlands			
1569			Union of Lublin	
1570	Elizabeth I excommunicated			
1571		Papal Congregation of the Index	battle of Lepanto	
1572	St. Bartholomew's Day Massacre			
1573			Compact of Warsaw	
1576		Rudolf II (1576–1612) Counter-Reformation in Germany		
1579	Union of Utrecht			
1580	Spain annexes Portugal			Brahe sets up observatory Bodin's *Six Books of the Commonwealth*

Date	Europe and Europe Overseas	Western Europe	Central Europe	Borderlands Europe	Arts, Letters, and Science
1582					Gregorian reform of the calendar
1584		murder of William the Silent			
1585			Pope Sixtus V reorganizes Curia		
1587		Maurice of Nassau (1587–1625)			
1588		Spanish Armada defeated		Christian IV (1588–1648)	
1589		Henry IV (1589–1610)			
1594		Henry IV's conversion to Catholicism			
1598		Edict of Nantes		Boris Godunov (1598–1605)	Botero's *Of the Reason of State*
1599		Philip III (1598–1621)		Charles IX (1599–1611)	
1600					Gilbert *On the Magnet*
1601	English East India Company incorporated				
1602	Dutch East India Company incorporated				
1603		James I (1603–25)			
1604			Brandenburg Privy Council set up	Time of Troubles (1604–13)	
1605		Gunpowder Plot			
1607	English settle Virginia		Protestant Union		Bacon's *Advancement of Learning*
1608	French settle Quebec		Catholic League		Monteverdi's "Orfeo"
1609		Spain and Netherlands truce			Kepler's first two laws

Year	Monarchs	Central Europe	Politics	Colonies / War	Arts & Sciences
1610			Louis XIII (1610–43)		Galileo's *Sidereal Messenger*
1611	Gustavus Adolphus (1611–34)				
1613	Michael Romanov (1613–33)				
1614					Cervantes's *Don Quixote*
1618				Thirty Years' War (1618–48)	
1619			execution of Jan van Oldenbarnevelt	Virginia assembly first slaves in British North America	
1620		Battle of White Mountain		Pilgrims settle Plymouth	Bacon's *New Organon*
1621			Spain and Netherlands at war		
1623					Velasquez painter to Spanish court
1624			Richelieu (1624–42)		Harvey's *Motion of Heart and Blood*
1625			Charles I (1625–49) Frederick Henry (1625–27)		Bernini architect at St. Peter's
1628			Petition of Right		
1629		Imperial Edict of Restitution	Charles I begins Personal Rule		
1630				Massachusetts Bay Colony established	
1632				battle of Lützen	
1633					trial of Galileo
1634	Christina (1634–54)			murder of Wallenstein	
1637			Scots's rebellion		Descartes's *Discourse on Method*

Date	Europe and Europe Overseas	Western Europe	Central Europe	Borderlands Europe	Arts, Letters, and Science
1640		revolt of Catalonia and Portugal Long Parliament (1640–60)	Frederick William, the Great Elector (1640–88)		
1642		English Civil Wars (1642–48) Mazarin (1642–61) fall of Olivares			
1643					Torricelli invents barometer
1648	Peace of Westphalia	the Fronde		"Deluge" of Poland (1648–67)	
1649		execution of Charles I the Commonwealth (1649–53) Cromwell (1649–58)			
1651	First English Navigation Act				Hobbes's *Leviathan*
1652		First Anglo-Dutch War (1652–54)			
1655				First Northern War (1655–60)	
1657	Dutch-Portuguese War over Brazil		Leopold I (1657–1705)		Pascal's *Provincial Letters*
1659		Peace of the Pyrenees			Boyle's chemical experiments
1660		Restoration of Charles II (1660–85)			Malpighi discovers capillaries
1661		Louis XIV (1643–1715) assumes control of government			

Year	America / British Isles	Western Europe	Turkish / Central Europe	Russia / Eastern Europe	Science & Culture
1662		Colbert (1662–83)			Royal Society founded; Petty's *Treatise on Ireland*
1664	English capture New Amsterdam		Imperial defeat of the Turks		
1665		Charles II of Spain (1665–1700); Second Anglo-Dutch War (1665–67)			Isaac Newton at Woolsthorpe
1666				deposition of Patriarch Nikon	French Academy of Sciences founded
1667		War of Devolution (1667–68)			
1670				Cossack rising under Razin	
1672		William III (1672–1702); Dutch War (1672–79)			
1675					Leibniz publishes his calculus
1679		Peace of Nijmegen			
1682		Declaration of Gallican Liberties		Peter the Great (1682–1725)	
1683			Sobieski saves Vienna from Turks		
1685		James II (1685–88); Edict of Nantes revoked			
1686					John Ray's natural history study
1687			Austrian subjugation of Hungary; Frederick I (1688–1713)		Newton's *Principia*
1688	War of the League of Augsburg (1688–97)	"Glorious Revolution"; William and Mary (1688–1702); Bill of Rights			

Date	Europe and Europe Overseas	Western Europe	Central Europe	Borderlands Europe	Arts, Letters, and Science
1690					Locke's *Essay on Human Understanding*
1692	battle of La Hogue				
1694		Bank of England founded			
1696					Gregory King's statistics
1697				Charles XII (1697–1718)	Bayle's *Historical Dictionary*
1698	Treaty of Ryswick				
1699					
1700		Philip V (1700–46)	Peace of Karlowitz	Great Northern War (1700–21)	Berlin Academy of Sciences founded
1701	War of the Spanish Succession (1701–13)				
1702		Anne (1702–14)			
1704	battle of Blenheim				
1706		Condemnation of Jansenism			
1707		Union of England and Scotland		Sweden invades Russia	Vauban's *Project for a Royal Tithe*
1711			Rakoczy's Hungarian rising defeated Charles VI (1711–40)	Peter reforms central administration	
1713	Treaty of Utrecht		Frederick William I (1713–40)		
1714		George I (1714–27)			
1715		Louis XV (1715–74)			
1717					London Freemason Grand Lodge

	International	Western Europe	Central Europe	Eastern Europe	Culture
1718	Quadruple Alliance (1718–33)				
1719			Pragmatic Sanction of Charles VI	Peter murders Prince Alexis	
1720		Mississippi Bubble			
1721		Walpole (1721–42)		Treaty of Nystadt	Montesquieu's *Persian Letters*
1722				Peter's Table of Ranks	Russian Academy of Sciences founded
1724					Vico's *New Science*
1725					
1726		Fleury (1726–42)			
1727		George II (1727–60)			
1733			War of the Polish Succession (1733–35)		Voltaire's *Letters on the English*
1738		Rev. John Wesley's "conversion"			
1739		War of Jenkins's Ear			
1740	War of the Austrian Succession (1740–48)		Maria Theresa (1740–80) Frederick II (1740–86)		Frederick II's *Anti-Machiavel*
1741				Elizabeth (1741–62)	
1745	Capture of Louisburg				
1746		Ferdinand VI (1746–59) William IV (1747–51)			
1747					
1748	Peace of Aix-la-Chapelle				Montesquieu's *Spirit of the Laws* First volume of *L'Encyclopedie*
1751	Clive takes Arcot in India				
1754	Washington's expedition Dupleix recalled from India				

Date	Europe and Europe Overseas	Western Europe	Central Europe	Borderlands Europe	Arts, Letters, and Science
1755		Charles III (1755–88)			
1756	Seven Years' War (1756–63)				
1757	battle of Plassey battle of Rossbach	Pitt the Elder (1757–61)			
1758					Quesnay's *Tableau Économique* Voltaire's *Candide*
1759	fall of Quebec	George III (1760–1820)			
1760	fall of Montreal				
1762				Catherine II, the Great (1762–96)	Rousseau's *Social Contract*
1763	Treaty of Paris				
1764				Russian church property secularized	Beccaria's *Crimes and Punishments*
1765	Stamp Act		Berlin State Bank founded		
1766		Revolt of the French parlements William V (1766–95)		Christian VII (1766–1808)	
1767					Hargreaves's spinning jenny
1769		Jesuits expelled from Spain			Watts patents his first steam engine
1770	Boston Massacre				
1771		Maupeou parlements in France		Gustavus III (1771–92)	Arkwright's first factory
1772				First Partition of Poland	
1773	Boston Tea Party			Pugachev's rising in Russia	

1774	First Continental Congress; Quebec Act	Wilkes seated in Parliament; Louis XVI of France (1774–92)	Austrian elementary school system established	Treaty of Kuchuk Kainarji	
1775	Lexington and Concord				
1776	Declaration of Independence				Smith's *Wealth of Nations*
1778			War of the Bavarian Succession (1778–79)		
1780			Joseph II (1780–90) personal liberty given to Austrian peasants		
1781	Cornwallis surrenders at Yorktown				Kant's *Critique of Pure Reason*; Rousseau's *Confessions*; "Sturm und Drang"
1783	Treaty of Paris	Pitt the Younger (1783–1806)			
1785				Russian Charter of Nobility	
1787		defeat of the Dutch "Patriots"; triumph of the parlements			
1788	U.S. Constitution ratified; first settlement of convicts in Australia				
1789		beginning of the French Revolution	Austrian agrarian law		Bentham's *Principles of Morals*
1790		Civil Constitution of the Clergy			
1791		Constitution of the First Republic			
1792	War of the French Revolution	the "Republic of Virtue" (1792–94)		Treaty of Jassy	
1793	coalition against France	the Terror (1793–94)		Second Partition of Poland	Condorcet's *Progress of the Human Mind*

Date	Europe and Europe Overseas	Western Europe	Central Europe	Borderlands Europe	Arts, Letters, and Science
1794	Thermidorean reaction				
1795		the Directory (1795–99)		Third Partition of Poland	
1796	Bonaparte's Italian victories				
1798	Bonaparte's Egyptian failure				Malthus's *Essay on Population*
1799		Bonaparte's coup of 18 Brumaire Consulate (1799–1804)			
1801		Napoleon's Concordat with Pope		Alexander I (1801–25)	
1802	Peace of Amiens				Chateaubriand's *Genius of Christianity*
1803	war resumes				
1804		Code Napoleon the Empire (1804–14)			Beethoven's 3rd Symphony ("Eroica")
1805	battle of Trafalgar battle of Austerlitz		Treaty of Pressburg		
1806	Berlin Decree		end of the Holy Roman Empire		
1807	battle of Jena-Auerstedt battle of Eylau		Treaties of Tilsit	Grand Duchy of Warsaw established	Fichte's lectures on *Volksgeist*
1808	Peninsular Campaign begins	Spanish constitution			Goethe's *Faust*
1812				Napoleon's Russian Campaign	
1813			War of Liberation battle of Leipzig		Sputhey poet laureate

1814	Congress of Vienna	French Charter of 1814	Metternich (1814–48)	Norway annexed to Sweden	
1815	Napoleon's defeat at Waterloo	Bourbon restoration "White Terror" in France Hundred Days			
1816	wars for Latin American liberation				
1817		English Coercion Acts	Wartburg Festival		Hegel at University of Berlin
1818	Congress of Aix-la-Chapelle				
1819		Peterloo massacre	Carlsbad Decrees		
1820	Congress of Troppau	French "Ultras" Spanish and Portuguese revolutions	Italian revolutions (1820–21)		
1821	Congress of Laibach			Greeks revolt against Turks	Ranke's *Zur Kritik* Stephenson's locomotive
1823	Monroe Doctrine promulgated				
1824		Charles X (1824–30)			
1825	Latin American independence achieved			Decembrist Revolution Nicholas I (1825–55) Treaty of Adrianople	
1829		Catholic emancipation in Britain			
1830	French occupy Algeria	July Monarchy Belgian independence	Italian revolutions (1830–32)	Polish revolution	Berlioz's "Symphonie Fantastique" Hugo's *Notre Dame de Paris*
1831				Mohamed Ali's Syrian coup	
1832		British Parliamentary Reform Act	Metternich's Six Acts Young Italy		
1833	Abolition of slavery in British empire	Carlist War in Spain		Official Nationality in Russia	

Date	Europe and Europe Overseas	Western Europe	Central Europe	Borderlands Europe	Arts, Letters, and Science
1834		Owen's Grand National Union	Zollverein		
1835		municipal reform in Britain			
1837	Durham Report (Canada)	Victoria (1837–1901)			
1838	regular trans-Atlantic steam service established	Chartism			Blanc's *Organization of Labor*
1839	Opium War (1839–42)				Stendhal's *Charterhouse of Parma*
1840	Union Act unites Canada first settlement of New Zealand			"Tanzimat" reform begins	
1841					List's *National System*
1846		British Corn Law Repeal	Pope Pius IX (Pio Nono) (1846–78)		
1847					
1848	Year of Revolution	Second French Republic			Mill's *Political Economy*
1849	Year of Reaction				Marx's *Communist Manifesto* Courbet and realism in painting
1850	Australia becomes self-governing Taiping Rebellion (1850–64)		Olmütz Humiliation		
1851		Amalgamated Society of Engineers		Christian shrine dispute in Holy Land	Crystal Palace Exhibition, London
1852		Napoleon III's Second Empire	Bach System Cavour (1852–61)		Comte's *Positivist Catechism*

1853	Crimean War				Gobineau's *Inequality of Human Races*
1854	Commodore Perry opens Japan				
1855	Paris Peace Conference			Alexander II (1855–81)	Spencer's *Principles of Psychology*
1856					Flaubert's *Madame Bovary*
1857	Sepoy Mutiny in India				invention of Bessemer steel process
1858	French occupy Saigon		Meeting at Plombieres War of Italian Unification		
1859					Darwin's *Origin of Species*
1860		Napoleon III's "Liberal Empire"	Treaty of Turin		
1861	American Civil War (1861–65)		William I (1861–88) Kingdom of Italy proclaimed	emancipation of Russian serfs	
1862			Bismarck (1862–90)		Turgenev's *Fathers and Sons*
1863	Maximilian becomes emperor of Mexico Syllabus of Errors			Polish rebellion	Renan's *Life of Jesus*
1864		First Communist International	Danish War	Zemstvos reforms in Russia	
1865					Tolstoi's *War and Peace*
1866			Seven Weeks' War Italy annexes Venetia		Dostoevski's *Crime and Punishment*
1867	Canadian Confederation	British Reform Act	North German Confederation Dual Monarchy		Marx's *Capital*
1868	Meiji Restoration Japan (1868–1912)	Gladstone vs. Disraeli Spanish Revolution			

Date	Europe and Europe Overseas	Western Europe	Central Europe	Borderlands Europe	Arts, Letters, and Science
1869	Suez Canal opened Vatican Council				
1870		Franco-Prussian War Third French Republic Paris Commune	German Empire Italy annexes Rome		
1871			Kulturkampf (1871–83) Second Reich (1871–1918)		
1872 1873		British secret ballot act			Maxwell's *Electricity and Magnetism*
1874		Spanish Bourbons restored Disraeli (1874–80) Organic Laws		Russian army reform	
1875			German Social Democratic Party		
1876	Belgian Congo Company incorporated			Turkish rebellion	
1877	Russo-Turkish War (1877–78)				
1878	Congress of Berlin	British Trades Union Congress	Bismarck outlaws Social Democratic Party		
1879			Dual Alliance (1879–1918) liberalization begins in Austrian Empire		
1880		workmen's compensation (Britain)			
1881	Alliance of Three Emperors (1881–87) French in Tunis			Alexander III (1881–94)	Zola's *Roman Experimental*

1882	Triple Alliance				
1883	British occupy Egypt; German colonial expansion				
1884	Berlin Conference	British Third Reform Act			Spencer's *Man Versus the State*; "Fin de Siecle" begins
1885	Spanish in Rio de Oro; British in Nigeria			Anti-Semitic pogroms in Russia	
1886					Hertz demonstrates electromagnetic waves
1887	Reinsurance Treaty				Michelson and Morley experiment; Strindberg's *Miss Julia*
1888		Boulanger challenge in France	Kaiser William II (1888–1918)		
1889		Second Communist International			
1890	Leo XIII's "Rerum Novarum"				
1891			German Social Democratic revolutionary platform	Trans-Siberian railway begun	
1892	Franco-Russian Alliance			Witte's industrialization	Lorentz posits electrons
1893		defeat of Gladstone's Irish home rule			
1894	Berlin Conference	Dreyfus Case in France (1894–1906)		Nicholas II (1894–1917)	
1895		French General Confederation of Labor			Durkheim's *Rules of Sociological Method*; Roentgen discovers X-Rays
1896	Jameson Raid; Italians defeated in Ethiopia				
1897	Germans occupy Kiao-Chow				
1898	Spanish-American War; Fashoda Crisis				

Date	Europe and Europe Overseas	Western Europe	Central Europe	Borderlands Europe	Arts, Letters, and Science
1899	Boer War Open Door Policy for China				Freud's *Interpretation of Dreams*
1900	Boxer Rebellion (1900–01)		Geman fleet expansion		Planck posits quantum theory Pareto's *Social Systems*
1902	British-Japanese Alliance	British Labor Party founded			
1903	Belgian Congo scandal			Bolshevik-Menshivik split	
1904	Russo-Japanese War Anglo-French Entente		Italian general strike		Chekhov's *Cherry Orchard*
1905	First Morroccan Crisis	separation of church and state in France British Liberal reform era (1906–11)	Schlieffen strategy drafted	Russian Revolution	Einstein's special theory of relativity
1906				Duma	
1907	Anglo-Russian entente				
1908	Second Moroccan Crisis		Austria annexes Bosnia and Herzegovina "Giolittism" in Italy	Revolt of the Young Turks	
1909		Lloyd George's social reforms British Parliament Bill			Peary reaches North Pole
1911	*Panther* Crisis Italy occupies Tripoli Third Moroccan Crisis			assassination of Stolypin	
1912	Sun Yat-Sen's revolution in China	Italian electoral reform	Socialist election victory in Germany	First Balkan War (1912–13)	
1913		defeat of Home Rule for Ireland		Second Balkan War	Stravinsky's "Sacre du Printemps" Gide's *Caves du Vatican*
1914	World War I (1914–19)		Ancona riots, Italy	assassination of Austrian heir in Sarajevo	

1915	stalemate on Western Front				Einstein's general theory of relativity; Lenin's *Imperialism*; Joyce's *Ulysses*
1916	battle of Verdun; battle of Somme; battle of Jutland; battle of Trentino	Lloyd George's cabinet		murder of Rasputin	
1917	U.S. enters war, Russia exits	Clemenceau (1917–20)	German electoral reform; Orlando (1917–19)	Russian Revolutions; Lenin (1917–24)	
1918	armistice		Rome Congress of Oppressed Nationalities	Treaty of Brest-Litovsk	Spengler's *Decline of the West*
1919	Peace of Paris (Treaty of Versailles)		Fascist party formed; Weimar Republic; Nazis founded	White War; allied intervention	Gropius founds Bauhaus
1920	League of Nations established		Czechoslovakian constitution	victory of the Red armies; NEP	
1921		Irish independence			
1922	Genoa Conference		destructive inflation in Germany; Mussolini (1922–45); Mussolini's "March on Rome"	USSR created; Kemel Ataturk's revolt	
1923			occupation of the Rhur; Munich *putsch*	Stalin (1923–53)	
1924	Dawes Plan for reparations	first British Labor government			
1925	Locarno Conference		Hindenburg elected German president		
1926	Germany admitted to League	British general strike		Pilsudski's coup in Poland	Klee founds Blue Four movement
1928	Kellogg-Briand Peace Pact			First Five Year Plan	

Date	Europe and Europe Overseas	Western Europe	Central Europe	Borderlands Europe	Arts, Letters, and Science
1929	Great Depression begins		Lateran Treaties	destruction of the kulaks	
1930	London Naval Conference				Gasset's *Revolt of the Masses*
1931	Japan invades Manchuria	Spanish Republic Statute of Westminster			
1932			Nazi election success		
1933	Japan and Germany leave League		Nazi coup Hitler (1933–45)	U.S. recognizes Soviet Russia; Russian Great Purge begins	
1934	Russia joins League	Stavisky riots in France	Nazi blood purge		
1935	Italy invades Ethiopia	Popular Front formed in France	Saar Plebescite; Nazi laws vs. Jews	Franco-Russian Alliance	
1936	Germany occupies Rhineland	Spanish Civil War; abdication of Edward VIII	Berlin-Rome Axis	new Russian constitution	
1937		fall of Blum's government			
1938	Anschluss; Munich Agreements			Arab-Jewish strife in Palestine	
1939	World War II (1939–45)		Germany annexes Czechoslovakia	German-Russian Pact; Russo-Finnish War (1939–40)	
1940	Fall of France; Battle of Britain	Churchill (1940–45)			penicillin applied
1941	Germany invades Russia; Japan attacks Pearl Harbor			siege of Leningrad	
1942	battle of Midway			siege of Stalingrad	Fermi's nuclear reaction

1943	North African campaign		overthrow of Mussolini		
1944	D-Day and the Russian drive west				
1945	United Nations formed	British Labor government (1945–51)	occupation of Germany		Atomic bomb dropped
1946	Truman Doctrine; Churchill's "Iron Curtain" speech	Fourth French Republic	Italian republic proclaimed; Nürnberg Trials of war criminals	Fourth Five Year Plan	
1947	Marshall Plan; Benelux established	Communist strikes in France and Italy		Cominform established	
1948	Berlin blockade and airlift	Britain gives India independence	Communist coup in Czechoslovakia	Tito breaks with Soviet Russia; Israeli-Arab conflict	World Health Organization established
1949	NATO established; Chinese Communists victorious		German Federal Republic (West Germany) established	COMECON	
1950	Korean War (1950–53)				
1951	beginning of African independence	Conservatives form British government			
1952		Elizabeth II (1952–)			
1953			East Germans riot vs. Russia		
1954	French defeated in Indo-China			Khrushchev (1954–64)	Ehrenburg's "The Thaw"
1955	Bandung Afro-Asian Conference; First Summit Conference		Austrian and German peace treaties	Warsaw Pact	
1956	Suez War		Hungarian Revolution	Twentieth Soviet Party Conference	

Date	Europe and Europe Overseas	Western Europe	Central Europe	Borderlands Europe	Arts, Letters, and Science
1957		Common Market European Free Trade Association			Pasternak's *Dr. Zhivago* Sputnik I
1958		De Gaulle forms Fifth French Republic	Pope John XXIII (1958–63)		
1959				Russian-Chinese tension Cyprus independent	
1960	U-2 incident Second Summit cancelled	De Gaulle's economic reforms			
1961			Berlin Wall erected Vatican Council (1962–65) Pope Paul VI (1963–)		
1962	Chinese threaten India			Russian-Chinese split	
1963	Nuclear disarmament treaty	De Gaulle vetoes Britain's entrance into Common Market			
1964	U.S. begins buildup in Vietnam				
1965					discovery of quasars
1967		Spanish student disturbances		Israeli-Arab "Six Day" War	
1968	Paris peace talks begin	Paris student riots	Russian repression of Czechoslovakian liberalization		
1969		De Gaulle resigns			United States lands men on moon

A Reading List

This reading list is designed to provide the interested student with suggestions for further reading and the titles of books with which he can begin research for course papers and independent work. With these purposes in mind we have restricted our recommendations to books in English. Most of the works listed contain bibliographical information that will provide the student with detailed assistance in further reading or research in the subject that interests him.

An asterisk before the title indicates that the book is available in a paperback edition.

BIBLIOGRAPHIES

The titles and authors of important works in every field of historical research, often with valuable critical comments, are contained in G. M. Dutcher and others, *A Guide to Historical Literature* (1931) and *The American Historical Association's Guide to Historical Literature* (1961). The annual *International Bibliography of the Historical Sciences* should also be consulted. There are many specialized bibliographies. Their titles can be found in T. Besterman, *A World Bibliography of Bibliographies* (4 vols., 1955–56), and C. M. Winchell, *Guide to Reference Books* (7th ed., 1951).

In 1957 the Service Center for Teachers of History of the American Historical Association began the publication of a series of pamphlets, each written by a specialist, that present concise summaries of publications reflecting recent research and new interpretations in a particular field of history. Historical periodicals, such as the *American Historical Review*, the *Journal of Modern History, Speculum,* and many others, contain book reviews and lists of new books and recently published articles.

REFERENCE WORKS

Useful reference works include W. L. Langer, ed., *An Encyclopedia of World History* (4th ed., 1968), a detailed collection of important events and dates from the beginning of recorded history; *The Columbia Encyclopedia* (3rd ed., 1963), the best of the one-volume encyclopedias. W. R. Shepherd, *Historical Atlas* (new ed., 1965) and R. R. Palmer, ed., *Atlas of World History* (1957) are helpful aids, as is *Lippincott's Pronouncing Gazetteer* (1962). Most important nations have their own multi-volume biographical dictionaries; in English the major ones are the *Dictionary of National Biography* (1885–1960) for Great Britain and the *Dictionary of American Biography* (1928–36).

The *Encyclopaedia Britannica* is still the most useful of the general encyclopedias; regrettably, its quality has declined in recent years. The *Encyclopedia of the Social Sciences* (1930–35) is still useful, but the new *International Encyclopedia of the Social Sciences* (1968) is more up to date. The *New Catholic Encyclopaedia*, the *Jewish Encyclopedia*, the *Encyclopedia of Philosophy* and the *Encyclopaedia of Islam* are among the most valuable of the specialized encyclopedias.

GENERAL HISTORIES

Historians have often joined together to write comprehensive histories that are published either as collaborative volumes, with each chapter written by a different author, or as individual volumes each by a single author. These works are of an uneven quality. The best known of the collaborative works in English are *The Cambridge Ancient History* (8 vols., 1923–39), *The Cambridge Mediaeval History* (8 vols., 1911–36), *The Cambridge Modern History* (13 vols., 1902–12), *The New Cambridge Modern History* (1957–   ), and *The Cambridge Economic History of Europe* (1941–   ). The last two are still incomplete. W. L. Langer is editing a series called *The Rise of Modern Europe,* in which each volume is written by a single historian. Nearly all of the projected twenty volumes have appeared. Many of them are listed in the following pages. E. Eyre, ed., *European Civilization, Its Origin and Development* (7 vols., 1934–39), is an often overlooked but useful collaborative work.

There are many general histories, in both single and multi-volume form, of the countries and of the institutions, ideas, economic life, and culture discussed in this book. A number of them are mentioned in the reading lists for the individual chapters. A useful beginning guide to general histories with excellent critical comments is provided in M. Faisler, *Key to the Past* (3rd ed., 1965), a publication of the Service Center for Teachers of History.

THE HERITAGE OF THE EUROPEAN WORLD   CHAPTER ONE

THE LEGACY OF ANCIENT CIVILIZATION

* W. F. Albright, *From the Stone Age to Christianity: Monotheism and the Historical Process* (1940). A thoughtful and informative inquiry into the development of man's ideas about God.

J. H. Breasted, *A History of Egypt from the Earliest Times to the Persian Conquest* (1905). Remains the standard work.

H. Breuil, *Four Hundred Centuries of Cave Art* (1952). The classic work on this subject.

J. B. Bury, *History of Greece to the Time of Alexander the Great* (3rd ed., 1951). One of the best one-volume surveys.

* V. G. Childe, *The Dawn of European Civilization* (5th ed., 1951). An imaginative reconstruction of the story of European man before recorded history.

L. Duchesne, *Early History of the Church* (2 vols., 1902–15). A valuable treatment of the spread of Christianity.

W. Jaeger, *Paedeia: The Ideals of Greek Culture* (3 vols., 1939–44). A masterly interpretation of Greek intellectual and spiritual life.

A. H. M. Jones, *The Decline of the Ancient World* (1957). A condensation of a distinguished two-volume work on the later Roman Empire.

THE SLOW BIRTH OF EUROPE

* J. Brønsted, *The Vikings* (1960). An outstanding account of the civilization of the Norsemen.

A Dopsch, *The Economic and Social Foundations of European Civilization* (1937). Argues that Roman civilization provided the basis for the revival of Western civilization in the eleventh century.

* H. Fichtenau, *The Carolingian Empire* (1957). A balanced estimate of Charlemagne's achievements.

* H. A. R. Gibb, *Mohammedanism: An Historical Survey* (2nd ed., 1953). The best introduction.

A. H. M. Jones, *The Later Roman Empire, 284–602* (2 vols., 1964). An outstanding work.

R. S. Lopez, *The Birth of Europe* (1967). A highly stimulating and well-written survey of the Middle Ages.

G. Ostrogorsky, *History of the Byzantine State* (1956). The most authoritative study.

F. W. Walbank, *The Decline of the Roman Empire in the West* (1946). A useful summary of the theories explaining the end of the classical world.

MEDIEVAL CIVILIZATION IN ITS PRIME

* G. Barraclough, *The Origins of Modern Germany* (1949). The best book in English on medieval Germany.

* M. Bloch, *Feudal Society* (1961). A brilliant analysis of the evolution and spread of feudalism and manorialism by a renowned French scholar.

R. H. C. Davis, *A History of Medieval Europe from Constantine to St. Louis* (1957). Especially valuable for its treatment of religious history.

R. Fawtier, *The Capetian Kings of France* (1960). A classic presentation of French medieval history.

P. Frankl, *Gothic: Literary Sources and Interpretations* (1960). A magnificent study of the Gothic style.

F. Ganshof, *Feudalism* (1961). A lucid, compact study.

C. H. Haskins, *The Normans in European History* (1915). Deals with the role of the Normans in the establishment of European states.

* ———, *The Renaissance of the Twelfth Century* (1927). The classic study of the revival of learning in medieval Europe.

E. Kantorowicz, *Frederick II* (1931). A penetrating analysis of relations between the papacy and the Hohenstaufen emperors.

D. Knowles, *The Evolution of Medieval Thought* (1962). A masterful survey from Greek origins to the fifteenth century.

* C. Petit-Dutaillis, *The Feudal Monarchy in France and England* (1936). The best comparative treatment of the Western feudal monarchies.
* H. Pirenne, *Medieval Cities* (1925) and *Economic and Social History of Medieval Europe* (1937). Ground-breaking reinterpretations by the famed Belgian scholar.
* S. Runciman, *A History of the Crusades* (3 vols., 1951–54). A fascinating account.

THE CRISIS OF THE MEDIEVAL ORDER

F. G. Heymann, *John Žižka and the Hussite Revolution* (1955) and *George of Bohemia, King of Heretics* (1965). Major contributions to the history of the religious troubles in Bohemia.
* K. B. McFarlane, *John Wycliffe and the Begininngs of English Non-Conformity* (1953). A useful brief account.
W. Ullman, *Origins of the Great Schism* (1948). The best study in English.

ECONOMIC CHANGE AND THE EXPANSION OF EUROPE   CHAPTER TWO

THE GREAT DEPRESSION OF THE LATER MIDDLE AGES

W. Kirchner, *The Rise of the Baltic Question* (1954). A well written scholarly study of an important area of Hanseatic activity.
P. Lindsay and R. Groves, *The Peasants' Revolt, 1381* (1950). A popular account of the English rural disturbances.
M. M. Postan and E. E. Rich, eds., *Trade and Industry in the Middle Ages* (1952). Vol. II of *The Cambridge Economic History*. Provides the now generally accepted view of the economic history of the later Middle Ages.
B. H. Slicher van Bath, *The Agrarian History of Western Europe* A.D. *500–1850* (1963). Contains a useful section on the agricultural depression of the fourteenth and fifteenth centuries.
* R. W. Southern, *The Making of the Middle Ages* (1953). A brilliant and evocative portrait of the twelfth century.

THE RISE OF MODERN CAPITALISM

* M. Dobb, *Studies in the Development of Capitalism* (rev. ed., 1964). A sophisticated Marxist analysis.
R. Ehrenburg, *Capital and Finance in the Age of the Renaissance* (1928). Informative about the activities of the Fugger banking family.
F. C. Lane, *Andrea Barberigo, Merchant of Venice, 1418–1449* (1944). A rare biography of a late medieval merchant.
B. N. Nelson, *The Idea of Usury: From Tribal Brotherhood to Universal Otherhood* (1949). Analysis of the religious, social, and psychological background of the prohibition against usury.
I. Origo, *The Merchant of Prato: Francesco di Marco Datini, 1335–1410* (1957). Unusually detailed biography based on archival sources.
R. A. de Roover, *The Rise and Decline of the Medici Bank, 1307–1494* (1963)

and *Money, Banking and Credit in Medieval Bruges* (1948). Two superb studies, based on intensive archival research.

H. See, *Modern Capitalism* (1926). A useful introduction.

THE GREAT DISCOVERIES

S. E. Morison, *Admiral of the Ocean Sea* (1942). By far the best book on Columbus.

A. P. Newton, ed., *The Great Age of Discovery* (1932). Account of the discoveries and early colonial policies of the European states.

J. H. Parry, *Europe and a Wider World* (1949) and *The Age of Reconnaissance, 1415–1650* (1963). Useful for an understanding of the organization and effects on Europe of European overseas expansion.

* B. Penrose, *Travel and Discovery in the Renaissance* (2nd ed., 1955). Scholarly account of exploration, navigation, and mapmaking.

E. Prestage, *The Portuguese Pioneers* (1933). The standard work covering Portuguese explorations up to the early sixteenth century.

R. L. Reynolds, *Europe Emerges* (1961). A thoughtful analysis of the emergence and growth of Europe and its expansion beyond its borders.

OVERSEAS EXPANSION AND ITS IMPACT ON EUROPE

E. J. Hamilton, *American Treasure and the Price Revolution in Spain, 1501–1650* (1934). A detailed analysis of the effects of American bullion on Spanish economic life.

* L. Hanke, *The Spanish Struggle for Justice in the Conquest of America* (1949). An objective study of the treatment accorded the Indians by the Spanish conquerors.

* F. A. Kirkpatrick, *The Spanish Conquistadores* (1934). A colorful account.

G. Masselman, *The Cradle of Colonialism* (1963). A study of Dutch colonialism from the 1590's to 1630, with special emphasis on the work of Jan Pieterszoon Coen.

R. B. Merriam, *The Rise of the Spanish Empire in the Old World and the New* (4 vols., 1918–34). A magisterial survey, though dated.

J. H. Parry, *The Spanish Theory of Empire in the Sixteenth Century* (1940). Traces the evolution of ideas about colonial government and the impact upon the Spanish government of the colonial forms of government.

W. H. Prescott, *History of the Conquest of Mexico* (3 vols., 1843) and *History of the Conquest of Peru* (2 vols., 1847). Historical classics.

H. R. Wagner, *The Rise of Hernando Cortés* (1944). A carefully done history of the conquest of Mexico.

THE RENAISSANCE CHAPTER THREE

THE RENAISSANCE IN ITALY

H. Baron, *The Crisis of the Early Italian Renaissance* (2 vols., 1955). Shows the shift in humanism in Florence from a medieval orientation to a realization of the value of freedom and of participation in civic life.

* J. C. Burckhardt, *The Civilization of the Renaissance* (1860). Still the point of departure for study of the Renaissance.

W. K. Ferguson, *The Renaissance in Historical Thought* (1948). A presentation of the concept of the Renaissance from the humanists to the mid-twentieth century.

* M. P. Gilmore, *The World of Humanism 1453–1517* (1952). A useful general survey.

D. Hay, *The Italian Renaissance in its Historical Background* (1961). Places the Renaissance in the stream of general historical development.

* E. F. Jacob, ed., *Italian Renaissance Studies* (1960). Essays on aspects of the Renaissance by leading British scholars.

G. R. Potter, ed., *The Renaissance, 1493–1520* (1957). Vol. I of *The New Cambridge Modern History.* Contains valuable essays by outstanding scholars on aspects of the era.

ITALIAN HUMANISM

P. O. Kristeller, *The Classics and Renaissance Thought* (1955) and *Studies in Renaissance Thought and Letters* (1956). Lucid and stimulating discussions of the philosophical thought of the Renaissance.

L. Martines, *The Social World of the Florentine Humanists 1390–1460* (1963). Shows that Florentine humanists came from the ruling classes and had independent means.

L. Olschki, *The Genius of Italy* (1949). Presents humanism as a movement supported by most of Italian lay society.

G. Toffanin, *History of Humanism* (1954). Views humanism as an orthodox Catholic movement rather than an irreligious break with the Middle Ages.

R. Weiss, *The Dawn of Humanism in Italy* (1947). A discussion of humanism before Petrarch.

ITALIAN ART

* B. Berenson, *The Italian Painters of the Renaissance* (rev. ed., 1952). A widely accepted interpretation of Renaissance painting.

K. M. Clark, *Leonardo da Vinci: An Account of His Development as an Artist* (2nd ed., 1952). A useful work.

E. Panofsky,* *Studies in Iconology: Humanistic Themes in the Art of the Renaissance* (1939) and *Renaissance and Renascences in Western Art* (2 vols., 1959). Works of great erudition and brilliant insights into the philosophical meaning of works of art.

C. de Tolnay, *Michelangelo* (5 vols., 1943–60). A monumental study.

R. Wittkower, *Architectural Principles in the Age of Humanism* (2nd ed., 1952). Discusses the relationships between architecture and philosophical ideas.

H. Wölfflin, *Classic Art: An Introduction to the Italian Renaissance* (new ed., 1952). Long-time standard work on the High Renaissance.

THE NORTHERN RENAISSANCE

O. Benesch, *The Art of the Renaissance in Northern Europe* (1945). Studies the connections between art and religious and philosophical thought.

R. H. Brinton, *Erasmus of Christendom* (1969). A biography that includes excerpts from Erasmus's works and letters.

* E. H. Harbison, *The Christian Scholar in the Age of the Reformation* (1956). A penetrating analysis of the effort to reconcile Christianity and learning.

* J. H. Hexter, *More's Utopia: The Biography of an Idea* (1952). Important for an understanding of More's famous book.

* J. Huizinga, *The Waning of the Middle Ages* (1924). A vivid assessment of French and Burgundian culture in the fourteenth and fifteenth centuries.

E. Panofsky, *Early Netherlandish Painting* (2 vols., 1953) and *Albrecht Dürer* (2 vols., 1948). The standard works on their respective subjects.

* M. M. Phillips, *Erasmus and the Northern Renaissance* (1950). A brief treatment.

RENAISSANCE SCIENCE

M. Boas, *The Scientific Renaissance 1450–1630* (1962). A valuable survey that stresses the relationship between humanism and the development of science.

* A. C. Crombie, *Medieval and Early Modern Science* (1958). An authoritative and comprehensive survey.

G. Sarton, *Six Wings: Men of Science in the Renaissance* (1957). A not wholly convincing reversal of Sarton's earlier claim that science lagged during the Renaissance.

V. P. Zubov, *Leonardo da Vinci* (1968). Discusses Leonardo's position in the history of scientific thought.

THE POLITICS OF THE RENAISSANCE   CHAPTER FOUR

POLITICAL THEORY

* F. Chabod, *Machiavelli and the Renaissance* (1958). Shows the influence of Italian history upon Machiavelli's thought. Has a remarkable bibliographical essay.

* J. N. Figgis, *Studies of Political Thought from Gerson to Grotius, 1414–1625* (2nd ed., 1916). The long-time standard work.

F. Gilbert, *Machiavelli and Guicciardini* (1965). A study of historical and political ideas in sixteenth-century Florence.

* J. R. Hale, *Machiavelli and Renaissance Italy* (1960). A short, skillfully done study.

* D. L. Jensen, *Machiavelli: Cynic, Patriot, or Political Scientist?* (1960). A selection of views of Machiavelli over four centuries, with a useful bibliography.

* F. Meinecke, *Machiavellism* (1957). Shows the contribution of Machiavelli's philosophy to the modern concept of the supremacy of the state's interests over moral law.

G. H. Sabine, *A History of Political Theory* (3rd ed., 1961). The appropriate sections in this outstanding book provide the best brief survey.

J. C. Whitfield, *Machiavelli* (1947). A sympathetic view of Machiavelli as a misunderstood and really moral philosopher.

ITALIAN POLITICS

* C. M. Ady, *Lorenzo de' Medici and Renaissance Italy* (1952). A useful short survey.

M. B. Becker, *Florence in Transition* (2 vols., 1967–68).

W. M. Bowsky, *Henry VII in Italy: The Conflict of Empire and City-State* (1960). A careful analysis of Italian politics at the start of the Renaissance.

G. A. Brucker, *Florentine Politics and Society, 1343–1378* (1962). An important study of a critical period in Florentine history.

C. S. Gutkind, *Cosimo de' Medici, Pater Patriae* (1938). A good biography, with valuable appendices on Florentine government and economic life.

D. Herlihy, *Pisa in the Early Renaissance: A Study in Urban Growth* (1958). A major contribution to the understanding of social and economic factors determining Italian city development.

* G. Mattingly, *Renaissance Diplomacy* (1955). Discusses the theory and practice of medieval and Renaissance diplomacy.

* F. Schevil, *History of Florence from the Founding of the City through the Renaissance* (1936). The best general history in English.

THE RISE OF THE NATION-STATES

P. Champion, *Louis XI* (1929). A popular biography.

* E. P. Cheyney, *The Dawn of a New Era, 1250–1453* (1936). Useful, though seriously dated in a number of respects, especially in economic and social history.

J. H. Elliott, *Imperial Spain, 1469–1716* (1964). Outstanding.

* G. R. Elton, *The Tudor Revolution in Government* (1953). Disputes the view that a new kind of monarchy began with the Tudors.

* M. P. Gilmore, *The World of Humanism, 1453–1517* (1952). A good general survey, with an extensive bibliographical essay.

H. Holborn, *A History of Modern Germany*, vol. I, *The Reformation* (1959). The first volume of a three-volume history; shows the transformation of medieval Germany.

J. D. Mackie, *The Early Tudors, 1485–1559* (1952). A volume in *The Oxford History of England*.

J. R. Major, *Representative Institutions in Renaissance France, 1421–1559* (1960) and *The Deputies to the Estates General in Renaissance France* (1960). Shows the close working relationship between the monarch and popular assemblies.

* A. R. Myers, *England in the Later Middle Ages, 1307–1536* (1952). A short and very readable volume in the *Pelican History of England*.

* A. J. Slavin, ed., *The "New Monarchies" and Representative Assemblies* (1964). A well-selected collection of essays with an excellent introduction by the editor.

REFORMATIONS, PROTESTANT AND CATHOLIC   CHAPTER FIVE

GENERAL ACCOUNTS

* Owen Chadwick, *The Reformation* (1964). The most sensitive and searching recent study of the Reformation.

* A. G. Dickens, *Reformation and Society in Sixteenth-Century Europe* (1966). A concise account of the social, political, and intellectual setting of the Reformation.

G. R. Elton, *Reformation Europe 1517–1559* (1967). A work of outstanding quality.

H. J. Grimm, *The Reformation Era* (1954). Especially good on Luther, and also has a lengthy critical bibliography.

* Joel Hurstfield, ed., *The Reformation Crisis* (1965). A collection of excellent varied and even contradictory lectures by current scholars of the period.

* G. Mosse, *The Reformation* (rev. ed., 1963). The best short survey.

THE ELEVENTH HOUR OF THE MEDIEVAL CHURCH

A. C. Flick, *The Decline of the Medieval Church* (2 vols., 1930). An informative and impressive presentation.

P. Hughes, *A History of the Church* (3 vols., 1947–49). Volume III provides a modern Catholic view on conditions in the Church on the eve of the Reformation.

J. Mackinnon, *The Origins of the Reformation* (1939). A useful survey.

L. Pastor, *The History of the Popes from the Close of the Middle Ages* (40 vols., 1891–1953). The standard work.

LUTHER AND THE GERMAN REFORMATION

* R. H. Bainton, *Here I Stand: A Life of Martin Luther* (1950). The best biography in English.

* E. H. Erikson, *Young Man Luther: A Study in Psychoanalysis and History* (1958). Attempts to explain Luther by means of modern psychoanalytical techniques, using Luther's own writings.

* H. Grisar, *Martin Luther* (1950). An unfavorable biography by a Jesuit scholar.

F. H. Littell, *The Anabaptist View of the Church* (1952) and *The Free Church* (1958). Useful for the Anabaptist movement.

C. L. Manschreck, *Melanchthon, the Quiet Reformer* (1958). A sensitive study of Luther's friend and fellow reformer.

E. G. Schwiebert, *Luther and his Times: The Reformation from a New Perspective* (1950). Stresses the influence of the University of Wittenberg in the spread of the Reformation.

G. Williams, *The Radical Reformation* (1962). A general survey of the left wing of the Reformation.

THE SWISS REFORMATION AND
THE RISE OF CALVINISM

* R. W. Green, *Protestantism and Capitalism. The Weber Thesis and Its Critics* (1959). Extracts from the major contributions to the debate, with a critical bibliography.

J. Mackinnon, *Calvin and the Reformation* (1936). A critical evaluation.

J. T. McNeill, *The History and Character of Calvinism* (1954). Discusses the diffusion of Calvinism.

* K. Samuelsson, *Religion and Economic Action* (1961). A sometimes overstated refutation of the Weber thesis.
* R. H. Tawney, *Religion and the Rise of Capitalism* (1926). Agrees with the essentials of Weber's thesis.
W. Walker, *John Calvin* (1906). Still the best biography.
* M. Weber, *The Protestant Ethic and the Spirit of Capitalism* (transl., 1930). The seminal study in the debate over the relationship between Protestantism and capitalism.

THE REFORMATION IN ENGLAND

* A. G. Dickens, *The English Reformation* (1964). Excellent survey.
P. Hughes, *The Reformation in England* (3 vols., 1950–54). An excellent work by a Catholic historian.
———, *Rome and the Counter Reformation in England* (1944). Includes a valuable analysis of Queen Mary's efforts to restore Catholicism.
M. M. Knappen, *Tudor Puritanism* (1939). Carefully works out the beginnings of English puritanism.
D. Knowles, *The Religious Orders in England* (3 vols., 1948–59). Volume III, *The Tudor Age,* is the most authoritative treatment of the dissolution of the monasteries.
* T. M. Parker, *The English Reformation to 1558* (1950). A good general account with too heavy a political emphasis.
J. J. Scarisbrick, *Henry VIII* (1968). A distinguished biography that is especially valuable for an understanding of the English Reformation.
H. M. Smith, *Henry VIII and the Reformation* (1948). Stresses the importance of state policy and minimizes the influence of the religious reformers.

THE CATHOLIC REFORMATION

H. Boehmer, *The Jesuits* (1928). The best study by a Protestant.
J. Brodrick, *The Economic Morals of the Jesuits* (1934); * *The Origins of the Jesuits* (1940); *The Progress of the Jesuits* (1947). Interesting studies by a Jesuit scholar.
* H. Daniel-Rops, *The Catholic Reformation* (transl., 2 vols., 1961). An outstanding work.
* A. G. Dickens, *The Counter-Reformation* (1969). A concise, scholarly, and well-written account.
P. Dudon, *St. Ignatius of Loyola* (1949). A good biography.

THE POLITICS OF THE REFORMATION   CHAPTER SIX

THE EMPIRE OF CHARLES V

K. Brandi, *The Emperor Charles V* (1939). The best biography.
B. Chudoba, *Spain and the Empire 1519–1643* (1952). An able analysis of Spanish imperialism on the Continent, particularly in central Europe.
R. B. Merriman, *The Rise of the Spanish Empire in the Old World and the New* (4 vols., 1918–34), and J. H. Elliott, *Imperial Spain, 1494–1716* (1964)

are the best works to consult; Elliott's book emphasizes social and economic development.

THE WARS OF RELIGION IN FRANCE

W. F. Church, *Constitutional Thought in Sixteenth Century France* (1941). A treatment of the conflict between medieval and modern ideas of government.
A. J. Grant, *The Huguenots* (1934). A useful study.
* J. E. Neale, *The Age of Catherine de' Medici* (1943). A valuable study.
H. Noguères, *The Massacre of St. Bartholomew* (1962). A very readable account.
F. C. Palm, *Calvinism and the Religious Wars* (1932). An excellent brief analysis.
H. Pearson, *Henry of Navarre* (1963). A good biography.

THE SPANISH PREDOMINANCE

See the books by Chudoba, Merriman, and Elliott listed above.

P. Geyl, *The Revolt of the Netherlands, 1555–1609* (1937). A major reinterpretation.
E. J. Hamilton, *American Treasure and the Price Revolution in Spain 1501–1650* (1934).
J. Klein, *The Mesta* (1920). The outstanding work on Spanish agricultural history.
* G. Mattingly, *The Armada* (1959). A brilliantly done account of international relations during the Anglo-Spanish war.
C. W. Oman, *A History of the Art of War in the Sixteenth Century* (1937). Study of the conduct of the wars of the era.
W. H. Prescott, *History of the Reign of Philip II* (1874). Still not superseded in comprehensive coverage.
R. S. Smith, *The Spanish Guild Merchant* (1940). A study of the social and economic life of the mercantile class.
C. V. Wedgewood, *William the Silent* (1944). Well written, though marred by excessive adulation of William.

ELIZABETHAN ENGLAND

* S. I. Bindoff, *Tudor England* (1959). An excellent brief survey.
J. B. Black, *The Reign of Elizabeth, 1558–1603* (2nd ed., 1959). A sound and comprehensive survey.
E. Lipson, *Economic History of England* (3 vols., 1956). Volume II presents the best overall treatment of economic life in Elizabethan England.
W. MacCaffrey, *The Shaping of the Elizabethan Regime* (1968). A careful analysis of the first fifteen years of Elizabeth's reign.
* J. E. Neale, *Queen Elizabeth I* (2nd ed., 1952). The best biography.
J. U. Nef, *The Rise of the British Coal Industry* (2 vols., 1932). An important study, though it tends to overstate the extent of industrialization in sixteenth–seventeenth century England.
C. Read, *Mr. Secretary Walsingham* (3 vols., 1925), *Mr. Secretary Cecil and Queen Elizabeth* (1955), *Lord Burghley and Queen Elizabeth* (1960). Thorough studies of English governmental policy.

A. L. Rowse, *The Elizabethan Age* (2 vols., 1950–55). Captures the color and excitement of the era.

R. H. Tawney, *The Agrarian Problem in the Sixteenth Century* (1912). A study of the effects of the growing commercialization of agriculture on noncapitalistic landowners.

THE BORDERLANDS OF EUROPE   CHAPTER SEVEN

THE CREATION OF THE RUSSIAN STATE

J. H. Billington, *The Icon and the Axe* (1966). A history of Russian culture written with imagination and verve.

* J. Blum, *Lord and Peasant in Russia from the Ninth to the Nineteenth Century* (1961). Deals with agrarian developments.

G. N. Lantzeff, *Siberia in the Seventeenth Century* (1943). An outstanding work on Russian expansion eastward.

P. I. Liashchenko, *History of the National Economy in Russia to the 1917 Revolution* (1949). A Soviet work of prime importance.

W. K. Medlin, *Moscow and East Rome* (1952). First-rate study of relations between church and state.

R. E. F. Smith, *The Enserfment of the Russian Peasantry* (1968). A scholarly analysis.

G. Vernadsky, *The Mongols and Russia* (1953) and *Russia at the Dawn of the Modern Age* (1959). Scholarly and well-written volumes.

R. I. Wipper, *Ivan Grozny* (1947). The official Soviet view of Ivan the Terrible as a great national hero.

POLAND TO 1660

O. Halecki, *Borderlands of Western Civilization: A History of East Central Europe* (1952). A political history of the region lying between Germany and Russia.

———, *A History of Poland* (1956). Has a strong Polish nationalistic bias.

W. F. Reddaway *et al.*, eds., *The Cambridge History of Poland* (2 vols., 1941–50). A useful collaborative work.

SCANDINAVIA TO 1660

N. G. Ahnlund, *Gustaf Adolf, the Great* (1940). A competent biography.

I. Andersson, *A History of Sweden* (1956). The standard general history in English.

J. H. S. Birch, *Denmark in History* (1938). A rather elementary survey.

E. F. Heckscher, *An Economic History of Sweden* (1954). Contains a brief treatment of the economic development of the era.

C. de Lannoy, *A History of Swedish Colonial Expansion* (1938). Deals with the Swedish Empire and its impact on Swedish domestic history.

K. Larsen, *A History of Norway* (1948). Competent and well written.

P. Lauring, *A History of the Kingdom of Denmark* (1960). A mediocre survey.

M. Roberts, *The Early Vasas: A History of Sweden, 1523–1611* (1968); *Gustavus*

Adolphus: A History of Sweden 1611–1632 (2 vols., 1953–58). These two works together provide a detailed history of Sweden's rise to great power status.

THE OTTOMAN EMPIRE TO 1656

A. D. Alderson, *The Structure of the Ottoman Dynasty* (1956). A careful study of the institution of the sultanate.

* C. Brockelman, *History of the Islamic Peoples* (1947). An attempt at a comprehensive history of the Middle East.

W. H. McNeill, *Europe's Steppe Frontier, 1500–1800* (1964). Sketches the history of the great eastern European plainland that was divided among the Ottoman, Austrian, and Russian empires.

R. B. Merriman, *Suleiman the Magnificent* (1944). Biography of the greatest Ottoman ruler.

A. Pallis, *In the Days of the Janissaries* (1951). An interesting account of Ottoman social history.

L. Stavrianos, *The Balkans Since 1453* (1958). An indispensable work.

D. M. Vaughan, *Europe and the Turk: A Pattern of Alliances, 1350–1700* (1954). Treats Turkey's role in international affairs.

P. Wittlek, *The Rise of the Ottoman Empire* (1958). An outstanding brief account.

SOCIAL, INTELLECTUAL, AND CULTURAL DYNAMISM, 1500–1660   CHAPTER EIGHT

SOCIETY AND SOCIAL DYNAMICS

M. Bloch, *French Rural History* (1966). A translation of a justly famed study first published in 1931.

F. L. Carsten, *The Origins of Prussia* (1954). Traces the main social and political development in the history of Brandenburg-Prussia to the mid-seventeenth century.

* G. N. Clark, *The Seventeenth Century* (1931). Analytical essays on aspects of the life of the period, including economic development, population, and cultural life.

J. C. Davis, *The Decline of the Venetian Nobility as a Ruling Class* (1962). Follows the fortunes of the Venetian aristocracy from the mid-sixteenth to the end of the eighteenth century.

H. P. R. Finberg, *The Agrarian History of England and Wales, 1500–1640* (vol. IV, 1967). A collaborative work of much value.

* C. J. Friedrich, *The Age of the Baroque, 1610–1660* (1952). An effort to relate politics to other aspects of life during this era.

* J. H. Hexter, *Reappraisals in History* (1961). Sparkling essays on Tudor and Stuart social history.

W. K. Jordan, *Philanthropy in England, 1480–1660* (1960). Traces with great skill the changes in social attitudes and aspirations as revealed by bequests to charity.

* J. U. Nef, *Industry and Government in France and England, 1540–1640* (1940). Shows the contrast in the relationships between government and business in the two countries, and helps explain why their forms of government differed.

A. Simpson, *The Wealth of the Gentry, 1540–1640* (1961). A careful analysis based on the records of five families.

* L. Stone, *The Crisis of the Aristocracy, 1558–1641* (1965). A monumental study of the long-term changes in the prestige and wealth of the English nobility.

THE SCIENTIFIC REVOLUTION

* H. Butterfield, *The Origins of Modern Science, 1300–1800* (1949). Well written essays for the general reader on selected topics.

M. Kaspar, *Kepler* (1959). A superb biography, translated from German.

* A. Koyré, *From the Closed World to the Infinite Universe* (1957). A brilliant discussion of the effects of the Scientific Revolution upon man's thoughts about God and the universe.

* T. S. Kuhn, *The Copernican Revolution* (1956). A vivid and illuminating analysis that makes difficult concepts understandable to the nonspecialist.

* G. de Santillana, *The Crime of Galileo* (1955). Fascinating account of Galileo's trial.

A. Wolf, *A History of Science, Technology, and Philosophy in the 16th and 17th Centuries* (1939). A storehouse of information.

THE BAROQUE

M. F. Bukofzer, *Music in the Baroque Era* (1947). Valuable critical account of the musical styles and ideas of the period.

F. Haskell, *Patrons and Painters* (1963). Gracefully written study of the relationships between the art and society of Italy in the age of the baroque.

A. Hausser, *Mannerism* (2 vols., 1965). A controversial effort to identify mannerism as the starting point for modern art.

* W. Sypher, *Four Stages of Renaissance Style* (1955). Considers baroque as later stage of Renaissance style.

V. L. Tapié, *The Age of Grandeur* (1960). Surveys the art, architecture, and civilization of the seventeenth century.

* H. Wölfflin, *Principles of Art History* (1932). Defines baroque and contrasts it with the classical Renaissance style.

AGE OF CRISIS, 1600–1660: ABSOLUTIST SOLUTION CHAPTER NINE

THE AGE OF CRISIS

E. Barker *et al.*, eds., *The European Inheritance* (3 vols., 1954). Volume II contains a valuable interpretative essay by Sir George Clark.

* T. Aston, ed., *Crisis in Europe 1560–1660* (1965). An anthology of articles from the English journal *Past and Present*.

* C. J. Friedrich and C. Blitzer, *The Age of Power* (1957). A survey focused on the search for power in political and intellectual life.

* D. Ogg, *Europe in the Seventeenth Century* (6th ed., 1954). A general survey, useful for political history.

THE THIRTY YEARS' WAR

* H. J. C. von Grimmelshausen, *The Adventurous Simplicissimus* (transl., 1912). Contemporary German novel that tells much about life during the war.

H. Holborn, *A History of Modern Germany: the Reformation* (1959). The third part of this useful study deals with the origins of the war and the war itself.

* T. K. Rabb, *The Thirty Years' War* (1964). Readings presenting differing points of view on the causes, nature, and effects of the war.

M. Roberts, *Gustavus Adolphus: A History of Sweden 1611-1632* (2 vols., 1953-58). A definitive study.

————, *The Military Revolution 1560-1660* (1956). A brief, stimulating reassessment.

F. Watson, *Wallenstein: Soldier under Saturn* (1938). A sometimes inaccurate account, but the best biography in English.

* C. V. Wedgewood, *The Thirty Years' War* (1938). The best general account in English.

THE DECLINE OF SPAIN, 1598-1665

B. Chudoba, *Spain and the Empire, 1519-1643* (1952). An excellent study of the connections between the Spanish and Austrian Hapsburgs.

J. H. Elliott, *Imperial Spain, 1469-1716* (New York, 1964). The best survey of Spanish history of the era.

J. H. Elliott, *The Revolt of the Catalans* (1963). A superb analysis of the causes of Spanish decline after Philip II's death.

L. Goldscheider, *El Greco* (1954). A magnificently illustrated study.

C. H. Haring, *Trade and Navigation between Spain and the Indies* (1918). The standard study of Spain's Atlantic trade during the era of the Spanish Hapsburgs.

M. A. S. Hume, *The Court of Philip IV* (1907). An account of the fantastic atmosphere of the royal court.

J. Lassaigne, *Spanish Painting* (2 vols., 1952). Excellent reproductions and a scholarly text.

THE RECONSTRUCTION OF FRANCE

* J. Boulenger, *The Seventeenth Century in France* (1963). Translation of an old standard French work.

D. Buisseret, *Sully and the Growth of Centralized Government in France, 1598-1610* (1968). An important revision, based on newly available manuscripts.

* C. J. Burckhardt, *Richelieu: His Rise to Power* (1964). Translation of an excellent German study.

P. R. Doolin, *The Fronde* (1935). A study of the revolt and the power of the monarchy.

* A. Huxley, *Grey Eminence* (1941). A stimulating if not scholarly biography of Richelieu's associate, the Capuchin Father Joseph.

* C. V. Wedgewood, *Richelieu and the French Monarchy* (1949). A brief, easily read study.

THE EMERGENCE OF ABSOLUTISM

W. A. Dunning, *A History of Political Theories from Luther to Montesquieu* (1905). Long the standard work, and still very useful.

C. C. Gillispie, *The Edge of Objectivity* (1960). A masterly study of the advance in science since Galileo through the use of mathematical logic and experiment.

* T. S. Kuhn, *The Structure of Scientific Revolutions* (1962). A philosophically oriented explanation of the process by which accepted scientific concepts are replaced by new concepts.

* J. G. A. Pocock, *The Ancient Constitution and the Feudal Law* (1957). Sparkling essay on the relationship of feudalism to absolutist and non-absolutist political theory.

G. H. Sabine, *A History of Political Theory* (3rd ed., 1961). The best general account.

* P. Smith, *A History of Modern Culture* (2 vols., 1930–34). The first volume of this now somewhat outdated but still very useful detailed account of European thought covers the period from 1543 to 1687.

* A. N. Whitehead, *Science and the Modern World* (1930). Places the scientific revolution in the context of Western culture.

ABSOLUTISM VERSUS OLIGARCHY: ENGLAND AND THE DUTCH REPUBLIC CHAPTER TEN

ENGLAND'S CONSTITUTIONAL CRISIS, 1603–1640

G. E. Aylmer, *The King's Servants* (1961). A detailed analysis of the social and economic status and political views of the men in the administration of Charles I.

T. G. Barnes, *Somerset 1625–1640: A County's Government During the Personal Rule* (1961). Details the breakdown of Charles I's attempt to rule without Parliament.

G. Davies, *The Early Stuarts, 1603–1660* (2nd ed., 1959). A useful survey.

S. R. Gardiner, *The History of England from the Accession of James I to the Outbreak of the Civil War 1603–1642* (10 vols., 1899–1901). An endlessly detailed narrative.

* W. Haller, *The Rise of Puritanism* (1938). Examination of the teachings of Puritanism up to the revolution.

J. H. Hexter, *The Rule of King Pym* (1941). A study of the political opposition to Charles I in the early months of the long Parliament.

C. Hill, *The Century of Revolution, 1603–1714* (1961). The first two parts of this valuable survey cover the period from James I to the Revolution.

M. A. Judson, *The Crisis of the Constitution* (1949). A valuable analysis of the conflicting political ideologies.

H. F. Kearney, *Strafford in Ireland* (1959). Revises some long-held views about Strafford's lord deputyship.

R. Lockyer, *Tudor and Stuart Britain 1471–1714* (1964). The best one-volume survey of the period.

* W. Notestein, *The English People on the Eve of Colonization, 1603–1660* (1954). Provides a survey of social life and institutions.

R. H. Tawney, *Business and Politics under James I* (1958). A study of economic life shown through the career of Lionel Cranfield, merchant and high government official.

H. R. Trevor-Roper, *Archbishop Laud* (2nd ed., 1962). A careful, objective work.

M. Walzer, *The Revolution of the Saints* (1965). Portrays Puritanism as a by-product of the social dislocation of the era.

D. H. Willson, *King James VI and I* (1956). An outstanding biography.

"ANOTHER PROTESTANT REPUBLIC"

A. M. Everitt, *The Community of Kent and the Great Rebellion, 1640–60* (1966). The revolution in its local context.

C. H. Firth, *Oliver Cromwell and the Rule of the Puritans* (1900). Still regarded as the best scholarly biography of Cromwell.

* W. Haller, *Liberty and Reformation in the Puritan Revolution* (1955). Recounts the development of Puritanism during the 1640's.

V. Pearl, *London and the Outbreak of the Puritan Revolution* (1961). Traces the ambivalent role of London in the opposition to Charles I.

C. V. Wedgewood, *The King's Peace* (1955), *The King's War* (1959), *A Coffin for King Charles* (1964). Successive volumes in a well written but traditional account of the history of the rebellion.

——, *Oliver Cromwell* (1939). A very readable biography.

P. Zagorin, *History of Political Thought in the English Revolution* (1954). A provocative survey.

THE RISE OF THE DUTCH REPUBLIC

* V. Barbour, *Capitalism in Amsterdam in the Seventeenth Century* (1959). A valuable study of the most important business center of the seventeenth century.

P. J. Blok, *History of the People of the Netherlands* (5 vols., 1898–1912). The standard general history. Volume III and the first part of volume IV cover the era from 1559 to 1660.

P. Geyl, *The Netherlands in the Seventeenth Century* (2 vols., 1961–64). A magisterial work by the great Dutch historian. Volume I goes to 1648.

THE FLOWERING OF DUTCH CULTURE

W. Bode, *Great Masters of Dutch and Flemish Painting* (1909). A useful general survey.

J. Rosenberg, *Rembrandt* (2 vols., 1948). The outstanding treatment.

THE PINNACLE OF FRENCH ABSOLUTISM   CHAPTER ELEVEN

"I AM THE STATE"

* M. Ashley, *Louis XIV and the Greatness of France* (1946). An introductory survey.

* W. F. Church, ed., *The Greatness of Louis XIV. Myth or Reality* (1959). Well chosen selection of differing views of Louis XIV.

J. E. King, *Science and Rationalism in the Government of Louis XIV, 1661–1683* (1949). Explains the technique of government as a reflection of Cartesian rationalism.

* W. H. Lewis, *The Splendid Century* (1953). A popular account of aspects of French social life.

H. Martin, *The Age of Louis XIV* (2 vols., 1865). Translated from French, this old work is still of prime importance.

The New Cambridge Modern History, vol. V, *The Ascendancy of France 1648–88* (1961). Useful essays by leading scholars on various aspects of the period.

* F. L. Nussbaum, *The Triumph of Science and Reason, 1660–1685* (1953). A good survey of European history pivoting around Louis XIV's France.

L. Rothkrug, *Opposition to Louis XIV: the Political and Social Origins of the French Enlightenment* (1965). A challenging study of interrelations between mercantilist policies and intellectual life.

F. Steegmuller, *The Grand Mademoiselle* (1956). A delightful biography based on the memoirs of Louis XIV's cousin who lived at the court.

J. B. Wolf, *Louis XIV* (1968). The best biography in English.

ABSOLUTISM IN ECONOMICS AND RELIGION

C. W. Cole, *Colbert and a Century of French Mercantilism* (2 vols., 1939) and *French Mercantilism, 1683–1700* (1943). Scholarly studies crammed with data.

E. Lodge, *Sully, Colbert and Turgot* (1931). A very general comparative treatment, presenting Colbert's mercantilism as a failure.

W. C. Scoville, *The Persecution of the Huguenots and French Economic Development, 1680–1720* (1960). Shows that Louis's anti-Huguenot policies were not responsible for French economic decline.

A. P. Usher, *The History of the Grain Trade in France, 1400–1710* (1913). Valuable chapter on the seventeenth century.

FRENCH PREDOMINANCE

R. B. Mowat, *A History of European Diplomacy, 1451–1789* (1928). A standard work.

* J. B. Wolf, *The Emergence of the Great Powers, 1685–1715* (1951). A valuable synthesis, especially good for the international diplomacy and wars of the era.

THE CULTURAL GLORY OF FRANCE

E. B. O. Borgerhoff, *The Freedom of French Classicism* (1950). An excellent study of seventeenth-century authors.

H. Brown, *Scientific Organizations in Seventeenth Century France* (1934). Shows the relationships between the government and the scientific community.

* A. Guérard, *The Life and Death of an Ideal* (1928). A scintillating analysis of the culture of seventeenth-century France.

J. Lough, *An Introduction to Seventeenth Century France* (1954). Shows the connections between literature and economic, social, and political life.

H. D. MacPherson, *Censorship under Louis XIV* (1929). Efforts at government control of literature.

ABSOLUTISM IN AUSTRIA, SPAIN, AND PRUSSIA CHAPTER TWELVE

For sketches of the history of these countries from 1660 to 1705 see the volumes by Nussbaum and Wolf cited in the reading list for Chapter Eleven. For the years from 1715 to the 1740's see the appropriate sections in the following general works:

M. S. Anderson, *Europe in the Eighteenth Century* (1961). A very good survey of comparative history.

* M. Beloff, *The Age of Absolutism* (1954). A brief, well-handled survey.

The New Cambridge Modern History, vol. VII, *The Old Regime, 1713–1763* (1957).

* P. Roberts, *The Quest for Security, 1715–1740* (1947). An uneven treatment.

THE AUSTRIAN HAPSBURGS

P. Frischauer, *The Imperial Crown* (1939). A history of the Hapsburgs to 1792.

————, *Prince Eugene, 1663–1736* (1934). The only biography in English of the great Austrian statesman and general.

R. A. Kann, *A Study in Austrian Intellectual History from Late Baroque to Romanticism* (1960). A skillful analysis.

L. P. Léger, *History of Austria-Hungary* (1889). Translated from French, this antiquated work is the only general history in English.

C. A. Macartney, *Hungary: A Short History* (1962). The best account in English.

H. F. Schwarz, *The Imperial Privy Council in the Seventeenth Century* (1943). A scholarly study of the chief administrative agency of Hapsburg centralization.

THE SPANISH BOURBONS

R. Altamira, *A History of Spain* (1949). An impressionistic short history, translated from Spanish.

R. Herr, *The Eighteenth Century Revolution in Spain* (1958). An important study of changes in Spanish life and thought under Bourbon rule.

* H. V. Livermore, *A History of Spain* (1958). Informative but uninspired.

HOHENZOLLERN PRUSSIA

W. H. Bruford, *Germany in the Eighteenth Century* (1935). A useful study of German society.

F. L. Carsten, *Princes and Parliaments in Germany from the Fifteenth to the Nineteenth Century* (1959). A study of the increase in princely power at the expense of the nobility and townsmen.

* G. A. Craig, *The Politics of the Prussian Army* (1955). Early chapters of this important book discuss the seventeenth and eighteenth centuries.

R. A. Dorwart, *The Administrative Reforms of Frederick William I of Prussia* (1953). A scholarly, valuable study.

R. R. Ergang, *The Potsdam Führer* (1941). A well done biography of the unpleasant Frederick William I.

S. B. Fay, *The Rise of Brandenburg-Prussia* (1937). A short, readable introduction.

G. P. Gooch, *Frederick the Great* (1947). A critical but still favorable treatment, told in large part through Frederick's own writings.

H. Holborn, *A History of Modern Germany: 1648–1840* (1964). The first section covers the confusing period in German history after 1648.

W. F. Reddaway, *Frederick the Great and the Rise of Prussia* (1904). A well written, favorable biography.

H. Rosenberg, *Bureaucracy, Aristocracy and Autocracy* (1958). A remarkable analysis of the emergence of the Prussian state bureaucracy and its impact on the Prussian social structure.

F. Schevill, *The Great Elector* (1947). A highly favorable and uncritical popular biography.

ABSOLUTISM AND OLIGARCHY IN
THE NORTH AND EAST   CHAPTER THIRTEEN

RUSSIA BECOMES A GREAT POWER

See the appropriate chapters in the books cited in the reading list for Chapter Seven.

G. P. Gooch, *Catherine the Great and Other Studies* (1954). An urbane and fascinating portrait of the empress and her influence.

V. Kliuchevsky, *Peter the Great* (1958). A good translation of a famed pre-Soviet treatment.

J. A. R. Marriott, *Anglo-Russian Relations 1689–1943* (1944). A useful survey.

H. Rogger, *National Consciousness in Eighteenth-Century Russia* (1960). An important monograph showing the development of national feeling as part of Westernization.

* B. H. Sumner, *Peter the Great and the Emergence of Russia* (1951). An excellent brief survey.

————, *Peter the Great and the Ottoman Empire* (1950). The beginnings of Russian imperialism in the Near East.

* G. S. Thomson, *Catherine the Great and the Expansion of Russia* (1950). A well written brief survey.

THE DECLINE AND DISAPPEARANCE OF POLAND

See the appropriate chapters in the books by Halecki cited in the reading list for Chapter Seven.

H. H. Kaplan, *The First Partition of Poland* (1962). A careful study showing the links between Poland's internal troubles and the intrigues of its powerful neighbors.

M. Kridl, *A Survey of Polish Literature and Culture* (1956). The first quarter of the book covers the period up to the end of the eighteenth century.

R. H. Lord, *The Second Partition of Poland* (1915). Long the standard work.

THE OTTOMAN EMPIRE, 1656–1792

See the appropriate chapters in the books cited in the readings for Chapter Seven.

H. A. R. Gibb and H. Bowen, *Islamic Society and the West* (2 vols., 1950–57). A detailed and comprehensive analysis of Ottoman governmental and religious institutions.

J. A. R. Marriott, *The Eastern Question* (4th ed., 1940). A survey of the Ottoman decline and the resulting effects in European international relations.

W. L. Wright, *Ottoman Statecraft: A Book of Counsel for Viziers and Governors* (1935). The long introduction is an excellent analysis of the Ottoman machinery of government.

CONSTITUTIONALISM AND OLIGARCHY IN THE WEST CHAPTER FOURTEEN

THE DUTCH OLIGARCHY, 1660–1766

P. Geyl, *The Netherlands in the Seventeenth Century, 1609–1715* (1961). Essential for an understanding of the era.

D. Ogg, *William III* (1956). An excellent biography.

H. H. Rowen, *The Ambassador Prepares for War: The Dutch Embassy of Arnauld de Pomponne, 1669–1671* (1957). Provides information about the Netherlands in De Witt's last years.

C. H. Wilson, *Profit and Power: A Study of England and the Dutch Wars* (1957) and *Anglo-Dutch Commerce and Finance in the Eighteenth Century* (1941). Important studies of economic aspects of Dutch-English relations.

THE TRIUMPH OF THE ENGLISH OLIGARCHY, 1660–1689

G. Davies, *The Restoration of Charles II, 1658–1660* (1955). A scholarly analysis of the background for the restoration of the English monarchy.

J. Locke, *Two Treatises on Government*, ed. by P. Laslett (1960). The lengthy introductory essay by the editor is of major importance for understanding Locke's political theory.

* C. B. Macpherson, *The Political Theory of Possessive Individualism, Hobbes to Locke* (1962). Brilliant study in political theory, especially Locke.

G. M. Trevelyan, *The English Revolution, 1688–1689* (1939). A defense of the Revolution as the critical turning point in modern English history.

F. C. Turner, *James II* (1948). A good biography.

C. H. Wilson, *England's Apprenticeship, 1603–1763* (1965). Preparation for great power status by a master historian.

THE AUGUSTAN AGE OF THE ENGLISH OLIGARCHY, 1689–1760

J. Carswell, *The Old Cause: Three Biographical Studies in Whiggism* (1954). Masterful studies of Whigs in action.

J. D. Chambers and G. E. Mingay, *The Agricultural Revolution 1750–1880* (1966). A useful survey.

P. G. M. Dickson, *The Financial Revolution in England: A Study in the Development of Public Credit, 1688–1756* (1967). The relationship between finance and politics.

D. Marshall, *English People in the Eighteenth Century* (1956). A study of the social structure of England.

G. E. Mingay, *English Landed Society in the Eighteenth Century* (1963). An excellent study based on recent scholarship.

J. H. Plumb, *Chatham* (1953). A readable and effective brief biography of the elder Pitt.

* ———, *England in the Eighteenth Century* (1951). An outstanding brief account.

———, *The First Four Georges* (1956). A very readable sketch of the first Hanoverian monarchs of Great Britain.

———, *Sir Robert Walpole* (2 vols., 1956–60). The standard work.

G. M. Trevelyan, *England Under Queen Anne* (3 vols., 1930–34). An exhaustive and dated examination of the period.

DUTCH AND BRITISH OLIGARCHY BESET, 1760–1790

C. Cone, *Burke and the Nature of Politics* (2 vols., 1957–64). A useful study.

S. Maccoby, *English Radicalism, 1762–1785* (1955). An exhaustive survey.

L. B. Namier, **The Structure of Politics at the Accession of George III* (2nd ed., 1957), and *England in the Age of the American Revolution* (2nd ed., 1961). Major studies that revise long-held views of English political history of the era.

R. Pares, *King George III and the Politicians* (1953). An outstanding analysis of the operations of politics.

G. Rudé, *Wilkes and Liberty: A Social Study of 1763 to 1774* (1962). Studies the social background of the times and the political movements associated with Wilkes.

J. S. Watson, *The Reign of George III, 1760–1815* (1960). The best general study.

WEALTH, WAR, AND EMPIRE   CHAPTER FIFTEEN

GENERAL SURVEYS

M. S. Anderson, *Europe in the Eighteenth Century* (1961). A very good survey of comparative history.

* W. L. Dorn, *Competition for Empire, 1740–1763* (1940). An extremely able synthesis; Rise of Modern Europe Series.

* L. Gershoy, *From Despotism to Revolution* (1944). Well written and authoritative; Rise of Modern Europe Series.

THE EUROPEAN ECONOMY

G. N. Clark, *The Wealth of England, 1496–1760* (1946). A brief, informative study.

E. Heckscher, *Mercantilism* (rev. ed., 2 vols., 1955). The standard work, recently under attack.

W. Letwin, *The Origins of Scientific Economics: English Economic Thought, 1660–1776* (1963). From merchant economists to political economists.

K. E. Knorr, *British Colonial Theories, 1570–1850* (1944). A clear, useful analysis.

EUROPE OVERSEAS: COLONIES AND COMMERCE

R. G. Albion, *Forests and Sea Power* (1926). A pioneering work showing the importance of naval stores in British colonial policy.

P. Bamford, *Forests and French Sea Power, 1660–1789* (1956). A first-rate study analyzing the rise and decline of French naval power.

C. R. Boxer, *The Dutch Seaborne Empire: 1600–1800* (1965). Definitive account by a leading authority.

The Cambridge History of the British Empire (9 vols., 1929–59). Vol. I of this collaborative work provides a detailed study of the empire in the seventeenth and eighteenth centuries.

* C. E. Carrington, *The British Overseas*, Vol. 1 (2nd ed., 1968). A lively account of British expansion from the seventeenth century to 1870.

K. Feiling, *Warren Hastings* (1954). A valuable account of the work of the first British governor-general of India, showing the confusion and corruption of British rule in the eighteenth century.

H. Furber, *John Company at Work* (1948). An account of the activities of the British East India Company and other companies in the second half of the eighteenth century.

* C. H. Haring, *The Spanish Empire in America* (1947). The best modern work on Spanish colonialism.

J. J. van Klaveren, *The Dutch Colonial System in the East Indies* (1953). A survey from the early seventeenth century to 1939.

* S. E. Morison, ed., *The Parkman Reader* (1955). Well chosen selections from the famed nineteenth-century multi-volume *France and England in North America*.

H. I. Priestley, *France Overseas through the Old Regime* (1939). Covers the history of the French Empire up to 1815.

* C. G. Robertson, *Chatham and the British Empire* (1948). An excellent brief survey of the work of the elder Pitt in building the empire.

* F. Tannenbaum, *Slave and Citizen: the Negro in the Americas* (1940). Maintains that the Spaniards were more considerate of their Negro slaves than were the English in North America.

DYNASTIC AND IMPERIAL STATECRAFT, 1700–1763

A. H. Buffington, *The Second Hundred Years' War, 1689–1815* (1929). A brief survey of French-British relations.

R. B. Mowat, *A History of European Diplomacy, 1451–1789* (1928). A useful survey.

* A. Sorel, *Europe under the Old Regime* (1947). Translation of a famed French study of the balance of power in the eighteenth century.

THE AMERICAN REVOLUTION, 1763–1783

* J. R. Alden, *The American Revolution* (1954). An excellent presentation.
* S. F. Bemis, *The Diplomacy of the American Revolution* (1935). A detailed and precise study.
* C. Bridenbaugh, *Cities in Revolt* (1955). Outstanding treatment of the urban dimension.
* O. M. Dickerson, *The Navigation Acts and the American Revolution* (1951). Questions the old view of the harmful effect of the Navigation Acts on colonial America.
* B. Knollenberg, *Origins of the American Revolution, 1759–1766* (1960). Emphasizes early tensions as a cause of the Revolution.
M. Kraus, *The Atlantic Civilization* (1949). Demonstrates the influence of European colonies in America upon European thought and political life.
* D. Lacy, *The Meaning of the American Revolution* (1964). Good narrative synthesis.
* E. S. Morgan, *The Birth of the Republic* (1956). A masterful, brief survey that incorporates new interpretations.
* E. Wright, *Causes and Consequences of the American Revolution* (1966). A broad range of representative articles by scholars.

SCIENCE: THE SEARCH FOR ORDER   CHAPTER SIXTEEN

THE SCIENTIFIC COMMUNITY OF INTELLECT

H. Brown, *Scientific Organization in Seventeenth Century France* (1934). Shows the relationships between the government and the scientific community.
* M. Nicolson, *Science and the Imagination* (1956). A study of the impact of the new science on literature.
M. Ornstein, *The Role of Scientific Societies in the Seventeenth Century* (3rd ed., 1938). The best and most thorough study.
M. Purver, *The Royal Society: Concept and Creation* (1967). Traces the origins of the Royal Society.
D. Stimson, *Scientists and Amateurs* (1948). A well written history of the Royal Society, emphasizing the seventeenth century.
* B. Willey, *The Seventeenth Century Background* (1934). Indicates the influence of the scientific revolution on writers and philosophers.

THE PHYSICAL WORLD

For general treatments see the works by Butterfield, Gillispie, and Wolf cited in the readings for Chapter Eight.

* E. N. daC. Andrade, *Sir Isaac Newton* (1950). The best brief biography.
A. E. Bell, *Christian Huygens and the Development of Science in the Seventeenth Century* (1947). A study of the Dutch scientist and his times.
M. Boas, *Robert Boyle and Seventeenth Century Chemistry* (1958). An important re-evaluation of Boyle's contribution.
A. R. Hall, *Galileo to Newton* (1963). A useful survey.

———, *The Scientific Revolution* (2nd ed., 1962). A closely reasoned analysis of scientific advance in the seventeenth and eighteenth centuries.

G. Holton and D. H. D. Roller, *Foundations of Modern Physical Science* (1958). An unusual textbook that combines physics and history, written by a physicist and a historian of science.

THE PSYCHIC WORLD

R. I. Aaron, *John Locke* (2nd ed., 1955). A biography and detailed analysis of Locke's political theory, moral philosophy, and teachings on education and religion.

* J. Bronowski and B. Mazlish, *The Western Intellectual Tradition* (1960). A stimulating survey; Part II covers the period of this chapter.

M. Cranston, *John Locke* (1957). An excellent biography.

THE WORLD OF FAITH

F. L. Baumer, *Religion and the Rise of Scepticism* (1960). The development of scepticism from the seventeenth century to the present.

M. Bishop, *Pascal, the Life of Genius* (1936). A beautifully written scholarly biography.

* S. Hampshire, *Spinoza* (1951). A first-rate introduction.

* P. Hazard, *The European Mind: the Critical Years, 1680–1715* (1935). A famous work, showing the conflict between Christian dogma and science and rationalism.

R. S. Westfall, *Science and Religion in 17th Century England* (1958). A study of interaction of science and religion as shown in the writings of the scientists.

THE SOCIAL WORLD

E. Beller and M. duP. Lee, Jr., *Selections from Bayle's Dictionary* (1952). Has a useful introduction.

M. A. Fitzsimons, A. G. Pundt, C. E. Nowell, eds., *The Development of Historiography* (1954). An encyclopedic survey of the development of historical writing.

R. F. Jones, *Ancients and Moderns* (1936). Treats the debates on the effect of increased scientific knowledge on human intellectual progress.

H. Robinson, *Bayle the Sceptic* (1931). The best work in English.

E. Roll, *A History of Economic Thought* (rev. ed., 1946). Contains a useful section on the early economists.

* P. Smith, *History of Modern Culture* (2 vols., 1930–34). A storehouse of information.

THE ENLIGHTENMENT CHAPTER SEVENTEEN

THE PHILOSOPHES

* C. Becker, *The Heavenly City of the Eighteenth Century Philosophers* (1932). Argues that the Age of Reason was really an age of faith.

D. D. Bien, *The Calas Affair* (1960). A well written and perceptive study of this famed episode in the history of toleration.

* H. N. Brailsford, *Voltaire* (1935). The best short biography in English.
* E. Cassirer, *The Philosophy of the Enlightenment* (1951). A major study of the basic philosophical ideas of the eighteenth century.
A. Cobban, *In Search of Humanity* (1960). A stimulating reassessment of the Enlightenment in relation to the present.
G. R. Cragg, *Reason and Authority in the Eighteenth Century* (1964). An excellent study of the Enlightenment in England.
P. Gay, *The Enlightenment: An Interpretation* (1966). A major work dealing with the intellectual origins of the Enlightenment.
* G. R. Havens, *The Age of Ideas: From Reaction to Revolution in Eighteenth-Century France* (1955). Uses the biographical approach to explain the ideas of the Enlightenment.
* P. Hazard, *European Thought in the Eighteenth Century* (1954). A treatment of the conflict between Christian doctrine and the Enlightenment.
* F. E. Manuel, *The Age of Reason* (1951). A very good introductory survey.
* K. Martin, *French Liberal Thought in the Eighteenth Century* (rev. ed., 1954). A study of political ideas from Bayle to Condorcet.
R. O. Rockwood, ed., *Carl Becker's Heavenly City Revisited* (1958). A symposium of differing views on Becker's thesis about the Age of Reason.
R. V. Sampson, *Progress in the Age of Reason* (1956). A treatment of the philosophies of history of the Enlightenment.
H. Vyverberg, *Historical Pessimism in the French Enlightenment* (1958). Argues that there was an undercurrent of pessimism in eighteenth-century thought hostile to the belief in progress.

THE ENCYCLOPEDISTS AND THE PROGRESS OF SCIENCE

A. and N. Clow, *The Chemical Revolution* (1952). A study of the chemical trade in eighteenth-century Scotland.
I. B. Cohen, *Franklin and Newton* (1956). An authoritative study of Franklin's work in electricity.
H. Guerlac, *Lavoisier, the Crucial Year* (1961). Explains the background and origin of Lavoisier's experiments in combustion in 1772.
* A. R. Hall, *The Scientific Revolution* (2nd ed., 1962). See the chapters on the eighteenth century.
A. Wilson, *Diderot, the Testing Years, 1713–1759* (1957). First of a planned two-volume biography.
A. Wolf, *A History of Science, Technology and Philosophy in the Eighteenth Century* (1939). A useful work of reference.

THE COUNTER-ENLIGHTENMENT

* E. Cassirer, *The Question of Jean Jacques Rousseau* (1954). An effort to show the essential unity of Rousseau's thought.
K. Epstein, *The Genesis of German Conservatism* (1966). The intellectual response in Germany to the challenge of the Enlightenment.
C. W. Hendel, *Jean Jacques Rousseau* (2nd ed., 1934). Traces the development of Rousseau's philosophy.
A. D. Lindsay, *Kant* (1934). A good introduction to Kant's philosophy.
N. K. Smith, *The Philosophy of David Hume* (1941). A useful study.

J. L. Talmon, *The Rise of Totalitarian Democracy* (1952). Finds the origins of modern totalitarianism in Rousseau's political thought.

THE CRISIS OF ABSOLUTISM CHAPTER EIGHTEEN

ENLIGHTENED DESPOTISM

For general surveys see the books by Dorn, Gershoy, and Anderson listed in the suggested readings for Chapter Fifteen. ˗

G. P. Gooch, *Maria Theresa and Other Studies* (1951). Ably shows the qualities of character and judgment of the Empress.

R. Herr, *The Eighteenth Century in Spain* (1958). Excellent for enlightened despotism in Spain.

F. Hertz, *The Development of the German Public Mind*, vol. II (1962). An important study, especially valuable for Frederick II and his political ideas.

R. J. Kerner, *Bohemia in the Eighteenth Century* (1932). Deals chiefly with the reigns of Joseph II and Leopold II.

The New Cambridge Modern History, vol. VII, *The Old Regime, 1713–1763* (1957). Contains useful chapters on all aspects of this period.

S. K. Padover, *The Revolutionary Emperor: Joseph the Second, 1741–1790* (1934). A useful biography, although uncritical at times.

W. E. Wright, *Serf, Seigneur, and Sovereign* (1966). A valuable study of agrarian problems and reforms in eighteenth-century Bohemia.

LOUIS XV AND FLEURY

* A. Cobban, *A History of Modern France* (2 vols., 1960). Vol. I covers the eighteenth century. Brilliant narrative and analysis.

P. Gaxotte, *Louis XV and his Times* (1934). A defense of the king.

G. P. Gooch, *Louis XV; the Monarchy in Decline* (1956). A condemnation of Louis' political ineptitude.

E. J. Lowell, *France under Louis XV* (2 vols., 1897). An old but still useful general treatment.

THE FAILURE TO RENOVATE FRANCE

M. Beer, *An Inquiry into Physiocracy* (1939). A very competent brief survey.

* C. B. A. Behrens, *The Ancien Regime* (1967). The best recent brief treatment.

P. Beik, *A Judgment of the Old Regime* (1944). A survey of economic and fiscal policies at the end of the Seven Years' War.

A. Bourde, *The Influence of England on the French Agronomes, 1750–1789* (1953). A Study of French agricultural developments.

G. T. Mathews, *The Royal General Farms in Eighteenth Century France* (1958). A careful study of the institution of tax farming.

W. Scoville, *Capitalism and French Glassmaking 1640–1789* (1950). An exemplary monograph, showing the transition to large-scale manufacturing.

FRANCE ON THE EVE OF REVOLUTION

E. Barber, *The Bourgeoisie in Eighteenth Century France* (1955). A study of the ideals and motivations of the middle classes.

D. Dakin, *Turgot and the Ancien Régime in France* (1939). Offers good description and analysis of the system of government.

F. L. Ford, *The Robe and the Sword* (1953). An analysis of the aristocratic resurgence.

R. Forster, *The Nobility of Toulouse in the Eighteenth Century* (1960). An excellent study of the economic and social activity of the nobility.

* G. Lefebvre, *The Coming of the French Revolution* (1947). A translation of the best survey of the social and economic history of the Old Regime.

* A. de Tocqueville, *The Old Regime and the French Revolution* (1955). A classic.

A. Young, *Travels in France during the Years 1787, 1788, 1789* (1929). An invaluable contemporary account by an observant Englishman.

THE FRENCH REVOLUTION   CHAPTER NINETEEN

GENERAL ACCOUNTS

* C. C. Brinton, *The Anatomy of Revolution* (1938). A comparative study of revolutions with emphasis on the French Revolution.

* ————, *A Decade of Revolution, 1789–1799* (1934). A well written survey, somewhat critical of the Revolution.

P. Farmer, *France Reviews its Revolutionary Origins* (1944). A survey of the changes in the interpretations of the Revolution.

N. Hampson, *A Social History of the French Revolution* (1963). A perceptive analysis of the interaction between social structure and political action.

G. Lefebvre, *The French Revolution* (2 vols., 1963–64). The best account, by a great French scholar.

THE COMING OF THE REVOLUTION AND
THE CONSTITUTIONAL MONARCHY, 1788–1792

R. M. Brace, *Bordeaux and the Gironde, 1789–1794* (1947). A study of middle-class involvement in the revolutionary movement.

C. C. Brinton, *The Jacobins* (1930). Portrays Jacobinism as a kind of religious movement.

R. K. Gooch, *Parliamentary Government in France: Revolutionary Origins, 1789–1791* (1960). A study of the abortive attempt to introduce parliamentary government.

* G. Lefebvre, *The Coming of the French Revolution* (1947). The best brief account of the background of the revolution through October, 1789.

* A. Mathiez, *The French Revolution* (1928). A strong defense of the revolution by a famous authority.

R. W. Phipps, *The Armies of the First French Republic and the Rise of the Marshals of Napoleon* (5 vols., 1926–39). An exhaustive account.

C. B. Rogers, *The Spirit of Revolution in 1789* (1949). Shows the unrest among the masses.

* G. Rudé, *The Crowd in the French Revolution* (1959). An examination of the composition and motives of the revolutionary mobs.

M. J. Sydenham, *The Girondins* (1961). A revisionist study that claims that there was no real difference between the policies of the Girondins and the Montagnards.

THE REPUBLIC OF VIRTUE, 1792–1794

* J. D. Godfrey, *Revolutionary Justice* (1951). Deals with the organization and procedures of the revolutionary tribunals.

D. Greer, *The Incidence of the Terror: A Statistical Interpretation* (1935) and *The Incidence of Emigration during the French Revolution* (1951). These studies show that members of all classes, not just nobles, suffered from the excesses of the Revolution.

W. F. Shepherd, *Price Control and the Reign of Terror* (1953). A careful, detailed monograph.

A. Soboul, *The Parisian Sans-Culottes and the French Revolution 1793–1794* (1964). An important study.

J. M. Thompson, *Robespierre* (2 vols., 1935). The best biography.

* ———, *Robespierre and the French Revolution* (1953). An excellent brief survey.

REACTION AND IRRESOLUTION, 1794–1799

J. C. Herold, *Bonaparte in Egypt* (1963). An exciting account, treated in depth.

G. Lefebvre, *The Thermidoreans and the Directory* (1964). A balanced treatment.

* A. Mathiez, *After Robespierre; the Thermidorean Reaction* (1931). An important study, especially valuable for the account of political retaliations.

B. Morton, *Brumaire, the Rise of Bonaparte* (1948). A well done, popular account.

D. Thomson, *The Babeuf Plot: The Making of a Republican Legend* (1947). A careful study of the leftist group.

THE IMPACT OF THE FRENCH REVOLUTION

* P. Amann, ed., *The Eighteenth-Century Revolution, French or Western?* (1963). Selections from writings reappraising the French Revolution as part of a Western revolution.

G. P. Gooch, *Germany and the French Revolution* (1920). A standard work.

R. R. Palmer, *The Age of the Democratic Revolution* (2 vols., 1959–64). Views the French Revolution as part of a revolution of the Western world.

E. Wangerman, *From Joseph II to the Jacobin Trials* (1959). Studies the impact of the French Revolution in Austria up to 1794.

THE NAPOLEONIC ERA CHAPTER TWENTY

NAPOLEON BONAPARTE

* G. Bruun, *Europe and the French Imperium 1799–1814* (rev. ed., 1957). The best one-volume survey, with an excellent bibliographical essay.

G. Lefebvre, *Napoleon* (2 vols., 1969). Translation of a justly renowned French work.

* F. Markham, *Napoleon and the Awakening of Europe* (1954). The best brief survey.

————, *Napoleon* (1964). An excellent brief biography.

F. Pratt, *The Road to Power* (1939) and *The Empire and the Glory: Napoleon Bonaparte, 1800–1806* (1949). Popular accounts by an outstanding American military historian.

J. H. Rose, *Life of Napoleon I* (2 vols., 1902). A detailed study.

S. Wilkinson, *Rise of General Bonaparte* (1930). An able discussion of Napoleon's military training and early career.

DOMESTIC REFORMER

J. B. Brissaud, *History of French Private Law* (1912) and *History of French Public Law* (1915). For detailed discussion of Napoleon's legal reforms.

R. B. Holtman, *Napoleonic Propaganda* (1950). A study of methods of "thought-control."

B. C. Poland, *French Protestantism and the French Revolution, 1685–1815* (1957). A useful study.

H. H. Walsh, *The Concordat of 1801* (1933). A study of Napoleon's agreement with the pope.

EMPIRE BUILDER

E. N. Anderson, *Nationalism and the Cultural Crisis in Prussia, 1806–1815* (1939). The growth of the idea of nationalism based on a study of seven leading figures.

* C. C. Brinton, *The Lives of Talleyrand* (1936). A very readable biography of Napoleon's foreign minister.

A. Bryant, *The Years of Endurance, 1793–1802* (1942); *The Years of Victory, 1802–1812* (1944); *The Age of Elegance, 1812–1822* (1950). Studies of Great Britain during the Revolutionary and Napoleonic eras.

H. C. Deutsch, *The Genesis of Napoleonic Imperialism* (1938). A valuable study up to 1805.

E. F. Kraehe, *Metternich's German Policy*, vol. I, *The Contest with Napoleon* (1963). A work of prime importance.

P. Paret, *Yorck and the Era of Prussian Reform, 1807–1815* (1966). An able analysis of military innovations and social change.

C. N. Parkinson, *The Trade Winds. A Study of British Overseas Trade during the French Wars, 1793–1815* (1948). A study in fluctuations and changing patterns in commerce.

R. J. Rath, *The Fall of the Napoleonic Kingdom of Italy* (1941). A superior study of the forces leading to the collapse of the Napoleonic Italian state.

W. O. Shanahan, *Prussian Military Reforms, 1786–1813* (1945). A careful and detailed study.

W. M. Simon, *The Failure of the Prussian Reform Movement, 1807–1819* (1955). A superior analysis of the obstacles to reform and the triumph of Prussian authoritarianism.

E. Tarlé, *Napoleon's Invasion of Russia, 1812* (1942). Written by a Soviet historian.

THE NAPOLEONIC LEGACY

* P. Geyl, *Napoleon: For and Against* (1949). A fascinating analysis of the changes in judgments of Napoleon since 1815.

A. L. Guérard, *Reflections on the Napoleonic Legend* (1923). A detached judgment of Napoleon and a study of the genesis and growth of his legend.

R. Korngold, *The Last Years of Napoleon* (1950). A sympathetic account.

ROMANTICISM AND REACTION   CHAPTER TWENTY-ONE

THE VIENNA SETTLEMENT AND THE CONCERT OF EUROPE

* F. B. Artz, *Reaction and Revolution, 1814–1832* (1934, 1950). A broad general survey of all aspects of the period; Rise of Modern Europe Series.

C. J. Bartlett, *Castlereagh* (1967). A biography of the man as well as a study of his policies.

* G. Ferrero, *The Reconstruction of Europe: Talleyrand and the Congress of Vienna, 1814–1815* (1941). An authoritative work by an Italian scholar.

H. A. Kissinger, *A World Restored: Metternich, Castlereagh and the Problems of Peace, 1812–1822* (1957). A study by a political scientist.

A. A. Lobanov-Rostovsky, *Russia and Europe, 1789–1825* (1947). Contains an account of Alexander I and his relations with the western powers.

G. de Bertier de Sauvigny, *France and the European Alliance, 1816–1821* (1958). A masterly study of the reintegration of France in the Concert of Europe.

* L. C. B. Seaman, *From Vienna to Versailles* (1955). A lively diplomatic history especially useful for the Congress system and its sequels.

C. K. Webster, *The Congress of Vienna, 1814–1815* (1934, 1963). A brief, classic treatment by one- of the wisest of modern historians. Originally written as background material for the plenipotentiaries at the Peace of Paris, 1919.

ROMANTICISM IN LITERATURE AND THE ARTS

* J. Barzun, *Berlioz and the Romantic Century* (2 vols., 1950). A detailed account of the most representative composer of the romantic period.

———, *Romanticism and the Modern Ego* (1943). Assesses the significance of romanticism for our own times.

* M. Berger, ed., *Madame de Staël on Politics, Literature and National Character* (1964). Selected writings of one of the central figures of the romantic movement.

K. Clark, *The Gothic Revival* (2nd ed., 1950). Shows the Neo-Gothic influence in England.

A. Einstein, *Music in the Romantic Era* (1947). A general survey by one of the leading historians of music.

J. C. Herold, *Mistress to an Age* (1958). A readable, fascinating biography of Madame de Staël.

T. H. von Laue, *Leopold Ranke, the Formative Years* (1950). A critique of the founder of "scientific" history.

* E. Newton, *Romantic Rebellion* (1962). A fresh treatment of romantic art.

ROMANTICISM IN PHILOSOPHY, POLITICS, AND RELIGION

C. C. Brinton, *English Political Thought in the Nineteenth Century* (2nd ed., 1949). Supersedes his earlier *Political Ideas of the English Romanticists* (1926).

* G. W. F. Hegel (R. S. Hartman, ed. and transl.), *Reason in History. A General Introduction to the Philosophy of History* (1962). Selections from the pen of the German idealist philosopher.

H. Kohn, *The Mind of Germany* (1960). An intellectual history of modern Germany concentrating on the romantic, liberal, and nationalist tendencies.

H. Marcuse, *Reason and Revolution: Hegel and the Rise of Social Theory* (1954). A study in the relationships of ideas and politics by an influential modern philosopher.

C. S. Phillips, *The Church in France, 1789–1848* (1929). A sympathetic account of the revival of the power of the Catholic Church.

H. S. Reiss, *The Political Thought of the German Romantics* (1955).

R. Soltau, *French Political Thought of the Nineteenth Century* (1931). Contains chapters on the writers of the romantic era.

J. L. Talmon, *Political Messianism: The Romantic Phase* (1960). A provocative interpretation of the origins of modern totalitarian movements.

P. Viereck, *Conservatism Revisited: the Revolt against Revolt, 1815–1949* (1949). Contains a sympathetic account of Metternich and his conservative contemporaries.

E. L. Woodward, *Three Studies in European Conservatism* (1929). An incisive analysis of Metternich, Guizot, and the Catholic Church.

RESTORATION POLITICS

A. Cecil, *Metternich, 1773–1859: A Study of His Period and Personality* (3rd ed., 1947). By a leading British biographer.

* E. Halevy, *England in 1815* (2nd ed., 1949). Vol. I of the celebrated French author's *History of the English People in the Nineteenth Century*.

N. E. Hudson, *Ultra-royalism and the French Restoration* (1936). A detailed study of French conservatism.

* A. J. May, *The Age of Metternich, 1814–1848* (1933). A useful brief introduction.

* L. Namier, *Vanished Supremacies* (1958). Selected essays on Talleyrand, Metternich, and related subjects by one of the most distinguished modern historians.

M. Raeff, *Michael Speransky, Statesman of Imperial Russia, 1772–1839* (1957). Biography of one of the chief ministers of Alexander I and Nicholas I.

D. Read, *Peterloo: The Massacre and Its Background* (1958).

W. Simon, *The Future of the Prussian Reform Movement, 1807–1819* (1955). Details the resurgence of conservatism.

L. I. Strankhovsky, *Alexander I of Russia* (1947).

R. J. White, *Waterloo to Peterloo* (1957).

THE RISING TIDE OF REVOLUTION CHAPTER TWENTY-TWO

REVOLUTIONARY CURRENTS: LIBERALISM AND NATIONALISM

G. Barany, *Stephen Szécheny and the Awakening of Hungarian Nationalism, 1791–1841* (1968). Outstanding study of Hungary's political, social, and economic evolution in the early nineteenth century.

* L. T. Hobhouse, *Liberalism* (1911). An early classic on English liberalism.

* H. Kohn, *The Idea of Nationalism: A Study in its Origins and Background* (1944). Traces the early development of nationalism. See also his *Mind of Germany* (1960).

L. Krieger, *The German Idea of Freedom* (1957). Discusses the dilemma of German intellectuals concerning liberalism and nationalism.

H. J. Laski, *The Rise of Liberalism* (1936, 1948). A provocative interpretation by a distinguished British socialist.

K. R. Minogue, *Nationalism* (1967). A stimulating brief treatment of nationalism as a political ideology.

* G. de Ruggiero, *The History of European Liberalism* (1927). A standard account by an Italian liberal.

* B. C. Shafer, *Nationalism: Myth and Reality* (1955). A clear, modern statement.

REVOLUTION AND SELF-GOVERNMENT
IN THE AMERICAS

J. B. Brebner, *North Atlantic Triangle* (1945). A charmingly written account of the relationships of the United States, Canada, and Great Britain.

J. L. Morison, *British Supremacy and Canadian Self-government, 1839–54* (1919). Old but valuable.

* D. Perkins, *Hands Off! A History of the Monroe Doctrine* (rev. ed., 1963). The authoritative work on its subject.

F. Thistlethwaite, *The Anglo-American Connection in the Early Nineteenth Century* (1959). Also appears as * *America and the Atlantic Community, 1790–1850*. Lucid, elegant interpretation.

* A. de Tocqueville, *Democracy in America* (1835). There are numerous editions of this classic.

J. B. Trend, *Bolivar and the Independence of Spanish America* (1948). A good introduction.

F. J. Turner, *The United States, 1830–1850* (1935). By the author of *The Frontier in American History* (1920).

C. K. Webster, *Britain and the Independence of Latin America, 1812–1830* (1944). A standard work.

A. P. Whittaker, *The United States and the Independence of Latin America* (1941). An authoritative study.

ROMANTIC REVOLUTION, 1820–1829

R. Carr. *Spain, 1808–1939* (1966). The most recent general history; the early chapters deal with Ferdinand VII and the revolution.

G. T. Romani, *The Neopolitan Revolution of 1820–1821* (1950).

R. H. Thomas, *Liberalism, Nationalism and the German Intellectuals, 1822–1847* (1952).

C. M. Woodhouse, *The Greek War of Independence* (1952). A short but well-written account.

M. Zetlin, *The Decembrists* (1958). The most recent study of the "first Russian revolution."

LIBERAL REVOLUTION, 1830–1834

G. L. Dickinson, *Revolution and Reaction in Modern France* (1892, 1927). A pioneering work, still worth reading. Covers the period from 1789 to 1871.

E. E. Y. Hales, *Mazzini and the Secret Societies* (1956). A sympathetic, facinating account of the dean of Italian revolutionaries.

* E. J. Hobsbawm, *The Age of Revolution: Europe, 1789–1848* (1962). A general survey from the viewpoint of a western Marxist, with chapters on the revolutions of 1830.

E. Holt, *The Carlist Wars in Spain* (1967). Well-written popular account.

R. F. Leslie, *Polish Politics and the Revolution of November 1830* (1956).

H. van der Linden, *Belgium: The Making of a Nation* (1920).

J. Plamenatz, *The Revolutionary Movement in France, 1815–1871* (1952). To be compared with Dickinson.

PARLIAMENTARY REFORM IN GREAT BRITAIN

B. Blackburn, *Noble Lord: The Seventh Earl of Shaftesbury* (1949). A biographical study of an aristocratic reformer.

A. Briggs, *The Age of Improvement* (1959). An interesting, well-rounded modern view of English life and society in the first half of the nineteenth century, with good treatment of the Great Reform.

G. D. H. Cole, *The Life of William Cobbett* (1924). A readable biography of one of the most colorful figures of the age.

N. Gash, *Politics in the Age of Peel* (1953). A detailed study of the techniques of parliamentary representation.

* E. Halevy, *The Triumph of Reform, 1830–1841* (2nd ed., 1950).

G. M. Trevelyan, *Lord Grey of the Reform Bill* (2nd ed., 1929). Standard work by a master of British history.

G. Wallas, *The Life of Francis Place, 1771–1854* (new ed., 1925). The standard biography of the leader of the London Workingmen's Association.

THE REVOLUTION IN ECONOMIC LIFE CHAPTER TWENTY-THREE

THE RISE OF MODERN INDUSTRY

* T. S. Ashton, *The Industrial Revolution, 1760–1830* (1948, 1962). A brief, balanced, lucid introduction by a leading authority. Excellent bibliography of specialized studies.

J. H. Clapham, *An Economic History of Modern Britain*, vol. I [1820–1850] (2nd ed., 1930). Compendious; the standard reference.

* P. Deane, *The First Industrial Revolution* (1965). A survey based on the most recent scholarly studies.

P. Deane and W. A. Cole, *British Economic Growth, 1688–1950* (1962). Recent and authoritative; analytical rather than narrative.

* R. M. Hartwell, *The Causes of the Industrial Revolution in England* (1967). An informed selection of recent scholarly articles. Debates in Economic History Series.

* E. L. Jones, *Agriculture and Economic Growth in England, 1650–1815* (1967). Companion to the previous volume.

* E. E. Lampard, *Industrial Revolution: Interpretations and Perspectives* (1957). An exceedingly brief but highly illuminating survey. AHA Service Center Series.

* P. Mantoux, *The Industrial Revolution in the Eighteenth Century* (1906, 1937). The pioneering work in the field, embodying prodigious research and great erudition. Still basic to a sound understanding of the phenomenon.

* W. W. Rostow, *The Stages of Economic Growth* (1961). A stimulating but controversial interpretation of the process of economic growth.

A. P. Usher, *A History of Mechanical Inventions* (1929, 1954). Unsurpassed for profundity of scholarship and insight.

EARLY INDUSTRIALISM IN EUROPE AND AMERICA

R. Cameron, *France and the Economic Development of Europe, 1800–1914* (1961, abridged ed., *1966). The migration of French capital, entrepreneurs, and engineers; also legal and institutional influences.

* J. H. Clapham, *The Economic Development of France and Germany, 1815–1914* (1920, 1936). A standard survey, but badly out of date.

A. L. Dunham, *The Industrial Revolution in France, 1815–1848* (1955). A detailed, slightly old-fashioned treatment.

* C. M. Green, *Eli Whitney and the Birth of American Technology* (1956). A solid account of the origins of American industrial supremacy.

H. J. Habakkuk, *American and British Technology in the 19th Century* (1962). A scholarly attempt to explain the causes of American industrial supremacy.

W. O. Henderson, *Britain and Industrial Europe, 1750–1870* (1954). The migration of British entrepreneurs and technicians.

D. C. North, *The Economic Growth of the United States, 1790–1860* (1961). Presents a stimulating, controversial thesis on the causes of American growth.

SOCIAL ASPECTS OF EARLY INDUSTRIALISM

D. Bythell, *The Handloom Weavers* (1969). An authoritative study of the most publicized "victims" of the Industrial Revolution.

F. Engels, *The Condition of the Working Classes in England in 1844* (1st German ed., 1845). A Marxist classic.

J. L. and B. Hammond, *The Rise of Modern Industry* (1925, 1939). A general account of the industrial revolution, with emphasis on its alleged ill effects. Compare von Hayek.

* F. A. von Hayek, ed., *Capitalism and the Historians* (1954). A spirited attack on the alleged "left wing bias" of historians dealing with the industrial revolution.

N. J. Smelser, *Social Change in the Industrial Revolution* (1960). By a sociologist.

E. P. Thompson, *The Making of the English Working Class* (1964). A detailed study by a leftist of the emergence of the English proletariat between 1790 and 1830.

A. F. Weber, *The Growth of Cities in the Nineteenth Century* (1899, 1964). A classic.

ECONOMIC LIBERALISM, LAISSEZ-FAIRE, AND FREE TRADE

D. G. Barnes, *A History of the English Corn Laws* (1930). Still the standard work.

* H. Girvetz, *From Wealth to Welfare: The Evolution of Liberalism* (1963). Points out the changing meaning of the concept of liberalism in the twentieth century.

W. D. Grampp, *The Manchester School of Economics* (1960). A concise, scholarly account.

F. A. Haight, *A History of French Commercial Policies* (1941). Good chapters on the nineteenth century.

* R. Heilbroner, *The Worldly Philosophers* (1952). A readable, popular, and sound review of the ideas of the great economists.

W. O. Henderson, *The Zollverein* (1939, 1959). The standard account in English.

F. List, *The National System of Political Economy* (1844). An influential book in both Europe and America.

* C. Woodham-Smith, *The Great Hunger: Ireland, 1845–1849* (1962). A vivid, well-written history of the Irish famine.

REVOLUTION AT FLOODTIDE   CHAPTER TWENTY-FOUR

CONTRASTING LIBERALISMS IN THE WEST

Louis Blanc, *The History of Ten Years, 1830–1840* (2 vols., 1844–45).

* J. F. C. Harrison, ed., *Society and Politics in England, 1780–1960* (1965). A selection of significant contemporary source materials with editorial comments.

* E. Halevy, *The Growth of Philosophic Radicalism* (rev. ed., 1949). A brilliant analysis of the doctrines of radical reform in England.

D. Johnson, *Guizot: Aspects of French History 1787–1874* (1963). A fresh evaluation of one of the major figures of the July Monarchy.

S. Mellon, *The Political Uses of History* (1958). An analysis of Guizot, Thiers, and other historians of the French Restoration period.

E. L. Woodward, *The Age of Reform, 1815–1870* (1938). Oxford History of England.

G. Wright, *France in Modern Times* (1960). Brilliant chapters on the July Monarchy and the revolution.

THE GROWTH OF SOCIAL PROTEST

* E. H. Carr, *Studies in Revolution* (1950). Essays on Socialist theorists and activists.

G. D. H. Cole, *Socialist Thought: The Forerunners, 1789–1850* (1953). Engagingly written by a master of the subject.

J. F. C. Harrison, *The Quest for a New Moral World* (1969). Robert Owen and the Owenites in Europe and America.

M. Hovell, *The Chartist Movement* (1918, 1925). An old but reliable account.

G. G. Iggers, *The Cult of Authority* (1958). A critical view of the Saint-Simonians.

F. E. Manuel, *The New World of Henri Saint-Simon* (1956). A sympathetic yet critical analysis.

* K. Marx and F. Engels, *The Communist Manifesto* (numerous eds.). Should be read by all educated persons.

R. Owen, *The Life of Robert Owen, by Himself* (1858). A delightful and informative if somewhat partisan autobiography.

E. Wilson, *To the Finland Station* (1953). An interesting study of socialism, utopianism, and Marxism by a master stylist.

THE REVOLUTION OF 1848 IN FRANCE

F. Fejto, ed., *The Opening of an Era: 1848* (1948). A reassessment of the revolutions on the occasion of their centenary.

A. de Lamartine, *History of the French Revolution of 1848* (transl., 1891). By a participant.

D. C. McKay, *The National Workshops* (1933). A well told story of an ill-fated experiment.

R. Postgate, *Story of a Year: 1848* (1955). A somewhat lighthearted view of the revolutions as seen from England.

* P. Robertson, *The Revolutions of 1848* (1952). An entertaining and scholarly comparative study of all the revolutionary movements of 1848.

F. A. Simpson, *The Rise of Louis Napoleon* (3rd ed., 1950). Traces the career of the future emperor from youth through the Second Republic.

OTHER REVOLUTIONARY MOVEMENTS

J. Blum, *Noble Landowners and Agriculture in Austria, 1815–1848* (1948). The background of the Austrian peasant emancipation.

T. S. Hamerow, *Restoration, Revolution, Reaction: Economics and Politics in Germany, 1815–1871* (1958). Centers on the revolutionary years.

B. King, *A History of Italian Unity* (2 vols., 1923). A standard work. Vol. I carries the story through 1849.

* Sir L. B. Namier, *1848: The Revolution of the Intellectuals* (1946). An attack upon German liberals, especially those in the Frankfurt Assembly.

R. Olden, *The History of Liberty in Germany* (1946). Covers the entire period 1807 to 1933.

R. J. Rath, *The Viennese Revolution of 1848* (1957). An able study.

C. Sproxton, *Palmerston and the Hungarian Revolution* (1919). A detailed, older study of England's foreign policy.

A. J. P. Taylor, *The Italian Problem in European Diplomacy* (1934).

THE REALIST REACTION   CHAPTER TWENTY-FIVE

EBB TIDE OF REVOLUTION, 1848–1851

* R. C. Binkley, *Realism and Nationalism 1852–1871* (1935). A good general account of all aspects of the period; Rise of Modern Europe Series.

* K. Marx, *The Eighteenth Brumaire of Louis Napoleon* (several eds.). Marx on the coup d'état of 1851.
A. Schwarzenberg, *Prince Felix zu Schwarzenberg, Prime Minister of Austria 1848–1852* (1947). A somewhat partisan study of the man who turned back the Austrian revolutionaries.
F. A. Simpson, *Louis Napoleon and the Recovery of France, 1848–1856* (3rd ed., 1951). Readable and reliable.

REALISM IN LITERATURE AND THE ARTS

G. M. C. Brandes, *Main Currents in Nineteenth Century Literature* (6 vols., 1901–1905). Dated but still useful.
H. R. Hitchcock, *Architecture: Nineteenth and Twentieth Centuries* (1958). A very good survey.
M. Raynal, *The Nineteenth Century: Goya to Gauguin* (1951) and *History of Modern Painting* (3 vols., 1949–50). Thorough coverage, excellent illustrations.
J. C. Sloane, *French Painting Between the Past and Present: Artists, Critics and Traditions from 1848 to 1870* (1951).

THE PROGRESS OF SCIENCE

A. Einstein and L. Infield, *The Evolution of Physics* (1938). A brief, semi-popular account of the major theoretical developments from Newton to the twentieth century.
J. C. Greene, *The Death of Adam: Evolution and Its Impact on Western Thought* (1959). A wide-ranging, closely reasoned study, with superb illustrations.
G. Himmelfarb, *Darwin and the Darwinian Revolution* (1959).
J. T. Merz, *A History of European Thought in the Nineteenth Century* (4 vols., 1896–1914). An indispensable reference work for the history of science.
W. P. D. Wightman, *The Growth of Scientific Ideas* (1951). A good general survey.

THE WARFARE OF SCIENCE WITH THEOLOGY

* C. C. Gillespie, *Genesis and Geology* (1951). Discusses the relation of science to religious belief in England from 1790 to 1850.
E. E. Y. Hales, *Pio Nono, a Study in European Politics and Religion in the Nineteenth Century* (1954).
W. Irvine, *Apes, Angels, and Victorians* (1955). Amusing.
A. D. White, *A History of the Warfare of Science and Theology* (several eds., 1896). A classic.

MATERIALISM AND POSITIVISM

* W. Bagehot, *Physics and Politics* (numerous eds., 1873, 1956).
* ———— (N. S. Stevas, ed.), *Walter Bagehot's Historical and Political Essays* (1959). A selection from the writings of one of the leading social and political analysts of the period.
* J. Barzun, *Darwin, Marx, Wagner* (1941). An attempt to show the similarities of three outwardly dissimilar individuals.

M. R. Davie, ed., *Sumner Today* (1940). A series of essays by William Graham Sumner, a leading Social Darwinist.

* G. P. Gooch, *History and Historians in the Nineteenth Century* (2nd ed., 1952). Critical essays by a master historian.

* R. Hofstadter, *Social Darwinism in American Thought* (1955). A well written study.

Z. A. Jordan, *The Evolution of Dialectical Materialism* (1967). Heavy reading, but highly illuminating.

W. M. Simon, *European Positivism in the Nineteenth Century* (1963). Deals with the theoretical aspects.

H. Spencer, *Man Versus the State;* also numerous other books by this outstanding exponent of Social Darwinism.

THE POLITICS OF POWER, 1852–1871   CHAPTER TWENTY-SIX

NAPOLEON III AND THE SECOND FRENCH EMPIRE

T. A. B. Corley, *Democratic Despot: A Life of Napoleon III* (1961). Highlights the contradictory features of the man.

D. Pinkney, *Napoleon III and the Rebuilding of Paris* (1958). A sound scholarly study of an important but neglected topic.

J. S. Schapiro, *Liberalism and the Challenge of Fascism: Social Forces in England and France, 1815–1870* (1949). A stimulating work that assigns to Napoleon III the role of precursor of fascism.

J. M. Thompson, *Louis Napoleon and The Second Empire* (1954). Well written, sympathetic.

* R. L. Williams, *Gaslight and Shadow: The World of Napoleon III, 1851–1870* (1957). Favorable to Napoleon III.

* C. Woodham-Smith, *The Reason Why: An Exposé of the Charge of the Light Brigade* (1953). A fascinating account of the Crimean War, exposing the incompetence and inefficiency of the British Army.

T. Zeldin, *The Political System of Napoleon III* (1958). Makes the emperor resemble a modern politician more than an absolute monarch.

THE RISORGIMENTO AND ITALIAN UNITY

K. R. Greenfield, *Economics and Liberalism in the Risorgimento: A Study of Nationalism in Lombardy, 1814–1848* (1934, 1964). A pioneering study, recently republished.

R. Grew, *A Sterner Plan for Italian Unity: The Italian National Society and the Risorgimento* (1963). An authoritative recent treatment.

D. Mack Smith, *Garibaldi* (1956). The best biography in English.

A. J. Whyte, *The Political Life and Letters of Cavour, 1848–1861* (1930). A standard biography.

FOUNDATIONS OF GERMAN UNITY

C. W. Clark, *Franz Joseph and Bismarck: The Diplomacy of Austria Before the War of 1866* (1934).

W. E. Mosse, *The European Powers and the German Question* (1958). Comprehensive and well balanced.

O. Pflanze, *Bismarck and the Development of Germany: The Period of Unification, 1815–1871* (1963). A major recent study.

A. J. P. Taylor, *The Struggle for Mastery in Europe, 1848–1918* (1954). Diplomatic history revolving about Prussia-Germany.

THE CLASH OF POWER IN NORTH AMERICA

* D. W. Brogan, *Abraham Lincoln* (1963). A sensitive brief biography and judgment on an age by a noted British historian.

D. G. Creighton, *Dominion of the North, a History of Canada* (1944).

H. M. Hyde, *Maximilian of Mexico* (1948). A good story.

J. G. Randall, *Civil War and Reconstruction* (2nd ed., 1961). A good history of this controversial period in American historiography.

THE WATERSHED OF 1867–1871

M. Howard, *The Franco-Prussian War* (1961). Mainly military history.

R. H. Lord, *The Origins of the War of 1870* (1924). An older, standard account.

L. D. Steefel, *Bismarck, the Hohenzollern Candidacy, and the Origins of the Franco-German War of 1870* (1962).

THE SPREAD OF MODERN INDUSTRY   CHAPTER TWENTY-SEVEN

TECHNOLOGICAL BASES OF THE NEW INDUSTRIALISM

T. K. Derry and T. I. Williams, *A Short History of Technology* (1961). An excellent one-volume work on technology.

L. F. Haber, *The Chemical Industry in the Nineteenth Century* (1958). Comprehensive, intelligible.

L. Mumford, *Technics and Civilization* (1933). A modern classic.

N. G. B. Pounds and W. N. Parker, *Coal and Steel in Western Europe* (1957). Covers the period from the mid-eighteenth to the mid-twentieth century; by a geographer and an economic historian.

C. Singer *et al., A History of Technology* (vols. 4 and 5, 1958, 1960). Primarily for reference.

BUSINESS ORGANIZATION AND THE WORLD MARKET SYSTEM

A. K. Cairncross, *Home and Foreign Investment, 1870–1913* (1953). A careful, detailed analysis.

H. Feis, *Europe, The World's Banker, 1870–1914* (1930). A basic work.

A. H. Imlah, *Economic Elements in the Pax Britannica, 1815–1914* (1958). Somewhat technical, but rewarding.

L. H. Jenks, *The Migration of British Capital to 1875* (1927). Sprightly and scholarly.

S. B. Saul, *Studies in British Overseas Trade 1870–1914* (1960).

B. Thomas, *Migration and Economic Growth* (1954). An analysis of British investment in and migration to America.

NATIONAL ECONOMIC STYLES

J. H. Clapham, *An Economic History of Modern Britain* (vols. 2 and 3, 1932–38).

S. B. Clough, *France: A History of National Economics, 1789–1939* (1939). Concentrates on economic policy.

* T. C. Cochran and W. Miller, *The Age of Enterprise: A Social History of Industrial America* (1942, 1961). A stimulating book.

* M. L. Hansen, *The Immigrant in American History* (1940). A landmark in its field.

C. P. Kindleberger, *Economic Growth in France and Britain, 1851–1950* (1963). Analytical rather than narrative and interestingly written.

G. Stolper *et al., The German Economy, 1870 to the Present* (1967). Best treatment in English.

T. Veblen, *Imperial Germany and the Industrial Revolution* (1919, 1939). Outdated facts but valuable interpretation.

ORGANIZED LABOR AND THE REVIVAL OF SOCIALISM

I. Berlin, *Karl Marx: His Life and Environment* (1948). Short but reliable.

E. Burns, *A Handbook of Marxism* (1935). A good introduction.

G. D. H. Cole, *Socialist Thought: Marxism and Anarchism, 1850–1880* (1954). Fundamental.

D. Footman, *Ferdinand Lassalle: Romantic Revolutionary* (1946). An interesting portrait of an early Socialist.

P. Gay, *The Dilemma of Democratic Socialism* (1952). A brilliant account of Bernstein's revisionism.

H. Goldberg, *The Life of Jean Jaurès* (1962). A monumental biography of the great French Socialist.

* P. Kropotkin, *Memoirs of a Revolutionist* (1896). Autobiography of an aristocratic Russian anarchist.

C. Landauer, *European Socialism* (2 vols., 1959). A comprehensive general study.

* G. Lichtheim, *Marxism: An Historical and Critical Study* (1961). Recent authoritative analysis.

V. R. Lorwin, *The French Labor Movement* (1954). Its historical chapters are unsurpassed in any language.

H. Pelling, *A History of British Trade Unionism* (1963). The most authoritative recent treatment.

DEMOCRATIC REFORM AND SOCIAL STRIFE, 1871–1914   CHAPTER TWENTY-EIGHT

THE TRIUMPH OF DEMOCRACY IN BRITAIN

J. C. Beckett, *A Short History of Ireland* (1952).

* A. Briggs, *Victorian People* (1955). Sketches of personalities of the period 1851 to 1867.

M. Cowling, *1867: Disraeli, Gladstone and Revolution; The Passing of the Second Reform Bill* (1967). Extremely detailed.

* E. Halevy, *Imperialism and the Rise of Labour, 1859–1905* (2nd ed., 1952). Vol. V of *History of the English People in the Nineteenth Century.*

* ———, *The Rule of Democracy, 1905–1914* (2nd ed., 1952). Vol. VI of *History of the English People in the Nineteenth Century.*

H. Pelling, *The Origins of the Labour Party* (1954). Authoritative.

* E. Wingfield-Stratford, *Those Earnest Victorians* (1930). Well written and entertaining.

* G. M. Young, *Victorian England: Portrait of an Age* (1954). A stimulating sketch of the period.

THE THIRD FRENCH REPUBLIC

G. Chapman, *The Dreyfus Case* (1955). A modern re-evaluation.

A. Horne, *The Fall of Paris* (1966). An exciting account of the siege of Paris and the Commune.

* K. Marx, *Class Struggles in France* (1872 and subsequent eds.). Marx's view of the Commune.

J. A. Scott, *Republican Ideas and the Liberal Tradition in France, 1870–1914* (1951).

P. Spencer, *The Politics of Belief in Nineteenth Century France* (1954). Deals with the role of the church.

* D. Thomson, *Democracy in France since 1870* (1946, 1964). An admirable synthesis.

THE SECOND GERMAN REICH

* G. A. Craig, *From Bismarck to Adenauer: Aspects of German Statecraft* (1958, 1964). Perceptive essays on statesmen and their problems.

* E. Eyck, *Bismarck and the German Empire* (1950). A short study by a noted liberal German historian.

A. Gerschenkron, *Bread and Democracy in Germany* (1943). A stimulating interpretation of German economic and political development.

V. L. Lidthe, *The Outlawed Party: Social Democracy in Germany 1878–1890* (1966). The best study in English of this critical period in the history of the party.

J. A. Nichols, *Germany after Bismarck* (1959).

THE LESSER STATES OF WESTERN EUROPE

E. Bonjour, H. S. Offler, and G. R. Potter, *A Short History of Modern Switzerland* (1952). Especially good on the nineteenth century.

R. Carr, *Spain, 1808–1939* (1966). Authoritative.

C. Seton-Watson, *Italy from Liberalism to Fascism, 1870–1925* (1967). A detailed sympathetic treatment of all aspects of Italian life, with emphasis on political history.

D. Verney, *Parliamentary Reform in Sweden, 1866–1921* (1957). Swedish democratic evolution was unusually calm.

THREE ARCHAIC EMPIRES CHAPTER TWENTY-NINE

RUSSIA IN THE NINETEENTH CENTURY

* J. Blum, *Lord and Peasant in Russia—from the 9th to the 19th century* (1961). The final chapters deal with the emancipation of the serfs.

* H. Kohn, ed., *The Mind of Modern Russia: Historical and Political Thought of Russia's Great Age* (1954). Selections from the great writers of the nineteenth century.

* W. E. Mosse, *Alexander II and the Modernization of Russia* (1962).

M. B. Petrovich, *The Emergence of Russian Pan-Slavism, 1856–1870* (1956). The definitive work in English.

W. Pinter, *Russian Economic Policy under Nicholas I* (1967). Analyzes the part played by governmental economic policy in the decline of Russia.

N. V. Riasanovsky, *A History of Russia* (1963). The best general account in English.

G. T. Robinson, *Rural Russia under the Old Regime* (1932, 1949). A survey of the changes brought about by the emancipation of the serfs.

* M. Rywkin, *Russia in Central Asia* (1964).

* H. Seton-Watson, *The Russian Empire, 1801–1917* (1967). Supersedes the author's *Decline of Imperial Russia, 1855–1914* (1952). An authoritative, readable history.

* A. Yarmolinsky, *Road to Revolution, A Century of Russian Radicalism* (1957, 1962).

AUSTRIA: THE MULTINATIONAL EMPIRE

* O. Jaszi, *The Dissolution of the Habsburg Monarchy* (1929). An older work, still valuable especially for its treatment of Hungary.

R. Kann, *The Multinational Empire: Nationalism and National Reform in the Hapsburg Monarchy, 1840–1918* (2 vols., 1950). A comprehensive study of the eroding forces of nationalism.

H. Kohn, *Pan-Slavism: Its History and Ideology* (1953).

C. A. Macartney, *The Hapsburg Empire, 1790–1918* (1969). The best survey.

A. J. P. Taylor, *The Habsburg Monarchy, 1809–1918* (2nd ed., 1948). A brief and well written study.

THE OTTOMAN EMPIRE

R. H. Davison, *Reform in the Ottoman Empire, 1856–1876* (1963). A thorough recent scholarly study.

J. Haslip, *The Sultan: The Life of Abdul Hamid II* (1958). An unusual kind of biography.

* W. Miller, *The Ottoman Empire and its Successors, 1801–1934* (1948). The standard work in English.

* L. S. Stavrianos, *The Balkans, 1815–1914* (1962). A valuable general survey of a troubled area.

THE REVIVAL OF WESTERN IMPERIALISM CHAPTER THIRTY

THE SECOND BRITISH EMPIRE

A. L. Burt. *The Evolution of the British Empire and Commonwealth from the American Revolution* (1956). A standard text.

E. Holt, *The Boer War* (1958). A recent general account.

F. G. Hutchins, *The Illusion of Permanence: British Imperialism in India* (1967). Lucidly and elegantly written.

P. Knaplund, *The British Empire, 1815–1939* (1941). An authoritative survey from the British viewpoint.

S. Sen, *Eighteen Fifty-seven* (1957). A centennial history of the Sepoy Mutiny by an Indian historian.

A. P. Thornton, *The Imperial Idea and Its Enemies: A Study in British Power* (1959). The rise and decline of the British belief in the "white man's burden."

B. Williams, *Botha, Smuts, and South Africa* (1948). Boers who became firm supporters of the British Empire.

THE OPENING OF ASIA

J. F. Cady, *The Roots of French Imperialism in Eastern Asia* (1954). Background of the Vietnam question.

T. F. Power, Jr., *Jules Ferry and the Renaissance of French Imperialism* (1944). Much broader than the title indicates.

J. Pratt, *The Expansion of Europe in the Far East* (1947). Good general account.

G. B. Sanson, *The Western World and Japan* (1950). A concise history by a leading authority.

Ssy-yu Teng and J. K. Fairbank, *China's Response to the West: A Documentary Survey, 1839–1923* (1954, 1963). A comprehensive survey using contemporary sources.

THE PARTITION OF AFRICA

P. Curtin, *The Image of Africa* (1964). British ideas about Africa from 1780 to 1850.

D. Forde and P. M. Kaberry, *West African Kingdoms in the Nineteenth Century* (1967). Reveals the diversity and complexity of indigenous African political and social life.

J. T. Gallager and R. I. Robinson, *Africa and the Victorians* (1961). A stimulating original interpretation of British strategy and tactics in Africa.

L. H. Gann and Peter Duignan, *Burden of Empire* (1967). A rebuttal of the argument that economic factors were of major importance in the colonization of Africa; traces the story to the epoch of de-colonization.

D. S. Landes, *Bankers and Pashas: International Finance and Economic Imperialism in Egypt* (1958). Reads like a novel.

H. I. Priestly, *France Overseas: A Study of Modern Imperialism* (1938). A detailed study of French imperialism from 1815 to 1930.

R. L. Tignor, *Modernization and British Colonial Rule in Egypt, 1882–1914* (1966). By a modern social scientist.

INTERPRETATIONS AND PERSPECTIVES

J. H. Hobson, *Imperialism: A Study* (1902). A pioneering study that attacked the traditional English idea of imperialism.

* V. I. Lenin, *Imperialism, the Highest Stage of Capitalism* (1916, 1939). The fundamental statement of the Marxist-Leninist theory of imperialism.

* A. T. Mahan, *The Influence of Seapower upon History* (numerous eds., 1893). A highly influential book in its day.

J. A. Schumpeter, *Imperialism and Social Classes* (1919, 1951). A refutation of the economic interpretation of imperialism.

E. Staley, *War and the Private Investor: A Study in the Relations of International Politics and International Investment* (1935). Shows the influence of government policies on foreign investment.

E. M. Winslow, *The Pattern of Imperialism* (1948). A study of the motives and interests of the imperial powers.

EUROPEAN CULTURE AND SOCIETY:
THE END OF THE GOLDEN AGE CHAPTER THIRTY-ONE

* C. J. H. Hayes, *A Generation of Materialism, 1871–1900* (1941). A general study of all aspects of the life of the times, including literature, art, social thought, and politics; Rise of Modern Europe Series.

The best way to appreciate the literature of the period is to read some of the books mentioned in the text. Illustrated histories of art are numerous.

FIN-DE-SIÈCLE LITERATURE AND ART

S. Giedion, *Mechanization Takes Command* (1948). Shows the influence of industrialization upon art.

A. Hauser, *The Social History of Art* (1952). The influence of art on society and vice versa.

* E. Neff, *The Poetry of History: The Contribution of Literature and Literary Scholarship to the Writing of History Since Voltaire* (1947).

N. Pevsner, *Pioneers of the Modern Movement from William Morris to Walter Gropius* (1936). A classic study of architecture and design by a noted authority.

H. A. Reyburn, *Nietzsche: The Story of a Human Philosopher* (1948).

M. Rheims, *The Age of Art Nouveau* (1967). Excellent illustrations.

* E. Wilson, *Axel's Castle, A Study in the Imaginative Literature of 1850–1930* (1931). A masterpiece of literary history.

POSITIVISM AND ITS CRITICS

H. Alpert, *Emile Durkheim and His Sociology* (1939). One of the best studies of the influential French sociologist.

S. Hughes, *Consciousness and Society: The Reorientation of European Social Thought, 1890–1920* (1958). A study of the influence of new ideas on man's view of society.

E. Jones, *Sigmund Freud* (1 vol. ed., 1961). An abridgment of the massive "authorized" biography.

* R. B. Perry, *The Thought and Character of William James* (1935, 1948). An abridged edition of this major work is available in paperback.

P. Rieff, *Freud: The Mind of the Moralist* (1959). A penetrating critique of one of the most influential personalities of modern times.

H. Vaihinger, *The Philosophy of "As If"* (transl., 1927). English translation of an important work in the philosophy of science.

THE NEW REVOLUTION IN SCIENCE

C. T. Chase, *The Evolution of Modern Physics* (1947).

* L. Infield, *Albert Einstein: His Work and Its Influence on Our World* (1950). A good introduction for the layman.

J. Mirsky, *To the North: The Story of Arctic Exploration* (1934, 1948).

W. Sullivan, *Quest for a Continent* (1957). A history of Antarctic exploration from the 1820's to the International Geophysical Year.

EUROPEAN SOCIETY AT THE END OF ITS GOLDEN AGE

G. Dangerfield, *The Strange Death of Liberal England* (1936). An examination of social and political changes in the decade preceding World War I.

* H. F. May, *End of American Innocence: A Study of the First Years of Our Time, 1912–1917* (1959).

J. H. Nichols, *A History of Christianity, 1650–1950* (1956). An authoritative modern work of scholarship with special attention to developments since about 1870.

J. G. J. Pulzer, *The Rise of Political Anti-Semitism in Germany and Austria* (1964).

* W. Rauschenbusch, *Christianity and the Social Crisis* (1907, 1963). A document of the times by the founder of American "social Christianity."

P. N. Stearns, *European Society in Upheaval: Social History since 1800* (1967). Also recommended for the earlier period.

THE FIRST WORLD WAR   CHAPTER THIRTY-TWO

THE DIPLOMATIC PRELUDE, 1871–1914

H. E. Barnes, *The Genesis of the World War: An Introduction to the Problem of War Guilt* (1926). Of special interest because of the author's revisionist approach.

E. Brandenburg, *From Bismarck to World War: A History of German Foreign Policy, 1870–1914* (1927). A German view of the origins of World War I.

* W. L. Langer, *European Alliances and Alignments, 1871–1890* (1931, 1950).

* ———, *The Diplomacy of Imperialism, 1890–1902* (2 vols., 1935). These volumes and the above constitute the definitive diplomatic history of their period.

N. Mansergh, *The Coming of the First World War* (1949). An authoritative study of the breakdown of the balance of power concept.

G. Monger, *The End of Isolation: British Foreign Policy, 1900–1907* (1963).

R. J. Sontag, *European Diplomatic History, 1871–1932* (1933). A standard text.

J. A. Thayer, *Italy and the Great War: Politics and Culture, 1870–1915* (1964). A penetrating recent study.

FROM THE EASTERN QUESTION TO THE BALKAN WARS

E. M. Earle, *Turkey, the Great Powers, and the Bagdad Railroad* (1923). A study of Western involvement in the Near East.

E. C. Helmreich, *The Diplomacy of the Balkan Wars, 1912–1913* (1938). Dry, factual, but reliable.

W. N. Medlicott, *The Congress of Berlin and After* (1938, 1963). The authoritative work on the Near Eastern settlement of 1878 to 1880.

J. Remak, *Sarajevo, The Story of a Political Murder* (1959). A gripping account of this explosive event.

C. Sforza, *Fifty Years of War and Diplomacy in the Balkans* (1941). By an Italian diplomat.

THE WAR

* H. Baldwin, *World War I* (1962). A brief, clear survey by a leading military analyst.

E. M. Coffman, *The War to End All Wars* (1968). American participation in the war.

J. Cameron, *1914* (1959). Recreates the atmosphere of the times.

F. Chambers, *The War Behind the War, 1914–1918* (1939). The home front in various countries.

* C. Falls, *The Great War, 1914–1918* (1959). Somewhat more detailed than Baldwin.

G. D. Feldman, *Army, Industry and Labor in Germany, 1914–1918* (1966). The home front in Germany.

A. Horne, *The Price of Glory: Verdun, 1916* (1963). The story of one of the costliest battles of the war.

A. Marwick, *The Deluge* (1965). A scholarly study of British society during World War I.

* A. Moorehead, *Gallipoli* (1958). The story of the disastrous British campaign to take the Dardanelles.

J. M. Read, *Atrocity Propaganda* (1941). A study of a crude form of psychological warfare.

G. Ritter, *The Schlieffen Plan* (transl., 1958). By a German historian.

H. R. Rudin, *Armistice, 1918* (1944). A standard account.

E. Taylor, *The Fall of the Dynasties* (1963). A popularized political history of the war and the years immediately preceding.

* B. Tuchman, *The Guns of August* (1962). Opening weeks of the war; reads like a novel.

R. M. Watt, *Dare Call It Treason* (1963). Mutinies in the French army in 1917, news of which was long suppressed.

DISINTEGRATION AND COLLAPSE   CHAPTER THIRTY-THREE

THE RUSSIAN REVOLUTION, 1917–1921

E. H. Carr, *The Bolshevik Revolution, 1917–1923* (1950–56). Vols. I–III of *A History of Soviet Russia,* the most comprehensive and detailed account in English.

I. Deutscher, *The Prophet Armed: Trotsky, 1879–1921* (1958). A sympathetic biography.

L. Fischer, *Lenin* (1964). The best biography.

C. Hill, *Lenin and the Russian Revolution* (1947). Good, brief introduction.

G. F. Kennan, *The Decision to Intervene* (1958). American involvement in the Russian Revolution.

* A. Moorehead, *The Russian Revolution* (1958). A well written, popular account, not entirely reliable.

* J. Reed, *Ten Days that Shook the World* (1919, 1960). Eyewitness account of the Bolshevik seizure of power by an American journalist.

L. Schapiro, *The Origins of the Communist Autocracy: Political Opposition in the Soviet State, 1917–1922* (1955).

L. Trotsky, *The History of the Russian Revolution* (2 vols., 1932, 1937). Trotsky was the Bolshevik War Commissar.

A. B. Ulam, *The Bolsheviks* (1965). An important study of the origins of Russian communism.

J. W. Wheeler-Bennett, *The Forgotten Peace: Brest-Litovsk, March, 1918* (1939). The negotiations between the Bolsheviks and the Germans.

* B. D. Wolfe, *Three Who Made a Revolution: A Biographical History* (1948, 1964). An exciting story of Lenin, Trotsky, and Stalin.

THE PEACE OF PARIS AND ITS AFTERMATH

T. A. Bailey, *Wilson and the Peacemakers* (1947). The U.S. role in the peace conference.

P. Birdsall, *Versailles Twenty Years After* (1941). An evaluation of two decades of controversy over the peace settlement.

T. Jones, *Lloyd-George* (1951). A sound biography.

F. S. Marston, *The Peace Conference of 1919* (1944). A brief guide to the conference.

I. Morrow, *The Peace Settlement in the German-Polish Borderlands* (1936). An especially important area.

ECONOMIC DISINTEGRATION AND COLLAPSE

A. L. Bowley, *Some Economic Consequences of the Great War* (1930). Written by an economist in the midst of the depression.

P. Einzig, *The World Economic Crisis, 1929–1931* (1931). The author was a financial journalist.

J. M. Keynes, *The Economic Consequences of the Peace* (1920). A most influential book.

E. Mantoux, *The Carthaginian Peace—or The Economic Consequences of Mr. Keynes* (1946). A sharp attack on the Keynesian thesis that the Treaty of Versailles was too harsh on Germany by a young Frenchman who died in World War II.

H. G. Moulton, and L. Pasvolsky, *War Debts and World Prosperity* (1932). The economists' view.

CRISIS OF THE SPIRIT

Just for fun, try J. Dos Passos's *U.S.A.*, E. Hemingway's *Farewell to Arms,* J. Steinbeck's *Grapes of Wrath*, A. Huxley's *Brave New World*, or A. Gide's *The Immoralist*.

LIBERAL ATTEMPTS AT RECONSTRUCTION CHAPTER THIRTY-FOUR

THE LEAGUE OF NATIONS AND COLLECTIVE SECURITY

E. H. Carr, *International Relations between the Two World Wars, 1919–1939* (rev. ed., 1948). A good survey of international affairs.

R. Dell, *The Geneva Racket, 1920–1939* (1941). A cynical view of the League.

R. H. Ferrell, *Peace in Their Time* (1952). A study of the origins of the Kellogg-Briand peace pact.

F. B. Walters, *A History of the League of Nations* (2 vols., 1952). A detailed study of the League.

A. Zimmern, *The League of Nations and the Rule of Law* (1936).

THE WEIMAR REPUBLIC IN GERMANY

K. Epstein, *Matthias Erzberger and the Dilemma of German Democracy* (1959). A sensitive, penetrating study.

E. Eyck, *A History of the Weimar Republic* (2 vols., transl., 1963). An authoritative study by a liberal German historian.

G. Freund, *Unholy Alliance* (1957). Germany's relations with the Soviet Union.

H. J. Gordon, *The Reichswehr and the German Republic, 1919–1926* (1957). The German army under the Weimar Republic.

* S. W. Halperin, *Germany Tried Democracy: A Political History of the Reich from 1918 to 1933* (1946). A well balanced scholarly history.

J. Plamenatz, *German Marxism and Russian Communism* (1954).

G. Scheele, *The Weimar Republic: Overture to the Third Reich* (1947).

* H. A. Turner, *Stresemann and the Politics of the Weimar Republic* (1963). A reappraisal of the role of the German statesman in domestic politics.

THE DEMOCRACIES OF WESTERN EUROPE

M. W. Childs, *Sweden, the Middle Way* (1947). Neither unbridled capitalism nor dogmatic socialism.

* R. Graves and A. Hodges, *The Long Weekend: A Social History of Great Britain, 1918–1939* (1940). A well written, somewhat satirical social history.

J. M. Keynes, *The End of Laissez-Faire* (1927). Brilliant essays by the noted economist. His *Essays in Persuasion* and *Essays in Biography* are also well worth reading.

* E. J. Knapton, *France since Versailles* (1952). A short, clear survey.
* L. C. B. Seaman, *Post-Victorian Britain, 1902–1951* (1966). A pithy reinterpretation of the first half of the twentieth century in Britain.
W. R. Sharp, *The Government of the French Republic* (1938). A valiant attempt to unravel the tangled skein of the Third Republic.
* D. Thomson, *England in the Twentieth Century, 1914–1963* (1964). An excellent brief survey.
S. H. Thomson, *Czechoslovakia in European History* (1943, 1953).
A. Werth, *The Twilight of France, 1933–1940* (1942). Highly recommended.

THE UNITED STATES: NEW ERA AND NEW DEAL

* F. L. Allen, *Only Yesterday* (1957) and *Since Yesterday* (1958). Lively social histories of conditions in the U.S. during the 1920's and 1930's.
D. Brogan, *The Era of Franklin D. Roosevelt* (1951). A perceptive account by a distinguished British historian.
* J. K. Galbraith, *The Great Crash* (1955). An exciting account of the stock market collapse of 1929.
* W. Leuchtenburg, *Franklin D. Roosevelt and the New Deal, 1932–1940* (1963).
* J. A. Schumpeter, *Capitalism, Socialism, and Democracy* (1942, 1952). A wise and penetrating analysis by a distinguished social scientist; applies to western Europe as well as the U.S.
* A. Sinclair, *Era of Excess: A Social History of the Prohibition Movement* (1962).
* E. Wilson, *American Earthquake: A Documentary of the Jazz Age, the Great Depression and the New Deal* (1958). Social history by a noted literary critic.

AUTHORITARIAN ATTEMPTS AT RECONSTRUCTION   CHAPTER THIRTY-FIVE

COMMUNISM IN RUSSIA, 1921–1938

* R. N. Carew Hunt, *The Theory and Practice of Communism* (1951). The international Communist movement.
E. H. Carr, *The Interregnum, 1923–1924,* and *Socialism in One Country, 1924–1926.* Vols. IV–VI of the monumental *A History of Soviet Russia.*
* I. Deutscher, ed., *The Age of Permanent Revolution: A Trotsky Anthology* (1964). A selection from the writings of Stalin's archrival.
* ————, *Stalin: A Political Biography* (1948).
L. Fischer, *The Life and Death of Stalin* (1953).
S. N. Harper and R. Thompson, *The Government of the Soviet Union* (1949). Its structure and functions.
G. F. Kennan, *Russia and the West under Lenin and Stalin* (1961). A perceptive analysis of Soviet foreign relations.
R. Pipes, *The Formation of the Soviet Union* (1954). A useful account of the minorities in Russia from 1917 to 1923.
H. Schwartz, *Russia's Soviet Economy* (1950, 1954). A good introduction.
* H. Seton-Watson, *From Lenin to Khrushchev: The History of World Communism* (1953, 1960).

FASCISM IN ITALY, 1922–1938

D. A. Binchy, *Church and State in Fascist Italy* (1941). A Catholic historian discusses the historical problem of church-state relations.

G. A. Borgese, *Goliath: The March of Fascism* (1937). By an antifascist.

C. F. Delzell, *Mussolini's Enemies: The Italian Anti-fascist Resistance* (1961). An able study of the Italian underground.

I. Kirkpatrick, *Mussolini: Study of a Demagogue* (1964). By far the best biography.

G. Megaro, *Mussolini in the Making* (1938). An excellent study of Mussolini's early life.

G. Salvemini, *Under the Axe of Fascism* (1936). A sound treatment of Italian fascism by a distinguished antifascist.

C. T. Schmidt, *The Corporate State in Action: Italy under Fascism* (1939).

NAZISM IN GERMANY, 1933–1938

* A. Bullock, *Hitler: A Study in Tyranny* (rev. ed., 1962). The best biography of Hitler.

* K. Jaspers, *The Question of German Guilt* (transl., 1961). An existentialist psychologist probes the question of public responsibility for Nazi atrocities.

* G. Lewy, *The Catholic Church in Nazi Germany* (1964).

F. Lilge, *The Abuse of Learning: The Failure of the German University* (1948). Shows the take-over of the German universities by the Nazis.

* H. Mau and H. Krausnick, *German History 1933–1945* (transl., 1958). A study by two young German historians.

* F. Meinecke, *The German Catastrophe: Reflections and Recollections* (1946, 1950). Personal reminiscences of a great German historian.

* G. L. Mosse, *The Crisis of German Ideology: Intellectual Origins of the Third Reich* (1964). An incisive analysis of the ideological background of National Socialism.

D. Schoenbaum, *Hitler's Social Revolution: Class and Status in Nazi Germany, 1933–1939* (1967). A penetrating study by a brilliant young historian.

* W. L. Shirer, *The Rise and Fall of the Third Reich* (1960). An account by an American journalist.

L. L. Snyder, *German Nationalism: The Tragedy of a People* (1952).

H. R. Trevor-Roper, *The Last Days of Hitler* (1947). A dramatic account of the end of National Socialism.

J. W. Wheeler-Bennett, *The Nemesis of Power: The German Army in Politics, 1918–1945* (1953). An indispensable analysis.

OTHER AUTHORITARIAN REGIMES

R. Benedict, *The Chrysanthemum and the Sword* (1946). The rise of militarism in Japan.

* G. Brenan, *The Spanish Labyrinth: An Account of the Social and Political Background of the Civil War* (1943). One of the best works of the events leading up to the Civil War.

D. M. Brown, *Nationalism in Japan* (1955).

C. A. Gulick, *Austria from Habsburg to Hitler* (2 vols., 1948). A detailed, comprehensive history.

M. MacDonald, *The Republic of Austria, 1918–1934: A Study in the Failure of Democratic Government* (1946).

H. Seton-Watson, *Eastern Europe between the Wars, 1918–1941* (1946). The best general account.

* H. Thomas, *The Spanish Civil War* (1961). The best history of the war.

G. O. Totten III, *The Social Democratic Movement in Prewar Japan* (1966). Covers many aspects of the period from 1925 to 1940.

THE COMMON ELEMENTS

A. Cobban, *Dictatorship: Its History and Theory* (1939).

* E. Fromm, *Escape from Freedom* (1941). A psychiatrist probes the reasons for submission to dictatorship.

D. Spearman, *Modern Dictatorship* (1939). A comparative survey.

THE SECOND WORLD WAR CHAPTER THIRTY-SIX

THE ORIGINS OF TOTALITARIAN AGGRESSION

G. W. Baer, *The Coming of the Italian-Ethiopian War* (1967). Detailed scholarly work.

G. Brook-Shepherd, *Anschluss: The Rape of Austria* (1963). A good recent study.

* W. Churchill, *The Gathering Storm* (1948) . Vol. I of Churchill's *History of the Second World War;* highly personal.

F. Gilbert and G. A. Craig, eds., *The Diplomats, 1919–1939* (1953). Penetrating studies of the principal diplomats of the era.

W. L. Langer and S. E. Gleason, *The Challenge to Isolation, 1937–1940* (1952) and *The Undeclared War, 1940–1941* (1953). A detailed history of the U.S. role leading up to 1941.

D. J. Lu, *From the Marco Polo Bridge to Pearl Harbor: Japan's Entry into World War II* (1961). A military-diplomatic history of Japanese aggression.

* L. B. Namier, *Diplomatic Prelude, 1938–1939* (1948). Perceptive essays on the origins of the war.

* A. J. P. Taylor, *The Origins of the Second World War* (1961, 1963). A revisionist view; highly controversial.

* J. W. Wheeler-Bennett, *Munich: Prologue to Tragedy* (1948, 1963). An outstanding contribution.

BLITZKRIEG, 1939–1941

H. F. Armstrong, *Chronology of Failure* (1940). An on-the-spot discussion of the collapse of France in 1940.

R. Aron, *The Vichy Regime* (1950). A critical history by a noted French author.

M. Bloch, *Strange Defeat* (1949). A distinguished French historian's perceptive study of France's surrender to Germany. (Bloch was executed by the Germans in 1944 for underground activities.)

B. Collier, *The Second World War: A Military History* (1967). Deals mainly with general fighting.

* C. Falls, *The Second World War* (2nd ed., 1950). A sound military history.
A. S. Milward, *The German Economy at War* (1965).
G. L. Weinberg, *Germany and the Soviet Union, 1939–1941* (1954). The diplomatic history of a strange alliance.
A. Werth, *The Year of Stalingrad* (1947). An interesting journalistic account.
D. Young, *Rommel: The Desert Fox* (1950). An absorbing story of the commanding German general in North Africa.

PEARL HARBOR AND THE WAR IN THE PACIFIC

R. J. C. Butow, *Japan's Decision to Surrender* (1961). The end of the war in the Pacific.
* D. Congdon, ed., *Combat: The War with Japan* (1962). A popular account of the war in the Pacific.
J. Creswell, *Sea Warfare, 1939–1945* (1967). Covers all naval operations.
S. E. Morison, *The Two-Ocean War: A Short History of the United States Navy in the Second World War* (1963). A one-volume abridgment of the multivolume history of U.S. naval operations, by one of the most distinguished American historians.

THE GRAND ALLIANCE

* W. Churchill, *Closing the Ring* (1951). Churchill's own account of the invasion of Europe.
* D. D. Eisenhower, *Crusade in Europe* (1949). By the Supreme Allied Commander.
* T. R. Fehrenbach, *The Battle of Anzio* (1962). A crucial battle of the invasion of Italy.
H. Feis, *Churchill, Roosevelt, Stalin* (1957). An interesting account of the relations between these three war leaders. See also Feis's other accounts of the diplomatic history of the war.
* C. Ryan, *The Longest Day* (1959). June 6, 1944, the Normandy invasion.
* C. Wilmont, *The Struggle for Europe* (1952). A critical account of American policy by an Australian scholar.

THE AFTERMATH OF WAR   CHAPTER THIRTY-SEVEN

EXHAUSTED VICTORS

R. A. Brady, *Crisis in Britain: Plans and Achievements of the Labour Government* (1950). An economist's account of the difficulties encountered by Britain's first Socialist government.
M. Einaudi *et al., Communism in Western Europe* (1951). A study of French and Italian Communists.
S. Hoffmann *et al., In Search of France* (1962). An interdisciplinary approach to a fascinating problem.
H. Luethy, *France Against Herself* (1954). An unusually lucid and penetrating analysis of French society, economy, and politics.
B. Ward, *The West at Bay* (1948). A trenchant and perceptive analysis of the situation of the former Great Powers of Europe in the aftermath of war.

F. Williams, *Socialist Britain* (1949).

P. M. Williams, *Politics in Postwar France* (1954). A sensible yet stimulating interpretation of the problems of the Fourth Republic.

G. Wright, *The Reshaping of French Democracy* (1948). A study of constitution making in postwar France.

DEFEATED ENEMIES

G. C. Allen, *Japan's Economic Recovery* (1958). By an economist well versed in Japanese affairs.

G. A. Almond, ed., *The Struggle for Democracy in Germany* (1949). Aspects of denazification, the occupation, and the founding of the Federal Republic.

E. Davidson, *The Death and Life of Germany* (1959). A study of the American occupation.

H. Feis, *Between War and Peace: The Potsdam Conference* (1960). An outstanding account of the first critical postwar meeting of the Big Three.

M. Grindrod, *The Rebuilding of Italy, 1945–1955* (1955). An interesting account of postwar reconstruction, economic and political.

K. Kawai, *Japan's American Interlude* (1960). A study of the postwar occupation.

R. Opie *et al., The Search for a Peace Settlement* (1951). A research study sponsored by the Brookings Institution.

F. W. Pick, *Peacemaking in Perspective: From Potsdam to Paris* (1950). An account of the negotiations leading up to the peace treaties of 1947.

E. O. Reischauer, *The United States and Japan* (rev. ed., 1957). By far the best introduction to American relations with Japan since the war.

THE FATE OF EASTERN EUROPE

H. F. Armstrong, *Tito and Goliath* (1951). Yugoslavia's defiance of the Soviet Union.

D. J. Dallin, *The New Soviet Empire* (1951). A distinctly anti-Soviet point of view.

J. Korbel, *The Communist Subversion of Czechoslovakia 1938–1948* (1964). The background of the *coup de Prague*.

J. P. Nettl, *The Eastern Zone and Soviet Policy in Germany, 1945–1950* (1951). The standard work on the subject.

H. Seton-Watson, *The East-European Revolution* (1950, 1956). The best account of the Communist take-over in Eastern Europe.

E. Wiskemann, *Germany's Eastern Neighbours* (1955).

R. L. Wolff, *The Balkans in Our Time* (1956). A detailed account of the Balkans before and after World War II.

THE UNITED NATIONS AND DIVIDED ALLIES

* H. W. Gatzke, *The Present in Perspective: A Look at the World since 1945* (1957, 1965). A general survey of the postwar period, especially useful for its perspective on the Cold War and international relations.

G. F. Kennan, *Realities of American Foreign Policy* (1954).

————, *Russia, the Atom, and the West* (1958). Two distinguished contributions by one of America's foremost scholar-diplomats.

J. Lukacs, *A History of the Cold War* (1961).

R. Leckie, *Conflict: The History of the Korean War 1950–1953* (1962).

* H. G. Nicholas, *The United Nations as a Political Institution* (1953).

R. B. Russell, *A History of the United Nations Charter* (1958). The ideas and compromises that made the charter, from the Atlantic Charter to the San Francisco conference.

THE END OF WESTERN HEGEMONY CHAPTER THIRTY-EIGHT

NEW NATIONALISMS

C. Dubois, *Social Forces in Southeast Asia* (1959). A good introduction.

R. N. Frye, *Iran* (1953). A brief general introduction to the modernization of a nation.

* J. D. Legge, *Indonesia* (1964). Modern Nations in Historical Perspective Series.

H. Z. Nuseibeh, *The Ideas of Arab Nationalism* (1956). By an Arab nationalist.

J. Romein, *The Asian Century: A History of Modern Nationalism in Asia* (1956, transl., 1962). A good general introduction to Asian nationalism.

* H. M. Sachar, *The Course of Modern Jewish History* (1958). Useful for understanding the historical background of the modern state of Israel.

H. Tinker, *Experiment with Freedom: India and Pakistan, 1947* (1967). Brief, synoptic account of the background of independence.

M. Zinkin, *Asia and the West* (1953). An interpretative study of the social and economic problems of Asian countries.

THE CHINESE REVOLUTIONS

O. E. Clubb, *Twentieth Century China* (1964). A general survey of the period since the first Chinese revolution of 1911.

J. K. Fairbank, *The United States and China* (1958). An authoritative account of American relations with China, including American involvement in the civil war and the stalemate with Communist China.

E. Hahn, *Chiang Kai-shek: An Unauthorized Biography* (1955). A perceptive human account by a skilled writer.

H. R. Isaacs, *The Tragedy of the Chinese Revolution* (1961).

* K. S. Latourette, *China* (1964). A brief general survey by a distinguished historian. Modern Nations in Historical Perspective Series.

B. Schwartz, *Chinese Communism and the Rise of Mao* (1951). An authoritative study of the leader of the Chinese Communists.

* R. Walker, *China Under Communism: The First Five Years* (1955). A severe critique of Chinese Communism.

THE EMERGENCE OF INDEPENDENT AFRICA

* R. M. Brace, *Morocco, Algeria, Tunisia* (1964). Modern Nations in Historical Perspective Series.

K. A. Busia, *Africa in Search of Democracy* (1967). By a noted Ghanian politician.

G. M. Carter, *The Politics of Inequality: South Africa since 1948* (1958). An analysis of racial tensions in South Africa.

* R. Emerson, *From Empire to Nation* (1960). A history of the crumbling of colonialism in both Asia and Africa.

R. Oliver and J. D. Fage, *A Short History of Africa* (1962). The emphasis is on the background of the independence movement.

C. E. Welch, Jr., *Dream of Unity: Pan-Africanism and Political Unity in West Africa* (1966). Only a dream.

LATIN AMERICA IN FERMENT

T. Draper, *Castro's Revolution: Myths and Realities* (1962).

A. O. Hirschman, *Journeys Toward Progress* (1963). Vivid, sympathetic accounts of Latin American efforts to achieve economic development.

H. L. Mathews, ed., *The United States and Latin America* (1963).

T. Szulc, *The Winds of Revolution: Latin America Today and Tomorrow* (1963). An unusually perceptive analysis by a skilled journalist.

THE STRUGGLE FOR A NEW
WORLD ORDER   CHAPTER THIRTY-NINE

RECOVERY AND REINTEGRATION IN WESTERN EUROPE

W. Diebold, Jr., *The Schuman Plan: A Study in Economic Cooperation* (1959). Detailed, comprehensive, and scholarly.

E. B. Haas, *The Uniting of Europe* (1958). A scholarly study of political, social, and economic forces.

* G. Lichtheim, *The New Europe Today—and Tomorrow* (1963). A good brief introduction by an incisive analyst and writer.

* K. Martin, *Britain in the Sixties: The Crown and the Establishment* (1964). Social commentary and critique by an "angry young man."

H. C. Wallich, *Mainsprings of the German Revival* (1955). The "economic miracle" in Germany.

P. M. Williams and M. Harrison, *De Gaulle's Republic* (1960). A penetrating, somewhat critical evaluation of the Fifth Republic.

* J. W. Wuorinen, *Scandinavia* (1964). Modern Nations in Historical Perspective Series.

THE ATLANTIC ALLIANCE

H. Borton, *Japan Between East and West* (1957). Cultural, political, and economic tensions.

* E. Goldman, *The Crucial Decade—And After: America, 1945–1960* (1960). A close scrutiny of the postwar United States and its role in world affairs.

* A. Grosser, *The Federal Republic of Germany: A Concise History* (1964).

* H. A. Kissinger, *Nuclear Weapons and American Foreign Policy* (1957). A controversial analysis of the bases of U.S. foreign policy by a political scientist of the "realistic" school, adviser to President Nixon.

Royal Institute of International Affairs, *Atlantic Alliance: NATO's Role in the Free World* (1952). A report explaining the aims, organization, and accomplishments of NATO.

COMMUNISM AFTER STALIN

A. Brumberg, ed., *Russia under Khrushchev* (1962). Essays on selected aspects of Soviet life.

* E. Crankshaw, *The New Cold War: Moscow vs. Peking* (1963). An analysis of the ideological split within the Communist bloc.

* M. Djilas, *The New Class: An Analysis of the Communist System* (1957). A critique of communism by a former Yugoslav Communist leader.

* S. Fischer-Galati, ed., *Eastern Europe in the Sixties* (1963). A country-by-country survey by experts.

* D. Granick, *The Red Executive: A Study of the Organization Man in Russian Industry* (1960). Excellent book on a little known subject.

R. Kolkowicz, *The Soviet Military and the Communist Party* (1967). Civil-military relations under communism.

C. A. Linden, *Khrushchev and the Soviet Leadership, 1957–1964* (1966). Highly informative.

* Z. K. Brzezinsky, *The Soviet Bloc: Unity and Conflict* (1963). A study of the relations between Russia and the satellite states.

BIRTH PANGS OF WORLD CIVILIZATION

* V. M. Dean, *The Nature of the Non-Western World* (1957). A useful introduction.

B. B. Fall, *The Two Viet-Nams* (1963). The split between North and South and its consequences for peace in Southeast Asia.

W. R. Fischel, *Vietnam: Anatomy of a Conflict* (1968). A collection of conflicting analyses and opinions on the war in Vietnam.

E. Fischer, *The Passing of the European Age: A Study of the Transfer of Western Civilization and Its Renewal in Other Continents* (1948). The subtitle indicates its scope.

A. L. George, *The Chinese Army in Action: The Korean War and its Aftermath* (1967). Based on interviews with captured Chinese soldiers.

* R. L. Heilbroner, *The Great Ascent: The Struggle for Economic Development in Our Time* (1963). An able, lucid explanation for the layman.

F. S. C. Northrop, *The Meeting of East and West* (1946). Cultural contrasts and similarities explored by a modern philosopher.

* H. Seton-Watson, *Neither War Nor Peace: The Struggle for Power in the Postwar World* (1960). One of the best accounts of the troubled state of international relations; wise and reflective.

A. J. Toynbee, *The World and the West* (1953). Reflections of one of the best known historians of civilization.

TENDENCIES OF TWENTIETH-CENTURY CIVILIZATION CHAPTER FORTY

SCIENCE, TECHNOLOGY, AND INDUSTRY

* R. Aron, *The Century of Total War* (1954). Analysis of the political and economic forces at work and their relations to science and technology.

* B. Barber, *Science and the Social Order* (1952). Examines the relationship between science and society.

P. M. S. Blackett, *Atomic Weapons and East-West Relations* (1956). An English scientist discusses the impact of nuclear weapons.

* J. Bronowski, *Science and Human Values* (1956). An informed discussion by a noted scientist.

V. Bush, *Modern Arms and Free Men: A Discussion of the Role of Science in Preserving Democracy* (1948). The author was President Truman's science adviser and played an important role in developing the atomic bomb.

* Sir A. Eddington, *The Expanding Universe* (1958). A popular exposition of the significance of recent discoveries in astronomy.

W. Esslinger, *Politics and Science* (1955).

* P. de Kruif, *The Microbe Hunters* (1926, 1939). A popular account of the progress of the biological and medical sciences in the first third of the twentieth century.

SOCIAL TRENDS

* T. C. Cochran, *The American Business System: A Historical Perspective, 1900–1955* (1956). Many of the changes in American business are being felt in Europe as well.

J. K. Galbraith, *The New Industrial State* (1967). How the "technostructure" is transforming society.

* C. B. Hoover, *The Economy, Liberty, and the State* (1959). A fine discussion of the relations between the economic system and fundamental human freedoms, with examples from recent history.

* V. O. Packard, *The Status Seekers* (1959). An examination of the class structure of American society, which has some parallels in Europe.

* D. Riesman, *The Lonely Crowd* (1947, 1953). A social-psychological interpretation of the individual in mass society.

A. Shonfield, *Modern Capitalism* (1965). A balanced survey of the changes in the economic system in Europe and America since the 1930's.

* W. H. Whyte, *The Organization Man* (1957). A study of the organizational compulsion in modern society and its effect on individual personality.

* C. Vann Woodward, *The Strange Career of Jim Crow* (rev. ed., 1957). The history of discrimination against Negroes in the United States.

THE ARTS IN TWENTIETH-CENTURY CIVILIZATION

A. H. Barr, *What Is Modern Painting?* (rev. ed., 1956). A useful introduction.

R. Brustein, *The Theater of Revolt* (1964). Modern tendencies in the theater by a noted critic.

T. M. Finney, *A History of Music* (1947).

K. London, *The Seven Soviet Arts* (1937). A critical survey of the arts under Stalin.

N. Lynton, *The Modern World* (1965). Landmarks of the World's Art Series.

C. Mauriac, *The New Literature* (1959). Essays on modern French authors.

* J. M. Richards, *An Introduction to Modern Architecture* (1951).

R. Richman, ed., *The Arts at Midcentury* (1954). Essays examining the status of the fine arts in Europe and the United States.

A. Webern, *The Path to the New Music* (1963). By a leading modern composer and theorist.

THE LIFE OF THE MIND IN THE TWENTIETH CENTURY

* J. Barzun, *The House of Intellect* (1959). A careful explanation and appraisal of the role of scholarship, education, and the higher culture.

R. Harper, *Existentialism: A Theory of Man* (1949). An introduction for the layman.

H. S. Hughes, *An Essay for Our Times* (1950). A thoughtful discussion of international politics and the future of man.

R. Niebuhr, *The Structure of Nations and Empires* (1959). A famous theologian's view of the problems of international politics.

* M. Polanyi, *Science, Faith, and Society* (1964). An essay on their relationships by a modern philosopher.

* K. R. Popper, *The Open Society and Its Enemies* (1950). A spirited, scholarly defense of pluralistic social systems.

D. D. Rune, ed., *Twentieth Century Philosophy* (1942). A series of stimulating essays on the main philosophical ideas of the twentieth century.

B. Russell, *The Autobiography of Bertrand Russell* (1967). It is different.

C. P. Snow, *The Two Cultures and a Second Look* (2nd ed., 1964). An examination of the sciences and the humanities and the lack of communication between them.

K. W. Thompson, *Political Realism and the Crisis of World Politics* (1960). A searching examination of the bases of world peace.

Try reading recent works of fiction, drama, and poetry by such authors as A. Camus, J. P. Sartre, W. Faulkner, B. Pasternak, D. Thomas, and B. Brecht.

Index